Dynamic Physical Education for Elementary School Children

Dynamic Physical Education for Elementary School Children

sixth edition

victor p. dauer
Washington State University
Pullman, Washington

robert p. pangrazi
Arizona State University
Tempe, Arizona

Burgess Publishing Company
Minneapolis, Minnesota

Editor: Wayne Schotanus
Production Manager: Morris Lundin
Art Director: Joan Gordon
Designer: Paula C. Gibbons
Sales/Marketing Manager: Travis Williams

Cover design by Paula C. Gibbons

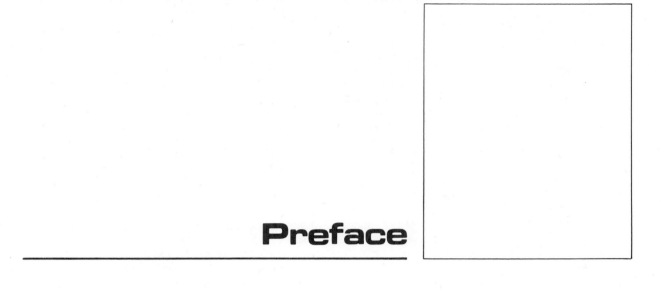

Preface

Elementary school physical education is a dynamic and rapidly changing field, a fact reflected by the number of textbooks that have appeared on the market in the last few years. The rapid growth and development of the field has required that old texts be revised in order to keep them in line with current thinking. The sixth edition of *Dynamic Physical Education for Elementary School Children* is no exception. Changes in physical education are inevitable and they contribute to a stronger profession.

The authors of *Dynamic Physical Education* have updated and expanded the material in an attempt to stay abreast of the changing needs of teachers and students. The strengths of the book have been maintained and refined. Emerging trends in the field of elementary school physical education have necessitated many changes from the fifth edition. An examination of the more dramatic changes initiates this discussion.

Consistent and up-to-date terminology, particularly in the area of movement, has been needed. In many cases, terms were used simultaneously to identify both methodology and content. All teaching methodology now is contained in one chapter, and teaching content is contained in other separate chapters. For the professor teaching methods classes, this arrangement should help simplify the task of teaching and delineating content and methodology. In the past, these were mixed together and were difficult for college students to study and comprehend. It is necessary to know content, necessary to understand methodology, and crucial to be able to diagnose the areas that need improvement in order to enhance the teaching environment.

In leafing through this curricular guide, readers will grasp quickly the strong import the authors place on the teaching process. The teacher has "go power" and can make any activity acceptable, interesting, and educational. Much coverage is devoted to teaching techniques, both in general and in specific sequences. The positive approach focusing on the success and accomplishment of children, with its attendant relationship to the development of satisfactory self-concepts, is featured. The hidden curriculum is brought out into the open.

It is held that successful teaching should employ a variety of teaching techniques and strategies, ranging from creative-exploratory to more defined approaches. The teacher, at the moment, selects the approach that best helps the children achieve their goals in relation to the goals of the program. The learning environment, the learner, and the activity suggest the most appropriate approach. The teacher should have at his or her command a range of instructional techniques that cover all the possible classroom situations.

The elements of movement (as proposed by Rudolph Laban) are recognized to be of vital importance and are integrated throughout the text. Laban's movement principles have a significant place in program theory and practice, but they must be regarded as a functional part within the whole program. To center the entire instructional process on Laban's approach, as is the tendency of some educators today, to the exclusion of other facets of the program is deemed by the authors educationally unsound. At the primary level, much emphasis can be focused on movement principles and body management, which for the sake of clarity, have been termed *educational movement*. However, as children advance to the intermediate grades, more attention should be placed on the acquisition of physical fitness and specialized skills in a variety of sports, rhythmics, stunts and tumbling, and other activities.

From this discussion should come a realization that physical education is concerned with two kinds of movement. The first is based on themes that lead to an understanding of movement factors and the development of effective body management skills. The second kind of movement converges on a particular skill, fundamental or specialized, with attention to technique points and the attendant methodology. The first type of movement can be termed *divergent movement,* since its goal is to extract broad movement potentials within the limitations of a particular theme. The second is called *convergent movement,* since it revolves around a specific skill.

The number of themes offered in the text has been broadened. The themes in the text can give teachers a starting point from which they can develop new and spontaneous lessons. More fundamental and specialized movements have been added, and a new section on nonlocomotor movements has been created.

Dynamic Physical Education has always been appreciated for the wealth of activities it offers to teachers. Today, however, presentation of activities is not enough. The reasons for teaching an activity and the theory behind the activity are becoming increasingly important. No longer are universities educating students who know a wealth of presentable and teachable activities but lack an understanding of the reasons why those activities are taught. Material has been added to this edition that presents, in readable and easily translatable terms, the reasons behind the need for fitness, the theory and practice necessary for optimum learning of motor skills, and the guidelines for competitive situations, among other topics. This knowledge, coupled with the activities, should help the professor to lead the students to a better understanding of the discipline so that they become better teachers.

Finally, the authors have long been advocates of individualized help for children with special needs. Material and guidelines for working with these youngsters have been lacking in past editions. In the new edition, this information has been developed in a separate chapter (nine). Programs for children with low fitness levels are discussed, as are possible solutions for the problems of obesity in children. Chapter nine offers directions that may be taken by schools so that they can conform to the requirements of Public Law 94-142, which mandates the way handicapped children are to be educated. Dr. Dauer has served as an advisor to the State of Washington Department of Education

during the past 2 years. His task has been to develop a program that seeks practical and teachable answers to the difficult questions about mainstreaming handicapped children.

The basic convictions of the authors are the foundations of the curriculum and activity sequences suggested in the text. Their first belief is that physical education, well taught and well conducted, can be an important medium for the child's total education. Benefits received from the program are not automatic, but they occur, in part, because of their manner of presentation in the children's learning experiences. Key points are careful planning and high-quality instruction.

Essentially, the authors hold that a broad program of physical education is the most educationally sound approach. A program of a broad nature, featuring balanced coverage and a variety of activities, is more likely to achieve a measure of satisfaction for all children, since each child has a better chance to find something to his or her liking among the variety of experiences offered.

The emphasis on the importance of a broad program has been incorporated as one of the general goals of the overall program. The elementary school years are a time for the children to explore and experiment in a variety of activities, a process that may be continued somewhat during their junior high school years. The modern high school program, however, usually centers on in-depth instruction in a choice of activities that can be enjoyed throughout the students' lifetimes.

Two general goals of physical education can be singled out as holding special significance: the achievement of a personalized level of physical fitness for each child and the acquisition of a broad range of fundamental and special skills. These goals are the heart of physical education, and all other goals are generated from them. Both fitness and skill development should be approached through systematically planned learning experiences rather than relegated to development as concomitant and secondary results of other program emphases.

The lesson plan format recommended is organized on this conviction: every teacher should teach from a lesson plan. The first two parts of the lesson plan should give particular attention to fitness, with the lesson focus (the third part) centering on progressive instruction. The lesson then can be terminated with a short game or relaxation activity.

Teachers are busy people who have many responsibilities, and to ask them to make daily lesson plans many times results in an unproductive experience. The lesson plan format recommended is structured so that the teacher makes out one overall lesson plan for each week. Not only is there a saving of the teacher's time, there is an opportunity for better progression and more effective learning experiences. The authors have employed this approach successfully in programs they have supervised, and Dr. Pangrazi continues this practice in the Phoenix (Arizona) area schools. Both classroom teachers who teach physical education and physical education specialists have found this type of lesson format an effective means of guiding the children's learning experiences. *Lesson Plans for Dynamic Physical Education* is based on the authors' experiences in supervising school programs. The lesson plans contain the precepts, activity sequences, and teaching progressions found in this edition of *Dynamic Physical Education for Elementary School Children.*

The authors are firm in their belief that the program should be largely of an instructional nature. Games are no longer the center of attention but rather play a more minor role than previously was assumed. The games included in this edition have been evaluated carefully, and only those that offer maximum activity for many children have been retained.

Progression in the presentation of activities is the soul of instruction. Activities are presented in logical sequences and progressions and constantly are being evaluated in public school programs. Progression naturally leads to the allocation of activities to grade levels, since experience with teachers has shown that this helps them select activities appropriate for the respective grade levels. The suggested levels of activities form a convenient base from which the teacher may depart upward or downward. Allocation also helps guarantee progression from grade to grade, since a teacher working with incoming students can have some knowledge of what has transpired in the students' past physical education experiences.

This leads to another important conviction: a physical education program should be a functional, child-tested program. With few exceptions, the activities in this text have been tested, modified, and adjusted as the authors' and readers' experiences with children have dictated. The input from many teachers and supervisors has been most valuable for putting movement experiences into their proper perspectives. This down-to-earth input is reflected in specialized instructional procedures for individual activities, which include teaching hints and stress points gleaned through practical experience. Variations within the activity material have been noted to give more breadth to learning experiences.

Almost all the photographs, sequence diagrams, and action sketches have been tailored for the book. Few outside sources are represented in the illustrative material.

A wide variety of practical suggestions for constructing inexpensive physical education supplies and equipment is presented in the last chapter of the book. Measurements and directions accompany the lists of suggested equipment and supplies for the elementary school physical education program.

In general, the sequence of activities has been expanded only where necessary. A new chapter (seventeen), "Activities with Jump Ropes," combines all the rope-jumping activities and the other activities with ropes. Activities with ropes are considered quite valuable in the educational process and merit this attention.

Perceptual-motor programs, including concepts, principles, and special activities, seem to have achieved a stable niche in the human movement picture. Much can be derived from this area that can provide higher-quality learning experiences for children within the regular program of activities. Giving attention, where relevant, to balance factors, coordination, laterality, directionality, spatial orientation, knowledge of body parts, and hand-eye and foot-eye coordination in the regular program is an important facet of the program to which the authors have given attention. Specialized perceptual-motor programs are remedial in nature and should be regarded as the domain of specialists in the perceptual-motor field.

The authors are indebted to many people who have provided many valuable suggestions and ideas. The Mesa, Arizona, Public Schools (Dr. Gene Peterson, director of elementary school physical education) have been most helpful in serving as a test laboratory for many phases of the program. The material on rope jumping to music is from the Seattle schools and was developed by Dennis Myer. The material was adapted and excerpted from original material by Paul Smith of the Shoreline School District, Seattle, Washington.

Credit for the photographs goes to Robert Bullis (formerly staff photographer at Washington State University) and William Hogg (Arizona State University).

Credits for many of the drawings and illustrations go to Dr. Julia Kiyoguchi and staff artists from Burgess Publishing Company. Original action sequences were drawn by Dr. Bruce Frederick (University of Wisconsin at Superior). The drawings for the sixth edition were prepared by members of the Burgess staff. The assistance of Dr. James Sweeney (Ohio State University) in earlier revisions is also gratefully acknowledged.

To my wife, Alice, whose help, inspiration, and encouragement have been of inestimable value in the writing of this book and its revisions.

Victor P. Dauer

This book is dedicated with love and respect to my family, without whose aid, patience, and understanding my efforts would not have been possible.

Robert P. Pangrazi

Contents

One

Introduction to Physical Education

The results of good physical education are not limited to the body alone, but extend even to the soul itself.

Aristotle, 350 B.C.

Without a doubt, physical education should be regarded as a vital and dynamic phase of every educational program. In fact, there is much more potential for child development in physical education than many educators realized even a decade ago, and the potential in each child for development goes far beyond what was imagined previously. The task becomes utilizing high-quality physical education learning experiences in order to foster the progress of which children are capable, including progress in psychomotor, cognitive, and affective learning.

If the overall mission of education is to foster the development of children who can achieve individual satisfaction as responsible, contributing citizens, then physical education, well planned and taught by understanding teachers, can make important contributions to this goal. In America's democratic society, this means serving all children—handicapped children, slow or delayed learners, gifted individuals, motor retardates, and those children called normal. The long-range goal is to provide opportunities for as many individuals as possible so that they can achieve their highest potentials.

Identifying the mission is only the beginning. The important question is what physical education *can* and *should* provide as a learning environment, so optimum development does take place. This predicates a narrowing of the gap between what is known and what is practiced.

It is the quality of teaching that makes the difference. Functioning more as a catalyst than as a director of learning, a teacher must be able to motivate a child to learn and to guide critically the child's learning experiences. Furthermore, learning to learn should be emphasized more, and problem-solving techniques should be used in the instructional process where they are applicable.

The term *the new physical education* is in vogue today and is used to describe the present direction of the field. However, the broad base represented by the age-old goals of physical education—fitness, motor skills, associated knowledges, and desirable attitudes—is still much the same as it has always been. But physical education has superimposed on this base many newer personalized goals that are to be achieved with methodology that is more flexible than the traditional approach. Even the traditional goals themselves have been broadened and expanded and made more relevant to today's needs.

Physical fitness, for example, has other values and directions besides providing raw body development. Cardiorespiratory factors are given a lot of attention today, as is the axiom that an active person leads a more productive and pleasurable life with less concern about cardiac problems. More attention is given to establishing a basis of lifelong activity, with instruction covering not only what to do but how and why it should be done. An appropriate level of fitness for an individual can lead to a more confident outlook, greater emotional stability, and better mental health.

It may be that physical vitality leads to increased intellectual vitality. Certainly, teachers have found that children with improved physical

1

conditions are more alert and, hence, more receptive to the educational process.

Much of the new emphasis on skills is centered on movement education, that is, learning through movement while learning to move. Efficient management of the body in a variety of movement challenges is an early goal on which the more advanced skills are based. In addition, the art of moving skillfully and efficiently has derived much from the perceptual-motor approach.

Rudolph Laban, with his concepts of movement, greatly influenced movement education. His movement factors of time, force, space, and flow have given new dimensions and terminology to physical education. Themes stressing Laban's movement principles provide the basis for learning experiences for many youngsters, especially preschool, kindergarten, and primary-level children. He has provided a new look and a stimulating emphasis.

Cognitive elements, once categorized as knowledges, are given high priority in the new physical education. Not only is the child to learn to move skillfully, but he or she is to gain an understanding of how and why he or she moves and of the movement principles underlying movement. Thus, the child conceptualizes as he or she learns through movement.

The affective domain also draws its share of attention, centered on the development of an appropriate self-concept for each child. In developing a self-concept, a child needs to acquire a sense of belonging, a degree of competency, and a feeling of being worthwhile. Instructional approaches have been modified so that children can better develop desirable self-concepts.

Much interest today is expressed in the relationship of skill, coordination, and related physical traits to academic performance. The evidence is inconclusive, but theorists emphasize the importance of successful perceptual-motor functioning as a basis of successful academic performance. The slow learner is, in some cases, a poor motor performer, so perceptual-motor tests can be used as a useful screening device for recognizing slow learners.

The following physical and motor attributes have been identified as the most important for children with learning difficulties: balance and postural control, temporal-spatial relationships, body image, and coordination. The essence of the perceptual-motor position is that the child goes through a sequence of learning stages involving these categories. Should development fail in any of the attributes, the child lacks the capacity to absorb complex learning, which is built upon initial progress. Most children are capable of learning; it is a matter of the right conditions. It may be that the development of perceptual-motor competency reflects the potential for educational development.

Is the improvement of a slow learner due to planned experiences in sensory-motor coordination, or is it centered on the process objectives? When a child improves his or her listening skills, learns to follow directions, improves task sequences, and can reproduce as directed (qualities important in academic progress), it can be said that he or she is learning to learn. Achieving success and satisfaction in a part of the school experience (physical education) can transfer and have positive effects on the child's overall progress in school.

The hidden curriculum in physical education embraces a broader range of learning in contrast to the stated curriculum and its aspects. Social, attitudinal, moral, and emotional learnings depend upon the way the instructional climate in physical education is organized. Such elements as the quality of the physical environment (cleanliness, space, ventilation, lighting, et cetera), a positive teaching approach (featuring praise and rewards), the moral tone in the classroom, and the personalized approach create deep and lasting impressions on the children.

One school administrator said that his school is a happier place because of its improved physical education program. The school has a higher morale, and he has fewer problems and fewer problem students. Teachers in the school reported that the students have found new interest in school because of their exciting and challenging physical education experiences.

WHAT IS PHYSICAL EDUCATION?

Physical education, then, is education of, by, and through human movement. It is that phase of general education that contributes to the total growth and development of the child, primarily through selected movement experiences and physical activities. The general goals of education and physical education are the same—the greatest possible development of each individual and education for responsible democratic citizenship.

The child must acquire the ability to move effectively if he or she is to achieve his or her potential. Physical education must be concerned with both the versatility and the quality of human motor performance. PE must not mean "poorer education." If PE is to be education, the physical education environment must be structured so that it stimulates the child to think. More and more evidence appears to demonstrate that physical education can effectively expand its function as an educational tool by focusing on exploration, creativity, thought and problem-solving processes, concept formation, and concomitant learnings, leading to self-confidence and a good self-image.

Health, vitality, and vigor are the bases for excellence in living. Physical education should be concerned with contributing to physical welfare and vigor, which are basic to a balanced life. If physical education does not provide the child with experiences with which to gain these attributes, no other area of the school curriculum will compensate for this loss.

As participants in physical education learning experiences, all children should be afforded the opportunity to clarify their basic values and to develop a commitment to act upon these values. The physical education setting should present a laboratory in group living in which this goal can be accomplished. Youngsters must learn to cooperate and to compete fairly. They need to solve the problems that face them or learn to live with them in a socially approved manner. The give-and-take situations in physical education can provide unique opportunities for guiding social growth in a desired direction. Physical education can provide experiences that aid the child in developing ways of working with himself or herself, with a partner, as a member of a group, as a contributing member of the class, and with the teacher.

Essentially, guiding physical education to *educate* children is the domain of the professional, the dedicated teacher. If physical education is to achieve acceptance as a full partner in the educational process, there is no place for inept or ineffective teachers.

EDUCATIONAL AND CULTURAL FORCES AFFECTING PHYSICAL EDUCATION

A better understanding of the current programs in physical education may be gained by first tracing the long history of physical education.

The Ancient Greeks and Subsequent Influences

The Greeks were the first ... the anci... to embrace the concept of ph... development of the whole hu... of developing citizens with a ... cal prowess so that they coul... land was basic to all cultu... included other ideals, one of ... and beauty of movement, ... sports participation. The concep... son as a moral person also was co... tant. Today's sports represent an imp... tage from the ancient Greeks and th... sports festivals, of which the Olympic Games ... the most important. The modern Olympic oath is a tribute to their ideals.

But degeneration set in and professionalism took over sports competition. Under the Romans, the sports festivals became brutal spectacles and the idealistic concepts of the Greeks were lost.

Little progress was made during the Dark Ages and the Middle Ages. Few practical programs appeared during the centuries that followed, although play and exercise began to be regarded as beneficial, primarily because of their value for good health.

Puritan Ethics and the Early American Settlers

For early settlers in America, there was little time to play. When schools were established, they attended to the serious business of "larnin'." From the Puritan point of view, play was not only a waste of time, it was downright sinful. Virtue rested in hard work.

But as frontier living became less demanding, hunting and fishing, which in earlier times had been necessary for survival, became leisure-time play. The English tradition of sports participation in archery, bowls, cricket, tennis, soccer, rugby, boxing, and track and field was important in the southern colonies. Still, the only physical activity found in schools remained free play during recess.

The German and Swedish Influence before World War I

During the 1800s, both Germany and Sweden established systems of physical education in the schools that were developmental in nature. In contrast, only a few sporadic attempts to develop similar programs were made in the United States. However, around the middle of the nineteenth century, the German and Swedish immigrants to this country brought with them their ideas about physical education.

The Germans proposed a system that favored a gymnastic approach and needed considerable equipment and special teachers. For this purpose, the first normal school for physical education in the United States was established by the Turners, a gymnastic society.

The Swedish system was based on the incorporation of an exercise program into its activities. The physical education program in the schools under this system consisted of a series of exercises that could be done outside or inside the classroom while the children stood beside their desks. The doctrine of dualism, according to which body and mind were separate and so physical education developed the body, prevailed.

For both systems, the need for equipment and gymnasiums posed problems, and the programs were questioned by many economy-minded citizens. A combination of games and calisthenics evolved and became a type of physical education that offered scheduled activity in a few American schools.

The Games and Sports Emphasis from World War I to 1953

During training programs for soldiers in World War I, it was established that a games and sports emphasis was more desirable than the strictly calisthenics type of training. A shift to the utilization of games and sports for physical development spawned school programs with the same emphasis. This development received impetus when two of John Dewey's cardinal aims of education stressed attention to physical activities. These aims were the promotion of health and the worthy use of leisure time, which became school curricular responsibilities. The school also was deemed to be responsible for molding social change, with a high value attached to games and sports.

When about one-third of the American men drafted in World War I were rejected as physically unfit for military service, a new demand for physical education in the schools resulted. State educational authorities legislated requirements for so many minutes of physical activity time per week in school programs. These laws legally established physical education as part of the school curriculum in many states.

Slowly a turn away from the concept of dualism became apparent. Physical education began to be concerned with more than just the physical. Strong programs of sports and games appeared in the secondary schools, and the elementary programs became miniature models of them. Literally, the programs could have been described by answering the question "what games are we going to play today?"

During the 1930s and the depression years, physical education was relegated to a minor role and, in many cases, was eliminated entirely. Equipment was difficult to secure, and special teachers were almost nonexistent.

During World War II, many new training programs for special groups appeared. New physical fitness development, hospital reconditioning programs, and other innovative approaches were supported by considerable research statistics.

An improvement in the quality of American physical education might have been expected after the war, but little effect was evident in the quality of elementary school programs. It seemed that American physical education on the elementary level reverted to "business as usual" routines, with emphasis on simple games and with some sports added for good measure.

The Surge of Physical Fitness from 1954 to the Present

Although physical fitness has always been considered an important goal in physical education, at times a renewal of the emphasis has occurred, following the social forces dominant at the time. Such a renewal occurred in 1954 following the publication of the comparative fitness levels of American and European children, which were based on the Kraus-Weber tests.[1] A study by Dr. Hans Kraus, comparing certain strength and flexibility measurements of 4000 New York-area school children with a comparable sample of Central European children, had far-reaching results. The American press became concerned about the comparative weakness of American children, and, with this concern, the present fitness movement was born.

One result of the furor over physical fitness was the establishment of the President's Council on Physical Fitness, a potent force in promoting good physical fitness not only among school children but also among citizens of all ages. The President's Council on Physical Fitness and Sports, as it is now called, through its many publications, services, and promotions, has had a major influence on school programs, leading to the development of better levels of physical fitness among children.

The results of this new emphasis on fitness have been evident in the elementary schools. Programs are of improved quality, and many have been established where none existed before. Administrators have become increasingly aware of the contributions that physical education can make to the growth and development of children. Other apparent effects are increased time allotments for physical education, better facilities and equipment, and provisions for consultant services and specialized teachers. The council's national physical fitness test has had widespread acceptance and has provided fitness comparisons on a country-wide basis.

Movement Education from 1960 to the Present

Movement education brought a fresh, new approach, a new methodology, and a new way of providing learning experiences for children. Movement education had its origins in England and evolved for a number of reasons. It was a revolt against more formal programs, which included calisthenics and were command oriented. It attempted to shift to the child the responsibility for his or her own progress. Methodology featured problem solving and an exploratory approach.

The real basis for movement education lies, however, in the incorporation into the meth-

---

[1]The Kraus-Weber tests served as an instrument in the study, but they are no longer regarded as a valid measurement of physical fitness for elementary school children.

odology of the concepts of Rudolph Laban.[2] The process of learning should be viewed as the acquisition of movement competency rather than as the mere accumulation of knowledge, absorption of subject matter, or development of certain skills. Programs center on the how as well as on the why. Emphasis is on developing versatility in movement and acquiring efficient body management competency. The elements of choice and self-selection are paramount. Children must have opportunities to practice freely, to choose freely, and to be creative.

To some, this approach seemed to be the panacea for the ills of physical education. It led, in some cases, to the rejection of physical-fitness-oriented activities, especially calisthenics, which were labeled as training and not as education. Controversy arose regarding the application of movement principles to the teaching of specific skills, particularly athletic skills. There was some tendency to apply the methodology to athletic skills without valid research evidence to support such practices. In England, movement methodology originally was centered mostly in the development of general body management and fundamental skills. It also had high value in the area of gymnastics, particularly in what the English call large apparatus.

Another interesting precept promulgated by some instructors is that the child must *first* experience the movement pattern, manipulative object, or piece of apparatus without direction or instruction and before any instructional sequences or challenges are imposed. The child must have a chance to try it out on his or her own. While there is little valid evidence that this principle results in the most beneficial educational progress, some defend it as the natural way of learning. Certainly, there are times when this approach yields benefits, but to superimpose a blanket rule of this type on all learning is not sound. The labeling confuses the picture and is unfortunate, as it establishes a bias that in turn tends to indicate that any other approach is unnatural.

Perceptual-Motor Programs from 1960 to the Present

All movement is essentially perceptual-motor movement, but the concern in perceptual-motor programs is corrective in nature and relates to remedying learning difficulties attributed to a breakdown in the perceptual-motor development of the child. Theorists hold that the child progresses through growth and developmental stages either from head to foot (cephalocaudal) or from the center of the body outward (proximodistal) in an orderly fashion. When there are disruptions, lags, or omissions in this process, certain underlying perceptual-motor bases fail to develop fully and can disturb the function of the input-integration-response monitoring sequence so important in complex learning.

A normal perceptual-motor reaction is defined as a *meaningful* and *consistent* response to the input stimuli, which connotes efficiency of process. In physical education, a normal perceptual-motor reaction is the ability of a young child to carry out in a skillful and accurate way simple motor acts.

Perceptual-motor programs grew out of concern for the slow learner, sometimes called the slow child or the delayed learner. Most children so identified show motor-coordination problems involving the movement factors (coordination, balance and postural control, image of the body and its parts, and relationships involving time and space). The most outstanding characteristic of slow learners is their poor coordination and poor motor planning.

Based on the theories of Montessori, Luria, Piaget, and others, educators outside of physical education (Getman, Delacato, Kephart, and others) developed tests by which motor deficiencies could be identified and programs through which they could be remedied. This in turn would contribute to better academic functioning.

When physical education people became involved in perceptual-motor programs, several national conferences were sponsored by the AAHPER and a considerable amount of literature appeared. Needed research and program studies were initiated, and emphasis finally has been placed on remedial programs for slow learners.

Perceptual-motor programs are important additions to the instructional strategies and content of regular physical education programs. A variety of movement demands and challenges should be included in regular physical education classes. Value lies both in the precise, limited movements and the exploratory, creative approach inherent in the movement education method. And there is a wide range of movement combinations between the two extremes.

TRENDS AND EVENTS AFFECTING PHYSICAL EDUCATION

The influences that tend to affect physical education have widened in scope over the last two

[2]Rudolph Laban immigrated to the British Isles from Germany in 1932. His theories first made their impact through dance. Laban's approach to movement was based on the theory that there were elements common to all movement and that these elements could be described. His movement analysis was adapted to physical education and led to the development of educational movement, a concept that at the time was both revolutionary and controversial.

decades. Among these appear some from general education sources, since physical education emphasizes education. Others spring from social and community forces and a number of influences come from other professional areas.

The American Medical Association

Strong formal approval and support of physical education programs in the schools came from the American Medical Association, which represents collectively the medical profession. The support followed a statement adopted at the AMA's national convention in 1960: "Resolved, That the American Medical Association through its various divisions and departments and its constituent and component medical societies do everything feasible to encourage effective instruction in physical education for all students in our schools and colleges."[3] The 1960 resolution was reaffirmed in 1969, strongly supported by the AMA Committee on Exercise and Physical Fitness, a body that was not in existence at the time of the 1960 resolution.

Cognitive Learning

Conceptual understanding (that is, the application of abstract ideas drawn from experience) also plays an important part in physical education today. Thus, in the process of movement, the child learns to distinguish between near and far, strong and weak, light and heavy, high and low. He or she should be given the opportunity to experiment and thereby establish an understanding of such other terms as curve, stretch, twist, turn, balance, and bounce. He or she also should be enabled to learn to work purposefully toward a designated goal or to be self-critical. Thus, the learning environment of physical education becomes an extension of the educational activities of the classroom.

In his or her movement patterns and skill-learning activities, the child not only learns to move but also should understand why he or she moves and the mechanical principles behind his or her movements. Within the instructional framework, basic kinesiological and mechanical principles are related to the movement patterns, so the child can grasp the underlying basis of efficient movement. In addition, instructional strategies focus on learning to learn through problem solving, inquiry, discovery, creativity, and working for success or toward a goal.

Affective Learning

A resurgence of interest in personal values and moral development appears to be a trend throughout educational circles. Physical education experiences can have a hand in molding val-

ues, either through participation in an environment serving as a laboratory for living or through incidental or planned instruction. Values, beliefs, feelings, and judgments are increasingly being stressed.

The Self-concept

Much emphasis centers on the development of self-concept as an important influence in shaping human behavior. The view that a child has of himself or herself is of vital importance in his or her relationships with peers and teachers and to his or her schoolwork. The ability to move with grace and confidence enhances a child's self-esteem; and, in contrast, the awkward, uncoordinated, or physically weak child is apt to be ridiculed for his or her shortcomings and made to feel different from his or her classmates. The child's view of himself or herself, positive or negative, can spill over into other areas of his or her life.

Experiences in which the child achieves and gains success can mold and shape a positive concept. Programs need to be guided, so each child can meet with some success and not be discouraged by failure.

The American Alliance for Health, Physical Education and Recreation

The American Alliance for Health, Physical Education and Recreation[4] has been a potent influence on physical education programs for children. Directed by staff consultant Dr. Margie Hanson, the association has met with success in striving to upgrade elementary school programs and shape philosophy by means of publications, staff services, conferences, workshops, and convention programs. The Elementary School Physical Education Commission, a group of professionals, functions with guidance from Dr. Hanson under the umbrella of the AAHPER. An interesting and potentially productive development is the interaction between the AAHPER and organizations also interested in the development of the elementary school child.

Personalized and Individualized Learning

A lot of lip service has been given to the concept of individualization, but, in practice, it has failed to achieve the status that an important educational principle should. One does not need to sell the idea. The problem is how it can be accomplished.

There is some confusion about the two terms *personalization* and *individualization*. Personalization is taken to mean adjusting what is learned to the needs and characteristics of the learner,

[3]Quoted from the proceedings of the 1960 Annual Convention of the American Medical Association (Chicago: American Medical Association, 1960).

[4]The abbreviation AAHPER will be used throughout this text to refer to the American Alliance for Health, Physical Education and Recreation.

regardless of the methodology employed. Individualization refers to any learning situation in which the learner operates on a noninteractive basis.

The AAHPER, through its constituent committees, has developed an informative handbook entitled *Personalized Learning in Physical Education*[5] and has promoted several conferences and workshops pertaining to the topic.

Increasingly, education centers on individual progress, with instruction, progressions, and achievements determined by the needs of the learner. More attention is being focused on individual activities in physical education, with less on competition between teams or individuals.

An individualized learning approach that has met with some success features the contract or learning package approach. Each student is given a learning packet that he or she completes as an individual project. Each student has certain goals to meet, which in some cases he or she can set; and, when ready, the student is tested to determine whether or not the stated goals have been satisfied. The approach provides specific (behavioral) objectives, a series of steps for meeting the goals, and self-direction. Utilized mostly on the intermediate level, this technique seems to be educationally sound, but it does demand a large amount of evaluation time.

Play cards are a less structured individualized approach, with the child selecting a play card and following the prescribed movement patterns. Play cards sometimes describe a number of levels of difficulty, challenging the child to go as far as he or she can or wishes.

Teacher's aides and parent volunteers can be helpful in conducting an individualized program. This instructional approach is also well suited to open-classroom schools, which are organized around a central learning area.

The Nongraded School

The nongraded school organization has important implications for physical education. To fit into this philosophy, a physical education program needs to have many alternatives so that individual differences can be met. No longer are classes scheduled for physical education. Groups of students appear for physical education experiences, or children may even come and go as individuals on a varied schedule. This may mean chronological age differences between students greater than those seen in the present program geared to the classroom schedule.

The Proliferation of Equipment

The availability of commercial equipment and supplies for operating a functional program is be-

[5]*Personalized Learning in Physical Education* (Washington, D.C.: AAHPER, 1976).

yond imagination. Before any equipment is purchased, a set of criteria should be established. Wall-attached climbing frames, portable floor apparatus, climbing ropes on tracks, balance-beam benches, parachutes, individual tug-of-war ropes, and various kinds of mats are items that should be strongly considered. However, there are many other pieces of equipment designed for tumbling, specialized movement patterns, and remedial work that need to be examined carefully before they are purchased.

Records are always in endless supply. No matter what the activity, it seems that someone has made a record to direct it.

Strong consideration also should be given to constructing equipment in the school rather than buying it ready-made. Suggestions for equipment that can be made by school personnel can be found in chapter thirty-four.

Sports and Related Activities

Increased opportunity for competition in sports, mostly from sources outside of the school, is available for children of elementary school age. In the past, schools have taken a strong stand against competition, but the reality is that children now compete with or without the permission or sanction of the schools. The question is not whether or not competition will occur but rather how a school can enhance the experience. Sports competition has good value when conducted in an educationally sound manner, with emphasis on wide participation and on a level commensurate with the age of the participants. The primary concern is one of proper supervision, and the schools can supply this.

Instruction in the lifetime sports is being stressed in secondary programs, and it is reaching down to the elementary level. Perhaps the most logical approach to this kind of instruction is to allocate these sports to the secondary program and have the elementary program give first importance to a wide variety of fundamental and introductory sports skills.

The tremendous public interest in jogging as a health and recreational activity and in long-distance running as a hobby should provide program directions for the elementary level. The widespread interest in tennis should indicate to educators the importance of related racket skills.

Fitness centers, too, have strong public support and are a going business in many communities. They stress mostly weight control and body contouring. Weight-control measures for individual children should be instituted early in remedial elementary programs.

The President's Council on Physical Fitness and Sports has instituted a sports award program that is within the reach of the average participant.

The award is based on a stipulated amount of participation and requires no achievement factor. Since stimulating consistent participation is a desirable goal, this type of awards program shows the way toward a new direction, one different from the normal varsity-type awards or those based on high levels of physical fitness or skill. Excellence still should receive attention, but the participation award offers needed recognition for effort.

Equal Opportunity for the Sexes

While most programs in the past have been coeducational, Title IX of the Education Amendments now calls for all curriculum offerings in physical education to be coeducational, ruling out any choice. It is no longer possible to exclude one sex from the type of activities participated in by the other. It is still possible to have separate competition for sexes in an activity, provided that it can be determined that mixed participation in that activity could be hazardous.

Another facet of equal opportunity for the sexes is the elimination of sexism and sex-role typing. Individuals should be allowed to attain their maximum development according to their own abilities, desires, and aspirations and not according to social or sexual roles arbitrarily prescribed by society. The labeling and sorting of individuals according to their sex should be eliminated from the educational process. Human needs must take precedence over the traditional sexual stereotypes of masculinity and femininity.

Equal Rights for the Handicapped

Public Law 94-142 mandates that handicapped children must have the right to a free and public education and that they must be educated in the least restrictive environment possible. No longer can they be swept under the table and out of sight in segregated classes or schools, unless a separate environment is determined *by due process* to be in the best interest of the child. Handicapped children are to be assigned to regular programs when they can participate reasonably well and to their advantage, and adapted programs are to be provided in regular schools to take care of those who need help. The physical education program for the handicapped, according to the law, must stress physical and motor fitness, fundamental motor skills and patterns, and skills in aquatics, dance, and a variety of games and sports. The challenge for fulfillment of the needs of the handicapped is considerable.

Culturally Deprived and Disadvantaged Children

Physical education also can provide culturally deprived and disadvantaged children with a new interest, lighting a spark that may help improve their attitudes regarding learning. While the problems and relationships are complicated and deep, physical education nevertheless can help youngsters to achieve status, enjoy respect, and succeed through improved peer regard. A long-range goal is to help stop children from dropping out of school by keeping their interest in schoolwork alive.

Semantics and Terminology

With the educational movement has come almost automatically a new terminology. The descriptive terminology employed includes such terms as *space-time relationships, bound* and *free flow, effort, force factors,* and so on. Most of the terminology was derived from the contributions of Rudolph Laban. While most of the terms are appropriate and useful, in extreme cases the use of the terms almost amounts to a jargon of the trade that is not easily understood by people outside the profession. For example, the word *space* is overused in much of the literature.

Another concern lies in the adoption of the British categories of program divisions—games, dance, and educational gymnastics. Track and field (athletics) and aquatics lie outside of these divisions. The question is whether or not this is the proper direction to take, since it would mean restructuring much of the present literature and guidelines.

Some of the newer approaches even take exception to the traditional term *physical education* and would substitute a more appropriate (to them) designation, such as *kinesiology, the art of movement, movement and learning,* or *the science of human movement.* Change may be desirable. The profession in the past changed its name from *physical training* to *physical education.*

Professional Preparation

The preparation of professionals in elementary school physical education is trying to keep pace with the changes in philosophy and science in the field. The emphasis is changing from producing instructors who emphasize content and methodology to producing teachers who teach children. In order to meet the needs of students in elementary schools today, teachers must extend their expertise to the handling of handicapped and retarded children; low-fitness individuals; children with motor deficiencies; and children from bilingual backgrounds, ghettos, and families of transient workers. The would-be teacher should acquire the expertise necessary to work with all kinds of children without giving them labels and to handle their differences without pigeonholing them. Physical education professionals should make the most of the time allotted them to help the regular elementary school classroom teacher acquire the necessary physical education skills.

During the last two decades, there have been cutbacks on service programs for college and upper-level secondary students. Whether this downgrading of physical education will carry over into professional preparation programs remains to be seen. But, when classroom teachers without preparation handle physical education, the child usually suffers from low-level physical experiences.

Educational Influences

The return to the basics in general education has affected physical education, also. Some state authorities are requiring that elementary schools spell out the fundamental academic skills and knowledges that children are expected to acquire as minimum achievements for each grade level. This, in turn, has challenged physical educators to come up with a similar set of basics.

The concept of accountability is based on the idea that progress in the achievement of basics is measurable and that teachers and schools can be held accountable for helping students attain a predetermined level of basic achievement. Accountability has both pros and cons. It is nice to be able to tell parents exactly what education is doing for their children, and schools can show that they are using the taxpayers' money well. But such accountability can mean discarding affective goals because they are difficult to measure. Goals such as the development of a healthy self-concept and the acquisition of desirable social goals defy numerical interpretation.

In the psychomotor area, for example, the development of a sense of balance is a needed quality, particularly in primary school children. Three kinds of balance are identified: static, dynamic, and airborne. Setting *valid* behavioral goals for a child's progress in balance is most difficult.

The problem of meeting accountability may drive the teacher in self-defense toward memorization, drill, rote learning, and practice in only those areas held important in accountability. In addition, evaluation can demand an inordinate amount of the teacher's time.

There is a trend toward extending education downward and upward. The downward aspects are of importance to the elementary school physical educator with the appearance of preschool education and child-care centers. Head Start programs are another extension of the educational system. Since much of the instruction is motor and physical, there must be concern with providing appropriate and effective movement experiences for preschool children.

To provide a more valid basis for programs, further research is needed. Considerable attention is being given the relationship between motor coordination and academic progress, particularly reading skills. Many studies follow the longitudinal format, a lengthy process covering a variety of growth and development factors. Interest in research is high, and valid evidence to support programs is accumulating.

A wide variety of instructional aids is available, including motion pictures, filmstrips, loop films, and sequence charts. Excellent projection equipment adaptable for use in gymnasiums also has been developed.

Influences from other cultures are an ongoing part of physical education programs. Games and dances from other lands, in particular, increase the child's opportunity for understanding and appreciating the life-styles of other people. Also, ideas from other countries are being experimented with and evaluated. As value judgments are approved, ideas find their way into American programs.

THE APPROACH TO ELEMENTARY SCHOOL PHYSICAL EDUCATION

A most important factor in presenting learning experiences to children is avoiding getting bogged down in a controversy over, or adherence to, specific lines of methodology. In selecting an approach to teaching physical education, three points stand out. The first is that excellent teaching is the principal ingredient of a quality program. Second, the learning situation, including the teacher, the learner, and the activity, suggests the appropriate methodology for attaining the expected outcomes. The third point is that studies show little if any difference in effectiveness between one method and another. The approach that is used should be the one that most readily and effectively accomplishes the goals of the lesson.

Most of the comparisons in methodology contrast the traditional (direct) methods to the indirect (flexible) methods. The traditional approach is defined as one that makes strong use of direct (command) teaching. On the other hand, the indirect approach distinguishes methodology that usually is associated with the movement approach and is characterized by problem-solving techniques, choice, self-direction, and creativity. It may appear that there are two contrasting methods employed in teaching, but, in reality, no such dichotomy exists.

In today's programs, much of the instruction is a mixture of the two. Even physical fitness development can utilize indirect techniques. The diagram

Methodology Used by the Teacher to Reach the Student

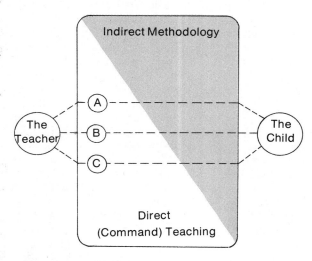

A. Mostly indirect but with some direct teaching.
B. A balance between direct and indirect approaches.
C. More emphasis on command approach than on indirect teaching methods.

above indicates how these two approaches can be combined for varied teaching, showing how the teacher uses different combinations to get through to the child.

At times, the direct approach may predominate, and, at other times, indirect approaches may take precedence. Between the two extremes lies a range of varied approaches that depend upon the degree of freedom a child is given to direct his or her own learning.

The right of the teacher to employ the approach he or she considers appropriate is fundamental and, of course, is based upon sound educational principles. However, a disproportionate use of the direct approach leaves much to be desired. More than 40 years ago, John Dewey commented on this.

A learning situation in which the learner can exercise no control in terms of his purposes teaches him to conform or rebel. A learning situation in which all the factors are under the learner's control leads to whimsical and undisciplined behavior. Desirable learning results from the learner recognizing factors in the situation to which he must adapt and others that he can manipulate in terms of his purposes. [6]

From a curricular standpoint, two types of physical education approaches are needed, one for children in grades kindergarten through two and another for those in grades three through six. A more flexible, movement-oriented program yields better educational results for younger children, while the upper grades can concentrate more on the development of specific skills and fitness qualities and still retain relative emphasis on movement methodology.

---

[6]Quoted in Ralph W. Tyler, "New Dimensions in Curriculum Development," *Phi Delta Kappan,* vol. XLVIII (September 1966), p. 26.

Two

The Basis of the Program

One step in personalizing physical education learning experiences is the examination of the basic urges of children and their effects on children's behavior. A second is the consideration of the cognitive, affective, and psychomotor characteristics and interests of children in relation to physical activity. A basic urge is an intense drive toward the attainment of certain personal goals, which the child seems to have in his or her natural makeup and in his or her relations with others. The urges apply in varying degrees to the different age groups and to both sexes. The last step in establishing a rational basis for a physical education program is the formulation of the program's goals.

BASIC URGES OF CHILDREN

The nature of the basic urges varies somewhat among children, but, for most children, the urges are important reasons for living and being. It is difficult to rank the urges in importance, and no attempt is made to do so here, since individual children themselves rank the urges differently. The importance of the urges lies in the implications and guidelines that can be drawn from them with respect to the content and methodology of each program.

The Urge for Movement

Children have an insatiable appetite for moving, performing, and being active. They run for the sheer joy of running. Activity for them is the essence of living. The physical education program must satisfy this craving for movement.

The Urge for Success and Approval

Children not only like to achieve but also desire recognition of achievement. They wilt under criticism and disapproval, whereas encouragement and friendly support promote growth and maximum development. Failure can lead to frustration, lack of interest, and inefficient learning. In extreme cases, failure can lead to an antipathy toward physical education that can have a profound effect on later participation in physical activities.

The Urge for Peer Acceptance and Social Competence

Peer acceptance is a basic human need. Children would like to be accepted, respected, and liked by others. The school has the role of finding ways through which peer acceptance can be gained. Children deeply resent situations in which they are shown to be inept, awkward, and objects of ridicule. Those who feel good about themselves are more at ease socially and are more assured in what they are attempting to do. To earn peer respect, children must achieve something that will gain for them this status.

The Urge to Contest

This is tied up with the prior urge and refers to the child's desire to match physical skill and strength with his or her peers. It means the urge to wrestle, to hit a ball, to pit skills, to overcome others, to take joy in competition, and to be successful in situations of stress.

The Urge for Physical Fitness and Attractiveness

Every teacher should understand how eager boys and girls are to be physically fit and to possess bodies that are agile and attractive. To be strong is both a joy and a glory. It gives dignity and confidence. Teachers should understand the humiliation suffered by the youngster who is weak, fat, crippled, or abnormal in any way.

The Urge for Adventure

This is the urge to participate in something different, romantic, or unusual. Children desire to climb to the heights, to be able to do something adventuresome, and to participate in activities that in themselves are interesting. It means a change from the old stuff to something new and exciting.

The Urge for Creative Satisfaction

Children like to try out different ways, experiment with different materials, and see what they can do creatively. Finding different ways of expressing themselves physically satisfies the urge for creative action. But it must be their ways, their ideas, and their accomplishments.

The Urge for Rhythmic Expression

Basically, all boys and girls enjoy rhythm. The program should offer a variety of rhythmic activities that all should learn well enough to give them many pleasant, satisfying hours. Rhythm is movement and children like to move. Dancing, rhythmic movements, rope-jumping skills, bouncing and dribbling ball routines, and similar activities are pleasing, exciting experiences, under competent leadership.

The Urge to Know

Young people live in a world of curiosity. They are interested not only in what they are doing but in why they are doing it. Knowing why is a great motivator. Lasting habits are established only when the individual is convinced that they are worthwhile.

CHARACTERISTICS AND INTERESTS OF CHILDREN IMPORTANT IN PROGRAM PLANNING

The table on pages 13-15 divides the characteristics and interests of youngsters into their respective learning domains. The characteristics and interests, coupled with the implications of the program, offer important considerations in program development. When program and curriculum are being developed, the table of characteristics and interests should be utilized. If an activity is not in line with the characteristics of a certain age group of children, the activity should be considered inappropriate or be modified to

meet their needs better. The implications of the program can take the form of movement experiences appropriate for the age group, pertinent approaches, and relevant instructional methodology.

THE PURPOSES OF PHYSICAL EDUCATION

While the general goal of physical education and, for that matter, all education—well-rounded development of children and youths as responsible citizens—is of a general nature, learning experiences should be provided to help the child attain more definable purposes or objectives. To be judged effective as an educational tool, physical education should help each child to: (1) develop and maintain a suitable level of physical fitness, (2) become competent in management of the body and acquire useful physical skills, (3) acquire desirable social standards and ethical concepts, (4) acquire needed safety skills and habits, (5) enjoy wholesome recreation, (6) acquire a desirable self-concept and an effective self-image, (7) derive personal and educational benefits from the program, and (8) acquire wide experience in a variety of physical education activities.

An examination of basic urges and characteristics of children will show that each of the objectives contributing to total development can be substantiated as meeting some portion of the basic growth and development needs of children.

PHYSICAL FITNESS

Purpose: The physical education program should provide every child with the opportunity to develop and maintain a level of physical fitness commensurate with individual needs.

An appropriate level of fitness is essential to the needs of both individuals and society and should, therefore, be a goal of education. Physical fitness is an important contribution of physical education toward educational goals and is accomplished in no other area of the curriculum.

A person who is physically fit possesses the strength and stamina to carry out daily tasks without undue fatigue and has enough energy left to enjoy leisure and meet unforeseen emergencies. Strength, power, endurance, agility, flexibility, and speed are qualities of fitness that should be developed through planned, progressive activity. An individual should be free of disease and remediable handicapping disorders. This implies a need for special examination and follow-up procedures.

Another concern of fitness is meeting the urge to have an attractive physique. The program can help by giving attention to posture and a balance of muscle-fat proportions. Proper nutritional habits can be reinforced.

Characteristics and Interests of Children

KINDERGARTEN AND FIRST GRADE

CHARACTERISTICS AND INTERESTS	*IMPLICATIONS FOR THE PROGRAM*
Cognitive Domain	
Short attention span.	Change activity often. Short explanations.
Is interested in what the body can do. Curious.	Movement experiences. Attention to educational movement.
Wants to know. Often asks why about movement.	Explain reasons for various activities and the basis of movement.
Expresses individual views and ideas.	Allow children time to do their own thing. Expect problems when children are lined up and asked to perform the same task.
Begins to understand the idea of teamwork.	Allow some opportunity for situations that require group cooperation. Discuss the importance of such.
Sense of humor expands.	Insert some humor into the teaching process.
Highly creative.	Allow opportunity for students to try new and different ways of performing activities. Sharing ideas with friends encourages them to create.
Affective Domain	
No sex differences in interest.	Same activities for both boys and girls.
Sensitive and individualistic. The I concept is very important. Accepts defeat poorly.	Need to teach taking turns, sharing with others, learning to win, lose, or be caught gracefully.
Likes small group activity.	Use entire class grouping sparingly. Break into small groups.
Sensitive to feelings of adults. Likes to please teacher.	Give praise and encouragement.
Can be reckless.	Stress sane approaches.
Enjoys rough-and-tumble activity.	Include rolling, dropping to the floor, et cetera, in both introductory and program activities. Stress simple stunts and tumbling.
Seeks personal attention.	Recognize children through both verbal and nonverbal means. See that all have a chance to be the center of attention.
Loves to climb and explore play environments.	Provide play materials, games, and apparatus for strengthening large muscles. Examples are climbing towers, wagons, tricycles, jump ropes, miniature Challenge Courses, and turning bars.
Psychomotor Domain	
Noisy, constantly active, egocentric, exhibitionistic. Imitative and imaginative. Wants attention.	Vigorous games and stunts. Games with individual roles (hunting, dramatic activities, story plays). Few team games or relays.
Large muscles more developed, game skills not developed.	Challenge with varied movement. Specialized skills of throwing, catching, bouncing balls.
Naturally rhythmical.	Music and rhythm with skills. Creative rhythms, folk dances, singing movement songs.
May become suddenly tired but soon recovers.	Use activities of brief duration. Provide short rest periods or include activities of moderate vigor.
Eye-hand coordination developing.	Give opportunity to handle objects such as balls, beanbags, hoops, et cetera.
Perceptual-motor areas important.	Give practice in balance, unilateral, bilateral, and cross-lateral movements.
Pelvic tilt can be pronounced.	Give attention to posture problems. Provide abdominal strengthening activities.

SECOND AND THIRD GRADES

CHARACTERISTICS AND INTERESTS	*IMPLICATIONS FOR THE PROGRAM*

Cognitive Domain

Still active but attention span longer. More interest in group play.	Active big-muscle program, including more group activity. Begin team concept in activity and relays.
Curious to see what they can do. Love to be challenged.	Offer challenges involving movement problems. More critical demands in stunts, tumbling, and apparatus work.
Interest begins in group activities and the ability to plan with, and for, others is developing.	Offer group activities and simple dances that involve cooperation with a partner or a team.
Enjoys challenges and will try anything.	Offer new activities in the form of challenges. Also place emphasis on teaching safety and good judgment in these matters.

Affective Domain

Likes physical contact and belligerent games.	Dodgeball games and other active games. Rolling stunts.
Developing more interest in skills. Wants to excel.	Organized practice in a variety of throwing, catching, and moving skills, as well as others.
Becoming more conscious socially.	Teach need to abide by rules and play fairly. Teach social customs and courtesy in rhythmic areas.
Likes to do things well and to be admired for accomplishments.	Begin to stress quality. Provide opportunity to achieve.
Essentially honest and truthful.	Accept their word. Give opportunity for trust in game and relay situations.
Does not lose willingly.	Provide opportunity for children to learn to accept defeat gracefully and to win with humility.
Sex differences are still of little importance.	No separation of sexes in any activity.

Psychomotor Domain

Capable of rhythmic movement.	Continue creative rhythms, singing movement songs, and folk dances.
Improved hand-eye and perceptual-motor coordination.	Give opportunity for handling hand apparatus. Movement experiences. Practice in perceptual-motor skills (right and left, unilateral, bilateral, and cross-lateral movements).
Becoming more interested in sports.	Introductory sports and related skills and simple lead-up activities.
Sports-related skill patterns mature in some cases.	Emphasize practice in these skill areas through simple ball games, stunts, and rhythmic patterns.
Reaction time is slow.	Avoid highly organized ball games that require and place a great premium on quickness and accuracy.

FOURTH, FIFTH, AND SIXTH GRADES

CHARACTERISTICS AND INTERESTS	*IMPLICATIONS FOR THE PROGRAM*

Cognitive Domain

Wants to know rules of games.	Include instruction on rules, regulations, and traditions.
Knowledgeable about and interested in sports and game strategy.	Place emphasis on strategy rather than on merely performing a skill without thought.
Questions the relevance and importance of various activities.	Explain regularly the reasons for performing activities and learning various skills.
Desires information about the importance of physical fitness and health-related topics.	Include in lesson plans brief explanations of how various activities enhance growth and development.

Affective Domain

Enjoys team and group activity. Competitive urge is strong.	Include many team games, relays, and combatives.
Interest in sports and sports-related activities is high.	Offer a good variety of sports in season, with emphasis on lead-up games.
Little interest in the opposite sex. Some antagonism may arise.	Offer coeducational activities, with emphasis placed on the individual differences of all participants, regardless of sex.
Acceptance of self-responsibility. Strong increase in the drive toward independence.	Provide on a regular basis leadership and followership opportunities. Involve students in evaluation procedures.
Intense desire to excel both in skill and physical capacity.	Stress physical fitness. Include fitness and skill surveys both to provide motivation and to check progress.
Sportsmanship a concern for both teachers and students.	Establish and enforce fair rules. Along with enforcement include an explanation of the need for rules and cooperation if games are to exist.
Peer group important. Wants to be part of the gang.	Stress group cooperation in play and among teams. Rotate team positions as well as squad makeup.

Psychomotor Domain

Steady growth. Girls often grow more rapidly than boys.	Continue vigorous program to enhance physical development. Stress correct movement fundamentals and posture.
Muscular coordination improving and skills are better. Interested in learning detailed techniques.	Continue emphasis on the teaching skills through drills, lead-up games, and free practice periods. Emphasize correct form.
Differences in physical capacity and skill development.	Offer flexible standards so all may find success. In team activities, match teams evenly so their skill levels are less apparent.
Posture problems may appear.	Include posture correction in activity and special posture instruction and emphasis on the effect body carriage has on the self-concept.
Girls (sixth) may show signs of maturity. May not wish to participate in all activities.	Need to have consideration for their particular problems. Encourage participation on a limited basis, if necessary.
Boys in the sixth grade are rougher and stronger.	Keep sexes together for skill development but separate for competition in certain rougher activities.

The physical fitness emphasis should be educational, so each child is stimulated to carry on physical activity beyond the scope of the school program. A long-range goal is the maintenance of an appropriate level of fitness of individuals in later years.

Each child should experience regular, vigorous activity based on good physiological principles. Each lesson should contribute to fitness.

Attention to fitness yields good values. Bones become stronger, musculature improves, and ligaments and tendons are strengthened to meet the demands of activity. The cardiorespiratory system, as well as other body systems, derives benefit from activity. The benefit from regular and systematic exercise in the prevention of heart disease should be established early in the child's education.

Fitness has other values. Peer status and relationships, particularly for boys, are better for those possessing suitable levels of physical fitness. Desirable fitness levels seem to lead to better social adjustment and a more buoyant, action-minded, optimistic personality. In turn, the child is better able to reach his or her academic potential.

The relationship between physical fitness and motor learning must be understood. The common elements of physical fitness—strength, endurance, and power, among others—are needed for optimum skill development.

MOVEMENT EXCELLENCE—USEFUL PHYSICAL SKILLS

Purpose: The physical education program should be so structured that each child can be-

come competent in management of the body and acquire useful physical skills.

To be graceful and skillful is a much sought-after goal. Movement education is defined as the process through which movement competency is obtained. The hierarchy of skill development rests on a base of competency in body management, from which evolve fundamental skills plus special and game skills. The following chart shows the relationship.

Competency in Body Management

Body management involves the body as a whole in meeting the challenges of the environment. Learning to manage the body leads to greater control over gross movements and increased skill.

The child controls his or her body in personal space, in general space in relation to others, in flight, and suspended on apparatus. The child needs to learn what the body can do and how he or she can manage the body effectively in a variety of movement situations and challenges. This understanding is termed *body awareness* and incorporates Laban's concepts of space, time, force, and flow.

Good body management practices also are related to the body's resistance to the forces of gravity. Children should be able to manage their bodies with efficiency and ease of movement and to accept good standards of posture and body mechanics as meaningful constituents of their movement patterns.

In addition to posture and body mechanics, another consideration in body management skill is perceptual-motor competency. The principles and concepts basic to perceptual-motor competency are strongly related and are applicable to body management. Good motor control requires sufficient neurological control and development, which can be aided by attention to perceptual-motor approaches and activities. Perceptual-motor approaches considered relevant to physical education include those that give attention to balance,

**Continuum of Program Development
Based on Skill Development and Attainment**

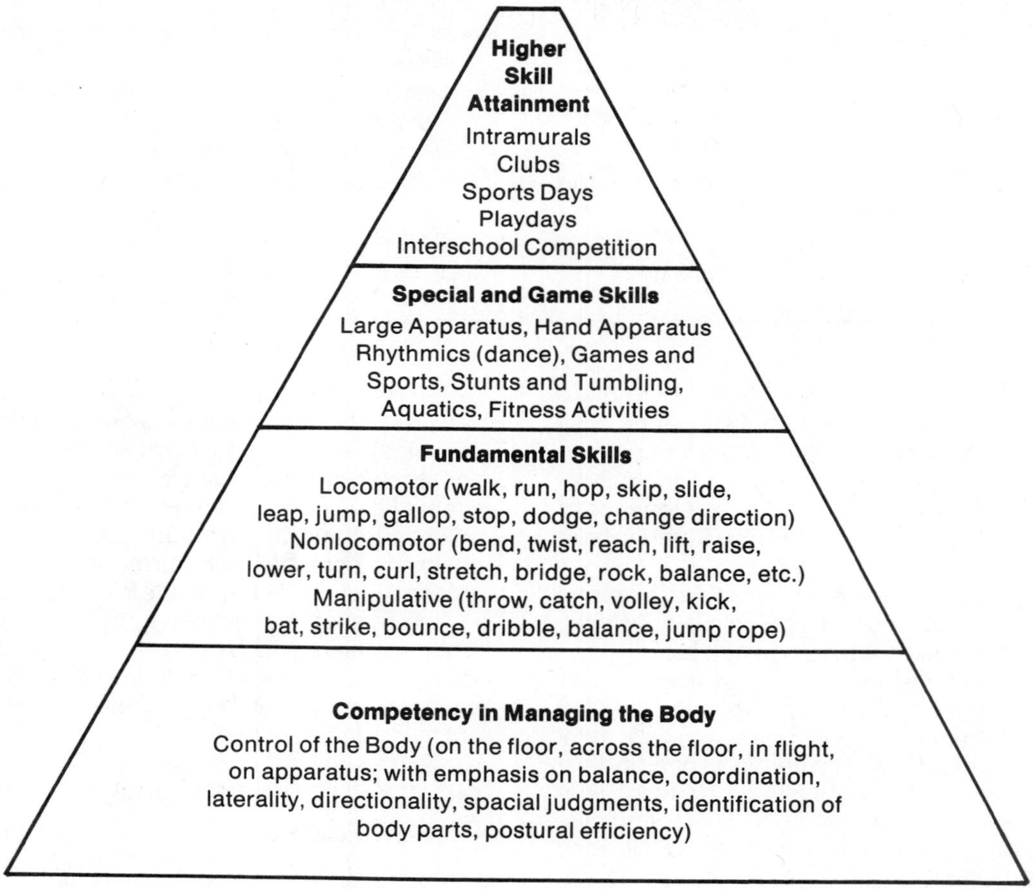

**Higher
Skill
Attainment**
Intramurals
Clubs
Sports Days
Playdays
Interschool Competition

Special and Game Skills
Large Apparatus, Hand Apparatus
Rhythmics (dance), Games and
Sports, Stunts and Tumbling,
Aquatics, Fitness Activities

Fundamental Skills
Locomotor (walk, run, hop, skip, slide,
leap, jump, gallop, stop, dodge, change direction)
Nonlocomotor (bend, twist, reach, lift, raise,
lower, turn, curl, stretch, bridge, rock, balance, etc.)
Manipulative (throw, catch, volley, kick,
bat, strike, bounce, dribble, balance, jump rope)

Competency in Managing the Body
Control of the Body (on the floor, across the floor, in flight,
on apparatus; with emphasis on balance, coordination,
laterality, directionality, spacial judgments, identification of
body parts, postural efficiency)

coordination, laterality, directionality, awareness of space, and knowledge of the body and its parts.

Fundamental Skills

Fundamental skills are those utilitarian skills a child needs for living and being. They are crucial to success in living and serve the child in maintaining his or her relationship to the environment.

This group of skills often is labeled the *basic* or *functional skills.* The term *fundamental skills* is preferable to the others, because the skills are the normal and characteristic attributes necessary for the child to function in the environment.

For purposes of discussion and application, it is convenient to divide the skills into three categories. It is possible for a child to isolate and perform a selected skill from a category. On the other hand, a movement pattern may include a number of skills from different categories. For example, a child may shake his or her body (a nonlocomotor activity) while running across the floor (a locomotor skill). Or, he or she may combine throwing and catching a beanbag (a manipulative skill) with hopping in various directions (a locomotor skill).

Locomotor Skills

Locomotor skills are those used to move the body from one place to another or to project the body upward, as in jumping and hopping. In addition to jumping and hopping, locomotor skills include walking, running, skipping, leaping, sliding, and galloping.

Nonlocomotor Skills

Nonlocomotor skills include those that the child does in place or without appreciable movement from place to place. Nonlocomotor skills are of a wider variety and are not as clearly defined as locomotor skills. Nonlocomotor skills include bending and stretching, pushing and pulling, raising and lowering, twisting and turning, shaking, bouncing, circling, and others.

Manipulative Skills

Manipulative skills are defined as those skills employed when the child handles some kind of a play object. Most of these skills involve the hands and feet, but other parts of the body can be used, also. Manipulative objects lead to better hand-eye and foot-eye coordination, particularly for tracking objects in space.

Propulsion (throwing, batting, kicking) and receipt (catching) of objects are important skills to be developed by using beanbags and a variety of balls. Rebounding or redirecting an object in flight, such as in volleyball, is another area of manipulative skills.

Control of an object such as a wand or a hoop also has a place in manipulative activity. Manipulative activities are the basis of the related game skills so important in the lives of children.

Specialized Skills

These are the skills related to the various sports and other physical education areas such as apparatus, tumbling, dance, and specific games. In the development of specialized skills, progression is obtained through planned instruction and drills. Many of the specialized skills have critical points of technique, with a heavy emphasis on conformance.

Deciding which specialized skills are to be taught for use in specific activities depends on the local interests and the cultural heritage of the schools. Specialized skills should be taught in a range of levels, and some arrangement for valid progressions can be employed.

THE SOCIAL GOAL

Purpose: The physical education environment should be such that children can acquire desirable social standards and ethical concepts.

Physical education is concerned with the development of desirable standards of ethical behavior and social and moral conduct. Many terms, such as *good citizenship* and *sportsmanship,* can be used to describe this goal. A child needs to be able to get along with others, to take turns, to win and lose gracefully, to work for the common good, and to respect the personality of his or her fellows. Every child should learn to exercise self-control in activities that are often emotionally intense. The child can be helped to act wisely, with courage and resourcefulness, in situations of stress.

Basically, the teacher's task is to help children discover the difference between acceptable and unacceptable ways of expressing feelings and to guide behavior on this basis. This should include establishing and enforcing limits of acceptable behavior.

A respect for the spirit as well as the letter of the rules should be developed. Physical education stresses the sportsmanlike viewpoint of sharing with the officials the responsibility for seeing to it that contests are played according to the spirit of the rules. As life is governed by social rules, customs, and traditions, so are the activities on the playfield and gymnasium floor. Fair play, honesty, and conformance with the rules can be stressed through physical activities.

Although youngsters need to learn to cooperate, they also must learn to compete with integrity, an important quality in today's society. They must learn to live with competition but to be fair about it.

Social growth occurs only when people communicate with, work with, compete against, or in some way relate to other people. The progressions in the lesson should provide an opportunity not only for the child to experiment and practice alone but also to work with a partner and to cooperate as a member of a group.

Social learning is influenced markedly by the child's unconscious imitation of peers, heroes, siblings, parents, and teachers. Imitation is part of the hidden curriculum, and it embodies the maxim that what one does speaks louder than what one says. The likes and dislikes of the teacher, the pressure of the group, and the power of the teacher influence the child's total development.

Physical education can help children develop a respect for facilities and equipment and an appreciation of the opportunity that is theirs through physical education.

While social goals are stressed throughout the program, a heavy emphasis should be placed on social learning in the kindergarten through third-grade levels. Adjusting to life in the school community is a goal of first importance.

SAFETY SKILLS AND ATTITUDES

Purpose: In physical education, children should acquire safety skills and habits and develop awareness regarding safety for themselves and for others.

The school has both a legal and a moral obligation to provide a safe environment. Safety must be actively sought. The teacher should carry out the activity only in a safe environment.

Instructional procedures in any activity should include the safety factors, so children may know and follow safe procedures. Good supervision is necessary to guide children in safe participation. Stress should be placed on safety for oneself and safety for others. Children need to understand that, because of the nature of physical education activities, rules are needed and safe procedures must be followed. Recklessness must be avoided, but, on the other hand, care must be taken not to create fear and overcautiousness.

Water safety is an important facet of physical education. Although few elementary schools provide opportunities for aquatic instruction, students should be encouraged to seek swimming instruction. Communities should look for cooperation among the various agencies to see that a swimming and water safety program is a part of the educational opportunities for children.

WHOLESOME RECREATION

Purpose: Through physical education, children should be stimulated to seek participation in,
and derive enjoyment from, wholesome recreation during their leisure time.

The basic considerations of wholesome recreation are these. First, the child must derive enjoyment in his or her play, so he or she will seek further participation. The child should become sufficiently skilled in a variety of activities, so his or her play meets with success and, hence, becomes more enjoyable. Second, a rational basis of play through orientation to varied activities that have carry-over possibilities should be established. Included should be a wide variety of games suitable for small groups and sports activities adapted to local situations. Rules, regulations, and strategies are of value in adapting school activities for leisure play. Ball activities are particularly important. Third, teaching children how to play should be considered. If children have good social rapport with partners and in small groups, the necessary social basis for play may already have been established. Children usually play with other children, not alone. Experience in the improvising or modifying of games in the school setting gives children ideas about directing their own play. Emphasizing the rules of currently popular activities is also helpful.

The inclusion of fitness concepts in leisure activity is essential. Jogging is to be encouraged, since it is valuable both as a personal and a family activity. If the youngster is interested in working out, he or she should have the knowledge necessary to develop his or her own level of fitness. The school can provide direction to families for home-constructed fitness and play areas.

In essence, play is play because it is a voluntary activity. Many children need little encouragement to play. However, for the children to derive the greatest benefit from play, the school can provide them with the background they will need to make the most of their playtime.

SELF-IMAGE AND SELF-CONCEPT

Purpose: Each child should develop a desirable self-concept through relevant physical education experiences.

The self-concept is the sum total of the image a child has of himself or herself. Not only is it important for the teacher to understand the learner, the learner should understand himself or herself, because self-concept is a powerful influence on human behavior. Individual self-concepts determine how children react in situations and how they interpret the actions of others.

The self-concept a child develops is vital in the learning process. It can make it possible for him or her to learn, or it can hinder or block his or her ability to learn. If a child can feel that he or she belongs, that he or she is loved and respected, and that his or her successes outweigh his or her failures, he or she is well on the way toward establishing a desirable self-concept. Nothing succeeds with a child like success. Security gives children a basis for the development of healthy personalities.

The diagram below illustrates how success and failure are related to the development of self-concept. The child approaches a task and, if there is failure, two undesirable directions are indicated. If there is success, certain effects can carry over positively to the self-concept.

By stressing comfortable physical experiences well within the emotional, physical, and intellectual limits of the child, physical education can do much to bring out the child and give him or her an opportunity to be expressive, to be creative, and to achieve success. Children retain substance from those experiences that hold personal significance and personal value. In the educational process, every child needs to feel that he or she is of value and worthy of respect in his or her own right.

The ability to move with grace, confidence, and ease can help a child to regard himself or herself in a favorable light. Achieving satisfactory (to them) levels of skill competency and fitness traits are factors that can make children feel good about themselves and become more assured in whatever they are trying to do. It is becoming more evident that the child's conception of self is partially related to the skills he or she has. The child needs to feel he or she is a worthwhile, functioning, learning person.

Peer comparisons should be kept on a healthy basis. Some competition among peers is desirable, but it should not limit the number of successful experiences available to the children. Doing one's best and recognizing that everyone cannot be a winner can help prevent *intense* frustration, even though there is usually some frustration in losing.

Achieving success in physical education can be especially valuable to the child who performs at a lower academic level but can achieve his or her measure of success in physical activities. This may be the place he or she blossoms.

PERSONAL VALUES

Purpose: Each child should acquire personal values from physical education that enable him or her to live a fuller and more productive life.

In addition to the many values for the child inherent in physical education experiences already mentioned, some others merit discussion. Developing creativity and imaginative play should be a sought-after goal. The urge for creative satisfaction is strong in all children but especially among kindergarten and primary-level youngsters. An opportunity to be creative should be a part of most, if not all, activity presentations. Versatility in movement and in play can be furthered only when the child is given occasions to "do his or her own thing." Too often, the teacher goes from one activity to the next without allowing the children to develop ideas of their own.

Children should be able to find satisfaction and release in play. The relief from tension and anxiety through play activity is important to the future well-being of the child. The simple ability to have fun, take part freely, and express joy in physical activities has high value in adjustment. It often is said that the school with an effective physical education program is a happy school.

Perhaps this concept should be taken further, and educators should teach children something about relaxation, about how to recognize tension, stress, and anxiety and what can be done to alleviate these feelings. Such instruction could include practice in controlling the body for relaxation and the elimination of tension. As living becomes more complicated and tense, the need for tension-reducing measures through physical activities grows.

The Child and His or Her Self-concept

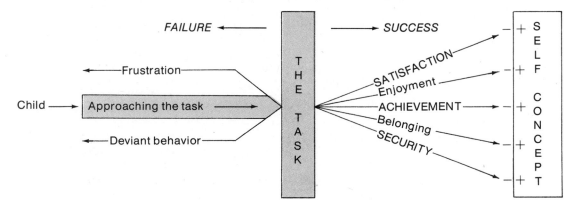

Some thinking processes can be exercised by the use of stipulated movement sequences that require auditory input, visual input, or memory recall. A number of contrasting terms can be introduced or reinforced through application with movement experiences, including up/down, forward/backward, fast/slow, and so on.

The development of reasoning powers can be furthered when the child is challenged with problem-solving experiences. The child should be encouraged to work out his or her own solutions to set problems, by using logical reasoning steps such as experimentation, selection, and consolidation.

Physical education should challenge levels of the child's conceptual thinking. Good teaching should concern itself with conceptual understanding, since it is an important ingredient in thinking. Selected concepts related to movement are important inclusions in the teaching process in physical education. Guidance should be given to the child as his or her conceptual thinking grows and as he or she makes personal interpretations along the way. The child should show versatility in movement, and he or she should show a basic understanding of his or her own movement.

WIDE EXPERIENCE

Purpose: Each child should acquire wide experience in a variety of skills, games, and fitness activities relevant to his or her level of competence.

With the change in high school physical education to more specialized and intensive development in selected activities, the burden of providing broad orientation to skills, games, and fitness activities falls to the elementary school program. In high school, the student increasingly will have choices and options as to how he or she can meet the activity requirements. Broad preparation and orientation in the elementary school years can provide a background upon which such choices can be made.

No longer can one expect to find in the specialized high school activity courses skills taught in the elementary school. So, the process becomes broad preparation in the elementary school program and specialization in the secondary program. Also, the elementary school program should stimulate interest in physical education courses, which are elective subjects in many senior high schools.

HOW CAN THESE PURPOSES BE FULFILLED?

Basically, to fulfill these purposes and objectives, physical education must be a planned de-velopmental program that takes into consideration the urges, needs, and interests of every child in the school. The following attributes characterize such a program.

1. There must be movement. Movement is the basis of physical education, and one way to judge the quality of a physical education program is to evaluate the degree of movement that each child experiences. Children learn by doing, and skills are taught by repetition. If there is practice, for example, in bouncing a ball, a child profits in direct relationship to how many times he or she is able to handle and bounce the ball. What the child does to the ball is important, but what the ball does to the child is more important.

   Physical education implies activity. The child profits little from an experience that is characterized by too much standing around, waiting for equipment to be arranged, listening to lengthy explanations by the teacher, and standing by while one or two children dominate the activity.

2. The selection of the activities must be based upon the needs and interests of the youngsters and geared to their level. This means preplanning and not just a "what-shall-we-do-today" type of program. If desirable learning is to result, the activities must be suited to the developmental level of the children.

3. The activities need to be directed and conducted in such a manner that the purposes of physical education can be fulfilled. The values of physical education are not gained automatically or accidentally. Physical activities need to be skillfully taught by understanding teachers who like children and have faith in their own ability to help children develop. This implies the application of educationally sound methods of teaching and the evaluation of the teaching process in terms of progress toward goals. Values in activity are not inherent in the activity but rather in the method of presentation. If a child is to achieve his or her potential in skilled movement, he or she must have quality teaching.

   Mere participation does not mean the child will attain the developmental level he or she should. This cannot be stressed too strongly. If quality of movement is to result, the learning process must be directed toward this end.

4. A program with balance in activities is more likely to accomplish the purposes of physical education and provide value for every participant. However, fitness qualities and the acquisition of skills are crucial, central, and unique to physical education. If the program is to contribute its best value to the general education of children, these goals must be re-

alized. These goals, however, should not be emphasized to the point of excluding other phases of the program.

Many diverse activities should be included and taught through a variety of methods. The concept of variety also applies to acquiring skills and achieving fitness. The goals children achieve from various facets of the pro-

gram are not the same. Different activities and approaches offer something of interest to all and allow for success and achievement in some phase of the program.

The program should offer something for every child. The next chapter enlarges on these concepts and discusses program planning.

Three

Developing a Physical Education Curriculum

Curriculum development should reflect the views of a wide variety of the school's personnel. A sound curriculum guide that is used by teachers throughout the school's district can serve as a foundation for the curriculum and its improvement. If the school system lacks a written curriculum guide, it could be asked how it would be possible to evaluate the effectiveness of both the teachers and the curriculum.

The guide should serve as a tool for teachers. In some cases, teachers have seen it to be a restriction that destroys effective and spontaneous teaching. It is difficult to understand this thinking, since the guide should be changed and re-evaluated each year, with both the teachers' comments and the introduction of new ideas. The written curriculum should be a guide for the coming year. It should help teachers avoid falling into old and boring patterns, deterring teachers from teaching a lesson because it is easy and familiar and minimizing the selection of activities simply because they are popular with the children.

The writing of the curriculum should not be for the express purpose of developing a completely new approach to physical education for youngsters; that would be an almost impossible task. In most cases, developing a new and innovative program requires a great deal of experience and expertise. Ultimately, a new approach should be researched and evaluated before it is declared to be the best answer to the needs of the children. Ideas that have been developed and found effective in the past should be integrated into the program guide. Gather ideas and activities, select those that make it possible to meet program objectives, and organize them systematically. The

following guidelines are important for establishing an educationally sound program that will help both teachers and students reach desired objectives.

GUIDELINES FOR CURRICULUM DEVELOPMENT

1. The major purpose of writing a curriculum is to give direction and continuity to the physical education program. If, for example, some activities are found to be inappropriate for a certain age group of children, they might be deleted from the next year's program. On the other hand, if youngsters are found to be exceptionally able in one of the objective areas, it might mean that less emphasis should be placed there and more time spent in areas where children are below par in performance. In all cases, the curriculum guide should be written with enough detail to provide direction and still retain a reasonable degree of flexibility.

2. The activities selected for the curriculum should be based on their potential to help teachers and students reach expected objectives. For example, selection should consider vigorous physical activity that promotes growth and physical fitness as well as instructional sequences that lead to a broad range of movement competencies and skill development. To further emphasize this point, it could be stated that the number-one program guideline should be developing a curriculum that ultimately provides for physical fitness and fundamental motor skills.

3. Teachers and administrators also should be

aware of the hidden curriculum when they write guides. The hidden curriculum contains a wide range of learnings that occur in the affective domain. For example, many attitudes, emotions, and social mores can be learned by students from what they perceive about the ways in which the school environment is organized. An attempt should be made to arrange the learning environment so that both the hidden and the formal, written curriculum facilitate the purposes of the program.

4. Planning should be done on a district-wide basis, with attendance by a representative sample of the population the guide is to serve. Teachers and supervisors from all levels should be included, so the scope and sequence can be carried out and the various program levels can be integrated. The program should be under the direction of a competent staff member, since the director coordinates the group's efforts as well as the implementation of the program. The curriculum committee should be ongoing in its function, meeting periodically to review and upgrade the program.

5. The curriculum should be broad and balanced. It should include a wide variety of activities and experiences to be taught through different approaches. The elementary school years are a time for experimentation, practice, and decision making about activities that are personally enjoyable for the children. The more activities a youngster can experience, the greater chance he or she has to experience success. It should be a premise of the program that it offer something for everyone.

6. The program should be of such a nature that it can be enjoyed by all youngsters, regardless of their individual skill levels. Activities that require a high level of skill are likely to be inappropriate for a large group of students. Along the same lines, consideration for exceptional children and others with special needs should be included in the planning of the program.

7. Program activities should be selected to make possible the achievement of desirable behavioral changes, associated educational values, and personal benefits. It is true that behavioral changes in children and the values they receive from participation are determined more by instructional procedures than by the program *per se.* However, the selection of activities should be such that the aforementioned changes and values *can* be achieved with appropriate methodology. For example, a program relying chiefly on exercises, games, sports, and relays would do little for the individual child in terms of self-direction, creativity, self-reliance, and individual level of progress.

8. Program content should rest on a foundation of efficient body management and fundamental movement skills geared to the developmental needs of the child. This implies an instructionally oriented program that leads toward a goal of reasonable movement competency and concept acquisition. The program should set aside sufficient time for skill instruction and practice. Practice must be systematically organized and based on good concepts of motor learning. The emphasis on instruction can be intense enough to lead to a reasonable mastery of skills.

9. Activities should be organized so that they can be presented to youngsters in a sequential fashion, arranged in meaningful progression beginning with easy experiences and proceeding to the more difficult. The curriculum also should reflect progression from grade to grade, within each grade, and within activities. The curriculum should ensure that the activities are taught in an orderly fashion rather than in a random, hit-or-miss fashion.

10. It is desirable to offer extended opportunities for children who are interested and skilled in particular areas. Intramural programs, sports days, playdays, special interest clubs, and recreational opportunities after school should be implemented and considered from the viewpoint of a total program for youngsters. Obviously, if these experiences are available for children who are interested and capable, the program could place more emphasis on developing skills and offering successful experiences for all children.

11. Activities in the program should be scheduled in line with the seasons of the year. Sports, in particular, are more readily accepted when they are offered during the time of the year when high schools, colleges, and professionals are actively involved in the same sports.

12. Specialized interests can affect the development of curriculum. For example, winter games might be inappropriate in the South and Southwest, and year-round swimming programs might be impossible in the North. Certain popular recreational activities should be considered when adults in the area participate in them regularly.

13. Climate is a factor that determines the extent of outdoor play. Some traditional outdoor activities may need to be modified to provide for a broad program of instruction indoors. Extremely hot weather and sunshine along the southern borders of the country have a

marked effect on what activities can be scheduled and how they can be taught.

14. School health instruction and physical education are separate areas of instruction and should be so regarded in the elementary school curriculum. The practice of teaching health instead of physical education during inclement weather may result in a dislike of health instruction. Time allocated for physical education should not be shared with health instruction. Each subject has its own place in the curriculum. This premise in no way rules out incidental health instruction within the physical education curriculum. Health and physical education instruction can complement and reinforce each other but not to the extent of sharing a designated time allotment.

15. The physical education program must have a climate of positive administrative support if it is to achieve its educational goals for children. The administration has an obligation to provide competent direction; efficient instruction; adequate indoor and outdoor facilities, including outdoor covered areas, hard-surfaced areas, and well-drained playing fields as needed; adequate budget for equipment and supplies; suitable storage space for supplies and equipment; dressing rooms and facilities for showers; and office or other space for the specialist. The degree of administrative support has a profound effect on the program.

16. Changes and trends in junior and senior high school physical education programs can have a significant effect on the makeup of the elementary school program. For example, at the present time, high school programs have limited requirements and place much emphasis on offering a broad spectrum of elective activities to students. The elementary school program needs to provide students with a background of activity, so they have the knowledge and experience to select activities later in their educational careers.

PLANNING THE CURRICULUM

The following sequence of steps should help teachers and administrators develop a program that is educationally sound. The steps may be interchangeable in some cases, but the sequence presented here is based on an orderly and logical progression.

Understanding the Basic Urges of Children

The people developing a curriculum should have a good understanding of the urges that motivate children. A program that runs contrary to these urges is doomed to mediocrity. Thus,

teachers should have an internalized standard that allows them to analyze activities for youngsters from the viewpoint of what urges the activities fulfill. For a review of the basic urges of children, as well as how each urge manifests itself in visible behavior, the preceding chapter can be consulted.

Identifying the Characteristics and Interests of Children

The characteristics and interests of children should be analyzed and compiled. Whereas basic urges are typical of all children in general, interests and characteristics are much more specific to various age groups. These may be affected by the geographical location or sociological background of the children. For example, children who live in poor areas may have different needs than those from upper-middle-class areas. Through careful consideration of research done by child development professionals and keen observation of the children in the program, a meaningful and useful list of characteristics and interests can be developed. In the preceding chapter, the authors compiled a list of the interests and characteristics that includes the implications for the program for each.

Developing Program Objectives

After the basic urges, characteristics, and interests of children have been gathered and the data have been analyzed, the foundation has been laid for developing meaningful program objectives. The objectives provide an overall statement of what the instructor and/or the institution would like to accomplish. Stated in another way, the question is "what will the program contribute to its participants?" These statements of direction are sometimes called goals, sometimes major instructional elements, and oftentimes objectives. Regardless of terminology, they serve as guidelines for the rest of the planning process. It would seem clear that meaningful objectives are possible for both the learner and the teacher when they are based on the urges and the basic qualities of individuals. This step is critical, since the objectives form evaluative criteria for the selection of activities and ideas that are to be included in the total curriculum.

Selecting Activities

Activities should be selected that enhance and aid accomplishment of the objectives of the program. It should be emphasized that the activities must be selected on the basis of what they can do for children rather than because they are fun or because the kids will enjoy them. In many cases, fun is a judgment based on the adults' feelings toward an activity. Children enjoy activities because teachers help to make the activities enjoyable and because the enjoyable activities meet their needs.

For example: if one of the objectives of the program is to develop a level of visual-motor coordination, then activities should be selected that do that. The larger the number of activities gathered, the more novelty and variation there will be in the approach to developing this objective.

Organizing Activities into Sequences or Units

After the many and varied activities have been selected, some scheme for organization should be carried out. A good approach is to organize the ideas and activities into units or sequences. The activities in the units should be organized in a continuum, from of the easiest to the most difficult, based on the judgment of teachers. As the ideas are taught and field-tested on the children, the order may be changed according to the demonstrated abilities of the students. The fact that the activities are organized in progression will (1) make it easier to ensure that the children will meet success rather than failure at the start of the unit, (2) ensure that safety and liability factors have been met due to the presentation of activities in proper sequence, and (3) aid teachers in finding a starting point for sound instruction by proceeding

through the activities until a significant number of students find difficulty performing adequately.

Another technique often valuable is developing pertinent instructional procedures that will remind the teachers using the unit to remember various points, such as safety hints, how to teach for quality as well as quantity, initial organization of equipment, ways to expand the activity for variety, and crucial factors to emphasize for proper motor-skill development.

Determining Broad Program Areas

At this point in the procedure, broad program areas can be established. These areas then can be allotted percentages of the program's time that are based upon the drives and needs of the students. This determination also answers the questions of parents and administrators about the program's emphasis.

The suggested percentages are to be regarded as approximate and subject to some adjustment. However, each area must have its proportionate share of instructional time, and too much shifting will destroy the balance of the program.

The percentages allotted to various program areas should reflect the characteristics of the children in the various grades. For example, depending on the emphasis and philosophy of the

Elementary School Physical Education Program Emphasis (Grade-Level Emphasis and Suggested Yearly Percentages)

KINDERGARTEN-PRIMARY GRADES	GRADES			
	K	1	2	3
Movement experiences and body mechanics	40	35	35	22
Rhythmic activities	30	25	25	22
Apparatus, stunts, tumbling	15	20	20	22
Simple game activities and relays	15	20	20	17
Sports skills and activities				14
Administration and testing				3
Fitness routines and activities				*
Swimming and water safety				†

INTERMEDIATE GRADES	4	5	6
Movement experiences and body mechanics	9	9	6
Rhythmic activities	18	18	18
Apparatus, stunts, tumbling, combatives	18	18	18
Simple game activities and relays	17	12	10
Sports skills and activities	35	40	45
Administration and testing	3	3	3
Fitness routines and activities	*	*	*
Swimming and water safety	†	†	†

*A short period of time (5-6 minutes) at the beginning of each class period usually is devoted to fitness activities. This does not affect the proportionate distribution of the other major elements of the program in a year's schedule, and for this reason, no specific percentages are included.

†Swimming and water safety is a recommended area of instruction for elementary school children. The amount allocated to this area would depend upon the facilities and instruction available. If swimming is included in the school program, it should reduce proportionately the percentage of time allotted to other activities.

program, there would probably be a larger percentage of time devoted to movement experiences at the first-grade level than the sixth-grade level. The table on page 25 lists the percentages recommended to offer a broad, balanced program. In a later step, the yearly plan can be analyzed to determine whether the weeks devoted to each area are in line with the time allotted for them.

Allocating Units of Activity According to Grade Levels

The broad allocations of activities developed in the preceding section are, in effect, a statement of the philosophy of the program. The next step is to list the specific units to be included within a category and specify the appropriate grade-level placement for each. The children's capability and

Suggested Allocation of Specific Activities According to Grade Level

	K	1	2	3	4	5	6
Movement Experiences and Body Mechanics	K	1	2	3	4	5	6
Fundamental movement—locomotor, nonlocomotor	K	1	2	3			
Magic ropes				3	4	5	6
Fundamental movement—manipulative	K	1	2	3	4	5	6
Beanbags	K	1	2	3	4	5	6
Yarn or fleece balls	K	1	2	3			
Playground balls (8½ inch)	K	1	2	3	4	5	6
Small balls (sponge, softball size)				3	4	5	6
Paddles and balls				3	4	5	6
Hoops	K	1	2	3	4	5	6
Jump ropes	K	1	2	3	4	5	6
Parachutes	K	1	2	3	4	5	6
Wands				3	4	5	6
Rhythmics (see chart page 199)	K	1	2	3	4	5	6
Rope jumping to music				3	4	5	6
Apparatus	K	1	2	3	4	5	6
Bounding boards	K	1	2				
Balance boards	K	1	2	3	4	5	6
Balance beams	K	1	2	3	4	5	6
Benches			2	3	4	5	6
Climbing ropes	K	1	2	3	4	5	6
Climbing frames	K	1	2	3	4	5	6
Individual mats	K	1	2	3			
Jumping boxes	K	1	2	3	4	5	6
Ladders and bars		1	2	3	4	5	6
Stunts and Tumbling	K	1	2	3	4	5	6
Pyramids					4	5	6
Combatives					4	5	6
Simple Games	K	1	2	3	4	5	6
Relays			2	3	4	5	6
Story games, poems, quiet play	K	1	2				
Sports Skills and Activities				3	4	5	6
Basketball				3	4	5	6
Flag football, speedball					4	5	6
Indoor and outdoor hockey					4	5	6
Soccer				3	4	5	6
Softball (mostly skills)				3	4	5	6
Track and field					4	5	6
Volleyball					4	5	6

readiness are the major considerations in the placement of specific activities at various levels. However, since a large number of activities are presented, some arbitrary decisions concerning grade placement must be made by the teacher or the supervisor. Adjustments upward or downward with respect to age level can be made later on an empirical basis after a period of class trial.

Another factor enters the picture. A skilled specialist usually has more success in achieving higher skill levels with youngsters than someone untrained in the area who has had limited preparation in physical education. However, the chart on page 26 can be used in program planning. Basically, it states that a particular unit should be part of a specific age-level program. The elements to be included, the approaches to be followed, and the instructional procedures to be utilized are discussed in later sections under the separate activity presentations.

PHYSICAL EDUCATION PROGRAMS FOR GRADE LEVELS

The material that follows presents descriptions of the type of program recommended for each grade level. Correlation should be evident between the recommended programs and (1) needs of children, (2) program guidelines, (3) broad category percentages, and (4) grade placement of specific activities.

The Physical Education Program for the Lower Grades

Some general comments concerning the program in the lower grades are made at the beginning, but the bulk of the program's description is presented under each grade level. The greatest change today is found in the program of the lower grades, which features individualism, self-direction, exploration, creativity, and movement theory. Perceptual-motor theory also has strong application up to the third grade. A suggested kindergarten program is presented, but, if there is no kindergarten, its function as an introduction to physical education needs to be shifted to the first grade.

One great change in today's programs is that the games program is now the frosting on the cake and is no longer the main dish. This is reflected in lower allocations to games and also in the format of the daily lesson plan, in which the game becomes an added feature rather than the focus of instructional procedures.

The increase in the number of recommended activities is apparent, broadening the program to the point where it is difficult to include all desirable activities to the extent that a reasonable level of competence can be developed.

The Kindergarten Program

There is a greater awareness of the characteristics of the learner at this level, a fact that results in more attention being focused on the learning process and the child. Play-type activities are highly important in the kindergarten program, since young children are naturally active and learn best when they enjoy what they are doing. For some children, kindergarten is a medium of adjustment, an attempt to ease the difficult transition from the security of the home to the uncertainty of the educational world. A child comes from a home where he or she is the center of attention to the classroom where he or she is just one of a group of children.

The large majority of suggested activities for kindergarten children are individual in nature, centering on movement experiences (40 percent) and rhythmics (30 percent). Some emphasis is given to simple stunts (15 percent) and to simple games (15 percent). While there is accent on cooperation with others, there is little emphasis on group or team play. The types of activities are such that the child has good opportunity to explore, try out, and create. He or she learns to express himself or herself through movement and continues to develop the skills of verbal communication (speaking and listening).

In movement, the child begins to lay the foundation of body management and fundamental skills, with attention to laterality, directionality, balance, and coordination. He or she seeks to further eye-hand coordination with simple manipulative activities. His or her fitness needs are taken care of within his or her movement experiences. Perceptual-motor competency theory has strong application to methodology on the kindergarten level.

The First-Grade Program

The first-grade program embraces the same four general areas as the kindergarten program, but with some shift of emphasis to the apparatus, stunts, and tumbling areas. The largest portion of the first-grade program is devoted to movement experiences (35 percent), which include attention to physical development through selected movement. As in kindergarten, there is emphasis on fundamental skills and efficient management of the body, stimulated through challenges to elicit a wide variety of movement. Locomotor skills are of prime importance, with some application to non-locomotor movements. Manipulative skills are stressed, with a foundation being laid for the important play skills of throwing and catching. Beanbags, yarn balls, and playground balls (8½ inches in diameter) are important tools for experimentation. Hoops and jump ropes also are included.

Good body mechanics and posture are important, with attention to specific movements leading to the development of the arm-shoulder girdle and the abdominal region. Perceptual-motor factors are an important consideration in conducting activities for the first-grade child.

The rhythmic program (25 percent) should provide an extension of movement to rhythm, reinforcing and relating to educational movement experiences. The creative aspects of rhythmic activities have a prominent place in the first grade. In more structured numbers, singing movement songs are stressed more than folk dance, although both are included.

The apparatus, tumbling, and stunts program is of material import (20 percent). Each school should have enough equipment, including climbing ropes, climbing frames, fixed or movable ladders, balance beams, bounding boards, benches, and individual mats, to have a well-rounded program. Floor and mat stunts give the children an opportunity to react to directions and achieve a specific movement pattern. Methodology in apparatus, stunts, and tumbling should be based on educational movement principles, seeking a wide and flexible response to the tasks.

The games program (20 percent) has its proportional place in the program but has yielded its traditional importance to movement experiences. In addition to the usual gymnasium-playground games for this level, story games, poems, and dramatic play have places.

The Second-Grade Program

In essence, the second-grade program follows the pattern of the first-grade program, with the exception of the introduction of simple relays based primarily on locomotor skills. Children are still encouraged to move in their own way, to experiment, and to explore, but specific patterns of coordination begin to appear. Continued practice in the locomotor, nonlocomotor, and manipulative skills (35 percent) is provided. Children also should be made aware of and encouraged to develop good posture. A few simple forms of systematic exercise may be introduced but not to the extent of the more formal fitness routines.

The rhythmic area (25 percent) moves toward more emphasis on folk dances, but action songs, creative rhythms, and basic rhythms receive good coverage. Ball bouncing and dribbling to rhythm are well accepted on this level, since the children are beginning to improve their manipulative competency.

Apparatus, stunts, and tumbling (20 percent) as an area receive continued attention. Youngsters begin to take pride in achievement and lay the basis for future activities.

Play is increasingly structured into some forms of group games (20 percent). The basic locomotor and ball-handling skills are combined with lines, circles, and other patterns to provide group experiences and an introduction to team play. This concept is furthered by the introduction of simple relays. The seeds of sports interest, which comes into its own in the third and fourth grades, are found in the late second-grade program.

The Third-Grade Program

Movement experiences (22 percent) still have an important function on this grade level. However, the emphasis on body management is secondary to improvement of fundamental skills, particularly of the manipulative type. It is here that the child begins to find himself or herself in skills. The third-grade program provides a transition between the simplified activity program of the lower grades and the sports interests and more advanced emphasis of the intermediate level.

The third-grade level is suggested for the introduction of the more precise fitness routines, such as exercise programs, circuit training, and the like. It is here that the child begins to absorb the concept that a systematic effort is necessary for him or her to realize good dividends from his or her fitness potential.

In the rhythmic area (22 percent), a transition from the casually organized dances of the previous grades to the concept of dancing with a partner is stressed as the children have opportunities to coordinate their own movements more precisely with those of their partners. The application of rhythm to ball skills and rope jumping is an important outlet for creativity, in addition to the retention of some emphasis on fundamental locomotor skills done to rhythm.

The stunt area (22 percent) becomes more complicated and more precise, with increased demands on balance, strength, and coordination. There is a shift toward more inclusion of what are regarded as the standard tumbling stunts. Apparatus work should stress a wide variety of movements built upon the foundation of the previous grades.

Simple games and relays (17 percent) become increasingly important for challenging the child with the newly acquired skills.

A major difference in activity for the third grade is the introduction of simple sports skills and activities (14 percent). The child uses a reasonable technique to roll, bounce, kick, bat, dribble, throw, and catch balls. Attention is directed to specific sports skills in softball, basketball, and soccer. Selected lead-up games provide a useful laboratory for the evaluation of the achievement of these simple skills.

An allocation for administration and testing is provided (3 percent). This permits introduction of some fitness or other testing. A fitness test for orientation purposes can be given late in the school year, a procedure that prepares the children for more formal testing in the fourth grade.

If swimming and water safety are to be included in the school program, the third grade is a likely level for this introduction. Ten percent of the allotted yearly time probably should be apportioned to this activity, with the time spent in the other activities reduced proportionately.

The Physical Education Program for the Intermediate Level

The principal change in the intermediate grades is a shift to more emphasis on specialized skills and sports activities. Football, volleyball, hockey, and track and field are additions to the basketball, soccer, and softball instruction introduced in the third grade.

More emphasis is placed on physical fitness and developmental activities. Physical fitness testing usually is introduced in the fourth grade. Fitness tests of the AAHPER and the President's Council on Physical Fitness and Sports reflect this practice.

Lesser emphasis is placed on movement experiences, which are concentrated on manipulative activity. Some perceptual-motor factors still are important, with attention paid to laterality and directionality. However, concentration should be on the dominant side (arm or leg), so that a functional skill for a sport—pitching, for example—can be developed.

Percentage allocations for both the rhythmic program and the program of apparatus, stunts, and tumbling are stable (18 percent) throughout the intermediate grades. Emphasis for movement experiences drops off in the fifth grade. Games decrease in percentage allocation from the fourth to the sixth grade, with the opposite being true for the sports area. Combatives form a new activity area for the intermediate grades, and, if possible, swimming should be a consideration.

The Fourth-Grade Program

The fourth grade sets the basis for the two grades that follow. Progression is the key word for the intermediate level, and the suggested program for the fourth grade must be the basis for the progressions at the fifth- and sixth-grade levels.

The first full experience with fitness activities, including a testing program, begins at this level, although some routines were introduced in the third grade.

More specialized skills are taught in all areas, particularly the selected sports (35 percent). A gradual involvement in the sports program is possible as the student learns the needed skills and participates in lead-up games in the fourth grade to the point in later grades at which he or she takes part in the sport itself, modified for the elementary grades.

In rhythmics (18 percent), a beginning in dance steps is made. Most of the dances specify partners, and social factors become important. Rope jumping to music also is emphasized.

The apparatus, tumbling, and stunts program (18 percent), continues the progressions of earlier grades. There is a strong shift to the standard tumbling items. Combatives are new.

Simple games and relays (17 percent) become more challenging in serving as a laboratory for the learned skills. Selected games show a balance between individual and team emphasis.

Swimming and water safety can be included at this level. Some movement experiences (9 percent) are retained, primarily in the manipulative area.

The Fifth-Grade Program

The fifth-grade program is much like that of the fourth grade, except for an increased percentage allotment for the sports program (40 percent) taken from the allotment for simple games and relays (12 percent). Increased interest in the sports program should be evident, since fifth graders generally have become eligible for participation in the intramural program.

Both movement experiences (9 percent) and fitness activities are continued at about the same pace as in the fourth grade. In rhythmics (18 percent), additional dance steps are introduced and dances become more intricate.

There is little change in the area of apparatus, stunts, and tumbling (18 percent). Stunts, naturally, become more challenging and are more difficult to achieve. More emphasis is centered on form.

The Sixth-Grade Program

Sports (45 percent) are the largest increment in the sixth-grade program. When the child finishes his or her sixth-grade program, he or she should have had experiences in regular or modified versions of basketball, softball, soccer, volleyball, flag football (touch), speedball, hockey, and track and field. He or she should have an extended opportunity in these activities in the intramural and interschool programs.

In rhythmics (18 percent), the waltz and square dance are new endeavors. A more adult touch is apparent in the rhythmic program. Rope jumping is still an important rhythmic tool.

Other areas are continued, with lesser emphasis on simple games (10 percent). Swimming can be a consideration, depending upon the overall school plan.

The sixth-grade program can be viewed as a transitional curriculum from the elementary to the junior high school program.

Planning the Yearly Program for Grades Kindergarten through Two

Planning the year's program for youngsters can be considered from a number of angles. With kindergarten through second-grade children, some teachers prefer a weekly schedule that reflects the broad activity percentages. The table that follows shows approximations of minutes based on the percentages of time allotted to each of the broad program areas. It illustrates a week of activities based upon 150 minutes per week to teach physical education. The specified minutes do not agree precisely with the percentages as listed, since the percentages are an approximation. Adherence to this weekly schedule does ensure that a broad, balanced variety of activities is included.

Progression can be incorporated into the instruction through the scheduling of specific activities on a weekly or a biweekly basis. Movement experiences could be scheduled for Mondays, Wednesdays, and Fridays. A specific activity, such as handling yarn balls, could be introduced on a Monday, with review and expansion of the instructional sequences on the following Wednesday and Friday. This is the antithesis of having a different movement experience each day. Similar planning can be accomplished in other areas. Some activities can be carried into a second week, as necessary.

A weekly schedule like the one that follows could be reproduced by ditto or mimeograph to provide a handy form for planning. The instructor could fill in the specific activities for each week, based on the suggested list on page 26 and on the recommended activities in rhythmics, games, apparatus, stunts, and tumbling. This schedule should be outlined for the school year so that there is some assurance that all of the activities will be taught. Oftentimes, teachers avoid the yearly plan and end up repeating certain units or running out of time to provide broad coverage of all activities.

In some cases, teachers prefer to set up a program around specific objectives. For example, two weeks might be devoted to perceptual-motor skills or creativity through movement. The organizational scheme would include selecting activities that enhance the chosen objective. Once the activities were selected, sequence and progression would have to be developed. This is a more difficult and time-consuming task, but some teachers find it a more meaningful one.

Planning the Yearly Program for Grades Three through Six

For the upper grades, some teachers prefer a more structured approach to organizing the yearly program. Many teachers have had experience with weekly units of activities and found the weekly approach superior to a daily schedule on which different activities are taught on different days. In a weekly unit, an activity is carried on over an entire week. There can be combinations of activities, games for variation, and flexible programs on the last day of the week. It might be mentioned that some physical education specialists have had good success with this approach for the primary grades, and the advantages of the approach outweigh its negative aspects.

First-Grade Program

ACTIVITY CATEGORY	PERCENTAGES (YEARLY)	TOTAL MINUTES (WEEKLY)	
Movement experiences	35	52.5	
Rhythmic activities	25	37.5	
Apparatus, stunts, and tumbling	20	30.0	
Simple games	20	30.0	
Totals	100%	150.0	minutes

Example of Proportional First-Grade Weekly Program

MONDAY	TUESDAY	WEDNESDAY	THURSDAY	FRIDAY
Movement 18 minutes	Rhythms 18 minutes	Movement 18 minutes	Rhythms 18 minutes	Movement 18 minutes
Games 12 minutes	Apparatus/Tumbling 12 minutes	Games 12 minutes	Apparatus/Tumbling 12 minutes	Choice Games and/or Apparatus/Tumbling 12 minutes

The advantages of the weekly plan are several. First, the teacher needs only one lesson plan for the week. The lesson plan should include sufficient material for the week. The teacher's objective in the lesson is to move the children along the path of learning at a comfortable rate. In a sense, what cannot quite be covered one day can wait until the next.

A second point is that little orientation is needed after the first day. Safety factors, instructional techniques, stress points, and concepts need only brief review in the day-to-day plan during a week. Equipment needs are quite similar from day to day.

The third advantage is that progression and learning sequences are quite evident, since both the teacher and the children can see progress. The teacher can begin a unit with the basics of an activity and progress to a point at which instruction and skill practice are again indicated. This procedure provides needed review and adapts the activity to the group. The sequence of activity for each day is built upon that of the preceding lesson. If the teacher has difficulty or needs to investigate an approach, he or she has time between lessons to clear up questionable points. Children also can be referred to resource material to study the activities for the next day or to clarify a point of difficulty from the past lesson.

The objection some have to a weekly unit program is that it does not have enough variety, and children tend to become tired of the same activities over a long period of time. Activities should be spaced so that not more than two or three weeks at the most of the same type of activity are practiced in successive weeks. The games and relay area can provide a change of pace when this seems to be indicated.

Some other combinations in weekly planning are in vogue. One is to have one type of activity on Monday, Wednesday, and Friday of a week, and another type on Tuesday and Thursday. Another is to reserve the games and relays for Friday of each week, utilizing the first four days for more sequential material. Both of these arrangements show good elements of progression.

The least desirable plan is to have a different program each day of the week, burdening the teacher with five different lesson plans.

In developing the yearly program, the table that illustrates the various emphases placed on the major program areas should be consulted (page 25). This table of percentages then is converted into weekly units. For example, fitness activities should be included in every lesson and should be scheduled for 36 weeks. For example, in the fourth grade, 35 percent of instructional time for the school year is devoted to sports. This would convert to roughly 13 weeks. Sports units then could be spread over the year, to total 13 weeks, and could include basketball, football, hockey, soccer, softball, track and field, and volleyball. The remaining areas then should be developed in the same manner.

Ultimately, as the curriculum becomes more organized, in addition to providing the activity emphasis for the week (lesson focus), introductory activities and fitness development activities also can be incorporated into the yearly plan. As in the lesson focus, this listing of the types of introductory and fitness activities helps to assure variety and broad coverage. The yearly plan on page 32 offers an example of parallel listing of introductory activities, fitness development activities, and the lesson focuses. A briefer plan would list only the lesson focuses. Note that the closing activity of the lesson is not included in the yearly plan, since this is subject to choice and is flexible.

SWIMMING AND WATER SAFETY

Swimming and water safety have been mentioned as an important adjunct to the physical education program. The emphasis should be on drownproofing, simple survival techniques, and basic swimming skills. Overcoming the children's fear of water should be emphasized throughout the instruction.

The community is responsible for making swimming instruction available to *every* child, since full participation is the goal. The school may cooperate in and supplement outside programs, but, in order to reach every child, a school-sponsored program may be necessary. The crux of the matter is that some agency must get the job done, and, if the school is involved in the program, a number of administrative decisions need to be made.

First of all, who is to participate? Should all children be given the opportunity for swimming instruction regardless of their ability? For some of the more skilled swimmers, participation in the program may result only in a pleasant diversion from class time. If only the nonswimmers or those with marginal skills are to take part, the situation merits several considerations, since some problems need solutions. Alternative activities and supervision need to be provided for the students who remain in school, since it is obvious that the classroom teacher cannot be both with the swimmers at the pool and with those remaining on the school premises. Also, careful handling is indicated so that those who are selected for the swimming program are not stigmatized for being inept and low skilled.

Material support must be forthcoming from the administration, since the swimming program usually involves busing and special fees. Sometimes,

Program Activities for the School Year
(Grades Three through Six)

WEEK	INTRODUCTORY ACTIVITY	FITNESS DEVELOPMENT ACTIVITY	LESSON FOCUS ACTIVITY
1	Orientation activities and games		
2	Fundamental movements and stopping	Teacher-leader activities	Football (week 1)
3	Move and assume pose on signal	Teacher-leader activities	Beanbags
4	Walk, Trot, and Sprint	Teacher-leader activities	Soccer (week 1)
5	Partner Over and Under	Teacher-leader activities	Soccer (week 2)
6	Run, Stop, and Pivot	Circuit Training	Paddles and balls
7	European Running	Circuit Training	Long rope jumping
8	European Running with variations	Circuit Training	Hockey (week 1)
9	Bend, Stretch, and Shake	Exercises to music	Playground balls
10	Marking	Exercises to music	Rhythms with equipment
11	Locomotor and manipulative activity	Exercises to music	Magic ropes
12	Movement varieties	Exercises to music	Hoops
13	New leader warm-up	Astronaut Drills	Benches
14	Group Over and Under	Astronaut Drills	Wands
15	Simple games	Astronaut Drills	Basketball (week 1)
16	Follow the leader	Astronaut Drills	Basketball (week 2)
17	Bend, Stretch, and Shake	Grass Drills and partner resistance	Recreational activities
18	Bridges by Three	Grass Drills and partner resistance	Hockey (week 2)
19	Jumping and hopping patterns	Grass Drills and partner resistance	Parachute activity
20	Milk Carton Fun	Challenge Course and isometrics	Climbing ropes
21	Simple games	Challenge Course and isometrics	Relays
22	Run, Stop, and Pivot	Challenge Course and isometrics	Balance-beam activities
23	European Running	Squad-leader exercises	Lummi sticks, schottische
24	Walk, Trot, and Sprint	Squad-leader exercises	Rhythms (Tinikling)
25	Locomotor movement variations	Squad-leader exercises	Individual rope jumping to music
26	Move, perform task on signal	Continuity Exercises	Stunts, tumbling, and combatives (week 1)
27	Partner Over and Under	Continuity Exercises	Stunts, tumbling, and combatives (week 2)
28	Combination movement patterns	Continuity Exercises	Jogging
29	Follow the leader	Continuity Exercises	Soccer (week 3)
30	Simple games	Animal movements	Softball (week 1)
31	Creative warm-up	Animal movements	Softball (week 2)
32	Stretching exercises and light-pace running	Stretching exercises and light-pace running	Track and field (week 1)
33	Stretching exercises and light-pace running	Stretching exercises and light-pace running	Track and field (week 2)
34	Four-corner movement	Walk, Trot, and Spring	Stunts and tumbling (week 3)
35	European Running with apparatus	Parachute exercises	Tug-of-war ropes
36	Squad-leader movement	Parachute exercises	Balance-beam activities with manipulative equipment

ALTERNATE LESSON	INTRODUCTORY ACTIVITY	FITNESS DEVELOPMENT ACTIVITY	LESSON FOCUS ACTIVITY
1	Simple games	Animal movements	Softball (week 1 for grades 3-4)
2	Substitute from any previous lesson	Substitute from any previous lesson	Flag football (week 2)

parents are expected to take care of the fees, but this poses a problem for students whose parents cannot, or will not, take care of this expense.

It is evident that facilities must be available for a swimming program to take place. Cooperation with the municipal recreation department, the YMCA and the YWCA, nearby colleges, and similar agencies can solve the facility problem. In some cases, weather permitting, the program can utilize outdoor facilities during the month of May, a lax period before heavy summer use. The pool should have the means to raise water temperatures to comfortable levels.

Portable pools, available from commercial sources, are one possible solution. The pools usually can be set up in a day's time. Pools vary in size. The program can make good use even of small pools, for example, a pool 24 by 24 feet, with a constant depth of 3 feet. Pools can be placed in one location for four to six weeks and moved to another location for a new group of students. Some states are recognizing the utility of portable pools and are authorizing the installation of both water valves and drainholes connected with a sewer system in new school construction.

Certified instruction is a must, and the instructional procedures should follow the Red Cross program or another valid format. It is suggested that the swimming program begin in the third grade, with a second program scheduled in either the fifth or the sixth grade.

THE PHYSICAL EDUCATION LESSON

The physical education lesson for a particular class period should grow out of a unit of instruction or be based on activity progressions. It is important that each lesson follow a written plan, especially for a beginning teacher. Written lesson plans vary in form and length, depending upon the activity and the background of the teacher. A written lesson plan ensures that thought has been given to the lesson before the children enter the activity area. It helps the teacher avoid spur-of-the-moment decisions and losing the unity and progression of the material. This does not mean a teacher cannot modify the lesson, but it does keep the central focus and purpose of the lesson intact.

Progression is more likely to occur in the forthcoming lesson when the teacher uses the previous lesson plan for a guide. In future years, the teacher also can refer to the collection of lesson plans for suggestions and improvements.

Portable Swimming Pool. Courtesy Port-A-Pool (Universal Bleacher Co.) and Los Angeles City Schools.

A lesson can be divided into the following parts, each of which is discussed.
1. Introductory activities (1-3 minutes).
2. Fitness development activities (4-8 minutes).
3. The lesson focus.
   a. Review of previously presented materials.
   b. New learning experiences.
4. Closing activity (2-5 minutes).

Except for the lesson focus, any of the parts may be omitted. In some cases, fitness development activities serve as introductory work.

The Introductory Activity

The introductory activity accomplishes in the lesson just what its name implies. Children come to the physical education class eager for movement, and the first part of the lesson is designed to meet this sheer appetite for movement. Once this is satisfied, the lesson can proceed toward the achievement of its specific objectives. A secondary purpose of introductory activity is to serve as warm-up activity that prepares the children's bodies for the activities that are to follow. While serving as introductory activity, the movement patterns also have fitness implications and should be related to and coordinated with fitness development activities, particularly for younger children in grades kindergarten through two.

Generally, some type of gross, unstructured movement is used for introductory activity, usually based on locomotor movements. An enterprising teacher can employ many different activities and variations effectively as introductory activity. Examples are included in chapter seven.

Quality in movement should be a consideration in introductory activities but not to the point of overshadowing the basic purposes of the activities. Correction, coaching, and, at times, direct instruction can help children achieve movement of reasonable quality during introductory activities, but these should not be overriding considerations.

The Fitness Development Activities

The second part of the lesson devotes time to fitness development activities, which are defined as activities that have as major objectives the physical development of the body and the various qualities of physical fitness (strength, power, endurance, agility, flexibility, and speed).

The lesson plan should include stated dosages, so a series of lessons shows increased loading. Physical fitness activities as they are to be included in the physical education lesson are discussed in chapter eight.

The Lesson Focus

The lesson focus is the heart and the meat of the lesson. Presented in it are the learning experiences growing out of the overall instructional plan.

The first consideration is to review and work with the activities of the preceding lesson until a satisfactory level of learning has been reached. In some instances, the entire lesson focus could be taken up with a repeat of the work of the preceding lesson.

After sufficient time has been given to the review, the new learning experiences are presented. Skill instruction, participation in a rhythmic activity, and a progression of stunts and tumbling are the kinds of things that are in the lesson focus.

The amount of time to be devoted to the lesson focus is determined by the time demands of the other three parts of the lesson. After introductory and fitness development activities have been done, the remainder of the time less that needed for the closing activity can be devoted to the lesson focus.

The Closing Activity

The closing activity can take many different forms. The lesson may be completed with a game that utilizes the skills under development in the lesson. Or it may emphasize the fun aspect, finishing up with a game or another activity that may be unrelated to the lesson focus. In either case, a pleasurable feeling should be gained from the day's experiences.

The closing activity also can include an evaluation of the lesson accomplishments that stresses and reinforces important technique points and concepts. Suggestions for future action in other lessons can be entertained.

A consideration in closing the lesson is returning equipment, apparatus, and supplies to their proper storage places. Definite assignments should be given, and student responsibility should be emphasized. Squads under the direction of leaders can take care of storing the equipment.

In some lessons, the closing activity may be minimal or it may be deleted entirely. This might be the case when a game or other activity as the focus of the lesson demands as much time as possible.

The Design of the Written Lesson Plan

Each physical education lesson should be based on a written lesson plan. The lesson plan should contain all the information necessary to provide a high-quality learning experience, including expected outcomes, progressions, means of organization, stress points, and reminders to the teacher. Following a well-structured lesson plan helps to make teaching a confident experience and provides unity, completeness, and depth to the movement experiences in the lesson.

A lesson plan can serve a single lesson, but it is more practical when used over several lessons.

During any one lesson, the instruction proceeds as far as educationally feasible and takes up again at that point for the next lesson. The same introductory activity, with some changes, and the same fitness development activity are repeated during the series of lessons. This simplifies the task of constructing the lesson plan and saves the teacher time.

The teacher may deviate from the lesson plan when the learning potential can be enhanced with changes in sequence or the addition of relevant material that was not evident when the lesson was planned.

A lesson plan format should be adopted that allows for the interchange of plans within a school district. If an adopted format is available, a supervisor can issue lesson plans for his or her district more readily.

The authors have had good success with this format, and it presents a workable and effective instrument for guiding the instructional process. The format contains the following kinds of information.

General Information

Name of school, classroom or class involved, date and activity are included.

Arrangement of the Necessary Supplies and Equipment

A list of materials that indicates the specific numbers needed of each item is presented, along with a description of the initial arrangement of what is to be ready before the class enters.

Lesson Evaluation

During and after the lesson, the teacher should note what was covered and with what success. The teacher should make notes to himself or herself for directions for future lessons.

Some teachers may question the feasibility of writing out lesson plans, saying that it takes too much time and effort and that it is not really needed. But a lesson plan need only be precise enough to be an effective guide for the learning experiences. It need not be long. The length depends upon the background of each instructor. Beginning teachers need to provide more detail than more experienced instructors. A lesson plan should be understandable as a functional tool. Some teachers may need only a word or a phrase to suggest an idea or a procedure, while others may need more written directions.

Description of the Lesson Plan

The lesson is divided into four activity parts—introductory activity, fitness development activity, lesson focus, and closing or game activity. Each of these areas should be further developed into the following parts for maximum teaching effectiveness—movement experience and/or content, organization and teaching hints, expected student objectives and outcomes, and notes and references.

Under the heading of movement experience and content should be included the amount of time allotted for the activity and a written description of the activities to be taught. The description of the activities should be concise and should be ordered in proper teaching progression. The column for organization and teaching hints specifies how the children are to be arranged, the points to be emphasized to offer children a quality experience, and the teaching stress points to emphasize when teaching skills.

The expected student objectives and outcomes column should include objectives from each of the three major domains: cognitive, psychomotor, and affective. These objectives may not be pure in a behavioral sense but should be statements that lend direction and continuity to the program. The outcomes should be a constant reminder to the teacher to teach toward these outcomes, so they will systematically be reached.

Finally, the notes and references column allows space for the teacher to write in comments about evaluation and to refer to a source that offers more in-depth description.

SAMPLE LESSON PLAN

A sample plan for a lesson using paddles and balls at the intermediate level begins on page 36. The plan incorporates the four parts of the lesson.

DEVELOPING UNIT PLANS

In a sense, the weekly lesson plan is a unit plan for the week. However, if an activity is carried on for more than one week, the unit plan should be considered. A unit plan is a sequence of learning experiences planned around a central theme or an area of activity that generally is designed to cover several weeks of work. Conceivably, a unit plan could cover materials for instruction from which lessons could be drawn for a week or less. Since the authors recommend the weekly lesson plan for a week or less of instruction, the unit plan is reserved for longer allocations of instructional time.

The program activities for the school year chart (page 32) includes examples of activities scheduled for more than one week during the school year: flag football (two weeks); soccer (three weeks); hockey (two weeks); stunts, tumbling, and combatives (three weeks); softball (two weeks); track and field (two weeks). In addition, rhythmic activities are scheduled over a number of weeks, but these are identified by individual topics and

Elementary School Physical Education Lesson Plan
Paddles and Balls
(Grades Three through Six)

Supplies and Equipment Needed
One paddle and ball per child
Seven jump ropes
Signs for circuit-training stations

MOVEMENT EXPERIENCE– CONTENT	ORGANIZATION AND TEACHING HINTS	EXPECTED STUDENT OBJECTIVES AND OUTCOMES	NOTES AND REFERENCES
INTRODUCTORY ACTIVITY (2-3 minutes)			
Run, Stop, and Pivot The class should run, stop on signal, and pivot. Vary the activity by having the class pivot on the left foot and on the right foot and increase the circumference of the pivot.	Emphasize correct form in stopping and absorbing force. Make sure students do not cross legs or lose balance while pivoting. Allow a few moments of free practice.	Cognitive: The pivot is used in many sports, such as basketball and baseball. Psychomotor: The student will be able to stop, pivot, and move by the end of the week.	*Dynamic Physical Education*, p. 87 (description of introductory activities)
FITNESS DEVELOPMENT ACTIVITY (7-8 minutes)			
Circuit Training (1) Rope jumping. (2) Push-ups. (3) Agility Run. (4) Arm Circles. (5) Rowing. (6) Crab Walk. (7) Tortoise and Hare (20 steps, alternate). (8) Bend and Stretch.	Establish starting stations and maintain them throughout the unit. Start with 15-20 seconds of exercise at each station, with 5-10 seconds rest between stations. Gradually decrease rest periods and increase exercise periods. Use signals such as "start," "stop," and "move up" to insure quick and effective movement from station to station.	Cognitive: Circuit Training should work all parts of the body, but no two similar parts in succession. Cognitive: The student will be able to describe how overload is achieved (by increasing the length of activity at each station and decreasing the rest between stations). Cognitive: In order that Circuit Training be effective, *quality* exercise must be performed at each station.	*Dynamic Physical Education*, pp. 112-15 (description of Circuit Training)
LESSON FOCUS (15-20 minutes)			
Paddles and Balls (1) Introduce proper method of holding paddle; forehand and backhand grip. (2) Place ball on paddle and attempt to roll it around the edge of the paddle without allowing it to fall off the paddle. (3) Balance the ball on the paddle, using both right and left	Scatter formation. Ping-pong paddles and old tennis balls with holes punched in them work well. Also, one can use the children's hands as paddles and a fleece ball can be used. This is a limited movement activity so break the activity into parts separated by some running, rope jumping, or similarly physically	Cognitive: The student will be able to name five sports in which paddle skills are used. Psychomotor: The student will be able to control the paddle and the ball in a variety of situations. Affective: One way to improve skills is to experiment with different ways of performing them. Discuss the value of	*Dynamic Physical Education*, pp. 264-65 (description of instructional procedures for paddles and balls)

MOVEMENT EXPERIENCE– CONTENT	ORGANIZATION AND TEACHING HINTS	EXPECTED STUDENT OBJECTIVES AND OUTCOMES	NOTES AND REFERENCES
hands as well as both grips while trying the following challenges. (a) Touch the floor with hand. (b) Move to knees and back to feet. (c) Sit down and get back to feet. (d) Lie down and get back to feet. (e) Skip or gallop or do any other locomotor movement. (f) Choice activity. (4) Bounce the ball in the air, using the paddle. (a) See how many times it can be bounced without it touching the floor. (b) Bounce it off the paddle and into the air and catch it with the other hand. (c) Increase the height of the bounce. (d) Kneel, sit down, take other positions (student choice). (e) Choice activity.	demanding activity. Concentrate on control of the ball and quality of movement. Take your time going through activities. Use left hands as well as right in developing the paddle skills.	trying new activities rather than always practicing areas in which we are already skilled. Psychomotor: Set a definite number (5, 10, 15, or 20). Control the ball with this number of bounces. Psychomotor: The student will be able to bounce the ball five times in succession from two selected positions.	
(5) Dribble the ball with the paddle. (a) From a kneeling position. (b) From a sitting position. (c) From a standing position. (d) Move in different directions —forward, sideways, circle. (e) Move using different	If students have a difficult time controlling the ball, it might be helpful to use fleece balls. Allow time for student choice. Give with the paddle.	Cognitive: The angle of the paddle when the ball is struck determines the direction that the ball travels. Cognitive: A paddle gives the student a longer lever with which to strike the ball and thus more force can be applied to the ball, which, in turn, increases its speed. Psychomotor: The	*Dynamic Physical Education,* pp. 264-65 (Description of activities for paddles and balls)

MOVEMENT EXPERIENCE– CONTENT	ORGANIZATION AND TEACHING HINTS	EXPECTED STUDENT OBJECTIVES AND OUTCOMES	NOTES AND REFERENCES
locomotor movements. (f) Exploratory activity. (6) Alternate bouncing the ball in the air and on the floor. (7) Bounce ball off the paddle into the air and catch it with the paddle. (a) Increase the height of the bounce. (b) Perform a Heel Click or a similar activity and catch the ball. (8) Bounce the ball continuously off the paddle into the air. (a) Bounce the ball on the side of the paddle. (b) Alternate sides of the paddle. (9) Partner activities. (a) Begin partner activities with controlled throwing (feeding) by one partner and the designated stroke return by the other. (b) Bounce the ball back and forth. (c) Increase the distance between partners and the height of the ball. (d) Catch the ball on your paddle after throw from your partner, then return throw. (e) Perform stunts while ball is in the air, such as catching ball behind back, under leg, above head, clapping	Partner activities are generally for students with a higher level of skill. Less talented youngsters may find them quite difficult.	student is able to perform three partner activities. Cognitive: Giving with the paddle is necessary if the ball is to be caught effectively. Psychomotor: Make three catches with the dominant hand and three with the nondominant hand. Affective: For partner work to be effective, cooperation is necessary. Discuss the need and importance of working effectively with others. Affective: Proper form is more important than immediate results. Discuss the importance of practicing skills using correct form without undue concern about results. Psychomotor: The feeder will get the ball to the striker on the bounce four out of five times. Psychomotor: The striker will return the ball to the feeder three out of five times.	

MOVEMENT EXPERIENCE– CONTENT	ORGANIZATION AND TEACHING HINTS	EXPECTED STUDENT OBJECTIVES AND OUTCOMES	NOTES AND REFERENCES
hands, clicking heels. (f) Use two balls. (g) Move and keep the balls going; try skipping, hopping, jumping, sliding.			

CLOSING ACTIVITY (5-7 minutes)

Since using paddles and balls is a moderately active skill, play a game that demands running and movement by all students. The following are suggested.

(1) Running Dodgeball	(p. 402)	
(2) Steal the Treasure	(p. 395)	
(3) Addition Tag	(p. 399)	

Dynamic Physical Education: pp. 377-412 (chapter on game-type activities)

---

can be handled feasibly in the weekly lesson format. The unit plan becomes a useful tool in those activities that feature critical progressions as well as related cognitive and affective target outcomes.

Sports units lend themselves very well to unit planning, with the instructional direction based in general on the charts included at the beginnings of the sports chapters. Some selection of lead-up activities and target games is necessary, since more games and materials than can be used usually are presented in the sports chapters. A target game is defined as the selected game that is to serve as the ultimate achievement of the unit. Sideline Basketball (page 460), for example, might be the target game for a unit in basketball at the fifth-grade level. The unit then would be organized so as to develop skill and techniques, so this game can be participated in successfully.

Other focuses could give direction to a unit. A particular kind of skill competency or a set of skills could be the overall goal of a unit. The skills, however, should be tested in a competitive situation, which takes one back to the target game or lead-up activity.

A day-by-day schedule or lesson plan should be formulated for the first week, with subsequent schedules determined on the basis of the progress made by the students.

Skill techniques and drills should dominate the early phases of a sports unit. In other activities, the fundamental skills for the activity should be established and reasonably achieved before more advanced activities are introduced. While the unit gives overall direction, progress is determined by the achievement of the students.

The format of a unit varies according to the activity and the educational thrusts within the unit.

The following format has been proven successful and is described in general terms and directions so that it can be adapted to various situations.

Format of the Unit Plan

General Purposes or Objectives of the Unit

Included here should be a statement in broad terms of what the unit is attempting to accomplish.

Specific or Target Goals

The specific objectives should be constituted so that, when they have been met individually and collectively, the general purpose of the unit has been accomplished.

Cognitive Understandings: These items are measured in terms of the children's part in the lessons and list knowledges and understandings to be acquired by them through the unit.

Affective Domain: What social and ethical concepts are to be an outgrowth of the learning experiences of the unit? What habits and attitudes are to be given attention?

Psychomotor Goals: Skills, techniques, and strategies to be included as parts of the learning experiences should be listed in proper progression as they appear in the unit.

Activity Experiences: In this section are listed the drills, the forms of competition, the formations, the races, the games, and other selected area experiences that contribute to the acquisition of the items under the specific goals listed above.

Facilities and Equipment Needed

List the items necessary for instructional purposes throughout the unit.

Instructional Procedures

Critical instructional procedures should be listed, with attention centered on the important approaches to be emphasized. Necessary safety measures should be stated. Any measures for evaluating the achievement of the specific goals should be identified.

Educational Media

Bibliographical materials for the students' use are to be listed. These should include items needed at the lesson site and those that should be available in the school library.

Materials in the form of pamphlets, mimeographed items, and other paperwork that are to be distributed to the students should be listed.

Audiovisual aids needed for the unit, including projection equipment and media, bulletin board materials, and the like, should be listed.

The Weekly Schedule

The schedule for the first week should be given in enough detail so that lesson plans can be made to conform to the unit sequencing.

The following basketball unit plan utilizes this format and is an example of plans that can be used to facilitate the teaching process.

Example: A Basketball Unit Plan

Grade Level: Fourth-grade boys and girls.
Unit Length: Three weeks.
General Objective of the Unit: The students will develop a basic understanding of the game as well as developing competency in the basic techniques and skills used in basketball.
Specific Goals
Cognitive Understandings: The students will be able to recognize dribbling and traveling violations and comprehend the out-of-bounds rule.
Affective Domain: (1) The students will develop an understanding and sensitivity toward differences in the individual abilities of their peers. (2) The students will value basketball as a team game rather than as an individual sport. (3) The students will learn to value sportsmanship when they compete in lead-up games.
Psychomotor Goals: The students will learn the following skills: Two-hand chest pass, one- and two-hand underhand pass, one-hand set shot, right- and left-hand lay-up shot, right- and left-hand stationary dribbling, right- and left-hand dribbling while moving.
Activity Experiences: The students will participate in the following skill drills: Shuttle Dribbling, Dribble and Pivot, lay-up shooting, Set-Shot Formation. The students will play the following lead-up games: Review End Ball, Birdie in the Cage, Captain Ball.

Facilities and Equipment Needed
1. One junior basketball or 8½-inch playground ball per student.
2. Six baskets adjusted to 8½-foot and 9-foot levels.
3. Eight hula hoops for Captain Ball.
4. Eight cones for drills.
5. Pinnies of different colors for opposing teams.

Instructional Procedures
1. Concentrate on skill development through the use of many drills to add variety and breadth.
2. Each child should have a chance to practice all skills. This is not possible if too much of the class time is used for playing the game.
3. Be sure all skills are performed with both sides of the body. It is important that children learn to dribble, pass, and shoot with either hand.
4. Use as many balls as possible when using drills for skill development.
5. If practical, the baskets should be lowered to 9 feet. This will allow the children to develop a proper shooting touch instead of throwing the ball at the basket.
6. Many basketball skills do not require the use of basketballs. Other balls, such as soccer and playground balls, can be used successfully.

Educational Media
Textbooks
Cousy, Bob. *Basketball Concepts and Techniques.* Allyn and Bacon, Boston, Mass., 1972.
Dauer, Victor P., and Pangrazi, Robert P. *Dynamic Physical Education for Elementary School Children.* 6th ed. Burgess Publishing, Minneapolis, Minn., 1979.
Wooden, John. *Practical Modern Basketball.* Ronald Press Company, New York, 1966.
Films
Cinema Eight. *Sport Films.* New York.
Eastman Kodak Company. *Basketball Teaching Films.* Rochester, N.Y.

Schedule (First Week)
Monday
    Introductory Activity
        Run and freeze on signal
    Fitness Development Activity
        Astronaut Drills
    Lesson Focus
        Basketball
            Introduce two-hand chest pass
            Introduce stationary dribbling
    Game or Drill
        Shuttle Dribbling Drill
Tuesday
    Introductory Activity
        Run and pivot on signal
    Fitness Development Activity
        Astronaut Drills

Lesson Focus
  Basketball
    Review two-hand chest pass
    Introduce one- and two-hand underhand pass
    Introduce one-hand set shot
Game or Drill
  Set-Shot Formation Drill

Wednesday
  Introductory Activity
    Run and change direction on signal
  Fitness Development Activity
    Astronaut Drills
  Lesson Focus
    Basketball
      Discuss the out-of-bounds rule
      Review stationary dribbling and the one-hand set shot
      Introduce dribbling right- and left-handed while moving
  Game or Drill
    End Ball

Thursday
  Introductory Activity
    Run and jump on signal
  Fitness Development Activity
    Astronaut Drills
  Lesson Focus
    Basketball
      Review dribbling while moving
      Introduce right-handed lay-up shot
      Introduce lay-up shooting drill
  Game or Drill
    Birdie in the Cage

Friday
  Introductory Activity
    Walk, trot, and run on signal
  Fitness Development Activity
    Astronaut Drills
  Lesson Focus
    Review the lay-up shot
    Introduce the Dribble and Pivot Drill
  Game or Drill
    Birdie in the Cage (emphasize quick, short passes)

Four

Organizing and Implementing the Program

Before proceeding with discussions of other aspects of organization, an examination of the patterns of teaching responsibility prevalent in today's school systems is useful. Plans vary from school district to district and, in some cases, vary within school districts.

PATTERNS OF TEACHING

Full Responsibility by the Classroom Teacher with No Consultant or Supervisory Services

This format generally results in a program of poor quality. Often, there is no curriculum, with the teachers deciding week by week what should be taught. The quality of any one part of the program depends entirely on the efforts and dedication of the individual teachers, who may have had one course or perhaps none in the physical education area. No qualified consultant is available to provide regular in-service education.

The tendency is to rely on games and activities the children like, particularly the dodgeball or "sock-em" types. Sports are overstressed.

If this system must be used, a teacher should be assigned to take charge of procuring, storing, and repairing the equipment for the program, at least.

Teaching by the Classroom Teacher with Consultant Aid

In this plan, the classroom teacher basically does the teaching, but there can be demonstration teaching by the consultant. The consultant works primarily with the teacher to improve the teaching process. In-service education is essential. Curricular materials and lesson plan formats should be provided for the teachers. The paperwork demanded of the classroom teacher should be held to a minimum.

Each school visited by the consultant should have a designated staff member responsible for the area. Such responsibilities should include coordinating procurement, care, and repair of instructional supplies and equipment. A major responsibility is supervision of the physical education storage room. All teachers share responsibility for orderliness, with most of the responsibility on the designated individual who provides liaison with the principal and the consultant.

Shared Teaching Responsibilities by the Classroom Teacher and the Specialist

To be successful, a partnership of effort is needed between the two teachers. The logistics of this arrangement are difficult. The specialist may teach the class only one day per week, a method used by districts to extend the umbrella of his or her services. He or she can introduce units and teach the more difficult elements, with the classroom teacher providing follow-up lessons. In a sense, the specialist must act as a consultant, but he or she rarely is given the time to do so. Each time he or she returns, he or she has little knowledge of what has transpired between visits, and the schedule rarely allows for the classroom teacher to enlighten him or her.

A definite lesson plan used by *both* the specialist and the classroom teacher provides better coordination and rational progression. The classroom teacher must observe and participate in the lead-off lesson so that the instruction has sequence. The specialist has difficulty learning personality characteristics of the children; in fact, he or she often has difficulty learning their names.

When the specialist teaches half the time (perhaps Tuesdays and Thursdays), a division of activities taught should be considered. From the district curriculum guide, activity allocations can be made, with the specialist teaching those that are more difficult and challenging. Care must be taken to make sure that the classroom teacher's presentations are not dominated by games and fun.

Teaching by the Specialist

This plan should produce the best results in terms of child progress toward the objectives of physical education. One of the administration's major objections to specialist teaching often is that it requires extra staff and hence extra budget allocation. In some systems, teachers' contracts specify a planning period, which is provided by having the specialist teach the class. The classroom teacher loses a valuable contact with the children and important observational opportunities.

The most prevalent practice is to assign the specialist responsibility for the intermediate classes, leaving the classroom teacher to teach the kindergarten and primary grades. Some districts, however, stress more attention to the lower grades and have reversed these responsibilities.

If a specialist is assigned to teach classes on all levels, he or she usually becomes a full-time member of the staff. He or she also can be given responsibility for the intramural and sports program.

It is difficult to see value in assigning a specialist to more than two schools. If he or she teaches part of the physical education classes in a school, he or she should be given time to provide resource help to those teachers who are teaching the other classes.

The specialist should become an intregral part of the school staff. Principals sometimes voice the objection that the specialist too often teaches in isolation and has little contact with other teachers.

Departmentalized Teaching (Differentiated Staffing) and Other Patterns

Departmentalized teaching involves a rotation of teachers and subject matter among classes on much the same plan as high school scheduling. During the morning (or afternoon), teachers usually work within the self-contained classroom; during the remainder of the day, they switch to departmentalized teaching. This pattern, sometimes called differentiated staffing, usually occurs at the intermediate level.

One teacher with special training or expertise in physical education teaches a succession of classes in physical education, compensated by other teachers teaching other subject matter in much the same manner. The teacher responsible for physical education also could coordinate the intramural and sports program.

This arrangement has value for small schools where there are one or two classes in each grade level. No additional expense for staff is involved, and children are exposed to more teachers and different methods.

A more modest plan is to trade or combine classes. Teachers can trade assignments; for instance, one teacher can teach successive lessons in physical education, while the other assumes responsibility for teaching another subject for both classrooms.

Differentiated staffing recognizes the unique strengths of individual staff members. Specialized positions can be established, and suitable staff can be appointed.

Utilizing Paraprofessionals, Assistants, and Other Teacher's Aides

Many different plans of providing assistance, paid or voluntary, to provide better-quality programs can be considered. The term *paraprofessional* is used to designate a person with some training but not full certification, who is employed to provide some expertise and assistance in the program. The position could be part- or full-time.

A full-time position could combine school and community recreational responsibility in the following fashion for an 8-hour day.

Noontime—supervise the cafeteria and/or noontime recreation or intramurals.

Afternoon school period—provide noncredentialed teaching assistance for physical education classes taught by the regular classroom teacher. Supervise recess.

After school—direct afterschool programs of recreation, intramurals, and sports.

Evening—direct adult or teenage community-type activities in the school.

A half-time position would not include the evening responsibilities. A person with recreation training is ideal for the position. However, unless the paraprofessional is certified, the classroom teacher must be present to provide legal supervision.

The paraprofessional should work with, and under, the classroom teacher to provide expertise in activities in which the average classroom teacher is limited. He or she can take the lead in directing fitness routines; teaching such activities as stunts, tumbling, and apparatus; and providing more effective instruction in track and field, sports skills, and rhythms. The premise of this method is that the teacher and the paraprofessional together can approximate what the specialist can accomplish.

Since most fathers are employed, parental help is almost entirely made up of mothers. Their value is higher in providing assistance in kindergarten and first and second grade, especially in perceptual-motor programs involving station teaching. Regular meetings and in-service education are necessary procedures.

Cross-Age Assistance

Cross-age teaching is defined as the utilization of older children as teacher's aides. The more emotionally mature the student, the better the results. Since most students are concerned with their own academic careers, not a great deal of time can be given by any one student. The use of junior or senior high school students in connection with a study of careers in education has been tried with some success. Orientation and periodic meetings are necessary. One district has found value in holding a weekly meeting each Monday before school begins to provide guidance for the week's program.

Better success is encountered when students can spend a block of time as a type of intern in such an assignment, similar to the practice in distributive education.

Junior high school and carefully selected elementary school students can be integrated with care into the instructional process but mostly as equipment monitors, demonstrators, and for providing incidental assistance. Returns are proportionate to the amount of prior planning time spent with the aides.

Assistance from College Education Students

A plan of mutual benefit to school districts and teacher-training institutions was initiated by the authors in the school district in Pullman, Washington, and continued by Dr. Pangrazi in his capacity at Arizona State University in conjunction with the Mesa, Arizona, schools and other nearby school districts. Upper-level college students, after sufficient preparation, are assigned blocks of time two or three days per week and function as specialist teachers of physical education with the classroom teacher present to fulfill the school's legal responsibility and assist with difficult problems. The experience runs for a full term or semester at a time and is under the direction of the school supervisor of physical education, who supplies the students with the local curriculum guide and a set of lesson plans. In-service educational meetings are held twice a month, with both school and university staff representation.

The public schools have been most receptive to the plan, since the plan supplies teachers of reasonable quality who are quite enthusiastic and are knowledgeable about the new trends and activities. The experience for the teaching students is invaluable. It is not a substitute for cadet teaching and generally is scheduled at an earlier period in the undergraduate program. Costs to the public school are minimal.

DEFINING RESPONSIBILITY

Fundamental to the success of a physical education program is acceptance by the school community of the idea that physical education is largely a developmental and instructional program that is an important part of the total educational experience of each child. A coordinated effort by the school administration, principals, supervisors, teachers, teacher's aides, custodians, school nurses, parents, and students is needed if the program is to achieve its stated goals. The responsibilities of each are defined in turn.[1]

Responsibilities of the School Administration

1. Determines the direction of the physical education program so that it meets at least statutory regulations.
2. Takes the lead in establishing a positive climate of approval and support of a comprehensive, quality program.
3. Provides facilities, equipment, and instructional supplies necessary for effective operation.
4. Assigns direction of the district program to a qualified staff member.
5. Provides qualified teaching personnel for the program.
6. Establishes a district-wide elementary physical education committee with broad representation, and empowers the physical education committee to make recommendations.
7. Encourages and provides the means for the development of an ongoing district curriculum guide for physical education, an integrated part of the physical education plan for all grades.
8. Provides district-level dissemination of program features to school patrons and general public.

[1]From *Administrator's Handbook, State Elementary Physical Education Guide* (Olympia, Wash.: State Superintendent of Public Instruction, 1973). Dr. Dauer assembled much of this material and edited it under the direction of Howard Schaub, state supervisor of physical education. By permission.

9. Establishes long-range goals for the program and periodically reviews and evaluates the progress toward these goals.
10. Asks for input from physical education staff in planning new construction or remodeling existing facilities.

Responsibilities of the Principal

1. Demands appropriate standards of curricular conformance and continuity, an educationally sound approach, and appropriate student play attire for activity.
2. Provides for effective scheduling of physical education instructional periods to ensure maximum utility of available teaching stations.
3. Provides for, or cooperates in, inventory, purchase, storage, care, and repair of equipment and instructional supplies.
4. Provides for continuous and periodic inspection of facilities and equipment, taking corrective action as needed.
5. Works with the custodial staff in establishing good standards of sanitation and health in physical education facilities.
6. Provides for, and cooperates with, in-service education for those classroom teachers teaching physical education.
7. Accepts or delegates responsibility for free-play periods (recess, noon, before and after school). Maintains a safety program for these play periods, with proper supervision and rules of conduct.
8. Provides an emergency care system to be followed in case of accidents (see page 50).
9. Establishes long-range plans for facility development and revolving equipment replacement.
10. Employs effective informational techniques, including newspaper notices, demonstrations, and other media to inform parents and the general public about the program.
11. Evaluates the physical education program periodically with teachers, supervisors, and other concerned individuals. May establish a physical education committee for this purpose.
12. Makes available to appropriate staff the physical restrictions of individual students as stated in school health records. This duty also can be delegated to the school nurse.
13. Negotiates with parents any excuse from physical education for religious or personal reasons.

Note: If a physical education supervisor or consultant is present, many of the duties of the principal can be delegated, but he or she should maintain his or her general supervision over the program.

Responsibilities of the Supervisor or Consultant

Careful selection of the individual who is to function as a supervisor or consultant is important.[2] He or she must be a fully qualified and superior teacher. His or her interpersonal relationships with the educational community are most important. He or she must be both knowledgeable and available. Good rapport must be established with principals, and he or she must enjoy the confidence of the teachers.

In working with a school, he or she should route most items through the principal. During visits, he or she should stop at the school office to make his or her presence known. Recognition by the supervisor that the principal is responsible for the total educational process of the school, including physical education, is important. All equipment and supplies should be routed through the principal's office, also, as a matter of courtesy and information.

The supervisor should keep his or her hand in teaching, and it is recommended that he or she teach one or two classes during one semester of the school year. The advantages are obvious.

The responsibilities of a supervisor or consultant are many. He or she:

1. Is charged with overall supervision of the program, including the following: maintaining continuity as determined by the curriculum guide, providing master teacher demonstrations, assisting teachers with instructional problems, and providing general encouragement to all phases of the program.
2. Functions as a delegate of the administration in establishing and maintaining a quality program in each of the assigned schools.
3. Maintains effective liaison with principals in (1) establishing a master list of equipment and supplies for each school; (2) purchase, care, storage, and repair of equipment and instructional supplies; (3) maintenance and repair of facilities; (4) arrangement of effective in-service education; and (5) work with custodians for good standards of cleanliness and sanitation.
4. Makes periodic inspections of the instructional process, facilities, and equipment, with emphasis on safety. Takes corrective action when necessary.
5. Provides a personal image consistent with good professional standards in personal conduct, fitness, skill attainment, and dress.

[2]A supervisor is one designated by the administration to be legally in charge of teaching the area of physical education and all its teachers. A consultant usually has lesser power of critical supervision and control, acting more as a resource person helping teachers with instructional problems. However, the terms sometimes are used interchangeably.

6. Sets and maintains good standards of dress for staff and other teachers.
7. Assists in the construction of inexpensive equipment and supplies.
8. Welcomes and provides for effective public relations through demonstrations, talks to groups, newspapers, radio, television, and other media.
9. Maintains an up-to-date library of books, files of material, and other educational media. Distributes material to keep teachers abreast of new ideas and approaches.
10. Is open-minded and receptive to, and experiments with, new ideas, innovations, and approaches that might be valuable in the educational process.
11. Provides for interchange of ideas with other districts and arranges for visitation by teachers to exemplary programs.
12. Maintains good accounting and housekeeping standards.
13. Makes a yearly report to the administration and such other reports as requested.
14. Keeps abreast professionally by maintaining contact with the state supervisor, membership in appropriate societies, and attendance at meetings, clinics, and other demonstrations.
15. Makes effective input into the design of new facilities and the renovation of existing facilities.
16. Maintains effective communication with staff. Is prompt in answering requests. Conducts efficient and purposeful staff meetings.

Responsibilities of the Physical Education Specialist

Physical education must be taught by teachers who like and understand children. Background in preparation should include teaching experience with children. Teachers who hold general classroom certification and have teaching experience in elementary education along with the special area of physical education have a better understanding of the total elementary educational experience of the child.

Considerable adaptation is necessary for the secondary teacher or coach who changes to the elementary level. Major changes must be made in the approach to children, activity emphasis, and methodology, or the elementary program becomes a watered down model of the secondary program.

The physical education specialist:
1. Functions as a contributing and participating member of the school staff in the schools he or she serves.
2. Provides a high-quality program based on the district guide.

3. Assumes pertinent and necessary duties included in the responsibilities of the physical education consultant and supervisor when they are not present.
4. Provides an effective personal image in fitness and skill attainment.
5. Teaches only when attired in a professional manner, consistent with the activity.
6. Maintains an adequate personal library and files of materials.
7. Observes approved safety standards in the conduct of activities.
8. Assists regularly classroom teachers who have the responsibility of teaching their own physical education classes.
9. Maintains suitable amounts of equipment and instructional supplies through either repair or replacement. Provides input for their selection and purchase.
10. Maintains good standards of sanitation and housekeeping.
11. Cooperates with guidance, counseling, and other school agencies in the solution of the problems of individual pupils. Consults and cooperates with parents, as needed.
12. Assists with determination of needs and planning of the program.
13. Demonstrates empathy and provides help for children with special needs (such as dealing with obesity, slow learners, underachievers, and those in special education classes).
14. Provides for student leadership training for squad leaders, captains, officials, and equipment monitors.
15. Provides for evaluation of the program by securing feedback from students, teachers, parents, and principals.

Responsibilities of the Paraprofessional or the Teacher's Aide

1. Assists the classroom teacher in all phases of the program.
2. Dresses appropriately for instruction.
3. Follows the curricular plan of the teacher and the district.
4. Takes part in in-service education.
5. Recognizes and stays within the limitations of his or her background training and position.
6. Functions as a contributing member of the school staff as defined in the scope of his or her position.

Responsibilities of the Classroom Teacher Who Teaches Physical Education Classes

1. Allots sufficient planning time for the physical education lesson.

2. Bases the instruction on an effective lesson plan.
3. Carries out the instructional program as prescribed by the district guide.
4. Provides for the students to change clothing and/or shoes as prescribed by school policy.
5. Dresses appropriately for the instruction, usually at least with a change to gymnasium shoes.
6. Provides for orderly issue and return of lesson equipment and supplies, with attention to good housekeeping practices.
7. Provides for quick and orderly movement of children between the classroom and the play area.
8. Takes part in in-service education. Asks for help and direction when in doubt or difficulty. Cooperates with the physical education consultant.
9. Gives attention to the needs of special students or those with restrictions.
10. Participates on committees organized to provide guidance for students with special needs.
11. Correlates the physical education area into the entire teacher-learning situation, with attention to relevant knowledges, skills, and values.

Responsibilities of the Custodian

1. Accepts and discharges the responsibility of providing a clean facility for the physical education program.
2. Makes available floor mops and other cleaning tools that can be used to clean the floor periodically during the day.
3. Gives ongoing attention to safety factors in facilities and equipment.
4. Participates with the principal in periodic inspection and repair of facilities and equipment.
5. Prepares or assists with the preparation of special facilities or lining of fields, as formally requested.

Responsibilities of the School Nurse

1. Makes sure that all staff members are aware of any student's physical restrictions that have bearing on his or her participation in physical education.
2. Passes judgment and makes recommendations with regard to excuses for physical education.
3. Takes charge of accident referrals, providing needed liaison with parents.
4. Interprets health records and makes recommendations for children in special programs (special education, slow learners, the obese, and underachievers in physical fitness).

5. Participates on committees organized to provide guidance for children with special needs.

Responsibilities of Parents

First, it must be recognized that the education of children is a joint venture of the parents and the schools. Parents can play a significant role by supporting efforts of the school and augmenting the child's development by efforts at home. To help in other ways, parents can:

1. See that each child is equipped with proper attire, as specified by district regulations for physical education classes.
2. Make rational decisions when writing or asking for children to be excused from activity, recognizing that this should be done only for valid reasons.
3. Become sufficiently informed of the philosophy and objectives of a modern-day physical education program and demand that the school operate a program of high standards.
4. Be able and willing to make suggestions for program modification or adjustment on the basis of the child's experiences.
5. Attend school demonstrations or participate in physical education nights.
6. Cooperate with the school on any remedial measures or necessary physical activity required to meet the child's special needs.
7. Encourage children and offer more opportunity for them to be physically active.
8. Be physically active, not only to set a good example but for their own well-being.

Responsibilities of Students

Students take on some general responsibilities when they:

1. Participate actively in classes to the best of their ability. Take part in all activities.
2. Take full advantage of the resources the school has for physical development.
3. Set rational goals for themselves and work to achieve them.
4. Dress properly for physical education activities.

SCHEDULING

A definite schedule for physical education classes should be established at each school, based on instructional time of at least 150 minutes per week, exclusive of recess or other supervised play. The standard is for instructional time and does not include time needed for moving to and from class, changing to gym clothing, visiting the washroom, and cleaning up.

Most national bodies recommend that physical education be scheduled on a daily basis. However, some consideration should be given on the intermediate level to another plan if the children change clothing and also shower after activity. A weekly schedule of three class sessions of a longer period of activity would tend to alleviate some of the dressing and showering problems and still meet the standard for time. Some teachers regard this as superior to the daily plan, since more efficient instruction is possible with emphasis on progression.

Where sufficient teaching stations exist, the scheduling problem is minimized. Caution is urged with outdoor scheduling where equipment is to be shared and conflicts can arise with limited supplies. Problems occur when too many classes are scheduled to use the physical education materials.

Class size should not exceed the normal limits of one class. The practice of sending out two or more classes with one teacher for physical education results in little more than a supervised play period.

The substitution of band, chorus, play practice, and athletic programs for physical education is not a recommended procedure. Teachers too frequently take the physical education period to practice special events for some or all of the children.

Some teachers regard the first period of the morning as prime learning and organizational time and so do not wish to have physical education scheduled at this time. Changing the schedule once or twice during the year to rotate classes is a solution. From another point of view, some teachers like to have physical education during the first period, because (to them) the activity period syphons off excess energy and makes the children ready to sit down and work rather than itch and look toward the clock for the time physical education is scheduled.

For the physical education specialist teaching consecutive classes, two suggestions are in order. The first is to schedule at least 5 minutes between classes. The second is to group like classes following each other to minimize the time needed to issue and set up equipment. Even with classroom teachers handling teaching chores, it is advantageous to have some time between classes to allow for flexibility.

HEALTH POLICIES

The quality of health affects the quality of learning. This tenet, together with the school's goal of optimum development, poses an educational responsibility for good health. Included within the concept of total development is the subgoal that each child should develop a favorable level of personal health. The school also has a legal responsibility to provide a healthful and safe environment for the child.

Periodic Health Examinations

A first concern for the student is the provision of a periodic health examination. This should determine, among other things, the extent of a child's participation in physical education. Health examinations should be required upon entrance (kindergarten or first grade) to school and from transfer students. Another examination is recommended at the fourth-grade level.

The examination should classify students in one of three categories: (1) normal participation in physical education, (2) participation subject to certain adaptations or restrictions, and (3) severe limitations or nonparticipation. The teacher must have access to the results of the examination in order that each student may receive the consideration stipulated in the examination.

An examination form approved by the local medical society makes for more consistent information. Agreement also can be reached with the local medical society with respect to a standard fee for the examination.

Screening by the Teacher

Periodic health examinations do not uncover every health problem related to physical activity participation. Some conditions may appear only after exercise. In other instances, the condition may develop between examinations or even shortly after an examination and have an important bearing on the health status of the individual.

The task of screening children who respond poorly to exercise is not difficult, since it involves noting certain observable conditions that are an indication of an abnormality. The Committee on Exercise and Fitness of the American Medical Association lists these observable signs that may accompany or follow exercise and that are indications for referral to a physician for further investigation.

Excessive Breathlessness: Some breathlessness is normal with exercise, but breathlessness that persists long after exercise is cause for medical referral.

Bluing of the Lips: Except in a cold, wet environment, bluing of the lips or nailbeds is an unnatural reaction to exercise. Its occurrence in the ordinary exercise setting is cause for medical referral.

Pale or Clammy Skin: Pale or clammy skin or cold sweating following or during exercise is not a normal reaction to physical activity within the usual temperature ranges of the gymnasium or playing field. Again, medical referral is recommended.

Unusual Fatigue: Excessive fatigue, as evidenced by unusual lack of endurance or early failure to maintain moderate activity, also suggests the need for medical referral. It is dangerous to attribute such reactions to malingering until possible organic causes have been ruled out.

Persistent Shakiness: Unusual weakness or shakiness that continues for more than 10 minutes following vigorous exercise is cause for medical referral. Normally, recovery should be reasonably prompt.

Muscle Twitching or Tetany: Muscular contractions such as twitching or tetany, whether localized or generalized, sometimes occur as an unusual reaction to exercise. It may be abnormal and warrants medical investigation.

In addition, such medical symptoms as headache, dizziness, fainting, broken sleep at night, digestive upset, pain not associated with injury, undue pounding or uneven heartbeat, disorientation, or personality changes are contraindications of normal functioning. The committee cautions that an occasional episode need not alarm the instructor, but recurring or persisting patterns of any of these symptoms, particularly when related to activity, indicate the need for medical review.

The instructor needs to be sensitive to these possible reactions of the children and note them in stride. He or she is further cautioned to remind himself or herself that *unusual* reactions are not necessarily *abnormal* reactions.

The specialist, with a scientific and health background, is in a better position to assess such health indications than is the classroom teacher. However, with concentration and practice, the classroom teacher can make effective use of the physical education period as a part of the daily health screening of the children.

Recent mandates that call for the placement of special children in regular classes add to the importance of screening procedures, since some special children have conditions that need monitoring.

Excuses and Readmittance

If a child is to be excused from physical education for a day or two for health reasons, the teacher can accept a note from the parent. If the excuse involves a significant length of time, it should be accepted only on the recommendation of a physician. Readmittance of children who have been out for a period of time also should be subject to a physician's recommendation. If there is a school nurse, excuse and readmittance cases should be routed through him or her, and he or she should, in turn, discuss the problem with the physical education teacher. In the absence of recommendations from both physician and nurse, consultation with the principal and the parent is probably the best solution. The latter procedure should be followed any time the parent wishes to have his or her child excused from physical education because of religious or personal reasons. At an early meeting with parents, regulations should be discussed and clarified.

Students who have been absent because of illness or some other condition should be observed closely for signs that might suggest that they are not ready to participate in unlimited physical activity. Girls should not be required to take part in vigorous activity during the early part of their menstrual periods.

Good rapport between physicians and schools is important in handling the health problems related to excuses and readmittances. One physician from the medical society should be designated to provide liaison among those responsible for physical education and the medical profession.

An unfortunate indictment of a few programs lies in the fact that some children ask for excuses because they dread the experience and have a fear of failure, a fear of ridicule, and a lack of sympathy from the teacher. The solution in this case lies with the program and not the child.

Healthful Environment for Physical Education

A healthful environment for physical education requires attention to standards for school safety, hygiene, and sanitation. In addition, the physical education setting should emphasize good standards of cleanliness, ventilation, and heating. Ventilation should be sufficient to remove objectionable odors. Temperatures, depending upon the extent of the activity, should range from 65 to 68 degrees. Generally, a temperature comfortable for an elderly teacher is too high for active youngsters.

A healthful environment also includes attention to mental hygiene. Proper student-teacher relationships in activity areas are important. Physical education should be a period during which students lose rather than acquire tensions.

Cleanliness of the gymnasium floor is particularly important in the present-day physical education program, since many of the movements require the children to place their hands or bodies on the floor. The floor should be swept in the morning just prior to the classes and as often as needed between classes. A wide dust mop should be handy for this purpose, and children can perform this chore. Adequate facilities should be available for cleaning up after class, and enough time should be allowed for the finishing up procedure.

SAFETY PROCEDURES

The school safety program consists of three aspects: (1) a safe school environment, (2) safety education, and (3) emergency care. Each is discussed in turn.

Safe Environment

The school must be certain that the school environment meets all the criteria for safety. This involves a number of aspects.

Health Status

As previously discussed, the health status of the children must be ascertained through a health examination, so no child may be placed in a physical environment beyond his or her capacity.

Provision for a Safe Teaching Place

This need is both quantitative and qualitative. There must be sufficient room and the area must be suitable for the intended purpose. The character of the activity determines the amount of space needed for safe play, including sufficient boundary clearance from walls, fences, and other obstructions. The area should be free from posts, wires, holes, and other hazards. The presence of broken glass or miscellaneous junk is a source of accidents. Sprinkler heads and pools of water also can cause serious injury.

Safe Equipment and Supplies

The equipment and supplies provided must be suitable for the level of the children and the selected activity. The equipment should be in good functioning condition.

Regular Inspection of Facilities and Equipment

Inspection of facilities should be made on a regular basis, perhaps monthly. This can be a shared duty for the principal, custodian, and physical education specialist. Items needing attention should be noted, and equipment should be taken out of service until properly repaired.

Supervision of Activities and Play Periods

All school-sponsored activities must be supervised, including recess, noontime recreation, and afterschool play. Much of this can be assigned to qualified teacher's aides, releasing the teacher for instructional duties. Under the law, a class may not be turned over to high school students or cadet teachers, since supervision must be supplied by a certified individual.

Proper Selection of Activities

The selected activity must stand up as a proper educational medium for the group involved. Teachers should avoid highly specialized or difficult games beyond the ability of the children. The scheduling of tackle football, for example, is a questionable one for the elementary level. The principal who sets rules for snowball fighting is encouraging an activity that is questionable and may cause injury.

Safety Education

Safety education as it relates to instructional procedures in physical education should be directed toward possible causes of accidents. An accident is caused when something or someone fails to function properly. The following represent causes of accidents inherent in the instructional process: (1) lack of skill; (2) lack of knowledge about hazards and needed safety precautions; (3) attitudinal problems (desire before good judgment, me-first attitude, show-off or dare complex, rudeness, or disrespect); and (4) presence of hazards.

Skills should be taught in sequential order so that safe participation is possible. The inherent hazards of each activity should be made clear to the children, as well as what safety precautions are needed to conduct the activity safely. Attention to developing proper attitudes should be included in the instructional process. Providing a safe environment was discussed in the preceding section.

Further discussion of safety considerations begins on page 63 and is included in the instructional procedures for the specific activity areas.

Emergency Care

The school has a responsibility to arrange a system of emergency care, so prompt and appropriate measures can be taken to protect the child in case of injury. Emergency care procedures should follow this sequence.

1. The administration of first aid is the first step. The problem of proper care is solved when a school nurse is present. If not, at least one person in the school should have first-aid certification. Some principals like to have the school secretary have such certification because that person is readily available. If a teacher has first-aid responsibilities, proper supervision must be supplied for his or her class when he or she is called to the scene of the accident. First-aid procedures should indicate whether the child can be moved and in what fashion.

2. Unless the injury is such that the child needs to be taken to a doctor without delay, the parents should be notified. The school should have on hand sufficient information pertaining to each student to give direction in case of an emergency. This should include the telephone numbers of the parents, both at home and at their places of employment. This also should include the name of the family doctor to whom the child can be referred. In addition, the name of a neighbor or a close friend to whom the child can be taken in case the parents cannot be contacted is helpful. The school should have ongoing arrangements with the local emergency care units, so a paramedic unit would be available for serious accidents.

3. The third step is to release the child to his or her parents or to another person designated

by them. Policies for transportation should be established.

4. A report of the accident should be filled out promptly, generally on a form adopted by the school system. The teacher and the principal should each retain copies, the additional specified copies being forwarded to the administration. The report should contain all necessary details with respect to full names of the child and the witnesses; details of the accident, including place, time, activity, circumstances, and possible causes; and disposition of the child. The injured part of the body should be identified and the kind of injury noted.
5. Follow-up procedures should be instituted to eliminate the causes of the accident and prevent future accidents of the same kind.

The Medicine Chest

Whether or not to have a medicine chest is a debatable point. The medical association for the area (local or county) should help make such a decision. Only those medications and materials approved by the association should be in the medicine chest, and approved directions for use of the contents should be prominently posted. Individual student's medications should be kept in another place.

Student Insurance

The school should make available accident insurance providing compensation in case of accident to a child. If a parent rejects the option of school accident insurance, he or she has little basis for objection to expenses that could have been partially or fully covered by insurance.

Other Safety Considerations

An important value emerging from a properly conducted physical education program is its positive effect on playground conduct. With good safety habits inculcated and attitudes directed toward productive lines, the level of playground conduct becomes more educationally sound.

Dogs and other animals should be kept from schoolyards. Children can trip over the animals, and the possibility of animal bites is always present. Whenever a child's skin is broken from an animal bite, the possibility of rabies must *always* be considered. The animal must be caught and held for the authorities. Only by observing the animal for a period of two weeks or so can the possibility of rabies be rejected.

The rubbish-burning area should be protected from the children. Children are naturally attracted to fire, and they love to handle burning materials.

Throwing stones and snowballs needs to be controlled. Other potentially dangerous rowdy habits need to be controlled, also.

Special rules need to be established for various areas, particularly in the use of various pieces of apparatus on the playground.

LEGAL RESPONSIBILITY FOR HEALTH AND SAFETY

The school has a legal responsibility of providing a healthy and safe environment for its students. Teachers, as individuals, share this responsibility. Teachers cannot be held accountable (financially liable) for injuries to children under their care unless negligence is legally determined. A person is deemed negligent when he or she has failed to act as a reasonably prudent person would have acted under the circumstances. Foreseeability is the key to negligence and the possibility of liability. If the teacher should have foreseen the causes leading to the injury and failed to take action as a prudent person would, a ruling of negligence can result. Negligence must *always* be established by court action.

In determining personal liability, three main questions are involved.

1. Did the teacher owe a duty of care to the child?
2. Was there a failure on the part of the teacher to observe such duty?
3. Was the failure the direct or proximate cause of any resulting injury?

If the answer is yes to all three questions, then liability can be ruled. Obviously, the answer to avoiding liability lies in providing proper care. This can involve any of the elements previously discussed under a safe school environment, safety education, and emergency care. A failure to observe any one of these safety recommendations that results in an injury can spell trouble.

Teachers need to be aware of the legal implications of certain flexible movement-oriented teaching methods that give the child an opportunity to explore and work with a piece of apparatus with little or no instruction. This theory proposes that the child needs to experiment and have a chance to explore as the first step in the learning process. If the child is injured, certain legal questions will be asked. Was the child instructed in the hazards of the activity? Were proper safety precautions taken? Were the skills or movement patterns presented in a progressive manner, so that the child mastered the simple skills before attempting the more complicated ones? Was there proper supervision?

It is evident that not all these questions can be answered affirmatively. Perhaps this method should be reserved for only those activities with a very low injury potential.

Liability insurance should be investigated. Perhaps the school has liability insurance that includes the teachers. Liability insurance is available in conjunction with memberships in some educational societies.

OPERATIONAL POLICIES

Coeducational Activity

Coeducational activity is activity in which boys and girls participate together. Formerly, some choice was involved, but Title IX of the Education Amendments of 1972 prohibits persons being excluded from educational programs and activities on the basis of sex. Interpretations call for all physical education programs to be coeducational.

This requirement represents no change for primary programs, since there has been little separation of sexes on that level. On the intermediate level, the implications of Title IX mean that both boys and girls have the right to participate in the same activities, and the curriculum must reflect this. No longer can there be separate boys' and girls' classes.

Within an activity, however, some consideration for separation of sexes may be made if the activity poses danger, usually to girls, because of the contact factor or rough nature of the activity. An individual's safety in this case would take precedence.

In an activity like soccer, all preliminary skills and practice should be conducted on a class basis without regard to sex. However, when competition is organized, there can be separate play.

Supervised Free-Play Periods

Legally, the school must provide a safe environment for periods of free play, including recess, before and after school, and during the noon hour. Supervision must be positive and directed toward the purposes of free play—the relief of tensions. Social behavior on the playground should be directed, so this purpose can be realized.

When intermediate children have a physical education lesson during a school session (morning or afternoon), a recess period may not be necessary.

The first part of the noontime program should be devoted to a supervised, happy, and restful lunch. After that, quiet types of activity are recommended. Children who eat lunch at home should not return to school until after a designated time.

Assignments for supervision generally are rotated among teachers, but a trend toward increased use of teacher's aides and specialized nonteaching personnel to assume these responsibilities has appeared recently.

It is recommended that aides do more than just provide a physical presence for control. They can help organize group activities, help the children with their movement patterns, and, in general, provide a positive influence on the play environment.

Student patrols can augment adult supervision during play periods. Patrol positions can be given status with some kind of organization and identifying clothing.

Students can be of help in setting playground conduct rules and implementing their establishment. Each year a student committee could review last year's rules with respect to accidents and make suggestions for changes, if they are needed. When students help make the rules, they are more likely to conform to them.

Attire

Ideally, all children should change to gym clothing for physical education classes, and children from the fifth grade on should shower after activity. Even if showers are not available, a better physical education class can be conducted when appropriate clothing is worn. It is particularly important that girls wear something other than dresses.

The solution to the problem of changing clothing for class is not easily found. Some teachers find it practical to have youngsters change when convenient and wear the play clothing during class sessions. Changing in washrooms has drawbacks, but at least it accomplishes the task.

The problem of storing the children's play clothing when lockers are not available needs a positive approach. The cooperation of the classroom teacher must be gained to establish some kind of a system. The system should preserve the ownership of each child's things, it should not be time consuming, and it should be a child-handled system.

As a basic minimum, children should wear gym shoes during the physical education class. The practice of having children skate around in stocking feet limits the children greatly in their responses to activity challenges. It would be better to have the children in bare feet than in stocking feet. Some educators even hold that children, during indoor participation, should have bare feet for superior tactile stimulation and foot development. Participation by the children with bare feet in some activities may be appropriate, but a blanket rule of this nature is not sound. Proper cleanup before putting on socks and shoes is an item with no easy solution.

THE EXTENDED ACTIVITY PROGRAM

Great concern has been expressed regarding the spread of organized athletics for children of elementary school age. It is obvious that these programs are here to stay, and they may even increase. Many of these programs are promoted outside of the schools. School authorities must decide whether and how they are going to be involved. The primary concerns are proper supervision and sanity in competition, and these are elements that the school can supply.

Another element enters the picture. No longer can one think in terms of a competitive program for males only. The equal opportunity provisions of Title IX mandate that competitive programs are to be designed for all children without regard to sex.

That programs of this nature have official approval is expressed by the AAHPER position paper on elementary school physical education.

Competition at the elementary school level is a vital and forceful educational tool. Properly used it can stimulate a keen desire for self-improvement as well as create environments in which children, motivated by common purpose, unite in an effort to accomplish goals in a manner not unlike the roles they will play as adults in a democratic, competitive society. [3]

This position also is supported by the American Medical Association. The plea is for moderation and a controlled program for both boys and girls, avoiding too much, too soon. Generally, educators react conservatively to competition, but parents react favorably.

Most important is the premise that a quality physical education program for all must be present to serve as the basis for the extended program. Extended opportunities for sports include intramural programs, interschool competition, playdays and sports days, and special interest clubs. Further discussion of the extended activity program is found in chapter twenty-five.

PROMOTIONAL IDEAS AND PUBLIC RELATIONS

Many people have little idea of what constitutes a quality physical education program or what physical education can really do for children. The purpose of good public relations is to get this message to the public, especially to school patrons. Good public relations do not just happen—they are planned. A variety of means should be devised and utilized, but the most important public relations factor is a quality program.

A Quality Program

A strong, well-directed program generates strong community support, and a program characterized by weak planning, poor teaching, and bad

judgment places such support in jeopardy. The old saying "you can't flay a dead horse" applies here. The children's informal reports to their parents must reflect joy, satisfaction, and value in the program, otherwise all efforts are in vain. With the children, the know-why is as important as the know-how and enables them to project values to others.

Changing the Image

The old popular identification of physical education as only a sports program must be dispelled. Education values must be stressed, and the image of the brawny individual with baggy sweat pants, whistle in mouth, baseball cap on head, and bat in hand erased. It is important that the physical educator give the impression of being a professional educator, as well as being one.

In One's Own Backyard

The importance of effective relationships between the specialist and other members of the school staff, with particular emphasis on rapport between the classroom teacher and the specialist, has been dealt with earlier in this chapter. Many classroom teachers do not understand the unique contributions physical education can make to the overall development of the child. If the specialist can learn to provide practical, sincere answers to common questions arising out of misinformation, this can help to establish physical education in a positive sense.

The specialist should be a partner in the counseling process, particularly in a positive manner, by informing the classroom teacher when a child or a class as a whole has been particularly receptive or achieved something distinctive. The specialist should cooperate in guiding children with special problems.

Faculty-family nights at the facilities, on a regular basis if possible, help to establish the good personal relations that are the basis of good public relations. Members of the administrative staff can be invited to local professional meetings where they can be introduced and given due recognition.

School-affiliated Methods

Many promotional ideas can utilize elements of the school program. The physical education program can contribute to assembly programs. Demonstrations can be used as halftime programs at athletic events. Sports days or playdays can be scheduled. Special events involving some competition, such as Junior Olympics, free-throw contests, gymnastic-type competitions, demonstrations, and the like, have value.

The district newsletter to school patrons should allot space for the physical education program.

Pictures have meaning when local children are identified.

Involving the Parents

Parents can be involved actively as participants or passively as spectators. One approach is to schedule a parents' night, which may take the following directions: (1) parents participating along with the children in regular class work, (2) parents observing a regular schedule of classes, (3) achievement night to show special attainments, or (4) demonstrations interpreting the main features of the year-round physical education program.

Community-school organizations, such as the PTA or the Friends of the School, should serve as vehicles for interpreting the program. Discussions, panel presentations, outside experts, and selected visual presentations are effective program elements. Parents should be given the opportunity to ask questions and resolve debatable points.

Involving parents as teacher's aides or as members of a fitness-testing team brings them into the heart of the program. Some events should be scheduled on Saturdays, so working parents can help.

Distributive materials and other contacts with parents should avoid "pedaguese." When parents are informed that their children are developing skillful movement, they can understand; but one wonders what they get out of a statement that their children are developing space-time-force-flow concepts.

Brochures covering yearly summaries, program descriptions, philosophies, and educational values are effective tools for better understanding.

One supervisor initiated a series of education pamphlets for parents, exploring the values of various fundamental skills, encouraging the parents to follow up school efforts. Another educator came up with the idea of a commercial-break system, in which children watching television do exercises or stunts during the commercials. Another teacher devised an effective means of public relations by calling the parents when the child did something outstanding. One parent remarked on how different this was, "because most calls from the school are complaints."

Community-oriented Informational Measures

The newspaper is probably the best source for publicity. The procedures that best serve the publication should be ascertained. How is new material to be submitted? What sizes and types of pictures are best? Are written articles to be submitted, or will reporters write them?

Having a good file of pictures is important. The standard 8-by-10-inch size is probably most practical, and it allows for portions of the picture to be used. Correct identification is essential.

A schedule of events should go to the newspaper at the beginning of each month. Feature articles should include announcements of coming events, reports of the event, and human interest stories. The editor should receive free tickets or at least an invitation.

Television and radio should be exploited. Events of special interest provide a second jolt of publicity through television coverage. Radio panel discussions have good value, also. Spot announcements make good public impact.

The support of service clubs should be enlisted through speeches, films, demonstrations, and other approaches. Service clubs often are anxious to provide material support in the form of sponsorship of some special event or the purchase of a special piece of equipment beyond the fiscal capacity of the school.

The physical educator should take part in community affairs, joining as many clubs and groups as feasible. He or she should be willing to help groups seeking the kind of school services for which he or she is responsible.

Motion picture films developed locally make excellent presentations. Super-Eight films are inexpensive, but attention to quality is important. The lighting for indoor shots must be adequate.

DEMONSTRATIONS AND ASSEMBLY PROGRAMS

Demonstrations are important mediums of public relations and vary from simple programs for PTAs to more elaborate all-city or all-district affairs. Emphasis should be on the values of physical education and should center on live demonstrations of the learned skills. The demonstration should attempt to dispel some of the false notions about physical education. It should not be just a bat-and-ball, free-play program or an athletic demonstration. The following guidelines should help structure an effective demonstration.

1. The activities should illustrate the attainment of the objectives of physical education; they should grow out of, and be typical of, the program.
2. The activities should not require a long period of preparation so that the physical education period becomes a training period for the demonstration. However, sufficient rehearsal must be conducted.
3. Children should be properly dressed for the activity, but elaborate and intricate costuming should be avoided. Simple costumes that can

be made by the children are most acceptable. No child should be left out because he or she does not have the right costume.

4. The demonstration should include a number of children. An attempt should be made to get all children in the groups involved in the program and to play fair by using typical groups. However, recognition can be given to children of superior ability by having them do specialty numbers.

5. A printed program is desirable.

6. The principal or another administrative official should open the program with a word of welcome to the parents and other visitors. His or her remarks should include mention of the educational importance of physical education and the district's administrative support of the program.

7. A microphone should be available, so running comments can be supplied as the activity unfolds. In this way, attention can be directed to the crucial points to be observed.

8. The opening number should be an eye-opener and attention-getter. The program should end with some sort of grand finale.

9. The program should be fast moving and contain activities of good audience appeal. Music is indispensable, and a well-balanced program contains several numbers with music.

10. The program should call attention to physical fitness, and some elements should be devoted to this area. A demonstration of physical fitness testing is always well-received.

11. Some part of the program can include a demonstration of instructional procedures, rather than centering all attention on accomplishments.

12. It is important to avoid tests of strength and skill that might lead to the embarrassment of those defeated.

13. While a high degree of performance is not needed, the activities should be done reasonably well, within the level of the children's abilities.

If large numbers of children are in the program, corresponding numbers of parents will attend. Some demonstrations are used as fund-raising devices to supply extra equipment and supplies beyond what the district furnishes.

Teachers sometimes are asked to put on assembly or convocation programs in physical education. These should be planned for students by students, although parents generally attend. One or two numbers usually are sufficient.

Five

The Teacher and the Learning Process

The learning environment is centered upon the teacher—his or her personality, his or her relationship with the learner, and his or her way of conducting the physical education activities.

THE TEACHER'S ROLE

Successful attainment of learning goals depends not so much on the choice of some specific methodology as it does on the effectiveness of the teacher. The teacher must be a highly skilled professional who knows how to direct learning toward selected goals. This requirement implies the ability to work with all types of learners and to handle their differences without applying labels to the children. Emphasis should be placed on helping children with different kinds of learning potentials and problems rather than on dealing with different kinds of children.

The teacher's role has a dual nature: first, as a catalyst of action that directs and guides children's efforts toward expected outcomes and, second, as a leader who provides a teacher image that projects desirable learning standards and human values.

In learning activities, a lot depends upon the teacher's ability to link the present learning status of the child with experiences that foster learning. Important, too, is the teacher's ability to energize and activate the children and keep their attention focused in a direction consistent with expected outcomes. Good observational techniques are a necessity.

In many ways, teaching reflects the personality, outlook, ideals, and background of the teacher. A good physical education teacher not only provides quality learning experiences, he or she communicates a zest for movement and learning that is bound to rub off on the children with whom he or she comes in contact.

First and foremost, the teacher must have the conviction that physical education is an important educational medium for the child's optimum development not only in the physical area but also in many other aspects of learning. To believe in physical education is the first essential for successful teaching.

A mother who is also a physical educator, in talking about the kinds of physical education experiences she wished for her daughter, described it this way: "I want her teacher to feel that physical education is important because my daughter understands that what is important to the teacher is important to her; and what the teacher doesn't bother with doesn't matter very much."[1]

Another aspect of teacher image is adequate preparation. Teachers need to realize that physical education is largely an instructional program for which certain preparation tenets are important. Lesson plans should provide the direction and grow out of an overall curriculum. A well-executed lesson is a joy for the children and a source of pleasure for the teacher.

The teacher should be a reasonable example of the health and physical fitness dictums the school is attempting to promote. Elderly teachers may feel this would be a difficult standard to meet.

[1]Margaret Miller, "Elementary School Physical Education," *The Physical Educator,* vol. 5, no. 3 (October 1968).

However, the teacher should be free of glaring departures from what are considered good healthful practices.

Children tend to imitate those whom they admire and respect. The teacher needs to be certain his or her personal example will not lay the basis for improper habits or attitudes. Teachers should be appropriately dressed for physical education teaching, at least to the extent of having proper footwear. Perhaps the old adage "if you don't live it, you don't believe it" is appropriate here.

The concern of the teacher must be with all children and particularly with those children who need help. It is true that the higher achievers in physical education generally progress satisfactorily in spite of the teaching. These are the most apt, the ones who learn largely by a self-directed process. But what about the ones who know that, no matter how hard they try, they just won't be good enough? For these children to make commendable progress both in motivation and skill attainment is a key challenge. They need special attention from a perceptive and sensitive teacher.

The teacher's ability to laugh, in its broadest context, is a needed quality—laughing with the children and at himself or herself. The smile is a most effective instrument of rapport.

The teacher can learn from the students. The ability to talk with the children and show respect for their views is important. Rather than attempting to provide all the guidelines for activity development, the teacher should seek the aid of the children for expanding development in an activity area or helping provide direction for the lesson.

Teachers often are concerned with a proper approach to teaching. A teacher, as a personality and an individual, has certain aptitudes that can indicate the direction and style of teaching with which he or she can expect the most success. The age level and readiness of the children, the type of activity, and the expected outcomes are also relevant factors. The proper approach is one that achieves the stated outcomes. Teachers, however, should develop expertise in a variety of methods and resources, so they can make choices that provide the best experiences for children. Flexibility is important.

Teachers are cautioned not to expect immediate or dramatic results. Securing control and developing good work habits is a long, steady, firm process. In the case where the children have had a poor background in physical education, this is especially true.

In an atmosphere of fairness and firmness, a friendly, sympathetic, understanding teacher can accomplish much, creating a climate of enjoyment and success. He or she must be a person deeply involved in the social aspect of the child's education and development. Conspicuous is the absence of sarcasm, threats, shaming embarrassment, and high-level competition that often result in frustrating failure.

The teacher as a person sometimes becomes angry when children display behavior that irritates him or her intensely. The important thing for the teacher to do at that point is to handle the anger constructively and not travel along a tangent the teacher might regret later.

Personal anger must be expressed in such a fashion that it does no damage and does not result in insults or name calling. Approach and attack the problem, not the child. Identify the deviant behavior, and then give the student a proper alternative to follow. Usually, remedial action should be taken only after careful thought.

The following example shows proper and improper ways to handle a common situation. The teacher has just asked the class to gather the balls and bring them to a designated spot, where they can be sacked for proper storage. Rather than carrying them, some students throw the balls and hit other students.

The teacher might say, "Now listen here, you bunch of dumb bunnies. Why can't you follow directions? You're the worst class I've ever had. Now get this mess cleaned up before I really get mad." This approach offers little solution and only serves to downgrade the students. Many times the students' self-concepts are so badly injured through this method that they no longer like physical education.

Instead of the above, a sound approach might be as follows: "I am disappointed with the way you brought the equipment to the area. Someone might get hurt when you throw things. Put the balls out again and let's practice bringing them in properly." This approach does not attack the students personally, but it does identify the deviant behavior and offer a proper alternative.

WORKING WITH CHILDREN

In the teacher's relations with the learner, a number of pedagogical considerations merit discussion. Each carries significance in the learning process: (1) developing creativity, (2) personalizing instruction, (3) coping with behavioral problems, (4) communicating with the learner, and (5) other instructional procedures.

Developing Creativity

If a teacher expects children to be creative, he or she must introduce originality and something of his or her personality into the teaching. Some personalities are more suited to such emphasis and methods than others.

Value in creativity lies in stimulating the child to become a self-propelled learner, developing habits of discovery and reflective thinking, and increasing the elements stored in the memory drum. With respect to the latter assumption, it is postulated that, when children discover with satisfaction cognitive elements, these are better retained and retrieved for future use.

This does not imply that creativity will be fostered by leaving children to their own devices, without instruction and without guidance. Constraining forces are still present, but the manner and form of instruction are changed. Children must have the freedom to explore and try out new and different patterns without fear of failure or criticism.

With individual children, the teacher needs to determine whether the child is following his or her instruction literally or whether it is subject to the child's interpretation. Unless there is interpretation, there is no creativity. This means that, if the teacher desires a creative response, he or she should not demonstrate, since this usually leads to imitative behavior.

There are several ways to inject creativity into the program. The teacher, in each case, must set the stage and know when to retire into the background. Excessive guidance stifles creativity, while too little direction leads to aimless movement.

Certain activities designated as creative in the program format provide one outlet. These include creative play (stories, poems, imitative behavior, and expressive movements), related creative dance, and, a more recent emphasis, creative games and dances. Each is discussed later, and appropriate instructional procedures and activities are outlined.

A second approach is for the teacher to designate time at the beginning of a movement experience for creative opportunity before the child receives instruction. This usually involves a manipulative object or a piece of apparatus. For example, a child might be given a hoop and told, "Experiment with the different kinds of things you can do with it." There are some who hold very strongly to this practice under the premise that direction stifles creativity and that the child should have the opportunity to try out, become familiar, and explore the range of possibilities *before* more defined instruction occurs. Opposing this viewpoint are those who hold that only a low level of learning occurs without direction and that more productive and *creative* activity is possible when the teacher transmits simple basics before the children experiment. This is likened to the position that the child should be guided so that he or she doesn't try to "rediscover the wheel" but rather learns to be creative about the way wheels can be used.

Another way is for the teacher to afford opportunity for creativity during appropriate segments of the instructional sequence. This can take the form of adding to or expanding on the presented progressions or moving off in an entirely new direction. Time for creativity should be designated in the lesson plan, and flexibility also should be practiced to allow for creativity at teachable moments. Certainly it is sound to allow opportunity for creativity after a few progressions have been established in order to give breadth to the movement patterns. Creativity also is furthered by the judicious use of movement factors, particularly sequence building and continuity.

Creativity means coming up with something worth saving because of its intrinsic or functional value. If one applies this to movement patterns, one can say that a pattern that is unique or different has intrinsic value (the performer derives satisfaction from doing something that has not been done before) while one that is more difficult and calls for more skill than has been needed previously has functional value (the performer derives satisfaction from having reached beyond his or her former competence level).

Teachers must have the ability to recognize original creative achievement. The teacher then can help the child to define and increase the alternatives for action. Direction should be positive and reinforcement sincere, and creativity should be recognized when it is truly displayed.

Stimulation can be injected into the creative process by a show-and-tell demonstration. After a period of exploration, the emphasis should be on what types of movement patterns are possible when one really thinks, rather than on imitative behavior. Children naturally observe others when they reach a block or are stymied in their thinking. Concentration should be on developing their own patterns. Ideas from others can be a base, however, on which to increase alternatives.

In moving from child to child, the teacher should ask questions that require reflective thinking rather than attempt to govern the direction and style of the child's response. Respect for the child's creative achievement is most important.

No attempt has been made to describe specific equipment or activities that foster creativity. Creativity is an umbrella that can be superimposed on all activity. Care must be taken to reject the premise that directed teaching is the antithesis of creativity and has no association with the creative process. For general movement patterns, much creativity (choice) can be injected. For the more precise, specific skills, creativity can enter after the skills have been reasonably acquired. At that point, an exploratory approach can lead to extension and better utilization of the practiced movement pattern.

It is the teacher's special responsibility to foster creativity in most, if not all, physical education activities. Give the child the opportunity at some point to "do his or her own thing."

Personalizing Learning

Personalization[2] means adjusting what is learned to the needs and characteristics of the learner. Learners differ in many significant ways, and human variability must be a consideration in the learning process. Children learn effectively at different rates and under different conditions. The task becomes pacing instruction at personalized rates and offering a variety of instructional strategies to provide different conditions.

One can reason, with respect to a certain grade level, that children are more alike than they are different and that, therefore, a core of appropriate learning activities can be provided and made flexible to consider individual differences. This appears to be a sound approach at this time.

One strong statement can be made. The traditional lockstep approach of the past, in which all children performed in the same manner to achieve the same goals, has little place in current methodology.

First of all, to personalize means that the teacher should physically and/or emotionally touch all children in the group. This means frequent movement among the children as opposed to the traditional teaching position at the front of the class. The teacher needs to interact effectively with each individual by using both verbal and non-verbal methods of motivation and by making a point to reach every child sometime during the presentation.

Allied with the previous point is the concept that the teacher should be perceptive and assistive in making comments. Comments should center on specific points of what is good and what can be improved, rather than relying exclusively on the usual approvals such as good, fine, et cetera.

Creativity is individual expression and as such is an element of personalization. Ways and means of incorporating creativity into the program have been discussed in another section of this chapter.

Another means of personalization is having enough equipment so that each student can work at his or her own task and presumably at his or her own rate. Along with this should be an opportunity for the child to extend the movement patterns in the direction he or she chooses. He or she may be told to come up with some new ways or ideas of his or her own.

The start-and-expand technique (page 253) provides personalization in the sense that every child achieves a measure of success. The slogan "there is always another way" gives children the opportunity to explore and find alternative solutions.

Personalization also can take the form of allowing options in the way responses to a challenge may be structured or the way a skill may be performed. Obviously, inept and faulty movement responses should receive corrective attention. It is important to give credit for a good effort and to call attention to the particular achievement.

Allow opportunities for children to set their own goals. This can obviate some of the justifiable criticism of the lockstep approach in fitness activities. In performing Curl-ups, for example, the children could be allowed to set their own limits and strive toward the goals they themselves set.

The employment of the problem-solving approach and the related guided discovery method allows children to guide their own learning into personal channels. These methods, together with exploration and creativity, reach into the heart of personalized learning.

Perhaps a minor point should be made here. Recognizing and calling each individual in the class by name is a matter of personalization. It shows that the teacher regards the students as individuals.

Coping with Behavioral Problems

Children who display overt deviant behavior or who have problems that get in the way of their learning are discussed in this section. Two points should be established to provide a frame of reference. The first is that parents are becoming increasingly concerned about the permissive climate of the schools and the apparent lack of good discipline in them[3] This concern puts pressure on the school administration, which, in turn, passes it on to the teachers, who are told to "make the children mind."

The attraction of the physical education environment is just too much for some children. They run around wildly and chase and wrestle with other children. Directions go in one ear and out the other, and action without inhibition is apparent. There are two programs: the one they are doing and the one the teacher is trying to accomplish. The obvious answer is to eliminate the first program. But how? A first approach would be to establish definite entry behavior, so random activity is kept to a minimum. A second suggestion is to provide vigorous introductory activity with the goal of siphoning off some of the excess energy. Early attention to the stop signal, hand or whistle, establishes better class control.

If disciplinary trouble develops, one must look first at the teacher and the program; that is, is there any reason for the deviant behavior? After this has

---

[2]*Personalized Learning in Physical Education* (Washington, D.C.: AAHPER, 1976). The reader is referred to this book for further information.

[3]Phi Delta Kappa. *The Gallup Polls of Attitudes toward Education,* and *Phi Delta Kappan,* September 1974 and December 1975.

been determined, attention can be turned to the children. Some aggression is normal with children, but it must be channeled into proper outlets.

The selection of membership for squads offers an opportunity to minimize certain problems of association. It offers a chance to separate children who might cause trouble by being in too close association.

The class clown is a nuisance and sometimes a disturbing problem. His or her chief aim in life is to get the other children to laugh. Care should be used in asking such an individual to demonstrate. His or her antics should receive no support from the teacher. Acceptable responses should be encouraged.

Because of the attractiveness of physical participation, classroom teachers on occasion use the exclusion from physical education as a disciplinary measure for breaches of conduct not related to physical education. This cannot be regarded as a sound educational practice, since every child has a right to the learning experience. However, within the physical education class framework, temporary exclusion is effectively practiced by teachers. Children who do something naughty are told, "You go over to the sidelines and sit down. You tell us when you are ready to come back and play according to the rules."

Some legal concerns involving students' rights in the above procedures and other disciplinary measures are now essential considerations in the teaching process. While minor infractions may be handled routinely, exclusion and other substantial punishments may only be imposed on the student after due process. The problem of students' rights is rather complicated and merits further study. Many school systems have established guidelines and procedures within which the physical education teacher must operate.

The specialist should discuss serious behavioral problems with the classroom teacher, since the behavior in the physical education class may be a part of an overall problem. A cooperative approach should provide a better solution. Sometimes, the teacher can approach the problem directly by discussing it with the child and asking for his or her cooperation. The child may be trying to be recognized by others. Leadership roles and recognition can help him or her secure peer regard. The role of the school is to help him or her understand what the problem is, get it into proper focus, and organize his or her capabilities to solve his or her own problem through constructive action. The child should be taken from class only when he or she is disruptive enough to interfere with the learning experiences of the other children. Sending a child out of class is a last resort and means that both the teacher and the child have failed.

Such types of deviant behavior as deliberate disobedience, refusal to carry out the teacher's legitimate request, threats made by a student, and open and continued disrespect are red flags and demand immediate action, but avoid public scolding and sarcasm. Try to maintain composure and avoid malice.

Correction should be handled privately. Do not belittle or berate a child in front of his or her classmates. He or she may be misbehaving just to receive attention, and to give him or her this attention may reinforce behavioral problems. Analysis of the possible causes of the behavior should be made to find what is triggering the behavior.

Corrective measures, to be effective, should be applied consistently, and the consequences should be instituted immediately after the student exhibits the behavior, instead of hours or days later. Some things to avoid are being vindictive, holding grudges, punishing when one can no longer stand the behavior, and using excessively harsh or inappropriate measures. The punishment should be designed to decrease the occurrence of the behavior in the future and should not be directed toward the child as an individual.

Punishing the group for the misbehavior of a few children is not only palpably unfair, it can trigger unwanted side effects. Students can become quite hostile toward students who cause their loss of privilege. This lowers the level of good social interaction. If the group as a whole is misbehaving, perhaps punishing the whole group is appropriate. However, it provides no remedial solution for the problem of undesirable group behavior. On the other hand, group reward can be used to reward commendable effort or achievement.

An important antidote for discipline problems is a teaching climate of warmth, understanding, friendliness, and firmness. Another factor is the achievement of success by all children. Children who are given a taste of success and who develop pride in achievement are less likely to become discipline problems. It is important that the progressions be fragmented into increments, each of which carries the aura of success. Important, too, is praise for recognizing the successes and letting the students know that they are doing well.

The effect of praise on the overall academic progress and general integration of individuals into the learning process often is discussed. Praise in the educational process should follow certain guidelines. Praise should be honest in its application, and it should be given without preference. Praise should be directed to both the individual and his or her performance, and it should be specific rather than general.

The use of praise should far exceed the frequency of critical comments, perhaps by a ratio of four or five to one. In addition to verbal comments, nonverbal signs of approval (smiles, nods, hand signals, pats on the head, and so forth) are effective.

In shaping behavior, the teacher needs to look for bits of appropriate behavior and reinforce these with approval. Sometimes, teachers tend to leave children alone when they are working well, supplying behavioral control only when something is amiss. A better approach is to establish the positive climate as being what it should be rather than just correcting negative aspects.

Simply reciting rules and telling the children what they should be doing has little lasting effect. Students need to live in a warm social environment if they are to learn desirable social habits. In dealing with children, the teacher should avoid the either-or type of statement, which issues an ultimatum—conform or else.

Labeling by peers and faculty is a serious, negative reinforcer for a problem child. Although it is difficult, try to start afresh each day with a student. Avoid statements like "are you doing that again?" and "why can't you ever act decently?" If the teacher can look at behavioral problems as a failure in the child's education rather than as a personality defect, a first step has been realized. Essentially, self-control is a major goal in the disciplinary area and should be a part of the maturing process.

An aggressive tendency that needs to be guided is when winning becomes an obsession. Some children go to any extreme to finish first and allow their competitive urges to run out of control. They compete so intensely, try so hard, that they often are disliked. Developing tolerance and respecting the rights of others are values to emphasize in this situation.

On the other side is the shy, timid, reluctant child who tends to withdraw and not participate. He or she, too, perhaps cannot stand to lose, so he or she simply withdraws. He or she is afraid of failure.

Younger children exhibit these characteristics to a greater degree, and special approaches are needed. For reluctant children, both physical and emotional security are essential. The reluctant child may first watch. If he or she sees others enjoying themselves, he or she may join in of his or her own accord. It is important to give him or her a piece of success and work on this. It is also important to tolerate some failure, so the child does not fear rejection.

Suppose a child says, "I can't do it." Ask him or her if he or she *wants* to do it. Then help by saying, "Let's do it together."

Shy and timid children are more likely to be comfortable in situations in which they can explore and develop in relative privacy rather than face peer pressure. This means the child must work at his or her own rate and achieve his or her own level of success.

The teacher should expect each child to do well within his or her capacities. If the teacher is satisfied with poor work from the child, poor work is what the teacher will get. Failures must be pushed aside and a climate of expectancy established.

Communicating with the Learner

Basically, the teacher needs to be able to communicate with each child at his or her level of need; that is, the communication must get through the child's filter. The teacher must look toward developing the children's listening skills and not just their hearing skills. Suggestions for effective communication follow.

1. Get the children's undivided attention. If attention is not secured and held, do some self-analysis. Are you talking at the wrong time, or are you talking too much? Beginning teachers often tend to oversimplify and talk too much.
2. Be brief and to the point. Avoid excessive verbalization.
3. Speak in terms consistent with the comprehension and the maturity of the children. Gradually develop their vocabulary, but avoid technical terms that would not be understood. In working with disadvantaged children, be sure the terms are appropriate and relevant to the group.
4. Wait until the children are reasonably quiet, and then use a voice with enough carry to cover the group, but do not shout. Develop an even, modulated tone.
5. Stand where you can see all the children. Avoid the center of the circle. Position the children so that you, the teacher, are facing the sun or the light source.
6. In phrasing instructional points of the lesson, accent the positive. Instead of saying, "Don't land so hard," say, "Land lightly."
7. Avoid excessive repetition and reliance on certain words and phrases, such as "okay," "all right," and that irritating "and-uh."
8. Avoid rhetorical questions that are meant to be commands, such as "shall we go in now?" or "would you like to . . .?"
9. An easy way to emphasize the why of activity is to say, "Do this because . . ."
10. Use characteristic terms. For example, instructing the children to sit in Indian fashion has more meaning than telling them to sit cross-legged and fold their arms. Many stunts, exercises, and other activities have colorful, descriptive names.
11. There should be emphasis on following directions. This is not to be interpreted as "do as I tell you" but rather as operating within the

limits of the problem framework, which can be either narrow, with some limitation, or broad, with considerable flexibility. Sequence building is an excellent device for giving practice in following directions.

12. In talking with a student, "eyeballing" is important. Provide direct eye contact and a physical posture that tells the child nonverbally that you are paying attention. Facial and verbal cues reinforce this indication of interest. Remember that children want to understand *and* be understood.

13. Look for opportunities for *honest* praise. Praise may apply to:
    a. Attitudinal items (industry, effort, concentration, cooperation).
    b. Choice of materials.
    c. Selection of appropriate, effective, or unique methods.
    d. Achievement (progress, subgoals, overall goals).
    e. Finishing up (putting away materials).

14. Judicious use of questioning can give direction, encourage new movements, discourage repetition of movements already found, and stress cognitive elements. Certain techniques in the use of questions to stimulate movement deserve consideration.
    a. Use divergent questions that call for a thoughtful answer as opposed to convergent questions to which the child merely answers with yes or no or with a specific answer. Follow-up questions such as "who has another idea?" "what else do we need to think about?" and similar queries serve to expand discussion.
    b. When asking questions, select an individual child. A question thrown at a group gets a chorus of responses. The teacher then needs to designate a child to be heard, a procedure that should have been used in the first place.
    c. Children should wait to be recognized before answering, usually by raising a hand.
    d. Try to stimulate a free flow of ideas by expanding the answer with probing phrases, such as "what are other points?" and "let's have another reason."
    e. Respect the students' opinions as long as they are sincere. Avoid humiliating or condemning a child by downgrading his or her answer to a question. Pass over smart-alecky answers quickly by directing attention to more appropriate responses.
    f. Avoid injecting your own opinion too soon, if at all, into the instructional process. However, a summary of important points may be of value at times.

g. Time taken out for questions and discussion is a period of inactivity. Get children back into activity quickly, avoiding protracted periods of discussion. The practice by some teachers of tossing in question-and-answer periods simply to be in tune with the times is to be deplored.

15. Some open-ended directives might better be made definite. Instead of saying, "How many times can you . . . ?" or "See how many times . . . ," use definite goals. Some children, particularly slow learners, like definite goals. A definite number can be set by the teacher, or the child can set his or her own.

16. When a child does not respond to directions, an assessment needs to be made as to whether the difficulty is in communication or lack of ability.

17. Children may stand during short periods of instruction. When they have articles in their hands, see that they give the teacher the courtesy of holding them still. When the children begin to fidget, they are becoming uncomfortable in the standing position and should be seated.

Other Instructional Procedures

Instructional procedures applicable to a broad range of activities are presented in this section. Procedures relevant to specific activity areas are treated in the respective sections for each activity area.

1. See that each child has an opportunity to be active in the learning situation. Self-activity is the basis of physical learning and—for that matter—all learning. There should be enough equipment so that there can be individual activity. In group work, the children should be divided into small enough groups so that there is little waiting for turns. Standing, watching, and waiting should be kept to a minimum.

2. Get young children into activity as quickly as possible.

3. Involve all children in the program, including the physical underachievers, the handicapped, the overweight, and the unskilled. Give them special attention to help meet their needs.

4. Provide individual contact. Look and smile at children in an attempt to give each one individual attention.

5. Recognize that self-concept is learned and modifiable. This is the first step in helping students achieve satisfactory levels of achievement.

6. Make a conscious effort (it takes that) to avoid stereotyping or labeling children. Some

teachers react unconsciously and negatively to children with rotund body builds, causing the children to start their associations with the teachers at a disadvantage. Other biases can cause prejudice, also.

7. If children are assigned as leaders, give them an actual opportunity to lead. Give children all the responsibility they can assume.

8. Little class time should be devoted to discussion of social values and mores. Treatment of these topics can be done at a more leisurely pace in the classroom setting. Far more impact comes from effective class organization and a sound social climate.

9. Devise ways of moving children easily and efficiently from one activity to another. Spots or numbers painted on the floor provide personal space for all the children and give them a home base for individual activity.

10. Have respect for the dignity of the child. Avoid laying hands on him or her, pushing or placing him or her in position when he or she does not understand the directions.

11. Each child should be expected to work at or near his or her potential. It is important that children gain the concept that success can be achieved only through good effort. The child who doesn't "put out" is selling himself or herself short. When a teacher expects poor effort and work from a child, he or she certainly gets them. Children should learn to "give it a good try."

12. Have some kind of predetermined means of selecting partners. Partners can be set for a period of time, with children matched according to size or some other factors.

13. Partners can be used to divide the class into fairly equal groups. Have the children within each pair decide which one is to be #1 and which is to be #2. The #1s form one group and the #2s form the other. This division also can be done by having one of the partners sit down. All standing form one team and those sitting form the other.

14. A sanitation problem is present when children share whistles for officiating. Enough whistles are needed so that each referee can have one to himself or herself. Provisions for washing and sanitizing whistles emphasize good health procedures. Thorough washing and immersing in alcohol is one method.

DIRECTING THE LEARNING EXPERIENCE

A number of topics should be considered when the direction of activities is being discussed. The list is headed by safety in the instructional pro-gram, since safety is a first and overriding concern in any instructional approach. These topics are discussed in this section: (1) safety in the instructional program, (2) utilizing squads for effective class management, (3) entry and exit behavior, (4) equipment-handling procedures, (5) teacher observation and coaching, (6) demonstrations, (7) other instructional procedures in directing activities, and (8) formations useful in educational movement and skills instruction.

Safety in the Instructional Program

Policies for health and safety as they relate to administrative responsibility were introduced in chapter four. Additional safety suggestions of instructional nature are offered here. Safety precautions and considerations with respect to the various activity areas are presented with the instructional sequences and procedures of the separate activities. For example, softball has definite need for safety rules such as not throwing the bat and having the waiting batters stand in a safe area. These items relate only to softball and are discussed under that unit.

There is nothing automatic about establishing a good safety climate. Instruction in safety must be given along with the other elements of the activity, and the lesson plan should reflect safety emphasis. The positive approach should be stressed, with emphasis on how to play safely in contrast to the scare approach that emphasizes possible injuries.

Once the rules have been established, good supervision and observation are needed to insist on correct and safe application of the rules. Some important general considerations for safety are these.

1. The first responsibility is to see that the playing area is a suitable and safe environment. A quick assessment by the teacher should note the presence of obstructions that might prove hazardous. The area should be of sufficient size.

2. Next, the teacher *must* consider the forthcoming activity and what is needed for safe participation. The children should know the basic and lead-up skills well enough for safe participation. They should be instructed in needed safety procedures and rules. The teacher needs to make sure the safety regulations are followed.

3. Where the children are in groups, leave sufficient space between them. The activity should not demand that the children of different groups run toward each other, since nasty collisions can occur. Also, where throws are employed, as in dodgeball, distances should be such that the throw has lost its force or hits

the ground before entering the territory of another group.

4. In ball activities, teach children to keep their eyes on the ball and not to throw the ball to another child unless he or she is watching.

5. Traffic rules in games and drills are important. Children should pass to the right when coming toward each other in games. Establish the time or distance when children follow each other, such as consecutive turns on a mat, high jumping, or the Challenge Course. One-way patterns should be established for other activities.

6. Establish rules for recovering balls that go out of play. A child may recover a ball as long as no one is between him or her and the ball. This avoids the competitive situation in which several children chase the ball.

7. Stringent rules are necessary regarding procedures in recovering balls that go into streets, areas of other groups, apparatus areas, and so forth. A stop-and-look pause should precede any action for recovery. Some teachers use the rule that a child may not go into a street unless given permission by the teacher.

8. Shoelaces should remain tied. Stop the play and see that this is done. Children should be required to wear shoes for outside activity. In some races and contests, children like to remove shoes because they feel they can travel faster, but this should not be permitted.

9. Maintain the instructional climate by not permitting horseplay and unnecessary roughness. Viciousness, such as vindictive tagging, has no place in physical education.

10. Children should be cautioned against bringing pencils or pens to the physical education class, and they should not be allowed to chew gum or munch on suckers.

11. During rough activity, glasses should be removed or glass guards made available. If glasses are removed, establish a safe place for them.

12. During the first week of the school year, a safety presentation should be part of the lesson. The children should be given a guided tour of both outdoor and indoor facilities, and safety considerations for each piece of apparatus and each play area should be explained. The items to be covered should be decided on before the tour; they should not be just offhand explanations by the teacher. Later, a description of what was covered, and in what fashion, may be needed if a liability suit is filed. The safety orientation must be directed to all the children in the school.

13. Teach children to keep their hands off other children, since this is not only annoying but can lead to conflict and possible injury.

Utilizing Squads for Effective Class Management

It is helpful for the teacher to organize youngsters into various formations in order to facilitate the teaching process and minimize management time. Squad formation, when it is used properly and is not overused, can be an effective means for arranging youngsters. Oftentimes, teachers fall into the habit of bringing the students into squad formation each time they want to communicate with them. This is not only unnecessary, it can waste a great deal of time. The following are some guidelines for using squad formation to maximize teaching effectiveness.

1. In selecting squads or groups, use methods of selection that do not embarrass a child chosen last. In no case should this be a slave-market type of selection, in which the leaders look over the group and visibly pick whom they wish. Some alternative ways for placing youngsters in groups might be for the teacher to select the squads ahead of time and arrange them so that there is a balance of ability levels in all squads; for the teacher to select some students to pick squads privately before class; and for the teacher to have students pick squads when they do not know which squads they are to be the captains of because the teacher assigns them to squads other than the ones they picked the members for.

2. A designated location should be used for assembling students in squad formation. When the teacher wants students to be in their squads, they should move to the predesignated location, with squad leaders in front and the rest of the squad trailing.

3. Squads are an effective device for providing opportunities for leadership and followership among peers. The teacher should make maximum use of squad leaders, so they feel that being a leader is a privilege that entails certain responsibilities. Examples of leadership activities might be gathering equipment for their squads, moving their squads to a specified location, leading their squads through squad-leader exercises or various introductory activities, and appointing members of the squads to certain positions in sport activities.

4. Squad leaders should be changed at least every three weeks, and the composition of squads altered every nine weeks. In all cases, every youngster should have an opportunity to lead.

5. In most cases, an even number of squads

should be formed. This allows the class to be quickly broken into halves for games. Six squads in a class of 30 students with only 5 members per squad means that in group activities there is a small number of students per piece of apparatus.

6. A creative teacher can make the use of squads an exciting and worthwhile activity instead of one that restricts movement and creativity. For example, cones are numbered and placed in different locations in the activity area. When students enter the gym, they are instructed to find their squad number and assemble. The numbers could be written in a different language or hidden in a mathematical equation or a story problem. Another idea that can make the use of squads an enjoyable experience is to spread out in an area task cards that specify how the squads are supposed to arrange themselves. The first squad to do so correctly should be awarded a point or some acknowledgment from the rest of the class. An example of some tasks for the squads might be arranging the members in a circle, sitting with their hands on their heads, and arranging themselves in crab position in a straight line facing northwest. The cards might specify what the children are to do for introductory activity or specify where they should go for their fitness development activity.

7. Allow the youngsters to find names for their squads. This can help them feel as though they are parts of select groups, and this feeling makes the activity more enjoyable for both teacher and students. Youngsters should be encouraged to develop pride in their squads.

Entry and Exit Behavior

Definite procedures are necessary for children to have a sense of security from knowing what to do when they enter the lesson area and exit after the lesson is over. The aim of definite entry behavior is to minimize management time and get the children into activity as soon as possible.

If the children need to change shoes in the gymnasium, this should be accomplished as expeditiously as possible, since little lesson activity can occur until all have made the change. For younger children in classes taught by specialists, help from classroom teachers for putting on shoes and tying laces conserves learning time. Instruction and practice in tying shoelaces is desirable.

Shoes may need to be marked for younger children, so right and left shoes can be identified. Position the shoes so that the inside edges are together and then place corresponding marks so that these come together when the correct shoe is on the foot. This avoids the right shoe being on the left foot and vice versa.

Having all shoes, both gymnasium and street, marked minimizes squabbles over ownership. A routine, orderly arrangement of street shoes should be established, so the child can find his or her own shoes quickly and without unnecessary scrambling. Some difficulties should be anticipated when children change back to street shoes. A few thoughtless children engage in playing tricks (such as hiding shoes, throwing them across the play area, tying knots in the laces, and so on) for their own amusement. This may take the character of a vendetta against one or two children, who are picked on by the others. Having squads put their shoes in different areas minimizes this prob-

A Class in Squad Formation

lem. If children change shoes in the classroom, a desirable procedure for younger children can be putting the shoes underneath the children's desks.

Some efficient means should be instituted for conveying to the specialist the names of children who are not to participate in the lesson. It is best if this decision is made before the children arrive at the lesson area. A note from the classroom teacher listing the names and health problems of those who are to watch or take part in modified activity can be delivered to the specialist as the children enter the room. The physical education teacher should accept the information at face value. This avoids the time-consuming procedure in which the teacher must question the students on the sidelines to determine what the problem is and what solution should be arrived at. Obviously, this procedure is not needed when the classroom teacher handles the teaching.

After the change to gym shoes has been made, the students should know their next moves. Equipment should be available and used until all shoe changing is completed, or the children can be directed to assemble for instruction in a specified area.

Some teachers like to have children assemble for instruction after they have changed their shoes, so that explanations of the lesson direction can be given. The teacher should understand that the children are excited over the opportunity to be active and that sitting quietly and listening at this point is not a satisfying experience. Explanations should be brief and to the point. Other teachers like to start with an introductory activity and then give any instructions necessary. A third plan is to have both the introductory activity and the fitness work before explanations are given. The children are glad for a moment's rest and to sit and listen while they recover from the strenuous activity.

Although children should move rapidly from station to station, wild and unruly running, particularly at the onset of the class, is hardly educational.

After the lesson is completed, exit procedures need to be enacted. Equipment procedures will be discussed in the next section. Changing shoes and forming for the return to the classroom may be the only items needing structuring.

Equipment-handling Procedures

Ideally, equipment should be made available and returned systematically without infringing too much on learning time. A system that has the children handle the equipment whenever possible is necessary. Instruction in the proper ways of handling, carrying, and moving equipment makes the process more efficient and safe. Respect for equipment should be taught, since the children should take care of equipment as if it were their own.

Sometimes, one or more children may be sent before the class to prepare the equipment and/or instructional supplies before the other children arrive. Or selected children might get the equipment ready while the rest of the class is participating in the introductory activity. Equipment monitors or squad leaders can take the lead in issuing and returning equipment. After the lesson is over, the teacher should assign children to put things back where they belong.

Observation and Coaching

Observation is a critical skill in prescriptive teaching, and effective observation provides the basis for productive coaching. Coaching is defined as assisting children to a higher level of movement competency while they are practicing the skill.

Observation and coaching are usually oriented toward individuals, but they can be group oriented. When the teacher circulates among the children to correct their shortcomings and suggest improvements, the teacher's approach is individual and yet the class is not interrupted. When the teacher notices that a particular point should be emphasized to the majority of the class, the teacher can stop the class and make a suggestion for the whole group. Opportunity for discussion and clarification are important in the group-coaching process.

Observation should be based on a valid frame of reference. The general principles of movement and skill in chapter six relate to all movement. Technique points pertaining to a particular skill form the second area for observation. Assessment needs to be made of the implementation of subskills and necessary progressions, with the goal of accepting the child where he or she is and guiding him or her to where he or she should be.

Coaching can help develop both the quality and the quantity of movement. Breadth of movement is stimulated through the use of different ways, directions, and alternatives, including motivation of the child toward full effort.

Coaching also must acknowledge individual differences. To expect all children to perform alike leads only to their frustration. Each child should be stimulated and encouraged to develop his or her pattern of success.

Communication in coaching must be kept on the child's level. Verbally and physically, the teacher should try to help as many children as possible. Care must be taken to avoid coaching too many points at one time, since this confuses and frustrates children. Concentrate on major points first, and leave minor refinements until later.

Demonstrations

Demonstrations serve the purpose of illustrating variety or depth of movement, showing something unique or different, pointing out items of good technique or approach, illustrating different acceptable styles, and showing progress or accomplishments.

Demonstrations can be performed by the teacher or selected students. Care must be taken that the selected student can accomplish the purpose of the demonstration. Rotating the demonstration among many students is a sound practice, but it is difficult to escape using the most skilled. Asking for volunteers tends to eliminate the stigma of teacher's favorite. All children should have the chance to demonstrate at some time.

The demonstration should be directed toward increasing the child's understanding and movement potential. A child needs to observe critically and analyze rather than just be entertained by the presented movements. In order that he or she may profit by what he or she has just viewed, the demonstration should be followed by a period of practice.

Be sure that all the children can see and hear and are paying attention to the performance. In explaining technique, the reasons behind the points should be brought out. The teacher can get into the habit of adding *because* to statements, for example, "hold the ball in the pads of the fingers *because* . . ."

It is a poor instructional procedure to demonstrate something the children already know. Sometimes, a period of observation as the children practice alerts the teacher to this.

Teacher demonstration to establish proper technique can take a number of forms. He or she can show only the proper starting position and then verbalize from that point. He or she can provide a more complete point-by-point demonstration, leading to better visualization by the students. Teacher demonstration should keep the terminology and demonstrated techniques on the children's level—it should not be an example of adult performance.

The more critical the skill, the more demonstration is needed. For more flexible movement patterns, demonstration may not be desirable. Demonstrations often lead to imitative behavior, which is a goal only when critical technique points are involved.

In educational movement, in which the goal is to develop variety and versatility in movement, demonstrations should be used only infrequently at the beginning of the lesson, and children should be given the opportunity to develop individual approaches rather than imitate the style of another child. However, a few basics might be presented early in the lesson or in the introductory phases of the lesson to give direction to the activity.

The question-and-answer technique has a place in the demonstration process, but it must not dominate it. Questions can be directed toward such learning elements as what is good, what factors are important, and what directions the efforts should take. Care must be taken so that the demonstration period does not become too protracted due to a lengthy question-and-answer period.

Demonstrations dwelling on uniqueness, variety, and achievement should come from the students. The pattern of demonstration from students can take several forms.

The Single Demonstration

As the students are practicing and moving, the class can be stopped for an individual to show what he or she has done. Comments should be positive, not derogatory, in nature. Should the demonstration be unsatisfactory, the teacher could go on to another child without comment or reprimand. The teacher might say, "Thank you, Carl. Let's see what Janet can do." Or he or she might direct the children to get back to work. The absence of positive reinforcement in this instance becomes the reprimand. Clowning and silliness should be cut off immediately.

Sometimes, only one child may be selected; however, it is usually better to select several children so that the students may observe varied approaches. If partner or small-group work is undertaken, the same principle holds. However, having each individual demonstrate his or her achievement is not efficient use of class time.

The single demonstration is a most effective teaching technique for interjecting children's ideas into the lesson sequences. A perceptive teacher circulating throughout the instructional area can pinpoint unique and different movement patterns that a child can show.

The Multiple Demonstration

The multiple demonstration has value for achievement demonstrations to show what has been accomplished after a period of practice or at the end of a unit. One convenient way to organize this is to have squads demonstrate. In utilizing squads, the teacher may select one or more squads to demonstrate and then direct the children to return to activity. Other squads could have turns later. The teacher might even use this as a motivational device by telling the children, "After a period of time, I am going to select the squad that I feel has made the best progress and ask them to demonstrate." Another way is to have half the class demonstrate while the other half watches.

The Teacher Who Cannot Demonstrate

There are teachers who, because of physical limitations, cannot demonstrate effectively. Few teachers who are not physical education specialists can do all physical activities well. Even the relatively skilled teacher at times needs to devise substitutions for an effective demonstration. For the teacher who has difficulty demonstrating activities, the following suggestions should prove helpful.

1. Through reading, study, analysis of movement, and other devices, arm yourself with an understanding and a knowledge of the activities that you have difficulty demonstrating. Even if you cannot perform, know how the activity is to be done.
2. Select skillful children to help demonstrate.
3. Be able to verbalize the skill so that you can coach the students and correct their errors.
4. Use effective visual aids at appropriate points in the unit.
5. Place more reliance on the squad leaders and use the squad formation in skill drills.

Other Instructional Procedures for Directing Activities

1. The teacher should use the daily lesson plan as the basis of the instruction. For the experienced teacher, the plan can be brief. Proper coverage of material is assured only through planned lessons.
2. Analyze each activity from the standpoint of how maximum movement can be a part of the activity. Activities are a means of development through movement, and as much movement as possible must be coaxed from them. A major technique to be acquired is the ability to change and vary an activity so that the most value can be secured from what is chosen for learning experiences. Be alert for changes that can increase interest and make more physical demands on the children. The children should be a source of suggestions for change and variations.
3. Use the whistle sparingly. Give one sharp blast and insist on the courtesy of attention. Early attention to this pays off later in the dividends of time saved. The whistle should be used only to halt activity. Starting commands for activities can be given with verbal signals. The whistle should mean stop, look (at the teacher), and listen.
4. Hand signals can be used to control activities that are not competitive. Raising one hand overhead means stop. Raising both arms overhead means assemble here. A thumb down means sit down. A thumb up means get up.
5. Use the more formal methods of organization only when needed. Stunts and tumbling are examples of activities in which good selection of formations is needed for safety and good teaching.

6. Background music can be played during many activities, particularly for stunts and tumbling. Music should be the quiet, relaxing type.
7. Techniques of evaluation should be a part of the program. Only through evaluative procedures can the degree of progress toward the objectives of the program be assessed.
8. At times, allow choice of activity.
9. Children love to run for the sheer zest of activity. Provide time in the program for this basic drive.
10. When referring to the use of one limb and then the other for young children, approach it just that way rather than making the designation of right and left. Right and left designations are important in establishing directionality and are to be used only for this reason. Say, "Step forward with one foot" rather than "Step forward with the right (or left) foot." When it makes no difference which limb is to be initially employed or which side they are to move, let the children choose.
11. At times, allow for experimentation and exploration by the children. The teacher may find it appropriate to give basic instruction in the topic or skill and then allow for exploration and creative activity based upon the material just presented.
12. When giving instructions for an activity, be explicit. If there are different, acceptable ways to perform the activity, show these and discuss with the children the reasons behind the various differences in technique. Explain enough to get the activity underway successfully.
13. Set up your procedures so that, when the explanation is completed, the activity can begin.
14. Know and emphasize the stress points in an activity. These are the critical points that are important to success in an activity.
15. A physical education class needs to be a happy medium between quiet and boisterousness. Youngsters should be able to let off steam but be under control. Two types of noise should be differentiated. The first is the noise growing out of purposeful activity, interest, and enjoyment. The second is noise that springs from disorder, lack of interest, rowdyism, and lack of control.
16. The teachers need to be careful that their own interests do not rule the program. Generally, adults drift toward those activities that they know and can do successfully.
17. While desirable learnings can result in a proper learning atmosphere, these are not automatic for activities but are the result of planning. Relays can be used as an example. In a good learning atmosphere, a child can

learn to cooperate, to observe rules, and to go along with the capacities of his or her teammates. On the other hand, in a poorly conducted class, he or she can learn to cheat, to become intolerant of the shortcomings of the members of his or her team, and to put winning above all other goals.

18. The development of courtesy, fair play, and honesty are important goals to be achieved by elementary school children. Teachers should note in their lesson plans where opportunities exist for the introduction of these social concepts. Their development must not be left to chance.

19. Conceptual understanding should be incorporated into the lesson. Skills should not be taught in isolation but should be coupled with the appropriate principles of movement and force.

20. In addition to alleviating the child's fear of failure, it is also important to tolerate some failure so that the child does not fear rejection. A child needs to feel capable and comfortable in what he or she is doing.

21. Teach children to wait for instruction before using equipment they have been issued. They should receive this instruction promptly. In some cases, it is well to tell the child what to get and what to do with it at the same time, so he or she can immediately begin to practice.

22. Before any challenge is posed to the children, the teacher should have some conception of the approximate movement responses that the challenge could elicit.

23. Try to sense when interest in an activity is waning and the activity should be modified or changed.

24. Take into consideration the children's fatigue level and modify activity accordingly.

25. When children cannot make responsible choices, options should be limited.

26. Very early in movement training, insist that the children not interfere with or touch each other.

27. If the classroom teacher has the responsibility for the physical education instruction, maximum use of activity time can be derived by giving time-consuming explanations in the classroom before the scheduled time for going to the play area. Rules can be explained, procedures and responsibilities outlined, and formations illustrated on the blackboard.

Formations Useful in Educational Movement and Skill Instruction

The instructional process should include consideration of an appropriate formation or arrangement for children that can best guide learning in the intended activity. The general type of activity has a bearing, because different formations are needed for activities in place (nonlocomotor), activities in which the children move (locomotor), and propelling and receiving activities (manipulative). In the latter classification are balls, beanbags, and other objects that are thrown or kicked and caught or received. A number of formations have usefulness in more than one area.

Mass or Scattered

Children are scattered throughout the area in random fashion to allow each student his or her own personal space. This formation is useful for in-place activities and individual movement in every direction. In locomotor movement, the children need to be cautioned about collisions and courtesy. The formation is basic for such activities as wands, hoops, individual rope jumping, and individual ball skills (nonpartner). One needs to watch for fringers, those children who go to the outskirts of the group, and close friends who gravitate together.

Extended Squad

This is a more structured formation based on squad organization that accomplishes about the same purpose. In the normal squad formation, members stand about a yard apart in a column. In extended formation, the squad column is maintained with more distance (10 to 15 feet) between members. The illustration shows both a regular and an extended squad formation.

Regular ⓛ X X X X X X

Extended ⓛ X X X X X X

Partner

This formation is most important in throwing, catching, kicking, and receiving skills. One ball or object is needed for each pair. On the playground, where there is sufficient room, pairs can scatter. Indoors, keeping the pairs in somewhat parallel fashion minimizes problems with flying balls.

Small Groups (by Twos, Threes, or Fours)

This is similar to partner arrangement but includes a few more children. Children work together with either a fundamental movement problem or ball skills.

Lane or File

This is the basic relay formation. It can be used for locomotor activity during which those in front move as prescribed and then take their places in the rear of the lane.

```
X  X  X  X
X  X  X  X
X  X  X  X
X  X  X  X
X  X  X  X
X̲  X̲  X̲  X̲
```

Squad with Leader (Lane plus One)

This is another useful relay formation, with possibly minor use in skill practice, but it has utility for throwing and catching skills. Each leader is positioned a short distance in front of his or her squad.

```
X  X  X  X
X  X  X  X
X  X  X  X
X  X  X  X
X̲  X̲  X̲  X̲
Ⓛ Ⓛ Ⓛ Ⓛ
```

Squad Formation, Re-forming at the Other End of the Space

The leading child in each squad begins his or her movement across the floor. When he or she is about halfway, the next child starts. The squads re-form at the other end and get ready for another movement.

SQUAD RE-FORMS
ON THIS END

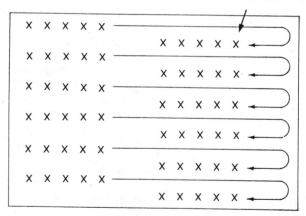

Squads in Crisscross Formation

Squads form as indicated, with two opposite squads moving at a time. In effect, they exchange places. Members of each squad move in turn when the child in front is far enough ahead. After the first two squads have performed, the other squads move similarly.

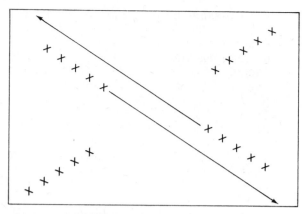

Line and Leader

This formation often is used for throwing and catching skills; the leader passes back and forth to each line player in turn. It makes a nice revolving relay.

Semicircle and Leader

This is a variation of line and leader.

Circle

This formation is one of long standing and is useful for ball-handling skills such as passing, kicking, and volleying.

```
    X  X
  X      X
  X      X
    X  X
```

Circle and Leader

This is another ball-handling formation, which also can serve as the basis for relays. The leader passes to each member of the circle in turn.

Double Line

This formation is good for passing and kicking. The illustration shows a zigzag formation that is more efficient than if corresponding players in each line were opposite each other. The ball is passed across from one line to the next.

Regular Shuttle

The movement of the players is similar to that of a shuttle of a loom, hence the name. It can be done with as few as three players, but more are generally used. It serves as the basis of dribbling (hockey, soccer, and basketball) skills, passing, and ball carrying (football). It also serves as a relay formation. Essentially, the player at the head of one line dribbles toward, or passes to, the player at the head of the other line. Each player keeps moving forward and takes his or her place at the end of the other half of the shuttle.

Shuttle Turn-back

This formation is used for passing, kicking, and volleying. The player at the head of one shuttle line passes to the player at the head of the other. After passing, each player goes to the back of his or her half of the shuttle.

Note: The remainder of the formations are useful mostly for locomotor movements, either around the room area or forward and backward. The formations are especially important in teaching fundamental locomotor skills in the educational movement program.

Around the Area in a Circular Fashion

The objection to this is that it creates competition and generates conformity. However, collisions are not likely, and the teacher can observe the children effectively.

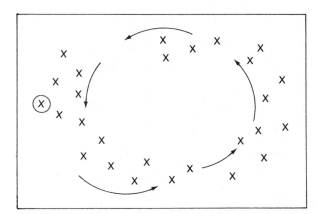

On Opposite Sides of the Room, Exchanging Positions

The children, on signal, cross to the opposite side of the area, passing through the opposite line.

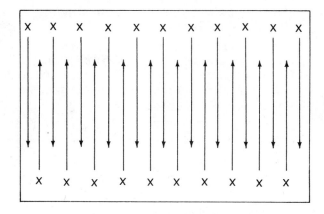

On Adjacent Sides, Crossing Over

On adjacent sides of the room or area, two lines of children take turns crossing to the other side.

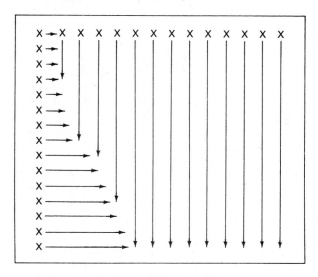

On Opposite Sides, Moving to the Center and Back

A center line can be formed with ropes, wands, or cones to mark the center limit. Children move to the center of the area and then return to place.

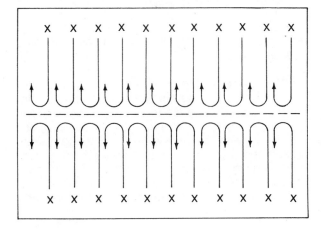

On Opposite Sides, One Line Moving Across and Back

The two sides alternate in their turns. The line of children from one side crosses to a point near the other line and then makes a turn, returning to place. After these children have completed the movement, the other group takes a turn.

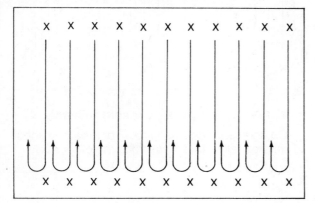

On Four Sides and Exchanging

The children on one pair of opposite sides exchange first, and then the others exchange. They alternate back and forth in this manner.

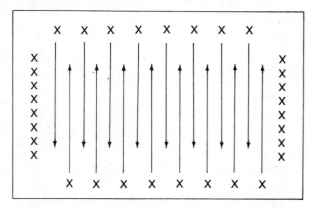

FURTHER CONSIDERATIONS IN THE LEARNING PROCESS

Included here is attention to such topics as leadership experiences, instructional aids, bulletin boards, and displays.

Leadership Experiences

If the goals of leadership and followership are to be realized, the program must provide social situations in which the students have real opportunities to lead. The very nature of the physical education program provides many jobs that can be distributed among students to give them real opportunities to assume responsibility. These experiences result on the one hand in an understanding of the nature of authority and responsibility and on the other in an acceptance by the children of the leadership authority so designated.

Guides for the Leadership Program

1. The jobs assigned should be realistic and definite and should be assigned over a designated time period. Job descriptions help orient the child to the proper performance of duties. A list of duties avoids overlapping and designates definite areas of responsibility.
2. The leadership program is not to be regarded as a time-saving device for the teacher. Furthermore, it is unfair to ask children to assume responsibilities without adequate guidance. The teacher must give due consideration to the training of the leaders and provide sufficient supervision. This takes both time and effort.
3. If leadership is considered a fine developmental opportunity, then it follows that it is good for all children. Jobs should be rotated at specified periods so that all children are given some type of responsibility during the year. It is recognized that jobs require different levels of ability and that the teacher must assign them carefully on the basis of the child's capacity.
4. The student should be held to a reasonable standard of job performance. He or she should be brought to the realization that to be a leader requires planning, and he or she must allot sufficient time to planning and discharging his or her duties.
5. The use of leaders actually should improve the efficiency of the class. The important element is not leadership but the quality of the physical education experience. A class should not suffer through an inferior experience because of the emphasis on leadership training.
6. Elementary school youngsters are not mature enough to be left in charge of a group for too long a period. Even a child with good leadership ability cannot cope with situations in depth.
7. Some consideration can be given to a leaders' club, which could include all the leaders for a given period. Such a club can be organized in a class or on an all-school basis. Leaders' clubs can meet during the club period in the regular curriculum or be scheduled for an afterschool session or a Saturday morning. The club organization provides for good discussion of duties, an improved *esprit de corps,* and definite discharge of duties.
8. While children gain from leadership experiences, care must be taken to ensure that the leaders are not kept too busy to participate in

the regular program. Also, assistant leaders could be appointed, assuming head duties during the next period. Continuity can be preserved in this manner.

Types of Leadership Experiences

Equipment Manager: Obtains, arranges, and returns equipment for the day's activities.

Area Supervisor: The duties of this individual include marking fields, setting up boundaries, and, in general, seeing that the area is ready for the activity. Indoors, this would entail duties like setting up mats or getting the public address system ready.

Squad Leaders: The possibilities in this area are numerous. Responsibilities vary from simple tasks like keeping the squad in proper order for relays or taking turns in stunt activities to supervisory responsibilities in the teaching of skills. Routine record keeping of individual performances and test scores can be a part of the duties.

Officials: Officials need to have a thorough knowledge of the rules of the games. Enough officials can be assigned so that each one gets a chance to play in the activity and still hold his or her position.

Game Leader, Demonstrator, Exercise Leader: Children can be assigned to choose and lead a game. If the activity or situation makes pupil demonstration desirable, the teacher can assign these duties to selected and properly directed students. Trained students also may lead exercises.

Monitors: Special responsibilities can be assigned to monitors. Turning lights on and off, supervising the cleanup after class, and making safety inspections are duties that monitors can assume.

Weekly Equipment Organizers: A solution to the vexing problem of keeping the equipment in order is to have from two to four students assigned to take responsibility for providing proper order. Rearranging can be done late in the school day on Friday or even after school. The equipment room is cleaned, materials are put away, and needed repairs are routed to the proper source. Each week begins with an orderly equipment room.

Playground Monitors: A group of students can be organized to help with the supervision of play areas. This assistance from students should augment but not substitute for the legally required adult supervision.

Instructional Aids in Physical Education

Visual Aids

Loop films, videotape recordings, motion pictures, filmstrips, slides, overhead projectors, and opaque projectors are beneficial. The visual aid should fit in with the learning situation and be appropriate for children. Visual aids that have children illustrating activities for children are more valuable than ones that do not.

Since the rental charge covers the use of the film for a period of time, coordination with other classes should be arranged for additional showings. Programs ought to be projected far enough ahead so films may be scheduled for correct placement in the program.

Visual aids emphasizing skill techniques should be shown early in a skill learning unit. Those illustrating strategies and game situations probably can come later.

Loop films have become an important medium of instruction. A wide variety of topics is available, including many movement techniques. Projectors utilizing plastic cartridges have made this an effective aid for instruction. Schools can make their own loop films using Super-Eight film and an inexpensive camera like the ones tourists use.

Videotape recorders provide both the students and the teacher with a visual record of class lessons, offering a critical instrument for analysis and evaluation. Sound and action can be recorded simultaneously, but conversation may be unintelligible.

Sound films and sound strips generally need to be shown without interruption. Discussion can be permitted during a slide presentation or with a filmstrip without sound.

Teachers should give some thought to the use of 35-millimeter slides as a teaching tool. Critical skills are difficult to illustrate, but formations, game boundaries, and field layouts lend themselves to the home slide projector.

The overhead projector uses transparencies to project images on a wall or screen. Children can help with the formulation of the transparencies.

Another useful tool to consider is the opaque projector. This device, like the old magic lantern, throws on the screen an enlarged version of the material. A teacher who uses a card system for games, rhythms, or other activities may find this an effective and useful time-saver.

Bulletin Boards

The class bulletin board should devote a proportionate space to physical education. Select a theme for the board and change it often. A theme could illustrate fitness, a unit, a sport, physical education in other areas, posture, or health practices. A particular skill could be selected for illustration. Pictures from magazines, newspapers, and other sources could be used for illustrations.

The board can be constructed of wall board or beaver board that holds thumbtacks or staples. A backdrop made of colored paper or colored muslin makes a nice display. The color scheme can be tied up with the theme and changed with the display. Some materials that can be used include these.

1. Pictures and diagrams make excellent displays. Snapshots can be included. Newspaper materials should be pasted or stapled to sturdy paper for better display.
2. Colored paper of all kinds and colors is needed. Construction paper is excellent.
3. Stick people can be made from pipe cleaners. These are interesting and provide an outlet for creative talent.
4. Yarn or string can make field outlines or provide borders for the displays.

The character of the bulletin board is limited only by the children's imaginations. The responsibility for the board could be assigned to groups of children on a rotating basis. An interesting bulletin board program also offers possibilities for integration with academic subjects.

Displays

Displays offer possibilities similar to bulletin boards. However, the display is generally done in three dimensions. The display should have the material organized around a theme. A display might be put in a showcase in the school hall. It could be arranged on a table in the classroom.

Six

The Basis of Movement Learning

Movement is an integral part of all learning. If children are going to enjoy movement, they need to understand the basis for movement, develop a positive feeling for activity, and achieve adequate levels of competency in their movement patterns. Elementary schools should place high priority on the development of a broad range of movement skills in children. Psychomotor skills, when attained at a reasonable level of competency, help children enjoy participation in various types of activity. Some educators believe that the critical variable in developing lifelong patterns of exercise depends on developing a satisfactory level of competency in physical activity for youngsters before they leave school.

It is important for a teacher to understand the nature of movement learning and to be able to apply the principles important in skill performance. A youngster needs a chance to explore and experiment with his or her physical capacities, and he or she can learn much through this process. However, the youngster must be taken beyond this stage by the teacher. The student needs the instructor to help him or her consolidate his or her gains, to add new insights, and to coach him or her to higher levels of performance.

A distinction should be made between what is movement and what is *educational* movement. Movement becomes learning when it accomplishes something for the child and helps him or her toward the realization of his or her educational potential. Progress in motor learning can be broken down into three areas.

1. The Acquisition of New Elements of Learning: The child has the opportunity to acquire new skills, knowledges, attitudes, and concepts.
2. Improvement and Consolidation of Learned Elements Deemed Desirable: What the child has that is good should be reinforced, consolidated, and expanded, so it becomes a part of his or her personal heritage.
3. Lessening and Elimination of Undesirable Learned Elements: In this area, the teacher needs to help the child rid himself or herself of habits that get in the way of his or her learning and cause conflict in his or her personal living. Substitution of the desirable for the undesirable is the key to this learning situation.

It is quite obvious that physical education activity not only is an end in itself, it is a learning environment for the achievement of other educational outcomes. It is equally apparent that the teacher is the key factor in guiding the movement experiences so that learning occurs.

Teaching methods and the selection of the activities in the program should be based on how children learn movement efficiently and so are able to achieve success and satisfaction in movement experiences.

PRINCIPLES OF LEARNING MOTOR SKILLS

The learning process involved in mastering motor skills can be made more productive when pertinent tenets from educational doctrine and motor learning research can be applied. The applications vary according to the stage of learning, the activities presented, and the maturity of the children.

Capability

Capability means that the learning task is within the physical capacity of the child, that he or she is capable of doing what he or she is expected to do. A number of factors affect capability, among them maturational level, previous experience, genetic endowment, and state of physical fitness. The key point is that the teacher's time is wasted having children try to perform a movement action or response before they are ready.

Maturational level involves the gross physical and neural body management competencies necessary for the child to have a basis for success and be challenged by the selected movement pattern. For example, a child must have the ability to track a moving object before he or she can become proficient in catching skills.

Capability can be modified by appropriate experience in movement. If the child lacks the capability to perform a task, the activity should be modified in a progressive manner. For example, if a child cannot catch a small, quickly moving object, it would be of little value to have him or her play a game of softball or baseball. It would be beneficial to bring out a larger, slower moving, and brightly colored object such as a beach ball for his or her practice sessions. The youngster must have the capability to perform the substitute activities of lesser challenge or further frustration will occur.

Readiness

Readiness is closely tied to capability in that readiness involves both the physical capability and the emotional aptitude for learning an activity. Most experts agree that an optimum state of readiness for each learner is defined as the level at which the child learns most efficiently with the least difficulty. Whenever possible, the teacher should recognize and utilize the optimum point for each learner. The point is difficult to recognize, since students mature at different rates. However, if attempts are not made to analyze each student's progress frequently and the teaching level is beyond the level of readiness, negative attitudes of frustration and withdrawal may appear. This again reaffirms the necessity of both individualizing instruction and personalizing the teaching methodology.

A good understanding of the characteristics and interests of youngsters should give the teacher an understanding of the student and his or her abilities. This understanding improves the selection of activities for meeting the child's readiness level.

In general, boys have been found to perform better in those gross motor skills that demand strength and large-body movements, while girls perform better in fine motor skills that require a high degree of coordination and precision. These tendencies may be attributed to the environmental setting rather than to genetic endowment, but it does point out the need for offering youngsters experience and participation in a wide variety of movement experiences in order to enhance their readiness to learn. Specific skill activities often are learned earlier when the child has had the advantage of enriched movement experiences during the preschool years.

Interest in activity plays a role in readiness levels, because people do things in which they are interested and, in turn, if they do well at an activity, they become ready to learn more about the activity. Often, interests and abilities go together. People want to do well in an activity because of the social rewards that are coupled with their success. Teachers have the responsibility of offering worthwhile experiences based on the student's existing interests, but they must go beyond this point to establish new interests and experiences. It also seems important for the teacher to attempt to curb interests that result in an unnecessary and unrewarding expenditure of time.

Motivation

Capability and readiness imply that the child can learn and is ready to learn. Being motivated means that the child wants to learn. Capability and readiness have both a physical and a neural basis, while motivation centers on psychological drives. The learner must have a need—some kind of drive to action—or little learning can take place. Children must want to learn, and the teacher can have a marked effect on the child's motivational level.

Physical education itself often is motivating to children simply because they associate it with recess and play, and play to them is fun. This feeling must not be lost. Students' faces always should light up when the teacher announces that it is time for physical education class. This excitement can be stirred up by something new, something different, or something challenging or perhaps by a new teaching style. Children enjoy losing themselves in the spirit of adventure and the novelty of something new or different, which can stimulate their desire and motivation to learn.

Children can be motivated by challenges. The teacher must make sure that the task is a challenge rather than a threat. A rule of thumb could be that, if the child thinks he or she can accomplish the task, it is a challenge. But, if the child feels he or she has little or no chance to be successful, it becomes a threat and a source of frustration.

There should be a shift in motivation from extrinsic to intrinsic. Emphasis should shift from teacher approval to personal satisfaction in task accomplishment. Teachers should expect that students will be successful so that students can reflect this confidence in their ability and have a set of realistic goals. On the other hand, if the teacher expects that students will fail, they probably will live up to the teacher's expectation.

Another area where teachers might consider the form of motivation is in establishing alternative forms of awards in testing or evaluation programs. For example, two types of awards can be given to students who are involved in an activity. One award could be based on achievement and the second award on participation. The President's Council on Physical Fitness and Sports presently offers both types of awards. One award stresses participation in a myriad of activities, and the other is awarded for high achievement in fitness.

Learning why they are doing things is a great motivator. Children learn more readily when they know the why of activities.

Children should be included in the planning often, thus capitalizing on the premise that those who participate in planning are more likely to support the activities.

The eagerness and enthusiasm that young people have for physical education should be exploited. They should be given immediate activity upon entering the teaching station. The introductory activities presented in chapter seven require little explanation and discussion, yet they offer a maximum amount of movement.

Goals

Learning can be aided by setting reasonable goals, because children are stimulated when they have a target that is both challenging and attainable. The teacher should make sure that the children understand the goals of the various activities. These goals can be expressed as behavioral objectives or can be defined in other ways. This attaches significance to the procedure and vests it with a personal value for the learner. Somewhere the child needs to get the feeling that he or she has met the challenge so that he or she can say, "I did it."

The goal should be stated clearly so that the learner knows what is necessary to reach it. Learning takes place more effectively when the learner actively participates in selecting and setting the goals of learning and in planning ways to attain them. Often, the teacher can hold discussions to allow students to help in setting goals. This encourages children to participate in deciding what are reasonable and desirable goals. Teaching aids such as movies, filmstrips, loop films, posters, and speakers help the teacher and students determine the goals they desire to attain.

If the overall goal can be broken into subgoals, the instructional sequence is enhanced. Subgoals are fragmented steps along the way to the overall goal that inform the child that he or she is making progress and give him or her pieces of the success ultimately possible.

Form and Technique

Technique in performing a skill is important and children should attempt to follow sound mechanical principles. But to expect all to perform skills in an identical manner is an error not in keeping with the principle of individual differences.

A teacher should emphasize the best way or ways to do things and what constitutes correct technique in a specific skill. However, he or she should point out to the student that there are performers who are successful even when they use what is considered incorrect form. Such performances should be regarded as exceptions developed after long periods of practice and participation.

If the child has a knowledge of basic mechanical principles and has practiced the skill for some time, he or she can be expected to develop his or her own unique style modified by his or her physiological and structural factors. Once the skill has been practiced and used for many years, attempts to change form and technique will meet with little success.

Learning a New Skill

When learning a new skill the student must first form a mental concept of the pattern of the skill. The teacher should provide effective verbalization, demonstration, or other means. For more critical skills, children learn from example, and effective demonstration can show youngsters how to perform skills. Many techniques lend themselves to slow-motion demonstrations. Selected children, properly directed, can provide suitable demonstrations. In addition, slides, filmstrips, motion pictures, pamphlets, posters, and other visual aids can be obtained from various sources. Loop films are of particular value in teaching skills, because they can be stopped and individual parts of the movement pattern analyzed.

The teacher should be able to verbalize skills (that is, to break a skill verbally into its component parts) so that children can follow the pattern of instruction.

The child then should be given the opportunity to perform the skill and compare it with his or her mental image. He or she should have an opportunity to explore, try out, and experiment with different ways of performing the skill as opposed to the autocratic "this is the way you do it" approach.

Speed in relation to final performance has several aspects. Children learn well at a speed that is just slightly slower than the normal speed of a skill, moving up to normal speed as soon as feasible. Too much emphasis on speed in a game or a relay before the child has absorbed the skill hardly helps learning.

Children need repeated trials to learn a skill. However, practice by itself does not ensure that learning is occurring, unless the practice is purposeful.

During practice sessions, the teacher needs to be able to coach and help youngsters attain good levels of skill by analyzing and making corrections. Students expect an intelligent answer to the question "what am I doing wrong?" Coaching depends on good powers of observation and on the development of keen recognition ability. Good coaching techniques also give the student the feeling of confidence. The student should have the feeling that, should he or she have difficulty, the instructor will help him or her discover a different solution.

Mimetics offer another important approach to the establishment of the basic concepts of a new motor skill. Students can be in mass formation and follow the directions of the leader. Since the student can concentrate on the skill without the implement (ball, bat, or other object), kinesthetic feeling for the skill can be acquired. Many can practice at one time, good form is emphasized in a short time, questions can be answered, and gross errors can be discovered at an early stage. In most cases this approach is effective with the intermediate grades or those youngsters who have some perception of the skill being performed.

Practice

Certain guidelines should ensure the maximum results from practice sessions.

1. Groups: Skills should be practiced with as small a group as possible considering the students' skill and the equipment available. Whenever possible and practical, *each* child should have a piece of equipment. In handling balls by throwing, catching, kicking, and other means of receipt and propulsion, maximum practice opportunity can be achieved by partner organization, with one object for two children.

2. Overlearning and Retention: There must be sufficient repetition to establish good retention. This involves the principle of overlearning. Correct form must be practiced until it becomes fixed. The more complex the skill and the higher the performance level, the more need for practice to establish and maintain the level. Repetition is effective only when it accomplishes something beyond what it did previously.

Overlearning has been achieved when there is a smooth, coordinated response or movement pattern with little thought or mental effort. The amount of retention of a learned skill depends on the degree of proficiency attained during practice and the degree of overlearning that has occurred.

3. Length of Practice Sessions: Relatively short practices (in time or in number of repetitions) usually make for more efficient learning than do longer practices. This is thought to be due to mental fatigue and lack of motivation on the part of the learner. The short attention span often attributed to youngsters is presently being questioned. Some educators feel that attention span is affected by motivation rather than the age of the learner. Using many approaches, challenges, and activities to develop the same skill helps maintain both the teacher's and the student's motivational level. An example is the many beanbag activities (page 255) that offer novelty to maintain motivation yet still focus on throwing and catching skills.

4. Distribution of Practice Sessions: Practice periods that are spread out over a long period of time are usually more effective than many sessions in a short length of time. The combination of practice and review appears to be more effective with youngsters. Activities can be taught in a short unit and then practiced through use of review sessions spaced throughout the school year. Particularly during the initial phases of skill learning, practice should be distributed. The skill should be practiced frequently but not for long durations. In the later stages, when success increases motivational levels, practice periods can be lengthened.

Progression

A logical progression of motor learning activities, based on the degree of difficulty (from single to complex movements, from gross to specific skills, and from large-muscle activity to fine motor activity) should be developed whenever possible. The teacher must remember, however, that individual differences occur among children and any one progression cannot satisfy the requirements of all children.

The start-and-expand technique is recommended to assure progression in skill learning. This means the skills presented are started at a low enough level so all children can meet with success and then expanded to more challenging skill performance. The best situation for the child would be to challenge him or her with a task that is just one stage above his or her present level.

Expansion *within an activity,* rather than too much progress up the ladder of progression, may be the approach indicated. The teacher must start at the children's level of competence and move upward from that point. If the lowest level of the activity does not meet this criterion of capability, then the activity is not a suitable educational experience for the group at that time.

The learner builds confidence when he or she meets with success and is ready to move to higher achievements. Success varies with children, since they progress at different rates and attain success differently.

Feedback and Reinforcement

Feedback and reinforcement are factors in modifying the learning process and maintaining receptiveness to learning. Unfortunately, detrimental effects can appear when feedback is unpleasant or negative. Feedback refers to the impressions, feelings, or concepts a child derives from the learning experiences in which he or she engages. Reinforcement implies a strengthening, a consolidation, and a shoring up of learning as a result of feedback.

Reinforcement is important in shaping the behavior of the learner. Whatever the child does that is reinforced probably will become a part of the child's behavioral pattern. The child is reinforced when he or she receives something pleasant (the teacher's attention, praise, and encouragement) or when something unpleasant is taken away (peer pressure, constant failure). On the other hand, it is punishment to a child when he or she receives something unpleasant or something pleasant is taken away from him or her.

Children thrive on praise and encouragement, and a positive approach is more meaningful to them than a negative one. With students who lack confidence in themselves, praise and encouragement are even more important. The feedback comes from the child's urge to seek status through approval, which should be reflected in the teacher's comments. Encouragement can help the child to progress by indicating to him or her that he or she is on the right track. It helps the child to overcome his or her fear of failure. Praise should be honest and give recognition where due.

Practice alone is not enough. The child must receive some feedback that tells him or her how his or her movement can be improved. In the early stages of learning a new skill, the amount of strict analysis should be minimal. The student should receive encouragement and information that assures him or her that he or she is developing properly. As the child's level of ability increases, more and more specific feedback can be offered the learner. If the movement pattern to be learned can be broken down into progressive increments, the possibility of positive feedback is increased. The teacher needs to be alert to small successes, so the child understands that he or she is making progress along the right lines.

Another method of offering feedback on the students' performance is for the teacher to discuss and stress the critical points of the skill with the students. The critique can be based upon a question such as "what are the important things we must remember to perform this skill efficiently?"

Finally, structured skill achievement tests to measure the students' progress can be used in the upper grades. The sports units lend themselves to this type of skill testing. Self-testing gives the students feedback about their personal improvements without the stigma of comparisons among classmates.

Transfer of Movement Learning

Simply defined, transfer of learning is the effect that previous practice or acquisition of movement skills and concepts has on the ability to learn new skills.

A child's efficiency of learning depends in part on how fast he or she can adapt and use previously learned skills and apply them to the new skill to be acquired. Transfer is not automatic, and it occurs more readily when the skill closely resembles previously learned patterns. When the teacher can apply a previously learned generalization to the new situation, effective transfer is likely.

Usually, if the teacher desires transfer of learning to occur, he or she must make a conscious teaching effort to discuss and apply generalizations about skills and their application in similar situations. Transfer also has a major limitation of which teachers must be aware; that is, it appears to be quite specific. For instance, learning to shoot a basketball will not make the student a better football passer. There seems to be more transfer from fundamental movement skills (walking, hopping, jumping, et cetera) to specific skills involving these components than between complex skills (shooting a basket, kicking a soccer ball, et cetera).

An interesting aspect of transfer is that some studies seem to support the Gestalt concept of transfer: that varied training encourages transfer and that learning how to learn is an important aspect of transfer. This concept points out the importance of offering a broad program of activity for elementary school youngsters, so they are more teachable and are ready to learn the specifics of highly developed activity at the junior and senior high school levels.

Part versus Whole Learning

There has been a great deal of discussion about teaching movement skills by either the part or the whole method. The whole method is the process of learning the entire skill or activity in one dose. The part method is learning parts separately until all parts are learned and can be combined into a unified whole. The choice of the whole or the part method depends upon the complexity of the skill or the activity to be learned. The teacher needs to decide whether or not the activity is simple enough to be taught as a whole or whether it should be broken down into parts. Ideally, the skill should be practiced as a whole. However, if the child is failing with the skill as a whole, it must be broken into subskills and each part practiced as such. Once the subskills have been mastered, they can be put together in proper sequence and practiced as a whole.

Stress and Anxiety

Various emotional conditions may have an effect on movement learning. Whatever threatens instead of challenges a child interferes with his or her learning process. Children feel challenged when they are confronted with a problem they can solve successfully, but they feel threatened when they are given a problem they do not feel capable of handling. The teacher must anticipate situations that may threaten students and cause them excessive stress and anxiety.

The teacher should concentrate on praise for progress and good performance, rather than dwelling on criticism and identifying performances of poor quality. Peer rejection is amplified when students are compelled to perform an activity before their classmates and the performance results in a "how not to do it" example. Enough equipment should be present so that each child is occupied in his or her own movement task and has no time to ridicule the less skilled, who then can progress at their own rates. This helps to reduce stress and anxiety.

Recent research indicates that competition is usually more disruptive when students are learning a complex skill as compared to a simple skill. When competition is introduced in the early stages of learning a skill, stress and anxiety are likely to cause more problems than when competition is introduced at a later stage.

Competition can enhance learning and performance. However, when competition becomes too heated, performance deteriorates. When excessive emotions are involved, learning ability usually suffers.

Implications for Teachers

1. Mounting evidence indicates that the early years of a child's life are when his or her attitudes and values are largely formed. A youngster who is active at an early age probably will be active in later stages of life. If youngsters are going to be expected to participate in activity throughout their lives, opportunities for activity must be available early in their lives and some emphasis must be placed on learning motor skills properly. Children often choose the activities they want to participate in according to their competency level in those specific activities, and teachers should try to give young children a reasonable competence level.

2. Both repetition and the opportunity to experiment with various movement patterns are crucial in motor learning. Single experiences and one-time exposures have little effect on motor learning. A child needs to be reared in an environment filled with a wide variety of sensual experiences and almost continuous activity. The child must be given the opportunity to repeat the same activity many times in reoccurring and varying explorations. The young child appears to have a natural desire to repeat, rework, and reiterate that represents a vital drive toward his or her development of new motor patterns.

3. Motor skills have a tendency to develop in a hierarchy from simple to complex. The complex skills are more difficult, if not impossible, to develop when the fundamental skills have not been learned previously. The fundamental motor skills demand considerable time and practice in order for the necessary refinement to take place. Motor skills must be overlearned, so they can be performed automatically and without conscious effort. This overlearning allows the child to direct his or her thought processes toward new movements to be learned and ultimately to the ability to think about strategy while performing sports activities.

4. The development of motor skills is an individual matter, and wide variation occurs among the members of any group of children of similar chronological ages. However, the sequence and direction of growth in all youngsters is much the same, and it progresses in an orderly fashion. Experts on motor learning have identified three patterns of development that typify the growth of children.

   a. Development, in general, proceeds from head to foot (cephalocaudal). Thus, coordination and management of body parts occur in the upper body before the lower. In effect, the child usually can throw before he or she can kick.

   b. Development occurs from inside to outside, or, in other words, the child develops from the center outward (proximodistal). For example, the child can control his or her arm before his or her hand and, therefore, can reach for objects before he or she can throw them.

   c. Development proceeds from the mass to the specific. Gross motor movements occur before fine motor coordination and refined patterns of movement. As the child learns motor skills better, there is a gradual elimination of most nonproductive movement.

5. The "start them young" viewpoint, as promoted by misguided parents and occasionally by athletic coaches, is to be deplored. These people tend to instruct children from the point of view that "the younger you start teaching refined skills, the better they will learn." This is reflected in the many organized sports programs that attempt to teach sports skills at an increasingly early age. Little evidence is available to show that teaching skills as early as possible produces a more proficient performer later. So many factors that affect the child's readiness (such as heredity, type of environment, parental pressure, et cetera) are involved that teachers may find the best key to readiness to be the individual child's interest in the activity.

   Certainly, many emotional blocks have been produced when children were forced into activities in which they were frustrated and possessed little interest and ability. A rich environment that offers many opportunities for children to explore and practice various skills is a far better training ground and a necessity rather than a luxury.

6. Most motor learning is specific. To broaden the development of motor learning patterns, a variety of movement experiences should be offered the child. For example, to help a child acquire the generalized motor competency labeled *locomotor movement* (walking, skipping, hopping, leaping, et cetera), experiences in many skills in a wide variety of situations should be planned. Not only should the child learn the separate movements, he or she also should put them in combination and sequence (flow) through experimentation, exploration, and sequencing.

7. Many motor skills, particularly complex skills that involve sequencing, should be practiced in the same sequence and over the same period of time as the natural act. Some skills can be slowed down a trifle, but to slow them down to the point where timing is lost inserts a negative factor that will have to be corrected later. One fundamental skill that can be slowed down effectively is skipping. The movement can be taught as a slow step-hop, with alternating feet. But, conversely, if a run is slowed down too much, it becomes an awkward movement with little meaning.

8. The addition of rhythm to a skills-learning situation not only enhances the quality of movement, it also adds breadth and motivation, capitalizing on the child's inherent love of rhythm. The rhythm must be appropriate for the movement pattern and the tempo of the movement. Another aid to learning motor patterns is the selection of cue words that help the student learn a new skill. An example would be to tell the child to say the words *step, hop* as he or she is learning how to skip.

9. In the early stages of learning, emphasis should be placed on exploration and experimentation with various skills. The approach should be a system of approximation and correction rather than trial and error. Success can be determined when the approximation begins to resemble the desired movement pattern.

10. Performance of *overlearned* skills generally is enhanced by a competitive situation, while the performance of poorly mastered skills or skills being learned is diminished by competition. An example would be the use of a relay to enhance the performance of a skill. If the skill is a simple one (such as running or skipping) being performed by a group of fourth graders, the competition probably would motivate the youngsters and cause them to give a better effort. On the other hand, if the skill is more complex (such as dribbling a soccer ball), the majority of students probably would be frustrated by the competition and do a poorer job of performing. Since a large majority of the skills youngsters are learning in elementary school are unrefined and *not* overlearned, competition should be used with caution, if it is used at all.

11. In the early stages of presenting a new skill, reasonable form should be stressed, so youngsters do not later have to relearn a skill because they learned an improper pattern. Proper patterns can be taught with individual differences still taken into consideration.

12. The activity should be changed when fatigue, boredom, and apparent lack of progress are evident among the children. Good teaching provides rest periods between practice sessions. Sometimes, a change of activity increases the student's desire to return to the original activity.

BASIC PRINCIPLES IMPORTANT IN MOVEMENT EXPERIENCES AND SKILL PERFORMANCE

Skills include both fundamental and specialized skills. Specialized skills need more precise and definitive approaches than fundamental skills, which can be taught through rhythmics and the exploratory approach of educational movement. For this reason, the instructional procedures for skill learning are more applicable to the specialized skills but still have a firm place in movement methodology.

To move more effectively and reach a better level of skill performance, the elementary school child should apply certain established principles to his or her movement patterns and skills. First of all, he or she should be made aware of the existence of such principles, and, second, he or she should learn how to apply these in his or her learning experiences. It is also important for the teacher to utilize the principles in coaching and helping youngsters improve their skills.

When effective patterns and correct techniques are established early in the learning process, the child should have little need to make a difficult adjustment later to correct an undesirable pattern.

The principles are general in nature, covering a variety of skills. A few, however, are specific and refer to certain types of skills. For elementary school children, the following principles in the performance of skills should be considered.

Starting and Moving the Body

The position of the body is important for facilitating various movements.

Ready Position

In the usual ready position, the feet should be spread to shoulder width. For some skills, one foot

Pushing

may be forward of the other. The knees are loose, the toes are pointed forward, and the weight is carried on the balls of the feet. There is a readiness for the legs to move easily in any direction. The back should be reasonably straight, the head up, and the hands ready for action.

Fast Starts

When a fast start is desired, the feet should be moved closer together (less than shoulder width) and the body should lean in the direction of the proposed movement. The center of gravity is moved forward and lowered somewhat by the body lean and more bend at the knees. This tends to cause a rapid release of stability in the direction of movement. Short steps should be used in the early phase of the start and gradually increased to longer strides.

Pushing and Pulling

Maximum stability is necessary for the powerful movements of pushing and pulling. To achieve a stable position, the following points are helpful.
1. The size of the base of support must be increased. This can be achieved by spreading the feet and pointing them in the direction of movement (one foot forward of the other).
2. The center of gravity must be lowered. Bending the knees and bending at the waist help accomplish this objective.
3. The center of gravity must be kept over the base of support. The head must be kept up and excessive body lean eliminated. After the push or pull has started, body weight may be

Ready Position

Pulling

shifted somewhat in the direction of the movement.

4. When resisting force, if the major body joints (knees, elbows, et cetera) are at right angles, maximum muscular effort is possible.

Stopping the Body

Sport and movement efficiency often require that an individual be able to stop quickly. Certain points aid in the performance of a more efficient stop.

Stability

The child should move into a stable position when stopping in order to avoid falling. Thus, the points listed above under the heading pushing and pulling are applicable to stability, also.

Absorbing Force

When the body is stopped quickly, the movement force must be absorbed. The ankles, knees, and hips should bend to absorb the force over as long a distance as possible. The bending movements should occur in succession from the ankles upward to prolong the time over which the force is absorbed.

Falling

Falling is usually an undesirable movement or at least an unplanned activity. However, it occurs often in many sports and movement activities and should be a subject of instruction. The force of the fall should be absorbed over as large an area as possible. Rolling helps to spread the impact and can be accomplished by tucking the head and doing a Forward or Shoulder Roll. The hands should be placed on the ground, with the wrists and elbows bent to absorb some of the force upon landing.

Propelling—Throwing, Striking, Kicking, Batting, Bowling

Many similarities exist between throwing, striking, kicking, batting, and bowling in that they all involve applying force to an object. The following principles govern these skills.

Visual Concentration

The eyes should be focused on some fixed or moving point in keeping with the skill. The child should watch the ball in striking, whereas in shooting a basket or in bowling the fixation should be on the target. In kicking, the child should keep his or her head down and watch the ball.

Pads of the Fingers

The pads of the fingers are the controlling elements in many manipulative skills, particularly in ball skills.

Opposition

Opposition refers to the coordinated use of the arms and legs. In right-handed throwing, the forward step should be made with the left foot. In walking or running, the movement of a leg is coordinated with that of the arm on the opposite side of the body. A step with the left foot means a forward swing with the right arm.

Weight Transfer

A transfer of weight from the back to the front foot is a critical element in throwing, batting, striking, and bowling skills. The initial weight of the body is on the back foot, with the transfer occurring during the execution of the skill.

Total Body Coordination

Many skills require the entire body to be brought into play in order to perform the skill effectively. A child who throws primarily with his or her arm should be taught to bring his or her whole body into play.

Development of Torque

Torque means bringing together a combination of body forces, employing twisting and rotating motions to achieve a high degree of force. It is related to total body coordination. In throwing or batting, the child should start with a forward motion of the hip and rotation of the body, thus adding force to the thrown or batted ball.

Follow-through

Follow-through refers to a smooth projection of the already initiated movement. The principle is vitally important in throwing, striking, batting, and kicking skills. In kicking, the movement is to kick *through* the ball, not at it. In batting, the normal swing must be fully completed, not arrested.

Relaxation

The child should be relaxed in his or her movements. To be relaxed means to use just enough muscular effort to perform the skill while avoiding an overuse, generally called tightening up, caus-

ing a distortion of the skill. This principle has particular application to critical target skills, such as shooting baskets and pitching.

Catching

This important skill is found in many activities and should be practiced with different objects, since each presents a different challenge.

Giving

The child should reach out for the object and then draw the arms toward the body as the catch is made. This giving with the arms allows the force to be absorbed over a longer period of time and helps prevent the object from rebounding out of the hands. Catching with the pads of the fingers also helps in making a successful catch. Fingers should be spread and relaxed.

Visual Concentration

The child must learn to follow the object with his or her eyes until it is caught. Larger balls, such as 8½-inch playground balls, rolled or thrown with a loft make it much easier for the young to practice tracking an object.

Body Position

The body should be moved so that it is positioned directly in line with the incoming object, and the weight should be transferred from the front to the rear foot. Knees should be bent and loose as the catch is made to aid in absorbing force. Feet should be spread to increase the stability of the body.

Protective Equipment

Baseball gloves are an example of the protective equipment that should be used when the object to be caught is moving at a high rate of speed. The glove increases the area over which the impact is absorbed, and the padding increases the time it takes to stop the ball.

Seven

Introductory Activities

Introductory activities are the first item of attention in the recommended lesson plan. They can take many forms, and teachers are urged to create and develop activities of their own. The chief characteristic of introductory activities is their vigorous nature. Gross movements (generally locomotor activities) are employed. They should challenge every student with movement, should not be rigidly structured, and should allow considerable freedom of movement.

Introductory activities should require only brief instructions, since their purpose is to get the children into activity quickly. Abrupt changes in direction, in the kinds of movements, and in the pace of activities predominate. Moving and then stopping is a pattern often used.

EUROPEAN RHYTHMIC RUNNING

Some type of Rhythmic Running is done in many countries of Europe to open the daily lesson. Essentially, this is light, rhythmic running to the accompaniment of some type of percussion, usually a drum or a tom-tom. Skilled runners do not need accompaniment but merely keep time with a leader.

Much of the running follows a circular path, but it can follow other patterns. To introduce a group of children to Rhythmic Running, have them stand in circular formation and clap to the beat of the drum. Next, as they clap, they can shuffle their feet in place, keeping time. Following this, have them run in place, omitting the clapping. The children then should be ready to move in a prescribed path with the run. That the run be light, bouncy, and rhythmic, keeping strict time with the beat, is es-

sential. A successful running pattern calls for the children to stay behind the person in front, maintain proper spacing, and lift the knees in a light, prancing step.

A number of movement ideas can be combined with the rhythmic running pattern.

1. On signal (whistle or double beat on the drum), runners freeze in place. Resume running when the regular beat begins again.
2. On signal, make a running full turn in four running steps. Lift knees high while turning.
3. Have children clap hands every fourth beat as they run. Instead of clapping, sound a brisk "hey" on the fourth beat, raising one arm and fist on the sound.
4. Run in squad formation. Follow the path set by the squad leader.
5. On signal, have them run in general space, exercising care not to bump or collide with each other. Return to circular running on the next signal.
6. Vary between running with high knee action and regular running.
7. Change to a light, soundless run and back to a heavier run. Let the tone of the drum control the quality of the movement.
8. Use Rhythmic Running while handling a parachute. (See page 267.)
9. On the command "center," run toward the center four steps, turn around (four steps) and resume circular running out to the original circular pattern.
10. On signal, run backward, changing direction of the circle.
11. Carry a beanbag or a ball. Every fourth step, toss the bag up and catch it while running.

Rhythmic Running, Circular Fashion

12. Assign a leader to move the class through various formations. A task that is enjoyable and challenging is crossing lines of children while they attempt to alternate one child from one line in front of a youngster from the other line.
13. Have the class move into various shapes upon signal. Examples might be to move into a square, rectangle, triangle, or pentagon. The Rhythmic Running must be continued while the youngsters are moving into position.
14. When a signal is given, each class member can change position with another student and then resume the activity. An example might be to change positions with the student opposite in the circle.
15. Since the movement is rhythmic, it can be used to practice certain skills, such as a full turn. The turn can be done to a four-count rhythm and should be more deliberate than a quick turning movement that lacks definition.
16. When the tom-tom stops, scatter and run in random fashion. When the beat of the tom-tom resumes, return to circular formation and proper rhythm.

GROSS MOVEMENTS AND CHANGES

Most of these movements stress locomotor activities, but some include manipulative and non-locomotor activities. The movements should involve the body as a whole and provide abrupt change from one movement pattern to another. A routine can begin with running and then change to another movement pattern that either is specified by the teacher or left up to the children.

Signals can be supplied with a voice command, whistle, drumbeat, or hand clap. Children love to be challenged by having to change with the signal. Each part of a routine should be continued long enough for there to be good body challenge and involvement but not so long that it becomes wearisome.

Running provides much of the basis for introductory activities, but other activities of a vigorous nature can be employed. The suggested introductory activities are classified roughly according to type and whether they are individual, partner, or group oriented.

Individual Running and Changing Movements

Free Running

Run in any direction, changing direction at will.

Running and Changing Direction

Run in any direction, changing direction on signal. As a progression, specify the type of angle (right, obtuse, 45 degree, 180 degree). Alternate right and left turns.

Running and Changing Level

Run high on toes, changing to a lower level on signal. Require runner to touch the floor at times when at lower level.

Running and Changing the Type of Locomotion

On signal, change the running to free choice or a specified type of locomotion (walking, jumping, hopping, skipping, sliding, galloping).

Running and Stopping

Run in various directions and, on signal, freeze. Stress stopping techniques and an immobilized position.

Running and Spiking

Run and, on signal, stop; jump as high as possible; and pretend to spike a volleyball. The jump can be repeated one or more times before the run resumes. A variation is using a basketball jump. On this, youngsters could pair up informally and jump against one another.

Run and Assume a Shape

Run and, on signal, assume a statue type of pose or position. Allow choice or specify a limitation.

Tortoise and Hare

When the teacher calls out the word "tortoise," the children run in place slowly. On the command "hare," they change to a rapid run, still in place. During the latter, stress good knee lift. This also could be conducted in general space.

Ponies in the Stable

Each child has a stable, his or her spot or place on the floor. This could be marked with a beanbag or a hula hoop. On the initial signal, gallop lightly (ponies) in general space. The next signal tells them to trot lightly to their stables and continue trotting lightly in place. As an added challenge, the teacher can place one less spot on the floor, so a youngster is left out each time.

Adding Fitness Challenges

Running (or other locomotor movements) can be combined with fitness activities. During the signaled stop, exercises such as Push-ups and Curl-ups could be done.

Move and Perform a Task on Signal

Tasks can be individual or partner activities. Examples are Seat Circles, Balances, Wring the Dishrag, Partner Hopping, Twister, and Chinese Get-up.

Run, Stop, and Pivot

This is an excellent activity for game skill development and is enjoyed by the youngsters when they are told to imagine they are basketball or football players.

Other Individual Movement Combinations

Upright Movement to All Fours

Begin with a movement in upright position and change to one on all fours.

Secret Movement

The teacher has written a number of movements on cards and selects one. Direction is given by saying, "I want you to show me the secret movement." Children select a movement and continue that movement without change until they are signaled to stop, whereupon the teacher identifies those who performed the movement of the card. Then, the movement is demonstrated by those who had chanced upon it, and then all perform the movement. If no one comes up with the movement pattern on the card, repeat the activity by asking children to change their responses.

Airplanes

Children pretend to be airplanes. When told to take off, they zoom with arms out, swooping, turning, and gliding. When they are commanded to land, they drop to the floor in prone position, simulating a plane at rest.

Combination Movement

Directives for sequence movement can establish specified continuity movement or allow some choice. The limitation can be to run, skip, and roll or to jump, twist, and shake. Another approach is to set a number for the sequence and let the children select the activities. Say, "Put three different kinds of movement together in a smooth pattern."

Countdown

The teacher begins a countdown for blastoff: "10-9-8-7-6-5-4-3-2-1-blast off." The children are scattered, and each makes an abrupt, jerky movement on each count. On the words "blast off," they blast off and run in different directions until the stop signal is given.

Magic Number Challenges

A challenge can be issued like this: "10, 10, and 10." The children put together 3 movements, doing 10 of each. Or the teacher could say, "Today we are going to play our version of twenty-one." Twenty-one becomes the magic number that is to be fulfilled with 3 movements, each of which is done seven times.

Crossing the River

The river can be the space between two parallel lines about 40 feet apart, or it can be the crosswise area in a gymnasium. Each time the children cross the river, a different type of locomotor movement is employed. Children can be encouraged not to repeat a movement. The play is continuous over a minute or so.

Four Corners

A square or a rectangle is laid out, with a marker at each corner. Basically, as the child turns each corner, he or she changes to a different locomotor movement. Sometimes, it is desirable to have a rectangular formation that has both short and long sides. More demanding movements can be specified for the short sides. Indoors, it may be advisable to set up two courses, each in half of the gymnasium.

Jumping and Hopping Patterns

Each child has a home spot. The basic idea is to provide jumping and hopping sequences away from and back to the spot. The teacher could say, "Move with three jumps, two hops, and a half-turn. Return back to place the same way." The teacher should have on hand a number of sequences. Action can extend beyond just jumping and hopping.

Individual Rhythmic Movements

Musical Relaxation

This activity can be conducted with a drum or with appropriate recorded music. The children run in time to the rhythm, and, when the rhythm stops, each assumes a reclining position quickly on his or her back, closes his or her eyes, and remains relaxed until the music begins again.

Moving to Rhythm

The possibilities with rhythm are many. The character of the rhythm guides the responses. The rhythm can guide locomotor movements. Changes in tempo can be a part of the activity. The intensity of the sound can be translated into light or heavy movements.

Moving to Music

Pieces such as "Bleking" and "Pop Goes the Weasel" can be used to provide a basis for creative movement. These are two-part pieces, and one type of nonlocomotor movement can be done to the first part and locomotor movement to the second.

Individual Movements with Manipulation

Individual Rope Jumping

Each child runs with rope in hand. On the change, the child stops and begins to jump rope.

Hoop Activities

Each child runs holding a hoop. When the signal is given to stop, either hula hooping is done or the hoop is laid on the floor and used for hopping and jumping patterns.

Wand Activities

Similar to the movements with jump ropes and hoops. After the run and stop, the children do wand stunts.

Milk Carton Fun

Each child has a milk carton, which has been stuffed with crumpled-up newspapers and secured with cellophane tape. The children may kick the cartons around in different directions for a minute.

Ball Activities

Balls can be dribbled as in basketball or (outside) as in soccer. When a change is signaled, stop, balance on one leg, pass the ball under leg, around back, and overhead, keeping both control and balance. Other challenges can be supplied, both in movement with the ball and the manipulative actions in place.

Partner and Group Activities

Partner and group activities offer excellent opportunities for introductory work.

Marking

The children can do what the English call marking. Each child has a partner who is somewhat equal in ability. One partner runs, dodges, and tries to lose the other partner, who must stay within a yard of him or her. On signal, both stop. The chaser must be able to touch his or her partner to say he or she has marked him or her.

Following Activity

One partner leads and performs various kinds of movements. The other partner must move in the same fashion. This idea also can be extended to squad organization.

Group Over and Under

Half of the children are scattered. Each is in a curled position. The other children leap or jump over the curled children. On signal, reverse the groups quickly. Instead of being curled, the children form arches or bridges and then the moving children go under these. A further extension is to have the children on the floor alternate between curled and bridge positions. If a moving child goes over the curled position, the floor child immediately changes to a bridge. The moving children react accordingly.

Bridges by Threes

Three children in a group can set up an interesting movement sequence using bridges. Two of the children make bridges and the third child goes under both bridges and sets up his or her own bridge. Each child in turn goes under the two bridges of the other two. Different kinds of bridges can be specified and the bridges can be arranged so that a change in direction is made. An over-and-under sequence also provides good interest. The child vaults or jumps over the first bridge and then goes under the next bridge before setting up his or her own bridge.

New Leader

Squads run around the area, following a leader. When the change is signaled, the last person goes to the head of the line and becomes the leader. Groups of three are ideal for this activity.

Manipulative Activity

Each child has a beanbag. The children move around the area, tossing the bags upward and catching them as they move. On signal, they drop the bags to the floor and jump, hop, or leap over as many bags as possible. On the next signal, they pick up any convenient bag and resume tossing to themselves. One less beanbag than children adds to the fun. Hoops also can be used in this manner. Children begin by using hoops in rope-jumping style or hula hooping. On signal, the hoops are placed on the floor, and the children jump in and out of as many hoops as they can. Next, they pick up a nearby hoop and resume the movement pattern. The activity can be done with jump ropes.

Body Part Identification

Enough beanbags for the whole class are scattered on the floor. The children either run between or jump over the beanbags. When a body part is called out, the children place that body part on the nearest beanbag.

Long Rope Routine

Four children form a loose column while holding on to the rope to the side. Each supports the rope with his or her right hand. On the first signal, the four in column formation run, led by the child at the head of the column. With the second signal, the rope is shifted overhead and put into the left hand, the shift being made without a pause in the running. At the third signal, the two inside children loose their grips on the rope and stand to one side. The other two children face each other and turn the rope for jumping by the two children who have stepped to one side. The next signal sets the four off again, running with the two jumpers holding the ends of the rope and the rope turners moving to the inside. The two pairs have exchanged places. The routine is repeated.

Leapfrog

Two, three, or four children can make up this sequence. The children form a straight or curved column, with all except the last child in line taking the leapfrog down position. The last child leaps over the other children in turn and, after going over the last child, gets down in position so that the others can go over him or her. Lines should curve around to avoid running into other jumpers.

Drill Sergeant

This movement is performed as a squad activity. The drill sergeant gives these kinds of commands for the movement sequence to be performed: "walk, jump twice, and roll"; "run, jump turn, and freeze (pose)"; "shake, jump turn, and roll"; and "seal walk, forward roll, and jump." The squad leader should be told about the activity ahead of time so that he or she can prepare some patterns, or he or she should be given cards with suggested patterns written on them. To add a realistic flavor, the sergeant can call the squad members to attention, give them the directions, and then call, "Move." Younger children, especially, love to play soldiers.

CREATIVE AND EXPLORATORY OPPORTUNITIES

Another approach of interest to children is providing creative and exploratory opportunities at the beginning of a lesson. Some examples follow.

1. Put out enough equipment of one type (hoops, balls, wands, or beanbags) for all the children to have a piece of equipment with which to explore. This can be open exploration, or it could follow the trend of a prior lesson, thus supplying extension to the progressions.
2. Have available a number of manipulative items. The children select the item with which they wish to play and decide whether to play alone, with a partner, or as a member of a small group.
3. Make available a range of apparatus, such as climbing ropes, climbing apparatus, mats, boxes, balance beams, balance boards, and similar items. Manipulative items could be a part of the package.

Tambourine-directed Activity

The tambourine can signal changes of movement, because it can produce two different kinds of sounds. The first sound is a tinny noise made by vigorous shaking. The second is a percussive sound made by striking the tambourine as a drum, either with the knuckles or the elbow. Movement changes are signaled by changing from one tambourine sound to the other. Suggestions are listed according to the types of sound.

Shaking Sound

1. The children remain in one spot but shake all over. These should be gross movements.
2. Same movement but the children gradually drop to the floor (level change).
3. The children scurry in every direction.
4. The children run very lightly with tiny steps.

Drum Sound

1. Jerky movements to the drumbeat.

2. Jumping in place or covering space.
3. Locomotor movements in keeping with the drumbeat.
4. Using three beats of the drum—collapse (beat one), roll (beat two), and form a shape (beat three).

To form a combination of movements, select one from each category. When the shaking sound is made, the children perform that movement. When the change is made to the drum sound, the children react accordingly.

Games

Selected games are quite suitable for introductory activities, provided that they keep all children active, are simple, and require little teaching. Usually, a familiar game is used so that little organizational time is needed. Some appropriate games are listed.

Addition Tag (page 399).
Back to Back (page 384).
Circus Master (page 384).
Couple Tag (page 393).
Hook On (page 404).
Loose Caboose (page 401).
One, Two, Button My Shoe (page 385).
Squad Tag (page 402).
Touchdown (page 407).
Whistle Mixer (page 403).

Miscellaneous Activities

Some running patterns can be established. Children can run laps. A Challenge Course or a cross-country type of circuit can be established.

Eight

Implementing Physical Fitness in the Program

Physical fitness is not only one of the most important keys to a healthy body; it is the basis of dynamic and creative intellectual activity.
John F. Kennedy
"The Soft American," Sports Illustrated,
December 26, 1960

All children have the right to become strong, sturdy, quick, agile, and flexible. It is the responsibility of the school to provide opportunities for them to achieve this physical goal — developing and maintaining a level of physical fitness that allows them to live fully and achieve well.

An examination of many sources indicates that the achievement of an optimum level of physical development appears in one form or another in all lists of both physical and general education goals. The school *must* be concerned with the child's physical well-being. The question that follows logically is how and to what extent the qualities of physical fitness should be pursued and attained.

Should this development be a by-product, a concomitant goal, of general program activities, or should it be achieved directly? The authors of this book take the position that both approaches should be employed in order to help each child develop and maintain a level of physical fitness commensurate with his or her needs. The key thought lies in motivating the child to take responsibility for his or her own fitness rather than forcing

upon him or her an external work program in which he or she has little interest. How much the school can accomplish toward this end depends upon the values placed on physical development in the curriculum. Physical fitness rarely occurs by chance. It usually is the result of an individual's knowing what to do to stay in top condition.

THE EFFECTS OF PHYSICAL FITNESS ON GROWTH AND DEVELOPMENT

In a study[1] conducted in the public schools of Iowa, more than 5000 children between the ages of 6 and 18 were examined over a 2-year period. Seventy percent of the children had some symptoms of coronary heart disease. Seven percent had extremely high cholesterol levels, a large percentage had developed high blood pressure, and at least 12 percent were overweight by at least 20 percent.

The life-styles of American children need to be changed before their eighth birthdays. It is well known that dietary and exercise patterns are relatively easy to change before a child's eighth birthday but they become increasingly difficult to change as the child grows older. In examining the

[1]Walter Glass, "Coronary Heart Disease Sessions Prove Vitally Interesting," *CAHPER Journal* (May/June 1973), p. 7.

developmental history of arteriosclerosis in humans, Dr. Kenneth Rose,[2] from the University of Nebraska, wrote, "The first signs appear around age two and the disease process is reversible until the age of nineteen. At about nineteen, the process of the disease is essentially irreversible, and from then on, it inexorably progresses until it becomes clinically manifest, usually in the 40s.

According to Dr. John Kimball,[3] a noted cardiologist from the University of Colorado, "Evidence is growing stronger that the earliest bodily changes leading to heart disease begin early in life." He points out that more and more autopsy reports on children show blood vessels that have already begun to clog with the fatty deposits that eventually can lead to heart attack. It is apparent that a child cannot be stimulated to start to exercise too early in life. In fact, if he or she is born into a family that shows a predisposition to heart disease, his or her salvation may be a carefully controlled diet coupled with exercise and movement.

Wilmore and McNamara[4] examined 95 boys, 8 to 12 years of age, in an effort to determine the extent to which coronary heart disease risk factors derived from an adult population were manifest in a group of young boys. They concluded that "coronary heart disease, once considered to be a geriatric problem, is now recognized as being largely of pediatric origin."

At this point, it might be well to address the question "can a child's heart be damaged by too much or too vigorous activity?" Evidence to date shows that a healthy heart cannot be damaged. This does not mean that the child is capable of the same physical work load as an adult; however, it does mean that a child can withstand a gradual increase in work load. Probably, in most cases, teachers and parents have expected too little of children for fear that overwork might permanently injure the children. Physical educators involved in programs with young children are of the opinion that adults have consistently underestimated the capacities of children and, consequently, have not challenged them to reach their optimum level of development. Children need exercise and movement for optimum development of the cardiovascular system. By gradually increasing the physical demands placed on children, researchers have found that youngsters are capable of high output and outstanding physical performance.

Activity also has an effect on skeletal growth.

Vigorous activity can result in an improved internal structure (the honeycomb structure at the ends of bones that is laid down in such a way that resistance to pressure and tension is assured). The bones also increase in diameter and mineralization in response to activity. Inactivity for prolonged periods causes demineralization of the bones and makes them more susceptible to fractures. Finally, it appears that vigorous activity causes the bones to grow to a shape that is mechanically advantageous for muscle attachments. This mechanical advantage should allow the child to perform physical challenges at a higher level in later years when sports activities become meaningful.[5]

Stronger bones are a response to an increased musculature and thus to increased strength. Muscles respond to overload and stress by increasing in strength, while bones respond to the increased work load the muscles are applying to them. Thus, in order to develop their strength, it is important to see that the work loads children are asked to carry are gradually increased.

How important is strength to a youngster's motor development? In their study, Rarick and Dobbins[6] attempted to identify and place in order of importance those factors that contribute to motor development in young children. The factor they identified as being most important was strength and/ or power in relationship to body size. Their study showed that those youngsters who demonstrated high levels of strength in relation to their body size were more capable of performing motor skills than those with lower levels of strength.

A negative factor, deadweight, was found to be the fourth-most important factor that has an effect on motor performance in children. Deadweight is synonymous with excess fat. Clearly, obesity is a factor that restricts the motor performance of young children. The study of childhood obesity has exposed some interesting implications. In many obese people, there is a decreased tendency for muscular activity, and it seems that, as weight increases, the impulse for physical exertion decreases. As the child becomes more obese, he or she finds himself or herself in a cycle that he or she often feels unable to control. Interestingly enough, movement and/or activity may be the crucial factor in weight control. In comparisons of diets of obese and normal children, usually no substantial difference in caloric consumption is

[2]Kenneth Rose, "To Keep the People in Health," *Journal of the American College Health Association,* vol. 22 (August 1973), p. 80.

[3]J. G. Albinson and G. M. Andrew, eds., *Child in Sport and Physical Activity* (Baltimore: University Park Press, 1976), p. 83.

[4]Jack H. Wilmore and John J. McNamara, "Prevalence of Coronary Heart Disease Risk Factors in Boys 8 to 12 Years of Age," *Journal of Pediatrics,* vol. 84, no. 4 (April 1974), p. 4.

[5]Lawrence G. Rarick, ed., *Physical Activity, Human Growth and Activity* (New York: Academic Press, 1973), p. 37, and Albinson and Andrew, eds., *Child in Sport and Physical Activity,* p. 82.

[6]Lawrence G. Rarick and D. Alan Dobbins, "Basic Components in the Motor Performances of Children Six to Nine Years of Age," *Medicine and Science in Sports,* vol. 7, no. 2 (1975), p. 2.

found. In fact, in some cases, obese and very heavy children actually consumed less food than normal-weight children. In a study[7] of high-school-age girls, it was found that girls who were obese ate less but exercised two-thirds less (in total time) than normal-weight girls. An examination[8] of children in an elementary school in Massachusetts showed that they gained more weight in winter when they were less active. Movies taken of normal and overweight children have demonstrated that there is a wide difference in activity levels of the two groups even though their diets are quite similar.[9]

People often have made the statement, "Don't worry about excessive weight; it'll come off when the child matures." But the opposite is usually true. The fat stays and continues to accumulate into adulthood, when it becomes difficult to lose. An overweight individual pays a tremendous psychological price and also finds himself or herself being threatened by an increased risk of disease and premature death. Some people now feel that there are two critical periods when fat cells multiply. One is from the third trimester of pregnancy through the fourth month of life and the other is during preadolescence. Certainly, if the fat cells multiply, it leaves the child with a tendency toward obesity for the rest of his or her life. The primary way to prevent the multiplication of fat cells is to keep the child from gaining excess weight at any stage of his or her growth and development. It seems as though childhood obesity must be challenged at an early age, and this challenge must come from increased movement and activity.

Before the subject of the physiological effects of activity and movement is left, it might be interesting to examine the long-term effects of activity in childhood. A well-known researcher, Dr. Saltin, did a study to find out whether any of the benefits of childhood activity carried over into adult life.[10] He compared the adjustability to effort of three groups of subjects in the 50-59-year-old age group. One group was made up of former athletes who had not participated in their sports for over 20 years and who worked in sedentary jobs. The second group included former athletes who had kept up their regular training during their adult years. And the third group consisted of individuals who had not

been athletes during their youthful years and who were inactive as adults. Interestingly enough, Saltin found that the group that included no athletes was capable of the least effort and that the group that was active during their youthful years, although then involved only in sedentary activities, scored significantly higher than the nonathletic group. Of course, the group that had maintained training scored a great deal higher than the other two groups. However, the main point is that, generally speaking, functional adult capacity appeared to be a partial function of activity during the growing years. The need for activity and movement in the formative years of life appears to be an important aid in the development of a strong and functional body.

GUIDELINES FOR ACHIEVING PHYSICAL FITNESS

The Health Appraisal

Each child should undergo a periodic health examination. This should determine, among other things, to what degree the child may participate in physical activities. It is not only a sensible educational approach but, in many cases, is a legal mandate to schools.

Improving Physical Fitness Levels

1. Physical fitness can be acquired only through muscular effort that is continued throughout the individual's lifetime. Gains made in fitness level can be lost in a span of six to eight weeks. Obviously, it is of little value to bring one's fitness level to an optimum state if it is not going to be maintained.

2. To raise levels of fitness, the youngster must exercise on a regular basis and participate in a program that progressively increases his or her work load. The basic principle important in this process is overloading all major muscle groups by gradually increasing the amount of work the child is to perform. As the work load is moderately increased, the strength of the child increases. In other words, in order to maintain their fitness level, children must be asked to do a greater amount of work over the school year, since they are maturing and have an increasing capacity for work.

3. The types of physical fitness challenges and activities must be geared to the children's ages and physical conditions, and, although children of all ages are capable of strenuous exercise, the types of activities that appeal to various age groups differ.

4. It is important that all parts of the body be exercised and developed. The harmonious relationship of the parts to each other (posture) is an important consideration. The ac-

[7]Mary L. Johnson, Bertha S. Burke, and Jean Mayer, "The Prevalence and Incidence of Obesity in a Cross Section of Elementary and Secondary School Children," *American Journal of Clinical Nutrition*, vol. 4, no. 3 (May/June 1956), p. 231.

[8]Ibid.

[9]Charles B. Corbin and Phillip Pletcher, "Diet and Activity Patterns of Obese and Non-obese Elementary School Children," *Research Quarterly*, vol. 39, no. 4 (December 1968), p. 922.

[10]B. Saltin and G. Grimby, "Physiological Analysis of Middle-Aged and Old Former Athletes, Comparison with Still Active Athletes of the Same Ages," *Circulation*, vol. 38, no. 6 (December 1968), p. 1104.

tivities and routines that follow in this chapter are grouped and organized so that all of the major muscle groups and all of the components of fitness are utilized.

5. Proper form must be used in developmental activities and routines in order for the children to realize their full potential in physical fitness. It is obvious that Push-ups done with the lower body flat on the floor have little value for developing strength.

6. Only when all of the components of fitness have been emphasized can *total* physical fitness be accomplished. Total fitness is particularly important for youngsters, who are increasingly aware of the fads and trends in adult exercise. For example, the jogging craze is good and certainly running is important, but children, as well as adults, also need development in the other components of fitness, such as strength and flexibility.

Components of Physical Fitness

The most important measurable components of physical fitness are strength, power, and cardiorespiratory endurance. Agility and flexibility are only slightly less important.

Speed, although a desirable attribute, is not sought *directly* in programs purporting to develop physical fitness. Some tests for physical fitness include a measurement of speed as one of their items, since measurements of speed may indirectly measure other components of fitness—strength, power, agility, and flexibility—in that the improvement of these qualities results in increased speed. Speed as a goal of the overall physical education program is sound, but little attention is paid *directly* to its development in fitness routines.

Strength refers to the ability of a muscle or muscle group to exert force. Among the child's learning experiences in physical education, there must be sufficient big-muscle activity over a wide range of activities done regularly and with enough intensity to develop strength.

Strength is necessary in skill performance, since, without strength, a low standard of performance can be expected because muscles give out before they can reach their skill potential.

Power implies the process of using strength to apply force for effective movement. Power is based on strength and its application to movement. Maximum strength effort is involved in providing an explosive movement for an all-out effort.

Endurance refers to the ability to carry on muscular effort over a period of time. It has a basis in strength in that a stronger person is able to keep up muscular effort longer than one without adequate strength. However, there are other involvements in the body. Primarily, endurance is a postponement of the stages of fatigue so that muscular work can be carried on. A person with good endurance has a well-conditioned cardiorespiratory system and other good deep-body mechanisms.

Agility refers to the ability to change direction swiftly, easily, and under good control. A particularly agile person is one who is hard to catch in a tag game. He or she can dodge and change direction well.

Agility is necessary for individual safety. Many persons today are alive and free from injury, because they were agile enough to get out of the way of a moving object.

Flexibility is a person's range of movement at the joints. A flexible child can stretch farther, touch his or her toes, bend farther, et cetera. He or she has more freedom of movement and can adjust his or her body more readily for various movements.

Speed, the ability to move quickly, is a necessary skill for many physical activities. Among fitness qualities, speed has a high prestige factor, as illustrated by the fame of track stars and Olympic runners. Every child should be given the opportunity to achieve his or her potential for speed.

FITNESS ELEMENTS IN SCHOOL PHYSICAL EDUCATION PROGRAMS

To accomplish the physical fitness objectives, a physical education program should channel its emphasis into five major elements of an overall program: (1) program activities and physical fitness; (2) fitness development activities, including postural considerations; (3) the testing program; (4) the program for physical underachievers; and (5) the extended program.

Program Activities and Physical Fitness

The types of activities included in a physical education program should be selected *and* conducted with the physical fitness goal in mind. The program should be rugged and demanding as measured by the criterion of how much physical work the individual child receives during the lesson. Children should be kept active.

Many of the usual physical education activities primarily involve the legs, lower back, hands, and arms. A good program would include hanging and arm-support activities, which generally are used insufficiently in programs. The inclusion of rope climbing, ladder work, horizontal bar stunts, and similar hanging activities is important in making sure that the upper torso is developed in proportion to other parts of the body.

Another approach to upper-body development, which has particular relevance to the kindergarten and primary level, is the principle of including activities during which the children get down on the floor in movements and positions in which the body is partially supported by the arms. Care must be taken to include a variety of positions, including the crab position in which the body is supported by the hands and feet but faces the ceiling.

The trend toward more stunts and tumbling activities in the program pays off in total body development. These activities also provide ample opportunity for upper-body development.

To achieve endurance, the program must make demands on the individual in the form of muscular effort that causes accelerated breathing. Generally, this involves activities including running or other sustained movement. No activity should be carried on to the point that the participants are breathless. However, the children need to push themselves beyond their first inclinations to stop.

Conditioning for endurance connotes increased doses. Many athletic coaches adhere to this principle by gradually increasing the doses of activity until the athletes can participate in a full-length game. Teachers are cautioned that a process of this nature takes time. If the children are to play an active game (like soccer), they must be brought up gradually to the level of endurance through increased doses of activity.

Rope skipping to music, Rhythmic Running (European style), and similar movements contribute to the development of endurance.

Agility can be developed in many games, relays, and similar activities. The development is not automatic, however, and children need to be taught how to stop, start, and change direction properly.

Flexibility can be furthered by stimulating children to extend the limits of joint movement in twisting, bending, and rotational movements, particularly in the stunts and tumbling program. Children need to be urged to extremes in joint movements by such directives as "see how far you can stretch" or "how far can you bend?"

Relays, simple games, and sports provide opportunities for practicing speedy movement. Chase and tag games are particularly valuable for this, as well as for reinforcing agility. Track and field activities teach proper running techniques.

Games that provide children many chances to run, dodge, chase, and tag should take precedence over circle games in which only one or two children are active. This principle of full participation reaches into movement pattern experiences and skill drills. Ample equipment and instructional supplies should be present so that there is little standing around and waiting for turns.

Combatives can stimulate all-out muscular effort. In particular, both individual and long tug-of-war ropes demand a high degree of effort. Parachute activity has high value for the development of fitness.

Fitness Development Activities

In the planning of a fitness program for the school year, it is well to establish variety in activities and to include a number of different approaches or means of fitness development. Reliance on a single approach for developing fitness is not sound, because children get tired of the same old stuff and lose motivation, an all-important factor in stimulating children to good effort. Variety is educational, promotes interest, and assures a broader approach to body development. Variety tends to minimize the inherent weaknesses of any one routine.

CRITERIA FOR FITNESS DRILLS AND ROUTINES

1. The activity should be capable of developing physical fitness and should lend itself to progressive doses.
2. It should not involve danger and should demand only simple skills.
3. It should require a minimum of equipment and be appropriate to the space demands of the modern school.
4. The activity should be demanding enough that fitness goals can be achieved in a reasonable amount of time. The point is that an activity is unacceptable when it requires the majority of the physical education period.
5. It should consider individual differences.
6. It should provide carry-over value to the child's daily living program.
7. It should allow opportunity for student leadership in conducting the drills.
8. In every drill or routine, there should be at least one activity centered on abdominal wall development and one pointed toward the arm-shoulder girdle.
9. The activity should be interesting so that the child will be motivated toward all-out effort.
10. The fitness participation should be both an educational and a physical experience. Discussions should cover the purposes of the drills and their parts, proper techniques with the emphasis on both how and why, and the results that can be expected.
11. Planning should consider two separate groups of children: kindergarten through grade two and grades three through six. The needs, characteristics, and capacities of younger children indicate a more informal approach in contrast to a more organized fitness program for the older children.

PLANNING THE FITNESS EMPHASIS FOR KINDERGARTEN THROUGH SECOND GRADE

A calisthenics-oriented fitness program is not suitable for children in grades kindergarten through two. Utilizing selected movement experiences is a more educationally sound approach. These experiences, which should have the potential of developing the components of physical fitness and which give attention to various body areas, provide a more informal and relaxed atmosphere for development.

The entire lesson for any one day should provide the recommended physical demands. In particular, introductory activity and fitness development activity, the first two parts of the lesson, should combine to provide broad developmental coverage by including activities from each of these four areas: (1) trunk development, (2) emphasis on the abdomen, (3) arm-shoulder-girdle emphasis, and (4) leg-agility development.

Suggested activities are listed under the four divisions, and there is a miscellaneous group of activities that are more general in nature. Some suggestions for general methodology to cover all activities are presented first.

Instructional Procedures

In working with the four body areas, it is recognized that many selected movement patterns contribute to more than one body area and, in some cases, to all four. However, a movement is listed under the area that is its main focus.

This example incorporates the four kinds of activities during the combined introductory-development phase of the lesson:

As the children enter the play area, the teacher says, "Run in different directions without touching or bumping into anyone. When I sound the whistle, stop immediately and balance on three parts of the body. Now, go." This is repeated several times and provides work mostly for one area of the body—the legs.

Next, the teacher says, "Now stand up, bend over, and pretend you are swimming. What would you do if an alligator were chasing you? Can you show me different ways to swim?" The teacher selects several children in turn to demonstrate, cuing the group to further and varied arm activity (arm-shoulder girdle).

"Let's sit down Indian fashion. Put your arms overhead and see how far you can sway back and forth. Put your arms out to the sides and see how far you can twist back and forth. How fast can you twist? Can you make circles with your arms while you are twisting?" (trunk emphasis).

The last movement experiences are directed as follows: "In your seated position, put your hands out to the back for support. Lift your knees and make your heels go pitty-pat. Can you turn in a complete circle with your heels bouncing fast?" (provides abdominal stress).

Inventiveness, imagination, and perceptiveness to utilize movement suggestions from the children are the keys to providing adequate experiences. Each child works individually on his or her own without regard to, or competition with, the others. It is important that the children be stimulated to good effort.

Selected exercises, particularly for the abdominal region, can be included, but the approach should be informal and avoid cadence.

To present activity based on the Partial Curl-up (page 106), the instructor, after getting the children into the starting position, can challenge them in this manner: "Work your fingers up to the top of your knees, raising your head and shoulders. Can you see your toes? Do this several times."

A way to develop movement sequences with the Push-up (page 104) is to begin with a controlled descent to the floor from the top position. "Let's pretend we are going to have a flat tire. When I say 'bang,' you lower yourself slowly to the floor as if you were a tire going flat. What kind of noise does air make when it is escaping from a tire?" The children can pretend it is a blowout (fast action) or a slow leak (very slow). "Can you push yourself back up, keeping your body pretty straight? If you have trouble, try doing it first on your knees." Other ways of working informally with the push-up position are presented on page 98.

Trunk Development

Movements that include bending, stretching, swaying, twisting, reaching, and forming shapes are important inclusions. No particular continuity exists, except that a specified approach should move from the simple to the more complex.

The more logical approach is to select one or more movements and use it or them as the theme for the day. Vary the position the child is to take—standing, lying, kneeling, sitting, et cetera. From the selected position, stimulate the child to varied movement based on the theme for the day. Examples of different types of trunk movements that can become both fitness and learning experiences for youngsters follow.

Bending

"Bend in different ways."

"Bend as many parts of the body as you can."

"Make different shapes by bending two, three, and four parts of the body."

"Bend the arms and knees in different ways and on different levels."

"Try different ways of bending the fingers and wrist of one hand with the other. Use some resistance. Add body bends."

Stretching

"Keeping one foot in place, stretch your arms in different directions, stepping as you move with the free foot. Stretch at different levels."

"On the floor, stretch one leg different ways in space. Stretch one leg in one direction and the other in another direction."

"Stretch slowly as you wish and then snap back to original position."

"Stretch with different arm-leg combinations in diverse directions."

"See how much space on the floor you can cover by stretching. Show us how big your space is."

"Combine bending and stretching movements."

Swaying and Twisting

"Sway your body back and forth in different directions. Change the position of your arms."

"Sway your body, bending over."

"Sway your head from side to side."

"Select a part of the body and twist it as far as you can in one direction and then in the opposite direction."

"Twist your body at different levels."

"Twist two or more parts of your body at the same time."

"Twist one part of your body while untwisting another."

"Twist your head to see as far back as you can."

"Twist like a spring; like a screwdriver."

"Stand on one foot and twist your body. Untwist."

"From a seated position, make different shapes by twisting."

Forming Shapes

Children love to form different shapes with their bodies, and this interest should be utilized to aid in trunk development. Shapes can be formed in most any position—standing, sitting, lying, balancing on parts of the body, and moving. Shapes can be curled or stretched, narrow or wide, big or little, symmetrical or asymmetrical, twisted or straight.

Emphasis on the Abdomen

The best position to ensure exercise of the abdominal muscles is with the child lying supine on the floor or a mat. Challenges should direct him or her to lift the upper and lower portions of the body from the floor, either singly or together. The following are examples of directives to a child lying on his or her back on the floor.

"Sit up and touch both toes with your hands."

"Sit up and touch your right toe with your left hand. Do it the other way."

"Bring up your toes to touch behind your head."

"With hands to the side, bring your feet up straight and then touch them by the right hand. By the left hand."

"Lift your feet up slowly an inch at a time, without bending your knees."

"Pick up your heels about 6 inches from the floor and swing them back and forth. Cross them and twist them."

"Lift your head from the floor and look at your toes. Wink your right eye and wiggle your left foot. Reverse."

Selected abdominal exercises (page 106) can be modified in approach to provide suitable challenges to children. The approach should be informal, using directives like "can you . . .?" or "show me how you can ... ," rather than staccato sequence counting.

Arm-Shoulder-Girdle Development

Movement experiences contributing to arm-shoulder-girdle development can be divided roughly into two groups of activities. The first group includes activities in which the hands and arms support the body weight either wholly or in part. In the second group of activities, the arms are free but are stimulated to move in many different ways.

Group 1. Arm-Support Activities

The teacher should make good use of the activities listed under the stunts and tumbling program. In addition, selected movement challenges can give direction to activities that place stress on the arm and shoulder girdle.

Animal Walks and Selected Stunts

Alligator (page 332).
Puppy Dog Run (page 323).
Cat Walk (page 323).
Rabbit Jump (page 328).
Lame Dog Walk (page 330).
Seal Crawl (page 336).
Crab Walk (page 330).
Turn Over (page 333).
Frog Jump (page 336).
Measuring Worm (page 336).
Frog Handstand (page 337).
Turtle (page 343).
Wheelbarrow (Partner Stunt) (page 348).

Movement Challenges

"Practice taking the weight completely on your hands."

"In crab position, keep your feet in place and make your body go in a big circle. Do this from push-up position."

"In crab position, let's see you go forward, backward, to the side, turn around, move real slow, and so on."

Movement Challenges Based on the Push-up Position

Each child is asked to assume the push-up position, which he or she uses as a base of operation. The challenges require a movement and then a return to the original push-up position.

Push-up Position

From this position, ask the children if they can:

"Lift one foot high. Now the other foot."

"Bounce both feet up and down. Move the feet out from each other while bouncing."

"Inch the feet up to the hands and go back again. Inch the feet up to the hands and then inch the hands out to return to the push-up position."

"Reach up with one hand and touch the other shoulder behind the back."

"Lift both hands from the floor. Try clapping the hands."

"Bounce from the floor with both hands and feet off the floor at the same time."

"Turn over so the back is to the floor. Complete the turn to push-up position."

"Lower the body an inch at a time until the chest touches the floor. Return."

There is value in maintaining the push-up position for a length of time. The various tasks to be done provide interest and challenge to the youngsters. The informal and individual approach stimulates the child to good effort in muscular work.

The crab position also should be utilized in a similar fashion. The side-leaning rest position is another that can be employed. Many of the same directives listed for the push-up position can be used with modification for the crab position.

Group 2. Free-Arm Activities

Swinging and Circling

"Swing one limb (arm or leg) at a time, different directions and levels."

"Combine two limb movements (arm-arm, leg-leg, or arm-leg combinations) in the same direction and in opposite directions. Vary levels."

"Swing arms or legs back and forth and go into giant circles."

"Swing arms as if swimming—bent-over position. Try a backstroke or a breaststroke. What does a sidestroke look like?"

"Make the arms go like a windmill. Go in different directions."

"How else can you circle your arms?"

"Pretend a swarm of bees is around your head. Brush them off and keep them away."

Reaching and Pulling

"Reach high into the sky and pull stars toward you. How quickly can you put a dozen stars in a basket?"

"Using both hands, pull something high, pull something low. Pull from different directions."

"Reach out and grab snowflakes. Did you get some? Gather a pile of snow together. Make snowballs. Throw snowballs."

"With your hands clasped behind your head, pull your head forward. See if you can make wind by waving your elbows back and forth."

"Reach up and climb a ladder to the sky, using only your hands and arms to climb. See how high you can reach."

Lifting

"Pretend you are lifting and throwing logs. Throw them in different directions. How high can you lift your log?"

"Stand with feet spread apart and arms outstretched to the side, palms up. Pretend you have a rock in one hand and you are tossing it overhead from side to side."

Leg-Agility Development Activities

Leg-agility development activities can include a wide range of leg movement challenges, either moving in general space or in place. The introductory phase of the lesson often includes a running type of activity.

Fundamental rhythmics using a drum or appropriate music are received well by the children. Listening skills are improved by the use of the drumbeat.

Running Patterns

Running in different directions. Running in place.

Tortoise and Hare (page 108).
Rhythmic Running (page 85).
Running and stopping.
Running laps.

Jumping and Hopping Patterns

Different directions back and forth over a spot. In, out, over, and around hoops, individual mats, or jump ropes laid on the floor.

Back and forth over lines. Down the lines.

Rope Jumping

Individual rope jumping.

Combinations

Many combinations of locomotor movements can be put together, such as run, leap, and roll; or run, jump turn, and shake. Other combinations can be devised.

Miniature Challenge Courses

A miniature Challenge Course can be set up either indoors across the floor sideways or outdoors. The distance between the start and finish lines depends upon the type of activity. A starting distance of about 30 feet is suggested; this can be adjusted. Cones can mark the course boundaries. The course should be wide enough for two children at a time to move down the course.

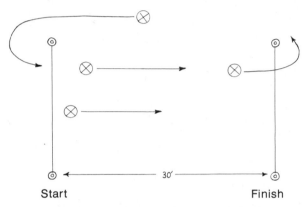

Start   Finish

Basically, each child performs the stipulated locomotor movement from the start to the finish line, turns left, and jogs back to the start. The movement is continuous, and directions should be given so that there is little delay. The number of children on each course should be limited to normal squad size or fewer.

The following movements can be stipulated:

All types of locomotor movements—running, jumping, hopping, sliding, et cetera.

Movements on the floor—crawling, Bear Walk, Seal Crawl, et cetera.

Over and under obstacles. Through tires or hoops.

A Challenge Course could be arranged like this: (1) crawling under two cone sets; (2) rolling down an inclined mat; (3) log rolling up an inclined mat; (4) moving up and down a three-step structure, and on final climb jumping and rolling; (5) crawling through a barrel or tire(s); (6) walking a balance beam; and, finally, (7) pulling body down a bench in prone position.

Circular and Figure-Eight Movements

Each child selects a spot on which he or she keeps his or her hands.

"Keeping the body straight, walk the feet in a full circle back to place. Change direction. Try with back to floor."

"Keep the feet in place and walk the hands in a full circle. Vary as in the previous movement."

Four cones or beanbags are placed in the following manner for a figure-eight hopping circuit. The children change feet at the end of each full circuit. Skipping, jumping, galloping, and sliding could be used in place of hopping.

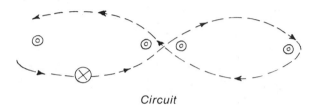

Circuit

Four-Corners Movement Formation

A rectangle is formed by four cones. The student moves around the rectangle, and each time he or she goes around a corner he or she changes the movement pattern. On the long sides, rapid movement such as running, skipping, or sliding should be designated. Moving along the short sides, the student can hop or jump.

Using the four-corner idea as a basis, other combinations can be devised. For example, in the following pattern, running is required along one of the long sides and sliding along the other. One of the short sides has mats and requires three forward rolls. An animal walk on all fours is required on the other side.

Measurements can vary according to the level of the children and the movement tasks included. Outdoors, four rectangles can be laid out. Indoors, at least two should be established. Too much

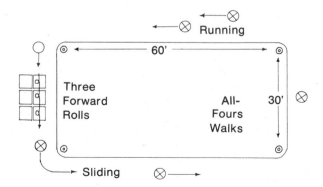

Four-Corners Movement Formation

crowding and interference occur when only one rectangle is used for the average-size class.

Other Activities

Parachute activities (page 267) provide many physical challenges for various body areas. Astronaut Drills (page 116) can be modified for good value for younger children. Circuit Training (page 112) also can be adapted to fit the needs of grades kindergarten through two. Stations can include some fun or manipulative activities on an informal basis in addition to exercise routines. Bounding boards (page 310) are highly recommended as a station activity. Others of value are going over and under hurdles, jumping boxes, manipulative activities with beanbags or balls, hula hoops, wand stunts, individual mats, climbing ropes, and tires in stands.

Hoops laid in floor patterns (page 274) provide excellent movement challenges. Bicycle or regular tires can serve the same purpose. Floor apparatus make excellent circuit stations.

PLANNING A YEAR'S FITNESS PROGRAM FOR GRADES THREE THROUGH SIX

In contrast to the program for the lower grades, the emphasis in fitness shifts to more structured drills and routines, with less stress on exploratory movement, in grades three through six. A well-established exercise program should be the basis for the fitness activities for these grades. Exercises must be learned well, since they are basic to other routines. Exercises should be given both with and without music. Other routines that are effective and add variety to fitness work are isometrics, Circuit Training, Continuity Exercises, Grass Drills, Astronaut Drills, Challenge Courses, jogging, and a number of miscellaneous activities. How a selection of these can be incorporated into a year's program is illustrated. Following the year's program, each of the fitness routines is discussed in turn.

Throughout the year, the teacher should keep in mind that the goal is to have children learn to develop fitness programs that are balanced foundations for total fitness. The teacher could have each student write out his or her own program for the week and couple this planning activity with a discussion about the values of different exercises. The results of each individual routine then could be evaluated and a progressive dosage developed for the following week.

Example of a Year's Program for Grades Three through Six

The following is an example of a year's program for grades three through six that includes different fitness routines scheduled over a 36-week period. Some adaptation to school schedules may be necessary.

Fitness Development Activity

Week	Activity
1-4	Exercises
5-8	Circuit Training
9-10	Astronaut Drills
11-12	Continuity Exercises
13-16	Exercises to music
17-18	Grass Drills and partner resistance
19-22	Squad-leader exercises
23-26	Circuit Training
27-28	Challenge Courses
29-30	Jogging
31-32	Selected movement sequences
33-34	Aerobic Dance
35-36	Parachute exercises and activities

Exercises

A program of fitness for the year should lead off with exercises, since these are the basis for many of the other drills. It is helpful if the exercises have catchy or descriptive names. Once the children associate the exercise with its characteristic name, little time is wasted in getting the activity underway.

Instructional Procedures

1. It is important for economy of time that the students move into an appropriate formation quickly. Some devices for accomplishing this include:
   a. Having the students scatter so each has sufficient personal space.
   b. Having students go to prearranged places. Spots or numbers painted on the floor help.
   c. Using extended squad formation. Squad stays in line but extends spacing between members from front to back (page 69).
2. In introducing a new exercise, show the children briefly how it is to be done. Give the purpose of the exercise and its value. Take the children through the exercise by parts (count by count) until it is mastered enough and then speed up to normal tempo. Remind the children about the key performance points.
3. Introduce a familiar exercise by its name, specify the work load in terms of repetitions or counts, sell it by restating its basic purpose, and remind students of the stress points to be observed.
4. The work load depends upon the number of repetitions and other factors. In setting repetitions, the instructor can be guided by the ranges specified under each exercise. Begin

with the lower figure and add one or two repetitions or sets each week. Lesson plans should reflect these figures.

Increasing the number of repetitions is only one way of providing progression by means of the overload principle. A second way is to change to a more demanding type of exercise of a similar nature. A third method is to increase the speed of the repetitions, and a fourth is to lessen the resting time between the exercises. Combinations of the above also can be used to increase the work load.

The development potential of certain exercises can be enhanced by incorporating positions that are held as in isometric exercises; that is to say, a position of the exercise is held for a period of time (6-8 seconds) with a near maximal contraction.

5. For some exercises, the instructor can allow students to set their own limits informally. This works well with Curl-ups, Push-ups, and similar exercises on which the limits can be based on individual capacity. The instructor simply requests the child to do as many repetitions as he or she can.

    Other challenges can be posed, such as asking the students to do as many repetitions as they are old or double their age.

    Suitable exercises of this nature have been labeled under cadence "at will."

6. Each instructor should develop some rhythmic means of starting exercises, such as "ready—begin." For halting, the voice is lowered and the tempo slowed during the last series of counts, which now becomes "1-2-and-halt." In simple analysis, stopping commands amount to substituting the words "and-halt" for the last two counts of the final series.

7. Each exercise has a rhythm or tempo that is most effective for its execution. Some experimentation is necessary to determine the appropriate rhythm. Children enjoy exercises when they are given in an even, rhythmic manner that is similar to the tone from a metronome.

8. A counting system should be employed in giving exercises that also keeps track of the number of repetitions. Series counting can include the repetitions in this fashion: "1-2-3-1, 1-2-3-2, 1-2-3-3." Or, it could be: "1-2-3-4, 2-2-3-4, 3-2-3-4."

    Another method of counting can be employed for such two-count exercises as the Curl-up and the Push-up, where a specified number of repetitions is desired. For the Curl-up, the cadence count can go "up—one, up—two, up—three." For the Push-up, it can go "down—one, down—two, down—three." This allows the accurate count so the specified number can be administered. The children can be involved in the counting by having the leader give the initiating command "down" or "up," and the children count in unison as they complete the movement.

9. Response cadence counting by the students adds a motivational factor and gives the students a role in the exercise routine. The leader names or describes the exercise, specifies the number of repetitions, and puts the group in starting position. The following dialogue exchange then takes place:
    Leader: "Ready—exercise."
    Group Response: "Ready—exercise."
    Group Cadence: "1-2-3-4, 2-2-3-4," et cetera (in unison).

    If eight repetitions are the desired number, the group stops itself like this:
    Group Response: "8-2-and-halt."

    The cadence counting should be clipped, sharp, and moderate in intensity. Avoid having the children shout while counting.

10. Good postural alignment should be maintained. In exercises where the arms are held in front, to the side, or overhead, the abdominal wall needs to be tensed and flattened to maintain the proper position of the pelvis. In most activities, the feet should be pointed reasonably straight ahead, the chest should be kept up, and the head and shoulders kept in good postural position.

11. Exercises in themselves are not sufficient to develop endurance. Additional activity in the form of running, rope jumping, or other such vigorous activity is needed to round out fitness development.

Precautions in Giving Exercises

Certain precautions should be observed in giving exercises. These also apply to other physical education activities.

1. The Curl-up, with the legs in a bent-knee position and feet flat on the floor, should be used in preference to the Sit-up, in which the legs are extended on the floor with the knees straight. The Curl-up tends to isolate the abdominal muscle group from the psoas muscle group. The straight-leg Sit-up develops the psoas muscle group, which can lead to increased lower-back curve, the opposite of the desired effect of strong abdominal muscles.

    In addition, when the upper part of the body comes up, as in the Curl-up, the movement should begin as a Roll-up, with the chin moving to touch or come close to the chest as the initial movement. This also helps to flatten out the lower-back curve.

2. In exercises using leg raising, such as marching in place and running in place, the knees

should be lifted to the point where the thigh is parallel to the floor. By lifting the knees high, more and different muscles are brought into play than ordinarily would be used with a moderate knee lift.

3. Some care should be taken in using exercises requiring a straight-leg position with no bending at the knee joint, such as forward-bending exercises. These activities tend to force the knee back in a hyperextended position, which contributes to posture faults. Some stretching of the leg muscles is excellent for flexibility, but the knee joint should be relaxed slightly rather than forced back to a back-kneed position.

4. Repeated deep-knee bending (Full Squats) is regarded by some as injurious to the knee joint. While an exercise or activity that demands an occasional deep-knee bend causes little harm, an activity that calls for repeated full knee-joint bending should be avoided. It is interesting to note that Japanese physical educators dispute the danger element of deep-knee bending. Their claim is that the Japanese people have sound and strong knees in spite of the many squatting positions that they assume as part of their living habits.

5. The so-called Bicycle Ride, in which the weight is carried high on the back of the neck, is not a recommended activity, especially for children with rounded shoulders.

6. Stretching exercises should be done in a controlled fashion, with constant pressure applied to the muscles being stretched. A good guideline is to ask youngsters to stretch until it hurts and then back off the pressure a small amount. Bouncing to further the range of motion is to be discouraged and actually may reduce the level of flexibility.

Student Leaders

At times, selected students should lead exercises—either single exercises or an entire routine. Careful instruction is needed, and students should realize that prior practice is essential to leading their peers effectively in a stimulating exercise session. Probably the greatest difficulty comes in maintaining a steady, even, and appropriate cadence. Starting and stopping the exercise are also sources of difficulty. The student leader should have directions concerning the number of repetitions and should use a counting system that keeps track of the progress. The teacher should ask for volunteers or make assignments, so students can practice ahead of time. No child should be forced to lead, since this can result in a disastrous failure, both for the child and for the class. A unique formation, which requires four student leaders, can be arranged in the following manner.

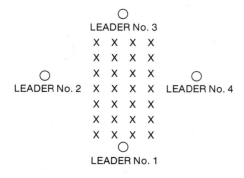

A student leader stands on each of the four sides of the formation. The sequence of leaders is generally clockwise, but it could be otherwise. The first leader, after he or she finishes an exercise, gives the command, "right—face." The children then are facing the second leader, who repeats the process. Two more exercises and changes bring the children back to the original leader. This formation could be adjusted to employ only two leaders, positioned on opposite sides of the formation. The command after the exercise led by the first leader would be "about—face."

Squad-Leader Exercises

Squad organization is also valuable for providing students with opportunities to lead exercises. Each leader takes his or her squad to a designated area and puts the squad through the exercises. The procedure works best as a planned activity with prior announcement to the squad leader rather than as a spur-of-the-moment approach. It is helpful if the squad leader has a card on which is specified the sequence of the exercises and the number of repetitions. The squad leader, if he or she wishes, can assign various members of the squad to lead exercises.

Combined Exercise Routines

An interesting fitness activity can be fashioned by combining exercises in the following manner: make it a rule that, after an exercise is given (in the normal way), the child immediately does a prescribed floor exercise, such as a Push-up or a Curl-up. A teacher's direction could be: "We are going to do a series of exercises. Just as soon as you finish an exercise, you will immediately do five Push-ups without waiting for any direction from me." This system works better when the directed exercises are given from a standing position so that either the Push-ups or the Curl-ups are a definite change. After the child has completed his or her floor exercise (on his or her own), he or she immediately stands and awaits the next directed exercise from the teacher.

Other combinations can be put together. Exercises can be alternated with running, jumping, and hopping in place.

Exercises to Music

Exercising to music adds another dimension to developmental experiences. While there are many commercial record sets with canned exercise programs available, the most effective approach is to rely on the tape recorder. The teacher has control over the selection, sequence, and number of repetitions, and the routine can be adapted to the needs and characteristics of the group. The usual starting and halting procedures are easily incorporated into tape sequences.

Appropriate music for taping can be found in basic movement record sets, polkas, waltzes, marches, jazz music, and other selections from the wide variety of records available. It is also possible to use a skilled pianist, a practice that is in vogue in some European countries.

A group of students can be assigned to make up an exercise routine to music and put it on tape. This gives them an input and a share in the program.

SELECTED EXERCISES

The recommended exercises in this section are presented under the following categories: (1) flexibility, (2) arm-shoulder girdle, (3) abdominal, (4) leg agility, and (5) trunk twisting and bending.

In any one class session, the number of exercises employed should be from 6 to 10. Included in each lesson should be 2 exercises from the arm-shoulder-girdle group and at least 1 from each of the other categories. Specific exercises should be changed at times, and a minimum of 12 to 15 exercises should be included in the overall year's experiences.

Several approaches are used to ensure a variety in exercise selection. One system is to select a basic group of exercises. Assume that 12 exercises are selected. These could be divided into two sets of 6 each, with the selection meeting the standards of category coverage as previously discussed. Some teachers like to alternate the sets day by day. Others prefer to have one set in effect for a week or two before changing.

As a time-saver, teachers can make up sets of exercises on cards, using a different-colored card for each of the categories. In this manner, the teacher can be assured of full developmental coverage by selecting a card from each color, with the stipulation of two from the arm-shoulder-girdle group.

Recommended exercises are presented under each of the five categories. Stress points or points critical to execution are presented where appropriate under the exercises. Teachers can supplement the listed exercises with those of their own choice, provided the exercises are fundamentally sound.

Flexibility Exercises

Many exercises in general can contribute to the development of flexibility. However, the main goal of those included in this section is the development of this ability. Flexibility exercises feature stretching of joints or muscle groups toward their limits. The flexibility exercises presented can be done in unison or done informally at each student's own pace and capacity.

Bend and Stretch

Starting Position: Standing erect, hands on hips, feet shoulder width apart and pointing forward.
Cadence: Slow.
Movement: Gradually bend down, taking three counts to touch the floor. Recover on the fourth count. Knees can be flexed somewhat if needed.
Beginning Dosage: Eight repetitions.

Cross-Foot Toe Touch

Directions: Same as Bend and Stretch, except cross one foot in front of the other. Do half the repetitions in this position and then reverse the feet.

Sitting Stretch

Starting Position: Sitting on the floor with legs extended forward and feet about a yard apart. Hands are clasped behind the neck, with the elbows pointed forward and kept close together.
Cadence: Slow or at will.
Movement: Gradually bend forward slowly, taking three counts to bend fully. Recover to sitting position on the fourth count.
Beginning Dosage: Eight repetitions.

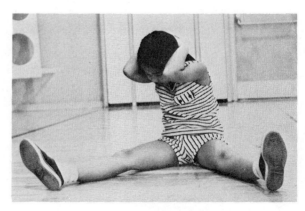

Sitting Stretch Position

Variation: Instead of bending straight forward, bend first toward the left knee, then forward, and then toward the right knee. Reverse the direction during the next sequence.
Stress Points: Because the legs are against the floor, there is little chance for hyperextended knee position, so the bending can be to the full limit.

Hurdle Stretch

Starting Position: One leg is pointed forward and fully extended. The other thigh is to the side, with the knee bent and the leg pointing to the rear. The position resembles that of a hurdler going over a hurdle. Both arms are pointed forward toward the extending foot.

Hurdle Stretch Position

Cadence: Slow or at will.
Movement: Bend forward slowly with the upper body and reach the hands toward the forward foot, taking three counts to bend fully. Recover to original position on the fourth count.
Beginning Dosage: Eight repetitions.
Stress Points: Attempt to keep the movements in an erect forward-backward direction, avoiding the tendency to lean away from the side of the back leg. The leg positions should be reversed after four repetitions.

Partner Rowing

Starting Position: Partners sit facing each other, holding hands with palms touching and fingers locked. Legs are spread and extended so that soles of each other's feet are touching.

Partner Rowing

Cadence: Slow and at will.
Movement: One partner bends forward, with the help of the other pulling backward, to try to bring

his or her chest as close to the floor as possible. Reverse direction. Pairs should work individually.
Beginning Dosage: Eight sets—forward and back.
Variation: *Steam Engine:* With both partners erect in the sitting position, alternate pulling hands back and forth like a pair of steam-engine pistons.
Beginning Dosage: Eight sets, right and left combined twists.

Arm-Shoulder-Girdle Exercises

Push-ups

Starting Position: Front-leaning rest. The body is straight from head to heels.
Cadence: Moderate or at will.
Movement: Keeping body straight:
1. Bend elbows and touch chest to ground.
2. Straighten elbows, raising body in straight line.
Beginning Dosage: Five repetitions.
Modification: If student is unable to perform the activity as described above, have him or her start with knees or hips in contact with the floor.
Stress Points: The only movement should be in the arms. The head should be up and the eyes looking ahead. The chest should touch the floor lightly, without receiving the weight of the body. The body should remain in a straight line throughout, without sagging or humping.

Push-up Position

Variation: After the children have some competence in doing Push-ups, have them try the following four-count sequence:
1. Halfway down.
2. All the way down.
3. Halfway up.
4. Up to starting position.
Teaching Hint: Controlled movement is the goal, speed is not desirable. Do most Push-ups at will, allowing each to achieve individually.

Reclining Pull-ups

Starting Position: One pupil lies on his or her back. His or her partner stands astride him or her,

with feet alongside the reclining partner's chest. Partners grasp hands with interlocking fingers or other suitable grip or with an interlocked wrist grip.
Cadence: Moderate to slow.
Movement: Partner on floor pulls up with arms until his or her chest touches partner's thighs. His or her body remains straight, with the weight resting on the heels. Return to position.
Beginning Dosage: Four to five repetitions.

Reclining Pull-ups

Variations
1. Raise as directed.
2 and 3. Hold the high position isometrically.
4. Return to position.

Another interesting variation is to have the children set a target number. On the last repetition, the raised (high) position is held for eight counts.
Stress Points: Supporting student should keep his or her center of gravity well over his or her feet by maintaining a lifted chest and good head position. The lower student should maintain a straight body during the Pull-up and move only the arms.

Arm Circling

Starting Position: Erect, feet apart, arms to the side with palms up.
Cadence: Moderate.
Movement
1. Eight forward 12-inch circles, moving both arms simultaneously, palms up.
2. Eight backward 12-inch circles, moving both arms simultaneously, palms down. The number of circles before changing can be varied.
Beginning Dosage: Three sets of forward and backward circles.
Stress Points: Good posture position should be maintained, with the abdominal wall flat and the head and shoulders held back.

Crab Position Exercises

Four developmental approaches that use the crab position as a basis are suggested.

Arm Circling

Starting Position: Crab position—the body is supported on hands and feet with the back to the floor. The knees are at right angles.

Crab Kicking

Cadence: Moderate.
Movement: Kick the right leg up and down (counts 1 and 2). Repeat with the left leg (counts 3 and 4).

Crab Alternate-Leg Extension

Cadence: Fast.

Crab Kick

Movement: On count 1, extend the right leg forward so it rests on the heel. On count 2, extend the left forward and bring the right back. Continue alternating.
Beginning Dosage: Ten sets, right and left combined.

Crab Full-Leg Extension

Cadence: Moderate.
Movement: On count 1, extend both legs forward

so the weight rests on the heels. On count 2, bring both feet back to crab position.

Beginning Dosage: Twelve extensions.

Crab Movements

Cadence: None. Informal movement.

Movement: Move forward, backward, sideward, and turn in a small circle right and left.

Flying Angel

Starting Position: Stand erect, feet together, arms at the side.

Cadence: Slow and under control. At will after the initiating command.

Movement: In a smooth, continuous motion, raise arms slowly forward with elbows extended and then upward, at the same time rising up progressively on the toes, lifting the chest, the eyes following the hands. The return is made lowering the arms sideward in a flying motion and returning to starting position. There is no counting; only an initiating signal is needed.

Beginning Dosage: Six repetitions.

Variation: The exercise can be done in a way similar to a breaststroke. The arms are raised with the hands in front of the chest and the elbows out slowly to full overhead extension. Otherwise, the movement is the same as the Flying Angel.

Stress Points: The abdominal wall must be kept flat throughout to minimize lower-back curvature. Head should be back and well up. The exercise

should be done slowly and smoothly, under good control.

Other Exercises

In addition to the preceding exercises, the following exercises included with the discussion of posture development should be considered.

Hook Lying (page 149).

The Swan (page 149).

Tailor Exercise (page 149).

Abdominal Exercises

For most exercises stressing abdominal development, the child lies on his or her back (supine position) on the floor or a mat as a basic starting position. To secure abdominal muscle involvement from this position, the child can bring his or her legs up, his or her upper body up, or both the legs and upper body up at the same time. If the upper body is brought up, the movement should begin with a Roll-up by moving the head first so that the chin makes contact or near contact with the chest, thus flattening and stabilizing the lower-back curve. The bent-knee position of the legs, either originally or in the execution of the movement, places more demands specifically on the abdominal muscles.

The isometric principle of utilizing a held position can be applied efficiently to abdominal exercises. The position should be held without movement for about 8 seconds at the point of the greatest contraction specified for the particular exercise.

Two excellent exercises for abdominal development that do not use the supine position are the Leg Extension and the Mad Cat.

Having three levels of Curl-up exercises allows for better adaptation to individual differences. At times, the instructor may specify that the group is to do Curl-up exercises and allow the individual students to choose the one they wish.

Partial Curl-up

Starting Position: On back with feet flat and

Flying Angel

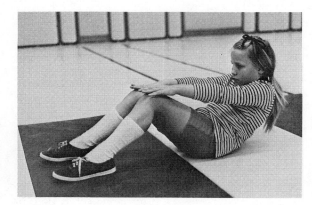

Partial Curl-up

knees bent, with hands flat down on top of thighs.
Cadence: Moderate or at will.
Movement: Leading with the chin, slide the hands forward until the fingers touch the kneecaps, lifting the head, shoulders, and upper body from the floor. Hold for eight counts and then return to position.
Beginning Dosage: Eight to 10 repetitions. The verbal count can be given as "up (lift), 2-3-4-5-6-7, down."

Another method of giving the exercise is to give only the "up" command. The students count to themselves and return to position individually.

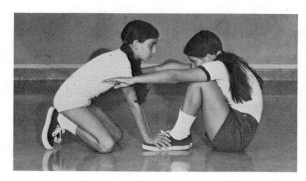

Curl-up

Curl-up (Arms Straight)

Starting Position: On back with feet flat and knees bent. Instep should be held by a helper. Hands are placed at side with palms down.
Cadence: Moderate or at will.
Movement: Two ways of doing the exercise are presented: (1) as a two-count exercise, up and down; (2) as an eight-count exercise, up, hold (2-3-4-5-6-7), and down.
Beginning Dosage: Five repetitions.
Stress Points: Roll up with the chest first: Move the chest as close to the knees as possible.
Variation: A second stage is to start with the arms along the floor overhead.

Curl-up with Twist

Starting Position: On back with feet flat and

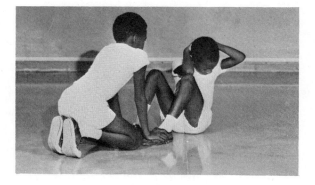

Curl-up with Twist

knees bent. Instep should be held by a helper. Fingers are clasped behind the head.
Cadence: Moderate or at will.
Movement: Curl up and touch the right knee with the left elbow. Repeat, alternating elbows.
Beginning Dosage: Five repetitions.
Variations
1. Touch the outside of the knee with the elbow.
2. Touch both knees in succession. The sequence is: up—touch left, touch right, and down.

Curl-ups for Time

Directions: Set a specified time—30 seconds is a good starting point. Each student attempts to do as many Curl-ups as he or she can during the time. A partner can count the repetitions. The body each time must make a full upward movement and return to the floor so the back of the hands touch. Otherwise, only half-credit should be given. When time is called, if the student has completed the upward movement but not the return, he or she is given half-credit.

Rowing

Starting Position: Lie on back with arms extended overhead along the floor.

Rowing

Cadence: Slow. Can be irregular.
Movement: Sit up in one continuous movement, bringing the knees to the chest and extending the arms beyond the knees, parallel to the floor. Hold for a moment, squeezing hard. Return to position.
Beginning Dosage: Five to seven repetitions.
Variation: Arms on the up movement can be held out to the sides, parallel to the floor.

Leg Extension

Starting Position: Sitting on floor with legs extended and hands on hips.
Cadence: Moderate.

Leg Extension

Movement

1. With a quick, vigorous action, raise the knees and bring both heels as close to the seat as possible. The movement is a drag with the toes touching lightly.
2. Return to position.

Beginning Dosages: Eight repetitions.
Variation: Alternate bringing the knees to the right and left of the head.

Toe Toucher

Starting Position: Flat on back, feet about 2 feet apart, arms extended overhead.
Cadence: Slow, irregular.
Movement

1. Roll up, thrust arms forward, and touch toes, keeping knees straight.
2. Roll back to original position.
3. Raise legs, swinging them overhead, keep knees straight, touch toes to ground behind head.
4. Lower legs to starting position, slowly.

Beginning Dosage: Three to four repetitions.

This exercise strengthens the muscles of the abdomen, thighs, and hips. It also stretches the hamstring muscles, which aid in the development of suppleness and flexibility. The massaging effect on the abdominal viscera is beneficial.

Mad Cat

Found on page 150 in the discussions of posture.

Leg-Agility Exercises

Leg-agility exercises should feature rhythmic, graceful motion with emphasis on control.

Running in Place

Starting Position: Standing with arms in loose thrust position.
Cadence: Slow, fast, slow.
Movement: Stationary run. Begin slowly (counting only on left foot). Speed up somewhat, raising knees to height of hips, then run at full speed,

raising knees hard, then slow down. Run should be on the toes.
Variations

1. *Tortoise and Hare:* Jog slowly in place. On the command "hare," double the speed. On the command "tortoise," slow the tempo to original jogging speed.
2. March in place, lifting knees high and swinging the arms up.
3. *Fast Stepping:* For a 10-second period, each child steps in place, just as rapidly as he or she can. Rest for 10 seconds and repeat. Watch for fatigue, since this exercise is quite strenuous.

Jumping Jack

Starting Position: At attention.
Cadence: Moderate.
Movement

1. On count 1, jump to a straddle position with arms overhead.
2. On count 2, recover to starting position.

The Jumping Jack is also a coordination exercise.
Beginning Dosage: Ten repetitions.
Variations

1. Begin with the feet in a stride position (forward and back). Change feet with the overhead movement.
2. Instead of bringing the feet together when the arms come down, cross the feet each time, alternating the cross.
3. On the completion of each set of eight counts, do a quarter-turn right. After four sets, the child will again be facing in the original direction.
4. *Modified Jumping Jack:* On count 1, jump to a straddle position with arms out to the sides parallel to the floor, with the palms down. On count 2, return to position.

Squat Thrust

Starting Position: Attention.
Cadence: Moderate.

The Squat Thrust

Movement

1. Bend markedly at the knees and sharply at the hips; place hands on the ground in front of the feet in a squat position with the knees inside the elbows.
2. Thrust feet and legs backward to a front-leaning rest position with body straight from

shoulders to feet, weight supported on hands and toes.
3. Return to the squat position.
4. Resume standing position.
Beginning Dosage: Eight thrusts.

The Squat Thrust is an excellent exercise for developing agility. It reaches and strengthens primarily the muscles of the trunk, thighs, and hips.
Stress Points: On the thrust to the rear, the body must be straight and the head up. On the completion of one full cycle of four counts, come back to a full standing position.

Treadmill

Starting Position: Push-up position, except that one leg is brought forward so that the knee is under the chest.
Cadence: Moderate.
Movement
1. Reverse position of the feet, bringing the other leg forward.
2. Change back with original foot forward. The exercise is continued rhythmically with feet alternating.

Treadmill

Beginning Dosage: Ten steps with the right foot.
Stress Points: Head should be kept up. A full exchange of the legs should be made with the forward knee coming well under the chest each time.

Other Leg-Agility Routines

While not really classed as exercises, several movement routines can be substituted to provide the challenge for leg-agility demands. General space is needed and the routines are probably more suited to outdoors, but they can be adapted for the gymnasium.

Walk, Trot, Sprint

Directions: Four cones can outline a square or rectangular area 30 to 40 yards on a side outdoors or the circumference of the gymnasium can be used. Children are scattered around the perimeter, all facing counterclockwise. The signals are given with a whistle. On the first whistle, the children begin to walk around in good posture. The next whistle signals a change to a trotting run. On the next whistle, the children run as rapidly as they can. Another whistle signals for them to walk again. The cycle is repeated as many times as the capacity of the children indicates.

Timed Activities

Children are stimulated to good effort if they know that they are being timed and are competing against other children. Timing can be done for 30, 45, or 60 seconds, or for some other interval. The following should be considered.
Rope Jumping for Time: The object is to turn the rope as fast as possible during the time limit. The number of successful jumps is counted.
Agility Run between Lines: Two lines are selected, any convenient distance between 10 and 20 feet just so all children are faced with the same distance. The child touches the lines alternately with the hands. He or she should touch one line with the left hand and the other with the right.

Additional Routines

European Rhythmic Running (page 85) is excellent.

Children can be required to run laps.

Rope jumping can be used with or without musical accompaniment.

The basketball group defensive drill (page 88) should be used at times.

Marking (page 88) also should be considered.

Trunk Twisting and Bending Exercises

A few of these exercises involve both bending and twisting motions, most either twisting or bending. Twisting and bending should be done to forceful limits. Movements should be large and vigorous.

Bear Hug

Starting Position: Standing, feet comfortably

Bear Hug

spread, hands on hips.

Cadence: Slow.

Movement

1. Take a long step diagonally right, keeping the left foot anchored in place; tackle the right leg around the thigh by encircling the thigh with both arms. Squeeze and stretch.
2. Return to position.
3. Tackle the left leg.
4. Return to position.

The value in flexibility comes from forcing a good stretch.

Beginning Dosage: Eight sets, right and left legs combined.

Side Flex

Starting Position: Lie on side, lower arm extended overhead. The head rests on the lower arm. Legs are extended fully, one on top of the other.

Cadence: Moderate.

Movement

1. Raise the upper arm and leg diagonally.
2. Repeat for several counts and change to the other side.

Side Flex

Beginning Dosage: Eight repetitions on each side.

Side Flex, Supported

Directions: This exercise is similar to the regular

Side Flex, Supported

Side Flex but more demanding. The body position of a side-leaning rest position is maintained throughout.

Body Circles

Starting Position: Feet shoulder width apart, hands on hips, body bent forward.

Cadence: Moderate.

Movement: The movement is a complete circle done by the upper body. A specified number of circles should be made to the right and the same number to the left.

Beginning Dosage: Five circles each way.

This exercise is done in free movement by directing the children to circle in one direction until told to stop. Direction then is reversed.

Variation: A more demanding exercise is structured by changing to the position at which the hands are clasped behind the neck and the elbows are kept wide. Otherwise, the exercise is the same.

Trunk Twister

Starting Position: Standing with feet shoulder width apart sideward, hands clasped behind head, elbows held backward, chin in.

Cadence: Slow.

Trunk Twister

Movement

1. Bend downward, knees straight. Recover slightly.
2. Bend downward but simultaneously rotate trunk sharply to left.
3. Same to the right.
4. Return to original position, pulling head back and chin in strongly.

Beginning Dosage: Eight sets.

The Trunk Twister reaches and strengthens all muscles of the trunk. It has excellent postural benefits. It results in increased flexibility in the lower-back region.

Windmill

Starting Position: Feet shoulder width apart, arms extended sideward with palms down.
Cadence: Moderate.
Movement
1. Bend and twist at the trunk, bringing the right hand down to the left toe.
2. Recover to starting position.
3. Same as #1, but bring the left hand to the right toe.
4. Recover to starting position.
Arms and legs should be kept straight throughout.
Beginning Dosage: Twelve sets, right and left combined.

Partner Resistance Exercises

Partner resistance exercises are useful for building strength, but they result in little development in the area of endurance or cardiovascular training. Their value lies in producing strength in a minimum amount of time. Since they primarily offer increases in strength, they should be regarded as an addition to the overall fitness program and not a substitute for any other phase of the program. Partner resistance exercises are especially valuable when used in conjunction with activities that demand a great deal of cardiovascu-

Arm Curl-up

lar endurance, such as Grass Drills, jogging, and Astronaut Drills.

Partner resistance exercises can strengthen specific muscle groups and so have value in posture work and helping the physically underdeveloped child. The exercises are simple, and children can do them as homework. Children should be made aware of the muscle group each exercise develops, so they are able to develop the body parts they need to.

Students should be somewhat matched in size and strength, so they can challenge each other. The exercises should be performed through the full range of motion at each joint, and they should take 8 to 12 seconds to be completed. The partner providing the resistance should say, "Ready" and begin the slow count. Positions then are reversed, and movements are made in opposite directions at appropriate times.

The following activities can be fun activities for children as well as excellent exercises for strength development. In addition to partner resistance exercises, similar resistance exercises can be performed with individual tug-of-war ropes (described in chapter sixteen).

Arm Curl-up

Directions: Exerciser keeps his or her upper arms against his or her sides with the palms up while his or her partner puts his or her fists in the palms. The exerciser attempts to curl his or her forearms upward to the shoulders. To develop the opposite set of muscles, push down in the opposite direction, starting at shoulder level.

Forearm Flex

Directions: Exerciser places his or her hands, palms down, on partner's shoulders. Exerciser attempts to push partner into the floor. The partner may slowly lower himself or herself to allow the exerciser movement through the range of motion. Try with the palms upward.

Fist Pull-apart

Directions: Exerciser places fists together in front of body at shoulder level. Exerciser attempts to pull hands apart while partner forces them together with pressure on the elbows. Try with fists apart and push them together; partner applies pressure by grasping the wrists.

Butterfly

Directions: Exerciser starts with arms straight and at sides. Partner attempts to hold the arms down while exerciser lifts with straight arms to the sides. Try with arms above the head and move them in opposite direction to sides.

Camelback

Directions: Exerciser is on all fours with head up.

Partner sits lightly or pushes on exerciser's back while he or she attempts to hump his or her back like a camel.

Back Builder

Directions: Exerciser spreads legs and bends forward at the waist with head up. Partner faces exerciser, clasps hands, and places them behind the exerciser's neck. The exerciser then attempts to stand upright while partner pulls downward.

Back Builder

Swan Diver

Directions: Exerciser lies in prone position with arms out to the sides and tries to arch back while partner applies pressure to the lower- and upper-back area.

Scissors

Directions: Exerciser lies on side while partner straddles exerciser and holds the upper leg down. Exerciser attempts to raise the top leg. Reverse sides and lift the other leg.

Bear Trap

Directions: Similar to the Scissors exercise, except the legs are spread first and an attempt is made to move them together.

Knee Bender

Directions: Exerciser lies in prone position with legs straight, arms ahead on the floor. Partner places hands on the back of ankle. Exerciser attempts to flex the knee while partner applies pressure. Try in the opposite direction. Repeat with the knee joint at a 90-degree angle.

Knee Bender

Push-up Position

Directions: One partner in push-up position with arms bent so that the body is about halfway up from the floor. The other partner straddles his or her head and puts pressure on top of his or her shoulders, pushing down. The amount of pressure takes judgment by the partner—too much will simply cause the bottom person to collapse. This exercise can be done as a resistive exercise where the Push-up is actually done with the top person supplying resistance.

Push-up Position

CIRCUIT TRAINING

In Circuit Training, there is a circuit of stations, each of which has a designated fitness task. The student moves from station to station, generally in a prescribed order, completing the designated fitness task at each station in turn.

Basic Theory

The exercise tasks composing the circuit should contribute to the development of all parts of the body. In addition, the activities should contribute to the various components of physical fitness (strength, power, endurance, agility, flexibility, and others). Thus, Circuit Training can be a valuable tool in the development of physical fitness.

Instructional Procedures

1. Each station should provide an exercise task

that is within the capacity of the children. The type of activity at each station should be one that each child can learn and do without the aid of another child. As the child moves from one station to the next, the exercises that directly follow each other should make demands on different parts of his or her body. In this way, the performance at any one station does not cause local fatigue that could affect the ability to perform the next task.

2. It is important that sufficient instruction in the activities be given, so the children can perform correctly at each station. The children should be taught to count the number of repetitions correctly, when a system of counting is employed.

3. The class can be divided, with some starting at each station. From the standpoint of supplying necessary equipment at each station, this method keeps the demands low. For example, if there are 30 children for a circuit of six stations, 5 children would start at each spot. The maximum equipment at each station in this case would be that necessary for 5 children.

4. A tape recorder can be used effectively to give directions for the circuit. Music, whistle signals, and even verbal directions can be prerecorded. The tape provides a rigid time control and gives a measure of consistency to the circuit. Using tapes also frees the teacher for supervisory duties.

Timing and Dosage

In general, a fixed time limit at each station seems to offer the best plan for circuit training on the elementary school level. Each child attempts to complete as many repetitions as he or she can during the time limit at each station. An increased work load can be accomplished by increasing the amount of time at each station. A suggested progressive time schedule is as follows.

Introduction	15 seconds at each station
First two weeks	20 seconds at each station
Second two weeks	25 seconds at each station
After four weeks	30 seconds at each station

Children need to be pushed, and the time limit is adjusted to accomplish this. A circuit that is too easy will contribute little to the development of fitness.

A 10-second interval should be established to allow children to move from one station to the next. Later, this can be lowered to 5 seconds. Students may start at any station, as designated, but they must follow the established order of stations.

A second method of timing is to sound only one signal for the change to the next station. Under this plan, the child ceases activity at one station, moves to the next, and *immediately* begins the task at that station without waiting for another signal.

Another means of increasing the activity demands of the circuit is to change the individual activities to more demanding types. For example, a station could specify Knee or Bench Push-ups and later change to regular Push-ups, a more demanding exercise.

Another means of adding effort is to have each child run a lap around the circuit area between changes.

Red, White, and Blue Circuits

This method of operating the circuit employs definite dosages at each of the stations. The repetitions at each of the stations are established under this kind of a formula:

Red: Modest challenge. Most children can do these.

White: Moderate challenge.

Blue: Considerable challenge.

Under this system, for example, the following could be established for the Push-ups:

Red: 10　　White: 15　　Blue: 20

Naturally, the number of repetitions and the progression would depend on the capacity of the children and their fitness level. Some experimentation is needed to set the repetition progressions at each of the stations.

Since the children progress at individual rates from station to station, the problem of sufficient equipment and space at each station is an important consideration. Signs at each station to designate the number of repetitions for each of the colors are valuable.

The Stations

The manners in which circuits are organized can vary. Equipment needed is also a consideration, and it is recommended that exercise tasks at the different stations be selected from those requiring a minimum of equipment.

The number of stations can vary but probably should not be fewer than six. Activities should be selected so that consecutive stations do not make demands on the same section of the body.

Signs at different stations can include the name of the activity and the necessary cautions or stress points for execution. Where children move between lines as limits (as in the Agility Run), traffic cones or beanbags can be used to mark the designated boundary lines.

A circuit should always include activities for exercising the arm and shoulder girdle and for strengthening the abdominal wall. A variety of activities are suggested and put into classifications, and one activity may be selected from each classification.

General Body Activities

Rope jumping: Use single-time speed.
Jumping Jack (page 108).
Running in place: Lift knees.

Crab Position – Arm and Shoulder Girdle

Crab Walk (see page 106 for description): Two parallel lines are drawn 6-8 feet apart. The child starts with hands on one line and feet in the direction of the other. He or she moves back and forth between the lines in crab position, touching one line with his or her heels and the other with his or her hands.

Crab Kicking (page 105): The child is in crab position and alternates with right and left foot kicking toward the ceiling.

Leg Exercises

Step-ups: A bench is needed for each three children who are at this station. The child begins in front of the bench, stepping up on the bench with the left foot and then up with the right foot. The child then steps down in rhythm, left and then right. The next class period when the child does the Step-ups, he or she should begin with the right foot to secure comparable development. The legs should be fully extended and the body erect when he or she is on the top of the bench.

Treadmill (page 109).

Straddle Bench Jumps: The child straddles a bench. He or she alternates jumping to the top of the bench and back to the floor. The activity is quite strenuous. Since the degree of effort is dependent upon the height of the bench, benches of various heights should be considered. These can be constructed in the form of small, elongated boxes 4 feet long, 10 inches wide and different heights between 8 inches and 10 inches. A 4-foot-long box accommodates two children at one time.

Fast Stepping (page 108).

Agility Runs – Legs and Endurance

Agility Run—Touch with the Toes: Two lines are established 15 feet apart. The child moves between the two lines as rapidly as possible, touching one line with the right foot and the other with the left.

Agility Run—Touch with the Hand: The same as above, except that the lines are touched with the hand instead of the foot.

Arm Circles – Arms and Shoulders

Standing Arm Circling (page 105).
Lying Arm Circling: The child lies facedown, with the arms out to the side. Alternate forward and backward arm circling, changing after five circles in each direction. The head and shoulders are lifted from the ground during the exercise.

Abdominal Exercises

Rowing (page 107).
Curl-ups (page 107).
Alternate Toe Touching: The child begins flat on his or her back with hands extended overhead. He or she alternates by touching the right toe with the left hand and vice versa. He or she should bring both the foot and the arm up at the same time and return to the flat position each time.

For Curl-ups, some means of anchoring the feet may be desirable. Mats can be used, so the child can hook his or her feet under the edge to provide support that ordinarily is given by another person holding the feet.

Bend and Stretch – Flexibility and Back

Bend and Stretch (page 103).

SAMPLE CIRCUIT TRAINING COURSES

Six-Station Course

1	2	3
Running in Place	Curl-ups	Arm Circling
6	5	4
Crab Walk	Trunk Twister	Agility Run

Supplies and Equipment: Mats for Curl-ups (to hook toes).
Time Needed: 4 minutes—based on 30-second activity limit, 10 seconds to move between stations.

Nine-Station Course

1	2	3	4
Rope Jumping	Push-ups	Agility Run	Arm Circling
8	7	6	5
Windmill	Treadmill	Crab Walk	Rowing

9   Hula Hooping (or any relaxing "fun" activity)

Supplies and Equipment: Jumping ropes, mats for knee Push-ups (if used), hoops (if used).
Time Needed: 6 minutes—based on 30-second activity limit, 10 seconds to move between stations.

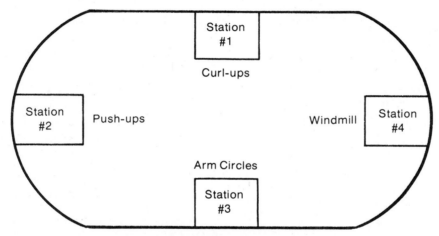

Outdoor Circuit Course

Windmill (page 111).
Trunk Twister (page 110).

Others

Many other exercises, stunts, and movements can be used. Some can be used in combination. In leg exercises, for example, the task can be designated as 25 running steps in place and then 5 pogo jumps into the air, with the whole task repeated.

If the gymnasium is equipped with chinning bars, horizontal ladders, and climbing ropes, circuits can make use of these. Some fun-type activities can be included to liven things up, too. Basketball dribbling, traveling over and under obstacles, tumbling stunts, and manipulative activities can be station tasks. Hula-hoop activities are attractive. Gym scooters add a different dimension to many routine movements.

Outdoor Circuits

An outdoor circuit around a 220-yard track or a comparable area can combine running and station tasks. Four stations are shown in the illustration above, but the number can be varied. Fewer sta-

tions are needed compared to previous examples, since demands on the legs are satisfied in the running.

Tasks are performed either for a specified time period or on a work-load basis. Work load can be set by counting the number of repetitions or sets a child can do in a minute for each of the exercise tasks and then using half of that figure as the dose.

When a time change is signaled, each participant runs one lap around the area counterclockwise past the station where he or she just performed and on to the next station. This is repeated for the number of stations. Stations should be located inside the track, so there is little interference with the runners. Laps should be run briskly at good speed.

This type of circuit could be utilized with a jogging trail, also. At specified points, different tasks could be performed.

CONTINUITY EXERCISES

Continuity drills have their origin in Europe. Continuity Exercises done snappily and with vigor are enjoyable experiences for youngsters.

The children are in an extended squad exercise formation or scattered. Each has a jump rope. The children alternate between rope jumping and exercises. A specified time period governs the length of the rope jumping, which should be done in fast time (single jumps). At the signal to stop the rope jumping, the children drop the ropes and immediately take the position for the selected exercise. The exercises all demand a down-body position and are in a two-count cadence. When the children are positioned for the exercise, the leader says, "Ready!" All children do one repetition of the exercise, counting out loud the two-count cadence with "one, two." For each repetition, then, the children wait until the leader initiates the repetition with a "ready" and each child replies with the action and the cadence count, "one, two."

The sequence of rope jumping and selected exercises forms this pattern.

First Signal: Children begin rope jumping.

Second Signal: Children drop ropes and take push-up position. (See page 104.) On each command of "ready," one Push-up is done to a two-count cadence.

Third Signal: Children resume rope jumping.

Fourth Signal: Children drop ropes and go into a supine position with arms overhead along the floor, preparatory to doing the Rowing exercise. (See page 107.) The command "ready" is given and each child performs the exercise to the two-count cadence.

Fifth Signal: Children resume jumping.

Sixth Signal: Children drop ropes and take a crab position, preparatory to doing a Crab Full-Leg Extension. On the signal "ready," both feet are thrust forward to an extended leg position with the weight momentarily on the heels and then back to the crab position, in a fast two-count cadence. (See page 105.)

Seventh Signal: Children resume rope jumping.

Eighth Signal: Children go into a side-lying position on their left sides for the Side Flex exercise. (See page 110.) On the "ready," each child performs a Side Flex in a two-count cadence. After performing one repetition, the child immediately rolls over to a right-side position. On the next command, he or she performs a Side Flex on the right side and again rolls back to the left position.

Ninth Signal: Finish, or one more session of rope jumping can be taken.

The number of repetitions should depend upon the age and physical condition of the group. Some experimentation may be necessary to determine the length of the rope-jumping periods.

As in Circuit Training, a tape recorder can signal changes of movement and also can supply appropriate music for rope jumping.

GRASS DRILLS

The name *Grass Drills* is apt, because the drills require the performer to alternate from the standing position to a down position, "on the grass." The drills are an adaptation of an old football drill, which is still used. The activities are strenuous and are performed in quick succession at top speed. Progression is gained by increasing the length of the work period. Alertness, quick reaction, and agility are needed in the drills. The drills are executed in place, so most any type of formation is appropriate as long as there is sufficient room between performers.

Basic Grass Drills

Grass Drills involve moving rapidly from one of three basic positions to another, using the command words "go," "front," and "back."

1. "Go"—run in place at top speed on the toes, knees raised high, arms pumping, and body bent forward slightly at the waist.
2. "Front"—drop to the floor in prone position, with hands underneath the body ready to push off to change position. Head should point toward the center of the circle or front of the room. Feet are extended back and kept together.
3. "Back"—the position is flat on the back, arms lying alongside the body with the palms down. The head-leg direction is opposite to the front position.

There are two ways to operate basic Grass Drills. The choice is after the "go" signal, which starts the children running in place.

1. Continuous Motion: In this method, when the command "front" is given, the child immediately goes to the prone position and comes back up to the running position without a second command. This also occurs when the "back" command is given.
2. Interrupted Motion: With this, instead of coming automatically back to the running position, the child stays in position (running, prone, or supine) until a change is called.

Variations: A number of different positions can be added to front and back, such as Push-up, Crab, V-up (page 355), Side-leaning Rest, Reverse Push-up, Turtle (page 343), and Seat Balance (full turn, right and left). Instead of running on "go," Fast Stepping can be substituted. Isometrics can be done while running.

Teaching Suggestion: Abdominal exercises should be added after the drills, since there is little abdominal development potential in Grass Drills.

ASTRONAUT DRILLS

These formerly were called Guerilla Exercises, but they have been updated. Children are spaced about 6 feet apart and walk around a circular pattern or the perimeter of the gymnasium. A succession of movement directives are given, which are interspersed with commands to walk. The circle may be stopped and the children told to perform certain movements in place. Walking then is resumed.

The following movements and tasks can be incorporated into the routine. The teacher can be creative in approach.

1. Various locomotor movements, such as hopping, jumping, running, sliding, skipping, giant steps, high on toes, et cetera.
2. On all fours, moving in the line of direction forward, backward, and sideward. Repeat backward and forward using crab position.
3. Stunt movements like the Seal Walk, Gorilla Walk, Bunny Jump, et cetera.
4. Upper torso movements and exercises that can be done while walking, such as Arm Circles, bending right and left, body twists, et cetera.
5. Various exercises in place. Always include an abdominal development activity.

Children who lag can move toward the inner part of the circle and allow more active children to pass them on the outside.

Enjoyment for children comes in being challenged through a variety of movements. The teacher should note the possibilities on a card or even have a full plan similar to the one that is given below.

Astronaut Drills can be adapted successfully to any level, kindergarten through the sixth grade. Careful selection of the movements is the key. While the emphasis is on physical development, educational implications must not be overlooked. Correct and coach form as the situation indicates.

Example of an Astronaut Drill

1. Walk.
2. On all fours, move.
3. Walk, again.
4. High on toes, walk. Reach arms high while walking on toes.
5. Feet first, Crab Walk.
6. Walk. Arms to the side, circle forward and backward. (Chest up, tummy flat.)
7. Stop, face center. Do some kind of Push-up activity.
8. Walk. Reach out with the hands, do a Hand Kick while walking.
9. Stop, face center. Do as many Curl-ups as you can in 10 seconds.
10. Hop. Change to other foot.
11. Stop, face center. Rock on tummy.
12. Jump, pogo-stick style (stiff knees).
13. Run, high knees.
14. Walk, giant steps.
15. Stop, face center. Do Windmills for 10 seconds.
16. Trot, run.

CHALLENGE COURSES

The Challenge Course is becoming increasingly popular as a tool for fitness development in the elementary school. Challenge Courses can be divided roughly into two types: the outdoor (generally permanent) and the indoor (portable).

The courses can be run against a time standard or done just for the exercise value. A course should be designed to exercise all parts of the body through a variety of activities. By including running, vaulting, agility, climbing, hanging, crawling, and other activities, good fitness demands are present when the child moves through the course as rapidly as he or she can.

Such physical education equipment as mats, parallel bars, horizontal ladders, high-jump standards, benches, and vaulting boxes can be used to make up effective Challenge Courses. A great variety of courses can be designed, depending upon the length and the different tasks to be included. Indoors, the space available would be an important factor. Some schools, fortunate enough to have a suitable wooded area, have established permanent courses.

An illustration of an indoor course is given on page 118; it is based on the assumption that a climbing rope is available. Items needed include:

3 benches (16 to 18 inches high)
3 tumbling mats (4 by 8 feet)
4 hoops or tires
1 set of high-jump standards (2) with a crossbar
1 climbing rope
1 36-inch vaulting box or wooden horse
5 chairs

MOVEMENT EXPERIENCES

Movement experiences, previously described in the program for younger children (pages 96-99), can be adapted effectively for older children. They are a welcome change of pace from other routines.

AEROBIC DANCE

Aerobic Dancing has the approval of the President's Council on Physical Fitness and Sports as an acceptable means of developing cardiorespiratory fitness, *provided* that the activity reaches moderate or high intensity. It also can develop some strength and flexibility, depending on the activities included. The basis of the activity is the idea that music increases interest, duration, and effort in the exercise, thus tending to eliminate

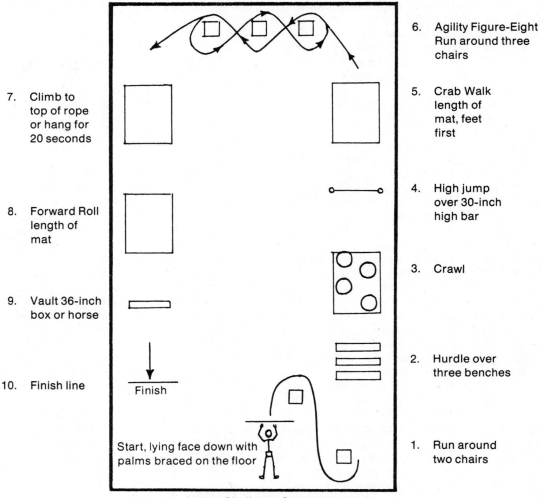

6. **Agility Figure-Eight**
   Run around three
   chairs

5. **Crab Walk**
   length of
   mat, feet
   first

4. **High jump**
   over 30-inch
   high bar

3. **Crawl**

2. **Hurdle over**
   three benches

1. **Run around**
   two chairs

7. **Climb to**
   top of rope
   or hang for
   20 seconds

8. **Forward Roll**
   length of
   mat

9. **Vault 36-inch**
   box or horse

10. **Finish line**

Finish

Start, lying face down with
palms braced on the floor

Indoor Challenge Course

some of the boredom associated with some fitness tasks.

Aerobic Dance consists of a mixture of Rhythmic Running, various fundamental movements (hopping, jumping, skipping, sliding, galloping), dance steps, swinging movements, and stretching challenges. Dances are choreographed for particular pieces of music, which should have a definite, pronounced beat and a swinging, stimulating character. Modern dance, ballroom dance, rock, cha-cha, Charleston, swing music, and others can be used. Music for rope jumping also serves well.

For elementary school children, the routines should be kept uncomplicated. When the music runs through a repetition or a change, the movement patterns should change. The following routine represents the type of movement continuity that can be structured. Routines can be designed effectively by children to music of their own or of the teacher's choice.

The suggested dance routine can be adapted to a piece of music with 120 to 140 beats per minute. The movement increments are organized by units of 16 counts.

1. Run in place (8).
   Jump in place (8).
   Repeat both (16).
2. Hop right (4), hop left (4).
   Pretend to push and step back with four step-close movements (8).
   Repeat the hopping pattern (8).
   Pretend to pull with both hands and step forward with four step-close movements (8).
3. Forward stride position, hands on hips.
   Change forward and back (8).
   Circle both arms to the right and step-close to the right four times (8).
   Repeat forward and back movements (8).
   Circle arms to the left and step-close to the left four times (8).
4. Do halfway Jumping Jacks in place, making a quarter-turn to the right on each 4 counts (16).
   Repeat making quarter-turns to the left (16).
   On these Jumping Jacks, the arms come up only to shoulder level. The entire dance can

be repeated, or additional routines can be added.

JOGGING FOR FUN AND FITNESS

Jogging, a fitness program for young and old, can provide a strong carry-over activity in the way of a personal jogging program, since it develops endurance and can lead to habits of regular activity.

Jogging is defined as easy, relaxed running at a pace that the person feels he or she can keep up for long distances without undue fatigue or strain. It is the first level above a walk.

The school should provide instruction in jogging techniques and planning a progressive program. Instruction can be offered during physical education time, but the activity itself should be done primarily during recess, the noon hour, after school, or during other free times.

Jogging is unique in that it takes no special equipment, can be done most anywhere, can be an individual activity, consumes relatively little time, and is not geared to any particular time of the day. For most people, it is an exercise in personal discipline. *For children,* it can enhance the self-image and raise confidence levels.

Types of Jogging Programs

Three types of jogging can be considered. The first is the jog-walk-jog method, which is generally employed during the early or introductory phases of jogging. One way to apply this system is for the child to cover a selected distance by a combination of jogging and walking. The child jogs until he or she feels the need to walk and walks until he or she feels like jogging again. Progression is realized by having the child eliminate as much of the walking as possible while maintaining the selected distance.

Another way to use the jog-walk-jog method is to divide the selected distance in specified increments of jogging and walking. For example, the jogger, to cover a quarter of a mile, could jog 110 yards, walk 55 yards, jog 110 yards, walk 55 yards, and jog the remaining 110 yards.

A second method is jogging all the way over a set distance, increasing or decreasing the pace in response to the body's reaction to the demands. Obviously, better endurance conditioning is needed for this procedure than in the jog-walk-jog method.

A third method is maintaining the pace but increasing the distance. Combinations of the three methods are also possible.

Instructional Procedures

Generally, authorities recommend that jogging be done on alternate days, to allow for recovery from the effects of the day's workout. Some joggers, however, like to run every day, alternating between heavy and light workouts.

The teacher should not be concerned much with foot action, since the child selects the means that is most comfortable for him or her. Arm movement should be easy and natural, with elbows bent, and the head and upper body should be in good postural position. Eyes should look ahead, and the body position in jogging generally should be erect but relaxed.

Beginning distances for elementary school children should offer sufficient challenge but not to the point of causing distress and undue fatigue. A suggested beginning distance is 440 yards, with the stipulation that the child can adjust to his or her individual requirements. Children should increase the distance gradually until they are running a mile or more.

Jogging should not be a competitive, timed activity, since each child should jog at his or her optimum pace. Racing belongs in the track program. A good technique for encouraging youngsters to run at a comfortable pace is to have them select a partner of equal ability with whom to jog. If they cannot visit with each other while running, they are probably running too fast. The teacher should not praise excessively the first youngsters finished with their jogging, because this encourages the children to race rather than to jog and those students without speed would seldom receive praise in this system. The other reason for not praising speed is that it keeps youngsters from learning to pace themselves. It is more important that they run for a longer time at a slower speed than run at top speed for a short distance when the object is developing endurance.

Many schools have enough room and suitable terrain for a jogging and cross-country course. This can be marked with a liner and lime so that the children run the course alongside the line. Check points every 220 yards give the runners convenient reference points. The course should be designed so that the circuit is a convenient unit, such as a quarter or a half of a mile or other multiples of 220 yards. The circuit should be laid out along the perimeter of the play area to minimize interference with other activities. Some schools have had good success with a program for cross-country running involving three separate courses. There are three distances and difficulty levels: beginning—½ mile, intermediate—1 mile, and advanced—2 miles. The more difficult courses can have hilly and sandy areas to increase the challenge. When the youngsters perform their jogging, they can go to the track that suits their ability and conditioning level. When youngsters do their cross-country running, they can select the course that suits their abilities and levels of conditioning. In most cases, the children select the course that challenges them appropriately.

In schools where physical education classes meet only two or three days a week, classroom teachers can help develop an effective conditioning program, the Random Running Program (RRP). In this program, the classroom teacher sends the youngsters outside to run randomly in any direction at their own speed. The only responsibility of the teacher is to clock the children for the specified time and encourage the youngsters to keep running. The following chart offers a good starting point for the intermediate grades. For primary-age children, the time element should be halved.

Week 1	3 minutes
Week 2	3½ minutes
Week 3	4 minutes
Week 4	5 minutes
Week 5	5½ minutes
Week 6	6 minutes
Week 7	6½ minutes
Week 8	7 minutes
Week 9	7½ minutes
Week 10	8 minutes
Week 11	9 minutes
Week 12	10 minutes

For indoor jogging, it can be determined how many laps of the gymnasium it takes to cover a quarter of a mile. A system to equalize the effect of direction is to jog counterclockwise on odd-numbered days and clockwise on even. Jogging, however, is better as an outdoor activity.

Motivational Techniques

A number of devices can be used to stimulate jogging. Record sheets can be kept by the teacher to record total distances jogged by individuals. Each student reports his or her jogging progress to the teacher. The individual mileage sheet could have a total of 100 miles recorded in increments of quarter-miles. Certificates of commendation could be given for totals of 50 or 100 miles of jogging.

Another motivator is the cross-country contest, during which one class may challenge others to jog a set distance. The first class to total the mileage is the winner. A United States map on which the children keep track of their class program helps to keep the contest alive. Each runner contributes his or her distance to the class total.

The song "California Here I Come" can provide the basis for a jogging song, with children making up verses.

Student artwork and posters illustrating such catchy phrases as "jog a bit and keep fit," "get the beat—use your feet," and "jogging is tops" can stimulate interest in the activity.

The use of manipulative equipment while jogging is sometimes a good technique for keeping youngsters moving. Examples include playing catch with a football or a frisbee while running, rolling a hoop, and running with a jump rope.

A good technique for helping youngsters understand pace is breaking down record times into short distances so that children can get a feel of how fast they would have to run to cover a longer distance in a certain time. Some examples follow.

To run a mile in	*you would have to run 44 40-yard dashes, with each dash run in*	*or run 17.6 100-yard dashes, with each dash run in*
3:48 minutes (world-record time)	5.18 seconds	12.95 seconds
5:00 minutes	6.81 seconds	17.04 seconds
6:00 minutes	8.18 seconds	20.45 seconds
7:00 minutes	9.55 seconds	23.87 seconds
8:00 minutes	10.90 seconds	27.25 seconds
10:00 minutes	13.62 seconds	34.08 seconds

Precautions for Jogging

Two cautions must be observed. Children with certain types of handicaps, such as cardiac abnormalities, asthma, and diabetes, should jog within stipulated medical limitations. Also, progression in jogging programs should be *slow*. The development of endurance for jogging is the result of a deep, systemic capacity, which changes slowly in response to the demands put upon it.

Jogging is a relatively safe physical education activity, since there is little chance for injury or physiological damage because the children's inborn "governors" stop them before any damage can occur.

TESTING FOR PHYSICAL FITNESS

A testing program is essential to the fitness program. Testing should uncover low-fitness students, measure the status of the rest of the students, determine needed areas for improvement, create motivation for the students, and provide material for public relations. Certainly, much of the effectiveness of the physical education program can be measured with respect to how it meets the challenge of fitness.

As a minimum, testing should take place at the beginning and end of the school year. Another testing period could be administered at the middle of the year to check progress at the halfway point. The progress of low-fitness children should be checked more often.

Fitness testing can be an enjoyable experience for children if the results are used for individual diagnosis rather than as comparative standards by which peers are graded. The teacher must be aware of the fact that, in some cases, striving to meet the goals of a test may motivate the able child but discourage the less able one. Tests and testing procedures for physical fitness can be found in appendix IV.

SPECIALIZED PROGRAMS FOR PHYSICAL UNDERACHIEVERS WITH WEIGHT PROBLEMS

After the underachiever in physical fitness has been identified, a remedial program should be instituted. The programs, together with measures to help overweight children, are described in the next chapter.

THE EXTENDED FITNESS PROGRAM

The school physical education program alone cannot provide all the necessary physical activity for proper development. It must provide, however, a good beginning and the necessary motivation toward improved fitness. The school can extend program experiences into other areas.

The school playground should provide suitable play space and be equipped with appropriate apparatus, so it can function as a laboratory for the learning experiences of the physical education program. Climbing structures, monkey rings, horizontal ladders, and exercise bars are examples of the kinds of playground equipment that have good fitness development potential.

A Challenge Course can be a part of the school's outdoor opportunities. Challenge Courses can be set up compactly or arranged on an extended layout. Schools also have found it profitable to lay out jogging courses on the school grounds.

For both boys and girls, an intramural program, growing out of the experiences of the physical education activities, should be operated. Saturday morning recreational programs also can extend the opportunities. A sound interschool competitive program is a further extension, mostly for the benefit of the more skilled. Special clubs, such as sports groups and tumbling clubs, provide outlets for special interests.

Municipal recreational programs, particularly during the summer-vacation months, can take up some of the slack when schools are not in session. Recreational groups also can cooperate with the school in making the school facilities available during the long Christmas and spring vacations.

The interest in, and motivation for, physical activity often carries over into the home. Basketball hoops and badminton courts are sometimes constructed. Climbing frames and chinning bars of home design can be made. More important than just providing equipment is the moral support and push that parents can provide to stimulate youngsters to become eager participants in regular activity.

MOTIVATION FOR PHYSICAL FITNESS

The physical education program can provide strong motivation, which is important in the fitness picture if the child is to be stimulated to good effort. Since fitness values are in proportion to the effort expended relative to the present status of physical fitness, educationally sound drives and incentives can provide reinforcement of the learning experiences of the gymnasium and playground. Some considerations for motivation follow.

1. The school can adopt the award system promoted nationally by the President's Council to recognize commendable levels of physical fitness as measured by the national physical fitness test of the council. However, the school system may wish to base its award system on another accepted test and can establish achievement levels similarly, using the 85th percentile as the minimum award standard. In the norms, a student must achieve the 85th percentile in all testing items to qualify for the award.

2. A second type of award is for commendable progress. This kind of award stimulates and serves to reward low achievers in physical development who are working toward satisfactory levels. The system also enables the school to recognize good achievement in terms of progress that is short of the higher standards set for awards like those of the President's Council.

3. The bulletin boards in the gymnasium and in the classrooms can be used to publicize items of interest about fitness. The material should be up-to-date and changed periodically.

4. Although it is misguided to try to get "everyone over the average," the publication of school norms and records gives the students a goal.

5. The use of visual aids should be exploited. A number of good films dealing with fitness are available. Write to the President's Council on Physical Fitness and Sports, Washington, D.C. 20201.

6. An excellent motivation for fitness is an understanding by each child of the values of physical fitness and how, physiologically, fitness can be developed and maintained.

7. As previously mentioned, cooperation at home is essential. Children are more likely to be fit when their parents are concerned about fitness.

8. School demonstrations for parents and physical education exhibitions can feature the topic of fitness.

9. The level of fitness should be an item on the periodic school report to the parents.

10. Some caution is urged in the use of contests among classes and/or schools based on fitness statistics. This can place undue pressure on low-fitness children and lead to undesirable peer relationships.

Nine

Children with Special Needs

Rebellion against your handicaps gets you nowhere. One must have the adventurous daring to accept one's self as a bundle of possibilities and undertake the most interesting game in the world—making the most of yourself.

Harry Emerson Fosdick

The current emphasis on equal education for all has focused attention on children with special needs. Most of this emphasis has been due to recent federal legislation, which mandates the educational services to which all handicapped children are entitled legally. There also has been increased interest in the problems for which physical education has unique solutions through the specialized attention physical education is able to give. Experience shows that an individualized program of physical activities can help handicapped children.

The discussions that follow dwell on the role of physical education in helping children overcome certain conditions and problems that can become impediments to learning and successful living.

The following subjects are treated in this chapter: (1) the program for mainstreaming handicapped children, (2) children with weight problems, and (3) underachievers in physical fitness. Discussions of children called slow learners, particularly as their problem is related to perceptual-motor competency, are found in chapter ten.

PROGRAM FOR HANDICAPPED CHILDREN

Handicapped children are defined as those who are mentally retarded, visually impaired (par-

tially sighted or blind), hearing impaired (hard of hearing or deaf), speech impaired, orthopedically impaired, learning disabled (with specific learning disabilities), seriously emotionally disturbed, or neurologically impaired (with epilepsy, palsy, or other nervous disabilities). Some children may have more than one of these handicaps.

On November 29, 1975, the Education for All Handicapped Children Act (Public Law 94-142) was signed into law. Effective October 1, 1977, it replaced former legislation for the handicapped. Several amendments and interpretations of the law have followed since 1977. The goal of the law is to provide full educational opportunities for every handicapped child. Handicapped children are to be educated in the least-restrictive environment possible and are to be educated as much as possible with children who are not handicapped. This requirement means children must be mainstreamed to the greatest extent their handicaps permit. Mainstreaming means integrating handicapped children with children who are not handicapped in regular classrooms, in contrast to segregating them in special classes. Mainstreaming can be total or partial, with the key being individual placement based on each child's physical and academic needs. When handicapped children are considered for mainstreaming, they can be grouped roughly into three classes: (1) those who can be mainstreamed fully, (2) those who can be mainstreamed partially, and (3) children for whom mainstreaming is not in the best interest.

The reasons for mainstreaming are three. Handicapped children function better academically and socially in the regular classroom. A second reason is that a regular school setting helps the handicapped child adjust and cope with the real world. Third, and from an opposite point of view, normal children learn to understand better and accept individual differences in people. However, in order to benefit from the experience, normal children need some preparation and education before handicapped individuals become members of their group.

Arguments against mainstreaming of handicapped youngsters begin with the supposition that the progress of regular students is diminished by the inclusion of special students in the class. Teachers also sometimes resist accepting handicapped children into regular classrooms, because they do not understand how to cope with the possible problems and how to provide educational progress geared to the special child. Supportive services are a part of the law, but some teachers feel that, once they have the handicapped children in their classrooms, the supportive services may be withdrawn, leaving them with nowhere to turn for help. There are also teachers who maintain that too much attention and special consideration must be given the handicapped, thus depriving the rest of the children of their share of their teacher's time.

What does mainstreaming mean to those teaching physical education classes? Handicapped children are to be part of these classes; and they must not only be considered, they must be included in the activities. No doubt after this class arrangement has been researched, practical suggestions for educationally sound approaches will appear. However, at this time, there is little on which to draw. But the following suggestions can be offered for now.

The law requires that each child have an individualized education program, which would include, among other things, a physical education program geared to meet the unique needs of that child. The program should include both recommendations and restrictions for activity. Goals can be set that will be realistic and attainable. Both pretests and posttests are a part of the process. Not all handicapped children can profit from being in regular physical education classes, but children with the following handicaps seem to be the most likely candidates.

Mildly Mentally Retarded Children

Mildly retarded children are those who have intelligence quotients roughly between 50 and 79. Generally, they are labeled *educable mentally retarded*. Some children remain permanently within this classification, but others whose retardation is due to environmental factors or deprivation can show improvement in mental capacity and functioning.

Physically, mildly retarded children differ little from their normal peers. They usually are able to compete with the rest of the children with little problem in fitness and skills. However, motor proficiency and skill attainment may lag behind those of normal children.

It is in the rate of learning and the ability to function academically that mildly retarded children show differences from their peer group. They may not absorb or follow directions as readily, or they may show slower reaction to problems requiring serialization or sequencing. When a retarded child seems to fail, it should be determined whether the result is due to failure to meet the challenge or to a problem in communication. A problem-solving situation designed for a normal child may be a bit too much for the special child to handle.

Consideration also must be made for the psychological and emotional characteristics of mentally retarded children. They may be accustomed to failure and to the fact that they do not measure up in the eyes of their peers. Their actions can be negative, resulting in withdrawal, passive resistance, or disruptive behavior. Some have been conditioned to think that their actions, no matter what they do, always result in failure, and so why should they try? They may have a low tolerance for frustration.

Since retarded youngsters have mental ages lower than their chronological ages, they may be more comfortable with younger children than with children their own ages. Overall, mentally retarded children are more likely to have poor self-concepts, low self-confidence, low tolerance for failure, and insufficient motivation for developing their potentials.

Children with Normal Mental Functioning but Handicapping Conditions

It is difficult to generalize about this group, since handicapping conditions appear in a variety of forms. The children are affected by hearing and visual impairments, neurological handicaps (resulting from cerebral palsy, epilepsy, muscular dystrophy), orthopedic handicaps (resulting from accidents, polio, birth defects), and health conditions (including diabetes, cardiac problems, asthma). Usually, these children are normal intellectually, although some can be retarded in addition to being physically handicapped. A mistaken impression exists that those afflicted with cerebral palsy are mentally retarded, also.

The majority of these children can function academically as well as, if not better than, their classmates, but they need special consideration for physical education experiences. Academically they can keep up, but their physical limitations must be considered.

Since many of these children are under some type of medical supervision, what they can and should do in physical education must first be determined by the limitations set by their physicians. It is extremely important that the teacher handling physical education experiences know and stay within the children's limits.

The children labeled as being emotionally disturbed or as having behavioral problems make up another group that can cause enigmatic problems for the physical educator. These children can function in the mainstream of physical education as long as their behavior is not disruptive, but they usually have been removed from regular classrooms because their behavior is disturbing for their classmates.

GUIDELINES FOR INTEGRATING THE HANDICAPPED INTO REGULAR PHYSICAL EDUCATION CLASSES

The type of handicap and the capabilities of each handicapped child determine in great measure the degree of success there can be in the integration process. Some other considerations include the following.

1. The Individualized Education Program (IEP) for each child, a legal requirement, is set by the child's guidance committee, which includes at least one parent. This program prescribes the focus for the education of each child. Physical and motor needs are essential parts of the IEP, and they give direction to a child's experiences in physical education. The needs must be substantiated and documented by assessment processes established by state education agencies and implemented by local education agencies.

2. A handicapped individual can be defined as one who has a physical or a mental impairment that substantially limits his or her participation in one or more major life activities, including his or her school environment. Obviously, there must be some restraint against full participation in physical activities for some handicapped children. These restraints need to be accepted by the child, the teacher, and his or her peers as *normal* in relation to the type of handicap with which the child is afflicted. In the process of mainstreaming, the child must be included in the regular program to the extent he or she is able, and provision for alternate activities must be made when that is not possible. Another approach is to alter the instructional approach or activity, so the handicapped child can be included. This brings up the age-old dilemma of the interests of the many versus the needs of a few. Decisions about changing the activities of whole classes must rest on the teacher's judgment, since there is no simple, easy solution.

3. Record keeping is essential and should include information from pretests and posttests, as well as anecdotal information. The records should show how each child is progressing with respect to his or her IEP. The program must be reviewed at least once a year.

4. In determining needs and designing the directions of students in physical education, levels of physical and motor fitness, performance in functional motor skills and motor patterns, and skills in aquatics, dance, individual and group games, and sports areas should be considered.

5. The more individualized the regular program is for all students, including the handicapped, the more likely it is that integration can occur.

6. While it is important to zero in on success, some tolerance for failure should be permitted. Activity sequences should begin at a low enough level that all students, including the handicapped, can attain a measure of success.

7. In the interest of normalizing, obvious labeling is to be avoided, even though overt labeling must be done in order to identify the children who need special help.

8. Genuine acceptance and empathy by their peers is a necessary basis for the successful mainstreaming of handicapped children, and so acceptance and empathy must be sought actively.

9. Each handicapped child requires personal attention and understanding. If these are lost in the process of mainstreaming, the child suffers. However, the child's needs should be met in a way that is part of the normal classroom situation.

10. Basically, the instructional approach is one of diagnosis and prescription. For mentally retarded children, this may mean more direct assistance and instruction from teachers.

11. Cross-age helpers and adult volunteers can provide assistance during times when the handicapped children cannot take part in the core activities and need help doing alternate activities.

12. The teacher must be alert to possible shortcomings in a special child's behavior (such as immaturity, hostility, or unsocial behavior) that can lead to problems with other children and rejection. Special children need to regard themselves as persons of worth before they can expect others to have the same feelings for them.

13. Peer regard can be influenced by excellent competency in a skill game situation or a fitness factor. The special child needs to do the

best he or she can in fitness and skills, since that is one way of gaining respect in the eyes of his or her peers. Above all, he or she needs to give forth a good effort.

14. Motivation for handicapped children is essential. Their goals must be realistic and attainable. Establishing confidence in their own ability to learn and function as individuals is important. On the other hand, the challenges must not be too easy or the child will be stigmatized as having special privileges.

15. In some cases, special equipment may be needed. For example, a lowered chinning bar helps a youngster confined to a wheelchair develop his or her arm-shoulder-girdle region.

16. Cooperative action for meeting the needs of the special child is most essential. Team effort should include the classroom teacher, the physical education specialist, the special education consultant, and one or both of the child's parents.

17. Low-fitness conditions and obesity in handicapped children can be given attention by following the guidelines set forth in the sections that follow.

REVERSE MAINSTREAMING

Reverse mainstreaming is the practice of bringing children without handicaps into classes of handicapped youngsters in order to help the handicapped youngsters attain social goals and to counter their isolation. This method is used in some school systems for children handicapped too severely to be mainstreamed successfully. Reverse mainstreaming is practiced on an occasional basis and usually is confined to use in the lower grades. Activities must be chosen so that *both* the regular and the special students can achieve success. The class sessions should be low-key, with emphasis on fun and enjoyment.

PUBLIC LAW 94-142: THE EDUCATION FOR ALL HANDICAPPED CHILDREN ACT

The authors have attempted to explain some of the more relevant and pertinent provisions of the law as they affect physical education, but the law has not been discussed in depth. The text of the law is long and complex, and every educator should study its provisions carefully.

It is interesting to note that the law mentions only physical education as a possible subject-area field that could focus attention on the importance of educationally sound programs for meeting the developmental and remedial needs of handicapped children.

OBESITY

Obesity is a common problem in America, and the solution for it is neither simple nor immediate. It is a difficult and sensitive problem, and its solutions are complex and have low rates of success. Each case is different, and the approach must fit the subject.

Obesity can be defined roughly in terms of percentages. A child who is between 10 and 20 percent over the weight designated appropriate for his or her age and height would be classed as overweight. A child 20 percent or more over the ideal is classed as obese. (However, these percentages vary from one source to another.) The advantage of a percentage definition is that it is meaningful to parents. Skinfold measures with calipers are a more recent and scientific means of identifying obese individuals. However, the simplest test is the appearance of the child; if the child looks obese, he or she is!

In any solution, the basic factors involved in obesity must be considered. These factors include genetics, emotional stability, hormonal functions, and diet-activity relationships.

The overwhelming odds are that a fat child will stay fat as he or she grows up. About 85 percent of fat children must fight fat for the rest of their lives.[1] The assumption that fat children normally grow out of their condition is a fallacy. Some parents rationalize the problem, maintaining that their child "still has some baby fat, but will grow out of it later." Unless active measures are taken, the chances of solving the child's problem are slim.

Heredity and environment may be difficult to separate as causes for obesity. Fat runs in families. If one parent is obese, about half of his or her children will end up as fat adults. This ratio jumps to 80 percent when both parents are obese.[2]

One theory supports the importance of an early solution for obesity. It is held that, during childhood, the obese child develops more fat cells than a child of normal weight, and the number of fat cells is carried over into adolescence and adulthood. An individual who has more fat cells is more prone to becoming overweight than a person who has fewer. The obvious implication is that weight-control measures should be taken early, so the fat cells cannot increase in number. During adult life, the number of fat cells is thought not to increase materially, if at all. Rather, the fat cells enlarge in size.

Obese children often experience physical activities in different ways than children of normal

[1]Alvin Eden, "How to Fat-Proof Your Child," *Reader's Digest,* December 1975.
[2]Ibid.

weight. Success is difficult for obese children to attain, and, when compared to their peers, heavy children often are physically inept. They can be made objects of ridicule and butts of jokes. Their peers often call them names, such as Fatso, Tubby, and Lard Bucket. The children can be hurt deeply and driven further away from active living, a direction opposite to the one they so desperately need to follow.

Not only does obesity impede the development of motor skills and limit the child's success in physical activities, it is a contributing factor to heart disease. Fat people are generally more inactive than their peers.

The most common factor in obesity is an imbalance in caloric intake and energy expenditure. Many obese children fail to involve themselves in enough physical activity to burn up the number of calories they ingest. Thus, the excess calories are stored in the fat cells and push the child further into obesity.

Identification of Obese Children

A practical method for determining obesity uses calipers to measure skinfolds. The skinfold of the triceps muscle is the most representative area of the body for indicating the fatness of the whole body. Calipers are relatively inexpensive, and the measurement can be made quickly. To measure the triceps skinfold, the skin on the back of the

child's upper arm is pinched with thumb and forefinger. The calipers then are applied to the skinfold, and they give a reading in millimeters. Three readings should be taken, and the results are averaged. The above chart can be consulted to see whether the child should be rated as obese.

Obesity Standards

MINIMUM THICKNESS OF TRICEPS SKINFOLD INDICATING OBESITY (IN MILLIMETERS)

Age (years)	Boys	Girls
5	12	14
6	12	15
7	13	16
8	14	17
9	15	18
10	16	20
11	17	21
12	18	22
13	18	23

SOURCE: C. C. Seltzer and J. Mayer, "A Simple Criterion of Obesity," *Postgraduate Medicine,* vol. 38, no. 2 (1965), pp. A–101.

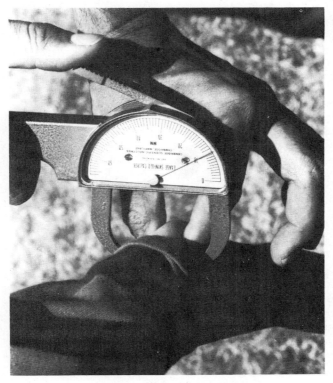

Measuring Skinfolds with Calipers

The Pinch Test

Another method is less scientific but can offer a reasonable estimate. It is called the pinch test. Several skinfold pinches can be made with the thumb and forefinger on such areas as the back of the upper arm, the side of the lower chest, the abdomen, and the back just below the shoulder blades. If a skinfold of more than an inch can be picked up, the child is considered obese. A skinfold between ½ inch and 1 inch is in the acceptable range. Some children are so obviously obese that measurement is hardly needed.

Working with the Obese Child

The solution of an obesity problem involves attention to diet and activity. Unfortunately, this means that the child must alter his or her life-style, requiring not only adjustment in his or her school life but also in his or her home life. Without these two factors a remedial program can have little success: a genuine commitment by the child to the program and the cooperation of the child's parents. For some children, commitment to the program is a relatively easy step, because they resent being fat and have wanted to do something about it but have not known quite what to do. A protracted time commitment is important, since the remedial program must turn into a program for

living or the child will revert to his or her old habits. Getting parents to cooperate can be more difficult, especially if they themselves are obese. The parents may give lip service to cooperation, but, in reality, they do not change the home life-style that contributes to the child's obesity.

Counseling is an important part of the program for fighting obesity, and it should include both conferences with the child and support through printed instructions. The program of activity for the underachiever in physical fitness is excellent for the obese child. (See page 129.)

Getting the child to follow the activity prescription is vital. This is where most of the physical educator's emphasis should lie. Dietary considerations should be secondary to the activity program.

Dealing with diet is an extremely complex problem and involves changing the eating habits not only of the obese child but of his or her parents and siblings. This is complicated by the fact that, in some cases, the obese child does not have a substantially different diet from, or eat more than, his or her classmates who have normal weights. Also, because it is difficult for a child to change the food he or she receives at home, diet control must be relegated to a minor role in the weight-control program. If the child can be influenced to eat more moderately at mealtime and to avoid snacking between meals, much has been accomplished. And, at least, the child's diet at school can be monitored.

Any weight-control project should include the whole school and involve the classroom teacher, since it is necessary to use some class time for conferences with the children in the program. Probably the intermediate level is the most feasible time to deal directly with the problem, since children at this level become more sensitive to their appearance and their relationships with their peers. And, should the program be instituted at the primary level, the children may have little motivation to deal with the problem.

Some points for consideration include the following. Is the child genuinely interested in helping himself or herself or is his or her interest primarily in getting an opportunity to escape the confines of the classroom or to receive special attention? Does the child have the time for the program, or is he or she involved in other remedial programs that already take a lot of time away from his or her classroom academic work? Has the individual been a part of other weight-control programs? If so, what was the program and what were the results? Does the specialist feel capable of helping the child reach the desired goals? A quick assessment needs to be made of the possibilities of achieving weight-control target goals, so a satisfactory interpersonal relationship can be established.

The program must achieve success, since nothing will kill it quicker than if it is "much ado about nothing." The group should be kept small (five to eight members), and it should include only those for whom there appears to be a good chance of success.

At the beginning of the program, height and weight should be taken to provide baseline data. A physical fitness test should be given to gather additional data. However, the walk-run test should be considered only for those children who feel they are ready for it. Heavy children who have been inactive find the walk-run test an unpleasant chore. Skinfold tests also should be taken and recorded. Weekly meetings should be held, during which weight, selected physical measures, and skinfold measures are taken and recorded. During the meetings, the consultant should review the child's achievements and, working with the child, lay out next week's schedule. The section on underachievers that follows contains other information valuable in weight-control programs.

UNDERACHIEVERS IN PHYSICAL FITNESS

Underachievers in physical fitness, often called low-fitness children, like handicapped and obese children, can be helped with prescriptive programs of physical activity tailored to their needs. The program for underachievers also can be used as part of the activity program for obese children. To a lesser degree, the program for the underachiever also can be applied to those handicapped children who have deficiencies in fitness qualities to the point of needing special attention. The discussions that follow deal primarily with underachievers in physical fitness, but they can be applied to the problems of obese and handicapped children as well.

The program is important, because it deals with children whose low physical achievement has affected their whole lives. Oftentimes, these children have enjoyed little success and are held in low regard by their classmates. Working with such children can be a rewarding experience, because the results, in many cases, are phenomenal, and the physical well-being and the personalities of such children are dramatically changed. Deep down, these children, with few exceptions, want to be helped and welcome both the impetus and the step-by-step program. In addition to helping children, the program can provide excellent public relations in that parents are generally impressed by the school's efforts to give attention to the special problems of their children.

The program for the underachiever usually is scheduled for the intermediate grades, but it can include the third grade. A basic concept is that the program is designed to help the children improve their fitness, in contrast to a program of activity forced on the children for their own good. The children need to accept the responsibility for their program and progress. This means that an underachiever should be in the program only if he or she wishes to help himself or herself. It is obvious that primary-level children usually do not have the maturity and the motivation to accept this personal responsibility.

There are several ways of identifying the underachiever in physical fitness. Underachievers can be identified by a screening test (page 580). On the modified national physical fitness test (page 581), they would score poorly on at least two tests or at marginal levels on all tests. If the school employs the AAHPER Test, an individual would be rated as an underachiever if two or more of his or her test items scored at or below the 30th percentile.[3]

Another means of selection instituted by one school system in the Northwest might be considered. Within a school, the teachers, principal, and specialist make a list of the names of children who might need attention. From this list, a number of children thought to have the greatest need are selected. The children are interviewed, screened, and then, if they are eligible, included in the program. The advantage of this method of selection is that the entire school population does not need to be tested in order to identify the underachievers. Teachers have remarked that they know through observation which children might need help and so testing obviously is not necessary.

Every school district should consider a special program for helping underachievers in physical fitness. Four forms that can be distributed as parts of the program are reproduced. If used, they can help make the program functional. The forms include a cover letter to parents, an outline of the program to be sent to parents, a sample letter to physicians that would be used to record the results of the health examination of each child, and a sample of the form students and teachers are to use to direct the activities of each child and to record his or her progress.

It is good procedure to have each child in the program examined by a physician. The school should absorb the cost of the examinations for those children whose parents have financial problems. An alternative but less acceptable method is

---

[3] *AAHPER Youth Fitness Test Manual* (Washington, D.C.: AAHPER, 1975).

having the parents certify that to their knowledge and according to previous physical examinations, the child has no disabilities that could prevent him or her from participating in the program.

The school district should explain either to a local medical association or to individual doctors, by letter, the nature of the program and the need for their cooperation. In this way, special arrangements and fees for the examinations might be arranged, and the physicians would be alerted to the purpose of the program when the children came in for their examinations.

Collectively, the four documents that follow provide an explanation of the program, and no further discussion of them should be necessary here.

COVER LETTER TO PARENTS

Date _____

A new approach now being considered in the _____ District schools is intended to take care of the needs of boys and girls whose physical fitness levels fall below what they should be, to the point that helpful action is indicated. In a recent assessment (testing) of fitness levels of all children, your youngster _____ scored low enough that we feel he or she can be benefited by a special program designed for his or her needs. The accompanying design of such a program explains its purposes and operation.

In order to help _____, we need your permission to have him or her take part in the program. As a part of this permission, it is important that _____ undergo a physical examination by your family physician in order to determine whether any health or physical conditions are present that need attention. It would be of no value to set up a program of physical activity for your youngster if the cause of his or her low achievement in physical fitness lies elsewhere. If the examination shows that your child is sound and can be helped by an activity program designed specially for him or her, this knowledge and reassurance would be of value to both you and the child.

If you have questions, please call your school principal or the district nurse. We feel that we can help your youngster, but, in order to do so, we need your permission and cooperation.

Signed _____

PROGRAM FOR CHILDREN WITH LOW PHYSICAL ACHIEVEMENT

A program for raising physical fitness levels of selected children is planned in the elementary schools of the _____ School District. This program will begin in _____, 19 _____, and operate for a period of 10-12 weeks. Boys and girls selected for the program are the ones whose levels of physical fitness are much lower than they should be in comparison to those of children of comparable age.

To a child, being physically fit means that he or she is in that physical condition that enables him or her to get the most out of daily living and helps him or her reach a proper growth potential. Being physically fit also means that each boy and girl is better equipped to meet the challenges and demands of school life. Further, it means being able to perform as well as his or her classmates in games and play, a quality that is invaluable in helping to establish confidence and a positive attitude toward living. It helps the child face that mysterious process of growing up—physically, mentally, and emotionally. We believe that the program can help your youngster become a better school citizen, and this will, in turn, have a beneficial effect on the quality of his or her schoolwork.

The Program

1. Children to be selected for the program are those whose levels of strength and power are abnormally low as determined by a physical fitness test.

2. After the boys and girls have been selected, it is important to secure a commitment from the youngster that he or she will participate in the program and will take responsibility for raising his or her level of fitness to acceptable norms. The physical education or classroom teacher will talk with the child, explain the program, and secure this commitment.

3. Parents' permission is to be obtained by letter. Parents agree to give permission for the child to participate in the program and promise that they will take the child to a physician to determine whether there are any physical or health problems that might be the cause or basis for the low-fitness condition. A special explanatory letter will be available that parents can give to a physician when seeking his or her advice. After the examination, the physician will specify that the child may undergo physical education without restriction or that his or her activities should have certain qualifications. Corrective action to remedy any health or physical conditions that the examination may uncover should be undertaken.

4. With the parents' permission and on the physician's recommendation, a special program of physical activity can be initiated. This will be based on the district directive, which will specify the kinds of activities designed to help the child. The physical education teacher will analyze the child's deficiencies and map out an appropriate help program. A consultation will be held each week, either singly or with others, to assess the progress each boy or girl is making and to introduce changes as indicated.

5. To improve the child's fitness, recommended physical activities that each youngster is to follow will be outlined. Your boy or girl will receive encouragement and special attention in regular physical education classes. In addition, he or she is to work on his or her own toward the objectives and is encouraged to utilize free time at home and school (recess, noontime, et cetera) to accomplish this. A basic understanding of maintaining good health and physical fitness will be a part of the program. The classroom teacher is also to help by providing informative materials for the child.

6. The parents' part in the special program should be one of encouragement and understanding rather than one of pressuring and forcing the child. It is essential that the child make a strong commitment to the program and take pride in accepting responsibility for personal improvement.

7. It is anticipated that the individual program for each child will cover from 10 to 12 weeks. After this period of time, boys and girls should continue on their own, with encouragement and occasional consultation with the contact person. A friendly follow-up interest by the classroom teacher is expected.

8. An evaluation of the effectiveness of the program for your child will be made by:
    a. Retesting the child's level of fitness after the program.
    b. Having the classroom teacher secure the child's reaction to his or her participation.
    c. Securing parents' reaction to the program, particularly with respect to the child's personality and enthusiasm, interest, attitude, and participation. Observation of any changes in the child's personality and behavior should be noted.
    d. Securing comments by the physical education teacher who supervises the child's activity program.

We hope that you will read this carefully and give approval to your child's participation in this program. Should you have questions, please call the school principal or the district nurse.

Sincerely,

Physical Education Supervisor

PHYSICAL EXAMINATION FORM

Date_____

To: family physician examining children in the special program for children with low physical achievement.

Your cooperation is asked to assist the _____ School District in working with selected children who are low in physical achievement to the point where special work is indicated.

It is important that an examination of the child be made so that it can be determined that no physical or health defects are present that preclude his or her working in a program of special activity. Upon completion of the examination, will you please note your findings and fill in the appropriate spaces below.

Please indicate one of three choices.

_____The youngster may participate fully in the program without restriction.

_____The youngster may participate in the program with the following restrictions:

_____

_____

_____

_____The youngster should not participate in this program because of the following reasons:

_____

_____

_____

Child's name_____
(Date)

_____
(Signature)

_____
(Address)

_____
(Phone)

STUDENT'S FORM

School District Individual Fitness Program

Step Up to Better Fitness

Name_____ Date_____

School_____ Grade_____ Circle: Boy   Girl

This is your program to help you become more physically fit. Please read it carefully, since it can help a great deal, depending upon how well you follow directions and work to improve.

What Is Physical Fitness?

Good physical fitness for you means that your body has enough strength, endurance, power, and flexibility to help you do better the things you like and get more fun and enjoyment out of living.

What Can Good Physical Fitness Do for You?

While being physically fit doesn't have the same value for everyone, most people agree that it can help you in these ways:

1. You get more fun out of what you are doing, because you can do things better without becoming tired so easily. You can play longer, jump farther, and do other kinds of things better.
2. You will enjoy your schoolwork and play better, because you are able to do the same things other boys and girls in your class can do and keep up with them.
3. You are helping yourself toward a better and fuller life. Becoming physically fit can make you look better and help you grow up to become the kind of person you want to be.
4. If you are interested in playing sports, becoming physically fit is most important.

How Can You Help Yourself to Better Fitness?

First of all, there must be a willingness by you to follow the work program as outlined for you and to try your best.

Second, you must think of how you help yourself toward better fitness by improving your eating, sleeping, and other daily living habits. Are you eating the right kinds of food and enough of them? Are you eating a variety of foods, including fruit, vegetables, and milk? Are you in bed and sleeping by at least 9:30 if you are in the primary grades or by 10:00 if in grades four, five, or six? Do you play outdoors and are you active generally, or do you just sit and watch TV programs?

To become physically fit means that you have to do more things and keep at them longer than you did before. These are the activities you should do to improve your fitness.

I. *General Activity (two items)*

Do at least two of the following:

	Weeks 1 2 3 4 5 6 7 8 9 10 11 12
1. Jogging	
2. Rope jumping	
3. Interval Running	
4. Side Straddle Hops	

II. *Increasing Arm Strength (three items)*

1. Do either:
   - Chins
   - Flexed-Arm Hang
2. Do Push-ups
3. Do one of the following:
   - Crab Walks
   - Rope climbing
   - Selected isometrics using a wand

III. *Helping Strengthen Abdominal (Tummy) Muscles (one item)*

Do one of the following:

1. Partial Curl-ups
2. Full Curl-ups
3. Full Curl-ups by time. Time limit _____ seconds

IV. *Body Twisting and Stretching Exercises (two items)*
   Do two of the following:

	Weeks 1 2 3 4 5 6 7 8 9 10 11 12
1. Toe Toucher	
2. Windmill	
3. Trunk Twister	
4. Body Circles (both directions)	
5. Side Flex	

V. *Take part in one or more of the following regularly in your leisure time:*

_____ Bicycling   _____ Skiing   _____ Bowling   _____ Roller skating

_____ Ice skating   _____ Soccer   _____ Hiking   _____ YMCA or YWCA activities

_____ Swimming   _____ Basketball _____ Baseball   _____ Scouting fitness activities

Description of Activities

I. *General Activities*
   1. Jogging.
      Set the distance and make it without stopping. Keep up as fast a pace as possible, but slow down if needed. Maintain a steady pace.
   2. Rope jumping.
      Use fast turning. Use basic two-foot jump or alternate feet. Set a bout of 50 or 100 turns. Stipulate the number of bouts. Can also be done by timing.
   3. Interval Running.
      Set a course of either 50 or 100 yards with two markers. Run down to the marker as fast as possible. Turn and walk back to original place. Repeat for one unit. Stipulate the number of units.
   4. Calisthenics.
      Stipulate eight-count sets and so many sets to a bout. Then set the number of bouts.

II. *Arm Strength*
   1. Set three trials for either Chins or a Flexed-Arm Hang. If no Pull-ups can be done, use the Flexed-Arm Hang.
   2. Push-ups.
      Should use regularly, if possible. Use the letdown first, then Push-up.
   3. Crab Walks can be done back and forth (round trips) between lines 5 yards apart. Touch one line with a foot and the other line with a hand.
   4. Rope climbing.
      Go up and down several times.
   5. Isometrics.
      Use a broom handle or a similar stick. Set three or four isometrics, using different arm positions.

III. *Abdominal Exercises*
   1. Partial Curl-ups.
      On back, feet flat and knees bent. Hands are flat down on top of thighs with arms stretched. Slide hands forward, leading first with the chin, until the head, shoulders, and upper body are off the floor. Hold for six counts and release.
   2. Curl-ups.
      On back with feet flat and knees bent. Fingers are clasped behind the head. Touch inside of opposite knee with elbow, alternating sides. Hook toes under something.
   3. Curl-ups by time.

IV. *Body Activities*
   1. Toe Toucher (four-count excercise).
      Standing position, feet spread, hands on hips. Reach down once, touching the toes; recover slightly and reach again; recover slightly and reach again; recover to position. Set the number of exercises.
   2. Windmill (four-count exercise).
      Standing, feet apart and arms out to the side, palms down. Twist down and touch one hand to the opposite foot. Recover. Repeat to the other side. Set the number of exercises.
   3. Trunk Twister (four-count exercise).
      Standing, feet apart, fingers clasped behind head, elbows out. Bend forward, twist one elbow down, twist the other down, recover. Set the number of exercises.
   4. Body Circles (eight-count exercise).
      Same position as #3, except body is bent forward at waist. Circle one way in four counts and then circle the other way in four counts. This is one complete set. Stipulate the number of sets.

5. Side Flex (two-count exercise).
   Lie on side with the lower arm extended along the floor to an overhead position. Upper arm is at side. Head rests on lower arm and legs are extended, one on top of the other. Lift upper arm and upper leg as high as possible. Lower. This is one repetition. Do so many right and so many left.

Ten

Perceptual-Motor Competency

Educational support for perceptual-motor programs appears still to be considerable, but currently there is little scientific evidence of their ability to affect academic achievement positively. There is some evidence that an association exists between perceptual-motor competency and certain academic skills, primarily reading readiness and achievement. This, however, is in a negative sense in that children who lack certain movement competencies identified in the perceptual-motor hierarchy have difficulty usually with reading, writing, and phases of drawing. Problems sometimes appear in speech. These children, though normal or above normal in intelligence, often fail to achieve success because of their learning disabilities.

The perceptual-motor educational concept is based on the theory that correlation of movement is centered in the brain stem and that reading, writing, spelling, and speech are controlled by this area of the neurological system. If the child has good perceptual-motor skills, then the motor-neural system has matured and developed to the point that it is not a negative factor in the learning process. Conversely, the theory holds that a child with deficient perceptual-motor development exhibits disability or fails to reach the normal level in one or more of the areas of reading, writing, spelling, and speech.

PERCEPTUAL-MOTOR COMPETENCY AND THE PHYSICAL EDUCATION PROGRAM

The earlier chapters on program planning should have made it clear that the perceptual-motor movements and activities discussed in this chapter should be incorporated already into the recommended program format. In fact, many of the activities labeled as perceptual-motor have been part of good physical education programs for many years.

The first basic concept is, therefore, that an effective physical education program includes in its normal format all the movement elements inherent in perceptual-motor competency, that is, that those elements are an important part of a very good physical education program and provide benefit for all children, particularly those in the lower grades. If the children have these experiences within the physical education program, there is little need to structure a separate perceptual-motor program or to substitute such a program for normal physical education activities for younger children.

The second concept is that a special program of perceptual-motor activities should be provided for children assessed as needing help with motor problems. These children would participate in the regular physical education program and in addition receive special help at another time.

A remedial program could be a cooperative effort of the perceptual-motor team, of which the physical educator is a member. Remedial activities would reach beyond accepted physical education activities and include visual tracking, tactile discrimination, chalkboard work, form recognition, and other specialized activities that are questionable inclusions in a regular physical education program. A specialized program would permit concentration on those children who need this help on an individual or a small-group basis.

Many perceptual-motor programs enlist help from the parents in order to assure attention on a one-to-one basis, which is not possible in regular physical education classes.

PERCEPTUAL-MOTOR FACTORS

Perceptual-motor competency is made up of a number of movement factors, which provide the basis for assessment and perceptual-motor development. Theory holds that, if one assesses each of these factors, collectively one has assessed perceptual-motor competency. Furthermore, if one selects activities that provide movement experiences purporting to develop each of the qualities, perceptual-movement competency is developed. The following factors generally are identified with perceptual-motor competency.

General coordination can be defined as the ability to move in good rhythm and muscular control (jump, hop, skip, slide, et cetera), the ability to use the different sides and parts of the body separately and in combination (laterality), and the ability to change from one movement pattern to another and to develop sequence of movement.

Spatial orientation is the development of directionality, internal and external. Internal directionality involves the concept of right and left parts. External deals with such directions as up and down, forward and backward, right and left in space, over and under. The child should be able to move in space with ease and not bump into objects or collide with other children.

A child with good *balance* should be able to exhibit good control of the center of gravity in all three aspects of balance—static (in place), dynamic (moving), and rotational (in flight).

Knowledge of the body parts and their location are essential elements of *body image*. The child should be able to identify and locate different body parts. He or she should be able to move these as directed. He or she should be able to imitate movement from a visual input, reproducing either from demonstrations, diagrams, or printed words.

Hand-eye and foot-eye coordination involve successfully tracking objects in throwing, catching, and kicking skills. Visual tracking is an important skill in reading—the ability to move the eyes across the printed pages in the right direction and at the proper speed, scanning words, phrases, and paragraphs to acquire quickly and correctly the information they contain. Other visual demands in the classroom are important, also.

Hearing discrimination is the ability of the child to move effectively and easily to rhythm. He or she should be able to reproduce auditory patterns. He or she should develop good listening skills as opposed to just hearing.

The child with good *form perception* is able to recognize different shapes and forms. Size and shape are of considerable importance in learning, and most tests of intelligence have items concerning them.

Tactile discrimination is a doubtful area for strong emphasis in physical education. It is true that children can have experiences that contribute to the sense of touch during movement experiences, but this experience belongs more properly in specialized programs.

Fitness elements are included by some educators as considerations in perceptual-motor programs. Usually included are strength, flexibility, and agility.

CHARACTERISTICS OF UNDERACHIEVERS AND SLOW LEARNERS

What characteristics does a child with poor or deficient perceptual-motor development exhibit? The child may have trouble holding or maintaining his or her balance. He or she appears clumsy and cannot carry himself or herself well in motion. The child may appear awkward in activities requiring coordination. He or she may show signs of dysfunction in lateral dominance. He or she can do things well or better with one side or one limb of the body. The child does not know right from left readily and may have to hesitate or think carefully before being able to come up with a definite movement or answer to a direction. In locomotor skills, he or she performs movements much more efficiently on one side than the other.

Kindergarten and first-grade children may not be able to hop or skip properly. They have difficulty making changes in, or combinations of, movement. After learning after a fashion to hop or skip, they cannot then hop or skip backward, nor can they hop well for a period of time.

Spatial orientation is another area in which indications can appear. The child has difficulty gauging space with respect to his or her body and bumps and collides with objects and other children. He or she may be accident-prone. Hand-eye coordination may be poor. He or she has trouble handling the simple tools of physical education—beanbags, balls, and other objects that involve a visual-motor perceptual relationship.

In the classroom, the child may show reversal of letters in words; that is, he or she may not recognize the difference between *b* and *d,* which to him or her look the same. The child's writing shows considerable irregularity and unevenness, and he or she has trouble reproducing forms.

HOW UNDERACHIEVERS AND SLOW LEARNERS CAN BE IDENTIFIED

If the teacher believes a child has a problem, some kind of testing procedures should be employed. A number of tests are currently being used, but there is little similarity in the items.

The problem is that no valid evidence is available in the form of a factor-analysis study to give weight and rank to the different perceptual-motor factors. Which are the most important and which should be stressed in the testing procedures? No ready answers are available.

Another problem is assessing the separate factors. Which is the best way to test a child's balance, or any other factors, for that matter? Little research evidence is available to provide direction in this area.

Current tests are based on the concept of including a variety of test items to cover most, if not all, of the perceptual-motor factors. Even though they lack a basis in valid research, these tests seem to be reasonably effective and can identify children with motor problems.

The one test that made a significant and original contribution in the area of perceptual-motor competency was the Perceptual Rating Scale, devised by Newell V. Kephart and presented in his book *The Purdue Perceptual-Motor Survey.*[1] Testing involves two aspects. The first is whether or not the child can do the task as specified, and the second is the assurance and confidence with which the child does the task. The test includes physical skills and hand-eye skills for using the chalkboard. Two areas from the test are presented for purposes of illustration.

Testing for Balance and Laterality

A walking board, which works on the same principle as the balance beam, is made of a 2-by-4-inch board 2 feet long. The 4-inch side is used for the test. The child is asked to walk forward, backward, and sideward (each way) without losing balance. Children should be able to move forward, backward, and sideward with ease and assurance. A child with a laterality problem will have difficulty moving one of the ways sideward, usually from left to right.

Skill Movements and Combinations

Combinations of hopping, jumping, and skipping movements on the floor are used in this part of the test. The child is given commands to demonstrate the following movements.

[1]Eugene Roach and Newell C. Kephart, *The Purdue Perceptual-Motor Survey* (Columbus, Ohio: Charles E. Merrill Books, Inc., 1966).

1. Put both feet together and jump forward one step.
2. Hop forward one step, using the right foot only.
3. Hop forward one step, using the left foot only.
4. Skip across the room.
5. Hop in place, first on the right foot and then on the left, continuing this pattern.
6. Same as the foregoing, but twice on the right and twice on the left.
7. Same procedure, but twice on the right and once on the left.
8. Same, but twice on the left and once on the right.

The child is carefully observed to see that he or she can make the movements and the changes with a smooth, rhythmical motion and with ease and assurance. Failure is indicated by a stiff, jerky motion, with pauses indicating that the child has taken time to think before moving.

Another test for consideration is the Sensory Motor Awareness Survey for Four- and Five-Year-Olds of the Dayton, Ohio, School System.

Dayton, Ohio, Sensory Motor Awareness Survey

Sensory motor training is an integral part of the curriculum of the Early Child Education Project of the Dayton (Ohio) Public Schools. The emphasis is on a preventative program for all children, rather than on a remedial one for a selected few. As a part of the program, the survey on the next page is used to provide information about each child.

The test is used in the Dayton schools as a screening device. If a child does not score well in any of the areas, he or she is given special help. Total score is not used.

INTEGRATING PERCEPTUAL-MOTOR ACTIVITIES INTO THE PHYSICAL EDUCATION PROGRAM

A perceptual-motor response is a response that is meaningful in relation to the input stimuli. The framework for the movement pattern is established, be it a single challenge or a sequence of movements. The child receives the input stimuli, perceives what is to be done, and comes up with the appropriate movement.

One of the basic purposes of the educational system is to enable the child to cope with the increasing academic demands of the school. The ability to follow directions and reproduce as specified are important for academic skills.

The implications that follow are relevant mainly to the early primary grades (kindergarten through second grade). Children beyond these grades need specialized attention if they have perceptual-motor problems.

DAYTON SENSORY MOTOR AWARENESS SURVEY FOR FOUR- AND FIVE-YEAR-OLDS

Date of Test _____

Name _____ Sex _____ Birth _____ Center _____

Body Image. One-half point for each correct part; nine points possible.

_____ 1. Ask the child to touch the following body parts:

Head_____	Ankles_____	Ears_____	Stomach_____	Elbows_____
Toes_____	Nose_____	Legs_____	Chin_____	Back_____
Eyes_____	Feet_____	Mouth_____	Waist_____	
Wrists_____	Chest_____	Fingers_____	Shoulders_____	

Space and Directions. One-half point for each correct direction; five points possible.

_____ 2. Ask the child to point to the following directions:

Front_____ Back_____ Up_____ Down_____ Beside you_____

Place two blocks on a table about 1 inch apart. Ask the child to point:

Under_____ Over_____ To the top_____ To the bottom_____ Between_____

Balance. Score two points if accomplished.

_____ 3. Have the child stand on tiptoes, on both feet, with eyes open for 8 seconds.

Balance and Laterality. Score two points for each foot; four points possible.

_____ 4. Have the child stand on one foot, eyes closed, for 5 seconds. Alternate feet.

Laterality. Score two points if the child keeps his feet together and does not lead off with one foot.

_____ 5. Have the child jump forward on two feet.

Rhythm and Neuromuscular Control. Score two points for each foot if accomplished six times; four points possible.

_____ 6. Have the child hop on one foot. Hop in place.

Rhythm and Neuromuscular Control. Score two points

_____ 7. Have the child skip forward. Child must be able to sustain this motion around the room for approximately 30 feet.

Integration of Right and Left Sides of the Body. Score two points if cross-patterning is evident for each.

_____ 8. Have the child creep forward.

_____ 9. Have the child creep backwards.

Eye-Foot Coordination. Score two points if done the length of tape or mark.

_____ 10. Use an 8 foot tape or chalk mark on the floor. The child walks in a crossover step the length of the tape or mark.

Fine Muscle Control. Score two points if paper is completely crumpled. Score one point if paper is partially crumpled. Score zero points if child needs assistance or changes hands.

_____ 11. Using a half sheet of newspaper, the child picks up the paper with one hand and puts the other hand behind his back. He then attempts to crumple the paper in his hand. He may not use his other hand, the table, or his body for assistance.

Form Perception. Score one point for each correct match.

_____ 12. Using a piece of paper with 2 inch circles, squares, and triangles, ask the child to point to two objects that are the same.

Form Perception. Score one point if circle is identified correctly. Score two points if the triangle and square are identified correctly.

_____ 13. Ask the child to identify by saying, "Point to the circle." "Point to the square." "Point to the triangle."

Hearing Discrimination. Score one point if the child taps correctly each time.

_____ 14. Ask the child to turn his back to you. Tap the table with a stick three times. Ask the child to turn around and tap the sticks the same way. Ask the child to turn his back to you. Tap the table again with the sticks (two quick taps, pause, then two more quick taps). Have the child turn back to you and tap out the rhythm.

Eye-Hand Coordination. Score one point for each successful completion.

_____ 15. A board is used with three holes in it. The holes are ¾, ⅝ and ½ inch in diameter. The child is asked to put his finger through the holes without touching the sides.

By permission of the Dayton, Ohio, Public Schools, W. T. Braley, consultant.

1. Testing and specialized remedial work in perceptual-motor training are within the province of specialists. Classroom teachers can cooperate with these specialists, but, generally, the work is outside the normal physical education program.

2. In the primary grades, two types of responses in movement work should be included—those that challenge the children with specific limitations and those that are mostly self-directed.

3. Balance activities, including the balance beam, balance boards, bounding boards, and other devices for bouncing, should have a prominent part. Conduct of balance activities should stress good control both in the movement and in the return to normal position.

4. Children should be given opportunities and practice in hand-eye and foot-eye coordination by frequent participation in activities in which they can handle balls, beanbags, hoops, ropes, rings, and the like.

5. A program emphasizing the development of fundamental locomotor skills should be instituted. This should be an instructional program.

6. Opportunity for management of the body in a variety of situations should be a part of the curriculum. Children should have activities on the floor, off the floor, across the floor, and on apparatus.

7. Spatial orientation should be emphasized, with many opportunities to go over, under, through, around, between, and along objects and apparatus.

8. Form concepts should be brought in wherever feasible. Children make different shapes, move in different figures, and select different forms in movement.

9. Success and self-concept development should have consideration. The movement patterns should start at a low enough level to provide the basis for more advanced patterns.

10. The concept of laterality should be included in all movement. The child should counter a move to the right with a similar move to the left. If he or she moves forward, stress a backward movement. No one side of the body nor direction of movement should dominate.

11. Movements should be further considered from the standpoint of unilateral, bilateral, or cross-lateral approach. Wherever possible, all should be used. A unilateral movement is one done by a single part or side of the body. Moving one arm forward would be a unilateral movement. A bilateral movement occurs when both arms or legs make corresponding movements. Moving both arms forward in a similar fashion is an example of a bilateral movement. A cross-lateral movement demands that parts of the body move in a different manner. Moving one arm forward and one backward at the same time would be a cross-lateral movement. This movement, however, is an opposed cross-lateral movement. An unrelated cross-lateral movement occurs when two corresponding parts move without relationship to each other. Lifting one arm up and the other arm forward would be unrelated movements.

12. A variety of movements and movement combinations should be presented as challenges to the child. The teacher needs the imagination and ability to take a simple movement and exhaust it completely with variety and combinations, thus giving play to many perceptual-motor-neural pathways.

13. Specialized activities designated specifically for perceptual-motor training should be included. These are bounding boards, Angels in the Snow, specialized movement sequences, cross-lateral crawling and movements, touching and naming body parts, left-right discrimination activities, and rope jumping.

There is evidence that perceptual-motor training can help perceptually deficient and mentally retarded children. Whether or not such training can help regular students increase their academic potential has not been resolved. However, the application of the movement principles of perceptual-motor work can enhance and give breadth to children's movement competencies. It is a new and exciting approach toward the concept of education for the whole child.

SPECIALIZED PERCEPTUAL-MOTOR ACTIVITIES

Included here are examples of activities that are only occasionally or casually included in the regular physical education program and are designated as perceptual-motor activities.

Angels in the Snow

The movement pattern Angels in the Snow receives the name from a traditional snow activity in which children lie in the snow on their backs and move their arms in an arc from a position overhead along the ground to their sides, thus outlining angels in the snow.

Children lie on the floor on their backs, with their legs together and arms at their sides. On command, the designated limbs move, the arms moving along the floor to a position above the head and the legs moving apart. Commands can single out one limb, two can be designated, or, in full bilateral action, both arms and both legs can be moved.

The commands are given as follows: "Right arm, left leg—move," (pause), "back." The words "out" and "back" are alternated so that the movement pattern is repeated 6 to 10 times.

The following movements generally comprise the patterns.

Bilateral—both arms, both legs, both arms and both legs.

Unilateral—right (or left) arm, right (or left) leg, right arm and right leg together, left arm and left leg together.

Cross-lateral—right arm and left leg, left arm and right leg.

The Angels in the Snow movement was originally designed as an individual exercise in which the leader pointed to an arm or a leg and said, "Move that arm (or leg)." This, however, proved unsuitable for group work.

Balloon Keep-it-up

Each child has a balloon and an instrument (small paddle, wand, baton) with which the balloon is kept in the air. This gives practice in ocular tracking. Sufficient space is needed, and extra balloons should be available.

Jumping, Hopping, and Turning

1. Jump forward, backward, sideward. Jump in patterns and combinations.
2. Hop forward, backward, sideward, stressing right and left in patterns and combinations.
3. Hop in various number combinations right and left: R-1, L-1; R-2, L-2; R-2, L-1; L-2, R-1; other combinations can be devised. The notation R-1, L-1 means to hop once on the right and once on the left foot.
4. Jump with quarter-turns, right and left; half-turns, right and left.
5. Establish the directions (east, south, west, north) and call out directions with the children making jump turns.

Command Movements in Standing Position

These movements follow the same command pattern as Angels in the Snow with the directive given first, followed by the execution command "move." The position is held until the leader says, "Back." Children should learn to exercise good control in waiting without preliminary movement until the command "move" is given, at which time they make the prescribed movement. The initial movement is held until the teacher can check the accuracy of the response. Two approaches can be used. The first is to change from one pattern into another, without repetition of any pattern. The other is to repeat a pattern, as when giving exercises. Repeat 6 to 10 times.

Types of movements that are effective are: right arm, right leg forward (unilateral); left arm, right leg forward (cross-lateral); both arms forward (bilateral); and both feet forward—a jump (bilateral).

Add the turn of the head to the movements. The head is usually turned toward the arm that is moved forward, but this can vary. Such a command would be "right arm and left foot forward, head right—move."

Side steps left and right can be used, with arms still moving forward and head turning as directed.

Crawling and Creeping Patterns

1. Unilateral crawling—crawling forward on hands and knees, using the arm and leg on the same side together.
2. Bilateral movement— moving forward, reaching out with both hands and then bringing the feet up to the hands (Bunny Jump).
3. Cross-lateral crawling—crawling forward, moving the right arm and the left leg at the same time, and vice versa.

Unilateral and cross-lateral creeping also can be employed. Creeping differs from crawling in that the child assumes a prone position in creeping, while he or she is on hands and knees in crawling. However, the terms often are used interchangeably.

Variations

1. Move forward, backward, sideward, make quarter-turns right and left.
2. Add turning the head first toward the leading hand and then opposite to it, coordinating with each step.

Form Recognition and Sequence Building with Geometric Forms

The geometric forms used are of at least two sizes (small and large) in each of the following shapes: circle, triangle, square, rectangle, and oval, among others. Sets should be painted in at least two colors with random selection from small and large shapes. A support for each shape is made from a piece of wood.

Two kinds of movement patterns can be employed with the shapes.

1. Shapes placed on the floor—directives or challenges of the following fashion can be given.
   "Can you walk around the larger circle and return?"
   "Jump once in the small oval and twice in the large triangle. Return."
   "Take the weight on the hands inside the red rectangle, balance on one foot inside the blue circle, and return."
   Other challenges can be used.
2. Shapes standing upright in supports—the purpose is to go through the shapes without

Going through Different Shapes

Reprinted by permission of © J. A. Preston Company, 1971.

touching them. Various means can be specified, such as headfirst, feetfirst, on the back, et cetera. Sequence building is important. Movement patterns can be specified in the following fashion.

"Go through the large circle and back through the small triangle."

"Go through the small circle headfirst, through the large triangle feetfirst, and return through the large rectangle as you wish."

"Crawl to the blue triangle, hop to the red rectangle, and skip to the blue circle. Return."

Imitation of Movements

This activity stresses visual input. Children face so that all can see the teacher. Children stand erect with arms at the sides. The teacher makes definite movements first with the arms, with the children following in imitation of the teacher's movements in mirror fashion (right for the teacher and left for the children). First movements should be made to the side, with forward-backward movements of the arms added later. Combinations of arm movements can be devised to challenge the children. Leg movements can be added.

Identifying Body Parts

Special practice should have the children learn the names and know the location of the various body parts. This is done by having the children touch the part or parts with both hands without looking at their bodies or getting hints from other children. Children stand or are seated facing the teacher, who says:

"Touch your shoulders."
"Touch your ankles."
"Touch your head."
"Touch your toes."
"Touch your ears."
"Touch your knees."
"Touch your eyes."

"Touch your hips."
"Touch your cheeks."
"Touch your forehead."
"Touch your thighs."

Early in the activity, during the learning phases, the children can repeat aloud the designated part of the body by saying, "I am touching my . . ." and inserting the correct term. Since this is a thinking-doing activity, the teacher should not perform the movements with the children.

A fun activity is for the teacher to touch incorrect parts deliberately on himself or herself in order to mislead the children.

Ladder Activities for Locomotor Movements

A wooden ladder is placed on mats and used to guide movements. The children begin at one end of the ladder and perform as they move down the length. Activity challenges that are of value are these.

1. Walk (run, hop, or jump) between the ladder rungs, moving forward (or sideward).
2. Walk on the rungs, balancing carefully on each. Do not touch the floor.
3. Walk on the ladder sides down the length.
4. Jump so one foot is always inside the ladder spaces.
5. Choice activities. Child creates his or her own patterns.

Movements should be done under good control, with enough repetition so that the movement patterns are reinforced.

An Arrangement of Obstacles

Challenge Courses

Miniature Challenge Courses can be set up so that the child has things to go over, under, and through. Constructed forms can be used.

Stepping Stones

The objective is to walk the squares of two colors arranged in a pattern with the right foot on one color and the left on the other. Use 20 to 30 tiles or cardboard squares of two colors, divided equally. Mark the child's feet with the correct colors with a ribbon or a chalk mark. The child walks on all the squares and steps as directed without skipping any or going back.

Trampoline

Some educators have had excellent success with reinforcing balance skills by using trampoline activities. However, the original cost, the storage problem, the inherent danger, and the necessary supervision make this impractical for most schools. Bounding boards and platform tubes are excellent substitutes (for bounding board activities, see page 310).

Games

Some games based on the imitation of movement are useful and fun for the children. Do This, Do That has its basis in fun in that the child imitates the movement as done when the leader says, "Do this!" When the leader says, "Do that!" no one is to move. Those caught can have points scored against them. The game Simon Says follows the same principle, with the children moving when the command is preceded by "Simon says."

Another similar game has the leader attempt to confuse the children by giving directions, which they are to follow, and making a different movement. For example, the leader can say, "Touch your shoulders," and at the same time put his or her hands on his or her hips. The children are to follow the verbal directions, not the visual cues.

Other Approaches

Specific activities designed to improve ocular pursuit are included in some specialized perceptual-motor programs. These involve a fixed posture of the head, with only the eyes following the pattern of movement.

One method of exercising ocular pursuit is to have the children watch a rolling ball. The children are seated about 10 yards away from the line of the path of the ball. A ball is rolled moderately fast back and forth along this line by two other children, each seated at an end of the line, the distance being about 10 yards. The children in exercising the eye muscles follow the ball back and forth along the line with their eyes.

Another method is to have the child hold out both arms forward with the thumbs up. The right thumb can be marked with a red tape. On commands of "red" and "white" the child switches his or her focus between the two thumbs. The thumbs should be first in a horizontal plane and later in vertical and diagonal planes.

A third method is to have a small ball on the end of a 3-foot string. The teacher holds the end of the string and allows the ball to swing back and forth in pendulum fashion, with the children following the path of the ball with their eyes.

Several devices for ocular pursuit using a ball on a series of inclined planes are on the market. The ball rolls down an incline and drops to the next incline, which reverses the direction. The effect is to have the ball move back on pretty much a vertical plane but drop to a lower level each time.

Chalkboard work, based on the original Kephart work, is another area of emphasis. The most likely chalkboard patterns to be made are circles. These are made by each hand in turn and both hands together. Repetition and conformity govern this line of movement training.

It can be questioned whether both ocular pursuit and chalkboard work should be regular class activities or whether they should be restricted to remedial situations. In addition, stressing ocular pursuit seems to trespass on optometry and the province of the oculist. Caution should be observed in the conduct of ocular pursuit exercises.

THE VALUE OF SPECIALIZED PERCEPTUAL-MOTOR PROGRAMS

Some feeling exists among educators that the value of a specialized or remedial perceptual-motor program lies not so much in the activities *per se* but in the process of learning. The value is thought to be in the following.
1. The child acquires a new interest and a new activity in school that, in turn, stimulate his or her overall effort and interest in classroom work.
2. There is ego involvement, the Hawthorne effect, in that most of the children in special programs have had little attention and in the programs are given special work and special attention, which carry over into academic work.
3. The child develops better listening habits.
4. The child learns to follow directions.
5. The child learns to reproduce as specified.
6. The child meets with success in a noncompetitive environment.

When the many programs that seem to be successful are analyzed, the wide variety of activities both in number and in kind is apparent, giving rise to the conclusion that the values listed above have some basis.

REMEDIAL PERCEPTUAL-MOTOR PROGRAMS

The topic of remedial programs is beyond the scope of this book. Reference is made to the following sources for specific programs.

Portland (Oregon) Public Schools. *Improving Motor-Perceptual Skills.* Corvallis, Ore.: Continuing Education Publications (Waldo Hall 100, Corvallis, Ore. 97331), 1970.

Braley, William T.; Konicki, Geraldine; and Leedy, Catherine. *Daily Sensorimotor Training Activities: A Handbook for Teachers and Parents of Pre-school and Primary Children.* Freeport, N.Y.: Educational Activities (P.O. Box 392, Freeport, N.Y. 11520), 1968.

Capon, Jack. *Motor-Perceptual Activities for Kindergarten and Primary Grades.* Write Mr. Capon, Supervisor of Physical Education, 400 Grand Street, Alameda, Calif. 94501.

Eleven

Postural Considerations

Posture refers to the habitual or assumed alignment and balance of the body segments while the body is standing, walking, sitting, or lying. In good posture, these parts are in proper relation to each other, and their good balance is reflected in ease, gracefulness, poise, and efficiency of carriage and bearing.

Posture is dependent primarily upon the strength of the muscles that hold the body in balance against the force of gravity. These muscles work continually and require strength and energy sufficient to hold the body in correct alignment.

However, from a mechanical standpoint, the musculature involved in good posture must be balanced in order to hold the bones and joints properly. Faulty alignment[1] can cause undue strain on supporting muscles and ligaments, leading to early fatigue, muscle strain, and progressive displacement of postural support. In extreme cases, pain may result and the position and function of vital organs, primarily those located in the abdomen, can be impaired.

The body, wonderful mechanism that it is, adjusts to the exterior forces applied to it. Unfortunately, this can result in poor posture. With elementary school children, poor posture may be a bad habit. But, as each child matures, poor posture becomes a growth characteristic. The result is that the muscles that activate the joints, of necessity, adapt both in length and function to the faulty positions of the body segments.

[1]In the interest of keeping the discussion in nontechnical terms, most technical terms have been omitted. Among these are *kyphosis,* which refers to a rounded upper back and forward shoulders; *lordosis,* which designates an excessive low back (lumbar) curve; and *scoliosis,* which refers to an undesirable lateral curvature of the spine.

ESTABLISHING GOOD POSTURAL HABITS

Most elementary school children are capable of assuming good posture. For them to maintain good posture depends upon a knowledge of the elements of good posture and a willingness to practice these, as well as balanced muscular development and sufficient stamina (muscle tone) to maintain good alignment. Emotional outlook and physical abnormalities also affect the child's ability to practice good postural habits. The following should be considered in helping children to develop better posture.

Motivation

The first and most important objective is to provide motivation for good posture. An understanding and appreciation of good posture must be developed through pictures, posters, demonstrations, and other media, so the youngsters consciously develop within themselves the desire for a body in good alignment.

The value of maintaining good posture can be stressed. For example, a teacher might say to the class, "A well-poised body will make you look more attractive, alert, and bright. It will help you feel and look like a winner. This is important when you look for a job or try to be selected for some school position." The teacher might add that good postural habits can prevent low-back and foot problems in later life, both of which are painful, annoying, and expensive in treatment. And, "You can be a better performer in sports if you keep your body in good alignment. With poor posture, fatigue and muscular strain can set in earlier, since bones

144

are out of line and muscles and ligaments take more strain than they should."

Muscular Development

The overall physical education program should include vigorous physical activities leading both to good general fitness and to strengthening the muscle groups that hold the body in proper alignment. Strengthening the abdominal wall and the musculature of the upper back and neck helps maintain proper body alignment.

Enough flexibility of the various body segments must be attained so the child is able to move his or her body segments with ease and assume good postural alignment.

If weak musculature is the cause of poor posture, exercises and other activities to strengthen affected areas of the body should be prescribed. Another factor is the development of good muscle tone, so fatigue, with its corresponding effect on body slump, sets in less readily.

Posture in the Instructional Process

Good posture is both a practice and a subject. The predominant emphasis should be on hints, corrections, reminders, and encouragement during all phases of the program. Even the most simple movements present postural challenges that give opportunities for incidental teaching. Strong postural implications can be derived from exercises when the children understand the why of the movement.

Where needed, more formal inspection of children's posture should be made. Applying the posture check (page 148) can provide important information for both the child and the parents and can provide motivation for the child. The perceptive teacher observing children in study and play can make a reasonably valid assessment of posture.

At times, posture can be a subject of direct study. Values and advantages of good posture should be stressed. Emphasis should be on helping the children accept the responsibility for their own good postures. Nagging and overzealousness on the part of the teacher or parents can have negative results.

Referrals

The classroom teacher needs to determine which children are to be referred to the nurse, physical education specialist, principal, or other appropriate agencies for help with posture problems. After a corrective program has been set up, the teacher's part is cooperating with the program and guiding the youngsters in fulfilling their prescribed corrective work.

Healthful School Environment

A healthful school environment encourages good posture. Attention should be given to assuring proper seating and good lighting, avoiding overfatigue, and eliminating tension in the classroom.

WHAT IS GOOD POSTURE?

Posture varies with the individual's age, sex, and body type. Very young children, in standing and walking, often toe out markedly to provide a wider, more stable base. Standing position exhibits an exaggerated lumbar curve and rounded shoulders, which are normal at this developmental stage. However, by the age of six or seven, the lumbar curve is lessening, with the prominent abdominal protrusion beginning to disappear. The feet and toes generally point ahead. Less rigid postural standards should be applied to the lower grades. The educational process should assist the child in making the transition from the normal exaggerated curves of young children to proper posture in adolescence.

The basic components for posture are much the same for all children and are illustrated in the chart on page 146.

Good posture position of the entire body is based on proper positioning of the feet, since, when the feet are positioned properly, it is more likely that the rest of the body will line up properly. If the weight is improperly placed on the heels with the knees in a back-kneed position, the pelvis is more likely to be tilted forward (down), with compensating increased lumbar curvature and rounded shoulders.

Proper and good-fitting shoes are very important for maintaining proper leg action during walking. Any shoe that distorts the normal shape and functioning of the foot should be avoided. Rundown heels, generally on the outside, cause the foot to adjust incorrectly. The normal foot has an inside straight line from the heel to and including the big toe. If worn long enough, any shoe that forces the big toe against the other toes can reshape the foot improperly. Tight, elastic socks also can force the big toe out of position.

Toeing out during walking or standing is undesirable, since it can lead to progressive arch trouble and cause other body compensations, such as less-efficient walking and off-balance standing. Another undesirable adaptation occurs in the heel cord, which may show an outward curve where it joins the heel. Further change occurs when the bony structure of the foot slides toward the inside. The change culminates in a prominent inside malleolus (bony protuberance).

Checking children for toeing out should be a part of every activity. The teacher should be sure that the children understand the anatomical reasons for keeping the feet parallel.

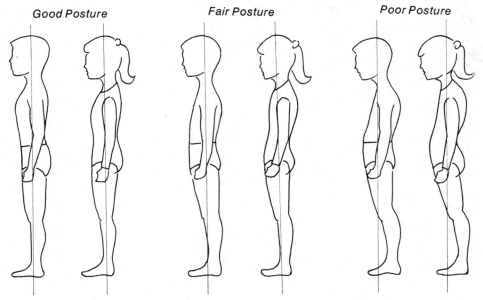

Good Posture   Fair Posture   Poor Posture

Good Posture	Fair Posture	Poor Posture
Head up, chin in, head balanced above the shoulders with the tip of the ear directly above the point of the shoulders, eyes ahead Shoulders back and easy with the chest up Lower abdomen in and flat Slight and normal curves in the upper and lower back Knees easy Weight balanced with toes pointed forward.	Head forward slightly Chest lowered slightly Lower abdomen in but not flat Back curves increased slightly Knees back slightly Weight a little too far back on heels	Head noticeably forward, eyes generally down Chest flat or depressed Shoulder blades show winged effect Abdomen relaxed and prominent Back curves exaggerated Knees forced back in back-kneed position Pelvis noticeably tilted down Weight improperly distributed

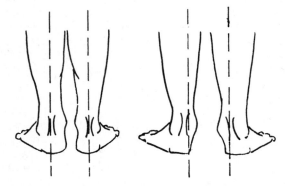

Normal Heel Cord   Pronated Heel Cord

THE FEEL OF GOOD POSTURE

Every child needs to feel when his or her body is in good postural alignment. One simple way to establish the kinesthetic feeling is to have the child assume proper foot and leg position, tuck the seat under, and lift the rib cage by taking a deep breath. At the same time, he or she stands tall, flattening the abdominal wall and keeping the head and shoulders in good position. Have the child release the air but maintain the position without tenseness.

Another method is to use a wall or a door. The child is instructed to "play wallpaper" against the wall, making contact with the heels, calves, seat, elbows, shoulders, and back of the head. An alternate way of getting into this position is to stand about 12 inches away from a wall and assume a modified Skier's Sit (page 356) position, with the thighs at about a 45-degree angle downward. In small increments, move the heels against the wall and, at the same time, slide the body upward until the legs are straight. The result is good standing posture. The children can be instructed to walk away from the wall without tenseness and return to the wall to check whether the proper position is held. A tom-tom can be used to provide rhythm for the walk.

Both of these means of securing a kinesthetic feel have good carry-over value, since they can be employed away from the school.

TEACHING CUES FOR GOOD POSTURE

The teacher should become skilled in providing the correct cues to help children. The following cues have value.

Feet—"Feet forward! Point feet straight ahead! Weight on entire foot!"

Knees—"Knees easy! Knees straight but not stiff!"

Lower back and abdomen—"Tuck your seat under! Flatten your tummy! Tummy flat! Hips under! Flatten lower back!"

Upper body—"Shoulders easy! Shoulder blades flat! Chest high! Raise chest!"

Neck and head—"Stand tall! Chin in! Head high! Stretch tall! Chin easy! Eyes ahead!"

Walking—"Walk tall! Feet forward! Eyes ahead! Arms relaxed!"

Sitting—"Seat back! Sit erect! Rest against the back! Bend forward at the hips when working!"

LATERAL DEVIATIONS IN POSTURE

Consideration to this point has concerned itself mostly with the forward-backward plane of body movement, generally assessed from the side. The body also must be in balance in the lateral plane, as viewed from either the front or back. The spinal column when viewed from the back should show a straight, vertical line that divides the body into two symmetrical halves.

A deviation occurs when this vertical line becomes either a single (C curve) or multiple (S curve) curvature. This is coupled with one or more of the following body adjustments: (1) one shoulder is higher than the other; (2) the head tilts to one side; (3) the hips are not level; and (4) the weight is obviously carried more on one leg than the other. Marked deviations are quite noticeable, but moderate deviations are difficult to detect, since children's bodies are covered with clothing and cannot be viewed critically.

One way that lateral curvature (scoliosis) can be detected is by having the child bend forward and touch his or her toes. A serious curvature is indicated when the ribs protrude on one side. Early attention to lateral curvature is important, since generally it gets worse instead of better with age. By the time the child gets into high school, the curvature has become well established and is difficult to remedy.

The teacher's efforts should be limited to instruction and practice in proper standing, with concentration on getting both the hips and shoulders level. Children at times stand so that the weight is more on one foot than the other, but one-sidedness should not become habitual.

Should the child's lateral deviation not respond after instruction, referral is indicated, since the cause may lie elsewhere. In some cases, one leg is shorter than the other, which causes a lateral tilt of the pelvis with the compensating lateral curvature of the spinal column even with the weight supported properly on both feet.

EVALUATING POSTURE

Since it is a responsibility of elementary school teachers to detect and report any physical problems of the children in their charge, some program

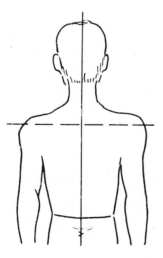

No Deviation

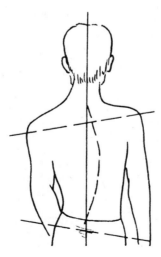

C Curve

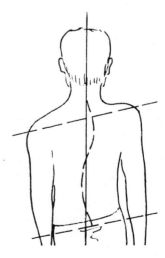

S Curve

POSTURE CHECK REPORT

Name_____ Grade_____ School_____

Date_____ Check made by_____

SIDE VIEW
Head
   Erect, chin in_____ Somewhat forward_____ Markedly forward_____
Upper Back
   Shoulders back_____ Slightly rounded_____ Round shoulders_____
Lower Back
   Slight natural curve_____ Moderate curve_____ Hollow back_____
Abdomen
   Flat_____ Slight protrusion_____ Protruding_____
Knees
   Relaxed_____ Slightly back_____ Hyperextended_____
Feet
   Pointed ahead_____ Somewhat out_____ Pointed out_____

FRONT AND BACK VIEW
Shoulders
   Level_____ Slightly uneven_____ Considerably
                                                  uneven_____
Hips
   Level_____ Slightly uneven_____ Considerably
                                                  uneven_____
Backs of Ankles and Feet
Heels and ankles   Turned out
   straight_____ somewhat_____ Pronated_____

REMARKS

CLASS POSTURE CHECK

Class_____ School_____

Date_____ Teacher_____

Code			Side Veiw						Front and Back View			
			Head and Neck	Upper Back	Lower Back	Abdomen	Knees	Feet	Level of Shoulders	Level of Hips	Feet and Ankles	Remarks
Meets good postural standards	1											
Slight but definite deviation	2											
Marked deviation	3											
Name												
1.												
2.												
3.												

of posture evaluation must be established. Evaluation can be done through observation, both formal and informal, and measurement devices. Concentration should be on those individuals who obviously exhibit posture deviations.

Posture Check Method

For youngsters with posture problems, the application of the posture check can be an educational experience. Two methods of recording are presented, an individual form and a form for recording the results for all of the children tested.

The teacher may prefer to use a single sheet including all of the class. But the individual form lends itself better to interpretation by parents and administrators. The class form is more adaptable for class analysis and comparisons. Each item can be rated 1, 2, and 3 on an ascending scale. By averaging the rating numbers, it is possible to come out with a mean rating for each child.

Some formal type of organization for the testing is needed. Children can be examined a few at a time. While it does present some difficulties, a better posture evaluation can be made if the children are in gym clothing or swimsuits. Any formal posture evaluation is an analysis of an assumed posture and not necessarily the one the child uses in daily living.

Informal Observation

Posture checks can be made of young people when they are participating in classroom and physical education activities. How does each child walk, stand, or sit when he or she is not conscious of an observer? The teacher can make notes and supplement the formal posture check.

Ear-Shoulder Method

In normal posture, the lobe of the ear is directly above the point of the shoulder. Any departure from this relationship indicates the degree of roundedness of back and shoulders and can be used as a measure of general posture deviation, since when one body area is out of alignment, other body segments compensate proportionally with abnormalities. This would mean then that, if the head were forward, there would be other parts of the body protruding to counterbalance the poor alignment. If one measures the degree the head is forward, then one has an estimate of general posture.

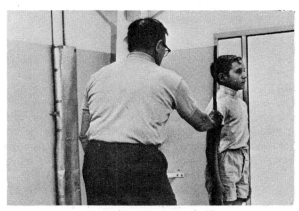
Ear-Shoulder Method

Measurement can be made with a wand or a pointer and can be expressed in the number of inches the lobe of the ear is away from (usually forward) the vertical line above the shoulder point.

Other Devices

An effective device to employ with children with obvious posture problems is to videotape and play back pictures of the children standing, walking, and in other positions, so they can observe themselves and make their own assessments using the posture check report. The same kind of an approach can be taken with a Polaroid camera.

SPECIAL POSTURE CORRECTION EXERCISES

Exercises to correct posture problems should be done slowly and under good control. Positions can be held, as in an isometric exercise, thus not only helping strengthen the designated muscle groups but also holding the body in proper alignment and helping develop the feel of good posture. Postural considerations for giving exercises found on page 101 under "Precautions in Giving Exercises" have strong application and should be incorporated into the methodology.

The recommended exercises for posture correction and maintenance are listed in two groups. The first group contains exercises of a special nature for the correction of posture. These are little used in the regular exercise program. The second group lists selected exercises often used in the regular program that have value for posture correction.

Head, Shoulder, and Upper Back Development

Hook Lying

Position: Lie on back with the feet flat on the floor, knees bent, and arms out in wing position, palms up.
Movement: Press elbows and head against the floor, keeping chin in. Hold for six to eight counts.
Beginning Dosage: Six to eight repetitions.

Swan Exercise

Position: Prone lying (facedown), arms extended sideward with palms down.
Movement: Raise upper back, head, and arms in an exaggerated swan dive position. The chin is kept in and the movement is limited to the upper back. Hold for two counts. Confine movement to upper back.
Beginning Dosage: Eight repetitions.

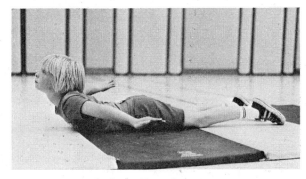
Swan Exercise

Tailor Exercise

Position: Sit tailor fashion (cross-legged) with

Tailor Exercise

trunk erect and locked fingers on middle of back of head, elbows out.
Movement: Force head and elbows back slowly against pressure. Be sure that there is no change in the erect body position.
Beginning Dosage: Ten repetitions.

Wall Sit Exercise

Position: Sitting as in the Tailor exercise but against a wall. Forearms rest naturally on the thighs.
Fixation Movements
1. Flatten upper back and shoulders against the wall and position the head properly, chin down and in.
2. Flatten the lower back, bringing it close to the wall by tensing the lower abdominal muscles and lifting up on the pelvis.

Movements: Holding the fixed position, perform the following movements slowly and smoothly.
1. Raise arms forward (pause) and overhead (pause). Return.
2. Raise arms forward (pause) and sideward to touch wall. Return.
3. Raise arms sideward to horizontal (pause) and then diagonally upward. Return. Palms are upward during entire movement.

Beginning Dosage: Five to seven repetitions.

Abdominal Muscle Development

Mad Cat

Position: On hands and knees, with the back somewhat sagging.
Movement: Arch the back as rounded as possible with a forcible contraction of the abdominal mus-

Mad Cat

cles. Hold for two counts and return to position.
Beginning Dosage: Six repetitions.

Hook Lying

Position: Lie on back with the feet flat on the floor, knees bent, and arms out in wing position with palms up.
Movement: Flatten lower back, bringing it closer to the floor by tensing the lower abdominals and lifting up on the pelvis. Hold for 8 seconds. Tense slowly and release slowly.
Beginning Dosage: Five to seven repetitions.

Foot Development

Floor Scratching (Sand Scraping)

Position: Sitting or standing, feet flat on floor.
Movement: Using the toes, scratch the floor by bringing the toes toward you forcibly on the floor.
Beginning Dosage: Ten repetitions.

Floor Creeping

Position: Sitting or standing, feet (bare) flat on the floor.
Movement: Using the toes, pull the foot forward with the heel sliding. Change to the other foot.
Beginning Dosage: Ten repetitions.

Marble Transfer

Position: Sitting on a chair or bench. A marble or a wadded piece of paper is needed.
Movement: Pick up the marble with the right foot and bring it up to the left hand. Transfer the marble to the right hand and bring up the left foot to put the marble back on the ground.
Beginning Dosage: Eight repetitions.

Knot Tying with Feet

Position: Standing.
Movement: Lay a jump rope on the floor. Tie a knot in the rope, using one foot only. Repeat with the other foot.

Foot Carry

Position: Standing.
Movement: A piece of rope or narrow felt tied in a loop about 1 foot in diameter is to be carried. Grasp the loop with the toes of one foot and hop a short distance. Repeat, changing the loop to the other foot.

Other Exercises

Exercises that have been included in the section on fitness development should be incorporated into the posture correction and remediation program. In each of the exercises used, strict attention to postural position is essential.

Flexibility Exercises

Partner Rowing (page 104).

Arm-Shoulder-Girdle Exercises

Arm Circling (page 105).
Flying Angel (page 106).

Abdominal Exercises

Curl-ups, three types (page 106-7).
Rowing (page 107).
Leg Extension (page 108).

Leg-Agility Exercises

Rope jumping (page 284).
Modified Jumping Jack (page 108).

Trunk Exercises

Trunk Twister (page 110).
Windmill (page 110).

Twelve

Instructional Approaches to Movement Education

The term *movement education* has been interpreted in a variety of ways. One definition is this: *movement education is education in, of, and through movement.* Compare this with a definition of *physical education* found in a recent article in an AAHPER journal[1]: *physical education is, in essence, a child's education in and through movement.* The definitions are much the same, and the similarity is leading to the position that the terms are interchangeable, a posture that is gaining in support. Movement education, then, has come to mean the sum total of all the child's experiences in movement and as such it has become synonymous with *physical education.*

An educationally sound physical education program incorporates movement philosophy, principles, and methodology throughout, giving attention to outcomes formerly not considered in traditional physical education approaches. A thorough understanding of, and practice in, the common elements of movement are essential to the development of good body-management competency and fundamental and special skills, qualities that together make up personal overall movement competency. Therefore, the Laban-oriented movement elements of space, time, force, and flow underlie the progression of skills and merit early attention in a program's focus. But, in order to round out and increase the program's scope, a fifth movement element must be added—body factors.

[1] Patricia Tanner and Kate Barrett, "Movement Education: What Does It Mean?" in *Echoes of Influence for Elementary School Education* (Washington, D.C.: AAHPER, 1977), p. 11.

COMPONENTS OF MOVEMENT EDUCATION

Educational Movement

Educational movement is carried on for its own sake, for increased understanding and awareness of the movement possibilities of the body. Understanding and awareness are developed through wide experience in movement that stresses the elements of movement, so that children may learn to move with ease, fluency, and versatility. A child should begin to develop his or her movement vocabulary of fundamental skills early in his or her educational life.

Fitness Considerations

Not only should a child learn to move and learn related concepts governing his or her movement, he or she should learn how to care for his or her body so that caring becomes a lifelong habit. He or she should become aware of how the body moves and how he or she can help in its development.

Fundamental and Specialized Skill Development

Included in the program are instructional procedures featuring the progression, drills, and repetition of movement that lead to the child's development of both fundamental and specialized skills. Skill development supplements and reinforces the early attention given to fundamental skills in educational movement. Children also should acquire the introductory skills necessary for selected sports, games, gymnastics, dance, and other activities, with focus on the how and why of known techniques.

152

Teaching the more specialized skills demands going *beyond* exploration and experimentation, since the learning process for specialized skills merits a more direct approach that uses defined techniques, progressions, and diligent practice. The stimulus-response bonds need to be solidified to the point where the target skill becomes over-learned and automatic.

The movement concepts, principles, and understandings, together with body-management competency as derived from educational movement, gives the learner a functional foundation on which skills can be based. Skills should not be taught in isolation but should be superimposed on what the learner brings with him or her from earlier movement experiences.

In addition, if educational movement can cause the child to expand his or her potential as a self-propelled learner, this learning to learn can carry over into later skill development. It is postulated that the child in his or her skills development program has a better basis for judgment, can sense more easily movement relationships, and can absorb the basic ideas and techniques of a skill more readily when he or she has a background in educational movement.

Posture and Body Mechanics

The posture component of educational movement concerns the child's achievement of good body alignment and carriage. A first concern for good posture is that sound mechanical principles be interwoven into all movement patterns. A second concern is incidental or direct instruction in the mechanics of good posture. Teachers must understand what constitutes good posture, how to observe and identify possible harmful deviations from it, and what approach should be taken for remediation. Proper body mechanics also should be stressed throughout the physical education program, giving heed to how to move efficiently and how to handle objects properly.

Perceptual-Motor Competency

In a sense, all movement is perceptual-motor movement. The term as used in this context refers to certain movement qualities that are somewhat related to the Laban-identified qualities but go beyond those concepts. The concern for perceptual-motor competency grew out of the study of the relationships between certain competencies and academic progress. Such qualities as coordination, balance, laterality, and identification of body parts are given emphasis in the program and integrated into the overall movement process. A second concern deals with the identification and remediation of children with deficient motor ability. The relationship between the general schoolwork of slower learners and certain motor coordination deficiencies opens new vistas.

In summary, movement education and physical education are held to be synonymous when movement education philosophy and concepts are integrated throughout the entire physical education program. The authors support the view that a new physical education has evolved and that the term *physical education* should be retained.

Another point is crucial. The five components of movement education are much interrelated, and, conceivably, all might be involved in some measure in a single lesson. The needs and objectives of the learners should determine the instructional approach.

EDUCATIONAL MOVEMENT

Educational movement is movement carried on for its own sake, for increased awareness and understanding of the body as a vehicle for movement, and for the acquisition of a personal vocabulary of movement skills. It is the foundation of movement experiences and competencies. But gains for children also come out of the teaching process by which movement goals are attained.

Two terms should be understood, since they are basic to educational movement. *Body awareness* is an understanding of the body as a whole and of the interplay and relationship of the body's individual parts to each other and to the body as a whole. *Body management* is the ability of an individual to manage his or her body in a variety of situations.

The following analysis of movement describes the overall movement patterns of the body as four general processes.

1. What Can the Body Do?

The possible movements of the body can be divided into two categories: locomotor and non-locomotor movements. Locomotor movements are those that transfer the weight from one body part to another in order to achieve linear movement. The ways that a child can move from here to there are innumerable and can provide many movement experiences. Nonlocomotor movements include the many ways that the body can be supported or balanced. One or more parts of the body can be anchored while other parts of the body move with or against each other. Reaching, pulling, twisting, contracting, raising, and lowering are just some of the nonlocomotor movements the child can experience.

The development of body awareness depends on a wide experience in movement that includes, in addition to locomotor and nonlocomotor movements, experimentation with what the body can do (for example, the various shapes it can assume: curled, stretched, twisted, wide, and narrow). Knowing the names and locations of the separate parts of the body must come before any understanding of the functions and possibilities of movement can be achieved.

2. With What and with Whom Does the Child Move?

A part of the child's movement experience is his or her relationship with the physical environment in which he or she moves (gymnasium, classroom, playground, et cetera), with the equipment he or she uses, and with the way he or she works (with other children or by himself or herself).

The child first learns to move with competency and to manage himself or herself and a piece of equipment without interfering with other children. Then, after he or she has learned to handle himself or herself reasonably well as an individual, he or she can learn to work with another child. Finally, the child can develop a sensitivity to others and work in a group, sharing experiences and judgments in a give-and-take situation that leads to better social maturity.

3. Where Can the Body Move?

Spatial factors have two aspects, general and personal. In general space, the child moves with consideration for others in locomotor movements. In personal space, the child is concerned only with *self* in his or her movements. Spatial factors are direction, level, pattern, size, and plane of movement.

4. How Can the Body Move?

Time factors, qualities of movement, flow, and the body factors are involved in movement. Time includes variation in speed, acceleration and deceleration, and rhythm. Qualities of movement, which some term *force,* include force of movement and expressive movement. Flow can either be sustained (free) flow or interrupted (bound) flow. Body factors describe the body and its parts in relation to the movement.

Themes of Educational Movement

In practice, educational movement is organized around themes, which can be categorized according to the general movement factors: space, time, force, flow, and body factors. A theme of spatial movement might ask the child to explore different ways of moving in a specific direction or level. Time could be featured in a theme asking the child to move at a fast or slow pace. Focus on force could be directed by such challenges as asking the child to link movements together in a particular way. Body factors could be related to the use of different parts of the body for support or movement.

Themes are seldom experienced in isolation. To some degree, the movement factors are

characteristic of all movements. At times, however, one or more factors are given special attention and become the core of a lesson.

With younger children, the movement experiences are quite general, and it is not easy to identify the different themes. During the primary years and later, the instruction can be guided more toward specific theme development.

The process of instruction must structure a learning environment in such a way that children learn to think for themselves and accept a large part of the responsibility for their own learning. Through the process of acquiring movement competency, children should learn to follow directions, to listen, to think, and to solve movement problems in their own ways. The teacher should not dominate the lesson but should stimulate the children to use their ideas to plan different ways to carry out the movement experiences. Each child should be encouraged to make what contributions he or she can to the whole. Since children have a desire to express themselves physically, as well as in other ways, satisfaction can only be obtained when the children have a measure of choice and an opportunity to exercise individuality.

Because the child expresses himself or herself individually in movement, he or she can achieve a satisfactory measure of success *for himself or herself* rather than to fulfill teacher-dominated or group standards. The child progresses according to his or her innate abilities, stimulated by the teacher and the learning situation. No child need feel awkward or self-conscious because he does not measure up to predetermined standards. The fact that children differ in size, shape, maturity, and motor ability does not preclude success and satisfaction. The child makes progress according to his or her rate and to his or her satisfaction.

The emphasis in educational movement should be on activity and movement of a *purposeful* nature, with *both* quantity and quality of movement promoted. Only then does movement become a sound educational experience. Too often, children undergo experiences without the necessary guidance or an insistence on their doing things as well as possible. Care must be taken so that doing things in different ways does not de-emphasize the value of doing things well.

A further point on guidance: the authors question the premise that it is paramount to the point of overriding all other elements of instruction that each child make his or her own choices about movement experiences. A child should be encouraged to continue to experiment even after he or she has arrived at a satisfactory (to him or her) solution. There may be other good ways and even a better way to do things, even though the initial selection is satisfying.

Some other values grow out of the process of

selection. Children should be able not only to move with ease and efficiency but also to analyze critically their own movements and those of others. As a result, it is postulated, a safer learning atmosphere will be achieved when children are neither forced nor urged to go beyond their capacities. They choose and perform individually when they have the inclination or when they have decided they are ready.

CLASSIFYING MOVEMENT PATTERNS

A major concept in selecting methodology educationally sound in terms of target goals is the consideration of movement patterns from two perspectives and, hence, as two categories. In any one lesson, the type of movement, its development, and its expected outcomes determine the teaching strategy to be followed. If the movement patterns were concentrated on theme development, the children's responses might show many different movements and flexibility of response might be the governing key. Should the concentration be on a more defined movement (a fundamental skill), more limitations would be in order as the selected pattern is experienced and refined.

Relevant instructional procedures must be applied to the two categories, which are termed respectively *divergent* and *convergent movement.* (The authors feel the terms *divergent* and *convergent* are more descriptive and appropriate than the terms, *unstructured* and *structured movement,* formerly used.)

Divergent Movement

Divergent movement aims toward the development of body awareness and efficient movement in a variety of situations. The key is wide experience in movement for gaining an understanding of the movement quality to be emphasized, whether it is space, time, force, flow, or body factors. The emphasis is on exploration, repetition, and creativity pointed toward the refinement of selected movement patterns. The instructional emphasis focuses on breadth of movement and versatility.

Two examples should illustrate. "Find a way you and your ball can travel in general space." This movement combines space factors and manipulation. "Reach out slowly in different directions and return to a curled position with a quick, forceful movement." A number of movement factors are implied in this theme.

There is no right or wrong response as long as the child solves the problem and stays within the focus of the challenge. The choice is the child's, and the teacher should accept the solution and build upon it for further development. Emphasis

should be on the concept that "there is always another way."[2]

Another approach in divergent movement is expressive and imitative movement. Expressive movement relies on feelings such as being happy, sad, angry, contrite, and gay. Imitative movement mimics animals, personalities, and other elements. Both expressive and imitative movements have a dual purpose in the movement program. First, they provide an opportunity for creative outlet and communication by movement. Second, they provide additional breadth and expansion of a movement's focus. An example of the latter approach could occur in a lesson focused on imitation; the child could be challenged to "advance like a soldier" or "move as if you are very tired after a hard day's work."

Themes are important in providing direction to divergent movement. Further discussion and examples of themes are found on page 170.

Convergent Movement

In convergent movement, the teacher guides the instruction toward the child's acquisition of a particular skill, which can be identified by name as opposed to general movement responses of wide choice in divergent movement. Children can practice such defined movements as walking, batting, bouncing, jumping, and pitching. A convergent movement can be identified by the fact that it usually ends in the suffix *ing.* Included are the fundamental and specialized skills, as well as the more precise skills on apparatus. Convergent movement implies a limitation; the child must conform to the specified target skill, but the activity can be accomplished or interpreted by various responses. The Laban movement factors are essential understandings as they apply to each particular skill.

The focus is on a particular skill, which includes the concept of acceptable and unacceptable ways of performing. The child should be guided to discover the best way or ways for him or her to perform the skill.

The more precise the skill, the more critical the need to establish good techniques. Good techniques should prevail even when the child feels more comfortable with a known departure from accepted form. A child who throws right-handed and steps with his or her right foot as he or she throws should be induced to change to a left-foot step, since the right-hand-right-foot throwing technique will establish an undesirable habit pattern that would need to be changed later. The child should be encouraged to change even if after ex-

[2]This statement was attributed to Ambrose Brazelton, former supervisor of physical education for the state of Ohio. Mr. Brazelton used this approach successfully in his work with children.

ploration and experimentation, he or she feels more comfortable with the right-hand-right-foot throw. As a minimum, the child should be made aware of the recommended techniques even if he or she chooses to retain the questionable (to the teacher) pattern.

For convergent movement, a somewhat different instructional approach than for divergent movement is indicated. The range of acceptable technique needs to be known and adhered to. In some cases, the range can be broad, and, in others, the choice can be quite limited. Perceptive guidance is essential in analyzing the child's performance in relation to the stress points of the skill. Progressions and pacing become important. Repetition aimed at establishing unconscious or automatic skill behavior is inherent in the lesson continuum.

EXPANDING MOVEMENT AND SECURING VARIETY OF RESPONSE

Space, time, qualities of movement (force), flow, and body factors are most important ingredients in educational movement as well as in other teaching approaches. Through their application by coaching and suggestion, they provide the means by which the teacher can bring out the movement potential of a child and develop his or her awareness of movement. Skill in their application is most essential when variety and depth of movement are to be attained.

The factors can enhance the value of *any* teaching approach or style of teaching. Frequent reference is made to them throughout this book.

Space Factors

Space factors involve level, direction, relationship, size, plane of movement, and pattern.

Level—low, high, or in-between.

Direction—straight, zigzag, circular, curved, forward, backward, sideward, upward, and downward.

Relationship—above, below, near, far, ahead, behind, over, under, through, in front, to the side, around, overhead, underneath.

Size—large or small.

Plane of movement—horizontal, vertical, or diagonal.

Pattern—squares, diamonds, triangles, circles, figure eights, and others.

Internal directionality—frontal plane, front and back; transverse plane, top and bottom; sagittal plane, sides, right-left discrimination.

Time Factor

The time factor may be varied as follows.

Different speeds—slow, moderate, or fast.

Acceleration or deceleration—increasing or decreasing the speed of movement.

Even or uneven time—sudden, jerky, smooth, or even movement; variation in rhythm.

Flow Factor

The flow factor establishes continuity of movement.

Interrupted flow (bound flow)—stopping at the end of a movement or part of a movement.

Sustained flow (free flow)—linking together smoothly different movements or parts of a movement.

Qualities of Movement

Three aspects of qualities of movement are important.

Force—light or heavy, strong or weak, sudden or sustained.

Expressive movement—happy or sad, gay or restrained, angry, rough.

Imitative—imitating animals, personalities, machines, fictitious characters.

Body Factors

A number of considerations in the use of the body can add variety to movement.

Shape—can be long or short, wide or narrow, straight or twisted, stretched or curled, symmetrical or asymmetrical.

Weight bearing—different parts of the body supporting the weight or receiving the weight; different numbers of body parts involved in a movement.

Execution—the movement may be done unilaterally (one-sided), bilaterally (both sides together), or cross-laterally (each side independently), performing with a different part of the body.

Body center oriented—leading with different parts of the body, movements away from and toward the center of the body.

Body zones—front, back, right side, left side, upper body, lower body, center of gravity.

Working on Apparatus

In addition to the factors just presented, variety in movement as the children work on large apparatus can be stimulated by the following considerations.

1. Apparatus can be arranged in different sequences, combinations, and numbers. Benches and balance beams, for example, can be placed on an incline, suspended higher than normal, or placed in combination with other equipment.

2. Variety can be promoted by viewing apparatus work as a three-step process, and

each step can be varied. Various ways to get on the apparatus can be stipulated. Things to do on or with apparatus can be outlined. Different means of getting down from apparatus can be specified.

3. Things to do on apparatus can be varied. The child can be challenged to go over, under, around, or through apparatus. He or she can support himself or herself in different fashions, using a variety of body factors.

4. Apparatus work can be combined with other activities and does not necessarily need to exist alone. An arrangement of combined activities might include one or more types of apparatus, and stations centering on manipulative activities or fitness challenges as a part of the circuit. Such combinations become a convenient approach when not enough apparatus are available to serve all the children in a single activity.

Extending Movement through Contrasting Terms

A means of increasing the child's understanding of movement possibilities is to employ terms stressing contrasts. The list that follows includes many common contrasting terms that can be used to stimulate different responses and provide variety. The contrasting terms express either relationships or descriptions of ways the children can move.

above—below, beneath, under
across—around, under
around clockwise—around counterclockwise
before—after
between—alongside of
big—little, small
close—far
crooked—straight
curved—flat, straight
diagonal—straight
fast—slow
forward—back, backward
front—back, behind
graceful—awkward
heavy—light
high—low
in—out
in front of—behind, in back of
inside—outside
into—out of
large—small
near—far
on—off
on top of—under, underneath
over—under, through
right—left
round—straight
separate—together
short—long, tall
sideways—forward, backward
smooth—rough

Climbing Frames Combined with Benches

sudden—sustained
swift—slow
tight—loose
tiny—big, large
top—bottom
to the right of—to the left of
up—down
upper—lower
upside down—right side up
upward—downward
wide—narrow, thin
zigzag—straight

Some of the terms may be grouped more rationally in three contrasts such as: forward—sideways—backward, up—down—in between, over—under—through. Word meanings also can be emphasized according to rank or degree: near—nearer—nearest, low—lower—lowest.

Contrasting terms are a fine basis for movement themes aimed at the child's understanding the terms and his or her ability to translate the meanings into movement. Contrasting terms also provide a valuable addition to ways of establishing variety. Instead of challenging a child to move fast, for example, the teacher could guide him or her to contrast a fast against a slow movement.

Phrasing the Challenge or the Question

Stimulating an effective movement response from children depends upon the manner in which the problems are phrased. Problems can be presented in the form of questions and statements, both of which should be of a nature that elicits and encourages variety, depth, and extent of movement. The teacher can secure ideas from the following directives but will no doubt develop his or her own style and approach. The form is given first, and a specific application of the form follows. The directives are divided into those that initially define the problem and those that have value in stimulating variety or imposing a particular limitation.

Presenting a Problem

1. Show me how a...moves.
   Show me how an alligator moves.
2. Have you seen a . . .?
   Have you seen a kangaroo jump?
3. What ways can you . . .?
   What ways can you hop over the jump rope?
4. How would you . . . or how can you . . .?
   How would you dribble a ball, changing hands frequently?
5. See how many different ways you can . . .
   See how many different ways you can hang from a ladder.
6. What can you do with a . . . or what kinds of things can you . . .?
   What can you do with a hoop?

7. Can you portray a . . .?
   Can you portray an automobile with a flat tire?
8. Discover different ways you can . . .
   Discover different ways you can volley a ball against a wall.
9. Can you . . .?
   Can you keep one foot up when you bounce the ball?
10. Who can . . . a . . . in such a way that . . .?
    Who can bounce a ball in such a way that it keeps time with the tom-tom?
11. What does a . . .?
    What does a cat do when it is wet?
12. Show . . . different ways to . . .
    Show (or discover) four different ways to move across the floor.

Securing Variety or Setting a Limitation

1. Try it again another way or try to . . .
   Try to jump higher.
2. See how far (many times, high, close, low, et cetera) . . .
   See how far you can reach with your arms.
3. Find a way to . . . or find a new way to . . .
   Find a new way to jump over the bench.
4. Apply . . . to . . .
   Apply a heavy movement to your run.
5. How else can you . . .?
   How else can you roll your hoop?
6. Make up a sequence . . .
   Make up a sequence of previous movements, changing smoothly from one movement to the other.
7. Now try to combine a . . . with . . .
   Now try to combine a locomotor movement with your catching.
8. Alternate . . . and . . .
   Alternate walking and hopping.
9. Repeat the last movement but add . . .
   Repeat the last movement but add a body twist as you move.
10. See if you can . . .
    See if you can do the movement with a partner.
11. Trace (or draw) a . . . with . . .
    Trace a circle with your hopping pattern.
12. Find another part of the body to . . . or find other ways to . . .
    Find another part of the body to take the weight.
13. Combine the . . . with . . .
    Combine the hopping with a body movement.
14. In how many different positions can you . . .?
    In how many different positions can you carry your arms while walking the balance beam?
15. How do you think the . . . would change if . . .?
    How do you think the balance we are doing would change if our eyes were closed?

16. On signal . . .
    On signal, speed up your movements.

Definitive Directives

Most of the directives illustrated are open-ended statements calling for indefinite responses. These should be alternated with challenges that ask for a specific number of responses. The directive might follow this form: "Find three different ways you can . . . ," or "Put together your sequence in two different ways." These offer a definite target objective, when the student might otherwise be concerned about how many ways he or she should discover.

Stimulating Effort

While stimulating variation does in a sense spur the children on to better effort, it is important for them to extend themselves within the movement itself. This is the idea of including in the movement problem incentives, such as asking them to carry out tasks as far as possible or with abrupt or definite changes. Although competition among individuals is not an accepted concept in movement education, some goals like "how far can you reach?" and "how far can you jump?" lend themselves to measurement. The number of floor boards covered or reached could be counted. There is also the idea of using beanbags or other markers and placing them "as far as you can." The device of having children stretch or reach until they pull themselves from their base makes them extend their limits.

INSTRUCTIONAL SEQUENCES FOR IMPLEMENTING EDUCATIONAL MOVEMENT

The unique nature of educational movement dictates specialized instructional sequences, so the greatest potential can be realized. Five steps are suggested for development of educational movement outcomes, with the target goals and the developing progressions determining the sequence and depth of each step. The first two steps in the sequence are reasonably fixed, but the other three can be varied or one or more of them can be omitted, depending on lesson development. The instructional process can be keyed by the following directions: explore, discover and expand, analyze and select, repeat and extend.

Step One: Setting and Defining the Problem

The first step defines the problem for the student, setting the stage, focus, and limitations. The focus could be within broad or narrow limitations. It might elicit an exploratory response. The what, where, and how need definition.

What is the child to do? An action word needs to be supplied. In divergent movement, is the child to move a certain way, go over and under, explore ways to . . . , or experiment with some nonlocomotor movement? He or she may be directed to run, jump, or use some fundamental skill (convergent movement) in some particular manner. With whom is the child to work—by himself or herself alone, with a partner, or as a member of a group? Is there a choice involved? With what equipment or on what apparatus is the child to perform?

Where is the child to move? This is the spatial aspect. What space is to be used—personal or general? What directional factors are to be employed—path, level?

How is the child to move? What are the force factors—light, heavy; sudden, sustained? What elements of time are involved—even, uneven; acceleration, deceleration? What are the relationships—over, under, across; in front of, behind? What body parts are involved—for support, for locomotion?

In initiating divergent movement patterns, the challenge can be stated like this: "Let's see you move across the floor, changing directions as you wish, with a quick movement with the one foot and a slow movement with the other."

As a basis for convergent movement, the teacher can say, "Show me how you can run in general space, changing directions and level at the same time when I sound the drumbeat." If they are deemed appropriate, hints on technique can be added, such as "remember to run lightly on your toes with a slight body lean and your head up."

Contrasting terms can be a part of the original theme format, or they can be introduced in the second step.

Step Two: Increasing Variety and Depth of Movement

The second step is to extend and challenge the creativity and thinking processes of the children, seeking to enhance their movements, provide depth to their experiences, increase variety of response, and encourage individual choices. Securing variety of response means that the teacher should be able to insert challenges and suggestions, which are based on the factors for expanding movement discussed earlier in this chapter (page 156).

The teacher needs effective observation, analysis, and perception techniques to modify and change the movement patterns through perceptive guidance. Coaching can be individual or group oriented.

In addition to using the factors for promoting variety, the teacher can encourage the children to expand their movement possibilities by asking them to find other ways to do the movement, since the original challenge may have been met by a single response. The teacher also can specify the number of responses desired rather than saying "Show me how many different ways you can respond."

Step Three: Developing Quality in Movement

Quality in movement is to be given attention in *all* steps at any teachable moment. Special attention to quality, however, is the hub of this step, whose purpose is to ensure that quality development is approached directly as well as incidentally. Too often, children are not encouraged to do things as well as they possibly can, and the movement experiences achieve as an end result only variety of movement and not quality.

It is important to understand that variety is necessary for setting a basis for the child's selection of his or her preferred movement pattern. Guide the child to select the movement pattern he or she deems most efficient or best for him or her. Since in divergent movement there is no right way, consideration becomes a matter of choice between such general qualities as lightness, smoothness, efficient use and flow of different body parts, rhythmic qualities, and coordination. Attention to mechanical principles as they relate to the selected movement themes is a part of the process.

In dealing with fundamental skills, stress points guiding the child toward the appropriate techniques are pertinent. General qualities in movement as mentioned in the preceding paragraph also prevail. Also the principles important in movement and skill performance (page 81) have relevance.

The key to developing quality is helping the children choose freely, practice freely, and reach an understanding of their movement possibilities; it is not in having them conform to artificial standards.

All the activities described in this text should be taught with emphasis on the quality of performance.

Step Four: Building Sequences and Combining Movement Patterns

The child can select certain movements that have been practiced and put them together in sequence, looking for good transition (flow) from one movement pattern to another. The child is challenged to think how he or she can put the movements together. This step can entail the child's selection of the movements and the number of movements he or she wishes to put in combination. Or some limitation can be specified with regard to the number of combinations, the type of movements, and the order of the sequence.

Achievement demonstrations are excellent for stimulating effort, since children love to show what they have put together. These demonstrations provide ideas and give the children a rough standard against which they can make comparisons of their movement patterns.

Here are two examples: "As you dribble the ball, move with different locomotor movements in various directions. Select some definite combinations and repeat them several times before changing to another combination." "You are to put together three movements in sequence as you dribble. First, dribble using one hand alone in general space while running lightly. Next, stop in a selected position with your feet wide apart and dribble, alternating hands in and around your body while maintaining the pose. Finally, dribble with the other hand while using a locomotor movement other than running."

The magic number principle is also excellent for developing sequences. "Today our magic number is 10. Put together a sequence in which you link 3 different types of movements together so that they total 10." (This could be 3 of one, 4 of another, and 3 of a third.) "You choose your combination." The teacher can say, "The magic number is 3. Put together 3 different types of movements, each of which is repeated three times."

Step Five: Culminating Activity

Partner and small-group work can expand instructional opportunities. Working with others is an important social goal and provides an extension of the opportunities to use skills.

Here are some suggestions for working with partners.

1. One child could serve as an obstacle while his or her partner utilizes him or her in the development of a theme. The moving partner could go over, under, or around the stationary partner.
2. Critique of movement between partners is another facet. Observation should center on points that have been discussed; otherwise the critique might be of low value. The critique could serve as a learning device to enhance cognitive elements for the observer and the performer.
3. Reproductive movement is another possibility. One child performs a pattern and the other reproduces it, either in a single pattern or a sequence. Some games utilize this reproduction factor.
4. A similar direction is to have children work together to develop parallel movements in which they are moving simultaneously in a

parallel fashion. A show-and-tell session is interesting.

5. Children can work cooperatively in forming different shapes, designs, forms, letters, and figures, either in upright positions or on the floor.
6. Much is to be gained in throwing and catching skills through partner work.
7. One partner can support the other wholly or in part.

Games and relays can serve as vehicles for participation in newly experienced skills. Creative games are another excellent medium for providing realistic extension of skill practice. An individual, a partner, or a small-group game can be created on the basis of the skill or movement factor just experienced.

In educational movement, groups should be kept small, ranging from three to six members in size. Otherwise, too much time is devoted to getting the group underway and too little is accomplished toward the movement goals. Group work should serve to accomplish something beyond what individuals or partners could do.

The order of the steps in the instructional sequence is not sacred or inflexible. As the problem develops and unfolds, changes will be indicated, and these should be made. Target goals relating to the children's progress are important, and the process becomes the agent toward that end.

TEACHING STYLES

In addition to the instructional approaches just presented, several different teaching styles merit consideration. It should be noted that all the styles can be employed in some manner to teach themes and fundamental skills.

Good teachers use more than one style of teaching and, in some cases, vary their styles a number of times during a single lesson. Factors that dictate the choice of the most effective teaching style are the expected outcomes for the students, the children themselves and their stage of progression, and the activity itself. Another important reason for using different styles is adding novelty and variation to the teaching and keeping both learner and teacher motivated. Teachers must make a strong effort to experiment with different styles of teaching and have the perseverance to make the various styles effective. For personalizing instruction for children, a variety of styles is most helpful. To some degree, each teacher's personality traits and aptitudes also determine which teaching styles and approaches are most suitable for him or her.

The nature of the activity should be considered also in choosing the teaching style to be used. For example, stunts and tumbling might lend themselves to an individualized style of teaching, whereas individual mat activities might present an excellent opportunity for the unlimited exploration approach.

No matter which style is employed, the child needs to know the answers to three questions.

1. Where am I going? What is it I am supposed to accomplish?
2. How do I get there? Is the teacher going to lead me, or do I have to attempt to find my own way?
3. How will I know when I have arrived? Do I evaluate myself, do I have a peer evaluate me, or is the teacher to judge my performance?

The where is found in the goals or expected outcomes of the unit or lesson, which outlines what the child is expected to accomplish. The goals can be expressed in terms of domains—psychomotor, cognitive, and affective. A point in favor of using the domain taxonomy is that many school systems have adopted the terminology and learning hierarchy implicit in the domains. Most educators have adequate background in the domains, and so only a minimum explanation will be offered here.

The psychomotor domain deals with body competency, skill, and developmental outcomes, with the lesson objectives making specific references to these areas. Cognitive elements considered pertinent are knowledges about activity and the development of conceptual understandings. Cognitive elements should go hand in hand with the development of psychomotor goals, and the teaching style selected should enhance this relationship.

The affective domain is currently receiving more consideration from physical educators. It deals with attitudes, feelings, and values. It is becoming increasingly evident that a person will avoid activity in later years if he or she develops a negative attitude during childhood. This antipathy can be countered by a positive teaching climate and a dedicated teacher. Many broad values, such as cooperation with others, sportsmanship, and the like, can be furthered by an effective teaching style.

The how involves the learning process by which the learner progresses in quest of his or her goals. This outlines to the learner how he or she is to proceed with respect to attainment of the anticipated goals.

Evaluation is a part of the instructional process, and children are vitally interested in knowing whether or not they have achieved the anticipated outcomes. Evaluation comes first from the child, with respect to how he or she feels about what he or she has done. More overt evaluation relies on established performance objectives, observation,

| Command | Task | Individualized | Problem Solving | Limited Exploration | Unlimited Exploration |

Direct (Teacher Controlled)   Indirect (Student Controlled)

Continuum of Teaching Styles

tests, and achievement demonstrations that afford informal comparison with peers.

Selecting the Appropriate Teaching Style

The teacher should select the style most likely to enhance the child's learning experiences. The basic selection criterion is the degree of control and direction the teacher or learner has while administering or accomplishing the objectives of the lesson. Teaching styles vary in the amount of control the teacher has over lesson preparation, lesson implementation, and evaluation of the lesson's results.

If time is short, the command style might be best for immediate but not long-term effects. On the other hand, limited exploration might serve well if time permits experimentation with alternatives. The ability of the children to accept responsibility for their own learning is a factor. The teacher must analyze carefully the class's status in the three domains and then decide on the appropriate teaching style.

Whatever style of teaching is selected, the teacher should remember that good teaching techniques cut across all teaching styles. For example, being prepared, keeping all the children active, and teaching with enthusiasm are points requisite to all teaching, regardless of style. No single style of teaching can be considered superior to another; each has its place and value in the hands of an effective teacher. However, one style may be more appropriate than another in a given situation.

Command Style

The command style is the most direct and teacher controlled. The teacher prepares all the facets of the lesson, is wholly responsible for the instruction, and, through direct methods, monitors the progress of the lesson. Basically, the process includes explanation, demonstration, and practice, the amount of time for each part being determined by the instructor. Evaluation usually is accomplished by the instructor, with preset standards that the teacher feels most, if not all, students are able to achieve. The children are guided along somewhat identical paths toward similar goals.

When the command style is being carried out,

instructions should be brief and to the point, with action following as much instruction as is feasible. Teachers can make the mistake of talking in depth with too many details about a skill. Students usually forget all but the last few points. Dry runs during which the students go through the motions of the skill without using the implements (ball or bat, for example) and get the feel of the activity are helpful. Demonstrations, either partial or full, can shorten the amount of time the teacher needs for explanation. During practice work, the teacher should circulate among the children to help and coach them.

When youngsters are being introduced to new pieces of equipment, it might be useful to allow them time for experimentation before giving directions. Any pertinent safety factors, however, should receive immediate attention.

The command style probably is used more consistently by many teachers than they imagine. Sometimes, it is selected because it is an efficient way to reach a teacher-selected goal. In situations in which discipline problems are a factor, the command style exercises tighter rein on class conduct. Teachers invariably use command-dominated approaches with large classes. Another valuable use of command style is in situations in which a precise skill or result is the goal. Such situations arise when specific measures are desirable during remediation of low fitness or perceptual-motor deficiencies. With children who have lower levels of comprehension (with retardates, for example), the command style is good for accomplishing specific increments of progress. The directions are definite, and the children get the practice needed in following directions.

The shortcomings of the command style are in the area of the learning process, since the children are given little chance to think or make choices regarding the learning process when they simply respond to command stimuli. Little consideration is given to what the child wishes to do or accomplish. It is evident that the usefulness of the command style is limited in cognitive and affective development of children.

If the command style is used, the perceptive teacher makes sure that it is personalized to the fullest extent possible. A good approach is to alternate or integrate other styles with it, so the directive is "do it this way" sometimes and other times it is "do it your way."

Task Style

When using the task style, the instructor is still responsible for setting the objectives of the lesson, selecting the activities, and determining the sequences for achieving the objectives. The basic difference between the task style and the command style is that the student becomes involved in the pace of the lesson and in the process of instruction in the task style. The teacher is no longer highly concerned about how the class is organized and about whether or not all of the children are working simultaneously on the same movement patterns. Instead, the teacher is more concerned that the students achieve the defined task. Whereas success in the command style may be judged on how successfully each child reaches the movement goal, difference in accomplishment is accepted by the instructor in the task style. This may motivate the less capable children who cannot achieve at the same level as the majority of the class.

Tasks may be presented verbally, or they may be contained on task cards. The student accomplishes the task at his or her own pace. He or she may find a partner to help, or he or she can function as a member of a small group. The format may call for all students to give attention to the same problem, or it could allow them to work on different problems.

Task cards are interesting devices for teaching children. A number of different cards can be made up to allow for progression. As a child completes the task on one card, another card can be issued with a new task for him or her to complete. Task cards for particular areas can be categorized according to the levels of skill required by the activities, from beginning (introductory) to intermediate to advanced skill levels. The following is an example of a task card.

Rope Jumping—Beginning Skills

Needed: one jump rope.

1. Check for proper size. The rope should come up to the armpits when the jumper is standing on it.
2. Forward turning to the side: Hold the rope handles in one hand. Turn the rope forward to the side.
3. Jump and rebound! Without the rope, practice the jump and rebound until it is in good rhythm.
4. Combine jump and rebound with turning the rope to the side.
5. Slow-time jumping! With the hands holding the rope in normal rope-jumping position and with the rope started behind the back, try to perform regular rope jumping to slow-time rhythm.
6. Turn the rope 5 turns without a miss.
7. Turn the rope 10 turns without a miss.

The strength of the task style of teaching lies in the fact that the students become involved in the learning process. A challenge is set up, and they are responsible for accomplishing the task in a manner that is meaningful to them.

Individualized Learning Package Style

The individualized learning package style is based on the concept of student-centered learning through an individualized curriculum consisting of many learning packages. This approach employs a variety of learning strategies and allows the student to progress at his or her own rate. Each student's needs are diagnosed, and a program is prescribed to facilitate those needs. The objectives are clear and are stated in behavioral terms. The student is required to learn cognitive factors before he or she moves on to psychomotor tasks.

Besides the learning packages, which are discussed later, other materials and hardware are necessary for establishing the proper learning environment. Materials needed are loop films, transparencies, audiotapes, reference books, wall charts, and cards for reporting the student's progress. Equipment such as slide and overhead projectors, cassette tape recorders, screens, and chalkboards are useful.

A learning center should be established that includes the materials and equipment that students need to direct their own learning. An example of a learning center is shown on page 164, and, clearly, many other arrangements are feasible.

This style of teaching basically follows five steps.

Step One: The student is tested to determine his or her present level of cognitive and psychomotor knowledge (diagnosis).

Step Two: Each student then is given a learning package based upon his or her present level of knowledge (prescription).

Step Three: The student next works on the tasks in the learning package until he or she feels able to perform them successfully. Self-testing is offered, so the student can decide whether he or she is ready for the next step (development).

Step Four: The student then goes to the teacher for his or her final evaluation. Both psychomotor and cognitive activities are evaluated at this point.

Step Five: The teacher finally determines whether or not the student has completed his or her tasks based upon the learning package. If the student has completed the tasks successfully, the teacher then (1) positively reinforces, (2) records the data on the student progress chart, and (3) prescribes a new learning package based on the needs of the student (evaluation).

If the student has not performed the task successfully, the teacher then can offer possible al-

Listening Viewing	Wall Charts		Listening Viewing	Reading Room
P R A C T I C E A R E A S				
Practice Areas	Teacher Diagnose Prescribe Evaluate	Practice Areas	Chalkboard	Resource Area
P R A C T I C E A R E A S				
Overhead Viewing	Wall Charts		Loop Viewing	Small-Group Discussion Area

Organization of Learning Center

ternatives for reaching the objective. This allows the teacher an excellent opportunity to counsel the student and reinforce critical points.

Learning Packages

Learning packages are the core of the individualized style of teaching. These packages basically are the student contracts that provide the ingredients the learner will need to accomplish the learning task.

The learning package consists of the following parts.

1. *Content classification* states the task or concept to be learned. This could be a psychomotor task, such as the Cartwheel, or a cognitive task, such as absorbing force.

2. *Purpose* provides the learner with an explanation of what the package will do for him or her. For instance, "This contract provides you with learning activities that will enable you to learn to perform the Cartwheel."

3. *Learning objectives* are the behavioral objectives that tell the learner under what conditions he or she will learn, what he or she is to learn, and how he or she will behave when he or she has learned.

4. *The diagnostic test (or pretest)* determines the student's knowledge and skill level. The student is given a cognitive test as well as psychomotor tasks to perform for assessment.

5. The students are given *learning activities* that offer many different ways to teach themselves the skill, concept, or activity. In each contract, different choices should be made available. This allows the student to select any or all of the strategies that will help him or her to teach himself or herself and learn. Some of the fol-

lowing methods can be used to enhance the student's learning: loop films and transparencies can be viewed and analyzed, an audiotape can be listened to for instruction in cognitive tasks, various books and manuals can be referenced so the student can easily read about the task, a videotape can offer demonstration and explanation of a skill to be performed, and wall charts can be used for visualization and breakdown of skills. Students also could be directed to ask other students who have successfully completed the activity to help them practice.

6. *Self-testing* is the phase that helps the students decide whether or not they are ready for the final test to be given by the teacher. Generally, the procedure consists of asking other students to check them out and tell them whether or not they are ready to ask the teacher for the final test.

7. The *final test* is an observable measure of the objectives. The psychomotor tests are usually an objective judgment made by the teacher, while the cognitive learnings usually are measured by a written exam.

In essence, the individualized style is a series of tasks put together in a meaningful sequence. The student controls the rate at which he or she learns and receives good feedback about his or her progress. The teacher controls the material by designing the packets and deciding the extent of the learning increments. The student is encouraged to investigate different approaches to learning the designated skills through written material, contacts with peers, and visual media. Acquiring experience in the learning process appears to be a valuable acquisition that an adult can use later to learn a new activity or skill.

Problem-solving Style

The problem-solving approach involves input, reflection, choice, and response. The problem structured must present a choice of alternatives for which there is no one prescribed, predetermined answer. When there is just one answer, problem solving becomes guided discovery.

Problems selected vary from simple types for primary-level children to more complex problems for intermediate-level children. A simple problem might be expressed like this: "What are the different ways you can bounce a ball and stay in your personal space?" There may or may not be emphasis on the best way.

A more complex problem involving deeper thinking would be a determination of the most effective ways to position and handle the feet while guarding an opponent in basketball. The solution could utilize an individual, a partner, or a group approach.

The following steps make up the problem-solving style.

1. Setting and Presenting the Problem: The problem should be presented in the form of a question or statement that provokes thought and reflection. No demonstration or explanation of the kinds of responses is desirable, since the solution should come from the children.
2. Determining Procedures: Some thought must be given the procedures necessary for arriving at a solution. For simple problems with younger children, this phase is minimal. However, cognitive values begin with an assessment of how one is to proceed in seeking the solution. Subproblems may need to be defined.
3. Experimentation and Exploration by the Children: Experimentation refers to trying out different solutions, evaluating them, and making a choice. Exploration has a slightly different meaning in that the goal is to seek breadth of activity. Self-direction is important, and the teacher acts in an advisory role, answering questions, helping, commenting, encouraging, but not providing solutions. Sufficient time must be allotted for this phase.
4. Observation, Evaluation, and Discussion: Each child should have the opportunity both to show his or her solution and to observe what others have discovered. Various kinds of achievement demonstrations can be utilized—individual, small group, squad, or part of the class. Discussion should center on justification for a particular solution.
5. Refining, Expanding, and Exploring: After observing what others have selected and evaluating the reasoning behind the chosen

solutions, the children should be given the opportunity to rework their own movement patterns (solutions), incorporating ideas from others.

A child must understand that there are problems and that they can be solved. He or she must be equipped with techniques, so he or she can proceed under self-direction toward a sound solution. It is essential that problems remain problems with possible solutions and that they do not become frustrations.

One of the more difficult procedures in the problem-solving style is designing problems to which students do not know the solutions. On the surface this sounds simple, but, if one student knows the answer or secures the solution ahead of time, he or she can pass it to the rest of the class and the process of solving and exploring is lost. The teacher should feel free to guide the youngsters, but the initiative for finding a solution should lie with the students. There are no limits to the areas that can be covered using problem solving; some of the following areas are offered as examples: concepts, relationships, strategies, and proper use of skills for specific situations.

Limited Exploration Style

In limited exploration, the teacher is responsible for lesson preparation, the subject matter selection, and the general direction of the responses. The choice of specific responses is the domain of the student, since there are choices but no one set response for each limitation.

In most cases, exploration styles are probably more germane for learning broad areas of movement and for developing multiple movement patterns of particular kinds of skills. In manipulative experiences, a child could show the different ways he or she can toss and catch a beanbag in place. The child can react as he or she wishes within the limitation of catching and tossing and remaining in place. Another example involving partners is in order. In learning ball skills, the partners could show the different ways they could bounce a ball back and forth between them. Fundamental movement could be stressed by asking the child to show the different ways he or she can jump back and forth over a jump rope on the floor. The method can center on exploring movement qualities (the limitation), such as space, time, force, and flow concepts.

Another facet of limited exploration is the guided discovery approach. A predetermined choice of which the teacher, but not the student, is aware is to be discovered. Let's say the teacher wishes to have the students acquire the concept that, in throwing a ball right-handed, the most efficient foot position is a stride position with the left foot forward. The students are given different foot patterns with which to experiment, with the goal of selecting the preferable pattern. The teacher should have them practice with the following limitations: feet together, feet in a straddle position, feet in a stride position with the left foot forward, feet in a stride position with the right foot forward. After practicing the four different foot positions, a choice is made about which position seems to be the best in terms of good throwing potential.

Limited exploration has good utility when one wishes to explore and develop versatility in a particular kind of movement pattern. Progressions in manipulative activities are particularly adaptable to this teaching style. Limited exploration is a flexible style in that, at any time during a lesson, the style can be used by giving the children an opportunity to explore in a particular situation. However, if the development of a particular skill is the goal, it is probably desirable to move to, or at least center on, the command teaching style or the task style.

Unlimited (Free) Exploration Style

In unlimited exploration, the only guidance from the teacher is his or her selection of the instructional materials to be used and designation of the area to be explored. Two directives might be these: "Today for the first part of the period you may select any piece of equipment you wish; see what you can do with it." "Get a jump rope and try anything you like with it." No limits are imposed on the children, except for pertinent safety factors. The teacher might need to forewarn or remind students how to use the equipment properly.

For the overall lesson, two schools of thought prevail with respect to when the exploratory style should be used. Some feel that a youngster should have the opportunity to explore with a piece of equipment or apparatus *before* he or she is given instruction or guided toward specific activities. It is claimed that the children get the feel of the equipment, which makes it easier for the teacher to explain how to use it. Also, the children might be more prone to want to learn about its use when they realize their limitations. Some teachers using this approach believe anything in the way of movement patterns is of good value, because the youngsters are creative and have discovered it themselves. Whether the activity has quality or value seems to be secondary.

On the other hand, some educators feel that opportunities for exploration should be offered after the students have learned the basics and then can create more realistically and to greater depth. There is also the thought that certain techniques are more desirable than others and that the child can explore after he or she has the proper patterns. Safety elements can be considered.

Undoubtedly, both approaches have merit and are useful in some situations. Occasionally, both approaches could be used in the same lesson.

With exploration, the teacher should avoid demonstrations and praising certain results too early, since this leads to imitative and noncreative behavior. In no sense does the teacher turn the children loose and then stand around uninvolved. The teacher should move among the students, encouraging, clarifying, and answering their questions on an individual basis. The teacher should concentrate on motivating effort, since the student has the responsibility for being a self-directed learner. It is sometimes wise to offer students the opportunity for self-direction in small doses, with the time allotted to self-direction increased as the children grow older and become more disciplined.

Exploratory opportunities should be offered frequently, for this phase of learning takes advantage of the child's love of movement experimentation and allows freedom for natural curiosity. Self-discovery is a necessary and an important part of learning, and students should have this reinforced by the joy of their creativity.

TEACHING ENVIRONMENTS

How the children are to be arranged or grouped for instruction is a decision that needs to be made early in the lesson-planning process. More than one of these patterns can be used in a single lesson. The objectives and nature of the movement experiences, together with the space and the equipment available, determine the type of grouping to be selected. Variations and subdivisions can be incorporated into three basic schemes.

Single-Challenge Format

All children are responding to the same challenge, whether as individuals, as partners, or as members of groups. This format allows the teacher to conduct the class according to a lesson plan that includes the elements of guided progression. The single-challenge format is convenient for coaching and demonstrating, since all the children are involved in similar activites.

Pacing is a problem with no easy solutions, since the instruction must be personalized for each child's needs. While it is recognized that individual children are different, the assumption is made that children of the same maturity are on similar levels, so a central core of activity can be emphasized in the program for all the children in a class.

Many of the instructional procedures already discussed are directed toward this format, and, for this reason, no further elaboration is made here.

Multiple-Group (Station) Format

In this arrangement, the class is divided into two or more groups, each working on a different movement challenge. Some system of rotation is provided, and children change from one activity to another.

Dividing a class into groups for station teaching is of value at times, particularly when supplies and apparatus are insufficient for an entire class working on single-challenge activities. This arrangement can save time for apparatus experiences, because, once the circuit is set, little change in apparatus is needed. The participants are changed, not the apparatus.

Some system of rotation must be instituted, with changes either on signal or at will. Sometimes, all stations can be visited during a class session, and, in some cases, only a few changes can be made.

Class control and guidance sometimes become a problem, since it is not practical to stop the class to provide instruction and guidance. Two techniques can help. The first is to conduct the children as a class around the circuit for a quick, preliminary orientation at each station. The second involves instruction using written guidelines outlining what to do and what considerations should be observed posted at each of the stations. The general instructions should include how students should put the station in orderly condition before moving on. These measures help make up for the fact that the teacher must divide his or her efforts over a number of stations. If there is a station with a safety hazard (such as rope climbing), the teacher may wish to devote more attention to that station.

Theme development is possible in that the stations can be selected and materials provided, so theme emphasis can be experienced at each station. If creativity, exploration, and varied movement are primary goals, station teaching meets these criteria.

A real question arises regarding skill development. There is no question that stations can be set up to provide experiences for expanding and increasing versatility in skills in which some expertise has already been acquired. But one wonders what is accomplished by handing a child a paddle and ball as an *initial* experience and telling him or her to bat it back and forth against a wall. The experience is an orientation, but perhaps it becomes the only accomplishment.

For effective movement, the children should have some basis on which to superimpose new experiences if they are to be given a number of activities in rotation. Dividing into groups usually should be done after the children have had experience in the kinds of movement experiences designated for the groups. Introductory and initial work can best be accomplished through single-activity organization.

Another problem is the time element. Each group, ideally, should have sufficient opportunity in the activity for full development. In some activities, children may finish and run out of things to do, while, in others, they may have too little time and too much to do.

Individual-Choice Format

Children select their movement experiences and rotate at will. They can get their own equipment out, or they can choose from pieces already provided.

This format should be used after the children have a good basis for further exploration and creativity. They should be encouraged to practice on needed areas or create beyond their present level. It should be a period of creativity, not just supervised free play.

Some teachers have found this format effective in introductory activities in a daily lesson. Occasionally, the teacher can give the following directions to a class upon entrance into the gymnasium: "For the first few minutes of our class period today, you may select and practice the movement pattern you wish." The teacher can qualify this by enumerating the possibilities: "You may practice movements without equipment; you may select from the available balls, beanbags, wands, or hoops; or you may work on the climbing ropes, balance beams, or mats."

A choice period also could be used to finish up a daily lesson or a unit of work. The choice could be limited to the activities and movements in the lesson or unit.

EVALUATION

Evaluation is the process of determining the extent to which the program in physical education meets its stated objectives. More valid information could be supplied if the evaluative techniques were based on measurement, but not all objectives lend themselves to feasible measurement.

Until behavioral objectives have been fully developed and refined to the point of practicability, the available objective means of assessment must be employed. These include fitness, posture, skill or achievement, and knowledge tests. But many of the outcomes deemed important in physical education cannot be measured by such devices. Reliance on other means of assessment is needed. For the purpose of discussion, evaluation is divided into four areas: (1) general standards for the program, (2) accepted tests, (3) teacher's observation, and (4) pupils' expression and opinion.

General Standards

Direction

Is there a competent supervisor or consultant providing direction? How does he or she function in relation to his or her specified duties (page 45)?

Planning

Is there a curriculum present upon which the program is based? Is there a year's program from which weekly and daily programs are derived? Are lesson plans required?

Time Element

Is there a daily program totaling at least 150 minutes of activity time for each child per week?

Facilities, Equipment, and Supplies

Is there an overall list of instructional supplies and equipment that stipulates adequate learning materials? Are these available during the year in sufficient quantity to sustain maximum activity? Are the quantity and quality of the teaching stations satisfactory?

Instruction

Is the instruction in the hands of capable and interested teachers? Is there regular in-service education? Do the teachers keep up-to-date with workshops and special courses?

Health and Safety

Are proper standards maintained for health and safety? Is participation based upon a regular medical examination? Is there provision for emergency care? Is there special consideration for those who cannot participate fully?

Testing Program

What objectives are evaluated by testing—physical fitness, knowledges and concepts, skills, motor competency?

Special Programs

Is there follow-up and special work for physical underachievers? For children with motor problems? For the obese? For those with handicaps?

Program Standards

Is there proportionate emphasis on movement experiences, fundamental and specialized skill development, rhythms, stunts and tumbling, sports and games activities, and fitness considerations?

Observation by the Teacher

The teacher can make reasonable judgments of the progress toward the goals of physical education by observing certain signs of individual student progress.

Physical Fitness

How well does a youngster meet the strength and endurance demands of activity?

How smoothly and adequately can he or she handle his or her body?

Is his or her posture and bearing satisfactory?

What about arm-and-shoulder-girdle development? Can he or she perform on the ladder and horizontal bar with reasonable success?

Does the child enjoy and thrive on vigorous activity?

Competency in Body Management

Can the child manage his or her body in a variety of movement situations? Does he or she move with ease? Can he or she go over, around, and under apparatus and obstacles?

Useful Skills

Has he or she mastered the fundamental skills of locomotion? Can he or she do these successfully to rhythm?

Does he or she show good form in specialized skills? Is he or she making satisfactory progress for his or her size and maturity?

Has he or she mastered throwing, kicking, and batting skills well enough to take part successfully in game-type activities?

Can he or she perform on apparatus the activities appropriate for his or her age?

On the intermediate level, can he or she integrate dance steps into dances?

Does he or she know and apply the appropriate mechanical principles to skill learning? Does he or she have the desire to practice for better performance?

Does he or she have a wide appreciation of skills rather than a concentration in a narrow area?

Social Learnings

Does the child behave democratically by entering wholeheartedly into activities chosen by the group?

Do children play together well and comfortably with wholesome boy-girl relationships? Are social graces the rule in the rhythmic program?

Is there evidence of good leadership and followership patterns? Do the children accept the decisions of the leader?

In competitive games, is there evidence of good sportsmanship in observing the rules, accepting the decisions of officials, and following the captain's suggestions? Can the youngsters win or lose in a sportsmanlike manner?

Can the child share with others and not try to dominate the play?

Safety

Have the children developed a safety consciousness?

Are they considerate of other children in dangerous situations?

Do they spot hazards and unsafe conditions and tend to correct them?

Recreational Objectives

During free play, can the child organize his or her own play either individually or with other children?

Does he or she learn the rules of activities so that he or she can enjoy these on his or her own time?

Can he or she play with assurance on various pieces of apparatus?

Does he or she know how to modify rules so that he or she can adapt games to small-group play and various places?

Is he or she motivated to take part in activity for activity's sake—that is, for the maintenance of fitness?

Developing a Realistic Self-image and Acquiring a Desirable Self-concept

Does the child belong to the group? Is he or she accepted by his or her peers? Is he or she achieving success in his or her play activities? Does he or she seem secure in his or her physical education experiences? Does he or she have a realistic (in terms of his or her capabilities) self-image?

Personal and Educational Values

Does the child take part joyously in play and find satisfaction in movement experiences? Can he or she react creatively when the call is for free rein to the imagination?

Does he or she approach problems with assurance and confidence? Does he or she give evidence of reasoning powers during problem-solving situations?

Is he or she learning terminology, acquiring understandings, and learning concepts as he or she participates in movement experiences? Does he or she understand the reasons behind what he or she is doing?

Students' Opinions and Discussions

After a class period or the completion of a unit, the teacher can organize an evaluating session with the children for the purpose of critical discussion of the merits of the experience. Discussion should be in terms of what was accomplished and how well they enjoyed the activity. Suggestions can be made on what needs to be done and how it can be accomplished.

A technique that can be used with intermediate children is the buzz group. The class is divided into four to six small groups, each with a chairperson and a recorder. The questions for discussion should be written on the board, and each group assigned to a section of the room to discuss them. The procedure gets its name from buzzing that goes on while groups are discussing values. After a specified period (there should be a preliminary warning), the class is brought together again for the reports from the recorders. Further discussion can be expanded on the class level.

Staff's Opinions

Fruitful information can be gathered from the school staff with respect to professional judgments and reactions of the students. The principal, counselors, and nurses should be included. Students tend to voice opinions and judgments more freely to others than to the physical education teacher. Considering staff judgments is an excellent device for good staff relationships.

Parents' Opinions

Since education is a partnership between the school and the home, the input of the parents is most desirable. A questionnaire with special questions and a minimum of writing brings best results. A summary of parents' opinions can be discussed at a community-school meeting.

Thirteen

Developing Movement Patterns and Fundamental Skills

In this chapter, movement patterns have been arranged in two categories—divergent and convergent movement—according to the target objectives of the movements. Discussions of manipulative activities (chapter sixteen), activities with jump ropes (chapter seventeen), apparatus activities (chapter eighteen), and fundamental rhythms (pages 200 to 204) include additional activities for rounding out and supplementing the types of theme-oriented and fundamental skills presented in this chapter.

DIVERGENT MOVEMENT AND MOVEMENT THEMES

Movement themes are the basis for developing divergent movement. A movement theme stresses a movement quality around which the youngsters build movement patterns and sequences. The purpose of the theme is to explore and experiment with the thrust of the theme, gain a good understanding of that movement quality, and develop body awareness in that movement area. Much of the execution employs fundamental skills, the development of which becomes concomitant to the concentration on the central movement theme.

Themes are identified according to the general movement concepts of space, time, qualities of movement (force), flow, and body factors. Some themes draw from more than one area.

In most cases, the formations or patterns of arrangement of the children are not specified. The teacher is referred to the section on teaching formations (page 69) for suggestions.

Care must be taken to express ideas and movement in correct terminology. Where terminology is new or unfamiliar to children, explanations should be made. The cognitive potential should be exploited where this is feasible. Note of this has been made in some of the movement descriptions, with particular attention given to explanation of prefixes.

Classifications of Divergent Movement Themes

Divergent movement themes are grouped into three classifications, based on the following rationale.

Basic Themes

Early attention in movement development and concept acquisition should dwell on establishing a knowledge of body parts and a good understanding of the different concepts of personal and general space. These themes are basic and provide background on which other themes can be superimposed.

Themes for Understanding Elements of Movement

In this area is contained the bulk of the themes, which collectively cover Laban's movement elements and some additional concepts. Some themes cover a single movement principle or factor, while others give attention to two or more.

Themes for Expanded Movement Combinations

Three broad thrusts are listed in the last category: (1) flow-sequencing and movement combinations, (2) cooperative partner activities, and (3) working as a member of a group. Flow-sequencing combinations can be flexible in nature, providing considerable choice, or they can be definitive in the activities designated for the sequence.

Good value can be garnered when children have the opportunity to interact with a partner or other members of a group. Some curriculum specialists like to include both partner and group interaction in the daily lesson regime. A basic tenet to follow, however, is that children should perform activities with a partner or as members of a group that ordinarily could not be done individually.

Basic Themes

Body Awareness

These are the body parts to be learned.

Head—forehead, face, eyes, cheeks, eyebrows, nose, mouth, ears, jaw, chin.

Upper body—neck, shoulders, chest, back, stomach, arms, forearms, elbows, wrists, hands, fingers, thumbs.

Lower body—waist, hips, seat, thighs, knees, ankles, feet, arches, toes, heels.

"We are going to see whether you can touch the body part I name" (kindergarten). "I will say, 'touch your hips.' As soon as you do this, you reply to me, 'I am touching my hips.'" Note that this works well when the teacher varies or alternates from the head and upper body to the lower body regions so that the children need to make gross motor changes.

"When I name a body part, let's see whether you can make this the highest part of your body in some stationary position. Now, the next task will be a little more difficult. Move in a straight line for a short distance, with the body part named kept above all other body parts. What body parts would be difficult to keep above all others?" (eyes, both ears, both hips).

"Now move around the room, traveling any way you wish" (could be limited) "and the signal to stop will be a word describing a body part. Can you stop and immediately put both hands on that part or parts?"

"Toss your beanbag into the air. When I call out a body part, sit down quickly, and put the beanbag on that part, or one of the corresponding parts named."

"This time, when I call out a body part, you are to move around the room as you wish, while holding with one hand a named body part. When I call out another name, you are to change the type of movement and hold the part with the other hand as you move." (Body awareness, space, level.)

Exploring Personal Space

A good way to illustrate to the child his or her personal space is to have him or her take an individual jump rope and double it. From a kneeling position, he or she should swing it in a full arc along the floor, and it should not touch another child or rope. "Show us how big your space is. Keeping one foot in place, outline how much space you can occupy. Sit Indian fashion and outline your space. Support the weight on different parts of the body and outline your space."

"Make yourself as wide as possible. Change to narrow, small, large, low, high, et cetera. Try these from different positions—kneeling, balancing on seat, and others. Show us what kinds of body positions you can assume while standing on one foot. Lying on your stomach. On your seat. Try the same with one foot and one hand touching the floor."

"Move from a lying position to a standing position without using your arms or hands. Return to lying."

"Can you stay in one place and move your whole self but not your feet? Sway back and forth first with your feet together and then with your feet apart. Which is better?"

"In a supine position (on your back) move your arms and legs from one position slowly and then move them back to where you started. Explore other positions."

"Keeping one part of your body in place, make just as big a circle as you can with the rest of your body."

"Explore different positions where one leg (foot) is higher than the rest of the body. Work out a smooth sequence of three different positions."

"Pump yourself up like a balloon, getting bigger and bigger. Hold until I say 'bang.'"

"In your personal space, show me how a top spins. Keep your feet together in place. With your arms wide to the sides, twist and make your feet turn."

Note: Children should adjust personal space, so they do not intrude on space of others. (Space, body factors.)

Moving in General Space

"Run lightly in the area, changing direction as you wish without bumping or touching anyone until I call 'stop.'" How many were able to do this without bumping into anyone?"

"Let's try running zigzag fashion in the area without touching anyone. This time when I blow the whistle, change direction abruptly and also change the type of locomotor movement."

"Run lightly in general space and pretend you are dodging someone. Can you run toward another runner and change direction to dodge him or her?"

"Get a beanbag and drop it to mark your personal space. See how lightly, while under control, you can run throughout the area. When the signal is given, run to your spot, pick up your beanbag, put it on your head, and sit down" (or some other challenge). "Try this skipping."

"We are going to practice orienteering" (explain). "Point to a spot on the wall, and see whether you can run directly to it in a straight line. You may have to stop and wait for others so as not to bump into anyone, but you cannot change direction. When you get to your selected spot, pick another spot, and repeat."

"What happens when the general space is decreased? You had no problem running without touching anyone in the large space. Now, let's divide the area in half with these cones. Run lightly within this area so as not to touch or bump anyone. Now it's going to get more difficult. I'm going to divide the space in half once more, but first let's try walking in the new area. Now, run lightly." Decrease the area as it is feasible.

"Get a beanbag and again mark personal space. Run around the beanbag until you hear 'bang,' and then 'explode' in a straight direction until the call 'stop.' Return to your personal space."

"From your beanbag, take five" (or more) "jumps" (hops, skips, gallops, slides) "and stop. Turn to face 'home' and return with the same number of movements. Take the longest steps you can and return with tiny steps."

"Show me how well you can move with these combinations in general space: run-jump-roll, skip-spin-collapse. You devise a series of three movements and practice them."

"Today our magic number is five. Can you move in any direction with five repetitions of a movement? Change direction, picking another movement to do five times. Continue."

"Blow yourself up just like a soap bubble. Can you huff and puff! Think of yourself as a big bubble that is floating around. When I touch you, the bubble breaks and you collapse to the ground. This time, blow up your bubble again, float around, and when you are ready, say 'pop' so the bubble bursts."

"I am going to challenge you on right and left movements. Show me how you can change to the correct direction when I say either 'right' or 'left.' Now begin running lightly."

"This time, see whether you can run rapidly toward another child, stop, and bow to each other. Instead of bowing, shake hands and say, 'How do you do!'"

"From your personal space, pick a spot on a wall. See whether you can run to the spot, touch it, and return without bumping anyone. This time, it's more difficult. You are asked to pick spots on two different walls, touch these in turn, and return."

Note: Target goals in these movement experiences, in addition to developing movement competency, should be: (1) the ability to share space with other children, (2) the ability to move through space without bumping anyone, and (3) the ability to develop consideration for the safety of others.

Themes for Understanding Elements of Movement

Exploring Flight

"Show me how many different ways you can go through space (flight). Try again using different levels. Lead with different parts of your body."

"See how high you can go as you go through space. What helps you get height?"

Note: Two parallel lines 2 feet apart can represent a creek to be crossed. Other objects such as cones (small), individual mats, and masking tape are useful. Avoid wands and jump ropes, which may cause falls. (Space, force, body factors.)

Use of Force—Light and Heavy, Sudden and Sustained

"Show me different kinds of sudden movements. Do a sudden movement and then repeat it slowly. Put together a series of sudden movements. Sustained movements. Mix sudden and sustained movements."

"Reach out in different directions with a strong, forceful movement. Crouch down as low as you can and explode upward. Try again exploding forward. Move as if you were pushing something very heavy. Pretend you are punching a heavy punching bag."

"What kinds of movements can you do that are light movements? Can you make movements light and sustained? Light and sudden? Heavy and sustained? Heavy and sudden? Which is easier? Why?"

"Can you combine heavy movements in a sequence of sudden and sustained movements? Can you make one part of your body move lightly and another heavily?" (Force.)

Body Shapes

"Let's try making shapes and see whether we can name them. Make any shape you wish and hold it. What is the name of your shape, John?" (Wide.) "Try to make different kinds of wide

Forming Different Shapes

shapes. Show me other shapes you can make. What is the name of your shape, Susie?" (Crooked.) "Show me different kinds of shapes that are crooked."

"Make yourself wide and narrow. Now tall and then small. How about tall/wide, small/narrow, tall/narrow, small/wide. Work out other combinations."

"Select three different kinds of shapes and move smoothly from one to another. This time I will clap my hands as a signal to change to a different shape."

Note: From the children, bring out the kinds of shapes and reinforce the concept by having the children practice each kind of shape. This could be divided into shapes while erect and shapes on the floor. (Body, flow factors.)

Over and Under Things

"Using your materials, explore the different ways you can go over and under what you have set up. Lead with different parts of the body."

Note: Cones, wands, blocks, ropes, baseball bats, chairs, et cetera, are examples of articles that can be used. This is an excellent partner or small-group activity. (Space, body factors.)

Developing a Theme (over and under things, using wands and cones)

Stretching and Curling

"In your own space, stretch out and curl. What different ways can you find to do this? Let's go slowly from a stretch to a curl and back to a stretch in a smooth, controlled movement. Curl your upper body and stretch your lower body. Now curl your lower body and stretch your upper body.

Work out a smooth sequence between the two combinations."

"Show different curled and stretched positions on body points and on body flat surfaces. Go from a curled position on a flat surface to a stretched position supported on body points. Explore how many different ways you can support your body in a curled position." (Time, force, body factors.)

Moving in Different Ways

"Discover different ways you can make progress along the floor without using your hands and feet. See whether you can walk with your seat. Better let your heels help you."

"What ways can you move sideways or backward? What rolling movements can you make? Look carefully before you move to make sure you have a clear space."

"With your hands fixed on the floor, move your feet in different ways. Cover as much space as possible. With your feet fixed, move your hands around in different ways as far as you can. Move around general space the way a skater does. The way a pogo stick does. Choose other ways. Change direction as you move, but keep facing in the same direction." (Space, body factors.)

Tension and Relaxation

"Make yourself as tense as possible. Now slowly relax. Take a deep breath, hold it tight. Expel the air and relax." "Reach as high as possible with both hands, slowly relax and droop to the floor. Tense one part of the body and relax another. Slowly shift the tension to the relaxed part, and vice versa."

"Run forward, stop suddenly in a tensed position, and then relax. Run in a tensed condition, change direction, and run in a relaxed manner."

Levels and Speed

"Use a jump rope, a portion of a line, or a board in the floor. Begin at the far end. Show me a slow, low-level movement down and back. What other ways can you go down and back slowly and at a low level? Change to a high-level, fast movement. In what other levels can you move?"

"Combine a low, fast movement down with a high, slow movement on the way back. Explore other ways and combinations you can invent. Vary by leading with different parts of your body."

Note: Each child has a path outlined by a rope, line, or board with a length from 8 to 10 feet. This activity also can be organized by means of selected formations (page 69). (Space, time, body factors.)

Acceleration and Deceleration

"Staying in your own personal space, begin with some kind of a movement and accelerate until you are moving as fast as you can. Reverse by beginning with a fast movement and slowing down until you are barely moving. Put together a sequence of two movements by beginning with one and accelerating and changing to another movement and decelerating. Try doing two different body movements at the same time, one that accelerates and one that decelerates."

Note: Time concepts can be stressed by relating this movement to a car with its accelerator and brakes, which decelerate. The prefixes of the two words can be explained. Acceleration and deceleration can be combined with many types of movements and challenges. (Time, flow.)

Receiving and Transferring Weight

"Project yourself into the air and practice receiving your weight in different fashions. Try landing without any noise. What do you have to do? See how high you can jump and land lightly."

"See how many different ways you can transfer weight smoothly from one part of the body to the other. Work up a sequence of three or four movements and go smoothly from one to the other, returning to original position." (Force, flow, body factors.)

Moving with the Weight Supported on Hands and Feet

"Pick a spot from your personal space and travel to and from that spot on your hands and feet. Try moving with your hands close to your feet. Far away from your feet. Show me bilateral, unilateral, and cross-lateral movements. Build up a sequence."

"What kinds of animals can you imitate? Move with springing types of jumps. What shapes can you assume while you are moving?"

Note: The terms *bilateral, unilateral,* and *cross-lateral* need explanation, including the significance of the prefixes. A selected movement formation is excellent for this activity. (Force, flow, body factors.)

Taking the Weight on the Hands

"Put your hands on the floor and see whether you can take the weight on your hands for a brief time. How do you get your body into the air? What

Taking the Weight on the Hands

is the importance of the center of gravity? What different things can you do with your feet while your weight is on your hands?"

"Begin from a standing position; take care not to go over. How should your fingers be placed for best support? Can you take the weight on your hands and return your feet to the floor in a different place?"

Note: Care must be taken so the children do not overbalance. (Force, body factors.)

Leading with Different Parts of the Body

"As you move between your..." (beanbags, lines, markers), "explore ways that different parts of your body can lead your movements. Add different means of locomotion. Work at different levels."

Leading with a Foot .

Note: Since this is locomotor activity, children need different spots or lines between which they can move. (Body factors.)

Balancing

"What are the ways you can balance on different surfaces of your body? Can you balance on three different parts of your body? Two? One? Put together sequences of three or four balance positions, using different parts or different numbers of body parts."

"Keep your feet together and sway in different directions without losing your balance. Can you balance on one foot with your eyes closed? Bend forward while balancing on one foot? Lift both sets of toes from the floor and balance on your heels? Show different ways you can balance on one foot and one hand. Sit on the floor. Can you lift your feet and balance on your seat without hand support? Can you balance on your tummy without your feet or hands touching the floor?"

"In a standing position, stick out one leg sideways and balance on the other foot."

Note: This theme is also called *Supporting the body weight.* Balance positions should be maintained from 3 to 5 seconds before changing. (Force, body factors.)

Bridges

"Show me a bridge made by using your hands and feet. What other kinds of bridges can you make? Can you make a bridge using only three body parts? Two?"

Making Bridges

"Show me a wide bridge. A narrow one. A short bridge. A long one. How about a high bridge? A low one? Can you make a bridge that opens when a boat goes through? Get a partner to be the boat and you be the bridge."

"Work up a sequence of bridge positions, going smoothly from one to the next." (Flow, body factors.)

Contrasting Movements

"Show me a wide shape. Now, an opposite one. A crooked shape. Now, its opposite. Show me a high-level movement, and its contrast. Can you do a fast movement? What is its opposite? Also, smooth/rough, light/heavy, and other terms."

"You pick two contrasting movements. When I clap my hands, do one and change to the other when I clap again. What are the movements you did?"

Note: Stimulate the children to think about and identify the opposite movements. One approach is to name one quality and then see whether the children can identify the opposite with a movement response. The second is to have the children match their own choices. Get further suggestions from the children.

Symmetrical and Asymmetrical Movements

"Show me different kinds of symmetrical movements. Asymmetrical movements. Put together sequences of symmetrical and asymmetrical movements."

Note: The terms need to be explained. The concept of the difference between these two types of movement can be utilized in many situations to provide another challenge to stimulate variety of movement. Take time, also, to give attention to the proper pronunciations of symmetrical and asymmetrical, since they are a little difficult.

Planes of Movement

"Show me a variety of movements on a horizontal plane. Vertical plane. Diagonal plane. Put together combinations so you go in sequence from one type of movement to another."

"Here is a challenge. When I call out a plane of movement, you respond with one that is correct. Ready?" (specify the plane of movement). (Space.)

Circles in the Body

"Can you make full circles with your hands and arms at different joints—wrist, elbow, and shoulder? Similarly, what circles can you make with your legs and feet? Try the second movement lying on your back. With what other body joints can you make circles?"

Forming Circles

"Can you keep two different circles going at the same time? Make a circle turning one way and another turning the other way."

"Repeat the above, using twisting actions."

Note: Carry this out far enough to get the children to explore most of their body and joint actions. (Body factors.)

Themes for Expanded Movement Combinations

Flow-Sequencing and Movement Combinations

The emphasis in sequencing should be on sustained (bound) flow. The sequences can be experienced individually or with partners (see partner activities).

The examples given here are in series of at least three challenges. If only two are pertinent to the situation, the teacher can select the first two movement patterns of a series. In introducing combinations, it may be best initially to give the first two movements and add the third in time.

This is an area of fruitful suggestions from the children. Be sure to let them arrange some of their own sequences.

Both locomotor and nonlocomotor movements can be put together in various combinations, such as the following.

1. Run, leap, and roll.
2. Shake (all over), gallop, and freeze.
3. Hop, collapse, explode.
4. Whirl, skip, sink slowly.
5. Creep, pounce, curl.
6. Lift, grin, and roll.
7. Kneel, sway, jump to feet.
8. Run, stop-look, explode.
9. All-fours run, roll, jump.
10. Jumping Jack, slide, jump turn.
11. Hop, collapse, creep.
12. Jump forward, shake, whirl.
13. Rock on heels, jump high, sit down.
14. Sink slowly, roll, jump turn.
15. Click heels right and left, jump half-turn, run backward.
16. Twist, skip, sit down, and smile.
17. Turn around three times, clap hands twice behind the back, run, balance on one foot.
18. Fast, tiny steps in place, fall forward to the hands, forward on all fours.
19. Take a deep breath, expel the air, saying, "Ah-h-h," jump forward, spin and sink.
20. Spin on your seat, roll forward, and take five jumps in the direction of your roll.

Students also should be challenged to put together combinations of their own choosing. The challenge can be open, asking them to put together two, three, or four kinds of movement, or the challenge could provide some limitation to the type of movement. In an example of the latter approach, the child could be directed to begin with some kind of a rapid movement, which is followed by a balance position and finished up with a movement on all fours. (Flow, space, body factors.)

COOPERATIVE PARTNER ACTIVITIES

Developing the ability to cooperate with others is an important educational goal. Problems should be realistic and give opportunity for discussion and decision making between partners. It is generally better, depending upon the activity, to pair together children of reasonably equal achievement; but, at other times, size, height, and weight can be pertinent factors to be considered.

How can children cooperate in solving problems? These approaches have merit as partner activities and are typical of the kinds of experiences that children could not have alone.

1. One child can be an obstacle, and his or her partner could devise ways of going over, under, and around the positions the "obstacle" takes. Additional challenges can be provided when one partner holds a piece of equipment such as a wand or a hoop to govern the movements.

Partner Work (going under an obstacle)

2. One partner supports the weight of the other, either wholly or in part. Or the two together can form different kinds of figures or shapes. Bridges can be built.

Supporting the Partner's Weight

3. There can be matching (copying) or contrasting movements. One child does a movement and the other copies it or provides a contrasting movement.
4. Shadow movements can be undertaken. One child moves and the other attempts to keep up with him or her with the same movements. This must be done slowly, with interrupted flow predominating.
5. There can be critiques of movement, with one child moving and the other providing the correction or critique.
6. Parallel sequence building can be undertaken in which the partners develop a sequence

with both moving together and in the same way.

7. Progressive sequence reproduction can be undertaken. The first child does a movement. The second child repeats the movement and adds another. The first child repeats both movements and adds a third. Some limit probably needs to be set on the number of movements.
8. Children can form letters or figures with their bodies on the floor or in erect positions.

WORKING AS A MEMBER OF A GROUP

Group work in movement education is defined as a group of children working together on a movement task. Groups should be kept small so that each child can make a significant contribution to the group effort. Much of the work can be confined to groups of three or four children, but groups up to squad size are practical. The task should be definite, so the interests and efforts are directed toward a common goal.

Most of the suggested ways children can work with a partner are applicable to small-group work, with modifications, of course. Designing, inventing, and modifying games are also excellent group problem-solving activities.

There may be some difficulty in coordinating group activity, because groups may work at different rates and may not be balanced with respect to the time they require to complete a task.

Group Making a Tower

Some movement challenges feasible for group work are these.

1. Exploring different ways of building a human tower.
2. Showing different ways some of the children can support the others wholly or in part.
3. Practicing copy activities. One child sets a movement pattern and the remainder of the children copy his or her actions.
4. Making a human merry-go-round.
5. Making up a pyramid of some kind.

CONVERGENT MOVEMENT AND LOCOMOTOR AND NONLOCOMOTOR SKILLS

Convergent movements have a place in the program when the teacher wishes to emphasize a particular movement and have the children explore this to its extent.

In this section, locomotor and nonlocomotor skills are analyzed, with stress points and teaching cues provided. Also, for each skill a number of suggested movement activities are described.

Fundamental Locomotor Movements

In the descriptions that follow, locomotor movement fundamentals are analyzed, and selected activities based on particular locomotor movements or combinations of movements are presented.

Walking

In walking, one is always in contact with the ground or floor, and the feet move alternately. This means that the stepping foot must be placed on the ground before the other foot is lifted for its step. Marching is a more precise type of walk, accompanied with lifted knees and swinging arms.

Many different ways of walking should be experienced, but the underlying motive should be to have children walk gracefully and efficiently in normal walking patterns. Experiencing different walking patterns offers an excellent opportunity to stress postural factors.

The weight of the body is transferred from the heel to the ball of the foot and then to the toes for the push-off for the next step. The toes are pointing straight ahead, with the arms swinging freely from the shoulders in opposition to the feet. The body is erect and the eyes are focused straight ahead at slightly below eye level. Legs are swung smoothly from the hips, with the knees bent only enough to clear the feet from the ground.

Stress Points
1. The toes should be pointed reasonably straight ahead.
2. Do not overswing the arms. The arm movement should feel natural.

3. The head should be kept up and the eyes focused ahead.
4. The stride length should not be excessive; unnecessary up-and-down motion is to be avoided.

Teaching Cues

1. Head up—eyes forward.
2. Point toes straight ahead.
3. Nice, easy, relaxed arm swing.
4. Walk quietly.
5. Hold tummy in, chest up.

Suggested Movement Patterns

1. Walk in different directions, changing direction on signal.
2. While walking, bring up the knees and slap with the hands on each step.
3. Walk on heels, toes, sides of the feet.
4. Gradually lower the body while walking (going downstairs) and raise yourself again slowly (going upstairs).
5. Walk with a smooth, gliding step.
6. Walk with a wide base on tiptoes, rocking from side to side.
7. Clap hands alternately front and behind. Clap hands under the thighs while walking.
8. Walk slowly and gradually increase the speed. Reverse the process.
9. Take long strides. Tiny steps.
10. On signal, change levels.
11. Walk quickly and quietly. Heavily and slowly.
12. Change direction on signal, but keep facing the same way.
13. Walk gaily, angrily, happily, and showing other moods.
14. Hold arms in different positions. Make an arm movement each time you step.
15. Walk different patterns—circle, square, triangle, figure eight, et cetera.
16. Walk through heavy mud, on ice or slick floor, on a rainy day.
17. Walk like a soldier on parade, a giant, a dwarf, a robot, et cetera.
18. Duck under trees or railings while walking.
19. Point toes in different positions—in, forward, and out.
20. Walk with high knees. Stiff knees. One stiff knee. Sore ankle.
21. Walk to a spot, turn in place while stepping, and take off in another direction.
22. Practice changing steps while walking.
23. Walk with a military goose step.

Running

Running, as contrasted to walking, is moving rapidly in such a manner that, for a brief moment, both feet are off the ground. Running varies from trotting (a slow run) to sprinting (a fast run for speed).

Running should be done lightly on the balls of the feet. It should be a controlled run and not a dash for speed. Children can cover some ground on the run, or they can run in place. Heels can take some weight in distance running and jogging.

Running should be done with a slight body lean. The knees are bent and lifted. The arms swing back and forth from the shoulders with a bend at the elbows.

Additional pointers for sprinting are found in the track and field unit (chapter thirty-one).

Stress Points

1. The balls of the feet should be used for running. This allows for shock absorption, which is important for comfort in running.
2. The faster one desires to run, the higher the knees must be lifted. The knees also must be bent more.
3. For distance running, little arm swing is used as compared to sprinting for speed. Also, less body lean is used in distance running, with comfort the key.

Teaching Cues

1. Run on the balls of the feet.
2. Head up—eyes forward.
3. Bend your knees.
4. Relax your upper body.
5. Breathe naturally.

Running

Suggested Movement Patterns

1. Run lightly throughout the area, changing directions as you wish, avoiding bumping anyone. Run zigzag throughout the area.
2. Run, stop on signal. Change direction on signal.
3. Run, turn around with running steps on signal, and continue in a new direction.
4. Pick a spot away from you, run to it, and return without bumping anyone.
5. Run low, gradually increasing the height. Reverse.
6. Run patterns. Run inside and around objects.
7. Run with high knee action. Slap knees as you run.

8. Run with different steps—tiny, long, light, heavy, crisscross, wide, and others.
9. Run with arms in different positions—circling, overhead, stiff at sides, et cetera.
10. Free running, concentrate on good knee lift.
11. Run different speeds.
12. Touch the ground at times with either hand as you run.
13. Run backward, sideward.
14. Run with exaggerated arm movements. Run with a high bounce.

Hopping

In hopping, the body is sent up and down by one foot. The body lean, the other foot, and the arms serve to balance the movement. Hopping on one foot should not be sustained too long. Children should change to the other foot after a short period. Hopping can be done in place or as a locomotor movement.

Stress Points
1. To increase the height of the hop, the arms need to be swung upward rapidly.
2. Hopping should be performed on the ball of the foot.
3. Start with small hops and gradually increase the height and distance of the hop.

Teaching Cues
1. Hop with good forward motion.
2. Stay on your toes.
3. Use your arms for balance.
4. Reach for the sky when you hop.
5. Land lightly.

Suggested Movement Patterns
1. Hop on one foot and then on the other, using numbered sequences such as 1-1, 2-2, 3-3, 4-4, 5-5, 2-1, 1-2, 3-2, 2-3. The first figure of a series indicates the number of hops on the right foot and the second specifies the hops for the left foot. Combinations should be done for 10 to 20 seconds.
2. Hop, increasing height. Reverse.
3. See how much space can be covered in two, three, or four hops.
4. Hop on one foot and do a heel and toe pattern with the other. Change to the other foot. See whether a consistent pattern can be set up.
5. Combine hopping in place with hopping ahead.
6. Hop forward, backward, sideward.
7. Hop different patterns on the floor.
8. Hop while holding the nonhopping leg (foot) with different hand positions.
9. Hold free foot forward or sideward while hopping. Explore other positions.
10. Hop with body in different positions—forward lean, backward lean, sideward balance.
11. Hop lightly, heavily.
12. While hopping, touch the floor with the hands, first one and then both.
13. Hop back and forth over a line, moving down the line as you hop.
14. Trace out numbers or letters by hopping.
15. Turn around while hopping in place.

Jumping

Jumping, as the term is used in fundamental movements, means to take off with both feet and land on *both* feet. The arms aid in the jump with an upswing, and the movement of the body helps lift the weight along with the force of the feet. A jumper lands lightly on the balls of his or her feet with his or her knees bent.

Stress Points
1. Bend the knees and ankles before taking off to achieve more force from muscle extension.
2. When landing, land on the toes and bend the knees to absorb the impact.
3. Swing the arms forward and upward in rhythm with the takeoff to add momentum to the jump and thus gain distance and height.
4. Keep the legs bent after jumping or the feet will touch the ground prematurely.

Teaching Cues
1. Swing your arms forward as fast as possible.
2. Bend your knees.
3. On your toes.
4. Land lightly with bent knees.
5. Jump up and try to touch the ceiling.

Jumping

Suggested Movement Patterns
1. Jump up and down, trying for height. Try small and high jumps. Mix in patterns.

2. Over a spot on the floor, jump forward, backward, and sideward.
3. Jump with the body stiff and arms held at sides. Jump like a pogo stick.
4. Practice jump turns in place—quarter-, half-, three-quarter-, and full turns.
5. Increase and decrease the speed of jumping. Increase and decrease height.
6. Land with the feet apart and together. Alternate the feet forward and backward.
7. Jump and land quietly. How is this done?
8. Jump, crossing and uncrossing feet.
9. See how far you can go in two, three, and four consecutive jumps.
10. Pretend you are a bouncing ball.
11. Clap hands or slap thighs while in the air. Try different arm positions.
12. Jump so the hands contact the floor.
13. Jump according to various patterns on the floor.
14. Pretend you are a basketball center jumping at a jump ball. Jump as high as you can. Jump from a crouched position.

Skipping

Skipping is actually a series of step-hops done with alternate feet. To teach a child to skip, ask him or her to take a step with one foot and then take a small hop on the same foot. He or she then takes a step and a hop with the other foot. Skipping should be done on the balls of the feet with the arms swinging to shoulder height in opposition to the feet.

Stress Points
1. Smoothness and rhythm are goals in skipping. Speed and distance are not.
2. The weight must be transferred from one foot to the other on the hop.
3. Arms are swung in opposition to the legs.
4. If having trouble skipping, it may help to slow the step-hop sequence and call out "step-hop" in rhythm.

Teaching Cues
1. Skip high.
2. Swing your arms.
3. Skip smoothly.
4. On your toes.

Suggested Movement Patterns: Many of the suggested movement patterns under walking and running can be applied to skipping, particularly with respect to changing direction, stopping, forming different floor patterns, moving at different speeds, and with different-size skips. Others that may be considered are:
1. Skip with exaggerated arm action and lifted knees.
2. Skip backward.
3. Clap as you skip.
4. Skip with a side-to-side motion.
5. Skip twice on one side (double skip).

Sliding

Sliding is done to the side. It is a one-count movement, with the leading foot stepping out to the side and the other foot following quickly. The same foot always leads, and the movement should be practiced in both directions. The movement should be done on the balls of the feet and the weight shifted from the lead foot to the trailing foot. Body bounce during the slide should be minimal.

Stress Points
1. Emphasis should be placed on moving sideways. Often, students move forward or backward, which is actually galloping.
2. Slide in both directions so both the right and left leg have a chance to lead as well as trail.
3. The slide should be a smooth, graceful, and controlled movement.

Teaching Cues
1. Move sideways.
2. Do not bounce.
3. Slide your feet.

Suggested Movement Patterns
1. An interesting way to slide is to lead in a direction with a definite number of slides, do a half-turn in the air, and continue the slide leading with the other leg, retaining the original direction. A four-plus-four combination is excellent.
2. Begin with short slides and increase length. Reverse.
3. Slide in a figure-eight pattern.
4. Change levels while sliding. Slide so the hands can touch the floor with each slide.
5. Slide quietly and smoothly.
6. Pretend to be a basketball defensive player and slide with good basketball position.
7. Slide with a partner.

Galloping

Galloping is similar to sliding, but the progress of the individual is in a forward direction. One foot leads and the other is brought up rapidly to it. There is more upward motion of the body than in sliding.

Stress Points: Same as for sliding.

Teaching Cues
1. Keep one foot in front of the other.
2. Lead with the other foot.
3. Make high gallops.

Suggested Movement Patterns
1. A most helpful way to teach the gallop is to have the children (holding hands) slide in a circle, either to verbal cues or to a drumbeat. Then gradually turn them to face the turn of the circle. This takes them naturally from the slide into the gallop. Next, drop hands and permit free movement in general space.
2. After a series of eight gallops with the same

foot leading, a change can be made to the other foot. The changes can be reduced to four gallops and finally to two gallops. Since later in the rhythmic program the gallop is used to teach the polka, it is important for the children to learn to change the leading foot.

3. Change the size of the gallops.
4. Gallop in a circle with a small group.
5. Pretend to hold reins and use a riding crop.
6. Gallop backward.

Leaping

Leaping is an elongated step designed to cover distance or to go over a low obstacle. Leaping usually is combined with running, since a series of leaps is difficult to maintain. Leaping should emphasize graceful flight through space.

Stress Points
1. Strive for height and graceful flight.
2. Land lightly and be relaxed.

Teaching Cues
1. Push off and reach.
2. Up and over, land lightly.
3. Use your arms to help you leap.

Leaping

Suggested Movement Patterns: Leaping is usually combined with a short preliminary run or is used during the course of a run.
1. Practice leaping in different directions.
2. See how high you can leap.
3. Practice soft landings.
4. Vary your arm position when you leap. Clap your hands as you leap.
5. Leap with the same arm and leg forward. Try the other way.
6. Show a leap in slow motion.
7. Leap and turn backward.
8. Leap over objects or across a specified space.
9. Practice Leaping the Brook (page 390).

Nonlocomotor Movements

Nonlocomotor movements include bending, twisting, turning (in place), movements toward and away from the center of the body, raising and lowering the parts of the body as a whole, and other body movements done in place. Nonlocomotor movements do not lend themselves as well to the distinction between divergent and con-vergent movement as do the locomotor and manipulative skills. Gross body movements to the limits of flexibility are important. Good control and a variety of body movements leading to effective body management are also important goals. Balance is another factor that should receive attention.

Bending

Bending is a movement at a joint (where the adjacent bones of the body are joined together). Emphasis should be placed on learning where the body bends, why it needs to bend, and how many different bends are combined for various movements.

Stress Points
1. Bending should be done as far as possible in order to increase flexibility and range of movement.
2. Explore the bending possibilities of as many joints as possible.
3. Add time factors—slow and rapid bending.

Teaching Cues
1. Bend as far as possible.
2. Bend one part while holding others steady.

Suggested Movement Experiences
1. Can you bend down and up?
2. Can you bend forward and backward, left to right, and north to south?
3. Bend as many ways as possible.
4. How many body parts can you bend below your waist? Above your waist? With your whole body?
5. Sit down and see whether you can bend differently than you did in a standing position.
6. Who can lie down and bend six body parts? Bend more or fewer parts?
7. Is it possible to bend one part quickly and one part slowly simultaneously?
8. Make a familiar shape by bending two body parts. Add two more parts.
9. Think of a toy that bends; see whether you can bend in a similar fashion.
10. Can you find a partner and bend with him or her? Have your partner make big bends while you make tiny bends.

Bending Movements

11. Show me how you would bend to look funny. Happy, sad, slow, quick.

Rocking

Rocking is a movement that occurs when balance is fluidly moved from one spot to another. The body weight is transferred to an adjacent body part in a gradual fashion. In rocking, the body should be in a rounded position in which it touches the floor. The term *swaying* implies a slower movement than rocking and is somewhat more controlled than rocking. In swaying, the base of support is unchanged.

Stress Points
1. Rocking is done best on a body surface that has been rounded. Arm and body part movements can help the rocking.
2. Rocking should be done smoothly and in good rhythm.
3. Rocking can be started with small movements, increasing in extent, or vice versa.
4. Rocking and swaying should be done to the full range of movement.
5. Swaying maintains a stable base.

Teaching Cues
1. Rock smoothly.
2. Rock in different directions. At varying speeds.
3. Rock higher (farther).
4. Sway until you almost lose your balance.

Suggested Movement Experiences
1. How many different ways can you rock?
2. Show me how you can rock slowly. Quickly, smoothly.
3. Can you be a rocking chair?
4. Lie on your back and rock. Point your arms and legs toward the ceiling.
5. Lie on your tummy and rock. Can you hold your ankles and make giant rocks?
6. Can you rock in a standing position?
7. Can you rock and twist at the same time?
8. Who can lie on his or her back, with knees up, and rock from side to side?
9. Show me two ways to rock with a partner.
10. From a standing position, sway back and forth, right and left. Experiment with different foot positions. Sway slowly and rapidly. What effect does rapid swaying have?
11. Repeat swaying movements from a kneeling position.

Swinging

Swinging can be described effectively as an action of body parts that resembles a rope swing. Another comparison is the pendulum of a clock. The teacher can put a weight on the end of a string about a yard long and demonstrate swinging motions. Note that most swinging movements are confined to the arms or the legs.

Swinging is a rhythmic, smooth motion that is fun to do to waltz-type music. It is also effective to combine this movement with stepping at the beginning of each measure of music. When experimenting with swinging movements, some children can carry the swings to extremes so that they make full circles instead. With a musical background, swinging and circular movements can form sequences. Music is important, since it gives the children the feeling of the swing.

Stress Points
1. Swinging should be a smooth, rhythmic action.
2. Body parts involved in swinging should be relaxed and loose.
3. Extent of the swing movement should be the same on both sides of the swing.
4. Make swinging movements as full as possible.

Teaching Cues
1. Loosen up; swing easy.
2. Swing fully; make a full movement.
3. Swing in rhythm.

Suggested Movement Experiences
1. Explore the different ways the arms and legs can be swung.
2. Work out swinging patterns with the arms. Combine them with a step pattern, forward and back.

Partner Swinging

3. Swing the arms back and forth and go into full circles at times.
4. With a partner, work out different swinging movements. Add circles.
5. Work out patterns and combinations to slow to moderate waltz music. Form sequences with swinging and full-circle movements.

Turning

Turning is considered a movement rotating around the long axis of the body. It involves the body as a whole. It is recognized that the terms *turning* and *twisting* sometimes are used interchangeably to designate movements of body parts, rather than the body as a whole. One can *turn* the head either way or *twist* the head.

In the suggested movement experiences, action is centered on the movement of the entire body. Movements of body parts, commonly called *turning,* are included under twisting.

Stress Points
1. Maintaining balance and body control is important.
2. Turning should be done in either direction, right or left.
3. Turns in standing position can be made by jumping, hopping, or shuffling with the feet.
4. Most turns should be made in increments or multiples of quarter-turns. Multiple turns should also be practiced.
5. Practice turns in body positions other than standing—seated, on tummy or back, and in other positions.

Teaching Cues
1. Keep your balance.
2. In jump turns, land in a relaxed way, with your knees easy.
3. Be definite in your turn—quarter-, half-, or full turn.

Suggested Movement Experiences
1. Turn your body to the left and right, clockwise and counterclockwise.
2. Post the directions on the wall and have the children turn to face north, east, south, and west. The teacher might even introduce some in-between directions, northwest, for example.
3. Can you stand on one foot and turn around slowly, quickly, with a series of small hops?
4. Show me how you can cross your legs with a turn and sit down. Can you get up again?
5. Every time you hear the signal, see whether you can turn once around, moving slowly. Can you turn two, three, or four times?
6. Lie on your tummy on the floor and turn your body slowly in an arc. Turn over so that you are on your back; turn back to your tummy again.
7. Find a friend and see how many different ways he or she can turn you and you can turn him or her.
8. Play follow the leader with your friend. You make a turn and he or she follows.

Twisting

Twisting is a rotation of a selected body part around its own long axis. The joints of the following body parts can be used for twisting: spine, neck, shoulders, hips, ankles, and wrists. Twisting differs from turning in that twisting involves movement around the body part itself, as compared to focusing on the space in which the body part turns in turning. Remember that the children are used to having some of these movements called turning.

Variations of Twisting Movements

Stress Points
1. Twist as far as possible, maintaining good control.
2. Fix or stabilize the body parts on which the twist is based.
3. Twist one way and then reverse the twist.
4. Explain why some joints are better for twisting than others.

Teaching Cues
1. Twist far (fully).
2. Twist the other way.
3. Hold the supporting parts firm.

Suggested Movement Experiences
1. Glue your feet to the floor; can you twist your body to the left and to the right? Can you twist it slowly, quickly? Can you bend and twist at the same time? How far can you turn your hands back and forth?
2. Twist two or more parts of the body at the same time.
3. Can you twist one body part in one direction and another in the opposite direction?
4. Is it possible to twist the lower half of your body without twisting the upper half?
5. What can you twist while sitting on the floor?
6. Can you twist one body part around another part? Is it possible to twist together even more parts?
7. Balance on one foot and twist your body. Can you bend and twist at the same time?
8. Show me some different shapes you can make by twisting your body.

9. Can you twist like a spring? Like a cord on a telephone?
10. Can you move and twist at the same time?

Stretching

Stretching is a movement that generally makes the body parts as long or as wide as possible. Stretching sometimes involves moving a joint through the range of movement. It is important that children understand that stretching the muscles involves some minor discomfort and controlled movement. The muscle-stretching process is necessary for maintaining and/or increasing flexibility.

Stress Points
1. Stretching should be made to the full range of movement.
2. Stretching exploration should involve many body parts.
3. Stretching should be done in many positions.
4. Stretching can be combined with opposite movements, such as curling.
5. Stretching should be done smoothly. Avoid jerky movements.

Teaching Cues
1. Stretch as far as possible. Make it hurt a little.
2. Find other ways to stretch the body part (joint).
3. Keep it smooth. Don't jerk.

Suggested Movement Experiences
1. Stretch as many body parts as you can.
2. Stretch your arms, legs, and feet in as many different directions as possible.
3. Can you stretch a body part quickly, slowly, smoothly?
4. Can you bend a body part and tell me which muscle(s) are being stretched?
5. How many ways can you stretch while sitting on the floor?
6. Lie on the floor and see whether you can stretch five body parts at once.
7. Is it possible to stretch one body part quickly while you stretch two others slowly?
8. From a kneeling position, see whether you can stretch to a mark on the floor without losing your balance.
9. Stretch your right arm while your left arm curls.
10. Find a friend and show me how many ways you can help each other stretch.
11. Can you stretch and become as tall as a giraffe? Name other animals.
12. Stretch and make a wide bridge. Find a partner to go under, around, and over your bridge.
13. Can you bend at the waist and touch your toes? See whether you can keep your legs straight while you are stretching them.
14. Combine stretching with opposite movements, such as curling or flexed-joint positions.

15. Can you stretch the muscles in your chest, back, tummy, ankles, wrist, fingers, et cetera?
16. Make a shape with your body. Now stretch the shape so it is larger.

Pushing

Pushing is a controlled and forceful movement used to push the body away from an object or to move the object in a desired direction by force against it.

Stress Points
1. The base of support should be broadened.
2. The body's center of gravity should be lowered.
3. The line of force should be directed toward the object.
4. The back should be kept in reasonable alignment, and the body forces gathered for a forceful push.
5. The push should be controlled and steady.

Teaching Cues
1. Broaden your foot base.
2. Use all your body forces.
3. Push steadily and evenly.
4. Lower yourself for a better push.

Suggested Movement Experiences
1. Stand near a wall and push it from an erect position; then push with the knees bent and one foot behind the other. In which position can you push with more force?
2. Push an imaginary object that is very light. Then imagine that you are pushing a very heavy object.
3. Try to push a partner who is sitting on a jumping box. Then try and push a partner who is sitting on a scooter. What changes must you make in your body position?
4. Can you push an object with your feet without using your arms and hands?
5. Sit down and push a heavy object with your feet. Can you put your back against the object and push it?
6. How many different ways can you find to push your object?
7. Find a friend and try to push him or her over a line.
8. Sit back to back with your partner and see whether you can move him or her.
9. Is it possible to lie on the floor and push?
10. Lie on the floor and push your body forward, backward, and sideward.
11. Lie on the floor and push yourself with one foot and one arm.
12. Put a beanbag on the floor and push it with your elbow, shoulder, nose, or another body part.
13. Can you move in crab position and push a beanbag?
14. Show me how you can push a ball to a friend.

15. Push the ball toward the ceiling in a very smooth manner.

Pulling

Pulling is a controlled and forceful movement made in an attempt to move an object closer toward the body. If the body moves, pulling causes the object to follow the body.

Stress Points
1. For forceful pulling, the base of support must be broadened and the body's center of gravity must be lowered.
2. The vertical axis of the body should provide a line of force away from the object.
3. Pulling should be a controlled movement with a minimum of jerking and tugging.
4. The hand grips must be comfortable if pulling is to be efficient. Gloves or other padding can help.
5. Pulling movements can be isolated in the body, with one part of the body pulling against the other.

Teaching Cues
1. Take a good grip.
2. Gather your body forces and pull steadily.
3. Get your body in line with the pull. Lower yourself.
4. Widen your base of support.

Suggested Movement Experiences
1. Reach for the ceiling and pull an imaginary object toward you quickly, or slowly and smoothly.
2. Use an individual tug-of-war rope and practice pulling at different levels with your hands and arms, against a partner.
3. From a kneeling position, pull an object.
4. Can you pull with your feet while sitting on the floor?
5. Pretend to pull a heavy object while you are lying on the floor.
6. Clasp your hands together and pull as hard as you can.
7. Try pulling an object while you are standing on only one foot.
8. Hold hands with a partner, and gradually pull as hard as you can.
9. Have your partner sit down, and then see how slowly you can pull him or her.
10. With your partner sitting on the floor, see whether you can pull him or her to his or her feet.
11. Can you pull with different body parts?

Pulling and Pushing

Combinations of pulling and pushing movements should be arranged in sequence. Musical phrases can signal changes from one movement to the other.

The selected partner resistance exercises on page 111 are also fruitful pulling and pushing experiences.

FUNDAMENTAL SPORTS-RELATED SKILLS

The fundamental sports-related skills involve catching, throwing, and kicking, among others. They are complex motor patterns, and, generally, children are not capable of exhibiting a mature pattern until the ages of eight or nine. Since motor patterns are learned at an early age and are difficult to change thereafter, it is important to teach the patterns correctly. An example of incorrect learning occurs in the area of throwing. Most girls never mature in throwing patterns, whereas many boys learn to throw correctly. Many factors contribute to this situation. Very little emphasis is placed on correct form for girls, and they are seldom encouraged to learn properly. Once the incorrect pattern has been practiced over and over for 8 to 10 years, it becomes next to impossible to change. Thus, if the skill-learning years do indeed occur early in life, it is crucial to teach and encourage correctness of performance in the specialized sports skills if proper development is to occur. Most complex skills must be practiced at near normal speed rather than in slow motion. The analysis of the following skills should give the teacher an idea of the sequence of development, which is more important than the chronological age at which children learn.

Throwing

In throwing, an object is thrust into space and is accelerated through the movement of the arm and the total coordination of the body. Teachers should be aware of two early stages of tossing that young children exhibit. It is difficult to determine whether these early stages of throwing fall into a pattern of development that is found generally in most children. However, the stages often can be seen in youngsters and merit some mention. The first toss is a two-handed underhand throw that involves little foot movement. A large ball, such as a beach ball, usually precipitates this type of throw that begins at waist level in front of the body. The child usually completes the toss using only his or her arms and sometimes has difficulty maintaining balance when encouraged to throw the ball for distance.

The second toss often found is the one-handed underhand toss. In this toss, which is similar to pitching a softball, the child begins to develop body torque and is able to shift his or her weight from the rear foot to the front foot. This toss requires a smaller object to throw, and beanbags, fleece balls, and small sponge balls work well for this toss.

The following skill analysis deals only with overhand throwing. The teacher should be concerned primarily about children developing proper form while throwing rather than the ability to throw for accuracy. A good rule to remember is that, if one is interested in developing patterns with full range of motion and speed of throw as the goals, accuracy should be a secondary goal. As the pattern matures, accuracy can be introduced gradually as a direction for accomplishment.

Stage One

Stage one generally can be observed between the ages of two and three years. This stage is basically restricted to arm movement in the anteroposterior plane. The feet remain stationary and spread shoulder width, with little or no trunk rotation occurring. Most of the movement force originates from flexing the hip, moving the shoulder forward, and extending the elbow.

Stage Two

Stage two usually develops between the ages of three and a half and five years. Some rotary motion is developed by the child in an attempt to increase the amount of force he or she can accumulate. This stage is characterized by a lateral fling of the arm, with much rotating occurring with the trunk. Often, the child takes a step in the direction in which he or she is throwing, although many children keep their feet stationary. This throwing style sometimes looks like a discus throw rather than a baseball throw.

Stage Three

This stage is typically found among children who are five to six years old. The starting position is similar to the other stages in that the body is facing the target area, the feet are parallel, and the child is erect. However, in this stage, the child steps toward the target with the foot on the same side of the body as his or her throwing arm. This allows for some rotation of the body and shifting of the body weight forward as the step occurs. The arm action is nearer the overhand style of throwing as compared to the fling in stage two, and there is also an increase in hip flexion. Many students never quite mature in their throwing pattern beyond this stage and exhibit many of the behaviors described in this stage.

Stage Four

This stage is the mature form of throwing and allows the child to apply more force to the object being accelerated. The thrower uses the rule of opposition in this stage, which means that he or she steps in the direction of the throw with the leg opposite his or her throwing arm. This allows him

or her to develop maximum body torque. The child addresses the target with the nonthrowing side of his or her body and strides toward the target to shift the body weight. The sequence of movement is: step toward the target, rotate the upper body, and throw with the arm. The cue words often used are "step, turn, and throw." The elbow should lead the way in the arm movement, followed by the forearm extension and finally a snapping of the wrist. This pattern must be practiced many times in an attempt to develop total body coordination. Through a combination of sound instruction and much practice, the majority of youngsters should be able to develop a mature pattern of throwing by the age of eight or nine.

Stage Four Throwing Pattern

Catching

Catching is a skill that involves using the hands to stop and control a moving object. Catching is much more difficult for children to learn than throwing due to the fact that they must be able to track the object with their eyes and learn to move their bodies into the path of the object at the same time. Another element that makes catching more difficult to master is the fear of the object to be caught. Teachers must be careful to use objects that cannot hurt the receiver when the early stages of catching are being taught. Balloons, fleece balls, and beach balls move slowly and encourage visual tracking and decrease the fear of being hit in the face.

Stage One

The child in this stage holds his or her arms in front of his or her body, with the elbows extended and the palms up. The arms are held in this position until the ball makes contact, and then they are quickly bent at the elbows. The catch is actually more of a trapping movement as the arms press the ball against the chest. Often the child turns his or her head or closes his or her eyes due to the fear response. Children should be encouraged to watch the object rather than the person throwing the object.

Stage Two

In this stage, the child repeats much of the same behavior as in stage one. However, rather than waiting for the ball to contact his or her arms, the child starts to make an anticipatory movement. The child cradles the ball somewhat, as compared to the straight-arm movement in stage one.

Stage Three

As the child matures in his or her catching pattern, he or she prepares for the catch by lifting his or her arms and bending them slightly. He or she still uses the chest as a backstop for the ball and cradles it with his or her arms and hands. As the child develops in this stage, an attempt is made to make contact with the hands first and then guide the object to the chest.

Stage Four

In the fourth and final stage of catching, which should occur at approximately nine years of age, mature form is characterized as the child catches with the hands. The child can be encouraged to catch with his or her hands by decreasing the size of the balls to be caught. As the child continues to improve his or her style, he or she reaches with the hands and then brings the object softly to the body; this is often termed *giving*. Also, the legs bend and the feet are moved in anticipation of the catch.

Catching a large object

Kicking

Kicking is a striking action carried out with the feet. There are different types of kicking: the punt (in which the ball is dropped from the hands and kicked before it touches the ground) and the place kick (kicking the ball on the ground in a stationary position) are two. A third is soccer kicking, probably the most difficult of the foot striking skills due to the fact that the ball is moving before the kick.

Stage One

The body is stationary and the kicking foot is flexed as the child prepares for the kick. The kicking motion is carried out primarily with a straight leg and little or no flexion at the knee. Very little movement occurs with the arms and trunk as the child concentrates on the ball.

Stage Two

In the second stage, the child lifts the kicking foot backward by flexing at the knee. Usually, the child displays opposition of the limbs; in other words, when the kicking leg goes forward, the child's opposite arm moves forward. As compared to stage one, the child's kicking leg moves forward farther as a follow-through motion.

Stage Three

The child then moves toward the object to be kicked in a run or walk. There is an increase in the distance the leg is moved, coupled with a movement of the upper body to counterbalance the leg.

Stage Four

The mature stage of kicking involves a preparatory extension at the hip in order to increase the range of motion. As the child runs to the ball and prepares to kick it, he or she takes a small leap to get the kicking foot into position. As the kicking foot is carried forward, the trunk leans backward and the child takes a small step forward on the support foot to regain balance.

Kicking a Soccer Ball

OTHER MOVEMENT IDEAS AND CHALLENGES

A number of ideas have value for stimulating children to purposeful movement.

Floor Targets

Lines can be used for jumping, hopping, and leaping activities. A jump rope laid lengthwise makes a fine floor target. Children begin at one end, go back and forth over the rope as they go down the line, and return down the rope back to place (page 289).

The Rope as a Floor Target for Jumping

A hoop on the floor is also an excellent stimulant to movement. Children can do different movements in and out, inside, and around the hoop. A number of hoops in line provide excellent motivation (page 274).

A wand or a beanbag can be carried during various locomotor movements. On signal, the object is placed on the ground and the child jumps back and forth across it.

Floor Patterns

Footprints can be painted or marked on the floor, with the children doing movements guided by them. Lines, mazes, and different kinds of figures can be painted on blacktop to provide guides for movement.

Sports

Different sports activities can provide the basis for creative movements. Being a hockey, football, or basketball player is meaningful to both boys and girls.

Individual Mats

Individual mats are excellent for basic movements, both nonlocomotor and locomotor challenges. The mat provides a place where the child can do things upon, across, and around (page 307).

Flash Cards

Flash cards can give direction to the movements. Flash cards can depict different patterns, such as circles, triangles, squares, and others. A flash card might read 2-3, which would give direction to hopping patterns. The flash card might depict any movement combination to be followed, such as run, leap, and roll.

AN EXAMPLE OF AN EXPLORATORY APPROACH EMPHASIZING RUNNING, LEAPING, AND STOPPING TECHNIQUES

The following routine illustrates how a locomotor movement such as running can be combined with leaping and stopping to provide meaningful experiences for children. Although the approach is primarily direct instruction, children have the opportunity to respond in individual patterns within the tasks as set. There is good control and opportunity for instruction in having the movement performed by squads in squad-column formation with the stipulation that each squad member follows when the member in front is halfway across the area. The children run across an area 20 to 30 yards in width, depending on their age level. When they have completed a run across the area, the squads re-form on the other side, awaiting directions to come back. Other movement formations can be used.

"Cross your feet over each time as you run."

"Run low, touching the ground on either side alternately."

"Run low, touching the ground with both hands as you go along."

"Run forward, looking back over your right shoulder."

"The same, except look back over the left shoulder."

"Run zigzag; that is, change direction every few steps."

"Run to the center, stop, and continue."

"Run forward, stop with the right side forward, and then stop again with the left side forward."

"Run forward and stop. Come back three steps and stop again. Continue in original direction."

"Try a two-count stop with a definite 'one, two' slap on the ground with the feet."

"Try a hop, step, and jump and then continue."

"Run sideways, leading the first time with one side. Next time, reverse the position."

"Mix in giant leaps with your run."

"Run backward."

"Run forward halfway and backward the rest."

"Run backward halfway and forward the rest."

"As you run across, turn around (right) completely and continue across."

"The same, but turn to the left."

"Run slowly and then suddenly change to running fast."

The children can devise other combinations to try out. Be sure the children understand and use good running form. Skipping, galloping, and other locomotor movements can be included in the combinations.

THE MOVEMENT SUGGESTION BOX

An idea that has been received enthusiastically by children is the movement suggestion box. This box, which should contain enough cards for the whole class, can be used in two ways.

The first approach is to have movement challenges written on the cards. Each child takes a card and responds to the challenge. This activity can be used well at the beginning of a lesson.

In the second approach, the child is offered some choice of the type of movement he or she may select. Cards covering three or more areas can be in different compartments. Suggested are mat activities, locomotor movements, non-locomotor movements, and manipulative activities. The child may choose a second area when he or she has finished the first task and there is still time left.

Fourteen

Creative Play—Story Games and Dramatic Play

Although creativity should be superimposed over the entire physical education program, there are activities that can be designed specifically for creative expression. Such activities generally are done without rhythmic accompaniment, but they can incorporate rhythmic action.

Creative activities should stimulate a flow of unique ideas and expressions from within individual children. Much of this activity is role playing, which requires the children to take on and act out the roles of real or imaginary characters. Their invented and improvised movements should result from original thought, experimentation, and considered evaluation. The limited and unlimited exploratory teaching styles should dominate, but other methodology can be used, also. The teacher structures the situation so that children can respond spontaneously and with feeling. Self-discovery is the key, and any response within the limits of the activity is acceptable. Alternatives must exist that provide the child with both a choice he or she can make and an opportunity to act upon that choice and respond creatively.

Creative play, as presented in this chapter, includes stories, poems, events, everyday happenings, objects, and ideas that can stimulate movement. The motivation must be sound, and it must kindle the urge for expression.

Most, if not all, of these creative movements should be used for younger children, including preschool children and children from kindergarten and first and second grade. This is not to say that creativity is not important from the third grade on, but creative opportunity can be furthered and realized in activities more relevant to the developmental levels of older children.

To be appropriate for physical education classes, the activities chosen should elicit gross motor actions. Those of a less active nature, such as finger plays, might be better employed in the regular classroom for relaxation or a change of pace.

Poems are excellent materials because of their catchy, rhythmic phrases and their foundations for interpretive action. Short rhymes and longer poems with several verses can be used.

Stories incite action as the children lose themselves in role playing to the story. Traditional stories and stories made up to fit particular actions can be used.

INSTRUCTIONAL PROCEDURES

1. Formations should be informal, with the children scattered or in a loose semicircle. All the children should be able to see and hear the leader. A good story basis is important, so probably the teacher needs to do the story telling. However, capable children can tell the stories, too.
2. Discuss the idea.
   a. What is it all about? What does it look like—size, shape, color, parts?
   b. How does it move—what can it do?
   c. What interpretations can we make—how can we move to show how it moves?
   d. What is the sequence of actions? What actions unfold as the story goes along?
   e. How can we put the different actions to-

gether? What people can act out different parts?
   f. Do we need any props? Sound effects?
3. Develop the idea.
   a. Begin to build up the unified whole— positions of people, groupings, cues for action, and a refined sequence.
   b. Experience the entire composition.
   c. Make evaluative comments—how did it make you feel? Were you motivated to express yourself? If we do this again, how can we improve our interpretations?
4. Respect the contribution of each child as long as it is sincere. Allow the children the integrity of their responses.
5. Encourage with both verbal and nonverbal reinforcement.
6. Be sure the children understand the words. It is difficult for a child to float like a balloon when he or she doesn't know what a balloon is.
7. The teacher needs to be perceptive—what is the next step to apply? What should be the next challenges to be developed? Provide suggestions and questions in such a manner that the children think the ideas are their own.
8. Remember that demonstrating how to move has little part in creative play if variety of response is desired.

STORIES

Children love to act out and dramatize many of the old, familiar stories. No doubt both the children and the teacher have favorites. Some of these might include:
"The Three Bears"
"The Three Pigs"
"Black Beauty"
"Cinderella"
"Rumpelstiltskin"
"The Shoemaker and the Elves"
"The Pied Piper"
"Mother Goose Stories"
"Henny Penny"
"The Sleeping Beauty"
"The Town Musicians"
"Peter Pan"

This list is only a starting point, but it is given to illustrate the kinds of stories that have possibilities.

Stories may need to be adapted and rewritten, with only the main points of the story used to direct the movement. As an example, the story "Jack the Giant Killer" is given with the story in the left-hand column and the *suggested* actions on the right. It should be emphasized that the actions grow out of the discussions with the children about how *they feel* the story should be interpreted.

Jack the Giant Killer

Once upon a time, a giant, called Caramaran, lived on top of a mountain in a cave. He was a very wicked giant, so the king of the country offered a large reward to the person who would kill the giant. So Jack, a country boy, decided he would try his luck.

The Words
1. One morning Jack took a shovel and pick and started toward the mountain. He hurried, because he wanted to climb the mountain before dark.
2. Jack finally reached the foot of the mountain and started to climb up.
3. He came to a place where he had to use his hands to help him climb.
4. Just as it grew dark, Jack reached the top of the mountain. When he was sure the giant was asleep in his bed, he took his pick and began to dig a hole outside the cave entrance.
5. After he had loosened the dirt with his pick, Jack took the shovel and threw the dirt up on all sides of the hole.
6. Then Jack covered up the hole with some long straws and sticks he had picked up.
7. After this was done, Jack waited until morning. Then he called loudly and wakened the giant, who strode angrily out of the cave. Since he was very tall, he took big steps.
8. The giant was so very angry that he didn't look where he was going and walked right

The Actions
1. Picking up pick and shovel and running around in a circle.

2. Walking around in a circle with high knee movements.
3. Climbing with motions using hands and arms.

4. Vigorous digging movements with trunk twisting, standing with feet apart.

5. Vigorous shoveling movements, first right, then left, throwing the dirt in various directions.
6. Forward, downward bending, picking up straws, twisting alternately left and right.
7. Arms overhead, stretching up tall, walking around in a circle on tiptoes.

8. Stooping quickly as if falling.

into the hole Jack had made. Down he fell and was killed.

9. Then Jack filled up the hole with the dirt he had taken out.

10. Jack went into the cave, got the giant's treasure, and ran home to tell his mother about it.

11. When he got home, he was so excited and tired he was all out of breath. Ever after this, Jack was called the Giant Killer.

9. Forward, downward movements, pushing dirt into hole, moving around in a circle, and doing the same thing over again.

10. Running around circle in the opposite directions, carrying the treasure.

11. Deep breathing.

DRAMATIC PLAY WITH POEMS

The field of poetry can be exploited to its fullest for source material for dramatic play. Mother Goose rhymes are particularly suited for activity, and there are many others. Poetry has some advantages over stories, because it uses catchy phrases and rhymes and because of the feeling that is in much of it.

Poems have an appeal particularly for kindergarten and first-grade children. Some examples of poems, together with suggested actions, follow.

The Giant

The Words

1. Once a giant came a-wandering

2. Late at night when the world was still

3. Seeking a stool to sit on

4. He climbed on a little, green hill.

5. "Giant, Giant! I am under you,

6. Move or this is the last of me."
7. But the giant answered, "Thank you,

8. I like it here, don't you see."

The Actions

1. Children wander around the room in a swaggering, giant type of step and movement.
2. Children become quiet and put a finger up to their lips to indicate silence.
3. Giant swaggers around looking for a place to sit.
4. All children perform climbing movements to get to the top of the hill.
5. Children crouch down and pretend they are stepped on.
6. Children try to push the giant away.
7. Children walk around surveying the countryside.
8. Giant swaggers around with thumbs under armpits.

Giants and Dwarfs

The Words

1. Let us all be little men,

2. Dwarfs so gay and tiny, then,
3. Let us stand up straight and tall
4. We'll be giants, one and all.

The Actions

1. Walk around like dwarfs, with body in a hunched position and arms and legs bent.
2. Continue walking. Be gay.
3. Walk on tiptoes, arms stretched upward.
4. Continue walking, occasionally turning around.

Pat-a-Cake

Each child has a partner; the children stand facing their partners.

The Words

1. Pat-a-cake, pat-a-cake, baker's man,

2. Bake me a cake as fast as you can,
3. Pat it, and mold it, and mark it with a T

4. And bring it safely home to baby and me.

The Actions

1. Clap own hands, clap hands to partner. Repeat. Shake forefinger at partner three times.
2. Stir the cake fast and vigorously.
3. Follow words with patting, molding, and putting a T on top of the cake.
4. Walk around in good balance carefully, so the cake will not be dropped.

The children find another partner during the walking, and the poem is repeated.

Hippity Hop

Each child has a partner; their inside hands are joined.

The Words	*The Actions*
1. Hippity hop to the barber shop,	1. Skip around the room with partner.
2. To buy a stick of candy.	2. Stop. Face partner. Reach in pocket for money, holding up one finger.
3. One for you and one for me,	3. Point to partner, point to self.
4. And one for cousin Andy.	4. Join inside hands and skip around the room.

Let's Pretend

The Words	*The Actions*
1. Now I'll be a telephone pole Standing up so tall.	1. Stretch up tall.
2. Now I'll be a jelly fish I can't stand up at all.	2. Melt down into a puddle.
3. Now I'll be a kangaroo Hopping on the ground.	3. Hop up and down in personal space.
4. Now I'll be a spinning top Whirling 'round and 'round.	4. Spin around.
5. Now I'll be a bouncing ball Bouncing up and down.	5. Bounce up and down like a ball.
6. Now I'll be a funny man And act like a clown.	6. Be a clown.
7. Now I'll be a monkey Climbing up a string.	7. Make climbing motions.
8. Now I'll be my own self I can do anything!	8. Select any action or pose.

Ripe Apples

The Words	*The Actions*
1. Lovely ripe apples on branches so high,	1. With arms stretched upward, sway back and forth.
2. I cannot reach them, way up in the sky.	2. Reach up high with one arm at a time.
3. I stretch up so tall, and I jump this way.	3. On tiptoes, stretch upward. Then jump upward to pick an apple.
4. I know when I've picked them, I'll eat them today.	4. Pretend to eat, raising hands alternately to mouth.
5. I'll sit down and rest, and eat them some more.	5. Sit down cross-legged and continue to eat.
6. "Um-m-m. Aren't they good?"	6. Shake heads, rub tummy while repeating in unison the last line.

Wallaby Kangaroo

The Words	*The Actions*
1. Wallaby, wallaby, kangaroo, How do you jump the way you do?	1. Have hands in front of shoulders to represent paws of the kangaroo. Look around from right to left but do not move.
2. I'm sure if I tried for a year and a day, I'd never be able to jump that way.	2. Jump around like a kangaroo.

Old Mother Hubbard

Old Mother Hubbard is a favorite with children. The teacher can select all or any of the verses. Informal organization is the key. The children can be in a circle or a semicircle about one or more selected Mother Hubbards. No specific action directions are necessary, and the children pantomime as the poem unfolds.

Old Mother Hubbard, she went to the cupboard,
To get her poor doggie a bone:
When she got there, the cupboard was bare,

And so the poor doggie had none.
She went to the baker's to buy him some bread,
But when she came back the poor doggie was dead.
She went to the undertaker's to buy him a coffin,
And when she came back the doggie was laughing.
She went to the butcher's to get him some tripe,
And when she came back he was smoking a pipe.
She went to the fish shop to buy him some fish,
And when she came back he was washing the dish.
She went to the hatter's to buy him a hat,
And when she came back he was feeding the cat.
She went to the tailor's to buy him a coat,
And when she came back he was riding the goat.
She went to the barber's to buy him a wig,
And when she came back he was dancing a jig.
She went to the draper's to buy him some linen,
And when she came back the good dog was spinning.
She went to the hosier's to buy him some hose,
And when she came back he was dressed in his clothes.
The dame made a curtsey, the dog made a bow,
The dame said, "Your servant," the dog said, "Bowwow."

I'm Very, Very Small

This little piece appears several places in this book, because it has good versatility. In this context, it can be used as the basis for creative play by getting the children to come up with different contrasting word combinations. The children act out the first three lines and assume whatever pose they wish during the last line.

I'm very, very small, or
I'm very, very tall,
Sometimes small, sometimes tall,
Guess what I am now?

Other combinations that can be used are low-high, thin-wide, hot-cold, happy-angry, and calm-edgy, among others.

MISCELLANEOUS EXPERIENCES AS A BASIS FOR DRAMATIC PLAY

Many everyday experiences from the childhood and adult world can form the basis for dramatic play. The children can help the teacher plan the story to guide the play. A simple idea like a railroad train can be a good basis. It could be developed in the following fashion.

Railroad Train

Each child is given the name of a part of a freight train. Several trains may be formed. The teacher tells a story in which the various parts of the train are mentioned. Several children are the engines, and the story usually begins with this portion of the train. After the story unfolds, the children form in line, one behind the other in the order named. After the trains have been assembled and all the "cars" are on the train, the story continues with the description of a train trip. The route is described in detail, with the train going slowly up and down grades and around curves, stopping at stations, and finishing up with a wreck. It also is possible to assemble the trains by having each of the parts of the train on "sidetracks" and the train backing up to hook onto the "cars."

Some attention should be given to the story, since the imagination of the teller is very important. Also, children can make suggestions for the train ride.

It is apparent that there is no dearth of material or ideas. Imagination plays a big part in widening the scope of dramatic play.

For another illustration of how an idea can be expanded, take the children on an imaginary hike. It should be noted that integration with other subject fields is possible. Conservation practices can be stressed. Safety in the woods can be emphasized.

The Hike

The Words

1. Today we are going on a hike. What are some of things we need to take?
2. We are going to roll our packs into a nice, neat bundle. Put down your tarp first, next arrange your blankets, and then put the rest of your things in. Now let's roll the pack and tie it up.
3. Off we go.

4. Time to rest.
5. Off again.
6. Make blazes so we can find our way back. Make trail markers.
7. Here we are. Pick out a good spot for the tent and put it up.
8. We need lots of wood for the camp fire. Will you see what you can find?
9. Build the fire and broil the steaks.
10. Bugle call for turning in.

The Actions

1. Children suggest various articles that should be included.
2. Children lay out packs and roll and tie them.

3. Children march two by two around the room, carrying packs.
4. All remove packs and sit down.
5. All resume marching.
6. Children make blazes in various manners and arrange stones for markers.
7. They cut stakes and poles, drive stakes and put up tents, arrange beds.
8. Children go out and drag in logs and wood. Some cutting may be needed.
9. As directed.
10. Children go to one side, brush their teeth, wash up, and then turn in. They crawl in tent, cover themselves carefully, and go to sleep.

Jack Frost and Mr. Sun

Children are scattered around the area and are doing nonlocomotor movements of their choice. Movements can be twisting, circling body parts, pushing and pulling movements, and similar movements. Two or three children are chosen to be Jack Frosts and another is Mr. Sun. The Jack Frosts scurry around the room, touching children and saying, "Freeze." The children freeze in whatever position they are caught.

Then, Mr. Sun walks around grandly, thawing out the children, who gradually resume their original movements.

The Toy Store

The Leader: I'm the owner of a toy store.
Class (in unison): What can we buy today?
The Leader: A pair of roller skates.
Action: The children then try to match their movements to the selected article. The action then is repeated with another article. Other things that can be named are a bicycle, pogo stick, kite, top, jump rope, basketball, football, shot put, discus, frisbee, and bowling ball.

The kind of business can be changed to a hardware store, a construction firm, a lumber company, a fishing boat, and the like.

Other Ideas

Some other suggestions for creative dramatic play follow.

1. Playing in the leaves; in the snow, making a snowman or sledding.
2. Going to a circus, a zoo, a toy shop, or a farm.
3. Doing common things like washing and hanging up clothes, washing dishes, trimming a Christmas tree, pitching hay, sowing grain, planting a garden, shaking and beating rugs, and cutting grain.
4. Pretending to be an animal (bear, deer, squirrel, giraffe, elephant, pony, et cetera), an imaginary creature (giant, witch, dwarf, troll, et cetera), or an official or a worker (conductor, police officer, engineer, et cetera).
5. Having fun at paddling a canoe or rowing a boat; playing baseball, football, track, basketball, et cetera; skiing, ice skating, roller skating, water skiing; swimming, using different strokes.
6. Celebrating holidays (Christmas, Halloween, Thanksgiving, Fourth of July), seasons (fall, winter, spring, summer).
7. Pretending to work in industries, such as lumbering, fishing, construction, and road building.

Fifteen

Rhythmic Movement

Music and other forms of rhythm add a great deal of enjoyment to physical education activities. While most movement can be conducted without rhythmic background, the accentuation of motor activity through rhythm stimulates the child toward higher intensity, increased enjoyment, and, often, longer participation in various activities.

Movement responses to rhythm should begin early in a child's school experiences and continue throughout the elementary school program. The teacher should capitalize on the child's natural love for rhythm and his or her need and desire for expressive movement in order to enhance the child's learning potential. Through participation in a broad rhythmic program, a child can develop an understanding of rhythm, can learn to move in rhythm, can increase his or her movement competency through rhythm, and can develop an appreciation of music and rhythm in modern culture.

For developing the child's rhythmic potential, a focus on considered listening as opposed to random hearing is important. The qualities and characteristics of the rhythmic background must be perceived by the child if they are to be translated into relevant movement. Gradually, through the span of the elementary grades, understanding and perception of the structure and meaning of rhythm evolve as the child gauges his or her movements to meter, accents, intensity, mood, and phrases. The child's ability to start and stop as the music or other rhythmic accompaniment dictates is a necessary requisite of body control for efficient rhythmic movement. Basically, the child must move in time and under control with the rhythm if the movement is to be classified as rhythmic.

Good social values can be derived from rhythmic participation in boy-girl relationships even though modern education tends to downgrade traditional male-female roles. The implementation of the principle of equal opportunity has long been overdue; however, it is hoped this new emphasis will not be carried to the extreme of eliminating the partner-type dances characteristic of many cultures. To be at ease with the opposite sex, to learn social graces, and to make common elements of courtesy a practice are important goals in the rhythmic program for both genders.

Fundamental locomotor skills are rhythmic in performance, and so the addition of rhythm in developing competency in these skills is of value. Furthermore, if a child can move in rhythm in selected locomotor skills, a good basis for successful participation in dance-type activities has been established. Children's dance should be a natural outgrowth of the movement activities with which they are already familiar.

When performing rhythmic activities children should move with reasonably good postures and with aimless and excessive movements of body parts kept to a minimum. Good opportunity is present for incidental and direct instruction in moving gracefully with good posture. The ability to move with others to form patterned movements is a challenge inherent in most intermediate-level dances.

Rhythmic activities also provide a vehicle for expressive movement, an area termed *creative rhythms.* In these activities, there is good opportunity for wide participation and personal satisfaction and achievement for all the participants, since the children personalize their responses within the framework of the idea. Opportunity also should be

196

offered for creating unique rhythmic responses within action songs and dances.

The vigorous nature of many rhythmic activities fulfills the criterion of developmental movement, particularly in gross motor activities for primary-level children and in rope skipping to music, which is emphasized mostly in the intermediate-level program. Exercises to music are another interesting fitness approach.

RHYTHMIC ACCOMPANIMENT

Essential to any rhythmic program is suitable rhythm that can stimulate or draw from the children the expected motor pattern and expressive movement. If children are to be asked to move to a rhythm, the rhythm must have stimulating characteristics, be appropriate for the expected responses, and have appeal to the learners. Characteristics of well-suited music include definite beat, accents, rousing quality, and definite phrasing that indicates the changes in the movement patterns. Relaxing mood music rarely stimulates movement.

Children should have exposure to different types of rhythmic accompaniment. The means through which rhythmic background can be supplied for movement in elementary school programs are discussed in the following paragraphs.

Dance Drum and Tom-Tom

Skillful use of a drum or a tom-tom adds much to rhythmic experiences, and the teacher can vary or interject drumbeats into many movement patterns. For example, many introductory lesson activities can be directed by drumbeats. Not only can the drumbeat guide movement, but it is useful for specifying moods and force in movement. Another use is guiding the flow of movement from one pattern to another by signaling tiny increments with light beats that stimulate the controlled transition.

Some practice and feel are necessary in order to beat a drum efficiently. The motion in striking is essentially a wrist action, not an arm movement. The beater can cue on a single apt performer to find the correct rhythm for beating. Some teachers have good success with a small, resonant, wooden tube struck with a hard striker. It provides a definite, piercing beat. Two bamboo sticks, each about 12 inches long, also provide a reasonable substitute for a drum.

Record Player

The second source of accompaniment is the record player. It should be of good quality and have a variable speed control. It should be adaptable to a range of records (33, 45, and 78 RPM). Some protection against needle bounce is needed. Either the player should have built-in protection, or it should be cushioned on foam rubber pads. The volume must be sufficient to carry the music over the competition of the activity's noise. The player also should have an input for a microphone. Better-quality sound reproduction can be obtained from players that have two speakers. A cart for holding the record player is also good to have.

Some kind of a permanent installation for both the record player and storage of records should be considered, particularly in new construction or renovation. Availability and convenience are the keys. Speakers placed overhead provide better-quality sound.

Each school and teacher should build up a collection of records. The physical education records should be stored in the physical education facility, rather than in the school library. Storage should be so arranged that each record has its place and is readily available. Keeping copies of the more frequently used records should be considered, too, especially in centralized equipment-distributing centers for larger school systems. Student operators of record players should be selected and given proper instruction, so record damage can be minimized.

Good record sets designed especially for physical education movement patterns and dances are available from a number of sources. Microgroove records (33 RPM) are more easily damaged than the others and also are difficult to start at the right place because of the tiny spaces between the selections. Also, microgroove records have more selections on them than other types of records, and the teachers may not find all of the selections useful. However, 33-RPM records do minimize the storage problems.

The smallest records (45 RPM) are preferred by some teachers because of their low expense and easy storage, while 78-RPM records are preferred by many because of their ease in handling, but they require more storage room. Many record players can no longer handle 78-RPM records, so teachers should be careful about choosing materials recorded at this speed.

Piano

The piano can provide excellent music when the player has a suitable degree of skill. It has one drawback: the teacher who plays and must read music is not able to observe the children as well, let alone help the children with their movement patterns.

Some simple rhythmic accompaniment can be done by playing only the black keys. Sounding simple chords, trills made with two adjacent black keys, and playing up and down the scale are forms of directing movement.

Tape Recorder

The tape recorder offers possibilities for rhythmic movement not found in other sources of accompaniment. It provides a means by which children can create and record their own accompaniment. Voice directions can be superimposed over music; this is useful for establishing a sequence of exercises to music.

Tape recorders are especially valuable for establishing a background for creative rhythms for which changes of music are desirable. Also, there are no delays in the activities that can be caused by changing records.

Many tape recorders provide better output when they can be amplified through the record player, since some recorders do not provide the necessary volume.

A disadvantage of the tape recorder is that tempo cannot be varied once a selection has been recorded.

Other Sources of Rhythm

Some other sources of rhythmic accompaniment merit consideration. In action songs, the children can learn the music and the words and so provide their own accompaniment.

The tambourine plays a useful role in the rhythmic program, since it can be used to provide two different types of percussive accompaniment. Shaking it gives a metallic, ringing type of noise, while striking it with the knuckles or on the elbow produces a drumlike sound. The metallic sound can stimulate the children to one kind of movement and the drumlike beat to a contrasting movement.

Sometimes, a chant or a poem recited in a rhythmic manner can provide the beat. Rhythm bands can give direction, also. Primary-level classrooms usually have the instruments for the rhythm band available.

CHARACTERISTICS OF RHYTHMIC BACKGROUND

Music has essential characteristics that the children should recognize, understand, and appreciate. These characteristics also are present in varying degrees in other types of rhythmic accompaniment.

The teacher should use the proper terminology when discussing the characteristics of a piece of music. The following terms should be employed.

Generally, *tempo* is the speed of the music. Tempo can be constant, show a gradual increase (acceleration), or show a decrease (deceleration).

Beat is the underlying rhythmic quality of the music. The beat can be even or uneven. Some musicians refer to the beat as the pulse of the music. Music with a pronounced beat is easier for children to follow.

Meter refers to the manner in which the beats are put together to form a measure of music. Common meters used in rhythmics are 2/4, 3/4, 4/4, and 6/8.

Certain notes or beats in a rhythmic pattern receive more force or a heavier emphasis, and this defines *accent.* Usually, the accent is applied to the first underlying beat of a measure and generally is expressed by a more forceful movement in a sequence of movements.

The *intensity* of the music can be loud, soft, light, or heavy.

Mood is related somewhat to intensity but carries the concept deeper into human feelings. Music can interpret many human moods, such as feeling cheerful, sad, happy, gay, warlike, fearful, stately, et cetera.

A *phrase* is a natural grouping of measures. In most cases, the group of measures totals eight underlying beats or counts.

Phrases of music are put together into rhythmic *patterns.* Children should recognize when the music pattern repeats or changes to another pattern.

THE RHYTHMIC MOVEMENT PROGRAM

Rhythmic activities should be scheduled in the same manner as other phases of the program and not regarded as fillers, rainy-day programs, or recreational outlets. A vast amount of rhythmic material from which to choose is available. The plea is for a balanced offering that includes activities from each of the categories of rhythmic movement over the school year.

The table on the next page shows the recommended types of rhythmic activities for each grade level. An examination of the table reveals that the program for grades kindergarten through two emphasizes fundamental rhythms, creative rhythms, and movement songs, with lesser attention to folk dances in the lower two grades. As the program moves into the third grade, movement songs are used less frequently and rope jumping and musical games enter the picture as well as simple folk dances. Mixers are used to a limited extent in the third grade.

The program for grades four through six is similar, except for square dancing. Square dancing is given some attention in the fifth grade with lead-up types of dances and is stressed in the sixth grade. For the intermediate level, folk dances, mixers, and rope jumping make up the bulk of the program, with some inclusion of musical games and fundamental rhythm activities of the manipulative

Types of Rhythmic Activity

ACTIVITY TYPE	K	1	2	3	4	5	6
Fundamental rhythms	X	X	X	X	S	S	S
Creative rhythms	X	X	X	X			
Singing Movement songs	X	X	X				
Folk dances	S	S	X	X	X	X	X
Mixers				S	X	X	X
Square dancing						S	X
Rope jumping to music			S	S	X	X	X
Musical games			S	S	S	S	S

KEY: X means the activity is an integral part of that grade level.
S means the activity is given only minor emphasis.

type. Movement sequences to music are enjoyable activities for intermediate-level children.

Skill Progressions

Another type of analysis can be made to note the progression of basic and specific dance steps as they are introduced into the program. Dances employing these steps appear in each of the respective grade-level programs.

Kingergarten: fundamental locomotor movements.

First Grade: fundamental locomotor movements.

Second Grade: fundamental locomotor movements, sliding, draw steps, Bleking step, step-hops.

Fourth Grade: two-step, Indian steps, marching, rope-jumping steps.

Fifth Grade: schottische, polka, Tinikling steps.

Sixth Grade: waltz, square dance, Varsouvienne.

From the standpoint of the child's competency, interest, progression, and learning potential, experience in the field has shown the above placement of skills to be sound. Early rhythmic experiences require only fundamental locomotor skills, and more defined steps are introduced as progression unfolds. Progression of this nature involves arbitrary decisions, but some placement of progression is necessary to avoid repetition and to ensure a wide variety of movements.

Instructional Procedures

Before the various segments of the rhythmic program are discussed, the instructional procedures common to all the segments should be outlined.

1. Establishing the correct tempo is of critical importance in most rhythmic activities, but tempo is often difficult to control. The tempo should be set at the rate considered best for the stage of learning, which during beginning instruction probably should be somewhat slow, so that the performers can be comfortable. However, the slow tempo cannot be so slow that it distorts the movement patterns. The proper speed is one at which the group as a whole can handle the expected movement patterns. Gradually, the tempo can be increased to what is considered the right speed. If the teacher has trouble establishing the right beat or count, he or she should zero in on a child with good rhythmic movement and pace the beat to that child's movements.

When the class is practicing patterns without music before performing them to a record, the tempo of practice should approximate that of the recorded music that is to follow. Practicing at one tempo and then performing at another adds an unnecessary challenge.

It is obvious that the record player should have a variable speed control. Also, since records have various tempos, the teacher should note on the record labels the correct speed settings for each, thus avoiding delays during classtime.

2. The teacher should have definite starting and stopping signals for the dancers, such as "ready and begin," "ready—now," and "stop." The signal for the dancers to begin should be given on the musical phrase just before the beginning of a full pattern. The phrase is usually eight beats in length, and the starting signals can be given on the fifth and seventh beats of the phrase in the following manner.

Beats

1	2	3	4	5	6	7	8
				"Ready and begin"			
				"Ready — now!"			

3. During the initial presentation of a rhythm, the children should be familiarized with what is to

follow. The teacher should try to analyze what the music stands for, that is, what its dominant quality is with respect to mood, tempo, accents, phrases, and meter.

4. Active listening, as differentiated from simple hearing, is vital. As the children listen for phrasing, they become aware of the changes in, and effects of, the music. While some counting of beats can be done initially, the ultimate goal is to have children alter movement patterns as indicated by changes in phrasing.

5. To gain a sense of the beat, children can follow the beat with hand or foot sounds. Hands can be clapped together or slapped lightly on parts of the body. In making foot sounds, the toes can be tapped against the floor, stamping can be done with the whole foot, heels can be pounded on the floor, or the soles or the sides of the feet can be brought together.

6. Spoken cues can help the children gain mastery of rhythmic patterns, but cueing techniques need practice. Spoken cues should be rhythmically correct, particularly when given before the introduction of music. Cues can vary in type. Some can involve simple counting (1, 2, 3, 4). Others can involve rhythm (slow, slow [or quick], fast, fast, fast). Another type utilizes descriptive words (step, step, step, hop as in the schottische or forward, side, close as in the waltz step). The cue for the next movement can be given when the prior movement is drawing to a close (1, 2, 3, and turn, or the word *turn* can be spoken alone at the appropriate time). As skills progress, cues should be shortened and finally eliminated.

7. Progression is important in teaching rhythmic activities. It is sound instructional procedure to progress from the simple to the more complex, from a slowed to a normal tempo, from solo to partner activity, from the familiar to the unfamiliar, and from a simple to a partner position.

8. In the lower grades, the teacher need not be too concerned with strict mechanics. Children should be held to reasonable standards appropriate for their ages. Too high standards breed frustration and kill some of the enjoyment in the activity.

9. Time is saved when a monitor can be sent into the dance room or area to warm up the record player before the other children come in. Third graders are quite capable of handling this chore. When the class comes in, the activity can proceed without undue delay. Newer record players with transistors need little warm up but should be made ready.

10. The teacher can be freed for better instructional duty when a child handles the record player. He or she should have definite signals for starting and stopping the music. Normally, music should be stopped at the completion of a full pattern. Volunteers from intermediate classes can help with primary-level rhythm classes.

11. Individual help should be given as needed, but the teacher should not hold the class to the pace of a slow learner. Whenever possible, corrections should be made to the whole group even when they are meant for individuals having difficulties.

12. Student demonstrations should be used when they are advantageous, but only in a positive sense. All the students should have a chance to demonstrate.

13. Postural points for graceful carriage, good form, and efficient movement should be included in the instruction.

14. The parachute provides an interesting addition or variation to many rhythmic activities. Where its addition seems practical for rhythmic-movement activities, the fact is noted in the variation sections of the activities in this book.

FUNDAMENTAL RHYTHMS

The fundamental rhythm program sets the basis for rhythmic movement in all forms of dance activities through its stress on fundamental skills done in rhythm. It centers on locomotor, non-locomotor, and manipulative skills, with most attention given the locomotor types.

Fundamental rhythms should be an outgrowth of the movement activities with which the children are already familiar, such as walking (stepping), running, jumping, and hopping. To these already acquired skills, rhythm then is added. Fundamental rhythms are emphasized in the primary grades and are extended into the intermediate level on a lesser scale.

The general purpose of a program of fundamental rhythms is to provide a variety of fundamental movement experiences, so the child can move effectively and efficiently and develop a sense of rhythm in connection with these movements. While the creative aspects of fundamental rhythms are important, it is necessary first to establish a vocabulary of movement competencies for each child, so he or she has a basis on which to create.

The skills in a fundamental rhythm program are important not only in providing background in creative dance but also in setting the basis for the more precise dance skills of folk, social, and square dances, which follow later in school programs. The fundamental skills also are related to effective movement in all forms of living and, in particular, to the activities in the physical education program.

The following fundamental movement patterns are basic to the program of fundamental rhythms.

Locomotor Movements

Even types: walking, running, hopping, leaping, jumping, draw steps, and such variations as marching, trotting, stamping, and twirling.

Uneven types: skipping, galloping, sliding.

Nonlocomotor Movements

Simple movements: bending, swaying, twisting, swinging, raising, lowering, circling, and rotating various parts of the body.

Mimetics: striking, lifting, throwing, pushing, pulling, hammering, and other common tasks.

Object handling: ball skills (other objects such as hoops, wands, and even chairs can be used).

Instructional Procedures

Instruction should begin with those fundamental movements that are natural to the children. In practice, success depends upon the teacher's initiating and guiding the simple patterns. It is important that the rhythms be conducted in an atmosphere of fun and enjoyment. Furthermore, the accompaniment should be suitable for the movements to be experienced.

The element of creativity must not be stifled in a program of fundamental movements. The instruction can be directed toward a specific movement (like walking), and a reasonable range of acceptability can be established. In other words, they are practicing walking, but they can walk in many different ways.

Teachers who feel awkward and insecure in developing rhythmic programs with a strong creative approach find the fundamental rhythms a good starting point. Combining the child's love of rhythmic movement with the basic movements he or she enjoys can be the beginning of a refreshing and stimulating experience for both teacher and child.

The approach to fundamental rhythms should be a mixture of direct and indirect teaching. For many of the movements, there are standard or preferred techniques. For example, there is a correct way to walk, and children should recognize and learn the correct fundamentals. Within the framework of good technique, a variety of movement experiences should be elicited.

Steps to be followed in the teaching format depend upon the lesson, whether it is an initial experience with a new movement or a review and an expansion of learned techniques. The following steps are suggested.

1. The teacher should gather the children together and explain what is to be done and provide just enough explanation to get the activity underway.
2. The children should listen and get the feel of the beat through hand or foot movements.
3. Then, they should move with the expected response to the rhythm provided, perhaps in a controlled fashion. As soon as possible, however, movement should be free, informal, and in every direction in general space.
4. The teacher should stop at times and ask questions that bring out important elements and key factors of the movement, supported by students' demonstrations. Critical observation by the teacher is a necessary ingredient for guiding the learning sequences.
5. Challenges should be issued to encourage variety and combinations of movement that allow for experimentation and creativity within the scope of the practiced movement.
6. At the completion of the lesson, pertinent points should be brought out from the children by asking, "What are we doing that was good and how can we improve our movement patterns?"

Creative Approach to Fundamental Rhythms

In a lesson emphasizing the creative aspects of fundamental rhythmics, the approach differs from one emphasizing specialized patterns. The purpose of the creative approach to fundamental learning is to have the child gain an interpretation or impression from the selected rhythm and then move creatively as he or she chooses, using fundamental skills.

As in the approach just discussed, the child listens to the music and gains a sense of the beat by clapping or other simple movements.

After the teacher discusses the characteristics of the music with the children, they are encouraged to select the kinds of movements the music suggests to them. Movement then is free and unstructured. Extension of movement experiences with variety and different combinations is then possible.

The drumbeat is a fine basis for creative movement. The teacher establishes a rhythm with the drumbeat, and the children follow with their choice of fundamental skills.

Ideas for Using Fundamental Rhythmic Movements

Presented in the following paragraphs are some ideas that should provide a basis for breadth and variety of movement in fundamental rhythmic movements. Children love change and the challenge of reacting to change. The children can change the movement pattern or some aspect of it (direction, level, body leads, et cetera) at the end of a musical phrase. The music provides the cue for changes, and the children must plan ahead for the upcoming change.

Changes also can be signaled by variations of the drumbeat. A heavy, accented beat, for example, could signal a change of direction or a kind of movement. Stops and starts, changes to different rhythms, and other innovations are within the scope of this process. The intensity and force of the drumbeat can call for light or heavy movements.

The use of different parts of the body singly and in various combinations is important in establishing variety. The different positions of the arms and legs provide many ways of moving. The child can perform high on the toes, with toes in or out, on the heels, with stiff knees kicking high in front or to the rear, with knees brought up high, in a crouched position, and in many other positions.

Arms can swing at the sides or be held stiff, be held out in front or overhead. Arms can move in circles or in different patterns and in other poses. The body can be bent forward, backward, and sideward, and it can be twisted and turned. By combining different positions of the arms, legs, and body, the children can assume many interesting variations of position. Changes in body level and patterns of movements for outlining circles, squares, triangles, and other shapes add interest.

Planned movement sequences are also effective vehicles for using fundamental skills and allowing creativity. This topic is further developed in the discussions of the various fundamental skills which follow.

Working with a Partner or a Group

A child can work with a partner or as a member of a group. Partner movements can be coordinated in a number of partner positions, side by side facing the same or opposite directions, partners facing each other with hands joined, or one partner directly behind the other with the back person having his or her hands on the shoulders of the forward partner. Some small-group work is possible, but it should be selected with care, since working in groups can stifle individual creativity.

Fundamental Locomotor Movements to Rhythm

Fundamental skills have been described together with teaching hints and stress points in chapter thirteen. These concerns are valuable also in fundamental rhythmic movements and should be applied in the instructional process. Many of the ideas and movement patterns should be examined for utility, since many of them can be adapted to rhythmic movement.

Some ideas of how rhythm may enhance fundamental movement skills follow.

Walking

1. Walk forward one phrase (8 counts) and change directions. Continue to change at the end of each phrase.
2. Use high steps during one phrase and low steps during the next.
3. Walk forward for one phrase and sideward during the next. The side step can be a draw step, or it can be of the grapevine type. To do a grapevine step to the left, lead with the left foot with a step directly to the side. The right foot crosses *behind* the left and then in front on the next step with that foot. The pattern is a step left, cross right (behind), step left, cross right (in front), and so on.
4. Find a partner; face each other and join hands. Pull your partner by walking backward as he or she resists somewhat (8 counts). Reverse roles. Try using pushing action by walking forward (8 counts) as partner resists when he or she moves backward. Reverse roles.
5. Walk slowly and gradually increase the tempo. Begin fast and decrease.
6. Walk in various directions while clapping hands alternately in front and behind. Try clapping hands under the thighs at each step, or clap hands above head in time with the beat.
7. Walk forward four steps, turn completely around in four steps. Repeat.
8. While walking, bring up the knees and slap with the hands on each step.
9. On any one phrase, take four fast steps (1 count to each step) and two slow steps (2 counts to each step).
10. Walk on heels or toes or with a heavy tramp. Change every four or eight beats.
11. Walk with a smooth, gliding step, or walk silently.
12. Use a waltz with good beat and walk to it, accenting the first beat of each measure. Add a sway of the body to the first beat of the measure.

Running

Many of the suggested movements for walking are equally applicable to running patterns. Some additional suggestions for running include the following three.

1. Walk during a phrase of music and then run for an equal length of time.
2. Run in different directions, changing direction on the sound of a heavy beat or a signal.
3. Lift the knees as high as possible while running.

Skipping

Almost all of the combinations suggested for walking and running are useful for skipping movements. Combinations of skipping, walking, and running can be devised in many different fashions.

Hopping

Some variations and combinations for hopping include these.
1. Hop like a bouncing ball. Hop very high, gradually reducing the height. The procedure can be reversed.
2. Hop along a line, crossing back and forth over the line each time.
3. Draw a small circle (about 18 inches across) on the floor. Hop across and in and out of the circle.
4. Hop in different figures like a circle, triangle, square, et cetera.
5. Trace out numbers by hopping. Try writing short words by hopping.
6. Alternate big and little hops. Form other combinations.
7. Hop on one foot a specific number of times and change to the other foot.
8. Turn around, hopping in place.

Jumping

The suggestions listed for hopping can be applied to jumping. In addition, the teacher can devise other movement patterns such as these.
1. Jump with the body stiff and arms held at the sides.
2. Jump and turn in the air. Quarter-, half-, and even full turns can be done to rhythm. Work gradually into full turns. Turn every four or eight counts.
3. Combine jumping in combination with hopping, walking, running, and skipping.
4. Increase and decrease the speed of jumping.
5. Land with feet apart or crossed. Alternate feet forward and back.

Leaping

Leaping is usually combined with running, since a series of leaps is difficult to maintain. It can be included in a running sequence, using the musical phrase as the cue. An excellent piece to use for leaping is "Pop Goes the Weasel." The youngsters can take a leap on the "pop" part of the piece.

Leaping provides a break in the movement pattern and is not readily performed to music with a steady beat. Special music in basic rhythm sets provides excellent rhythm cueing for leaping. A drumbeat pattern can be modified for running and leaping sequences.

Sliding

A novel way to adapt sliding patterns to rhythm is to move sideways in one direction for a number of slides and then do a half-turn in the air, continuing the slide in the same direction but leading with the other foot.

Galloping

Because the gallop provides a foundation for, and a means to teach, the polka, it is important that the children learn to change the leading foot. First, the leading foot can be maintained for a series of eight gallops and then changed. Later, the changes can be reduced to four and finally to two gallops. Changes of this nature have value in perceptual-motor development.

Draw Step

The draw step is a two-count movement to either side. A step is made directly to the side, and on the second count the other foot is drawn up to it. The cue is "left (or right), close; left close," and so on.

Fundamental Nonlocomotor Movements to Rhythm

Nonlocomotor movements include those movements the body is able to execute while the feet remain in place. They provide for dramatic and expressive movement and involve movements by the arms, legs, head, and torso, singly or in combination. Specific movements used in this portion of the rhythmic program include swinging, circling, rotating, twisting, lowering, raising, bending, extending, flexing, and combinations of the movements. Large, free, unhampered movements to the full range of flexibility are a goal. Instruction can range from specific movements to creative opportunity of free choice.

Combination Movement Routines

Children love combination movement routines of their own or those outlined by the teacher that are guided by a drumbeat, a record, or a created tape. A few examples are given below.

With a Drumbeat

1. Walk eight steps (eight moderate beats).
2. Run seven steps and stop (eight quick beats accenting the last beat for a stop).
3. Turn one way in place, partially crouched (four light taps on the rim of the drum, making a wooden sound).
4. Unturn (opposite direction) (four light taps repeated).
5. Explosive movements in place; reach and grab, repeat (two fast, heavy beats).
6. Repeat, using the other hand (two fast, heavy beats).

7. Hold specified shape (very fast, light beats for 5 seconds).

Innumerable combinations are possible. The routine can be repeated, and members of the class can make up their own combinations.

With a Record

Movements are done in personal space, with each group of movements requiring 32 counts or beats of the music. The record can be a polka, a schottische, a Tijuana Brass number, or a piece from the jazz age; any piece that has a definite, stimulating rhythm is appropriate.

Group 1: 32 counts—clap 8, rest 8, clap 8, rest 8.

Group 2: 32 counts—jump in place 8, rest 8, and repeat 16.

Group 3: 32 counts—clap 8, jump in place 8, and repeat 16.

Group 4: 32 counts—repeat group 3.

This generally completes one full pattern of the music for pieces that have a verse part and a chorus.

Other variations of movement in place can be employed, including hopping on one foot either free or with the other foot tapping, hopping with the knee up and slapping that thigh, hopping with a forward or backward lean, turning in place, and others.

Rhythmic Object Handling and Manipulative Activities

An area of challenge for developing manipulative skills lies in applying rhythm to ball skills, rope-jumping routines, and (occasionally) hoops, wands, and chairs. Since these activities extend the learning sequences in the areas mentioned, they are presented in conjunction with those progressions (ball skills, page 258; rope jumping, page 283; and hoops, page 274).

CREATIVE RHYTHMS

Creativity should be a part, in some degree, of all dance and rhythmic activities, with the scope of the activity determining the degree of freedom.

Creative rhythms, however, provide a special area in the rhythmic program where creativity is the goal and functional movement is secondary. The emphasis is on the process and not the movement outcomes. A flow of ideas comes from within the individual and is expressed in movement language. The goal is to communicate feelings through movement guided by rhythm. Creativity can take several discernible forms.

Creativity for the child manifests itself in the opportunity to respond with self-expression within the scope of the movement area, which can range from total freedom to movements within previously stated limits. As long as the child stays within the general lesson guidelines set by the teacher, in creativity there is no wrong or right. The child's judgment should be respected, and one looks for original interpretations. Stimulation should be positive in nature, guiding the movement patterns by suggestions, questions, encouragement, and challenges, helping the children to structure their ideas, and helping them to change and add variety. Careful guidance is necessary to fan the spark of self-direction, since freedom in itself does not automatically develop creativity. Direction and structure are needed to help each child express himself or herself with a flow of unique ideas, encouraging him or her to explore, interpret, and express himself or herself in varied and original movements as he or she reacts to the rhythm.

Instructional Procedures

Appropriate music or rhythmic background is important; otherwise, movement can become stilted or artificial. There are many specialized record sets on the market today that provide excellent background in a variety of creative approaches. In addition, selected records can be adapted to creative movement. The drum or tom-tom can be used effectively, as well as other percussion instruments. A rhythm band can be organized for a particular creative presentation. Tape recorders allow children to structure their own rhythmic background as they wish.

An atmosphere of creative freedom must be established. The class should be comfortable, relaxed, and free from artificial restraints.

The problem-solving approach has good merit in teaching creative dance.

1. Presenting the Setting: What is the basic idea? What expressive movements can be expected? What are the guidelines or boundaries of movement? What space are they to use?
2. Acquiring the Mood or Impact of the Rhythm: Listening is an important element, since children must get the mood or sense of the rhythmic background. Some questions that can be posed to the children are "what does the music make us think of?" and "what does the music tell us to do?"

If the movement or interpretation is preselected, then little time should be wasted in getting action underway. Provide enough of the music so that the children can grasp the impact; have the children clap the beat if necessary and then move into action. Action-directing statements can be: "Let's pretend we are . . . ," "Let's try being like a . . . ," "Try to feel like a . . . ," and "Make believe you are . . ."

In some lessons, the focus may be partially on the selection of appropriate rhythmic background. This is true when the children formulate a creative rhythm of the dramatic type and seek suitable music for their dance.

3. Developing the Idea: The children are given time to develop and try out their ideas and come up with their own solutions. This is an open-ended approach, with a variety of solutions expected. Coaching and guidance are important aspects at this point. Application of the concepts of time, space, force, body factors, and flow is essential. The key is for the teacher to aid the child in self-discovery.

4. Selecting and Consolidating Movements: This step emphasizes the aspect of quality and should stress to children the need for them to come up with a pattern of their choice with emphasis on quality movement that stresses aesthetic elements. Children will be asked to put together a series of movements in a sustained pattern with emphasis on grace, smoothness, rhythmic movement, and attractiveness.

5. Demonstrating Movement Patterns: This step must be guided carefully, so there is respect for each child and his or her created movement patterns. Demonstration can be made by individuals, groups, or the entire class. Note that the teacher's demonstrations or demonstrations early in creative development are undesirable and can lead to imitative instead of creative behavior.

Suggestions for Creative Rhythms

Six different approaches are outlined, and suggestions and ideas for development are presented. The approaches necessarily overlap, and a creative idea can employ one or more of them. Suggestions are meant to serve as starting points for illustrating the kinds of ideas that can be developed.

Understanding and Relating to Rhythm

The teacher should bring in the idea of meter (2/4, 3/4, 4/4, and 6/8 times) and have children move in time to the meter. Other movements can illustrate even and uneven time, accents, phrasing, and other elements stressing the structure of rhythm.

Fundamental Motor Rhythms

Creativity can be developed through problem-solving activities involving the incorporation of various locomotor movements into varied patterns, changes in direction, changes to other kinds of activities, and the like.

The use of the tom-tom is recommended. A skillful teacher can vary the tempo, signal movement changes, and provide a variety of interesting activities. The teacher can pound out a beat, with the boys and girls moving according to the rhythm provided. Some variety can be added by the following devices: (1) upon a single loud beat, each student abruptly changes direction, or turns around, or jumps into the air, or leaps into the air; (2) a very quick, heavy double beat is given, signaling the children to stop in place without any movement or to fall to the floor; (3) various changes in beat patterns and accents can be given, with the children following the pattern with movement.

Records especially designed for fundamental movements are excellent teaching aids. Records should have sections featuring separate skills and sections guiding combinations of movement. Records can be used for both instruction and creative activities.

One teacher came up with the unique idea of having her children, seated in a circle, tap out a rhythm with lummi sticks. After the rhythm was sufficiently established, half of the class arose and moved in general space to the rhythm that was continued by those who remained seated.

Expressive Movement

Children can express moods and feelings and show their reactions to colors and sounds by improvising dances, movements that demonstrate different aspects of force, and gestures that depict different feelings. A piece of music is played, generally on a recording, and the children discuss its qualities and how it makes them feel. Children interpret the music differently, however. Moods that can be expressed are being happy, gay, sad, brave, fearful, cheerful, angry, solemn, silly, stately, sleepy, funny, cautious, bold, and nonchalant.

Identification

There are endless sources of subjects for identification interpretations, with the child in his or her own mind taking on the identity of a familiar character, creature, or object. The following ideas should be useful.

1. Animals—elephants, ducks, seals, chickens, dogs, rabbits, lions, and other animals.
2. People—soldiers, Indians, firefighters, sailors, nurses, various kinds of workers, forest rangers, teachers, cowboys, et cetera.
3. Play objects—seesaws, swings, rowboats, balls, various toys, and many common articles with which the children play.
4. Make-believe world—giants, dwarfs, gnomes, witches, trolls, dragons, pixies, and fairies, among others.
5. Machines—trains, planes, jets, rockets, automobiles, bicycles, motorcycles, tractors, elevators, et cetera.
6. Circus—clowns, various trained animals,

trapeze artists, tight- and slack-wire performers, jugglers, acrobats, and bands.

7. Nature—fluttering leaves, grain, flowers, rain, snow, clouds, wind, tornadoes, hurricanes, and others.

Dramatization

Many rhythmic movements are fine vehicles for group development. Suitable background music or rhythmic accompaniment is a necessary ingredient. Excellent recordings are also available, from short numbers lasting a minute or two to more elaborate productions like those found in the Dance-a-Story Series.

Some ideas useful for dramatic rhythms are these.

1. Building a house, a garage, or another project.
2. Making a snowman, throwing snowballs, going skiing.
3. Flying a kite, going hunting or fishing, going camping.
4. Acting out stories about Indians, cowboys, firefighters, engineers.
5. Interpreting familiar stories—"Sleeping Beauty," "The Three Bears," "Little Red Riding Hood," and others.
6. Household tasks—chopping wood, picking fruit, mowing the lawn, cleaning the yard.
7. Celebrating holidays like Halloween, the Fourth of July, Thanksgiving, Christmas.
8. Ideas using the seasons.
9. Sports activities—football, basketball, baseball, track and field, swimming, tennis, golf, and others.

An example showing how an idea can be exploited for a rhythmic lesson of creativity is called The Wind and the Leaves. One or more children are chosen to be the wind, and the remainder of the children are the leaves. Two kinds of rhythm are needed. The first indicates the blowing wind. The second rhythm is quieter and stimulates the leaves to flutter to the ground after the wind has stopped. Thus, the story divides itself into two parts, each of which offers many possibilities of creativity.

Rhythm 1: fast, high, shrill, indicating the blowing of the wind. The intensity and the tempo illustrate the speed and force of the wind. Rhythm 2: slow, measured, light beat to match the leaves fluttering in the still air and finally coming to rest at various positions on the ground. During the first rhythm, the children representing the wind can show how they would represent a heavy gust. While this is going on, the leaves can show what they feel it means to be blown about. During the second rhythm, the wind is still and the leaves are fluttering to the ground. Other characterizations could be added. Street sweepers could come along and sweep the leaves up.

Two other ideas may be of help. One teacher had success with her class by devising a game called "Guess What." The class was divided into groups, and each was given the task of acting out an idea, with percussion accompaniment. Each group put on its performance before the others, and at the completion the other groups guessed what the interpretation was. In this game, the interpretations should not be too long.

A tape recorder also can be of value in dramatic rhythms. Bits of music and other accompaniment can be put together as desired. This procedure allows for the story or the idea to be structured with its own individually designed rhythmic background.

Creating Dances

A wide field of creative endeavor is possible in this dimension. Considerable reference has already been made to this line of creativity. Efforts in creativity can vary from the structuring of simple routines to the formulation of a complete dance to a new or a familiar piece of music. Probably, the small-group method is most applicable. Students need to analyze the characteristics of the piece, determine the kinds of movements best suited to the musical elements, and design an appropriate movement routine or dance.

Creative Rhythms in the Intermediate Grades

While children at the intermediate level generally have outgrown those activities that imitate animals and objects, some creative activities appropriate to the intermediate grades are desirable. Based on the creative approach, rhythms involving fundamental skills can be valuable learning experiences for these children. The movements should be vigorous and challenging, so there is good acceptance by the more skilled, particularly the boys. Ball bouncing and dribbling routines to music have strong appeal.

Some caution should be exercised in utilizing creative activities of a dramatic and expressive nature in the upper grades. The acceptance by intermediate-level boys has been marginal at best. At a time when children are looking forward to becoming more adult, activities of this nature *seem to them* like turning the clock backward. With the abundance of suitable rhythmic materials for intermediate-level children, a repeat of the experiences of the primary grades, even if upgraded, would seem poor utilization of instructional time.

SINGING MOVEMENT SONGS

Singing movement songs include action songs and singing games. The latter term is losing favor in present-day terminology, since few of the songs really can be labeled games. In these rhythmic activities, the children usually sing verses, and the verses tell the children how to move. Considerable latitude in the resulting movements is usually the case, since the children follow and interpret the action picture of the words. A singing movement song is usually an interpretation of an old story, a fable, a celebration, or some kind of a task.

Instructional Procedures

In presenting a singing movement song, the following steps provide a logical sequence of progression. Seat the children on the floor.

1. Background: Tell something about the song, discussing its nature and meaning.
2. Analyzing the Music: Have the children listen critically to the music. They can clap to the beat.
3. Learning the Verses: Writing the verses on a blackboard or on a poster card speeds learning and saves time. It is generally better to learn one verse at a time and put it into action before proceeding with the others; but, if the verses are learned in the classroom before the activity period, then all should be learned. Sometimes, the music teacher and the physical education teacher can cooperate. The children can learn the music and the verses during the music period and add the action during the activity period.
4. Adding the Action: Arrange the children in formation quickly and proceed with the action. Encourage creative interpretation as determined by the framework of the singing movement song. Begin with the largest workable part of the activity the children can handle at one time. After this is learned, add other increments. In most cases there should be little need to practice a step pattern to be used in the activity, since most action songs involve only simple basic steps, which are subject to individual interpretation.
5. Including Variations: The teacher should be alert to possible variations that may be suggested by the children.
6. Other Suggestions: The source of music must be loud enough for the children to hear as they sing; otherwise, the singing will be out of time with the music. After the children learn the verses and can sing reasonably well, the music source may not be necessary, since the children's singing can carry the activity.

Where a key figure is the center of attention, several children may assume the part; thus, the attention is spread out and more children are involved. In activities in which children select partners during the course of the action, have the boys select girls, and vice versa. However, this is not critical for younger children, since boys can dance with boy partners and girls with girls.

Occasionally allow the children to alter the last line of a song and provide a surprise ending. A different last line can be composed, and the children can match their actions to it accordingly.

FOLK DANCE AND OTHER DANCE ACTIVITIES

A folk dance is defined as a traditional dance of a given people. In this form, a definite pattern of dance routine usually is specified and followed. In the original form, little variation from the traditional dance pattern was permitted, but elementary school physical education programs utilize many variations.

Few folk dances for kindergarten and primary children involve special dance steps. Rather, the simple fundamental locomotor movements are the basis for the dances. The more specialized steps, such as the two-step, polka, schottische, and waltz, are parts of the intermediate-level program.

A first consideration in teaching folk dance is whether or not the basic step important to a dance is known well enough to serve as the basis of the dance. If instruction is indicated, this can be handled in one of two ways. The first way is to teach the step separately before teaching the dance. The second way is to teach the dance in its normal sequence, giving specific instruction on each step as it comes up. The first way is generally more efficient, since the children can concentrate on one element, the step, at a time. The mastery of the step does not become a stumbling block for the dance, since the dance would not be introduced until sufficient skill had been acquired in the step. In some instances, the step can be learned one day and incorporated into the dance during the next class session. Children experiencing difficulty can be helped between classes and can be encouraged to practice at home.

Introducing New Steps

The ability level of the group and the degree of difficulty of the dance step concerned influence the manner in which the instruction proceeds. Several approaches may be necessary to ensure that everyone has acquired sufficient skill in the step. The following considerations are important.

Analysis of the Step

Explain and discuss the characteristics of the rhythm, the accents, and the foot pattern in relation to the rhythm.

1. Listen to the music.
2. Clap hands or tap feet to the rhythm. Emphasize the accents with a heavier clap or tap.
3. Use the blackboard to illustrate the relationship of the step to the music.
4. Demonstrate the step.

Selection of Formation: Select the formation most suitable for teaching. Progression can follow this pattern with regard to formation:

1. Scattered around the room: This is the simplest of arrangements. Children can concentrate on their own movements without the worry of coordinating with a partner or group.
2. Line or lines: A series of lines can be formed. Children move in this formation.
3. Single circle: No partners.
4. Double circle: With a partner.

Position of the Dancers: In general, each child practices first individually and later with a partner. When starting with a partner, the children can assume the side-by-side position first and then assume the closed position later if that position is the goal. Another approach to reaching the closed dance position is having the partners face each other but stay at arm's length, with hands joined.

Method of Presentation: The sequence of presentation can be repeated as often as indicated as the dancers move from individual instruction to working with partners.

1. Use a walk-through, talk-through approach without music. Let the dancers move slowly (by the numbers) as the instructor puts them through the step.
2. Increase the practice speed, still without music.
3. Practice with the music. The tempo can be slowed, so it approximates the practice speed.
4. Apply the step to a simple sequence.

The relation of cues to the accompaniment is important. The tempo of the cues should be increased to approximate the tempo of the music. It is confusing to children to practice a dance with cues given at one speed and find they need to adjust the speed of their dancing to a different tempo when the music is introduced. Music should be a slow and comfortable learning tempo, which can be increased gradually.

Movement Patterns: Steps usually should be done in place first, followed with forward, backward, or other movements. Half-turns and full turns round out the movement possibilities.

Introducing New Dances

Most dances are taught by the whole-part-whole method, wherein the largest whole part of the dance the children can grasp at one time is taught. Much of the procedure in teaching a new step is applicable to a folk dance but with modifications. The following steps are presented with the assumption that a new step has been learned and the class is then ready to proceed with the dance itself.

1. With the children sitting informally or in the formation for the dance, tell them about the dance and its characteristics.
2. Have the children listen to and analyze music for accents, phrases, or changes.
3. Singly or with partners (as indicated), the children should walk through as much of the dance as they can absorb. Practice without and then with the music, using a slowed tempo until enough has been learned to proceed to the next part. Provide at this point only the basics needed for the dance, since too many details and refinements tend to cause confusion.
4. A technique of value in the whole-part-whole method of presentation is having the children learn half of a two-part dance or a third of a three-part dance and then putting this to music. When the music comes to the part the children do not know, have them stand and listen while waiting for the repetition of the portion they have learned. Listening to the music during the unknown part of the piece emphasizes the changes and fixes the relationship of the parts to the whole in the children's minds.
5. Teach the remaining portions of the dance and put the whole together, beginning at a slow tempo and then gradually increasing the tempo to the normal tempo of the dance.
6. Add such refinements as partner changes (if the dance is a mixer), needed points of technique, and other details.
7. Change partners, and repeat the dance.

Instructional Procedures

In addition to the instructional procedures for all rhythmic activities (page 199), some procedures especially for folk dance should be followed.

1. The instructor should know the dance, have the instructional sequences determined in advance, and have the music already geared to the right tempo.
2. Get the group into formation as quickly as possible, since children can grasp the dance better when they are in formation.
3. Arrange for partners quickly and efficiently. Change partners frequently. Boys or girls can move forward or back one place.
4. Extras on the sideline should be rotated into partner dances. A good way to change is to have the dancers stand in place at the completion of the dance and leave that place *only* when replaced by an extra.
5. Give individual help with caution. Assign the more able as partners to those having difficulty.
6. Watch for fatigue, particularly when the dance patterns are quite demanding, since fatigue destroys the enjoyment of the dance. Shorten the number of repetitions.
7. Conduct activities as informally as possible in

a good social environment. Remind the dancers that courtesy is a two-way street between boys and girls.

8. Make frequent use of mixers, since they make for better sociability, add interest, and give everyone an equal opportunity to have good dancing partners.

9. Let the group know the number of repetitions the dance will go through before stopping. Either make an announcement before the dance begins or have a means by which they can know they are on the last repetition. Cue with something like "once more" or "last time," or use a hand signal of some kind.

10. Caution should be observed in stressing too heavily dancing as entertainment. Too often, dance has become only an object for adult entertainment at demonstrations.

11. Stress the enjoyment and relaxation that comes from knowing a dance well and achieving a sense of pride in its execution.

12. At times, a class can invite another class to join in a dance party, usually to do dances they both have learned. Courtesy and good social conduct can be a part.

Arranging for Partners

Arranging for partners can be a source of deep hurt or embarrassment for some children. To be acceptable, a method of arranging partners must avoid the situation in which children are looked over and overlooked. Some suggestions follow.

1. Have the children walk down the center of the room by twos. The boys are on the right side of the room and girls on the left, both facing the same direction toward one end of the room. All march forward to the end of the room, turn toward each other, and march down the center by twos and into a circle formation.

2. Boys join hands in a circle formation, and each girl steps behind a boy.

3. Boys stand in a circle facing counterclockwise, while the girls form a circle around them facing clockwise. Both circles move in the direction they are facing and stop

on signal. The boy takes the girl nearest him as his partner.

4. For square dances, take the first four couples from any of the previous formations to form a set. Continue until all sets are formed.

5. Two squads can be assigned to establish partners. The boys in one squad are paired off with the girls in the other. The squad leaders can supervise this chore.

6. The names of all girls can be put into a box, and the boys can draw names from the box to determine partners. For variety, the names can be drawn in the classroom, and the boys can escort their partners to the activity area. This process should be carried out without ostentation and in a dignified manner.

Both boys and girls should accept partners with grace and courtesy. Allow them to discuss and help set their own standards in this area. It is important to help them be at ease with the opposite sex. Courtesy should be stressed, and the children, while participating in the above methods of determining partners, must avoid changing or jockeying positions in order to try to offset the element of chance.

Formations for Singing Movement Songs and Folk Dances

The formations illustrated below and on the next page cover almost all of the action songs and dances. The teacher should be able to verbalize the formations, and the children should be able to take their places in formations without confusion. The formations are listed under single circle, double circle, and other categories.

Dance Positions

In most dance positions, the boy holds his hand or hands palms up and the girl joins the grip with a palms-down position. The following dance positions for partners are common to many dances.

Partners Facing Position

Partners are facing. The boy extends his hands forward with palms up and elbows slightly bent. The girl places her hands in the boy's hands.

Single Circle

1. All facing center, no partners.
2. All facing counterclockwise.

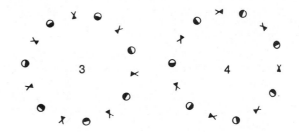

3. By partners, all facing center.
4. By partners, with partners facing.

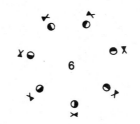

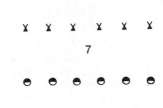

Double Circle
5. Partners facing each other.

6. Partners side by side,
   facing counterclockwise.

Other Formations
7. Longways set.

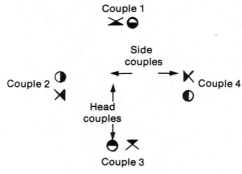

8. Square dance formation.

Side-by-Side Position

Partners stand side by side, boys usually to the left of the girls. The boy offers his partner his right hand, held above waist level, palms up. The girl places her left hand in the raised hand.

Closed Position

This is the social dance position. The boy faces the girl, holding her right hand in his left hand out to the side about shoulder level, with elbows bent. His right hand is on the girl's back just below her left shoulder blade. Her left arm rests lightly on the top of his right arm, with her left hand on his shoulder.

Open Position

From the closed position, the boy turns to his left and the girl to her right, with their arms remaining about the same. Both face in the same direction and are side by side.

Varsouvienne Position

Boy and girl stand side by side, facing the same direction. The boy holds the girl's left hand with his left hand in front. She brings her right hand directly back over her right shoulder, and the boy reaches behind her back at shoulder height and grasps this hand with his right.

Skaters' Position

This is the crossed-arm position in which the dancers stand side by side, facing the same direction, with the right hand held by the right, and the left by the left.

Example of a Lesson Plan

A guide for a rhythmic lesson in folk dance is shown on the next page.

Varsouvienne Position

Skaters' Position

Minutes	Activity
5	Introductory dance. Generally, a dance the children know and enjoy. Or it could be rope jumping to music.
5-10	Review of material from preceding class. A dance that needs practice and refinement. Time would vary according to how much review is needed.
10-15	Presentation of new material.
5-10	Older dances already mastered with emphasis on enjoyment. On occasion, finish up the period with a musical game (page 250) or a favorite game.

Kindergarten

The kindergarten list is made up primarily of singing movement songs. The list of suggested activities is not extensive, since the kindergarten program should make good use of the activities listed under the first grade. Some of the dances are individual, and some require partners. The movements demand only the simplest kind of locomotor steps. The following are suggested rhythms for kindergarten, for which the required skills are specified.

Dances	Skills
Farmer in the Dell	Walking
Baa Baa Blacksheep	Stamping, walking
Twinkle, Twinkle, Little Star	Tiptoe steps
Mulberry Bush	Walking or skipping
Bluebird	Walking
Let Your Feet Go Tap, Tap, Tap	Skipping
Ten Little Indians	Walking, Indian dancing
Pease Porridge Hot	Turning in a circle, running
Touch Your Shoulders	Identification of body parts
Put Your Hands	Identification of body parts, simple movement skills

Farmer in the Dell (English)

Records: Victor 21618 and 45-5066 (Album WE 87); Folkraft 1182.
Skill: Walking.
Formation: Children are in single circle, with hands joined and facing the center. One child is chosen to be the farmer and stands inside the circle.

Verses
1. The farmer in the dell
   The farmer in the dell
   Heigh-ho! the dairy-o!
   The farmer in the dell.
2. The farmer takes a wife.
3. The wife takes a child.
4. The child takes a nurse.
5. The nurse takes a dog.
6. The dog takes a cat.
7. The cat takes a rat.
8. The rat takes the cheese.
9. The cheese stands alone.

Directions

Verse 1: The circle players walk to the left with hands joined while the farmer is deciding on a child to be selected for the wife.

Verse 2: The farmer chooses another child, who is led to the center and becomes the wife. The child that has been selected joins hands with the farmer, and they walk around the inside of the circle in the opposite direction from that of the big circle.

Verses 3 to 8: Each child selected in turn joins the center group.

Verse 9: All children in the center with the exception of the child who is the cheese return to the outside circle. The circle stops and the children face the center clapping hands during this verse.
Suggestions: The game should be repeated until several children have had an opportunity to be in the center.

Variations

1. Several farmers may be chosen to start. When the outer circle gets smaller, the children can no longer join hands.
2. Verse 8 can be: "The cat chases the rat." During this, the cat does chase the rat in and out of the circle with the children raising and lowering their joined hands to help the rat and hinder the cat. If the cat catches the rat, the cat gets to be the farmer for the next game. If not, the rat becomes the farmer. The rat must be caught during the singing of the verse.

Baa Baa Blacksheep (English)

Records: Folkraft 1191; Russell 700A; Victor E-83.
Skills: Stamping, walking.
Formation: Single circle, all facing center.
Verse
Baa Baa Blacksheep, have you any wool?
Yes sir, yes sir, three bags full.
One for my master and one for my dame,
And one for the little boy who lives down the lane.
Directions
Line 1: Stamp three times, shake forefinger three times.
Line 2: Nod head twice and hold up three fingers.
Line 3: Bow to the person on the right and then to the left.
Line 4: Hold one finger up high and walk around in a tiny circle, again facing the center.

Twinkle, Twinkle, Little Star (English)

Record: Childcraft EP-C4.
Formation: Children are in a single circle, facing in.
Skills: Tiptoe steps.
Verse
Twinkle, twinkle, little star.
How I wonder what you are.
Up above the world so high
Like a diamond in the sky.
Twinkle, twinkle, little star.
How I wonder what you are.
Directions: Children are in a large enough circle so they can come forward seven short steps without crowding.
Line 1: Children have arms extended overhead and fingers extended and moving. Each child takes seven tiptoe steps toward the center of the circle.
Line 2: Continue with seven tiptoe steps in place making a full turn around.
Line 3: Each child makes an overhead circle with his or her arms, rocking back and forth.
Line 4: All form a diamond with the fingers in front of the face.

Line 5: With the arms overhead and the fingers extended, move backward to original place with seven tiptoe steps.
Line 6: Turn in place with seven tiptoe steps.

Mulberry Bush (English)

Records: Victor 20806, 45-5065; Columbia 90037-V; Folkraft 1183.
Skill: Walking or skipping.
Formation: Single circle, facing center, hands joined.
Chorus
Here we go round the mulberry bush,
The mulberry bush, the mulberry bush,
Here we go round the mulberry bush,
So early in the morning.
Verses
1. This is the way we wash our clothes,
   Wash our clothes, wash our clothes,
   This is the way we wash our clothes
   So early Monday morning.
2. This is the way we iron our clothes,
   (Tuesday morning).
3. This is the way we mend our clothes,
   (Wednesday morning).
4. This is the way we sweep our floor,
   (Thursday morning).
5. This is the way we scrub our floor,
   (Friday morning).
6. This is the way we make a cake,
   (Saturday morning).
7. This is the way we go to church,
   (Sunday morning).

Directions: The action song begins with the chorus, which also is sung after each verse. As each chorus is sung, the children skip (or walk) to the right. On the words "so early in the morning," each child drops hands and makes a complete turn in place.

During the verses, the children pantomime the actions suggested by the words. Encourage the children to use large and vigorous movements. Encourage the children to select other actions, such as building a house, running a farm, mixing concrete, or mixing bread.

Bluebird (American)

Record: Folkraft 1180.
Skill: Walking.
Formation: Single circle, hands joined and facing the center. One child stands outside the circle and is the bluebird.
Verse
Bluebird, bluebird, through my window,
Bluebird, bluebird, through my window,
Bluebird, bluebird, through my window,
Hi diddle dum dum dee.

Chorus

Take a little boy (girl) and tap him (her) on
   the shoulder (repeat twice more).
Hi diddle dum dum dee.

Directions: During the verse, all children in the circle lift joined hands high, forming arches, under which the bluebird weaves in and out. At the completion of the verse, the bluebird should stand directly behind one of the circle players. During the chorus, the bluebird taps the child in front of him or her lightly on the shoulders with both hands. This child becomes the new bluebird with the old bluebird keeping his or her hands on his or her shoulders, forming a train. As the chorus is sung, the bluebird train moves around in various directions in the center of the circle. When the verse is sung again, the train moves in and out of the arches. Continue the action until seven or eight children form the train. Return the train children to the circle formation and begin anew with a new bluebird.

Let Your Feet Go Tap, Tap, Tap (German)

Record: Folkraft 1184.
Skill: Skipping.
Formation: Double circle, partners facing.

Verse

Let your feet go tap, tap, tap,
Let your hands go clap, clap, clap,
Let your finger beckon me,
Come, dear partner, dance with me.

Chorus

Tra, la, la, la, la, la, la, et cetera.

Directions

Line 1: Tap foot three times.
Line 2: Clap hands three times.
Line 3: Beckon and bow to partner.
Line 4: Join inside hands and face counterclockwise.
Chorus: All sing and skip counterclockwise.
Note: This can be sung to "Merrily We Roll Along," with a little adjustment for line 2.

Ten Little Indians (American)

Record: Folkraft 1197.
Skills: Walking, simulated Indian dancing.
Formation: Children are in a circle. Ten children are selected and numbered consecutively from 1 to 10, but they remain in the circle.
Sequence: The piece is played four times to allow a complete sequence of the dance.

1. One little, two little, three little Indians,
   Four little, five little, six little Indians,
   Seven little, eight little, nine little Indians,
   Ten little Indian braves (squaws).

   During this verse, the Indians as numbered go from the circle to the center when their number is mentioned in the singing, while the remainder of the circle children clap lightly.

2. During the second repetition of the music, the Indians in the center do an Indian dance, each in his or her own way.

3. The verse under #1 is again sung, but this time the Indians in the center return to the circle when their numbers are sung.

4. During the last rendition of the piece, all children dance as Indians, moving in any direction they wish.

   The dance is repeated with another set of Indians.

Pease Porridge Hot (English)

Record: Folkraft 1190.
Skills: Running, turning in a circle.
Formation: Double circle, partners facing.

Verse

Pease porridge hot
Pease porridge cold
Pease porridge in a pot
Nine days old!
Some like it hot,
Some like it cold,
Some like it in a pot,
Nine days old!

Directions

   The dance is in two parts. The first is a pat-a-cake rhythm done while the children sing the above verse. During the second part, the children dance in a circular movement.

Part I

Line 1: Clap own hands to thighs, clap own hands together, clap own hands to partner's hands.

Line 2: Repeat action of line 1.

Line 3: Clap hands to thighs, clap own hands together, clap right hand against partner's right, clap own hands together.

Line 4: Clap left hand to partner's left, clap own hands together, clap both hands against partner's hands.

Lines 5-8: Repeat lines 1-4.

Part II

   Join both hands with partner and run around in a small circle, turning counterclockwise for the first four lines and ending with the word "old!" Reverse direction and run clockwise for the remainder of the verse. Move one step to the left for a new partner.

Variation

Part I: Children are seated on the floor, facing partners with hands braced in back for support. The movements are done with the feet instead of the hands. Instead of clapping hands to thighs, knock both heels against the floor. Otherwise, the feet do the work of the hands.

Part II: Have each child spin on his or her seat in one direction during the first eight measures and spin the other way during the next eight. Each child must keep his or her knees up and his or her heels near his or her seat while spinning to avoid contact with his or her partner. Or, during part II, have the children crawl around until they are ready to select another partner for the next sequence of the song.

Touch Your Shoulders (American)

Music: Verses are sung to the tune of "Mary Had a Little Lamb."
Skill: Identification of body parts.
Formation: None needed; children can be in any arrangement.
Verses
1. Touch your shoulders and your knees.
   Touch your shoulders and your knees.
   Touch your shoulders and your knees.
   Make your feet go stamp, stamp, stamp.
2. Touch your elbows and your toes, et cetera.
   Make your hands go clap, clap, clap.
3. Touch your ankles, reach up high, et cetera.
   Shake yourself up in the sky.
4. Touch your hips and touch your heels, et cetera.
   Jump up high; one, two, three.

Directions: The verses describe the action. Children use both hands in touching. Additional verses can be devised by the children, using body parts not previously mentioned and a different finishing line.

Put Your Hands (American)

Music: The verses are sung to this traditional American tune. The two asterisks (**) indicate the places at which the staccato-type movements occur.
Skills: Identification of body parts, simple movement skills.
Formation: None needed; children can be in any arrangement.
Note: This little piece has been utilized for a variety of singing movement songs that stress touching stipulated body parts. The following verses are suggested. The children will be able to come up with others.
Verses
1. Put your hands on your head, then your knees (clap, clap).
   Put your hands on your head, then your knees (clap, clap).
   Put your hands on your head, put your hands on your knees,
   Put your hands on your head, then your knees (clap, clap).
2. Put your hands on your shoulders, turn around (turn).
   Put your hands on your shoulders, turn around (turn).
   Put your hands on your shoulders, put your hands on your hips.
   Put your hands on your shoulders, turn around (turn).
3. Put your hands on your toes, then your nose (stamp, stamp).
   Put your hands on your toes, then your nose (stamp, stamp).
   Put your hands on your toes, put your hands on your nose.
   Put your hands on your toes, then your nose (stamp, stamp).

Put Your Hands

Teaching Hint: Encourage the children to formulate other verses.

First Grade

The first-grade singing movement songs and folk dances are introductory in nature and involve simple formations and uncomplicated changes. The movements are primarily walking, skipping, and running. Only a few of the dances are done with partners, so the problem of getting the boys and girls paired off as partners is not important. Most of the activities are quite flexible, and the children can interpret the words and music in various ways.

The rhythmic activities listed under the kindergarten program should be added to the list of suggested activities.

Dances	Skills
Guess What I Am Now!	Levels, shapes
The Farmer in the Wheat	Skipping, walking
London Bridge	Walking
The Muffin Man	Skipping
Oats, Peas, Beans, and Barley Grow	Walking, skipping
Looby Loo	Skipping
Pussy Cat	Walking, draw step, jumping
The Thread Follows the Needle	Walking
I See You	Skipping, two-handed swing
Sing a Song of Sixpence	Walking
Dance of Greeting	Running, bowing, curtsying
Hickory Dickory Dock	Running
Chimes of Dunkirk	Sliding

Guess What I Am Now! (American)

Music: The following is played.
Skills: Changes in level, shapes.
Formation: Single circle, facing center. One child, the guesser, is blindfolded and stands in the center of the circle. Another child, a member of the circle, is designated as the leader of the action.
Verse
I'm very, very tall,
I'm very, very small.
Sometimes tall, sometimes small,
Guess what I am now!
Action
Circle members stretch tall.
Make themselves as small as possible.
Stretch tall and then small.
Hold either tall or small.
Directions: Just before the last line, the leader points up or down and the circle members take the position indicated. The guesser (blindfolded) then attempts to guess whether the group is tall or small. If he or she guesses correctly, he or she then chooses another child. If he or she guesses incorrectly, he or she gets another turn. At the completion of the second turn, whether the guesser is right or wrong, another child becomes the guesser.
Variations
1. Use other terms such as wide/thin, fast/slow, happy/sad, crooked/straight.
2. Have the children hold a parachute. The guesser must stand outside the circle. At the completion of each of the four lines, the children shake the parachute.

The Farmer in the Wheat (American)

Records: Victor 21618 and 45-5066; Folkraft 1182. Same music as "Farmer in the Dell."
Skills: Skipping, walking.
Formation: Single circle, facing center. Three children—the farmer, the sun, and the rain—stand in the center.
Verses
1. The farmer in the wheat.
   The farmer in the wheat.
   Heigh-ho, the dairy-o,
   The farmer in the wheat.
2. The farmer sows his wheat, et cetera.
3. He covers them with dirt, et cetera.
4. The sun begins to shine, et cetera.

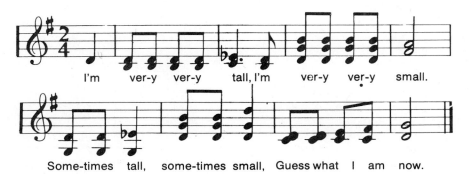

I'm Very, Very Small

5. The rain begins to fall, et cetera.
6. The wheat begins to grow, et cetera.
7. The farmer cuts his grain, et cetera.
8. The farmer stacks his grain, et cetera.
9. They all begin to dance, et cetera.

Directions

Verse 1: Children in the circle walk to the left with hands joined.

Verse 2: The farmer skips around the inside of the circle counterclockwise and sows his or her wheat, while the children continue to walk.

Verse 3: The children stop, drop hands, and face the center. The farmer skips around the circle, tapping each child on the head; as he or she is touched, the child sinks down to the ground, becoming a wheat stalk.

Verse 4: The sun skips around spreading sunshine.

Verse 5: The rain skips around showering the wheat.

Verse 6: Children rise slowly and jerkily to a standing position, with arms overhead to simulate the heads of wheat.

Verse 7: The farmer skips around the inside of the circle and cuts the grain. Each child falls to the ground.

Verse 8: The farmer skips around the group, arranging children by pairs to lean against each other to form stacks.

Verse 9: Paired children, inside hands joined, skip counterclockwise around the circle. The farmer, sun, and rain form a small circle and skip clockwise.

Teaching Hint: It may be necessary to repeat verse 8, since it takes time to stack the grain.

London Bridge (English)

Record: Victor 20806.
Skill: Walking.
Formation: Single circle moving either clockwise or counterclockwise. Two children are chosen to form the bridge. They face and join hands, holding them high in the air to represent a bridge ready to fall.

Verses

1. London Bridge is falling down,
   Falling down, falling down.
   London Bridge is falling down,
   My fair lady.
2. Build it up with iron bars, et cetera.
3. Iron bars will rust away, et cetera.
4. Build it up with gold and silver, et cetera.
5. Gold and silver I have not, et cetera.
6. Build it up with pins and needles, et cetera.
7. Pins and needles rust and bend, et cetera.
8. Build it up with penny loaves, et cetera.
9. Penny loaves will tumble down, et cetera.
10. Here's a prisoner I have got, et cetera.

11. What's the prisoner done to you? et cetera.
12. Stole my watch and bracelet too, et cetera.
13. What'll you take to set him free? et cetera.
14. One hundred pounds will set him free, et cetera.
15. One hundred pounds we don't have, et cetera.
16. Then off to prison he (or she) must go, et cetera.

Directions: All children pass under the bridge in a single line. When the words "my fair lady" are sung, the bridge falls and the child caught is a prisoner. He or she must choose either gold or silver and must stand behind the side of the bridge that represents his or her choice. No one must know which side is gold and which silver until after he or she has made the choice as a prisoner. When all have been caught, the game ends with a tug-of-war.

Variations

1. Use two or three bridges to speed up the action.
2. The game can be played in a way similar to Arches (page 251). There is no tug-of-war in this version, since the children just form more arches.
3. In Head and Shoulders, Knees and Toes, the tune of "London Bridge" is used for a body-parts action song. The following is an example of the kind of action verses the children themselves can compose.

   Head and shoulders, knees and toes,
   Knees and toes, knees and toes;
   Head and shoulders, knees and toes,
   Turn yourself around.

   Movements of the hands touch the body parts as indicated by the words.

The Muffin Man (English)

Record: Folkraft 1188.
Skill: Skipping.
Formation: Children are in a single circle, facing the center, with hands joined. One child, the muffin man, is in the center.

Verses

1. Oh, do you know the muffin man,
   The muffin man, the muffin man?
   Oh, do you know the muffin man,
   Who lives in Drury Lane?
2. Oh, yes we know the muffin man, et cetera.
3. Four of us know the muffin man, et cetera.
4. Eight of us know the muffin man, et cetera.
5. Sixteen of us know the muffin man, et cetera.
6. All of us know the muffin man, et cetera.

Directions

Verse 1: The children in the circle stand still and sing, while the muffin man skips around the circle. He or she chooses a partner by skipping in place in front of him or her. On the last line of the verse, "Who lives in Drury Lane," the muffin man and partner go to the center.

Verse 2: The action is the same, except two children skip around in the circle and choose two partners.

Verse 3: The action is repeated with four skipping and four partners being chosen.

The verses continue until all the children have been chosen. When all have been chosen, the last verse is sung while the children skip around the room.

Oats, Peas, Beans, and Barley Grow (American-English)

Records: Victor 20214; Folkraft 1182.
Skills: Walking, skipping.
Formation: Single circle with a farmer in the center.
Verses
1. Oats, peas, beans, and barley grow,
   Oats, peas, beans, and barley grow.
   Do you and I, or anyone know, how
   Oats, peas, beans, and barley grow?
2. First, the farmer sows the seed,
   Then he stands and takes his ease,
   He stamps his foot and claps his hands
   And turns around to view his lands.
3. Waiting for a partner,
   Waiting for a partner,
   Open the ring and choose one in
   While we all gaily dance and sing.
4. Now you're married, you must obey,
   You must be kind in all you say.
   You must be kind, you must be good,
   And keep your wife in kindling wood.

Directions

Verse 1: The children walk clockwise around the farmer.

Verse 2: All stand in place and follow the actions suggested by the words of the verse.

Verse 3: Circle players again move clockwise, while the farmer chooses a partner, which should be done before the end of the verse.

Verse 4: Everyone skips during this verse. The circle continues in the same direction it has been while the farmer and his or her partner (wife) skip in the opposite direction.

Looby Loo (English)

Records: Victor 20214; Russell 702; Folkraft 1102, 1184; Columbia 10008D.
Skill: Skipping.
Formation: Single circle, all facing center, with hands joined.
Chorus: A chorus is repeated before each verse. During the chorus all children skip around the circle to the left.

Here we dance looby loo
Here we dance looby light
Here we dance looby loo
All on a Saturday night.
Verses
1. I put my right hand in
   I take my right hand out
   I give my right hand a shake, shake, shake,
   And turn myself about.
2. I put my left hand in, et cetera.
3. I put my right foot in, et cetera.
4. I put my left foot in, et cetera.
5. I put my head way in, et cetera.
6. I put my whole self in, et cetera.

Directions: On the verse part of the dance, the children stand still facing the center and follow the directions of the words. On the words "And turn myself about," they make a complete turn in place and get ready to skip around the circle.

The movements should be definite and vigorous. On the last verse, the child jumps forward and then backwards, shakes himself or herself vigorously, and then turns about.

Pussy Cat (English)

Record: Russell 700B.
Skills: Walking, draw steps, jumping.
Formation: Single circle, all facing center, with hands joined. One player, the pussy cat, is in the center. If desired, more than one pussy cat can be in the center.
Verse
Pussy Cat, Pussy Cat, where have you been?
I've been to London to visit the Queen!
Pussy Cat, Pussy Cat, what did you there?
I frightened a mouse from under her chair!
Chorus: The chorus is a repeat of the same music, but the children sing tra la, la, la instead of the words.

Directions

Line 1: Sung by the circle children as they walk counterclockwise around the circle.

Line 2: Sung by the cat as the children reverse the direction and walk around the other way.

Line 3: Sung by the children as they drop hands, walk toward the center, and shake a finger at the cat.

Line 4: Sung by the cat, who on the last word, "chair," jumps high into the air, and the others pretend fright and run back to the circle.
Chorus

Line 1: Children take two draw steps (one to each measure) to the right followed by four stamps.

Line 2: Repeat to the left.

Line 3: Four steps (one to each measure) to the center.

Line 4: Three steps backward in the same tempo as line 3, followed by a jump.

A draw step is made by stepping directly to the side with one foot and bringing the other foot toward it in a closing movement. It is a step with one foot and a close with the other.

Variation: Have more than one pussy cat in the circle, or have a number of smaller circles, each with a pussy cat.

The Thread Follows the Needle (English)

Records: RCA Victor 22760 (Album E87); Pioneer 3015.

Skill: Walking.

Formation: A single line with about eight children is formed. Hands are joined and each child is numbered consecutively.

Verse

The thread follows the needle
The thread follows the needle
In and out the needle goes
As mother mends the children's clothes.

Directions: The first child (#1) is the needle and leads the children, forming stitches until the entire line has been sewn. When the music starts, the needle leads the line under the raised arms of the last two children (#7 and #8). When the line has passed under their arms, they turn and face the opposite direction, letting their arms cross in front of them. This forms the stitch.

The leader then repeats the movement and passes under the next pair of raised arms (#6 and #7). Number 6 then is added to the stitch when he or she reverses direction. This is repeated until the entire line has been stitched, with the leader turning under his or her own arm to complete the last stitch.

To "rip" the stitch, children raise their arms overhead and turn back to original positions.

The game can be repeated with a new leader.

I See You (Swedish)

Records: Victor 20432; Russell 726; Folkraft 1197.

Skills: Skipping, two-handed swing.

Formation: The boys and girls stand in two longways sets as follows.

(1)	X	X	X	X	X	X	X	boys
(2)	O	O	O	O	O	O	O	girls
(3)	X	X	X	X	X	X	X	boys
(4)	O	O	O	O	O	O	O	girls

Lines 1 and 2 are facing lines 3 and 4. The space between the two middle lines (2 and 3) should be from 10 to 12 feet. Lines 1 and 4 are the active players. Each active player's partner is directly in front of him or her and stands with hands on hips.

Verse

I see you, I see you
Tra, la, la, la, la, la.
I see you, I see you
Tra, la, la, la, la, la.

Chorus

I see you and you see me,
I take you and you take me (repeats).

Directions

Verse

Line 1: On the first "I see you," each active player looks over partner's left shoulder in peekaboo fashion. On the second "I see you," each active player looks over partner's right shoulder in same peekaboo fashion.

Line 2: Tempo is doubled and active players make three fast peekaboo movements, left, right, left.

Line 3: Repeat the action of line 1, except the first peekaboo is made to the right.

Line 4: Repeat the action of line 2, except the movements are right, left, right.

Chorus

Line 1: All children clap on the first note, and the active players, passing to the left of their partners, meet in the center with a two-handed swing, skipping around once in a circle, clockwise.

Line 2: All children clap again and each active player then faces his or her own partner, skipping around him or her once in a circle, clockwise.

Partners then have changed places with the active players, and the entire pattern is repeated with a new set of players in the active roles.

Sing a Song of Sixpence (English)

Records: Folkraft 1180; Victor 22760; Russell 700.

Skill: Walking.

Formation: Players are in circle formation, facing the center. Six to eight players are crouched in the center as blackbirds.

Verses

1. Sing a song of sixpence, a pocket full of rye,
   Four and twenty blackbirds, baked in a pie,
   When the pie was opened the birds began to sing.
   Wasn't that a dainty dish to set before the king?
2. The king was in his counting house, counting out his money,
   The queen was in the pantry, eating bread and honey,
   The maid was in the garden, hanging out the clothes,
   And down came a blackbird and snipped off her nose!

Directions

Verse 1

Line 1: Players walk around in a circle.

Line 2: Circle players walk with shortened steps toward the center of the circle, with arms outstretched forward.

Line 3: Players walk backward with arms up. The blackbirds in the center fly around.

Line 4: Circle players kneel as if presenting a dish (blackbirds continue to fly around).

Verse 2

Lines 1, 2, and 3: Pantomime action of words, counting out money, eating, and hanging up clothes.

Line 4: Each blackbird snips off the nose of a circle player who then becomes a blackbird for the next game.

Dance of Greeting (Danish)

Records: Victor 45-6183, 20432; Folkraft 1187; Russell 726.

Skills: Running, bowing, curtsying, sliding.

Formation: Single circle, all facing center. Each boy stands to the left of his partner.

Measures

1	All clap, clap, and bow to partner (girl curtsies).
2	Repeat but turn back to partner and bow to neighbor.
3	Stamp right, stamp left.
4	Each player turns around in four running steps.
5-8	Repeat action of measures 1-4.
9-12	All join hands and run to the left for four measures (16 counts).
13-16	Repeat action of measures 9-12, with light running steps in the opposite direction.

Variation: Instead of using a light running step, use a light slide.

Hickory Dickory Dock (American)

Record: Victor 22760.

Skill: Running.

Formation: Children are in a double circle, partners facing.

Verse

Hickory Dickory Dock, tick tock,

The mouse ran up the clock, tick tock.

The clock struck one, the mouse ran down.

Hickory, Dickory, Dock, tick tock.

Directions

Line 1: Stretch arms overhead and bend the body from side to side like a pendulum; finish with two stamps on "tick, tock."

Line 2: Repeat action of line 1.

Line 3: Clap hands on "one." Join hands with partner and run to the right in a little circle.

Line 4: Repeat the pendulum swing with the two stamps.

Chimes of Dunkirk (French)

Records: Victor 45-6176, 17327; Folkraft 1188; Columbia A-3016.

Skill: Sliding.

Formation: A single circle with boys and girls alternating. Partners face each other. Hands are on own hips.

Measures

1-2	All stamp lightly left, right, left.
3-4	Clap hands overhead, swaying back and forth.
5-8	Join hands with partner and make one complete turn in place clockwise.
9-16	All join hands in a single circle, facing the center, and slide to the left (16 slides).

Second Grade

The second-grade program includes many activities similar to those taught in the first grade. In addition, there is more emphasis on partner-type dances and changes of partners. The dance patterns tend to become more definite, and more folk dances are included. The movements still are confined primarily to the simple locomotor types, with additional and varied emphasis in more complicated formations.

Dances	*Skills*
Down the Mississippi	Bending, scooter movements
Did You Ever See a Lassie	Walking
Go Round and Round the Village	Walking
Shoemaker's Dance	Skipping
Jolly Is the Miller	Marching
Shoo Fly	Walking, skipping
Ach Ja	Walking, sliding
A-Hunting We Will Go	Sliding, skipping
How D'ye Do, My Partner	Bowing, curtsying, skipping
Rig-a-Jig-Jig	Walking, skipping
The Popcorn Man	Jumping, skipping

Down the Mississippi (American)

Records: To the tune "Here We Go Round the Mulberry Bush." Victor 20806, 45-5065; Columbia 90037-V; Folkraft 1183.

Skills: Bending, scooter movements.

Formation: None. Children can be scattered or in a circle, as desired. Each child is seated on the floor, with his or her legs together and extended forward.

Verses

1. This is the way we row our boat, row our boat, row our boat,

This is the way we row our boat,
Down the Mississippi!
2. This is the way we glide along, et cetera.
3. This is the way we rock the boat, et cetera.
4. This is the way we turn around, et cetera.
5. This is the way we float for home, et cetera.
6. This is the way we spell Mississippi, spell Mississippi, spell Mississippi. This is the way we spell Mississippi, M-I-S-S-I-S-S-I-P-P-I WOW!

Directions

Verse 1: Each child rows his or her boat in time to the music.

Verse 2: Each child folds his or her arms across his or her chest and bends forward and backward.

Verse 3: Each child, with arms outstretched to the side, bends from side to side.

Verse 4: Each child by rowing with one "oar" only, turns in place in stages, pivoting on his or her seat.

Verse 5: Each child folds his or her arms across his or her chest and moves in any direction he or she wishes using scooter movements, reaching out with the heels and pulling the seat up to the heels.

Verse 6: Children sing the first three lines (no action) and then sound out (spell) Mississippi in staccato fashion.

(May they never misspell Mississippi!)

Did You Ever See a Lassie (Scottish)

Records: Victor 45-5066, 21618; Folkraft 1183; Columbia 10008D.
Skill: Walking.
Formation: Children are in a single circle, facing halfway left, with hands joined. One child is in the center.

Verse

Did you ever see a lassie, a lassie, a lassie?
Did you ever see a lassie do this way
and that?
Do this way and that way, and this way and
that way?
Did you ever see a lassie do this way
and that?

Directions

Measures

1-8 Children with hands joined walk to the left in a circle. Since this is fast waltz time, there should be one step to each measure. The child in the center gets ready to demonstrate some type of movement.

9-16 All stop and follow the movement suggested by the child in the center.

As the verse starts over, the center child selects another to do some action in the center and changes places with him or her. The word "laddie"

should be substituted when the center person is a boy.

Go Round and Round the Village (English)

Records: Folkraft 1191; RCA Victor EPA 4144.
Skill: Walking.
Formation: Single circle, hands joined. Several extra players stand outside, scattered around the circle.

Verses

1. Go round and round the village,
   Go round and round the village,
   Go round and round the village,
   As we have done before.
2. Go in and out the windows, et cetera.
3. Now stand and face your partner, et cetera.
4. Now follow me to London, et cetera.

Directions

Verse 1: Circle players move to the right, and the extra players on the outside go the other way. All skip.

Verse 2: Circle players stop and lift joined hands, forming the windows. Extra players go in and out the windows, finishing inside the circle.

Verse 3: Extra players select partners of the opposite sex by standing in front of them.

Verse 4: The extra players and partners then skip around the inside of the circle, while the outside circle skips the opposite way.

Variations

1. All chosen players continue and repeat the game until the entire circle has been chosen.
2. An excellent way is having the boys in the circle and the girls as extra players. In this way, everyone will select and be selected as a partner. Reverse and put the girls in the circle and leave the boys as the extras.
3. Add a parachute for the single-circle children to hold. Children circle during verse 1, holding the parachute with both hands at shoulder height on verses 2 and 3, and again circle on verse 4. Have five or six children as extras. After they choose partners and are skipping with partners during verse 4, those chosen as partners become the new extras and the former return to the circle. During verse 4, students may have to shift positions so that they are spaced around the parachute after partners leave.
4. The dance can be done with partners, who promenade around the outside on verse 1. During verse 2, the boy leads the partner through. Verse 3 is the same, but the partners divide to find new partners. Verse 4 is a repeat of verse 2. Verse 5 is "Now promenade to London, et cetera." New partners promenade as in verse 1.

Shoemaker's Dance (English)

Records: Victor 20450, 45-6171; Russell 750; Folkraft 1187; Columbia A-3038.
Skill: Skipping.
Formation: Double circle, partners facing, boys on the inside.

Verse

See the cobbler wind his thread,
Snip, snap, tap, tap, tap.
That's the way he earns his bread,
Snip, snap, tap, tap, tap.

Chorus

So the cobbler blithe and gay
Works from morn to close of day
At his shoes he pegs away,
Whistling cheerily his lay.

Directions

Measures

1-2 Clenched fists are held in front about chest high. On "See the cobbler," one fist is rolled forward over the other three times. On "wind his thread," roll the fists over each other backward three times.

3 Fingers of the right hand form a scissors and make two cuts on "Snip, snap."

4 Double up fists and hammer one on top of the other three times.

5-8 Same action, except finish up with three claps instead of hammering fists.

Chorus: Partners join inside hands, outside hands on hips. All skip in a counterclockwise direction around the circle. Near the end of the chorus, all slow down and face each other. All children take one step to the left to secure a new partner.

Variation: For the chorus, a more modernized version can be substituted.

Shoemaker, shoemaker, mend my shoe,
Have it back by half past two.
Stitch it up and stitch it down
Make the finest shoes in town.

Jolly Is the Miller (American)

Records: Victor 45-5067 or 20214; Old Timer 8089; Folkraft 1192; American Play Party 1185.
Skill: Marching.
Formation: Double circle, partners with joined inside hands, facing counterclockwise. Boys are on the inside. A miller is in the center of the circle.

Verse

Jolly is the Miller who lives by the mill;
The wheel goes round with a right good will.
One hand on the hopper and the other on
   the sack;
The right steps forward and the left steps
   back.

Chorus: The children march counterclockwise, with inside hands joined. During the second line when the "wheel goes round," the dancers make their outside arms go in a circle to form a wheel. Children change partners at the words "right steps forward and the left steps back." The miller then has a chance to get a partner. The child left without a partner becomes the miller.

Variation: The dance can be adapted to the use of a parachute. However, the miller in the center may have to be eliminated.

Shoo Fly (American)

Records: Folkraft 1102, 1185; Decca 18222.
Skills: Walking, skipping.
Formation: All are in a circle, with hands joined, facing in. Boy stands with his girl on right.

Verse

Shoo fly, don't bother me,
Shoo fly, don't bother me,
Shoo fly, don't bother me,
I belong to Company G.
I feel, I feel, I feel like a morning star,
I feel, I feel, I feel like a morning star.

Directions

The dance is in two parts and finishes with a change of partners.

Measures

1-2 Walk forward four steps toward the center of the circle, swinging arms back and forth.

3-4 Walk four steps backward to place, with arms swinging.

5-8 Repeat all of above.

9-16 Each boy turns to the girl on his right, takes hold of both her hands, and skips around in a small circle, finishing so the partners have exchanged places, which means that the boy is where the girl was and vice versa. The circle then is re-formed, and the boy's new partner is on his right. The dance is repeated with new partners.

Variation: For the second part of the dance, the following is an interesting substitute for the two-handed swing.

Designate one couple to form an arch by lifting joined hands. This couple then moves forward toward the center of the circle. The couple on the opposite side moves forward, under the arch, drawing the circle after it. When all have passed through the arch, the couple forming the arch turns under their own joined hands. The dancers then move forward to form a circle, with everyone facing out. The dance is repeated with all facing out.

To have the circle face in again, the same couple again makes an arch and the lead couple backs through the arch, drawing the circle after them. The arch couple turns under their own arms.

In this version, there is no change of partners.

Ach Ja (German)

Record: Evans, Child Rhythms VII.
Skills: Walking, sliding.
Formation: Double circle, partners facing counterclockwise, boys on the inside.

Verse

When my father and my mother take the
    children to the fair,
Ach Ja! Ach Ja!
Oh, they haven't any money, but it's little
    that they care,
Ach Ja! Ach Ja!
Tra la la, tra la la, tra la la la la la la
Tra la la, tra la la, tra la la la la la la
Ach Ja! Ach Ja!

Directions
Measures

1-2	Partners walk eight steps in line of direction.
3	Partners drop hands and bow to each other.
4	Each boy then bows to the girl on his left, who returns the bow.
5-8	Measures 1-4 are repeated.
9-10	Partners face each other, join hands, and take four slides in line of direction (counterclockwise).
11-12	Four slides are taken clockwise.
13	Partners bow to each other.
14	Boy bows to girl on his left, who returns the bow. To start the next dance, the boy moves quickly toward this girl, who is his next partner.

Variation: In a simplified version, the children walk around as individuals, bow once, and continue. On the second bow, they take the partner's hand and walk in the line of direction until the final bow. Partners then separate.

A-Hunting We Will Go (English)

Records: Folkraft 1191; Victor 45-5064, 22759.
Skills: Sliding, skipping.
Formation: Longways set with the children in two lines facing each other, boys in one line and girls in the other.

Verse

Oh, a-hunting we will go.
A-hunting we will go,
We'll catch a fox and put him in a box
And then we'll let him go!

Chorus

Tra, la, la, la, la, la, la, et cetera.

Directions

Everyone sings.
Lines 1 and 2: Head couple, with hands joined, slides between the two lines to the foot of the set (8 counts).
Lines 3 and 4: Head couple slides to original position (8 counts).

Chorus: Couples join hands and skip in a circle to the left, following the head couple. When the head couple reaches the place formerly occupied by the last couple in the line (foot couple), they form an arch under which the other couples skip. A new couple is the head couple; the dance is repeated until each couple has been at the head.

Variation

1. On the chorus, the head couple separates, and each leads his or her own line down the outside to the foot of the set. The head couple meets at the foot and forms an arch for the other couples. The other dancers meet two by two and skip under the arch back to place.
2. The first two couples slide down the center and back on lines 1, 2, 3, and 4. Otherwise the dance is the same.

How D'ye Do, My Partner (Swedish)

Records: Victor 21685; Folkraft 1190.
Skills: Bowing, curtsying, skipping.
Formation: Double circle, partners facing, boys on the inside.

Verse

How d'ye do, my partner?
How d'ye do today?
Will you dance in the circle?
I will show you the way.

Directions
Measures

1-2	Boys bow to their partners.
3-4	Girls curtsy.
5-6	Boys offer right hand to girl, who takes it with her right hand. Both turn to face counterclockwise.
7-8	Couples join left hands and are then in a skaters' position. They get ready to skip when the music changes.
9-16	Partners skip counterclockwise in the circle, slowing down on measure 15. On measure 16, the girls stop and the boys move ahead to secure new partners.

Rig-a-Jig-Jig (American)

Record: Ruth Evans, Childhood Rhythms, Series VI, Folkraft 1199.
Skills: Walking, skipping.
Formation: Single circle, all facing center, boys and girls alternating. One child is in the center.

Verse

As I was walking down the street,
Heigh-ho, heigh-ho, heigh-ho, heigh-ho,
A pretty girl I chanced to meet,
Heigh-ho, heigh-ho, heigh-ho.

Chorus

Rig-a-jig-jig, and away we go,
Away we go, away we go.
Rig-a-jig-jig, and away we go,
Heigh-ho, heigh-ho, heigh-ho.

Directions: While all the children sing, the center player walks around the inside of the circle until the words "A pretty girl" and then stands in front of a partner. Girls choose boys and boys choose girls. The boy then bows to the girl on the last line of the verse.

He takes her hand in skaters' position, and during the chorus they skip around the inside of the circle while the circle players clap hands in time.

The dance is repeated, with the partners separating and choosing new partners until all have been chosen.

The second time the verse is sung, the words "A nice young man" or "A handsome man" can be substituted for "A pretty girl."

Variations

1. The dance can be done by alternating boys and girls and using the appropriate verses. Select four or five boys to begin in the center. They choose partners and, after the skip, return to the circle. The girls continue the dance, choosing five more boys, and so on.
2. For smaller children, an informal dance can be devised. On the verse, the children walk around individually, singing as they walk. When they come to the words "a pretty girl," the name of an animal can be substituted. On the chorus part, they imitate the selected animal. Suggest horse, pony, elephant, lion, camel, and so on.

The Popcorn Man (American)

Record: Folkraft 1180 ("The Muffin Man").
Skills: Jumping, skipping.
Formation: Children are in a single circle, facing the center, with hands at sides. One child, the popcorn man, stands in front of another child of opposite sex.
Verses

1. Oh, have you seen the Popcorn Man,
   The Popcorn Man, the Popcorn Man?
   Oh, have you seen the Popcorn Man,
   Who lives on _____ Street?
2. Oh, yes, we've seen the Popcorn Man,
   The Popcorn Man, the Popcorn Man.
   Oh yes, we've seen the Popcorn Man,
   Who lives on _____ Street.

Directions

Verse 1: The children stand still and clap hands lightly, with the exception of the popcorn man and his or her partner. These two join hands and jump lightly in place while keeping time to the music. On the first beat of each measure, a normal jump is taken, followed by a bounce in place (rebound) on the second beat.

Verse 2: The popcorn man and his or her partner then skip around the inside of the circle individually, and, near the end of the verse, each

stands in front of a child, thus choosing new partners.

Verse 1 then is repeated with two sets of partners doing the jumping. During the repetition of verse 2, four children skip around the inside of the circle and choose partners. This continues until all the children have been chosen.

The children choose the name of a street they would like to put into the verses.

Third Grade

In the third grade, most of the emphasis shifts to the folk dance. Simple locomotor skills are still the basis of the movement patterns. Continued emphasis is on the simple skills, with more attention to sliding and draw steps. The formations tend to be more the partner type, with partner changes included in many of the dances. Some basic formations are introduced that will be used in more advanced dances in the intermediate grades.

Most of the steps used in the dances—draw steps, sliding, and skipping—have been previously described and employed in dances. To these are added the step-hop and the Bleking step. To do the step-hop, the child takes a short step with one foot and hops on that foot. He or she then takes a step with the other foot and hops on it. A description of the Bleking step is found in the dance directions for the Bleking dance.

Dances	*Skills*
Paw Paw Patch	Skipping
Three Blind Mice	Skipping
Jump Jim Joe	Jumping, running, draw steps
Hokey Pokey	Turning, shaking
Carrousel	Draw steps, sliding
Children's Polka	Draw steps, running
Bleking	Bleking steps, step-hops
Crested Hen	Step-hops, turning under
Gustaf's Skoal	Walking, skipping turning
Csebogar	Skipping, sliding draw steps, elbow swing

Lummi sticks (see page 249)
Rope jumping to music (see page 287)

Paw Paw Patch (American)

Records: Victor 45-5066; Folkraft 1181, Honor Your Partner 103.
Skill: Skipping.
Formation: Children are in a longways set of five or six couples; boys are in one line and the girls are in another on the boys' right, all facing forward.
Verses

1. Where, oh where is sweet little Nellie,
   Where, oh where is sweet little Nellie,

Where, oh where is sweet little Nellie,
Way down yonder in the paw paw patch.
2. Come on, boys, let's go find her, et cetera.
3. Pickin' up paw paws, puttin' in your basket, et cetera.

Description

Verse 1: Girl at the head of her line turns to her right and skips around the entire group and back to place. All others remain in place, clap, and sing.

Verse 2: The first girl turns to her right again and follows the same path as in verse 1. This time she is followed by the entire line of boys, who beckon to each other.

Verse 3: Partners join inside hands and skip around in a circle to the right, following the head couple. When the head couple is at the foot of the line, they make an arch under which the other couples skip back to original formation, with a new head couple.

The entire dance is repeated until each couple has had a chance to be the head couple.

Instead of using the name Nellie, the name of the girl at the head of the line can be sung.

Variation: The dance can be arranged to feature the boys instead of the girls. In verse 1, substitute the name of Freddie for Nellie. In verse 2, change to "Come on, girls, let's go find him." The action is changed as follows.

Verse 1: Boy at the head of the line turns to his left and skips around the group.

Verse 2: The boy turns again to the left, followed by the entire line of girls.

Verse 3: Partners turn to the left.

Three Blind Mice (American)

Record: None.
Skill: Skipping.
Formation: Children are in a hollow square formation, facing the inside of the square, with six to eight on each side of the square. Each of the sides performs independently in turn as one part of the four-part round.

Verse (all sing)
Three blind mice,
Three blind mice,
See how they run,
See how they run,
They all ran after the farmer's wife,
Who cut off their tails with a carving knife.
Did you ever see such a sight in your life,
As three blind mice?

Description

Sides of the square are numbered 1, 2, 3, and 4. Each acts as one part of the round and begins in turn. All perform the same movements when their turn comes up as part of the round.

Line 1: Clap hands three times.
Line 2: Stamp the floor three times.
Line 3: Four skips forward.

Line 4: Four skips backward to place.
Line 5: Turn in place with four light steps.
Line 6: Face the center, raising one hand above the other, and make a cutting motion.
Line 7: Put both hands over the ears with a rocking motion sideways.
Line 8: Clap hands three times.

Sing through twice. Do not overlap the lines at the corners or there will be crowding when the children skip forward.

Jump Jim Joe (American)

Record: Folkraft 1180.
Skills: Jumping, running, draw steps.
Formation: Double circle, partners facing. Boys are on the inside. Both hands are joined.

Verse
Jump, jump, and jump, Jim Joe,
Take a little twirl and away we go,
Slide, slide, and stamp just so—and
Take another partner and jump, Jim Joe.

Description

Line 1: Two slow and then three fast jumps in place.

Line 2: Partners run around each other clockwise in a small circle in place and return to position.

Line 3: With hands on hips, each person moves to his or her left with two draw steps (step left, close right, step left, close right), followed by three stamps. Each person then has a new partner.

Line 4: Join hands with the new partner and run around each other back to place, finishing the turn with three light jumps on the words, "jump, Jim Joe."

It should be pointed out to the children that the word "slide" in line 3 results in a draw step.

Hokey Pokey (American)

Records: Capitol 2427, 6026; McGregor 6995; Old Timer 8086, 8163.
Skills: Nonlocomotor movements, including turning and shaking.
Formation: Single circle, all facing center.

Verse
You put your right foot in,
You put your right foot out,
You put your right foot in
And you shake it all about;
You do the hokey pokey
And you turn yourself around.
That's what it's all about.

Directions: During the first four lines, the children act out the words. During lines 5 and 6, they hold their hands overhead with palms forward and do a kind of a hula while turning around in place. During line 7, they stand in place and clap hands three times.

The basic verse is repeated by substituting successively left foot, right arm, left arm, right elbow, left elbow, head, right hip, left hip, whole self, and backside. The final verse finishes off with the following.

You do the hokey pokey,
You do the hokey pokey,
You do the hokey pokey.
That's what it's all about.

On each of the first two lines, each child raises his or her arms overhead, performing a bowing motion with arms and upper body. On line 3, all kneel and bow forward to touch the hands to the floor. During line 4, they slap the floor six times, alternating hands in time with the words.

Teaching Hints: Encourage the youngsters to make large and vigorous motions during the hokey pokey portions and the turn around. This adds to the fun. The records feature singing calls, but there is some variation in the action sequences of the various records. The children should sing lightly as they follow the directions given on the record.

Carrousel (Swedish)

Records: Victor 45-6179; Folkraft 1183.
Skills: Draw steps, sliding.
Formation: Children are in a double circle, all facing inward. The inner circle, representing a merry-go-round, joins hands. The outer players, representing the riders, place hands on the hips of the partner in front of them.
Verse
Little children, sweet and gay, carrousel is
    running. It will run to evening.
Little ones a nickel, big ones a dime.
Hurry up, get a mate, or you'll surely be too late.
Chorus
Ha, ha, ha, happy are we,
Anderson and Peterson and Henderson
    and me,
Ha, ha, ha, happy are we,
Anderson and Peterson and Henderson
    and me.
Description: During the verse, the children take slow draw steps (step, close) to the left. This is done by taking a step to the side with the left foot and closing with the right on count 2. This gets the merry-go-round underway slowly. Four slow stamps replace the draw steps with the words "Hurry *up,* get a *mate,* or you'll *surely* be too *late.*" A stamp is made on each of the italicized words. The circle then has come to a halt.

During the chorus, the tempo is increased and the movement is changed to a slide. Be sure to have the children take short, light slides. Otherwise the circle gets out of control.

All sing during the dance.
Variation: This dance can be done very well with a parachute. Try it first with single children (no riders) and then with riders.

Children's Polka (Kinderpolka) (German)

Records: Victor 45-6179, 2042; Russell 750; Folkraft 1187.
Skills: Draw steps, running.
Formation: Single circle, partners facing. Hands are joined and extended sideways.
  Note: Although this dance is called a polka, it does not use the polka step.
Measures

1-2	Take two draw steps to the center—step, close, step, close. Finish with three light stamps.
3-4	Repeat, moving away from the center.
5-8	Repeat measures 1-4.
9-10	Clap thighs with the hands and then the hands together in slow tempo. Clap hands to partner's hands in three fast claps.
11-12	Repeat 9-10.
13	Extend the right foot forward on the heel, place the right elbow in left hand, and shake the forefinger three times at partner.
14	Repeat, extending the left foot and using the left forefinger.
15	Turn self around in place, using four running steps.
16	Face partner and stamp lightly three times.

Bleking (Swedish)

Records: Victor 45-6169, 20989; Folkraft 1188.
Skills: Bleking step, step-hops.
Formation: Single circle, partners facing with both hands joined. Boys are facing counterclockwise and girls clockwise.
Part I: The Bleking Step
Measures

1	Hop on the left foot and extend the right heel forward with the right leg straight. At the same time, thrust the right hand forward. Hop on the right foot, reversing the arm action and extending the left foot to rest on the heel.
2	Repeat the action with three quick changes—left, right, left.
3-4	Beginning on the right foot, repeat the movements of measures 1 and 2.
5-8	Repeat measures 1-4. Cue by calling: "Slow-slow; fast, fast, fast."

Part II: The Windmills
Partners extend their joined hands sideways shoulder high.
Measures

9-16	Partners turn in place with a repeated

step-hop. At the same time, the arms move up and down like a windmill. The turning is done clockwise, with the boy starting on his right foot and the girl on her left. At the completion of the step-hops (16), the partners should be in the original places ready for part I again.

Variations: Change original position to double circle, partners facing, the boys with backs to the center.

Part I: As above.

Part II: All face counterclockwise, partners with inside hands joined. Partners do the basic schottische of "step, step, step, hop" throughout part II (see page 234).

Another excellent variation is to have the dance done by partners scattered throughout general space. Part I is as described. On part II, the children leave their partners and step-hop in various directions around the dancing area. When the music is about to change back to part I, each finds a partner wherever he or she can and the dance is repeated.

Creative Possibilities: Bleking is excellent music for creative dance with the stipulation that the children maintain the Bleking rhythm of "slow-slow; fast, fast, fast" during part I and do any kinds of movements in place that they wish. During part II, they may do any locomotor or other movements that they wish.

Crested Hen (Danish)

Records: Victor 45-6176, 21619; Methodist M-108; Folkraft 1159, 1194.
Skills: Step-hops, turning under.
Formation: Children are in sets of three, which can be two girls and a boy, two boys and a girl, or three of the same sex. One child is designated as the center child.
Part I
Measures

1-8   Dancers in each set form a circle. Starting with a stamp with the left foot, each set circles to the left, using step-hops.

1-8   (Repeated). Dancers reverse direction, beginning again with a stamp with the left foot and following with step-hops. The change of direction should be vigorous and definite, with the left foot crossing over the right in changing the direction.

Part II

During this part, the dancers use the step-hop continuously while making the pattern figures. The outside dancers release their hands to break the circle and stand on each side of the center person, forming a line of threes with the center dancer while retaining joined hands with him or her.

Measures

9-10   The dancer on the right moves forward in an arc to the left and dances under the arch formed by the other two.

11-12   After the right dancer has gone through, the two forming the arch turn under (dishrag), forming again a line of threes.

13-16   The dancer on the left then repeats the same pattern, moving forward in an arc under the arch formed by the other two, who turn under to unravel the line.

As soon as part II is completed, dancers again join hands in a small circle. The entire dance is repeated. Another of the three can be designated at the center dancer.

Gustaf's Skoal (Swedish)

Records: Methodist M-108; Victor 45-6170, 20988; Folkraft 1175; Linden 701; RCA Victor EPA-4135.
Skills: Walking (stately), skipping, turning.
Formation: Similar to a square dance set of four couples, each facing the center. Boy is to the left of his partner. Couples join inside hands and outside hands are on the hips. Two of the couples facing each other are designated as the head couples. The other two couples, also facing each other, are the side couples.
Note: The dance is in two parts. During part I, the music is slow and stately. The dancers perform with great dignity. Part II is light and represents fun.
Part I
Measures

1-2   Head couples holding inside hands walk forward three steps and bow to the opposite couple.

3-4   Head couples take three steps backward to place and bow to each other. During all of this, the side couples hold their places.

5-8   Side couples perform the same movements, while head couples hold places.

1-8   Dancers repeat entire figure.

Part II
Measures

9-12   Side couples raise joined hands, forming an arch. Head couples skip to the center, where they meet opposite partners. Each, after dropping his or her own partner's hand, takes the hand of the dancer facing him or her and skips under the nearest arch. After going under the arch, they drop hands and head back to home spot to original partner.

13-16   Clap hands smartly on the first note of measure 13 while skipping. Skip toward partner, take both hands, and skip once around in place.

9-16 (Repeated.) Head couples form the arches; side couples repeat the pattern just finished by the head couples.

Variation: During the first part of part I, where the dancers take three steps and bow, a shout of "Skoal" at the same time raising the right fist about head high as a salute can be substituted for the bow. The word *Skoal* means a toast.

Csebogar (Hungarian)

Records: Victor 45-6182, 20992; Kismet 141; Methodist M-101; Folkraft 1195.
Skills: Skipping, sliding, draw steps, elbow swing.
Formation: Single circle with partners. Girls are on the right; all are facing center with hands joined.

Part I

Measures

1-4 Take seven slides to the left.

5-8 Seven slides to the right.

9-12 Take four skips to the center and four backward to place.

13-16 Hook right elbows with partner and turn around twice in place, skipping.

Part II

Partners are facing each other in a single circle with hands joined.

Measures

17-20 Holding both hands of the partner, take four draw steps (step, close) toward the center of the circle.

21-24 Four draw steps back to place.

25-26 Toward the center of the circle with two draw steps.

27-28 Two draw steps back to place.

29-32 Hook elbows and repeat the elbow swing, finishing up with a shout, facing the center of the circle in the original formation.

Variation: Instead of the elbow turn, partners may use the Hungarian turn. Partners stand side by side and put the right arm around the partner's waist. The left arm is held out to the side, elbow bent, with the hand pointing up and the palm facing the dancer.

Fourth Grade

Basic Dance Steps

Two-step, Indian steps, marching, rope-jumping steps

Suggested Dances

Bingo
American Indian Dances
Glow Worm Mixer
Grand March
Tunnel Under
Tantoli
Horah
Little Brown Jug
Norwegian Mountain March
Oh Susanna
Pop Goes the Weasel
Virginia Reel
Circle Virginia Reel
Green Sleeves
Five-Foot-Two Mixer
Lummi sticks (see page 249)
Rope jumping (see page 287)

Teaching the Two-Step

The forward two-step can be taught simply by moving forward on the cue "step, close, step," starting on the left foot and alternating thereafter.

The close step is made by bringing the toe of the closing foot to a point even with the instep of the other foot. All steps are almost slides, a kind of shuffle step.

Begin the instruction in a single circle, and have all dancers begin the two-step on the left foot, moving counterclockwise. Next, arrange children by couples in a circle formation, boys on the inside, all facing counterclockwise. Repeat the instruction, with both partners beginning on the left foot. Next, practice the two-step with partners, with the boy beginning on his left foot and the girl starting on her right. The next progression is having them move face to face and back to back.

Bingo (American)

Records: Victor 45-6172 or 41-6172; Folkraft 1189.
Skills: Walking, right and left grand.
Formation: Double circle, partners side by side, facing counterclockwise, inside hands joined, boy on the inside.
Note: Bingo is a favorite of young people. The singing must be brisk and loud. The dance is in three parts.

Part I

Partners walk counterclockwise around the circle, singing.

A big brown dog sat on the back porch
  and Bingo was his name.
A big brown dog sat on the back porch
  and Bingo was his name.

Part II

All join hands to form a single circle, girls on partner's right. They sing (spelling out) as follows with these actions.

Song	Action
B-I-N-G-O,	All take four steps into the center.
B-I-N-G-O,	All take four steps backward.
B-I-N-G-O,	All take four steps forward again.

And Bingo was his name.

Take four steps backward, drop hands, and face partner.

Part III

Shake right hands with partner, calling out *B* on the first heavy note. All walk forward, passing partners, to meet oncoming persons with a left handshake, calling out *I* on the next chord. Continue to the third persons with a right handshake, sounding out the *N*. Pass on to the fourth persons, giving a left handshake and a *G*. Instead of a handshake to the fifth persons, face each other, raise arms high above the head, shake all over, and sound out a long, drawn-out *O*. The fifth persons are the new partners and the dance is repeated.

Variations

1. There actually was a desperado by the name of Ringo who had quite a reputation as a gunman, whose name could be used in the dance. The wording of the verses could be changed as follows.

    There was a fast gunman in the West and Ringo was his name! (et cetera) R-I-N-G-O.

2. The dance can be adapted to the use of a parachute. At the end of part II, the end of the line "And Bingo was his name," boys face the parachute and hold it with both hands, lifting it to shoulder level. The girls drop hands from the parachute, getting ready to move clockwise. On each of the letters B-I-N-G-O, they move inside the first boys, outside the next, and so on for five changes. They then take the hands of the boys facing them and get ready to repeat the dance. The next sequence can have the girls remain in place and the boys move counterclockwise.

American Indian Dances

Most tribal civilizations included dance as an important part of their living. This is especially true of the American Indians. Dances were done in preparation for war, in harvest and other kinds of celebrations, in animal pantomimes like the buffalo and eagle dances, and in religious ceremonies. In many cases, the dance routines were quite precise, while, in other cases, there was little conformity. Many different types of steps are used in the many American Indian tribal dances. Five of these steps are described. Body positions in the dances should be exaggerated, with much bending, twisting, and turning and grotesque movements. Arms generally dangle. A tom-tom provides the rhythmic background.

The Shuffle: This is a light, one-count movement in which the pressure is on the balls of the feet, with the feet dragging on the floor. The dancers shuffle forward, backward, turn around, and move in various directions.

The Follow Step: The left foot always remains forward. First step is with the left, and the right is brought up to it. The beat is an even count.

The Toe-Heel Step: This is a two-count movement that is done from a crouched position at moderate rhythm. On the first part of the step, the foot comes down on the toes with the heel kept high in the air. On the second count, the heel is dropped to the ground.

The Heel-Toe Step: This step is similar to the toe-heel, except that the weight first is on the heel (count 1) and then the toe is brought down (count 2).

The Three-in-One Step: Four counts are needed to complete this step. With the weight completely on the left foot, the right toe is touched out to the side (count 1), moved forward (count 2), and further forward (count 3). Each of these are taps, with no weight placed on the tapping foot. On the fourth count, a step forward is taken with the right foot. The weight is then on the right foot, and the step is repeated with the left foot. The cue is "tap, tap, tap, step."

The War Dance Step: The war dance step is done to a fast beat and can be either a fast step-hop or a double bounce. The latter is in the nature of two flat-footed bounces on each foot alternating. It is fast and vigorous and accompanied with exaggerated body movements. Extreme facial contortions are a part of the war dance.

To work with these steps, have the children scatter and go through them one after another.

No attempt is made to put the steps together in a sequence. This could be a movement problem for children that uses these steps as well as others. Decide on the type of dance and let the children establish the routines together with the basic beats.

Glow Worm Mixer (American)

Records: Folkraft E1158; Imperial 1044; MacGregor 310, 3105B; Windsor 4613.
Skills: Walking, elbow swing.
Formation: Double circle by partners, all facing counterclockwise. Partners have inside hands joined and boys are on the left.

The dance is done in 16 steps and is best described in terms of four patterns of 4 steps each.

Steps	Action
4	1. Four walking steps forward.
4	2. Face partner and back away four steps. Steps should be short.

4   3. Boy changes partner by walking four steps to the girl of the couple ahead of him. The girl of that couple moves forward to meet him.

4   4. Join right elbows with the girl and make a four-step turn. At the end of the turn, release elbows immediately, join inside hands, and get ready to repeat the dance.

Variation: This can be made a get-acquainted activity. Change #4 of the above to the following: Meet the girl, stop, shake hands, and say, "How do you do?"

Grand March (American)

Record: Any good march or square dance record.
Skills: Controlled walking, grand-march figures.
Formation: Girls on left side of the room, facing the end. Boys on the right side, facing the same direction (end). This is the foot of the hall. The teacher or caller stands at the other end of the room, the head of the hall.

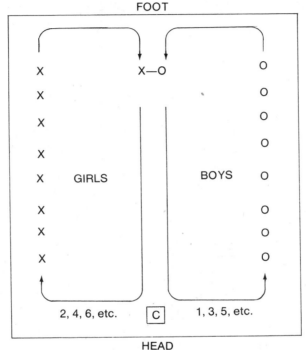

Call		Action
1. Down the center by twos.		1. Lines march forward to the foot of the hall, turn the corner, meet at the center of the foot of the hall, and march in couples toward the caller, with inside hands joined. The girls' line should be on the proper side, so that, when the couples come down the center, the boy is on the girl's left. Odd couples are #1, 3, 5, et cetera. Even couples are #2, 4, 6, et cetera.
2. Twos left and right.		2. Odd couples go left and even couples right around the room and meet at the foot of the hall.
3. Down the center by fours.		3. Couples walk down the center, four abreast. When they approach the caller—
4. Separate by twos.		4. Odd couples go left and even couples right. They meet again at the foot.
5. Form arches.		5. Instead of coming down the center, the odd couples form arches and the even couples tunnel under. Each continues around the sides of the hall to meet at the head.
6. Other couples arch.		6. The even couples arch, and the odd couples tunnel under. Each continues around the sides of the room to the foot.
7. Over and under.		7. The first odd couple arches over the first even couple and then ducks under the second even couple's arch. Each couple goes over the first couple and under the next. Continue around to the head of the hall.

8. Pass right through.	8. As the lines come toward each other, they mesh and pass through each other in the following fashion. All drop handholds. Each girl walks between the boy and girl of the opposite couple. Continue to the foot of the hall.
9. Down the center by fours.	9. Down the center four abreast.
10. Fours left and right.	10. The first four go left around the room and the second four right. Fours meet at the foot.
11. Down the center by eights.	11. Eight abreast down the center.
12. Grapevine.	12. All persons join hands in each line and keep them joined. The leader takes either end of the first line and starts around the room with the line trailing. The other lines hook on and form one long line.
13. Wind it up.	13. The leader winds up the group in a spiral formation like a clock spring. The leader makes the circles smaller and smaller until he is in the center.
14. Reverse (unwind).	14. The leader turns and faces in the opposite direction and walks between the lines of the winding dancers. He unwinds the line and leads it around the room.
15. Everybody swing.	15. After the line is unwound, everybody swings.

Teaching Suggestions: The leaders (couples #1 and #2) should maintain an even, steady pace and not hurry, or else the march becomes a race.

When one set of couples forms arches, as in movements 5 and 6, for the other set of couples to tunnel under, arches should be made with the inside arms and the couples should continue marching while they form the arches.

Tunnel Under (American)

Record: Any good march or square dance record.
Skills: Walking, making tunnels.
Directions: This is an informal, fun activity that is thoroughly enjoyed by the children. It can be used for entering or leaving the room at the beginning or finish of a rhythmic lesson. The children are in a column or partners with the girl on the right of the boy and inside hands joined. To begin—the boy and girl in the lead couple face each other and form an arch by both hands joined overhead. The next couple goes under the arch and immediately forms a second arch. The remainder of the couples in turn go through the tunnel and form arches. Just as soon as the last couple passes under, the original lead couple follows through the tunnel. The teacher should direct the tunnel so that it forms turns and corners, ending at the selected point. If the children are leaving the room, the tunnel can head eventually in the direction of the door. As the couples reach the door, they pass directly out without forming any more arches.

The tunnel can be unraveled at any time by having the lead couple, after passing under the tunnel, walk forward with the other couples following.

Tantoli (Swedish)

Record: Victor 45-6183.
Skills: Heel-and-toe polka, step-hops, two-step.
Formation: Double circle, girl on right of partner in open social dance position, both facing counterclockwise. Boy puts his right arm around the girl's waist, and the girl's left hand is on the boy's right shoulder. Outside hands are on hips. A simplified position has partners just join inside hands.

Part I

Measures	Directions	Action
1-2	Heel and toe. Step, close, step.	Tilt body backward and place left heel (right for girls) forward on floor with toe pointing up. Tilt body forward and place the left toe (right for girls) backward on the floor. Do a two-step (step, close, step).
3-4	Heel and toe. Step, close, step.	Repeat, starting with the other foot.
5-8	Repeat measures 1-4.	

Part II

Measures	Directions	Action
9-12	Step-hop.	With inside hands joined, partners take eight step-hops forward, swinging arms back and forth.

| 13-16 | Turn away. | The boys turn to the inside (left), making a small circle with eight step-hops to the girls behind them for a new partner. The girls turn to the outside (right) and step-hop one turn in place, awaiting new partners. |

Part II can be done using a two-step.

Horah (Israeli)

Records: Folkraft 1110; Folk Dancers MH 1052.
Skills: Stepping sideward, step-swing.
Formation: Single circle hands joined, all facing center. Can be a partial circle.
Directions: Horah is regarded as the national dance of Israel. It is a simple dance, designed to express joy. The traditional dance is done in circle formation, with the arms extended sideward, hands on the neighbors' shoulders. It is best to introduce the dance with hands joined in a circle. The dance can progress counterclockwise or clockwise. The clockwise version is presented. The entire pattern takes only three measures and is repeated over and over again.

Measures	Action
1	Step sideward on left foot, moving directly left.
	Step behind left with right foot (grapevine step).
2	Step sideward again on left foot.
	Hop on left foot and swing right across in front.
3	Step sideward on right foot.
	Hop on right foot and swing left across.

Teaching Suggestion: Cue by saying, "Step, step, step, swing; step, swing." Begin with individual movement and progress to circle formation.

Little Brown Jug (American)

Records: Columbia 52007; Folkraft F1304A; Columbia 36021; Imperial 1213; MacGregor 5003; Windsor 4624.
Skills: Sliding, skipping, elbow swings.
Formation: Double circle, partners facing with boys on the inside. Partners join hands shoulder high. Directions are given for the boys; girls use the opposite foot.

Measures	Action
1-4	Boys touch left toe to the side and then bring the foot back beside the right foot.
	Repeat. Three slides to the left and close.
5-8	Repeat to the opposite direction, leading with the right foot. The three slides bring the dancers back to the original position.
9-12	All clap hands to thighs three times.
	Clap partner's left hand three times.
	Clap partner's right hand three times.
	Partners clap both hands three times.
13-14	Partners hook right elbows and skip around until the boy faces the next girl, the one who *was* on his right in the original formation.
15-16	Boy hooks left elbow with this girl who is his new partner. He skips completely around her with a left elbow swing, back to the center of the circle, and all get ready to repeat the dance.

Teaching Suggestion: When the boy hooks right elbow, he has only to make about a three-quarter-turn until he faces the girl who is to be his new partner. When hooking elbows, hands should be pointed toward the floor.

Norwegian Mountain March

Records: Victor 45-6173, 20151; Folkraft 1177.
Skills: Waltz run, turning under.
Formation: Sets of threes, one boy and two girls or one girl and two boys. The boy stands in front with the two girls behind him, forming a triangle. The girls join inside hands and the boy reaches back to take the girls' outside hands. The dance portrays a guide leading two climbers up a mountain.
Note: The basic step of the dance is a fast waltz run with the first beat of each measure accented, and the bodies of the dancers should sway to the music. Throughout the dance, the dancers keep their hands joined.

Measures	Directions	Action
1-8	Waltz run.	Run forward 24 steps, bending with and accenting the first note of each measure, beginning with the left foot.

9-16	Waltz run.	Repeat action of measures 1-8.
17-18	Boy under.	The boy moves backward under the girls' raised arms for six steps.
19-20	Left girl under.	The girl on the boy's left takes six steps to cross in front of the boy and go under his raised *right* arm.
21-22	Right girl turn.	The girl on the right with six steps turns under the boy's right arm.
23-24	Boy turn.	The boy turns under his own right arm. The dancers should be in the original triangle.
25-32		A repeat of measures 17 to 24 is made, except that the right girl goes under the boy's left arm, followed by the left girl turning under the same left arm. The boy turns under this arm to unwind the group.

Teaching Suggestion: Time must be taken to practice the turns. Plan a demonstration group.

Oh Susanna (American)

Records: Victor 45-6178, 20638; Folkraft 1186; Decca 18222; Imperial 1080, 1146.
Skills: Sliding, skipping, grand right and left.
Formation: Couples in a single circle, facing the center, with the boy on the left of the girl; all hands are joined.

Measures	Directions	Action
1-4	Slide left.	All take eight slides to the left.
5-8	Slide right.	All take eight slides to the right.
9-12	To the center and back.	Four skips to the center and four skips back.
13-16	Grand right and left	Partners face, touch right hands, walk past each other right shoulder to right shoulder and give a left to the next. Continue grand right and left until the music changes. Pick the next girl for partner.
17-24	Promenade.	Promenade or two-step around the circle.

Note: The dancers should promenade until the verse portion of the piece begins again for a repeat of the dance. During the grand right and left, if a dancer does not secure a partner, he or she should come to the center of the circle. After finding a partner, the couple joins the promenade.

Pop Goes the Weasel (American)

Records: Victor 45-6180, 20151; RCA Victor LPM-1623; Folkraft 1329; Folk Dancer MH 1501; Columbia A3078.
Skills: Walking, skipping, turning under.
Formation: Double circle, couples facing. In each set of two couples, #1 couple is facing clockwise and #2 counterclockwise.

Measures	Action
1-4	Couples walk or skip four steps forward and then four backwards.
5-6	Each set of two couples joins hands and skips clockwise one full turn, returning to position.
7-8	#1 couple lifts joined hands and #2 couple skips under to move forward (counterclockwise) to meet the next #1 couple. Repeat as long as desired.

Variation

Formation: Dancers are in sets of threes, all facing counterclockwise. Each forms a triangle with one child in front and the other two with joined hands forming the base of the triangle. The front dancer reaches back and holds the outside hands of the other two dancers. The groups of three are in a large circle formation.

Measures	Action
1-6	Dancers skip around the circle for the first six measures.
7-8	On the "Pop goes the weasel," the two back dancers raise their joined hands and the front dancer backs up underneath to the next set. This set, in the meantime, has "popped" its front dancer back to the set behind it.

Virginia Reel (American)

Record: Any good reel. Methodist M104; Imperial 1092; Folkraft 1141, 1249; Columbia A-3079; MacGregor 789; Victor 41-6180.
Skills: Walking, forward and back, arm turns, dos-a-dos, sliding, reeling.
Formation: Six couples in a longways set of two lines, facing each other, boys in one line and girls in the other. The boy on the left of his line and the girl across from him are the head couple. During the first part of the dance, all perform the same movements.

Measures	Calls	Action
1-4	All go forward and back.	Take three steps forward, curtsy or bow. Take three steps back and close.
5-8	Right hands around.	Move forward to partner, join right hands, turn once in place, and return to position. Use forearm grasp.
9-12	Left hands around.	Repeat the action with the left hands joined.
13-16	Both hands around.	Partners join both hands and turn once in clockwise direction and back to place.
17-20	Dos-a-do your partner.	Partners pass each other right shoulder to right shoulder and then back to back, and move backwards to place.
21-24	All go forward and back.	Same as measures 1-4.
25-32	Head couple sashay.	Head couple with hands joined slides eight slides down to the foot of the set and eight slides back to position.
33-64	Head couple reel.	The head couple begins the reel with linked right elbows and turns one and a half times. The boy is then facing the next girl and his partner is facing the next boy. The head couple then each link left elbows with the person facing them and turn once in place. Head couple meets again in the center and turns once with a right elbow swing. The next dancers down the line are turned with a left elbow swing and then back to the center for another right elbow turn. Thus, the head couple progresses down the line, turning each dancer in order. After the head couple has turned the last dancers, they meet with a right elbow swing but turn only halfway around and sashay back to the head of the set.
65-96	Everybody march.	All couples face toward the head of the set, with the head couple in front. The head girl turns to her right and the head boy to his left, and each goes behind the line of dancers followed by the other dancers. When the head couple reaches the foot of the set, they join hands and make an arch, under which all other couples pass. The head couple is then at the foot of the set and the dance is repeated with a new head couple. The dance can be repeated until each couple has had a chance to be the head couple.

Circle Virginia Reel (American)

Variation: A similar dance using some of the same principles can be done in a circle formation.
Skills: As listed.
Formation: Double circle, boys on the inside, with partners facing.
Action: The dancers follow the calls given and, after a series of patterns, change partners by having the boy move to the next girl to his left. The calls can come in any order, and the change of partner is made with "on to the next." The following calls work effectively:

Forward and back.	Left hand swing.	Dos-a-do your partner.	Left elbow swing.
Right hand swing.	Both hands swing.	Right elbow swing.	Swing your partner.

Green Sleeves (English)

Record: Victor 45-6175, Honor Your Partner Album #13.
Skills: Walking, star formation, over and under.
Formation: Couples are in circle formation, all facing counterclockwise. Boys are on the inside and inside hands are joined. Couples are numbered #1 and #2. Two couples form a set.

Measures	Directions	Action
1-8	Walk.	Walk forward for 16 steps.
9-12	Right hand star.	Each member of couple #1 turns individually to face the couple behind them. All join right hands and circle clockwise (star) for eight steps.
13-16	Left hand star.	Reverse and form a left-hand star. Circle counterclockwise. This should bring couple #1 back to place and they face in original position (counterclockwise).
17-20	Over and under.	Couple #2 arches and couple #1 backs under four steps while couple #2 moves forward four steps. Couple #1 then arches and

		couple #2 backs under—four steps for each.
21-24	Over and under.	Repeat measures 17-20.

Five-Foot-Two Mixer (American)

Record: Ed Durlacher Album, Series III, Record 301, Honor Your Partner Album.
Skills: Two-step, walking, turning, balancing.
Formation: Couples are in a double-circle formation, facing counterclockwise, boys on the inside holding partner in a skaters' position.

Measures	Directions	Action
1-2	Two-steps.	Take two two-steps in line of direction, beginning on the left foot for *both* boy and girl.
3-4	Walk.	Four walking steps.
5-6	Two-steps.	Two two-steps in line of direction.
7-8	Walk and turn.	The girl turns in with four walking steps, while the boy walks forward four steps. The left-hand grip is dropped and the right-hand grip is retained. A single circle then is formed, with the boys facing out and the girls facing in.
9-10	Balance forward and balance back.	Each does a two-step balance forward and a two-step balance back.
11-12	Walk around your partner.	Drop neighbor's left hand, continue grip with partner's right hand, walk four steps to make a half-circle to face the opposite direction. A new single circle then is formed, with the boy facing in and the girl facing out. This maneuver amounts simply to the partners exchanging places.
13-14	Balance forward and balance back.	All do a two-step balance forward and a two-step balance back.
15-16	Walk with a new partner.	Drop right-hand grip (with partner), keep hold of new partner with left hand, and use the four steps to walk into skaters' position with the new partner. Everyone is then in the original formation but with a new partner.

Fifth Grade

Basic Dance Steps

Schottische, tinikling steps, polka

Suggested Dances

Schottische
Schottische Mixer
Horse and Buggy Schottische
Tinikling
Ace of Diamonds
Heel-and-Toe Polka
Klappdans
Come Let Us Be Joyful
Seven Jumps
Sicilian Circle
La Raspa
Lummi sticks (see page 249)
Rope jumping (see page 287)

Teaching the Schottische

The schottische is actually a light run, but, when it is being learned, it should be made a walking step. This is also true in polka instruction. Active music will quicken the step later. The cue is "step, step, step, hop; step, step, step, hop; step-hop, step-hop, step-hop, step-hop." A full pattern of the schottische then, is three steps and a hop, re-peated and followed by four step-hops. Boy starts on the left foot and partner on opposite foot. The step can be learned first in a single circle and later practiced by couples in a double-circle formation.

Teaching the Step-Swing

The step-swing is done in the following manner. Step with one foot, usually the left for boys, and swing the free leg across. A little knee snap gives the maneuver a rhythmic action.

Teaching the Polka Step

The polka step can be broken down into four movements: (1) step forward left; (2) close the right foot to the left, bringing up the toe even with the left instep; (3) step forward left; and (4) hop on the left. The next series begins on the right foot.

Several methods can be used to teach the polka.

1. Step-by-Step Rhythm Approach: Analyzing the step slowly, have class walk through the steps together in even rhythm. Cue is "step, close, step, hop." Accelerate the tempo to normal polka time and add the music.
2. Two-Step Approach: Beginning with the left foot, two-step with the music, moving forward in the line of direction in a single circle. Gradually accelerate the tempo to a fast

two-step and take smaller steps. Without stopping, change to a polka rhythm by following each two-step with a hop. Use a polka record for the two-step, but slow it down considerably to start.
3. The Gallop Approach: Form the students in lines of six to eight on one end of the room. Have them cross the floor by taking eight gallops on the left and then eight on the right. Repeat several times. In a change from a gallop with the left foot leading to one with the right foot (and vice versa), a hop is needed. Repeat the gallops across the room, alternating four at a time. Repeat later, alternating two on each side. This is the polka step.
4. By Skipping: The polka movement also can be taught as based on skipping. If children skip twice on the same side and alternate these movements, they are doing the polka.
5. By Partners: After the polka step has been learned individually by one of the four methods, the step should be practiced by partners in a double-circle formation, boys on the inside and all facing counterclockwise with inside hands joined. Boys begin with the left foot and girls with the right.

Schottische

Record: Victor 26-0017, or any good schottische.
Skill: Schottische step.
Formation: The dance is done by couples facing line of direction (counterclockwise). The boy is on the girl's left and inside hands are joined.

There are many variations of the schottische, based upon the basic pattern of the schottische step. The pattern can be divided into part I and part II.

Part I

Measures	Action
1-2	Partners start with the outside feet and run lightly forward three steps and hop on the outside foot.
3-4	Beginning with the inside foot, run forward three steps and hop with the inside foot.

Part II

Measures	Action
5-8	Four step-hops are taken, beginning with the outside feet. A number of different movement patterns may be done while the four step-hops are taken.

1. Drop hands, turn away from each other on the four step-hops, and rejoin hands again in original position.
2. Turn in peasant position, clockwise direction.
3. Join both hands and dishrag (turn under the joined hands).
4. Boy kneels and girl takes the step-hops around him counterclockwise.

Schottische Mixer

Record: Victor 26-0017, or any schottische music preferred.
Skill: Schottische step.
Formation: Double circle by partners, all facing counterclockwise. Boys are on the left of the girls. Inside hands are joined.

Action

Two full patterns of the schottische step are done with each exchange of partners.

Part I — Four measures. All run forward three steps and hop. Repeat.
Four measures. All do four step-hops moving forward.

Part II — Four measures. All run forward three steps and hop. Repeat.
Four measures.
Boy turns in a small circle to the inside on the four step-hops to circle to the girl immediately behind him. This is his new partner.
Girl turns to the outside (right) in a small circle *in place* on the four step-hops and looks for the boy circling to her from the couple ahead.

Horse and Buggy Schottische (American)

Record: Any good schottische. MacGregor 400; Imperial 1046.
Skill: Schottische step.
Formation: Couples are in sets of fours in a double circle, all facing counterclockwise. Couples join hands and give the outside hands to the other couple.

Action

Part I — All run forward step, step, step, hop; step, step, step, hop.
Part II — During the four step-hops, one of two movement patterns can be done.

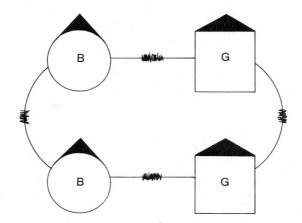

1. The lead couple drops inside hands and step-hops around the outside of the back couple, who move forward during the step-hops. The lead couple then joins hands behind the other couple, and the positions are reversed.
2. The lead couple continues to hold hands and move backward under the upraised hands of the back couple, who untwist by turning away from each other.
3. Alternate 1 and 2.

Variation: During part I, the grapevine step provides a nice challenge. Step left diagonally, right behind left, left and hop; step right diagonally, left behind right, left and hop. Part II is the same.

Tinikling (Philippine Islands)

Records: RCA Victor LPM-1619; Mico TM-006.
Skills: Tinikling steps.
Formation: Sets of fours scattered around the room. Each set has two strikers and two dancers.
Note: The dance represents a rice bird as it steps with its long legs from one rice paddy to another. The dance is popular in many countries in Southeast Asia, where different versions have arisen.
Description: Two 8-foot bamboo poles and two crossbars on which the poles rest are needed for the dance. One striker kneels at one end of the poles, the other at the other end, both holding the end of a pole in each hand. The music is in waltz meter, ¾ time, with an accent on the first beat. The strikers slide and strike the poles together on count 1. On the other two beats of the waltz measure, the poles are opened about 15 inches apart, lifted an inch or so, and tapped twice on the crossbars in time with counts 2 and 3. The rhythm "close, tap, tap" is continued throughout the dance.

A Tinikling Set

Basically, the dance requires a step be done *outside* the poles on the close (count 1) and two steps done *inside* the poles (counts 2 and 3) when the poles are tapped on the crossbars. Many step combinations can be devised.

The basic tinikling step should be practiced until it is mastered. The step is done singly, although both dancers are performing. Each dancer takes a position at an opposite end and on opposite sides so his or her right side is to the bamboo poles. This means each dancer is on the left side of the poles with respect to his or her position.

Count 1: Step slightly forward with the left foot.
Count 2: Step with the right between the poles.
Count 3: Step with the left between the poles.
Count 4: Step with the right outside to the right (for them).
Count 5: Step with the left between the poles.
Count 6: Step with the right between the poles.
Count 7: Step with the left outside the original position.

The initial step (count 1) is used only to get the dance underway. The last step (count 7) to original position is actually the beginning of a new series (7, 8, 9—10, 11, 12).

The dancer can go from side to side, or he or she can return to the side from which he or she entered.

The dance can be done singly with the two dancers moving in opposite directions from side to side, or they can enter from and leave toward the same sides. Dancers can do the same step patterns or do different movements. The dancers can dance as partners moving side by side with inside hands joined, or they can face each other and have both hands joined.

Teaching Suggestions: Steps should be practiced first with stationary poles or with lines drawn on the floor. Wands or jump ropes can be used as stationary objects over which to practice. Since the dance is popular and lots of fun, there should be a number of sets of equipment so many children can be active.

Other Tinikling Steps and Routines

1. Crossover Step: Same as the basic Tinikling step, except that the dancer begins with the right foot (forward step) and steps inside poles with the left, with a cross-foot step. Each time the dancer steps out he or she has to use a cross-step.

2. Rocker Step: Dancer faces poles and begins with either foot. As he or she steps in and out (forward and backward) his or her body uses a rocker motion.

3. Circling Poles: Dancer positions himself or herself as in the basic Tinikling step.

Measure 1
Count 1: Step slightly forward with left foot.
Count 2: Step with right between poles.
Count 3: Step with left between poles.

Measure 2
Count 1: Step with right outside poles to the right.
Counts 2 and 3: With light running steps, make a half-turn to a position for return movement.

Measures 3 and 4
Return to original position using the same movements as in measures 1 and 2.

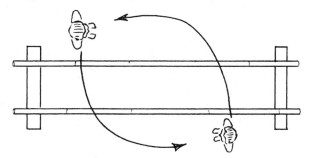

4. Fast Tinikling Trot: This is similar to circling the poles, except that it goes twice as fast, requiring only two sets of three counts. Instead of having the side of the body to the poles, as in the basic Tinikling step, the dancers face the poles. The following steps are taken.

Measure 1
Count 1: Shift weight to left foot, raise right foot.
Count 2: Step right foot between the poles.
Count 3: Step left foot outside the poles; begin turning to the left.

Measure 2
Count 1: Step with the right foot outside the poles, completing the left turn to face the poles again.
Count 2: Step with the left foot inside the poles.
Count 3: Step outside with the right foot.
 The next step is done with the left foot to begin a new cycle. The movement is a light trot with quick turns. Note that the step outside the poles on each of the count 3s is made with the poles apart.
 5. Side Jump: Begin with the side toward the poles. The dancer can begin on either side.
Measure 1
Count 1: Jump lightly in place.
Counts 2 and 3: Jump twice between the poles.
Measure 2
Count 1: Jump outside the poles, either side.
Counts 2 and 3: Jump twice between the poles.
 The feet should be kept close together to fit between the poles. The dancer can exit to the same side he or she entered or can alternate sides. Another way to do this is by facing the poles and jumping forward and backward rather than sideward. When jumping sideward, one foot can be kept ahead of the other in a stride position. The stride position can be reversed on the second jump inside.
 6. Cross Step: Beginning with the basic Tinikling position, use this sequence.
Count 1: Cross step across both poles with left foot, hopping on the right side.
Counts 2 and 3: Hop twice on right foot between the poles.
Count 4: Hop on left outside the poles to the left.
Counts 5 and 6: Hop twice again on right foot between the poles.
 7. Straddle Step: Basically, the dancer does a straddle jump outside the poles on count 1 and two movements inside the poles on counts 2 and 3. Let the dancers explore the different combinations. Jump turns are possible.
 8. Line of Poles: Three or more sets of poles are about 6 feet apart. The object is to dance down the sets, make a circling movement (as in #3), and return in the opposite direction down the line. The dancer keeps his or her right side to the poles throughout.

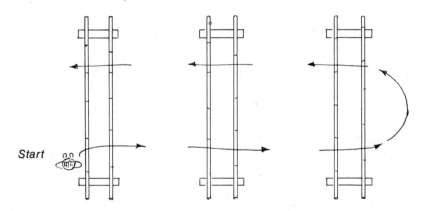

Start

 During measure 1 (three counts), the dancer does a basic Tinikling step, finishing on the right side of the first set of poles. During measure 2 (three counts), he or she uses three light running steps to position himself or herself for the Tinikling step at the next set of poles. When he or she gets to the end, he or she circles with three steps to get into position for the return journey.
 9. Square Formation: Four sets of poles can be placed in a square formation for an interesting dancing sequence.
 Four dancers are positioned as shown below. The movements are as follows.
Measure 1: Each dancer does a Tinikling step, crossing to the outside of the square.
Measure 2: Dancers circle to position for a return Tinikling step.
Measure 3: Dancers do a Tinikling step, returning to the inside of the square.
Measure 4: With three running steps, dancers rotate counterclockwise to the next set.
 Teaching Suggestions: The basic Tinikling step must be mastered if the children are to enjoy the activity. Have the children look forward, so they learn by thinking and doing and not by trying to gauge the poles visually.
 Most Tinikling music has an introduction, which the children should count out mentally in order to begin at the correct point in the musical sequence. The original dance and accompanying music calls for the

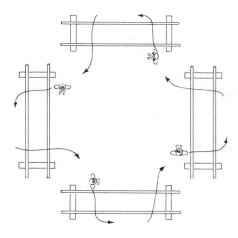

dancers to approach with four waltz steps and then four measures of the following sequence: step in place left, tap right toe between the poles, step outside with the right.

Variation: The dance can also be done to 4/4 time. Schottische music with a good beat is appropriate. Since the basic movements were originally in waltz time (three beats), adjustment of the movements to conform to four beats needs to be made.

Ace of Diamonds (Danish)

Records: Victor 45-6169, 20989; Folkraft 1176; Methodist M-102.
Skills: Walking, elbow swing, step-hops, polka.
Formation: Couples are in a double circle, partners facing, with boys on the inside of the circle. Girls, with hands on hips, are facing the center.

Measures	Action
1-4	Clap hands once, hook right arms with partners, and walk around partner clockwise for six steps.
5-8	Clap hands once, hook left elbows, and walk around partner for six steps in counterclockwise direction. Partners should be back to original places.
9-12	With arms folded high, all take four slow step-hops toward the center. The boy moves backward and begins with the left foot, while the girl moves forward and begins with the right foot. The step is made on the first beat of the measure and the hop on the second.
13-16	Four step-hops back to place.
17-24	Join inside hands and polka counterclockwise around the circle.

Variation: For measures 9-16, Bleking-type step. Partners should hop on the left foot and thrust the right heel forward. Hop on the right and put the left heel forward. Three more changes are made rapidly. The rhythm is slow, slow, fast, fast, fast. Repeat.

Heel-and-Toe Polka (American)

Records: Old Timer 8005; MacGregor 400.
Skills: Heel-and-toe polka, step-hops, two-step, polka.
Formation: Double circle, all facing counterclockwise. Boys are on the inside, and partners have inside hands joined.

Directions are for the boy. Girl uses opposite foot.

Measures	Directions	Action
1-2	Heel-toe, step-close-step.	With weight on the inside foot, extend the outside heel forward on the floor. On toe, bring the toe alongside the instep. Weight is still on the inside foot. Step left, right, left.
3-4	Heel-toe, step-close-step.	With weight on the outside foot, repeat measures 1-2, beginning with the inside heel and toe. Step right, left, right.
5-6	Heel-toe, step-close-step.	Repeat measures 1-2.
7-8	Heel-toe, step-close-step.	Repeat measures 3-4.
9-16		With inside hands joined and partners side by side, do eight two-steps in line of direction.

Variations

1. The dance can be done as a couple dance in social dance position. During the eight two-steps, the dancers can do two-step turns.
2. The polka step can be substituted for the two-step.
3. Heel-and-Toe Polka Mixer: A mixer can be made out of the dance in the following manner. The entire dance is done as described above (measures 1-16). During the next repetition of the dance, measures 1-8 are not changed. During measures 9-16, the dancers change partners by the boys turning in a small circle to the left to the girl behind them while the girl turns to her right in a small circle, returning to her position. She looks for the boy coming from the couple ahead of her.

Klappdans (Swedish)

Records: Victor 45-6171; Folkraft 1175.
Skills: Heel-and-toe polka, polka.
Formation: Double circle, all facing counterclockwise. Boys on the inside. Inside hands are joined and the other hands are on the hips.

Measures	Action
1-8	Beginning with the outside foot, partners polka around the circle.
9-16	All do the heel-and-toe polka, leaning back on the heel and forward on the toe.
17-20	Partners face each other and bow. Clap hands three times. Repeat.
21-22	Clap partner's right hand, own hands, partner's left hand, and own hands.
23	Each makes a complete turn *in place* to the left, striking right hand against right hand in turning, which is a pivot on the left foot.
24	Stamp three times.
25-32	Repeat measures 17-24.

A mixer can be made out of the dance by having the dancers on measures 23 and 24 progress one partner to the left while whirling. There would be two changes of partners for each complete pattern of the dance.

Come Let Us Be Joyful (German)

Records: Victor 45-6177; Folkraft 1195.
Skills: Walking, elbow turn.
Formation: A set is composed of two lines of three facing each other. Sets are in a circle formation. Each line of three has hands joined.

Measures	Action
1-2	All walk forward and bow—three steps and a bow.
3-4	Walk backward three steps and close (bring feet together).
5-8	Repeat measures 1-4.
9-10	Center dancer in each set hooks right elbow with partner on the right hand and turns her in place by walking around her.
11-12	Hooks left elbow with the other partner and turns her in place.
13-16	Repeats measures 9-12.
17-20	All walk forward three steps and bow, walk backward three steps and close.
21-24	Both lines advance again but, instead of bowing and retiring, move through (right shoulders pass each other) to the oncoming group of three to form a new set.

The dance is repeated.

Seven Jumps (Danish)

Records: Methodist M-108; Victor 45-6172, 21617.
Skills: Controlled movements, light step-hops, balance control.
Formation: Single circle, with hands joined.
Directions: There are seven jumps to the dance. Each jump is preceded by the following.

Measures	Action
1-8	The circle moves to the right with seven step-hops, one to each measure. On the eighth measure, all jump high in the air and reverse direction.
9-16	Circle to the left with seven step-hops. Stop on measure 16 and face the center.
	First Jump
17	All drop hands, place them on hips, and lift the right knee upward, toe pointed downward.
18	All stamp right foot to the ground on the first note, and then they join hands on the second note.

	Second Jump
1-18	Repeat measures 1-18, except do not join hands.
19	Lift left knee, stamp, and join hands.
	Third Jump
1-19	Repeat measures 1-19. Do not join hands.
20	Put right toe backward and kneel on right knee. Stand, join hands.
	Fourth Jump
1-20	Repeat measures 1-20. Do not join hands.
21	Kneel on left knee. Stand, join hands.
	Fifth Jump
1-21	Repeat measures 1-21. Do not join hands.
22	Put right elbow to floor with cheek on fist. Stand, join hands.
	Sixth Jump
1-22	Repeat measures 1-22. Do not join hands.
23	Put left elbow to floor with cheek on fist. Stand, join hands.
	Seventh Jump
24	Repeat measures 1-23. Do not join hands.
	Forehead on floor. Stand, join hands.
	Finale
1-16	Repeat measures 1-16

Teaching Suggestion: This dance was performed originally in Denmark by men as a control-elimination dance. Those who made unnecessary movements or mistakes were eliminated. Stress good control.

Variation: An excellent variation is to do the dance with a parachute. Dancers hold the parachute taut with one hand during the step-hops. The chute is kept taut with both hands for all jumps except the last one during which the forehead touches the chute on the floor.

Sicilian Circle (American)

Records: Methodist 104; Columbia 52007 ("Little Brown Jug"); Folkraft 1115, 1242 (with calls).

Skills: As listed, square dance movements.

Formation: Dancers are in sets of two couples, one of which is facing clockwise and the other counterclockwise. The sets are in circle formation.

Measures	Directions	Action
1-4	Go forward and back.	Couples with inside hands joined move forward (four steps) toward the opposite couple and return.
5-8	Circle four hands round.	Couples circle once around clockwise.
9-12	Right and left through.	Couples give right hands to the persons opposite and pass the persons opposite. Couples join inside hands and turn in place to the left so they face each other.
13-16	Right and left back.	Couples repeat and return to original positions.
17-20	Ladies chain.	Girls cross to opposite places by giving each other their right hands as they start and dropping hands as they pass each other. They give left hands to the opposite boys, who take the hands with their right. The couple then turns around in place.
21-24	Chain right back.	Repeat, chaining back to original partner.
25-28	Go forward and back.	Repeat measures 1-4.
29-32	Go forward and pass through.	Couples walk forward toward opposite couple, drop hands, and pass through. The girl walks through between the two members of the opposite couple.
		Each couple walks forward after passing through to meet an oncoming couple, forming a new set. The dance is repeated.

La Raspa (Mexican)

Records: Imperial 1084; Folkraft 1190; World of Fun M106; Columbia 38185.

Skills: Bleking step, running, elbow turn.

Formation: A partner dance, with couples scattered around the room.

Measures	Action
1-4	Partners face in opposite directions, standing left shoulder to left shoulder. Boy clasps his hands behind his back, girl holds skirt. Do one Bleking step, beginning with the right.

5-8	Couples then face the other way, with right shoulder to right shoulder. Do one Bleking step, beginning with the left.
9-16	Repeat measures 1-8.
17-20	Hook right elbows, turning with eight running steps. Clap hands on the eighth step.
21-24	Hook left elbows and repeat in the reverse direction.
25-32	Repeat measures 17-24.

Variation: This is another of those dances that can feature an informal atmosphere. During the first part, youngsters can be scattered around the room doing the Bleking step with or without a partner. During the second part, they can skip in a general space, clapping on each eighth count.

Sixth Grade

Dance activities for the sixth grade introduce three important new elements. These are the waltz, Varsouvienne, and square dancing. These, in turn, mean that more emphasis is placed on individual couple dances. The teacher must be more concerned with the change of partners, because, in some dances, the children are in a scattered formation and the usual technique of having each partner move forward so many places may need to be modified. One simple solution is to have the nearest couples exchange partners, with the stipulation that no one can dance a second time with the same partner.

Introductory material for square dancing is found in many of the dances already presented. While not actually having the dancers in a square dance set, many of the basic square dance maneuvers have been used in dances like the Sicilian Circle, which employs many of the skills needed in square dancing.

Dance Steps

Waltz, square dancing, Varsouvienne

Suggested Dances

Rye Waltz
Little Man in a Fix
Lili Marlene
Brown-eyed Mary Mixer
Teton Mountain Stomp (Mixer)
Varsouvienne
Varsouvienne Mixer
Oh Johnny, Oh
My Little Girl
Hot Time
Lummi sticks (see page 249)
Rope jumping (see page 287)

Teaching the Waltz

The waltz consists of three walking steps to a measure, one long (on the first count) and two short. The first count should always be emphasized. This gives the waltz its characteristic swing. The waltz generally is written with two measures coming together. One measure is heavy and the other light. The boy should start on the heavy beat with his left foot. The progression of teaching the waltz is the rhythm, the waltz balance, the waltz box, and the waltz turn.

The Rhythm: Have the class clap hands to accent the first beat of each measure. Work out combinations in which half the class claps the first beat and the other half the second and third beats of each measure. Let them tap with their feet.

Put the class in circle formation, with all facing in and holding hands. Have them step in place with an accent on the first beat of each measure. Start with the left foot. In the learning stages, both boys and girls follow the same directions. The cue is "*step,* step, step; *step,* step, step."

The Waltz Balance: After the dancers have learned to identify the first beat and have gotten the feel of waltz music, the waltz balance can be introduced. Retain the circle formation for this instruction. The balance is performed forward and backward first.

Step forward (count 1) with the left foot, close with the right foot alongside the left (count 2), and step in place (count 3) with the left foot. Step backward with the right foot (count 1), close with the left foot (count 2), and step in place with the right foot (count 3). Later the students will step very lightly on the third count or simply balance during this count.

The balance should be practiced to the side. The movement is step left (to the side), close right, step left in place. Step right (to the side), close left, and step right in place.

The patterns of the waltz balance should be done with partners. Both hands are joined, partners facing and boys on the inside. The boy steps forward with his left foot, while the girl steps backward right. The next progression is to perform the balance in social dance position. After some practice in the circle formation, the couples can be scattered around the room for practice.

The Waltz Box: The waltz box is the soul of waltz dancing and makes waltzing a pleasure. The box pattern should be learned individually and then practiced either in a line formation or in a large single circle. A six-count sequence, comprising two waltz measures of three counts each, is executed to complete the box, with the boy stepping either forward or backward on the first count. The forward movement is the accepted basis for learning the box.

Moving as individuals, all dancers step directly forward on the left foot, with a sliding step. On the second count, the next movement is forward and to the right with the right foot. On the third count, the left foot closes to the right. The movements for the first three counts are as follows.

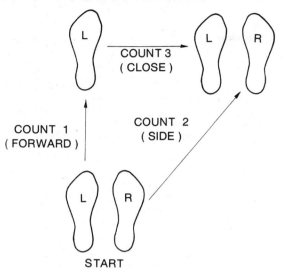

Waltz Step (three counts)

The next three movements reverse direction and laterality. The fourth count of the sequence directs the right foot to move directly backward. The left foot moves backward and out. On the sixth count, the right foot closes to the left, at which point the dancer has returned to original position. This is a diagram of the entire sequence. The cue is "forward, side close; back, side close."

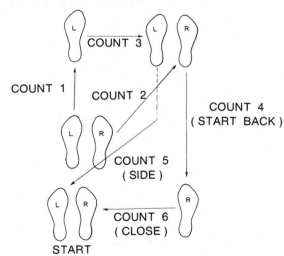

Waltz Box Steps (six counts)

Next, the box should be practiced with a partner in extended-arm position. Partners face each other and reach out and join hands. Following this, the pattern of the box should be practiced in social dance position.

The forward step movement should be practiced until it has been reasonably mastered before the initial backward step is introduced. When the students are dancing with partners on their own, they can practice informal turns before proceeding to the formal waltz turn.

The Waltz Turn: When teaching the waltz turn, it is a pivot (left), step (right), close (left); pivot (right), step (left), close (right). To pivot, the boy turns his *leading* foot to the outside, when the step is forward.

At first the children should make quarter-turns. They can check this by facing each wall in turn in a clockwise direction. Later, a complete turn is made in six counts (two measures).

The turn should be practiced individually and then with a partner. It is important to master the clockwise turn also, since many of the dances call for this turn. The dancers should learn to make progression around the room in the line of direction (counterclockwise), while the couples themselves are turning clockwise. This is accomplished easily when the boy takes the initial backward step in the line of direction.

Teaching Square Dance

Introductory square dancing is fun and a challenge for youngsters because of the adult slant of the activity. In many cases, the children have come into contact with the activity because their parents belong to square dance clubs or have been square dancers.

The teacher sometimes is concerned about being able to call square dance figures. The skill of calling does take practice and study, but, in some instances, the youngsters can call successfully. However, the fun of square dancing begins with a good, solid caller.

Singing calls, however, requires a slightly different approach. Children can learn the music and the words together with the movements. The entire group can sing while dancing, or one or more children can provide the singing call.

Innumerable square dance records with calls are on the market, and the teacher should have a variety of simple dances. Some records duplicate the music on the two sides. One side presents the music with calls, and the other, without the calls.

The fundamental skills should be a challenge but not a chore to the children. It needs to be emphasized that square dancing is continued throughout the junior high school program and the sixth grade work is only an introduction.

Teaching Suggestions
1. Teach youngsters to listen to the call. It is equally important for them to know what the call means. Youngsters are to have fun but must be quiet enough to hear the call.
2. Generally, the caller explains the figures, has the children walk through the patterns, and calls the figure.
3. It is important to follow the directions of the

caller and not to move too soon. Children should be ready for the call and move at the proper time.

4. The teacher should remember that there are many different ways of doing different turns, swings, hand positions, et cetera, and as many opinions on how they should be done. Settle on good principles and stick with them.

5. When a set becomes confused, the dancers should return to home positions (for each couple) and try to pick up from that point. Otherwise, the choice is to wait until the dance is over or a new sequence has started.

6. Change partners at times through the dancing. Have each boy move one place to his right and take a new partner. Another way is to have the girls (or boys) keep positions, and the partners change to another set.

7. The shuffle step, rather than a skipping or running step beginners usually tend to use, should be used. The shuffle step makes a smoother and more graceful dance, has better carry-over values for dancing, and conserves energy. The shuffle step is a quick walk or about a half-glide in time to the music. It is done by reaching out with the toes in a gliding motion. The body should be in good posture and not be bouncing up and down on each step.

Square Dance Formation

Each couple is numbered around the set in a counterclockwise direction. It is important to have the couples know their positions. The couple with their backs to the music is generally couple #1, or the head couple. The couple to the right is #2, et cetera. While the head couple is #1, the term *head couples* includes both #1 and #3. In some dances, couples #2 and #4 are the side couples. (See page 210.)

With respect to any one boy (gent), the following terms are used.

Partner: the girl at his side.

Corner lady: the girl on the boy's left.

Right-hand lady: the girl in the couple to the boy's right.

Opposite or opposite lady: the girl directly across the set.

Other terms that are used include these.

Home: the original or starting position.

Active or leading couple: the couple leading or visiting the other couples for different figures.

American Square Dance Figures

Honor Your Partner: Partners bow to each other.

Honor Your Corner: Boy bows to his corner, who returns the bow.

Elbow Swing: Boy turns his girl with a right-hand swing, using a forearm grasp.

Allemande Left: Face your corner, grasp corner with a left forearm grip, walk around your corner, and return to your partner. Generally, the next figure is a right and left grand.

Right and Left Grand: Face your partner, touch right hands with partner, walk past your partner, and touch left hands with the next person in the ring, and so on down the line. This causes the boys to go in one direction around the circle and the girls in the other, alternately touching right and left hands until partners meet. The girl reverses direction by turning under uplifted joined right hands, and the couple promenades home.

Promenade: Walk side by side with your partner with the right hand joined to the right hand and left to left in a crossed-arm (skaters') position. Walk around once to home position.

Swing Your Partner (or Corner): The boy and girl stand side by side with right hip against right hip. The dancers are in social dance position, except that the boy's right arm is more around to the side than back at the shoulder blade. The dancers walk around each other until they return to starting position.

Right and Left Through (and Back): Two couples pass through each other, girls to the inside, touching right hands passing through. After passing through, the boy takes the girl's left hand in his left, puts his right hand around her waist, and turns her in place so that the couples are again facing each other. On "right and left back," the figure is repeated, and the couples return to place.

Ladies Chain: From a position with two couples facing each other, the ladies cross over to the opposite gents, touching right hands as they pass each other. When they reach the opposite boys, they join left hands with them. At the same time, the gent places his right arm around the lady's waist and turns her once around to face the other couple. On "chain right back," the ladies cross back to partners in a similar figure.

Dos-a-do Your Partner (or Corner): Walk around your partner, passing right shoulder to right shoulder. Return to place by partner.

All Around Your Left-Hand Lady, See-Saw Your Pretty Little Taw: Boy does a dos-a-do with his corner girl and then passes around his partner, left shoulder to left shoulder.

Do-pass-so: Give the left hand to your partner and walk around your partner. Release your partner and, with right hands joined, walk around your corner. Return to partner, take left hand in left hand, and turn her in place with the arm around the waist. The turning movement is similar to the figure used in right and left through and ladies chain.

Circle Right (or Left): All eight dancers join hands and circle. You can add "into the center with a great big yell." The circle usually is broken up with a swing at home base.

Other Calls: There are many other calls that can be used. The figures presented are basic and provide enough material for sixth-grade square dancing. However, other sequences are needed for special dances. These can be learned as the dances are learned.

Rye Waltz (American)

Records: MacGregor 298; Old Timer 8009; Imperial 1044; Folk Dancer 3012.
Skills: Waltz step, sliding.
Formation: Couples in a closed position, forming a circle with the boys' backs to the center of the circle.
Note: Directions are for the boys; girls use opposite feet.
Part I: The Slide
1. Point left toe to side (count 1) and return to the instep of the other foot (count 2). Repeat (counts 3 and 4).
2. Take three slides to the boy's left and dip (counts 5, 6, 7, and 8). The dip is made by placing the right toe behind the left foot.
3. Repeat #1, using the right foot for pointing.
4. Repeat #2, but sliding to the right. (Some records repeat 1-4.)

Part II: The Waltz
5. Starting with the boy stepping *backward* on the left foot, waltz for 16 measures, turning clockwise.
6. At the end of the waltz, some records repeat part II. This means that the couple waltzes until the music changes and then does three slides to the left and a dip.

Little Man in a Fix (Danish)

Records: Michael Herman 1053; Folk Dancer MH 1054; RCA Victor 20449.
Skills: Waltz steps, Tyrolean Waltz step, running in waltz time.
Formation: Two couples form a set; sets are scattered out on the floor. The two boys lock or hook left elbows, having right arms around the girls' waists. The girl places her left hand on the boy's shoulder and her free hand on her hip.

Measures	Action
1-8	Turn in place counterclockwise, using 24 little running steps (three to a measure).
9-16	Without stopping, boys grasp left hands, and each takes the left hand of the partner in his right hand. The object is to form a wheel. The boys raise joined hands, forming an arch under which the girls pass right shoulder to right shoulder. After they pass under, the girls turn left, face each other, and join hands over the boys' joined left hands. The wheel continues to turn left to complete a total of 24 running steps.
17-20	Boys release left hands, and girls release joined right hands, separating the couples. The boy of each couple stands on the left of the girl, with inside hands joined. Each couple does four Tyrolean Waltz steps. The Tyrolean Waltz step leads off with the outside foot into a side-by-side waltz step. On the first measure (1-2-3), the joined hands are swung forward. On the second measure, leading off with the inside foot, a second waltz step is done side by side with the hands swinging backward. This completes two waltz steps, one to a measure. The next two waltz steps are similar.
21-24	In regular social dance position, waltz four measures with partner.
25-32	Repeat measures 17-24.

The music starts anew, and each couple seeks another couple to form a set. There should be an extra couple, whose man is the "Little Man in a Fix," since he was not able to link up with another couple to form a set. The extra couple stands by itself until the Tyrolean Waltzes are danced, at which time they join the others on the floor.

Lili Marlene (American)

Records: Western Jubilee 725; MacGregor 310.
Skills: Two-step, slides, step-swing, step and turn.
Formation: Couples in circle formation, facing counterclockwise. Inside hands are joined. Directions are for the boys. Girls use the opposite feet.

Measures	Directions	Action
1-4	Walk-2-3-4, slide, slide, slide, close.	Starting with the left foot, walk forward four steps, turn and face partner, join both hands, take three slides in line of direction and close.

5-8	Walk-2-3-4, slide, slide, slide, close.	Repeat measures 1-4, but start with the right foot and travel in the opposite direction.
9-12	Step-swing, step-swing.	Still with joined hands, step to the left and swing the right foot across the left. Step to the right and swing the left across. Repeat.
13-16	1-2-3 turn, 1-2-3 turn.	Facing counterclockwise with inside hands joined, take three steps in line of direction, beginning with the left foot, and pivot on the third count with the right foot pointed clockwise on the fourth count. Repeat, beginning with the right foot and turning (pivot) on the right foot. Couples then should be facing line of direction, with inside hands joined.
17-20	Two-step.	Take four two-steps forward.
21-24	Two-step away.	Drop inside hands and, on four two-steps, circle away from partner. Boy makes a larger circle to the girl behind him. Girl circles back to place, meeting the boy from the couple ahead.

Brown-eyed Mary Mixer (American)

Records: "Little Brown Jug," Columbia 52007; Old Timer 8051.
Skills: Two-step, elbow turn (forearm grasp).
Formation: Couples facing counterclockwise, boys on the inside. Right hands and left hands are joined in crossed-arms position (skaters'). Directions are opposite for the girl.

Measures	Directions	Action
1-4	Two-step left and two-step right, walk-2-3-4.	Do a two-step left and a two-step right and take four walking steps forward.
5-8	Repeat measures 1-4.	
9-10	Turn your partner with the right.	Boy takes girl's right hand with his right and walks around this girl to face the girl behind him.
11-12	Now your corner with your left.	Turns girl behind him with the left.
13-14	Turn your partner all the way around.	Turns own partner with the right, going all the way around.
15-16	And pick up the forward lady.	Boy steps up one place to the girl ahead of him, who becomes his new partner.

Teaching Hint: When the boy turns the girl, he should slide his hand along the girl's wrist and use a forearm grasp for turns.

Teton Mountain Stomp Mixer (American)

Records: Windsor 4615; Western Jubilee 725.
Skill: Walking.
Formation: Double circle, partners facing, with both hands joined. Boys are on the inside of the circle.
Note: Directions are described for the boys. The girls use the opposite feet.

Measures	Directions	Action
1-4	Left, right, left, stamp. Right, left, right, stamp.	Step left, close right, step left, stamp right. Repeat, beginning with the right foot.
5-6	Left, stamp, right, stamp.	Step left, stamp right, step right, stamp left.
7-8	Walk—turn.	Both face line of direction, join inside hands and walk four steps. On the last step, the boy turns around.
9-10	Walk—turn.	The boy backs four steps, while the girl moves forward four steps. Both are moving counterclockwise, the girl facing and the boy with his back to the line of direction. Both turn around on the last step. The girl then has her back to line of direction.
11-12	Walk.	Each takes four steps *forward*. The boy walks in line of direction, but the girl is walking clockwise. Each skips one person and meets the next for a new partner.
13-16	Two-step, two-step,	Both face counterclockwise, with inside hands joined. They

walk. take two two-steps, beginning on the outside foot, and then four steps in line of direction.

Variation: For measures 13-16, when the boy meets his new partner, he swings her for eight counts (twice around).

Varsouvienne (American-Swedish)

Records: MacGregor 398; Old Timer 8077; Folkraft 1034, 1165; Windsor 7615.
Skills: Varsouvienne step and variations.
Formation: Couples in Varsouvienne position. Directions are the same for both partners.

Measures	Action
1	Bend left knee and bring left foot in front of right leg on the upbeat. Step forward with the left and close with the right, taking the weight on the right foot.
2	Repeat measure 1.
3-4	Cross left foot over right instep and then step in place with the left foot. Step with the right foot to the right (behind partner), step forward with the left (alongside partner), and point right toe forward. The girl in the meantime does the same steps but almost in place, moving slightly to her left. The girl is then on the left side of the boy, still in Varsouvienne position.
5-8	Repeat measures 1-4, beginning with the crossing of the right foot.
9-10	Cross left, step left, step right, step left, point right. Retaining only the left-hand grip, the boy does the stepping in place while the girl rolls out to the left away from the boy.
11-12	Cross right, step right, step left, step right, point left. Still retaining the left hands, the girl turns under the boy's lifted left hand and walks back into the Varsouvienne position.
13-16	Repeat measures 9-12.

Varsouvienne Mixer (American)

Record: Same as preceding dance.
Formation: Couples are in circle formation, all facing counterclockwise, in Varsouvienne position.

Measures	Action
1-12	The first 12 measures are the same as the previous dance.
13-14	The girl rolls to the center with the cross, step, step, step, point. Left hands are still held.
15-16	The girl walks to the boy of the couple behind her, crossing in front of him to Varsouvienne position. They both finish with the left foot pointed.

Teaching Suggestion: The girl should look behind her to see who her next partner will be.

Oh Johnny, Oh (American)

Records: Folkraft 1037; Old Timer 8041, 8043; Decca 954; MacGregor 652 or 2042.
Skills: Square dance figures as listed.
Formation: Square dance set of four couples.

Call (All Sing)	Action
1. All join hands and you circle the ring.	1. Circle of eight moving left.
2. Stop where you are and you give her a swing.	2. Swing your partner.
3. And now you swing that girl behind you.	3. Swing the corner lady (on man's left).
4. Now swing your own if you have time and then you'll find an—	4. Swing your partner.
5. Allemande left on your corners all	5. Turn the corner lady with the left hand.
6. And do-si-do your own	6. Pass right shoulders and move back to back around partner.
7. And all promenade with the sweet corner maid singing, "Oh Johnny, Oh Johnny, Oh!"	7. Promenade with new (corner) lady.

The dance is repeated three more times until original partners are together again.

Variation: The dance can be done in a circle formation, with couples facing counterclockwise, girls on the right. The corner girl is the one from the couple immediately in back.

Teaching Suggestion: In the circle formation, couples should swing around only once.

My Little Girl (American)

Record: Folkraft 1036.

Skills: Square dance figures.
Formation: Square dance set of four couples. The caller sings the call.

Call	Action
1. First couple promenade the outside, around outside of the ring.	1. The first couple promenades around the outside of the set, while the other couples move into the center.
2. Head ladies chain right down the center and they chain right back again.	2. Ladies #1 and #3 chain and chain right back.
3. Head ladies chain the right-hand couple and they chain right back again.	3. Ladies #1 and #3 chain and chain back with the right-hand ladies.
4. Head ladies chain the left-hand couple and they chain right back again.	4. Chain with the left-hand ladies.
5. Now it's all the way around your left-hand lady—oh boy! what a baby!	5. The four boys move around their corner girls, returning to position.
6. Seesaw your pretty little taw—prettiest girl I ever saw.	6. Move around behind partners and return to position.
7. Allemande with your left hand—right to your honey and a right and left grand.	7. Self-explanatory.
8. Deedle—I, Deedle—I, Deedle—I, Do—you meet your gal and promenade.	8. Self-explanatory.
9. And listen while I roar—you swing your honey till she feels she feels funny—she's the gal that you adore.	

The dance is repeated three times, with the second, third, and fourth couples promenading. For couples #2 and #4, substitute the word *side* for *head* in lines 2, 3, and 4.

Hot Time (American)

Records: Folkraft 1037; Windsor 7115.
Skills: Usual square dance figures plus allemande right.
Formation: Square dance set of four couples.
Note: This is a singing call, and everyone should sing. Much of the action is self-explanatory.

Call	Action
Introduction	
All join hands and circle left the ring.	Circle left.
Stop where you are and everybody swing.	All swing.
Promenade that girl all around the ring.	All promenade.
There'll be a hot time in the old town tonight.	
The Figure	
First couple out and circle four hands 'round.	First couple goes to couple on the right and circle four.
Pick up two and circle six hands 'round.	Take second couple to third and circle.
Pick two more and circle eight hands 'round.	All three couples move to the fourth and circle.
	Circle eight.
There'll be a hot time in the old town tonight, my baby!	
Allemande right with the lady on the left.	Break and do a left allemande. Pass by partner (right shoulders) to next lady.
Allemande right with the lady on the right,	Allemande right is the opposite of allemande left and is done with the right hand.
Allemande left with the lady on the left,	Again pass partner by, without touching, to corner lady.
And a grand old right and left around the town.	Self-explanatory.
When you meet your honey, it's dos-a-do around,	At the end of the grand right and left, partners go back to back.
Take her in your arms and swing her 'round and 'round.	All swing.
Promenade home, you promenade the town—	All promenade.
There'll be a hot time in the old town tonight, my baby!	Continue to promenade.

Repeat three more times, with the second, third, and fourth couples leading out. Do not repeat the introduction.

Finale

All join hands and circle left the floor.	Circle left.
Swing her 'round and 'round, just like you did before.	All swing.
Because that's all, there isn't any more.	Continue swinging.
There'll be a hot time in the old town tonight.	

Teaching Suggestion: Emphasize in the allemande sequences that the allemande left is done with the left-hand girl and the allemande right with the right-hand girl. In moving from the left-hand girl to the right-hand girl and back, partners pass each other right shoulder to right shoulder and do not touch.

Additional Square Dances

For additional dances to round out the program, the following are suggested.

Take a Little Peek
Birdie in the Cage—Seven Hands Round
Forward Six and Fall Back Six
Dive for the Oyster
Red River Valley
Star by the Right
Divide That Ring

These and others are available from a number of sources in the form of single records or albums. In addition, the square dance patterns and steps, previously described in this chapter, are on records with simple walk-through instructions. Square dance records with or without calls can be found.

The following sources, among others, have excellent square dance records and albums suitable for the elementary school program.

Educational Record Albums	David McKay Company 119 West 40th Street New York, N.Y. 10018
Honor Your Partner Records	Educational Activities, Inc. P.O. Box 392 Freeport, N.Y. 11520
Square Dance Records	Teaching Aids Service 31 Union Square West New York, N.Y. 10003

LUMMI STICKS (AMERICAN INDIAN)

Activities that use lummi sticks are appropriate for grades three through six. Lummi sticks are smaller versions of wands and are 12 to 15 inches long. Some believe that the lummi sticks were a part of the culture of the Lummi Indians in northwest Washington, but their actual origin is obscure.

The chant sets the basis for the movements and should be learned first, so it becomes automatic as a basis of the stick actions. Most lummi stick activities are done by partners, although some can be done individually. Each child sits Indian fashion, facing his or her partner at a distance of 18 to 20 inches. Children adjust as the activities demand. The sticks are held in the thumb and fingers (not the fist) at about the bottom third of the stick.

Routines are based on sets of six movements; each movement is completed in one count. Many different routines are possible, and only basic ones are presented. The following one-count movements are used to make up routines.

Vertical tap: tap both upright sticks to the floor.

Partner tap: tap partner's stick right to right or left to left.

End tap: tilt sticks forward or sideward and tap ends to floor.

Cross tap: cross hands and tap upper ends to floor.

Side tap: tap upper ends to side.

Flip: toss stick in air, giving it a half-turn. Catch other end.

Tap together: hold sticks parallel and tap together.

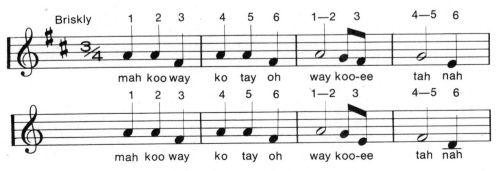

The Lummi Stick Chant

Toss right (or left): toss right-hand stick to partner's right hand, at the same time receiving partner's right-hand stick.

Pass: lay stick on the floor and pick up partner's stick.

Toss right and left: toss quickly right to right and left to left, all in a time of one count.

Routines

A number of routines are presented in sequence of difficulty, incorporating the activities just named. Each routine is to be done four times to complete the 24 beats of the chant.

1. Vertical tap, tap together, partner tap right. Vertical tap, tap together, partner tap left.
2. Vertical tap, tap together, pass right stick. Vertical tap, tap together, pass left stick.
3. Vertical tap, tap together, toss right stick. Vertical tap, tap together, toss left stick.
4. Repeat 1, 2, and 3, except substitute end tap, flip, and then the stated movement.
5. Vertical tap, tap together, toss right and left quickly.
6. End tap, flip, toss right and left quickly.
7. Cross tap, cross flip, uncross arms for vertical tap. Cross tap, cross flip, uncross arms for vertical tap.
8. Right flip side—left flip in front, vertical tap in place, partner tap right. Left flip side—right flip in front, vertical tap in place, partner tap left.
9. End tap in front, flip, vertical tap. Tap together, toss right, toss left.
10. Vertical tap, tap together, right stick to partner's left hand, tossing your left stick to your own right hand. Repeat. This is the circle throw.
11. Same as #10, but reverse the circle.

Lummi stick activities are another example of movement patterns that can be the basis for creativity. Let the children design their own sequences.

The activity can be done by fours, with a change in the timing. One set of partners begins at the start, and the other two start on the third beat. All sing together. In this way, the sticks are flying alternately.

GAMES USING RHYTHMIC BACKGROUNDS

There are a number of interesting games that use music as a part of the game. Most of them are simple in principle and are based on the idea of movement changes when the music changes or stops. Some of them are similar to the old, old game of Musical Chairs.

Grades Kindergarten through Two

Circle Stoop

Children are in a single circle, facing counterclockwise. A march, or similar music, can be used, or the game can be played to the beat of a tom-tom. The children march in good posture until the music is stopped. As soon as the child no longer hears the music or beat of the tom-tom, he or she stoops and touches both hands to the ground without losing his or her balance. The last child to touch both hands to the ground successfully pays a penalty by going into the mush-pot (center of the circle) or being eliminated. Children should march in good posture, and anyone stooping, even partially, before the music is stopped should be penalized. The duration of the music should be varied, and the children should not be able to observe the stopping process if a record player is used.

Variations

1. Employ different locomotor movements, such as skipping, hopping, or galloping, while using suitable music.
2. Use different positions for stopping instead of stooping. Positions like the push-up, crab, lame dog, balance on one foot, or touch with one hand and one foot add to the interest and fun.

Freeze

Children are scattered around the room. When the music is started, they move around the room, guided by the character of the music. They walk, run, jump, or use other locomotor movements, depending upon the selected music or beat. When the music is stopped, they freeze and do not move. Any child caught moving after the cessation of the rhythm pays a penalty.

A tom-tom or a piano provides a fine base for this game, since the rhythmic beat can be varied easily and the rhythm can be stopped at any time. In place of a tom-tom or a drum, two sticks or Indian clubs can be knocked together to provide the beat.

Variations

1. Specify the level at which the child must freeze.
2. Have the child fall to the ground or go into one of the different positions, such as push-up, crab, lame dog, balance, or some other defined position.

Statues

This is a musical game similar to Freeze. When the music stops, all children become statues and hold for a count of five. If a child moves during the count, he or she must stay out of the game during the next sequence and help the teacher judge whether any of the statues move. The type of statues can be specified: for example, funny, pretty, ugly, or balancing statues.

Right Angle

A tom-tom can be used to provide the rhythm for this activity. Some of the basic rhythm records also have suitable music. The children change direction at right angles on each heavy beat or change of music. The object of the game is to make the right-angle changes on signal and not bump into other children.

Grades Three through Six

Arches

The game is similar to London Bridge. Arches are placed around the playing area. To form an arch, two players stand facing one another with hands joined. When the music starts, the players move in a circle, passing under the arch. Suddenly, the music stops and the arches come down by dropping the hands. All players caught in an arch immediately pair off together to form other arches, keeping in a general circle formation. If a caught player does not have a partner, he or she should wait in the center of the circle until one is available. The last players caught (or left) form arches for the next game.

The arches should be warned not to bring down their hands and arms too forcefully, so the children passing under them will not be pummeled. Also, children with glasses need consideration. Glasses should be removed, or children with glasses can begin as parts of the arches.

Variation: Different types of music can be used, and the children can move according to the pattern of the music.

Whistle March

A record with a brisk march is needed. The children are scattered around the room, individually walking in various directions and keeping time to the music. A whistle is blown a number of times; at the signal, lines are formed of that precise number, no more and no fewer. The lines are formed by having the children stand side by side with locked elbows. As soon as a line of the proper number is formed, it begins to march to the music counterclockwise around the room. Any children left over go to the center of the room and remain until the next signal. On the next whistle signal (single blast), the lines break up and all walk individually around the room in various directions.

Teaching Hint: It may be well to make a rule that children may not form the same combination as in the previous line.

Partner Stoop

The game follows the same basic principle of stooping as in Circle Stoop, but it is done with partners. The group forms a double circle, with partners facing counterclockwise, which means that one partner is on the inside and one on the outside. When the music begins, all march in the line of direction. After a short period of marching, a signal (whistle) is sounded, and the inside circle reverses direction and marches the other way —clockwise. Partners are then separated. When the music stops, the outer circle stands still, and the partners making up the inside circle *walk* to rejoin their respective partners. As soon as a child reaches his or her partner, they join inside hands and stoop without losing balance. The last couple to stoop and those who lose balance go to the center of the circle and wait out the next round.

Variation: The game can be played with groups of three, instead of partners. The game begins with the groups of three marching abreast and holding hands and facing counterclockwise. On the signal, the outside player of the three continues marching in the same direction. The middle player of the three stops and stands still. The inside player reverses direction and marches clockwise. When the music stops, the groups of three attempt to reunite at the spot where the middle player stopped. The last three to join hands and stoop are put into the center for the next round.

Squad-Leader Dance

Each squad forms a spaced column. The child in front is the leader. When the music starts, the leader does movements in time to the rhythm, leading the squad around the room, with all squad members performing as the leader does. When the music is stopped, all stop and the leader goes to the rear of the squad. The child in front of the squad is then the new leader, and the activity is repeated. Change leaders until all have had a chance.

Follow Me

The game has its basis in the phrasing of the music. The children are in circle formation, facing in, with a leader in the center. The leader performs a series of movements of his or her choice, either locomotor or nonlocomotor, for the duration of one phrase of music (eight beats). The children imitate his or her movements during the next phrase. The leader takes over for another set of movements, and the children imitate during the next phrase. After a few changes, the leader picks another child to take his or her place.

Variations

1. A popular way to play this game is to have the

children follow the leader as he or she performs. This means changing movement as the leader changes and performing as the leader does, with everyone keeping the rhythm. A change is made as soon as the leader falters or loses his or her patterns or ideas.

2. The game can be done with partners. One partner performs during one phrase, and the other partner imitates his or her movements during the next phrase. The teacher can decide which couple is making the most vivid and imaginative movements and is doing the best job of following the partner's movements.

Sixteen

Manipulative Activities

A manipulative activity is one in which a child handles some kind of a play object, usually with the hands, but it can involve the feet and other parts of the body. As fundamental skills, manipulative activities invite strong application of educational movement methodology, adding an important dimension to movement experiences. Manipulative activities can strengthen both hand-eye and foot-eye coordination, as well as develop dexterity in handling a variety of play objects.

Activities utilizing hoops, wands, beanbags, balls of various types, tug-of-war ropes, and parachutes round out a basic program. Deck tennis rings, rubber horseshoes, lummi sticks, frisbees, and scoops also can enrich the offerings.

Activities with jump ropes are important in the program, since they offer multiple movement possibilities—manipulative activity, rhythmic activity, and fundamental movement opportunity. Because of the complexity and interrelatedness of the activities, a separate chapter (chapter seventeen) is devoted to activities with jump ropes.

The supply factor is critical to a program of manipulative activities. For individual work, one item should be on hand for each child. In partner work, one item should be present for every two children. The demands for group work are smaller. However, most manipulative activity consists of individual and partner work, except, of course, for parachute play. One parachute is sufficient for a normal-size class.

Beanbags and yarn balls provide the first throwing and catching skills for younger children. A softer object instills confidence and tends to eliminate the fear younger children have of catching a hard or an unyielding object. After the introductory skills have been mastered, other types of balls can be added and more demanding skills can be brought in.

Since early competency in handling objects provides a basis for later, specialized skills, basic principles of skill performance (page 81) should have strong application, particularly as related to throwing and catching skills.

The start-and-expand approach is sound for manipulative activities. Start the children at a low level of challenge, so all can achieve success, and expand the skills and experiences from that base. In progression, most activities begin with the individual approach and later move to partner activity. Partners should be of comparable ability.

PROGRESSION AND MOVEMENT THEMES

The activities in the manipulative area are presented in progression, in the form of either movement themes or movement tasks and challenges. Rather than just listing a series of activities in progression, the reliance on movement themes permits greater flexibility for the teacher. The teacher can develop as many activities or approaches as seem feasible in a particular theme and then move to the next theme in the progression.

For example, the first movement theme in beanbag activities is under individual activity on page 255 and is entitled "in place, tossing to self." Suggestions for the development of this theme follow. The teacher has two approaches. He or she can develop one or two themes in depth, exhausting all the possibilities, or he or she can take a few activities from a number of themes, moving from one to the other with more dispatch. In the latter case, when the lesson is repeated the following day, the teacher can use the same themes but pose different challenges.

The children should be given opportunities to "do their own thing" and come up with new and different activities.

SKILL PRACTICE THROUGH CREATIVE GAMES

Manipulative activities offer an excellent opportunity to extend skill development through creative games. After a period of practice or experimentation, children can work out a game situation in which the skill just practiced or experienced can be organized into a game situation. This can be an open situation in which the children integrate the skill into a game of their choosing, or the teacher can specify certain limiting factors that are to be included in the game.

The game can be oriented toward individuals, partners, or groups. Groups must be kept small; otherwise, the individual input would be insignificant. The emphasis should be on the children practicing the skill in a game of their choosing, which generally should follow immediately after the skill has been experienced.

ACTIVITIES WITH BALLOONS

Balloons can be used to provide interesting movement experiences that give practice for hand-eye coordination in particular. Keeping a balloon afloat is a particularly valuable challenge, since the activity is within the reach of young children and special education students. Success can be achieved with balloons when the students are not quite ready for ball skills. However, the activities can be expanded to challenge first- and second-grade children.

Since balloons are inexpensive and readily available, the expense factor is low. Of course, extras are needed, since there always is breakage. Balloons should be spherical in shape and of good quality. At times, however, odd-shaped balloons can provide a change of pace.

Balloons should be inflated only moderately, since high inflation increases the chance of breakage. Sometimes, a penny or a small washer can be put inside a balloon to give it an odd and different flight pattern.

Instructional Procedures

1. After blowing up each balloon, twist the neck and fix it with a twist tie used to tie plastic bags. This permits the balloon to be deflated easily and reused. Tying a knot in the neck is effective in preventing air loss, but it makes deflating the balloon difficult.
2. Blowing up balloons for a class is quite a chore. With help, the children can learn to do this, but some problems usually occur. Some children may get their balloons inflated quickly, while others may require some help from the teacher. This leaves some children ready and waiting, while others are still preparing for the activity. As soon as a child has successfully blown up a balloon, he or she then can practice keeping it in the air.
3. Stress fingertip control and tactile contact.
4. Tell the children to play only with their own balloons and leave alone any that come into their personal spaces, since someone will be coming after the lost balloon.

Recommended Activities

1. Begin with free exploration, having the children play *under control* with their balloons. Emphasize good manners, that is, not bursting or interfering with other children's balloons. The objective is to have the children gain a sense of the balloons' flight.
2. Introduce specific hand, finger, and arm contacts. Some things that can be introduced include using alternate hands; contacting at different levels (low, high, and in between) and jumping and making high contact with the balloon; using different hand contacts (palm, back, side, and different fist positions); using finger combinations (two fingers, index finger, thumb only, others); and using arms, elbows, and shoulders.
3. Expand the activity to using other body parts. Establish sequences.
4. Bat from different body positions (kneeling, sitting, lying).
5. Use an object to control the balloon (a lummi stick, a ball, or a stocking paddle).

Batting Balloons from Different Body Positions

6. Stress some movement restrictions. Keep one foot in place. Keep one foot or both feet within a hoop, on an individual mat, or on a carpet square.
7. Work with a partner by alternating turns, batting the balloon back and forth, employing follow patterns, et cetera.
8. Introduce some aspects of volleyball technique, including the overhand pass, the underhand pass, and the dig pass. Begin with a volleyball serve. Make this informal and on a "let's pretend" basis. Check the volleyball unit (page 535-538) for technique suggestions.
9. If balloons can be spared, a fun game is to have each child tie an inflated balloon to an ankle. With a lead of 1 or 2 feet, they can be turned loose in an area to try to burst each other's balloons. As soon as a child has had his or her balloon burst, he or she is eliminated. This also can be a squad contest.

ACTIVITIES WITH BEANBAGS

Activities based on beanbags provide valuable learning experiences for children at all levels in the elementary school. They provide a good introduction to throwing and catching skills for kindergarten and primary-level children and should precede instruction with inflated balls. All parts of the body can be brought into play with beanbag activities.

Instructional Procedures

1. Beanbags should be at least 6 inches square. This size beanbag balances and can be controlled better on various parts of the body, offering a greater measure of success for intermediate-level children.
2. Throwing and catching skills involve many intricate elements. Emphasize the skill performance principles of opposition, eye focus, weight transfer, and follow-through. It is important for children to keep an eye on the object being caught and on the target when they are throwing.
3. Stress laterality and directionality when teaching throwing and catching skills. This means children should be taught to throw, catch, strike, and balance the beanbags with both the left and right sides of their bodies. Also, they should learn to catch and throw at different levels.
4. Children should throw about chest high to a partner, unless a different type of throw is specified. Teach all types of returns—low, medium, high, left, and right.
5. In early practice, stress a soft receipt of the beanbag when catching by giving with the hands, arms, and legs. Softness is created by having the hands go out toward the incoming beanbag and bring it in for a soft landing.
6. In partner work, keep distances between partners reasonable, especially in introductory phases. Fifteen feet or so seems to be a reasonable starting distance.
7. In partner work, emphasize skillful throwing, catching, and handling of the beanbag. Hard and difficult throwing, the purpose of which is to cause the partner to miss, should be avoided.
8. Beanbags should not be kicked, since few can stand this kind of abuse.

Recommended Activities

Activities are generally classified as individual or partner activities. A few activities are done in groups of three or more.

Individual Activities

In Place, Tossing to Self: Toss with both hands, right hand, left hand. Catch the same way. Catch with back of the hands.

Toss the beanbag progressively higher.

Hold the beanbag in each hand and make large arm circles (windmill). Release the bag so it flies upward, and catch it.

Toss from side to side, right to left (reverse), front to back, back to front, around various parts of the body, different combinations.

Toss two beanbags upward, and catch a bag in each hand.

Toss upward, catch with hands behind back.

Toss upward from behind the body, and catch in front.

Toss upward, and catch on the back, on the knees, on the toes, on other parts of the body.

Hold the bag at arm's length in front of body, with palms up. Withdraw hands quickly from under bag, and catch it from on top with a palms-down stroke before it falls to the floor.

Toss upward and catch as high as possible. As low as possible. Work out a sequence of high, low, and in between.

Toss upward and catch with the body off the floor. Try tossing as well as catching with the body off the ground.

Toss the beanbag in various fashions while seated and while lying.

In Place, Adding Stunts: Toss overhead to the rear, turn around, and catch. Toss, and do a full turn, and catch.

Toss, clap hands, and catch. Clap hands more than once. Clap hands around different parts of the body, and catch.

Toss, do pretend activities (comb your hair, wash your face, brush your teeth, shine your shoes), and catch.

Toss, touch different body parts with both hands, and catch. Touch two different body parts, and catch. Touch two body parts, clap your hands, and catch.

Toss, kneel on one knee, and catch. Try this going to a seated or lying position. Reverse the order, coming from a lying or sitting position to a standing position to catch.

Toss, touch the floor, and catch. Explore with other challenges. Use heel clicks or balance positions.

Bend, reach between legs, and toss bag onto back and onto shoulders.

Reach one hand over the shoulder, and catch with the other hand behind the back. Reverse the hands. Drop the beanbag from one hand behind the back, and catch with the other hand between the legs. Put the beanbag on the head, lean back, and catch it with both hands behind the back. Catch it with one hand.

Locomotor Movements: Toss to self, moving to another spot to catch. Toss forward, run, and catch. Move from side to side. Toss overhead to the rear, run back, and catch. Add various stunts and challenges previously described.

Vary with different locomotor movements.

Balancing Beanbag on Various Parts of the Body: Balance on head. Move around, maintaining balance of beanbag. Sit down, lie down, turn around, et cetera.

Balance the beanbag on various parts of the body and move around in this fashion. Balance on top of instep, between knees, on shoulders, on elbows, under chin, et cetera. Use more than one beanbag for balancing.

Propelling Beanbag with Various Parts of the Body: Toss to self from various parts of the body—elbow, instep, between feet, between heels, knees, shoulders.

Sit and toss bag from the feet to self. Practice from a supine position. From a supine position, pick up the bag between the toes, place it behind the head, using a full curl position. Go back and pick it up, returning it to original place.

Manipulating with Bare Feet: The children are barefooted. The bag should be picked up by curling the toes. This has value in strengthening the muscles supporting the arch.

Pick up with one foot. Hop to another spot. Change feet.

Toss to self from either foot. Using a target (hoop), toss the beanbag into the target.

Juggling: Begin with two bags and keep them in the air alternately. Juggle three bags. (See page 261 for instructions on juggling.)

Other Activities: From a wide straddle position, push the beanbag between the legs as far back as possible. Jump into the air with a half-turn and repeat.

Take the same position as above. Push the bag back as far as possible between the legs, bending

the knees. Without moving the legs, turn to the right and pick up the bag. Repeat the maneuver, turning to the left the next time.

Stand with feet apart, holding the beanbag with both hands. Reach up as high as possible (both hands), bend over backward, and drop the bag. Reach between the legs, and pick up the bag.

Get down on all fours in kneeling position, and put the bag in the small of the back. Wiggle and force the bag off the back without moving the hands and knees from place.

In crab position, place the beanbag on the stomach, and try to shake it off. Put the beanbag on the back and do a Mule Kick.

Push the beanbag across the floor with different body parts, such as nose, shoulder, and knee.

Drop the beanbag onto the floor. See how many different ways you can move over, around, and between the beanbags. As an example, jump three bags, Crab Walk around two others, and Cartwheel over one bag.

Spread the legs about shoulder width. Bend over, throw the beanbag between the legs and onto the back. Next, throw the beanbag all the way over the head, and catch it.

Partner Activities

Tossing Back and Forth: Begin with various kinds of two-handed throws—underhand, overhead, side, and over-the-shoulder. Change to one-handed tossing and throwing.

Throw at different levels, also at different targets—right and left.

Throw under leg, around the body. Center as in football. Try imitating the shot put and the discus throw. Try the softball windmill (full arc) throw.

Have partners sit tailor (cross-legged) fashion about 10 feet apart. Throw and catch in various styles, seated in this fashion.

Use follow activities, in which one partner leads with a throw and the other follows with the same kind of a throw.

Run, leap, and toss to partner while in flight.

Jump, turn in the air, and pass to partner.

Toss to partner from unexpected positions and from around and under different parts of the body.

Stand back to back and pass bag around both partners from hand to hand as quickly as possible. Also, try moving bag around and through various body parts.

Toss in various directions to make partner move and catch.

With one partner standing still, the other partner runs around him or her in a circle as the bag is tossed back and forth.

Propel two beanbags back and forth. Each partner has a bag, and the bags go in opposite directions at the same time. Try tossing both bags at once in the same direction, using various types of throws. Try to keep three bags going at the same time.

Propelling Back and Forth with Different Parts of the Body: Toss bag to partner with foot, toe, both feet (on top and held between), elbow, shoulder, head, and any other part of the body that can be used. Use a sitting position.

With back to partner, take a bunny jump position. With bag held between the feet, kick bag back to partner. Try from a standing position.

Partners lie supine on floor with heads pointing toward each other, heads about 3 inches apart. One partner has a beanbag between his or her feet and deposits it in back of his or her head. The other partner picks up the bag with his or her feet (which are over his or her head) and returns the bag to the floor after returning to a lying position. Try to transfer the bag directly from one partner to the other with the feet, with both partners in backward curl position.

Group Activities and Games

Split-Vision Drill: A split-vision drill from basketball can be adapted to beanbags. An active player faces two partners about 15 feet away. They are standing side by side, a short distance apart, in this fashion.

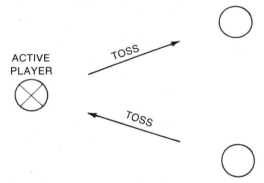

Two beanbags, one in the hands of the active player and the other with one of the partners, are needed for the drill. The active player tosses his or her bag to the open partner and *at the same time*

Beanbag Toss Target

receives the other bag from the other partner. The two bags move back and forth between the active player and the two others, alternately. After a period of time, change positions.

Target Games: Wastebaskets, hoops, circles drawn on the floor, and other objects can be used as targets for beanbag tossing. Target boards with cutout holes are available on the commercial market. Holes can be triangles, circles, squares, and rectangles, thus stressing form concepts.

Beanbag Quoits: The game is played in the same way as horseshoes. A court is drawn with two spots on the floor about 20 feet apart. Spots can be made from masking tape and should be 1 inch in diameter. Each competitor gets two bags. There is a different color for each player. Tosses are made from behind one spot to the other. The object is to get one or both bags closer to the mark than the opponents. If the bag completely blocks out the spot, as viewed from directly overhead, this bag scores 3 points. Otherwise any bag nearer to the spot than the opponent's bag scores 1 point. Games are 11, 15, or 21 points. The player winning the previous point tosses first.

Other Games: The children love to play One Step (page 398). Teacher Ball (page 386) is readily adaptable to beanbag tossing.

Shuffleboard: If the gym floor has a shuffleboard court, beanbags can be used as substitutes for regular shuffleboard equipment. However, it may be necessary to shorten the tossing distance.

FUNDAMENTAL BALL SKILLS

Included in this section are the fundamental ball skills in which the child handles balls without the aid of other equipment, such as a bat or a paddle. Ball skills are mostly of two types:

Hand-Eye Skills: throwing, catching, bouncing, dribbling (as in basketball), batting (as in volleyball), and rolling (as in bowling).

Foot-Eye Skills: kicking, trapping, and dribbling (as in soccer).

Other parts of the body are used on occasion, but the main emphasis centers on ball handling with the hands and feet.

Ball skills are of vital importance to children in their play experiences. A good basis for these skills must be laid in the lower grades, with continued development in the upper grades. Not only should the children acquire skill through varied experiences in handling balls, but they also should gain knowledge of the skill principles essential to competency in ball-handling skills.

Types of Balls

For younger children, yarn and fleece balls are excellent for introductory throwing and catching skills, since they help overcome the fear factor. Balls cut out of sponge rubber are also excellent. (See chapter thirty-four for instructions for making balls from yarn and sponge rubber.) The innovative teacher also can come up with other suitable objects, such as crumpled-up-newspaper balls formed with cellophane tape, papier-mâché balls, stitched rolled-up socks, and stuffed balloons.

The whiffle ball is also valuable. This is a plastic, hollow ball with holes and other figures cut out of the cover. Scoops, either commercial or home constructed, provide an extension of the activities.

Another type of ball that has value is a soft softball, a much softer version of the regular softball. It has advantages for catching thrown balls and fielding grounders but does not hold up well if batted.

The inflated rubber playground ball (8½ inches) should be the ball used for most of the children's ball-handling experiences. Skill work should start with this size ball and move to smaller items later. Balls should be moderately inflated so that they will bounce well, but not to the point of overinflation, which causes difficulty in catching. Overinflation also can distort the balls' spherical shape.

Some concern should be given to the color of the balls. In a study comparing blue, yellow, and white balls against a black background and a white background, "blue and yellow balls produced significantly higher catching scores than did a white ball."[1] However, no data were provided for the common playground balls of red color.

Types of Organization

Instruction in lower grades should begin with individual work and progress to partner and group activities. After the children have acquired some skill, a lesson can include both individual and partner activities.

In propelling the ball back and forth between partners, children can progress from rolling the ball to throwing the ball on first bounce, to throwing the ball on the fly. Be sure a disparity in skill between partners does not cause a problem for either partner. A skilled child can aid a less skilled child to better performance, but the more skilled individual may resent being restricted in more complex skills by an inept child.

Group work should be confined to small groups (three to six), so each child can be actively involved. Group work should include activities and approaches that are not possible in individual or partner activity.

[1]Gordon S. Morris, "Effects Ball and Background Color Have upon the Catching Performance of Elementary School Children," *Research Quarterly*, vol. 47, no. 3 (October 1976), pp. 409-15.

Other Factors

Distance between partners should be short at first and then gradually lengthened. The conception of targets is introduced by directing the children to throw the ball to specific points. Later, a change from a stationary target to a moving target maintains progression. Relays are useful for reinforcing skill learning but the skills should have been learned reasonably well before they are applied in a relay.

Instructional Procedures

1. The principles of skill performance (page 81) have strong application to ball skills, particularly visual concentration, follow-through, arm-leg opposition, weight transfer, and total body coordination. The principles should be incorporated into the instructional sequences and, in addition, be an important part of the coaching process. Balls should be handled with the pads of the fingers and should not be palmed.
2. In catching, a soft receipt of the ball should be created by a giving movement with hands and arms. Hands should reach out somewhat to receive the ball and then cushion the impact by bringing the ball in toward the body with loose and relaxed hands.
3. In catching a throw above the waist, the hands should be positioned so that the thumbs are together. To receive a throw below the waist, the catch is made by the hands with the little fingers toward each other and the thumbs out.
4. In throwing to a partner, unless otherwise specified, the throw should reach the partner about chest high. At times, a variety of target points should be specified—high, low, right, left, knee-high, et cetera.
5. A lesson should begin with simple basic skills within the reach of all children and progress to more challenging activities.
6. Laterality is an important consideration. Right and left members of the body should be given practice in turn in somewhat equal time allotments.
7. Practice in split vision should be incorporated into bouncing and dribbling skills. Children should learn to look somewhat forward, not at the ball, in bouncing and dribbling work. A split-vision drill (page 257) is of value in throwing patterns.
8. Tactile senses can be brought into play by having the children dribble or bounce the ball with eyes closed, allowing practice in getting the feel of the ball.
9. Rhythmic accompaniment, particularly for bouncing and dribbling activities, adds another dimension to ball skills.

10. It is desirable that there be enough balls for each child to have a ball. However, in case there are only enough balls for each two children, the first child does the prescribed routine and then bounces, tosses, or passes the ball to the second child, who repeats the designated routine.

11. The vexing problem of loose balls can be solved in the following fashion. Tell children to leave the balls alone, since someone is sure to be coming after them. To bat, kick, or throw it out of the area simply compounds the problem.

Recommended Activities

Activities with balls are presented with the 8½-inch rubber playground ball in mind. Some modification is needed if the balls are smaller or are of the type that does not bounce, as in the case of yarn or fleece balls.

Individual Activities

Each child has a ball and practices by himself or herself. In the first group of individual activities, the child remains in the same spot. Next, he or she utilizes a wall to rebound the ball to himself or herself. The wall should be reasonably free of projections and irregular surfaces so that the ball can return directly to the student. If the ball is to bounce after contact with the wall, the children can stand back farther than if they are to handle the return on the fly. In the third group of activities, the children are performing alone while on the move.

In Place, Controlled Rolling and Handling: The child assumes a wide straddle position, places the ball on the floor, and rolls it with constant hand guidance between and around the legs.

Roll the ball in a figure-eight path in and out of the legs.

Reach as far to the left as possible with the ball and roll it in front of you to the other side. Catch it as far to the right of the body as possible.

Turn in place and roll the ball around with one hand.

Other positions are seated with outstretched legs, cross-legged sitting, and push-up position.

Can you roll the ball lying on top of it? Can you roll the ball around the floor while on all fours, guiding it with your nose and forehead?

With a moderately bent back, release the ball behind the head, let it roll down the back, and catch it with both hands.

Make different kinds of bridges over the ball, using the ball as partial support for the bridge.

Roll the ball down one arm, behind the back, and down the other arm, and then catch it.

In Place, Bouncing and Catching: Beginning with two hands, bounce and catch. Bounce a given number of times. Bounce at different levels. Bounce one-handed in a variety of fashions. Bounce under the legs. Close eyes, bounce and catch.

Bounce, perform various stunts, such as heel click, body turns, and hand claps, and catch.

Bounce the ball around body, under body, and over body.

Practice various kinds of bounces with catches made with the eyes closed.

Bounce the ball with various body parts, such as head, elbow, and knee.

Bounce the ball, using consecutive body parts (for example, elbow and then knee), and catch.

In Place, Tossing and Catching: Toss and catch, increasing height gradually. Toss from side to side. Toss underneath the legs, around the body, from behind. Add challenges while tossing and catching: clap hands one or more times, make body turns (quarter, half, or full), touch the floor, click heels, sit down, lie down, et cetera.

To enhance body-part identification, toss and perform some of the following challenges. Touch your back with both hands, touch your back with both hands by reaching over both shoulders, touch both elbows, touch both knees with crossed hands, touch both heels with a heel slap, and touch your toes. Be sure and catch the ball after completing each challenge. To aid in this learning process, the teacher or a leader can quickly call out the body parts and the class must respond with a toss, touch, and catch.

Toss upward and let bounce. Add various challenges as above.

Toss upward and catch the descending ball at as high a level as possible; at a low level. Work out other levels and put into combinations. Catch with crossed arms.

From a seated position, toss ball to self from various directions. Lie down and do the same.

Practice catching by looking away after the ball is tossed upward. Experiment with different ways of catching with the eyes closed.

In Place, Batting the Ball (as in Volleyball) to Self: Bat the ball, using the fist, open hand, or side of hand.

Bat and let ball bounce. Catch the different fashions.

Rebound the ball upward, using different parts of body. Let it bounce. Practice serving to self.

Bat the ball so it is not allowed to touch the ground. Can you change your position while you do this?

Bat the ball, perform a stunt, and bat again.

In-Place Foot Skills: Put toe on top of ball. Roll ball in different directions, keeping the other foot in place and retaining control of the ball.

Use two-footed pickup, front and back.

From a sitting position with the legs extended, toss the ball with the feet to the hands.

Try doing a full curl, retaining control of the ball until it is again placed on the floor without losing its position between the feet. Try bringing the ball between the feet to a point directly over the body. With the arms outstretched for support, lower the feet with the ball to the right and left.

Hold ball overhead along the floor in supine position and do a Curl-up, bring the ball forward, touch the toes with it, and return to supine position.

Drop the ball, and immediately trap it against the floor with one foot.

Try and bounce the ball with one foot.

In-Place Dribbling Skills: Dribble the ball first with both hands and then with the right and the left. Emphasize that the dribble is a push with good wrist action. Children should not bat the ball downward. Use various number combinations with the right and left hands. Dribble under the legs in turn, back around the body. Kneel and dribble. Go from standing to lying position, maintaining a dribble. Return to standing position.

Dribble the ball at different levels and at various tempos.

Dribble without looking at the ball. Dribble and change hands without stopping the dribble. Dribble with the eyes closed.

Dribble the way the Harlem Globetrotters do.

Throwing against a Wall (Catching on the First Bounce): Throw the ball against the wall, and catch the return after a bounce. Practice various kinds of throws—two-handed, one-handed, overhead, side, baseball, chest-pass, et cetera.

Throwing against a Wall, (Catching on the Fly): Repeat the throws used above, but catch the return on the fly. It may be necessary to move close and have the ball contact the wall higher.

Batting against a Wall and Handball Skills: Drop the ball, and bat it after it bounces. Keep the ball going as in handball. Serve the ball against the wall as in volleyball. Experiment with different means of serving.

Kicking against a Wall and Trapping (Foot-Eye Skills): Practice different ways of controlled kicking against the wall and stopping (trapping) the ball on the return. Try keeping the ball going with the foot on the bounce against the wall.

Kick the ball against the wall, and return it to the hands with a foot pickup.

Put some targets on the wall and see how many points you can score after 15 kicks.

Rolling While Moving: Roll the ball, run alongside it, and guide it with the hands in different directions. Roll the ball forward, run and catch up with it.

Tossing and Catching While Moving: Toss the ball upward and forward. Run forward, and catch after a bounce. Toss the ball upward in various directions—forward, sideward, backward—run under ball, and catch on fly. Add various stunts and challenges such as touching the floor, heel clicks, turning around, et cetera.

Batting the Ball While Moving: Bat the ball with the hand upward in different directions, catch ball on first bounce or on fly.

Practicing Foot Skills (Soccer Dribble) While Moving: Dribble ball forward, backward, and in other directions. Dribble around an imaginary point. Make various patterns while dribbling, such as a circle, square, triangle, figure eight, et cetera.

Dribbling (as in Basketball) While Moving: Dribble forward using one hand, and back to place with the other. Change directions on whistle. Dribble in various directions, describing different pathways. Dribble in and around cones, milk cartons, or chairs.

Each child has a hoop, which he or she lays on the floor. Each child then dribbles inside his or her hoop until the change signal is sounded, and then he or she dribbles to another hoop and continues the dribble inside that hoop. Children must avoid dribbling on the hoop itself.

Practicing Locomotor Movements While Holding Ball: Hold the ball between the legs and perform various locomotor movements. Try holding the ball in various positions with different body parts.

Partner Activities

In-Place Rolling: Roll the ball back and forth to partner. Begin with two-handed rolls and proceed to one-handed rolls. Roll the ball to partner, and the partner picks up the ball with his or her toe and snaps it up into his or her hands.

In-Place Throwing and Catching: Toss the ball to partner on first bounce, using various kinds of tosses. Practice various kinds of throws and passes to partner. Throw to specific points—high, low, right, left, knee-high, et cetera. Try various odd throws such as under leg, around the body,

Throwing at a Wall-mounted Target

backward tosses, centering as in football. Throw and catch over a volleyball net. Work in a threesome, having someone hold a hoop between the two partners playing catch. Throw the ball through the hoop held at various levels. Try throwing through a moving hoop.

In-Place Batting and Volleyball Skills: Serve as in volleyball. Serve to partner, who catches. Toss to partner and have him or her make a volleyball return. Keep distances short and the ball under good control. Bat back and forth on first bounce. Bat back and forth over a line or over a bench.

In-Place Kicking: Practice different ways of controlled kicking between partners and different ways of stopping the ball (trapping). Practice a controlled punt, preceding the kick with a step from the nonkicking foot. Place ball between feet and propel forward or backward to partner. Practice foot pickups. One partner rolls the ball, and the other hoists ball to self with extended toe.

In-Place Throwing from Various Positions: Practice different throws from a kneeling, sitting, or lying position. Allow the children freedom for creativity in selecting positions.

In-Place Two-Ball Activities: Using two balls, pass back and forth, with balls going in opposite directions.

In-Place Follow Activities: One partner throws or propels the ball in any manner he or she wishes, and his or her partner returns the ball in the same fashion.

Throwing and Catching against a Wall: Alternate throwing and catching against a wall. Alternate returning the ball after a bounce as in handball.

Throwing on the Move: Spatial judgments must be good to anticipate where the moving child should be to receive the ball. Moderate distances should be maintained between children.

One child remains in place and tosses to the other child, who changes position. The moving child can trace different patterns, such as back and forth between two spots and in a circle around the stationary child.

Practice different kinds of throws and passes as both children move in different patterns. Considerable space is needed for this type of class work. Practice foot skills of dribbling and passing.

Hold the ball between the bodies without using the hands or arms. Experiment with different ways to move.

JUGGLING BALLS

Professional juggling is done with special balls, but sponge balls serve quite well for physical education classes. Small, tight beanbags (2 to 3 inches square) can serve as substitutes, too.

Juggling two balls can be done with one hand and three balls can be juggled with two hands. Juggling can be done in a crisscross fashion, which is called *cascading,* and it can be done in a circular fashion, called *showering.* Cascading is considered the easier of the two methods and represents the first approach.

Much practice is necessary, and there will be a lot of misses during the course of acquiring this skill. The object is to eliminate the misses gradually until the student acquires the art of keeping the balls in the air. If the students are to juggle successfully, certain procedures should be given attention.

Instructional Procedures

1. Juggling involves accurate, consistent tossing. This should be the first emphasis. The toss should be from 2 to 2½ feet upward and usually inward, as the ball is tossed from one hand to the other.
2. The fingers, not the palms of the hands, should be used in tossing and catching, with a relaxed wrist action stressed.
3. The student should look upward to watch the balls at the peak of their flight, rather than watching the hands.
4. Balls should be caught about waist high and released a little above this level.
5. Two balls must be carried in the starting hand, and the art of releasing one while retaining the other must be mastered.
6. Progression involves working successively with one ball, two balls, and then three balls.

Recommended Progressions for Cascading

One Ball

Using one hand only, toss upward and catch with the same hand. Begin with the dominant hand, and then practice with the other. Stress quick tossing.

Handle the ball alternately with right and left hands. This involves an inward toss from one hand to the other.

Two Balls

With a ball in each hand, alternate tossing the ball upward and catching in the *same* hand. One ball is always in the air.

Begin again with a ball in each hand. Toss on an inward path to the other hand. To keep the balls from colliding, toss under the incoming ball.

After some expertise has been acquired, alternate the two kinds of tosses by doing a set number (four or six) of each type before shifting to the other type of path.

Three Balls – Cascading

Hold two balls in the starting hand and one in the other. Toss one of the balls in the starting hand, toss the ball from the other hand, and then toss the third ball. This is juggling!

Recommended Progressions for Showering

Two Balls

The motion should be counterclockwise. Hold a ball in each hand. Begin by tossing with the right hand on an inward path and then immediately tossing the other ball from the left directly across the body to the right hand. Continue this until the action is smooth.

Three Balls

Hold two balls in the right hand and one in the left. Toss the first ball from the right hand on an inward path and immediately toss the second on the same path. At about the same time, toss the ball from the left hand to the right hand directly across the body.

Combining Patterns

A few children may be able to change from cascading to showering and vice versa. This is a skill of considerable challenge.

ACTIVITIES WITH SCOOPS AND BALLS

Scoops made out of bleach bottles or similar containers (see chapter thirty-four) can add another dimension to throwing and catching skills. It is possible to use 3-pound coffee cans for catching beanbags and balls, but they do not offer as many possibilities as scoops. Scoops should follow playground ball activity, since they use a smaller ball, such as a tennis ball or a 2¼-inch sponge rubber ball.

Recommended Activities

Individual Activities

Put the ball on the floor, and pick it up with the scoop. Throw the ball in the air, and catch it with the scoop. Throw the ball against the wall, and catch it in the scoop. Put the ball in the scoop, throw it in the air, and catch it. Throw the ball against the wall with the scoop, and catch it with the scoop. Switch the scoop to the opposite hand after ball has been thrown.

Throw the ball in the air from the scoop, perform a stunt, such as a heel click or a body turn, and catch the ball.

Toss upward, and catch the ball as low as possible; as high as possible. Toss it a little higher each time, and catch it in the scoop. Toss so that you have to stretch to catch the ball.

Note that most activity should begin with a toss from the free hand and later employ a toss from the scoop.

Partner Activities

One partner rolls the ball on the floor, and the other catches it in the scoop.

Partners throw the ball back and forth and catch it in the scoop. Play One Step (page 398) while playing catch to add some challenge to the activity.

One partner throws the ball in the air from his or her scoop, and the other partner catches it.

Throw the ball from the scoop at different levels, and catch it at different levels.

Follow or matching activities are also excellent for scoops.

Throw and catch from various positions, such as sitting, back to back, prone position, and kneeling.

Partner Work (catching a fleece ball with scoops)

Work with more than one partner, with more than one ball, and with a scoop in each hand.

Games and Relays

Many games and relays can be carried out using the scoops. Many school districts are now playing lacrosse with the scoops and a whiffle ball.

Set up a lesson in which the children devise games for themselves that use the scoop and ball.

BOWLING

Children in kindergarten and the two lower grades should practice informal rolling. In about the third grade, the emphasis should change from informal rolling to bowling skills: this emphasis should continue through the sixth grade.

Bowling skills should begin with a two-handed roll and progress to one-handed rolls using both right and left hands. Various targets can be utilized, including Indian clubs, milk cartons, small cones, blocks, and human targets.

The regular (8½-inch) rubber playground ball is excellent for bowling skills. Volleyballs and soccer balls also can be used. Stress moderate speed in the moving ball.

Bowling activities are organized mostly into partner or group work. When targets are being used, two children on the target end are desirable. One child resets the target, while the other recovers the ball.

The ball should roll off the tips of the fingers and have good follow-through.

Bowling Skills (Partner Activity Unless Otherwise Noted)

1. Begin with two-handed rolls from between the legs, employing a wide straddle stance.
2. Roll the ball right-handed and left-handed. The receiver can employ the foot pickup, done by hoisting the ball to self (hands) with the extended toe.
3. Practice different kinds of spin (English) on the ball. For a right-handed bowler, a curve to the left is called a hook ball and a curve to the right is a *backup ball.*
4. Employ human straddle targets. Organize children in groups of four, two on each end. One child on each end becomes the target, and the other the ball chaser. Using a stick 2 feet long, make chalk marks on the floor for the target child. He or she stands so that the inside edges of his or her shoes are on the marks, thus standardizing the target spread. Require the targets to keep their legs straight and motionless during the bowling. Otherwise, children can make or avoid contact with the ball and upset the scoring system.

Stress moderate bowling distances (15 to 20 feet) at first, and adjust as the children become more proficient. Scoring can be based on two points scored for a ball that goes through the legs without touching and one point scored for a ball that goes through but touches the leg.

5. Indian clubs, milk cartons, or even regular bowling pins can be used as targets. Begin with one and move up to two or three. Plastic bowling pins are available for this purpose. Other targets can be made by laying a wastebasket on its side and rolling into it or using the 3-pound coffee can for the smaller ball.
6. The four-step approach is the accepted form for ten-pin bowling, and its basis can be set in class work. The teacher is referred to bowling manuals for more details, but here is the technique in a brief form for a right-handed bowler.

    Position: Stand with both feet together and the ball held in both hands comfortably in front of the body.

    Step 1: Step forward with the right foot, and at the same time push the ball directly forward and a little to the right.

    Step 2: Step with the left foot, and allow the ball to swing down alongside the leg on its way into the backswing.

    Step 3: Step with the right foot. The ball reaches the height of the backswing with this step.

    Step 4: Step with the left foot, and bowl the ball forward.

    As cues, the teacher can call out the following sequence for the four steps: (1)"out," (2)"down," (3)"back," (4)"roll."
7. A fine game for rounding off the activities is Bowling One Step (page 392).

Bowling through Human Straddle Targets

ACTIVITIES WITH PADDLES AND BALLS

The present popularity of racket sports makes it imperative that the schools give attention to providing a basis for the activity. The emphasis is divided into two approaches. For the primary-level children, the nylon-stocking paddle (page 563) can be used to introduce the racket sports. Much of this early activity is devoted to informal, exploratory play. Different types of objects can be batted—table tennis balls, newspaper balls, shuttlecocks, and tennis balls.

For children in the third through sixth grades, wooden paddles (page 568) and appropriate balls are used, with instruction laying a basis for future play in racquet ball, table tennis, squash, and regular tennis.

The activities, particularly paddle tennis, take considerable space. If played outdoors, balls roll hither and thither. The emphasis must be on controlled stroking.

Instructional Procedures— Nylon-Stocking Paddles

1. Most of the stroking should be volleys, although, when the balls do bounce, some ground strokes can be done.
2. See that there is good individual control before proceeding to partner work. Remember that rallies for young children tend to be quite brief.
3. Teach something about grip, but let the children experiment in the kinds of things they wish to do.

Recommended Activities

1. Toss the ball, and hit it upward. See if it can be hit a second time. Hit it forward, chase it, and hit it back. Explore different ways of stroking.
2. Hit it against a wall, retrieve it, and continue. Try different strokes.
3. Work with a partner. One can toss it to the other, who hits it back.
4. Use a spherical balloon. Keep it up individually, or propel it back and forth between partners.

Instructional Procedures—Wooden Paddles

1. All paddles should have leather wrist thongs. The hand should go through the leather loop before grasping the paddle. No play should be permitted without this safety precaution.
2. Proper grip must be emphasized, and seeing that children maintain this is a constant battle. The easiest method of teaching the proper grip is to advise the student to hold his or her paddle perpendicular to the floor and then shake hands with it. Young people tend to revert to the inefficient hammer grip, which is similar to the grip used on a hammer.
3. Accuracy and control should be the goals of this activity, and the children should not be concerned with force or distance.
4. The wrist should be held reasonably stiff, and

Holding the Paddle Properly—The Handshake Grip

Incorrectly Holding the Paddle—The Hammer Grip

the arm action should be a stroking motion.

5. Early activities can be attempted with both right and left hands, but the dominant hand should be developed in critical skills.

6. During a lesson, related information about racket sports may be quite relevant.

7. Practice in racket work should move from individual to partner work as quickly as feasible, since this is the basic reality of the racket sports.

8. For the forehand stroke, turn the body sideways (meaning that, for a right-handed player, the left side is toward the direction he or she wishes to hit).

9. For the backhand stroke, put the thumb against the handle of the racket for added support and force. Turn sideways so that the shoulder on the side of the racket hand leads toward the direction of the stroke.

10. A step is made with the leading foot in the direction of the stroke as the stroke is made.

11. A volley is made with the racket faced in a sort of punch stroke. The important element is a firm surface on which the ball can rebound. The racket is pushed forward rather than being stroked.

Recommended Activities

Individual Activities

1. Place ball on paddle, and attempt to balance it to prevent it from falling off. As skill increases, attempt to roll the ball around the edges of the paddle.

2. Bounce the ball in the air, using the paddle. See how many times it can be bounced without touching the floor. Bounce it off the paddle upward, and catch it with the other hand. Increase the height of the bounce.

3. Dribble the ball with the paddle, from a stationary position; moving. Change the paddle from hand to hand while the ball is in the air.

4. Alternate bouncing the ball in the air and on the floor.

5. Bounce the ball off the paddle upward and catch it with the paddle. This requires one to give with the paddle and create a soft home for the ball.

6. Put the ball on the floor and scoop it up with the paddle; start dribbling the ball without touching it; and put a reverse spin on it, and scoop it up into the air.

7. Bounce the ball off the paddle into the air and alternate sides of the paddle as you bounce the ball.

8. Bat the ball into the air and perform the following stunts while the ball is in the air: touch the floor; do a heel click (single and double); clap hands; turn completely around; and do various combinations of these activities.

9. Stroke the ball against the wall. This is a good lead-up to tennis and paddleball. Have the children practice both the forehand and backhand strokes.

Partner Activities

All partner activity should begin with controlled throwing (feeding) by one partner and the designated stroke return by the other. In this way, the child concentrates on his or her stroke without worrying about the competitive aspects of the activity.

1. Forehand: Toss and return stroke. Stroking back and forth with partner.

2. Backhand: Toss and return stroke. Stroking back and forth with partner.

3. Continuous Play: Back and forth play over a net. Improvised nets can be set up by laying a jump rope on the floor crosswise to the field of play, or by supporting a wand on blocks or cones, or by utilizing a bench for the barrier. (See chapter thirty-four for a diagram of a home-constructed net.)

4. Volleying: Toss and return stroke. Volley back and forth. In the volley, the ball does not touch the floor. The volley is a punching type of stroke, with the racket remaining faced against the ball.

5. Partner Play: This is doubles play. Partners on each side alternate turns returning the ball.

6. Volley Tennis: Use a whiffle ball. It moves slowly and allows children the time to position their feet properly. Catch with a partner: Allow the ball to bounce before returning it. Perform stunts while the ball is in the air.

7. Dribble Flag Pull: Dribble the ball with your paddle and try to pull your flag without losing control of the ball.

8. Keep the Ball Aloft: While you move, keep the ball in the air with a partner by alternating bounces.

ACTIVITIES WITH FRISBEES (FLYING DISCS)

Instructional Procedures

1. When the disc is thrown, it should be kept parallel to the ground at release. If it is tilted, a curved throw will result.

2. Good throwing principles should be followed by stepping into the throw and following through upon release of the disc.

3. If space is limited, the frisbees should be thrown in the same direction. Students, divided into two groups, can throw across the area to each other.

4. There should be at least one disc for each child, so practice time can be maximized. However, the majority of activities are best

practiced by students in pairs using one disc.

5. Youngsters can develop both sides of their bodies by learning to throw and catch the discs with either hand. The teacher should design the activities so that youngsters have time for both types of practice.

6. In the early stages of throwing the disc, distance should not be a goal; rather, emphasis should be on proper form and technique.

7. Since a frisbee is somewhat different from the other implements children usually throw, an adequate amount of time should be devoted to teaching form and style in throwing and catching. Avoid drills that reward speed in throwing and catching.

Throwing the Disc

Backhand Throw

The backhand grip is used most often. The thumb is on top of the disc, the index finger along the rim, and the other fingers placed under the disc. To throw the frisbee, stand with the lead foot toward the target in a sideways position. The lead foot is on the same side of the body as the throwing arm. Step toward the target, and throw the frisbee in a sideways motion across the body. Snap the wrist and try to keep the disc flat upon release.

Underhand Throw

Use the same grip as in the backhand throw, except that you face your target. The disc is held at the side of the body. Step forward with the leg opposite the throwing arm as the frisbee is brought forward. When the throwing arm is moved out to the front of the body (parallel to the ground), the frisbee is released. The trick to this throw is learning to release it so that it is parallel to the ground.

Catching the Disc

Thumbs-down Catch

This catch is used to catch the disc when it is thrown at waist level or above. The thumb is pointing toward the ground when this catch is made. With all catches, the frisbee should be tracked from the thrower's hand. This clues the catcher as to whether there is a tilt on the disc that will cause it to curve.

Thumbs-up Catch

Used for catching the frisbee when it is thrown below waist level. The thumb points up, and the fingers are spread in preparation for receiving the disc.

Gripping the Frisbee for a Throw   *A Thumps-up Catch*

Trick Catches

The disc can be caught in different positions. The two most popular are behind the back and the between the legs. In the behind-the-back catch, the thumbs-up catch is used and the disc is caught with the arm that is farthest away from the thrower. For the between-the-legs catch, the thumbs-up catch is used and a leg can be lifted to facilitate the catch.

Recommended Activities

1. Throw the frisbee at different levels to your partner.
2. Catch the frisbee, using various catching and hand positions.
3. Throw a curve with the disc. Try curving it to the left, the right, and upward. Throw a slow curve and then a fast slider.
4. Throw a bounce pass to your partner. Throw a fast, low bounce. Throw a high, slow bounce.
5. When you are the catcher, do various stunts after the disc has left your partner's hand. Examples are full turns, heel clicks, clapping your hands, and touching the ground.
6. Throw the disc with your nondominant hand. Try to throw for accuracy first and then strive for distance.
7. Make the disc respond like a boomerang. Throw into the wind at a steep angle and see whether it comes back to you.
8. Throw the frisbee into the air, run, and catch it. See whether you can increase the distance the disc can be thrown and caught before it touches the ground.
9. Have your partner hold a hoop as a target. See how many times you can throw the frisbee through the hoop. Play a game of One Step in which you move back a step each time you throw the disc through the hoop. When you make two misses in a row, your partner gets a chance to try it.
10. Place a series of hoops on the ground. Different colors of hoops can signify different point values. Have a contest with your partner to see who can earn more points in five throws.
11. Play catch with a partner while you are both moving. Try to throw the disc in front of your partner so that he or she does not have to break stride to catch the disc.
12. Throw for distance. Try to throw farther than your partner, using a series of four throws.
13. Throw for both distance and accuracy. Using a series of four or more throws, try to reach a goal that is a specified distance away. Many different objects can be used as goals, such as basket standards, fence posts, and trees. This could be the start of playing frisbee golf, which is becoming a popular recreational sport.
14. Set a time limit of 30 seconds. Within this time, see how many successful throws and catches can be made. A certain distance apart for all the pairs must be set, and missed catches do not count as throws.
15. Working in groups of three, see whether you can keep the disc away from the person in the middle. Establish your own set of rules as to when someone else must move into the middle, et cetera.
16. In groups of three, with one person in the middle, try to throw the frisbee through the middle person's legs. A point is scored each time the disc is thrown through the legs without touching them. Legs must be spread about shoulder width.

PARACHUTE PLAY

Parachute play can be enjoyed by all children from the first through the sixth grades. Activities must be selected carefully for younger children, since some of the skills presented will be difficult for them. One parachute is generally sufficient for the normal-size class of 30 children.

Parachutes come in different sizes, but those with diameters ranging from 24 to 28 feet are suitable for a regular class. Small parachutes 10 or 12 feet in diameter are available for small groups and function particularly well for smaller-size classes in special education.

Each parachute has an opening near the top to allow trapped air to escape and keep the parachute properly shaped. Most parachutes are constructed of nylon. A parachute also should have the facility of stretching tight when it is pulled on by children. A parachute that does not stretch taut when handled by children spaced around it has limited usefulness.

Values of Parachute Play

Parachutes provide a new and interesting medium of accomplishing physical fitness goals, with good development of strength, agility, coordination, and endurance. Strength development is especially centered on the arms, hands, and shoulder girdle. However, at times, strength demands are made on the entire body.

A wide variety of movement possibilities, some of which are rhythmic, can be employed in parachute play. Locomotor skills used while manipulating the parachute are much in evidence. Rhythmic beats of the tom-tom or appropriate music can guide locomotor movements.

Parachute play provides many excellent group learning experiences, and individuality disappears in much of this type of play.

Terminology

As the activities unfold, certain terms peculiar to the activity must be carefully explained. Terms such as *inflate, deflate, float, dome, mushroom,* and others need to be clarified when they are introduced.

Grips

The grips used in handling the parachute are comparable to those employed in hanging activities on apparatus. Grips can be with one or two hands, overhand (palms facing away), underhand (palms facing), or mixed, a combination of underhand and overhand grips. The grips should be varied.

Instructional Procedures

1. For preliminary explanations, the parachute can be stretched out on the ground in its circular pattern with the children seated back just far enough so that they cannot touch the parachute during instructions. During explanations when the parachute is held by the children, they should retain their hold lightly, letting the center of the parachute drop to the ground. Children must be taught to exercise control, so they do not manipulate the parachute while explanations are in progress.
2. The teacher explains the activity, demonstrating as needed. If there are no questions, he or she initiates the activity with a command such as "ready—begin!" Best success occurs when children start together on signal. At times, the teacher may wish to have the children lay the parachute down, back off a step or two, and sit down for further instructions or for a short rest.
3. Squads can be used in forming the parachute circle. Each squad occupies a quarter of the parachute's circumference. Squads are useful for competitive units in game activity.
4. Watch carefully for fatigue, particularly with younger children.

Activities

Activities are presented according to type, with variations and suggestions for supplementary activities included. Unless otherwise specified, activities begin and halt on signal. Pupils' suggestions can broaden the scope of activity.

Exercise-Type Activities

Exercises should be done vigorously and with enough repetitions to challenge the children. In addition to the exercises presented, others can be adapted to parachute play.

Toe Toucher: Sit with feet extended under the parachute and the chute held taut with a two-hand grip, drawn up to the chin. Bend forward, and touch the grip to the toes. Return to stretched parachute.

Curl-ups: Extend the body under the parachute in curl-up position, so the stretched parachute comes up to the chin when held taut. Perform Curl-ups, each time returning to the tight parachute.

Dorsal Lifts: Lie prone, head toward the parachute, and feet pointed back away from it. Grip the chute and slide backward until there is some tension on it. Raise the chute off the ground by a vigorous lift of the arms, with the head and chest off the ground. Return.

V-Sit: Lie in a position similar to that for dorsal lifts, but supine. Do a V-up by raising both the upper and lower parts of the body simultaneously to form the V position. Knees should be kept straight.

Backward Pulls: Backward Pulls are made facing the parachute and pulling back, away from its center. Pulls can be made from sitting, kneeling, or standing positions.

Other Pulls: Side Pulls using a flexed-arm position can be structured. Other variations of pulling can be devised.

Hip Walk and Scooter: Begin with the parachute taut. Move forward with the Scooter (page 340) and the Hip Walk (page 340). Move back to place with the same movement until the chute is taut again.

Elevator: Begin with the chute taut and at ground level. On the words, "elevator up," students lift the chute overhead while keeping it stretched tight. On the command, "elevator down," the class quickly lowers the chute to starting position. Lower or raise in increments.

Levels also can bring in body-identification factors, as the children hold the chute even with their heads, noses, chins, shoulders, chests, waists, thighs, knees, ankles, and toes.

Running in Place: Students can run in place while holding the chute at different levels. Grass Drills (page 116) can be performed while holding on to the chute.

Isometrics: It is possible to perform isometrics with the chute. For example, hold the chute taut at shoulder level and try to stretch it for 10 seconds. Many other exercises can be performed to develop all parts of the body.

Merry-go-round Movements

Merry-go-round movements, in which the center hole in the parachute remains above the same spot, offer many opportunities for locomotor movements, either free or to the beat of a tom-tom. Rhythmic Running, European style, is particularly appropriate. Holds can be one- or two-handed.

Many fundamental movements can be utilized while children move in a circular fashion, such as walking, running, hopping, skipping, galloping, sliding, draw steps, grapevine steps, and others. The parachute can be held at different levels.

Shaking the Rug and Making Waves

Shaking the Rug involves rapid movements, either light or heavy. Making Waves are large movements to send billows of cloth up and down like waves. Waves can be small, medium, or high.

Different types of waves can be made by having children alternate their up and down motion or by having the class work in small groups around the chute. Various patterns can be made by having these small groups take turns showing what they can do. Children can perform locomotor movements while they shake the rug for a more demanding activity.

Making a Dome

Begin with the parachute on the floor, children holding with two hands and kneeling on one knee. To trap the air under the chute and make a dome shape, each child stands up quickly, thrusting his

or her arms above the head and returning to starting position. Vary by having all or some of the children change to the inside of the chute on the down movement, as in a cave. Domes also can be made while moving in a circle.

Stunts under the Chute

Number Exchange: Children are numbered from 1 to 4. The teacher calls a number as the dome is made, and those with the number called must exchange positions before the chute comes down. Locomotor movements can be varied. Tasks under the chute can be specified, such as turning a certain number of turns with a jump rope, throwing and catching a beanbag, bouncing a ball a number of times, et cetera. The needed objects should be under the chute before the dome is made.

Chute Crawl: Half of the class, either standing or kneeling, stretches the chute out level with the

Making a Dome

The Dome

ground. The remaining children crawl under the chute to the opposite side from their starting positions.

Mushroom Activities

With the chute on the ground and students on one knee and holding with two hands, stand up quickly, thrusting arms overhead. Keeping the arms overhead, each walks forward three or four steps toward the center. The arms are held overhead until the chute is deflated.

Mushroom Release: All children release at the peak of inflation and either run out from under the chute or move to the center and sit down, with the chute descending on top of them.

Mushroom Run: Children make a mushroom, move into the center, and, without further delay, release holds and run once around the inside dome of the chute, counterclockwise, back to place.

Kite Run

Half of the class holds the chute on one side with one hand. The leader points in the direction they are to run, and they do so, holding the chute aloft as a kite.

Activities with Balls and Beanbags

Ball Circle: Place a basketball or a cage ball on the raised chute. Make the ball roll around the chute in a large circle, controlling it by raising or lowering the chute. Try the same with two balls. A beach ball is also excellent.

Popcorn: Place a number of beanbags (6-10) on the chute. Shake the chute to make them rise like popping corn.

Team Ball: Divide the chute players in half, so each team defends half of the chute. Using two to six balls, any variety, try to bounce the balls off the opponents' side, thus scoring one point for the attacking side.

Poison Snake: Place 6 to 10 Olympic jump ropes on the chute. By shaking the chute, try to make them hit players on the other side, who have a point scored against them for each touch. The team with the lowest score is the winner.

Circular Dribble: Each child has a ball suitable for dribbling. The object is to run in circular fashion counterclockwise, holding to the chute with the left hand and dribbling with the right hand, retaining control of the ball. This is the preferred direction for right-handers but is more difficult for left-handers. As an equalizer, try the dribbling clockwise.

The dribble should be started first. Then on signal, each starts to run. If a ball is lost, the child must recover the ball and try to hook on at his or her original place.

Hole in One: Use four or more plastic whiffle balls the size of golf balls. The balls should be of two different colors. The class is divided into two teams on opposite sides of the chute. The object is to shake the other team's balls into the hole in the center of the chute.

Other Activities

Running Number Game: Have the children around the chute and count off by fours. Start them running lightly, holding the chute in one hand. Call out one of the numbers. Children holding the number immediately release their grip on the chute and run forward to the next vacated place. This means that they must put on a burst of speed to move ahead to the next vacated place.

Routines to Music: Like other routines,

Popping Popcorn (Beanbags) in the Chute

parachute activities can be adapted to music. A sequence should be based on eight counts, with the routine made up of an appropriate number of sequences.

Tug-of-War: For a team tug-of-war, divide the class into two equal teams. On signal, they pull against each other and try to reach a restraining line. Another tug-of-war that is often more enjoyable for primary-age children is an individual pull, where all children tug in any direction they desire.

Action Songs and Dances: A number of action songs and dances can be performed while children hold on to a parachute. The following are suggested.

I'm Very, Very Small (page 215)
Go Round and Round the Village (page 220)
Carrousel (page 225)
Bingo (page 227)
Seven Jumps (page 240)

ACTIVITIES WITH WANDS

Wands have been used in physical education programs for many years, but it has only been recently that a wide variety of interesting and challenging activities have appeared. Wands can be made from ¾-inch maple dowels or from a variety of broom and mop handles. If two sizes are chosen, make them 36 inches and 42 inches. If only one size is to be used, a wand length of 1 meter is advised. This is not only an appropriate length, but it ties in with metric concepts.

Wands are more interesting when they are painted with imaginative designs, a chore that can be a class project.

Wands serve the physical education program in four ways: (1) challenge activities, (2) wand stunts, (3) exercises using wands, and (4) combative activities. Challenge activities, wand stunts, and exercises are presented here, and combatives are found in the section under that title (page 372).

Wands are noisy when they hit the floor. Putting rubber crutch tips on each end of the wand alleviates most of the noise and makes it easier to pick up wands from the floor. The tips should be put on with mucilage.

The year's supply of wands should include five or six extra beyond the number needed to have one for each child. There will be some breakage.

The recommended level of introduction for wand stunts is the third grade; however, the challenge activities may be introduced earlier.

Instructional Procedures

1. Since wands are noisy, it is helpful during instruction to have the child hold his or her wand with both hands or put it on the floor.
2. Many wand activities require great flexibility, which means not all children will be able to do

them. Girls usually perform flexibility stunts better than boys.
3. An adequate amount of space is needed for each individual, since wand stunts demand room.
4. Wands are not to be used as fencing foils. Stop this nonsense at once.
5. When balancing a wand, look at the top of the wand to secure cues on how to move to retain the balance.

Challenge Activities

Challenge activities can be used to offer a less structured approach and to allow for problem solving. The following are just a few of the many possible challenges. Many ideas can be developed by the children.

1. Can you reach down and pick up your wand without bending your knees?
2. Can you balance your wand on different parts of your body?
3. Can you hold your stick against the wall and move over and under it?
4. Let's see whether you can hold the stick at both ends and move through the gap.
5. Can you spin the wand and keep it going like a windmill?
6. Let's see how many different ways you can move over and around your wand when it is on the floor.
7. Put one end of the wand on the floor and hold the other end. How many times can you run around your wand without getting dizzy?
8. Place the wand between your feet and hop around as though you are on a pogo stick.
9. Throw your wand in the air and catch it.
10. Hold the wand vertically near the middle. Can you release your grip and catch the wand before it falls to the floor?
11. Have a partner hold a wand horizontally above the floor. Jump, leap, and hop over the wand. Gradually raise the height of the wand.
12. Try making different kinds of bridges over your wand.
13. Place the wand on the floor. Curl alongside it, just touching it. Curl at one end of the wand.
14. Balance the wand on the floor. Release the wand and try different stunts such as clapping hands, doing a heel click, and touching different body parts.
15. Put the wand on the floor and see how many different ways you can push it, using different body parts.

Wand Stunts

Individual Stunts

Wand Catch: Stand a wand on one end and hold it in place with the fingers on top. Bring the foot quickly over the stick, letting it go and catching

Beginning the Grapevine

Back Scratcher (wand has been passed overhead and is now being forced down the back)

Grapevine—Second Stage (head ducks under and wand is passed down the back)

the stick with the fingers before it falls. Do this right and left, inward and outward, for a complete set. Try to catch it with just the index finger.

Thread the Needle—V-Seat: Maintaining a V-seat position, with the wand held in front of the body with both hands, bend the knees between the arms and pass the wand over them and return, *without touching* the wand to the legs. Try with the ankles crossed.

Thread the Needle—Standing: Holding wand in both hands, step through stick one leg at a time and return without touching stick. Step through again, but this time bring the wand up the back, over the head, and around in front. Reverse. Try from side to side with the stick held front and back.

Grapevine: Holding wand near the ends, step with right foot *around* right arm and over wand inward toward the body. Pass the wand backward over the head and right shoulder until you are standing erect with wand between legs. Reverse back to original position. Try with the left foot leading.

Back Scratcher: Hold wand with underhand grip (palms up), with arms crossed in front of the body. Bend the elbows so that the wand can go over and behind the head. Attempt to pass the wand down the length of the body from the back of the shoulders to the heels. Do not release grip on wand. The wand is worked down behind the back while the arms stay in front of the body.

Wand Whirl: Stand wand upright in front of you. Turn around quickly and grasp wand before it falls. Do it right and left. Try making two full turns and catch the wand.

Twist Under: Grasp upright-standing wand with right hand. Twist around under the right arm without letting go of wand, taking it off the floor, or touching knee to floor. Repeat, using the left arm.

Jump Wand: Holding the wand in front with both hands, jump over the wand. Jumping back is not recommended, since the wand can hit the heels and cause an awkward fall. The wand passes under the body during the jump. Hold the wand with the tips of the fingers. (A rope or a towel can be substituted for children having difficulty.)

Balancing the Wand: Balance the wand vertically with one hand. Experiment with different hand and finger positions. Walk forward, backward, and sideward. Sit down, lie down, and move into other positions while keeping the wand balanced. Keep the eyes on the top of the wand.

Try balancing the wand horizontally in a variety of ways on the hands, arms, feet, and thighs. Balance it across the back of the neck. In crab position, balance it across the tummy.

The Sprinter: Get into a sprinter's position, with the wand on the floor perpendicular to the direction of the sprint and between the feet. Change the feet rapidly, alternating over the wand. Try moving both feet forward and backward.

Crab Leap: Place the wand on the floor. Get in crab position, and attempt to move the feet back and forth over the wand without touching the wand. Also try it with alternating feet.

Long Reach: Stand with the legs extended and the feet spread about 12 inches apart. Hold a wand in the left hand, and use it like a third limb. With a piece of chalk in the right hand, reach forward as far as possible and make a mark. Use the wand as a support and see whether the mark can be bettered.

Merry-go-wand: Place the wand vertically on the floor about 2 feet in front of the body. Bend over, and place the forehead on the upper end of the wand. Using a crossover step, go all the way around the wand without letting it fall to the floor. Hands must be kept on the small of the back.

Wand Bridge: Start with a straddle stance and the legs straight. Hold a wand near one end, with the other end pointed toward the ceiling and above the head. Bend backward and place the wand on the mat behind you, and walk the hands down the wand. Return to standing position.

Wand Twirl: Perhaps some children in the class have baton-twirling experience and can show the class some points of technique.

Partner Stunts

Partner Catch: Partners face each other a short distance (5 feet) apart, each holding his or her wand in the right hand. On signal, each throws the wand to the partner with the right hand and catches the incoming wand with the left. Distances can be increased somewhat.

Partner Change: Partners face each other a short distance (5 feet) apart, each with his or her wand standing upright, held by the right hand on top. On signal, each runs to the other's wand to catch it before it falls. This also can be done in the same way as the Wand Whirl, with each whirling to the other's wand. Proper positioning needs to be determined. Try with a small group of five or six. On signal, all move to the next wand.

Turn the Dishrag: Both partners face each other and grasp the wand. When ready, they perform a dishrag turn (page 327).

Jump the Wand: One partner moves the wand back and forth along the floor, while the other partner jumps it. To add challenge, partners should change the tempo of movement and raise the level of the wand.

Partner Carry: Partners face each other and place one end of the wand against their foreheads. By applying pressure to the wand, they can move around the area without dropping it. Challenge can be added by kneeling, sitting, and moving into push-up position. The wand also can be held with other body parts, such as tummies, knees, and elbows.

Wand Reaction: One partner holds the wand horizontally. The other partner places his or her hand directly above the wand palm down. When the wand is dropped, the person with his or her hand over the wand tries to catch it before it strikes the floor.

Isometric Exercises

The isometric exercises with wands presented here are mainly grip exercises.

A variety of grips should be employed. With the wand level, use either the overhand or underhand grip. With the wand in vertical position, a grip can be taken so that the thumbs are pointed up, pointed down, or pointed toward each other. Repeat each exercise with a different grip. The exercise can be repeated with the wand in different positions: in front of the body, held level; overhead; behind the back; or front of the body, held vertical.

Pull the Wand Apart: Place the hands 6 inches apart near the center of the wand. With a tight grip to prevent slippage and the arms extended, pull the hands apart. Change grips and position.

Push the Wand Together: Same as the previous exercise, except push the hands together.

Wand Twist: Same hand positioning. Twist the hands in opposite direction.

Bicycle: With the wand level throughout and using an overhand grip, extend the wand out and downward. Bring it upward near the body, completing a circular movement. On the downward movement, push the wand together, and, on the upward movement, pull the wand apart.

Arm Spreader: Hold the wand overhead with the hands spread wide. Attempt to compress the stick. Reverse force, and attempt to pull the stick apart.

Dead Lift: Partially squat and place the wand under the thighs. Place the hands between the legs and try to lift. Also try with the hands on the outside of the legs.

Abdominal Tightener: From a standing position, place the wand behind the buttocks. With both hands on the outside of the buttocks, pull forward and contract the abdominal muscles.

Stretching Exercises

Physical educators have been using wands for a long time for stretching, bending, and twisting movements.

Side Bender: Grip wand and extend arms overhead. Feet are apart. Bend sideways as far as possible, maintaining straight arms and legs. Recover, and bend to the other side.

Slave Twist: Place the wand behind the neck, with the arms draped over the wand from behind, forming the slave position. Rotate the upper body first right as far as possible and then left. Both feet and hips should remain in position. The twist is at the waist.

Slave Twist to Knee: Same position as above. Bend the trunk forward and twist so the right end of the wand touches the left knee. Recover, and touch the left to the right knee.

Slave Twist to Knee

Shoulder Stretcher: Grip the stick at the ends in a regular grip. Extend the arms overhead and rotate the stick, arms, and shoulders backward until the stick touches the back of the legs. When

done correctly, the arms should be kept straight. Those who find it too easy should move their arms closer toward the center of the wand.

Toe Touch: Grip the stick with hands about shoulder width apart. Bend forward, reaching down as far forward as possible without bending the knees. The movement should be slow and controlled. As a variation, try the same activity from a sitting position.

Over the Toes: Sit down, flex the knees, place the stick over the toes, and rest the stick against the middle of your arch. Grip the stick with the fingers just outside of the feet. Slowly extend the legs forward, pushing against the stick and trying for a full extension of the legs.

ACTIVITIES WITH HOOPS

Most American hoops are made from plastic, but Europeans use some made from wood. The plastic variety is less durable, but it is more versatile. Extra hoops are needed, since there will be breakage. The standard hoop is 42 inches in diameter, but it is desirable to have smaller hoops for younger children (36 inches). The hoop with the lead shot inside is of no advantage.

Instructional Procedures

1. Hoops are a noisy activity. The teacher might find it helpful to have the children lay the hoops on the floor when they are to listen.
2. Hoops can be a medium of creativity for children. Allow them free time to explore their own ideas.
3. Allow the children an adequate amount of space in which to perform, since hoops require much movement.
4. In activities that require children to jump through hoops, instruct the child holding the hoop to grasp it lightly, so it will not cause an awkward fall when a performer hits the hoop.
5. Hoops can serve as a "home" for various activities. For instance, the children might leave their hoops to gallop in all directions and quickly return to them upon command.
6. Hoops make good targets. They can be made to stand by an individual mat placed through the hoop and over its base (see page 565).
7. When teaching the reverse spin with the hoop, have the students throw the hoop up in place rather than forward on the floor. After they learn the upward throw, they can progress to the forward throw for distance.

Hoops as Floor Targets

Each child has a hoop, which he or she places on the floor. A number of movement challenges can give direction to the activity.

1. Show what different patterns you can make jumping or hopping in and out of the hoops.
2. Do a Bunny Jump and a Frog Jump into the center and out to the other side.
3. Show what ways you can cross from one side of the hoop to the other by taking the weight on your hands inside the hoop.
4. What kinds of animal walks can you do around your hoop?
5. On all fours, show the kinds of movements you can do, with your feet inside the hoop and your hands outside; with your hands inside the hoop and your feet outside; or with one foot and a hand inside and one foot and a hand outside.
6. See how many times you can jump in and out of your hoop during the time limit (15, 20, or 30 seconds). Try this with hopping.
7. Balance and walk around the hoop, trying to keep your feet from touching the floor.
8. Curl inside your hoop. Bridge over your hoop. Stretch across your hoop. See how many different ways you can move.
9. Pick up your hoop and see how many different machines you can invent. Let your hoop be a steering wheel of a car. What could it be on a train or a boat?
10. Jump in and out of the hoops, using the alphabet. Jump in on the vowels and out on the consonants. Use odd and even numbers in the same way. Vary the locomotor movements.
11. Get into the hoop by using two body parts. Move out by using three parts. Vary the number of body parts used.

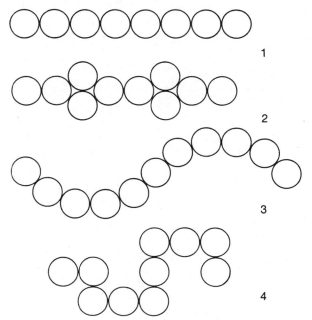

Hoop Floor Patterns for Exploratory Activity

12. Organize the class by squads or comparable groups, and divide the hoops among them. Using some of the formations shown at the bottom of the page for ideas, try different locomotor movements, animal walks, and other feasible ways of maneuvering through the maze of hoops. After the children have gained some experience, this can become a follow-the-leader activity.

Hoop-handling Activities

1. Spin the hoop like a top. See how long you can make it spin. Spin it again, and see how many times you can run around the spinning hoop before it falls to the floor.
2. Hula hoop using various body parts such as waist, legs, arms, and fingers. While hula hooping on the arms, try to change the hoop from one arm to the other. Lie on the back with one or both legs pointed toward the ceiling; explore different ways the legs can twirl the hula hoop. Hula hoop with two or more hoops.
3. Jump or hop through a hoop held by a partner. Further challenge can be added by varying the height and angle of the hoop.
4. Roll the hoop and run alongside it. Change directions when a command is given.
5. Hula hoop on one arm. Throw the hoop into the air, and catch it on the other arm.
6. Hold the hoop and swing it like a pendulum. Jump and hop in and out of the hoop.
7. Use the hoop like a jump rope. Jump forward, backward, and sideward. Do a crossover with the hands.
8. Roll the hoop with a reverse spin to make it return to the thrower. The key to the reverse spin is to pull down (toward the floor) on the hoop as it is released. Roll the hoop with a reverse spin, and jump over the hoop and catch it as it returns. Roll the hoop with a reverse spin, and, as it returns, hoist it with the foot and catch it. Roll the hoop with a reverse spin, kick it up with the toe, and go through the hoop. Roll the hoop with a reverse spin, run around it, and catch it. Roll the hoop with a reverse spin, pick it up, and begin hooping on the arm in one motion.
9. Many partner stunts can be performed, such as these: Play catch with a partner. Play catch with two or more hoops. Hula hoop and attempt to change the hoops from one partner to another. One partner rolls the hoop with a reverse spin, and the other attempts to crawl through the hoop. This is done most easily just after the hoop reverses direction and begins to return to the spinner. Some children can go in and out of the hoop twice. Partners can spin the hoops like tops and see who can keep the hoop spinning longer.

Games with Hoops

Hoops can be used for some simple games.

Musical Hoops

Hoops, one less than the number of children, are placed on the floor. Players are given a locomotor movement challenge to do, and, on signal, they find a hoop and sit Indian fashion in the center of it. Music can be employed, with the children moving to the music and seeking a hoop when the music stops.

Around the Hoop

The class is divided into groups of threes, with children in each group numbered 1, 2, and 3. Each group of three sits back to back inside a hoop. Their heels may need to be outside the hoop. The leader calls out a direction (right or left) and names one of the numbers. The child with that number immediately gets up, runs in the stipulated direction around the hoop, and then runs back to his or her place and sits down. The winner is the group that is sitting in good position after the child returns to his or her place.

Hula Hoop Circle

Four to six children hold hands in a circle, facing in, with a hoop dangling on a pair of joined hands. They move the hoop completely around the circle and back to the starting point. This requires all bodies to go through the hoop. Hands may help the hoop move, but handholds cannot be released.

INDIVIDUAL TUG-OF-WAR ROPES

An individual tug-of-war rope consists of a rope about 5 feet long, including two loops, one on each end. For making the rope, a sturdy piece of rope about 10 feet long and two pieces of garden hose (each about 24 inches long) are needed. The pieces of hose are used to encase the loops. Braided nylon cord ¼ to ⅜ inches thick works quite well for the rope; sash cord is also excellent. Thread the rope through a piece of hose on each end, and tie each loop securely (see page 565 for instructions). The hose cushions the handholds.

Tug-of-war ropes help in the development of strength, since the contestants must utilize maximum or near-maximum strength in the contests. These strength demands may continue over a short period of time. Since considerable effort is demanded in some cases, force concepts are concomitant learnings.

Instructional Procedures

1. Contests should be among opponents who have comparable ability. Each child should have a chance to win part of the time.

2. Plan a system of rotation, so children meet different opponents.
3. Caution students not to let go of the ropes. If the grip is slipping, they should inform the other student, renew the grip, and start over.
4. Individual ropes are excellent for partner resistance activities. Suggested activities are included in this unit, and it is recommended that a few of them be practiced each time the children use the ropes.
5. Make clear the starting routine, so it is fair to each contestant. Make definite what constitutes a win and how long a contest must endure to be called a tie.
6. A line on the floor perpendicular to the direction of the rope makes a satisfactory goal for determining a win. Pegs could be placed behind the children, and they might pick up the pegs to win. One child pulls the other forward until he or she is over the line. If the distance to be pulled (over the line) seems not far enough, two parallel lines can be drawn from 8 to 10 feet apart. The object is to pull the opponent out of the area between the lines.

An in-depth discussion of instructional procedures and formations for conducting combative activities is found in chapter twenty.

Recommended Activities

Try the following ways of pulling.
1. Right hand only, left hand only, both hands.
2. Grasp with the right hand, with the body supported on three points (the left hand and the feet). Change hands.

Pulling on Three Points

3. Pull with backs toward each other, with the rope between the legs, holding only with one hand.
4. Opponents are face down on all fours, with the feet toward each other. Hook the loops around one foot of each opponent. The force is provided with both hands and the foot that is on the floor for each contestant.
5. Opponents are in crab position. The rope is pulled by hooking a foot through the loop.

Pulling in Crab Position

6. The tug-of-war rope offers good possibilities in movement exploration. Let the children try to devise ways other than those mentioned by which they can pull against each other.
7. Opponents face each other, standing on one foot only. Each contestant tries to pull the other off balance without losing his or her own balance. If the raised foot touches the floor, the other person is declared the winner.
8. Contestants stand with opposite sides toward each other. They hold a tug-of-war rope with opposite hands and move apart until the rope is taut. The goal is to make the other person move his or her feet by pulling and giving on the rope. Legs must be kept straight, and only the arms can be used in the contest.
9. Students stand 10 feet away from the ropes, which are on the floor. On signal, they run to the ropes, pick them up, and have a tug-of-war. Contestants can be started from different positions, such as push-up, sit-up, crab, et cetera.
10. Peg Pickup: Instead of having opponents pull each other across a line, put a peg (Indian club) behind each opponent at a suitable distance. Each one then tries to pull the other toward his or her own peg so that he or she can pick it up.
11. Four-Corner Peg Pickup: Tie two individual ropes together at the center so four loops are available for pulling. Put four pegs in the form of a square, and let four children compete to see who can pick up his or her peg. (See page 566.)
12. Doubles: Have two children pull against two. The loops should be big enough so that both can secure handholds on them. Use right hands only, left hands only, et cetera.
13. Japanese Tug-of-War: Two children take hold of a rope, each with both hands on a loop. The children are positioned close enough together so that there is some slack in the rope. A third party grasps the rope to make a 6-inch bend at the center. The contestants pull the rope so that there is no slack. On the signal "go," the third party drops the loop and the opponents try to pull the other off balance. To move a foot is to lose.
14. Group contests are possible. See page 566 for a diagram of rope arrangements suitable for groups.

A Game with Individual Tug-of-War Ropes

Hawaiian Tug-of-War

Playing Area: Gymnasium playground. Two parallel lines are drawn about 20 feet apart.
Players: The game is between two people, but as many pairs as are in a class can play.
Supplies: An individual tug-of-war rope for each pair.

An individual tug-of-war rope is laid on the floor at right angles to, and midway between, the two parallel lines. The two children playing position themselves so that each is standing about 1 foot from one of the loops of the rope. This means that they are in position to pick up the rope and pull against each other on signal.

Hawaiian Tug-of-War

The object of the game is to pull the other child, so the winner can touch the line behind him or her. The magic word is *hula.* This signals that both children should pick up the rope and begin to pull. They must not reach down and pick up the rope unless "hula" is called. The teacher can use commands such as "go" and "begin" to deceive the children.

Partner Resistance Activities with Ropes

The children should follow good exercise principles, exerting sufficient force (near maximum), maintaining resistance for 8 to 10 seconds and stabilizing the base so that the selected part of the body can be exercised.

As in other activities, grips can be varied. The upper grip (palms away) and the lower grip (palms toward performer) are utilized. Occasionally, a mixed grip with one hand in upper position and one hand in lower position can be used.

The force is a controlled pull, not a tug. The partner should not be forced to move his or her position. Much of the exercise is centered on the hands and arms, but other parts of the body come in as braces. In the suggested exercises, partners work together. The position is the same for both partners. The exercises also could be done by one person, with the other end of the rope attached firmly to some part of the building. One or more basic activities are suggested for each position, and the teacher and the children can devise others. Laterality must be kept in mind, so the right and the left sides of the body receive equal treatment.

Partners Standing with Sides toward Each Other

1. Lower grip. Flexed-arm pull, elbow at right angles.
2. Upper grip. Extended arm at 45 degrees from side. Pull toward side.
3. Lower grip. Arm extended completely overhead. Pull overhead.
4. Loop around ankle. Feet are apart. Pull with closer foot.

Lower Grip, Flexed-Arm Isometric

Partners Facing, Standing

1. Lower grip. Flexed-arm pull, one hand and two hands.
2. Upper grip. Arm extended at side or down. Pull toward the rear.
3. Upper grip. Pull both hands straight toward chest.
4. Upper grip. Arms above head. Pull backward.

Partners Facing, Sitting

1. Repeat activities described above.
2. Hook on with both feet. Pull with both feet.

Partners Facing, Prone Position

1. Upper grip. Pull directly toward chest.
2. Lower grip. Flexed-arm pull.

Partners in Prone Position, Feet toward Each Other

1. Hook around one ankle. With knee joint at a right angle, pull.
2. Try with both feet together.

Pushing and Pulling Resistive Exercises

Using mostly the standing positions, work out resistive exercises in the following manner. One child pulls and makes progress with eight steps. The other child then pulls him or her back for eight counts. The addition of music makes this an interesting activity for children. The child being pulled out must provide the right amount of resistance to make the puller work reasonably hard.

MANIPULATIVE ACTIVITIES WITH FOOTSIES

The program of manipulative activities can be expanded with a number of activities that have limited or local popularity. Activities with footsies are one category of these. A description of the construction of a footsie can be found on page
. Some things that can be done while twirling the footsie include these.

1. Turn it with the right foot and then the left foot, clockwise and counterclockwise.
2. Travel forward, backward, and sideward while twirling the footsie.
3. Turn around in place in the same direction as the footsie. The opposite way.
4. Bounce a ball while twirling. Toss the ball and catch it. Play catch with a partner.

Twirling the Footsie

Seventeen

Long-Rope Jumping **Individual Rope Jumping** **Movements Guided by Rope Patterns**

Activities with Jump Ropes

Rope jumping is an excellent activity for the whole body. It increases coordination, rhythm, and timing. It tones up the cardiorespiratory system and increases both speed and endurance. It makes a contribution to weight control and total physical condition. It can contribute to good posture habits. It has good carry-over values.

Some people prefer to refer to rope jumping as *rope skipping*. In the material that follows, the terms are used interchangeably.

From an educational standpoint, rope jumping has good value in the school program. It allows a maximum amount of student activity within a minimum amount of time and space. The activities are in good progression. The teacher can begin at the student's level and develop from that point. It is inexpensive and easily taught.

It provides a creative activity that has unlimited possibilities for new material. The further youngsters progress, the more they tend to invent steps and routines of their own. The activity is not seasonal in character.

For the teacher and the administrator, it provides excellent program material for PTA meetings and other demonstrations.

Because it is a learned activity, the material is not allocated to grades. Teachers should begin the year with a review of all fundamentals and such other material as the children have mastered.

The rope jumping activities in this chapter are grouped into three categories: (1) long-rope jumping, (2) individual rope jumping, and (3) movements guided by rope patterns.

Some teachers like to teach primary-age children long-rope jumping first. This allows them to establish a jumping rhythm without the added burden of having to turn the rope.

LONG-ROPE JUMPING

Groups of five children form convenient clusters for practicing long-rope skills. Two of the group become turners and the others are jumpers. Rotate the positions regularly. Take time to teach the students how to turn the rope effectively. Jumpers should enter the rope from an angle, establishing an entry path that is comfortable. One end of the rope can be tied to a table leg, so that more youngsters can be actively jumping.

The rope should be heavy enough to carry the rhythm, and it should be from 9 to 16 feet in length (the length depends on the ages of the children). The newer Olympic-type ropes with plastic links are excellent jump ropes.

Two important concepts need to be understood. *Front door* means that the child enters from the side where the rope is coming down. This is the easier entry. *Back door* is identified as the side where the rope is coming up. To enter front door, the jumper follows the rope in and jumps when it completes the turn. For back door, the timing is made so that the jumper jumps the rope as it is coming toward him or her.

Chants are suggested for certain of the jumping sequences. There are many chants that represent a cultural heritage from years of rope jumping. No doubt children have their own favorites. Most chants are geared to girls' names, an old custom from the time when jumping was considered a feminine activity. In today's physical education, both sexes participate in the activity, and appropriate chants should be substituted for the boys. In some of the chants presented, a suitable substitute is provided.

Introductory Skills

1. Hold the rope 6 inches from the ground. Children jump over, back and forth. Raise the rope a little each time. Be sure to hold the rope loosely in the hands. This is called Building a House.
2. The Ocean Wave is another stationary jumping activity. The turners make waves in the rope by moving the arms up and down. The children try to time it so as to jump over a low part of the wave.
3. Snake in the Grass: The holders stoop down and wiggle the rope back and forth on the floor. Children try to jump over the rope and not touch it as it moves.
4. Swing the rope in a pendulum fashion. Children jump the rope as it passes under them. This establishes basic jumping patterns and should have good development.
5. Have the child stand in the center between the turners. Carefully turn the rope in a complete arc over the jumper's head. As the rope completes the turn, the jumper jumps over it. He or she immediately exits in the same direction as the rope is turned.
6. Run through the turning rope without jumping, following the rope through.
7. While the rope is being turned, the jumper runs in and jumps once. He or she runs out immediately. The rope must be coming toward the jumper (front door). Youngsters also like to play school: they go through the following sequence trying to pass to the sixth grade. Kindergarten—run through the turning rope. First grade—run in the rope, take one jump, and run out. Second through sixth grade—increase the number of jumps by one. When the jumper misses, he or she becomes a holder, and the sequence begins anew.
8. When they have difficulty with the rhythm, the children can practice to one side without actually jumping to the rope. A drumbeat can be used to reinforce the rhythm with alternate heavy (jump) and light (rebound) beats.
9. A fun activity is to turn the rope under a bouncing ball, which must be lively. The turners stand ready, and a third child tosses a ball upward so that it remains in one spot while bouncing. The turners adjust the speed of the turning as the bounces become smaller and more rapid. Count can be kept of the number of successful turns before the ball ceases bouncing.

Intermediate Skills, Routines, and Chants

Intermediate skills are based on the ability of the jumper to go in front door, jump, and exit first front door and then go through the same sequence back door. The ability to enter back door should be developed quickly. Enough practice in executing the simple jumping skills and exits should be held so that confidence is fortified; the students then can turn to more intricate and interesting routines. Entries and exits should be varied.

1. Run in, jump a specified number of times, and exit.
2. Add chants that dictate the number of jumps, which are to be followed by an exit.

   Tick tock, tick tock,
   What's the time by the clock?
   It's one, two, et cetera (up to midnight).

   I like coffee, I like tea,
   How many boys (girls) are wild about me?
   One, two, three, et cetera (up to a certain number).

   Hippity hop to the barber shop,
   How many times before I stop?
   One, two, three, et cetera.

   Bulldog, poodle, bow wow wow,
   How many doggies have we now?
   One, two, three, et cetera.

   Lady, lady at the gate
   Eating cherries from a plate.
   How many cherries did she eat?
   One, two, three, et cetera.

3. Children can label their first jump "kindergarten" and exit at any "grade." To graduate from high school, the exit would be at the twelfth grade. Each grade should be sounded crisply in succession.
4. Kangaroo or White Horse gets its name from the jump required for back-door entry. When this is performed, the jumper resembles a kangaroo or a leaping horse. The student calls out, "Kangaroo," takes the entry jump through back door, and exits. Next time, he or she calls out, "Kangaroo one!" and adds a single jump. Successive jumps are called and added until a designated number is reached.
5. Try different kinds of steps. Vary the two-footed jump with right and left hops and heel-and-toe steps. Another challenge is to turn the rope over a line parallel to the rope and have the jumper jump back and forth over the line, adding foot positions such as feet together, feet apart, and stride forward and back.

6. Vary the jumping patterns with turns. Make four quarter-turns until the jumpers again face the original direction. Reverse the direction of the turns.
7. Add stunts as directed by selected chants.

> Teddy Bear, Teddy Bear, turn around.
> Teddy Bear, Teddy Bear, touch the ground.
> Teddy Bear, Teddy Bear, show your shoe.
> Teddy Bear, Teddy Bear, you better skidoo.
>
> Teddy Bear, Teddy Bear, say your prayers.
> Teddy Bear, Teddy Bear, go upstairs.
> Teddy Bear, Teddy Bear, turn out the light.
> Teddy Bear, Teddy Bear, say good night.
>
> Mama, mama, I am sick.
> Get the doctor quick, quick, quick.
> Mama, mama, turn around.
> Mama, mama, touch the ground.
> Mama, mama, are you through?
> Mama, mama, spell your name.
> (Use Daddy if the jumper is a boy.)

8. Hot Pepper: Turners turn the rope faster and faster, with the performer trying to keep up with the increased speed. The following chants are good for Hot Pepper.

> Mabel, Mabel, set the table,
> Bring the plates if you are able,
> Don't forget the salt and
> Red hot pepper!
> (On the words "Red hot pepper," the rope is turned as fast as possible until the jumper misses.)
>
> Pease porridge hot, pease porridge cold,
> Pease porridge in a pot, nine days old.
> Some like it hot, hot, hot!
>
> Ice cream, ginger ale, soda water, pop.
> You get ready 'cause we're gonna turn hot!

9. Calling In: The first player enters the rope and calls in a second player by name. Both jump three times holding hands, and then the first runs out. The second player then calls in a third player by name. Both jump three times holding hands, and the second player exits. Players should be in an informal line, waiting to be called in, since the fun comes from the uncertainty of when one is to enter.
10. Children can enter and exit according to the call in a chant. The initial performer enters, and the next jumper waits.

> In the shade and under a tree,
> I'd like . . . to come in with me.
> He's (she's) too fat and I'm too stout.
> He stays in and I'm getting out.
>
> Calling in and calling out,
> I call . . . in and I'm getting out.

11. High Water: The rope is turned so that it becomes gradually higher and higher off the ground.

> At the beach, at the sea,
> The waves come almost to the knee.
> Higher, higher, et cetera.

12. Stopping the Rope: During the chant, the rope is stopped by the jumper in a designated fashion. Stops can include (1) the jumper stops and the rope hits him or her; (2) the jumper stops the rope by straddling it; (3) the stop is made with the legs crossed and the rope between the feet; and (4) the stop is made by stamping on the rope.

> Mister, mister, kiss your sister
> (Mother, mother, kiss your brother).
> If you don't, you stop like this!
>
> Junior, junior, climb the tree (make climbing motions).
> Junior, junior, slap your knee (slap knees).
> Junior, junior, throw a kiss (as indicated).
> Junior, junior, time to miss (stop the rope).
> (For girls, use "baby doll.")

13. Two, three, or four children jump at a time. After some skill has been reached, children in combination can run in, jump a specified number of times, and run out, keeping hands joined all the time.
14. Circling with two, three, or four at a time: start as a small circle, run in, and jump in a circle. Keep the circle moving in one direction. Run out as a circle.
15. Have the rope held at high jumping height. Practice high jumping skills — scissors, Western roll, modified Western (belly) roll. Jump for form and not for height. Be sure the rope is held loosely. If mats are available, these are a help.
16. Take a ball with you. Bounce the ball while jumping. Try balancing a beanbag on a body part while jumping.
17. Have a partner ready with a ball. Toss the ball back and forth to your partner as you jump.
18. Chase the Rabbit: Four or five jumpers are in single file with a leader, the rabbit, at the head. The rabbit jumps in any manner he or she wishes, and all others must match his or her

movements. If anyone misses, he or she must go to the end of the line. If the rabbit misses or stops the rope, he or she goes to the end of the line and the next child becomes the new rabbit. Set a limit on how long a rabbit can stay at the head of the line.

19. On Four Cylinders: The challenge is to do activities in series of fours—four of one kind of jump, four of another, et cetera. The number of series can be specified, and the child has a choice of what he or she wishes to include. Tell the children that their "engines are running on four cylinders."

20. The "jumper" jumps with an individual rope while jumping under the long rope. Both ropes should be turned the same way. Later, the long rope can be turned in the opposite direction. Partners can try jumping under both the individual and long ropes simultaneously.

21. Begging: A jumper runs in and works his or her way up the rope toward one of the turners. As he or she jumps, he or she says, "Father, father, give me a dollar." The turner replies, "Go see your mother." The jumper works his or her way toward the other turner and says, "Mother, mother, give me a dollar." The turner replies, "Go to your father." This continues until a miss or one of the turners says in reply, "Get out" or "Get lost," at which the jumper exits.

22. Setting the Table: A jumper enters and starts jumping. A partner stands ready with at least four beanbags. The following verse is recited, during which the partner tosses in the beanbags one at a time and they are placed in a row by the jumper on the side, with the upward swing of the rope.

   Mabel, Mabel, set the table (toss in one bag),
   Bring the plates if you are able (toss in another bag),
   Don't forget the bread and butter (toss in the other two bags).

The jumper exits. Another jumper can reverse the routine and take out the bags.

23. Partners can go in and perform a number of stunts. Wring the Dishrag (page 327) is nice. Partner Hopping (page 341) also works. The Bouncing Ball (page 327) is another suggestion. Examine the partner stunts and make other selections.

24. Quadruped is a good term for the children to learn—it means on four (quadru) feet (ped). Children enter and begin with a hop (one foot), then make a jump (two feet), add a hand touch next (three feet), and then jump with both hands and feet (four feet). Selected

movements on hands and feet can be executed, such as the Rabbit Jump and the Push-up.

25. Blind Man: Single or multiple jumpers enter and begin jumping to this chant.

   Peanuts, popcorn, soda pop,
   How many jumps before you stop.
   Close your eyes and you will see
   How many jumps that this will be!

The eyes remain closed during the continued jumping, which can be to a target number or until a miss occurs.

26. One or both holders can go inside and jump, turning with their outside hands. First attempts can begin with a pendulum swing and then proceed to a full turn.

Making Up Chants

The children can be encouraged to make up chants. They can begin from scratch or can fill in blank spaces in a rough format. The material to be inserted is in parentheses.

   (Suzy, Suzy) dressed in (yellow)
   Went upstairs to (kiss a fellow).
   How many (kisses) did she (get)?
   One, two, et cetera.

   (Joe, Joe) dressed in (white)
   Went upstairs to (say "good night").
   How many (steps) did he (take)?
   One, two, et cetera.

Fitness Routine with Ropes

Four children are in column formation, holding the rope on one side of the body with the hand on that side. There are three signals for changes in the maneuver. On the first signal, the four children run in column formation (as in follow the leader) holding the rope on one side (right or left). The leader takes them in various directions. On the second signal, the rope is shifted overhead quickly to the other side and the running continues. The third signal causes the four to stop and form a jumping group. The two on the outside (front and rear) become the turners, and the two in the center perform as jumpers. On the next signal, the routine is repeated, except the jumpers then take the front and rear positions with the rope, so they become turners on the next jumping.

Jumping Two Ropes

Turning two ropes simultaneously requires practice, and time must be allotted for this. Handling two ropes is quite fatiguing, and turners should be rotated frequently.

1. Double Dutch: Two ropes are turned alternately; rope near the jumper is turned front

door; rope away from jumper is turned back door.

2. Double Irish: Two ropes are turned alternately, the reverse of Double Dutch.
3. Egg Beater: Two large ropes are turned at right angles simultaneously by four turners. Try three or four ropes simultaneously.

The Egg Beater

4. Fence Jumping: Two ropes are held motionless about 2 feet apart, parallel to each other and each about 12 inches above the ground. Have the players jump or hop in and out of the ropes in various combinations. The children can devise many different methods.
5. Try two-rope combinations, with the jumper using an individual rope. The jumper must jump fast time with the individual rope.
6. The turners can move to the inside of the rope and turn and jump simultaneously.

Formation Jumping

Four to six long ropes with turners can be placed in various patterns, with tasks specified for the ropes. Ropes can be turned in the same direction (front door or back door), or the turning directions can be mixed. Formations are suggested below.

INDIVIDUAL ROPE JUMPING

The emphasis in teaching rope jumping should be on establishing the basic turning skills and letting the children create their own routines and progress on their own. Rope jumping is a fine body developer and health builder. It provides good challenge for the cardiorespiratory system and makes for fine aerobic exercise. It has good carry-over values, since the activity can be done anywhere and can be carried on throughout life. It is particularly valuable as part of the conditioning process for certain sports. It lends itself to prescribed dosages through the number of turns, the length of participation, the speed of the turning rope, and the different steps.

The teaching approach can center on rope jumping with or without music. Since rope jumping is of a rhythmic nature, the addition of music is a natural progression. Music adds much to the activity and enables the jumper to create and organize routines to be performed to the musical pieces. The best approach is probably a combination of experiences with and without music.

The Rope

The authors prefer the Olympic-style rope, which is made of plastic links and turning handles. Sash cord and hard-weave synthetic rope prove quite satisfactory, also.

To determine the proper length of a rope, have the child stand on the center of the rope. The ends, when drawn up alongside the body, should reach the armpits or slightly higher.

Preschool children generally use 6-foot ropes, while the primary-level group needs mostly 7-foot ropes and some 6-foot and 8-foot lengths. Grades three through six need a mixture of 7-foot and 8-foot ropes. A 9-foot rope serves well for most instructors.

Spoke   Zigzag   Line

Correct Jump Rope Length

Weight is a factor in choosing ropes, too. They must be heavy enough to maintain the momentum of turning. The center of the rope can be weighted with some cord to give it added momentum for sideways skipping.

Body Position and Form

Good posture is a consideration in rope skipping. The body should be in good alignment, with the head up so that the eyes look ahead at eye level. The jump is made with the body in a straight, erect position and with a slight straightening of the knees providing the lift for the jump, which should be of minimal height (about 1 inch).

The wrists should supply the force to turn the rope, with the elbows kept close to the body. Avoid unnecessary pumping action and lifting of the arms.

The landing should be made on the balls of the feet, with the knees bent slightly to cushion the shock. Usually, the feet, ankles, and legs should be kept together, except when a specific step calls for a different position.

Explanation of Terminology

Most steps can be done in three different rhythms: slow time, fast time, and double time.

Rebound

This is simply a hop in place as the rope passes over the head. Better jumpers only bend the knees slightly without actually leaving the floor. It is used only in slow-time jumping (explained below), and its object is to carry the rhythm between steps.

Slow Time

In slow-time rhythm, the performer jumps over the rope, rebounds, jumps in place as the rope passes over the head, and then executes the second step or repeats the original step a second time on the second jump.

The performer actually jumps over the rope to every other beat of the music in slow-time rhythm. The odd beat occurs as the rope passes over the head. The rhythm is carried by the rebound.

The rope is rotating slowly (passes under the feet on every other beat) and the feet also move slowly, since there is a rebound between each jump.

Slow-time rhythm—slow rope, slow feet, with a rebound.

Fast Time

In fast-time rhythm, we have the opposite of slow time. The rope rotates in time with the music, which means twice the number of rope turns for the same time as in slow time. The rope turns fast (120 to 180 turns per minute, depending upon the tune's tempo), and the performer executes a step only when the rope is passing under the feet.

Fast-time rhythm—fast rope, fast feet.

Double Time

In double-time rhythm, the rope is turned at the same speed as for slow time, but, rather than taking the rebound, the performer executes another step while the rope is passing over the head.

Double time is the most difficult to master. When the feet are speeded up, there is a tendency also to speed the rope up (which is wrong).

Double-time rhythm—slow rope, fast feet.

Instructional Procedures

1. Enough ropes should be available for each child to have a rope appropriate for his or her size. Ropes can be color-coded for length.
2. Where there are no handles on the ropes, the ends of the ropes should be wrapped in tape or dipped in wax to prevent fraying.
3. A system for storage should be devised; otherwise, there can be tangles. Ropes can be hung or individually bundled for storage.
4. Begin with the rope behind the feet for forward jumping and in front of the feet for backward turning.
5. Begin with slow-time rhythm and the basic two-footed jump.

6. Two steps can be taken before the actual jumping. The first is to jump without the rope to the correct rhythm. For slow time, this would be a jump and then a rebound step. The child can pretend he or she is turning the rope. The second is to take both ends of the rope in one hand and turn the rope *without* jumping. The rope is turned in a forward arc to one side of the body. The two steps then can be combined, so the child is simulating jumping while the rope is turned at the side. The next step is regular jumping.

7. Add music as soon as the jumpers have gotten through the first stages of jumping. Music provides a challenge for continued jumping.

8. In the kindergarten-through-grade-two group, there usually are some children who cannot jump, but, by the third grade, if the children *have had* previous experience, all the children should be able to jump. Some children who cannot jump may be helped by the pendulum swing of the long rope. The teacher or an older student can have them jump with him or her inside an individual rope. Cue words such as "jump" or "ready, jump" should be used, too.

9. Numerous combinations are possible in rope jumping. These are discussed in the next section.

10. To collect ropes at the completion of a rope-jumping activity, have the squad leaders or two or three other children act as monitors. They should put both of their arms out to the front or to the side at shoulder level. The other children then drape the ropes over their arms. The monitors return the ropes to the correct storage area.

Collecting the Ropes

Combination Possibilities in Rope Jumping

1. Changes in the speed of the turn, utilizing slow-time, fast-time, and double-time routines can be made. Children should be able to shift from one routine to another, particularly when changes appear in the music.

2. Developing expertise in various foot patterns and steps (see the next section) is another possibility. The ability to change from one foot pattern to another is a needed skill.

3. Use the cross-hands position forward and backward.

4. Go from a forward to a backward turn, and return.

5. Do double turns, during which the rope passes under the feet twice before the jumper lands. A few children may be able to do a triple turn.

6. Progress forward, backward, or sideward, employing a variety of steps.

7. Backward jumping is quite difficult, but it can be explored. Most steps can be done or modified for the backward turn.

8. Speedy turns can be practiced. See how fast the rope can be turned in 15 or 30 seconds.

9. Many interesting routines can be done with partners. These are discussed later (page 287).

Basic Steps

Remember, most steps[1] can be done in three different rhythms—slow time, fast time, and double time. After the youngsters have mastered the first six steps in slow time, the teacher may wish to introduce fast and double time. The alternate-foot basic step and spread legs, forward and backward, are two steps that seem to work well for introducing double-time jumping.

Two-Foot Basic Step

With feet together, jump over the rope as it passes under the feet and take a preparatory rebound while the rope is over the head.

Alternate-Foot Basic Step

As the rope passes under the feet, the weight is shifted alternately from one foot to the other, raising the unweighted foot in a running position.

Swing-Step Forward

Same as alternate-foot basic step, except the free leg swings forward. Keep knee loose, and let foot swing naturally.

Swing-Step Sideward

Same as swing-step forward, except the free leg is swung to the side. Knee should be kept stiff.

---

[1]A color film, *Rope Skipping—Basic Steps,* featuring the system and steps in the text, may be ordered from Martin Moyer Productions, 900 Federal Avenue, Seattle, Washington 98102.

Rocker Step

One leg is always forward in a walking stride position in executing the rocker step. As the rope passes under the feet, the weight is shifted from the back foot to the forward foot. The rebound is taken on the forward foot while the rope is above the head. On the next turn of the rope, the weight is shifted from the forward foot to the back foot, repeating the rebound on the back foot.

Spread Legs Forward and Backward

Start in a stride position as in the rocker, with weight equally distributed on both feet. As the rope passes under the feet, jump into the air and reverse feet position.

Cross Legs Sideward

As the rope passes under the feet, spread legs in a straddle position (sideward). Take the rebound in this position. As the rope passes under the feet on the next turn, jump into the air and cross feet with right foot forward. Repeat with left foot forward. Continue to alternate forward foot.

Toe Touch Forward

As the rope passes under the feet, swing right foot forward. Alternate, landing on right foot and touching left toe forward.

Toe Touch Backward

Similar to the swing-step sideward, except the toe of the free foot touches to the back at the end of the swing.

Shuffle Step

As the rope passes under the feet, push off with right foot, side stepping to the left. Land with weight on left foot, and touch right toe beside left heel. Repeat in opposite direction.

Heel-Toe

As the rope passes under the feet, jump with weight landing on right foot, touching left heel forward. On next turn of the rope, jump, landing on the same foot, and touch left toe beside right heel. Repeat, using opposite foot.

Heel Click

Do two or three swing-steps sideward in preparation for the heel click. When the right foot swings sideward, instead of a hop or rebound when the rope is above the head, raise the left foot to click the heel of the right foot. Repeat on the left side.

Step-Tap

As the rope passes under the feet, push off with right foot and land on left. While the rope is turning above the head, brush the sole of the right foot forward and then backward. As the rope passes

under the feet for the second turn, push off with the left foot, landing on the right, and repeat.

Schottische Step

The schottische step can be done to double-time rhythm, or it can be done with a varied rhythm. The pattern is step-step-step-hop, step-step-step-hop, step-hop, step-hop, step-hop, step-hop. In varied rhythm, three quick turns in fast time are made to conform to the three steps and then double-time rhythm prevails. The step should be practiced first in place and then in general space. Schottische music should be introduced.

Bleking Step

The Bleking step has the time pattern of slow, slow, fast, fast, fast. The rope should turn to conform to this time pattern. The step begins with a hop on the left foot with the right heel forward. Next, hop on the right and extend the left heel forward. Repeat the action with three quick changes right, left, right. The pattern is repeated with a bounce on the right foot and the left heel extended. If done to the music for Bleking, four Bleking steps of slow, slow, fast, fast, fast are done. The second part of the music (chorus) allows the children to organize a different routine of their own. Remind the children to listen for changes in the music.

Crossing Arms

Crossing arms while turning the rope provides an interesting variation. Crossing arms during forward turning is easier than crossing behind the back during backward turning.

Tell the children that, during crossing, the hands exchange places. This means that, during forward crossing, the inside of the elbows are close to each other. This is not possible during backward crossing.

Crossing and uncrossing can be done at determined points after a stipulated number of turns (4, 2, 1). Crossing can be accomplished during any of the routines.

Double Turn of the Rope

Do a few basic steps in preparation for the double turn. As the rope approaches the feet, give an extremely hard flip of the rope from the wrists. Jump from 6 to 8 inches into the air, and allow the rope to pass under the feet twice before landing. A substantial challenge for advanced rope jumpers is to see how many consecutive double turn jumps they can do.

Going from Forward to Backward Jumping without Stopping the Rope

1. As the rope starts downward in forward jumping, rather than allowing it to pass under the

feet, the performer swings both arms to the left (or right) and makes a half-turn of his or her body in that direction (turn facing the rope). On the next turn, spread the arms and start turning in the opposite direction. This method can be used from forward to backward jumping and vice versa.

2. When the rope is directly above the head, the performer can extend both arms, causing the rope to hesitate momentarily. At the same time as he or she extends both arms, he or she makes a half-turn in either direction and continues skipping with the rope turning in an opposite direction from the start.

3. From a crossed-arm position as the rope is going above the performer's head, he or she may uncross the arms and turn simultaneously. This starts the rope turning and the performer skipping in the opposite direction.

Sideways Skipping

The rope is turned laterally with one hand held high and the other extended downward. The rope is swung around the body sideways.

Start with the right hand held high overhead and the left hand extended down the center of the body. Swing the rope to the left, at the same time raising the left leg sideways. Usually the speed is slow time, with the rebound taken on each leg in turn. Later, better jumpers may progress to fast-time speed.

Rope passes under the left leg, and jumper then is straddling the rope as the rope moves around his or her body behind him or her.

Take the weight on the left foot, raising the right foot sideways. Take a rebound step on the left as the rope moves back to the front, the original position.

Mystery Rope Jumping

The following is a challenging sequence that children enjoy trying as a change-of-pace activity.
1. Rope is held with both hands at the right side of the body.
2. Swing the rope slightly forward in a pendular arc. Carry the rope backward and over the head in front of the body. Cross the arms, and step inside the rope with the left leg.
3. Move the right arm overhead, and step out with right leg.
4. Swing the rope in a pendulum swing to the left side. Finally, return the rope to the right side, and repeat.

Individual Rope Jumping with Partners

Many interesting combinations are possible in which one child turns the rope and one or more children jump with him or her. In those routines in which directions call for a child to run into a jumping pattern, it may be well to begin with the child already in before proceeding to the run-in stages.

1. The first child turns the rope and the other stands in front ready to run in.
   a. Run in, face partner, and both jump. Try with hands on the waist, hands on the shoulder.
   b. Run in, turn back to partner, and both jump.
   c. Decide on which steps are to be done. Run in, match steps.
   d. Repeat with the rope turning backwards.
   e. Run in with a ball, and bounce it during the jumping.
2. Partners stand side by side, clasp inside hands, and turn the rope with outside hands.
   a. Face the same direction, and turn the rope.
   b. Face opposite directions, clasp left hands, and turn the rope.
   c. Face opposite directions, clasp right hands, and turn the rope.
   d. Repeat routines with inside knees raised.
   e. Repeat all, with elbows locked. Try other arm positions.
3. First child turns the rope and the second is in back of him or her ready to run in. Run in, grasp waist, and jump (engine and caboose). Put hands on shoulders.
4. Children stand back to back, holding a single rope in right hands.
   a. Turn in one direction—forward for one and backward for the other.
   b. Reverse direction.
   c. Change to left hands, and repeat.
5. Three partners jump: #1 turns the rope forward, #2 runs in front, #3 runs in behind, and all three jump. Try with the rope turning backward.
6. Two jumpers, each with a single rope, face each other and turn both ropes together, forward for one and backward for the other, jumping over both ropes at once. Turn the rope alternately, jumping each rope in turn.
7. Partner turning #1 jumps in a usual individual rope pattern. #2 is positioned to the side. #1 hands #2 one end of the rope, and #2 maintains the turning rhythm. Hand the rope back.
   a. Try from the other side.
   b. Turn the rope backward.

Movement Sequences to Music

The opportunities for creative activity in movement sequences with music are unlimited. Good music is essential, and it must have a definite beat and a bouncy quality. Those pieces with a two-part format, usually labeled the verse part and the chorus, are excellent. The changes from the verse to the chorus part and back signal changes in rope-jumping patterns.

Many of the records listed in chapter fifteen can be used quite successfully for rope jumping to music. Schottisches, marches, and polkas provide good background. Jazz music, rock-and-roll pieces, and similar music also serve well. In addition, special records designed for rope jumping are available from commercial sources. Some that have proved successful include those listed below.

1. Records listed in the rhythmic program (chapter fifteen) include these:
   The Mulberry Bush (page 212)
   The Muffin Man (page 216)
   Looby Loo (page 217)
   Go Round and Round the Village (page 220)
   Bleking (page 225)
   Little Brown Jug (page 231)
   Oh Susanna (page 232)
   Pop Goes the Weasel (page 232)
   Schottische (page 235)
   Polka (page 234)
   Square Dance (page 247)
2. Rope-jumping records, including Ball Bouncing and Rope Skipping, Album #12, Durlacher PR280. The teacher will discover many other records and albums that work well as the children progress and become more familiar with the various rope-skipping activities and techniques.
3. Rock-and-roll, disco, and modern jazz records are good for intermediate children who love to structure routines to modern music. Many of them have favorites that they can bring from home. Listed are some appropriate suggestions:
   "Waiting for the Robert E. Lee," Jack Barbour, Accent Sunny Hills AC 102-S.
   "Wheels and Orange Blossom Special," Billy Vaughn, Dot 45-161774.
   "Sweet Georgia Brown," Harlem Globetrotters theme song.
   Herb Alpert and the Tijuana Brass records.

Devising Sequences to Music

Devising jumping sequences to be done to music can provide good opportunity for the children to make up their own routines for selected records. Simple changes from slow time to fast time can introduce this activity. Later, different steps can be incorporated, crossing and uncrossing arms can be included, and then the turning direction can be varied. Partner rope-jumping stunts also can be adapted to music. Some suggestions of how different steps can be incorporated into the sequences follow.

1. "Pop Goes the Weasel": This has a definite verse and chorus change. Direct the children to change from slow-time jumping to fast-time jumping on the chorus.
2. Bleking: This offers an interesting change in rope speed. The rhythm is slow, slow, fast, fast, fast (four times). The rope should be turned in keeping with the beat. Later, the Bleking step can be added. The chorus part allows for considerable latitude.
3. Schottische: Do the schottische step in place (four times), and on the chorus part do moving step-hops in different directions.
4. "Little Brown Jug": Here is a four-part routine that can be done to four rounds of the music.
   First verse part—two-foot basic step (slow time).
   Chorus—two-foot basic step (fast time).
   Second verse part—alternate foot basic step (slow time).
   Chorus—alternate foot basic step (fast time).
   Third verse part—swing-step forward (slow time).
   Chorus—swing-step forward (fast time).
   Fourth verse part—swing-step sideward (slow time).
   Chorus—swing-step sideward (fast time).

Assessment of Individual Rope Jumping

Individual rope-jumping stunts, because of their specificity and individualism, can be adapted easily for learning packages and contract teaching. It is easy to set up skill assessment based on the accomplishment of a stated maneuver in so many turns of the rope.

Skill assessment can be organized progressively, or it can be grouped into beginning, intermediate, and advanced tests. An example of a beginning test follows.

Level-one (beginners) test (slow time and fast time):

1. Basic two-footed jump—10 turns.
2. Alternate-foot step—10 turns.
3. Turning rope backward—10 turns.
4. Alternate crossing arms—10 turns.
5. Running forward—20 turns.

Another approach is to put the items in some kind of a sequence:

1. Two-foot basic step—slow time (20 turns).
2. Two-foot basic step—fast time (20 turns).
3. Two-foot basic step—four steps slow time, four steps fast time, repeat (16 turns).
4. Alternate-foot basic step—slow time (20 turns).
5. Alternate-foot basic step—fast time (20 turns).
6. Turning the rope backward—slow time (10 turns).
7. Turning the rope backward—fast time (10 turns).
8. Going from forward to backward turning—slow time (as needed).

9. Going from forward to backward turning—fast time (as needed).
10. From forward to backward turning and return (as needed).
11. Cross hands turning—slow time (10 turns).
12. Cross hands turning—fast time (10 turns).
13. Run in place (20 turns).
14. Run forward (20 turns).
15. Double jumps to one turn, do two (as needed).
16. Demonstrate at least two of the following: swing-step forward, swing-step sideward, rocker step, spread legs forward and backward, cross legs sideward, Bleking step, schottische step (16 turns).

The above items provide a rather comprehensive analysis and can be shortened. In order to be successful, the child must complete the prescribed maneuver for the duration of the turns specified.

MOVEMENTS GUIDED BY ROPE PATTERNS

Ropes can be placed on the floor in various fashions to serve as stimuli for various locomotor and nonlocomotor movements. The activities should stress creative responses within the limits of the challenge. The educational movement factors of space, time, flow, and force can be interwoven with the activity. The key is the ingenuity of the teacher in providing direction to the movement patterns. The child can move as an individual, with a partner, or as a member of a small group.

Generally, a rope is placed in a straight line or in a circle. However, geometric figures can be formed and numbers or letters of the alphabet featured. The discussions are organized around these patterns.

Rope Forming a Straight Line

One approach is for the child to begin at one end of the line and perform activities as he or she moves down the line. Much of this can be based on hopping or jumping. The child then returns up the line to the original starting point.

1. Hop back and forth, moving down the line. Return using the other foot.
2. Jump lightly back and forth down the line. Return.
3. Hop slowly under control down the line. Hop rapidly back.
4. Jump so the rope is between the feet each time, crossing and uncrossing the feet alternately.
5. Move on all fours, leading with different parts of the body.
6. Do crouch jumps back and forth across the rope. Vary with three points and then two points of contact.
7. Jump as high as you can down the line and as low as possible back.
8. Hop with a narrow shape down and a different shape back.
9. Walk the rope like a tightrope.
10. Begin with a bridge and move the bridge down the line. Return with a different bridge.
11. Lie across the rope, holding one end. Roll down the line, causing the rope to roll around the body. Unroll the rope back to position.
12. Do a movement slow-slow, fast-fast-fast down the line, and repeat back.
13. "Pull" yourself down the line, and "push" yourself back.

The child is positioned close to the center of the line and simply moves back and forth across the line without materially changing his or her relative position.

1. Hop back and forth across the line. Jump back and forth.
2. Go over with a high movement; come back with a low.
3. Do a Bunny Jump across and back. A Frog Jump. A Crouch Jump.
4. Lead with different parts of the body back and forth. Propel with different parts.
5. Get into a moderate crouched position over the rope. Jump the feet back and forth over the rope.
6. Take a sprinter's start so that the rope is between the feet. Alternate the feet back and forth over the rope.
7. Jump back and forth lightly on tiptoes.
8. Go back and forth over the rope, employing different shapes.
9. With your toes touching the rope, drop the body forward across the rope, taking the weight on both hands. Walk out the hands forward to the limit.
10. Pretend the rope is a river. Show different kinds of bridges that you can make over the river.

Rope Forming a Circle

Do movements around the outside of the rope clockwise and counterclockwise—walk, skip, hop, slide (facing and back to circle), jump, run, gallop. (These activities can be done with hoops, also.)

1. Hop in and out of the circle, moving around. Jump.
2. Jump directly in and then across. Jump backward.
3. Jump in, collapse, and jump out without touching the rope.
4. Begin in the circle. Jump forward, backward, and sideward, each time returning to the center of the circle.
5. Place feet in the circle and walk the hands the

full circumference outside the circle. Place hands inside and feet outside. Face the floor, the ceiling, and to the side.

6. Inside the circle, make a small shape. Make a large shape, so you are touching all sides of the circle.

7. Do a Tightrope Walk clockwise and counterclockwise.

8. Jump and click the heels, lighting inside the circle. Repeat going out.

9. Do jump turns inside the circle without touching the rope; do quarter-turns, half-turns, and full turns.

10. Jump in with a Bunny Jump. Jump out. Try with a Frog Jump.

11. Take the weight on the hands inside the circle, so the feet land on the other side. Try a Cartwheel.

Rope Forming Various Figures

Have the rope form different figures, such as geometric figures, letters, and numbers. Many of the challenges previously described apply here, too.

1. With the rope and yourself, form a triangle, a square, a rectangle, a diamond shape, and a figure eight.

2. With the rope and yourself, form a two-letter word. Form other words.

3. Get a second rope, and make your own patterns for hopping and jumping.

Partner Activity

Partner activity with ropes is excellent. Partners can work with one or two ropes. There can be matching, following, or contrasting movements by the partners. Add-on is an interesting game, in which one partner does an activity and the other adds an activity to form a sequence.

Group Activity

Group activity with jump ropes also has good possibilities. Each child brings his or her rope to the group. Patterns for hopping, jumping, and other locomotor movements can be arranged with the ropes. An achievement demonstration after a period of practice allows each group to show the patterns they have arranged and the movements that can be done in the patterns. A further extension is to leave the patterns where they are and rotate the groups to different locations so that they can experience movements in patterns formed by others.

Eighteen

Apparatus Activities

Children possess an innate desire for the physical expression that apparatus allows them. Apparatus plays a large role in the child's overall physical development. It is a part of the fundamental makeup of children to want to run, jump, throw, swing, and climb. Educators are beginning to realize that, despite old prejudices, what a child likes to do and will do, naturally and spontaneously, usually fits into the educational scheme.

Activities on apparatus play an important part in today's physical education programs. A wider variety of apparatus than ever before is now available from commercial sources and through school construction. Exercising on overhead and climbing apparatus has strong physical effects on the grip, arm, and shoulder girdle. Flexibility and stretching effects have value in the maintenance of posture. The child learns to manage his or her body free of ground support.

Equipment placed on the floor provides important extensions for educational movement. Exploratory and creative activity, as well as wide experience in body management, should characterize the approach to instructional procedures. Individual response in movement should be stressed, with the emphasis on doing but not on conformity. Variety in apparatus activity can be enhanced by the addition of hand apparatus such as beanbags, balls, wands, hoops, blocks, and other items. Individual or partner manipulative activities that are performed as the children move on apparatus add another dimension to the movement possibilities.

Combinations of different pieces of apparatus often offer more challenges to children than a single piece. For example, jumping boxes used with balance beams and individual mats allow for a wider variety of activities than boxes alone could.

Traffic rules should be established to stipulate when the child next in turn starts. His or her return route to the starting point can be established, too. In addition, children should be instructed in spotting techniques in addition to the performance items.

Attention to form is relative to the type of activity. Most stunt-type movements involve three sequences in the instructional process: (1) mounting, or getting on, the apparatus; (2) doing a skill or meeting a challenge; (3) dismounting. Emphasis should be on giving it a good try and doing things as well as one can. The teacher can think in terms of minimal and maximal performance standards, taking individual differences into consideration. On the lower end of the skill scale, children like to know "did I do it?" On the upper end, they like to know they achieved success.

The start-and-expand technique (see page 291) reinforces this kind of an approach by starting at a low point on the progression of skills. Achieving some measure of success is important. Serious enjoyment and fun should keynote the instructional climate in apparatus activities.

Some attention should be given to the dismount as determined by the character of the apparatus. The dismount should be a controlled movement, with a landing in a bent-knee position and the weight balanced over the balls of the feet. The child should land in good control and hold the position momentarily to show control. Many challenges, such as shapes through the air, turns, stunts following the landing, and others, can be structured into dismounts.

RETURN ACTIVITY

The employment of return activity can increase the movement potential of mat work, balance beams, benches, and other selected pieces of apparatus. In this technique, the child performs some kind of movement task on his or her way back (return) to his or her place in line. The return-activity technique avoids having children stand in line after they have finished their task on the apparatus. To increase the challenge of the return activity, a marker can be placed some distance in front of the apparatus. Students then must perform their return activity on the way to the marker and back to the end of the line. The return activity is usually something different, a change of pace, from the instructional emphasis. The instructional concentration is centered on the lesson activities, so the return movements should demand little supervision. Choice and exploration should characterize return activities.

An illustration of return activity in combination with the balance-beam bench follows. In this, the child performs on the bench, accomplishes his or her dismount, and does a forward roll on the way back to place. Three children are in place, illustrating the three aspects of the activity. One child is performing, another is dismounting, and the third child is rolling.

Return Activity

HANDLING EQUIPMENT

Children should be instructed in the proper setup and storage of apparatus and mats. Guidelines can be established for the children, with the following points in mind. Usually children should handle apparatus under a teacher's guidance.

1. The order of assembly should be (1) bring out large pieces first, and then position and assemble them; (2) attach smaller pieces or position small parts; (3) position mats for safety or dismounting; and (4) make available hand apparatus as called for.
2. In removing apparatus, this procedure is reversed. Return to proper storage area.
3. Materials should be carried and not dragged over the floor. For particular pieces that need cooperation among children, designate the number of children and the means of carrying. Safety considerations are very important.
4. Traffic patterns should be established when they are needed. Where materials need to go through a doorway into a storage room, consider having one piece brought in at a time, with the children exiting before the next piece is brought in by another group of children.
5. If the entire class is not needed for removal of the apparatus, appoint a squad or a similar group to handle things. In the meantime, send the other children on their way.

Establishing a school policy for handling equipment by students is a sound procedure. The teacher then operates within the established policy.

TYPES OF APPARATUS

The following types of apparatus are included in the instructional material that follows.

Climbing and Hanging (Body Support) Types

Climbing ropes, horizontal ladders, climbing frames, cargo net, the exercise bar.

Apparatus Placed on the Floor

Balance beam, benches, tires, jumping boxes, magic ropes, individual mats, balance boards, bounding boards, gym scooters, combination sets, stilts, bongo board.

ROPE CLIMBING

Rope climbing offers high-level developmental possibilities for the upper trunk and arms, as well as good training in the coordination of the different parts of the body. Adequate grip and arm strength are necessary prerequisites to climbing. Becoming accustomed to the rope and gaining confidence are important goals in early work on the ropes. Many children need to overcome a natural fear of height.

Instructional Procedures

1. Mats should be under all ropes.
2. The hand-over-hand method should be used for climbing and the hand-under-hand method for descending.
3. Children should be cautioned not to slide, or

they may get rope burns on the hands and skinned places on the legs.

4. If a climber becomes tired, he or she should stop and rest. Proper resting stops should be taught with the climbing.
5. Always leave enough margin to descend safely. No child should go higher than his or her strength allows.
6. Spotters should be used initially for activities in which the body is inverted in stunts. Spotters may hold the rope steady while the child climbs.
7. Rosin in powdered form and magnesium chalk are aids to better gripping. It is particularly important that they be used when the rope becomes slippery after use.
8. Children swinging on the ropes should make sure the other children are out of the way.
9. Marks to limit the climb can be put on the rope with adhesive tape. A mark 8 to 10 feet above the floor is the limit for all children until they can demonstrate sufficient proficiency to be allowed to climb higher.

Rope Climbing on a 10-Rope Set

10. If the ceiling is over 15 or 16 feet in height, a wooden stop (circle) to limit climbing beyond that height is suggested.

Preliminary Sequences

Progression is important in rope climbing, and the fundamental skill progressions should be followed.

Supported Pull-ups

In these activities, a part of the body remains in contact with the floor. Pull up hand-over-hand and return hand-under-hand.

1. Kneel directly under the rope. Pull up until on tiptoes and return to position.
2. Start in a sitting position. Pull up; legs are supported on the heels. Return to sitting position.
3. Start in a standing position. Grasp rope, rock back on heels, and lower body to floor. Keep a straight body. Return to the standing position.

Hangs

In a hang, the child pulls himself or herself up in one motion and holds the position for a length of time—5, 10, or 20 seconds. Stress progression.

1. From a seated position, reach up as high as possible and pull the body from the floor except for the heels; hold.
2. Same as previous stunt, except pull the body completely free of the floor, and hold.
3. From a standing position, jump up, grasp, and hang. This should be a Bent-Arm Hang with the hands about even with the mouth. Hold.
4. Repeat previous stunt, but add leg movements. One or both knees up; bicycling movement of the legs; half-lever—leg (one or both) comes up parallel to the floor; full lever—bring feet up to face.

Pull-ups

In the Pull-up, the child raises and lowers his or her body repeatedly. The initial challenge should be to accomplish one Pull-up in the defined position. Increase the number of repetitions with care. Repeat all activities described for hangs, except substitute the Pull-up for the hang. Pull up each time till the chin touches the hands.

Inverted Hang

Reach up high with both hands. Keep the rope to one side. Jump to a bent-arm position and, at the same time, bring the knees to the nose, inverting the body, which is in a curled position. In a continuation of the motion, bring the feet higher than the hands and lock the legs around the rope. The body then should be straight and upside down. In the learning phases, the teacher should spot.

Swinging and Jumping

Use a bench, box, or stool for a takeoff point. To take off, the child should reach high and jump to a bent-arm position while swinging. Landing should be done in a Bent-Knee Drop.

1. Swing and jump. Add half- and full turns.
2. Swing and return to perch. Add Single and Double Knee Bends.
3. Jump for distance, over a high jump bar or through a hoop.
4. Swing and pick up an Indian club, and return it to perch.
5. Carry articles—beanbags, balls, deck tennis rings. Partner stands on side away from

takeoff bench and puts articles to be carried back to perch between knees or feet.

6. Not using takeoff devices, children can run toward a swinging rope, grasp it high up, and secure momentum for swinging.

Climbing the Rope

Scissors Grip

Approach the rope and reach as high as possible, standing with the right leg forward of the left. Raise the back leg, bend at the knee, and place the rope *inside* of the knee and *outside* of the foot. Cross the forward leg over the back leg, and straighten the legs out with the toes pointed down. This should give a secure hold. The teacher should check the position.

The Scissors Grip

Climbing Using the Scissors Grip: From the scissors-grip position, raise the knees up close to the chest, with the rope sliding between them, while supporting the body with the hand grip. Then lock the rope between the legs, and climb up with the hand-over-hand method as high as the hands can reach. Bring the knees up to the chest, and repeat the process until the following goals are reached. Climb halfway. Climb three-quarters of the way. Climb to the top mark.

A top mark should be established beyond which the children should not be permitted to climb.

Leg-around Rest

Using the left leg and keeping the rope between the thighs, wrap the left leg completely around the rope. The bottom of the rope then crosses over the instep of the left foot *from the outside.* The right foot stands on the rope as it crosses over the instep, providing pressure to prevent slippage. To provide additional pressure, release the hands and wrap the arms around the rope, leaning from the rope at the same time. If the right leg is used, the above instructions should be reversed.

The Leg-around Rest

Climbing Using the Leg-around Rest: Climbing with the leg-around rest is similar to climbing with the scissors grip, except the leg-around rest grip needs to be loosened each time and reformed higher up on the rope.

Descending the Rope

There are four methods of descending the rope. The only differences are in the use of the leg locks, since the hand-under-hand is used for all descents.

Reverse of the Scissors Climb

From an extended position, lock the legs and lower the body with hands until the knees are against the chest. Hold with the hands, and lower the legs to a new position.

Using the Leg-around Rest

From the Leg-around Rest, lower hand-under-hand until the knees are against the chest.

Lift the top foot, and let the rope slide loosely to a lower position. Again secure with the top foot. Repeat until down.

Instep Squeeze

The rope is squeezed between the insteps by keeping the heels together. The hand-under-hand movement lowers the body while the rope slides against the instep.

Stirrup Descent

The rope is on the outside of the right foot and is carried under the instep of the foot and over the toe of the left foot. Pressure from the left foot holds the position. To get into position, let the rope trail along the right leg, reach under, and hook it with the left toe. When the force of the left leg is varied, the rope can slide smoothly while the descent is made with the hands.

Other Climbing Activities

Climbing for Time

A stopwatch and a definite mark on the rope are needed. The height of the mark depends upon the children's skill and capacity. Each child should have three trials (not in succession, however) and the best time is recorded as his or her score. He or she should start from a standing position with hands reaching as high as he or she wishes. The descent should not be included in the timing, since too much emphasis on speed in the descent causes children to drop from too great a height or promotes rope burns on the hands and other parts of the body.

Climbing without Using the Feet

This strenuous activity should be attempted only by the more skillful. During early sessions, the mark set should not be too high. Start from a sitting position. This activity also can be timed.

Organizing a Tarzan Club

Put a marker at the top limit of the rope, and make each child who can climb and touch the marker a member of the Tarzan Club. Form a Super-Tarzan Club for those who can climb to the marker without using their feet. The climber must start from a sitting position on the floor.

Stunts Using Two Ropes

Two ropes, hanging close together, are needed for these activities.

Straight-Arm Hang

Jump up, grasp one rope with each hand, and hang with the arms straight.

Bent-Arm Hang

Same as above, except that the arms are bent at the elbows.

Arm Hangs with Different Leg Positions

1. Single and Double Knee Lifts.
2. Half-lever—bring feet up parallel to floor, toes pointed.
3. Full Lever—bring feet up to face and keep knees straight.
4. Bicycle—pedal like a bicycle.

Pull-ups

Same as a Pull-up on a single rope.

Inverted Hangs

1. With the feet wrapped around the ropes.
2. With feet against the inside of the ropes.
3. With the toes pointed and the feet not touching the ropes.

Spotting for Inverted Hangs on Double Ropes (holding the performer's hands on the rope gives confidence in learning stages)

Skin the Cat

From a bent-arm position, kick feet overhead and continue the roll until the feet touch the mat. Return to the starting position. A more difficult stunt is to start from a higher position, so the feet do not touch the mat. Reverse to original position.

Climbing

1. Climb up one rope, transfer to another, and descend.
2. Climb halfway up one rope, cross over to another rope, and continue to climb to the top.

3. Climb both ropes together without legs. This is difficult and requires the climber to slide one hand at a time up the ropes without completely releasing the grip.
4. Climb as in on a single rope, with hands on one rope and feet on the other rope.

Activity Sequences

Rope-climbing activities are conducive to forming sequences through which the child can progress. The following sequence represents the kinds of progressive challenges that can be met.

1. Jump and hang (10 seconds).
2. Pull-up and hold (10 seconds).
3. Scissors Climb to blue mark (10 feet).
4. Scissors Climb to top (15 feet).
5. Demonstrate Leg-around Rest (10 feet).
6. Inverted Hang, body straight (5 seconds).

It is also possible to structure three levels from the activities included in the chapter. Perhaps each level could be given a characteristic name. Each of the levels could be organized as a task card or a contract project.

HORIZONTAL LADDERS AND CLIMBING FRAMES

Horizontal ladders and climbing frames are manufactured in a variety of models. The most usable ladder is one that can be stored against the wall out of the way. If the ladder can be adjusted so it is inclined, the movement possibilities are extended.

The climbing frame pictured below is manufactured by Centaur Athletics and offers youngsters an exciting climbing environment. It is stored against the wall and can be moved into position by students. The frame can be purchased in two or three sections and offers a great deal of flexibility for climbing activities. Climbing ropes, horizontal ladders, balance beams and rope climbing lad-

Exploring on Climbing Frames

ders can be attached to the frame. The climbing frames can be combined with climbing ropes for instructional purposes, with half the class on each

type of apparatus. Climbing frames can be purchased from Centaur Athletics, Inc., P.O. Box 178, Custer, Wash. 98240.

Horizontal ladders and climbing frames provide a good lead-up activity for climbing ropes, since they are rigid and stationary and thus easier to climb. Grip strength and arm-shoulder-girdle development are enhanced due to the suspension of body weight. This development can help toward better posture.

Instructional Procedures

1. The opposed-thumb grip, in which the thumb goes around the bar, is important. In most activities, the back of the hands should face the child. Vary the grip, however, using other holds. Use other grips, such as the lower grip (palms toward the face) and the mixed grip (one hand facing one way and one the other) for variety.

Upper (Monkey)   Lower   Mixed

2. Whenever the child is doing an Inverted Hang, spotters should be present.
3. Speed is not the goal of this activity. In fact, the longer the child is hanging from the ladder, the more beneficial the activity is. There is value in just hanging.
4. In activities involving movement across the ladder, all children should travel in the same direction.
5. Mats always should be placed under the climbing apparatus when it is in use.
6. When dismounting from ladders, the children should be instructed to land in a bent-leg position, on the balls of the feet.
7. Do not force children to climb the wall-attached climbing frames. Many children have a natural fear of height and need much reassurance before they will climb. If necessary, climb the frame with the child until he or she is confident.
8. Bars placed out-of-doors should not be used when they are wet since they become slippery.

Activities with Horizontal Ladders

Hangs

The hangs should be performed with the opposed-thumb grip and usually with straight arms. Encourage the children to hang in a bent-arm position, however, to involve more muscles in the upper arms. The following hang variations are suggested.

1. Straight Leg—keep legs straight and point toes toward ground.
2. Knees up—lift the knees as high as possible toward the chest.
3. Bicycle—lift the knees and pedal the bicycle.
4. Half-lever—bring the legs up parallel to the ground, with the knees straight and the toes pointed.
5. Hang with the hands on a rung. Touch one or both toes to a rung or the side of the ladder.
6. Inverted—hang with the hands on a rung. Bring the feet up and over the next rung and hook the toes under a second rung. Release the hand grip, and hang in an inverted position.

Note: A spotter should be present during the child's first few attempts at inverted stunts.

7. Flexed Arm—stand on a box if necessary to get in position. Hang as long as possible with the chin even with the hands.
8. Swinging—hang from a rung with both hands, and swing the body back and forth.
9. Swing back and forth and jump as far as possible. Vary with turns.
10. Hang from the ladder first with one hand and then with the other.

Traveling Activities

1. Travel the length of the ladder, using the rungs. Start by traveling one rung at a time, and then skip one or more rungs to add challenge.
2. Travel the length of the ladder, using both side rails; also use just one rail to travel the ladder.
3. Hang with both hands on the side rails. Progress the length of the ladder by jumping both hands forward at once.
4. Travel along the ladder with both hands on the same rung. Progress by jumping forward with both hands simultaneously from one rung to the next.
5. Travel underneath the ladder in a monkey-crawl position, with both hands and feet on the rungs. Try with the feet on the side rails.
6. Travel the length of the ladder, carrying a beanbag, a ball, or any other similar object.
7. Travel the length of the ladder sideways and backward.
8. Travel the length of the ladder, doing a half-body turn each time a move is made to a new rung.
9. Partners start at each end of the ladder and pass each other along the way, doing the above activity.

Activities with Wall-attached or Floor-supported Climbing Frames

Wall-attached climbing frames (see page 558 for photographs of some frames) are excellent pieces of equipment because of the movement possibilities on them and the ease of getting them into action. Floor-supported apparatus are available in considerable variety and combinations, but they necessitate more time and effort in assembly and disassembly.

The use of different parts of the body for supporting, moving, and leading should be explored. Different shapes can be a part of the experiences. As the body moves upward, across, and downward, different parts of the body can lead. The body can hang free or be supported in balance in different fashions. The key is to provide different challenges and encourage imaginative and clever responses. A perceptive teacher can do much to stimulate varied climbing patterns.

Ways of Getting on the Frame

If other apparatus are attached (such as a bench) to the frame, the way the entry onto the bench is to be made can be defined. The entry also could be a climb, or it could be a jump to a hanging position. The entry could be by means of an attached climbing rope. In getting onto the frame, certain body parts can lead or leave the floor last. "Can you get on so your hands are the last to leave the floor?" "See whether you can get on so your seat is the last to touch the floor." "Explore getting on with your body lying on the floor sideways, prone, or on your back."

Partner activity also can be employed. "Work out different ways your partner can help you get onto the frame."

What to Do on the Frame

Obviously, the activities vary according to the type of frame being used. In general, these guides provide a good beginning.

1. What the child does as he or she climbs upward can be defined.
2. Challenges to be met as the child moves at the same level on the frame can be set.
3. Positions that can be assumed, hangs that can be held, balances that can be made, and other static or held movements can be specified.
4. If multiple frames are present with bars, ladders, or poles between them, how to move from one section to another can be defined.
5. Movement possibilities as the descent is made can be specified.

It is not feasible to list all the possible challenges, since the possibilities are too numerous and are limited only by the versatility of the teacher. A few examples should suffice.

"Try moving up the ladder so your hands move first in any change of position and are followed by foot movement. Descend so your feet move first. Next time, reverse the procedure."

"Go halfway up the frame on one side, and then go in and out the openings as you move at the same level across the frame. Continue upward, and move back across the frame as you wish. Move downward to the halfway mark, repeating the in-and-out movements but leading with a different part of the body. Descend as you wish."

"Climb until you can cross to the next section. Do so by using the hands only. Descend."

"Climb upward, and, as you go up, hang for a few seconds with your feet free before going up the next rung. Descend by using only your hands."

Follow-the-leader-type activities are excellent. The magic number can be employed. If the magic number is five, for example, the child does five different kinds of movements in total, or he or she can do five on the upward path and five on the descent.

How to Dismount from (Get Off) the Frame

Dismounting can be varied to include jumping down, drops from a hanging position, touching the ground first with a specified part of the body, or adding stunts after the dismount.

"Can you dismount so your hands touch first?" "See whether you can dismount with a jump that includes a half-turn." "When you drop to the mat, finish with a forward or backward roll." "In your jump dismount, show us different shapes."

ACTIVITIES WITH CARGO NETS

Cargo nets provide experiences similar to those with climbing frames, except the stability of fixed apparatus is missing. The same general approaches can be applied to cargo nets as to climbing frames. It must be remembered that the movements of one child can affect those of the others, since the net's position changes with the weight on it.

Nets can be dropped like window shades from the ceiling, or they can be suspended on four corners to provide different kinds of experiences. Those dropped from the ceiling can be anchored to the floor to give them some stretch and stability. Cargo nets are also available with some wall-attached frames, notably the Hampton Frame.

Storage of nets presents problems, since they are heavy and cumbersome.

EXERCISE BAR (LOW HORIZONTAL BAR)

Horizontal bars should be installed on the playground in a series of at least three at different heights. Indoor bars can be freestanding and have adjustable heights. Care must be taken to see they are properly secured.

The primary program should be limited to simple hangs and climbs. To perform many of the more complicated stunts on the bar, it is necessary to have sufficient arm strength to pull the body up and over the bar. Some of the youngsters in the third grade will begin to have this capacity, but the emphasis in the primary grades should be on a more limited program.

In the intermediate program, attention should be turned toward more gymnastic stunts. However, the advanced skills are difficult, and the teacher should not be discouraged by the children's apparent lack of progress.

Instructional Procedures

1. Only one child should be on a bar at a time.
2. Do not use the bar when it is wet.
3. The basic grip is the opposed-thumb grip, upper style (see page 296 for grip description). The lower and mixed grips also should be used.

Sequence of Activities

Hangs

Feet pointed, one or both knees up, half- or full lever. Bring toes up to touch the bar inside the hands; outside the hands.

Swings

Swing back and forth, propelling the body forward to a stand.

Moving along the Bar

Begin at one side and move hand against hand to the other end of the bar. Move with crossed hands.

Sloth Travel

Face end of bar, standing underneath. Grasp bar with both hands, and hook the legs over the bar at the knees. In this position, move along the bar to the other end. Return by reversing the movement.

Arm and Leg Hang

Grasp bar with upper grip. Bring one of the legs between the arms and hook the knee over the bar.

Double-Leg Hang

Same as in the previous stunt, but bring both legs between the hands and hook the knees over the bar. Release the hands, and hang in the inverted position. If the hands touch or are near the ground, a dismount can be made by releasing the legs and dropping to a crouched position on the ground.

Skin the Cat

Bring both knees up between the arms as in the previous stunt, but continue the direction of the knees until the body is turned over backward. Release grip and drop to ground.

Skin-the-Cat Return

Same as the preceding stunt, except do not release the hands. Bring the legs back through the hands to original position.

Front Support

Grasp the bar with an upper grip, and jump to a straight-arm support on the bar. Jump down.

Front Support Push-off

Mount the bar in the same way as for a front support. In returning to the ground, push off straight with the arms and jump as far back as possible.

Tummy Balance

Jump to the bar as in the preceding stunt. Position the body so that you can balance on the tummy with the hands released.

Sitting Balance

Jump to the bar as for a front support. Work the legs across the bar, so you can maintain a sitting balance. If balance is lost backward, grasp the bar quickly and bend the knees.

Tumble Over

Jump to a front support position. Change the grip to an under grip. Bend forward and roll over to a standing position under the bar.

Single-Knee Swing

Using the upper grip, swing one leg forward so there is a Single-Knee Hang. Using the free leg to gain momentum, swing back and forth.

Side Arc

Sit on the bar with one leg on each side of the bar, both hands gripping the bar in front of the body. Lock the legs, and fall sideways. Try to make a complete circle back to position. Good momentum is needed.

Single-Leg Rise

Using the position in a Single-Knee Swing, on the backswing and upswing, rise to the top of the bar. The down leg must be kept straight. Swing forward (down) first, and, on the backswing, push

down hard with straight arms. A spotter can assist by pushing down on the straight leg with one hand and lifting on the back with the other.

Knee Circles

Sit on top of the bar, with one leg over and one under. Lock the feet. With the hands in an upper grip, shift the weight backward, so the body describes a circle under the bar and back to place. Try this with a forward circle, with the hands in an under grip. Note that considerable initial momentum must be developed in order for the circle to be completed.

BALANCE BEAM

Balance-beam activities are valuable in contributing to the control of balance in both static (stationary) and dynamic (moving) balance situations. The balance-beam side of a balance-beam bench is ideal for this activity, with its 2-inch-wide and 12-foot-long beam. However, balance beams come in many sizes and can be constructed from common lumber materials (see chapter thirty-four). Some teachers prefer a wider beam for kindergarten and first-grade children and, in particular, special education children. Children should graduate to the narrower beam as soon as the activities on the wider beam no longer seem to challenge them.

Some other ideas are interesting. A pole with ends shaped to fit the supports can be substituted for the flat balance beam. The pole is more challenging. Another idea is constructing a beam that begins with a 2-inch width and narrows to a 1-inch width at the other end. Beams of varying widths (4 inches, 3 inches, 2 inches, and 1 inch) can be used, also. The children progress from the wider to the narrower beams. A variety of widths is preferable for handicapped children.

Walking on Balance-Beam Benches

Learning good control of balance demands a considerable amount of practice and concentration. The teacher should not be discouraged by apparent slow progress. Proper practice in time greatly increases the children's proficiency.

Instructional Procedures

1. Children should move with controlled, deliberate movements. Speedy movement is not a goal. Advise the performer to recover his or her balance before taking another step or making another movement.
2. In keeping with the principle of control, children should step slowly on the beam, pause momentarily in good balance at the end of the activity, and dismount with a small, controlled jump from the end of the beam when the routine is completed.
3. Mats can be placed at the end of the bench to cushion the dismount and allow for rolls and stunts after the dismount.
4. Visual fixation is important. Children should look ahead at eye level, rather than down at the feet. Eye targets can be marked or attached to walls to assist them in visual fixation. Visual fixation allows balance controls other than vision to function more effectively. From time to time, movements can be done with the eyes closed, entirely eliminating visual control of balance.
5. Children should step off the beam when they lose balance, rather than teeter and fall off awkwardly. Allow the performer to step back on the beam and continue his or her routine.
6. Success early in a balance-beam activity can be based on two levels. The lower level allows the performer to step off the beam once during his or her routine. The higher level demands he or she remain on the beam throughout. In both levels, he or she must pause at the end of the beam *in good balance* before dismounting.
7. Both laterality and directionality are important. Corresponding parts of the body (right and left feet) should be given reasonably equal treatment. For example, if the performer does follow steps leading with the right foot, the next effort should be made leading with the left foot. Directions right and left should be given equal weight. A child naturally uses his or her dominant side and direction, with which he or she feels more skillful and confident, but must be encouraged to perform otherwise.
8. The child next in turn begins when the performer ahead is about three-quarters of the distance across the beam.
9. Return activities should be a consideration for enhancing the breadth of activity. (See page 292 for an explanation of return activity.)
10. A child or the teacher can provide assistance on a single beam with the performer. The assistant should hold his or her assisting hand palm up, so the performer can use the help if and when he or she needs it.

Activities

The activities for the balance beam are presented according to general movement themes. The first theme is activities on parallel beams. The second theme emphasizes moving across the full length of the beam. Others follow.

One approach is to develop fully all the activities and possibilities within a theme before proceeding to the next. A second approach is to take a few activities from each theme and cover more territory.

Activities on two parallel beams are presented first as lead-up practice for the single-beam tasks. The beams should be placed about 10 to 30 inches apart. The parallel-beam activities can be done alone or with a partner when more security is desired.

Activities on Parallel Beams

1. With a partner and inside hands joined walk forward, backward, and sideways; walk sideways, using a grapevine step; hold a beanbag in the free hand.
2. Without a partner perform various animal walks, such as Crab Walk, Bear Walk, Measuring Worm, and Elephant Walk.
3. With one foot on each beam, walk forward, backward, and sideways.
4. Step to the opposite beam with each step taken.

Activities on the Parallel Beams

5. Progress the length of the beams with hands on one beam and feet on the other.
6. Progress to the middle of the beams, and perform various turns and stunts, such as picking up a beanbag, moving through a hoop, and stepping over a wand.

Moving across the Full Length of the Beam

1. Perform various locomotor tasks, such as walk, follow steps, heel-and-toe steps, side-steps, tiptoes, step behind, grapevine (step behind, step across), et cetera.
2. Follow different directions—forward, backward, sideward.
3. Use different arm positions—on hips, on head, behind back, out to the sides, pointing to the ceiling, folded across chest, et cetera.
4. Balance objects (beanbags or erasers) on various parts of the body—one, two, or three on the head, back of hands, shoulders.

Half-and-Half Movements

These repeat the movements, arm positions, and balance objects as previously described, except the performer goes halfway across the beam using a selected movement, and then changes to another type of movement at the center and does that on the second half of the beam.

ChallengeTasks or Stunts

The performer moves along the beam to the center with a selected movement, performs a particular challenge or stunt at the center, and finishes out his or her movements on the second half of the beam. Examples of challenges or stunts that can be performed at the center of the beam are these.

1. Balances—Front Balance, Back Layout, Stork Stand, Seat Balance, Knee Balance, Side-leaning Rest.
2. Stunts—Knee Dip, Heel Sit, Forward Leg Extension, Back Finger Touch.
3. Challenges—full turn, pick up beanbag at center, pick up paper at center with teeth, do a Push-up.

More Difficult Movements across the Beam

1. Hop the length of the beam forward, sideward, and backward.
2. Cat Walk (page 323), Rabbit Jump (page 328), Lame Dog Walk (page 330), Seal Crawl (page 336), Crab Walk (page 330).
3. Do various locomotor movements with eyes closed.
4. Walk to the center of the beam, and do a Side-leaning Rest. Try on the other side as well.
5. Walk to center, and do a complete body turn on one foot only.

Using Wands and Hoops

1. Carry wand or hoop. Step over wand or through hoop—various fashions.
2. Step over or go under wands held by partner. Same with hoop.
3. Use a hula hoop twirling on arms or around the body while moving across the beam.
4. Balance a wand on various body parts while moving across the beam.
5. Balance a wand in one hand and twirl a hoop on the other hand and proceed across the beam.

Manipulative Activities to Self

1. Using one or two beanbags, toss to self in various fashions—around the body, under the legs, et cetera.
2. Using a ball, toss to self. Circle ball around body, under the legs.
3. Bounce ball on the floor and on the beam. Dribble on floor.
4. Roll ball along the beam.

Manipulative Activities with a Partner

With partner standing beyond far end of beam—toss and throw a beanbag or ball back and forth. Have partner toss to performer for a volleyball return. Bat ball (as in volleyball serve) to partner.

Partner Stunts

1. Regular and reverse Wheelbarrows (page 348) with the supporting performer keeping feet on floor.
2. Partners start on opposite ends of beam and move toward each other with the same kind of movement, do a balance pose together in the center, and return to respective ends of the beam.
3. Partners start on opposite ends of the beam and attempt to pass each other without losing their balance and touching the floor. Challenge them to find different ways of passing.

ACTIVITIES ON BENCHES

The balance-beam bench is an effective piece of apparatus for strength and balance development. Bench activities are interesting and challenging to children and offer a variety of movement possibilities.

Instructional Procedures

1. All activities on the benches should contain three distinct parts: the approach and lead up to the bench, the actual activity on the bench, and, lastly, the dismount off the bench.
2. Mats should be placed at the end of the benches to facilitate the dismount and allow for various rolls and stunts after the dismount.
3. Benches may be positioned horizontally, inclined, or in combination with other equipment for variation and greater challenge.
4. Four to five children assigned to a bench for activity should be the maximum number assigned to one bench.

A Class in Bench Activities

5. The child next in turn begins when the performer ahead has reached about the three-quarters distance on the bench.
6. Return activities (page 292) for the child to perform as he or she returns to his or her place in line add to the activity potential.
7. Speed is *not* a goal in bench activities. Movements should be done deliberately and carefully, with attention given to good body control and management.
8. Attention should be given to use of corresponding parts of the body and directional movements. For example, if a child hops on the right foot, the next effort should be made on the left foot. In jump turns, both right and left movements should be utilized. A child naturally uses the stronger or preferred part of his or her body. See that he or she has a balance in the demands.

Activities

Animal Walks

Perform various animal walks on the bench.
1. Seal Crawl (page 336).
2. Cat Walk (page 323).
3. Lame Dog Walk (page 330).
4. Rabbit Jump (page 328).

Locomotor Movements

Perform various locomotor movements along the length of the bench.
1. Stepping on and off the side of the bench.
2. Jumping on and off the side of the bench.
3. Hopping on and off the side of the bench.
4. Skipping on the bench.
5. Galloping on the bench.

Pulls

Pull the body along the bench, using different combinations of body parts. For instance, use arms only, legs only, right leg and left arm, or left leg and left arm. Pull along the bench, using the following positions.
1. Prone position (headfirst and feetfirst).
2. Supine position (headfirst and feetfirst).
3. Side position (headfirst and feetfirst).

Prone Movements—Headfirst

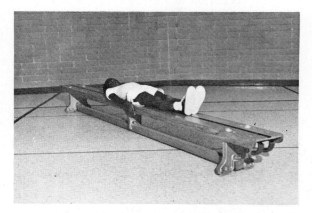

Supine Movements—Feetfirst

Note: Various leg positions (such as legs up in a half-lever position, knees bent, et cetera) should be used while performing pulls and pushes. Those body parts not being used to pull can be used to carry a piece of manipulative equipment, such as a beanbag, ball, or wand.

Pushes

Push the body along the bench, using different parts of the body as discussed earlier. Push the body, using the following positions.
1. Prone position (headfirst and feetfirst).
2. Supine position (headfirst and feetfirst).
3. Side position (headfirst and feetfirst).

Movements along the Side of the Bench

Proceed alongside the bench in the following positions (keep the limbs on the floor as far from the bench as possible).
1. Prone position (hands on bench).
2. Supine position (hands on bench).
3. Turnover (proceed along the bench, changing from prone to supine positions, hands on bench).

All of the above positions are performed with the feet on the bench.

Scooter Movements

Sit on the bench and proceed along the bench without using hands.
1. Regular Scooter: Proceed with the feet leading the body. Try to pull the body along with the feet.
2. Reverse Scooter: Proceed as above, but with the legs trailing and pushing the body along the bench.
3. Seat Walk: Proceed forward by walking on the buttocks. Use the legs as little as possible.

Crouch Jumps

Place both hands on the bench and jump back and forth over the bench. Progress the length of the bench by moving the hands forward a few inches after each jump.
1. Straddle Jump: A variation of the crouch jump. Straddle the bench with the legs. Take the weight on the hands and jump with the legs as high as possible.
2. Regular: Use both hands and both feet. Jump as high as possible.

Crouch Jumps

3. One Hand and Two Feet: Same as above, except eliminate the use of one hand.
4. One Hand and One Foot: Perform the crouch jump, using only one hand and one foot.

Basic Tumbling Stunts

Basic tumbling stunts can be incorporated into bench activities.
1. Back Roller (page 324).
2. Backward Curl (page 330).
3. Forward Roll (page 337).
4. Backward Roll (page 331).
5. Cartwheel (page 354).

A Forward Roll

Dismounts

As stated earlier, all bench activities in which the child moves from one end of the bench to the

Dismounting from a Bench

other should end with a dismount. The following are suggested dismounts that can be used. Many other stunts can be used.

1. Single Jump—forward or backward.
2. Jump with turns—half-, three-quarter, or full turn.
3. Jackknife—jump, kick legs up, and touch toes with the fingertips. Keep feet together.
4. Jackknife (Split)—same as above, except spread legs as far as possible.
5. Jump to a Forward Roll.
6. Backward Jump to a Backward Roll.
7. Side Jump to a Side Roll.
8. Judo Roll.
9. Jump with combinations of the above stunts.

Additional Experiences for Expanding Bench Activities

1. The range of activities can be extended with the addition of balls, beanbags, hoops, and wands. Wands and hoops can be used as obstacles to go over, under, around, or through. Basic balance and manipulative skills can be incorporated into the activity with balls and beanbags.
2. Different balance positions on the benches can be done. Two children should perform at a time, each near one end of the bench.
3. Children love to go over and under a series of benches in a row, in a kind of obstacle course. Some of the benches can be supported on jumping boxes, making them excellent for vaulting activities.

Four benches can be placed in a large rectangle with a squad standing at attention on top of each bench. On signal, each squad gets off its own bench and then runs around the outside of the other three benches and back to the attention position on its own bench. The first squad back and at attention can be declared the winner.

Another enjoyable activity is arranging the benches as illustrated below. A student is chosen to lead the squad or class through the course. A different activity must be performed at each bench.

4. Benches can be placed in a hollow square formation, with children moving around the sequence of the square, doing a different movement on each bench.
5. Place one end of the bench on a jumping box or another bench. Children can get good jumping practice by running up the incline and going for good height at the end of the bench.
6. Benches are appropriate for some partner activities. Children can start on each end and pass through or around each other, reversing original positions. Wheelbarrow Walks are quite suitable.
7. A bench can be supported on two jumping boxes and used as a vaulting box. The bench is long enough to accommodate three children. Children can jump off it, Mule Kick on it, and vault over it.

JUMPING BOXES

Jumping boxes can be constructed or purchased. They provide opportunities for children to secure experiences with jumping from a height and propelling the body through space.

Boxes can be of two heights. For kindergarten and first grade, boxes of 8 inches and 16 inches are suggested. For the second and third grades, 12-inch and 24-inch heights are more suitable. Activities with jumping boxes generally are confined to the primary grades.

Boxes can be built with 18-by-18-inch sides for the higher height and 16-by-16-inch sides for the lower. This enables the smaller box to be stored

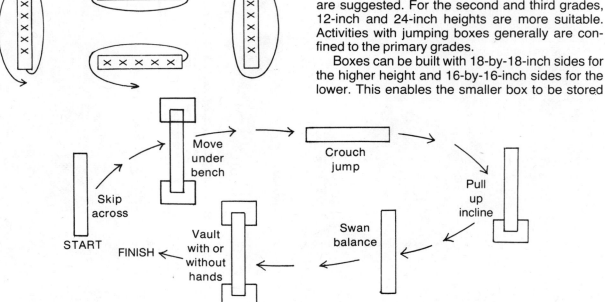

inside the larger. The top should be padded and covered with durable leather or plastic cloth. A rubber floor pad can be placed under the box to offer good floor protection and security from sliding. Plans for constructing boxes are found in chapter thirty-four.

Boxes can be combined with other pieces of equipment. A box raising one end of a balance-beam bench can provide a slope. Boxes on both ends can raise a bench high enough for vaulting activities.

Many of the suggested activities can be done from a step platform. Heavy wooden chairs (never folding chairs) with backs removed, can be used as higher platforms.

Instructional Procedures

1. Attention should be given to "meeting the ground" in proper form, stressing lightness, bent-knee action, balance, and body control.
2. Mats should be used to cushion the landing.
3. The exploratory and creative approach is important, since there are few standard stunts in jumping box activities.
4. A group of not more than four or five children should be assigned to each series of boxes.
5. Additional challenge can be incorporated into the activity by the use of hoops, wands, balls, et cetera. In addition, rolling stunts after the dismount extend the possibilities of movement.
6. Return activities work well with boxes.
7. Children should strive for height and learn to relax as they go through space.
8. The suggested activities that follow can be augmented with a little imagination. Let the children help expand the activity.

Sequence of Activities

Mounting the Box

Many different combinations can be used to get onto the box.

1. Practice stepping onto the box (mounting) by having the child take the full weight on the stepping foot and hold it for a few seconds. This develops a sense of balance and tends to stabilize the support foot.
2. Mount the box, using locomotor movements such as step, jump, leap, and hop. Perform quarter-, half-, three-quarter-, and full-body turns while jumping onto the box.
3. Use a crouch jump to get onto the box.
4. Back up to the box and mount it without looking at it.
5. Mount the box while a partner throws you a beanbag on the way up to the top of the box.
6. Place various targets on top of the box with a piece of chalk, and try and land on the spot when mounting.

Dismounting the Box

The following dismounts can be used to develop body control.

1. Jump off with a quarter-, half-, or full turn.
2. Jump off with different body shapes, such as stretch, curl up into a ball, jackknife, et cetera.
3. Jump over, under, or through various objects.
4. Jump off, and do a Forward or Backward Roll.
5. Change the above dismounts by substituting a hop or leap in place of the jump.
6. Increase the height and distance of the dismount.

Jump Dismounts from a 16-Inch Box

7. Dismount in various directions, such as forward, backward, sideways, northward, and southward.
8. Jump off, and use a jackknife or wide straddle dismount.
9. Perform a balance stunt on the box and then dismount.

Various Approaches to the Boxes

The approach to the box can be varied by performing various movements, such as these.

1. Fundamental locomotor movements: run, gallop, skip, and hop.
2. Animal walks: Bear Walk, Crab Walk, et cetera.
3. Various obstacles can be set up to move over and under; for instance, jump over a bench, move through a hoop held upright by a mat, and do a Backward Roll on the mat.
4. Jump rope to the box, and see whether you can continue jumping while mounting and dismounting the box.
5. Use continuous squad motion after the class has learned the basic movements used with jumping boxes. The squad captain is responsible for leading the class through different approaches, mounts, and dismounts with the boxes. The same activity cannot be used twice in succession.

Addition of Equipment

Use various pieces of equipment to enhance the box activities. The following are some suggestions.

1. Beanbags—throw them up while dismounting, or try to keep them on your head while mounting or dismounting the box.
2. Balls—try to dribble a playground ball while performing the box routine.
3. Hoops—jump through a stationary hoop (held by a partner) while dismounting, or use the hoop as a jump rope and see how many times you can jump it while dismounting.

Through the Hoop!

4. Wands—jump over or under the wand.

Box Combinations

Boxes can be arranged in a straight line and in other patterns. The child does a different movement over each box as though running a Challenge Course.

MAGIC ROPES

Magic ropes come from Germany. Each rope is similar to a long rubber band. Ropes can be made by knitting wide rubber bands together, or they can be constructed from ordinary ¾-inch, white elastic tape, available in most clothing stores. Loops on each end enable the child to thrust his or her hand through and grasp the rope. Ropes should be long enough to stretch to between 30 and 40 feet (see chapter thirty-four).

A major advantage of the magic rope is its flexibility; children have no fear of hitting or tripping on it while they are performing. Ropes should be stretched tight enough so there is little sag.

Instructional Procedures

1. Two or more children need to be rope holders while the others are jumping. Develop some type of rotation plan, so all children participate.
2. Many variations can be achieved with the magic ropes by varying their height and by raising and lowering opposite ends of the ropes.
3. The jumping activities are strenuous; therefore alternate between jumping activities and those activities that involve crawling under the ropes, et cetera.
4. Emphasize to the class that they should concentrate on *not* touching the rope. The magic ropes can help develop the child's perception of his or her body in space if he or she regards the rope as an obstacle to be avoided.
5. Better use can be made of the ropes with an oblique approach, which involves starting at one end of the rope and progressing to the other end using jumping and hopping activities, et cetera. By comparison, the straight-on approach allows the child to jump the rope only once.
6. A total of eight ropes is needed for a class, two to each squad. Squads make excellent groups for this activity, since the leader can control the rotation of the rope holders.
7. The child next in turn should begin his or her movements when the child ahead is almost to the end of the rope.

Sequence of Activities

Activities with Single Ropes

Start the ropes at a 6-inch height and progressively raise them to add challenge.

1. Jump the rope.
2. Hop the rope.
3. Jump the rope, and perform various body turns while jumping.
4. Change body shapes and sizes while jumping.
5. Crawl or slide under the rope.
6. Alternate going over and under the rope.
7. Crouch jump over the rope.
8. Hold the rope overhead, and have others jump up and touch it with their foreheads.

Over a Single Magic Rope

9. Gradually lower the rope, and "limbo" under it without touching the floor with the hands.
10. Jump the rope backward without looking at it.
11. Perform a Scissors Jump over the rope.

Activities with Double Ropes

Vary the height and spread of the ropes. Do these activities with ropes parallel to each other.

1. Jump in one side and out the other.
2. Hop in one side and out the other.
3. Crouch Jump in and out.
4. Perform various animal walks in and out of the ropes.
5. Long jump over both of the ropes.
6. Perform a stunt when jumping in between the two ropes. Possible stunts could be a Heel Click, body turn, hand clap, and Straddle Jump.
7. Jump or leap over one rope and land on the other rope.

With ropes crossed at right angles to each other, do these activities.

1. Perform various movements from one area to the next.
2. Jump into one area and crawl out of that area into another.

With one rope above the other to create a barbed-wire-fence effect, do these activities.

1. Step through the ropes without touching.
2. Crouch Jump through.
3. Vary the height and the distance apart at which the ropes are placed. This adds much excitement to the activity, since children are challenged not to touch the ropes.

Over Double Magic Ropes

These miscellaneous activities are useful, too.

1. Perform the various activities with a beanbag balanced on the head while bouncing a ball.
2. Use four or more ropes to create various floor patterns.
3. Use a follow-the-leader plan to add variety to the activity.

4. Create a Challenge Course with many ropes for a relay.
5. Allow the class time to create their own ideas with the ropes and other pieces of equipment.

INDIVIDUAL MATS

Individual mats have an English origin and are the basis for many exploratory and creative movements. Essentially, the mat serves the child as a home base of operation and as an obstacle that he or she goes over or around.

Mats can vary in size, but 20 by 40 inches and 24 by 48 inches seem to be the most popular sizes. Three-quarter-inch thick mats are standard, but the thickness of the mats also varies. The mat should have a rubber backing, which prevents mat slippage on the floor. Foam-backed indoor-outdoor carpeting of good quality makes an excellent mat. In some cases, chaise-lounge pads can be used as a substitute for individual mats.

Instructional Procedures

1. Educational movement techniques are very important in mat work.
2. Much emphasis should be centered on body management and basic skills of locomotor and nonlocomotor movement.

Balance Activities on Individual Mats

3. Mats should be far enough apart to allow for free movement around them.
4. Each child should have a mat.

Sequence of Activities

Rigid adherence to the sequence presented below is not necessary, since the activities are quite flexible and demand only fundamental skills.

Command Movements

In this the child changes movements on command. Commands used are:

"Stretch": Stretch your body out in all directions as wide as possible.

"Curl": Curl into a little, tight ball.

"Balance": Form some kind of a balance.

"Bridge": Make a bridge over the mat.

"Reach": Keeping one toe on the mat, reach out as far as possible along the floor in a chosen direction.

"Rock": Rock on any part of the body.

"Roll": Do some kind of a roll on the mat.

"Twist": Make a shape with a part of the body twisted.

"Prone": Lie facedown on the mat.

"Melt": Sink down slowly into a little puddle of water on the mat.

"Shake": Shake all over, or shake whatever parts of the body are designated.

"Fall": Fall to the mat.

"Collapse": Similar to a fall, but follows nicely after a bridge.

Sequencing can be established in several fashions. The child can emphasize flow factors by moving at will from one selected movement to another. Or changes can be made on a verbal signal or a beat of a drum. A magic number can be injected by asking the children to change in keeping with that number.

Another means of exploration is selecting one of the movement challenges—stretch, balance, bridge. If stretch were selected, the child would change from one type of stretch position to another. In balance, the movement sequence could begin with balancing on six parts and reduce this number one at a time on signal until the child balances on one part. Different kinds of shapes can be explored.

Movements on and off the Mat

The children do different locomotor movements on and off the mat in different directions. Turns and shapes can be added. Levels are another good challenge.

1. Take the weight on the hands as you go across the mat.
2. Lead with different parts as you go on and off the mat. Move on and off the mat with specified number of body parts (one, two, three, four, five) used for landing.
3. Jump backward, forward, sideward. Make up a rhythmic sequence. Move around the area jumping from mat to mat.

Movements over the Mat

This is similar to the preceding movements, except the child goes completely over the mat each time.

Movements around the Mat

Locomotor movements around the mat are done both clockwise and counterclockwise.

1. Do movements around the mat, keeping hands on the mat. Do the same, but keep the feet on the mat.
2. Change to one foot and one hand on the mat. Vary with crab position.
3. Work out combinations of stunt movements and locomotor activities in going around the mats. Reverse direction often and regularly. Move throughout the area, running between the mats, and on signal jump over a specified number of mats.

Using Mats as a Base

1. Stretch and reach in different directions to show how big the space is.
2. Do combination movements away from and back to the mat, such as two jumps and two hops, or six steps and two jumps.
3. Use the magic-number concept. See how many letters you can make. Find a partner, put your mats together, and make your body into different letters and numbers.

Mat Games

Each child is seated on his or her mat. On signal, each child arises and jumps over as many different mats as he or she can. On the next signal, each child takes a seat on the nearest mat. The last child to get seated can be designated or pay a penalty. The game also can be played by eliminating one or two mats and thus having one or two children left without a home base. This is done by the teacher standing on a mat or by turning over mats and putting them out of the game. To control roughness, make a rule that the first child to touch a mat gets to sit on it.

A variation of this game is to have each child touch at least 10 mats and then sit Indian fashion on his or her own mat. Or a child could be required to alternate touching a mat and jumping over the next until a total of 10 is reached. "See how many mats you can Cartwheel or jump over in 10 seconds." Change the challenge and try again.

Developmental Challenges

Have the children experiment with partial or full Curl-ups. Keep this informal and on a challenge basis.

From a sitting position on the mat, the child picks up the short sides of the mat and raises the feet and upper body off the floor. See whether anyone can do variations of the V-up (page 355).

Manipulative Activities

Keeping one foot on the mat, maintain control of a balloon in the air, either with a hand, a nylon-stocking paddle, or a lummi stick. Try this with a stocking paddle and a paper ball. The number of touches, or strokes, can be counted. Try with both feet on the mat.

Carpet Squares

These are store carpet samples that are usually 12-by-12-inches or 16-by-16-inches square, although they also come in rectangular shapes. Most kinds of carpet slide readily on the floor.

One child can pull another with either a wand or a jump rope, with the rider seated or kneeling on the square. Another activity is to use the squares "crossing the river on ice cakes." One child can do this individually and shift squares, or he or she can be helped by a partner who shifts the squares for him or her.

BALANCE BOARDS

Balance boards are small devices on which the child tries to stand and keep the board in balance. Generally, they have either a circular or square platform about 15 inches wide and a rounded bottom to provide the challenge for balance. A rubber pad should protect the floor.

Some instructors like to begin with a single-axis board (page 562). This is simpler in its demands and has use for handicapped children and those having difficulty with the board with the rounded bottom. Another type of board has a 4-by-4-inch square bottom that provides a flat surface for better stability. If this seems too easy, the bottom square can be reduced in size (page 562). Having a variety of boards is an excellent idea. The activities are somewhat limited, consisting of maintaining balance with a variety of challenges.

Two Types of Balance Boards

The balance boards are quite useful when a lot of apparatus is put out and the children are allowed to explore on the various pieces.

Sequence of Activities

1. Secure a balanced position on the board. Change position of arms.
2. Secure balance, and gradually lower the body to touch the board.
3. Change from a two-foot to a one-foot balance. Change from one foot to the other. Turn completely around on the board. Move the feet together and move them apart. Stand on tiptoes. Close eyes and balance.

Balancing on Different Balance Boards

4. Tilt forward until the front edge of the board touches the floor, and return to the starting position. Also try tilting backward, right, and left.

Hold and maintain balance while performing tasks 5-11.

5. Bounce and catch a ball with two hands.
6. Toss a ball into the air, and catch it with both hands.
7. Try both of the above stunts with one hand.
8. Dribble a ball, and keep track of the number of successful bounces made without losing balance.
9. Twirl a hoop on various body parts, and maintain balance.
10. Jump rope on the board.
11. Do some of the above activities with eyes closed.
12. Balance on various body parts, such as knees, tummy, and seat. Getting back up is difficult.
13. Touch different body parts as specified while balanced. Touch opposites (touch the right shoulder with the left hand; the left ear with the right hand, et cetera).
14. Pick up a beanbag from the board.
15. Balance on the board with a partner.
16. Start from a standing position on the board and move to a kneeling position. Reverse and move to standing position.
17. Toss and catch beanbags, balls, or hoops with a partner. Change a hoop from performer's arm to partner, without stopping the twirling or losing balance.

BONGO BOARDS

The bongo board features a single-axis-type balance board with a movable cylinder that allows the board to be shifted back and forth over the cylinder. Edges are fixed completely around the board underneath to prevent the cylinder from moving out from under the board. Commercial varieties generally feature a track in the center to keep the roller in line.

The suggested activities, with the exception of #2, can be accomplished on a single-axis balance board (fixed cylinder). This may be an appropriate place to start before progressing to the bongo board.

Sequence of Activities

1. To mount, place the board on the roller so one end is on the floor. Step on this end first, and then place the other foot on the high end. Bring the lower end off the floor, and shift the board along the roller until the roller is in the center. Hold and balance. This is the basic position.
2. Shift the board back and forth on the roller with easy motion, beginning with a small shift and increasing somewhat, under control.
3. Take basic position. Turn on the balls of the feet and face one end. Face back to basic position. Turn the other way.
4. Assume basic position. Slowly bring the feet together, and widen them out again.
5. Begin with basic position. Make a turn as in #3. Gradually move the feet until they are positioned together over the roller. Return to original position.
6. From basic stance, jump lightly and land. Increase the height of the jumps.
7. Toss and receive beanbags and balls from a partner while in basic stance. Do same while in a turned position (#3).
8. Maintaining the basic position, stoop and touch the board. Try picking up a beanbag from the board.
9. Handle hoops or juggle beanbags or balls while in balance.
10. Touching body parts as specified also can be done on the bongo board. Remember to include opposite touching; that is, touch the left knee with the right hand, et cetera.

BOUNDING BOARDS

Bounding boards provide a unique type of movement similar to that of a child bouncing on a trampoline. They can be constructed easily from a piece of ¾-inch plywood, size 2-by-6-feet. The board is supported on pieces of 4-by-4-inch lumber, which are padded with carpet to protect the floor. The plywood must be a quality product with few knots. Marine plywood, though expensive, is the best (see chapter thirty-four).

Two children can work on one board, with the performer moving forward to leave the board and return back to place. Emphasis should be on lightness, height, and relaxation during the bounding. Bounding for the most part should be done in the center of the board. The activity is for younger children only. Older children can damage and break the boards.

Sequence of Activities

1. Bound in the center; two feet, one foot.
2. Bound in the center, using turns and different arm positions. Add hand clapping.
3. Move across the board, using jumping and hopping. Return. Add turns and hand clapping.
4. Bound with numbered foot combinations, alternating two, three, or four hops on one foot and then changing to the other. These are called twoseys, threeseys, and fourseys.
5. To the previous skills, add forward and backward leg extensions and leg changes sideward.
6. Use different numbers of hops when alternating, such as hopping once on the right foot and twice on the left. Use other combinations, such as 2-3, 2-4, et cetera.
7. Add rope jumping with slow time and fast time. Use hoops.

Bouncing on Bounding Boards

8. The teacher calls out a specific body part, and the child holds this while bouncing.

GYM SCOOTERS

Gym scooters make excellent devices for developmental activity when properly used. The minimum number for a class should be one scooter for each two children. However, if the scooters are used only for relays, four or six will suffice.

Two rules are important in the use of scooters. The first is: the children are not to stand on them as they would on skate boards. The second rule is: scooters, with or without passengers, are not to be used as missiles.

Scooters can be used by children working individually or with partners. A child working alone can do many variations by combining the method of propulsion and the method of supporting the body. The child can propel the scooter with his or her feet, hands, or both. His or her body position can be kneeling, sitting, prone, supine, or even sideways. His or her weight can be wholly or partially supported on the scooter. Variation in space factors, particularly direction, adds to the interest.

On a Gym Scooter

When children work in pairs, one child rides and the other pushes. The rider's weight may be wholly or partially supported by the scooter. If only partially by the scooter, the remainder of the weight is supported by the partner.

Educational movement methodology is applicable to scooter work, but care should be exercised so that it is a developmental period and not just a fun session.

Scooters are excellent for relays, and many games can be adapted to their use. See the chapter on game-type activities for suggested scooter games (page 377).

ACTIVITIES WITH TIRES

Activities with tires are challenging to children and easy on the school budget. Tires of different sizes can be used. The tires should be washed, and they can be painted to make them more appealing to children. Make the painting a school project in conjunction with the classroom teacher or art specialist.

Tires generally are used outside, since considerable space is needed. Holes around an inch in diameter should be bored through the treads, with four of them spaced around the outside to facilitate water drainage. Storage is a problem that can be solved with a rack similar to the ones used in tire shops. A chain and a lock help prevent theft and vandalism.

Tire stands for keeping tires upright can be made (page 569). Tires can be placed on the ground singly or in combinations, or they can be handled as moving objects by the children.

Activities with Tires Placed on the Ground

1. Jump in and out of the tire forward and backward, side to side.
2. Stand in the tire, and jump out as far as possible.
3. Take a push-up position with hands on the tire and the feet outstretched. Walk the feet in a large clockwise and counterclockwise circle. Reverse and put the feet on the tire and walk the hands.
4. Run, hop, skip, gallop, and slide around the tire clockwise and counterclockwise. Add different animal movements.
5. Run and jump into the center of the tire without touching it. Sink down and exit like a frog.
6. Use the Bunny Jump, the Frog Hop, and the Pogo Stick to move into the center and out.
7. Balance on one foot inside the tire, close the eyes, hold for a few seconds, and hop out with the eyes closed.
8. Can you Straddle Jump in and out of the tire?
9. Gradually increase and decrease the height of jumps inside the tire.
10. Make a bridge with the hands inside the tire and the feet out. Move the bridge around the tire. Explore with different kinds of bridges, some with the feet inside the tire. Can you make a bridge completely across the tire? Try turning the bridge completely around.
11. Show the different kinds of things you can do by moving or standing on the sides of the tire.
12. Stack two tires, and leap, jump, or otherwise move in and out. Add a third if you think you can make it.

Activities with the Tires Placed in Patterns and Combinations

Tires can be placed in various combinations, either touching one another or spaced a bit apart, depending upon the movement challenges. They can be placed in a straight line or in different curved patterns.

1. Run, jump, hop, and use various animal walks through the patterns.
2. Jump through the patterns with one foot on the tire sides.
3. Experiment with straddle-jumping patterns so

one foot is outside and one inside the tires. Try some crisscross jumping.

4. Jump through, touching only the sides. Run through on the sides. Form different figure-eight and circular movements on the sides while walking or running lightly.
5. Increase the height of the jump slightly each time as you move down the line of tires.
6. In the patterns, add tires to make some double heights to add challenge.

Handling the Tires

This can include both in-place activities and those that involve rolling the tire. Partner activities should be a part of the experiences.

1. Spin the tire, and see what you can do while moving around the tire as it spins.
2. Roll the tire. See whether you can get in front of it and stop it. Try getting in front of it and jumping over it as it rolls. Roll at a target.
3. Experiment with different ways you can lift and hold the tire in the air. Can you get it overhead?
4. With a partner, roll the tire back and forth. Roll so your partner can jump the tire. Set a target in between, and see which of you can hit the target.
5. Work out a few contests with your partner. Try a tug-of-war with a tire. Devise other contests, either pulling or pushing.
6. Let your partner roll his or her tire on a crossing path, and see whether you can hit his or her tire with yours.

Other Activities with Tires

1. Play Beanbag Horseshoes with the tires as targets. Scoring systems: one point for each beanbag that lands inside the tire or two points for landing it inside the tire and one for on the sides.
2. Different relays can use the tire as a rolling relay, or the tires can be obstacles to jump in or run around, through, or on.
3. Tires can be mounted on stands, and the children can explore different ways to go through, over, or around the tires.

STILTS

Stilts are made in different fashions and heights, with the step providing about a 4-inch support. A step of 6 to 12 inches is suitable for beginners, and mounting is less of a problem with the shorter steps. Higher heights of 18, 24, and 30 inches can be used to challenge the more skilled. It may be necessary to use a jumping box, a sturdy chair, or a ladder to mount some of the higher heights. The length of the stilts should reach a foot or two above the shoulders, measured when the student is on the stilts.

Stilts made from tin cans have some value for younger children, but the challenge for balance is not as meaningful as with regular stilts. Activities on tin-can stilts can follow the described patterns, in most cases.

Stilts are regarded mostly as outdoor equipment. If they are used indoors, the stilts should have rubber pads at the bottoms to minimize slippage.

The exploratory approach should predominate, since children need to move at their own pace in these activities. The following activities are suggested.

Sequence of Activities

1. Mounting and initial stepping must be mastered. Mounting can be done from the ground or from a raised surface.
2. Movement in different directions should be practiced—forward, backward, and sideward. Try moving while keeping one stilt always forward or backward.
3. Pattern walking can offer more challenge. Using tires or other obstacles, challenge the child to walk in various patterns.
4. Walk the stilts apart with small increments. Bring them back together again.
5. Try to balance momentarily on one stilt and pivot on one stilt.
6. Can you jump in place with the stilts? Can you move while jumping? Try hopping (a bit more difficult).
7. Using a low (8-inch) jumping box, step up on the box and down again. (The top of the box should have a nonslip surface. A stair platform of two or three steps also can be negotiated by the more skilled, provided again that there is provision against slipping. Spot as necessary.)

MISCELLANEOUS APPARATUS IDEAS

Solid chairs (not the folding type) can provide the base for jumping and climbing patterns. The backs can be removed to make them stools.

Unicycles are unique and attractive instruments for movement. These are not mastered easily, but they intrigue the children. Expense is a factor. The high school shop could make them as a project.

Skate boards are a fact of life, and perhaps some attention to technique and safety can be included in the physical education program. This could be an afterschool activity.

Roller skating has been found to be an excellent activity for both handicapped and normal children. Fitting and fastening on skates, however, is quite time consuming.

Some schools have had success with springboards and mini-trampolines. Simple bouncing and jumping stunts seem in line, but the more advanced tumbling stunts should be confined to special groups working under trained instructors and with expert supervision.

The authors question the use of the regular trampoline for elementary school physical education classes. With only one child bouncing at a time, the other children stand inactive. The hazards posed by trampolines have caused some administrators to take a hard look at the trampoline for inclusion in the school program on any level. It is difficult to justify the inclusion of the trampoline in the elementary school program because of the space it takes up when not used, and the difficulty of moving or storing the apparatus. Most trampolines in elementary school programs seem to have been inherited from high school programs, since the expense of purchase can hardly ever be justified. Perhaps the logical use of the trampoline is with a special interest group in a gymnastics-type program under qualified supervision.

Nineteen

Stunts and Tumbling

Stunts and tumbling are important parts of every child's overall experience in physical education, and they make significant contributions toward the achievement of the goals of physical education.

THE STUNTS AND TUMBLING PROGRAM

Through the stunts and tumbling program, such personal characteristics as dedication and perseverance toward a goal can be furthered, since stunts seldom are mastered quickly or in a few attempts. Since much of the work is individual, the child faces his or her own challenge and has the opportunity to develop resourcefulness, self-confidence, and courage. On the other hand, disregard for safety must be avoided.

Social interplay is provided by the various partner and group stunts requiring cooperative effort. The social attributes of tolerance, helpfulness, courtesy, and appreciation for the ability of others grow out of the lessons when the methodology is educationally sound. Further group consciousness develops from the child's own increased concern for his or her own safety and that of others. Children should use proper spotting techniques and be ready to help others execute stunts.

When a child masters a challenging stunt, his or her satisfaction, pride of achievement, and sense of accomplishment contribute to a gain in self-respect and an improvement in self-image.

Physical Values

Important physical values can emerge from an instructionally sound program of stunts and tumbling. Exercise in good body management can be

provided, thus fulfilling the objective of offering opportunities for a child to manage his or her body effectively in a variety of situations. Coordination, flexibility, and agility can be enhanced.

The opportunity to practice control of balance is present in many stunt activities and is particularly featured in some. Visual control of balance can be eliminated occasionally by having the children close their eyes during balance stunts, thus centering demands on the other balance controls.

The raw physical demands of held positions and stunt execution contribute to the development of strength and power of many diverse parts of the body. The many stunts that demand support by the arms, wholly or in part, provide needed development for the often weak musculature of the arm-shoulder-girdle region. Stunts and tumbling activities contribute to all areas of physical fitness.

Educational Values

As well as introducing new terminology into children's lives, stunts and tumbling activities offer a wonderful opportunity for children to acquire fundamental concepts, such as those of right and left, near and far, wide and narrow, up and down, and forward and backward.

PROGRESSION AND GRADE-LEVEL PLACEMENT

Progression is the soul of learning experiences in the stunts and tumbling program, and, in this text, the activities in this program are allocated in progression within grades. It is essential for the order of those stunts, which lead from one grade to the next, to be reasonably maintained. Adherence to grade-level placement is secondary to this principle. If, on the other hand, children come with little or no experience in these activities, the teacher should start them off with activities specified for a lower grade level.

Another key point in the organization of these activities lies in the fact that they are divided into six basic groups: (1) animal movements, (2) tumbling and inverted balances, (3) balance stunts, (4) individual stunts, (5) partner and group stunts, and (6) partner support activities. This arrangement allows the teacher to pick some activities from each group for a well-balanced lesson. Too often, teachers concentrate on tumbling activities and children become bored and tired of this approach. Selecting stunts from all of the groups allows more students to meet success, due to the wide range of activities being offered.

Standard Tumbling Stunts

The essentials of a stunts and tumbling program consist of the standard tumbling activities, such as rolls, stands, springs, and related stunts commonly accepted as basic to such a program. The suggested progression of these *basic* gymnastic-type activities is presented in the following list. Descriptions of the stunts are found in the programs at the indicated grade levels.

Sequence and Grade-Level Chart

Kindergarten and First Grade
  Side Roll
  Forward Roll
  Back Roller
  Backward Roll (Handclasp Position)
Second Grade
  Forward Roll Practice
  Climb-up
  Three-Point Tip-up
  Backward Curl
  Backward Roll (Regular)
Third Grade
  Forward Roll Variations
  Frog Handstand
  Headstand
Fourth Grade
  Forward Roll Combinations
  Backward Roll Combinations
  Headstand Variations
Fifth Grade
  Forward and Backward Roll Combinations
  Neckspring
  Handstand
  Cartwheel
  Judo Roll
  Eskimo Roll
Sixth Grade
  Forward and Backward Roll Combinations
  Cartwheel and Round-off

Headstand Variations
Headspring
Dive Forward Roll
Handstand
Forearm Headstand
Forearm Stand
Straddle Press to Headstand
Walk-over

Kindergarten and Primary-Level Program

The kindergarten and primary-level program relies on simple stunts with good developmental possibilities, with a gradual introduction to those tumbling stunts that are classified as lead-ups or preliminaries to more advanced stunts. Stunts requiring exceptional body control, critical balancing, or the need for substantial strength should be left for higher grades. The program of stunts and tumbling in the lower grades should include the following: (1) a variety of simple stunts involving gross body movements, opportunity for creative expression, control of balance, and directional concepts; (2) a progressive introduction to the basic tumbling stunts, such as the Forward and Backward Rolls and basic stands; and (3) introductory work performed with a partner in partner stunts.

Intermediate-Level Program

The intermediate-level program is built upon the activities and progressions from the primary-level program. More emphasis is placed on the standard tumbling stunts, with the accompanying need for appropriate spotting techniques. While most stunts in the primary level can be performed with a greater degree of choice, the intermediate level is based on a somewhat different emphasis. More conformance to the stunt pattern or design is desired. The stunts make higher demands on strength, control, form, agility, balance, and flexibility.

While many of the stunts on the lower level can be done at least in some fashion, the teacher will find on the intermediate level certain stunts that will be too much challenge for some of the children. An attempt is made to arrange stunts for the upper grades so that the list includes stunts everyone can do, stunts that are somewhat challenging, and more difficult stunts that the less skillful will find quite challenging. The range of stunts provides something for all levels of ability in any grade level. For the intermediate level the program includes: (1) basic tumbling stunts, with emphasis on progression; (2) stunts demanding critical balance; (3) stunts demanding considerable flexibility; (4) partner support stunts; (5) miscellaneous stunts demanding agility or strength; and (6) a program of simple pyramids.

PRESENTING ACTIVITIES

Steps in presenting activities in the daily lesson plan for stunts and tumbling should include the following considerations.

1. Provide warm-up activity as needed.
2. Consider appropriate physical fitness development activity.
3. Arrange children in suitable formations for teaching.
4. Review previously learned materials and practice lead-up activities to the stunts to be presented.
5. Present the new activity with appropriate description and demonstration.
6. Provide opportunity for practice and improvement of performance.
7. Establish a basis for variety through appropriate movement methodology.
8. Evaluate progress and, as needed, repeat directions. Bring in stress points, and work toward refining and perfecting performance.

Warm-up Activity

For the most part, introductory activity and the fitness movement patterns usually supply sufficient warm-up for the stunts and tumbling lesson. If additional stretching seems warranted, the following routine can be followed.

Take a wide straddle position with the feet about 3 feet apart and the toes pointed ahead. With the arms out to the sides, bend, twist, and generally stretch in all directions. Next, touch the floor with the hands to the front, sides, and back, with little bending of the knees.

Organizing the Children for the Lesson

One of the justifiable criticisms of stunts and tumbling lessons is that the children must wait in line for lengthy turns on the mat. Taking turns in itself is not wrong, but this must be controlled to the point where everyone is reasonably active. Sometimes, it is desirable for students to watch what others are doing.

The arrangement of children should depend upon the stunts selected and whether or not mats are required. Priorities should be established in this order.

1. Whenever possible, all children should be active and performing at the same time. Where mats are not required for the activities, there is little problem. Individual mats can be used for many of the simple balances and rolling stunts, particularly for the kindergarten and first grade. When mats are required, teachers must be more ingenious. Ideally, there are enough mats for groups of three students to take turns. When return activities are used, there is little standing around within the groups of three. When spotting and cooperation are needed, small groups function well.
2. When the number of mats is limited, children can work across the mats sideways. On a 6-foot-long mat, two children can tumble across sideways. An 8-foot-long mat can be used by three performers working crossways at the same time. The ends of the mats can be used for various kinds of stands, as long as care is taken so that children do not fall toward each other. In this arrangement, the learning centers on single rolls, but this does not rule out occasional series of rolls lengthwise on the mats.
3. If the children are to do a lot of tumbling lengthwise down mats, there should be at least six mats per class; this allows six groups to practice at one time. When there are eight mats available the squad formation can be used, with a squad having access to two mats. Return activity should be a consideration for providing additional activity demands.
4. Station teaching should be considered, especially when the amount of equipment is limited. Careful planning is necessary to assure that the experience stresses progress and diligence. All stations could revolve around stunts and tumbling experiences, or one or two tumbling and stunts stations could be included with other activities.

Wall charts listing the activities in progression provide excellent guidance. The chart illustrated with stick figures could be made as a class project. The station arrangement could be:

Station 1: Forward and Backward Rolls.
Station 2: Headstands.
Station 3: Cartwheels.
Station 4: partner stunts.

5. The contract or task card approach is made to order for tumbling and stunts. The stunts could be arranged in one progression or in levels. The student would do his or her reading and investigating from wall charts or other sources and media. He or she could get another student to give him or her preliminary approval before the child demonstrates the stunt for the teacher.

Formations for Teaching

Formations that have value in organizing a class for conducting stunts and tumbling instruction follow.

Squad Line Formation: Mats are placed in a line, with the squads lined up behind the mats. Each child takes a turn and goes to the end of his or her line, with the others moving up. An alternative method is for each child to perform and then return to his or her position. The children can be seated.

Squad File Formation: By positioning the mats so the children approach the mats from the ends, a file formation can be arranged. The teacher is in front, and the children perform toward him or her. As soon as a child has completed his or her turn, he or she goes to the end of the line.

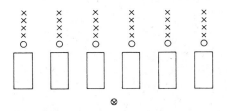

A weakness of this formation is that, at times, some children may be hidden from the teacher by other children, posing problems of control.

Semicircular Formation: The squad file formation can be changed readily to a semicircular arrangement. This formation focuses attention on the teacher, who is in the center. Groups are more separated than in the squad file formation.

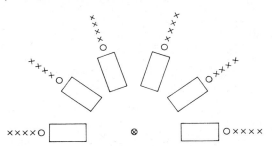

Hollow Rectangle: The squads perform on the sides of a hollow rectangle. The advantage of this formation is that the children can watch each other. If the teacher is in the center, some portion of the class will be behind his or her back.

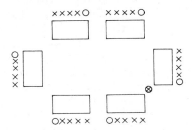

U-shaped Formation: The mats are formed in the shape of a U. The formation has good visual control possibilities for the teacher, and the chil-

dren are able to see what their classmates are doing.

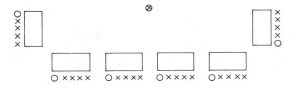

Double Row Formation: In this formation, three groups form a row on one side and three on the other. The teacher is never far from any group. Children can see each other.

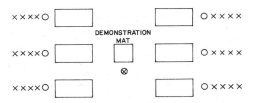

Demonstration Mat: When sufficient mats are available, one mat can be placed in an appropriate central position, so little movement of the children is necessary to see the demonstrations. The mat should be used exclusively for demonstrations.

Return Activities

Return activities are discussed on page 292. They have a place in the stunts and tumbling program and work best in the lesson activities in which children perform lengthwise down the mat. Each child should turn in a designated direction (right or left) at the end of the mat and use that pathway to do his or her return task. A popular return activity is to make use of a magic number. Instructions for the return are given in this way: "Today, our magic number for return activity is five." For example, children may solve this problem by doing three jumps and two hops on the way back, or they may do four Push-ups and one Frog Jump.

Return Activities (children are doing Forward Rolls on the mats and doing an animal walk back to place as return activity)

Review

Review of the learning experiences from the previous lesson or lessons is important in maintaining good continuity. Points of difficulty from previous lessons should be brought out and solved. Variety beyond that which was secured previously can be developed. Quality of performance should be given consideration. "What was good?" and "how can we make our performance better?" should be key questions. It is possible that much of the new lesson could be devoted to the review and improvement of previously presented experiences. It is pointless to go on to a new lesson and leave activities in which reasonable results have not been secured. Caution should be used to avoid "driving the activities into the ground." The teacher can always return to them at a later date, if necessary.

Description and Demonstration

The teacher can describe and demonstrate simultaneously. While the teacher may wish to demonstrate some stunts, the children love to help and can provide effective demonstration. In presenting a stunt, the following pattern should prove helpful.

1. The Significance of the Name

Most of the stunts have a characteristic name, and this should be a consideration in the teaching. If the stunt is of an imitative type, the animal or character represented should be described and discussed.

2. The Stunt's Description

Stunts can be approached by following these steps.

Starting Position: Most stunts have a definite starting position. To perform properly, the child should understand what position he or she is to assume as the first step in doing a stunt.

Execution: Based on the starting position, the key movements for good performance in the stunt should be stressed. Such other factors as how far to travel, how long to balance, and how many times a movement should be done should be clarified for the student.

Finishing Position: In some stunts, a definite finishing position or act is a part of the stunt. In balancing stunts, for example, it is important that the child return to a standing (or some other) position without losing his or her balance or moving his or her feet.

Safety Considerations: Each child is entitled to know the inherent dangers of any stunt or tumbling activity. The safety rules to be followed and the duties of the spotters or helpers should be a part of the instruction.

The Demonstration

As the teacher describes the stunt, a student can demonstrate under the teacher's direction. If the stunt is one that is similar to, or based upon, a previously learned stunt, the description should be as brief as possible. There may be little need for demonstration in such cases. For primary-level children, the stunts are varied and can take many forms. The teacher should look for children to demonstrate unique and interesting variations of the stunt.

Three levels of demonstration are recognized: (1) provide minimal demonstration in the form of the starting position, and let the children progress from this point; (2) go through the entire stunt slowly, step by step, explaining what is involved; (3) execute the stunt as it would be done by the students normally. Since children need to analyze and solve problems, too much demonstration defeats this purpose.

Explanation and demonstration should cover only one or two points. Do not try to demonstrate too far in advance. Show the points necessary to get the activity underway. Add further details and refinements as the instruction progresses.

Demonstrations also have a place later in the sequence of instruction. Demonstrations partway through the instruction can show successful execution of something others do not understand or with which they are having difficulty. Demonstrations at the end of a unit can show what has been achieved. Each squad or group can demonstrate its achievements in turn.

Opportunities for Practice and Improvement

The character of each stunt determines the amount of practice needed and the number of times it should be performed. The teacher should analyze a stunt to the point where he or she can verbalize the various small points necessary for good performance. Such directions as "point your toes forward," "tuck your chin down," and "fingers spread wide" are examples of cues for successful performance.

A reasonable standard of performance should be a part of the teaching. The teacher must answer the child's question, "did I do it?" Some stunts are on a pass-fail basis, while others can be evaluated in terms of quality. A child needs standards that are both challenging and attainable. The instruction must make clear to the child what is involved in the performance criterion of the stunt, so he or she knows whether or not he or she is within these bounds.

Quality in movement should be stressed throughout, but early emphasis should be on *doing the stunt.* Caution should be exercised in giving the child too many directions and details at the beginning that only tend to confuse him or her. Directions added a few at a time stimulate the child to continued practice and improvement.

Many of the stunts require a position to be held for a short time. At first, have the child merely do the stunt. Later, have him or her hold for 3 and then 5 seconds.

Practice and repetition are essential in establishing effective movement patterns. Often, a teacher leaves an activity too soon to allow for needed progress. The following system is suggested.

Whenever explanations and demonstrations are completed and the children begin practice, each child in a group should go through the stunt at least twice. When each child in the group has had two turns at an activity, the group remains in formation, waiting for the next instruction. If this system is to function properly, groups need to be of about the same size and move at about the same speed. A teacher can ascertain in a glance whether the children are ready for the next instructions. This avoids the necessity of whistle blowing to clear the mats.

How closely should children follow one another on the mat? A child should start his or her routine when the child ahead is just leaving the mat.

Variety of Response

Variety of movement can be secured in two general ways. The first is to make use of the suggestions for variety incorporated in the stunt descriptions. The second is to use educational movement principles to establish problems, limitations, and suggestions that stimulate the children to extended experiences. The activity potential of any one stunt can be extended by use of time factors, body factors, space factors, flow factors, and expressive factors.

Since most stunts have a starting position, an execution routine, and a finishing position, one or more of these could be varied to stimulate variety of movement and provide exploratory activity. For example, for variety in the Forward Roll, a child could begin with a Rabbit Jump, execute the Forward Roll with arms folded across the chest, and finish with a jump and a half-turn.

Laterality is a factor that must be emphasized. In practice, the children's attention needs to be called to using the side or member of the body that normally is not used.

The concept of directionality should be established in children, so they approach performance of stunts with the principle of right and left usage without waiting to be so instructed. If a balancing stunt is done on one foot, then the next time it should be tried on the other. If a roll is made to the right, a comparable roll should be made to the left. A teacher may wish to develop the stunt thoroughly on one side before making the change to the other side, but the change should be made.

SAFETY CONSIDERATIONS

Safety is a foremost consideration in the program of stunts and tumbling. The inherent hazards of an activity and how to avoid them must be included in the instructional procedures. Spotting techniques are particularly needed in the intermediate-level program. Only a few kindergarten and primary-level stunts are hazardous enough to require spotting techniques.

Spotting

As the complexity of the activities is increased, more attention must be given to spotting. The purpose of the spotter is to assist the performer, help receive the weight, and prevent a hazardous fall. The first two purposes can be anticipated and included in the instruction, since the stunt determines what assistance can be given and where the spotter should aid in receiving the weight. Saving the performer from a fall is more difficult, since it cannot be anticipated.

In assisting, the spotter should take a firm hold on the performer and position himself or herself in relation to the direction of the stunt, since he or she may need to move with the performer as he or she executes the stunt. The spotter must be careful to assist but not to provide too much help that becomes a hindrance. The spotters should avoid "wrestling" the performer into position.

In stunts where the body is inverted, spotting is an important consideration. In stunts such as the Headstand and the Handstand, it is important to control the child's movement, so he or she returns to the floor in the same direction from which he or she got into position for the stunt.

Receiving the weight of a performer is needed only infrequently in the elementary school program. It is used in activities during which the child goes through the air in some kind of a jumping or vaulting stunt, some assistance being given to help cushion his or her return to the floor. For cautious children, this type of help will enable them to do the stunt and get the feel of it. Later, as they become more sure of themselves, they dispense with the help.

Each stunt should be analyzed with safety in mind, and a trained spotter should be assigned routinely. It is important for spotters to know both the stunt and the spotting techniques. Sufficient time must be allotted for teaching correct spotting techniques.

Children should ask others to spot when they are learning a new stunt. They should be willing, in turn, to assist in spotting as needed.

Other Safety Considerations

1. Emphasis should be placed on how to fall. Children should be taught to roll out of a stunt when balance is lost. When doing Headstands and Handstands children should try to return to the floor in the direction from which they started. The return is facilitated by bending both at the waist and at the knees.
2. Pockets should be emptied, and lockets, glasses, watches, and other articles of this nature should be removed. A special depository for these articles should be provided, or, better yet, they should be left in the classroom.
3. No practice periods should be conducted without the presence of a teacher or a proper supervisor.
4. Fatigue and strain in young children should be guarded against.
5. Children should be encouraged but not forced to try stunts. Care should be taken not to use peer pressure to stimulate participation.
6. Control is a basic element of the stunts and tumbling program. Children should learn to use controlled movements. Speed is secondary and, in some cases, even undesirable.

ADDITIONAL CONSIDERATIONS IN METHODOLOGY

Instructional Emphasis

1. While some stunts do not require mats, it is well to include stunts requiring mats in every lesson. Children like to perform on mats, and rolling stunts using mats are vital.
2. In selecting students for demonstration, be sure the student understands and can perform reasonably correctly.
3. Many partner stunts work well only when the partners are of about the same size. However, if the stunt is of the partner support type, then the support child should be strong enough to hold the weight of the other. This usually means a larger and stronger child on the bottom to provide the support.
4. The instruction should include, in addition to safety considerations, the points to be stressed that are critical to performance. Be sure the performer understands the stress points before he or she proceeds.
5. No two children perform alike. Respect individual differences, and allow for different levels of success.
6. While some emphasis on form and control should be established in the lower grades, children on the intermediate level should be made more conscious of the need to refine and perfect performance. This, however, should be within the capacity of the children.
7. It is important to relate new activities to those learned previously. A good practice is to review the lead-up stunt for an activity.
8. Horseplay and ridicule have no place in a program of stunts and tumbling. See that the children have fun but also that they respect the efforts of their classmates.
9. Proper gym shoes are a help in the program. However, children can tumble in bare feet.
10. When a stunt calls for a position to be held for a number of counts, use a standard counting system like "one thousand and one, one thousand and two," or "monkey one, monkey two," et cetera.
11. When children are asked to reach out or place objects a distance along the floor, distances can be specified by having the children count boards on the floor away from a line or base position. Generally, the start should be made at a modest distance, so all can achieve success, with appropriate increases to follow. In Balance Touch (page 331), for example, the teacher can specify that the beanbag should be placed a certain number of board widths away from a line. Distances then can be varied by increasing the number of boards between the line and the object.
12. At times, the teacher can have children work in pairs, with one child performing and the second providing a critique.
13. In using small hand apparatus (wands, hoops, et cetera) with stunts, it is best to have one item for each child. If this is not possible, a minimum of two pieces is needed for each group, so the child next in line does not have to wait for the return of the needed object. One person, generally the leader of the group, should be designated to secure and return hand apparatus.
14. In planning a series of stunts, the position at the completion of one stunt determines what the next stunt can be. The child must anticipate, so he or she can finish one stunt in the appropriate position that allows him or her to go naturally and smoothly into the next stunt.
15. There should be little shifting of mats during the course of instruction. In arranging a sequence of stunts for a day's lesson, it is well to put the mat stunts together.
16. Occasionally soft background music contributes to a pleasant atmosphere, but it should be low enough in volume so as not to interfere with the instruction. Long-play records or tapes are excellent, since little attention is needed for the music sources.
17. The beat of a drum or a tom-tom can be

utilized to direct controlled movements. Children change position in small increments as guided by a beat. In Lowering the Boom (page 321), for example, children can lower themselves a little each time the drum sounds.

Start-and-Expand Technique

The start-and-expand technique should be applied to stunts, when it is feasible. Take the example of teaching a simple Heel Click (page 327). The instructor can begin by saying, "Let's see all of you jump high into the air and click your heels together before you come down" (the start). "Now, to do the stunt properly, you should jump into the air, click your heels, and land with your feet apart with a nice bent-knee action to absorb the shock" (expansion). Further expansion can be adding quarter- or half-turns before landing, clapping hands overhead while clicking heels, and clicking heels twice before landing.

The start is made so simple that all children can experience some measure of success. The instruction then expands to other elements of the stunt, with variations and movement factors added and refined as indicated.

Social Factors

1. Proper attire is essential for eliminating a modesty problem. On days when stunts are scheduled, girls can change to slacks or shorts. The best solution, however, is to have all children change to gymnasium-type uniforms.
2. Children should have fun *with* their friends in these types of activities, but they should not be allowed to laugh *at* an inept child.
3. Social goals that should be stressed for the children are cooperating with a partner, a small group, the entire class, and the teacher. Showing consideration in taking turns is important.
4. Children should be taught to have respect for equipment and to care for it. Mats should be lifted clear of the ground and not dragged when being moved.

Basic Mechanical Principles

Certain simple mechanical and kinesiological principles should be established as the foundations of an effective program. If children can build upon these basic principles, instruction is facilitated.

1. Momentum needs to be developed and applied, particularly for rolls. Tucking, starting from a higher point, and preliminary raising of the arms are examples of devices to increase momentum.
2. The center of weight must be positioned over the center of support in balance stunts, particularly the inverted stands.

3. In certain stunts, such as the Neckspring and the Headspring, the hips should be projected upward and forward to raise the center of gravity for better execution.
4. In stunts where the body is wholly or partially supported by the hands, proper positioning of the hands is essential for good performance. The hands should be spread to approximately shoulder width, and the fingers should be spread and pointed forward. The pads of the fingers apply pressure for a good basis of support. This hand position generally should be employed unless there is a specific reason to depart from it.

Stunt Check-off System

Some teachers find value in establishing a check-off system to keep track of the student's progress. Two systems are suggested. The first simply checks those stunts the student has completed. The second differentiates between a stunt done well and one that meets minimum requirements. In the latter system, the teacher can make a diagonal line (/) for a stunt meeting minimum requirements and a cross over that line, making an X, for a stunt done well. The lists of the stunts with the children's names by squads can be posted on the bulletin board or kept on squad cards for convenient use in the stunt lesson.

A glance at the cards enables the teacher to know which stunts need to be reviewed and practiced. An analysis of this type makes for a better educational experience for the children. However, care must be taken that the check-off system does not take too much teaching-learning time.

Some cautions need to be observed while using these systems. The lists should not result in peer pressure on students. Also, the student's sense of achievement may be distorted if he or she becomes interested only in getting stunts marked on the list.

Wave (or Ripple) Effect

An interesting movement and sequence pattern can be injected into the instruction with the use of wave (or ripple) effect. These should be used only after the students have achieved a reasonable mastery of the movements.

A squad makes a suitable size group to carry out the wave effect. The children in the group form a line alongside a series of mats laid lengthwise. The formation would look like this.

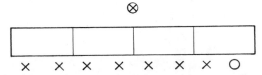

The wave effect can go in either direction but generally moves from right to left (for performers).

The Wave Effect Employing the Dead Body Fall

The child on the right begins a stunt, followed in turn by each successive child in the line. The stunt movement appears to move along the line like a wave. The timing must be constant with each child in succession following the child to his or her right.

The wave effect is an excellent culmination of a unit or a series of lessons. It also has good value in demonstrations for PTAs and other groups.

KINDERGARTEN AND FIRST-GRADE PROGRAM

The kindergarten and first-grade program consists primarily of simple, imitative walks and movements, plus selected balance stunts and rolls. The Forward Roll is practiced, but its refinement is left to later grades. The Back Roller and Backward Roll from a handclasped position show the children some of the possibilities in these kinds of movements.

The teacher should be concerned with the creative aspects of the activities as well as performance standards. Children in this grade level tend to do stunts in different ways because of their different interpretations of what is required.

The establishment of good directional concepts and a basic understanding of common movement terminology should have a prominent place in the instruction. The why of activity should be answered for the children.

Activities for Kindergarten and First Grade

Animal Movements

Alligator Crawl
Kangaroo Jump
Puppy Dog Run
Cat Walk
Monkey Run
Bear Walk

Tumbling and Inverted Balances

Rolling Log
Side Roll
Forward Roll
Back Roller
Backward Roll (Handclasp Position)

Balance Stunts

One-Leg Balance
Double-Knee Balance
Head Touch
Head Balance
One-legged Balance Stands

Individual Stunts

Directional Walk
Line Walking
Fluttering Leaf
Elevator
Cross-legged Stand
Walking in Place
Jump Turns
Rubber Band
Rising Sun
Heel Click

Partner and Group Stunts

Bouncing Ball
Seesaw
Wring the Dishrag

Animal Movements

Alligator Crawl

Lie facedown on the floor with the elbows bent. Move along the floor alligator fashion, keeping the hands close to the body and the feet pointed out.

First, stress unilateral movements, that is, right arm and leg moving together. Then, change to cross-lateral movements, with the right arm moving with the left leg, and vice versa.

Alligator Crawl

Kangaroo Jump

The arms are carried close to the chest with the palms facing forward. A beanbag is placed between the knees. Move in different directions employing small jumps without losing the beanbag.

Puppy Dog Run

Place hands on the floor, bending the arms and legs slightly. Walk and run like a happy puppy. The teacher should make sure the youngsters look ahead. By keeping the head up in good position, the neck muscles are strengthened.

Variations

1. *Cat Walk:* Children also may use the same position to imitate a cat. Walk softly, stretch at times like a cat. Be smooth and deliberate.
2. *Monkey Run:* Turn the hands so the fingers point in (toward each other).
3. Go sideward, backward, et cetera. Turn around in place.

Puppy Dog Run

Bear Walk

Bend forward and touch the ground with both hands. Travel forward slowly by moving the hands and foot on the *same side together;* that is, the right hand and foot are moved together and then the left hand and foot. Make deliberate movements. This movement is classified as unilateral, since the arm and leg on the same side move together.

Bear Walk

Variation: Lift the free foot and arm high while the support is on the other side.

Tumbling and Inverted Balances

Rolling Log

Lie on back with arms stretched overhead. Roll sideways the length of the mat. The next time roll with the hands pointed toward the other side of the mat. To roll in a straight line, keep the feet slightly apart.

Rolling Log

Variation: Alternately curl and stretch while rolling.

Side Roll

Start on hands and knees, with the side selected for the roll toward the direction of the roll. By dropping the shoulder and tucking both the elbow and knee under, roll over completely on the shoulders and hips, coming again to the hands-and-knees position. Momentum is needed to return to the original position. Children should practice rolling back and forth from one hand-and-knee position to another.

Forward Roll

Stand facing forward, with the feet apart. Squat and place the hands on the mat, shoulder width apart, with the elbows against the insides of the thighs. Tuck the chin to the chest and make a rounded back. A push-off with the hands and feet provides the force for the roll. The child should carry the weight on his or her hands, with the elbows bearing the weight of the thighs. If the elbows are kept against the thighs and the weight

Forward Roll Position (note the position of the elbows on the insides of the thighs)

is assumed there, the force of the roll is easily transferred to the rounded back. The child should try to roll forward to his or her feet. Later, try with the knees together and no weight on the elbows.

Forward Roll

Spotting the Forward Roll (one hand is on the back of the head and one is under the thigh)

Kneeling alongside the child, the instructor can help by placing one hand on the back of the child's head and the other under the thigh for a push, finishing the assist with an upward lift on the back of the neck.

Back Roller

This stunt is a lead-up to the regular Backward Roll. Begin in a crouched position, knees together and hands resting lightly on the floor. Roll backward, securing momentum by bringing the knees to the chest and clasping them with the arms. Roll back and forth rhythmically. On the backward movement, the roll should go well back

on the neck and head. Try to roll forward to original position. Where children have difficulty in rolling back to original position, have them cross the legs and roll to a crossed-leg standing position.

Back Roller

Backward Roll – Handclasp Position

Teachers can have good success teaching the backward roll by beginning with this approach. The child clasps his or her fingers behind the neck, with the elbows held out to the sides. From a crouched position, he or she sits down rapidly, bringing the knees to the chest for a tuck to secure momentum. He or she rolls completely over backward, taking much of the weight on his or her forearms. In this method, the neck is protected and the pressure is taken by the forearms.

Rolling Backward in the Handclasp Position

Remind the children to keep their elbows back and out to the sides to gain maximum support and assure minimal neck strain.

Backward Roll

Balance Stunts

The child should begin to learn the concept of balance stunts, that is, that the position should be held for a specified length of time without undue movement or loss of balance *and* a recovery must be made to the original position. Hold for 3 and 5 seconds. Also perform with the eyes closed.

One-Leg Balance

Begin with lifting one leg from the floor. Later, bring the knee up. Arms should be free at first; then proceed to specified arm positions, such as folded across the chest, on hips, on the head, or behind the back.

Double-Knee Balance

Kneel on both knees, with the feet pointed to the rear. Lift the feet from the ground and balance on the knees. Vary the position of the arms.

Allow the children to experiment with different positions for balance.

Head Touch

Kneel on a mat with both knees, with the feet pointed backward. Arms are outstretched backward for balance. Lean forward slowly and touch the forehead to the mat. Recover to position. Vary the arm position.

Head Touch

Head Balance

Place a beanbag, block, or book on the child's head. Have him or her walk, stoop, turn around, sit down, get up, et cetera.

The object should be balanced so that the upper body is in good posture. Use hands out to

Head Balance

the side for balance. Later, vary the position of the arms—folded across the chest or placed behind the back or down at the sides.

Structure problems by having the children link together a series of movements.

One-legged Balance Stands

Each balance stunt should be done with different arm positions. Begin first with the arms out to the side and then have them folded across the chest. Have the children devise other arm positions.

Each stunt can be held first for 3 seconds and then for 5 seconds. Later, eyes should be closed during the count. The child should recover to original position without loss of balance or excessive movement. Stunts should be repeated, using the other leg.

Kimbo Stand: With the left foot kept flat on the ground, cross the right leg over the left to a position where the foot is pointed partially down and the toe is touching the ground. Hold this position for a specified count and return to standing position.

Knee-Lift Balance: From a standing position, lift one knee up so the thigh is parallel to the ground, with toe pointed down. Hold. Return to starting position.

Knee-Lift Balance

Stork Stand: From a standing position, shift all the weight to one foot. The other foot is placed so the sole of the foot is against the calf of the standing leg. Hold. Recover to standing position.

Individual Stunts

Directional Walk

Stand with side toward the desired direction, arms at sides. Take a sidestep in the desired direction (right or left), simultaneously lifting the arm and pointing in the direction of movement. At the same time, turn head in the direction of movement and sound off the direction. Complete the sidestep by closing with the other foot, dropping the arm to the side, and turning the head back to normal position. The movements should be definite and forceful, and the directional command should be called out crisply. After a number of sidesteps in one direction, reverse.

Directional Walk

The walk serves to reinforce the concept of right and left.

Line Walking

Use a line on the floor, a chalked line, or a board. Children walk forward and backward on the line, as follows.
1. Regular steps.
2. Follow steps—the front foot moves forward and the back foot moves up. One foot always leads.
3. Heel and toe—take regular steps but on each step bring the heel against the toe.
4. Hopping on the line—change to the other foot.

Fluttering Leaf

Keeping the feet in place and the body relaxed, flutter to the ground slowly just as a falling leaf would do in the fall. The arms can swing back and forth loosely to accentuate the fluttering movements.

Elevator

With the arms out level to the sides, pretend to be an elevator going down. Lower the body a little at a time by bending the knees, keeping the upper body erect and eyes forward. Return to position. Add a body twist to the downward movement.

Cross-legged Stand

Sit with the legs crossed and the body partially bent forward. Six commands are given.
1. "Touch the right foot with the right hand."
2. "Touch the left foot with the right hand."
3. "Touch the right foot with the left hand."
4. "Touch the left foot with the left hand."
5. "Touch both feet with the hands."
6. "Touch the feet with crossed hands."

The commands should be given in varied sequences. The child must interpret that his or her right foot is on the left side and vice versa.

If this seems too difficult, have the child start with the feet in normal position (uncrossed).
Variation: The stunt can be done as a partner activity. One child gives the commands, and the other responds as directed.

Walking in Place

Pretend to walk vigorously by using the same movements as in walking but not making any progress. This is done by shifting the feet back and forth. Exaggerated arm movement should be made. Children can gain or lose a little ground. Two children can walk alongside each other, with first one going ahead and then the other.

Jump Turns

Jump turns reinforce directional concepts. Use quarter- and half-turns, right and left. Arms should be kept along the sides of the body. Stress landing lightly without a second movement.

Number concepts can be utilized. The teacher calls out the number as a preparatory command and then says, "Move." Number signals are: one—left quarter-turn, two—right quarter-turn, three—left half-turn, and four—right half-turn. Give the children a moment after the number is called before moving.
Variation: Have the arms outstretched to the sides.

Rubber Band

Children are down in a squat position with the hands and arms clasped around the knees. The teacher says, "Stretch, stretch, stretch," until the children are stretched as tall and as wide as they can be. The teacher then says, "Snap," and the children snap back to original position.

Variation: This can be called Pumping up the Balloon. Have a child stand in front of the children so all can see him or her. He or she is the pumper. He or she pretends to be using a bicycle pump and gives a "shoosh" every time he or she pumps. When the pumper feels he or she has reached the limit, the pumper shouts, "Bang," whereupon the children react as above.

Rising Sun

Lie on back. Using only the arms for balance, rise to a standing position.

Variation: Have the children fold arms over the chest. Experiment with different positions of the feet. Feet can be crossed, spread wide, both to one side, et cetera.

Heel Click

Stand with feet slightly apart, jump up and click heels, coming down with feet apart. Try with a quarter-turn right and left.

Variations

1. Have the child clap hands overhead as he or she clicks heels.
2. Another variation is to have the child join hands with one or more children. A signal is. needed. The children can count, "One, two, THREE," jumping on the third count.

Heel Click

3. Some children may be able to click their heels twice before landing. Landing should be with the feet apart.
4. Begin with a cross step to the side, and then click heels. Try both right and left.

Partner and Group Stunts

Bouncing Ball (Partner Stunt)

Toss a *lively* utility ball into the air and let the children watch how it bounces lower and lower until it finally comes to rest on the floor. From a bent-knee position, with the upper body erect, each child imitates a ball by beginning with a high "bounce" and gradually lowering the height of the jump to simulate a ball coming to rest. Children should absorb part of the body weight with their hands as well as push off the floor with the hands to gain additional height.

Bouncing Ball

Variations

1. Have the children do this as a partner stunt, with one partner serving as the "bouncer" and the other as the "ball." Reverse positions. Try having one partner dribble the "ball" in various positions.
2. Toss the ball into the air and have the children move with the ball as it bounces lower and lower.

Seesaw (Partner Stunt)

Two children face each other and join hands. One child stoops down. The seesaw moves up and down, with one child stooping while the other rises. The children can recite the words to this version of "Seesaw, Margery Daw" as they move.

Seesaw, Margery Daw,
Maw and Paw, like a saw,
Seesaw, Margery Daw.

Variation: Have the rising child jump into the air at the end of the rise.

Wring the Dishrag (Partner Stunt)

Two children face each other and join hands. Raise one pair of arms (right for one and left for the other) and turn under that pair of arms, continuing a full turn until back to original position. Care must be taken to avoid bumping heads.

Wring the Dishrag

Variation: Try the stunt at a lower level, using a crouched position.

SECOND-GRADE PROGRAM

Begin with a review of the kindergarten and first-grade stunts. Continued practice should be held in the Forward Roll. The Backward Curl and the regular Backward Roll are significant inclusions at this grade level. Additional balance stunts expand the practice opportunities for this quality.

Children of this age group are more amenable to coaching, compared to the previous level, and some attention to performance factors can be stressed. However, the children's attention span is short, and performance factors should be introduced as opportunities arise.

Activities for the Second Grade

Animal and Character Movements

Rabbit Jump
Elephant Walk
Siamese Twin Walk
Tightrope Walk
Gorilla Walk
Lame Dog Walk
Crab Walk

Tumbling and Inverted Balances

Forward Roll Review and Practice
Climb-up
Three-Point Tip-up
Backward Curl
Backward Roll—Regular

Balance Stunts

Balance Touch
Single-Leg Balances
Hand-and-Knee Balance
Single-Knee Balance

Individual Stunts

Lowering the Boom
Turn-over
Thread the Needle
Heel Slap
Pogo Stick
Top
Turk Stand
Push-up
Crazy Walk
Seat Circle

Partner and Group Stunts

Toe Toucher
Double Top
Rolly Polly

Animal and Character Movements

Rabbit Jump

Crouch to the floor with the knees apart. The arms are between the knees, with the hands placed on the floor ahead of the feet. Move forward by reaching out first with both hands and then bringing both feet up to the hands. Eyes should look ahead.

Emphasize to the children that this is called a jump rather than a hop because both feet move at once. Note that the jump is a bilateral movement.

Variations

1. Try with the knees kept together and the arms on the outside. Try alternating the knees together and apart on successive jumps. Go over a low hurdle or through a hoop.

Rabbit Jump

2. Experiment with taking considerable weight on the hands before the feet move forward. This can be aided by raising the seat higher in the air when the hands move forward.

Elephant Walk

"The elephant's walk is steady and slow.
His trunk like a pendulum swings to and fro."
Bend well forward, clasping the hands together to form a trunk. The end of the trunk should swing close to the ground. Walk in a slow, deliberate, dignified manner, keeping the legs straight and swinging the trunk from side to side. Stop and throw water over the back with the trunk.

"But when there are children with peanuts
    around
He swings it up and he swings it down."

Elephant Walk

Variation: Arrange children in pairs, one as the mahout (elephant keeper) and the other as the elephant. The mahout walks to the side and a little to the front of the elephant, with one hand touching the elephant's shoulder. The mahout leads the elephant around during the first two lines of the poem, and then during the last two lines he or she releases the touch, walks to a spot in front of the elephant, and "tosses" the elephant a peanut when the trunk is swept up. The mahout returns to the elephant's side, and the action is repeated.

Siamese Twin Walk

Partners stand back to back, with elbows locked. Walk forward, backward, sideward in unison.

Tightrope Walk

In the Tightrope Walk, children should give good play to the imagination. Set the stage by discussing what a circus performer on the wire might do. Have the children select a line, board, or chalked line on the floor for the "wire." They can pretend to be on the high wire, doing various tasks

Siamese Twin Walk

with exaggerated loss and control of balance. Add tasks like jumping rope, juggling balls, and riding a bicycle on the wire. Some could pretend to hold a parasol or a balancing pole while performing.

Gorilla Walk

Bend knees and carry the trunk forward. Arms hang at the side. As the child walks forward, he or she should touch his or her fingers to the ground.

Gorilla Walk

Variation: Let the children stop and beat on their chests like gorillas. Also, bounce up and down on all fours with hands and feet touching the floor simultaneously.

Lame Dog Walk

Walk on both hands and one foot. The other foot is held in the air as if injured. Walk a distance and change feet. Eyes should be forward. Also move backward, in other combinations. See whether the children can move with an "injured" front leg.

Crab Walk

Squat down and reach back, putting both hands on the floor without sitting down. With head, neck, and body level and in a straight line, walk forward, backward, and sideward.

Children have a tendency to lower the hips. See that the body is kept in a straight line.

Crab Walk

Variations

1. As each step is taken with a hand, the other hand can slap the chest or seat.
2. Move the hand and foot on the same side simultaneously (unilateral movement).
3. ·Try balancing on one leg and opposite hand. Hold for 5 seconds.

Tumbling and Inverted Balances

Forward Roll Review and Practice

Review the Forward Roll (first grade). Spot and assist as necessary. Work on getting the children to come out of the roll to their feet. Grasping knees at the end of the roll is of help.

Variations

1. Roll to the feet with the ankles crossed.
2. Some children can try to roll with the knees together.

Climb-up

Get down on a mat on hands and knees, with the hands placed about shoulder width apart and the fingers spread and pointed forward. Place the head forward of the hands, so the head and the hands form a triangle on the mat. Walk the body weight forward so most of it rests on the hands and head. Climb the knees to the top of the elbows. This stunt is lead-up to the Headstand (third grade).

Variation: Raise the knees off the elbows. In the Climb-up as well as the Three-Point Tip-up, it may be necessary to spot the overweight or weak child. Spotting should be done with one hand on the shoulder and the other on the back of the thigh. The main concern is to support the body weight in order to prevent excessive pressure on the neck and head.

Three-Point Tip-up

The Three-Point Tip-up ends up in the same general position as the Climb-up, but with the elbows on the inside of the thighs. Squat down on the mat, placing the hands flat, fingers pointing forward, with the elbows inside and pressed against the inner part of the lower thighs. Lean forward, slowly transferring the weight of the body to the bent elbows and hands until the forehead touches the mat. Return to starting position.

Three-Point Tip-up

This stunt also provides a background for the Headstand and for the Handstand given at later grades.

Some children may have better success by turning the fingers in slightly, thus causing the elbows to point out more and offering better support to the thigh contact.

Children can tuck their heads and do a Forward Roll as an alternate method of returning to the starting position.

Backward Curl

This stunt has three stages.

1. Begin in a sitting position, with the knees drawn up to the chest and the chin tucked down. The arms are placed out to the sides as the shoulders make contact with the mat. Roll backward until the weight is on the shoulders and the feet and legs come back over the head so the toes touch the mat. Roll back to starting position.

Backward Curl

2. Same action as in #1, except the hands are placed alongside the head on the mat as the child rolls back. The fingers are pointed in the

direction of the roll, with the palms down on the mat. A good direction to the children is "point your thumbs toward your ears and keep your elbows reasonably close to your body."

3. The third stage is similar to #2, except the child starts in a crouched position on his or her feet. He or she is in a deep-knee-bend position, with the back toward the direction of the roll. He or she secures momentum by sitting down quickly and bringing the knees to the chest.

The teacher has to recognize this, like the Back Roller, as a lead-up to the Backward Roll. The hand pressure is an important item to be stressed. Teach the children to push hard against the floor to take the pressure from the back of the neck.

Variations

1. Touch the knees behind the head instead of the toes.
2. Another interesting challenge can be made using a beanbag. Have the child keep a beanbag between his or her feet and deposit it behind the head, returning to position. Next, curl back and pick up the beanbag, returning it to original position.
3. A more difficult Backward Curl, which some children may be able to do, starts with the child sitting with legs crossed and the hands grasping the feet. Roll backward, touching the floor overhead with the feet. Return to position.

Backward Roll–Regular

Start with the back to the direction of the roll in the same squat position as in the forward roll. Push off with the hands quickly, sit down, and start rolling over on the back.

The knees should be brought to the chest, so the body is tucked and momentum is increased. Quickly bring the hands up over the shoulders, palms up, fingers pointed backward. Continue rolling backward with the knees close to the chest. The hands then touch the mat at about the same time as the head. It is vitally important at this point to push hard with the hands. Continue to roll over the top of the head and push off the mat until ready to stand.

Backward Roll

Proper hand position can be emphasized by telling the children to point their thumbs toward their ears and to spread their fingers for better push-off control.

Spotting: Care must be taken never to push a child from the hip, thus forcing him or her to roll over. This puts undue pressure on the back of the neck.

Spotting the Backward Roll (the lift is at the hips of the roller; lift, but do not force the child over)

The proper method of aiding the child who has difficulty with the stunt is as follows. The spotter stands in a straddle position, with his or her near foot alongside at about the spot where the performer's hands and head will make contact with the mat. His or her other foot is one stride in the direction of the roll. The critical point is for the spotter to lift the hips just as the head and hands of the performer make contact with the mat. This is accomplished by taking the back hand and reaching across to the far hip of the performer, getting under the near hip with the near hand. The lift is applied on the front of the hips just below the beltline. The object is to relieve the pressure on the neck.

Balance Stunts

Balance Touch

An object (eraser, block, or beanbag) is placed a yard away from a line. Balancing on one foot, the

Balance Touch

child reaches out with the other foot, touches the object, and recovers to the starting position. He or she does not place weight on the object but merely touches it. Reach sideward, backward.

Variation: Try at various distances. On a gymnasium floor, count the number of boards to establish the distance for the touch.

Single-Leg Balances

Forward: Extend the leg backward until it is parallel to the floor. Keeping eyes forward and arms out to the side, bend forward, balancing on the other leg. Hold for 5 seconds without moving.

Forward Leg Balance

Backward: With the knee straight, extend one leg forward, with the toe pointed so it is level to the floor. Balance on the other leg for 5 seconds. Use arms out to the side for balance. Lean back as far as possible. The bend should be far enough back so that the eyes are looking at the ceiling.

Side: Stand on the left foot with enough side bend to the left so the right (top) side of the body is parallel to the floor. Put the right arm alongside the head in a line with the rest of the body. Reverse, using the right leg for support. (Support may be needed momentarily to get into position.)

Hand-and-Knee Balance

Get down on all fours, with support on hands, knees, and feet, with toes pointed backward. Lift one hand and the opposite leg from the floor and balance on the other hand and knee. Keep the foot from touching during the hold. Reverse hand and knee positions.

Single-Knee Balance

Similar to the previous stunt, except that the balance is made on one knee (and leg), with the arms outstretched to sides. Reverse positions.

Hand-and-Knee Balance

Single-Knee Balance

Individual Stunts

Lowering the Boom

Start in push-up position (front-leaning rest position). Lower the body slowly to the floor. The movement should be controlled, so the body remains rigid.

Variations

1. Have the children pause halfway down.
2. Have them come down in stages, inch by inch. Be sure they understand the concept of an inch as a measure of distance.
3. Call this a flat tire. Children let themselves down slowly to the accompaniment of noise simulating air escaping from a punctured tire. See how they react to a blowout, initiated by an appropriate noise.
4. Go down in stages by alternating movements of the right and left arms.
5. Vary the stunt with different hand-base posi-

tions, such as fingers pointed in, thumbs touching, and others.

Turn-over

From a front-leaning rest position (as in Lowering the Boom), turn over so the back is to the floor. The body should not touch the floor. Continue the turn until the original position is assumed. Reverse the direction. Turn back and forth several times.

The body should be kept straight and rigid throughout the turn.

Thread the Needle

Touch the fingertips together in front of the body. Step through with one foot at a time without the tips losing contact. Step back to original position. Then lock the fingers in front of the body, and repeat the stunt. Finally, see whether children can step through the clasped hands without touching the hands.

Thread the Needle

Heel Slap

From an erect position with hands at the sides, jump into the air and slap both heels with the hands.

Heel Slap

Variation: Use a one-two-three rhythm with small preliminary jumps on *one* and *two*. Make a quarter- or half-turn in the air. During a jump, slap the heels twice before landing.

Pogo Stick

Pretend to be a pogo stick by keeping a stiff body and jumping on the toes. Hold the hands in front as if grasping the stick. Progress in various directions.

Stress upward propelling action by the ankles and toes, with the body kept stiff, particularly at the knee joint.

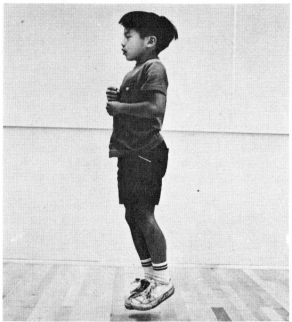

Pogo Stick

Top

From a standing position with arms at the sides, try jumping, turning to face the opposite direction, turning three-quarters of the way around, and making a full turn facing the original direction. Number concepts can be stressed in having the children do half-, three-quarter-, and full turns.

Successful execution of the stunt should call for the child to land in good balance with hands near the sides. No movement of the feet should occur after landing.

Children should turn right and left.

Variation: Fold arms across chest.

Turk Stand

Stand with feet apart and arms folded in front. Pivot on the balls of *both* feet, and face the opposite direction. The legs then are crossed. Sit down in this position. Reverse the process. Get up without using the hands for aid, and uncross the legs with a pivot to face original direction.

Turk Stand

Very little change should occur in the position of the feet.

Push-up

From a front-leaning rest position, lower the body and push up back to original position. Be sure the only movement is in the arms, with the body kept rigid and straight.

Variation: Stop halfway down and halfway up. Go up and down by inches.

Note: Since the Push-up is used in many exercises and testing programs, it is important for the children to learn proper execution early.

Crazy Walk

The child makes progress forward in an erect position by bringing one foot behind *and* around the other to gain a little ground each time. Set up a specified distance, and see which children can cover this with the fewest steps.

Variation: Reverse the movements, and go backward. This means bringing the foot in front and around to gain distance in back.

Seat Circle

Sit on the floor, knees bent and hands braced behind. Lift the feet off the floor and push with the hands, so the body spins in a circle on the seat as a pivot. Spin right and left.

Variation: Place a beanbag between the knees or on the toes, and spin without dropping it.

Partner and Group Stunts

Toe Toucher (Partner Stunt)

Partners lie on their backs with their heads near each other and their feet in opposite directions. They grasp each other, using a hand-wrist grip, and bring up their legs (both partners) so their toes touch. Keep high on the shoulders and touch the feet high.

Crazy Walk

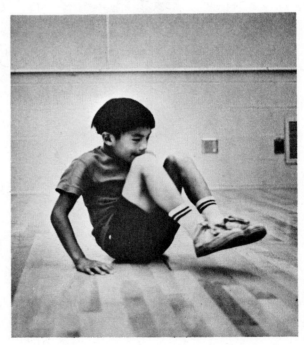

Seat Circle

Partners should be of about the same height. Strive to attain the high shoulder position, since this is the point of most difficulty.

Variation: One partner carries a beanbag, a ball, or some other article between his or her feet. The article is transferred to the other partner, who lowers it to the floor.

Toe Toucher

Double Top (Partner Stunt)

Face partner and join hands. Experiment to see which type of grip works best. With straight arms, lean away from each other and at the same time move toes close to partner's. Spin around slowly in either direction, taking tiny steps. Increase speed.

Double Top

Variations
1. Use a stooped position.
2. Instead of holding hands, hold a wand and increase the body lean backward. Try the stunt standing right side to right side.

Rolly Polly (Group Stunt)

Review the Log Roll. Four or five children lie facedown on the floor, side by side. The last child does a Log Roll over the others and then takes his or her place at the end. Continue until all the children have rolled twice.

THIRD-GRADE PROGRAM

In the third grade, in comparison to kindergarten through grade two, more emphasis on form and quality of performance is centered in stunt execution. More partner and group stunts are included in the third-grade program.

The Headstand, an individual stunt, is an important addition to the tumbling area. Stunts such as the Frog Handstand and the Mule Kick give the children experience in taking the weight totally on the hands.

Activities for the Third Grade

Animal Movements

Cricket Walk
Seal Crawl
Seal Crawl Variations
Frog Jump
Measuring Worm
Walrus Walk
Mule Kick

Tumbling and Inverted Balances

Forward Roll Variations
Backward Roll Practice
Frog Handstand (Tip-up)
Headstand

Balance Stunts

One-Leg Balance Reverse
Tummy Balance
Knee Dip

Individual Stunts

Squat Thrust
Reach-under
Stiff Person Bend
Coffee Grinder
Curl-up
Scooter
Hip Walk
Long Bridge
Heelstand
Wicket Walk

Partner and Group Stunts

Partner Hopping
Twister
Partner Pull-up
Chinese Get-up
Rowboat

Animal Movements

Cricket Walk

Squat. Spread the knees. Put the arms between the knees, and grasp the outside of the ankles with the hands. In this position, walk forward or backward. Chirp like a cricket. Turn around right and left.

See what happens when both feet are moved at once!

Seal Crawl

The child is in the front-leaning (push-up) position, the weight supported on straightened arms and toes. Keeping the body straight, he or she walks forward, using his or her hands for propelling force and dragging his or her feet.

Watch to see that the body is straight and the head is up.

Seal Crawl

Variation: Let the child crawl forward a short distance and then roll over on his or her back, clapping his or her hands like a seal, with appropriate seal grunts.

Seal Crawl Variations

Review the Seal Crawl; include the following variations.
1. Crawl with the fingers pointed in different directions—out and in.
2. Reverse Seal Crawl: Turn over, and attempt the crawl dragging the heels.
3. Elbow Crawl: Assume the original position but with the weight on the elbows. Crawl forward on the elbows.
4. The Seal Crawl also can be made more challenging by using the crossed-arm position.

Elbow Crawl

Frog Jump

From a squatting position, with the hands placed on the floor slightly in front of the feet, jump forward a short distance, lighting on the hands and feet simultaneously. Note the difference between this stunt and the Rabbit Jump (first grade).

Frog Jump

Emphasis eventually should be on both height and distance. The hands and arms should absorb part of the landing impact to prevent excessive strain on the knees.

Measuring Worm

From a front-leaning rest position, keeping the knees stiff, bring up the feet as close as possible to the hands by inching forward with the feet. Regain position by inching forward with the hands. Emphasize keeping the knees straight, with necessary bending occurring at the hips.

Measuring Worm

Walrus Walk

Similar to the Seal Crawl (see opposite). Begin with a front-leaning rest position, with fingers pointed outward. Make progress by moving both hands forward at the same time. Some children may be able to clap hands as they take each step.

Before giving this stunt, review the Seal Crawl and variations.

Walrus Walk

Variation: Move sideways so that the upper part of the body describes an arc while the feet hold position.

Mule Kick

Stoop down and place the hands on the floor in front of the feet. The arms are the front legs of the mule. Kick out with the legs while the weight is supported momentarily by the arms. Taking the weight on the hands is important.

The stunt can be taught in two stages. First, practice taking the weight momentarily on the hands. Next, add the kick.

Variation: Make two kicks before the feet return to the ground.

Mule Kick

Tumbling and Inverted Balances

Forward Roll Variations

In the kindergarten, first-grade, and second-grade programs, the emphasis was on the simple accomplishment of the Forward Roll. The third grade is a good level to begin giving some attention to elements of form in performing the Forward Roll. And a new starting position for the roll, with the knees held together inside the arms, is introduced.

Stress the fact that the fingers should be spread and pointed ahead in the direction of the roll. Increased momentum through a quicker roll and push-off with the feet should help the child to his or her feet at the end of the roll. There should be little or no pressure on the head. A smooth, tight roll is the goal at this level.

Children experiencing difficulty can go back to the introductory method of elbows inside the thighs, or they might be helped by holding a beanbag under their chins.

During the roll, the performer can cross his or her legs and come to his or her feet in this position. The legs can be uncrossed with a pivot that will face him or her in the direction from which he or she came. The child then can roll back to position.

Backward Roll Practice

Continue practice with the Backward Roll. Spot as needed. Practice the Backward Roll both with the hands clasped behind the neck (first grade) and in the regular manner.

Frog Handstand (Tip-up)

The stunt follows the same directions as the Three-Point Tip-up (second grade). Squat down on the mat, placing the hands flat, fingers pointing forward, with the elbows inside and pressed against the inner part of the knees. Lean forward using the leverage of the elbows against the knees and balance on the hands. Hold for 5 seconds. Return to position.

Frog Handstand

The head does not touch the mat at any time. Hands may be turned in slightly if this makes better contact between the elbows and the insides of the thighs.

Headstand

Two approaches are suggested for the Headstand. The first is to relate the Headstand to the Climb-up, and the second is to go directly into a Headstand using a kick-up to achieve the inverted position. With either method, it is essential for the triangle position of the hands and the head to be maintained as diagrammed on the next page.

In this position, the hands are placed about shoulder width apart, with the fingers pointed forward, spread, and slightly cupped. The head is positioned on the mat 10 to 12 inches forward of the hands, with the weight taken on the forward part of the head, near the hairline.

In the final inverted position, the feet should be together, with the legs straight and the toes pointed. The back is arched, with the weight evenly distributed among the hands and the forward part of the head.

The safest way to come down from the inverted position is to return to the mat in the direction that was used in going up. Recovery is helped by bending at both the waist and the knees. If the child overbalances and falls forward, he or she should tuck the head under and go into a Forward Roll.

Both methods of recovery from the inverted position should be included in the instructional sequences early in the presentation.

Basing the Headstand on the Climb-up: A spotter is stationed directly in front of the performer and steadies him or her as needed. However, if the spotter cannot control the performer, he or she must be alert to move out of the way if the performer goes into a Forward Roll coming out of the inverted position.

Headstand Based on the Climb-up

The child takes the inverted position of the Climb-up (page 330) and slowly moves his or her feet upward to the headstand position, steadied by the spotter only as needed. The spotter can first apply support to the hips and then transfer to the ankles as the climb-up position is lengthened into a Headstand.

Basing the Headstand on the Kick-up: The goal of the kick-up method is to establish a pattern that can be related to other inverted stunts, as well as to serve for the Headstand. Keeping the weight on the forward part of the head and maintaining the triangle base, walk the feet forward until the hips are high over the body, somewhat similar to the climb-up position. Keep one foot on the mat, with the knee of that leg bent and the other leg somewhat extended backward. Kick the back leg up to the inverted position, following quickly with a push by the other leg, thus bringing the two legs together in the inverted position. The timing is a quick one-two movement.

Headstand Based on the Kick-up

When learning, children should work in units of three students. One child attempts the stunt with a spotter on either side. Positions are rotated. Each spotter kneels, placing his or her near hand under the shoulder of the performer. The performer then "walks" his or her weight above the head and kicks up to position. The spotter on each side supports by grasping a leg.

Teaching Points: The triangle formed by the hands and the head is important, as is the weight centered on the forward part of the head. The majority of the troubles that occur during the Headstand come from incorrect head-hand relationship. The correct placement can be ensured by making sure that the head is placed the length of the performer's forearm from the knees and the hands are placed at the knees.

Spotting the Headstand

A good teaching technique to aid children in finding the proper triangle is to mark the three spots on the mat with chalk (more lasting spots can be made with paint).

Do not let children stay too long in the inverted position or hold contests to see who can stand on his or her head the longest.

Most of the responsibility for getting into the inverted position should rest on the performer. Spotters may help some, but they should avoid "wrestling up" the performer.

Balance Stunts

One-Leg Balance Reverse

Assume a forward-balance position. In this, the body leans forward, the arms are out to the sides, the weight is on one leg, with the other leg extended behind. In a quick movement, swing the free leg down to give momentum to change to the

One-Leg Balance Reverse

same forward-balance position facing in the *opposite* direction (180-degree turn). No unnecessary movement of the supporting foot should be made after the turn is complete. The swinging foot should not touch the floor.

Tummy Balance

The child lies prone on the floor with arms outstretched forward or to the sides palms down. He or she raises the arms, head, chest, and legs from the floor, balancing on his or her tummy. Knees should be kept straight.

Tummy Balance

Knee Dip

Grasp the right instep behind the back with the left hand, balancing on the left foot. With the other arm out for balance, lower and touch the floor with the bent knee. Regain balance. During the learning stages, the teacher can place a book under the knee being lowered, making an easier stunt. Try with the other leg.

If there is difficulty, another child can support from behind. This activity should be done on a tumbling mat to protect the knee.

Knee Dip

Variation: Hold the right foot with the right hand, and vice versa.

Individual Stunts

Squat Thrust

While the Squat Thrust is used later as an exercise, the act of completing the cycle successfully is classified as a stunt. The stunt is done in four definite movements. Starting from the posi-

tion of attention, on count *one,* the child squats down on the floor, placing the hands flat (shoulder width) on the floor, with the elbows inside the knees. On count *two,* the feet and legs are thrust back so that the body is perfectly straight from head to toe in push-up position. On count *three,* the child returns to squat position and, on the *last* count, returns to the position of attention.

Squat Thrust

Girls should do three in 10 seconds and boys four in the same amount of time.

First teach proper positioning during each of the four phases. Then stress the rhythmic nature of the movements. Music may be added.

Reach-under

Take a position with the feet pointed ahead and spaced about 2 feet apart, toes against a line or a board of the floor. Place a beanbag two boards in front of, and midway between, the feet. Without changing the position of the feet, reach one hand behind and between the legs and pick up the beanbag. Pick up with the other hand. Move the beanbag a board out at a time and repeat.
Variation: Allow the heels to be lifted from the floor.

Stiff Person Bend

Take a standing position with the feet about shoulder width apart and pointed forward. Place a

Stiff Person Bend

beanbag 6 inches behind the left heel. Grasp the right toe with the right hand, thumb on top. Without bending the knees, reach the left hand outside the left leg and pick up the beanbag without releasing the toe's hold on the right hand. Increase the distance slowly. Reverse positions.

Coffee Grinder

Put one hand on the floor, and extend the body with that side to the floor in a side-leaning position. The child walks around his or her hand, making a complete circle while keeping his or her body straight.

The stunt should be done slowly with controlled movements. The straight body alignment should remain constant throughout the complete circle movement.

Coffee Grinder

Curl-up

Two children work together, with one child holding the other's feet. The performer lies on his or her back, with the knees up so an angle of 90 degrees is formed at the knee joints. The feet are flat (soles down) on the floor. The hands, with the fingers interlaced, are behind the lower part of the head.

The child curls up, alternately touching the right and left elbows to the opposite knees. One touch is made on each Curl-up.

Students should be encouraged to find different ways of performing the Curl-up and to make it more challenging.

Be sure the child returns the head completely to the floor each time. No rest should be allowed, since the Curl-ups must be continuous. The child may move at his or her own pace, however. (See page 107 for a description of the Curl-up.)

Scooter

The Scooter is an excellent movement for abdominal development. The child is on the floor in extended sitting position, with arms folded in front of the chest but held chin high. To scoot, he or she pulls his or her seat toward the heels, using heel pressure and lifting the seat slightly. He or she then extends the legs forward again and repeats the process.

Scooter

Hip Walk

The child sits in the same position as in the Scooter, but the arms are in thrust position, with the hand making a partial fist. The child makes forward progress by alternate leg movements. The arm-leg coordination should be unilateral.

Long Bridge

Begin in a crouched position with the hands on the floor, knees between the arms. Push the hands forward a little at a time until you are in an extended push-up position. Return to position.

Long Bridge

Challenge children to extend out as far forward as they can and still retain the support.
Variation: Begin with a forward movement and then change to sideward movement, establishing as wide a spread as possible. Another variation is to work from a crossed-hands position.

Heelstand

Begin in a full squat position with the arms dangling at the sides. Jump upward to full leg extension with the weight on both heels, flinging the arms out diagonally. Hold momentarily, and return to position. Several movements can be done rhythmically in succession.

Heel Stand

Wicket Walk

Children bend over and touch the floor with their weight *evenly* distributed on hands and feet.

If the knees are kept straight, a wicket can be formed. Walk the wicket forward, backward, and sideward. Keep arms and legs as nearly vertical as possible.

Be sure the knees are kept reasonably straight, since the stunt loses much of its flexibility value if the knees are bent too much.

The stunt gets its name from the child's position, which resembles a wicket in a croquet game.

A common error in the execution of this stunt is to keep the hands positioned too far forward of the feet.

Partner Hopping

Wicket Walk

Partner and Group Stunts

Partner Hopping (Partner Stunt)

Children coordinate hopping movements for short distances and in different directions. Three combinations are suggested.

1. Stand facing each other. Extend the left leg forward to be grasped at the ankle by the partner. Each partner then hops on his or her right leg.
2. Stand back to back. Lift the leg backward (bend knee), and have the partner grasp the ankle. Hop as before.
3. Stand side by side with inside arms around each other's waist. Lift the inside foot from the floor, and make progress by hopping on the outside foot.

If either partner begins to fall, the other should release the leg immediately. Vary by moving in different directions and patterns. Reverse foot positions.

Twister (Partner Stunt)

Partners face and grasp right hands as if shaking hands. The first partner swings his or her right leg over the head of #2 and turns around, taking a straddle position over his or her own arm. Number two swings his or her left leg over #1, who has bent over, and the partners are then back to back. Number one then continues with his or her left leg

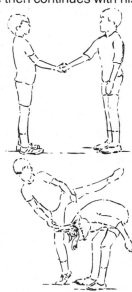

Twister

and faces in the original direction. Number two swings his or her right leg over back to the original face-to-face position.

Partners need to duck to avoid being kicked by each other's feet as the legs are swung over.

Variation: The stunt can be introduced by grasping a wand instead of holding hands.

Partner Pull-up (Partner Stunt)

Partners sit down facing each other in a bent-knee position, with the heels on the floor and the toes touching. Pulling cooperatively, both come to a standing position. Return to the floor.

Partner Pull-up

This stunt can be performed with the feet flat on the floor as a variation.

Chinese Get-up (Partner or Group Stunt)

Two children sit back to back and lock arms. From this position, both try to stand by pushing against each other's backs. Sit down again. If the feet are sliding, do the stunt on a mat.

Chinese Get-up

Variations
1. Try the stunt with three or four children.
2. From a halfway-down position, move like a spider.

Rowboat (Partner Stunt)

Children sit on the floor or on a mat, facing each other with legs apart and feet touching. A wand is grasped with both hands by each, and they pretend to row the boat. Seek a wide range of movement in the forward-backward rowing movement.

The stunt can be done without a wand by having the children grasp hands.

FOURTH-GRADE PROGRAM

The fourth-grade program continues emphasis on the Forward and Backward Rolls with variations and combinations. Partner support stunts are introduced. Flops or falls are another addition. More emphasis should be placed on form and "dressing up" the stunt.

Activities for the Fourth Grade

Animal Movements

Double Lame Dog
Turtle
Walrus Slap

Tumbling and Inverted Balances

Forward Roll Combinations
Backward Roll Combinations
Headstand Practice and Variations

Balance Stunts

Leg Dip
Balance Jump
Seat Balance
Face to Knee Touch
Finger Touch

Individual Stunts

Knee Jump to Standing
Knee Drop
Forward Drop
Dead Body Fall
Stoop and Stretch
Squat Jumps
Tanglefoot
Egg Roll
Toe Touch Nose
Toe Tug Walk

Partner and Group Stunts

Leapfrog
Wheelbarrow
Wheelbarrow Lifting
Camel Lift and Walk
Dump the Wheelbarrow
Dromedary Walk
Centipede
Double Wheelbarrow

Partner Support Stunts

Double Bear
Table
Statue
Lighthouse
Hip-Shoulder Stand

Animal Movements

Double Lame Dog

Support the body on a hand and leg (same side). Move forward in this position, maintaining balance. The distance should be short (5 to 10 feet), since this stunt is strenuous.

Four leg-arm combinations should be employed. Cross-lateral movements of right arm-left leg and left arm-right leg should be varied with unilateral movements of right arm-right leg and left arm-left leg.

Double Lame Dog

Variation: Keep the free arm on the hip or out to the side.

Turtle

With the feet apart and the hands widely spread, the body is in a wide push-up position about halfway up from the floor (elbows somewhat bent). From this position, move in various directions, keeping the plane of the body always about the same distance from the floor. Movements of the hands and feet should occur only in small increments.

Turtle

Walrus Slap

Review the Seal Crawl and the Walrus Walk (page 336) from previous grades. From the same position (front-leaning rest), push the body up in the air by quick force of the arms, clap the hands together, and recover to position.

Variation
1. Try clapping the hands more than once.
2. Move forward while clapping the hands.
3. Reverse Walrus Walk. Turn over, and do a Walrus Walk while facing the ceiling. Clapping the hands is quite difficult in this position and should be attempted only by the more skilled. Work on a mat.

Tumbling and Inverted Balances

Forward Roll Combinations

The Forward Roll should be reviewed, and there should be increased emphasis on proper form. Combinations that can be introduced are these.
1. Forward Roll to standing position.
2. Forward Roll preceded by a short run.
3. Two Forward Rolls in succession.
4. Leapfrog and Forward Roll.
5. Forward Roll to a vertical jump in the air, and repeat.
6. Rabbit Jump and Forward Roll.
7. Hold the toes while rolling.
8. Forward Roll through a hoop.

Backward Roll Combinations

The Backward Roll technique should be reviewed. Continued emphasis on the push-off by the hands has to be made. Combinations to be taught are these.
1. Backward Roll to standing position. Correct use of the hands must be emphasized. A strong push by the hands is necessary to provide enough momentum to land on the feet.
2. Two Backward Rolls in succession.
3. Crab Walk into a Backward Roll.
4. Children can add a jump into the air at the completion of the roll combination.

Headstand Practice and Variations

Continue work on the Headstand. Stress correct body arch and proper foot position. Spot as needed.

Variations
1. Clap hands and recover. The weight must be shifted momentarily to the head for the clap. Some children will be able to clap the hands twice before recovery.
2. Employ different variations of leg positions, such as the split sideward, split forward and backward, bent knees, et cetera.

Headstand Variation

Balance Jump—Starting Position

3. Holding a utility ball between the legs, go into the Headstand, retaining control of the ball.

Balance Stunts

Leg Dip

Extend both hands and one leg forward, balancing on the other leg. Lower body to heel seat and return without losing the balance or touching the floor with any part of the body. Try with the other foot.

Another child can assist from the back by applying upward pressure to the elbows.

Balance Jump

With the hands and arms out to the side and the body parallel to the ground, one leg is extended behind and the weight is balanced on the other leg. Quickly change balance to the other foot, resuming the initial position with the feet exchanged. Be sure the body is maintained parallel to the ground during the change of legs. Try with the hands outstretched forward.

It might be helpful to work in pairs and have one student critique the performance of the other child to make sure the limbs are straight and parallel to the floor.

Leg Dip

Seat Balance

Sit on the floor, holding the ankles in front, with the elbows inside the knees. The feet are flat on the floor, and the knees are bent at approximately a right angle. Raise the legs so the knees are straight, with the toes pointed, and balance on the seat for 5 seconds.

Seat Balance

Face to Knee Touch

Begin in a standing position with feet together. Placing hands on the hips, balance on one foot, with the other leg extended backward. Bend the trunk forward, and touch the knee of the supporting leg with the forehead. Recover to original standing position. Teachers can begin by having the children use their arms away from their sides for balance and then later stipulate the hands-on-hips position.

Face to Knee Touch

In the learning stages, an assist can be given from behind by supporting the leg that is extended backward or by placing one hand against a wall.

Finger Touch

Put the right hand behind you with the index finger straight and pointed down. Grasp the right wrist with the left hand. From an erect position with the feet about 6 inches apart, squat down and touch the floor with the index finger. Regain erect position without losing balance. In learning the stunt, the teacher can use a book or a corner of a mat to decrease the distance, making the touch easier.

Finger Touch

Individual Stunts

Knee Jump to Standing

The starting position is kneeling with seat touching the heels and toes pointing backward (shoelaces against the floor). Jump to a standing position with a vigorous upward swing of the arms. It is easier to jump from a smooth floor than from a mat, since the toes slide more readily on the floor. If a child has difficulty, allow him or her to come to a standing position with the feet well spread.

Knee Jump to Standing

Variation: Jump to a standing position, and, at the same time, face the side direction with a quarter-turn in the air. This is a jump and turn in the air in one quick motion. Try a half-turn.

Individual Drops (Falls)

A number of drops or falls can challenge children to good body control. Mats should be used. The impact of a forward fall should be absorbed with the hands and the arms. During the fall, the body should maintain a straight-line position. Look to make sure there is no change in any of the body angles, particularly at the knees and waist.

Knee Drop

Kneel on a mat, with the body upright. Pick the feet off the floor and fall forward, breaking the fall with the hands and arms.

Knee Drop

Forward Drop

From a forward-balance position on one leg with the other leg extended backward and the arms extended forward and up, lean forward slowly, bringing the arms toward the floor. Continue to drop forward slowly until overbalanced, and let the hands and arms absorb the shock to break the fall. Head is up, and the extended leg to the rear is raised high, with the knee joints maintained reasonably straight. Repeat changing position of the legs.

Forward Drop

Dead Body Fall

The idea of the stunt is to fall forward from an erect position to a down push-up position. A slight bend at the waist is permissible, but the knees should be kept straight, and there should be no forward movement by the feet.

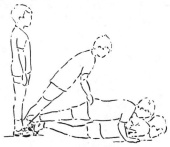

Dead Body Fall

Stoop and Stretch

Hold a beanbag with *both* hands. Stand with the heels against a line and feet about shoulder

width apart. Keeping the knees straight, reach between the legs with the beanbag, *placing* it as far back as possible. Reach back and pick it up with both hands.

Stoop and Stretch

Variations

1. Bend at the knees, using more of a squatting position during the reach.
2. Use a piece of chalk instead of a beanbag. Reach back and make a mark on the floor. Try writing a number or drawing a small circle or some other figure.

Squat Jumps

Take a three-quarter-squat position, with the trunk erect and one foot slightly ahead of the other so the heel of the front foot is even with the toe of the back foot. Hands are placed palms down on top of the head. Spring into the air, and change the relative position of the feet. Make 5, 10, and 15 changes, clearing the floor by 4 inches. Children should avoid going down to a full squat position. The knees are completely straightened on each jump.

Squat Jump

Tanglefoot

Tanglefoot

Stand with the heels together and the toes pointed out. Bend the trunk forward and extend both arms down between the knees and around behind the ankles. Bring the hands around the outside of the ankles from behind and touch the fingers to each other, holding for a 5-second count.

Variation: Instead of touching, clasp the fingers in front of the ankles. Hold this position in good balance for 5 seconds without releasing the handclasp.

Egg Roll

In a sitting position, assume the same clasped-hands position as in Tanglefoot. Roll sideways over one shoulder, then to the back, followed by the other shoulder, and back up to the sitting position. The movements are repeated in turn to make a full circle back to place. The secret is a vigorous sideward movement to secure initial momentum. If mats are used, two should be placed side by side to cover the extent of the roll. Some children can do this stunt better from a crossed-ankle position.

Egg Roll

Toe Touch Nose

From a sitting position on the floor, try to touch the toe of either foot to the nose with the help of both hands. More flexible youngsters will even be able to bring the foot on top of the head or behind the neck. While this is a flexibility exercise, caution should be used in forcing the leg too far. Do first with one foot and then the other.

Variation: Perform from a standing position. Begin from an erect position with the feet together. Touch the toe to the nose, and return the foot to its original position without losing balance. Try the standing version with the eyes closed.

Toe Tug Walk

Bend over and grasp the toes with the thumb on top. Knees are bent slightly, and the eyes are forward. Walk forward without losing the grip on the toes. Walk backward and sideward to provide more challenge. Also, walk in various geometric patterns, such as a circle, triangle, or square. This stunt can be introduced in an easier version by having the children grasp the ankles, thumbs to the insides, and perform the desired movements.

Toe Tug Walk

Variation: Try doing the walk with the right hand grasping the left foot, and vice versa.

Partner and Group Stunts

Leapfrog

A *back* is formed by one student so a leaper with a running start can lay his or her hands flat on the back at the shoulders and vault over him or her. Backs are formed in these following progressive heights.

Low Back: The child crouches down on his or her knees, curling into a tight ball with his or her head tucked well down.

Medium Back: From a standing position, the child reaches down the outside of his or her legs and grasps the ankles. His or her feet should be reasonably spread and the knees bent. The child should assume a stable position, in order to absorb the shock of the leaper.

High Back: The child stands stiff-legged, bends over, and braces his or her arms against the knees. The feet should be well spread, the head down, and the body braced in order to absorb the vault.

High, Medium, Low Leapfrog Positions

Leapfrog is a traditional physical education activity, but the movement is actually a jump-and-vault pattern. The takeoff must be made with both feet. At the height of the jump, the chest and head must be held erect to avoid a forward fall. Emphasize a forceful jump to achieve height, coordinated with light hand pressure to vault over the back. Landing should be done lightly with a bent-knee action under good control.

Leapfrog

Variations
1. Work in pairs. The children alternate in leaping and forming backs as they progress around the room.
2. Have more than one back for a series of jumps.
3. Using the medium back as described, vault from the side rather than from the front. Legs of the vaulter must be well spread, and the back must keep his or her head well tucked down.
4. Combine with a Forward Roll on a mat following the Leapfrog.

Wheelbarrow (Partner Stunt)

One partner gets down on his or her hands with his or her feet extended to the rear, legs apart. The other partner (the pusher) grasps his or her legs halfway between the ankles and the knees. The wheelbarrow walks forward on his or her hands, supported by the pusher. Movements should be under good control.

Wheelbarrow Lifting

Camel Lift and Walk (Partner Stunt)

The wheelbarrow raises his or her seat as high as he or she can, forming a camel. He or she can lower himself or herself down or go on to walk in the raised position.

Dump the Wheelbarrow (Partner Stunt)

Walk the wheelbarrow over to a mat. The lower child ducks his or her head (chin to chest), raises his or her seat (bend at the waist), and exits from the stunt with a Forward Roll. A little push and lift with the feet are given by the pusher.

Dromedary Walk (Partner Stunt)

The first child (support) gets down on hands and knees. The second (top) child sits on him or

Wheelbarrow

Children have a tendency to grasp the feet too low. The pusher must not push too fast. The wheelbarrow should have his or her head up and look forward.

Fingers should be pointed forward and well spread, with the pads of the fingers supporting much of the weight. Holder should carry the legs low, keeping the arms extended.

Wheelbarrow Lifting (Partner Stunt)

Partners assume the wheelbarrow position as described. The pusher lifts his or her partner's legs up as high as he or she can without changing his or her hand position. He or she should be able to lift so the angle of the body of the lower child is about 45 degrees with the floor.
Variation: The pusher brings the legs up to the previous level as described, changes his or her handgrip to a pushing position and continues to raise the lower child toward a handstand position. The lower child should keep his or her arms straight and the head well against the back of the neck.

Dromedary Walk

her, facing to the rear, and fixes his or her own legs around the chest of support. The top child leans forward, so he or she can grasp the back of the support's ankles. Arms are reasonably extended. The support takes the weight off the knees and walks forward with the top child's help.

Centipede (Partner or Group Stunt)

The support player should be the stronger and larger individual. He or she gets down on his or her hands and knees. The top player faces the same direction, placing his or her hands about 2 feet in front of those of the support player. Then, he or she places his or her legs and body on top of the support. The knees should be spread apart and the heels locked together.

The centipede walks with the top player using hands only and the support player using both hands and feet. The support child should gather his or her legs well under him or her while walking and thus should be off his or her knees.

Centipede Walk

Variation: More than two can do this stunt. After getting in position, the players should keep step by calling right and left out loud.

Double Wheelbarrow (Group Stunt)

This stunt usually is done by three children but can be done by one or two more. Two children assume about the same position as in the previous stunt, Centipede, except the under child has his or her legs extended to the rear, feet apart. The third child stands between the legs of the under child, reaches down, and picks up the legs of the lower child, forming the Double Wheelbarrow. The double wheelbarrow moves forward with right and left arms moving together.

An easy way to get into position for this activity is to form the front of the wheelbarrow first and then pick up the legs of the second child.

Double Wheelbarrow

Partner Support Stunts

Several considerations are important in the conduct of partner support stunts. The lower child (support) should keep his or her body as level as possible. This means widening the hand base, so the shoulders can be more nearly level with the hips. The support performer must be strong enough to handle the support chores. Spotters are needed, particularly where the top position involves a final erect or inverted pose. Avoid stepping on the small of the lower child's back.

In the Lighthouse and the Hip-Shoulder Stand, the top performer can remove his or her shoes, which makes the standing position more comfortable for the support. When he or she holds the final pose, the top child should fix his or her gaze forward at a spot level with his or her eyes and relax as much as he or she can while maintaining the position.

There are many different ways in which children can support a partner.

Double Bear

The bottom child is down on his or her hands and knees. Top child assumes the same position directly above, with hands on the shoulders and knees on the hips of the bottom child. Touch up the final position by holding heads up and backs straight.

Table

Bottom performer assumes crab position (base). Top performer straddles base, facing to the rear, and positions his or her hands on base's shoulders, fingers pointing toward the feet. His or her feet then are placed on top of the base's knees, forming one crab position on top of another. As a final touch, the heads are positioned so the eyes look up toward the ceiling and the seats are lifted so that the backs are straight.

Double Bear

Statue

and should not be eliminated until the stunt is mastered.

The Lighthouse

The support is down on hands and knees. The top child completes the figure by standing on *the*

Table

Statue

First child gets down in crab position. The second child straddles one foot (either), facing the child in crab position. With the help of a third person, he or she mounts each knee of the base child in turn so he or she is standing erect. Hold for a few seconds.

Partners should be facing each other. Do not have the top child mount with his or her back toward the base child. Spotters are important here

Lighthouse

shoulders of the support facing the same direction. He or she stands erect with hands out to the sides.

Variation: Have the support turn around in a small circle, with the partner keeping his or her standing balance.

Hip-Shoulder Stand

Support is on his or her hands and knees, with hands positioned out somewhat so his or her back is level. Top child faces to the side and steps up, first with one foot on support's hips, and then with the other on his or her shoulders. A spotter should stand on the opposite side and aid in the mounting. Care must be taken to avoid stepping on the small of the back.

Hip-Shoulder Stand

FIFTH-GRADE PROGRAM

The teacher should review all the stunts from the fourth grade. Repetition is valuable, because many of the fifth-grade activities have their basis in the simpler stunts performed in the fourth grade.

The children at this stage should be quite skillful in doing both the Forward and Backward Rolls. Additional routines are added. The Judo Roll, Cartwheel, and Eskimo Roll continue the mat-type activities. Improvement in the Headstand should be expected. The Handstand is an important in-

troduction. The following stunts make up the suggested fifth-grade program. Except for review, animal movements have little place in this level program.

Activities for the Fifth Grade

Tumbling and Inverted Balances

Forward and Backward Roll Combinations
Neckspring
Headstand Review and Variations
Wall Arch
Handstand
Cartwheel
Judo Roll

Balance Stunts

Fish Hawk Dive
High Dive
V-up
Push-up Variations
Turn-over and Flip-flop

Individual Stunts

Wall Walk-up
Skier's Sit
Curl-up Practice
Rocking Horse
Heel Click (Side)
Walk-through
Jump-through
Circular Rope Skip

Partner and Group Stunts

Double Scooter
Eskimo Roll
Tandem Bicycle
Circle High Jump
Stick Carries
Two-Way Wheelbarrow

Partner Support Stunts

Back Layout
Front Sit
Flying Dutchman

Tumbling and Inverted Balances

Forward and Backward Roll Combinations

Combinations from the fourth grade should be reviewed. The following routines can be added.

1. Alternating Forward and Backward Rolls: Begin the combination with a Forward Roll, coming to the standing position with the feet crossed, pivoting the body to uncross the feet, thus bringing the back in the line of direction for a Backward Roll.
2. Back Extension: Carry the Backward Roll to the point where the feet are above the head

Alternating Forward and Backward Rolls

and slightly over. Push off vigorously with the hands, and shoot the feet into the air, landing on the feet.

3. A number of variations and different body positions can be added to the rolls. Holding toes, heels, ankles, or a wand can be incorporated. Utilizing different arm positions such as out to the sides or folded across the chest gives variety. Use a wide straddle position for both the Forward and Backward Rolls. Try a Stiff-legged Sitdown leading into a Backward Roll.

Neckspring

The stunt is related to the Backward Curl. The performer goes into a backward-curl position with the feet kept over the head. The feet are brought sharply forward toward the mat. As the shoulders come off the mat, the arms are extended with good push-off by the hands, and there is an upward snap to standing position. The Neckspring can be followed by a Forward Roll.

Neckspring

Spotting: Kneel alongside the child. Place one hand under the back and the other under the *near* shoulder blade. Attention must be given to preventing a backward fall in case of improper lunging by the performer. As a precaution, it is a good idea to start the Neckspring with the student placed in the middle of the mat. The lower hand under the back acts as a pivot, while a good lift is given by the

hand under the shoulder. If the spotters lack strength, it is possible to use two children, placing one on each side of the performer.

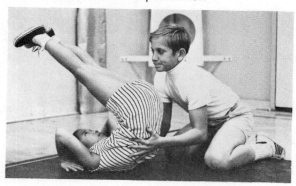

Spotting the Neckspring

Headstand Review and Variations

Review the various aspects of the Headstand, using the single-spotter technique as needed. Vary with different leg positions. Add the following.

Develop a two-foot recovery. After the stand has been held, recover by bending at the waist and knees, pushing off with the hands and landing on the feet back to where you started.

Wall Arch

Take a position with the shoulders against a wall and the feet about 2 feet out. Place the hands against the wall, employing the position used in the Backward Roll. Without moving the feet, work the hands downward to give the body an arch shape. Recover to position. If the activity is too

Wall Arch

difficult, students may move their feet or make other adjustments. It may be necessary to spot the performer and gradually lower him or her to the arched position.

Handstand

The first two phases of the Handstand are introduced in the fifth grade. Initially, the Handstand should be done with the aid of two spotters (double spotting). The second method is to perform the stunt with one spotter, employing knee pressure as a part of the spotting technique. To do the stunt, place hands on the mat, shoulder width apart, fingers spread, slightly cupped and pointed

Double Spotting for the Handstand, First Stage (note the hand support under the shoulders)

Double Spotting for the Handstand, Second Stage

straight ahead. Keeping one leg straight and the shoulders well forward of the hands, kick up with the straight leg and push off with the bent leg. With the back arched, the shoulders are brought back to a point directly over the hands.

Double Spotting: Spotters should be stationed on both sides of the performer. It is important that the spotter on each side have a firm grip beneath the shoulders of the performer. The other hand of each spotter can assist the lift by upward pressure on the thigh. The performer walks his or her hips forward until they are over his or her hands. He or she kicks up with one foot, pushes off with the other, and raises that leg to join the other in the inverted position. The rhythm is a one-two count.

Single Spotting (Knee Pressure): Spotter takes a stride position, with the forward knee somewhat bent. The performer kneels on one knee, with his or her shoulder against the spotter's leg. The weight is transferred over the hands, and the body goes into the handstand position with one-two kick-up. Spotter catches the legs and holds the performer in an inverted position.

Alternate Spotting for the Handstand (Double Spotting): Two children are used to spot a third. The first child sits on a mat with legs out straight in a wide V. The Handstand is done between his or her legs. He or she catches the performer at the sides of the waist. The second spotter stands directly behind the seated spotter and

Single Spotting for the Handstand, First Stage (performer's shoulder is against the spotter's leg)

*Single Spotting for Handstand, Second Stage
(note knee pressure against performer's shoulder)*

Alternate Spotting for the Handstand

catches the performer's ankles. *The performer must keep elbows straight, head up, and back arched to avoid falling toward the spotter.*

Stress Point: Before the child can go up into the handstand position, the center of gravity must be placed well over the hands.

Cartwheel

Begin with the legs and arms spread, with the left side toward the direction of wheeling. For a preliminary movement (windup), swing the left arm up and keep the right arm at the side. Then throw the weight smoothly to the left side, bringing the right arm up and the left arm down so that the hand takes a position about 2 feet from the left leg. The right arm then comes down to the mat, and the right leg follows upward.

Just before the right hand touches the floor, there is a push-off with the left foot to give momentum to the roll: Swing both legs up and over the head. The right foot touches first, followed by the left. As the left foot approaches, a good push is given with the right hand to return the individual to standing position. It is important to keep the head up throughout the stunt.

Cartwheel

The entire body must be in the same plane throughout the stunt, and feet must pass directly overhead.

In teaching the Cartwheel to children who are having difficulty, concentrate on taking the weight of the body on the hands in succession. The children need to get the feel of the weight support, and then they can concentrate on getting the body into proper position.

After the class has had some practice in doing Cartwheels, try adding a running approach with a skip just prior to takeoff.

Spotting: A spotter stands behind the performer and moves with him or her. The spotter grasps the performer at the waist with a crossed-arm position. This position allows the arms to become uncrossed as the performer wheels and is given assistance.

Judo Roll

The Judo Roll is a basic safety device to prevent injury from tripping and falling. Rolling and "taking the fall" lessen the chances of injury.

The Judo Roll is essentially a Forward Roll with the head turned to one side. The point of impact is on the back of one shoulder and the finish is back to a standing position.

For a left Judo Roll, the child should stand facing the mat with his or her feet well apart and the left arm extended at shoulder height. Bring the arm down, and throw the left shoulder toward the mat in a rolling motion, with the roll made on the shoulder and upper part of the back.

Both right and left Judo Rolls should be practiced. Later, a short run and double-foot takeoff should precede the roll.

Judo Roll

Variations

1. Roll to the feet and a walk-out position.
2. Place a beanbag about 3 feet in front of the performer and have him or her go beyond the bag as he or she starts the roll.

Balance Stunts

Fish Hawk Dive

Place a folded paper on the floor, with the edge up so the performer can pick it up with his or her teeth. Kneel on one leg, with the other leg extended behind and the arms out for balance. Lean forward, pick up the paper with the teeth, and return to position without losing balance.

Begin the stunt using an 8½-by-11-inch piece of paper folded lengthwise. It may be necessary to have someone hold the paper. If the stunt is done successfully, fold the paper a second time so a lower target is presented.

High Dive

Fold a piece of paper that the performer can pick up with his or her teeth. Using the arms for balance and standing on one foot only, try to pick

High Dive

up the paper with the teeth. If this seems too difficult, shorten the distance to the paper by elevating it on a box or book.

Begin with a regular sheet of notepaper folded lengthwise; it may have to be steadied by another child.

V-up

The child is on his or her back, with the arms overhead and extended. Keeping the knees straight and the feet pointed, the legs and upper body are brought up at the same time to form a V. The entire weight is balanced on the seat and should be held for five counts.

This exercise, like the Curl-up, is excellent for the development of the abdominal muscles. It is quite similar to the seat balance, except for the variation in the starting position.

V-up

Variation: Those who have trouble can do an easier version of the stunt by placing the hands in back on the floor for support.

Push-up Variations

Begin the development of Push-up variations by reviewing proper Push-up techniques. Stress that the only movement is in the arm and that the body should come close to, but not touch, the floor. The following variations can be explored.

Monkey Push-up: Point fingers toward each other. Next, bring the hands close enough so the fingertips touch.

Circle-O Push-up: Thumbs and forefingers form a Circle-O.

Fingertip Push-up: Get up high on the fingertips.

Different Finger Combinations: Do a Push-up using four, three, two fingers.

Extended Push-up: Extend the position of the hands progressively forward or to the sides.

Crossed Push-up: Cross the arms. Cross the legs. Cross both.

One-legged Push-up: Lift one leg from the floor.

One-handed Push-up: Use only one hand, with the other outstretched or on the hips.

Exploratory Approach: Opportunity should be given to see what other types of push-ups or combinations the students can create.

Turn-over and Flip-Flop

The object is to turn completely over from a front-leaning rest (push-up) position, using only the arms and hands. The remainder of the body is kept straight. The feet, particularly, must be stiffened.

Lift one hand, depending upon the way the turn is to be made, and at the same time turn the body so the back is to the floor. The lifted hand returns quickly to the floor for support. The weight is then on the hands and heels. Continue with the other hand, and complete the turn. Return by reversing the direction and making a complete turn back the other way.

Turn-over

Flip-Flop: Do a Flip-Flop by propelling the body into the air and reversing the body position as in the Turn-over. Flip back. The stunt should be done on a mat.

Individual Stunts

Wall Walk-up

From a push-up position with feet against a wall, walk up the wall backward to a handstand position. Walk down again.

Wall Walk-up

Skier's Sit

The Skier's Sit is an isometric type of activity that is excellent for developing the knee extensor muscles. The child assumes a sitting position against a wall, so that the thighs are parallel to the floor and there is a right angle at the knee joint. The child's body position is the same as if he or she were sitting in a chair, but, of course, there is no chair. The arms are folded across the chest. The feet should be flat on the floor and the legs straight up and down. Children should try to sit for 30 seconds, 45 seconds, and 1 minute. This exercise is done by skiers to develop muscles used in skiing.

Skier's Sit

Variation: Support the body with crossed legs. A more difficult stunt is to support the body on one leg, with the other leg extended forward.

Curl-up Practice

The child is on his or her back, with feet apart, flat on the floor. The knees are bent at approximately a right angle. The stunt can be done two ways.

1. With the arms folded in front of the chest, Curl-ups are done so the folded arms touch the knees each time.
2. The hands, with fingers interlaced, are grasped behind the lower part of the head. The left elbow touches the right knee on the first Curl-up and the right elbow touches the left knee on the next.

Curl-up Position

Boys should do from 15 to 20, while girls should do 10 to 15. Gradually increase the number during the year. Done properly and regularly, this exercise has good value in the maintenance of proper posture.

Rocking Horse

The child is face down on a mat with the arms extended overhead, palms down. With the back arched, rock back and forth. Some children may need to have someone start them rocking.

Rocking Horse

Variation: The stunt can be done by reaching back and grasping the insteps with the hands. The body arch is more difficult to maintain with this position. Also, try rocking from a side position.

Heel Click (Side)

Balance on one foot, with the other out to the side. Hop on the supporting foot, click heels, and return to balance. Try with the other foot. Insist on good balance.

The child should recover to the one-foot balance position without excessive foot movement.

Variations

1. The stunt also can be done moving. Take a short lead step with the right foot. Follow with a cross step with the left and then a hop on the left foot. During the hop, click the heels together. To hop on the right foot, reverse the above directions.
2. See how high the children can jump into the air before clicking heels.
3. Combine right and left clicks.

Walk-through

From a front-leaning rest position, walk the feet through the hands, using tiny steps until the body is fully extended with the back to the floor. Reverse the body to original position. Hands stay in contact with the floor throughout.

Walk-through

Jump-through

This is related to the Walk-through except that, instead of walking through, jump the feet through with one motion. Reverse with a jump, and return to original position. The hands must push sharply off the floor, so the body is high enough from the floor to allow the legs to jump under.

Jump-through

The child may find it easier to swing a little to the side with one leg, going under the lifted hand. This is indicated in the diagram above, where the youngster swings a little to one side.

Circular Rope Skip

Crouch down in a three-quarter knee bend, holding a folded skipping rope in one hand. Swing the rope under the feet in circular fashion, jumping it each time. Reverse the direction of the rope. Work from both right and left sides with either a counterclockwise or clockwise turn of the rope.

Circular Rope Skip

Variations

1. Perform the rope skip with a partner.
2. Jump using different foot patterns, such as one foot and alternate feet, and slow and fast time.
3. Establish standards to declare a class champion in different areas. Maximum number of turns in 30 seconds, most unique routine, and the most jumps without a miss are possible ideas.

Partner and Group Stunts

Double Scooter (Partner Stunt)

First review the Scooter, page 340.

The Double Scooter is done by two children of about the same size. The children sit facing each other, sitting on each other's feet. With arms joined, they scoot forward or backward with cooperative movements. When one child moves his or her seat, the other child should help by lifting with his or her feet. Progress is made by alternately flexing and extending the knees and hips.

Double Scooter

Eskimo Roll (Double Roll)

This is one of the older stunts and a favorite of many youngsters. The stunt is done with two children who are designated as #1 and #2. Number one lies on the mat with feet in the direction of the roll. Number two takes a position with his or her feet on either side of #1's head. Number one reaches back and grasps #2's ankles with the thumbs on the inside. Number one raises his or

her feet, so #2 can similarly grasp his or her ankles.

Number two propels his or her hunched body forward, while #1 sits up and takes the position originally held by #2. Positions then are reversed. The roll continues. Be sure the top child hunches well and ducks his or her head to cushion the roll on the back of the neck and shoulders. Also, when the top child propels himself or herself forward, his or her bent arms should momentarily take his or her weight. It is important that the underneath child keep his or her knees in a bent-knee position.

Variation: Roll backward after reaching the end of the mat. To begin a reverse roll, the top child sits backward and pulls vigorously on the legs of the bottom child. In finishing at the end of the mat, one performer comes to his or her feet and releases his or her hold on the ankles of the lower child, who then straightens out on the floor.

Tandem Bicycle (Group Stunt)

As with a tandem bicycle, the stunt can be done with two or more players. A Bicycle is formed by the first player with back against a wall in bent-knee position as if sitting. The feet should be placed so they are under the body. The second player backs up and sits down lightly on the knees. Other children may be added in the same fashion. The hands are around the waist of the player immediately in front for support. Forward progress is made by moving the feet on the same side together.

Tandem Bicycle

Eskimo Roll

Circle High Jump (Group Stunt)

Children are in circles of three, each circle having children of somewhat equal height. Hands are joined, and one child tries to jump over the opposite pair of joined hands. Each circle to be completely successful must have each child jump forward over the opposite pair of joined hands. Jumping backward is not recommended.

To reach good height in jumping, an upward lift of the joined hands is necessary. The jumper may try two small preliminary jumps before exploding into the jump over the joined hands.

Circle High Jump

Variation: Precede the jump with a short run by the group. A signal needs to be sounded so that all of the participants know when the jump is to occur during the run.

Stick Carries (Group Stunt)

Children are in groups of three, with each group having a sturdy broom handle about 4 feet long. Using movement exploration techniques, two of the children are to carry the third with the broom handle. The child carried may be partially supported on or completely off the ground. Children should be of similar weight. Exchange positions. It is better to use special sticks for this purpose, since ordinary wands may break.

Stick Carry

Two-Way Wheelbarrow (Group Stunt)

Review the various Wheelbarrow activities in the fourth grade (page 348). Add the Double Wheelbarrow, a stunt done by three children. In essence, one child is holding two wheelbarrows, one in front of him or her and one behind him or her. The child secures the front position first in a normal wheelbarrow position. The child behind in wheelbarrow position secures his or her position by placing his or her ankles over the already established hand position of the holder.

Two-Way Wheelbarrow

Partner Support Stunts

Back Layout

The under, or support, partner lies on his or her back, with arms outstretched, palms down, for support. His or her legs are raised, and his or her feet are positioned as if pushing up the ceiling. He or she bends his or her knees, and his or her partner lies back, resting the small of his or her back on support's soles. Thus, the top partner is balanced in a layout position with his or her arms out to the sides for balance and his or her body in a slight curve. The support partner can reach up and give support to the top's arms to provide better stability. A spotter should aid in positioning the top partner.

Back Layout

Front Sit

The support gets down in the same position as for the Back Layout. The top partner straddles the support, facing so that support and top partner are looking at each other. The top partner backs up to sit on the support's feet. As the support raises the top partner in a seated position, the top partner extends his or her legs forward, so the support can reach up and support them to stabilize the seated position. Spot from behind.

Flying Dutchman

Front Sit

Flying Dutchman

The under, or support, person takes a position as in the Back Layout. The top person takes a position facing the support, grasping his or her hands, and at the same time bending over his or her feet. The top person then is raised from the floor by extending his or her knees, arching his or her back, and resting on the feet of the support person. He or she can release his or her grip and put his or her arms out level to the side in a flying position. A little experimentation determines the best spot for the foot support. Spot as needed to get into position and for safety.

SIXTH-GRADE PROGRAM

Continued practice should be held on the basic rolls, with attention centered on variations and combinations. The Cartwheel, Headstand, Handstand, and Round-off follow logically in the progressions. The stunts from the fifth grade should be reviewed. The sixth-grade program adds a number of stunts that the children find quite challenging. Such stunts as the Dive Forward Roll, Headspring, Forearm Headstand, Forearm Stand, Front Seat Support, Elbow Balance, Straddle Press to Headstand, and the Walk-over provide sufficient breadth for even the most skilled. It is difficult for all the children to accomplish all the stunts listed.

Particular attention should be paid to the lead-up stunts for the gymnastic-type stunts. While there is still opportunity for exploration and individual expression, more emphasis is placed on execution, conformity, and form. Animal movements are of little importance in the sixth grade.

Activities for the Sixth Grade

Tumbling and Inverted Balances

Forward and Backward Roll Variations
Cartwheel and Round-off
Movement Sequences
Headstand Variations
Headspring
Dive Forward Roll
Handstand
Handstand against a Wall
Walking on Hands
Freestanding Handstand
Forearm Headstand
Forearm Stand
Straddle Press to Headstand
Walk-over

Balance Stunts

Long Reach
Wrestler's Bridge
Toe Jump
Handstand Stunts
Front Seat Support
Elbow Balance

Individual Stunts

Bouncer
Pretzel
Jackknife
Heel-and-Toe Spring
Single-Leg Circle

Partner and Group Stunts

Partner Rising Sun
Triple Roll
Quintuplet Roll
Dead Person Lift
Injured Person Carry
Merry-go-round

Partner Support Stunts

Knee-and-Shoulder Balance
Press
All-Fours Support
Angel
Side Stand

Tumbling and Inverted Balances

Putting together different combinations of forward and backward rolls should be stressed, with emphasis on choice, exploration, and self-discovery. Variations can be instituted that use different kinds of approaches, execution acts, and finishes.

Forward Roll Variations

1. Hold toes, heels, ankles, or a wand.
2. With hands crossed, roll as in (#1) above.
3. Roll with hands on knees or a ball between the knees.
4. Roll with the arms at sides, folded across the chest, or back of the thighs.
5. Finish with a Walk-out by ending the roll with one leg extended forward to walk out of the stunt. Or finish on one knee.
6. Start with a standing broad jump, a jump over a low object, or some other jumping, hopping, or leaping movement.
7. Place a low jumping box or bench under a mat and roll from, and to, the higher elevations.
8. Place a bench or jumping box on, or before, the mat and work out various possibilities with these pieces of equipment.
9. Roll from a wide-straddle position (feet as wide apart sideways as possible), holding on to ankles.
10. Press forward from a front-leaning rest position, and go into the roll.

Backward Roll Variations

1. Begin with a Stiff-legged Sitdown, and go into the roll.
2. Push off into a Backward Extension, lighting on the feet.
3. Roll to a finish on one foot only.
4. Roll with hands and arms in various positions—out to the sides, clasped behind the neck, et cetera.
5. Roll with a ball between the knees.
6. Walk backward with a crab movement and then roll.
7. Combine Forward and Backward Rolls.

Cartwheel and Round-off

Continued practice on the Cartwheel should be held, and a light run with a skip as a takeoff for the Cartwheel should be developed. To change to a Round-off, the hands are placed somewhat closer together during the early Cartwheel action. Bring the feet together and make a quarter-turn to land on both feet, with the body facing the starting point. The Round-off can be followed by a Backward Roll.

Movement Sequences

Set up problems so that the children can use and put together in sequence the stunts they have learned and other movements. Some problems that can be structured are these.

1. Specify the number, the kinds of stunts and movements to be done, and the sequence to be followed. For example, tell the child to do a balance stunt, a locomotor movement, and a rolling stunt.
2. Mats can be arranged so that they become the key for the movement problems to be solved. Arrange the mats in some prescribed order, such as two or three in succession, in a U shape (three or four mats), or in a hollow square formation. There should be some space between mats, depending on the conditions as stated in the problem. The problem could be set up like this: "On the first mat, do a Forward Roll variation and then a movement to the next mat on all fours. On the second mat, do some kind of a balance stunt, and then proceed to the next mat with a jumping or hopping movement. On the third mat, you have a choice of activity." The problem also could be stated in more general terms, and the children could do a different stunt or variation on each mat and a different movement between mats.
3. Have children work with a partner and work out a series of partner stunts. This can be done with two children of equal size and strength, so they can alternate as support for stunts; or it might be two children of different sizes, and the larger child would provide the support for the smaller. A third child may act as a spotter to take care of safety factors. After the children have practiced for a period of time, each partnership can demonstrate the routines that they have developed.

Headstand Variations

Practice the movement from a Headstand into a Forward Roll to feet. Do the Headstand with a beanbag or a ball between the ankles.

Headspring

With forehead and hands on the mat and the knees bent, the performer leans forward until he or she is almost overbalanced. As the weight begins to overbalance, the feet are raised sharply and snapped forward, coupled with a push of the hands. As the feet begin to touch, the body is snapped forward to a bent-knee position. The performer keeps his or her balance and rises to a standing position.

Headspring

Two spotters placed on each side of the performer should be used. One hand from each spotter should be placed under the back of the performer and the other hand under the shoulder. The spotters should give the performer a lift under the shoulders to help him or her snap to a standing position. A slight run may be needed to get proper momentum.

Some instructors like to introduce this stunt going over a rolled-up mat, providing more height for the turn.

Dive Forward Roll

The stunt is similar to the regular Forward Roll, except the roll is preceded by a run and a short dive. The child should take a short run and take off with both feet, so he or she is already partially turning in the air as his or her hands come down to cushion the fall. The head should be tucked under, and the roll should be made on the back of the neck and shoulders.

Dive Forward Roll

The teacher should avoid contests to see how far a student can dive. The stunt described is actually only an elongated Forward Roll during which the player is off the ground for a short period of time.

Dives over objects or other students should be used with caution and reserved only for the more skilled.

Handstand

The Handstand can be developed by taking it through these stages.
1. Double spotting (fifth grade).
2. Single spotting, knee support (fifth grade).
3. Single spotting, catch ankles.
4. Handstand against a Wall.
5. Free Handstand.
6. Walking on hands.
7. Stunts against a wall.
8. Other stunts.

The first two stages of the Handstand, presented in the fifth-grade program (page 353), should be reviewed. Progression then can follow this order.

Single Spotting (without Knee Support): Performers should begin to use the extended starting position. The performer and spotter face each other 4 or 5 feet apart. The performer lifts both arms and the left leg upward as a preliminary move, with the weight shifted to the right leg. The lifted arms and forward leg come down forcefully to the ground, with the weight shifted in succession to the left leg and then to the arms. The right leg is kicked backward and upward to establish initial momentum, quickly followed by the left leg. The downward thrust of the arms, coupled with the

Single Spotting for Handstand

upward thrust of the legs, inverts the body to the handstand position. The hands should have been placed about 2 feet in front of the spotter, who reaches forward and catches the performer's ankles as they come up in the handstand position.

Handstand against a Wall

Mats should be used. It is better in the beginning to place the hands too close to the wall than to have them too far from it. The extended starting position is used. Some performers may have better success in bending the knees so that the flat of the foot is against the wall. The arms must be held straight, the back arched, and the head up in order to avoid collapsing into the wall.

Handstand against a Wall

Walking on Hands

Hand walking generally should be in a forward direction. Some may find it more comfortable to walk with knees slightly bent for balance. Walking can be done first with a spotter supporting. This support should be minimal.

A unique way to walk on hands is to utilize a partner. The performer does a Handstand, and the partner catches his or her feet. The performer walks his or her hands forward until they are on the partner's feet. Cooperatively the two walk in different directions.

Freestanding Handstand

The performer should learn to turn the body when he or she feels he or she is falling and land on his or her feet. Spotters can be used to prevent an awkward fall. The hands may need to move to help control the balance.

Forearm Headstand

The stunt is similar to a Headstand, except for the way the supporting base is formed. Take a kneeling position, with both elbows on the mat and the forepart of the head in the cupped hands. From this position, support the body in an inverted upright position. Spotters are needed on both sides of the performer.

Forearm Headstand

Variation: A second way to arrange the hand position for support is to have the hands on the floor, with the palms down. A rest is made for the head by the thumbs and forefingers forming a small circle. The remainder of the fingers are spread, and the elbows are out so the base is a triangle formed by the hands and elbows. Spot in front.

Forearm Stand

Place the forearms down on the mat, with the palms down and the elbows out, forming a triangular base. Do a Forearm Stand, so the forearms and hands support the weight of the inverted body. Stress getting the center of gravity over the support base. There is more body curve in this stunt compared with the Headstand and Handstand. Spot to avoid a forward fall.

Forearm Stand

Straddle Press to Headstand

A more difficult stunt than a regular Headstand is the Straddle Press to Headstand. Begin by placing the hands and head in the triangular headstand position. The feet are in a wide straddle position, with the hips up. First raise the hips slowly by pressing to a point over the head-hands support. Slowly raise the legs to a Straddle Headstand, and finish with the legs brought together in regular headstand position. All movement is done under slow, controlled action.

Walk-over

Bend the body forward as in the Handstand, placing the hands on the floor. Extend one leg backward, and fix the other with the knee bent as the push-off foot. Swing the extended leg upward, at the same time pushing off with the other foot. Good body arch is needed as the extended foot leads and touches the floor first. Push off with the hands and walk out. One leg always leads the other in the Walk-over.

Balance Stunts

Long Reach

Place a beanbag 3 or 4 feet in front of a line. Keeping toes behind the line, lean forward on one hand and reach out with the other hand to touch the beanbag. The recovery to the original position must be made with one quick motion. In this, the supporting hand comes off the floor in one clean movement. Increase the distance of the bag from the line.

Long Reach

Variations

1. A piece of chalk can be used to mark a more precise distance. Since the distance the child can reach is dependent upon his or her height, measure how far he or she can reach beyond his or her height. With the child lying on the floor, make a mark on the floor and make a mark at his heels and at the top of his or her head. Then see how far he or she can reach in relation to his or her height while keeping his or her feet behind the restraining line.
2. Try the Long Reach from a crab position.

Wrestler's Bridge

Lie on the mat, bringing up the feet so that they are flat on the mat. Push up with the body, and arch the neck so that the support is on the feet and head.

Wrestler's Bridge

Variations

1. Pass a ball or a beanbag around the body, or toss it from side to side. Toss it from one partner to another or to a series of partners.

2. Place hands back on floor, with the thumbs near the ears, and raise the body to a full arch, lifting the head from the floor.
3. Reverse the body position, still keeping the hands away from the floor.
4. Do a Headstand, and fall forward to a Wrestler's Bridge. During the fall, the knees are bent for landing on the soles of the feet. After falling into the bridge position, the hands can be removed from the support position.
5. Work in pairs, and have one partner make an arch (facedown) and the other make a Wrestler's Bridge underneath him or her.

Toe Jump

Hold the left toe with the right hand. Jump the right foot through without losing the grip on the toe. Jump back again. Try with the other foot. The teacher should not be discouraged if only a few can do this stunt, since it is quite difficult.

Toe Jump

Handstand Stunts

A number of challenging activities can be done from the handstand position against a wall. The first is to turn the body in a complete circle, maintaining foot contact with the wall throughout. Another stunt is to shift the support to one hand, holding it for a short period of time. A stunt demanding considerable arm strength is an Inverted Push-up. The body is lowered by bending the elbows and then returned to handstand position with a straightening of the elbows (Push-up).

Do a Handstand to a single spotter. Turn in a circle, with the spotter providing support. From a handstand position with a single spotter, hand walk forward until hands are on the toes of the spotter. Cooperative walking can be done with the performer maintaining his or her support on the spotter's toes.

Front Seat Support

Sit on the floor, with the legs together and forward. The hands are placed flat on the floor, fingers pointed forward, somewhat between the hips and the knees. The stunt is in two stages.
1. Push down so the hips come off the floor, with the weight supported on the hands and heels.

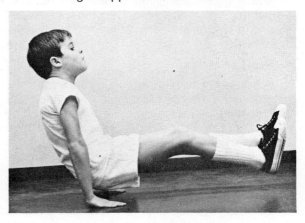

Front Seat Support

2. Support the entire weight of the body on the hands for 3 to 5 seconds. Assistance can be given with slight support under the heels to get into position.

Elbow Balance

The object of this stunt is to balance the body facedown horizontally on two hands, with the elbows supporting the body in the hip area. To get into position, support the arched body with the

Elbow Balance

toes and forehead. Work the forearms underneath the body for support, with the fingers spread and pointed to the back. Try to support the body completely on the hands for 3 seconds, with the elbows providing the leverage under the body. Assist by slight support under the toes.

The Elbow Balance presents a considerable challenge. Take time to discuss center of gravity location so that the elbow support point divides upper and lower body mass.

Individual Stunts

Bouncer

Start in push-up position. Bounce up and down with both the hands and the feet leaving the ground at the same time. Try clapping while doing this. Move in various directions.

Pretzel

The object of the stunt is to touch the back of the head with the toes by raising the head and trunk and bringing the feet to the back of the head. The stunt should be done in two levels. First, challenge the child to bring his or her toes close enough to his or her head so that the distance can be measured by another child with a handspan (thumb-little finger distance when spread). If this distance is met, then try touching one or both feet to the back of the head.

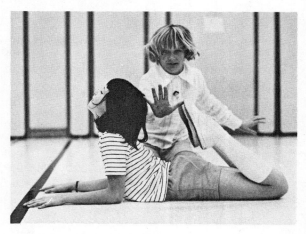

Pretzel

Jackknife

Stand erect with the hands out level to the front and a little to the side. Jump up and bring the feet up to touch the hands quickly. Vary by starting with a short run. Be sure the feet come up to the hands rather than the hands moving down to touch the feet. Do several Jackknives in succession. The takeoff must be with both feet, and good height must be reached.

Jackknife

Heel-and-Toe Spring

The heels are against a line. The object of the stunt is to jump backward over the line while bent over and grasping the toes. Lean forward slightly to allow for impetus and then jump backward over the line. Try jumping forward to original position. To be successful, the child should retain the grasp on the toes.

Introduce the stunt by having the children grasp their ankles when they are making the jumps. This is less difficult.

Heel-and-Toe Spring

Single-Leg Circle

Assume a squatting position, with both hands on the floor, left knee between the arms, and right leg extended to the side. Swing the right leg forward and under the lifted right arm, under the left leg and arm, and back to starting position. Several circles should be made in succession. Reverse position, and try with the left leg.

Single-Leg Circle

Partner and Group Stunts

Partner Rising Sun (Partner Stunt)

Partners lie facedown on the floor, with heads together and feet in opposite directions. A volleyball, a basketball, or a ball of similar size is held between their heads. Working together, they stand up and return to position while retaining control of the ball without touching the ball with the hands.

Partner Rising Sun

A slightly deflated ball works best. Some caution is necessary to prevent bumping heads if the ball is suddenly squeezed out.

Triple Roll

Practice and review the Side Roll (page 323). Three children get down on their hands and knees on a mat, with heads all in the same direction to one of the sides. The performers are about 4 feet apart.

The performers are numbered 1, 2, and 3, with the #1 child in the center. The action always starts with the center child. Number two is on the right and #3 on the left. Number one starts rolling toward and under #2, who projects himself or herself upward and over the player underneath him or her. Number two then is in the center and rolls toward #3, who projects himself or herself upward and over #2. Number three, in the center, rolls toward and under #1, who, after clearing #3, is back in the center. Thus, each performer in the center rolls toward and under the outside performer. The children should be taught that, just as soon as they roll to the outside, they must get ready immediately to go over the oncoming child from the center. There is little time for delay. The

upward projection of the body to allow the rolling child to go under is important.

Triple Roll

Quintuplet Roll

Five persons can make up a roll series. The pattern below starts the series. Numbers three and five begin by going over #2 and #4, who roll under. Number one goes over #3 as soon as he or she appears. Each then continues to go alternately over and under.

Dead Person Lift (Group Stunt)

One child lies on his or her back on the floor, with body stiff and arms at the side. Two helpers

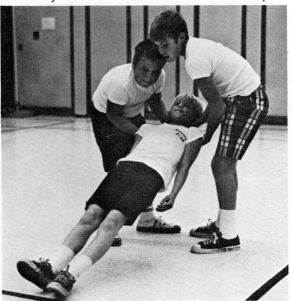

Dead Person Lift

stand, one on either side of the "dead person," with hands at the back of his or her neck and fingers touching. Working together, they lift the "dead person" in his or her rigid body position to a standing position. From this position, the "dead person" can be released and fall forward with a Dead Body Fall.

Injured Person Carry (Group Stunt)

The "injured" child is lying on the ground on his or her back. Six children, three on each side, kneel down to lift him or her up. The injured child must maintain a stiff position. The lifters work their hands, palms upward, under him or her to form a human stretcher and lift him or her up. They walk a short distance and set the injured person down carefully.

Injured Person Carry

Merry-go-round (Group Stunt)

Eight to 12 children are needed to form the Merry-go-round. Half of the children form a circle with joined hands, using a wrist grip. Each of the remaining children drapes himself or herself over

Merry-go-round

a pair of joined hands in the following fashion to become a rider. The rider stretches out his or her body, faceup, toward the center of the circle, with his or her weight on the heels. Then the rider leans back on a pair of joined hands and connects his or her hands, *behind* the circle of standing children, with the hands of the riders on either side of him or her. Thus, there are two sets of joined hands, the first circle, or Merry-go-round, and the riders.

Movement of the Merry-go-round is counterclockwise. The circle children providing the support use side steps. The riders keep pace with small steps taken with their heels.

Partner Support Stunts

The basic instructions for partner support stunts (page 349) should be reviewed.

Knee-and-Shoulder Balance

The support partner is on his or her back, knees well up and feet flat on the floor. He or she puts his or her hands out, ready to support the shoulders of the top child, who takes a position in front of the support's knees, on which he or she places his or her hands. He or she leans forward so that his or her shoulders are supported by the hands of the bottom partner and kicks up to a Knee-and-Shoulder Stand.

Spotters are needed on both sides of the pair. If the top child begins to fall, the support partner should maintain the support under his or her shoulders so the top child will light on his or her feet.

Knee-and-Shoulder Balance

Key points for the top partner are to keep the arms straight and the head up, so he or she can look directly into the support partner's eyes.

Press

The bottom partner lies on his or her back, with knees bent and feet flat on the floor. The top partner takes a straddle position over the bottom partner. Both performers then join hands with each other. The top partner sits on the joined hands, supported by the bottom partner, and rests his or her legs across the bottom partner's knees. Both performers need to keep elbows straight. Hold for a specified time.

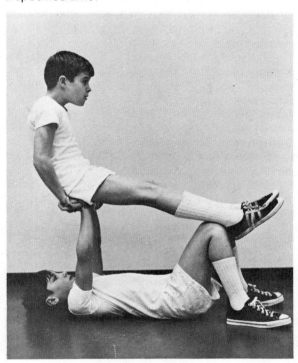

Press

All-Fours Support

The bottom performer lies on his or her back, with legs apart and knees up. His or her hands are

All-Fours Support

positioned close to his or her shoulders, with the palms up. The top performer stands on these hands and leans forward, placing his or her hands on the support performer's knees. The support raises the top performer up by lifting him or her up with his or her arms. The top performer is then in an all-fours position, with his or her feet supported by the bottom performer's extended arms and his or her hands supported on the bottom performer's knees.

Angel

The Angel is formed by the top performer standing erect on the support's knees, with his or her arms level out to the side. The bottom performer takes hold of the top's thighs and leans back to place the figure in balance. Hold for 5 seconds.

To get into this position, the top performer stands in front of the support partner. Support squats down and places his or her head between the legs of the top performer. Support raises up so that top is sitting on his or her shoulders. As the top performer proceeds to take his or her position on support's knees, support must lean well back for balance, removing his or her head from between the top performer's legs. Children need to experiment with each other to determine the best way to achieve the final position.

Angel

Side Stand

Support gets down on hands and knees to form a rigid base. Top performer stands to the side,

Side Stand

hooks his or her hands, palms up, well underneath the chest and waist. He or she leans across, steadying with his or her hands, kicking up to an inverted stand. Spotters are needed on the far side.

Variation: The top performer, instead of hooking his or her hands underneath, supports himself or herself by grasping the bottom performer's arm and leg.

PYRAMIDS

Making pyramids is a pleasurable activity for children and provides a use for many of the skills and abilities learned in the stunts and tumbling program. The emphasis in this section is on smaller pyramid groups. A larger pyramid can be formed by utilizing three of the smaller groups. Pyramids provide the opportunity for movement

exploration, since the variety of figures that can be made is endless. While the figures presented are composed of three performers, four and five performers can be combined into similar formations.

Selected Pyramids

A pyramid is composed of a center group and two side groups, usually similar to give balance and symmetry to the entire group. Pyramid building is an excellent squad activity. The class also can be divided into larger groups, each with a leader.

Each group or squad is given the task of assembling a pyramid. After a period of practice, the groups can exhibit their pyramids. The teacher can circulate from group to group, giving help as needed.

Should the teacher wish to use pyramids for demonstration purposes, whistle signals or spoken commands can use the following pattern. Children should be at attention along a line or at the edge of the mats (if used).

Signal 1: All base performers get into position and top performers move to place.

Signal 2: All top performers mount and get into position.

Signal 3: Hands are out to the sides or up for the finishing touch. This signal is used to show the pyramid in all of its glory.

Signal 4: Pyramid is disassembled, and children move to line and stand at attention.

Children should not do pyramids unless the appropriate balance skills have been mastered. Stunts using only one performer or pairs also should be considered in pyramid building.

The authors recommend that the problem-solving approach be used in having the children devise different pyramid groups. Begin with groups of threes and move to larger numbers. Smaller groups, however, provide more opportunity for contributions by individual children.

Some types of pyramids made by groups of three follow. Four and five performers can be combined into similar formations.

Pyramid

Pyramid

Pyramids

Twenty

Combative Activities

Combatives are natural for the physical education program, since children love to pit their strength and wits against their fellow students. The cultural foundations for such activities as wrestling, boxing, judo, and fencing lie deep in the social structure. Combatives, the authors feel, should begin in the fourth grade and continue through the school years.

Contests can be between individuals or groups. Most of the emphasis in the program is on individual competition, but some group activity is included.

Combatives can be used quite effectively in conjunction with the stunts and tumbling unit. Often, the tumbling activities are not too physically demanding, and combatives can provide a change of pace and more excitement for the lesson. Furthermore, a day's lesson dealing wholly with combatives is usually too exhausting for the children and interest can be lost.

The individual tug-of-war-rope activities (page 276) should be part of combative experiences. Intermingle them with the suggested combative activities described in this chapter.

INSTRUCTIONAL PROCEDURES

1. The instructions for the contest should be as explicit as necessary. The starting position should be defined, so both contestants begin from an equal, neutral position, neither having an unfair initial advantage. This concept is carried into the contest rules. What constitutes a win must be defined also, as well as the number of trials permitted.

2. When contestants of somewhat equal ability are matched, contests become more interesting because of the uncertainty of the outcome. Matching of the contestants should be done in a way that ensures that all children can win at least part of the time.

3. Sportsmanship should be stressed. Children should be encouraged to find all possible strategies and maneuvers to gain success, but only within the framework of the rules.

4. Safety factors are a greater consideration in group contests than in individual combat. Good supervision and a quick whistle are needed. Children should learn to freeze when the whistle is blown. In tug-of-war contests, no one should let go suddenly and send the other child or children sprawling backward.

5. Contests can be conducted en masse on signal by the teacher, or more flexibility can be incorporated into class activity by allowing children to start contests on their own.

6. Laterality is a factor. Contests should be done with the right side (arm or leg), the left side, and the neutral position (both arms or both legs).

7. Body position can be varied. Children can utilize standing, crouching, sitting, and lying positions for the same contest.

8. Work out a system of rotation, so each contestant has more than one evenly matched opponent.

9. Where a stick is required for the contest, a strong broomstick is a better implement than a wand. Wands should be used only when they are sturdy.

FORMATIONS FOR CONDUCTING COMBATIVE ACTIVITIES

Because of their nature, combative activities need special consideration when children are being arranged for participation. Except in the first formation, the emphasis is on some kind of rotation.

By Pairs

Each child is paired with another of comparable ability. Direction can be by signal or at will of the contestants. This formation keeps everyone active and is more informal than those that follow.

Groups of Threes

The children are divided into groups of threes. In any three, two players compete against each other and the third child acts as the referee. Opponents are changed and another child referees. One more change completes a round.

Winner-Loser Eliminations by Groups of Fours

Four evenly matched contestants are grouped together. In each activity, they are matched by pairs, with the winners competing against each other and the losers competing for third place. To save time, in the next combative activity, each individual should compete against the partner with whom he or she just finished. Winners again compete against winners and losers against losers.

Double Line by Teams

Two teams of four or six children each compete against each other. The teams are in lines facing each other. Each child pairs off with an opponent facing him or her. After competing against opponents, the children in one of the teams rotate in the following manner: The child on the left moves behind his or her team and takes a new position on the right side of his or her team's line. All other members of his or her team move down one place to the left to face a new opponent. The members of the other team maintain their positions.

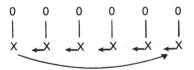

Double Circle by Teams

The team forms a large circle, with the members facing the center of the circle. The members of the other team pair off against this team on the inside, in effect forming another circle. After each bout, the contestants move to the next opponent on the left. One of the circles can remain stationary, with the other moving to the left to find new partners.

ACTIVITIES BY GRADE LEVEL

Fourth Grade

Hand Wrestle

Starting Position: Contestants place right foot against right foot and grasp right hands in a handshake grip. The left foot is firmly implanted to the rear for support.
Action: Each contestant tries to force the other by hand and arm pressure to move either foot. Any movement by either foot loses.
Variations
1. Stand left foot against left foot, and contest with the left hands.
2. Each contestant stands balanced on his or her right foot. Clasp right hands. A player loses if his or her right foot is moved or his or her back foot touches the ground. Try with the left foot and left hand. The foot off the ground can be held with the free hand.

Finger Fencing

Starting Position: Contestants stand on right foot and hold the left foot with the left hand.
Action: Hook index fingers of the right hands, and try to push opponent off balance. Change feet and hands. Any movement of the supporting foot means a loss.

Touch Knees

Starting Position: On feet, facing each other.
Action: The object is to touch one of the opponent's knees without having one's own knee touched in turn. Allow five touches to determine victor.
Variations
1. Grasp left hands, and try to touch the knees with the right hand. First one to touch wins that bout.
2. Either with hands free or with left hands grasped, try to step *lightly* on the other's toes.

Grab the Flag

Starting Position: Opponents are on their knees, facing each other on a tumbling mat. Each has a flag tucked in his or her belt near the middle of the back.
Action: Players must remain on their knees at all times. Each tries to grab the flag from the other.
Variation: This could be used as a group contest in which contestants pull flags until a champion is established.

Rooster Fight

Starting Position: Players stoop down and clasp hands behind the knees.

Action: The object is to upset the other player or make him or her lose his or her handhold.

Variation: Squat down and hold the heels with the hands. Player loses when he or she is upset or his or her hands come loose from his or her heels.

Rooster Fight (Group Contest)

Starting Position: Rooster position, as described in the previous contest. The children can be divided into two or more teams, or the group can work on an individual basis and see which child can be the last one left.

Action: Place children around the edges of an area large enough to contain the group. On signal, the children come forward and compete team against team or as individuals. A child that is pushed out of the area also is eliminated.

Palm Push

Starting Position: Contestants face each other standing 12 inches apart. They place the palms of their hands together and must keep them together during the course of the contest.

Action: By varying the strength and intensity of the push, try to force the opponent to move one foot. Hands only may be used for pushing.

Variation: A wand could be used instead of pushing the palms together.

Bulldozer

Starting Position: Opponents are on their hands and feet (not knees) facing each other, with their right shoulders touching.

Action: Contestants try to push (not bump) each other backward. Pushing across the mat or a restraining line determines a winner. Have students change shoulders and repeat.

Individual Tug-of-War-Rope Activities

Individual tug-of-war-rope activities (page 276) should be included in a lesson on combative activities.

Fifth Grade

Breakdown

Starting Position: Both opponents are in front-leaning rest position, facing each other. This is the push-up position.

Action: The object is to break down the other's position with the use of a hand by pushing or dislodging the support and still maintain one's own position.

Variation: Try the contest with each contestant having a partner holding his or her teammate's legs up in the wheelbarrow position.

Elbow Wrestle

Starting Position: Lying on the floor or sitting at a table, facing each other. Right hands are clasped, with elbows held against each other.

Action: The object is to force the other's arm down while keeping elbows together. It is a loss to raise the elbow from the original position.

Variation: Change to a position using left arms.

Indian Wrestle (Leg Wrestle)

Starting Position: Two opponents lie on their backs on the floor or a mat, with heads in opposite directions, trunks close, and near arms locked at the elbows.

Action: Three counts are given. On the first two counts, each player lifts the leg nearest the opponent to a vertical position. On the third count, he or she hooks his or her opponent's leg near the foot with his or her heel and attempts to roll him or her over backward.

Variation: Use right and left legs in turn.

Catch and Pull Tug-of-War (Group Contest)

Starting Position: Two teams face each other across a line.

Action: The object is to catch hold of and pull any opponent across the line. When a player is pulled across the line, he or she waits back of the opponent's team until time is called. The team capturing the most players wins.

Variation: Have those pulled across the line join the other team. This keeps the children in the game but sometimes makes the players careless.

Teaching Suggestions: Pulling by catching hold of clothing or hair is not permitted. The penalty is disqualification. Players may cross the line to pull only if they are securely held by a teammate or chain of players. Stop immediately if a leg split appears.

Stick Twist

Starting Position: Contestants face each other with their feet approximately 12 inches apart. They hold a wand above their heads with both hands and with their arms completely extended.

Action: On signal, they slowly bring the wand down without changing their grip position. The object is to maintain the original grip and not let the wand twist in the hands. The wand does not have to be forced down but rather moved down by mutual agreement. It can be moved completely down only if one player allows it to slip in his or her hands.

Toe Touch

Starting Position: Contestants face each other; each places both hands on his or her opponent's shoulders.

Action: On signal, each contestant tries to step on the opponent's toes without letting him or her step on his or her toes. Score may be kept by counting the number of touches made.

Variation: Groups of four or more opponents can touch each other's toes.

Crab Contest

Starting Position: Both contestants are in crab position with their seats held high.

Action: On signal, opponents try by jostling and pushing to force the other to touch his or her seat to the mat.

Variation: Beanbags can be placed on the contestants' tummies, and a winner can be declared when one knocks his or her opponent's beanbag to the floor.

Individual Tug-of-War Contests

Include also in the fifth-grade program a variety of individual tug-of-war contests. (See page 276.)

Sixth Grade

Most of the combatives for fourth- and fifth-grade students are beneficial and enjoyable at this level. A review is in order and adds a wider variety of activities to the sixth-grade program.

Shoulder Shove

Starting Position: Raise the left leg so the ankle is held by the right hand. Hold the right elbow with the left hand.

Action: Try to bump the other person off balance with the left shoulder so that one of the hands releases its position.

Teaching Suggestion: Encourage contestants to call a loss when the left hand releases the right elbow, since this is difficult for the opponents to see. Dropping the hold on the ankle is definite and visible.

Variations

1. Have each child stand on one foot and fold his or her arms. The aim is to knock the other player off balance, so the uplifted foot touches the ground.
2. Using a 6- or 8-foot circle, see which player can force the other out of the circle.
3. Use the kangaroo theme; each contestant must carry a volleyball between his or her legs at the knees. The object is to get him or her to lose control of the ball.

Shoulder Shove (Group Contest)

Starting Position: Children may compete by teams or as individuals in a group contest. Have each take a position at the edges of a defined area.

Action: Any player losing his or her handhold or touching the uplifted foot is eliminated. The team or individual lasting the longest wins.

Teaching Suggestion: Children may bump others from the front or side but not from the back on penalty of elimination.

Variation: *King of the Circle:* Draw a circle large enough to accommodate the group. Using the shoulder-shove position, the children try to shove each other out of the circle or make others lose their shoulder-shove positions. A quick whistle is needed to stop the action in case any player is down on the ground. The fallen players should be removed from the circle before the game is continued. No player may contact another from behind.

Wand Wrestle

Starting Position: Two players face each other, grasping a wand between them. Be sure that the grips are fair, and that each child has an outside hand.

Action: By twisting and applying pressure on the wand, either player tries to get the other to relinquish his or her grip.

Variations

1. *Basketball Wrestle:* Use a basketball instead of a wand. Be sure each has the same grasp advantage at the start.
2. Have both players squat down while holding on to the wand. The object is to take away the wand or upset the opponent.

Chinese Pull-up

Starting Position: Opponents sit on the floor, facing each other, with knees straight and the soles of the feet against the opponent's soles. Each bends forward until he or she can grasp a wand between them.

Action: By a straight pull only, the object is to pull the other player forward to make him or her release his or her grip.

Teaching Suggestions: To provide a straight pull, one player should have both hands on the inside and the other both hands on the outside, rather than having alternate grip positions.

Wand Lift

Starting Position: Two contestants stand facing each other and holding a 3-foot-long stick or wand in the following manner. Each holds the end of the stick with the right hand, using an underhand grip. Each then places his or her left hand with an overhand grip next to and touching the opponent's right-hand grip. The elbows are bent at approximately a right angle.

Action: This is meant to be a test of pure strength. The object is to press down with the left hand and lift with the right to bring the stick up to a vertical position. The body can be braced for action, but body motion should be minimal.

Variation: Try with a left-hand lift.

Sitting Elbow Wrestle

Starting Position: Partners sit on a mat, back to back, with elbows locked. Feet are spread wide.
Action: Each pulls to his or her left in an attempt to tip the opponent over.
Variations
1. Reverse direction.
2. Position the legs so that the knees are bent and the soles of the feet are flat on the mat.

Power Pull

Starting Position: One contestant stands with fingers touching in front of, and close to, his or her chest. The other person stands facing him or her and grasps his or her wrists.
Action: On signal, the contestant holding the wrists attempts to pull the opponent's fingers apart. A straight pull (no jerking) is the action.

Individual Tug-of-War Contests

Individual tug-of-war contests also should be utilized in the sixth-grade program. (See page 276.)

Rope Tug-of-War

Starting Position: Two equal teams face each other on opposite ends of a rope. A piece of tape marks the center of the rope. Two parallel lines are drawn about 10 feet apart. At the start, the center marker is midway between the lines.
Action: Each team tries to pull the center marker over its near line.
Teaching Suggestions: The rope should be long enough to accommodate the children without crowding. It should be at least three-quarters of an inch in diameter. Never permit a child to wrap the rope around his or her hands, arms, or body in any manner.
Variation: Changes in the contest can be made by having the children in different positions for pulling. The following positions are suggested.
1. Pulling with the rope overhead. The teams have their backs toward each other.
2. Pulling with one hand on the ground.
3. Pulling from a seated position, with feet braced on the floor.

Four-Team Tug-of-War

Starting Position: Four teams line up as in the diagram. A special rope is needed—the size and extent depend upon the number of children. A cone, an Indian club, or a beanbag is behind each team at an equal distance to provide the winning effort.

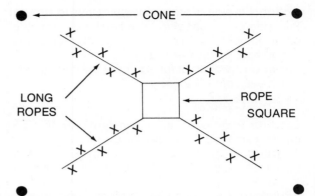

Action: Each team pulls on signal in the direction of its cone. A team wins when the player on the end of the rope can knock over the cone without losing his or her contact with the rope.
Variation: This can be a three-team contest, with the center figure a triangle.
Teaching Suggestion: An automobile tire can be substituted for the center rope square. It is necessary only to tie four tug-of-war ropes to the tire to provide the basis for the contest.

Circle-Rope Tug-of-War

Starting Position: A circular rope is needed. This can be formed by taking a rope 1 inch or more in diameter and 60 to 65 feet in length and making it into a circular rope. A line is needed, and the players on each team are placed as in the diagram.

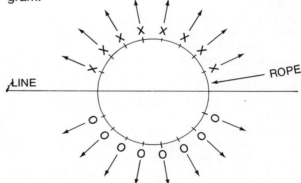

Action: The object is to pull all members of the opposing team completely across the line. Players must pull and are not permitted on the inside of the rope.
Teaching Suggestion: Outside players of each team should pull to the side to help maintain the circle. Otherwise, the two sides come together and the contest becomes nothing but a straight-rope pull.

Twenty-one

Game-Type Activities

Physical educators, including the authors of this text, are taking a long, hard look at how the games program fits into the overall elementary school physical education program. Some of the traditional elements incorporated into the games program are being reevaluated in terms of their contributions to child development. If the games program can make significant contributions to the development of children, then games activities should be selected and guided in a way that allows these values to emerge. The following discussion presents a rationale for deciding what can be derived from a well-conducted program of games.

The major objective of the games program is to provide experiences by which children can learn to participate successfully in a game situation (this means playing with others in a socially sound manner without bickering, quarreling, or fighting). Further, it means that the children observe and appreciate fair play and sportsmanship. Educationally sound subobjectives can be listed, too.

1. To provide vigorous large-muscle activity with developmental potential.
2. To serve as a laboratory for selected skills.
3. To develop the ability to run, maneuver, dodge, start, stop, and, in general, manage the body under control when sharing general space with others.
4. To learn to manage and control oneself under stress.
5. To improve listening skills.
6. To be able to understand and follow rules and directions.
7. To foster alertness in reacting strategically to the game situation.

8. To understand oneself and others better.
9. To provide outlets for dramatization and imagination.

It is apparent that children must be actively engaged as participants in a game to derive any of these values. Games in which one or two children are active while the remainder stand around and watch cannot make contributions to all of the children in terms of the target goals. Games dominated by a few of the more skilled students do little for those who need help the most.

In the selection of the games suggested for each grade level, the potential for activity was the dominant consideration. Generally excluded were such old traditional favorites as Two-Deep, Three-Deep, Cat and Rat, Duck-Duck-Goose, and Slap Jack. These games feature a runner and a chaser, with the balance of the children providing a stationary background for the game. Rotation does involve many of the children, but there usually are still some who can justifiably say, "Gee! I didn't even get a chance to run."

Certain of the games selected may seem to be of marginal value since only some of the children are active at any given time. This is recognized, but teachers can handle such games so as to maximize the benefits for all participants.

Educational values in the games program can be enhanced by providing the opportunity for children to create their own games. Children need help inventing games, since they must have some kind of a rough structure on which to build. For example, the teacher could indicate what equipment is to be used, some space limitations, and the skills to be included. The game could be indi-

377

vidual, partner, or group oriented. Further discussion of this topic is included later in this chapter.

Each game should be analyzed from the standpoint of whether or not it requires a skill that the children should practice before playing the game. When practice is indicated, the teacher selects the appropriate drills and brings the children to the point of skill necessary to play the game pleasurably. Drills and the acquisition of necessary skills become more meaningful when the children see their purposes.

The games for kindergarten through second grade do not require a high degree of skill, and the less skilled children can participate successfully without peer pressures.

Manipulative skills become more important factors in game success with third graders and older children. Ball skills, in particular, are challenged through the medium of game activity. Movement skills with emphasis on agility become important. Starting and stopping, escape and capture, changing direction, and reacting swiftly are competencies important in game participation. Failure as a competitor can be identified with the lack of good execution in one or more of these skills.

Games for the intermediate grades are included in two sections in this book. This chapter presents tag-type and general games that do not fall under any of the sports-type activities. The lead-up activities to basketball, football, hockey, volleyball, soccer, softball, and track are found with the discussions of each sport.

The intermediate grades should make use of all the primary games that are suitable or can be adapted to the intermediate program. Children in the intermediate grades enjoy and play many of the games that were introduced earlier, particularly in the third grade.

INTRODUCING VARIATIONS

The introduction of variations is an important instructional device which the games leader can use effectively. One can see the children's faces light up when the instructor says, "Let's try playing the game *this* way," and introduces an interesting variation. Variations can revive interest when it lags, and they can help the teacher to extract more mileage from an activity.

The following are effective devices that can be used to vary activities.

1. Change the distance to be run by shortening or lengthening it. For example, in Circle Chase, instead of having the runners go once around, double the distance.
2. Change the method of locomotion. Use hopping, walking, skipping, or galloping instead of running.
3. Play the game with partners. Have two children join inside hands and act as a single person.
4. Change the method of tagging. Limit where on the body a player may be tagged or with which hand he or she may be tagged.
5. Change the formation. For example, in Circle Soccer, make a square.
6. Vary the boundaries. Make the formation larger or smaller.
7. Include penalties. A person who is caught a number of times (say, three) has to undergo a penalty.
8. Increase the number of key players, taggers, or runners. This gets the game moving a little faster.
9. In tag or chase games, call out, "Reverse," to signal the chaser to become the runner and the runner to become the chaser.
10. Change the method or means of scoring.
11. Make goals larger or smaller.

Over the years the authors and other teachers have come up with ideas on how to vary and change many of the traditional games. Pertinent and worthwhile suggestions of this nature are presented with the descriptions of the games.

SAFETY SUGGESTIONS FOR GAMES

Because of the competitive spirit aroused, games have some built-in hazards that must be anticipated and for which safety considerations need to be established.

Slipping and Falling

Emphasis should be placed on running properly and turning and changing direction properly. The playing area should be kept free of dangerous objects. The teacher should make certain that all players are aware of hazardous conditions of the playing area, such as slickness, holes, or loose pebbles.

Collisions and Tripping

Stress the need for all players to be alert. Goal games, in which the children are divided and begin to run through each other from opposite goals, are collision-prone. When there is more than one chaser or catcher, the danger is multiplied. The group should be scattered to avoid collisions. If players are running in opposite directions, they should pass each other to the right. Children should be taught to tag by touching, not shoving, and the teacher should insist that tagging be done properly.

Hitting Each Other with Wands, Beanbags, or Balls

Proper use of supplies should be taught.

Playing Dodgeball Games Safely

Dodgeball games for children provide much enjoyment and competition. Some controls are necessary, however. Glasses should be removed whenever possible. A soft, slightly deflated volleyball or a rubber playground ball should be used. Avoid a basketball or a heavy ball that can hurt players. Hits should be made below the waist or at least below the shoulders. A penalty should be imposed on any throw that hits a player on the head. Restraining lines, if carefully marked and observed, prevent the thrower from getting too close to the targets. Good supervision prevents vicious throwing and ganging up on certain individuals. A better game results when teams are balanced and one or two players do not monopolize the throwing.

Maintaining Control

Participants should be coached to stop immediately when the whistle blows. A child may be down, or some other safety hazard may need attention. The whistle should be used for stopping the action. Start the action with a verbal command.

Spatial Factors

Sufficient room for the games should be established. Colliding with fences and walls during running and chasing games is an ever-present danger. Establish boundaries far enough from those and other obstacles to preserve safety. When separate groups of children are playing games, keep them far enough apart so that they do not overrun each other.

MAINTAINING COMPETITIVE BALANCE IN GAMES

Balance between offense and defense or success and failure in games is important. In the tag and capture games, there should be good opportunity to remain safe and still provide a strong challenge of being caught. This means the teacher should look carefully at the basic rules concerning boundaries and other restraints. The distance to be run to a base or between goal lines can be lengthened or shortened as indicated.

Balance in games involving teams is important. The sides should be reasonably equal, so one side does not annihilate the other. When there is no chance of winning, children can hardly be expected to give it a good try. Rotate positions so that one or two very skilled children do not dominate the game. On the other hand, take measures to see the team does not lose continually because of the presence of a low-skilled or inept child; this avoids creating resentment against that child.

INSTRUCTIONAL PROCEDURES FOR CONDUCTING GAMES

1. The principal ingredient of successful games leadership is a vigorous, snappy approach. A hustling attitude combined with a spirit of enthusiasm do much toward producing the desired results.
2. Know the game well before attempting to teach it. This means identifying the safety hazards, anticipating the difficulties, and adapting the game to the group and the situation.
3. Most games can be modified to use the equipment and supplies available. Some games, however, are best played with the equipment and supplies designed for them.
4. Complete all preparations before starting to introduce the game. Establish lines and boundaries and have supplies ready for distribution.
5. Put the group in formation with all possible speed. Be careful of too-formal methods of organization. Use a modified close formation for explanations and then allow the children to fall back to game positions to start the activity.
6. Every unit or group should have a leader or someone in charge. Use these people to secure the equipment needed for the game.
7. Where mingling of teams can cause confusion, identify a team with pinnies, crepe armbands, colored shoulder loops, or similar devices.
8. For maximum participation, organize the class into a number of groups as determined by the character of the activity. Many games play best with 10 to 15 players.
9. When explaining the game, talk briefly and to the point. Tell what is to be done and what is to be avoided. Demonstrate or diagram as needed. Students should be comfortable during explanations.
10. To clear up hazy points, ask for questions and then reply so that all can hear. If desirable, repeat the question before supplying the answer.
11. Do not attempt to cover all the possible rule infractions prior to participation. Cover enough to get the game underway, and fill in with additional rules as needed. Minor faults can be corrected during the game.
12. Sometimes, it is well to have a trial period, so children can understand the game before playing for real. Children resent losing a point or getting caught when they feel this is due to their lack of understanding of the game.
13. Enforce the rules impartially once they have been established. Discuss the reasons for the rules with the children.

14. Where lines and limits are important, establish them definitely, so there is no question when a child is out-of-bounds or beyond the limits. Make clear and enforce the penalty for an infraction.

15. Suggestions for better performance and coaching hints should be a part of the instructional procedures in games. "Lean forward a little for a faster start" and "give with your knees when you want to stop" are examples of appropriate comments by the teacher.

16. Play with the class occasionally. They like to have the teacher play with them. Do not dominate the play, however.

17. Watch the game carefully for a decrease of interest. Kill or change the game before it dies a natural death. Sometimes, the teacher can stop a game even at the height of interest, and children then look forward to the activity at a later time.

18. Stress social learning in game experiences. Allow children to call infractions or hits on themselves. Insist on respect for decisions by officials, particularly in judgment calls.

19. Watch for deliberate cheating and consistent disregard for the rules. These are red flags that must be handled. Children expect the teacher to enforce fairness in play, and the teacher's doing otherwise can cause them to lose respect for the teacher.

20. Allied to the previous point is the action of a child so obsessed with winning or being first that he or she cannot stand to lose and so will do anything to win. He or she blames himself or herself and castigates his or her teammates for the catastrophe of losing. This can be a strong, personal feeling, and the roots may be deep. Counseling in private may suggest methods by which the child can be helped.

21. When arguments or disputes arise during a game, taking sides puts the teacher in a situation in which he or she cannot win. It is best to try to get the children to resolve their own differences, even though this is difficult. Any decision the teacher makes should be based on fact and not hearsay or guessing.

22. Be careful of the situation in which some child is made the butt of jokes. The child's psychological hurt may be deep and permanent. The possibility of physical hurt must not be ruled out. The slow, heavy child who cannot move readily is at a disadvantage in dodgeball games and other activities demanding mobility.

23. Avoid overemphasis on competition. Centering too much attention on winning makes the skilled resent being on the same team with the less skilled.

24. Arrange for full participation. Rotate with a planned system.

25. In number-calling games, in which children compete against each other in some specified task, all teams can be given points for successful performance so that any disqualification results in loss of the possible place points, even for last place.

26. Help and encourage the losing side, but avoid biased officiating to aid the losing side. Children should be good losers but not easy losers.

27. Be sure everyone has had a chance to participate or take a turn. Ask children to raise their hands or use some other device to identify those who have not had a turn.

28. Use with caution games that eliminate children. A good rule is that a child should lay out for one or two turns and then reenter the game quickly. Another device is to play only until a few of the children have been eliminated and then declare the remainder the winners. Elimination should not be carried down to the bitter end.

CREATIVE GAMES

As a change of pace from being required to conform to established rules and play structured games, children can be given the opportunity to create games; this challenges their inventiveness and originality. Few children can devise games without some assistance, so the problem for the teacher is to provide a fundamental basis upon which the children can build their own games. There are several approaches through which this can be accomplished.

1. Make the game relevant to a skill just practiced. Specify that the children are to use the equipment with which they have just been practicing and that they are to create an original game with only this equipment. The guidelines for the game should reflect and be built upon the progressions just experienced. The skills should have been reasonably well acquired, so the game becomes a laboratory for the skills and not just a means of competition.

2. A second approach is to set certain limitations in the form of specified pieces of equipment to be used, space limitations to be observed, movements or skills to be included, and whether the game is to be oriented toward individual, partner, or small-group play. For example, the directions could include the following: (1) equipment—use two hoops, two balls, and an Indian club; (2) space—step off or outline a space about 25 by 25 feet; (3) skills—include bouncing and striking; and

(4) organize one against one or two against two.

3. A third means uses already named or established games. The children could insert variations or completely restructure the games. The focus also could be on taking the elements of two games and combining them into one original, creative game.

It is important to accept the fact that original and creative games cannot replace traditional games. Both traditional and creative games should be integral parts of the games program, and they should be pointed toward the general objective of successful participation in games play. At times and with respect to certain skills, original games can better meet the physical needs of the children and satisfy their desire to test their skills against others.

Although the goal of developing skills in game playing should be stressed, some concomitant educational values can be derived, too. The structuring of the game is generally an experience shared with others, and it should include a free flow of original and creative ideas, with evaluation and selection of the game elements as parts of the problem-solving process.

Most of the stress should be on original games as natural outgrowths of skill development experiences. Oftentimes, teachers are puzzled about how a skill can be enhanced by putting it into a related game situation. The game grows out of the skills just experienced; this is different than in the lead-up-game approach, since the necessary skills for the lead-up game are chosen and practiced so that the lead-up game can have successful participation. In a sense, the children select their lead-up games to suit their skill levels when they devise original games.

THE GAMES PROGRAM FOR KINDERGARTEN

The games program for the kindergarten level features mostly individual and creative play. Little emphasis is centered on team play or on games that demand a scoring system. The games are simple, easily taught, and not demanding in special skills. Beanbags are used in some of the activities, but ball games are not particularly appropriate for this level.

Dramatic elements are present in many of the games, and others help establish number concepts and symbol recognition. Games based on stories or poems are popular with children at this level.

In addition to the games presented in this section, the teacher should make use of first-grade games and also those presented in chapter fourteen.

Kindergarten Games

Colors
Fireman
Kneeling Tag
Magic Fountain
Marching Ponies
Mother Goose
Mother, May I?
Popcorn
The Scarecrow and the Crows
Statues
Tommy Tucker's Land

The Games

Colors

Playing Area: Playground, gymnasium, classroom.
Players: Entire class.
Supplies: Colored paper or colored construction paper cut into circles, squares, or triangles for markers.
Skills: Perceptual concepts, running.

Five or six different colors of markers should be used, with a number of children having the same color. The children are seated in a circle. Each places his or her marker in front of him or her.

The teacher calls out one of the colors, upon which all having that color run counterclockwise around the circle and back to place. The first one seated upright and motionless is declared the winner. Different kinds of locomotor movements can be specified, such as skipping, galloping, walking, et cetera.

After a period of play, leave the markers on the floor and have the children move one place to the left.

Variations
1. Use shapes, instead of colors. Use a circle, triangle, square, rectangle, star, diamond.
2. Use numbers.

Note: Many other articles or categories, such as animals, birds, or fishes, can be used. The game has value in teaching elements of identification and recognition.

Fireman

Playing Area: Playground, gymnasium, classroom.
Players: Entire class.
Supplies: None.
Skill: Running.

A fire chief is appointed. He or she runs around the outside of a circle of children and taps a number of them on the back, saying, "Fireman," each time. After making the round of the circle, the chief goes to the center. When he or she says, "Fire," the "firemen" run counterclockwise around the circle and back to place. The one who returns first and is able to stand in place motionless is declared the winner and the new chief.

The chief can use other words in an attempt to fool the firemen, but they run only on the word "fire." This merely provides a fun aspect, since there is no penalty for a false start. To add to the gaiety, the circle children can sound the siren as the firemen run.

Kneeling Tag

Playing Area: Playground, gymnasium.
Players: Entire class.
Supplies: None.
Skills: Running, right and left discrimination.

Two or more children are it. They attempt to tag the other children, who can be safe by kneeling on one knee. The child tagged changes places with it.

The teacher should specify which knee is to be used. This should be changed partway through the game. The game can be played progressively, with the children tagged joining the taggers, but it cannot be played until all children are tagged because of its safe position feature. Play until about half the children are tagged and then reorganize.

Children need to be encouraged to dare a little, since they cannot be caught if they kneel all the time. Players kneeling on the wrong knee are not safe.

Variation: Color concepts can be stressed by selecting a color for safety. This is more appropriate for a gymnasium, where lines of different colors are already on the floor, but construction paper in different colors can be taped to the floor as safe bases. Markers of this type are not likely to survive long, however.

Magic Fountain

Playing Area: Playground, gymnasium, classroom.
Players: Entire class.
Supplies: Pictures of animals, a box, and a stool or table.
Skill: Imagery.

A supply of animal pictures (10-15) is placed in a box on a stool or table to one side. This is the magic fountain. The children are seated in a circle on the floor. Four or five children are selected by the teacher; one of them is designated to draw out a picture from the magic fountain. He or she shows the picture to the rest of his or her group, keeps it hidden from the remainder of the children in the circle, but gives it to the teacher.

As soon as all the chosen children have seen the picture, they return to the circle area and imitate the animal they saw in the picture. When the circle players guess the animals, the entire class then goes through appropriate, imitative movements of the animal or the object. The entire group should develop their movements thoroughly;

otherwise, the game becomes one with action for a few and sitting for the rest.

Marching Ponies

Playing Area: Playground, gymnasium, classroom.
Players: Entire class.
Supplies: None.
Skills: Marching, running.

One child is the ringmaster and crouches in the center of a circle of ponies formed by the other children. Two goal lines on opposite sides of the circle are established as safe areas. The ponies march around the circle in step, counting consecutively as they step. At a predetermined number (which has been whispered to the ringmaster by the teacher), the ringmaster jumps from his or her crouched position and attempts to tag the others before they can reach the safety lines. Anyone tagged must join the ringmaster in the center and help him or her catch the other children the next time.

The game should be reorganized after six to eight children have been caught. Those left in the circle are declared the winners.

Variations

1. A safe area for the ponies can be designated.
2. Add other characterizations, such as lumbering elephants, jumping kangaroos, et cetera. A child could be allowed to be the ringmaster when he or she comes up with a unique movement.

Mother Goose

Playing Area: Gymnasium, classroom, playground.
Players: 8 to 10.
Supplies: None, but some props can be used.
Skill: Imagery.

A leader is selected who is called Mother Goose if a girl and Papa Goose if a boy. The children are seated in a circle, with the leader in the center. The leader says, "Try to guess who I am." He or she acts out a nursery rhyme, and the children try to guess who he or she is. He or she is replaced by the one who guesses correctly. Children should raise hands to be recognized.

After a correct guess is made, all children arise and act out the character or rhyme that has been identified.

Mother, May I?

Playing Area: Playground, gymnasium.
Players: 8 to 10.
Supplies: None.
Skills: Fundamental locomotor movements.

Starting and finishing lines are established about 40 feet apart. In a gymnasium, the game can proceed sideways across the floor. One child is it and stands between the two lines. The remainder of the children stand on the starting line. The object of the game is to reach the finish line first.

It tells one of the players how many steps he or she can take and what kind. The player must ask, "Mother, may I?" and await the answer before he or she moves. If he or she fails to ask the question, he or she goes back to the starting line. Even when the question is asked, it may say "no."

The steps should be varied to provide different kinds of movements. Steps such as baby steps, scissors steps, giant steps, hopping steps, bunny steps (jumps), and others are appropriate for the game. The first to the finish line is it for the next game.

If a boy is in the center, the call is "Daddy, may I?"

Popcorn

Playing Area: Playground, gymnasium, classroom.
Players: Entire class, divided into two groups.
Supplies: None.
Skills: Curling, stretching, jumping.

The children should be given a short preliminary explanation of how popcorn pops in response to the heat applied. Half the children are designated as popcorn and crouch down in the center of the circle formed by the rest of the children. The circle children represent the heat. One of them should be designated the leader; the leader's actions serve as a guide to the other children. The circle children, who also are crouched down, gradually rise to a standing position, extend their arms overhead, and shake them vigorously to indicate high heat. In the meantime, the popcorn in the center begins to pop. This should begin at a slow pace and increase in speed and height as the heat is applied. In the final stages, the children are popping up rapidly.

Change groups, and repeat.

The Scarecrow and the Crows

Playing Area: Playground, gymnasium, classroom.
Players: Entire class.
Supplies: None.
Skills: Dodging, running.

The children form a large circle to represent the garden, which the scarecrow is guarding. Six to eight crows scatter on the outside of the circle. The scarecrow assumes a characteristic pose inside the circle. The circle children raise their joined hands and let the crows run through into the garden, where they pretend to eat. The scarecrow tries to tag one of the crows, and the circle children help the crows by raising their joined hands, allowing them to leave the circle but trying to hinder the scarecrow. If the scarecrow runs out of the circle,

all the crows immediately run into the garden and start to nibble at the vegetables, while the circle children hinder the scarecrow's reentry.

When the scarecrow has caught one or two crows (the teacher can decide), a new group of children is selected to be scarecrow and crows. If after a reasonable period of time the scarecrow has failed to catch any crows, a change should be made.

Statues

Playing Area: Playground, gymnasium.
Players: Entire class, organized by pairs.
Supplies: None.
Skills: Body management, applying force, balance.

Children by pairs are scattered around the area. One child is the swinger and the other the statue. The teacher voices a directive such as "pretty," "funny," "happy," "angry," or "ugly." The swinger takes the statue by one or two hands, swings it around in a small circle two or three times (specify), and releases it. The statue takes a pose in keeping with the directive, and the swinger sits down on the floor.

The teacher or a committee of children can determine which children are the best statues. The statue must hold the position without moving or be disqualified.

After the winners have been announced, the partners reverse positions. Children should be cautioned that the purpose of the swinging is to position the statues, but it must be controlled.
Variation: In the original game, the swinging is done until a directive is called. The swinger immediately releases the statue, who takes the pose as called. This gives very little time for the statue to react, and better and more creative statues are made if the directive is given earlier.

Tommy Tucker's Land

Playing Area: Playground, gymnasium, classroom.
Players: 8 to 10.
Supplies: About 10 beanbags for each game.
Skills: Dodging, running.

One child is Tommy Tucker and stands in the center of a 15-foot square, within which the beanbags are scattered. Tommy is guarding his land and the treasure. The other children chant:

I'm on Tommy Tucker's land,
Picking up gold and silver.

The children attempt to pick up as much of the treasure as they can while avoiding being tagged by Tommy. Any child who is tagged must bring back his or her treasure and retire from the game. The game is over when there is only one child left or all the beanbags have been successfully filched. The teacher may wish to call a halt to the game earlier if it reaches a stalemate. In this case, the child with the most treasure becomes the new Tommy.

Variation: This game can be played with a restraining line, but there must be boundaries that limit movement.

THE GAMES PROGRAM FOR THE FIRST GRADE

The games for the first grade can be divided into two categories: running and tag games and ball games. Few team activities are included, since at this level children are quite individualistic and team play is beyond their capacities. The ball games should require only the simple skills of throwing and catching.

First-Grade Games

Review Kindergarten Games
Animal Tag
Back to Back
Charlie over the Water
Circus Master
Midnight
Old Man (Old Lady)
One, Two, Button My Shoe
Squirrel in the Trees
Tag Games—Simple
Where's My Partner?
Ball Passing
Ball Toss
Stop Ball
Teacher Ball (Leader Ball)

The Games

Animal Tag

Playing Area: Playground, gymnasium. Two parallel lines are drawn about 40 feet apart.
Players: Entire class.
Supplies: None.
Skills: Imagery, running, dodging.

The children are divided into two groups, each of which takes position on one of the lines. The children of group 1 get together with their leader and decide what animal they wish to imitate. Having selected the animal, they move over to within 5 feet or so of the other line. There they imitate the animal, and group 2 tries to guess the animal correctly. If they guess correctly, they chase group 1 back to its line, trying to tag as many as possible. Those caught must go over to the other team.

Group 2 then selects an animal, and the roles are reversed. However, if the guessing team cannot guess the animal, the performing team gets another try.

To avoid confusion, have the children raise hands to take turns naming the animal. Otherwise, there will be many false chases.

If the children have trouble guessing, then have the leader of the performing team give the initial of the animal.

Back to Back

Playing Area: Playground, gymnasium, classroom.
Players: Entire class.
Supplies: None.
Skills: Fundamental locomotor movements.

The number of children should be uneven. If the number is even, the teacher can play. On signal, each child stands back to back with another child. One child will be without a partner. This child can clap his or her hands for the next signal, and all children change partners with the extra player seeking a partner.

Variation: Considerably more activity can be secured by putting in an extra command. After the children are in partner formation back to back, the teacher can say, "Everybody—run!" (or skip, hop, jump, slide, et cetera). Other commands can be given, such as "Walk like an elephant." The children move around the room in the prescribed manner. When the whistle is blown, they immediately find a partner and stand back to back.

Charlie over the Water

Playing Area: Playground, gymnasium, classroom.
Players: 15 to 20.
Supplies: None.
Skills: Skipping, body management.

The children are in circle formation, with hands joined. One or more extra children are in the center, depending on the number of children in the circle. The one in the center is Charlie. The circle children skip around the circle to the following chant:

Charlie over the water, Charlie over the sea,
Charlie caught a bluebird, but can't catch *me!*

On the word *me,* all circle children drop hands, stoop, and touch the ground with both hands. The center players try to tag the circle players before they stoop. Any player tagged changes places with the center player. The game then continues.

Children should be held to retaining their balance while stooping. If they fall, they can be tagged.

The following chant can be used if a girl is in the center: "Sally over the river, Sally over the sea," et cetera.

Other positions can be stipulated instead of stooping. Balancing on one foot, crab position, push-up position, and others can be used.

Circus Master

Playing Area: Playground, gymnasium, classroom.
Players: 10 to 40.

Supplies: None.
Skills: Imagery, fundamental locomotor movements.

One child, the circus master, is in the center of the circle formed by the other children. He or she stands in the center, pretends to have a whip, and gets ready to have the animals perform. He or she gives a direction like the following, "We are going to walk as elephants do, like this!" He or she then demonstrates in a small circle how he or she wishes the children to perform. He or she commands, "Elephants ready—walk." The children imitate an elephant walking around the large circle, while the circus master performs in a small circle in the center. When ready, the circus master calls, "Halt." Then he or she takes a place in the circle, and another child comes forward to the center.

A prearranged order for circus masters can be established; this is excellent for young children, since they can be prepared with a particular animal imitation. However, interest would die long before all the children could be in the center. Make arrangements for other children to be in the center when the game is played at a later date.

Midnight

Playing Area: Playground.
Players: 6 to 15.
Supplies: None.
Skills: Running, dodging.

A safety line is established about 40 feet from a den in which one player is standing as the fox. The others stand behind the safety line and move forward slowly, asking, "Please, Mr. Fox, what time is it?" The fox answers in various fashions, such as "bedtime," "pretty late," "three-thirty," and so on. He or she continues to draw the players toward him or her. At some point, the fox answers the question with "midnight," and chases the others back to the safety line. Any player caught joins the fox in the den and helps catch others. However, no player in the den can leave until the fox calls out, "Midnight."

Old Man (Old Lady)

Playing Area: Playground, gymnasium, classroom.
Players: Entire class.
Supplies: None.
Skills: Fundamental locomotor movements.

A line is drawn through the middle of the area. Any convenient line can be used. Half the children are on one side and half on the other. The children hold hands with a partner across the center line. There must be an odd person, the teacher or another child. The teacher gives a signal for the children to move as directed on their side of the line. They can be directed to run, hop, skip, et cetera. At a whistle, the children run to the center line, and each reaches across to join hands with a child from the opposite group. The one left out is the old man (if a boy) or the old lady (if a girl). Children may reach over but not cross the line. The odd person should alternate sides, so the old man can be on the other side at times.

The game also can be done to music, with the players rushing to the center line to find partners when the rhythm stops.

One, Two, Button My Shoe

Playing Area: Playground, gymnasium. Two parallel lines are drawn about 50 feet apart.
Players: Entire class.
Supplies: None.
Skill: Running.

One child is the leader and stands to one side. The remainder of the children are behind one of the lines. The leader says, "Ready." The following dialogue takes place between the leader and the children.

Children	Leader's Response
One, two	Button my shoe.
Three, four	Close the door.
Five, six	Pick up sticks.
Seven, eight	Run or you'll be *late!*

The children carry on the above conversation with the leader and are toeing the line, ready to run. When the word *"late"* is given by the leader, the children run to the other line and return. The first child across the original line is the winner and becomes the new leader.

The leader can give the last response in any timing he or she wishes by pausing or dragging out the words. No child is to leave before the *"late."*

Squirrel in the Trees

Playing Area: Playground, gymnasium.
Players: 15 to 35.
Supplies: None.
Skills: Fundamental locomotor movements.

A tree is formed by two players facing each other with hands held or on each other's shoulders. A squirrel is in the center of each tree, and one or two extra squirrels are outside. A signal to change is given. All squirrels move out of their trees to another, and the extra players try to find trees. Only one squirrel is allowed in a tree.

As a system of rotation, when each squirrel moves into a tree, he or she changes places with one of the two players forming the tree. The system of rotation is important, since it ensures that all children automatically and eventually rotate into being active players.

Tag Games—Simple

Playing Area: Playground with established boundaries, gymnasium.
Players: Any number.
Supplies: None.

Skills: Fundamental locomotor movements, dodging.

Tag is played in many different ways. Children are scattered about the area. One child is it and chases others to tag one of them. When he or she does, he or she says, "You're it." The new it chases other children. Different tag games are listed.

1. Being safe through touching a specified object or color: touching wood, iron, the floor, or a specified color can make a runner safe.
2. Seeking safety by a particular action or pose: some actions used to become safe are these.
   Stoop—touch both hands to the ground.
   Stork—stand on one foot (the other cannot touch).
   Turtle—be on one's back, feet pointed toward the ceiling.
   Hindoo—make an obeisance with forehead to the ground.
   Nose and toe—nose must be touched by the toe.
   Back to back—stand back to back with any other child.
   Skunk—reach an arm under one knee and hold onto the nose.
3. *Locomotor Tag:* It specifies how the children shall move. It also must use the same kind of movement, that is, skip, hop, jump, et cetera.
4. *Frozen Tag:* Two children are it. The rest are scattered over the area. When caught they are "frozen" and must keep both feet in place. Any free player can tag a "frozen" player and release him or her. The object of the taggers is to freeze all the players.

Where's My Partner?

Playing Area: Playground, gymnasium, classroom.
Players: Entire class.
Supplies: None.
Skills: Fundamental locomotor movements.

Children are arranged in a double circle by couples, with partners facing. The inside circle has one more player than the outside. When the signal is given, the circles skip to the right. This means they are skipping in opposite directions. When the command "halt" is given, the circles face each other to find partners. The player left without a partner is in the "mush pot."

Children can gallop, walk, run, or hop instead of skipping. Reverse circles.
Variation: The game also can be played with music. When the music stops, the players seek partners.

Ball Passing

Playing Area: Playground, gymnasium, classroom.

Players: Entire class, divided into two or more circles.
Supplies: Five or six different kinds of balls for each circle.
Skill: Object handling.

The basis of this game is the child's love of handling objects. Not over 15 children should be in any one circle. Two or more squads combine to form a circle. The children need not be in any particular order.

The teacher starts a ball around the circle; the ball is passed from player to player in the same direction. The teacher introduces more balls until five or six are moving around in the circle at the same time in the same direction. If a child drops a ball, he or she must retrieve it and a point is scored against his or her team. After a period of time, a whistle is blown, and the points against each team are totaled. The team with the lowest score wins.

Beanbags, large blocks, or softballs can be substituted for balls.

Ball Toss

Playing Area: Playground, gymnasium, classroom.
Players: Groups of six to eight.
Supplies: A ball or a beanbag for each group.
Skills: Throwing, catching.

The children form a circle with one child in the center. The center player throws the ball to each child in turn around the circle. The ball is returned to the center player each time. The object of the game is to make good throws and catches completely around the circle. After each child has had a turn in the center, the teacher can ask each circle to total the number of center players that were able to complete their throws without any errors.

Good form should be stressed.

Stop Ball

Playing Area: Playground, gymnasium.
Players: About half the class.
Supplies: Ball.
Skills: Tossing and catching.

One child, with hands over eyes, stands in the center of the circle of children. A ball is passed clockwise or counterclockwise from child to child around the circle. Failure to catch or making a bad toss penalizes the child by making him or her step back one long step. He or she stays out of the game for two turns.

At a time of his or her own selection, the center player calls, "Stop." The player caught with the ball steps back and stays out for two turns. The center player should take three or four turns and then be changed.

Teacher Ball (Leader Ball)

Playing Area: Playground, gymnasium.

Players: Five to eight.
Supplies: Volleyball or rubber playground ball.
Skills: Throwing and catching.

One child is the teacher or leader and stands about 10 feet in front of the others, who are lined up facing him or her. The object of the game is to move up to the teacher's spot by not making any bad throws or missing any catches.

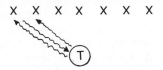

The teacher throws to each child in turn, beginning with the child on his or her left, who must catch and return the ball. Any child making a throwing or catching error goes to the foot of the line, on the teacher's right. Those in the line move up, filling the vacated space.

If the teacher makes a mistake, he or she goes to the foot of the line, and the child at the head of the line becomes the new teacher.

The teacher scores a point for himself or herself when he or she remains in position for three rounds (three throws to each child). He or she takes a position at the foot of the line, and another child becomes the teacher.

This game should be used only after the children have practiced throwing and catching skills. It can be worked in as a part of the skill-teaching program.

Variation: Provide specific methods of throwing and catching, such as "catch with the right hand only" or "catch with one hand and don't let the ball touch your body."

THE GAMES PROGRAM FOR THE SECOND GRADE

The games program for the second grade is quite similar to that for the first grade. The second-grade teacher should make use of all games presented in the first grade. The simple ball games of the first grade have particularly good values and should be included as a regular part of the second-grade program.

Second-Grade Games

Review First-Grade Games
Automobiles
Caged Lion
Cat and Mice
Change Sides
Charlie over the Water—Ball Version
Flowers and Wind
Forest Ranger
Hill Dill
Hot Potatoes

Hound and Rabbit
I Can Do What You Can!
In the Creek
Leap the Brook
March Attack
May I Chase You?
Mouse Trap
Red Light
Snowball
Stop and Start
Circle Straddle Ball
Exchange Dodgeball
Roll Dodgeball
Straddle Bowling

The Games

Automobiles

Playing Area: Playground, gymnasium.
Players: Entire class.
Supplies: Each child has a "steering wheel."
Skills: Color concepts, running, stopping.

Each child is to be a driver of an automobile and needs a "steering wheel." This can be a hoop, a deck tennis ring, or something the child has made out of cardboard. The teacher has three flash cards, colored red, green, and yellow. These are the traffic-control colors.

The children drive around the area, steering various paths, and responding as the teacher raises the cards aloft one at a time. The children follow the traffic directions: red—stop, green—go, and yellow—caution.

An ambulance station and a fire station can be established with appropriate "cars." When one of these comes forward with the characteristic siren noise (made by the driver), all other cars pull over to the side of the road and wait until the ambulance or fire engine has gone by.

Teaching Suggestion: Have the children use the proper hand signals for making turns, slowing down, and stopping.

Caged Lion

Playing Area: Classroom, gymnasium. A 10-foot square is drawn.
Players: 10 to 20.
Supplies: None.
Skills: Running, dodging.

One child is selected to be the lion and takes a position on hands and knees inside the 10-foot square. Other players tantalize the lion by standing in the cage area or running through it. The lion tries to tag any of the children. Any child who is tagged by the lion trades places with him or her.
Variation: *The King's Land:* The forbidden area, consisting of a 20-foot square, is known as the king's land. A warden is appointed who tries to catch (tag) anyone who is on the king's land. When

successful, he or she is released and the tagged player becomes the new warden. Children taunt the warden by saying, "I'm on the king's land!"

Cat and Mice

Playing Area: Playground, gymnasium, classroom.
Players: 10 to 30.
Supplies: None.
Skills: Running, dodging.

The children form a large circle. One child is chosen to be the cat and four others are the mice. The mice cannot leave the circle. On signal, the cat chases the mice inside the circle. As they are caught, they join the circle. The last mouse caught becomes the cat for the next round. The teacher should start at one point in the circle and go round the circle selecting mice so each child gets a chance to be in the center.

Sometimes, one child has difficulty catching the last mouse or any of the mice, for that matter. Have the circle children take a step toward the center, thus narrowing the running room. Repeat the narrowing, if necessary. Cut off any prolonged chase sequence.

Change Sides

Playing Area: Two parallel lines about 30 feet apart.
Players: Entire class.
Supplies: None.
Skill: Body management competency.

Half the children are on each line. On signal, all cross to the other line, face the center, and stand at attention. The first group to do this correctly wins a point. Children must be cautioned to use care when passing through the opposite group. Space the children well along each line; this allows room for them to move through each group.

The locomotor movements should be varied. The teacher can say, "Ready—walk!" Skipping, hopping, long steps, sliding, and other forms of locomotion can be specified. The position to be assumed at the finish also can be varied.
Variation: The competition can be by squads, with two squads on each line.
Teaching Suggestion: Because success depends upon getting across first, watch for shortcutting of the rules. Talk this problem over with the children.

Charlie over the Water – Ball Version

Playing Area: Playground, gymnasium.
Players: 8 to 12.
Supplies: One volleyball or playground ball.
Skills: Skipping, running, stopping, bowling.

The children are in circle formation with hands joined. One child, Charlie, is in the center of the circle, holding a ball in his or her hands. The children skip around the circle to the following chant:

Charlie over the water,
Charlie over the sea,
Charlie caught a bluebird,
But can't catch *me!*

On the word *"me,"* the children drop hands and scatter. On the same signal, Charlie tosses the ball into the air. He or she then catches it and shouts, "Stop!" All children stop immediately and must not move their feet. Charlie rolls the ball in an attempt to hit one of the children. If he or she hits a child, that child becomes Charlie, and, if Charlie misses, he or she must remain as Charlie, and the game is repeated. However, if he misses twice, he or she should pick another child.

If a girl is in the center, the chant should go: "Sally over the river, Sally over the sea," et cetera.

Flowers and Wind

Playing Area: Two parallel lines are drawn long enough to accommodate the children. The lines are about 30 feet apart.
Players: 10 to 30.
Supplies: None.
Skill: Running.

The children are divided into two equal groups: one is the wind and the other the flowers. Each of the teams takes a position on one of the lines, facing the other. The flowers secretly select the name of a common flower. When ready, they walk over to the other line and stand about 3 feet away from the wind. The players on the wind begin to call out, trying to guess the flower chosen. When the chosen flower has been guessed, the flowers take off and run to their goal line, chased by the players of the other team.

Any player caught must join the other side. The roles are reversed, and the other team chooses a flower.

If one side has trouble guessing, then give the first letter, the color, or the size of the flower as a clue.

Forest Ranger

Playing Area: Playground, gymnasium, classroom.
Players: Entire class.
Supplies: None.
Skill: Running.

Half of the children form a circle facing in. These are the trees. The other half of the children are the forest rangers and stand behind the trees. An extra child, the forest lookout, is in the center. The forest lookout starts the game with the command "Fire in the forest. *Run, run, run!*" Immediately, the forest rangers run around the outside of the circle to the right (counterclockwise). After a few moments, the lookout steps in *front* of one of the trees. This is the signal for each of the rangers to step in front of a tree. One player is left out, and he or she then becomes the new forest lookout. The trees become rangers, and the rangers become trees. Each time the game is played, the circle must be moved out somewhat, since the formation narrows when the rangers step in front of the trees.

Hill Dill

Playing Area: Playground. Two parallel lines are drawn about 50 feet apart.
Players: 10 to 50.
Supplies: None.
Skills: Running, dodging.

One player is chosen to be it and stands in the center. The other children stand on one of the parallel lines. The center player calls, "Hill Dill! Come over the hill!" The children run across the open space to the other line, while the one in the center tries to tag them. Anyone caught helps it in the center. The last child caught is in the center for the next game.

Once the children cross over to the other line, they must await the next call.

Hot Potatoes

Playing Area: Gymnasium, playground, classroom.
Players: 8 to 12 in each group.
Supplies: Six balls, six beanbags.
Skill: Object handling.

Children are seated in a small circle close enough together so objects can be handed from one to another around the circle. Balls and/or beanbags are passed around the circle, a few being introduced at a time. The object of the game is to pass the balls or beanbags rapidly so no one gets stuck with more than one object at a time. If he or she does, the game is stopped, and he or she moves back and waits. After three are out of the circle, the game starts over.

Start the game with two or three objects and gradually add objects until someone has more than one at a time.
Variation: Reverse the direction of passing on signal.

Hound and Rabbit

Playing Area: Playground, gymnasium.
Players: 15 to 30.
Supplies: None.
Skills: Running, dodging, alertness.

Players are scattered around the area in groups of three. Two of the three make a tree by facing each other and putting their hands on each other's shoulders. The third child, who has the part of a rabbit, stands between them (in the tree). Two extra rabbits are outside and are chased by a hound. The hound chases one of the rabbits, who takes refuge in any tree. No tree may hold more than one rabbit, so the other child must leave and look for another tree to be safe. When the hound

catches either rabbit, the hound and the rabbit exchange places, and the game continues.

A rotation system is important and should be used whenever a rabbit enters a tree. The three in any one group should rotate, so the entering rabbit becomes a part of the tree and one of the children making up the tree becomes a rabbit.
Teaching Suggestion: Changes should be made frequently; that is the fun of the game.

I Can Do What You Can!

Playing Area: Playground, gymnasium, classroom.
Players: Not more than six or seven in a group. Any number of groups can play.
Supplies: Usually none. The game can be played with each child using the same piece of equipment, such as a ball, wand, or beanbag.
Skills: Many—depending on the leaders.

This is primarily a follow-the-leader type of game. Each group works independently of the others. Each group forms a semicircle, with the leader in front. The leader starts any type of activity he or she wishes, and the other children attempt to make the same moves. After a brief period, the teacher blows the whistle, and another leader takes his or her place in front of the group.

This works well with selected pieces of hand apparatus, provided each child in the group has the same type of equipment. Tossing, throwing, catching, and bouncing balls, wand stunts, and beanbag tricks are some activities that are easily adapted to the game. Caution children not to demand outlandish or silly performances from the group.

In the Creek

Playing Area: Playground, gymnasium, classroom.
Players: Entire class.
Supplies: None.
Skills: Jumping, leaping, hopping.

A creek is formed by drawing two parallel lines 2 to 3 feet apart, depending upon the ability of the children. The lines should be long enough to accommodate the children comfortably with enough room for each to jump. If necessary, two or three sets of lines can be drawn.

The children line up on one of the banks, all facing the creek and facing the same direction. The object of the game is to make the children commit an error in the jumping.

The teacher or leader gives one of two directions: "in the creek" or "on the bank." Children then on the bank jump into the creek or over to the other bank, depending upon the command. When they jump on the bank, they immediately turn around and get ready for the next command.

If children are in the creek and the command "in the creek" is repeated, they must not move.

Errors are committed when a child steps on a line, makes a wrong jump, or moves when he or she should have remained still. Children who make a mistake can be sent to another game, and this keeps them in activity.

After a period of time, the original directions may not challenge the children. Different combinations can be set up. "In the creek" means to jump and land with both feet. "On the bank" one way is a leap. "On the bank" the other way is a hop. Also, false commands can be given, such as "in the ocean" or "in the lake." No one is to move on these commands under penalty of elimination.

Keep things moving fast with crisp commands. Children should be charged with judging their own errors.

Leap the Brook

Playing Area: Gymnasium or other flat surface.
Players: Entire class.
Supplies: None.
Skills: Leaping, jumping, hopping, turning.

A brook is marked off on the floor for a distance of about 30 feet. For the first 10 feet, it is 3 feet wide; for the second 10 feet, 4 feet wide; and for the last 10 feet, the width becomes 5 feet.

The children form a single file and jump over the narrowest part of the brook. They should be encouraged to do this several times, using different styles of jumping and leaping.

Stress landing as lightly as possible on the balls of the feet in a bent-knee position. Good form should be stressed throughout the game.

3′	4′	5′
X	X	30′ X
X	X	X
X	X	X
X	X	X
X	X	X

After they have satisfactorily negotiated the narrow part, the children move up to the next width, and so on.

The selection of the distances is arbitrary, and they may be changed if they seem unsuitable for any particular group of children.

Variations: Use different means of crossing the brook—leaping, jumping, hopping. Also, specify the kinds of turns to be made—right or left; quarter-, half-, three-quarter, or full turns. Have the children use different body shapes, arm positions, et cetera.

March Attack

Playing Area: Playground, gymnasium. Two parallel lines are drawn about 60 feet apart.
Players: 25 to 40, divided between two teams.

Supplies: None.
Skills: Marching, running.

One team takes a position on one of the lines, with their backs to the area. These are the chasers. The other team is on the other line, facing the area. This is the marching team.

The marching team moves forward on signal, marching in good order toward the chasers. When they get reasonably close, a whistle or some other signal is given and the marchers turn and run back to their line, chased by the other team. If some of the marchers are caught before reaching their line, they change to the other team. The game is repeated, with the roles of marcher and chaser exchanged.

May I Chase You?

Playing Area: Playground.
Players: 10 to 30.
Supplies: None.
Skills: Running, dodging.

The class stands behind a line long enough to accommodate all. The runner stands about 5 feet in front of the line. One child in the line asks, "May I chase you?" The runner replies, "Yes, if you are wearing..." He or she can name a color, an article of clothing, or a combination of the two. All who qualify immediately chase the runner until one tags him or her. This person becomes it.

The children will think of other ways to identify those who may run.

Mouse Trap

Playing Area: Playground, gymnasium, classroom.
Players: 20 to 40.
Supplies: None.
Skills: Skipping, running, dodging.

Half of the children form a circle, with hands joined, facing the center. The other children are on the outside of the circle. Three signals are given for the game. These can be given by word cues or whistle.

The circle players represent the mouse trap, and the outer players are the mice.

Signal 1: The mice skip around the circle, playing happily.

Signal 2: The trap is opened; that is, the circle players raise their joined hands to form arches. The mice run in and out of the trap.

Signal 3: The trap snaps shut (the arms come down). All mice caught join the circle.

The game is repeated until all or most of the mice are caught. The players exchange places, and the game begins anew. Do not allow children to run in and out through adjacent openings.

Red Light

Playing Area: An area 60 to 100 feet across, with a goal toward which the players move.

Players: Entire class.
Supplies: None.
Skills: Fundamental locomotor movements, stopping.

The object of the game is to be able to move across the area successfully without getting caught. One player is the leader and stands on the goal line.

The leader turns his or her back to the players, claps hands five times, and turns around on the fifth clap. In the meantime, the players move toward the goal line, timing their movements to end on the fifth clap. If the leader catches any movement by any person, that person is required to return to the starting line and begin anew. When the leader turns his or her back, he or she should be permitted to turn around immediately to catch movement before clapping. However, once he or she begins clapping, he or she must complete it before turning around. The first child to reach the goal line successfully without being caught with illegal movement is the winner and becomes the leader for the next game.

Variations
1. An excellent variation of the game is to have the leader face the oncoming players. He or she calls out, "Green light," for them to move and, "Red light," for them to stop. When he or she calls other colors, the players should not move.
2. Different types of locomotion can be worked in. The leader names the type of movement (hop, crawl, et cetera) before turning his or her back to the group.
3. The leader can specify how those caught must go back to place—walk, hop, skip, slide, crawl, et cetera.

Note: In the original game of Red Light, the leader counted rapidly, "1-2-3-4-5-6-7-8-9-10-red light," instead of clapping five times. This has proved impractical in most gymnasiums, because the children moving forward cannot hear the counting; so clapping, which provides both a visual and an auditory signal, has been substituted.

Snowball

Playing Area: Gymnasium or hard-surfaced area, inside preferable to outside. A playing area 50 to 60 feet long and approximately 30 feet wide divided by a center line—at the rear of each half of the area is an end line connecting the side lines.
Players: Any number.
Supplies: Fleece balls, yarn balls, paper balls.
Skill: Throwing.

Divide the group into two equal teams. Each team takes any position desired on each side of the center line. Any number of snowballs may be used, with balls divided equally between both teams. Five to six balls for each team provide the best action. (The more balls used, the faster the game.) Start game on signal and have players throw balls at opponents across the center line. A ball striking any part of a player retires that player to the bench or sidelines. (These players retrieve balls thrown out of court for their team but may not throw at opponents.) Game ends when one team is reduced to only one player (more or less optional).

Rules
1. All players must remain inside boundary lines (unless permitted to retrieve ball) and must make all throws from within boundaries. Penalty: out of game for stepping over, or throwing from out of, boundary lines. Center line may not be crossed.
2. Balls that bounce from floor and hit a player are not counted as hits.
3. A player who attempts to catch a ball and misses is out. A caught ball puts the thrower out of the game, providing the ball was caught on a fly.
4. A player may have only one ball in his or her hands at a time, unless there are less than five players on his or her side.

Teaching Suggestions
1. Players should be encouraged to throw from as close to center line as possible in order to ensure a better chance of a hit.
2. Encourage several players to direct throws at one player at same time.
3. Encourage aggressive offensive action.

Stop and Start

Playing Area: Playground.
Players: Any number can play.
Supplies: None.
Skill: Locomotion.

The children are in the center of the playground, scattered enough so each has room to maneuver. The teacher or leader stands a little to one side and gives directions. He or she points in a direction and calls "gallop." Any other locomotor movement can be used. Suddenly, he or she calls, "Stop." All children must stop immediately without further movement. Anyone moving can be sent to the rear of the group.

Circle Straddle Ball

Playing Area: Playground, gymnasium, classroom.
Players: 10 to 15.
Supplies: Two volleyballs or rubber playground balls.
Skills: Ball rolling, catching.

Children are in circle formation, facing in. Each stands in wide straddle step with the side of his or her foot against the neighbor's. The hands are on the knees.

Two balls are used. The object of the game is to roll one of the balls between the legs of any player before he or she can get his or her hands down to stop it. Each time the ball goes between the legs of an individual, a point is scored against him or her. The players having the fewest points against them are the v:inners.

Be sure the children catch and roll the ball rather than bat it. Children must keep their hands on their knees until a ball is rolled at them.

After practice, the following variation should be played.

Variation: One child is in the center with a ball and is it. The other children are in the same formation as above. One ball is used. The center player tries to roll the ball through the legs of any child he or she chooses. He or she should mask his or her intent, using feints and changes of direction. Any child allowing the ball to go through his or her legs becomes it. All players start with hands on knees until the ball is thrown.

Exchange Dodgeball

Playing Area: Playground, gymnasium.
Players: 12 to 20.
Supplies: Volleyball or rubber playground ball.
Skills: Throwing, dodging.

Children form a large circle with one child, it, in the center. The children are numbered off by fours or fives, so there are groups of three or four children who have the same number. The center player also has a number that he or she uses when he or she is not it.

The center player has a ball that he or she places at his or her feet. He or she calls a number, picks up the ball, and tries to hit one of the children who are exchanging places. When a number is called, all children with that number exchange places. The center player remains it until he or she can hit one of the children below the waist.

Variation: Have the children use animal names instead of numbers.

Roll Dodgeball

Playing Area: Playground, gymnasium.
Players: 20 to 30, divided into two teams.
Supplies: Two volleyballs or rubber playground balls.
Skills: Ball rolling, dodging.

Half of the children form a circle, and the other half are in the center. Two balls are given to the circle players. The circle players roll the balls at the feet and shoes of the center players, trying to hit them. The center players move around to dodge the balls. When a center player is hit, he or she leaves the circle.

After a period of time or when all the children have been hit, the teams trade places. If a specified time limit is used, the team having the fewest players hit wins. Or the team that puts out all the opponents in the shortest time wins.

Variation: Center players are down on hands and

feet. Only one ball is used; otherwise the game is the same. Do not play too long in this position, since it is quite strenuous.

Teaching Suggestion: Be sure to have practice in rolling a ball first. Balls that stop in the center are dead and must be taken back to the circle before being put into play. It is best to have the player who recovers a ball roll it to one of his or her teammates rather than to have him or her return to his or her place with the ball.

Straddle Bowling

Playing Area: Playground, gymnasium.
Players: Four to six.
Supplies: Volleyball or rubber playground ball.
Skill: Bowling for accuracy.

Children may compete within a group, or teams can compete against each other. One child is the bowling target and stands in straddle position with his or her feet wide enough apart so the ball can pass through easily. Another child is the ball chaser and stands behind him or her.

A foul line is drawn 15 to 25 feet away from the target, depending upon the ability of the children. The bowlers line up behind this line for turns.

Children can be given one chance or a number of tries. To score a point, the ball must go between the legs of the target. When the children on the throwing line have bowled, two of them relieve the target and chaser.

Variations

1. Scoring can be changed to allow two points if the ball goes through the legs and one point if it hits a leg.
2. Other targets can be used. A box lying on its side with the opening pointed toward the bowler is a good target. Two or three Indian clubs at each station make excellent targets. Scoring could be varied to suit the target.
3. *Bowling One Step:* In groups of squad size or smaller, each of the players in turn gets a chance to roll at an Indian club or a bowling pin. A minimum distance is set up, short enough so most bowlers can hit the pin (10 to 15 feet). The player keeps rolling until he or she misses. The object is to take a step backward each time the pin is knocked down. The winner is the one who has moved the farthest back.

Children should be cautioned that accuracy, not speed, is the goal. Also, the players should experiment with different spin effects to curve the ball.

THE GAMES PROGRAM FOR THE THIRD GRADE

Compared with the first two grades, the third grade undergoes a definite change in the games program. The chase and tag games become more complex and demand more maneuvering. Introductory lead-up games make an appearance. The interests of the children are turning toward games that have a sports slant. Kicking, throwing, catching, batting, and other sports skills are beginning to mature.

Third-Grade Games

Review Second-Grade Games
Busy Bee
Couple Tag
Crows and Cranes
The Eagle and the Sparrows
Fly Trap
Follow Me
Frog in the Sea
Galloping Lizzie
Jump the Shot
Nonda's Car Lot
Poison Circle
Steal the Treasure
Triple Change
Weathervane
Balance Dodgeball
Bat Ball
Bounce Ball
Circle Team Dodgeball
Club Guard
Competitive Circle Contests
Newcomb
One Step

The Games

Busy Bee

Playing Area: Playground, gymnasium, classroom.
Players: Entire class.
Supplies: None.
Skills: Fundamental locomotor movements.

Half of the children form a large circle, facing in, and are designated as the stationary players. The other children seek partners from this group, and each stands in front of one of the stationary players. An extra child is in the center and is the busy bee.

The bee calls out directions that are followed by the children:

"Back to back."
"Face to face."
"Shake hands."
"Kneel on one knee" (or both).
"Hop on one foot."

The center child then calls out, "Busy bee." Stationary players stand still, and all inner circle players seek other partners while the center player also tries to get a partner. The child without a partner becomes the busy bee.

Children should be thinking of the different movements they might have the class do if they should become the busy bee. In changing partners, children should be required to select a partner other than the stationary player next to them.

After a period of time, rotate the active and stationary players. Also, vary by using different methods of locomotion.

Variations

1. Select a definite number of changes—10 for example. All children who have not repeated any partner during the 10 exchanges and who have not been caught as the busy bee are declared winners.
2. Instead of having the children stand back to back, have them lock elbows and sit down as in the Chinese Get-up. After they sit down and are declared safe, they can get up, and the game proceeds as described above.

Couple Tag

Playing Area: Playground, gymnasium. Two goal lines are established about 50 feet apart.
Players: Any number.
Supplies: None.
Skills: Running, dodging.

Children run by pairs, with inside hands joined. All pairs, except one, line up on one of the goal lines. A pair is in the center and is it.

The pair in the center calls, "Come," and the children run to the other goal line, keeping hands joined. The pair in the center tries to tag any pair, using *only* the joined hands. As soon as a couple is caught, it helps the center couple. The game continues until all are caught. The last couple caught is it for the next game.

Variation: *Triplet Tag:* Play the game with sets of threes. Tagging is done with any pair of joined hands. If the triplet breaks joined hands, it is caught.

Crows and Cranes

Playing Area: Playground, gymnasium. Two goals are drawn about 50 feet apart.
Players: Any number.
Supplies: None.
Skills: Running, dodging.

Children are divided into two groups, the crows and the cranes. The groups face each other at the center of the area about 5 feet apart. The leader calls out either "crows" or "cranes," using a cr-r-r-r-r sound at the start of either word to mask the result.

If "crows" is the call, the crows chase the cranes to the goal. If "cranes" is given, then the cranes chase. Any child caught goes over to the other side. The team that has the most players when the game ends is the winner.

Variations

1. Have the children stand back to back in the center about a foot apart.

2. The game can be played with the two sides designated as black and white. A piece of plywood painted black on one side and white on the other can be thrown into the air between the teams instead of having anyone give calls. If black comes up, the black team chases, and vice versa.

3. The game also can be played as Blue, Black, and Baloney. On the commands "blue" and "black," the game proceeds as described above. On the command "baloney," no one is to move. The caller should be sure to sound the bl-l-l-l before ending with one of the three commands.

4. Another variation of the game is to have a leader tell a story using as many words beginning with "cr" as possible. The players run only when the words *crows* and *cranes* are spoken. Words that can be incorporated into a story are *crazy, crunch, crust, crown, crude, crowd, crouch, cross, croak, critter.* Each time one of these words is spoken, the beginning of the words is lengthened with the cr-r-r-r sound. No one may move on any of the words except *crows* or *cranes.*

The Eagle and the Sparrows

Playing Area: Playground, with two parallel lines drawn about 50 feet apart. A circle representing the eagle's nest is drawn in the center.
Players: Entire class.
Supplies: None.
Skills: Running, hopping, dodging.

One player is the eagle and is down on one knee in the nest. The other players circle around, flying like sparrows, until the eagle suddenly gets up and chases the sparrows to either line. Any sparrow caught joins the eagle and helps him or her catch others. However, no center player can chase until the eagle starts first.

If the group is large, begin with two or three eagles in the center.
Variation: All sparrows must take three hops before they can start running.

Fly Trap

Playing Area: Playground, gymnasium.
Players: Entire class.
Supplies: None.
Skills: Fundamental locomotor movements.

Half of the class is scattered around the playing area, sitting on the floor in Indian (cross-legged) fashion. These children form the trap. The other children are the flies and buzz around the seated children. When a whistle is blown, the flies must freeze at the spot. If any of the trappers can touch a fly, that fly sits down at that spot and becomes a trapper. To reach legally, the trapper must keep his or her seat on the ground.

The game continues until all the flies have been caught. Some realism is given to the game if the flies make buzzing sounds and move with their arms out as wings.

A little experience with the game enables the teacher to determine how far apart to place the seated children. In tagging, the children must keep their seats on the ground.

After all the flies have been caught, the children trade places.

Change the method of locomotion occasionally.

Follow Me

Playing Area: Playground, gymnasium.
Players: 8 to 30.
Supplies: A marker for each child. Squares of cardboard or plywood can be used. Individual mats work very well.
Skills: All locomotor movements, stopping.

Children are arranged in a rough circle, each standing or sitting with one foot on his or her marker. An extra player is the guide. He or she moves about the circle and points at different players and asks them to follow. Each player as chosen falls in behind the guide. The guide then takes his or her group on a tour, and the members of the group perform just as the guide does. The guide may hop, skip, do stunts, or perform other movements, and the children following must do likewise. At the signal "home," all run for places at the markers. One child will be without a marker. This child chooses another guide.

It is not a good idea to make the last child the new leader, since this causes some children to lag and try to be last. In this version, the last child gets to choose a new leader. Another way to overcome the tendency to lag would be to make the first one back the leader. Or there could be a special leader marker; the first one to this marker becomes the new leader.

A penalty can be imposed on the one who does not find a marker.

Frog in the Sea

Playing Area: Any small area indoors or outdoors.
Players: Six to eight in each game.
Supplies: None.
Skills: Fundamental locomotor movements.

One player is the frog and sits down Indian fashion (crossed legs). The others mill about, trying to touch the frog but, at the same time, keeping out of his or her reach. They can call, "Frog in the sea, can't catch me." The frog must remain sitting and try to tag those tantalizing him or her. Anyone tagged exchanges places with the frog.

Care should be taken so the children do not punish the frog unnecessarily.

Variations
1. The frog may not tag anyone until the teacher says, "Jump frog."
2. The game proceeds as described for the regular game. When the teacher says "jump frog," the frog can project himself or herself in any direction with a jump. He or she is permitted to tag both during the original part of the game and at the jump.

Galloping Lizzie

Playing Area: Playground.
Players: 10 to 15.
Supplies: Beanbag or fleece ball.
Skills: Throwing, dodging, running.

This is a version of the game of tag. One player is it and has a beanbag or fleece ball. The other players are scattered around the playground. The player with the beanbag or fleece ball runs after the others and attempts to hit one below the shoulders with the beanbag or fleece ball. The person hit becomes it, and the game continues. Be sure that it throws the bag or ball and does not merely touch another person with it.

Variation: The game can be played by children in pairs, and a pair of children becomes it, with one of the players handling the beanbag or ball. A specific kind of a toss can be called for (overhand, underhand, left hand, et cetera).

Jump the Shot

Playing Area: Playground, gymnasium.
Players: 10 to 20.
Supplies: A jump-the-shot rope.
Skill: Jumping over a rope.

The players stand in circle formation. One player with a long rope stands in the center. A soft object is tied to the free end of the rope to give it some weight. An old, deflated ball makes a good weight.

The center player turns the rope under the feet of the circle players, who must jump over it. Anyone who touches the rope with the feet is eliminated and must stand back from the circle. Reform the circle after three or four children have been eliminated.

The center player should be cautioned to keep the rope along the ground. The speed can be varied. A good way to turn the rope is to sit cross-legged and turn the rope over the head.

Nonda's Car Lot

Playing Area: Playground, gymnasium.
Players: 20 to 35.
Supplies: None.
Skills: Running, dodging.

One player is it and stands in the center of the area between the two lines. The class selects four models of cars (for example, Dodge, Chevy,

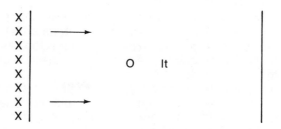

Volkswagon, Ford). Each student selects a car from the four models but does not tell anyone what it is.

It calls out a car model. All students who selected that model attempt to run to the other line without getting tagged by it. It calls out the cars until all the students have run. When a child (car) gets tagged, he or she must sit down where he or she got tagged. The child cannot move but may tag other students.

When it calls out, "Car lot," all the cars must go. The game is played until all the students (cars) have been tagged.

Poison Circle

Playing Area: Playground, gymnasium.
Players: 8 to 12 in each circle.
Supplies: Volleyball or rubber playground ball.
Skills: Pushing and pulling, running, throwing, dodging.

Players form a circle, with hands joined with good solid grips. Inside the circle of players, another circle is drawn on the floor with chalk. This should be a foot or two smaller than the circle of children. The ball is placed in the center of this area.

At a signal, the circle pulls and pushes, trying to force a child to step into the inner circle. When this occurs, everyone yells, "Poison," and the children scatter. The one who stepped in the circle quickly picks up the ball and tries to hit one of the other children below the waist. He or she must throw from within the circle. If he or she hits a child, it is a "dud" against the child. If he or she misses, it is a "dud" against the thrower. Anyone with three "duds" pays a penalty.

Steal the Treasure

Playing Area: Playground, gymnasium, classroom.
Players: 8 to 12.
Supplies: Indian club.
Skill: Dodging.

A playing area 20 feet square is outlined, with a small circle in the center. An Indian club is the treasure and is placed in the circle. A guard is set to protect the treasure. Players then enter the square and try to steal the treasure without getting caught. The guard tries to tag them. Anyone tagged must retire from the circle and wait for the next game. The player who gets the treasure is the next guard. If getting the treasure seems too easy, make a rule requiring the child to carry the treasure to the boundaries of the square.

Variation: *Bear and Keeper:* This game is similar in action. Instead of a treasure, a bear is seated cross-legged on the ground and is protected by a keeper. Anyone who touches the bear without being tagged becomes the new keeper, with the present keeper becoming the bear. In a rougher version of this game, the bear stands crouched over and the children try to swat him or her on the seat without getting tagged.

Triple Change

Playing Area: Playground, gymnasium.
Players: 15 to 30.
Supplies: None.
Skill: Running.

Players form a large circle, facing in. Three children stand in the center. Those forming the circle and those in the center are numbered off by threes. The players in the center take turns, each calling out his or her own number. When a number is called, all those with that number change places. The one in the center *with this number* tries to find a place. The child without a place goes to the center and waits until the other center players have had their turns.

Variation: The teacher could call out the numbers, not necessarily in order, to add an element of suspense to the game.

Weathervane

Playing Area: Playground, gymnasium, classroom.
Players: Entire class.
Supplies: None.
Skills: Jumping, turning.

Children stand alongside their desks or are scattered throughout the area. A leader stands at the front of the class and gives the directions. He or she calls out the four main compass directions—north, south, east, and west. The children jump in place, making the necessary turn in the air to face the called direction. This could involve a quarter-, half-, or three-quarter-turn. If the direction that the children are facing is called, then each child jumps in the air with no turn. All turns should be in the same direction for a period of time to avoid confusion.

A child could have to sit down after a stipulated number of errors. An alternate method would be for each child to keep track of the number of errors he or she made.

Variations: After the children become skillful in turning, a number of variations could be used.

1. A full turn could be required when a direction is repeated.
2. Right and left turning could be alternated.

Balance Dodgeball

Playing Area: Playground, gymnasium.
Players: Entire class.
Supplies: A ball for each child who is it.
Skills: Throwing, dodging.

Children are scattered over the area. One or more children have a ball and are it. Children are safe from being hit when they are balanced on one foot. This means that one foot must be off the ground and the other foot that supports the weight must not be moved on penalty of being hit. Hits should be made below the shoulders. Anyone legally hit becomes it.

Teaching Suggestion: To avoid having it stand by a child waiting for the child to lose his or her balance or touch a foot to the ground, have the child count rapidly up to 10. It then must leave and seek another child.

Variation: *Footsie Dodgeball:* To be safe from being hit, the child must have both feet off the ground.

Bat Ball

Playing Area: A serving line is drawn across one end of a field that is approximately 70 by 70 feet. A 3-by-3-foot base is drawn in the center of the playing field about 50 feet from the serving line.
Players: Two teams, 8 to 15 on each team.
Supplies: Volleyball or similar ball.
Skills: Batting, running, catching, throwing.

One team is scattered out across the playing area. The other team is behind the serving line, with one player up at bat. The batter puts the ball in play by batting it with his or her hand into the playing area. The ball must land in the playing area or be touched by a member of the fielding team to be counted as a fair ball. As soon as the ball is hit, the batter runs to the base and back across the serving line. In the meantime, the fielding team fields the ball and attempts to hit the runner below the shoulders.

Scoring: The batter scores a run each time a fair ball is hit and he or she touches the base and gets across the serving line before being hit by the ball. He or she also scores a run if the fielding team commits a foul.

Out: The batter is out when the ball is caught on a fly. Two consecutive foul balls also put the batter out. The batter is out when hit by a thrown ball in the field of play. Sides change when three outs are made.

Fouls: Fielders, in recovering the ball and attempting to hit the batter, may not run with the ball. The ball must be passed from fielder to fielder until thrown at the batter. A pass may not be returned to the fielder from whom it was received.

Variation: *Shotgun Ball:* The entire batting team runs each time there is a fair ball. The defensive team tries to hit as many of the runners as possible. Instead of touching the base, the runners run around it from either direction and back to the serving line. Each safe runner scores one run. More outs (6 to 10) should be scored in this version before the teams change sides.

Bounce Ball

Playing Area: A rectangular court 40 by 60 feet, divided into two halves by a center line. Each half is 30 by 40 feet.
Players: Two teams, 8 to 15 players on each.
Supplies: Two volleyballs or rubber playground balls of about the same size.
Skills: Throwing, ball rolling.

Each team occupies one of the halves of the court and is given a volleyball. One or two players from each team should be assigned as ball chasers to retrieve balls behind their own end lines.

The object of the game is to bounce or roll the ball over the opponent's end line. A ball thrown across the line on a fly does not count.

Two scorers are needed, one at each end line. Players can move wherever they wish in their own areas but cannot cross the center line. After the starting signal, the balls are thrown back and forth at will.

Variation: Use a row of benches across the center line. Throws must go over the benches and bounce in the other team's area to score.

Circle Team Dodgeball

Playing Area: Playground, gymnasium.
Players: 20 to 40.
Supplies: Volleyball or rubber playground ball.
Skills: Throwing, dodging.

The children are divided into two teams, one of which forms a large circle. The other team grouped together is in the center of the circle. One of the circle players has the ball.

When the starting signal is given, the circle players try to hit the center players with the ball. Any center player hit below the shoulders is eliminated and leaves the circle. Scoring can be done in several ways.

1. Establish a throwing time of 1 minute. Count the number of center players remaining.
2. Play until all center players have been eliminated. Score is determined by the number of seconds it takes to eliminate the players.
3. Allow a throwing time of 1 minute. Do not eliminate any center players but give one point to the circle players for each successful hit.

4. Limit the number of throws a team can take. After the specified number of throws, count the remaining center players.

The teams trade places, and the scores are compared to determine the winner.

Teaching Suggestion: When some children tend to hog the action, a rule that no player may throw more than three times in any one action can be used to spread the throws among the children.

Club Guard

Playing Area: Gymnasium, outdoor smooth surface.
Players: 8 to 10 in each game.
Supplies: Indian club, volleyball.
Skill: Throwing.

A circle about 15 feet in diameter is drawn. Inside this circle at the center, an 18-inch circle is drawn. The Indian club is put in the center of the small circle. One child guards the club. The other children are back of the larger circle, which is the restraining line for them. This circle should be definite.

The circle players throw the ball at the club and try to knock it down. The guard tries to block the throws with his or her legs and body. He or she must, however, stay out of the smaller inner circle.

The outer circle players pass the ball around rapidly so one of the players can get an opening to throw, since the guard needs to maneuver to protect the club. Whoever knocks down the club becomes the new guard.

If the guard steps in the inner circle, he or she loses his or her place to whoever has the ball at that time.

A small circle cut from plywood or similar material makes a definite circle so it can be seen when the guard steps inside. A hoop can be used, too.

Variation: Set up more than one club to be guarded.

Competitive Circle Contests

Playing Area: Playground, gymnasium.
Players: Two teams, 10 to 15 on each.
Supplies: Two volleyballs or rubber playground balls, two Indian clubs.
Skills: Throwing, catching.

Two teams can compete against each other in the form of independent circles. The circles should be of the same size, and lines can be drawn on the floor to assure this. The players of each team are numbered consecutively, so there is a player in each circle with a corresponding number.

These numbered players go to the center of the opponent's circle in turn and compete for their team against the circle of opponents.

For individual Dodgeball and Club Guard, make a rule that there must be three passes made to three different people before the ball can be thrown at an individual or the club.

To begin, the #1 players go to the opponent's circle. Three different contests are suggested, using the above arrangement as the basis.

Individual Dodgeball: The circle players throw at the center players, who represent the other team. The circle that hits the center player first wins a point.

Club Guard: In this contest, the center player guards an Indian club as in Club Guard. Whichever circle knocks down the club first wins a point.

Touch Ball: The circle players pass the ball from one to another while the center players try to touch it. Whichever center player touches the ball first wins a point for his or her team.

After the #1 players have competed, they return to their own team's circle and the #2s go to the opponent's circles. This is continued until all players have competed. The team with the most points wins.

Newcomb

Playing Area: Volleyball court.
Players: Two teams, 8 to 10 on each.
Supplies: One to four volleyballs.
Skills: Throwing, catching.

Each team occupies one side of the court. The children may be positioned in two or three lines of players, depending upon the number of children and the size of the court. There is no rotation system, and service is informal.

The object of the game is for one team to throw the ball underhanded over the net in such a way that it will not be caught. The game starts with a member of one team throwing the ball into the opposite court. The ball is thrown back and forth until an error is committed. Each time a team commits an error, a point is scored for the opposite team. Errors are (1) failure to catch a ball, (2) not throwing the ball across the net successfully, and (3) throwing the ball so it falls out-of-bounds on the other side of the net. The first team reaching a score of 15 is the winner.

There is no formal rotation, but the teacher can change the lines from front to back at times. The child nearest to a ball that touched the floor or went out-of-bounds starts the play with a throw. The ball may be passed from one player to another before it is thrown across the net.

As the children learn the game, introduce more balls. An official may be needed on each side.

One Step

Playing Area: Playground.
Players: Two. Any number of pairs can compete against each other, depending upon the space available.

Supplies: Ball or beanbag.
Skills: Throwing, catching.

The game is excellent for practicing throwing and catching skills. Two children stand facing each other about 3 feet apart. One has a ball or a beanbag. The object of the game is to throw or toss the ball in the stipulated manner, so the partner can catch it *without moving his or her feet* from their position on the floor. When the throw is completed successfully, the thrower takes one step backward. He or she waits for the throw from his or her partner. Limits can be established back to which the partners step, or the two children who can move to the greatest distance apart as compared to other couples are the winners. Variables to provide interest and challenge are (1) the type of throw, (2) the type of catching, and (3) the kind of a step. Throwing can be underhand, overhand, two-handed, under one leg, around the back, et cetera. Catching can be two-handed, left-handed, right-handed, to the side, et cetera. The step can be a giant step, a tiny step, a hop, a jump, or some similar movement.

When either child misses, moves the feet, or fails to follow directions, the partners move forward and start over. A line of children facing each other makes a satisfactory formation for having a number of pairs compete at the same time.

GAMES FOR INTERMEDIATE-LEVEL CHILDREN

In contrast to games for the lower grades, the activities for the intermediate level are more difficult to allocate with precision to specific grade levels. In many cases, the allocation involve arbitrary decisions, based on both judgment and choice. However, it is felt the allocation of games to grade levels is important, since it assures the children of new experiences for each school year.

The intermediate program should make good use of all the games from the lower grades that can be utilized for older children. Modifications of the games with respect to rules and boundaries allow use on many levels, even in junior and senior high school programs.

The intermediate-level games presented here should be supplemented by the lead-up games found in chapters twenty-six through thirty and thirty-two and thirty-three.

THE GAMES PROGRAM FOR THE FOURTH GRADE

Fourth-Grade Games

Review Third-Grade Games
Addition Tag
Alaska Baseball
Box Ball

Cageball Kick-over
Circle Chase
Hand Hockey
Islands
Jump the Shot Variations
Loose Caboose
Nine Lives
Running Dodgeball
Squad Tag
Squeeze
Trades
Trees
Whistle Mixer

The Games

Addition Tag

Playing Area: Playground.
Players: Entire class.
Supplies: None.
Skills: Running, dodging.

The object of the game is to catch all the children by tagging. Two couples are it, and each stands with inside hands joined. These are the taggers. The other children run individually. The couples move around the playground, trying to tag with the free hands. Anyone tagged joins the couple, making a trio. The three then chase until they catch a fourth. Once a fourth person is caught, the four divide and form two couples, adding another set of taggers to the game. This continues until all the children are tagged.

Some limitation of area should be established, enough to enable the couples to catch the runners. If the children are scattered to distant parts of a playground, the game moves slowly and is fatiguing. A legal tap is made only when the couples or groups of three keep their hands joined.

The game can be used as an introductory activity, since all the children are active.

Alaska Baseball

Playing Area: Playground.
Players: Entire class.
Supplies: Volleyball or soccer ball.
Skills: Kicking, batting, running, ball handling.

The players are organized into two teams, one of which is at bat and the other in the field. A straight line provides the only out-of-bounds, and the team at bat is behind this line at about the middle. The other team is scattered around the fair territory.

One player propels the ball by either batting (as in volleyball) or kicking a stationary soccer ball. His or her teammates are in a close file just behind him or her. As soon as he or she sends the ball into the playing area, he or she starts to run around his or her own team. Each time the runner passes the head of the file, the team gives a loud count.

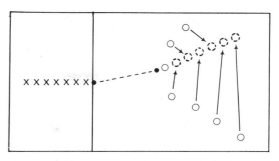

There are no outs. The first fielder to get the ball stands still and starts to pass the ball back over his or her head to the nearest teammate, who moves directly behind him or her to receive the ball. The remainder of the team in the field must run to the ball and form a file behind it. The ball is passed back overhead, with each player handling the ball until the last player in line has a firm grip on it. He or she shouts, "Stop." At this signal, a count is made of the number of times the batter ran around his or her own team. In order to score a little more sharply, half rounds should be counted. Allow five batters, or half of the team, to bat and then change the teams. This is better than allowing one entire team to bat before changing to the field, since the players in the field get quite tired from many consecutive runs.

Variation: Set up regular bases. Have the batter run the bases instead of scoring as indicated. Scoring can be in terms of a home run made or not, or the batter can continue around the bases, getting a point for each base.

Box Ball

Playing Area: Playground, gymnasium.
Players: Four teams, 6 to 10 on each team.
Supplies: A sturdy box, 2 by 2 feet and about 12 inches deep. One volleyball or similar type of ball for each team.
Skills: Running, ball handling.

Any number of teams can play the game, but four makes a convenient number. Each team occupies one side of a hollow square at an equal distance from the center. Each team is facing inward and is numbered off consecutively from right to left. The teams should have an even number of players.

A box containing as many balls as there are teams is put in the center. The instructor calls a number, and the player from each team who has that number runs forward to the box and takes a ball. He or she then runs to the head of his or her line and takes the place of #1. In the meantime, the players in his or her line have moved to the left just enough to fill in the space left by the runner. Upon reaching the head of the line, the runner passes the ball to #1 and so on down the line to the end child. The last child runs forward and

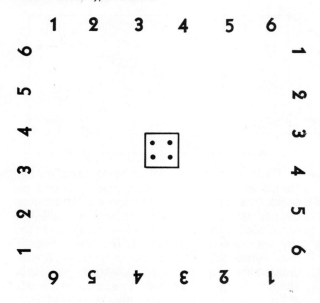

returns the ball to the box. The first team to return the ball to the box scores 1 point.

The runner must not pass the ball down the line until he or she takes his or her place at the head. The ball must be caught and passed by each child. Failure to conform to these rules results in disqualification.

The runner then stays at the head of the line. He or she retains his or her number, but it is not important to maintain the line in consecutive number sequence.

Cageball Kick-over

Playing Area: Playground (grassy area), gymnasium.
Players: Two teams, 7 to 10 on each team.
Supplies: A cageball, 18-inch, 24-inch, or 30-inch size.
Skill: Kicking.

The two teams sit facing each other, with their legs outstretched and the soles of the feet about 3 feet apart. Each player supports his or her weight on his or her hands, which are placed slightly back of him or her, while maintaining the sitting position.

The teacher rolls the cageball between the two teams. The object of the game is to kick the ball over the other team. After a point is scored, the teacher rolls the ball into play again. A system of rotation can be used whereby, when a point is scored, the player on the left side of the line takes a place on the right side, moving all the other players one position to the left.

When the ball is kicked out at either end, no score results and the ball is put into play again by the teacher.

Variation: Allow the children to use their hands to stop the ball from going over them.

Circle Chase

Playing Area: Playground, gymnasium.
Players: 20 to 40.
Supplies: None.
Skill: Running.

The group is arranged in the circle, standing elbow distance apart and facing the center. Depending upon the size of the group, count off by threes, fours, or fives around the circle. The teacher calls out a number. All players with that number start running around the circle. Players try to catch and tag the player ahead. Those tagged drop out of the game, while those not tagged make one lap around the circle and back to place. Players should try both to tag and keep from being tagged.

After all of the numbers have been called, the remaining players re-form the circle and count off to get new numbers. The game then is repeated until a designated number of children remains.

The game is interesting and competitive but has the basic weakness that those who are eliminated, the slower children, probably need the running the most. It is best to get them back into the game as soon as practical.

Variation: Instead of having each player run around once, let him or her run around two or three times before stopping.

Hand Hockey

Playing Area: Field about 100 by 100 feet.
Players: Two teams composed of 12 to 15 each.
Supplies: Soccer ball or volleyball.
Skills: Striking, volleying.

Half of the players of each team are guards and are stationed on the goal line they are defending. The other half of the players on each team are active players and are scattered throughout the playing area.

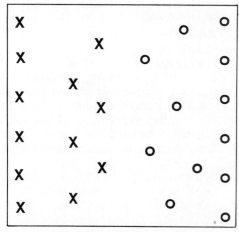

The object of the game is to bat or push the ball with either hand so it crosses the goal line the other team is defending. Players may move the ball as in hockey but may not throw, hoist, or kick it. The defensive goal line players are limited to one step into the playing field when playing the ball.

The ball is put in play by rolling it into the field at about the center. After a goal has been scored or after a definite time period, guards become active players, and vice versa.

An out-of-bounds ball goes to the opposite team and is put in play by being rolled from the sidelines into the playing area. If the ball becomes entrapped among the players, play is stopped and the ball is put into play again by a roll from the referee.

Players must play the ball and not resort to rough tactics. A player who is called for unnecessary roughness or illegally handling the ball must go to the sidelines (as in hockey) and remain in the penalty area until the players change positions.

Players should scatter and attempt to pass to each other rather than bunch around the ball.

Variation: *Scooter Hockey:* The game is played in the same way as described, except the active players from each team in the center are on gym scooters. The position each child takes on the gym scooter can be specified or it can be free choice. If specified, some positions that can be used are kneeling, seated, or using a tummy balance. A hard surface is needed; usually played indoors using a basketball floor.

Islands

Playing Area: Gymnasium, hardtop surface outside.
Players: Entire class.
Supplies: None.
Skills: Leaping, jumping, hopping.

With chalk, a number of patterns of islands are laid out on the floor in the following fashion.

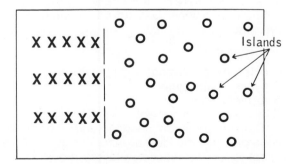

The object of the game is for the children to step, jump, or hop from island to island without error. Errors occur by stepping on a line or outside of an island. Islands can be of different sizes and in different arrangements, depending upon the ability of the children. Courses can be laid out under two plans. The first would be to establish courses

in order of increasing difficulty. The children would move to a more difficult course after completing one successfully. The other plan would be to make each course reasonably easy at the start and increase the difficulty as the course progresses. Children can leap, jump, or hop from island to island.

The teacher should review and play Leap the Brook, a game in the second-grade list, before introducing Islands.

Jump the Shot Variations

Playing Area: Playground, gymnasium, classroom.
Players: 10 to 30.
Supplies: A jump-the-shot rope.
Skill: Rope jumping.

Review the Jump the Shot as described in the third-grade games.

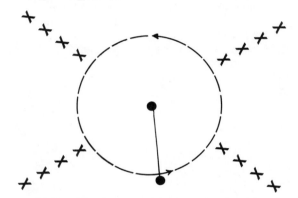

Squads line up in the following fashion in spoke formation. Each member is given a definite number of jumps (3, 4, or 5). The next squad member in line must come in immediately without missing a turn of the rope. A player scores a point for his or her squad when he or she comes in *on time,* jumps the prescribed number of turns, and exits successfully. The squad with the most points wins.

Try with couples. Couples must join inside hands and stand side by side when jumping.

Loose Caboose

Playing Area: Playground, gymnasium.
Players: 12 to 30.
Supplies: None.
Skills: Running, dodging.

One child is designated as the loose caboose and tries to hook on to a train. Trains are formed by three or four children standing in a column formation with each child placing his or hands on the waist of the child immediately in front. The trains, by twisting and turning, endeavor to keep the caboose from hooking on to the back. Should the caboose manage to hook on, the front child in the train becomes the new caboose. Each train should attempt to keep together. If the number of children is 20 or more or there seems to be difficulty in hooking the caboose to the end of a train, there should be two cabooses.

Nine Lives

Playing Area: Any gymnasium or room or hard-surfaced area.
Players: Any number.
Supplies: Fleece balls.
Skills: Throwing, dodging.

Any number of fleece balls may be used. The more the better. At the signal, the players get a ball and hit as many people as possible. When a player counts that he or she has been hit anywhere nine times, he or she goes out of the game and stands against a wall until a new game is started. The following rules should be enforced.

1. Only one fleece ball in possession at a time.
2. A player may run anywhere with a ball or to get a ball.
3. A player may not be hit in the head. This puts the thrower out.

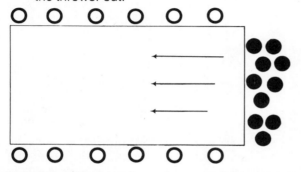

Teaching Hints: Many times, children cheat about the number of times they have been hit. A few words about sportsmanship may be necessary, but a high degree of activity is the important element.
Variations
1. For a ball caught on a fly, a designated number of hits may be taken away.
2. Specify throwing either left- or right-handed.

Running Dodgeball

Playing Area: Playground, gymnasium. Two parallel lines are drawn about 40 feet apart to form a gauntlet. The gauntlet is about 60 feet in length.
Players: Two teams, 10 to 15 on each team.
Supplies: Four volleyballs or rubber playground balls suitable for dodgeball.
Skills: Running, throwing, dodging.

Team A does the throwing and team B runs the gauntlet. Team A's players are divided, with half on one side of the gauntlet and half on the other. Four volleyballs are split between them.

Team B's players line up at one end of the gauntlet. They are to run through the gauntlet be-

tween members of team A without getting hit. In moving through, they can run separately or all together.

The throwing team may recover the volleyballs lying in the running area but must return to the sides before throwing. After a count is made of the successful runners, the teams trade places, and the game is repeated.
Variations
1. Instead of having the team run once across, have the players run across and immediately start back. They score a point only when they make the round trip without being hit.
2. A good active game can be played by having the ball rolled instead of thrown. This causes the players to jump high into the air to avoid being hit.

Squad Tag

Playing Area: Playground, gymnasium.
Players: Entire class.
Supplies: Pinnies or markers for a squad. Stopwatch.
Skills: Running, dodging.

This is a straight tag game with the entire squad acting as taggers. The object is to see which squad can tag the remainder of the class members in the shortest time. The tagging squad should be marked.

The tagging squad stands in a football huddle formation in the center of the area. Heads are down and hands are joined in the huddle. The remainder of the class is scattered as they wish throughout the area. On signal, the tagging squad scatters and tags the other class members. When a class member is tagged, he or she stoops in place and remains there. Time is taken when the last member is tagged. Each squad gets a turn.

Children need to be cautioned to watch for collisions, since there is much chasing and dodging in different directions. Definite boundaries need to be established.

Squeeze

Playing Area: Gymnasium, playground.
Players: Entire class.
Supplies: None.
Skill: Body management.

Definite lines are needed, and a basketball court provides the ideal area for this game. At the direction of the teacher, players move as prescribed within the defined area, generally the entire basketball court. They must keep moving by using the stipulated locomotor movement. A player may not fall, step on a boundary line, or collide with another child. Those who do so are out and stand (freeze) as obstacles in the movement area to be avoided by active players.

After a period of movement, the playing area is halved, and the game continues. This is repeated two more times, so finally the children are moving in one-eighth the original space. Throughout, the children must avoid colliding or bumping into each other.

When two children bump into each other, both are out, regardless of fault. Vary the kinds of prescribed locomotor movements. Agile children have fun seeing how close they can come without touching anyone.

Variation: An alternate penalty for colliding can be established by having the children who collided move to the sidelines and count up to 10 slowly. The purpose is to have them think about better control of their bodies. They reenter the game as soon as they have finished their counting.

Trades

Playing Area: Playground, gymnasium, classroom. Two parallel lines are drawn 60 feet apart.
Players: Entire class.
Supplies: None.
Skills: Imagery, running, dodging.

The class is divided into two teams of equal numbers, each of which has a goal line. Team B, the chasers, remains behind its goal line. Team A approaches from its goal line, marching to the following dialogue.

Team A: "Here we come."
Team B: "Where from?"
Team A: "New Orleans."
Team B: "What's your trade?"
Team A: "Lemonade."
Team B: "Show us some."

Team A moves up close to team B's goal line and proceeds to act out the motions of an activity, occupation, or specific task, which they have chosen previously. The members of team B make as many guesses as necessary to guess what the pantomime represents. Team A gives the initials of the activity to help. A correct guess means that team A must run back to its goal line chased by team B. Any member caught must join team B. The game is repeated with the roles reversed. The team ending with the greater number of players is the winner.

Teaching Hint: If one team has trouble guessing, the other players should provide hints. Also, teams should be encouraged to have a number of activities chosen so little time is consumed in the huddle for choosing the next activity to be guessed.

Trees

Playing Area: Playground, gymnasium. Two parallel lines are drawn 60 feet apart.
Players: Entire class.
Supplies: None.
Skills: Running, dodging.

All players except it are on one side of the area. On the signal "trees," the players run to the other side of the court. It tries to catch as many as possible. Any player tagged by it becomes a tree and must stop where he or she was tagged and keep both feet in place. He or she cannot move his or her feet but can tag any of the runners who come close enough. It continues to chase the players as they cross on signal until all but one are caught. This player becomes the tagger for the next game.

To speed things up, two taggers may be chosen. Also, the taggers should have reasonable ability to catch the others, or the game will move slowly. Children cross from side to side only on the signal "trees."

Whistle Mixer

Playing Area: Playground, gymnasium, classroom.
Players: Any number.
Supplies: Whistle.
Skills: All basic locomotor movements.

Children are scattered throughout the area. To begin, they walk around in any direction they wish. The teacher blows a whistle a number of times in succession with short, sharp blasts. Whatever the number of blasts, the children form small circles with the number in the circles equal to the number established by the whistle signal. Thus, if there are four blasts, the children form circles of four—no more, no less. Any children left out are eliminated. Also, if a circle is formed with more than the specified number, the entire circle is eliminated.

After the circles have been formed and the eliminated children have been moved to the sidelines, the teacher calls, "Walk," and the game continues. In walking, the children should move in different directions.

Variation: A fine version of this game can be done with the aid of a tom-tom. Different beats of the tom-tom would indicate various locomotor movements—skipping, galloping, slow walk, normal walk, running. The whistle would still be used to set the number to be in each circle.

THE GAMES PROGRAM FOR THE FIFTH GRADE

Fifth-Grade Games

Review Fourth-Grade Games
Battle Dodgeball
Bombardment
Bronco Dodgeball
Circle Hook-on
Circle Tug-of-War
Jolly Ball
Mickey Mouse
Right Dress, Left Dress
Right Face, Left Face (Maze Tag)
Scooter Kick Ball

Sunday
Touchdown
Whistle Ball

The Games

Battle Dodgeball

Playing Area: Playground, gymnasium.
Players: Two teams, 10 to 15 on each team.
Supplies: Two volleyball or rubber playground balls.
Skills: Throwing, dodging.

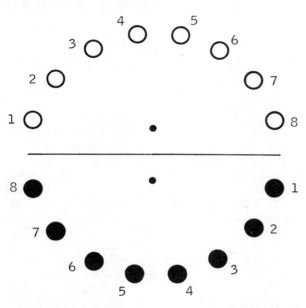

The teams form one circle, each occupying half of the circle. Players on each team are numbered consecutively. For any one number, there is a player on each team. Two volleyballs are placed about 5 feet apart in the center of the circle, one on each side of a center line that separates the teams from each other.

The teacher calls out the number he or she chooses. The two players with that number run forward; each picks up a ball and tries to hit the other with it. Players on the sides of the circle may retrieve balls and throw them to their teammates in the center. However, each competing player must stay in his or her half of the circle.

The winning player scores a point for his or her team. Play for a certain number of points or until each player has had a turn.
Variation: Call two numbers, which means two compete against two. Compete until one or both are hit.

Bombardment

Playing Area: Gymnasium.
Players: Two teams, 10 to 15 on each team.
Supplies: 12 Indian clubs for each team. Four volleyballs or rubber playground balls.

Skill: Throwing.

A line is drawn across the center of the floor from wall to wall. This divides the floor into two courts, each of which is occupied by one team. Another line is drawn 25 feet from the center line in each court. This is the club line. Each team sets its Indian clubs on this line. These should be spaced. Each team is given two of the balls. More balls can be used.

The object of the game is to knock over the other team's clubs. Players throw the balls back and forth but cannot cross the center line. Whenever a club is knocked over by a ball or accidentally by a player, the club is removed. The team with the most clubs standing is declared the winner.

Out-of-bounds balls can be recovered but must be thrown from the court.
Variation: Instead of removing the clubs, they can be reset. Two scorers, one for each club line, are needed for this version.

Bronco Dodgeball

Playing Area: Playground, gymnasium.
Players: 15 to 20.
Supplies: Volleyball or rubber playground ball.
Skills: Catching, passing, throwing, dodging.

Half of the children form a circle about 10 yards across. These are the throwers. The other children are in the center and form a bronco, made by the children standing in file formation, each with hands placed on the hips of the child immediately in front. The object of the game is to hit the rear member of the bronco with the ball. This is the only child who may be legally hit. The bronco moves around, protected by the child at the head of the file. He or she, however, is not permitted to use his or her hands.

As soon as the child at the rear of the bronco is hit, he or she leaves the circle and the next child on the end becomes the target. If the bronco breaks during the maneuvering, all the children to the rear of the break are eliminated. Exchange the circle and bronco players.

Five or six children may be as many as can conveniently maneuver as a bronco. Have two broncos in the center if the group is large. Stress quick passing and throwing, since this is the key to reducing the number in the bronco.

Circle Hook-on

Playing Area: Playground, gymnasium, classroom.
Players: Four.
Supplies: None.
Skills: Dodging, body management.

This is a game of one child against three, who form a small circle with joined hands. The object of the game is for the lone child to tag a designated child in the circle. The other two children in the circle, by dodging and maneuvering around, attempt to keep the tagger away from the third member of the circle. The circle players may maneuver and circle in any direction they wish but must not release hand grips. The tagger, in attempting to touch the protected circle player, must go around the outside of the circle. He or she is not permitted to go underneath or through the joined hands of the circle players.

Circle Hook-on (the teacher plays with the children)

Variations

1. Use a piece of cloth, a handkerchief, or a flag tucked in the belt in back of the child opposite. The fourth child tries to pull the flag from the belt.
2. Instead of tagging, the chaser tries to hook on the child being protected.

Teaching Hints: Watch for roughness by the two in the circle protecting the third. The game works better if the children are of about equal physical ability. Allow a period of time and rotate if the chaser is not successful. In any case, the children should rotate so each has a chance to be the tagger.

Circle Tug-of-War

Playing Area: Playground, gymnasium.
Players: 10 to 15 in each circle.
Supplies: 12 to 15 Indian clubs.
Skills: Pushing, pulling.

The object of the tug-of-war is to have the other players break a grip or knock over a club. A circle is formed by the players, who join hands with good grips. In the center of the circle, the Indian clubs are placed in a scattered formation. After the starting signal, the players pull or push to eliminate other players. Both players who break a grip are eliminated, and any player who knocks over a club in the struggle is out. After about half are eliminated, re-form the circle and start anew.

Variation: The game also can be played with the players facing out. With their backs to the center, they have more trouble dodging the Indian clubs.

Jolly Ball

Playing Area: Playground, gymnasium.
Players: 20 to 30.
Supplies: Cageball 24 inches or larger, or a pushball 36 to 48 inches.
Skill: Kicking.

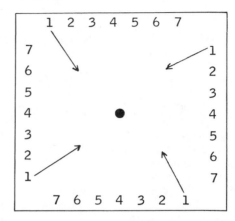

Four teams are organized, each of which forms one side of a hollow square. The children are sitting down, facing in, with hands braced behind them (crab position). On each team, the children are numbered consecutively from one to as far as needed. Each child waits until his or her number is called. The four active players (one from each team) move forward in crab position and try to kick the cageball over the heads of any one of the three opposing teams. The players on the teams also can kick the ball. Ordinarily, the hands are not to be used, but this could be allowed among less skilled children and in the learning stages of the game.

A point is scored against a team that allows the ball to go over its line. A ball that goes out at the corner between teams is dead and must be replayed. When a point is scored, the active children retire back to their teams, and another number is called. The team with the fewest points wins the game. This game is quite strenuous for the active players in the center, and time should be called after a reasonable length of time when there are no scores.

Variation: The game also can be played by allowing two children at a time from each team to be active.

Mickey Mouse

Playing Area: Playground, gymnasium, classroom.
Players: Entire class.
Supplies: Four Indian clubs.
Skill: Running.

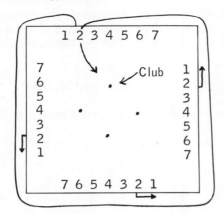

A hollow square, about 10 yards on each side, is formed by four teams, each of which occupies one side, facing in. The teams should be even in numbers. Each team is numbered consecutively from right to left. This means that there is one person on each team with the same number. The children are seated cross-legged.

A number is called by the teacher. The four children with the number run to the right all the way around the square and through their *own* vacated space toward the center of the square. Near the center in front of each team stands an Indian club. The first child to put the Indian club down on the floor is the winner. The clubs should be at an equal distance in front of the teams and far enough away from each other to avoid collisions in the center.

Scoring is kept by the words "Mickey Mouse." The player who puts the club down first gets to write two letters of the name. The player who is second gets to put down one letter. The lettering can be done in a space in front of each team, where the name would be reasonably protected from the runners. The first team to complete the name is the winner.

In number games of this type, the numbers are not called in order. The teacher should keep some kind of a tally to make sure every number is called.

Teaching Suggestion: Caution children not to slide on their knees when they put the club down.

Variation: Instead of having the group seated, have each one take a prone position, ready to do a Push-up. The teacher gives a preliminary command, such as "ready." Each child comes up to a push-up position. The teacher then calls the number. The children not running then return to the prone position on the floor. In this manner, each time a number is called, each child does a Push-up.

Right Dress, Left Dress

Playing Area: Playground, gymnasium.
Players: By squads or teams.
Supplies: None.

Skills: Body management, right-left concepts.

Competition is by teams, each of which has a leader. A predetermined order for lining up is established for each team.

The simplified version of the game calls for only two commands, "dress right" and "dress left." As directed by the teacher, the children move in the area, using the announced locomotor movement. On the command "dress right," each leader stops and his or her team lines up to his or her right in the prescribed order and stands at attention. The first team to do so wins a point. The command "dress left" calls for the children to line up to the left of the leader, again, in the prescribed order.

A slightly more complicated game adds the factor of direction to the challenge. The commands are preceded by one of the four directions. For example, if the challenge is "south, dress right," the leader faces south and the game is as before.

Teams bunch up together during movement, but this is expected. Judicious selection of direction and right-left combinations nullifies any maneuvering by the teams.

Right Face, Left Face (Maze Tag)

Playing Area: Playground, gymnasium.
Players: 25 to 35.
Supplies: None.
Skills: Running, dodging.

Children stand in rows straight both from front to rear and side to side. A runner and a chaser are picked. The children all face the same way and join hands with the players on each side. The chaser tries to tag the runner going up and down the rows but not breaking through or under the arms. The teacher can help the runner by calling "right face" or "left face" at the proper time. At this command, the children drop hands, face the new direction, and again grasp hands with those who are then on each side. New passages are then available to the runner and chaser. When the runner is caught or the children become tired, a new runner and chaser are chosen.

Variations
1. Directions can be used instead of the facing commands. The teacher can call out north, south, east, or west.
2. The original game from which the game above was taken is called Streets and Alleys. In this version, the teacher calls out, "Streets" and the children face in one direction. The call "alleys" causes them to face at right angles.
3. The command "air raid" can be given, which means the children drop to their knees and make themselves into small balls, tucking their heads and seats down.
4. Try with one runner and two chasers.

Scooter Kick Ball

Playing Area: Gymnasium, basketball court.
Players: 20 to 30, divided into two teams.
Supplies: Cageball, gym scooters for active players.
Skill: Striking with various body parts.

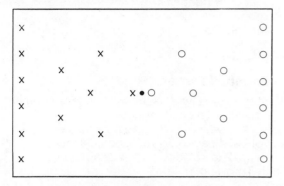

Each team is divided into active players (on scooters) and goal defenders. The active players are seated on the scooters, and the goal defenders are seated on the goal line, with feet extended. The object of the game is to kick the cageball over the goal line defended by the opposite team. The players are positioned as follows.

The game is started with a face-off of two opposing players on scooters at the center of the court. This position also is used after a goal is scored. The active players on scooters may propel the ball only with their feet. Touching the ball with the hands in an attempt to stop or propel the ball is a foul and results in a free kick by the opposition at the spot of the foul. A player may use his or her head and body to stop and propel the ball.

The players defending the goal are seated on the goal line. The first rule is to limit their defense by applying the same rule as for scooter players—not permitting use of the hands to stop the ball. The feet, body, and head may be used.

If scoring seems too easy, then permit the defenders to use their hands. Defenders should be restricted to the seated position at the goal line and not permitted to enter the field of play to propel or stop the ball.

If the sidelines are close to the walls of the gymnasium, there is little need to call out-of-bounds balls since the ball can rebound from the wall.

The number of scooters determines the number of active players. The game works well if half of the players from each team are in the center on scooters and the other half are goal defenders. After a goal or a stipulated period of time, active players and goal defenders exchange places.

Some consideration for glasses should be made, since the ball moves quite suddenly and glasses might be broken. One other problem arises with the active player who falls off his or her scooter. He or she should be required to seat himself or herself on the scooter before he or she can be eligible to propel the ball.

Variation: If there are enough scooters so each child in the game can have one, the game can be played under much the same rules as in soccer. A more restricted goal (perhaps half of the end line) can be set up with standards. A goalie can defend this area. All other players are active and can move to any spot on the floor.

The floor space should be large enough to allow some freedom for playing the game. Putting too many active players in a relatively small space causes a jamming up of the players.

Sunday

Playing Area: Two parallel lines are drawn about 50 feet apart.
Players: Entire class.
Supplies: None.
Skills: Running, dodging.

One player is it and stands in the center of the area between the two lines. All other children are on one of the two lines. The object is to cross to the other line without being tagged or making a false start.

Players stand with their front feet on the line. They must run across immediately when it calls out, "Sunday." Anyone who does not come immediately is considered caught. It may call out other days of the week to confuse the runners. No player may make a start if another day of the week is called. What "making a start" is must be defined. At the beginning, define it as a player moving either foot. Later, when the children get better at the game, a forward movement of the body can make one caught.

It must be careful to pronounce *Monday* in such a way that it cannot be confused with *Sunday*. If trouble develops here, eliminate *Monday* from the signals for the false start.

Touchdown

Playing Area: Playground, gymnasium. Two parallel lines about 60 feet apart are needed.
Players: Two teams, 10 to 15 on each team.
Supplies: Small object that can be concealed in the hand.
Skills: Running, dodging.

Two teams face each other, each standing on one of the parallel lines. One team goes into a huddle and the members decide which player is to carry an object to the opponent's goal line. The team moves out of the huddle and takes a position like a football team. On the charge signal "hike," the players run toward the opponent's goal line, each player holding his or her hands as if he or she were carrying the object. On the charge signal, the opponents also run forward and tag the players. When a player is tagged, he or she must stop immediately and open both hands to show whether or not he or she has the object.

When the player carrying the object reaches the goal line without being tagged, he or she calls, "Touchdown" and scores six points for his or her team. The team scoring retains possession of the object and gets another try. If the player carrying the object is tagged in the center area, the object is given to the other team. They go into a huddle and try to run it across the field and score.

Whistle Ball

Playing Area: Playground, gymnasium, classroom.
Players: Groups of six to eight.
Supplies: A ball for each group.
Skills: Passing, catching.

A group of not more than eight children stands in a circle formation. A ball is passed rapidly back and forth among them in any order. The object is to stay in the game the longest. Children sit down in place when they do any of the following:

1. They have the ball when the whistle blows. (The teacher should set a predetermined time period, at the end of which a whistle is blown. This can be anywhere from 5 to 20 seconds, with the time periods varied.)
2. A child makes a bad throw or fails to catch a good throw.
3. A player returns the ball directly to the person from whom he or she received it.

When the game gets down to two or three players, the time limits should be short.

Teaching Suggestions: One way to control the time periods is to appoint a child as timer, giving him or her a list of the time periods, a whistle, and a stopwatch. The timer should be cautioned not to give any advance indication of when he or she will blow the stop signal. An automatic timer enhances the game.

THE GAMES PROGRAM FOR THE SIXTH GRADE

Comparatively fewer games are listed for the sixth grade than for each of the other grades. Good use should be made of any of the games for the other grades. The children in the sixth grade are more sophisticated, and much of their games experience comes from the sports program.

Sixth-Grade Games

Review Fifth-Grade Games
Cageball Target Throw
Chain Tag

Jump the Shot Variations
Low Bridge Limbo
One-Base Dodgeball
Over the Wall
Pin Dodgeball
Prisoner's Base
Scatter Dodgeball
Spud
Triangle Dodgeball

The Games

Cageball Target Throw

Playing Area: Gymnasium with a space about the size of a small basketball court.
Players: Two teams, 5 to 15 on each team.
Supplies: 1 cageball (18 inches, 24 inches, or 30 inches), 12 to 15 balls of various sizes.
Skill: Throwing.

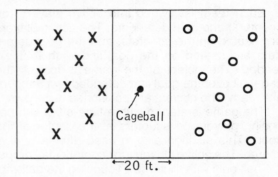

An area about 20 feet wide is marked across the center of the playing area, with a cageball in the center. The object of the game is to throw the smaller balls against the cageball, forcing it across the line in front of the other team. Players may come up to the line to throw but may not throw while inside the cageball area. However, a player may enter the area to recover a ball. No one is to touch the cageball at any time, nor may the cageball be pushed by a ball in the hands of a player.

If the cageball seems to roll too easily, it should be deflated slightly. The throwing balls can be of almost any size—soccer balls, volleyballs, playground balls, et cetera.

Variation: Have two rovers in the center area, one from each team, to retrieve balls. These players cannot block throws or prevent a ball from hitting the target but are there for the sole purpose of retrieving balls for their teams.

Chain Tag

Playing Area: Playground with two parallel lines about 50 feet apart.
Players: 20 to 40.
Supplies: None.
Skills: Running, dodging.

Essentially, this game is like other goal-exchange games, except in the manner players can be caught. In this game, the center is occupied by three players who form a chain with joined hands. The free hands on either side of the chain do the tagging.

The players in the center call, "Come," and the other children cross from one line to another. The chain tries to tag any of the runners. Anyone caught joins the chain. When the chain becomes too large, it should be divided into several smaller chains.

Variation: *Catch of Fish:* In this game, chain catches the children by surrounding them like a fish net. The runners cannot run under or through the links of the net.

Jump the Shot Variations

The sixth-grade teacher should emphasize the Jump the Shot routines and variations as listed in the fourth-grade program. The following should be added to the activity routines.

Skill: Rope jumping.

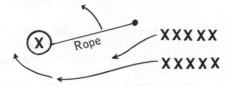

Two squads are in file formation and face the rope turner.

1. Each player runs clockwise (against the turn of the rope), jumping the rope as often as necessary to return to the squad.
2. Each player runs counterclockwise in the same direction as the rope is turning and tries to run around the circle before the rope can catch up with him or her. If this happens, he or she must jump to allow the rope to go under him or her. The best time for a player to start is just after the rope has passed.
3. Try some of the stunts in which the hands and feet are on the ground, and see whether the players can have the rope pass under them. The Rabbit Jump, push-up position, Lame Dog, and others offer possibilities.

Low Bridge (Limbo)

Playing Area: Gymnasium, classroom.
Players: 5 to 10.
Supplies: Wand, low standards.
Skill: Body management.

This game is popular in many lands, and some players develop a fine degree of skill in the task required. The object of the game is to move under a bar supported like a high jump bar without dislodging the bar or touching the ground with the hands or body. The bar should be started high enough so all children can go under it successfully. Each child is to get three tries to go under the bar. If he or she fails, he or she is eliminated and acts as an official for the event.

Blocks could be used together with different sizes of boxes to support the wand. Some kind of a system is needed so the wand can be lowered a little at a time for each repetition of the event. The wand is lowered after all children have gone under or have had three misses. Two miniature standards similar to the type used for the high jump make the event precise and easy to administer. (See page 599.)

One-Base Dodgeball

Playing Area: Playground, gymnasium. A home line is drawn at one end of the playing space. A base or standard is placed about 50 feet in front of the home line.
Players: Two teams, 8 to 15 on each team.
Supplies: Base (or standard), volleyball or playground ball.
Skills: Running, dodging, throwing.

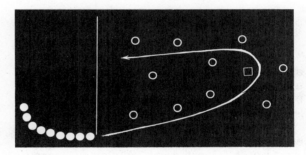

One team is scattered around the fielding area. The boundaries of this area are determined by the number of children. The other team is lined up in single file behind the home line. Two children are running at a time.

The object of the game for the fielding team is to hit the players with the ball, who try to round the base and head back for the home line without being hit. The game is continuous, meaning that, as soon as a running team player is hit or crosses the home line, another player starts immediately.

The fielding team may not run with the ball but must pass it from player to player, trying to hit one of the runners.

The running team scores a point for each player who successfully runs around the base and back to the home line.

At the start of the game, the running team has two players ready at the right side of the home line. The others on the team are in line, waiting for a turn. The teacher throws the ball anywhere in the field, and the first two runners start toward the base. They must run around the base from the right side. After all the players have run, the teams exchange places. The team scoring the most runs wins.

Teaching Suggestions: Players on the fielding team should make short passes to a person close to a runner, so the runner can be hit. They must be alert, because two children are running at a time. The next player on the running team must watch carefully, so he or she can start the instant one of the two preceding runners is back safely or has been hit.

Over the Wall

Playing Area: Playground.
Players: Entire class.
Supplies: None.
Skills: Running, dodging.

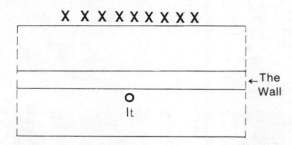

Two parallel goal lines are drawn about 60 feet apart. Two additional parallel lines about 3 feet apart are laid out parallel to the goal lines in the middle of the game area. This is the wall. Side limits have to be established.

One player is it and stands on, or behind, the wall. All other players are behind one of the goal lines. It calls, "Over the wall." All players then must run across the wall to the other goal line. It tries to tag any player he or she can, who, if caught, helps catch the others. Players also are considered caught when they step on the wall. They must clear it with a leap or jump and cannot step on it anywhere, including the lines. After crossing over to the other side safely, players must wait for the next call.

The game can be made more difficult by increasing the width of the wall. It can step on, or run through, the wall at will.

Pin Dodgeball

Playing Area: Gymnasium.
Players: Entire class.
Supplies: Two volleyballs, six Indian clubs.
Skills: Throwing, dodging, catching.

Two teams of equal number play the game. Each team is given one volleyball and three Indian clubs. A court 30 by 60 feet or larger with a center line is needed. The size of the court depends upon the number of children in the game. The object of the game is to eliminate all players on the opposing team or to knock down their Indian clubs. The

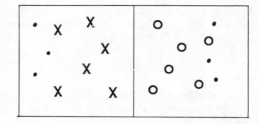

volleyballs are used to throw at the opposing team members or to knock down the clubs. Each team stays in its half of the court.

A player is eliminated if he or she does any of the following.

1. He or she is hit *on the fly* by a ball he or she does not catch.
2. He or she steps over the center line to throw or retrieve a ball. Any opposing team member hit under these circumstances is not eliminated.
3. He or she attempts to block a thrown ball with a ball in his or her hand, and the thrown ball touches him or her in any manner. A player can legally block a thrown ball with a ball held in his or her hand.

A foul is called when a player holds a ball longer than 10 seconds without throwing at the opposing team. The ball is given immediately to the opposing team.

Players who are eliminated should move to the sidelines and sit down, so it can be clearly determined who is still active.

The Indian clubs are put any place in the team area. Players may guard the clubs but must not touch them. When a club is knocked down, it is removed immediately from the game. If a club is knocked down unintentionally by a member of the defending team, the club is counted as down.

A player can be saved if the ball hits him or her and is caught by a teammate before it touches the ground.

A referee should take position at the side of the court near the center line. When a foul is called for holding the ball over 10 seconds, play stops, and the ball is rolled to the offended team.

The game is won when all players from one team have been eliminated or all three clubs on one side have been knocked down.

Prisoner's Base

Playing Area: A rectangular area marked off as in the diagram. The size of the area depends somewhat upon the number of children playing.
Players: Two teams with 5 to 15 on each side. Each team has a captain.
Supplies: None.
Skills: Running, dodging.

To win the game, a team must have one of its players enter the opponent's goal area without being tagged or one team must capture all players from the opposing team.

The one-way tagging rule dominates the game, and the time a player crosses his or her own goal line to enter the playing area is critical. A player may tag and capture an opponent who was already in the playing area when the player crossed his or her own goal line to enter the playing area. This player is immune from being tagged by any opponent who *preceded him or her* into the playing area.

Players move into the playing field and later retreat behind their own goal line to establish new eligibility to tag. The basic idea is to try to capture an opponent and avoid being captured. If a player has been captured, both he or she and the captor may go to the appropriate prison and goal line without interference.

An illustration utilizing players from two opposing teams, the reds and the blues, may help to clarify. Player #1 (reds) is in the playing field attempting to set a foot inside the opponent's prison without being tagged. As he or she gets near, player A (blues) crosses the goal line and tries to tag him. Player #1 retreats, chased by player A. As player A gets closer to the red goal line, player #2 (reds) enters the playing area to try to tag player A. As player #2 approaches, player B (blues) crosses his or her line and tries to tag player #2. Thus, each player tries to tag and avoid being tagged.

A prisoner must keep one foot in the prison and can stretch forward as far as he or she is able to make rescue easier. To be rescued, a prisoner must be tagged by his or her own teammate who has been able to reach him or her without being tagged. The rescued and the rescuer return to their own goal line without the penalty of being tagged. Both are then active players.

If more than one prisoner is captured, they may form a chain by holding hands, the last prisoner caught acting as anchor and keeping one foot in the prison. Only the first prisoner at the end of the chain can be released.

The captain directs his or her team strategy: as some players guard the goal, others guard the prisoners, and another group acts as taggers.

Any player who crosses the sidelines to avoid being tagged is considered a prisoner.

Variation: A popular version of this game is called Stealing Sticks. The game is played in the same manner, except that 10 sticks or Indian clubs are added. These are divided, with five going to each team. Any player crossing the opponent's goal area without being tagged is eligible to take home one stick. The game continues until one side has lost its sticks. If the play is ended before either side has possession of all the sticks, the team with the most sticks wins.

Scatter Dodgeball

Playing Area: Playground, gymnasium. If outside, definite boundaries should be set.
Players: Any number can play.
Supplies: Two or three volleyballs or rubber balls suitable for dodgeball.
Skills: Throwing, dodging.

The children are scattered throughout the area. The teacher rolls the two balls into the playing area. Anyone may pick up a ball and throw it at anyone else. If a person is hit or the ball in his or her hand is struck with a ball, he or she goes to the sidelines. If he or she has a ball in his or her hand, he or she should drop it immediately and not attempt to throw. If two children throw at each other and both are hit, both are eliminated.

No player may have possession of all the volleyballs. The ball must be actually thrown, since touching another player while the ball is held in the hand does not put the player out.

Children should be cautioned not to punish others unnecessarily with hard hits. Throws should be below the waist whenever possible, and a throw hitting the head puts the thrower out of the game.

Spud

Playing Area: Playground.
Players: 8 to 12.
Supplies: Rubber playground ball (6 to 8½ inches) or volleyball.
Skills: Throwing, running, stopping.

Players are numbered consecutively and stand in a small circle. One player is in the center, holding the ball. He or she tosses the ball straight up moderately high, at the same time calling the number of one of the other players. All players scatter immediately, except the player whose number was called. He or she goes to the center of the circle, catches the ball, and immediately calls, "Stop." All players stop at once in place and must not move their feet from the fixed positions. The player with the ball takes three steps in any direction and selects a player whom he or she wishes to hit. He or she throws the ball at this player, trying to hit him or her. If he or she misses, he or she gets a point (dud) against him or her. If he or she hits a player or the player moves his or her feet, the player gets one point against him or her. The player against whom the point was scored throws up the ball for the next game. When a player gets a stipulated number of points (three or four), he or she is out of the game or pays a penalty.

Teaching Suggestion: Some control must be made on the toss of the ball into the air. It should be of moderate height and go straight up and down. There also should be control over the order of the numbers to avoid favoritism or collusion. If there is a problem, make a rule that a number may not be called more than twice during the course of a game. When one or two players have been eliminated, re-form the game. If the throwing is too successful, make it a rule that the children must keep only one foot in place or that they must decrease or shorten the number of steps that can be taken after catching.

Variations

1. Use a fleece ball instead of the playground ball or volleyball. With a fleece ball, do not allow any steps by the thrower.
2. The game can be played by partners, who have the same number. One partner catches the ball, while the other partner runs out with the scattering players. On "stop," he or she also must hold his or her place. The partner with the ball throws to his or her partner, who must keep both feet in place while catching.

He or she in turn tries to hit any of the other players.

Triangle Dodgeball

Playing Area: Playground, gymnasium.
Players: Four.
Supplies: Ball for dodgeball.
Skills: Throwing and catching, dodging.

Three players stand in a triangular formation, about 8 yards apart. One of the three players has a ball. The fourth player is the dodger and stands in the center of the triangle.

To start the game, three passes must be made between the triangle players. After these, the players attempt to hit the dodger, who must stay within the confines of the triangle. When a hit is made on the dodger below the shoulders, the successful thrower becomes the dodger.

Twenty-two

Relays

Relays are enjoyable activities that add interest and competition to some phases of physical education. When conducted properly, they can provide good values in helping develop fitness, movement skills, and social objectives. Children can learn to cooperate with others in the interest of winning, to conform to rules and directions, and to use skills in situations of stress and competition. On the other hand, if the relays are not conducted in a sound, educational way, the child learns that he or she can win by cheating.

Relays should not be overworked in the program. In some cases, instructors turn to these in an attempt to solve activity motivation problems, because relays hold a high interest for children. No hard sell is necessary.

Relays serve as a laboratory for skills and, in some cases, are a part of skill methodology. Usually, it is sound to have children show reasonable competence in skills before racing; otherwise, they forget to perform the skills correctly in their haste to win. Overemphasis on winning compounds this problem. To win is the goal, but not at any cost.

A few special instructional supplies such as blocks, pie plates, and standing pegs are needed for relays. These can be kept in a special container. Otherwise, items for relay races are taken from the regular physical education supplies.

TYPES OF RELAYS

Three types can be identified according to the participation of the players.

Regular Relays

In regular relays, each player completes the chore when it is his or her turn and then retires from action.

Revolving Relays

In a revolving relay, each player participates both when it is his or her turn and also as part of the relay task. An example of this is a ball-handling relay in which each player handles the ball on each turn (Arch Ball and Corner Fly, for example).

Modified Relays

Modified relays are number-calling relays. They are not true relays in the sense of one player completing a chore and tagging off the next player. However, they have their place in the program, providing opportunity for alertness and quick reaction when the child's number is called.

INSTRUCTIONAL PROCEDURES

1. Place from four to eight players on a team. Too many on a team drags out the race and the children lose interest.
2. If the teams have uneven numbers, either some players on the smaller teams should run twice or a rotation system should be set up by which the extra players wait out in turn. Make sure that the rotation system is fair and that each player on the team, not just the unskilled, lays out in turn. This principle also should apply to the teams with fewer mem-

bers; otherwise, the more skilled runners will always run twice. See that running is rotated fully.

3. Appoint a captain for each team. Let him or her arrange the order, be responsible for the application of the rules, and help keep things under control. Also place responsibility on him or her to call fouls on his or her team. After the race, captains can be asked about their teams' conformity to the rules.

4. It helps in relays, particularly of the revolving type, when the last runner or finishing player is identified with an armband, pinny, or colored shirt. The captain generally should be the finishing player, but this role can be assigned to another member of the team. Obvious identification of the finishing player keeps the teacher informed of the progress of the race and allows him or her to anticipate the finish.

5. Infractions of the rules should be penalized. It is good social learning for the children to experience a situation in which they must conform to rules or be assessed a penalty. A team could be disqualified, points could be deducted, or other penalties could be imposed. All teams and players should be penalized on an equal basis.

6. It is important that the finishing order be determined properly. In the instructions, one must be definite about the start, turning point, and finishing act. In some races, crossing the line can be the finishing act. In others, some definite act, held position, or specified formation can be used. A definite finishing act helps to determine winners more validly.

7. Some definite marker or object should be used as a turning point to eliminate arguments. A turning point could be children running to a line and back. Cones, chairs, Indian clubs, jump standards, and beanbags are examples of things that can be used. If cones or Indian clubs are used, knocking over the turning point is disqualification unless the runner resets the marker before proceeding.

8. To encourage teams to win is fundamental, since this is the children's chief goal. However, too much emphasis on winning makes the skilled resent being on teams with those of lesser ability. The idea of winning at any cost must be squelched.

9. Distances need to be modified when restricted movements are used, such as the Puppy Dog Run, the Crab Walk, and others in which the physical demands are heavy. When hopping is used, a change to the other foot should be made halfway through the race.

10. Demonstrate a relay just enough so each team understands the procedures. This can entail a simple demonstration by one individual or having the entire team practice the routine. If the new relay does not seem to be started properly, stop the group and review the instructions.

11. For modified relays, the teacher should make up a card with a list of numbers to ensure that all numbers will be called without the need to stop the activity to make this determination.

12. Set some procedures about the handling of supplies. Have a central source, and appoint one person from each team to secure and return equipment.

13. Some procedures for ensuring fair tagging off for the next runner should be instituted. Runners should not leave the restraining line before being tagged. Exchanging a baton or a beanbag can assure fair play.

14. Place the responsibility for monitoring the run of the preceding runner on the next runner. If the runner has made an error that needs correction, the next runner should hold up both hands, palms forward, and direct the runner to return and make the needed correction.

15. Traffic rules should be clear. In most cases, the way to the right governs. When the runner goes around the turning point, he or she does it from the right (counterclockwise), returning past the finish line on the right side also as he or she faces the line of team members. He or she tags the left hand of the next runner with his or her left hand.

16. To avoid putting too much stigma on the less skilled players, place these members in the middle of the team. This is preferred to a starting or finishing position, where other students can easily see their lack of skill.

17. Any dropped or mishandled ball must be retrieved by the person dropping it. It must be started by him or her in the proper sequence at the point where it was dropped.

KINDERGARTEN AND FIRST-GRADE APPROACH

While relays, as such, are a little beyond the capacity of most kindergarten and first-grade children, some experience in handling beanbags and yarn balls in relay sequences is of value. Place the children in a line (side-by-side) formation, and have them pass the articles down to the end; or arrange them in a circle formation, and have them pass the beanbag around the circle. The object of the activity is to pass well and not drop the article. Some attention can be given to seeing which group can do it first, but this should not be the goal. The objective should be learning to participate in this kind of activity and to cooperate with others.

Another way to develop relay concepts is to place the squads or teams in a squad file formation and then proceed as follows.

1. The first child (head of the file) in each team moves toward and around a given turning point a short distance away and is asked to return to his or her place. The first child to complete this action successfully wins a point for his or her team.
2. The child is asked to go to the rear of the line, and the next child has his or her turn.
3. The next step would be for the child to move directly without delay to the rear of the line after he or she has completed his or her turn. Learning to go around the designated side of the turning point and returning up the correct aisle for safety purposes can be conceptualized.
4. When simple relays are run with kindergarten and first-grade children, it is recommended that a beanbag be exchanged between runners. Children can be instructed not to run unless they have the beanbag.

SELECTED RELAYS

Most of the relays presented can be experienced successfully by children from grades three through six, depending upon their previous experience and skill level. Relays may be introduced into the second-grade experiences, but they need to be selected carefully.

Outside of the foregoing statements, no attempt is made to classify relays by grade level, because that would be an exceedingly difficult process. An attempt has been made to arrange the relay movements roughly according to increasing difficulty.

Beanbag Relays

Beanbags make a good starting point for younger children in relay competition. They can be handled more easily than balls.

Beanbag Pass Relay

Players are in a line, standing side by side. The player on the right starts the beanbag, which is passed from one player to the next down the line. When it gets to the end of the line, the race is over. Be sure each player handles the bag or ball. Rotate.

The next stage is to operate this as a revolving relay, in which each member of the team must rotate from the front of the squad to the rear. When each child has had an opportunity to be the lead member of the group, the relay is finished. Vary with an underleg pass, in which the beanbag is passed underneath one leg of the child to the next player.

Circle Beanbag Pass Relay

Players stand in a circle, facing out, close enough so the beanbag can be handed from player to player. Begin and end one circuit with the same player. Use the underleg pass here also.

Carry and Fetch Relay

The formation is a lane with a hoop or circle up to 30 feet in front of each team. The first runner of the team has a beanbag. On "go," he or she carries the beanbag forward and puts it inside the hoop, returning and tagging off the next runner. The second runner goes forward, picks up the beanbag, and hands it off to the third runner. Thus, one runner carries the beanbag and the next runner fetches it back. Different locomotor movements can be specified.

Beanbag Circle Change Relay

Players are in lane formation. Two hoops or circles are about 15 and 30 feet in front of the runners. A beanbag is in the far hoop.

The initial runner of the team runs forward, picks up the beanbag, and moves it to the other hoop. The next player picks it up and takes it back. The beanbag must rest inside the hoop.

The Farmer and the Crow Relay

Runners are in lane formation. A line is drawn about 20 feet in front of the teams. The first runner of each team is the farmer, the second runner the crow, and so on. The farmer has five beanbags. On "go," the farmer hops forward and drops the five beanbags reasonably spaced with the last beanbag placed beyond the drawn line. He or she runs back and tags the next player, the crow. The crow runs to the farthest beanbag, begins hopping, and as he or she hops picks up the beanbags. He or she hands the five beanbags to the third runner, the farmer, who puts the objects out again.

Note: Whenever a player has a beanbag in his or her hand, he or she should hop. He or she runs when he or she has no beanbags. The race can be run with hopping required during its entirety. The last beanbag should be placed beyond the far line, since this determines how far each player will need to move.

Lane Relays without Equipment

The basic lane formation is this:

Each runner runs in turn. The race is over when the last runner finishes his or her turn. Lane relays

are usually regular relays. Different types of movements can challenge the runners.

Locomotor movements: walking, running, skipping, hopping, galloping, sliding, jumping.

Stunt and animal movements: Puppy Dog Run, Seal Walk, Bear Walk, Rabbit Jump, Frog Jump, Crab Walk, et cetera.

Restricted movements: heel and toe, sore toe (hold left foot with right hand), walk on heels, Crazy Walk (page 334), Toe Tug Walk (page 347), et cetera.

Partner Relays

1. Children run with partners (inside hands joined) just as a single runner would using running, walking, skipping, hopping, and galloping.
2. Children face each other with both hands joined (as partners) and slide one way to a turning point, sliding back to starting point leading with the other side.
3. Wheelbarrow Relay: One person walks on his or her hands while the partner holds him or her by the *lower legs,* wheeling him or her down to a mark. Change positions for the return.

Chariot Relay

Three children run as a single unit. Two of them stand side by side with inside hands joined, forming the chariot. The driver stands behind and grasps the outside hands of the chariot. Two or more chariots form a relay team. In front of each team is a turning point, around which the chariot must travel on its leg of the race. The chariot whose turn is next starts when the prior chariot crosses the original starting line. Running lanes must be spaced far enough apart to avoid collisions, since chariots demand considerable space while running.

Sedan Carry Relay

Three children run at one time, two to carry and one to ride. To form a seat for the carry, two children face each other. Each grasps his or her own left wrist with his or her right hand. The open hand then grasps the partner's wrist. The person carried sits on the seat and puts his or her hands around the necks of the carriers.

Other Lane Relays

Indian Club Relays

There are a number of relays that can be run using Indian clubs.

1. All Up, All Down Relay: Three Indian clubs are set in a small circle about 20 feet in front of each team. The first player runs forward and puts the Indian clubs down. The second runner goes forward and sets the clubs up one at a time, using only one hand. The clubs must stand. The next player puts them down, and so on.
2. Draw a short (24-inch) line about 20 feet in front of each team. An Indian club is standing on one side of the line. Each player must run forward and stand the Indian club on the other side of the line, using one hand only.
3. Two adjacent circles are drawn about 20 feet in front of each team. Three Indian clubs are standing in one of the circles. Each runner in turn runs forward and moves the clubs one at a time so they will stand in the other circle. The next player moves the clubs back one at a time to the original circle.
4. Roll and Set Relay: Each team has a mat and an Indian club. The mat is placed lengthwise in front of the team, and the club is on the floor by the edge of the mat nearest to the team. The starting mark is about 5 feet from the edge of the mat. The first player runs toward the mat, picking up the club. With the club carried in his or her hand, he or she does a forward roll and sets the club beyond the far edge. He or she runs back and tags off the next player. This player runs to the club, picks it up, does a Forward Roll on the way back, and sets the club in the original spot. The players alternate in this fashion until all have run. The club must stand each time, or the player must return and make it stand.

Three Spot Relay

Three parallel lines are drawn in front of the teams to provide three spots for each team. Lines can be 10 to 15 feet apart.

Each player is given three tasks to perform, one at each spot. He or she then runs back and tags off the next player, who repeats the performance. Suggestions for the task are these.

1. Prone (facedown on the floor).
2. Back (lie on back on floor).
3. Obeisance (touch forehead to floor).
4. Nose and toe (touch toe to nose from sitting position).
5. Do a specified number of hops, jumps, Push-ups, Curl-ups, et cetera.

6. Perform a designated stunt, such as the Coffee Grinder, Knee Dip, et cetera.
7. Rope jumping with specified turns.

Teaching Suggestions: It must be made clear that the runner must perform according to the designated directions at each spot. He or she must complete the performance before moving to the next spot. Other task ideas can be used. The winning team can select the requirements for the next race.

Gym Scooter Relays

Each team has a gym scooter. Scooters lend themselves to a wide variety of movements, both with individuals and partners. However, scooters should not be used as skateboards.

Some suggestions for individual movements are these.
1. Seated, propelling with the hands or the feet.
2. Kneeling, propelling with the hands.
3. Facedown, moving in alligator or swimming fashion.

In work with partners, the system can be employed where one partner pushes or pulls the other on the scooter to the turning point and a change is made of rider and pusher there. The other system is to have the child supplying the moving force become the next rider at the return to the team's restraining line, where the next relay member becomes the pusher.

Some partner actions are these.
1. Rider kneeling, partner pushing or pulling.
2. Rider in a Seat Balance, partner pushing or pulling on the feet of the rider.
3. Rider doing a Tummy Balance, partner pushing on the feet.

The Wheelbarrow Race also can be done with the down person supporting his or her hands on a scooter.

Potato-Type Relays

A small box about a foot square is placed 5 feet in front of each lane. Four 12-inch circles are drawn at intervals of 5 feet beyond the box. This makes the last circle 25 feet from the starting point. Four blocks or beanbags are needed for each team.

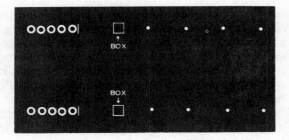

To start, the blocks for each team are placed in the box in front of it. The first runner goes to the box, takes a single block, and puts it in one of the circles. He or she returns to the box each time and places the blocks one at a time in the circles. When the four blocks are in the circles, he or she tags off the second runner. This runner brings the blocks back to the box one at a time and tags off the third runner, who returns the blocks to the circles, and so on.

Variation: The race can be run by using Indian clubs. Instead of using a box, draw a circle large enough to contain four Indian clubs.

Teaching Suggestions: The use of the box to receive the blocks makes a definite target for the blocks to be placed. When the blocks are returned to the circles, some regulation must be made regarding the placement. The blocks should be considered placed only when they are inside or touching a line. Blocks outside need to be replaced before the runner can continue. Paper plates can be used in place of the circles drawn on the floor.

Sack Race

The Sack Race has long been a popular picnic event and holds strong attraction for the children. Each team has a sack, and the runners must progress while their feet are inside the sack. Either lane or shuttle formations can be employed.

In lane formation, the sacked runner goes around a marker, returns to his or her team, and gives the sack to the next participant. Another way of running the race is to have the runner move while in the sack to a marker, get out of the sack, and run back to the head of his or her line. In the shuttle formation, the first runner moves in the sack across the area and gives the sack to the next runner.

Sturdy grain sacks made of burlap hold up well. Large plastic garbage bags can be used, but they are more breakable, especially on rough surfaces.

Three-legged Race

This is another old favorite. Two children run together as a single unit in the following fashion. The children stand side by side, facing the same direction. Adjacent ankles are tied together with a 3-to-4-foot-long piece of rope. Arms around the body and/or waist help provide balance. With ankles tied together, the two children must cooperate in their leg rhythm. The race can be organized as a lane relay or a shuttle relay. Allow the children a period of practice before running the race.

Obstacle-Type Relays

These races involve some kind of task the runners must do.

Over and Under

Stretch a magic rope about 18 inches above the floor at the point where the turning point would be normally. Each runner jumps over the rope and immediately starts back by going under the rope.

Figure Eight

Space three or four cones evenly in front of each team. Players weave in and out in figure-eight fashion.

Bench Relays

A balance-beam bench or an ordinary bench is in front of each two teams. Teams are in lane formation.

Several interesting races can be run using benches. The following are suggested.

1. Run forward, jump over the bench, jump back again, return, and tag off.
2. Each team has a beanbag. Run to the bench, pass the beanbag underneath, and return to the team, giving the beanbag to the next player, who repeats the run.
3. Each team has a beanbag, which is placed about 3 feet in front of the bench. The first player runs forward, picks up the beanbag, and jumps over the bench, carrying the bag with him or her. He or she drops it on the far side of the bench. He or she then jumps back over the bench and tags off. The next runner jumps over the bench, picks up the bag, jumps back over the bench with the bag, and places the bag on the floor near original position. The players alternate carrying the bag over and bringing it to the near side.

Eskimo Relay

Teams are in lane formation, with each team having two squares of cardboard about 2 by 2 feet. Players race two at a time. The cardboards represent cakes of ice, and the task is to use the cardboards as stepping stones. One player is the stepper, and one handles the cardboards. The stepper may not touch the floor. There are two ways this can be operated in lane formation. The first is to have the cardboard player handle the cardboards to a turning point and then exchange places. The second is to operate on a crossover basis, where the cardboard player conveys the stepper to the distant mark. The stepper and the card holder then exchange roles. The cardboards are given to the next player at the head of the line, and the old cardboard player becomes the new stepper to be conveyed across.

Variation: The race can be run in shuttle formation, with the children working in pairs. The children should go both ways (a second trip) during the race, so the stepper and cardboard handler exchange places.

Jack Rabbit Relay (Jump Stick Relay)

Each runner carries a broomstick or wand 3½ to 4 feet long. A turning point is established about 30 feet in front of each lane.

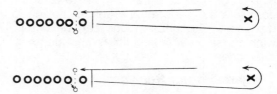

The race starts with the first player in line running forward around the turning point and back to the head of the line. In the meantime, the next player takes a short step to the right and gets ready to help with the stick. The runner with the stick is then returning on the left side and shifts the stick to his or her left hand. The second player reaches out his or her right hand and takes the other end of the stick at the head of the line. The stick then is carried under the others, who must jump up to let the stick go past. When the stick has passed under all the players, the original player releases his or her grip and remains at the end of the line. The second runner runs around the turning point, and the next player in line helps him or her with the stick, becoming the next runner when the stick has gone under all the jumpers. Each player repeats until all have run.

To end the race properly takes a little doing. The simplest way is to call the race complete when the last runner crosses the line with the wand. A second way is to have him or her carry the wand under the team helped by the original first runner, who has been rotated to the front of the line. The last runner releases the wand and the first runner with the held wand takes his or her place at the head of the line. The team is then as it was at the start.

Teaching Suggestion: If the children are unfamiliar with the relay, practice is needed. When the children carry the stick back under the jumpers, it should be quite close to the ground.

Hula Hoop Relay

Each team consists of a file of five or six children who have their hands joined. The leader in front holds a hoop in his or her free hand. The object is to pass the hoop down the line so that all the bodies go through the hoop until the last person holds the hoop. The last person takes the hoop to the head of the line and the process is repeated until the original leader is again at the head.

The hoop may be manipulated by the hands as long as the children retain joined hands, even to the point of locking little fingers. All bodies must pass through the hoop, including the last person's.

Variation: Moving the hoop can be done in a circle of children (all the children's hands are joined). Hang the hoop on a pair of joined hands; when the hoop has gone around the circle through all the bodies and back to the same spot, the race is over.

Lane Relays with Balls

There are many interesting ball relays that utilize a variety of formations and actions, including bouncing, dribbling, passing, and rolling. Lane formations can feature ball skills. Revolving-team ball relays are those in which the teams stand in a lane-type formation with the player in front of each team having the ball. The patterns of ball handling can become races.

Bounce Ball Relay

A circle is drawn 10 to 15 feet in front of each team. The first player runs to the circle, bounces the ball once, runs back to his or her team, and *gives* the ball to the second player, who repeats the same routine. Each player has a turn, and the team having the last child to carry his or her ball back over the finish line first wins. To vary, have the players bounce the ball more than once.

Kangaroo Relay

The first player in each lane has a ball between his or her knees held by knee pressure. He or she jumps forward, retaining control of the ball, rounds the turning point, and jumps back to the head of the file, where he or she gives the ball to the next player, who repeats. If he or she loses the ball from between the knees, he or she must stop and replace it. Slightly deflated balls are easier to retain.

Basketball or Soccer Ball Dribbling Relays

See chapters twenty-six and twenty-nine for some suggested patterns.

Bowling Relay

The player at the head of each team has a ball. A line is drawn 15 to 20 feet in front of each team. The first player runs to the line, turns, and rolls the ball back to the second player. The second player must wait behind the starting line to catch the ball, and then he or she repeats the pattern of the first player. The race is over when the last player has received the ball and carried it over the forward line.

Crossover Relay (Lane Relay)

This relay is similar to Bowling Relay, except the ball is thrown instead of rolled.

Arch Ball Relay (Revolving-Team Relay)

Each player, using both hands, passes the ball overhead to the next person, and so on to the back player. The back player on receiving the ball, runs to the head of his or her line, and the activity is repeated. The race is over when the original front player comes back to his or her spot at the front of the line. Each player must clearly handle the ball.

Right and Left Relay (Revolving-Team Relay)

Same general action as Arch Ball, except the ball is handed to the person behind with a side turn. The first turn is to the right, and the next person turns to the left.

Straddle Ball Relay (Revolving-Team Relay)

Each player takes a wide straddle stance, forming an alley with the legs. The ball is passed down the alley to the back person, who runs to the front with the ball and repeats the activity. Players may handle the ball to help it down the alley, but it is not required that each person do so.

Over and Under Relay (Revolving-Team Relay)

Players take a straddle position. The first player hands the ball over his or her head with both hands to the player behind, who in turn hands the ball between his or her legs to the next player. The ball goes over and under down the line.

Pass and Squat Relay (Revolving-Team Relay)

This is an interesting relay, but some practice is necessary to see that it functions properly. One player (#1) with a ball stands behind a line 10 feet in front of his or her teammates, who are in lane formation.

⑥ ⑤ ④ ③ ②|←— 10′ —→|①

Number one passes the ball to #2, who returns the ball to #1; #2 squats down as soon as he or she has returned the ball to #1, so the throw can be made to #3; and so on down the file to #6. When the last person in line receives the ball, he or she does not return it but carries it forward, straddling the members of his or her team including #1, who has taken a place at the head of the file. The player carrying the ball forward then acts as the passer. The race is over for a team when the original #1 player receives the ball in the back position and straddles the players back to the original position.

Some care must be taken that the front player in the file is behind the team line as the passing starts. After the straddling, it is necessary to reposition the file. Each player should make himself or herself into a compact ball during the straddling activity.

Circle Pass Relays

Simple Circle Relay

Each team forms a separate circle of the same size. At first, the circle should be small enough so the players can hand the ball to each other. Later, as skill increases, the circles can be enlarged.

The leader of each group starts the ball around the circle by handing the ball to the player on his or her right. As soon as the ball gets back to the leader, the entire team sits down. The first team to be seated in good formation wins.

Later, the circle can be enlarged and the ball passed from player to player. More than one circuit of the circle can be specified. An alternate way to finish is to have the leader hold the ball aloft to signal the completion of his or her team.

Circle and Leader Relay

A circle 15 to 20 feet in diameter is formed. One player is in the center with a ball. He or she passes in succession to each of the players. The race is over when the ball is returned to the center player from the last player. Different passes can be specified.

Corner Fly (Spry) Relay

The players are in a line, facing the leader, who has a ball that he or she passes to and receives from each player, beginning with the player on his or her left, with the exception of the last player (on his or her right). When this player receives the ball, he or she calls out, "Corner fly." He or she runs forward and takes the spot of the leader, who takes a place in the line to the left. In the meantime, all players adjust positions, moving over one place to fill the spot vacated by the new leader. The relay continues, with each player becoming the leader in turn. When the original leader returns to his or her spot with the ball, the relay is over.

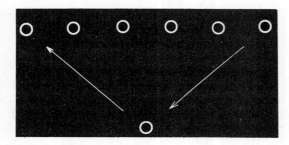

Variation: A marker can be placed behind the leader so that the last player in line, when he or she receives the ball, runs around the marker to the leader's spot. This gives a little more time for the team to shift places and get ready for the new leader.

Teaching Hint: If a team is one person short of the number of players on the other teams, two adjust-

ments can be made. First, two consecutive passes could be made by the leader to the first (on the left) person. Secondly, the initial leader might take two turns (first and last), which means another person comes forward after his or her second turn to provide the finish.

Tadpole Relay

One team forms a circle, facing in, and has a ball. Another team is in lane formation, with the head of the lane 10 feet from the circle.

The objective of the game is to see how many times the ball can make a complete circuit of the circle by passing to each player while the other team completes a relay. The other team is in lane formation, facing the circle, and lined up behind a line 10 feet from the circle. Each player in turn runs around the outside of the circle and tags off the next runner until all have run. In the meantime, the ball is being passed around the circle on the inside. Each time the ball makes a complete circuit, the circle players count the number loudly. After the relay has been completed and the count established, the teams trade places and the relay is repeated. The team making the highest number of circuits by passing is the winner. The relay gets its name from the shape of the formation, which resembles a tadpole.

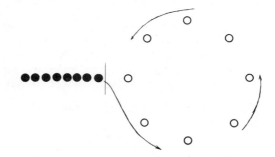

Variation: Vary with different types of passes and different methods of locomotion by the running team.

Miscellaneous Relays

Pass the Buck Relay

Players are facing sideways, with teams about 5 feet apart. All players of a team are linked by joining hands. The leader is on the right of each team. On signal, the leader "passes the buck" to the next player (by squeezing his or her hand), who in turn passes the squeeze to the next, and so on down the line. The end player, when he or she receives the buck, runs across the front of his or her team and becomes the new leader. He or she starts the squeeze, which is passed down the line. Each player, in turn, comes around to the end of the line, with the original leader finally returning to his or her original position.

Hip-hiking Relay

Teams are in shuttle relay formation, about 10 feet apart. Children take a position sitting on the floor, with the legs forward, the weight of the legs on the heels, and the knees bent at about 90 degrees. The arms are crossed in front and held out at shoulder level. Progress is made by reaching out with the heels and then bringing the seat forward. The first child of one shuttle line hikes forward to the other shuttle half, tagging off a child who hikes back.

Teaching Suggestions: Hip-hiking Relay has good posture values in the development of the pelvic region. However, it is a strenuous exercise, and children should not hike too far during the early stages of practice.

Rescue Relay

Lane formation is used, with the first runner at a line about 30 feet in front of his or her team.

The runner who is in front of his or her team runs back to the team, takes the first player in line by the hand, and "rescues" him or her to the 30-foot line. The player who has just been rescued runs back and gets the next player, and so on until the last player has been conducted to the line.

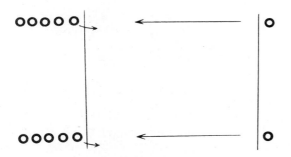

Around the Bases Relay

Four bases are laid out like a baseball diamond. Two teams, lined up at opposite bases on the inside of the diamond, compete at a time.

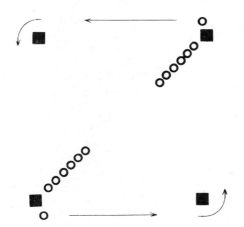

The lead-off player for each team makes one complete circuit of the bases and is followed by each player in turn.

Variation: The same type of relay can be run indoors by using chairs or Indian clubs at the four corners. Further variation can be made by requiring the children to run more than one lap or circuit on a turn.

Modified Relays

In modified relays, players are numbered and run as individuals. These are not relays in the true sense of the word.

Attention Relay

Players of each team are facing forward in lane formation about arm's distance apart. The distance between teams should be about 10 feet. Two turning points should be placed for each team. One is 10 feet in front of and the other 10 feet behind each team. Players are numbered consecutively from front to rear. The teacher calls, "Attention." All come to the position of attention. The teacher calls out a number. The player on each team holding that number steps to the right, runs around the front and the back marker, and returns to place. The first team to have all members of the team at attention, including the returning runner, wins a point.

Teaching Suggestion: The numbers should not be called in consecutive order, but all numbers should be called. Be sure there is enough distance between teams so the runners will not collide in the spaces between teams.

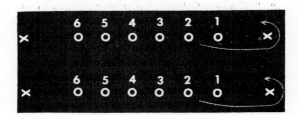

Variations

1. Use different means of locomotion.
2. Organize the teams by pairs and have two run at a time, holding inside hands.
3. *Under the Arch:* The leader calls two consecutive numbers, for example, 3 and 4. Immediately, #3 and #4 on each team face each other and form an arch by raising both hands. The players in front of the arch (#1 and #2) run forward, go around the front marker, run to the back marker and around it, and then run back to place, passing under the arch. The players behind the arch run under the arch first, run around the front marker, around the back marker, and back to place. When all have returned to place, the arch

players drop hands and resume position. The first team to be at attention is the winner.

Note: The running is always forward at the start. Each player follows the person ahead of him, keeping in place. Each goes around the front marker, around the back marker, and back to place. At the appropriate time, while taking this path, the players pass under the arch.

4. Each team stands on a bench. With the teams standing at attention, a number is called out, and that member of the team jumps down from the bench, runs completely around it, and runs back to his or her place on top of the bench.

Circular Attention Relay

Two teams form a circle, facing counterclockwise, each team occupying half the circle. The players of each team are numbered consecutively.

The teacher calls the group to attention. Then, a number is called. The children holding that number (one on each team) immediately run forward (counterclockwise) around the circle and back to place, and stand at attention. The first to get back at attention scores a point for his or her team. Call numbers until all have run.

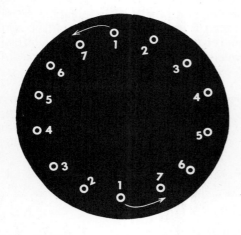

Variation: *Circle Leapfrog:* All players are crouched down on their knees, with their foreheads supported in cupped hands on the floor, facing counterclockwise. When a number is called, the runner straddles or leapfrogs all the children around the circle and back to place and resumes the original position. Scoring is the same as in Circular Attention.

Prone Relays

Players are lying facedown on the floor, in a circle, with their heads toward the center of the circle and hands joined.

Players on each team are numbered consecutively. When a number is called, the player with that number runs around or over the players on his or her team and back to place in prone position, with hands rejoined. The first player back scores a point for his or her team. Play for a definite score or until all the numbers have been called.

Human Hurdle Relay

Variations

1. *Human Hurdle:* Each team forms a small circle, sitting with backs to the center of the circle. Otherwise, the procedure is the same.

2. *Cyclone:* This is a team race, and the team getting back to the original place first is the winner. At the starting signal, the #1 player gets up and starts around the group. Immediately after #1 passes him or her, the second player follows. The third player follows just as soon as #1 and #2 have passed him or her. The remainder of the players follow in the same manner. When #1 gets back to place, he or she takes his or her original position. Each player in turn goes around until he or she gets back to his or her original place.

   Note: The last player cannot move until all the other players have gone by him or her. Only then does he or she start the trip around the circle. When he or she gets back to place, the race is over. This race can be done from the original prone position or from the sitting position.

Twenty-three

Classroom
and
Limited-Area
Activities

One of the most difficult problems confronting physical education teachers is conducting programs when adverse weather forces the activity inside and the gymnasium facilities are not adequate to handle the load. When no appropriate gymnasium facility is available, it may be necessary to use classroom and other limited spaces, such as the hall or the cafeteria.

INDOOR PHYSICAL EDUCATION

The Relaxation Period

This is designed to provide a break in the day's routine, and, in a sense, it is like recess. It is a kind of safety valve that allows the children to let off steam, but it also can be used to enrich their experiences while it offers them relaxation. Since it is a supplement to regular physical education experiences, the relaxation period should provide different activities from those in the regular program. The relaxation period is usually short, not more than 10 minutes or so.

Although the suggested classroom activities found in this chapter are appropriate for the purpose of relaxation, the amount of physical challenge they offer is quite limited. Activities requiring more physical effort are listed under program suggestions (page 424).

The Occasional Classroom Physical Education Lesson

This is an emergency situation when the physical education lesson must be taught in the classroom or related facility, because the usual facility is not available. For this reason, it is the most difficult type to plan. The program emphasis usually has to be shifted, since the rather rugged, active program of the gymnasium or playground is not suitable for the classroom conditions.

The Split Gymnasium-Classroom Program

Where facilities are available but not adequate for a daily program, the classes held in regular physical education facilities have to be supplemented by classroom physical education. For example, in a school where 20 classrooms share one gymnasium, a particular classroom is scheduled only twice a week for regular physical education. The classes in the gymnasium can be supplemented by lessons in the classroom in order to meet the weekly time requirement.

Planning must include both aspects, the regular and the classroom programs. The more rugged activities and instructional emphasis on skills are centered in the regular physical education program. To the classroom are allocated those activity areas that are suitable for limited spaces. When weather permits outdoor scheduling, this problem is alleviated.

Classroom Physical Education

In this situation, no suitable gymnasium facilities are present at all, and so all physical education that cannot be conducted on the playground must be carried on in the classroom, or no program is possible. Planning for this situation must include two programs, one for the playground and one for the classroom. The classroom program should be in sequential lessons, which means the lesson order is established and followed consecutively as the indoor program days come up.

GUIDELINES FOR CONDUCTING CLASSROOM AND LIMITED-SPACE ACTIVITIES

The following are considerations that have relevance in some degree to one or more of the situations just described.

The Noise Problem

The noise problem must be solved. Several suggestions are offered. The children must recognize that the activity is a privilege and that their cooperation is essential. They need to keep their exuberance under control to the point where the class activity does not interfere with other classes. Another solution is for the same section of the school to have physical education periods at the same time. When all classes in the same part of the building are playing at the same time, there is little chance that they will disturb each other. This would be particularly true if one class were directly above the other. The noise, particularly from shuffling and moving feet, would seriously interfere with the academic activities of the class below.

Equipment and Supplies

If there is to be an appreciable amount of classroom physical education, a set of equipment and supplies separate from that used in the regular physical education program is needed. A supply cart that contains most of the usual items needed is an efficient answer. It can be rolled directly into the classroom and so saves sending monitors to a central point to carry items back to the classroom. Equipment carts containing balance beams (portable), light folding mats, balance boards, individual mats, and other equipment are also timesavers.

Each classroom also should have a special collection of games, targets, manipulative objects, and other special items for indoor play. Many of the items can be constructed by the children.

Only supplies that will not damage the classroom should be used. Small sacks stuffed with excelsior, fleece balls, beanbags, yarn balls, rolled-up socks sewn together, balloons, and articles of this nature can be used with little danger to the facilities.

Preparing the Facilities

When the classroom desks and chairs are movable, there is enough flexibility for a variety of activities. Furniture can be pushed together to permit circle activities and rhythms. Chairs and desks can be pushed to one side to form an open space. If mats, balance beams, or benches are to be used, several wider aisles can be made by pushing adjacent rows together. Instruction should be given in how to prepare desks for moving. All personal items must be put away; desk tops should be cleared; and books and other things stacked underneath, so they will not fall out when the desks are moved. Items and projections that might cause tripping or damage should be placed in safe positions. Windows should be opened and the temperature lowered.

If the desks and chairs are fixed, then space is more limited. The aisles as established should be used. As much space as possible should be cleared.

Halls have a low priority for use. The noise permeates the entire building, and the activity interferes with the passage of students.

Program Suggestions

Too many teachers look for special classroom activities when the necessity to use the room for physical education occurs. Some end up with a program of trivial games, which only provide entertainment and relief from tension. Granted, these do play a part in the program, but their importance is minor compared to that of other purposes.

The activities of the regular physical education program should be carefully examined to determine which can be utilized and which can be modified for the classroom program. Stunts and tumbling, certain pieces of apparatus (movable), selected manipulative equipment, rhythmic activities, and movement experiences should be considered.

Six tumbling mats (4 by 7 feet) can be positioned in the available space. Four balance beams fit easily into the regular aisles or any available space. Benches can be used in the classroom, but these present a problem in getting them in and out of the area.

Target activities with beanbags, yarn balls, and regular rubber playground balls can be used. Targets can be placed at the end of the rows. Balls can be rolled or bounced. Ring toss games also contribute to skills.

Rhythmic activities are excellent for classroom work. The formations depend upon the size of the room and whether or not the desks are movable. Nonlocomotor creative rhythms and ball-bouncing rhythms are valuable.

Relays, particularly the modified (number-calling) type, have a place in classroom activities. Many can be modified for the classroom environment. Regular rows can be used, with the last child performing first and the leader positioned at the head of the row. Fast walking should be substituted for running.

Movement experiences are also an important inclusion. Traffic patterns are important for locomotor movements. Story plays and poems also have a place. These should require only limited locomotor movement.

Fitness activities can be adapted to classroom work. Many exercises are quite appropriate for this. Isometric exercises without equipment or with wands can be done readily in the classroom.

Individual isometric exercises are included at the end of this chapter and are useful for developing strength. Partner resistance exercises require little space and tend to motivate students to strive for higher levels of fitness. Jumping and hopping in place cause few spatial problems.

Many of the regular physical education games can be adapted for the space available. In addition, other activities, identified as classroom-type games, should be included. These vary from reasonably active games to quiet games.

The authors question a heavy emphasis and reliance on social recreation and intellectual games. Movement is the key to physical education, and the games should induce movement and provide an opportunity to practice skills.

Other Considerations

To a considerable degree, children should accept responsibility for their own conduct. They should realize and accept the limitations of classroom physical education.

Multiple activity play has a place in classroom activity. A number of groups scattered around the room may be involved in different activities.

Rules, strategies, and techniques of sports activities sometimes can be covered in indoor sessions. Good visual aids are also invaluable.

As many children as possible should engage in activity at one time, since activity is the key to physical education. Some system of rotation should be established to assure all children a proportionate share of the activity time.

Watch for overheating. Have the children remove excess clothing. Allow them to wear gym shoes for appropriate activities.

Stress safety. Caution players about colliding with chairs and desks. If the aisles are used for activity, tell the children to keep their feet well under their desks to avoid tripping players.

THE FITNESS CORNER

The fitness corner is gaining popularity in classrooms. Essentially, it is a multiple-apparatus installation placed out of the way in a classroom in order to provide a place where children can do some climbing and hanging exercises. Included may be bars, climbing ropes, ladders, and rings. Some type of climbing apparatus, either freestanding or wall-supported, is the basis of the fitness corner. The area is generally small, meant for only a few children at a time. The installation usually is

fixed, so the apparatus is available at all times. Mats should be placed under the apparatus.

A number of rubber bands made from inner tubes cut in two sizes (1½ inches and 2 inches) can be made available for resistance exercises. A chart describing the kinds of resistive exercises the children can do could be posted. Some means of storage must be devised, or the articles will be scattered around the classroom.

SUGGESTED CLASSROOM ACTIVITIES

Popular Games

Add and Subtract

Formation: Informal or by rows.
Players: Two to four.
Supplies: Two rubber heels or blocks of wood for each player. One is marked with a plus sign and one with a minus sign. Different colors of beanbags could be used.

1	5	3
7	9	8
4	6	2

Lay out a nine-square diagram, with each square 12 inches wide. The squares are numbered 1 through 9. Each player tosses two rubber heels (or beanbags) toward the target on the floor, one at a time. He or she adds the score made by the plus throw and subtracts the score of the minus throw. Scores are determined by where the heel rests on the target. If the heel rests on a line between two squares, the higher value is taken. Any throws falling completely outside the target area are scored minus 5.

The game adapts itself well to the classroom, since a target can be drawn at the front of each aisle.

Alphabet Mix

Formation: Circle, children standing.
Players: Entire class.
Supplies: Flash cards (optional).

One player is chosen to be the leader. All the players are given a letter of the alphabet. The leader calls out two letters, and the circle players having these letters must change places. The leader then tries to get into one of their places before they can complete the exchange. The player left without a place becomes the leader.

As a variation, the teacher can make a set of flash cards with letters on them. The children then change places when their letter is flashed. It is also possible to assign a word to each player and then flash two words to enhance their word-recognition skill. Also, more leaders may be used, and more than two letters or words may be called.

Animals Move

Formation: Players stand in the aisles between desks or are scattered.
Players: Entire class.
Supplies: None.

The player who is it stands in the front of the room and calls out a mammal, a bird, a fish, or a reptile and a movement. For instance, the leader might call out, "Horses fly, birds crawl, or salmon swim." When the leader states a correct relationship, the class must move accordingly. In this case, they would make a swimming movement. If an incorrect relationship is given, the children should not move. Those who move at the wrong time can sit down and wait until a new leader is selected. Games should be kept short, so all children get a chance to lead and do not have to sit out too long.

As the children become skilled at the game, the teacher should stress quality of movement. Encourage the children to improve their hopping, flying, jumping, and other types of movement patterns.

Around the Row

Formation: Row in a classroom.
Players: Whatever number there are in a row.
Supplies: None.

The game is played by rows, with an extra player for each row. The children form a row plus the extra player on the command "march" and walk around the row. At a signal, they stop marching and attempt to get a seat. One player is left out. The game continues to the next row, using the player left out as the extra. Watch for roughness. Walking only is permitted, no running.

Balloon Football

Formation: Teams are arranged in two lines facing each other 4 to 6 feet apart.
Players: Entire class divided into two equal teams.
Supplies: Balloon or light beach ball.

Players must sit in their chairs and keep one hand on the back of the chair throughout the game. The balloom or light beach ball is tossed between the two teams. Both teams try to bat it over the heads of their opponents so that it touches the floor behind the opposite team. Each

touchdown scores a point. To facilitate play, a student should be placed behind each team to serve as a scorekeeper and retriever. Put the balloon into play at different places along the two lines to prevent action from concentrating among a few players.

Balloon Volleyball

Formation: A rope is stretched across the middle of the classroom.
Players: Entire class.
Supplies: Two balloons. Extras should be available since there is breakage.

This is an informal game with the children trying to bat the ball back and forth across the rope. Two balloons should be used at once to provide good action. Several variations are possible.
1. All children standing. Rope should be stretched just over their reach.
2. All children sitting on the floor. Rope about 3 feet from the floor.
3. Children in seats that cannot be moved. Rope should be about 5 feet high.

In each case, a system of rotation should be set up. Scoring is done when a side fails to control a balloon and allows it to touch the floor or a wall. The balloon can be batted as often as possible.
Variation: When a small marble or button is put *inside* the balloon, the balloon takes an erratic path, adding to the interest.

Basketball Bounce

Formation: Individual or by team formation.
Players: Two to six for each basket.
Supplies: Basketball, volleyball, or other rubber ball and a wastepaper basket.

Each player in turn stands behind a line that is 5 to 10 feet from a wastepaper basket. Five chances are allowed to bounce the ball on the floor in such a fashion that it goes into the basket. Score five points for each successful basket.

Beanbag Pitch

Formation: File by rows.
Players: Two to six for each target.
Supplies: Beanbags and a small box for target for each team.

A target box is placed at the head of each row. A pitch line is drawn 10 to 15 feet back of the target. Each player takes a specified number of pitches at the box. Scores are taken for each player, and the team with the highest score wins. Many other targets are possible. Have the children design targets.

Bicycle Race

Formation: Alternate rows perform at a time.
Players: Half of the class.
Supplies: The desks are needed.

The children stand in the aisle between two rows of desks. Each child places one hand on his or her own desk and one on the desk next to him or her. Upon the signal "go," each child imitates riding a bicycle with his or her legs while supported by his or her hands. The child who rides the longest without touching the floor with his or her feet is the winner for the row. Winners can compete later for the champion bicycle rider of the room.

Blind Man's Bluff

Formation: Small circle, with one child in the center.
Players: 8 to 10.
Supplies: One blindfold for each game.

Blind Man's Bluff is one of the old, traditional games. One child is blindfolded and stands in the center of a small circle formed by the other children. Another child is chosen to be inside the circle, and the blind man tries to catch him or her. As the quarry dodges him or her, the blind man calls out, "Where are you?" whereupon the other must respond immediately by making a sound like that of a baby chick, "cheep, cheep!"

When the blind man has caught the other player, he or she tries to identify him or her by feeling the face, arms, and clothes. Identification does not affect the outcome of the game but simply adds to the fun. Two other children are chosen to replace the first two players.

Circles should be kept small, otherwise catching is difficult and protracted. The blindfold should be effective, since the game is spoiled if the child can see under it. The game is usually confined to the kindergarten through second grades.
Variation: The circle children can make a buzzing sound (z-z-z-z-z-z), which becomes louder as the blind man nears the quarry.

Boiler Burst

Formation: The children are seated at their desks or chairs.
Players: Entire class.
Supplies: None.

The seats are arranged so there will be one less seat than players. The extra player stands at the front of the class and begins a story. At a dramatic moment, he or she says, "And the boiler burst!" The children exchange seats, and the narrator tries to secure a seat. If he or she is successful, another child replaces him or her. The new narrator may develop his or her own story or continue that begun by the predecessor.

The game can be adapted to an outdoor situation by having markers for each child. To make the game more vigorous, the children could be required to walk to a turning point and back. The child who does not secure a marker is the new storyteller.

Bowling

Formation: File by rows.
Players: Two to six.
Supplies: Bowling pin or pins and balls for rolling.

Many bowling games are possible in the classroom, with the aisles used as the alleys. Various kinds of balls can be used for rolling. The target can be a single pin or a group of pins. Competition can be between individuals in a row or between rows.

Give the children opportunities to design their own bowling games.

Cat and Mice (Classroom Game)

Formation: Children are at their desks.
Players: 5 to 20.
Supplies: None.

This is an excellent activity for the classroom. One player designated as the cat sits at the front desk (teacher's) and puts his or her head down on his or her hands on the desk so he or she cannot see. The remainder of the children are the mice. One mouse from each row comes to the front, stealthily approaches the desk, and scratches on the desk. When he or she is ready, the cat gets up and chases the mice back to their seats. Any child caught joins the cat at the desk and helps catch the others. The game is over when each of the players has had a chance to approach the desk.

Chair Quoits

Formation: File.
Players: Two to six.
Supplies: Chair for each group; five deck tennis rings or rope rings.

A line is established about 10 feet from a chair turned upside down so the legs are pointed toward the thrower. Each throws the five rings for the following scores.

Ringer on back legs: 10 points.
Ringer on front legs: 5 points.

Make a score sheet, and keep score for several rounds.
Variation: Fruit jar rings can be used with the chair or with other targets. Special peg targets can be constructed. (Diagram, page 568.)

Change Seats

Formation: Children are in their seats.
Players: Entire class.
Supplies: None.

All seats either should be occupied or should be removed or marked with books to indicate that they are not to be used. The teacher gives the command "change left," "change right," "change front," or "change back." one or more children are it and do not have seats.

At each command, the children move *one seat* in the direction of the call. The children who are it try to move into any seat they can. When the command "change front" is given, the child in the front seat must turn and move to the rear seat of his or her row. Similarly, those on the outside rows on "change left" or "change right" must move around to the other side of the room to get their proper seats.

It needs to be emphasized that on command each child is to move to the designated seat in keeping with the command. If he or she is in error, one of the players who is it takes his or her seat.

If the game seems to become too boisterous, the children should be made to walk between the seats.

Do This, Do That

Formation: Children scattered around the room.
Players: Entire class.
Supplies: None.

One child is the leader and performs various movements, which are accompanied by either "do this" or "do that." All players must execute the movements that are accompanied by "do this." If the directions are "do that," no one is to move. Those who move at the wrong time are eliminated and sit down in place.

Play until some of the children have been eliminated and then re-form the game with another leader, selected from the children who were not caught.

Flag Chase

Formation: Hollow square, children seated in chairs.
Players: Four teams of equal number.
Supplies: Four flags and one chair per person arranged in a square facing the center, with one chair in the center of the square.

The four equal-size teams are seated on the sides of the square, facing the center. The first player at the left end of each line is given a flag. On signal, the player with the flag runs to the center, around the chair, and back to the other end of his or her line. Meanwhile, all of the players on his or her team have moved up one seat toward the head of the line, leaving a vacant chair. The runner sits in the vacant chair, and the flag is passed down the line. When the player at the head of the line receives the flag, he or she runs the same pattern as his or her teammate. The object of the game is to be the first team to have all its players circle the center chair and get back in original position. Establish traffic rules so that all children are going around the chair in the same direction (counterclockwise).

Floor Pingpong

Formation: Regular table tennis court marked off on the floor.
Players: Two to four.

Supplies: Table tennis ball, a paddle for each player.

Play as in regular table tennis. Games should be short (10 points), so many children can be accommodated. A makeshift net can be set up with blocks and a wand.

Geronimo

Formation: Children seated in regular classroom arrangement.
Players: Entire class.
Supplies: None.

One child is the leader and walks among the children seated in the classroom. He or she suddenly points to a child and says, "Geronimo." This child must immediately put both hands to his or her ears. The child directly behind him or her must put both hands on top of his or her head. The children on either side must cover the ear next to Geronimo with the near hand and the nose with the other hand. Play with duds as penalties. Three duds mean out.

The game can be made harder by adding more intricate movement tasks. Change the movement of the child on either side to holding the near ear with the opposite hand and holding the nose with the other hand.

Variation: The Spanish word *Bandito* can be substituted for Geronimo.

Teaching Suggestion: Explain who Geronimo was and also the use of the word by the United States Marines as their battle cry.

Hide the Beanbag

Formation: Children scattered around the room.
Players: 15 to 20.
Supplies: Beanbag (small).

One child is the searcher and stands to the side with eyes covered. The remainder of the children are scattered, and are sitting in Indian style. One child is given the beanbag and must hide it by sitting on it.

The searcher uncovers his or her eyes and moves among the group, trying to find the child who has the beanbag. He or she is aided by the children who clap softly as he or she moves, clapping louder when he or she gets close to the one with the beanbag. The searcher is allowed three guesses to identify the one with the bag. When he or she is correct, he or she chooses another child to be the searcher. When he or she fails to guess the correct child in three tries, the child with the beanbag becomes the new searcher.

The teacher should choose the child to hide the beanbag. This offers an excellent opportunity to involve shy children in the game.

Hunter, Gun, Rabbit

Formation: Two lines facing each other.
Players: Entire class.

Supplies: None.

The children are divided into two teams, which line up facing each other. They can be sitting or standing. Each team has a captain. Each team privately decides on one of the following three imitations.

Hunter—bring hands up to the eyes and pretend to be looking through binoculars.

Gun—bring hands and arms up to a shooting position and pretend to shoot.

Rabbit—put hands in back of head with fingers pointed up. Move hands back and forth like moving rabbit ears.

A signal "go" is given, and each team pantomimes its choice. To score, the following priorities have been set up.

1. If one side is the hunter and the other the gun, the hunter wins since the hunter shoots the gun.
2. If one team selects the gun and the other imitates a rabbit, the gun wins since the gun overcomes the rabbit.
3. If one side is the rabbit and the other the hunter, the rabbit wins since it can run away from the hunter.
4. If both teams have the same selection, no point is scored.

The first team scoring 10 points wins.

Teaching Suggestion: Keep things moving. One way to do this is to have the child on the right of each line go down the line and whisper the choice to the children of the team. The child then positions himself or herself on the left, with a new child at the right of each line ready for selecting and initiating the next choice.

Imitation

Formation: Children scattered around the room. The leader is in front.
Players: Entire class.
Supplies: Record player, records.

The game is based on the musical phrase length of eight counts. The leader performs for eight counts with any kind of movement he or she wishes. For the next eight counts, the children imitate his or her movements in the same sequence. The leader sets another round of movements, and the children imitate.

After a period of imitation, the leader selects another child to be in front as leader.

Lost Children

Formation: Children scattered around the room. Desks are in place.
Players: Entire class.
Supplies: None.

One child is chosen to be the policeman or policewoman and leaves the room. The other children walk around the room. The teacher or leader calls the police officer in and says, "The children are lost. Will you please take them home safely?"

The police officer then takes each child to his or her seat. The players stay where they are until the police officer seats them. Success for the police officer is determined by the number of children he or she can seat correctly. He or she is not permitted to look in the desks or in books for clues to correct seating.

O'Grady Says

Formation: Children scattered around the room.
Players: Entire class.
Supplies: None.

This game is borrowed from the United States Army. Different directions are given, such as "right face," "left face," and "about face." Also, calling to attention and standing at ease can be used. A leader stands in front and calls out the various commands. The players are to follow *only* when the command is preceded by "O'Grady says." Any one moving at the wrong time is eliminated and should sit down.

Additional commands involving other movements can be used. To be effective, the commands must be given rapidly.

Orienteering

Formation: Players stand to the right of their desks.
Players: Entire class.
Supplies: Chart of compass face.

Either the teacher or a chosen student stands facing the class. This person then calls out various directions, such as north, southwest, et cetera. The rest of the class must quickly face in the proper direction. When students face the wrong direction, they can either sit down or have a point scored against them.

In an attempt to introduce them to a compass and simple orienteering skills, a chart with the face and directional needle of a compass can be used. The leader can turn away from the class, place the needle in a certain direction, and then show it to the class. The class then responds by turning toward the proper direction.

Variation: Regular orienteering can be done on a modified basis by setting up a course with compass directions and distance using steps, with the object of arriving at a final destination spot. However, in some buildings, compasses are not accurate.

Overhead Relay

Formation: File by rows.
Players: Each row in a classroom forms a team.
Supplies: Beanbag, eraser, or similar object for each team.

The first person in each row has in front of him or her the object that is to be passed to the desk behind. At the signal to pass, he or she claps hands, picks up the object, and passes it overhead to the child behind. This child places the object on the desk, claps hands, and passes overhead. When the last child in the row receives the object, he or she runs forward to the head of the row, using the aisle to his or her right. *After* he or she has passed by, each child, using the *same* aisle, moves back one seat. The child who has come to the front then sits down in the first seat, places the object on the desk, claps hands, and passes overhead.

This continues until the children are back in their original seats and the object is on the front desk. The first row done wins.

Put Hands

Formation: Students are standing or seated. They can be scattered around the room.
Players: Entire class.
Supplies: None.

One child is the leader and stands in front of the class. He or she gives certain directions verbally and tries to confuse the class by doing something else. He or she could say, "Put your hands on top of your head." He or she might put his or her own hands on top of his or her shoulders. Those who are in error have a point scored against them. Directions he or she could give, to which he or she should make other movements, are:

"Put your hands on—shoulders, toes, knees, head, chest," et cetera.

"Reach out to the—side, front, back, high."

"Put your right hand (or left) on your shoulder, behind your back," et cetera.

After a short time, the leader should be changed.

Variation: Other movements can be introduced, such as "right hand point west," "left hand forward, right hand to the sky," "head right, jump left," and others.

Simon Says

Formation: Children seated or scattered around the room.
Players: Entire class.
Supplies: None.

One player is selected to be Simon and stands in front of the class. He or she gives a variety of commands like "stand up," "clap your hands," "turn around," and others. He or she may or may not precede a command by the words "Simon says." No one is to move unless the command is preceded by these words. Those who move at the wrong time are eliminated and must sit out the game.

The leader gives commands rapidly, changing to different movements. He or she tries to confuse the class by doing all of the movements.

Snap

Formation: Children seated in a circle.
Players: 10 to 15.
Supplies: None.

This is a rhythm game involving a three-count rhythm. The children must practice the rhythm well before the game can be successful. The action is as follows.

Count 1: Slap knees.
Count 2: Clap hands.
Count 3: Snap fingers.

Each child in the circle has a number. The leader calls a number on the third count (snap fingers). The player whose number was called then calls another when he or she snaps his or her fingers. The object of the game is to keep the precise rhythm and keep the numbers called back and forth across the circle.

Errors
1. Breaking the rhythm.
2. Not calling another number after yours has been called.
3. Calling when your number has not been called.
4. Calling a number of a player who has been eliminated.

Players are eliminated after they have made three errors. The number of an eliminated player is dead and cannot be called.

Ten, Ten, Double Ten

Formation: Informal.
Players: Entire class.
Supplies: Small object.

All the children except one leave the classroom. The child left in the room places the object in some place visible but not too easily found. The children come back into the room. As soon as a child sees the object, he or she continues searching for another moment so as not to give away the position. Then, he or she calls out, "Ten, ten, double ten, forty-five, fifteen, buckskin six," and sits down in his or her seat. The child who found the object first gets to place it for the next game. The children who were last finding it, or any who did not, must remain in their seats for the next turn.

Tic-Tac-Toe

Formation: None.
Players: Two to four.
Supplies: Tic-tac-toe target board, six beanbags of one color and six of another. Yarn balls can be used in place of beanbags.

The tic-tac-toe target is made from 1-by-4-inch boards, which make a throwing target a little less than 4 inches deep, with each of the nine squares 1 foot square. The target is mounted on a 4-

by-4-foot piece of sturdy plywood. A prop should be placed behind the board so that it tilts about 45 degrees.

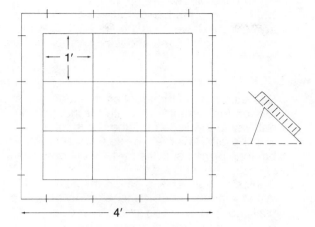

The object of Tic-tac-toe is to get three squares covered in a line in any direction. Only one beanbag is permitted in a square. If a second beanbag lands inside a square, it is removed. The game can be played one against one or partners against partners. Alternate sides toss at the target.

The teacher might consider setting the general outline of the game and letting the children make up their own rules and scoring system.

Where, Oh Where?

Formation: Children are seated in regular seats or in a circle on the floor.
Players: Entire class.
Supplies: Spool or other small object that can be hidden in a closed hand.

One child is chosen to be it and turns his or her back to the group while hiding his or her eyes.

The object is passed among the children from hand to hand until a signal is given. It turns around and attempts to guess who has the object. He or she gets three guesses. All children, including the one who has the object, do various movements and stunts to confuse the guesser. The object must be held in the hand, however. If the guess is correct, the child with the object becomes the new guesser. If not, it tries again. If a child misses on three turns in a row, he or she should choose another child to be it.

If the number of children in the class is large, two children can be it, thus doubling the chances of guessing, since each should be allowed three guesses.

Who's Leading?

Formation: Children are in a circle formation, either sitting in chairs or on the floor. They can be standing, but this becomes tiring.

Players: Entire class.
Supplies: None.

One child is it. He or she steps away from the circle and covers his or her eyes. The teacher points to one child, who is the leader. The leader starts any motion he or she chooses with his or her hands, feet, body, et cetera. All the children follow the movements. The child who is it watches the group as they change from one motion to another to try to determine who is leading. Players should cover up for the leader, who also tries to confuse it by looking at other players.

It gets three guesses. If not successful, he or she chooses another child to be it. If he or she guesses correctly, he or she gets another turn (limit of three turns).

The game seems to work best when the guesser is positioned in the center of the circle, since he or she then cannot observe all the children at once.

Zoo

Formation: Children are in regular seats.
Players: Entire class.
Supplies: None.

Seven children are chosen to stand in front of the class, and one of them is selected as the leader. The leader directs each of the other six children to choose a favorite animal and then places them in a line, saying the names of the animals as he or she does so.

On signal 1, the six children, performing in the order in which they were just announced by the leader, imitate the animal they have chosen. Ten to 15 seconds should be allowed for this.

On signal 2, the rest of the children stand, wave their arms, jump or hop in place, turning round if they wish, and then sit down, close their eyes, cover them with their hands, and put their heads down on the desks.

The leader then arranges the six animals in a different order. When this has been done, the seated children return to sitting position. Another signal is given, and the animals perform once again for a short period.

Once this has been completed, any seated child can volunteer to place the six children in their original positions, naming the animal in each case. If the child succeeds in placing the animals in their original standing position and calling them by their chosen name, he or she may become an animal in the zoo and choose a name for himself or herself. The child then takes his or her place among the animals, and the game continues until 12 or some other designated number of children are in the zoo.

Other categories such as flowers, Mother Goose characters, play characters, and so on can be used.

Other Games

The teacher should examine the section on games for both the primary and the intermediate levels for activities of possible use.

ISOMETRIC CONDITIONING EXERCISES FOR CLASSROOM USE

An isometric exercise is characterized by having virtually no movement of the body part but a high degree of muscular tension. In this type of activity, the muscles should undergo a holding contraction of eight slow counts. To prevent movement, the pulling, pushing, or twisting action is braced against some external stabilizing force. This can be against a desk, a chair, a wall, the floor, the sides of a door frame, or a special isometric apparatus. Or an individual could work one set of muscles against another, so that there is no movement. In addition, isometric exercise can be done with partners, with one partner providing the stabilizing action.

In the regular classroom, where the narrow confines and furniture limit activity, an isometric program has value because of the no movement feature. Furthermore, many of the activities can be done by children seated at desks, with the desks themselves used as braces to prevent movement.

It should be stressed that maximum or near-maximum tension of the muscle group to be developed must be achieved and held for approximately 8 seconds, hence the eight slow counts. There is no need for repetition of an exercise at any one session, since maximum strength development is gained from one contraction at an exercise session. Contractions should be repeated three or four times per week.

Individual Isometric Exercises

Arms

Standing or seated. With the left palm up and the right palm down, clasp the hands in front of the body, chest high. Press down with the right hand, resisting with the left. Reverse.

Fingers and Grips

Seated. Two ordinary books are needed so that together the thickness is 1 inch. Grasp the books in an opposed thumb grip. Squeeze hard with the fingers of both hands.

Arms and Shoulders

1. Standing or seated. Clasp the fingers together in front of the chest with the forearms held level to the floor (elbows out). Pull against the fingers to force the elbows out. Be sure to keep the chest up, the shoulders back, and the head erect.

2. Standing or seated. Using a grip with the palms together, the fingers interlocked (knuckles upward), push the palms together. Be sure the elbows are up and out.

3. Seated. Drop the hands to the sides so they are straight down. Curl the fingers under the seat. Pull up with the shoulders, keeping the body erect.

Legs

1. Seated. With the right foot on the floor, move the left foot on top of it, with the heel about halfway to the ankle. Lift the right foot, resist with the left. Reverse. The same exercise can be done by crossing the feet, so the pressure is ankle against ankle.

2. Against a wall. This is called the Skier's Sit. With the heels about 12 inches away from the wall, go into a sitting position (no chair or bench), so the back is against the wall and the thighs are parallel to the floor. A right angle is formed by the thighs and the body and again at the knee joints. Hold for 30 seconds. The arms are folded across the chest. The head and shoulders are up and maintain contact against the wall.

Legs, Arms, Abdominals

Seated. Place hands, palms down, with fingers extended, on the lower portion of the top of the thighs. Press down with the hands and up with the legs.

Neck and Arms

Standing or seated. Clasp the hands behind the back of the head. Keeping the elbows well out, force the head back against the pressure of the hands.

Back, Arms, Thighs

Seated. Sitting as erect as possible, place both hands under the thighs close to the knees. Pull up with the hands against downward pressure of the thighs.

Arms, Abdominals, General Body

Stand about 3 feet behind a chair. Bend forward at the waist until the hands can be put on the back of the chair (elbows are straight). With a strong downward pull from the abdominal wall and the arms, pull down against the chair.

FINGER PLAYS

Finger plays are relaxation and manipulative experiences that can be utilized in the classroom, because they can be done while the children are seated. Finger plays represent a long and rich heritage of many cultures, and it is not feasible to include a large number. Several examples are included below. The spoken lines are at the left and the suggested actions are at the right. The lines can be recited by the children in unison.

The Church

Here is the church	Fold hands as in prayer in front of chest.
Here is the steeple	Raise both forefingers up high.
Open the doors and	Reverse the hands so palms are up, fingers spread.
See the people.	Wiggle the fingers.

Fingers

Thumbkin, pointer man, middle man tall—	Fingers of left hand are extended on top of desk.
	Beginning with the thumb, lift each finger with the right
Ring man, wee man, great men all.	hand and let fall heavily.

The Rain

Pitter, patter, pitter, patter,	Light finger drumming action on desks.
Hear the raindrops say.	
But, if a sunbeam should peep out,	Fingers touch overhead, making a sun.
They'd make a rainbow gay.	Separate arms with a wide sweep, showing the rainbow.
Rumble, rumble, rumble, rumble,	Fists doubled up, roll knuckles on desk.
Hear the thunder say.	
But soon the clouds will all be gone,	Arms overhead, fingers touching.
And we'll go out to play.	Bring hands down to desk, move fingertips rapidly back and forth.

Open and Close

Open, close them; open, close them.	Hold arms out diagonally upward, open and close fingers.
Give a little slap.	Slap thighs.
Open, close them; open, close them.	As before.
Lay them in your lap!	As directed.

Twenty-four

Integration
with
Other
Subjects

Art
Geography
Health and Safety
History
Language Arts
Music
Number Concepts (Mathematics)
Projects

Many physical education experiences and learning situations provide opportunities for the use of, and combination with, other subject areas for the purpose of broadening the learning environment. Conversely, other subject areas can be of use in broadening and enriching the physical education program.

Even in the unit-of-work study program, physical education should be considered for its contributions. Take the example of a class that is studying the Oregon Trail as its unit of work. Combined with the geographical, historical, home economics, health, musical, and social studies approaches, the unit also can study the recreational life of the pioneers. Games and dances used by the pioneer youngsters and Indian games and dances can be a part of the study.

The opportunities for integrating physical education activities with other subjects are numerous and limited only by the ingenuity of the teacher and the interests of the children. Classroom teachers play an important role in a successful physical education program. Integrating physical education experiences with other areas of the curriculum not only demonstrates to children that the teacher values the program but also makes physical activity more meaningful to them. Without good support of the classroom teacher, it is difficult to develop a really successful physical education program.

Some suggestions about the ways in which physical education can relate to and complement other subject areas are presented. These introduce the topic and provide some examples. Many other integrations could be devised.

ART

Children like to make things for their own programs. Posters, decorations, and costumes bring together art and physical education. Some other ideas for integrating art and physical education include these.

1. Illustrate features of various games, such as ball toss targets, shuffleboard courts, hopscotch, and four square.
2. Make bulletin boards and other displays for classrooms, halls, and gymnasiums. Some ideas for creating useful themes might be good diets for fitness, activity and physical fitness, examples of great athletes at work, lifetime sports and leisure activity, and basic skills needed for specific sports.
3. Select a skill (such as throwing) and illustrate the various phases of a successful throw. For instance, the rule of opposition, proper arm position, body rotation, and the follow-through could be drawn and analyzed by students.
4. Watch another class participating in a sport and create some action figures that capture the flavor of the sport. Basic movements in various sports and games could be analyzed for their basic similarities and differences.
5. Develop costumes for a mock Olympiad. Insignias of various countries could be studied and placed on the uniforms.
6. Carry out a contest to develop a school insignia and slogan. Various posters could be painted and entered in the competition. When a selected insignia is identified, it could be

434

silk-screened onto T-shirts for school teams.

7. Design charts of athletic fields or game areas, and illustrate where players should be placed for various game strategies.
8. A similar project might be to draw athletic fields and game areas to scale. Students could visit a ball park and attempt to draw the facility to scale and include different parts such as bleachers, dugouts, dressing rooms, and showers.
9. Students could make programs for upcoming pageants, gymkhanas, and physical education demonstrations. The programs could be illustrated, contain maps on how to find the school, and provide a description of the evening's program.
10. Posters of encouragement could be painted and put up to show support for intramural teams, classroom competitions, and afterschool sports programs.
11. Progress charts for activities such as jogging, Push-ups, and Curl-ups could be made. High achievers could be given an award for achievement, and other students could be rewarded for participating. These awards could be designed and painted by students.

GEOGRAPHY

Since the origins of physical education materials are diverse and scattered, geographical associations provide the classroom teacher with another source of learning experiences. It is possible to find clues about the play and sports habits of people in their location, terrain, and other geographical factors. Some areas of study could be these.

1. The climate in different areas of the United States could be studied to ascertain how climatic factors affect the play habits of people. Factors such as altitude and weather could be studied.
2. Games of different countries could be played and studied in an attempt to see how others play. Cultural factors such as dress, folklore, mores, and industries might be related to the games they participate in and enjoy.
3. During a rhythms unit in which folk dances were being taught, the origin of the dance and the characteristics of the country and its people could be discussed. Costumes used in specific dances could be made to make the dances more authentic.
4. Students from other countries could visit the class to explain their play habits and games.
5. The Olympics could be studied to see which countries dominate certain sports in the competition. This would give a clue to the emphasis certain countries place on various sports

and might be traced to the type of physical education found in the schools.

6. Geographical and climatic factors of various areas could be studied to see how they affect the performance of athletes. For instance, altitude at the Mexico Olympic Games (1968) seriously affected long-distance runners but aided long jumpers—why?
7. Language barriers during international competition often cause problems for officials and referees. Attempts made to remedy this problem might be discussed.

HEALTH AND SAFETY

It is difficult to separate health and safety from physical education. Physical education should be carried on in a healthful and safe atmosphere. Many opportunities for incidental teaching of health concepts arise. Safety considerations for each activity are important in the planning. Here are some more examples.

1. Physical fitness concepts could be discussed. For example, the basic steps in developing physical fitness and their relationship to the general health of individuals should be clearly understood.
2. The value of exercise for good mental and physical health should be emphasized to children. The detrimental effects of smoking, alcohol, and drugs on the body could be brought into the discussion.
3. A safety week could be declared for the school. Students could develop a list of safety standards for the school building and playground. Posters that illustrate proper safety techniques also might be developed.
4. Activities and skills learned in physical education should be related to leisure and recreation. Students should realize the value of learning skills at an early age so they will be able to use the skills in recreational activity later in life.
5. When physical examinations are given to classes, it is an opportune time to discuss the reasons why they are given. Discussion should cover congenital as well as acquired defects, conditions caused by disease, and the problems of contagious disease.
6. The value of exercise in promoting healing and improving certain health conditions should be discussed when the opportunity arises. Students with asthma, if their situation is faced openly, can learn to gauge how much activity they can participate in. When a child's limb is broken, the problem of muscle atrophy can be discussed to demonstrate the need for exercise and use of muscles.
7. A class could conduct a posture checkup day.

The mechanics of posture could be discussed, with emphasis on methods of improving posture conditions found in the class.

8. Nutrition, rest, and body care should be analyzed to enable students to see the role they play in daily living and a healthy body.

9. Students could take a period to check and inspect equipment and facilities for safety standards. After the inspection, a discussion of existing conditions could be covered and new standards presented.

10. Simple experiments to show the immediate effects of exercise on the body could be developed. For instance, pulse rates before and after exercise could be measured, air exhaled at rest and after exercise could be collected in plastic bags, and breathing rate before and after exercise could be measured. Reasons for the body adaptations should be discussed.

11. The crucial balance between caloric intake and exercise is a valuable concept for students to acquire. Children must understand that obesity is controlled through a combination of proper diet and adequate exercise.

12. Students could plan their daily and weekly schedule for work, rest, and play, and then compare the plan with recommended time allotments and with other students' schedules.

HISTORY

Physical education is rich in historical background. Many of today's activities have a traditional basis. The historical aspects of physical education offer many possibilities for historical study and should be developed. An appreciation of physical education could be furthered if children understood the background of an activity. Some suggestions for incorporating history are these.

1. The origins of activities could be studied— events such as the discus throw, the shot put, and the pole vault are performed now only because of the tradition behind them.

2. The origin and adaptation of present-day sports such as baseball, basketball, and American football could be explored. The relationship between rule changes and the higher athletic achievements of modern athletes could be analyzed.

3. The study of the ethnic background, historical context, and meaning of dances often makes them more interesting to children.

4. The fitness of different peoples could be compared—the ancient Greek, Persian, and Roman civilizations placed much emphasis on fitness as do modern-day countries such as the USSR and the United States.

5. The history and development of sports equipment and facilities is often interesting and revealing. For example, the Roman Colosseum could be compared with present-day stadiums, or comparisons between performance and poles used for vaulting might be made.

6. The history of the Olympics is fascinating. The evolution from the ancient games to the present-day Olympics offers many insights into the values of different societies.

7. Medieval knighthood and the jousting tournaments could make for interesting study.

LANGUAGE ARTS

Physical education materials make useful subjects for written and oral expression. The world of sports and games provides many examples of outstanding individuals who can serve as topics for presentations. Additional suggestions follow.

1. To increase their motivation to read, children could read game descriptions, rules of various sports, autobiographies of famous sports heroes, newspaper reports of game scores, and books oriented toward self-improvement in a given sport.

2. Writing activities that could be used include the following: write an autobiography about your sports career to date; write a summary of a game program your school has conducted; go to an intramural contest, and report the happenings and results for the school newspaper; find out as much as you can about your sports hero, and write a short story about him or her.

3. Practice in oral expression could occur through pupils giving demonstrations and describing various points of the performance, explaining rules of various activities to other students, reporting the results of a school contest to students who were unable to attend, and working in small groups to evaluate each other's performances.

4. To add some interest to spelling, words that are going to be used in the coming physical education lesson could be learned, a few difficult sports terms could be added to the weekly spelling list, and a spelling bee using only terms and words found in sports and physical education could be conducted.

5. Students could write plays about famous sports heroes, about the origin and development of games, or about imaginary athletes. Children also could pantomime various sports and games activities, and other members of the class could attempt to guess the activity being pantomimed.

6. Terminology used in physical education could make an interesting study of word origins. Words like *gymnasium, calisthenics,* and *exercise* have special origins.
7. When playdays or demonstrations are to be organized, students could be assigned to write the script to be used by the announcers. The basics of public speaking and the use of public address systems could be covered also.
8. Stories about athletes, important people in the history of sports, and famous referees and officials could be dramatized. Students could work in small groups and then give their presentations to the rest of the class.
9. Choral readings of well-known poems about sports, such as "Casey at the Bat," could be conducted.

MUSIC

Rhythm is an integral part of physical education, and much of the program features both music and rhythm. Musical training should not be isolated from physical education. The two areas overlap and should blend in the children's experiences. Examples of combining musical and physical education include the following.

1. Students could learn the characteristics of music and rhythm and then, through physical education and movement, interpret this learning.
2. When action songs are presented, the words and music could be taught by the music teacher and the movement patterns taught later in the physical education class.
3. To understand more about music, students could learn the names of different musical selections and become familiar with the heritage of music.
4. Rope-jumping and ball-bouncing routines created to a selected piece of music could be developed by students.
5. Exercises to music could help students understand the different tempos found in music, as well as learn to move to the tempo.
6. The tom-tom should be used often in introductory activities. Students could learn the basic locomotor movements and do them to the beat of the drum.
7. In an activity like European Rhythmic Running (page 85), students could make their own rhythm by chanting, clapping their hands, and stamping their feet.
8. Students could make tapes for exercises to music.
9. Students could make up movement sequences (page 118).

NUMBER CONCEPTS (MATHEMATICS)

Concepts of numbers can be strengthened. Practical application of the processes of addition, subtraction, division, multiplication, percentage computation, and measurement can be demonstrated through selected physical education procedures. Ways in which number concepts can be related to physical education include the following examples.

1. Students could measure their own and other students' performances. They could learn to read a tape measure and a stopwatch to enable them to evaluate performances in terms of distance, time, and height.
2. After a self-test or standardized fitness test, students could work out the class averages.
3. Students could learn to work with percentages by working out batting averages, team standings, and field goal accuracy. This might be a good task for the student who cannot participate because of an injury or illness.
4. For a study of geometric principles, students could analyze the layout of fields and game areas. Rectangles, diamonds, and circles are used often as playing areas.
5. To understand the metric system better, students could compare European (metric system) and American performances. Measurements at a track meet might be made with the metric system.
6. Basic arithmetic skills could be enhanced by games in which numbers are used as signals. For example, instead of calling out "8," the teacher could say, "36 divided by 3 minus 4."
7. Games such as number hopscotch are useful for developing number recognition as well as remembering a sequence of numbers. A large square containing 16 to 25 smaller squares could be drawn on the playground, and a number could be placed in each of the smaller squares. The leader then could call out a sequence of numbers and the player would hop into each of the squares containing the numbers called.
8. Children could measure and lay out a playing field. For instance, laying out a track and areas for field events could be a class project.

PROJECTS

Class projects in physical education and related areas form excellent educational opportunities. The teacher and the children should plan together. Many ideas can be found for these projects. Playdays are an excellent area. A playday could be organized with one or more classes in the same school, with a class in another school, or just among the children of the class itself. Demonstrations and exhibitions for parents are fruitful projects. A convocation program or demonstration in the gymnasium before other children merits consideration.

A foreign country day can be planned, involving all specialists and teachers in the school. The physical education specialist could be responsible for preparing a show of games played in the country, the art teacher might prepare costumes, and the music teacher could prepare a class to sing songs unique to the selected country. It also might be possible to cook a lunch that resembles food eaten in the foreign land, and the foreign language teacher might prepare a short play or skit in a foreign language.

Another suggestion is to invite another class to have a rhythmic party. The program can be planned, invitations written, committees formed, and all the necessary details arranged.

The enterprising teacher will think of many other ideas that can be used as projects for the children. The projects could be done every season or every year.

Twenty-five

General Considerations for Sports Activities

Sports activities are so much a part of the American and international social scene that little justification for inclusion in the elementary school program is needed. The games and sports programs have been major parts of the elementary curriculum for a long time. Although for years attention was focused mostly on boys, today's sports program should emphasize activity that provides challenge for all—boys and girls, the skilled and the unskilled, the normal and the handicapped.

Few elementary school administrators would tolerate heavy emphasis on the development of those few boys who promise to become high school varsity players. The need for a rational, educationally sound approach is apparent; the program must meet the needs and interests of elementary school children and be geared to their development. Inherent in sports activities are many physical, educational, personal, and social values that schools should exploit for the best interests of children.

The sports selected for inclusion in the program are basketball, touch football, hockey, soccer, softball, track and field, and volleyball. These activities are modified for the elementary school curriculum. The broad goal of the sports program is to provide children with the background and the interest for immediate and future sports participation. Instructional sequences should be organized so children can develop a reasonable level of skill, have the opportunity for controlled competition in lead-up and modified sports, and acquire the necessary cognitive elements with regard to accepted techniques and appropriate game strategy.

COORDINATING THE PROGRAM

The emphasis on sports activities can have a three-pronged approach. Class instruction provides opportunities for all to learn the basics of a sport. Intramurals grow out of this base and provide additional instruction, practice, and opportunities for competition. Finally, a controlled interschool competitive program can provide additional experiences for the more skilled and interested children.

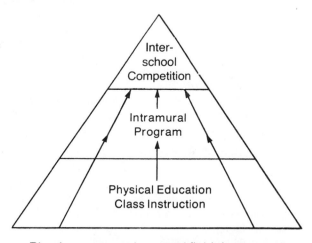

Playdays, sports days, and field days are more informal types of competition among groups and can be intramural or interschool. The term *intramural* is used to define a program entirely within the framework of a school. Special interest clubs are also a desirable extension.

The guiding principles underlying the sports program are these: (1) a school should have a good physical education program before undertaking an intramural program, and (2) both physical education and intramural programs must be sound operations before interschool competition is initiated. Intramural and interschool competitions come under the term *extended program* and grow out of the physical education experiences of all children.

IMPLEMENTING THE PHYSICAL EDUCATION SPORTS PROGRAM

This section discusses organizational and instructional elements common to all the sports selected to be parts of the elementary class instructional program. Specifics are found under the separate sports.

Safety

Good physical conditioning is an important prerequisite to game-type play. Fatigue must be controlled, and attention must be given to matters of physical and mental stress. Safety instruction is essential, since each sport has its particular hazards. Proper safety equipment and supplies are also prime considerations. Equated competition has safety implications.

Coeducational Considerations

In many of the lead-up games and most of the drills, coeducational participation is possible and desirable. Certain activities mandate separation of sexes because of the nature of the activities. Parallel competition can be held on different sections of the field or indoor facility.

Facilities

Preparation of facilities, particularly outdoors, must be anticipated. Fields should be laid out and lined. Additional discussions about the requirements for facilities of specific sports are found in each separate sports chapter.

Instructional Supplies

An adequate quantity of instructional supplies should be available, so little standing around and waiting for turns occurs. In ball skills, it is desirable to have one ball for every two children. Official balls, in many cases, are not needed, and many substitutes can be used.

Grouping for Instruction and Competition

The squad, with a designated leader, is an effective unit for instructional purposes, particularly for rotating (or station) instruction. Smaller group organization within squads, where units are composed of not more than four children, allows maximum activity. Most introductory phases of instruction should utilize small groups. More formal drill work can follow.

Teams should be made up of individuals with comparable abilities if the youngsters are expected to enjoy competition. The makeups of the teams should be changed often, so the youngsters have the opportunity to compete with all of their peers rather than always playing against the same children. When selecting groups, the teacher should use methods that alleviate the sting felt by children who might be chosen last because of their poor skill levels. If the teacher is going to select the teams ahead of time, he or she should weigh such variables as fitness tests, skill tests, height, weight, and opportunities of youngsters for outside sports participation. The teacher then should arrange the teams before the youngsters come to class. A list could be posted, and the class could be given a few minutes to organize into teams.

Homogeneous and heterogeneous groups have both advantages and disadvantages. For example, it is often a disadvantage to have skilled and unskilled players together when the skill demands a great deal of progression and ability. An example would be a relay involving basket shooting. It might be possible that a team could never win because of the poor performance of one player on the team. Such a problem would be better solved by letting the good players play on a team together and compete against another team of good shooters. In this case, the competition and winning or losing would be more meaningful for the two teams. The other side of the coin is that, in many situations, playing with athletes that are somewhat more skilled improves the performance and success of the less skilled players. Heterogeneous grouping might increase the opportunities for youngsters to help each other reach the goals of the team or the group.

A good guideline to follow might be to avoid keeping the same teams for too long a time. The same team might lose over and over if it had the least ability and, in turn, the poorly skilled youngsters would again receive the blame for the losses. Frequent rotation of team members appears to give the students the opportunity to play with all of their peers and at the same time minimizes the effects of competition and frequent losing.

Choosing teams can be done in any of the following ways.
1. Draw names out of a hat. Using colored tags with names written on them, the teacher could have the youngsters grouped by color.
2. Leaders could be elected by students who, in turn, would go to the captain of their choice. Obviously, the number of members on a team would have to be limited.

3. Four to six leaders could be elected or selected by the teacher. They then would select teams in a private session outside of the classroom.

4. Depending on the activity, the class could be arranged by height or weight and then separated by counting off. This is particularly useful in activities that give the advantage to the heavier and stronger children.

Instructional Aids

The library of every elementary school should contain a special section featuring sports books, pamphlets, magazines, and stories. Students could be assigned to report on a particular skill or phase of a sport.

Slide sets and loop film collections can be developed. These require proper viewing equipment, which many schools have. The school district should acquire a number of how-to-do-it films. Many good sports films, both loop and regular, can be purchased from commercial sources. Super-Eight films can be made as a school project and put into loop film packets; this is an interesting educational experience.

The children can make posters illustrating techniques. Some commercial sources have posters, but it is an effective educational experience for the students to make them. Posters not only can show techniques but also can stress healthful living (diet, rest, smoking, drugs) as important in sports.

Newspapers and magazines are fruitful sources of stories, pictures, and other illustrations. Keeping the gymnasium or hall bulletin board up-to-date could be a rotating class project.

Competition

Without a doubt, sports activities give rise to many problems about dealing with competition. The precedent set by professional, college, and high school sports programs often gives reason to advocate a similar philosophy ("win at all costs") at the elementary school level. AAHPER has published guidelines for competition among elementary children. Another recent publication also should be examined: it is a coaching manual titled *Youth Sports Guide for Coaches and Parents*.[1] Both publications offer sound advice about this controversial subject. The following guidelines are useful for examining the effects of competition. The teacher should remember that competition is inherently neither good nor bad. Rather, it is the way in which it is handled by the teacher that makes it a rewarding or a negative experience for the children involved.

1. Competitive situations can be rewarding only for those students capable of winning regularly. Highly skilled children usually enjoy competition, since they have a good chance of finding success. Thus, the teacher should use the feelings of *low-achieving* youngsters as guides in evaluating the effect competition has on a healthy environment for all children.

2. When children compete against each other, the teacher should emphasize the enjoyment of the activity for everyone. It would seem a worthwhile endeavor to discuss how all children are valuable and important, regardless of their performance in a game situation. In some unfortunate cases, children receive the teacher's attention and approval only when they are winners. This obviously places a heavy premium on winning at all costs.

3. There is some evidence to show that rewarding winners with extrinsic rewards actually may decrease a child's intrinsic motivation to participate in an activity.[2] When the extrinsic motivation is removed, the child may no longer want to participate for the fun of it. In some cases, this feeling may generalize to all physical activity. Emphasis should be placed on the joy of participation rather than on the importance of receiving a reward, such as a ribbon or a trophy.

4. All children should have a chance for success. This might be accomplished by careful grouping, by pairing children with others of their own ability, and by making comparisons based on improvement and effort rather than on sheer ability and skill. For example, competition might be varied by matching individuals against peers of somewhat equal ability, thus keeping the goals of competition within the students' level of aspiration. Another useful form of competition is autocompetition, in which the students compete against themselves and try to improve upon their own individual past performances.

In summary, competition is a part of the American way of life. Used wisely by a caring teacher, it can be a useful ingredient in balanced human development. An environment in which teachers are warm and friendly and firm but consistent in their judgment, and one in which children can explore their personal skill levels without fear of failure, fosters sound personal growth.

---

[1]Jerry R. Thomas, editor, *Youth Sports Guide for Coaches and Parents* (Washington, D.C.: The Manufacturer's Life Insurance Company and the National Association for Sport and Physical Education, 1977), p. 98.

[2]D. Greene and M. R. Lepper, "Intrinsic Motivation: How to Turn Play into Work," *Psychology Today,* no. 8 (September 1974), p. 52.

Lead-up Games

Most lead-up games emphasize one or two skills and serve as a laboratory for the skill being practiced. Each lead-up game should be analyzed with respect to the skills necessary to play it successfully. When a lead-up game is included in a unit, it becomes the focal game for the unit. More than one lead-up game may be included in a unit as the focus. The desired skills are practiced and applied in the focal game, with the game becoming both a goal and an evaluation.

Some of the following points should be kept in mind when lead-up games are being used.

1. Lead-up games should not replace drills. Drills are used when students have not learned specific skills, whereas lead-up games are used for skills that have been learned.
2. Drills usually maximize the amount of practice time each student can receive in a period of time. Lead-up games are for the purpose of putting skills to use in a competitive situation. Thus, the amount of time each student practices a skill will vary, depending on that student's skill level and aggressiveness. Skills are best learned when the pressure of competing and avoiding mistakes is absent.
3. When skills have been learned well, lead-up games are an excellent medium for practice, since they offer the student a chance to practice under pressure. Since lead-up games closely approximate a game situation, they motivate many youngsters.
4. Lead-up games should involve as many youngsters as possible at one time and utilize as much equipment as possible. The more times a youngster can participate, practice, and have a successful experience, the more he or she will develop a positive attitude toward the sport involved.

The sports chapters that follow generally offer more lead-up games than it is possible to cover in most elementary school sports units.

Sports Skill Practice through Creative Games

Creative games made up by the children are an excellent supplement to sports skill practice, and the result is usually a realistic game at the level of the children. Creative games are not to be regarded as substitutes for lead-up games, but they do offer a quick and convenient laboratory situation in which the skills can be experienced.

The creative game may be based on an open situation in which the children set up a game of their own design. It could, on the other hand, include certain limiting factors or elements that the teacher specifies. The emphasis is on the skill and its extended development. It may be organized on an individual, partner, or team basis, as specified by the teacher or chosen by the students.

Creative games also supply an important opportunity for observation. The teacher can determine through observation the direction the skill practice should take. The teacher may find that the skill development is sufficient for the gamelike activities offered or that further practice or attention to certain details is indicated.

Modifying Activities

Most sports activities need modification to adapt them so that elementary children can derive enjoyment and achieve success in participation. Changing selected elements increases the probability of successful participation. The most important consideration for modifying a sport is allowing the children to use and learn proper movement patterns. For example, many children learn to throw a basketball at a 10-foot high basket rather than learning to shoot properly. A proper modification would be to lower the basket and reduce the size and weight of the ball, so the children could learn to shoot correctly. Patterns learned and practiced for a period of 2 or 3 years can sometimes be difficult, if not impossible, to alter. The following ideas may be useful in making the activity more effective.

1. Decrease the number of players on a side, particularly in soccer- and football-type games.
2. Shorten field or court sizes.
3. Shorten time periods.
4. Lower nets and baskets.
5. Make scoring easier by increasing the size of goals, removing goalies, or substituting a different kind of scoring.
6. Change to more appropriate equipment, such as softer softballs, a beach ball in place of a volleyball, and junior-size footballs and basketballs.
7. Use zones to guarantee more position play.
8. Change rules to increase successful play, such as moving up the serving distance or allowing an assist on the serve in volleyball.

Officiating

When children are to officiate, some instructional time must be spent on this phase. Rules should be clarified and posted, and simple officiating techniques should be covered. Impartial enforcement teaches respect for rules.

Some self-officiating is desirable, particularly in out-of-bounds decisions. A child can clarify an out-of-bounds decision by saying, "I touched it last."

Instructional Procedures

The principles of motor learning (chapter six) have a direct bearing on the acquisition of sports skills. Where appropriate, these should be incorporated into both the instruction and the coaching during practice.

The how and why of activity are inseparable in sports instruction. If a child is asked to perform a skill in a certain manner, he or she should know why.

Each student in physical education classes should practice all skills, and the organization pattern of skill practice should reflect this. Rotation during lead-up games should be made, so each child receives experience at all positions and so the play is not dominated by one or two skilled individuals.

Instruction should include the critical points of the skill. Noting similarities with other skills teaches transfer and helps establish basic concepts.

Individual coaching during practice is a vital part of the instruction. Students should be encouraged to concentrate on correct execution, and the instructor should circulate among students to see that this occurs. Positive correction keys this process, providing reinforcement with a word, a smile, a nod, or another means by which students are motivated toward quality performance.

The problem of the skilled performer who is advanced because of outside practice in Little League Baseball, Pop Warner Football, and Biddy Basketball can be partially alleviated by utilizing skilled players as peer instructors. Keeping them interested is a challenge.

Some organization by skill level for practice can be done. Care must be taken not to reinforce the label that hangs on some poorly skilled children.

Students should be encouraged to participate, evaluate, and make adjustments to movement patterns during skill practice. This implies many opportunities to try the various skill elements and the right to make individual decisions with regard to the style they wish to adopt. Small-group practice permits this kind of experimentation without undue peer or performance pressure.

Relays that function as skill drills should be used with caution, since students in their haste to win often revert to sloppy and inept skill performance.

Critique sessions can be a valuable instructional procedure. Part of the group (half of the class or one squad) can demonstrate what has been achieved, with emphasis centered on positive elements. Critiques between two individuals in which one shows achievement and the other provides correction should be considered.

A skilled performer can be introduced to motivate, provide technique help, and answer questions. Another motivational device is to arrange a trip to a ball game. Special ticket arrangements for groups usually can be made, including arrangements for those children who cannot buy tickets.

Most sports have an interesting origin and history, and the school library should contain materials about sports. A presentation by a student of the basic background of a sport stimulates interest.

General safety considerations (page 63) and specific safety features for particular sports should be incorporated into the instructional plan.

The sections on general methodology should be reviewed.

Planning the Schedule

Prior discussion of the physical education program (chapter four) covered the allocations of time to the sports program in general as it is related to other program areas in the total physical education program. Using these figures as a basis, specific allocations of time in terms of weeks can be made to each sports activity with respect to grade level. The third grade is the recommended grade level at which the sports program should be initiated.

If it is not possible to include all recommended sports in the class program, the following priorities can be a guide.

Lowest priority for inclusion in the program should go to softball and volleyball, in that order. In

Allocation of Time to Specific Sports According to Grade Level (Three through Six) by Weeks

GRADE LEVEL	3	4	5	6
MEASURE OF TIME	WEEKS	WEEKS	WEEKS	WEEKS
Basketball	2	3	3	3
Football		2	2	2
Hockey (floor or field)		1	1	2
Soccer	1	2	3	3
Softball	2	2	1	1
Track and field		2	3	3
Volleyball		1	1½	2
Total allocation	5	13	14½	16

most schools, children participate in softball during recess, the lunch period, and at other times. It can be argued that the absence of softball from the instructional program is compensated to an extent by recreational softball experiences.

Volleyball usually is included in the junior high school curriculum, and elimination from the elementary school program generally means only postponement of participation and instruction.

Football activities should rank above softball and volleyball in priority in the instructional program but below the other sports—basketball, hockey, soccer, and track and field. Football experiences are slanted mostly toward the boys. Boys, particularly, undergo many football experiences in later school years.

During the year, sports should be scheduled on a block-time plan, meaning that each sport should be taught for a specified length of time, one or more weeks, without interruption. A unit plan on which the progressions and experiences are based should be made for each sport.

TOURNAMENTS

Depending on the preference of the teacher, the ability level of students, the available time, and the limitations on facilities and equipment, tournaments can be an enjoyable way to culminate a sport unit. Various types of tournament drawings can be used with good success.

Round Robin Tournament

This type of drawing is probably the most useful when there is adequate time to play the necessary games or matches. In round robin play, every team or individual plays each team or individual once. Final standings are based on the win-loss percentages. In order to determine the amount of time the tournament will take to complete, the following formula can be used (TI = number of teams or individuals):

$$\frac{TI\,(TI-1)}{2}$$

For example, if there are five teams in a volleyball unit, 5(5-1)/2 = 10 games to be scheduled.

For arranging a tournament for an odd number of teams, each team should be assigned a number. Number the teams down the right column and up the left column. When an odd number of teams is being used, all numbers rotate and the last number each time draws a bye. An example using seven teams follows.

Round 1	Round 2	Round 3	Round 4
7	6	5	4
6-1	5-7	4-6	3-5
5-2	4-1	3-7	2-6
4-3	3-2	2-1	1-7

Round 5	Round 6	Round 7
3	2	1
2-4	1-3	7-2
1-5	7-4	6-3
7-6	6-5	5-4

When an even number of teams is being arranged, the plan is similar, except the position of team #1 remains stationary and the other teams revolve around it until the combinations are completed. An example of an eight-team tournament follows.

Round 1	Round 2	Round 3	Round 4
1-2	1-8	1-7	1-6
8-3	7-2	6-8	5-7
7-4	6-3	5-2	4-8
6-5	5-4	4-3	3-2

Round 5	Round 6	Round 7
1-5	1-4	1-3
4-6	3-5	2-4
3-7	2-6	8-5
2-8	8-7	7-6

Ladder Tournament

A ladder tournament can be used as sort of an ongoing tournament, which either is administered formally by the teacher or is used informally by the students. Competition occurs by challenge and is minimally supervised. Various arrangements can be used, but usually one participant can only challenge opponents who are two steps above his or her present ranking. If the challenger wins, he or she changes places with the loser. The teacher could establish an initial ranking, or positions could be drawn out of a hat.

```
+-------------------------------------+
|                                     |
|            Shuffleboard             |
|            Tournament               |
|                                     |
|     1. _____      |
|                                     |
|     2. _____      |
|                                     |
|     3. _____      |
|                                     |
|     4. _____      |
|                                     |
|     5. _____      |
|                                     |
|     6. _____      |
|                                     |
|     7. _____      |
|                                     |
+-------------------------------------+
```

Pyramid Tournament

A pyramid tournament is very similar to a ladder tournament, except that there is more challenge and variety due to a wider choice of opponents. In the pyramid tournament, a player may challenge any opponent one level above his or her present

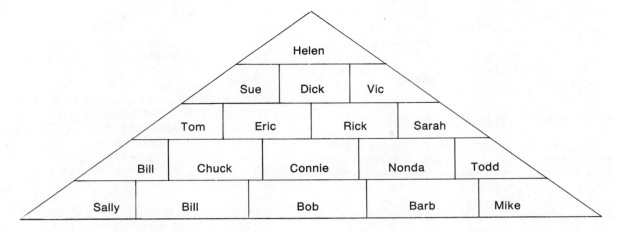

ranking. Another variation is that a player must challenge someone on his or her level and beat that person before he or she can challenge another person at a higher level.

Elimination Tournament

This type of tournament is not the best format for elementary school youngsters because of the fact that the teams that lose early have to sit out and observe. In many cases, these are the teams that need more participation and success rather than less. An example of a simple elimination tournament for six teams follows.

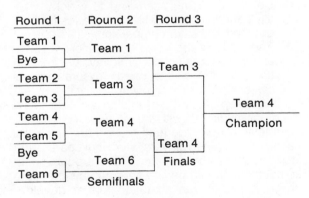

CLUBS AND SPECIAL INTEREST GROUPS

It is the opinion of the authors that this type of organization has not been exploited enough. Club work not only can provide extra opportunity in activities in the class instructional program but can cater to special interests—archery, backpacking, swimming, gymnastics, rhythmics (dancing), baton twirling, cycling, tennis, skiing, skating, bowling, golf, and wrestling, among others. Competent leadership is vital and may be found outside of the school family.

Two types of emphases seem to emerge. One is to satisfy the urge for adventure, something different and new. The other is to provide the highly skilled an opportunity for effective participation.

Clubs can be organized within a school, but the most effective special interest groups are organized in larger systems. Meeting perhaps on a weekly basis, one of the district schools can be specified for an interest group supervised by qualified personnel. Parents need to assume the responsibility for getting interested children in the district to the school and back home.

PLAYDAYS

A playday is a festival-type setting where children of a school or different schools meet to take part in physical education activities. The emphasis is on social values, rather than on competition. Yet, competition is important in that teams made up from different participating schools can play against each other.

A playday may be entirely within a particular school. However, the usual pattern is for a playday between schools. It may be carried on during the school day, after school, or on a Saturday.

The program may consist of sports-type activities, or it may include the more simple games, relays, and contests. Stunts, individual athletic events, and even rhythms are the bases of activities in some meets. The programs vary according to the size of the schools and the grade levels of the children.

Playdays that attempt to emphasize champions or that glorify the star performers from each school are undesirable. The real purpose of a playday is to have everyone on a team and a team for everyone.

Children should have a large part in the planning, and the experience gives them a fruitful opportunity to act as hosts or as guests in a social situation. The program emphasis may be on activities that have been previously practiced or rehearsed, or it may include new and unique events broadening the scope of the physical education experience.

THE INTRAMURAL PROGRAM

The intramural program should provide opportunity to extend and expand skills and knowledges gained from the physical education program and supply the element of competition. The emphasis in the program should be on competing and participating and not on determining champions. Generally, the program is carried on after school, but some schools find it feasible to use other times. Adult leadership is essential, but students should have an important part in the planning and execution of the program.

Teams may be chosen on the basis of classrooms, by a classification system, or by lot. Equitable competition is needed to maintain interest. The program should be an opportunity for all boys and girls and not just the more skilled.

Whoever directs the program should receive special compensation. To ask a teacher to assume this responsibility in addition to regular duties without remuneration seldom produces the desired results.

Rules should specify that all players play at least a portion of the time. The program should be open to all with no cutting from the team, regardless of level of skill. Since this is an extracurricular activity, having parents' permission is desirable. The problem of working around the school bus schedules must be faced. In some schools, parents not only give permission for children to participate but accept the responsibility of providing transportation.

INTERSCHOOL COMPETITION

In launching and operating interschool sports competition for elementary school children, the school system must make a number of commitments.

1. The program should be under the control of the school, and the competition level should be appropriate to the maturity of elementary school boys and girls. Schedules should be limited and based on providing friendly competition between nearby schools. In short, it should not be a miniature secondary school program. There is little place for pep rallies, ornate uniforms, victory celebrations, elaborate recognition ceremonies, excessive publicity, play-offs, and bowl contests. Contests should be after school or on Saturdays, so academic time is not sacrificed. Admission should be free. Publicity should focus on team achievement rather than individual performances.

2. The safety and welfare of the children are paramount, and certain controls are vital. Parents' permission should be required. Qualified leadership, under the general supervision of the principal, is an essential ingredient. Medical examination or screening should be required prior to participation. Insurance coverage is a consideration. Emergency care procedures and attention to counteracting the hazards of the sport are of utmost importance.

3. Suitable equipment and facilities need to be provided. Properly fitted protective equipment is a strong consideration. Junior-sized equipment is easier for children to handle and usually costs less than the regulation sizes.

4. Proper physical conditioning should be established prior to competition.

5. Careful grouping according to weight, size, skill, and physical maturation makes for both equated and safer competition.

6. The program should be stressed for both boys and girls. Coeducational volleyball competition has met with success in some school systems.

One acceptable way to function is to coordinate the program directly with the intramural operation. Competition would be held first on an intramural basis, and selected players later would participate in interschool competition. This introduction to competition should be in a relaxed, low-pressure program, which can stimulate further development. Admittedly, it is difficult to escape the fact that the purpose of competition is to win, but— "Win with the code and your head and your honor held high."

Twenty-six

Basketball Activities

American youngsters need little incentive to participate in basketball, because this sport is already part of their social scene. Although it was previously considered a male preserve, basketball now is included in the schema of sports for girls, and this opens up a new perspective. Skill practice and lead-up games can be structured to give *both* girls and boys the educational benefits of basketball instruction.

Basketball in the elementary schools should not be regarded as a proving ground for future high school stars, either girls or boys. It should be an instructional program for *all* students. The fundamentals are to be stressed in physical education classes, with emphasis on developmental and lead-up activities. There must be many opportunities for all children to have experiences in the many phases of the game of basketball.

When the emphasis in class is on instruction and skill development, little time is left for the playing of unmodified basketball games during school hours. The more skilled and interested students should be given additional opportunities through an intramural program, recreational periods (on weekends, holidays, and vacations), or an educationally sound interschool competitive league.

Ball-handling skills should be developed slowly and should be an outgrowth of the instruction in fundamental skills on the primary level. In the primary grades, the children learn the elements of catching, bouncing, passing, and dribbling many kinds of balls. Later, in the intermediate grades, shooting, offensive and defensive play, and rules are added to this base. The suggested program begins in the third grade, and the program for this grade is included in the plan of progression that follows.

EMPHASIS IN EACH GRADE LEVEL

Third Grade

Little actual basketball playing is done in the third grade. Concentration should be on the simple fundamental skills of passing, catching, shooting, and dribbling. The lead-up game, End Ball, permits the youngsters to use their basic skills in a game in which the children are more or less stationary.

Fourth Grade

Fourth grade is the starting point for actual basketball practice. The instructional emphasis is based on fundamental skills developed at the primary level, with modification and improvement of these skills for more specialized use. Emphasis is focused on developing a broad range of skill in passing, catching, dribbling, and shooting. The lay-up shot and the one-hand push shot also receive attention. Captain Ball adds the elements of simple defense, jump balls, and accurate passing. Basic rules covering traveling and dribbling violations also should be taught.

Fifth Grade

In the fifth grade, different kinds of basketball games are introduced. Shooting games, such as Around the Key and Twenty-one, are popular. Sideline Basketball and Captain Basketball supply new experiences for the children. Continued prac-

Suggested Basketball Program

GRADE	THIRD	FOURTH	FIFTH	SIXTH
Skills				
Passing	Chest or push Baseball Bounce	Underhand One-hand Two-hand One-hand push	All passes to moving targets	Two-hand overhead Long passes
Catching	Above waist Below waist		While moving	
Shooting	Two-hand chest shot	Two-hand chest shot Lay-up, right and left One-hand push shot	Free throws	One-hand jump shot Two-hand jump shot
Dribbling	Standing and moving	Down and back Right and left hands	Figure eight Pivoting	Practice with eyes closed
Guarding and Stopping			Feinting Pivoting	Parallel stop Stride stop Three-player weave
Knowledges Rules	Dribbling	Violations Dribbling Traveling Out-of-bounds	Held ball Personal fouls Holding Hacking Charging Blocking Pushing etc.	Conducting the game Officiating
Activities	End Ball Birdie in the Cage	Captain Ball Softball Basketball Dribbling Tag	Captain Basketball Sideline Basketball Twenty-one Around the Key Freeze Out	Flag Dribble One-Goal Basketball One-on-One Five Passes Basketball Snatch Ball Three-on-Three Basketrama
Skill Tests		Dribble	Figure-eight dribble Wall pass test	Figure-eight dribble Baskets per minute Free throws

tice on all the fundamental skills previously introduced is necessary for good progression. More basketball skills are added to the already growing group. Selected rules necessary to play the simple version of basketball should be covered.

Sixth Grade

The sixth grade should continue practice on all skills. Shooting games from the other grades can be continued. Basketball Snatch Ball and One-Goal Basketball give opportunity to use skills that have been acquired. Regular basketball with its formations, lineup, and other details should be covered, so the children can be ready to participate in basketball played as a regular game. Officiating should be taught, because it is a valuable experience for children to officiate their scrimmages and games.

SKILLS IN BASKETBALL

The skills needed in basketball in the elementary school instruction program can be divided into passing, catching, dribbling, shooting, defending, stopping, and pivoting. Feinting also should be taught as a part of passing, dribbling, and offensive maneuvers.

Passing

Regardless of which pass is used, certain factors are common to all passes. The ball should be handled with the thumb and finger pads and not with the palms of the hands. Firm control is obtained by the pressure of the pads of the fingers and thumbs. The passer should step forward in the direction of the receiver. Passes should be made with a quick arm extension and a snap of the wrists, with the thumbs and fingers providing the momentum. At the finish, the palms should be facing the floor.

The passer should avoid telegraphing the direction of the pass. He or she should develop peripheral vision and keep his or her eyes moving from place to place to develop an awareness of his or her teammates' positions, at the same time anticipating the spot toward which a teammate will be moving to take the pass away from the opponent.

Chest (or Two-Hand) Push Pass

Generally, one foot is ahead of the other, with the knees flexed slightly. The ball is held at chest level, with the fingers spread on each side of the ball. Elbows remain close to the body, and the ball is sent out by the extended arms and proper wrist snap as one foot moves toward the receiver.

Baseball (or One-Hand) Pass

The passer should imitate the action of a baseball catcher throwing the ball to second base.

Ready for a Push Pass or a Two-Hand Push Shot

Push Pass

Baseball Pass

Body weight shifts from back to front foot. A sidearm motion is to be avoided, since it puts an improper spin on the ball. The illustration on page 449 shows a left-hander throwing the pass.

One-Hand Push Pass

The passer holds the ball with both hands but supports with the left more than with the right, which is a little back of the ball. The ball is pushed forward with a quick wrist snap by the right hand.

Bounce Passes

Any of the three preceding passes can be adapted to make a bounce pass. The object is to get the pass to the receiver on first bounce, so the ball comes to the receiver's outstretched hands about waist high. A little experimentation determines that the ball should be bounced a little more than halfway between the two players to make it come efficiently to the receiver.

Underhand Pass

For the two-hand pass, the ball should be held to one side in both hands, with the foot on the other side toward the receiver. The ball is somewhat "shoveled" toward the receiver with a step made with the leading foot. The one-hand variety is made like an underhanded toss in baseball.

Underhand Pass

Two-Hand Overhead Pass

The two-hand overhead pass is effective for a player against a shorter opponent. Passer is generally in a short stride position, with the ball held overhead. It is important for the momentum of the pass to come from a forceful wrist and finger snap. The arms should remain relatively in place. The pass should take a slight downward path to be most effective.

Catching

Receiving the ball is a most important fundamental to be mastered, since many turnovers involve failure to handle a pass properly. The receiver should move toward the pass. His or her fingers are spread and relaxed. He or she is reaching somewhat for the ball with bent elbows and a relaxed wrist. He or she attempts to cushion the pass by causing his or her hands to give as the ball comes in. He or she should squeeze the ball with

Overhead Pass—Ready Position

Overhead Pass—Finishing Position

the fingertips for control before starting any other maneuver.

Dribbling

Dribbling is used to advance the ball, break for a basket, or maneuver out of a difficult situation.

The dribbler's knees and trunk should be slightly flexed, with the head and eyes forward, utilizing peripheral vision. He or she should look beyond the ball and see it in the lower part of the visual area. The ball is propelled with a cupped, relaxed hand by using fingertips, a relaxed wrist, and little overall arm motion. Younger children tend to slap at the ball rather than push it.

Good Dribbling Form

Dribbling should be done with hand and practice in changing from one hand to the other is essential. Some practice in the style of the Harlem Globetrotters is of value, but fancy behind-the-back and between-the-legs dribbling is of dubious value at this stage of development.

Dribbling

Shooting

Shooting involves intricate skills, and students should be encouraged to develop consistent techniques rather than to be satisfied because the ball happened to go into the basket. There are some common factors for all types of shots, and these should be learned and practiced.

1. Good body position is important. Both the toes and the shoulders should face the basket. The weight should be evenly distributed on both feet. The ball should be held in preliminary phases between shoulder and eye levels.
2. Utilize a comfortable grip, with the fingers well spread and the ball resting on the pads of the fingers. One should be able to see daylight between the palm of the hand and the ball. The shooting elbow for one-hand shots is directly below the ball.
3. Immediately, when the decision is made to shoot, fix the eye on the target (rim or backboard) during all phases of the shot.
4. Cock the wrist as the shot starts.
5. Follow through well, imparting a slight backspin on the ball. Be sure the arms are fully extended, the wrist completely flexed, and the hand dropping down toward the floor. The arc should be 45 degrees or a little above.

Good Hand and Finger Positions on a One-Hand Shot

6. Children should begin (third grade) with the two-hand push shot and move to the one-hand shot (fourth grade) as soon as control is evident.

Push Shot, Two Hands

The feet can be together or one can be leading; knees are slightly bent. The hands are placed more to the back, with the thumbs a few inches apart. The wrist is cocked slightly, and the ball is propelled with good follow-through.

Two-handed Push Shot

Push Shot, One Hand

This is usually a jump shot for short distances and a set shot for longer distances. The ball is held at shoulder-eye level with both hands, the body erect, and knees slightly flexed in preparation for a jump. The shooter executes a vertical jump, leaving the floor slightly. The supporting (nonshooting) hand remains in contact with the ball until the top of the jump is reached. The shooting hand takes over with fingertip control, with the ball rolling off the center three fingers. The hand and wrist follow through, as previously described. Visual concentration on the target is maintained throughout. Proper technique should be emphasized rather than accuracy. In using this as a set shot, the shooter rises up on his or her toes.

One-handed Push Shot

Lay-up Shot

The lay-up is a short shot taken when going into the basket either after receiving a pass or at the end of a dribble. It involves the principle of opposition, in that, when shooting from the right side, the

takeoff is with the left foot, and vice versa. The ball should be carried with both hands early in the shot and then shifted to one hand for the final push. The ball should be laid against the backboard with a minimum of spin and should be guided by fingertip control.

Free-Throw Shot

Free-throw shooting can be performed successfully with different types of shots. The one-hand foul shot now is the most popular. Needed are complete concentration, complete relaxation, and a rhythmic, consistent delivery. Some players find it helpful to bounce the ball several times before shooting to relieve tension. Other shooters like to take a deep breath and exhale completely just prior to shooting.

The specific mechanics of the shot do not differ materially from shooting from other spots on the floor from comparable distances. Smoothness and consistency are most important.

Jump Shot, One Hand

The jump shot has the same upper-body mechanics as the one-handed push shot already described. The primary difference is the height of the jump. The jump should be straight up, rather than at a forward or backward angle. The ball should be released at the height of the jump. Since the legs cannot be used to increase the force applied to the ball in the jump shot, it is difficult for those youngsters who lack strength. Therefore, for developing proper shooting habits, the basket should be at low level and a junior-size basketball should be used.

One-handed Jump Shot

Jump Shot, Two Hands

Some children may find the two-handed jump shot preferable to the one-handed technique because of their lack of size and strength. Many varieties are used by good basketball players today. Some seem to involve more control by one hand than the other. The key is a comfortable, controlled shot at the height of the jump, with both hands controlling the ball for a longer period of time.

Defending

The player, with his or her knees slightly bent and the feet comfortably spread, should face the opponent. The weight should be evenly distributed on both feet to allow for movement in any direction. A defensive player should stand about 3 feet from the opponent and wave one hand to distract or block passes and shots. Movement sideward is done with a sliding motion. A defensive player should be loose and able to move quickly so as not to be caught flat-footed.

In Defensive Position

Stopping

To stop quickly, the weight of the body should be dropped to lower the center of gravity and the feet applied as brakes. In the parallel stop, the body turns sideward and the feet act together as brakes. The stride stop comes from a forward movement and is done in a one-two count. The stopping begins with one foot hitting the ground with braking action and the other foot firmly planted *ahead* on the second count. The knees are bent, and the body center of gravity is lowered. From a stride stop, the movement can become a pivot by picking up the front foot and carrying it to the rear and at the same time fading to the rear.

Stopping

Pivoting

Pivoting is used by a player with the ball to protect the ball by keeping his or her body between himself or herself and the defensive player. The ball is held firmly in both hands, with the elbows out to protect the ball. One foot, the pivot foot, must always be in contact with the floor. It is permissible to turn on the ball of that foot, but the pivot foot must not be dragged away from the pivot spot. The lead foot may, however, step in any direction.

Pivoting

If the player has received the ball in a stationary position or during a jump where both feet hit the ground simultaneously, either foot may become the pivot foot. If a player stops after a dribble on a one-two count, the pivot foot is the foot that made contact on the first count.

Feinting

Feinting is used to mask the intent of a maneuver or pass and is essential to basketball. Feinting can be done with the eyes, the head, a foot, or the whole body. It is a deceptive motion in one direction when the intent to move in another direction is accomplished. In passing, it means faking a pass in one manner or direction and then passing in another.

INSTRUCTIONAL PROCEDURES

1. Many basketball skills, particularly on the third-grade level, do not stipulate the use of basketballs. Other balls such as volleyballs, playground balls, and rubber balls can be used successfully.
2. Many of the skills can be practiced individually or in pairs with playground balls or similar balls. For instance, dribbling, passing, and catching skills receive more practice time when as many balls as possible are utilized. This allows all children to develop at their own pace, regardless of their skill levels.
3. Baskets should be lowered to 7 feet, 8 feet, or 9 feet, depending on the size of the youngsters. If the facility also is used for community purposes, adjustable baskets—preferably power driven—are the key. Lowering baskets to 5 or 6 feet for use by children in wheelchairs is desirable; this height also is useful for experimentation by younger children. These low baskets can be mounted directly on a wall, so they can be set up and removed as needed. No backboard is necessary. When the baskets are mounted to one side, children confined to wheelchairs and other handicapped individuals can shoot baskets even though they are not able to participate in many basketball activities.
4. The program should concentrate on skills and include many drills. Basketball offers endless possibilities, and drills should be utilized to give variety and breadth to the instructional program. Each child should have an opportunity to practice all the skills. This is not possible when a considerable portion of the class time is devoted to playing the game with official rules on a full-length court.

DRILLS IN BASKETBALL

In working with the different drills, the instructor should utilize the technique suggestions for the skill being practiced and also apply the movement principles (page 81). Drills cover both single skills and combinations of skills.

Passing Drills

Good use should be made of selected skill formations (page 69) for passing practice, including two line, circle, circle and leader, line and leader, shuttle turnback, and regular shuttle. A number of other drills should be considered for passing drills.

Slide Circle Drill

A circle of four to six players slide around a person in the center. The center person passes and receives to and from the sliding players. After the ball has gone around the circle twice, another player takes the center position.

Circle-Star Formation

With only five players in a circle formation, a star drill is particularly effective. Players pass to every other player, and the path of the ball in a full round forms a star. The star drill works well as a ball-passing relay.

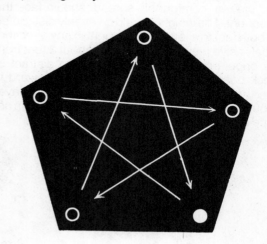

Triangle Drill

From four to eight players can be used in this formation. The ball begins at the head of the line and is passed forward. Each player passes and moves to the spot to which he or she passed, thus making a continual change of positions.

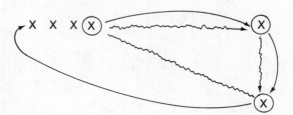

Three-Player Weave

Another valuable drill is the three-player weave. This drill needs sufficient explanation and must be practiced. It should be remembered that the player in the center always starts the drill. The drill has two other key points. The first to remember is that "you always go behind the player to whom you threw the ball." The second is that "just as soon as you go behind and around the player, head diagonally across the floor until you receive the ball." The pass from the center player can start to either side.

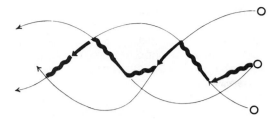

Dribbling Drills

Dribbling can be practiced as a single skill or in combination with others.

File Dribbling

Players dribble forward around an obstacle and back to the line, where the next player repeats. The obstacle can be an Indian club, a cone, or a chair. A variation of value is to have each player dribble down with one hand and back with the other.

Shuttle Dribbling

Dribbling begins at the head of file A. The player dribbles to file B, handing off the ball to the player at the head. He or she then takes his or her place at the end of file B. The player receiving the ball then is dribbling back to file A. A number of shuttles can be arranged for dribbling crossways over a basketball court.

Obstacle or Figure-Eight Dribbling

Three or more obstacles are set out about 5 feet apart. The first player at the head of each file dribbles in and around each obstacle, changing hands so the hand opposite the obstacle is used.

Dribble and Pivot Drills

In these drills, there is emphasis on stopping and pivoting.

File Drill

Each player in turn dribbles forward to the designated line, stops, pivots so he or she faces the

file, and then passes back to the next player, who repeats. The first player runs to a place at the end of the line.

Dribble and Pivot Drill

Players are organized by pairs and scattered around the basketball floor in the following fashion. One ball is required for each pair. On the first whistle, the front player of the pair dribbles in any direction and fashion on the court. On the second whistle, he or she stops where he or she is and pivots back and forth. On the third whistle, he or she dribbles back to where he or she can pass to his or her partner, who immediately dribbles forward, and the routine is repeated.

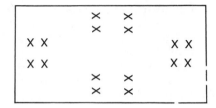

Shooting Drills

These are simple shooting drills or combinations of shooting and other skills.

Simple Shooting Drill

Players form files of not more than four people and take turns shooting a long and a short or some other prescribed series of shots.

File and Leader

The first player in each file has a ball and is the shooter. He or she passes the ball to the leader, who returns the ball to him or her to the spot he or she has selected for the shot. This usually is a floor shot and not a lay-in.

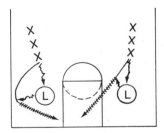

Dribble and Shoot

Two files are established on one end of the floor. One file has a ball. The player dribbles in and shoots the lay-in. A member from the other file recovers the ball and passes it to the next dribbler. When both have finished, each goes to the rear of the other file. After some expertise in the drill has

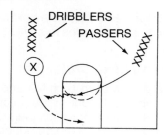

been developed, two balls can be used, allowing more shooting opportunities.

Set-Shot Formation

Players can be scattered around a basket in a semicircle, with a leader in charge. Players should be close enough so that they can shoot well. The leader passes to each in turn to take a shot. The leader chases the ball after the shot. A bit of competition can be injected by allowing a *successful* shooter to take one step back for the next shot. Or a player gets to repeat his or her shot when he or she makes it.

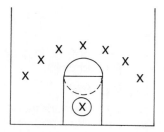

Lay-up Drill

This is one of the favorite drills in basketball. One line simply passes to the other line for lay-up shots. Come in from the right side first (the easiest), then from the left, and last down the center. Each player goes to the end of the other line.

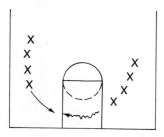

Jump-Shot Drill

This is similar to the lay-up drill, except the incoming shooter receives the ball, stops, and takes his or her jump shot. The line of shooters should move back, so there is forward movement to the shooting spot. As soon as the passer passes the ball to the shooter, he or she takes his or her

place at the end of the shooter's line. The shooter goes to the passer's line after shooting.

One extension of this drill is to allow a second jump shot when the shooter makes the first. In this case, the incoming passer passes to the shooter taking a second shot, as well as to the next shooter.

Another extension that establishes a gamelike play situation is having both the shooter and the incoming passer follow up the shot when the basket has not been made. As soon as the follow shot is made or there are three misses by the followers, the passer passes the ball to the new shooter.

The avenues by which the shooters approach should be varied, so there is variety in the shooting spots.

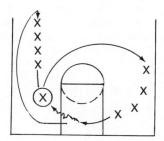

Offense and Defense Drills

Group Defensive Drill

The entire class is scattered on a basketball floor, facing one of the sides. The instructor or the student leader stands on the side, near the center.

The drill can be done a number of ways.

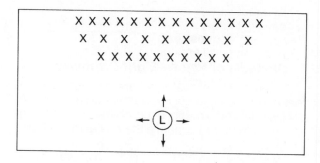

1. The leader points in one direction (forward, backward, or to one side) and gives the command "move." When the students have moved a short distance, he or she commands, "Stop." Players keep good defensive position throughout.
2. Commands can be changed so that movement can be continuous. Commands are "right," "left," "forward," "backward," and "stop." The leader must watch that movement is not so far in any one direction that it causes players to run into obstructions. Commands

can be given in order. Pointing can accompany commands.

3. The leader is a dribbler with a ball. He or she moves forward, backward, or to either side, with the defensive players reacting accordingly.

Teaching Points: Good defensive position and movement should be stressed. Movement from side to side should be a slide. Movement forward and backward is also a two-step movement with one foot always leading.

Offense-Defense Drills with a Post

Basically, the drill consists of an offensive player, a defensive player, and another player acting as a passing post. The post player generally remains stationary and receives the ball from, and passes to, the offensive player, who tries to maneuver around or past the defensive player and secure a good shot. Play can be confined to one side of an offensive basket area, thus allowing two drills to go on at the same time on one end of the basketball floor. If there are side baskets, many drills can be operated at the same time.

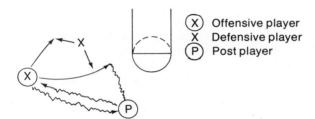

Ⓧ Offensive player
X Defensive player
Ⓟ Post player

After a basket has been attempted a rotation of players, including any waiting players, is made.

Teaching Suggestions: The defensive player should cover well enough to prevent shots in front of him or her. Some matching of ability must be made or the drill will be meaningless.

BASKETBALL ACTIVITIES

Third Grade

End Ball

Players on each team are divided into three groups: forwards, guards, and ends. The object is for a forward to throw successfully to one of the end-zone players.

Playing Area: A court 20 by 40 feet is divided in half by a center line. End zones are marked 3 feet wide, completely across the court at each end.

Players: 9 to 12 on each team.

Supplies: Basketball or 8½-inch rubber playground ball.

Skills: Passing and catching, jumping at jump balls.

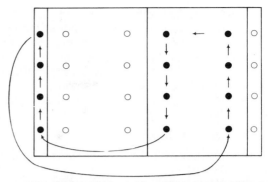

The players from each team are positioned as diagrammed. The end-zone players take positions in one of the end zones. Their forwards and guards then occupy the half of the court farthest from this end zone. The forwards are near the center line, and the guards are back near the end zone of that half.

The ball is put in play with a center jump between the two tallest opposite forwards. When a team gets the ball, the forwards try to throw over the heads of the opposing team to an end-zone player. To score, the ball must be caught by an end-zone player with *both* feet inside the zone. No dribbling or moving with the ball is permitted by any player. After each score, play is resumed by a jump ball at the center line.

Fouls: Fouls result in loss of the ball to the other team. Fouls are:

1. Holding a ball more than 5 seconds.
2. Stepping over the end line or stepping over the center line into the opponent's territory.
3. Walking (traveling) with the ball.
4. Pushing or holding another player.

Out-of-Bounds: The ball belongs to the team that did not cause it to go out-of-bounds. The nearest player retrieves the ball out at the sideline and returns it to the guard of the proper team.

Teaching Suggestions: Encourage fast, accurate passing. Players in the end zones must practice jumping high to catch and still land with both feet inside the end-zone area. A system of rotation is desirable. Each time a score is made, players on that team can rotate one person. (See diagram.)

To outline the end zones, some instructors have had excellent success using folding mats (4 by 7 feet or 4 by 8 feet). Three or four mats forming each end zone make a definite area and serve to eliminate the problem of defensive players (guards) intruding into the end zone.

Variations

1. A game that carries the progression one step further is Free-Throw End Ball. In keeping with the rules, the end-zone player scores one point when he or she catches the ball. He or she is allotted one free throw, which gives him or her the chance to score an additional point. This is an actual free throw.

2. *Corner Ball:* This differs from End Ball in that scoring is made with a pass only to the corners instead of a complete end zone. Four folding mats are needed, one placed at each corner. This imposes the limitation that only two players from each team are in position to receive the ball, one in each corner. Otherwise, the play is the same as in End Ball.

Birdie in the Cage

Formation: Circle with one player in the center.
Players: 8 to 15.
Supplies: Soccer ball, basketball, volleyball.
Skills: Passing and catching, intercepting.

The object of the game is for the center player to try to touch the ball. The ball is passed from player to player in the circle, and the center player attempts to touch the ball on one of these passes. The player who threw the ball that was touched takes the place in the center. Also, in case of a bad press resulting in the ball leaving the circle area, the player whose fault caused the error changes to the center of the ring.

Teaching Suggestions: The ball should move promptly and rapidly. Passes to a neighboring player should not be allowed. If there is difficulty in touching the ball, a second center may join the first. Play can be limited to a specific type of pass, such as bounce, two-hand, et cetera.

Variation: This can be played with as few as three children, with the ball passed back and forth between the two while a third child tries to touch the ball. An excellent version of this game calls for four players, with three forming a triangle formation, positioning themselves about 15 feet apart.

Fourth Grade

Captain Ball

Captain Ball is a very popular game that is played with many variations. In this version, a team is composed of a captain, three forwards, and three guards. The guards throw the ball to the forwards, who attempt to pass the ball to their captain.

Playing Area: About 30 by 40 feet; two games can be played crosswise on a basketball court. A center line is needed; otherwise, the normal out-of-bounds lines can be used. Hoops are used to provide the circles for the forwards and the captains.

Players: Seven on each side.
Supplies: Basketball, pinnies, eight hoops.
Skills: Passing and catching, elementary guarding.

The captain and the three forwards are each assigned to respective circles and must always keep one foot inside the circle. Guarding these four circle players are three guards.

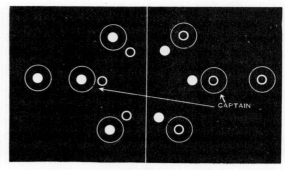

The game is started by a jump at the center line by two guards from opposing teams. The guards can rove in their half of the court but must not enter the circles of the opposing players. The ball is put into play after each score in much the same manner as in regular basketball. The team scored upon puts the ball into play by a guard throwing the ball inbounds from the side of the court.

As soon as a guard gets the ball, he or she throws it to one of the forwards who must maneuver to be open. The forward then tries to throw it to the other forwards or in to the captain. Scoring is as follows.

Two points—all three forwards handle the ball, and then it is passed to the captain.

One point—the ball is passed to the captain but has not been handled by all forwards.

Fouls

1. Stepping over the center line, or stepping into circle by guard.
2. Traveling, running, or kicking the ball.

Penalty: Free throw. Ball is given to one of the forwards, who is unguarded and gets a throw to the guarded captain. If the throw is successful, it scores one point. If it is not successful, the ball is in play.

Out-of-Bounds: As in basketball, the ball is awarded to the team that did not cause the ball to go out.

Out of the Circle: If a forward or a captain catches a ball with *both* feet out of his or her circle, the ball is taken out-of-bounds by the opposing guard.

Teaching Suggestions

1. Some instruction is necessary for children to absorb the basic strategy of the game. The most effective offensive formation seems to

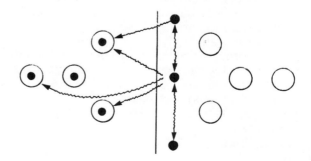

be one where the guards are spaced along the center line, as shown. Only the offensive team is diagrammed.

By passing the ball back and forth among the guards, the forwards have more opportunity to be open, since the passing makes the guards shift position.

2. The guards may dribble, but this should be held to a minimum and used for advancing the ball only when necessary. Otherwise, dribbling accomplishes little.
3. The forwards and the captain should learn to shift back and forth to become open for passes. Considerable latitude is available, since they need keep only one foot in the hoop.
4. Teach short and accurate passing by using both high and bounce passes. Circle players may jump for the ball but must come down with one foot in the circle.

Variations
1. Four guards may be used, but this makes it more difficult to score.
2. A five-circle formation may be used, forming a five spot like that on a die. Nine players on each team are needed—four forwards, four guards, and one captain.
3. A platform 6 to 8 inches high and 20 inches square can be used for the captain to elevate him or her enough to make reception of the ball easier.

Softball Basketball

Playing Area: Playground or gymnasium with basket.
Players: 10 to 30.
Supplies: Playground ball or basketball, bases.
Skills: Running, passing, catching, shooting.

Half of the players (●) are scattered in the field. The other half of the players are batters (X) and

are positioned behind home plate. The players on each team are numbered consecutively. For each number, there is a player on each team. Players in the field must be behind the restraining line until the ball is batted.

The teacher calls out any number he or she chooses. The player in the field whose number is called positions himself or herself under or near the basket, while the home player picks up the ball and bats it with his or her hand. The ball must stay within the base boundaries. As soon as the ball is struck, the batter runs around the bases. The fielding team gets the ball and passes it to the player positioned near the basket.

The object is to make a basket before the runner makes it around the bases. If the basket is made before the runner reaches home plate, he or she is out. When a team has three outs, they change positions. If the runner runs around the bases before the basket is made, then a point is scored for the home team. Players in the field may not travel with the ball.

Variation: Specify what type of pass the field players must make. Specify the number of passes that must be made before the ball goes to the shooting player.

Dribbling Tag

Playing Area: Any smooth, hard-surfaced playing area.
Players: Whole class.
Supplies: Basketball or playground ball for each player.
Skills: Dribbling, dodging while dribbling.

Two to five players are designated to be it. They chase the rest of the players. Players can only move when they are dribbling under control. Players tagged by those chasing become chasers. Emphasis should be placed on dribbling under control.

Variation: Players can find a partner and play one-on-one. The object is to steal the ball or cause a bad dribble. Use a time limit, and have the players change positions on signal.

Fifth Grade

Captain Basketball

Captain Basketball is closer to the game of basketball than Captain Ball. Captain Ball has limited movements of the forwards because of the circle restrictions. Captain Basketball brings in more natural passing and guarding situations similar to those found in the basketball scrimmage.

Playing Area: Basketball court with center line. A captain's area is laid out by drawing a line between the two foul restraining lines 4 feet out from the end line. The captain must keep one foot in this area.
Players: Six or eight on each team.

Supplies: Basketball pinnies.
Skills: All basketball skills except shooting.

The game is played much the same way as basketball. A throw by one of the forwards in to the captain scores two points. A free throw scores one point.

A team normally is composed of three forwards, one captain, and four guards. The captain must keep one foot in his or her area under the basket.

The game is started with a jump ball, after which the players advance the ball as in basketball. However, none may cross the center line. Thus, the guards must bring the ball up to the center line and throw it to one of their forwards. The forwards maneuver and attempt to pass successfully in to the captain.

Fouls: As in basketball. Stepping over the center line or a guard stepping into the captain's area draws a free throw.

Free Throw: The ball is given to a forward at the free-throw line. He or she is unguarded and has 5 seconds to pass successfully to his or her captain, who is guarded by one player. The ball is in play if the free throw is unsuccessful.

Teaching Suggestions

1. A folding tumbling mat can be used to designate the captain's area at each end of the court. Use of a mat tends to discourage intrusion by guards into the captain's area.
2. The game provides a good opportunity to learn both the rules and the techniques of basketball.
3. While players are required to remain in their own half of the court, they should be taught to move freely in that area.
4. Stress short, quick passes, since long passes are not effective.
5. Stress proper guarding techniques.
6. If only six play on each team, the team should have three guards, two forwards, and one captain.

Sideline Basketball

Playing Area: Basketball court.
Players: Class is divided into two teams, each team lining up on one side of the court, facing the other.
Supplies: Basketball, pinnies.
Skills: All basketball skills.

The game can be played by three or four active players from each team. The remainder of the players stand on the sideline and catch and pass the ball to the active players. They may not shoot, nor may they enter the playing floor. This can be defined as requiring sideline players to keep one foot completely out-of-bounds at all times.

Active players play regular basketball, except that they may pass and receive the ball from sideline players. The game starts with the active players occupying their own half of the court. Initially, the game begins with a center jump. After that, the ball is taken out-of-bounds under its own basket by the team that was scored upon. Regular basketball is played by the active players until one team scores or a period of time elapses (2 or 3 minutes). When either occurs, the active players take places in the line on the left side of their line and three new active players come out from the right. All other players move down three places in the line.

No official out-of-bounds on the sides is called. The players on that side of the floor simply recover the ball and put it in play by a pass to an active player without delay or waiting for a signal. Out-of-bounds on the ends is the same as in regular basketball. If one of the sideline players enters the court and touches the ball, it is a violation and the ball is awarded out-of-bounds on the other side to a sideline player of the other team. Free throws are awarded when a player is fouled.

Sideline players may not pass to each other but must pass back to an active player. Sideline players should be well spaced along the side.

Twenty-one

Playing Area: One end of a basketball court.
Players: Three to eight in each game, with a number of games played on one end of the floor. Players are in file formation.
Supplies: Basketball.
Skill: Shooting.

Each child is permitted a long shot (from a specified distance) and a follow-up shot. The long shot, if made, counts two points and the short shot, one. The follow-up shot must be made from the spot where the ball was recovered from the first shot. The normal one-two-step rhythm is permitted on the short shot from the place where the ball was recovered.

The first player scoring a total of 21 points is the winner. If the ball misses the backboard and basket altogether on the first shot, the second shot must be taken from the corner.

Variations

1. For a simpler game, allow dribbling before the second shot.
2. A player continues to shoot as long as he or she makes every shot. This means that, if he or she makes *both* the long and the short shot, he or she goes back out to the original position for a third shot. All shots made count, and he or she continues until he or she misses.
3. The game works very well as team competition, with each player contributing his or her total to the team score.
4. Various combinations and types of shots may be used.

Around the Key

Playing Area: One end of a basketball floor.
Players: Three to eight players.
Supplies: Basketball.
Skill: Shooting.

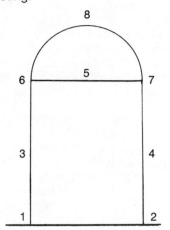

Spots are arranged for shooting as indicated in the diagram. A player begins at the first spot and continues to shoot as long as he or she makes the shot. When he or she misses, he or she has two choices. The first is to wait for his or her next turn and continue from the place where he or she missed. The second is to "risk it," which means he or she gets another shot from where the miss occurred. If the player makes this, he or she continues. If the player misses, he or she starts over from the beginning on his or her next turn. The winner is the one who completes the key first or who has made the farthest progress.

In the beginning, it is well to give each child two shots from each spot.

Variations

1. Each child shoots from each spot until he or she makes the basket. A limit of three shots from any one spot should be set. The child finishing the round of nine spots with the lowest number is the winner.
2. The order of the spots can be changed. A player can start on one side of the key and continue back along the line, around the free-throw circle, and back down the other side.
3. An easier version of the game can be played by permitting two shots from each spot. This permits more success.

Freeze Out

There are many types of freeze-out shooting games. This version is an interesting shooting game that culminates quickly and allows players back in the game reasonably quickly.
Playing Area: One end of the basketball court.
Players: Four to eight.
Supplies: Basketball.

Skill: Shooting under pressure.

Each player can have three misses before he or she is out. After the first miss, he or she gets an O; after the second, a U; and, after the third, the T; this spells OUT and puts him or her out until all but one player have been eliminated, leaving that player the winner.

The players are in file formation. The first player shoots a basket from any spot he or she wishes. If he or she misses the basket, there is no penalty and the next player shoots. If he or she makes the basket, the following player must make a basket from the same spot or he or she is scored a miss. Each player keeps track of his or her own misses.

Players should remember that, if the player ahead of them makes a basket, they must do likewise or have a miss scored against them. If the player ahead of them misses, they may shoot from any spot they wish without penalty.

Sixth Grade

Flag Dribble

Playing Area: One end of a basketball floor or a hard-surfaced area outside with boundaries.
Players: 4 to 15.
Supplies: Each player has a basketball and a flag tucked in the belt at the back.
Skill: Dribbling.

To play this game, children must have reasonable skill in dribbling. The object of the game is to eliminate the other players while avoiding being eliminated. A player is eliminated if he or she loses control of the ball, if his or her flag is pulled, or if he or she goes out-of-bounds. Keeping control of the ball by dribbling is interpreted to mean continuous dribbling without missing a bounce. A double dribble (both hands) is regarded as a loss of control.

The game starts with the players scattered around the playing area near the sidelines. Each has a ball. The extra players wait outside the area. On signal, each player begins to dribble in the area. While keeping control of his or her own dribble and staying in bounds, he or she attempts to pull a flag from any other player's back. He or she also can knock aside any other player's ball to eliminate that player. As soon as the game in progress is down to one player, that player is declared the winner. There are times when two players lose control of their basketballs at about the same time. In this case, both are eliminated. Sometimes, two players are left and the game results in a stalemate. In this case, declare both winners and start anew.

Variations

1. If it is impractical to use flags, the game can be played without this feature. The objective becomes only to knock aside or deflect the other

basketballs while retaining control of one's own ball.
2. This can be played by teams or squads. In this case, mark each squad or team well.

One-Goal Basketball

Playing Area: An area with one basketball goal.
Players: Two teams, two to four on each.
Supplies: Basketball. Pinnies can be used.
Skills: All basketball skills.

If a gymnasium has as many as four basketball goals, many children can be kept active with this game. If only two goals are present, a system of rotation can be worked out.

The game is played according to the regular rules with the following exceptions.
1. The game begins with a jump at the free-throw mark, with the centers facing the sidelines.
2. When a defensive player recovers the ball, either from the backboard or on an interception, the ball must be taken out beyond the foul-line circle before offensive play is started and an attempt at a goal can be made.
3. After a basket is made, the ball is taken in the same fashion away from the basket to the center of the floor, where the other team starts offensive play.
4. Regular free-throw shooting can be observed after a foul, or some use the rule whereby the offended team takes the ball out-of-bounds.
5. If an offensive player is tied up in a jump ball, he or she loses the ball to the other team.

Fouls are somewhat of a problem, since they are called on individuals by themselves. An official can be used, however.

Variation: A system of rotation can be instituted wherein the team that scores a basket holds the floor and the losing team must retire in favor of a waiting team. For more experienced players, a score of three or more points can be required for eliminating the opponents.

One-on-One

This is a variation of One-Goal Basketball and differs primarily in the number of players. Only two players play; otherwise the rules are about the same. Stress must be placed on the honor system, since generally no officials are present and players call fouls on themselves. There is more personal contact in this game than in One-Goal Basketball. The game has value because of its backyard recreational possibilities. It has popularity because it has been featured on television broadcasts of professional basketball players.

Five Passes

Playing Area: Half of a basketball floor.
Players: Two teams, four or five on each team.

Supplies: Basketball and colored shirts, markers, or pinnies.
Skills: Passing, guarding.

The object of the game is to complete five consecutive passes, which scores a point. On one basketball floor, two games can go on at the same time, one in each half.

The game is started with a jump ball at the free-throw line. The teams observe regular basketball rules in ball handling, traveling, and fouling. Five consecutive passes must be made by a team, which counts out loud as the passes are completed.

The ball must not be passed back to the person from whom it was received.

No dribbling is allowed. If for any reason the ball is fumbled and recovered or improperly passed, a new count is started. After a successful score, the ball can be thrown up again at a center jump at the free-throw line. A foul gives a free throw, which can score a point. Teams should be well marked to avoid confusion.

Variations
1. After each successful point (five passes), the team is awarded a free throw, which can score an additional point.
2. After a team has scored a point, the ball can be given to the other team out-of-bounds to start play again.
3. Passes must be made so all players handle the ball.

Basketball Snatch Ball

Playing Area: Basketball court.
Players: Two teams, 6 to 15 on each team.
Supplies: Two basketballs, two hoops.
Skills: Passing, dribbling, shooting.

Each team occupies one side of a basketball floor. The players on each team are numbered consecutively and must stand in this order. The two balls are laid in two hoops, placed one on each side of the center line. When the teacher calls a number, the player from each team whose number was called runs to the ball, dribbles it to the basket on his or her right, and tries to make the basket. As soon as the basket has been made, he or she dribbles back and places the ball on the spot where he or she picked it up. The first player to return the ball after making a basket scores a point for his or her team. The teacher should use some system of keeping track of the numbers, so all children have a turn. Numbers can be called in any order.

Teaching Suggestion: In returning the ball after making a basket, emphasis should be placed on legal dribbling or passing. In the hurry to get back, sometimes illegal traveling occurs.

Variations
1. Players can run by pairs with either a pair of

players assigned the same number or the teacher calling two numbers. In this case, a total of three passes must be made before the shot is taken and three passes are required before the ball is replaced inside the hoop.

2. Three players can run at a time, with the stipulation that the player who picks up the ball from the hoop must be the one who takes the first shot. All players must handle the ball on the way down and on the way back.

3. A more challenging spot to return the ball can be made by using a deck tennis ring. This demands more critical control than placing the ball in to a hoop. In either case, the ball must rest within the designated area to score.

4. A more challenging task for a single player can be made by having him or her pass the ball to each of his or her teammates successively on the way down and on the way back. Teammates scatter themselves along the sideline after the number has been called.

Three-on-Three

Playing Area: Half of a basketball court.
Players: Teams of three, three to five teams.
Supplies: Basketball.
Skills: All basketball skills.

An offensive team of three stands just forward of the center line, facing the basket. The center player has a basketball. Another team of three is on defense and awaits the offensive team in the area near the foul line.

The remaining teams await their turns and stand beyond the end line.

Regular basketball rules are used. At a signal, the offensive team advances to score. A scrimmage is over when a score is made or the ball is recovered by the defense. In either case, the defensive team moves to the center of the floor and becomes the offensive unit. A waiting team comes out on the floor and gets ready for defense. The old offensive team goes to the rear of the line of waiting players. Each of the teams should keep its own score.

Two games can be carried on at the same time, one in each half of the court.

Variations
1. If the offensive team scores, it remains on the floor and the defensive team drops off in favor of the next team. If the defense recovers the ball, the offensive team rotates off the floor.
2. If a team makes a foul (by one of the players), that team rotates off the floor in favor of the next team.
3. A team wins when it scores three points. The contest becomes a regular scrimmage in which the defensive team becomes the offensive team when recovering the ball. When a team scores three points, the other team is rotated off the floor. Rules for One-Goal Basketball (page 462) prevail.
4. The game can be played with four against four.

Basketrama

Playing Area: Area around one basket.
Players: Usually two.
Supplies: A basketball for each player.
Skill: Shooting under pressure.

Two players, each with a basketball, on signal, shoot individually as rapidly as possible, taking any kind of shots they wish until one scores 10 baskets and becomes the winner. Each player must handle his or her own basketball and must not impede or interfere with the other's ball. Naturally, the balls do collide at times, but deliberate interference by knocking the ball out of the way or kicking it means disqualification.

Balls should be marked, so that there is no argument as to ownership. This can be done by using different types of basketballs or by marking with chalk or tape.

Variations
1. The game can be played with more than two players, but this causes confusion and mix-ups of the respective basketballs.
2. Scoring can be done by each player counting out loud each basket he or she makes or by having another student keep score for each contestant.
3. The method of scoring can be varied. A time limit can be set and the player's score is the number of baskets he or she makes during that time. Another method is to time the player to see how many seconds it takes him or her to make 10 baskets.

THE GAME OF BASKETBALL

For elementary school children, the game of basketball is similar to the official game played in the junior and senior high schools, but it has modifications in keeping with the capacities of the children. The following basic rules apply to the game for elementary school children.

Teams

A team is made up of five players, including two guards, one center, and two forwards.

Timing

The game is divided into four quarters; each is 6 minutes in length.

Officials

The game is under the control of a referee and an umpire, both of whom have an equal right to call violations and fouls. They work on opposite sides of the floor and are assisted by a timer and a scorer.

Putting the Ball in Play

Each quarter is started with a jump ball at the center circle. Throughout the game, the jump ball is used when the ball is tied up between two players or when it is uncertain who caused an out-of-bounds ball to go out.

After each successful basket or free throw, the ball is put in play at the end of the court under the basket by the team against whom the score was made.

Violations

The penalty for a violation is the award of the ball to the opponents at a near out-of-bounds point. The following are violations.

1. Traveling—taking more than one step with the ball without passing, dribbling, or shooting. Sometimes called walking or steps.
2. Stepping out-of-bounds or causing the ball to go out-of-bounds.
3. Taking more than 10 seconds to cross the center line from the back to the front court. Once in the forward court, the ball may not be returned to the back court by the team in control.
4. Double dribble—a second series of dribbling without another player handling the ball; palming (not clearly batting) the ball; or dribbling the ball with both hands at once.
5. Stepping on or over a restraining line during a jump ball or free throw.
6. Kicking the ball intentionally.
7. Remaining more than 3 seconds in the area under the offensive basket, bounded by the two sides of the free-throw lane, the free-throw line, and the end of the court.

Personal Fouls

Personal fouls are holding, pushing, hacking (striking), tripping, charging, blocking, and unnecessary roughness.

When a foul is called, the person who was fouled receives one free throw. If he or she was fouled in the act of shooting (basket missed), he or she receives two shots. If the basket was made, the score counts and one free throw is awarded.

Technical Fouls

Technical fouls include failure of substitutes to report to the proper officials, delay of game, and unsportsmanlike conduct.

Disqualification

A player who has five personal fouls called against him or her is out of the game and must go to the sidelines. Disqualification can result from extreme unsportsmanlike conduct or a vicious personal foul.

Scoring

A basket from the field scores two points and a free throw one point. The team that is ahead at the end of the game is declared the winner. If the score is tied, an overtime period of 2 minutes is played. If the score is still tied after this period, the next team to score (one or two points) is declared the winner.

Substitutes

Substitutes must report to the official scorer and await a signal from the referee or umpire before entering the game. The scorer will sound the signal at a time when the ball is not in play, so the official on the floor can signal for the player to enter the game.

Offensive Time Limit

Consideration can be given to establishing a time limit (30 seconds) during which the offensive team must score or give up the ball.

BASKETBALL SKILL TESTS

The tests in basketball presented cover dribbling, passing, shooting, and making free throws. For each of the first four tests, a stopwatch is needed.

Straight Dribble

A marker is placed 15 yards down the floor from the starting point. The dribbler must dribble around the marker and back to the starting position, where he or she finishes by crossing the starting line. The marker must remain standing or disqualification results. Allow two or three trials and take the best time.

Figure-Eight Dribble

Four obstacles (Indian clubs, bases, or cones) are placed 5 feet apart in a straight line beginning 5 feet from the starting line. The player must dribble in and out of the markers in the path of a figure eight, finishing at the point where he or she started. Allow two or three trials and take the best time.

Wall Ball Test

A player stands 5 feet from a smooth wall. He or she is given 30 seconds to make as many catches as he or she can from throws or passes against the wall. Generally, the two-hand or chest pass is used. Balls must be caught on the fly to count. Another student should do the counting. Allow only one trial. Use a board or mat to provide a definite restraining line.

Baskets for 30 Seconds

A player stands near the basket in any position he or she wishes. On signal, he or she shoots and continues shooting for a period of 30 seconds. His or her score is the number of baskets he or she made during the time period. Another student should do the counting. Allow only one trial.

Free Throws

Score is kept of the number of free throws made out of 10 attempts. Give three or four warm-up trials before the player announces he or she is ready. Score should be kept by another student with pencil and paper; an X is marked for a made try and an O for a miss.

Twenty-seven

Football-Type Activities

Football is truly the great American game. With television exposure to professional football keyed by the game of the week and culminating in the Super Bowl, public interest in this game has grown considerably. The names of professional football players have become household words.

The shape of the football makes throwing and catching more difficult than with a round ball. Specialized skill development is needed, which means the teacher must spend sufficient time with football skills if the children are to enjoy the instruction and participation.

Touch and Flag Football are modifications of the game of American football. A ball carrier is considered down in Touch Football when he or she is touched with one hand. Some rules call for a two-handed touch, while others require a player to wear one or two flags that the opponents must seize in order to down the ball carrier (hence, the name Flag Football).

Flag Football has advantages over Touch Football in that the ball carrier is not stopped by a touch but must lose a flag. This means there can be more twisting and dodging, making the game

Suggested Football Program

GRADE	FOURTH	FIFTH	SIXTH
Skills	Passing Centering Catching	Stance Pass receiving Punting	Blocking Carrying the ball Running and dodging Ball exchange Lateral passing
Knowledges			Football rules Plays and formations
Activities	Five Passes Football End Ball	Kick Over Fourth Down	Football Boxball Flag Football Pass Ball
Tests	Passing for distance Centering	Kicking for distance Passing for distance	Passing for accuracy Passing for distance

more interesting and challenging. In addition, there is little argument over whether or not the ball carrier was downed.

EMPHASIS IN EACH GRADE LEVEL

Fourth Grade

Passing, centering, and catching should comprise the fourth-grade program. Most of the time should be spent on skills. The two lead-up games of Five Passes and Football End Ball make use of the skills listed.

Fifth Grade

The fifth grade should review the skills learned on the fourth-grade level. The emphasis then shifts to passing skills, with moving receivers in football drills. Punting and kicking games are introduced.

Sixth Grade

More specialized skills like blocking, carrying the ball, ball exchanges, and football agility skills feature the lead-up work for the game of Flag Football.

FOOTBALL SKILLS

Passing

Skillful forward passing is needed in Flag Football and the lead-up games; passing is a potent weapon. The ball should be gripped lightly behind

Good Position for Passing

the middle with the fingers on the lace. The thumb and fingers should be relaxed.

When throwing, the off foot should be placed so that it points in the direction of the pass, with the body turned sideward. The ball is raised with two hands up and over the shoulders. The ball is delivered directly forward with an overhand movement of the arm, with the index finger pointing toward the line of flight. A left-hander is used in the illustration.

Holding the Ball—Ready to Pass

Passing

Lateral Passing

Lateral passing is pitching the ball under-handed to a teammate. The ball must be tossed sideward or backward. The ball should be tossed with an easy motion, and no attempt should be made to make it spiral like a forward pass.

Ready for a Direct Catch

Ready for a Lateral Pass

Catching

The receiver should keep his or her eyes on the ball and catch it in his or her hands with a slight giving movement. As soon as the ball is caught, it should be tucked in to carrying position. The little fingers should be together for most catches.

Carrying the Ball

The ball should be carried with the arm on the outside and the end of the ball into the notch formed by the elbow and arm. The fingers add support for the carry.

Centering

The player takes a position with his or her feet well spread and toes pointed straight ahead. His or her knees are bent, and he or she should be close enough to the ball to reach it with a slight stretch. The right hand takes about the same grip as would be used for passing. The other hand is on the side near the back and merely acts as a guide. Center passing for the T-formation is with one hand, however. The other arm rests on the inside of the thigh.

Catching on the Move

Protecting the Ball during Carrying

Centering (note hand and finger positions)

Stance

The three-point stance is the one most generally used in Flag Football. Feet are about shoulder width apart, toes pointing straight ahead, with the toe of one foot even with the heel of the other. The hand on the side of the foot that is back is used for support; the knuckles rest on the ground. The player should look straight ahead and always take the same stance irrespective of the direction he or she is to move.

Offensive Three-Point Stance

Some players prefer the parallel stance, wherein the feet, instead of being in the heel-and-toe position, are lined up even. In this case, either hand can be placed down for support. Some defensive players like to use a four-point stance, as shown. Both hands are in contact with the ground.

Defensive Four-Point Stance

Blocking

In blocking in Flag Football, the blocker must stay on his or her feet. The block should be more of an obstruction than a takeout. He or she should set with his or her shoulder against the opponent's shoulder or upper body. Making contact from any direction from the rear not only is a foul but can cause injury. Elbows are out and hands are held near the chest.

Blocking Position

Ball Exchanges

Children love to work plays where the ball is exchanged from one player to another (a reverse). The object is to start the play in one direction and then give the ball to another player heading in the opposite direction. The ball can be handed backward or forward. The player with the ball always makes the exchange with the inside hand, the one near the receiving player. The ball is held with both hands until the receiver is about 6 feet away. The ball then is shifted to the hand on that side, with the elbow bent partially away from the body. The receiver comes toward the exchange player with his or her near arm with bent elbow carried in front of his or her chest, with the palm down. The other arm has the palm up and is carried about waist high. As the ball is given (not tossed) to the receiver, the receiver clamps down on the ball to secure it. Then, as quickly as he or she can, he or she changes it to normal carrying position.

A fake reverse, sometimes called a bootleg, is made when the ball carrier pretends to make the exchange but keeps the ball. He or she can hide the ball momentarily behind the leg.

Punting

Punting should be practiced first with a soccer ball or a rubber playground ball of that size. The kicker should stand with the kicking foot slightly forward. The fingers should be extended in the

Bootleg or Fake Reverse

Punting

direction of the center. The eyes should be on the ball from the time it is centered until it is kicked. The kicker should actually see his or her foot kick the ball. After the ball is received, the kicker should take a short step with his or her kicking foot. A second step is taken with the other foot. The kicking leg is swung forward, and, at the impact, the knee is straightened to provide maximum force. The toes are pointed, and the long axis of the ball makes contact high and on the outside of the instep. The leg should follow through well after the kick.

INSTRUCTIONAL PROCEDURES

To ensure a high-level educational experience for boys and girls in football-type activities, the following procedures are suggested.

1. All of the children should have a chance to practice all the skills, and a system of rotation should be set up to ensure this.
2. Drills and play should not be dominated by one or two individuals. Rotation of players to different positions should make sure such domination does not occur.
3. Drills should be carried out with attention to proper form, and they should approximate game conditions. When going out for passes is being practiced, proper stance should be employed.
4. Junior-size footballs should be used.
5. Roughness and unfair play must be controlled by strict enforcement of the rules and through good supervision.

ORGANIZING FOR INSTRUCTION

The differences between the sexes in athletic contests should be allowed for in football activities. The instruction may follow one of several patterns.

1. The instruction for boys and girls may be entirely separate.
2. Skills may be taught together, but sexes are separated for other phases.
3. Skills and selected simple lead-up games may have coeducational participation.

Any type of blocking and rough, forceful scrimmage-type play may not be suitable for mixed participation. When boys are participating in Flag Football, Fourth Down, or Pass Ball, girls might do likewise in another area. Noncontact games like Football Endball, Five Passes, or Football Box Ball may have mixed participation. Speedball (page 498) is an excellent alternate activity for girls, if the game of Flag Football seems unsuitable for them.

There should be at least six to eight footballs for football drills. The ideal is one football per two children, but this is seldom attained.

Passing and catching skills can be practiced informally. More room is needed for kicking skills. Ball exchange drills work well with three or four children. Informal work gives children a chance to experiment and explore without the pressure of performing at a designated level.

For more effective instruction, groups can be organized by skill ability.

Combining two or more skills into a drill means the practice will be a little more structured. Numbers still should be kept small.

FOOTBALL DRILLS

These structured drills supplement the suggested organizational patterns discussed in the preceding section.

Ball Carrying

Formation: Regular zone flag football field with 20-yard interval lines.
Players: Four to six.
Supplies: Football, flags for each player. Cones to mark zones.

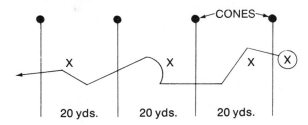

The ball carrier stands on the goal line ready to run. Three defensive players await him or her at 20-yard intervals, each one stationed on a zone line, facing the ball carrier.

Each defender is assigned to the zone he or she faces and must down the ball carrier by pulling a flag while the carrier is still in the zone. The ball carrier runs and dodges, trying to get by each defender in turn without having any of the flags pulled. If one flag is pulled, the runner continues. If both flags are pulled, the last defender uses a two-hand touch to down the ball carrier. After the runner has completed his or her run, he or she goes to the end of the defender's line and rotates to the defending position.

Ball Exchange

Formation: Shuttle, with the halves about 15 yards apart.
Players: 4 to 10.
Supplies: Football.

The two halves of the shuttle face each other across the 15-yard distance. A player at the head of one of the files has a ball and carries it over to the other file, where he or she makes an exchange with the front player of that file. The ball is carried back and forth between the shuttle files. The receiving player should not start until the ball carrier is almost up to him or her. A player, after handing the ball to the front player of the other file, continues around and joins that file.

Combination

Formation: Regular offensive formation with passer, center, end, and ball chaser.
Players: Four to eight.
Supplies: Football.

Passing, centering, and receiving skills are combined into one drill. Each player, as soon as he or she has taken his or her turn, rotates to the next spot. A minimum of four players is needed. The four positions are:

Center—centers the ball to the passer.

Passer—passes the ball to the end.

End—receives the pass.

Ball chaser—retrieves the ball if missed by the receiver (end) or takes a pass from the end (if he or she caught the ball) and carries the ball to the center spot, which is his or her next assignment.

The rotation follows the path of the ball. This means that the rotation system moves from center to passer to end to ball chaser to center. Extra players should be stationed behind the passer for turns.

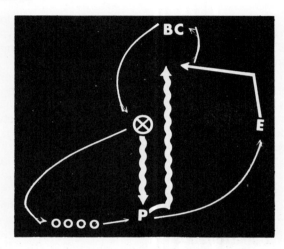

One-on-One Defensive Drill

Formation: Center, passer, end, defender.
Players: 8 to 10.
Supplies: Football.

The drill is as old as football itself. A defensive player stands about 8 yards back, waiting for an approaching end. The passer tries to complete the pass to the end while the defender tries to stop or intercept the ball. Have one defender practice against all the players and then change defenders.

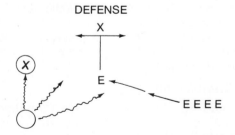

It is important for the passer to be able to pass well, or the drill has little value.
Variation: Have two ends and two defenders. Passer throws to the end that appears to be the most unguarded.

Punt Return

Formation: A center, a kicker, two lines of ends, and receivers.
Players: 10 to 20.
Supplies: Football, flags for each player.

The object of the drill is for the receiver to catch a punted ball and return it to the line of scrimmage while two ends attempt to pull a flag or make a tag.

Two ends are ready to run downfield. The center centers the ball to the kicker, who punts the ball downfield to the punt receiver. The ends cannot cross the line of scrimmage until the ball has been kicked. Each end makes two trips downfield as a "tackler" before rotating to the punt receiver position.

A good punter is necessary for this drill. Only selected children with the degree of skill to punt the ball far enough downfield should be permitted to kick. It is also important that the ends wait until the ball is kicked, or they will be downfield too soon to give the receiver a fair chance to make a return run.

Stance

Formation: Squads in extended file formation.
Players: Six to eight in each file.
Supplies: None.

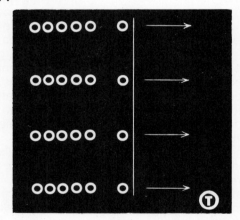

The first person in each file performs and, when finished with his or her chores, goes to the end of his or her file. On the command "ready," the first person in each file assumes a football stance. The teacher can correct and make observations. On the command "hip," the players charge forward for about 5 yards. The new players at the head of the line get ready.

FOOTBALL ACTIVITIES

Fourth Grade

Football End Ball

The only difference between this game and Basketball End Ball is that a football is used. Distances children are to throw from the forwards to the end players should be governed by the children's capacity. See page 457 for a description of End Ball.

Five Passes (Football)

Playing Area: Football field or other defined area.
Players: 6 to 10 on each team.
Supplies: Football, pinnies or other identification.
Skills: Passing and catching.

Players scatter on the field. The object of the game is for one team to make five consecutive passes to five different players without losing control of the ball. This scores one point.

Defense may play the ball only and not make personal contact. No player may take more than three steps when in possession of the ball. More than three steps is called traveling, and the ball is awarded to the other team.

The ball is given the opponents at the nearest out-of-bounds for traveling, minor contact fouls, after a point has been scored, and for causing the ball to go out-of-bounds.

There is no penalty when the ball hits the ground. It remains in play, but this interrupts the five-pass sequence, which must begin anew. Jump balls are called when the ball is tied up or there is a pileup. The official should call out the pass sequence.

Fifth Grade

Kick Over

Playing Area: Football field with a 10-yard end zone.
Players: 6 to 10 on each team.
Supplies: Football.
Skills: Kicking, catching.

Teams are scattered on opposite ends of the field. The object is to punt the ball over the other team's goal line. If the ball is caught in the end zone, no score results. If the ball is kicked beyond the end zone on the fly, a score is made regardless of whether or not the ball was caught. A ball kicked *into* the end zone on the fly and not caught also scores a goal.

Play is started by one team with a punt from a point 20 to 30 feet in front of the goal line it is defending. On a punt, if the ball is not caught, the team must kick from the spot of recovery. If the ball is caught, three long strides are allowed to advance the ball for a kick. Players should be numbered and kick in rotation. If the players do not kick in rotation, one or two aggressive players will dominate the game.
Variation: Scoring can be made only by a drop-kick across the goal line.
Teaching Suggestion: The player whose turn it is to kick should move fast to the area from which the ball is to be kicked.

Fourth Down

Playing Area: Football field (use only one-half) or equivalent space.
Players: Two teams, six to eight on each team.
Supplies: Football.
Skills: Most football skills, except kicking and blocking.

Every play is a fourth down, which means the play must score or the team loses the ball. No kicking is permitted, and players may pass any time from any spot in any direction. There can be a series of passes on any play either from behind or beyond the line of scrimmage.

The teams line up in an offensive football formation. The ball is put in play by centering. The back receiving the ball runs or passes to any of his or her teammates. The one receiving the ball has the same privilege. No blocking is permitted.

To start the game, the ball is placed in the center of the field and the team that wins the toss has the chance to put the ball into play. After each touchdown, the ball is brought to the center of the field and the team against which the score was made puts the ball into play.

To down a runner or pass receiver, a two-handed touch above the waist is made. The back first receiving the ball from the center has immunity against tagging, provided he or she does not try to run. All defensive players must stay 10 feet away from him or her unless he or she runs. The referee should wait a reasonable length of time for the back to pass or run, and, if he or she holds the ball beyond that, the referee should call out "10 seconds." The back then must throw or run within 10 seconds, or the defensive players can tag him or her.

The defensive players scatter to cover the receivers. They can use a one-on-one defense, with each player covering an offensive player, or employ a zone defense.

Since the team with the ball loses possession after each play, rules for determining where the ball is to be placed when the other team takes possession are needed.

If a player is tagged with two hands above the waist, the ball goes to the other team at this spot.

If an incomplete pass is made from *behind* the line of scrimmage, the ball is given to the other team at the spot where the ball was put into play.

Should an incomplete pass be made by a player while *beyond* the line of scrimmage, the ball is brought to the spot from which it was thrown.
Variation: The game could be called Third Down, and two downs would be allowed to score.
Teaching Suggestions
1. The team in possession should be encouraged to pass as soon as practical, since children become tired from running around to become free for a pass.

2. The defensive team can score by intercepting a pass. Since passes can be made at any time, upon interception the player should look down the field for a pass to one of his or her teammates.

Sixth Grade

Football Box Ball

Playing Area: Football field 50 yards long. Five yards beyond each goal is a 6-by-6-foot square, which is the box.
Players: Two teams, 8 to 16 on each.
Supplies: Football, team colors.
Skills: Passing, catching.

The teams should be marked, so they can be distinguished. The object of the game is similar to End Ball in that the team tries to make a successful pass to the captain in the box.

To begin the play, players are onside, which means they are on opposite ends of the field. One team, losing the toss, kicks off from their own 10-yard line to the other team. The game then becomes a kind of a keep away, with either team trying to secure and retain possession of the ball until a successful pass can be made to the captain in the box. The captain must catch the ball on the fly and still stay with both feet in the box. This scores a touchdown.

Rules: A player may run sideward or backward when in possession of the ball. He or she may not run forward but is allowed momentum (two steps) if receiving or intercepting a ball. Penalty for illegal forward movement while in possession of the ball—loss of ball to opponents, who take the ball out-of-bounds.

The captain is allowed only three attempts or one goal. If either occurs, another player is rotated to the box.

On any pass or attempt to get the ball to the captain, the team loses the ball. If a touchdown (successful pass) is made, the team brings the ball back to its 10-yard line and kicks off to the other team. If the attempt is not successful, the ball is given out-of-bounds on the end line to the other team.

Any out-of-bounds ball is put in play by the team that did not cause the ball to go out-of-bounds. No team can score from a throw-in from out-of-bounds.

In case of a tie ball, a jump ball is called at the spot. The players face off in a jump ball as in basketball.

Players must play the ball and not the individual. For unnecessary roughness, the player is sidelined until a pass is thrown to the other team's captain. The ball is awarded to the offended team out-of-bounds.

On the kickoff, all players must be onside, that is, behind the ball when it is kicked. Penalty is loss of ball to the other team out-of-bounds at the center line. After the kickoff, players may move to any part of the field.

On the kickoff, the ball must travel 10 yards before it can be recovered by either team. A kickoff outside or over the end line is treated as any other out-of-bounds ball.

A ball hitting the ground remains in play as long as it is inbounds. Players may not bat or kick a free ball. Penalty is loss of ball to the other team out-of-bounds.

Falling on the ball means loss of ball to the other team.

Teaching Suggestion: A 4-by-7-foot or a 4-by-8-foot folding tumbling mat can be used to define the box where the captain must stand to catch the ball for a score.

Flag Football

Flag Football should be played with two flags on each player. The flag is a length of cloth that is hung from the side at the waist of each player. To down (stop) a player with the ball, one of the flags must be pulled.

Flag Football should rarely, if ever, be played with 11 players on a side. This results in a crowded field and leaves little room to maneuver.

Specifying 25 plays per half eliminates the need for timing and lessens arguments about a team taking too much time in a huddle.

Using the zone system makes the first down yardage point definite and eliminates the need for a 10-yard down chain.

Playing Area: A field 30 by 60 yards, marked off in 20-yard intervals with lines parallel to the goal line. This divides the field into three zones. There also should be two defined end zones, from 5 to 10 yards in width, defining the area behind the goal in which passes may be caught.

Numbers: Six to nine on a team. If six or seven are on a team, four players are required to be on the line of scrimmage. For eight or nine players, five offensive players must be on the line.

Supplies: Football, two flags for each player (flags should be about 3 inches wide and 24 inches long).

Timing: The game shall consist of two halves. A total of 25 plays shall make up each half. All plays count in the 25, except the try for one point after a touchdown and a kickoff out-of-bounds.

Scoring: Touchdown—six points. Point after touchdown—one point. Safety—two points. A point after touchdown is made from a distance of 3 feet from the goal line. One play (pass or run) is allowed for the extra point.

Kickoff: The game is started with a kickoff. The

team winning the toss has the option of selecting the goal it wishes to defend or choosing to kick or receive. The loser of the toss takes the option not exercised by the first team.

The kickoff is from the goal line, and all players on the kicking team must be onside. The kick must cross the first zone line or it does not count as a play. A kick that is kicked out-of-bounds (not touched by the receiving team) must be kicked over. A second consecutive kick out-of-bounds gives the ball to the receiving team in the center of the field. The kickoff may not be recovered by the kicking team unless caught and fumbled by the receivers.

Downs and Yardage: The field is divided into three 20-yard zones. A team has four downs to move the ball into the next zone or lose the ball. For example, a team that secures the ball in the center has four downs to move the ball into the next zone or score. If the ball is legally advanced into the last zone, then the team has four downs to score. A ball on the line between zones is considered in the more forward zone.

Time-outs: Time-outs are permitted only for injuries or when called by the officials.

Substitutions: Unlimited substitutions are permitted. Each must report to the official.

Forward Pass: All forward passes must be thrown from behind the line of scrimmage. All players on the field are eligible to receive and intercept passes.

Huddle: The team in possession of the ball usually huddles to make up the play. After any play, the team has 30 seconds to put the ball into play after the referee gives the "in play" signal.

Blocking: Blocking is done with the arms close to the body. Blocking must be done from the front or side, and blockers must stay on their feet.

Tackling: A player is down if one of his or her flags has been pulled. The ball carrier must make an attempt to avoid the defensive player and is not permitted to run over or through the defensive player. The tackler must play the flags and not the ball carrier. Good officiating is needed, since defensive players may attempt to hold or grasp the ball carrier until they are able to remove one of the flags.

Punting: All punts must be announced. Neither team can cross the line of scrimmage until the ball is kicked. Kick receivers may run or use a lateral pass. They cannot make a forward pass after receiving a kick.

Fumbles: All fumbles are dead at the spot of the fumble. The first player who touches the ball on the ground is deemed to have recovered the fumble. When the ball is centered to a back, he or she must gain definite possession of the ball before a fumble can be called. He or she is allowed to pick up a bad

pass from the center or a ball of which he or she did not have possession.

End Zone: A pass caught in an end zone scores a touchdown. The player must have control of the ball in the end zone. A ball caught beyond the end zone is out-of-bounds and is considered an incomplete pass.

Touchback: Any ball kicked over the goal line is ruled a touchback and is brought out to the 20-yard line to be put in play by the receiving team. A pass intercepted behind the goal line can be a touchback if the player does not run it out. It is a touchback even if he or she is tagged behind his or her own goal line.

Safety: A safety occurs when the team *defending* a goal line causes the ball to go back over the goal line by fumbling, running, or being caught during a scrimmage play behind its own goal line.

Penalties: Loss of 5 yards for:
1. Offside.
2. Delay of game (too long in huddle).
3. Failure of substitute to report.
4. Passing from spot not behind line of scrimmage (also loss of down).
5. Stiff arming by ball carrier, or not avoiding a defensive player.
6. Failure to announce intention to punt.
7. Shortening the flag in the belt, playing without flags in proper position.
8. Faking the ball by the center (he or she must center the pass on the first motion).

Loss of 15 yards for:
1. Holding, illegal tackling.
2. Illegal blocking.
3. Unsportsmanlike conduct (can result in a disqualification).

Pass Ball

Pass Ball is a more open game than Flag Football. The game is similar to Flag Football with these differences.
1. The ball may be passed at any time. This means it can be thrown at any time beyond the line of scrimmage, during an interception, during a kickoff, or during a received kick.
2. Four downs are given to score a touchdown.
3. A two-handed touch on the back is used instead of pulling a flag. However, flags can be used.
4. If the ball is thrown from behind the line of scrimmage and results in an incomplete pass, the ball is down at the previous spot on the line of scrimmage. If the pass originates otherwise and is incomplete, the ball is placed at the spot from where this pass was thrown.
5. Since the ball can be passed at any time, no downfield blocking is permitted. A player may screen the ball carrier but cannot make a

block. Screening is defined as running between the ball carrier and the defense.

FOOTBALL SKILL TESTS

Tests for football skills include the skills of centering, passing, and kicking (punting).

Centering

Each player is given five trials centering at a target. The target should be stationed 6 yards behind the center. Targets that can be used include these.

1. An old tire suspended from the ground so the bottom of the tire is about 2 feet from the ground. Scoring: for centering the ball through the tire—2 points; for hitting the tire but not going through it—1 point. Possible total—10 points.
2. A baseball pitching target used in the softball program is quite suitable for a centering target. Scoring is the same as with the tire target.
3. A 2-by-3-foot piece of plywood is needed. This is held by a player at the target line in front of his or her body, with the upper edge even with the shoulders. The target is held stationary and is not to be moved during the centering. Scoring: For hitting the target—1 point. Possible total—5 points. Other targets can be devised.

Passing for Accuracy

Suspend a tire about shoulder height, so it is fairly stable. The tire can be suspended from goal posts or by the use of volleyball standards. Each player is given five throws from a minimum distance of 15 yards. As skill increases, increase the distance.

Scoring: for throwing through the tire—2 points; for hitting the tire but not passing through—1 point. Possible total—10 points.

Passing for Distance

Each player is allotted three passes to determine how far he or she can throw a football. The longest throw is measured to the nearest foot. It is important to reserve the test for a relatively calm day, since the wind can be quite a factor (for or against the player) in the test.

The passes should be made on a field marked off in 5-yard intervals. Markers made from tongue depressors mark the first pass distance. If a later throw is longer, the marker should be moved to that point. When markers are used, the members of a squad can complete the passing turns before measuring, which can then be done at one time for all members of a squad.

Kicking for Distance

Punting, place-kicking, and drop-kicking can be measured for distance with techniques similar to those described for passing for distance.

FLAG FOOTBALL FORMATIONS

A variety of offensive formations are shown, including the T-formation. The T-formation has limited strategical use in Flag Football, since the passer (the quarterback) is handicapped by being up close to the center. Emphasis should be on variety and spread formations, with flankers and ends positioned out beyond normal placement.

The following formations are based upon a nine-player team, with four backs and five linemen. The formations would vary if the number on each team were decreased. A variety of formations can be presented to the children, making a varied and more interesting game. Backfield formations can be right or left. Only the formation to the right is presented.

Key: Center X   Back   B
      End   E   Lineman O

Offensive Line Formations
Balanced (tight ends):
    E O X O E
Unbalanced Right (tight ends):
    E X O O E
Line over Right (tight end):
    X E O O E
Right End Out (can be one or both):
    E O X O (5 yds) E
Right End Wide (can be one or both):
    E O X O (15 yds) E
Right End Wide, Left End Out (can be reversed):
    E (5 yds) O X O (15 yds) E
Spread (3 to 5 yards between each lineman):
    E O X O E

Offensive Formations

The formations diagrammed can be combined with any of the offensive line formations. For purposes of clarity, a balanced line with tight ends is used for all formations. However, a variety of line formations can be used with each of the backfield formations.

Single Wing:

    E O X O E
                  B
              B
           B
        B

Double Wing:

```
      E  O  X  O  E
  B           B        B
              B
```

Punt:

```
      E  O  X  O  E
      B  B
              B
              B
```

Flanker Right:

```
      E  O  X  O  E
                 B
              B        B
           B
```

Wing Right, Flanker Left:

```
      E  O  X  O  E
                    B
     B           B
              B
```

Wing Right, Flanker Right:

```
      E  O  X  O  E
                 B     B
              B
           B
```

T-Formation (regular):

```
      E  O  X  O  E
              B
           B  B  B
```

Wing T:

```
      E  O  X  O  E
              B           B
           B  B
```

Spread:

```
      E  O  X  O  E
    B           B           B
              B
```

Pass Patterns

The following pass patterns may be run by the individual pass catcher, whether he or she is a lineman or a back. They are particularly valuable to use in practice, when the pass receiver informs the passer of his or her pattern.

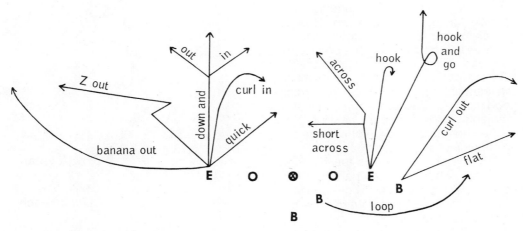

Twenty-eight

Hockey

Hockey is a fast-moving game that can be adapted for use in the elementary school. When played with a plastic puck, it can be played indoors. Outdoors, a plastic fun ball can be used. Hockey played in the elementary school is a lead-up to ice hockey as well as field hockey, which is popular for girls and women.

Hockey is a valuable sport that demands much running and team play for success. While learning to play good hockey, children should develop good fundamental skills and learn position play rather than the unorganized "everyone chase the puck" style often played in schools.

Another advantage of hockey is the fact that children of all sizes and ability can participate on even terms. Play can be mixed, with boys and girls playing on an equal basis. Shin guards are not needed in elementary school hockey.

The object of the game is to advance the puck by using a hockey stick into the opponent's goal.

EMPHASIS IN EACH GRADE LEVEL

Fourth Grade

Emphasis is on the fundamental skills needed to play the game of hockey. Little strategy is introduced, and drills are used to develop the fundamental skills. Learning to dribble loosely, fielding the ball, and making short passes should receive most of the attention.

Fifth Grade

Emphasis continues on skill development, with more emphasis on puck control and passing accuracy. Lead-up games that use skills utilized in

Hockey Equipment

regulation hockey are played. Team play is advocated, and drills to develop this phase of the game are practiced.

Sixth Grade

At this level, strategy for successful play is emphasized. Rules of regulation hockey are intro-

478

Suggested Hockey Program

GRADE	FOURTH	FIFTH	SIXTH
Skills	Grip and carry of the stick Loose dribble Front field Quick hit Goalkeeping	Controlled dribble Side field Tackle Dodging Face-off	Driving Jab shot
Knowledges	Simple rules	Puck handling and passing strategy	The game of hockey Team play and strategy
Activities	Circle Keep Away Hockey Race Away Mickey Mouse Hockey Modified Hockey	Goalkeeper Hockey Sideline Hockey	Regulation Elementary Hockey
Tests		Pass for accuracy Dribble for speed	Fielding Driving for distance

duced, and the actual game is played. Skills should be reviewed and practiced through the use of selected drills and lead-up games.

HOCKEY SKILLS

Grip and Carry of Stick

The hockey stick should be held with both hands and carried as low as possible to the ground. The basic grip puts the left hand at the top of the stick and the right hand 8 to 12 inches below the left hand. The player should learn to carry the stick to the right of the body, with the blade close to the ground while running. To assure accuracy as well as safety, the stick must not be swung above waist height.

Loose Dribble

The loose dribble is an elementary form of moving the puck under control by an individual player. It demands less skill in stick handling than controlled dribbling. In loose dribbling, the ball or puck is pushed 10 to 15 feet in front of the player. The player then runs to the ball and gives it another push, repeating the sequence. This type of dribble is used in open field play when there is little fear of an opponent's intercepting the ball. It also is used to allow skilled players to run at maximum speed. The ball must be pushed with the flat side of the blade and kept in front of the body.

Front Field

Fielding refers to stopping the ball and controlling it. Fielding the ball or puck in hockey is as important as catching the ball is in basketball and

as a skill demands much practice in order that the player can field the ball and move it smoothly in the desired direction. The student must keep his or her eye on the ball, move to a point in line with the path of the ball, and extend the flat side of the blade forward to meet it. The faster the ball approaches, the more the student must learn to give with the

Grip and Carry

Front Field Position

Starting the Dribble

stick to absorb the ball's momentum. The player should field the ball in front of his or her body and not permit it to get too close to his or her feet.

Quick Hit

The quick hit is a short pass that usually occurs from the dribble. The quick hit should be taught before driving, since it emphasizes accuracy but not distance. The player has his or her feet spread with the toes pointed slightly forward when striking. He or she approaches the puck with the stick held low and brings the stick straight back in line with the intended direction of the hit. The hands should be the same distance apart as in the carry position, and the stick should not be lifted higher than waist level. The player's right hand guides the stick down and through the ball. The head should be kept down to maintain eye contact with the ball. A short follow-through in a forward motion occurs after contact with the ball.

Controlled Dribble

The controlled dribble consists of a series of short taps in the direction the player desires to move. The hands should be spread 10 to 14 inches apart, so more control of the stick can be gained. As the player becomes more skilled, the hands can be moved closer together. The stick is turned so the blade faces the ball. The grip should not be changed but rather the hands rotated until

the back of the left hand and the palm of the right hand face the ball. The ball then can be tapped in front of the player just far enough to keep it away from the feet but not more than one full stride away from the stick. Emphasis is on controlling the ball during heavy traffic so that opposing players cannot easily intercept the ball.

Side Field

A ball approaching from the left or right side is more difficult to field than one approaching from the front. When the ball is approaching from the player's left, he or she must allow the ball to travel in front of the body before fielding it. If the ball is approaching from the right, it must be intercepted before it crosses in front of the body. The player's feet must be pointed in the direction he or she desires to move after controlling the ball. Regardless of the direction of the ball, the side of the blade must always be used to field it.

Tackle

The tackle is a means of taking the ball away from an opponent. The tackler moves toward the opponent with the stick held low. The tackle is timed so that the blade of the stick is placed against the ball when it is off the opponent's stick. The tackler then quickly dribbles or passes the ball in the direction of his or her goal. Throwing the stick or carelessly striking at the ball should be

instant, the ball is pushed to either side of the tackler, depending on the direction the player is planning to dodge. If the ball is pushed to the left, the player should move around the right side of the opponent, and vice versa. Learning to select the proper instant to push the ball ensures the player success at dodging. Dodging should not be attempted if a pass would be more effective.

Side Field

Tackling (opponent tries to intercept the ball from the boy with the white stick)

discouraged. Timing is extremely important for a successful tackle. Players should be reminded that it is impossible to make a successful tackle on every attempt.

Dodging

Dodging is a means of evading a tackler while maintaining control of the ball. The secret is to retain possession of the ball as long as possible while running directly at the opponent. At the last

Driving

Driving is used to hit the ball moderate to long distances and for shots at the goal. It differs from the quick hit in that the hands are brought together more toward the end of the stick. This gives the player longer leverage to apply greater force to the ball and results in long distance and faster hits. The swing and hit are similar to the quick hit. Emphasis on stick control should be made, so wild swinging does not occur.

Driving

Face-off

The face-off is used to start the game, after a goal has been scored, or in situations where the ball is stopped from further play by opposing players. The face-off is taken by two players, each facing a sideline, with right sides facing their respective goal lines. Each player hits the ground on his or her side of the ball and his or her opponent's stick over the ball alternately three times. After the third hit, the ball can be played, and each opponent attempts to control the ball or pass it to a teammate. An alternate means of starting action is to have a referee drop the ball between the opposing players' sticks. The right hand can be moved down the stick to facilitate a quick, powerful movement.

Jab Shot

The jab shot is used only when a tackle is not possible. It is a one-handed poking shot that attempts to knock the ball away from an opponent. It should be used only as a last resort.

Goalkeeping

The goalkeeper may kick the ball, stop it with any part of the body, or allow it to rebound off the body or hand. However, he or she may not hold the ball or throw it toward the other end of the playing area. The goalkeeper is positioned in front of the goal line and moves between the goal posts. When a ball is hit toward the goal, the goalkeeper should attempt to move in front of the ball and keep his or her feet together. This allows him or her to block with his or her body should he or she miss the ball with the stick. After the ball is blocked, it should be passed to a teammate immediately.

An 8-foot folding mat set on end makes a satisfactory goal.

INSTRUCTIONAL PROCEDURES

1. For many children, hockey is a new experience, since few have played the game and many may have never seen a game. It may be helpful to show a film of a game to introduce the unit.
2. Since few children have had the opportunity to develop skills elsewhere, it is necessary to teach the basic skills in a sequential manner and allow ample time in practice sessions for development.
3. Hockey is a rough game when children are not taught the proper methods of stick handling. They need to be reminded often to use caution and good judgment when handling sticks in close quarters.
4. Ample equipment allows for more practice time and skill development per individual. If possible, a stick and a puck for each child are desirable.
5. If hockey is played on a gym floor, a plastic puck should be used. If played on a carpeted area or outdoors, use a Cosom fun ball.
6. Hockey is a team game that is more enjoyable for all the children when the players are taught to pass to open teammates. Excessive control of the puck by an individual should be discouraged.
7. An individual who is restricted to limited activity can be designated as a goalkeeper. This would provide an opportunity for him or her to participate and receive reinforcement from his or her peers. An asthmatic child is an example of the type of child who might serve as a goalkeeper.
8. Excessive fatigue must be considered, since hockey is a running game demanding agility and endurance. Children should be in reasonably good physical condition before participating in this highly active game. Rotation of substitutes into the game and spaced rest periods are other ways to prevent overfatigue.

HOCKEY DRILLS

Dribble Drills

1. Successful hockey play demands good footwork and proper stick handling. All players can spread out on the field, carrying the stick

in proper position in a group mimetic drill. On command by the instructor, players can move forward, backward, and to either side. Concentrate on quick reactions and good footwork.
2. Each player with a ball practices dribbling on his or her own. Dribbling should be practiced first at controlled speeds and then at faster speeds as skill develops.
3. Players can practice in pairs, the partners standing about 20 feet apart. One player dribbles the ball toward his or her partner, goes around the partner, and returns to the starting spot. He or she then passes the ball to the partner, who moves in a similar manner. A shuttle type of formation can be used with three players.

Passing and Fielding Drills

1. In pairs, about 20 feet apart, players pass the ball *quickly* back and forth. Emphasis should be on an immediate pass after the field. Cue words might be "field-pass," "pass-field."
2. One player passes the ball to his or her partner, who fields the ball, dribbles twice, and passes back to the other. Passes should be fielded from various angles and sides of the players.
3. The shuttle turnback formation can be used where two files of four or five players face each other. The first person in the file passes to the first person in the other file, who in turn fields the ball and returns the pass. Each player, when finished fielding and passing, goes to the end of the file.
4. The downfield drill is useful for polishing passing and fielding skills while moving. Three files of players start at one end of the field. One player from each file proceeds downfield, passing to and fielding from the others until the other end of the field is reached. A goal shot can be made at this point. Keep the players close together for short passes until a higher skill level is reached.
5. Driving for distance and accuracy can be practiced with a partner. Partners can begin about 15 yards apart. The first player drives off. If the ball stops in a position that makes it necessary for his or her partner to move three steps or less, the partner is allowed to take four steps backward before returning the drive. If, however, the first player's drive causes the partner to move a distance of more than four steps, the partner must return to his or her starting (original) position. The same conditions apply throughout. This can be turned into a game situation when goals

are placed just behind the players, who attempt to score by making accurate drives.

Dodging and Tackling Drills

1. Players are spread out on the field, each with a ball. On command, they dribble left, right, forward, and backward. On the command "dodge," the players dodge an imaginary tackler. Players should concentrate on ball control and dodging in both directions.
2. Three players form a shuttle-type drill as diagrammed. Player #1 has the puck or ball in front of him or her. He or she approaches a cone (a defensive player), dodges around the cone, and passes to player #2, who repeats the dodging maneuver in the opposite direction. Player #2 passes to #3, and the drill continues in that manner.

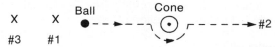

3. Players work in pairs. One partner dribbles toward the other player, who attempts to make a tackle. If the tackle is successful, roles are reversed. This drill should be practiced at moderate speed in the early stages of learning.
4. A three-on-three drill can be used to practice many of the skills presented. Three players are on offense and three on defense. The offense can concentrate on passing, dribbling, and dodging, while the defense concentrates on tackling. A point can be given to the offense when they reach one side of the field. The defensive team becomes the offensive team after a score.

HOCKEY ACTIVITIES

Fourth Grade

Circle Keep Away

Playing Area: 20-to-25-foot circle.
Players: 8 to 10, with one in the center of the circle.
Supplies: One stick per person and a puck or ball.
Skills: Passing, fielding.

Players are evenly spaced around the circle. The object of the game is to keep the player in the center from touching the puck. The puck is passed back and forth, with emphasis on accurate passing and fielding skills. If the player in the center touches the puck, the player who last passed the puck takes the place of the center player. A change of players also can be made on a passing or fielding error.

Hockey Race Away

Playing Area: Two or more 20-to-25-foot circles.
Players: 8 to 10 players spread around in each

circle. It is necessary to have an equal number of players in each circle.
Supplies: One stick per player, and a puck or ball per circle.
Skill: Dribbling.

The object of this activity is to dribble the puck or ball around the circle as quickly as possible. After a player dribbles around the circle, he or she passes to the player on his or her right. This player then dribbles around the circle. The first circle to have all players complete their turns is declared the winner.

Teaching Suggestions

1. Emphasis should be on control of the puck. This is a good opportunity to develop the skill of controlled dribbling.
2. A player who has finished dribbling should sit down. This will indicate that the player has completed his or her turn.

Mickey Mouse Hockey

Playing Area: Playground, gymnasium.
Players: Four teams of equal size, with each team forming one side of a square formation.
Supplies: One stick per player and four pucks or balls.
Skill: Dribbling.

The game is similar to Mickey Mouse (page 405), with the following exceptions.

1. Four pucks are used instead of Indian clubs. When a number is called, each player with the called number goes to his or her puck, dribbles it back out of the square through the spot he or she occupied, around the square counterclockwise, and back through his or her place to his or her original puck spot. Circles 12 inches in diameter are drawn on the floor to provide a definite place to which the puck must be returned.
2. If the game is played outdoors, hoops can be used as spots to which the pucks or balls must be returned. No player is permitted to use anything other than the stick in making the circuit and returning the ball to the inside of the hoop. The penalty for infractions is disqualification of his or her circuit.

Modified Hockey

Playing Area: Gymnasium, hockey field.
Players: 7 to 11 on each team.
Supplies: One stick per person and a puck or a ball.
Skills: Dribbling, passing, dodging, tackling, and face-off.

The teams may take any position on the field as long as they remain inside the boundaries. The object of the game is to hit the ball through the opponent's goal. No goalies are used in this game. At the start of the game and after each score, play is started with a face-off. One point is given for each goal scored.

Teaching Suggestions: The distance between goal lines is flexible but should be on the long side. If making goals is too easy or too difficult, adjustment of the distance between goal lines can be made accordingly.

Fifth Grade

Goalkeeper Hockey

Playing Area: A square about 40 by 40 feet.
Players: Two teams of equal size, each team occupying two sides of the square.
Supplies: One stick per player and one puck or ball.
Skills: Passing, fielding, goalkeeping.

Team members are numbered consecutively from left to right. Two or three numbers are called by the instructor. These players enter the playing area, attempt to capture the puck that is placed in the center of the square, and attempt to pass it through the opposing team. A point is scored when the puck does go through the opponent's side. Sideline players should concentrate on goalkeeping skills. When a score is made, the active players return to their positions, and new players are called.

Teaching Suggestion: Keep track of the numbers that are called, so all players have an equal opportunity to play. Different number combinations can be called.

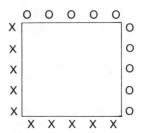

Sideline Hockey

Playing Area: Gymnasium, hockey playing area, 60 by 100 feet.
Players: 6 to 12 players on each team.
Supplies: One hockey stick per player, puck or ball, two 4-by-8-foot folding tumbling mats.
Skills: Most hockey skills, except goaltending.

Each team is divided into two groups. They are positioned as indicated in the diagram, with eight players on each team as an example.

Half of each team is in the court; these are the active players. The others stand on the sidelines. No goalkeeper is used in the game. A face-off at the center starts the game and puts the ball in play after each score. Each team attempts to score a goal, aided by the sideline players. Sideline players help in keeping the ball inbounds and can pass it into the court to the active players. Sideline players must pass only to an active player and not to each other.

Any out-of-bounds plays on the sidelines belong to the team guarding that sideline and are put in play with a pass. An out-of-bounds over the endline that does not score a goal is put in play by the team defending the goal.

The halves of the teams change playing places as soon as a goal is scored or after a specified time limit.
Fouls and Penalties: Illegal touch, sideline violations, and other minor fouls—loss of puck to the opposition. Roughing fouls and illegal sticking—banishment to the sideline for the remainder of the competitive period.
Teaching Suggestions: Some attention must be given to team play and passing rather than just ganging up in the play. Teams should use the sideline players by passing to them and receiving the pass in return. Rotation of teams can be made, so the same two teams do not face each other continually.

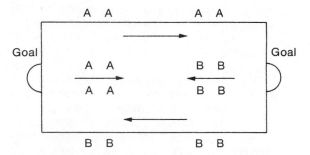

Sixth Grade

Regulation Elementary Hockey

Playing Area: A basic playing area of approximately 40 to 50 feet by 75 to 90 feet can be used. Small gymnasiums can be used, with the walls serving as the boundaries. If a large gymnasium or an outdoor field is used, the playing area should be delineated with traffic cones. The playing area can be divided in half, with a 12-foot restraining circle centered on the midline. This is where play begins at the start of periods, after goals, or after foul shots. The official goal is 2 feet high by 6 feet wide, with a restraining area 4 feet by 8 feet around the goal for protecting the goalie.

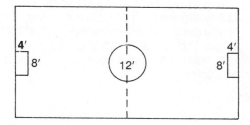

Players: Each team consists of six players: one goalkeeper, who stops shots with hands, feet, or stick; one center, who is the only player allowed to move full court and who leads offensive play (the center has his or her stick striped with black tape); two guards, who cannot go past the center line into the offensive area and whose responsibility it is to keep the puck out of their defensive half of the field; and two forwards, who work with the center on offensive play and cannot go past the center line into their defensive area.

Playing Time: A game consists of three periods of 8 minutes each, with a 3-minute rest between periods. Play is started with a face-off by the centers at mid-court. Other players cannot enter the restraining circle until the puck or ball has been hit by the centers. The clock starts when the puck is put into play and runs continuously until a goal is scored or a foul is called. Substitutions can only be made when the clock is stopped. If the puck goes out-of-bounds, it is put back into play by the team that did not hit it last.

Scoring: Whenever the puck passes through the goal, on the ground, one point is scored. But, if the puck crosses the goal line while in the air, it must strike against the mat or back wall to count for a score. Under no circumstances can a goal be scored on a foul. The puck can deflect off a player or equipment to score, but it cannot be kicked into the goal.

Goalkeeping: The goalkeeper may use his or her hands to clear the puck away from the goal, but he or she may not hold or throw the puck toward the other end of the playing area. (He or she would be charged with a foul for holding the puck.) The goalkeeper may be pulled from the goal area but is restricted up to the center line. No other player may enter the restraining area without being charged with a foul.

Fouls, Playing: The following are fouls and are penalized by loss of the puck or ball at the spot of the foul:

1. Illegally touching the puck with the hands.
2. Swinging the stick above waist height (called sticking).
3. Guards or forwards moving across the center line.
4. Player other than the goalie entering the restraining area.
5. Goalie throwing the puck.
6. Play stopped by a player holding, stepping on, or lying on the puck.

Defenders must be 5 yards back when the puck is put into play. If the spot where the foul occurred is closer than 5 yards to the goal, only the goalkeeper may defend. This shot is put in play 5 yards out directly in front of the goal.

Fouls, Personal: This includes any action or rough play considered dangerous to other players. A player is banished from the game and must retire to the sidelines for 2 minutes.

1. Hacking or striking with a stick.
2. Tripping either with the foot or stick.
3. Pushing, blocking.

TESTS FOR HOCKEY SKILLS

Pass for Accuracy

The player has five attempts to pass the ball or puck into a 3-by-3-foot target. He or she must pass from a distance of 30 feet. The target can be drawn or taped on the wall, or a 3-foot square of cardboard can be utilized. A player can approach the 30-foot restraining line in whatever fashion he or she desires. Two points are awarded for each successful pass.

Dribble for Speed

Three cones are placed in line 8 feet apart. The first cone is 16 feet from the starting line, and the finish line is 16 feet from the last cone. The player dribbles around the cones in a figure-eight fashion to the finish line. A stopwatch is used for timing, and the score is recorded to the nearest tenth of a second. Two trials are given, and the faster trial is recorded as the score.

Fielding

Three players are designated as passers and pass to the person being tested from different angles. The ball or puck must be definitely stopped and controlled. The instructor can judge whether the throw was a good opportunity for the player to field. Six passes, two from each angle, are given, and one point is given for each successful field.

Driving for Distance (Outside Only)

A restraining line can be made as a starting point for this test. Each player is given five trials, and the longest two attempts are recorded as the player's score. Distance is measured to the nearest foot. Players can be lined up in four or five squads behind the restraining line. One-third of the class can be used to measure distances and return the balls. After players have taken their five trials, they can exchange places with someone who is measuring and/or returning the balls.

The test should be done on grass, since solid ground permits unrestrained rolling.

Twenty-nine

Soccer

Interest and participation in soccer in the United States are growing by leaps and bounds. Its popularity in America has begun to rival that in other countries. Opportunities for learning the game and competing are increasingly being made available to children of elementary school age in leagues and clubs not connected with the schools.

Soccer is a game for "educated feet." The purpose is to advance the ball without the use of hands or arms down the field and into the goal. The official goal consists of two goal posts 24 feet apart with a crossbar 8 feet high. The ball must go under the crossbar and between the posts in order to score. However, in the lead-up games, goals are modified so that the ball merely crosses a line below shoulder height or is kicked through a line of defenders.

Success in soccer depends upon how well individual skills are coordinated in team play. Good soccer also stresses position play rather than groups of individuals dashing about chasing a ball.

Soccer rates high in its contributions to fitness and offers many opportunities to develop mature social and emotional qualities.

EMPHASIS IN EACH GRADE LEVEL

Fourth Grade

Before the fourth grade, the children should have played Circle Kick Ball and had some experience in kicking skills on an elementary level. Circle Kick Ball is to be reviewed. Fourth-grade material primarily stresses kicking and its use in simple lead-up games. Simple rules regarding touching the ball with the hands or arms and what constitutes fouling can be introduced on this level. Traps are taught, so children can control the ball without the use of hands.

Fifth Grade

Continued emphasis and expansion of kicking skills together with the skills of dribbling and passing make up the bulk of the fifth-grade program. Simple elements of team play are brought in. The children should play a modified form of soccer, Mini-Soccer, in the fifth grade.

Sixth Grade

The skills designated for the fourth and fifth grades should be reviewed and practiced, with additional challenges and combinations brought in.

The sixth-grade children can be *introduced* to regular soccer, but the regular game is not suitable for class work. The seven-player game is a much better substitute, since it brings out vigorous action for all players. A unit of study on soccer as an international game is of value, since few American children realize how important this game is in the lives of the people of other lands. Speedball can be added to the sixth-grade program, and it uses most of the soccer skills as well as other ball-handling techniques.

BASIC SOCCER RULES FOR LEAD-UP GAMES

1. The ball may not be deliberately played with the hands, forearms, or arms. Mere incidental touching should be disregarded. If the arms

Suggested Soccer Program

GRADE	FOURTH	FIFTH	SIXTH
Skills	Instep kick Inside of foot kick Toe trap Foot trap	Heel kick Dribbling Outside foot kick Body trap Passing	Kicking goals Kickoff (place kick) Punt Volleying Heading
Knowledges	Simple rules	Ball control and passing	The game of soccer Team play and rules
Activities	Soccer Croquet Ball Soccer Touch Ball Circle Kick Ball (Review) Soccer Dodgeball Diagonal Soccer Sideline Soccer	Pin Kick Ball Line Soccer Three-Line Soccer Mini-Soccer Milk Carton Soccer	Mini-Soccer Modified Speedball Regulation Soccer
Tests	Toe trap Accuracy kick (stationary position)	Dribbling Trapping (three types) Accuracy kick	Dribbling Punt Placekick Penalty kick Accuracy kick

are in contact with the body and are used only to block or stop the ball from this position, there is no violation. The free kick is the normal penalty for a touch violation. The ball is placed on the ground, with defenders not closer than a specified distance (10 feet, for example), depending on the game. A goal cannot be scored from a free kick of this type. The ball must not be kicked before the referee signals. In some games in which the free kick is not practical, a score can be awarded for an illegal touch.

2. The goalkeeper is exempt from the illegal touch rule. He or she may handle the ball *within his or her own area* by catching, batting, or deflecting with the hands. If the goalie has caught the ball, he or she may not be charged by the opponents, and, while he or she is holding the ball, he or she is limited to four steps by official rules. In elementary school play, the teacher should insist on the goalkeeper getting rid of the ball immediately by throwing or kicking. This removes the temptation to rough up the goalie. In some lead-up games, a number of students may have the same privileges as the goalie in handling the ball. The rules need to be clear, and the ball handling should be done within a specified area.

3. For serious fouls like tripping, striking, kicking, holding, or pushing an opponent, a direct free kick is awarded. A goal *may be* scored from such a kick. In soccer, if the team commits one of these fouls within its own penalty area (defensive), a penalty kick should be awarded. Only the goalkeeper may defend against this kick, which is from 12 yards out. All other players must be outside the penalty area until the ball is kicked. In lead-up games, consideration should be given to penalty-type fouls. These would be committed in a limited area by the defensive team near the goal it is defending. A kick can be awarded or a goal can be scored for the attacking team for the foul.

4. The ball is out of play and the whistle should blow when the ball crosses any of the boundaries, when a goal is scored, or when a foul is called. When a team last touches or causes the ball to go out-of-bounds on the sides, the other team is awarded the ball. The ball is put in play with an overhead throw-in by both hands.

5. If the ball is caused to go over the end line *by the attacking side,* the defending team receives a kick from any point desired near the end line of that half of the field. If the defense last touched the ball going over the end line, then the attacking team is awarded a corner kick. The ball is taken to the corner on the side

Soccer Throw-in from Out-of-bounds

where the ball went over the end line, and a direct free kick is executed. A goal may be scored from this kick.

6. The game is started by a kickoff with both teams onside. In lead-up games, the kickoff can be used or the ball can be dropped for a free ball. In some games, the teacher may find it advisable simply to award the ball for a free kick in the back court to the team not making the score.
7. Playing time in lead-up games can be determined by halves or by reaching a predetermined score. In a regular soccer game, the play is by halves.
8. When the ball is trapped or ensnarled among a number of players or when someone has fallen, a quick whistle is needed. The ball can be put in play by dropping it between players of opposite teams.
9. While the offside rule is of little value in elementary school play, the children should understand the rule and the reasons for it. Its purpose is to prevent the "cheap" goal (a player on offense waits near the goal to take a pass behind the defenders and score easily against the goalkeeper). While there are a

number of details to the concept of offside, essentially a player on offense ahead of the ball must have two players between him or her and the goal. One of these players is the goalkeeper, of course. The offside rule does not apply when the player receives the ball directly from an attempted goal kick, an opponent, a throw-in, or a corner kick.

SOCCER SKILLS

Skills recommended for inclusion in the instructional sequences are kicking, dribbling, trapping, passing, volleying, and heading. Tackling, a move by a player to gain possession of the ball from an opponent who is dribbling, usually involves deliberate use of a leg to block or take away the ball. While an accepted part of the game for older players, it can lead to undesirable roughness and possible injury for children, and, therefore, its inclusion in the teaching program is not recommended for elementary school.

Basic Soccer Kicks

Certain fundamentals apply to all soccer kicks and are presented first. Early stress should be on accuracy, since distance seems to take care of itself.

1. The eyes must be focused on the part of the ball to be kicked.
2. From a mechanical standpoint, the lower the point of contact by the foot on the ball, the more elevation the kick will have.
3. The arms and body should be used in coordination with the legs and feet to maintain good balance.
4. The ball will move with better accuracy if the plane of the foot is directly through the ball in line with the target.
5. Most kicking skills should be developed in both feet.
6. Kicking with the toe as in the straight-on football kickoff has little value in the game of soccer.

Instep Kick

The instep kick is the basic soccer kick. The kicker is two or three steps back of the ball at an angle. The nonkicking foot is placed alongside the ball 6 to 8 inches away, with the kicking leg cocked for the kick. Just before contact, the kicking foot is locked so that the toe is down. Contact is made with the lower part of the shoe around the lower laces, with good forward snap of the lower leg at the knee. A normal follow-through is desirable.

A variation of this kick is made with the inside of the foot just above the great toe to provide a kind of easy loft shot to elevate the ball over a player.

Inside Foot Kick

Instep Kick

Instep Kick

Inside Foot Kick

Generally, the inside foot kick is used for accurate passing, but it can be used for volleying and shooting (scoring). The nonkicking foot is placed alongside the ball. As the kicking foot is drawn back, the toe is turned out. During the kick, the toe remains turned out so the inside of the foot is perpendicular to the line of flight. The sole is kept parallel to the ground. The distance of the kick determines the amount of follow-through.

Outside of the Foot Kick

This kick is used almost exclusively for short, chop-like passes. The nonkicking foot steps more to the side than for the inside foot kick, with the backswing of the kicking foot taken across that leg. Contact with the kick is on the outside of the foot along the sole line.

Heel Kick

The heel kick has occasional use for a short pass to a teammate behind the player. The player steps slightly ahead of the ball with the nonkicking foot and with a short snappy punch of the heel propels the ball backward.

Punt

Used by the goalkeeper only, the punt can be stationary or done on the run. The ball is held in both hands waist-high in front of the body directly over the kicking leg. In the stationary position, the kicking foot is forward. A short step is taken with the kicking foot and then a full step on the other leg. With the knee bent and the toe extended, the kicking foot swings forward and upward. As contact is made with the ball at the instep, the knee straightens, and additional power is secured from

Punt

the other leg through a coordinated rising on the toes or a hop.

Trapping

In the elementary school, three types of trapping should be taught. Relaxation and giving with the ball are important in all traps.

1. Sole of the Foot Trap: This involves stopping a rolling ball by putting the sole of the foot on the ball and holding it to the ground.

2. Foot Trap: Using the inside of the foot or leg and giving with the ball, the motion of the ball is stopped by the inside of the foot.

3. Body Trap: This can be accomplished with the chest or thighs acting as the ball stop. The ball is deflected downward and controlled by the feet. Generally, only one thigh is used in trapping. The thigh is lifted and pulls away from the ball, giving with it to decelerate the ball, so it drops to the ground. Girls should cross arms across the chest for protection.

Dribbling

Dribbling is moving the ball with a series of taps or pushes to cover ground and still retain control of the ball. The best contact point is the inside of the big toe. Both the inside and outside of the foot can be used to move the ball.

Trapping the Ball—Side of the Foot

Trapping the Ball—Sole of the Foot

Dribbling—Ball-Foot Relationship

Volleying

The change of the direction of a ball on the fly is called volleying. This can be done by stiffening a part of the body, so the ball rebounds in the desired direction. Volleying can be done with the instep, knee, thigh, hip, or shoulder.

Heading

Heading is a special kind of volleying in which the direction of flight is changed through an impact with the head. The neck muscles can be used to aid in the blow. The eye must be kept on the ball until the moment of impact, which is made at the top of the forehead at the hairline.

In preparing to contact the ball with the head, the player should stand in a stride position, with the knees relaxed and the trunk bent backward at the hips. At the moment of contact, the trunk moves forward abruptly and the front of the forehead is driven at the ball.

Out-of-Bounds Throw-in

This move may be executed from a standing position or from a run, but it must be an overhead motion. No foot position is specified, but generally a stride position is employed. The ball is held

Heading—Contacting the Ball

overhead and is propelled with a final flick of the wrist and with minor arm motion.

INSTRUCTIONAL PROCEDURES

1. Planning instructional sequences for soccer should be based on two premises. The first is that soccer skills must be developed and stressed in order that children may participate successfully. The skill of controlling the ball with the feet comes slowly, and sufficient drills and opportunities are needed to develop the appropriate ball-control skills. The second is that lead-up games and introductory activities should feature give-and-take between competitors. A few of the early lead-up games presented feature primarily kicking skills, but the majority of the activities include some kind of competitive play between opponents.

2. Use balls smaller than the regular soccer ball. Molded rubber balls or partially deflated rubber playground balls (8½ inches) can be used, provided their quality is good enough to withstand the constant kicking. The key to soccer practices is to have plenty of balls available. Rubber balls mean more fun, since they can be kicked farther, controlled more easily, and even headed without discomfort. Junior-size soccer balls are also excellent.

3. Smaller fields and smaller teams (in comparison to regulation soccer sizes) should be used. This means more activity and also permits separation of sexes when vigorous competitive game play is scheduled. Most skills and many lead-up games can be taught coeducationally, but separation in heavy competition should be made, particularly on the sixth-grade level. The game with 11 players on each team has little place in the elementary school program.

4. Soccer, with its attack and defense, can be a rough game. Rough play like pushing, shoving, kicking, and tripping must be controlled. Rules need to be strictly enforced. Good execution of skills leading to good ball control helps eliminate knots of players. Attention to proper heading, volleying, and kicking skills helps eliminate injuries that result from contacts with the ball. Players need to watch for kicked balls, since these may strike players in the face or head unexpectedly. Glasses should be removed when possible, or glass guards should be provided.

5. Children need to be watched carefully for fatigue, since soccer is a vigorous game. The teacher should use methods of rotation to help rest players. Rotate children in and out of

the position of goalkeeper (generally the least-demanding position).

6. Soccer plays best on a grass surface. However, if a hard surface is used, the balls can be deflated slightly so that they do not bounce too readily.

7. Scoring can be modified for children in keeping with their capacities. Scoring must be a challenge but should be neither too easy nor too difficult. In order to avoid arguments in situations when the ball is to be kicked through a line of children, the height of the kicks should be limited to shoulder level or below. This tends to emphasize an important soccer principle: control of the ball on the ground. Cones, jump standards, and similar devices can be used to mark goal outlines. Formal soccer goals are not necessary items for the elementary school program.

SOCCER DRILLS

Drills for soccer skills should stress kicking, passing, trapping, dribbling, volleying, heading, and scoring (shooting). Trapping generally is combined with kicking and passing, while other skills may be practiced either by themselves or in combination. Experiences in which a defensive player participates add realism to the drills.

Individual Work

If enough balls are available, some individual work is profitable, particularly in the early phases of development. Children can develop an awareness of self with relation to handling the ball with the feet. Dribbling skills are particularly appropriate. By tossing the ball to oneself, one can accomplish heading practice. The ball can be dropped in front of the body and caught as it bounces on the top of the foot. Body (chest) traps can be practiced. Juggling possibilities can be explored by volleying from the head, thigh, or instep. Smothering the ball with the sole of the foot on the low bounce is also possible.

Informal Drills between Two Players

One ball is needed for each two children. Most soccer skills can be practiced in this manner, thus allowing good exploration of the skills and development of awareness of a partner. The instructional pattern is particularly appropriate for introductory phases of the sport. Children can be scattered, with space needs determined by the type of skill being practiced.

With children scattered, verbal instructions are difficult. A solution is to have a central pair to demonstrate the patterns and skills to be practiced and explored. When the class is called for central instructions, each pair can leave its ball at its own space, move to the central area for necessary

direction, and return to its area to implement the instructions. During the conduct of general practice, the instructor should circulate among the groups and provide help and encouragement.

Besides cooperation in the development of skills, one player can explore the techniques of keeping the ball away from the other. Dribbling practice is also possible where one player acts as a home base while the other dribbles in general space. Roles then are reversed.

Two small goals can be established and informal competition held. Allow the children to set up their own rules. The diagram shows some suggested dimensions.

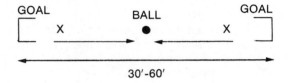

Two-Line Drill

Two lines with three or four children in each line face each other across a 30- to 45-foot distance. Following the pattern of the previous design, one ball can be utilized for two players or one ball for the group.

```
x x x x  ↑
         │  30'-15'
x x x x  ↓
```

Drills for Three Players

With one ball for each three players, many of the possibilities suggested for pair practice are possible. The three can set up a triangle and kick, pass, and trap in this fashion. Keep away, where two keep the ball away from the third player, offers excellent ball-handling possibilities. An excellent shuttle-type dribbling drill can be structured, as shown in the diagram. Players keep going back and forth continuously.

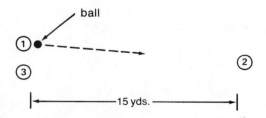

Player #1 has the ball and dribbles to #2, who dribbles the ball back to #3. The drill can be conducted in several ways. The first is to dribble the entire distance. A second way is to dribble a portion of the distance and then pass the ball to the end player. Also, obstacles can be placed, so it is necessary to dribble in and out of each obstacle.

A scoring situation can be set up with three players. Player #1 has the ball and attempts to maneuver by player #2, so that he or she can shoot a goal through the goalposts guarded by #3. A system of rotation is necessary.

Circle

The circle formation can be used for kicking, passing, and trapping. The ball may be kicked back and forth across the circle or may be passed from player to player in a circular direction. Trapping may be included in the skills.

Circle and Leader

The circle and leader formation lends itself well to the development of soccer skills. The use of the leader in the center allows for more controlled skill practice. The leader passes and receives the ball from each circle player in turn. After completing a round to all the players, the leader takes his or her place in the circle, and another child becomes the leader.

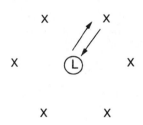

An effective pattern of kicking can be executed by having the leader pass to one of the circle players, who in turn sends the ball to another player and then back to the leader. An element of competition can be introduced when the leader tries to intercept this pass across the circle. Rotation is the same as in the previous drill.

File (Lane) Formation Drills

Each team is in a relay formation to practice the skills. A standard or base should be placed about 15 feet in front of the file. The following patterns of drills illustrate some of the possibilities from this formation.

1. Player dribbles forward, around the base, and back to the file.
2. Player dribbles forward and around the base and from this point passes back to the head of the file. Use three obstacles, 12 feet apart. The player dribbles in and out of the obstacles in a weaving motion, forming a figure-eight pattern.

Passing Drill

A double shuttle formation, which is the equivalent of two teams alongside each other in shuttle formation, is used for this drill. The shuttle halves are about 25 to 30 yards apart.

Two players, one from each file, move at a time. One player has the soccer ball. A short dribble is taken forward and then the ball is passed to the other player moving forward with him or her. The second player takes a short dribble forward and passes the ball back. This continues until they reach the other files, where two players repeat the maneuver and return the ball to its original starting place. The ball is shuttled back and forth by two players at a time.

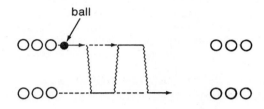

Line and Leader

A leader in front of a line can feed the ball to each player in turn for trapping and heading. Each player, after taking his or her turn, goes to the end of the line. Keep lines small.

Shuttle Dribbling

Dribbling, passing, and trapping can be practiced in the regular shuttle drill. The first player dribbles to the other file. The ball continues to be dribbled back and forth in turn. Each dribbler joins the rear of the file toward which he or she dribbled. The player can dribble part way toward the other file and, when about 5 yards away, pass to the head of the other file.

Two-Way Goal Practice

Two to six players are divided, half of them on each side of the goal. The width of the goal can vary, depending upon the skill of the players. Two types of scoring practice should be done: (1) kicking a stationary ball from 10 to 20 yards out; and (2) preceding the scoring kick with a dribble. In the

1. Stationary ball   GOAL   2. Dribble and shoot

cones
restraining line

X X X   ● —→ 10'-20' ◄— | ----O X X X

10-20 yds.   12-15 yds.

second, a restraining line 12 to 15 yards out is needed. This can be marked by cones.

Scoring with a Goalkeeper

Use a goal 20 feet wide, guarded by a goalkeeper. There needs to be a ball chaser, and two balls are used in the drill.

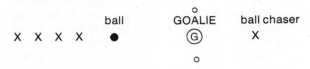

In a way similar to the preceding drill, practice should be done with a stationary ball 12 yards out (penalty distance) and with kicks preceded by a dribble. The goalie and chaser should remain for one complete round and then rotate. The second ball is advised, since it can be put into play while the chaser is recovering the previous kicked ball.

Competitive Practice with a Goalie

Many designs can be organized to utilize one goal guarded by a goalie. Some possibilities are these.

1. One offensive player against one defensive player plus the goalie.
2. Two offensive players against one defensive player plus the goalie.
3. Two offensive players against two defensive players plus the goalie.
4. Three offensive players against two defensive players plus the goalie.

Relays

Almost all soccer drills can be organized as relays. Relays should be introduced only after the children have mastered the skills sufficiently to have a reasonable control of the path of the soccer ball. Insistence on procedure in soccer relays is important. The ball should always be under good control, and a relay should finish with the ball in the possession of the team, not just kicked through or past some line. Touching the ball with the hands or arms should mean disqualification.

SOCCER ACTIVITIES

Third Grade

Circle Kick Ball

Formation: Circle.
Players: 10 to 20.
Supplies: Soccer ball or 8½-inch playground ball.
Skills: Kicking and trapping.

Players kick the ball (with the side of the foot) back and forth inside of the circle. The object is to kick the ball out of the circle *beneath* the shoulder level of the circle players. A point is scored against each of the players where the ball left the circle.

However, if the lost ball is clearly the fault of a single player, then the point is scored against him or her only. Any player who kicks the ball over the shoulders of the circle players has a point scored against him or her. Players with the fewest points scored against them win.

Variation: Instead of having points scored against them, the offending players can drop out of the circle until the next players have erred and then change places with them. Score can be kept, or this can be just informal play.

Fourth Grade

Soccer Croquet Ball

Formation: A grassy space. A number of games can be played in the same general area.
Players: Two or three.
Supplies: A soccer ball or another ball per child.
Skill: Kicking.

The game is played like croquet; the object is for one ball to hit the other. Each hit scores a point. The first player kicks his or her ball out 10 to 15 yards ahead. The next player kicks his or her ball and tries to hit the ball lying ahead. Alternate kicking continues until a hit is made, scoring one point for the kicker. The game continues until a player scores a specified number of points (10 to 15).

If three play, turns in sequence are taken. If a successful hit is made on one ball, the kicker gets a try immediately at the other.

Soccer Touch Ball

Formation: Circle with player in center.
Players: 8 to 10.
Supplies: Soccer ball.
Skills: Kicking and trapping.

Players are spaced around a circle about 10 yards in diameter. The object of the game is to keep the player in the center from touching the ball. The ball is passed back and forth as in soccer. If the center player touches the ball with a foot, the person who kicked the ball goes to the center. Also, if there is an error (a missed ball), the person responsible changes places with the one in the center.

Soccer Dodgeball

Formation: One team forms a circle, with the other team grouped in the center.
Players: 20 to 30.
Supplies: Soccer ball, slightly deflated.
Skills: Kicking (controlled), trapping, dodging.

This is a variation of Team Dodgeball (page 397), except that the ball is kicked instead of thrown at the center players. Players may not use their hands to control or retrieve the ball. A point is scored for the kicking team for each time a person in the center is hit. Hit players can be eliminated or remain to be hit again. A point is deducted from the team score for every violation by touching with the hands.

The ball should be deflated slightly and kicked with the side of the foot.

Diagonal Soccer

Playing Area: A square about 60 by 60 feet. Two corners are marked off with diagonals, outlining dead areas 5 feet from the corners on both the sides.
Players: 20 to 30.
Supplies: Soccer ball. Pinnies can be used.
Skills: Kicking, passing, dribbling, some trapping; defending and blocking shots.

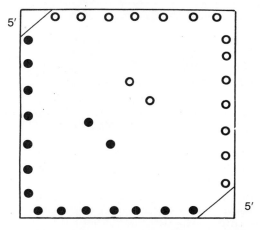

Each team lines up as illustrated and protects two adjacent sides of the square. Dead areas on opposite corners are used to divide the opposing teams' goal lines. These can be marked off with a series of cones. To begin competition, three players from each team move into the playing area in their own half of the space. These are the active players, who during play may roam anywhere in the square. The other players act as line guards.

The object of the game is for the active players to maneuver and kick the ball through (beneath shoulder height) the opposing team's line to score.

When a score is made, the active players rotate to the sidelines, and new players take their places.

Players on the sidelines may block the ball with their bodies but cannot use their hands. The team against whom the point was scored starts the ball for the next point.

Scoring: Only active players may score. Scoring is much the same as in Circle Soccer in that a point is scored for the opponents when:

1. A team allows the ball to go through its line below the shoulders.
2. A team touches the ball illegally.
3. A team kicks the ball over the other team above shoulder height.

Variations

1. If the class is large, enlarge the area and use more active players.

2. If scoring seems too easy, allow the line defenders to use their hands to stop the ball.

Sideline Soccer

Playing Area: Rectangle about 100 by 60 feet.
Players: 10 to 15 on each team.
Supplies: Soccer ball, four cones. Pinnies can be used.
Skills: Most soccer skills, competitive play.

The teams line up on the sidelines of the square with the end lines open. Three active players from each team are called from the end of the team line. These players remain active until a point is scored and then are rotated to the other end of the line.

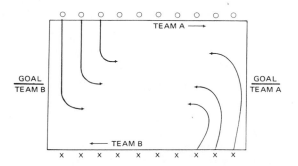

The object is to kick the ball over the end line, which has no defenders. The three compete against each other, helped by the players on the sidelines. To score, a ball must go over the end line at or below shoulder height. It counts one point. None of the players may play the ball with the hands. The active players follow the restrictions of no pushing, holding, kicking, or other rough play. Rough play constitutes a foul and causes a point to be awarded to the other team.

The ball must be kicked last by an active player to score. If the ball is out-of-bounds or does not score, play continues until a point is scored by the group of active players. Cones should be put at the corners to define the scoring area.

Play is started by the referee's dropping the ball between two players from opposite teams. Out-of-bounds is given to the team on that side. This is a free kick but cannot score a goal directly from the kick. Violation of the touch rule is also a free kick at the spot of the foul.

A second stage of this game is needed. After some expertise is reached, move in the corner cones, narrowing the goal area. If the ball goes over the end line but not through the goal area, the ball is put into play by a defender with a kick.

Teaching Suggestions: Establish a system of rotation in which the active players move to the opposite end of the sideline and new players come forth. Add more active players when the class is large. The distance between goals can be increased.

Fifth Grade

Pin Kick Ball

Formation: Two teams starting about 20 yards apart and facing each other.
Players: 7 to 10 on each team.
Supplies: Six or more pins (cones, Indian clubs, or bowling pins), two soccer balls.
Skills: Kicking, trapping.

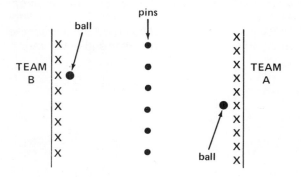

This is quite a flexible game in which the number of pins, balls, and players can be varied. At least six pins are placed between two lines of players. Two balls are used, one of which is given to each team at the start of the kicking. Kicks should be made from the line behind which the team is standing. Players should trap and concentrate on accuracy. Each pin knocked down scores a point for that team.

The type of kick can be specified, or it can be left up to the player's choice. Be careful of one or two players dominating the game. This can be controlled somewhat by having those who just scored go to either end of the line. More soccer balls can be added when the game seems slow. As accuracy improves, the distance between teams can be increased.

Line Soccer

Playing Area: Two goal lines from 80 to 120 feet apart. A restraining line is drawn 15 feet parallel to and in front of each goal line.
Players: 10 to 15 players on each team.
Supplies: Soccer ball, four cones. Pinnies are desirable.
Skills: Most soccer skills, competitive play.

Each team stands on one goal line, which it is to defend. The referee stands in the center of the field, holding a ball. At the whistle, three players (more if the teams are large) from the right side of each line of players run to the center and become the active players. The referee drops the ball to the ground, and the players try to kick it through the other team defending the goal line. The players in the field may advance by kicking only. A score is made when an active player kicks the ball through

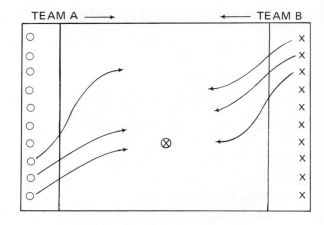

the opposite team on the end line, provided the kick was made outside the restraining line. Cones should be put on the field corners to define the goal line. A system of player rotation should be set up.

The line players act as goalies and are permitted to catch the ball. The ball must be laid down immediately and either rolled or kicked. It cannot be punted or drop-kicked.

Scoring: One point is scored when the ball is kicked through the opponent's goal below shoulder level. One point is also scored in case of a personal foul involving pushing, kicking, tripping, et cetera.

Penalties: For illegal touching by the active players, a direct free kick from a point 12 yards in front of the penalized team's goal line is given. All active players on the defending team must be to one side until the ball is kicked. Goalies only defend.

Time Limit: A time limit of 2 minutes for any set of players should be set. When no goal is scored during this time, a halt is called and players are changed.

Out-of-Bounds: The ball is awarded to the opponents of the team last touching it out-of-bounds. The regular soccer throw-in from out-of-bounds should be used. If the ball goes over the shoulders of the defenders at the end line, any end-line player may retrieve the ball and put it in play with a throw or kick.

Teaching Suggestions: Line Soccer should be played with the rules of soccer where possible. If boys and girls play together, girls should compete only against girls as active players. Arrange the rotation so this occurs.

Variations

1. If there is enough space, the teams can be divided into fourths (1s, 2s, 3s, and 4s). They need not keep any particular order at the end lines but simply come out as active players when called. By the use of numbers, the teacher can pit different groups against each other.

2. Instead of giving a score for a personal foul, a penalty kick can be awarded. The kicker kicks from 12 yards out and only three defenders are permitted on the line.

Three-Line Soccer

Playing Area: Soccer field 80 to 120 feet long, 60 to 100 feet wide. A center line bisects the field.
Number: 15 to 20 on each team.
Supplies: Soccer ball, pinnies.
Skills: Most soccer skills, position play.

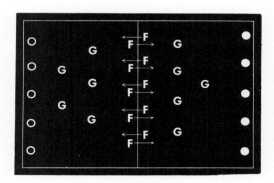

This game follows the same general rules as Line Soccer. Each team is divided into three equal groups, who line up as forwards, guards, and goalies.

Play begins with a kickoff, with both teams onside. The forwards stand at the center line for the kickoff and then for play move into the forward (for them) portion of the field. The guards are scattered in the back half of the field, and the goalies are on the goal lines. Thus, forwards compete against guards of the other team, while the goalies guard the goal.

The goalies may use their hands to defend their goal, but the other players follow regular soccer rules.

To score, the ball is driven past the line of goalies below shoulder level. After each score, the team that did not score gets to kick off. Rotation is by complete position, that is, forwards become guards, guards become goalies, and goalies become forwards. Rotation is generally done after each score but can be on a time basis. Out-of-bounds balls are put in play with the regular soccer throw-in.

Penalties

1. Free kick—for illegal touch and from the spot of the foul.
2. Direct free kick—personal foul by a team in its front court.
3. Penalty kick—personal foul by a team in its back court (defense). The ball is placed 12 yards from the goal line and only the goalies may defend.

Mini-Soccer (Seven-Player Game)

Playing Area: Any large area 100 by 150 feet, with goals.
Players: Seven on each team.
Supplies: Soccer ball, pinnies or colors to mark teams, four cones for the corners.
Skills: All soccer skills.

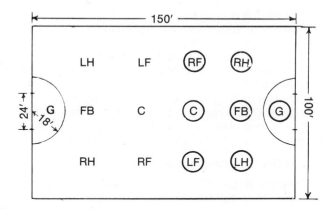

This should be the basic game for soccer play in elementary schools. It provides much more activity than the 11-player- per-team game, in which there can be a considerable lack of activity when the ball is at the other end of the field.

In a physical education class, the teacher should plan one game for the girls and one for the boys. This occupies a total of 28 children and is convenient for class instruction, provided the balance of boys and girls permits this. If not, the numbers can be reduced and the field size should be smaller.

A goal, 24 feet wide, is on each end of the field, marked by jumping standards. A 12-yard semicircle on each end outlines the penalty area. The center of the semicircle is at the center of the goal.

The game follows the general rules of soccer, with one goalie for each side. One new feature needs to be introduced, the corner kick. This kick is used when the ball goes over the end line but not through the goal and is last touched by the defense. If the attacking team last touched the ball, the goalkeeper kick is awarded. The goalie puts the ball down and place-kicks it forward. If the defenders last touch a ball going over the end line, the ball is taken to the nearest corner for a corner kick. This is a direct free kick, and a goal can be scored from the kick.

Most soccer rules apply to this version of the game.

The forwards play in the front half of the field, and the guards are in the back half. However, neither position is restricted to these areas entirely but may cross the center line without penalty.

A foul by the defense within its penalty area (semicircle) results in a penalty kick, taken from a point 12 yards distant, directly in front of the goal. Only the goalie is allowed to defend. The ball is in play, with the others waiting outside the penalty area.

The players are designated as center forward, outside right, outside left, right halfback, left halfback, fullback, and goalie. Players should rotate positions at times.

Teaching Suggestions: Position play should be emphasized. The lines of three should be encouraged to be spread and hold reasonable position.

Variation: The object of this game is to provide a miniature game of soccer. The number of players can vary, with games using as few as three on a side in a more restricted area. If teams have more than seven players, arrange for frequent substitutions but maintain the seven-player game.

Milk Carton Soccer

Playing Area: 60-by-100-foot area outdoors, a basketball court indoors.

Players: 6 to 10 on each side.

Supplies: Two to four gallon milk cartons.

Skills: Kicking, dribbling, stopping (trapping) the ball.

Several gallon cartons should be available. These should be filled with soft, light foam building insulation or chunks of foam rubber. The cartons should be taped to make them more durable. Cartons break and substitutes are needed.

Goals, 6 to 8 feet wide, should be established on each end of the field. Jump standards make excellent goals.

Regular soccer rules (see page 486) prevail, except for the following.

1. The penalty kick is from a spot 10 feet in front of a goal, which is guarded by the goalkeeper only.
2. No corner kick is called. A ball that goes over an end line and does not score a goal is put in play by the defending goalkeeper with a kick.
3. The goalkeeper must use a ground ball kick when putting the ball into play. He or she is not permitted to punt or drop-kick.
4. The carton is not suitable for heading. Heading should be called a foul and a free kick awarded.

Teaching Suggestions: The game is vigorous and must be controlled, since it can get rough. Since a carton cannot be kicked as far as a soccer ball (nor will it roll well), there is a tendency for the players to group together too closely in play. Encourage players to spread out and utilize passing and team play. It is better to use smaller numbers on each team and put in substitutes periodically. Play is quite strenuous and demanding.

Sixth Grade

Mini-Soccer (Seven-Player Game)

This game, introduced in the fifth grade, should be an important part of the sixth-grade program.

Modified Speedball

Playing Area: Any large area about 100 by 150 feet, with two goals. Three parallel lines are drawn on each end, 15 feet apart. Soccer goals are 24 feet in width. Cones or standards can be used. Soccer goals are placed on the middle of the three lines.

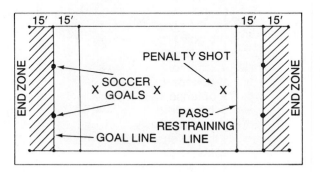

Players: Two teams of six to eight players each.

Supplies: Soccer ball or other appropriate ball, pinnies.

Skills: Combines soccer and some basketball skills, foot pickups.

Speedball combines the techniques of soccer and basketball. The ball may be advanced and scored as in soccer or passed as in basketball.

Air Ball and Ground Ball: A distinction must be made between an air ball and a ground ball, as this determines the manner in which a ball may be advanced. An air ball results from a player catching a kicked ball on the fly—or on first bounce. Passes thrown from one player to another are air balls. If a thrown pass touches the ground, it becomes a ground ball. Only an air ball may be touched with the hands.

A player may convert a ground ball (rolling or stationary) to an air ball by hoisting it to himself or other player with his foot. Conversely, a player may change an air ball to a ground ball by dropping it to the ground.

Scoring: Three methods of scoring are proposed.

1. Field goal—a ground ball kicked through the goal as in soccer scores two points.
2. Touchdown—an air ball passed from beyond the pass-restraining line to a teammate positioned in the end zone scores one point.
3. Penalty score—a ground ball kicked through the goal from a penalty shot taken 12 yards in front of the goal scores one point.

Basic Rules

1. A ground ball may not be touched with the hands but must be played as in soccer.
2. An air ball may not be kicked. However, a kicked ball, whether on first bounce or on the fly, may be kicked, since it has not been converted to an air ball until caught.
3. Only a ground ball may score a goal. If a player has the ball in his or her hands (air ball), the ball must touch the ground before it can be kicked.
4. One player on each team is the goalie and positions himself or herself to protect the goal. He or she may handle any ball with his or her hands (as in soccer), but this handling must be done in the area between the restraining line and the goal line.
5. Any ball crossing the goal line is out-of-bounds, except for those that make a score. If the out-of-bounds is the fault of the offensive team, the defense throws the ball in from the end zone. If the defense caused the ball to go out-of-bounds or last touched it, the ball is given to the offense for a throw-in at the nearest corner of the field. Any out-of-bounds along the sideline is given to the team that did not touch it last or cause it to go out-of-bounds. The throw-in may be made in any manner. As in basketball, if there is doubt about the fault with an out-of-bounds, a jump ball is called.
6. After a score, the ball is put in play by the goalie either with a throw or a kick.
7. A player catching the ball is allowed only two steps or traveling is called, giving the other team the ball outside. Jump ball may be called, as in basketball, when the ball is tied up with two opposing players.
8. One air dribble is allowed in advancing the ball. To make an air dribble, a player throws the ball into the air ahead of himself or herself, runs forward, and catches the ball before it hits the ground. Dribbling the ball by bouncing, as in basketball, is not permitted.
9. For violations for traveling and illegal handling of the ball, the other team is awarded the ball out-of-bounds for a throw-in.
10. A penalty shot is given for illegal touching by the defense within its restraining line, holding, pushing, and other unnecessary roughness. The shot is a kick from a stationary ball placed 12 yards in front of the goal. It must be a single kick at the goal and cannot be touched or played by the offense until the defense (goalie or other player) touches the ball. No interference with the kick is permitted. Defensive players must be to the side, and offensive players must stay behind the restraining line until the ball is kicked.
11. Play is by halves, with the teams exchanging goals for the second half.

Teaching Suggestions

1. Unless there is an overhead bar like a regular soccer goal, the limit of the height of the ball for the field goal or penalty score should be shoulder high.
2. Some practice in having a player hoist a ground ball to the hands is needed. To hoist a rolling ball, the player extends one foot forward, with the toes held close to the ground, and nudges the ball as it comes to him or her into his or her hands. Two methods of hoisting a stationary ball to the hands are suggested. The first is to straddle the ball, with the feet inverted and holding the ball. A jump with a quick pickup of both feet is made, hoisting the

Hoisting to the Hands

Hoisting to the Hands

ball to the hands. The second method with a stationary ball is called the toe-roll-back method. The player places one foot (the toes) on top of the ball. He or she rolls the ball back with the toes, slides the top of the toes under the ball, and nudges the ball up to his or her hands.

3. Another unique technique valuable in speedball is kicking the ball lightly with the side of the foot near the big toe, so that the ball is hoisted to a teammate.

4. The usual speedball rules do not permit converting a kicked ball (ground ball) to an air ball by catching it on the first bounce. If this is allowed, it makes for a faster game with fewer interruptions.

Regulation Soccer

Players: 11 on each side, including 5 forwards, 3 halfbacks, 2 fullbacks, and 1 goalkeeper.

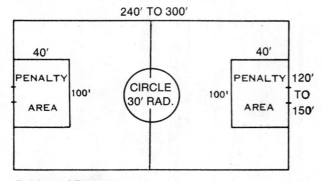

Duties of Players

1. Forwards—advance the ball into scoring territory and attempt to score.
2. Halfbacks—work both as offense and defense. Must do a great deal of running. Must back up both offense and defense.
3. Fullbacks—primarily defense. Must be skilled in defensive movements.
4. Goalkeeper—the last line of defense. Must be agile and skillful in blocking the ball. May use hands on defense within own penalty area.

The Kickoff: On the toss of the coin, the winner gets the choice of kicking off or selecting his or her goal. The loser exercises the option not selected by the winner.

The ball must travel forward about 1 yard by the kicker, and he or she cannot touch it again until another player has kicked it. The defensive team must be 10 yards away from the kicker. After each score, the team not winning the point gets to kick off. Both teams must be onside at the kickoff. The defensive team must stay onside and out of the center circle until the ball is kicked.

Scoring: Regular soccer rules call for scoring by counting the number of goals made.

Playing Time: Elementary school children should play not more than 6-minute quarters. There should be a rest period of 1 minute between periods and 10 minutes between halves.

Out-of-Bounds: When the ball goes out-of-bounds on the sides, it is put in play with a throw-in from the spot where it crossed the line. No goal may be scored, nor may the thrower play the ball a second time until it has been touched by another player. All opponents are to be 10 yards back at the time of the throw.

If the ball is caused to go out-of-bounds on the end line by the attacking team, a goal kick is awarded. The ball is placed in the goal area and kicked beyond the penalty area by a defending player. He or she may not touch the ball twice in succession, and all defensive players are to be 10 yards back.

Corner Kick: If the ball is caused to go out-of-bounds over the end line by the defensive team, a corner kick shall be awarded. The ball shall be placed 1 yard from the corner of the field and kicked into the field of play by an attacking player. The 10-yard restriction also applies to the defensive player.

Dropped Ball: If the ball is touched by two opponents at the same time and caused to go out-of-bounds, a drop ball shall be called. The referee drops the ball between two opponents, who cannot kick the ball before it touches the ground. A drop ball also is called when the ball is trapped among downed players.

Offside: If a player is closer to the opponent's goal line than the ball at the time the ball is played, he or she is offside. Exceptions occur and the player is not offside (1) when he or she is in his or her half of the playing field; (2) when two opponents are nearer their goal line than the attacking player at the moment the ball is played; and (3) when the ball is received directly from a corner kick, a throw-in, or a goal kick.

Fouls: Personal fouls involving unnecessary roughness are penalized. Tripping, striking, charging, holding, pushing, and jumping an opponent intentionally are forbidden.

It is a foul for any player except the goalkeeper to handle the ball with the hands or arms. The goalkeeper is allowed only four steps and then must get rid of the ball. Other fouls include these.

1. Playing the ball again when it should be contacted first by another player, as in a throw-in or a penalty kick.
2. Failure to kick the ball the proper distance on a kickoff or a penalty kick.
3. Goalkeeper carrying the ball more than four steps.
4. Kicking the ball before it hits the ground on an official drop ball.

Penalties

1. A penalty kick is awarded when a personal foul is committed by the defense within its own

penalty area. The ball is placed 12 yards from the goal, and only the goalkeeper can be in the penalty area.

2. A direct free kick is awarded at the spot for a personal foul and illegal touching. This kick may score a goal.

3. A free kick is awarded for the other infractions listed. Another player must play the ball after the free kick in order that a goal can be scored.

Teaching Suggestions

1. Players should be taught to play their positions, staying on their side of the field.
2. They should wear pinnies or shirts, so that the teams can be distinguished from each other.
3. Teams should attempt to develop control and accuracy. The ball is better advanced by passing than by long kicking.
4. The lines should be spread to avoid crowding.
5. Halfbacks should take most free kicks so that the forwards can be in position.
6. Eyeglass protectors must be worn by those with glasses.
7. After some skill has been acquired, the offside rule may be applied.

Note: Regular soccer is described because the children should play it occasionally so that they get the flavor of the regular competitive game.

TESTS FOR SOCCER SKILLS

The tests for soccer skills cover various kinds of kicks, dribbling, and trapping.

Dribbling—Figure Eight

Three obstacles or markers are arranged in line, 4 yards apart with the first positioned 4 yards from the starting line. The starting line is 4 yards wide. A stopwatch is used, and the timing is done to the nearest tenth of a second.

Three trials are given each player, with the fastest trial taken as the score. On each trial, the contestant dribbles over the figure-eight course and finishes by kicking or dribbling the ball over the 4-yard finish line, at which time the watch is stopped.

The test is best done on a grass surface, but, if a hard surface must be used, the ball should be deflated somewhat, so it can be controlled.

Trapping

The formation is a file plus one. The one in front of the file is the thrower. The thrower stands 15 to 20 feet in front of the file and rolls or bounces the ball to the player at the head of the file. Three trials each for the toe trap, foot trap, and body trap are given. The ball must be definitely stopped and controlled. A score of nine points is possible, one point awarded for each successful trap.

The thrower should adopt one type of throw that is to be used for all traps and all players. If the scorer judges that the roll was not a proper opportunity, the trial is taken over. For the fourth grade, the only trap taught is the toe trap. Five trials can be allowed.

Soccer Punt for Distance

A football or other field, marked in gridiron fashion at 5- or 10-yard intervals, is needed. One soccer ball is needed, but, when three can be used, considerable time is saved. A measuring tape (25 feet or 50 feet) plus individual markers round out the supply list.

Each player is given three kicks from behind a restraining line over which he or she cannot cross during the kicks. One child marks the kick for distance, while one or two other children act as ball chasers.

After the three kicks, the player's marker is left at the spot of the longest kick. This is determined by the point where the ball *first touched* after the kick. Measurement is taken to the nearest foot.

The squad or small group should all kick before the measurements are taken. The punt must be from a standing, not running, start. If a child crosses the line during the kick, it is ruled a foul and counts as a trial. No measurement is taken.

Soccer Place Kick for Distance

The directions are the same for this test as for the punt for distance, with two exceptions. The ball is kicked from a stationary position. It must be laid on a flat surface and not elevated by dirt, grass, or other means. The second difference is that the child is given credit for the entire distance of the kick, including the roll. The kicking should be done to a grassy surface, since the ball will roll indefinitely on a smooth, hard surface. If the surface presents a problem, the test can be limited to the distance the ball has traveled in flight.

Penalty Kick

The child faces a target area from behind a point 12 yards out where the ball has been placed. The child stands behind the ball. The target area is formed by a rope stretched tight, so it is 6 feet above the ground. Four ropes are dropped from this, at distances 5 feet apart. This outlines three target areas 6 feet high and 5 feet wide. The center

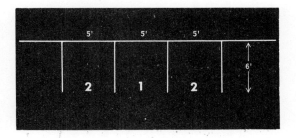

target area scores 1 point and the side areas, 2. This is in keeping with the principle that a penalty kick should be directed away from a goalkeeper toward either corner of the goal. Each child is allotted five kicks at the target. A score of 10 points is possible.

Accuracy Kick

The same target is used for this kick as for the penalty kick. However, the center area scores 2 points and the side areas 1 each. A balkline is drawn about 20 feet from the target. The child is back another 20 feet for a start. He or she dribbles the ball forward and then must kick the ball as it is moving but before it crosses the balkline. Five trials are given and a score of 10 points is possible.

Variation: The test also can be used with a stationary kick (placekick). The kicking distance would depend upon the capacities of the group.

Thirty

Softball

The major emphasis in softball should be on instruction and lead-up games. Children have adequate opportunities during recess, noon hour, and other times to play the regular game. In the physical education class, too much of the softball participation is of the "choose sides and let em go" variety. Youngsters love softball and a good instruction program should make use of this drive. Softball instruction should begin in the third grade and progress through the sixth. By the time the children are in the fifth grade, they should be playing regular softball modified for their level.

Since the experiences with softball of individual children vary so much, it is difficult to allocate with sureness the various skills and knowledges for a progressive program. The third-grade program is outlined, because it is felt that planned instruction in the game should begin on this level. It is recognized that second graders should throw and catch with softballs along with other types of balls.

EMPHASIS IN EACH GRADE LEVEL

Third Grade

Teaching the fundamental skills of batting, throwing, and catching is the emphasis in the third grade. Batting must receive its share of attention, since softball is little fun unless children can hit. Proper form and techniques in all three fundamental skills should be parts of the instruction, with attention not only to the how but also the why. A wide range in skills should be expected.

The lead-up games for the third grade are simple, but they provide an introduction to the game of softball. There is little emphasis on the pitcher or the catcher. A few basic rules of the game are learned.

Fourth Grade

In the fourth grade, specific skills for pitching, infield play, base running, and batting provide the material. Proper pitching techniques in keeping with the pitching rules are important to the budding softball player.

Fifth Grade

The fifth-grade student should be provided with the background to play the game of regulation softball designed for his or her age level. The material for instruction is pointed toward this end. An expansion of the fourth-grade program is emphasized, with additional techniques useful in the regular game of softball added. Tee Ball provides good opportunity for the softball skills, except for pitching and catching. Home Run and the ever-popular Scrub (Work-up) provide a variety of experiences. Batter Ball stresses hitting skills.

Sixth Grade

Experiences with batting, throwing, catching, and infield skills are continued. New pitching techniques, situation play, and double-play work are added. Slow-Pitch Softball provides lots of action. Babe Ruth Ball emphasizes selective hitting. The other games stress a variety of skills.

BASIC SOFTBALL RULES

Most sporting goods establishments have copies of the official rules for softball available.

503

Suggested Softball Program

GRADE	THIRD	FOURTH	FIFTH	SIXTH
Skills				
Throwing	Gripping the ball Overhand throw Underhand toss	Continued practice Around the bases	Throw-in from outfield Side-arm throw	Continued practice

*Catching
and
Fielding*
	Catching thrown
	  balls
	Catching fly balls
	Grounders
		Continued practice
		Fielding grounders
		  in infield
		Sure stop for
		  outfield
			Catching flies from
			  fungo batting
			Infield practice
				Flies and infield
				  practice

Batting	Simple skills Tee batting	Fungo hitting Continued practice Tee batting	Different positions at plate Tee batting	Bunting
Fielding positions		Infield practice How to catch	Infield positions Backing up other players	Double play

*Base
running*
	To first base	To first bass and
		  turning
		Circling the base
			Getting a good
			  start off base
			Tagging up on
			  fly ball
				Sacrifice

Pitching	Simple underhand	Application of pitching rule	Target pitching	Slow pitches
Coaching			Coaching at bases	
Knowledges				

Rules	Strike zone
	Foul and fair ball
	Safe and out
		Foul tip
		Bunt rule
		When the batter is
		  safe or out
			Pitching rule
			  Position
			  Illegal pitches
			Infield fly
			Keeping score
			Base running
				Review all rules
				Situation type quiz

Activities	Throw It and Run
	Two-Pitch Softball
		Two-Pitch Softball
		  (from 3rd grade)
		Hit and Run
		Kick Softball
		Hit the Bat
		In a Pickle
			Tee Ball
			Home Run
			Kick Pin Softball
			Five Hundred
			Batter Ball
			Scrub (Work-up)
				Slow-Pitch Softball
				Hurry Baseball
				Three-Team Softball
				Base-circling
				  Contest
				Babe Ruth Ball

Tests	None	Target throw Throw for distance	Old Woody (strike target) Throw for distance Circling the bases	Tee batting Old Woody Throw for distance Circling the bases Fielding grounders

Although an official rule guide should, of course, be used by students when they are studying the rules, a general idea of the basic rules of the game can be obtained from the following discussion.

Playing Area

The official diamond has 60-foot base lines and a pitching distance of 46 feet. Play in the intermediate grades should be with base lines no longer than 45 feet and a pitching distance of 35 feet or shorter.

Players

The nine players on a softball team are the catcher, pitcher, first baseman, second baseman, shortstop, third baseman, left fielder, center fielder, and right fielder. The right fielder is the outfielder nearest first base.

Batting Order

Players may bat in any order, although at times it is convenient in class play to have them bat according to their positions in the field. Once the batting order has been established, it may not be changed even if the player changes to another position in the field.

Pitching Rules

The pitcher must observe the following rules.
1. Face the batter with both feet on the pitching rubber, with the ball held in front with both hands.
2. The pitcher is allowed one step toward the batter and must deliver the ball while taking that step.
3. The ball must be pitched underhanded.
4. He or she cannot fake a pitch or make any motion toward the plate without delivering the ball.
5. He or she cannot roll or bounce the ball to the batter to keep him or her from hitting it.
6. No quick return before the batter is ready is allowed.
7. To be called a strike, a pitch must be over the plate and between the knees and shoulders of the batter. A ball is a pitch that does not go through this area.

Batting

The bat must be a softball bat. The batter cannot cross to the other side of the plate when the pitcher is ready to pitch. If a player bats out of turn, he or she is out. A bunt foul on the third strike is out. A pitched ball that touches or hits the batter entitles the batter to first base, provided he or she does not strike or bunt at the ball.

Striking Out

A batter is out when he or she misses the ball three times. This is called striking out.

Batter Safe

The batter is safe when he or she reaches first base after hitting a ground ball before the fielding team can get the ball to the first baseman with his or her foot on the base.

Fair Ball

A fair ball is any ball that settles on fair territory between home and first base and between home and third base. A ball that rolls over a base or through the infield into fair territory is a fair ball. A fly ball (including line drives) that drops into fair territory beyond the infield is a fair ball. Foul lines are considered to be in fair territory.

Foul Ball

A foul ball is a batted ball that settles outside the foul lines between home and first or between home and third. Also, a fly ball that drops into foul territory beyond the bases is a foul fly.

Fly Ball

Any fly ball, foul or fair, when caught is out. A foul fly, however, must be over the head of the batter or it is ruled as a foul tip. A foul tip caught counts as a strike, and the ball is in play. A foul tip, then, caught on the third strike makes the batter out.

Base Running

No lead-off is permitted. The runner must hold his or her base until the ball leaves the pitcher's hands on the penalty of being called out. On an overthrow where the ball goes into foul territory *and* out of play, runners advance one base beyond the base to which they were headed at the time of the overthrow. On an overthrow at second base by the catcher with the ball rolling into center field, the runners may advance as far as they can. To avoid being tagged on a base line, the runner is limited to a 3-foot distance on either side of a direct line from base to base. A runner hit by a batted ball while *off* the base is out. The batter, however, is entitled to first base. Base runners must touch all bases. If a runner fails to touch a base, it is an appeal play, which means the fielding team must call the oversight to the attention of the umpire, who will then (and not before) rule on the play.

Runners may overrun first base on the initial run to first base without penalty. On all other bases the runner must maintain contact with the base or he or she can be tagged out. To score, he or she must make contact with home plate.

Scoring

A run is scored when the base runner makes the circuit of bases (first, second, third, and home) before the batting team has three outs. If the third out is a force out, no run is scored even if the runner crossed home plate before the out was actually made.

The situation needing the most clarification occurs when a runner is on base with one out and the batter hits a fly ball that is caught, making the second out. The runner is forced to return to the base he or she occupied before the ball reaches that base and puts him or her out. If he makes the *third* out as the result of failure to return to his or her base in time, no run scores.

SOFTBALL SKILLS

Children can find many ways to execute softball skills effectively by trial and error, by accident, and through instruction. Care must be taken not to try to mold every child into a prescribed form, but rather the lesson should work toward helping him or her make the most of his or her pattern of movement.

*Gripping the Ball—
Full Grip (little finger
supports on the side)*

*Gripping the Ball—
Two-Finger Grip*

Gripping the Ball

The standard grip for softball calls for the thumb to be on one side, the index and middle fingers on top, and the other fingers supporting on the other side. Younger children with small hands may find it more comfortable to use a full-hand grip, wherein the thumb and fingers are spaced rather evenly in controlling the ball. Regardless of the grip used, the pads of the fingers should control the ball.

Throwing, Overhand

The first motions involve securing a firm grip on the ball, raising the throwing arm to shoulder height, and bringing the elbow back. The hand with the ball then is brought back, so the hand is well behind the shoulder at about that height. The left side of the body is turned in the direction of the throw, and the left arm is raised and in front of the body. The weight is on the back (right) foot with the left foot advanced, with the toe touching the ground. The arm comes forward with the elbow leading, and the ball is thrown with a downward snap of the wrist. The weight of the body is brought forward into the throw, with the weight shifting to the front foot. There should be a good follow-through, ending so the palm of the throwing hand is facing the ground. The eye should be on the

Throwing Overhand

target throughout, and the arm should be kept free and loose during the throw.

Throwing, Side-Arm

The delivery of the side-arm throw is much the same as for the overhand throw, except the entire motion is kept near a horizontal plane. The side-arm throw is used for shorter, quicker throws than the overhand throw and employs a quick, whiplike action. On a long throw, the side-arm throw curves more than the overhand, since usually a side-spinning action is imparted to the ball on release. There is generally some body lean toward the side of the throwing arm.

Underhand Toss

The hand and arm are brought back with the palms facing forward in a pendulum swing. The elbow is held slightly bent. The weight is mostly on the back foot. The arm comes forward almost in a bowling motion, and the ball is tossed. The weight shifts to the front foot during the toss. The flight of the ball should remain low and arrive about waist high.

Pitching

The official rule calls for the pitcher to have both feet in contact with the pitcher's rubber; however,

Preliminary Position—Pitcher

few if any elementary schools possess a rubber. The pitcher can stand with both feet about even, facing the batter, and holding the ball momentarily in front of him or her with both hands. The pitcher takes one hand from the ball, extends the right arm forward, and brings it back with a pendulum swing, positioning the ball well back of the body. A normal stride is taken toward the batter with the left foot to begin the throwing sequence. The arm is brought forward with a slingshot motion underhanded with the weight transferred to the leading foot. Only one step is permitted. The follow-through motion is important.

The windmill motion is the alternate pitching motion in which the arm describes a full arc overhead to behind the body and forward to the batter. The arm goes into full extension on the downward swing in the back, gathering momentum as the forward motion begins. Otherwise, the pitch is the same as the normal windup. This is generally a difficult style for youngsters to master.

Ready Position—Infielder

Pitching

Ready Position for Fielders

Infielders should assume a ready position, which is a semicrouch, with the legs spread shoulder width apart, knees bent slightly, and hands on or in front of the knees. As the ball is delivered, weight is shifted to the balls of the feet. The outfielder's position is also a semicrouch but a little more erect.

Catching Fly Balls

There are two methods for catching a fly ball.
1. For a low ball, the fielder keeps his or her little fingers together and forms a basket with his or her hands.
2. For a higher ball, the thumbs are together, and the ball is caught just in front of the chin.

There should be give with the catching hands. Care should be taken with a spinning ball to provide sufficient squeeze of the hands to stop the spinning.

The eye is on the ball continually until it hits the glove or hands. The knees are flexed slightly in receiving and aid in the give when the ball is caught.

Catching a Low Fly Ball

Catching a High Fly Ball

Fielding a Grounder

Fielding Grounders

The fielder should move first as quickly as possible to the path of the ball. He or she then should move forward and attempt to play the ball on the good hop. The eye must be kept on the ball and see the ball into the hands or glove. The feet are spread, the seat is kept down, and the hands carried low but in front. The weight is on the balls of the feet or the toes, and the knees are bent to lower the body. As the ball is caught, the fielder straightens up, takes a step in the direction of the throw, and makes the throw.

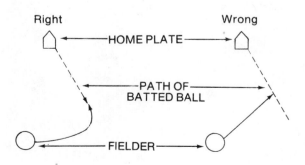

Sure Stop—Outfielder

Sure Stop for Outfield Balls

To keep the ball from going through an outfielder and allowing extra bases, a type of stop can be used that uses the body as a barrier in case the ball is missed by the hands. The fielder turns half right and lowers a knee to the ground at the point where the ball is coming. The hands attempt to catch the rolling ball, but, if it is missed, the body will generally stop the ball.

First Base Positioning

When a ball is hit to the infield, the first baseman moves to the base until his or her heels are touching the base. He or she then judges the path of the ball, stepping toward the ball with one foot

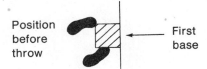

Position before throw → First base

First Baseman Stretching for the Throw

and stretching forward. The other foot remains in contact with the base.

Catcher's Position

The catcher takes a crouch position, feet about shoulder width apart, with the left foot slightly ahead of the right. He or she can use a glove and should wear a mask. He or she is positioned back just beyond the range of the swing of the bat. A body protector is desirable.

Catcher in Position

Batter's Position

Batting (Right-handed)

Stand with the left side of the body toward the pitcher, with the feet spread and the weight on both feet. The body should be facing the plate. Hold the bat with the trademark up, so the left hand (for right-handed batters) grasps the bat lower than the right. The bat is held over the right shoulder, pointing both back and up. The elbows are away from the body for free swinging.

The swing begins with a hip roll and a short step forward in the direction of the pitcher. The bat then is swung level with the ground at the height of the pitch. Eyes are kept on the ball until it is hit. After the hit, there is good follow-through.

Points the batter should avoid are lifting the front foot high off the ground, stepping back with the rear foot, dropping the rear shoulder, chopping down on the ball (or golfing), dropping the elbows, crouching or bending forward, and failing to keep eyes on the ball.

Youngsters should have experience with different grips on the bat—the long, choke, and middle grips. Stress a light grip on the bat, since

Choke Grip　　　*Long Grip*　　　*Middle or Modified Grip*

this relaxes the forearm muscles. Beginning batters should start with the choke grip.

Bunting

The batter turns to almost face the pitcher, with his or her right foot alongside home plate. As the pitcher releases the ball, the upper hand is run about halfway up the bat. He or she holds the bat loosely in front of the body and parallel to the ground and just meets the ball. The ball can be directed down either the first or the third base line.

Regular Bunt Position

The surprise (or drag) bunt is done without the squaring around or facing the pitcher. The batter holds the bat in a choke grip and, when the pitcher lets go of the ball, runs the right hand up on the bat. He or she directs the ball down either foul line, keeping it inside as close to the line as possible.

Base Running

When the batter hits the ball, he or she should run hard and purposefully toward first base, no matter what kind of hit. He or she should run through (past) the bag, tagging it in the process. He or she should step on the foul-line side of the base to avoid a collision with the first baseman.

Since a runner on base must hold the base position until the pitcher releases the ball, securing a fast start away from the base is essential. With either toe in contact with the base, the runner assumes a body lean, with the weight on the ball of the leading foot and the eyes on the pitcher. After the pitch is made, the runner takes a few steps away from the base in the direction of the next base.

INSTRUCTIONAL PROCEDURES

1. Safety is of utmost importance. The following precautions should be observed.
    a. Throwing the bat is a constant danger. The members of the batting team should stand on the side opposite the batter. For a right-handed batter, the batting team members should be on the first base side and vice versa.
    b. To keep the batter from throwing the bat:
        (1) Have the batter touch the bat to the ground before dropping it.

     (2) Call the batter out if he or she throws the bat.

     (3) Have the batter carry the bat to first base.

     (4) Have the batter change ends with the bat before dropping it.

     (5) Have the batter place the bat in a 3-foot circle before running.

  c. Sliding leads to both injury and destruction of clothing. No sliding should be permitted. Runners should be called out when they slide into base.

  d. If a catcher stands close behind the plate while catching, he or she must wear a mask. A body protector is recommended, especially for girls.

  e. Colliding while running for the ball can be held to a minimum if players are taught to call for the ball and not to trespass on other players' areas.

  f. When changing fields at the beginning of an inning, the batting team moves toward first base, staying on the first base side of second base. The fielding team goes to bat via the third-base side of the infield.

  g. Soft softballs should be used, particularly in the lower grades. Fleece balls are excellent for introductory throwing skills.

  h. All bats should be taped. Broken or cracked bats should not be used, even when taped.

2. Batting skills must be stressed. There is no more ego-shattering experience for a youngster than to stand at the plate and demonstrate an ineptness that draws scorn and ridicule from his or her peers. First make sure he or she knows the correct stance and proper mechanics of batting. Improved hitting then will come with practice.

3. The spoiler of many games of the softball type is the pitcher-batter duel. If this is prolonged with few hits by the batter, the remainder of the players justifiably become bored from standing around. Having a member of the batting team pitch is one method of eliminating the problem.

4. Players should rotate positions often. A good rule in physical education classes is that everyone, including the pitcher, should rotate to another position at the start of a new inning.

5. The distance between the bases has a heavy effect on the game. The distance should be lessened or increased according to the game and the capacities of the children.

6. Umpires can be appointed, or the team at bat can umpire. A rule that can be followed is that the person who made the last out of the previous inning is the umpire for the coming inning. There should be instruction for all in umpiring. To expect a child to umpire properly without proper instruction is poor teaching.

7. Encourage good players to recognize and give approval to those who are less skillful. Since there are many differences in ability, an opportunity for a lesson in tolerance is present. It is important not to let an error become a tragedy to a child.

8. Each player should run out his or her hit, no matter how hopeless it seems.

9. Analyze each of the lead-up games for its purpose, and practice the needed skills before their inclusion in the game.

10. Insist on conformance to the rules. Copies of the *Official Guide for Softball* should be available in the classroom.

11. Children must recognize that perfection in softball skills comes only through good practice sessions.

12. Teach respect for officials and acceptance of the umpire's judgment. The disreputable practice of baiting the umpire should be no part of the child's softball experiences.

13. Care of equipment is the responsibility of all. The trademark of the bat should be kept up when the ball is contacted in the middle of the swing. The bat should be used to bat softballs only. Hitting rocks and sticks with the bat injures the bat and lessens its effectiveness and life expectancy. The bat should be carried, not thrown, from one person to another.

DEVELOPING SOFTBALL SKILLS AND KNOWLEDGES

It is essential that students not only develop skills in softball but acquire many knowledges about the various phases of the game. The amount of field space and the equipment available determine the instructional organization. To cover the many phases of the game, a multiple-activity pattern seems best. It should incorporate the following guidelines into the instructional patterns.

1. The children should have many opportunities to practice the skills. Even in rotating groups, there should be as many small groups as possible. Throwing practice and fielding grounders can be between just two children, for example.

2. The basis of the rotational system can be the squad, with responsibility centered on the captain for the conduct of the practice at the different stations. He or she can be aided by others, as in the next point.

3. The Little League problem cannot be ignored. These "stars" generally have skill levels above those desirable in class instruction. Their skills can be utilized for helping with various phases of the instruction, provided

sufficient direction for these efforts is given. In most cases, the boys are more likely to have Little League experience than the girls, but in the future this may change.

4. The activities and procedures to be stressed at each station should be carefully planned and communicated to the participants. Prior meetings with the captains and other helpers are valuable. Appropriate softball rules should be covered.

5. Complete rotation of stations is not necessary at each class session. During a class session, teams may practice at one station for a part of the time and then use the remainder of the time to participate in an appropriate lead-up game.

6. Not only must there be direction at each station, the individuals must assume responsibility for cooperating with the planned activities and making the most of the skill development opportunities.

7. The use of the rotational station system does not rule out all class activities as a unit. Mimetic drills (drills without equipment) are valuable for establishing fundamental movement patterns for most skills. Students can go through the motions, simultaneously practicing such techniques as batting, pitching, throwing, and fielding without worry concerning results. Correct technique can be emphasized. Discussions of rules and various demonstrations for the entire class are fruitful.

8. Station teaching provides an excellent opportunity for visiting high school students to provide assistance. In many systems, high school students visit elementary schools on a regular basis for observation and educational experiences, some of which are admittedly sterile. Here is an opportunity to make good use of these visitors.

9. The teacher's part in the rotational system is to circulate from one station to another, providing encouragement, correction, coaching, and motivation for the learning experiences.

10. A motivational factor can be introduced in comparing the rotational system to varsity or major league practices. This gives it an adult flavor.

11. Selection can be made from the list of lead-up games, particularly for those that are suitable for squad play or fewer children.

Suggested Skill Development Activities for Stations

Skill activities and opportunities for participation at each of the stations can consist of emphasis on a single skill or a combination of skills. They also can involve situational drills. Children should

realize that constant repetition is necessary to develop, maintain, and sharpen softball skills.

The multitude of softball skills to be practiced allows for many different combinations and instructional organizations. The following are examples of the kinds of combinations and organizations that can be used in station teaching.

1. Batting can be organized many ways. The key is to see that each child has many opportunities to hit the ball successfully. Sufficient area is needed.
   a. Use a batting tee. For a station, two tees are needed, with a bat and at least two balls for each tee. Three to five children are assigned to each tee. There should be a batter, a catcher to handle incoming balls, and fielders. When only three children are in a unit, the catcher should be eliminated. Each batter is allowed a certain number of swings before being rotated to the field. The catcher becomes the next batter and a fielder moves up to catcher.
   b. Organize informal hitting practice. Needed are the batter, pitcher, and fielders. Two batting groups should be organized at each station. A catcher is optional.
   c. Early practice in hitting can use a thrown (underhand) playground rubber ball. The larger ball is easier to hit.
   d. Bunting practice can be held with groups of three—a pitcher, batter, and fielder.

2. One ball is needed per two children for practice at throwing and catching.
   a. Throw back and forth, practicing various throws.
   b. Throw ground balls back and forth for fielding practice.
   c. One player acts as a first baseman, throws grounders to the other, and receives the put-out throw.
   d. Throw flies back and forth.
   e. One player bats out flies, with two or three fielders catching flies.
   f. Four bases are established, and throws from base to base are made.

3. Use proper pitching form and an effective catcher's position for pitching practice.
   a. One player pitches to the other over a plate.
   b. One player is the pitcher, the second is the catcher, and the third the umpire. Call balls and strikes. A fourth player can be a stationary batter, providing a more realistic pitching target.
   c. Pitch toward pitching targets, either a wooden target (page 520) or a similar area outlined on a wall.

4. For infield drill, the children are placed in the

normal infield positions of catcher, first, second, third, and shortstop. One child acts as batter and gives directions. The play should begin with practice of throwing around the bases either way. After this, the batter rolls the ball to the different infielders, beginning with the third baseman and continuing in turn around the infield, with each throwing to first to retire an imaginary runner. Various play situations can be developed.

If the batter is skillful enough, he or she can hit the ball to the infielders instead of rolling the ball, making a more realistic drill. Using a second softball saves time when the ball is thrown or batted past an infielder, because the players do not have to wait for the ball to be retrieved before going on with the next play.

After the ball has been thrown to the first baseman, other throws around the infield can take place. The drill can be used with a partial infield.

5. Different situations for practicing base running can be set up.
   a. Bunt and run to first. Needed are a pitcher, a batter, an infielder, and a first baseman. The pitcher serves the ball up for a bunt, and the batter after bunting takes off for first base. A fielding play can be made on the runner.
   b. Bunt and run to second base. Batter bunts the ball, runs to first and then on to second base, making a proper turn at first base.
6. The game of Pepper can be played. This is one of the older skill games in baseball. A line of three or four players is about 10 yards in front of, and facing, a batter. The players toss the ball to the batter, who attempts to hit *controlled* grounders back to them. A batter stays at bat for a period of time and then rotates to the field.

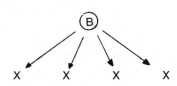

7. Some of the game-type activities such as Batter Ball, Hit the Bat, In a Pickle, Five Hundred, and Scrub can be scheduled activities at stations.

Putting Together a Station Program

Generally, four squads are formed from a regular class of around 30 students, with 7 or 8 students assigned to each squad. Some illustrations of the way stations can be organized follow.

Illustration 1

Station 1: Batting—see 1a.
Station 2: Throwing, fielding grounders—see 2c.
Station 3: Base running—In a Pickle, page 515.
Station 4: Bunting and base running—see 5a.

Illustration 2

Station 1: Batting and fielding—game of Pepper—see 6.
Station 2: Pitching and umpiring—see 3b.
Station 3: Infield practice—see 4.
Station 4: Batting practice—see 1b.

Illustration 3

Station 1: Fungo hitting, fielding, throwing—Hit the Bat, page 515.
Station 2: Bunting and fielding—see 1d.
Station 3: Pitching to targets—see 3c.
Station 4: Batting—see 1a and 2b.

SOFTBALL ACTIVITIES

Third Grade

Throw It and Run Softball

Playing Area: Softball diamond reduced in size.
Players: Two teams of 7 to 11 each (usually 9 players are on a side).
Supplies: Softball or similar ball.
Skills: Throwing, catching, fielding, base running.

The game is played like softball with the following exception. With one team in the field at regular positions, the pitcher throws the ball to the batter, who, instead of batting the ball, catches it, and immediately throws it out into the field. The ball then is treated as a batted ball, and regular softball rules prevail. However, no stealing is permitted, and the runners must hold bases until the batter throws the ball. A foul ball is out.

Variations

1. *Under-Leg Throw:* Instead of having the batter throw directly, have him or her turn to the right, lift his or her left leg, and throw the ball under the leg into the playing field.
2. *Beat-Ball Throw:* The fielders, instead of playing regular softball rules, throw the ball directly home to the catcher. The batter, in the meantime, runs around the bases. He or she gets one point for each base he or she touches before the catcher gets the ball and calls out "Stop." There are no outs, and each batter gets a turn before changing sides to the field. A fly ball caught would mean no score. Similarly, a foul ball would score no points but would count as a turn at bat.

Two-Pitch Softball

Playing Area: Softball diamond.
Players: Regular softball teams, but the numbers can vary.
Supplies: Softball, bat.
Skills: Most softball skills, except regular pitching.

This introductory game is played like regular softball, with the following changes.

1. A member of the team at bat is the pitcher. Some system of rotation should be set up so every child takes a turn as pitcher.
2. The batter has only two pitches in which to hit the ball. He or she must hit a fair ball on either of these pitches or he or she is out. He or she can foul the first ball, but, if he or she fouls the second, he or she is out. There is no need to call balls or strikes.
3. The pitcher, because he or she is a member of the team at bat, does not field the ball. A member of the team at field acts as the fielding pitcher.
4. If the batter hits the ball, regular softball rules are followed. However, no stealing is permitted.

Variation: *Three Strikes:* In this game, the batter is allowed three pitches (strikes) to hit the ball. Otherwise, the game proceeds as in Two-Pitch.

Teaching Suggestion: Since it is the responsibility of the pitcher to pitch a ball that can be hit, shorten the pitching distance, so the batter has ample opportunity to hit the ball. The instructor also can act as the pitcher.

Fourth Grade

Two-Pitch Softball

Described in the third-grade program, the game should be emphasized in the fourth grade, also.

Hit and Run

Playing Area: Softball field, gymnasium.
Players: Two teams, 6 to 15 players on each team.
Supplies: Volleyball, soccer ball, or playground ball, home plate and base marker.
Skills: Catching, throwing, running, dodging.

One team is at bat, and the other is scattered out in the field. Out-of-bounds must be established, but the area does not need to be shaped like a baseball diamond. The batter stands at home plate with the ball. In front of him or her, 12 feet away, is a short line over which the ball must be hit to be in play. In the center of the field about 40 feet away is the base marker.

The batter bats the ball with his or her hands or fists so that it crosses the short line and lights inside the area. He or she then attempts to run

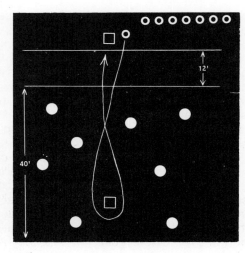

down the field, around the base marker, and back to home plate without being hit by the ball. The members of the other team field the ball and attempt to hit the runner. The fielder may not run or walk with the ball but may throw to a teammate closer to the runner.

A run is scored for each successful run around the marker and back to home plate without getting hit with the ball. A run also is scored if a foul is called on the fielding team for walking or running with the ball.

The batter is out when:

1. A fly ball is caught.
2. He or she is hit below the shoulders with the ball.
3. The ball is not hit beyond the short line.
4. The team touches home plate with the ball before the runner does. This may be used *only* when the runner stops in the field and does not continue.

The game can be played in innings of three outs each, or a change of team positions can be made after all from one team have batted.

Variation: *Five Passes:* The batter is out when:

1. A fly ball is caught.
2. The ball is passed among five different players of the team in the field with the last pass to a player at home plate beating the runner to the plate. The passes must not touch the ground and must be among five different players.

Teaching Hint: The distance the batter runs around the base marker may have to be shortened or lengthened, depending upon the children's ability.

Kick Softball

Playing Area: Regular softball field with a home base 3-feet square.
Players: Regular softball teams, but numbers can vary.

Supplies: Soccer ball or another ball to be kicked.
Skills: Kicking a rolling ball, throwing, catching, running bases.

The batter stands in the kicking area, a 3-foot-square home plate. The batter kicks the ball rolled on the ground by the pitcher. The ball should be rolled only with moderate speed. An umpire calls balls and strikes. A strike is a ball that rolls over the 3-foot square. A ball is one that rolls outside this area. Strikeouts and walks are called the same as in softball. The number of foul balls allowed should be limited. No base stealing is permitted. Otherwise, the game is played like softball.

Variations

1. The batter kicks a stationary ball. This saves time, since there is no pitching.
2. *Punch Ball:* Using a volleyball, the batter can hit a ball as in a volleyball serve or he or she can punch a ball pitched by the pitcher. The latter sometimes causes some pain when the pitch is too hard.

Hit the Bat

Playing Area: Open field for fungo batting.
Players: 3 to 10 children.
Supplies: Softball, bat.
Skills: Fungo hitting, fielding, throwing.

Children, except the batter, are scattered in the field. The batter tosses the ball to himself or herself and hits the ball to the fielders. The object of each fielder is to become the batter. The fielder becomes the batter if:

1. He or she catches three flies from the *present* batter.
2. He or she can hit the bat with the ball.

To become eligible to throw to the bat, the fielder must field the ball cleanly. The batter lays the bat down on the ground facing the throw, so it presents the largest possible target.

If a fielder catches a fly ball, he or she gets 10 steps toward the bat from where he or she caught the ball. If he or she catches the ball on first bounce, he or she gets 5 steps. He or she tries to hit the bat.

Variations

1. If hitting the bat seems to be difficult, count a throw as successful when the ball goes directly over the bat.
2. Two balls caught on first bounce can count as one fly ball caught.
3. The batter is not put out if he or she can catch the ball as it rebounds from the bat after being hit by a rolling ball.

In a Pickle

Playing Area: Any flat surface with 60 feet of room.

Players: Three or more.
Supplies: Two bases 45 to 55 feet apart, softball.
Skills: Throwing, catching, running down a base runner, and tagging.

When a base runner gets caught between two bases, he or she is in danger of being run down and tagged; literally, he or she is "in a pickle." Two fielders attempt to run down a runner between bases. To begin, both fielders are on bases, one with a ball. The runner is positioned 10 to 15 feet in the base path away from the fielder with the ball. The two fielders attempt to run down the runner between the bases and tag him or her.

If the runner escapes and secures a base, he or she gets to try again. Otherwise, a system of rotation is established, including any sideline (waiting) players. No sliding is permitted.

Fifth Grade

Five Hundred

Playing Area: Field big enough for fungo hitting.
Players: 3 to 12, although more can play.
Supplies: Softball, bat.
Skills: Fungo batting, catching flies, fielding grounders.

There are many versions of this old game. A batter stands on one side of the field and bats the ball out to a number of fielders, who are scattered. The fielders attempt to become batter by reaching a score of 500. To do this, the fielder is granted points for the following.

200—catching a ball on the fly.
100—catching a ball on first bounce.
50—fielding a grounder cleanly.

Whenever a change of batters is made, all fielders lose their points and must start over.

Variations

1. The fielder's points must total exactly 500.
2. Points are subtracted from the fielder's score if he or she fails to handle a ball properly. Thus, if he or she drops a fly ball, he or she loses 200 points.

Batter Ball

Playing Area: Softball diamond lines as in the diagram on the next page.
Players: Two teams, 8 to 12 on each.
Supplies: Softball, bat, mask.
Skills: Slow pitching, hitting, fielding, catching flies.

Batter Ball involves batting and fielding but no base running. It is much like batting practice but adds the element of competition.

A line is drawn directly from first to third base. This is the balkline over which a batted ball must travel to be fielded. Another line is drawn from a point on the foul line 3½ feet behind third base to a

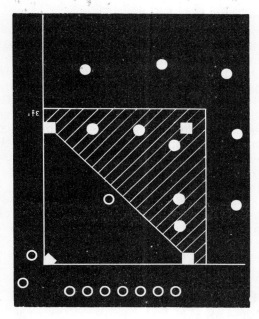

point 5 feet behind second base (in line with home plate). Another line connects this point with a point on the first base line 3½ feet behind that base. The scored space is the infield area.

Each batter is given three pitches by a member of his or her own team to hit the ball into fair territory across the balkline. The pitcher may stop any ground ball he or she wishes before it crosses the balkline. The batter then gets another turn at bat.

Scoring

1. Successful grounder—one point. The batter scores one point when an infielder fails to handle cleanly his or her grounder within the infield area. Only one player may field the ball. If the ball is fielded properly, the batter is out.
2. Line drive in infield area—one point. A ball from the bat that lands first in the infield area can be handled only on the first bounce for an out. If it bounces in front of the balkline, it is classed as a grounder and can be handled on any bounce. Any line drive caught on the fly also is an out.
3. Fly ball in infield area—one point. Any fly ball in the infield area must be caught or the batter scores one point. The ball must be caught legally by the first person touching it.
4. Two-bagger—two points. Any fly ball, line drive or not, that lights fairly in the outfield area without being caught scores two points. If it is caught, the batter is out.
5. Home run—three points. Any fly ball driven over the heads of the farthest outfielder in that area scores a home run.

Three outs can constitute an inning, or all batters can be allowed one turn at bat and then change to the field.

A new set of infielders should be in place for each inning. The old set goes to the outfield. Pitchers should be limited to one inning. They also take a turn at bat.

Teaching Suggestions

1. Many games of this type take special fields, either rectangular or a narrowed-angle type. This game was selected because it uses the regular softball field with the added lines. The lines can be drawn with a stick or can be marked with regular marking methods.
2. The pitcher has to decide whether or not he or she should stop the ball. If the ball goes beyond the restraining line, even though he or she touched it, the ball is in play.

Station Organization: Batter Ball can be modified to use as a station in rotational teaching with the emphasis on individual batting and squad organization. One member of the squad would be at bat and gets a definite number (say, five) chances to score. He or she keeps his or her own point total. The other squad members occupy the necessary game positions.

Home Run

Playing Area: Softball diamond (only first base is used).
Players: 4 to 10.
Supplies: Softball, bat.
Skills: Most softball skills, modified base running.

This game can be played with as few as four children. The needed players are a batter, a catcher, a pitcher, and one fielder. The other players are fielders, although some can take positions in the infield.

The batter hits a regular pitch and on a fair ball must run to first base and back home before the ball can be returned to the catcher.

The batter is out when:

1. A fly ball, fair or foul, is caught.
2. He or she strikes out.
3. On a fair ball, the ball beats him or her back to home plate.

To keep skillful players from staying in too long at bat, a rule can be made that, after a certain number of home runs, the batter automatically must take a place in the field.

A rotation (work-up) system should be set up. The batter should go to right field, move to center, and then to left field. The rotation continues through the third-base position, shortstop, second base, first base, pitcher, and catcher. The catcher becomes the next batter. Naturally, the number of positions is dependent upon the number of players in the game. If there are enough players, there can be an additional batter waiting to take his or her turn.

The game can be played with three youngsters, eliminating the catcher. With only one fielder, the pitcher covers home plate.

The first-base distance should be far enough to be a challenge but close enough so a well-hit ball scores a home run. The distance would be dependent on the number playing and the capacity of the children.

Variations
1. It is possible to play this game more like softball, allowing the batter to stop at first if another batter is up.
2. A fly ball caught by a player puts the fielder directly to bat. The batter then takes his or her place at the end of the rotation, and the other players rotate up to the position of the fielder who caught the ball. The rule may cause children to scramble and fight for fly balls, which is a situation not desired in softball. It should be ruled that the ball belongs to the player into whose territory it falls.
3. *Triangle Ball:* For this game, first base and third base are brought in toward each other, narrowing the playing field. Second base is not used. Thus, the game gets its name from the triangle formed by home plate and the two bases. The batter must circle first and third bases and return home before the ball reaches home plate. The game also can be played with as few as three players, with the pitcher covering home plate.

Tee Ball

Playing Area: Softball field.
Players: Two regular softball teams, but numbers can vary.

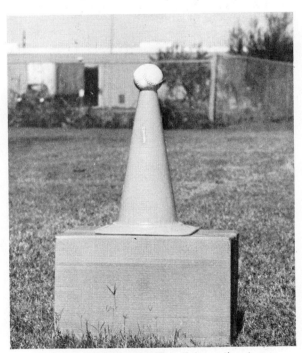

An Improvised Batting Tee (for another type, see page 562)

Supplies: Softball, bat, batting tee.
Skills: Most softball skills (except pitching and stealing bases), hitting a ball from a tee.

The game is an excellent variation of softball and is played under its rules, with the following exceptions.

Instead of hitting a pitched ball, the batter hits the ball from a tee. The catcher places the ball on the tee. After the batter hits the ball, the play is the same as softball. With no pitching, there is no stealing. A runner stays on the base until the ball is hit by the batter.

A fielder occupies the position normally held by the pitcher. His or her primary duty is to field bunts and any ground balls he or she can reach and to back up the positions in the field on throws in the same way a pitcher would normally position himself or herself.

Teams can play regular innings for three outs or change to the field after each player has had a turn at bat.

A tee can be purchased or made from radiator hose. If the tee is not adjustable, it would be better to have three different sizes available.

Tee Ball has many advantages. There are no strikeouts, every child hits the ball, there is no waiting for the pitcher-catcher duel, and there are many opportunities for fielding.

The batter should take his or her position far enough back of the tee so that, in stepping forward to swing, he or she will hit the ball slightly in front of himself or herself.

Kick Pin Softball

Playing Area: Softball diamond; 45-foot base distances; 20-foot pitching distance.
Players: Two teams, 8 to 12 on a side (catcher, pitcher, three basemen, and the rest fielders).
Supplies: One soccer ball, four Indian clubs or cones.
Skills: Kicking a rolling ball, throwing, catching, running bases.

The Indian clubs or cones are placed on the outside corner of each base and in the middle of home plate. The batter kicks a ball rolled by the pitcher (who aims at the Indian club or cone on home plate). The kick must be a fair ball. The batter *circles around* the outside of the bases and finally touches home plate. In the meantime, the fielders retrieve the ball and pass it successively to the basemen on first, second, third, and then home. As each baseman receives the ball, he or she kicks the club down and passes to the next base.

The batter is out when:
1. A pitched ball knocks down the club on home plate.
2. The ball is caught on the fly by a fielder.
3. The batter knocks over any club during his or her time at bat.

4. A second foul ball occurs any time at bat.
5. If the ball, in its rotation from first base to the other bases in succession, gets ahead of the runner and the baseman kicks the club down.

The batter scores a run only on a home run, that is, beating the ball to home plate.

The game can be played by innings with three outs, or it can be played so each player of the team at bat gets a turn before changing to the field.

Teaching Suggestions
1. Indian clubs stand with difficulty outside. A 3-inch square of plywood screwed to the bottom of each club will make it stand easily. Cones stand better.
2. Old bowling pins generally can be secured from a local bowling alley. The industrial arts department can aid in restoring a flat bottom for better standing. (See page 563.) The pitcher should use judgment in rolling the ball. The fun comes in the kick and the resultant run and not the duel between the batter and the pitcher. This can be controlled somewhat by the addition of a rule that if a certain number of balls (not hitting the club if the batters let the ball go by) are thrown, the batter gets a free kick. The kick would be a placekick with the ball placed just to the left of home plate where the batting box for the right-handed batter is located.

Variations
1. Hit Pin Softball is about the same game, except, instead of kicking the club, the club is knocked over with the ball held in the hands.
2. Instead of counting home runs, a point can be given for each base rounded before the club is kicked by the baseman holding the ball. A home run scores four points under this counting system.

Scrub (Work-up)

Playing Area: Softball field.
Players: 7 to 15.
Supplies: Softball, bat.
Skills: Most softball skills.

The predominant feature of Scrub is the rotation of the players. The game is played with regular softball rules, with each individual more or less playing for himself or herself. There are at least two batters, generally three. A catcher, pitcher, and first baseman are essential. The remainder of the players assume the other positions. Whenever the batter is out, he or she goes to a position in right field. All other players move up one position, with the catcher becoming a batter. Thus, the first baseman becomes a pitcher, the pitcher moves to the catcher, and all others move up one place.

Variations
1. If there are only two batters, then one base is

sufficient. The runners use only first base and return back to home plate.
2. If a fly ball is caught, the fielder and batter exchange positions.

Sixth Grade

Slow-Pitch Softball

The major differences between regular softball and Slow-Pitch Softball lie in the pitching, but there are other modifications to the game. With slower pitching, there is more hitting and thus more action on the bases and in the field as well. Outfielders are a very important part of the game, since there are many long drives. Rule changes from the game of official softball are as follows.
1. The pitch must be a slow pitch. Any other pitch is illegal and is called a ball. The pitch must be slow with an arc of 1 foot. However, it must not rise over 10 feet from the ground. The legality of the pitch depends upon the umpire's judgment call.
2. There are 10 players instead of 9, the extra player playing in the outfield and called the roving fielder. The extra player positions himself or herself to handle line drives hit just over the infielders.
3. The batter must take a full swing at the ball. He or she is out if he or she chops at the ball or bunts.
4. If the batter is hit by a pitched ball, the batter is not entitled to first base. The pitch is merely called a ball.
5. Balls and strikes are called as in softball.
6. The runner must hold base until the pitch has reached or passed home plate. No stealing is permitted.

Teaching Suggestion: It may be desirable to shorten the pitching distance somewhat. Much of the success of the game depends upon the pitcher's ability to get the ball over the plate.

Babe Ruth Ball

Babe Ruth, the former New York Yankee Sultan of Swat, held the all-time total home run record (714) until it was broken recently by Hank Aaron of the Atlanta Braves. The home run that most people remember occurred during the 1932 World Series games at the Chicago Cubs' ball park. The Chicago fans had been riding the Babe quite hard. In anger, he dramatically pointed to the center field stands and proceeded to drive the ball into the center field stands. Players can imitate Babe Ruth by pointing to the direction they wish to hit.

Playing Area: Baseball diamond.
Players: Batter, pitcher, three outfielders.
Supplies: Bat, ball, four cones or other markers.
Skills: Batting, pitching, fielding.

The normal three outfield zones—left field, center field, and right field—are divided by four cones. It is helpful when the foul lines have been lined, but the cones can define them.

The batter calls the field to which he or she intends to hit. The pitcher throws controlled pitches so the batter can hit. The batter remains in position as long as he or she can hit to the designated field. Field choices must be rotated. The batter gets only one swing to make a successful hit. The batter may allow a ball to go by, but, if he or she swings, it counts as a try. There is no base running. Rotate players.

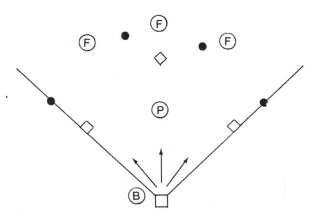

Teaching Suggestions: Children play this informally on sandlots, with a variety of rules. Some possibilities to consider—what happens when a fly ball is caught? What limitations should be made on hitting easy grounders? Let the players decide about these points and others not covered by the stated rules.

Hurry Baseball (One Pitch)

Playing Area: Softball diamond. Shortened pitching distance.
Players: Two teams, 8 to 12 on each team.
Supplies: Softball, bat.
Skills: Slow pitch, most baseball skills, except stealing bases and bunting.

Hurry Baseball demands rapid changes from batting to fielding, and vice versa. The game is like regular softball, with the following exceptions.

1. The pitcher is from the team at bat. He or she must not interfere with, or touch, a batted ball on the penalty of the batter being called out.
2. The team coming to bat does not wait for the fielding team to get set. Since it has its own pitcher, the pitcher gets the ball to the batter just as quickly as the batter can grab a bat and get ready. The fielding team has to hustle to get out to their places.
3. Only one pitch is allowed to a batter. He or she

must hit a fair ball or he or she is out. The pitch is made from about two-thirds of the normal pitching distance.
4. No stealing is permitted.
5. No bunting is permitted. The batter must take a full swing.

The game is good fun and provides fast activity in the fast changes that need to be made immediately when the third out has been made. Teams in the field learn to put the next hitter as catcher, so he or she can immediately take his or her place in the batter's box when the third out is made. Batters must bat in order. Scoring follows regular softball rules.

Three-Team Softball

Playing Area: Softball diamond.
Players: 12 to 15, divided into three teams.
Supplies: Mask, ball, bat.
Skills: All softball skills.

This version of softball works well with 12 players, a number considered too few to divide into two effective fielding teams. The players are divided into three teams. The rules of softball apply, with the following exceptions.

1. One team is at bat, one team covers the infield (including the catcher), and the third team provides the outfielders and the pitcher.
2. The team at bat must bat in a definite order. This means that instances, due to the few batters on each side, could occur when the person due to bat is on a base. He or she must be replaced by a player not on base, so he or she can take a turn at bat.
3. After three outs, the teams rotate, with the outfield moving to the infield, the infield taking a turn at bat, and the batters going to the outfield.
4. An inning is over when all three teams have batted.
5. The pitcher should be limited to pitching one inning only. A player may repeat as pitcher only after all members of his or her team have had a chance to pitch.

Base-circling Contests

Playing Area: Softball diamond.
Players: Four squads (entire class).
Supplies: Track starter.
Skill: Base running.

Each squad is assigned one of the bases of a diamond, with runners of each squad running as individuals in turn. For best results, all bases should be the same. Bases should be anchored or be the nonslip-rubber type.

The squad leader arranges his or her players in a definite numerical sequence without respect to the order of other squads. Once arranged, the order may not be changed. This avoids jockeying of positions for best advantage.

The number-one runner from each of the squads takes his or her place on the base paths. Runners may start in any manner they wish but must be in contact with the base.

Scoring

First place—four points.
Second place—three points.
Third place—two points.
Fourth place—one point.

Players must touch all bases on penalty of disqualification. Each player scores points for his or her team according to the place he or she finishes in his or her heat.

Teaching Suggestions

1. The bases need to be fastened securely to avoid inequities and falls. Having bases painted on a black or hardtop surface is a solution.
2. Judging the four place finishers at the four bases, scattered as they are, must be anticipated. The instructor should stand behind one base, out of the way, sight toward the opposite base, and see the other bases out of the sides of his or her field of vision. A second judge viewing from the opposite diagonal would be of help. Captains from each squad can judge whether or not the runner touched the particular base assigned. The purpose of giving a point for fourth place differentiates between a successful and an unsuccessful run.

Variation: If four stopwatches are available, places can be determined by time.

TESTS FOR SOFTBALL SKILLS

Tests for softball skills include throwing (accuracy and distance), fielding grounders, circling the bases, and pitching.

Throw for Accuracy

A target with three concentric circles of 18, 36, and 54 inches is drawn on a wall. Scoring is three, two and one point, respectively for the circles.

Five throws are given to each child for a possible score of 15. Balls hitting a line score for the higher number.

Instead of the suggested target, a tire could be hung. Scoring would allow 2 points for a throw through the tire and 1 point for just hitting the tire. A maximum score of 10 points is possible with this system.

Throw for Distance

Each child is allowed three throws, and the longest throw on the fly is recorded as his or her distance.

Fielding Grounders

A file of players is stationed behind a restraining line. A thrower is about 30 feet in front of this line. Each player in turn fields five ground balls. His or her score is the number of balls he or she fields cleanly.

It is recognized there will be inconsistencies in the throw and bounce of the ground balls served up for fielding. If the opportunity obviously was not a fair one, the child should get another opportunity.

Circling the Bases

A diamond with four bases is needed, plus a stopwatch for timing. The object is to time the runner circling the bases. Two runners can run at one time by starting from opposite corners of the diamond. Two watches are needed with this system.

Variation: The batter can bunt a pitched ball and run around the bases. The timing starts with the bunt and finishes when the batter touches home plate.

Pitching

Pitching is one of the easier skills to test in softball and certainly is one of the most popular with children. There are two basic methods used for testing.

1. Allow a certain number of pitches at a target. Scoring is on the basis of the number of strikes that can be thrown out of a designated number of pitches.
2. Regular pitching, as if to a batter, counting balls and strikes. Batters would be either struck out or walked. The test score would be how many batters the child was able to strike

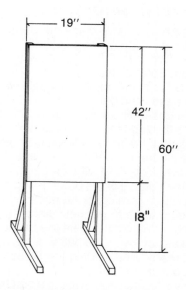

Old Woody Pitching Target

out from a given number at bat. This could be expressed as a percentage.

A target is needed and should be 19 inches wide and 42 inches high. This can be devised in a number of ways. It can be outlined temporarily on a wall with chalk, or a more permanent means would be to use paint. The lower portion of the target should be about 18 inches above the ground or floor. The target could be constructed from plywood or wood. Some means of support or hanging would be needed.

Scoring is based upon whether or not the pitch entered the strike zone as shown by the target. The boundaries of the target should be counted as good. The pitching distance should be normal (35 feet), and regular pitching rules should be observed.

Old Woody

Old Woody is the name of a pitching target that is in the form of a stand that can be moved from school to school. The target size is shown on the opposite page. A sturdy frame holds the target and allows it to be used in most any spot. The contest is based upon the number of strikeouts a pitcher can throw to an imaginary batter. He or she continues pitching until he or she walks the batter. Other variations could be used.

Thirty-one

Track and Field Activities

Track and field activities carry much of their own motivation. Extensive television coverage, international competitions, and the impact of the Olympics all lift track and field to a high status as a prestige activity. These factors, coupled with the urge in boys and girls to run, jump, hurdle, and race against others, make track and field activities an exciting part of the program.

In particular, sprinting techniques are important, with instruction centering on the correct form for starting, accelerating, and sprinting. Speed and quickness are important movement attributes that govern the degree of success in many play and sports activities. In many nations, children are taught to sprint just as they are taught to write.

All children can benefit from track and field instruction. Personal values and goals for individuals are many. A child can:

1. Learn proper techniques for better performance, leading to more enjoyment and improved motor patterns.
2. Seek improvement over prior performances and derive satisfaction from such self-improvement. Since all track and field performances are measurable, noting and recording improvement is quite feasible.
3. Be stimulated to practice and run on his or her own. Track and field activities, except for relays, are individual events and have carry-over value into the child's free time. Jogging habits can be established.
4. Make an individual contribution to a team or group achievement.
5. Win an event or beat a selected opponent.
6. Recognize that success in track and field activities comes only through proper effort involving physical accomplishments, emotional dedication, and healthful living habits.

Competition is important but must not be overemphasized. More attention should be given to improvement and progress toward a personal goal than toward beating fellow classmates. However, the basic emphasis of track and field—the desire to come out on top—must not be lost. The instructional program should have as one of its goals the stimulation of each student to good effort and "giving it a good try."

The program for the elementary grades in track and field should consist of short sprints (40 to 100 yards), running and standing long jumps, high jumps, hop-step-and-jumps, and relays. Jogging and distance running should be encouraged throughout the program. The stress should be primarily on practice and accomplishment, but some modified competition as in cross-country is quite acceptable. The idea that distance running is harmful for children is fast disappearing. Children should learn to stride for distance to establish pace. Relays should be an important inclusion. Hurdling can be included when the equipment problem can be solved.

Children should learn the difference between walking, sprinting, running, striding (pace), and jogging. Rules for the different events also should be covered.

Since few elementary schools have a permanent track, laying out and lining the track (see page 529) each year can be a valuable educational experience.

Some type of culminating meet is desirable to provide a goal for participants and a finishing touch to the track and field instruction. A discussion of meets of this nature is included at the end of this chapter.

EMPHASIS IN EACH GRADE LEVEL

Fourth Grade

The fourth-grade program should stress running short distances, learning starts, and participating in the two long jumps. Some light running for distance, similar to jogging, can be included.

Fifth Grade

More serious efforts for form begin in the fifth grade. The high jump, scissors style, can introduce the students to this activity. Experimentation can be made with other styles. Students should begin to use check marks with the running long jump. Striding for distance should be started, as well as relay work, including baton passing. The sprinter's start should be emphasized.

Sixth Grade

Hurdling, primarily for practice, is an addition to the list of activities learned in the fourth and fifth grades. This activity should use modified hurdles. In the high jump, the critical techniques in the Straddle Roll and the Western Roll should be brought out.

An effort should be made to develop pace in distance running without strong elements of competition. Relaxed, flowing running should be the goal.

The hop-step-and-jump extends the range of jumping activities. Relays and baton exchange are given attention. Sprinting should emphasize the start, acceleration, and drive for the finish line. The Potato Shuttle Race adds a novel event to the program.

INSTRUCTIONAL PROCEDURES

1. Spiked running shoes should not be permitted. Many light gym or running shoes are available and are quite suitable. Spiked shoes create a safety problem and also give an unfair advantage to children whose parents can afford them. Running in bare feet is not recommended.

2. Form should be stressed at all times, but it should be appropriate to the individual. The child should be brought to the realization that good results in track and field are due to good form and diligent practice. Each child should be encouraged to develop good technique within his or her own style. Observation of any event at a track meet bears out the fact that many individual styles are successful.

3. The program should offer something for all—boys and girls, highly skilled and low skilled, and those with physical problems. Children with weight problems need particular attention and may need special goals. Particularly, they need to be stimulated and encouraged, since their participation will be minimal if little attention is paid to them. Special events and goals could be established for children with handicaps.

4. The amount of activity, particularly distance work, should be built up progressively. A period of conditioning should precede any competition or all-out performance, such as the 1600-meter run-walk test. If this procedure is followed, the children will show few adverse effects.

5. Warm-up activity should precede track and field work. This should include jogging and bending and stretching exercises.

6. Pits for long and high jumping must be main-

Suggested Track and Field Program

GRADE	FOURTH	FIFTH	SIXTH
Skills Track	40-60 yard dashes Standing start Sprinter's start Jogging and cross-country running	50-80 yard dashes Sprinter's start Baton passing Relays Striding for distance Jogging and cross-country running	60-100 yard dashes Sprinter's start Baton passing Relays Striding for distance Potato Shuttle Race Hurdling Jogging and cross-country running
Skills Field	Long jump Standing long jump	Long jump Standing long jump High jump	Long jump Standing long jump High jump Hop-step-and-jump

tained properly. They should contain sand, sawdust mixtures, or loose dirt for long jumping. For high jumping, mats by themselves or placed over secured inner tubes or tires are satisfactory. Commercial landing platforms are excellent but expensive.

7. The metal high jump crossbar is economical in the long run, but it will bend. Sometimes, bamboo poles can be secured from rug and carpet establishments, where they are used in the center of rolls of carpet during shipment. A satisfactory substitute can be made from nylon cord with a weight on each end to keep it taut and still allow it to be displaced. In Europe, small leather bags with shot are used as weights to keep the ropes level. Magic ropes (rubberized stretch ropes) also can be adapted for low-level jumping practice.

8. The use of a track starter signal is recommended. In most competitions, starting is with a starter's gun. The clapboard track starter approximates the sound and does not have the drawback of requiring expensive ammunition. See page 569 for diagram that shows how to construct this starting device.

9. The goal of the program should be to allow each student to develop at his or her own individual rate. The instructional sessions should be strenuous enough to assure some overload but not to the point where the students become discouraged or physically ill. The instructor needs to be perceptive enough to determine whether the students are working too hard or too little. Attention must be given to those who appear disinterested, dejected, emotionally upset, or wishing to withdraw or quit the activity.

ORGANIZING FOR INSTRUCTION

Prior Preparation

Track and field differs from other areas in the elementary school program in that considerable prior preparation must be made before the classes begin.

1. A track must be laid out when there is no permanent one. This can be done with marking lime. Lanes for sprints are of value but not an absolute requirement.

2. A hurdling area should be similarly outlined in an appropriate area.

3. Separate pits should be placed for the running long jump, the high jump, and the hop-step-and-jump. These should be spaced, so there is a minimum of interference between activities.

4. High jump equipment should be checked. Needed are standards with pins, crossbars

(or cord substitute), and impact-absorbing pads.

5. Takeoff boards for both the long jump and the hop-step-and-jump should be in place. Jumping without the use of a takeoff board is not a satisfying experience. Pits should have fresh building sand of a coarse variety.

6. Accessory materials should be assembled, including batons, starter clapboards, watches, hurdles, and finish line yarn.

7. Starting blocks are a debatable item. There is no doubt they add interest to the program, but their use and adjustment are sometimes difficult for the elementary school student.

Organizing the Students

Height and weight are factors affecting the degree of physical performance in an activity like track and field. More efficient instruction is possible when the children are grouped on some basis of height and weight. They also should be arranged by sex. The following groups can be formed to serve as a basis of the instruction.

Group 1: Heavier and taller boys.
Group 2: Shorter and lighter boys.
Group 3: Heavier and taller girls.
Group 4: Shorter and lighter girls.

A simple way to form groups is to rank the boys and girls separately according to the following formula, which yields a standard number.

Score = 10 × the age (nearest half-year)
+ weight in pounds

After the boys have been ranked, the upper 50 percent are assigned to group 1 and the remainder to group 2. A similar division is made with the girls. Some decisions regarding borderline cases must be made.

Some track and field skills can be practiced with single-activity organization. Starting skills can be practiced with perhaps one-quarter of the children at a time. The four groups can practice baton-passing skills at one time. Striding for distance can be practiced with the selected groups running as a unit in turn.

The predominant plan of organization should be multiple activity. Four stations can utilize selected group organization, but more stations are desirable. If eight stations are used, two stations can be assigned to each group. Stations can be selected from the following skills: (1) starting and sprinting; (2) baton passing; (3) standing long jump; (4) running long jump; (5) hop-step-and-jump; (6) high jump; (7) hurdles; (8) striding for distance, pace judgment; and (9) Potato Shuttle Race.

In any one class session, it is generally not educationally sound to have children practice at all stations. The entire circuit can be completed during additional class sessions. It is helpful to have written directions at each station which state what is to be accomplished as well as technique points to be observed.

In the later instructional sequences of the activity, on choice days the student can select the skills he or she desires to practice. With guidance, the choice system could embrace the entire program, with children on each day determining those areas in which they would like to concentrate. This can be related to the individualized or contract type of instruction.

TRACK AND FIELD SKILLS

Standing Start

The standing start should be practiced and the best techniques employed, since this type of start has a variety of uses in physical education activities. Many children find it more comfortable to use this start, rather than the sprint start. However, as soon as practical, children should accept and employ the sprint start for track work.

The feet, in the standing start, should be in a comfortable half-stride position. Avoid an extremely long stride position. The body leans forward, so the body center of gravity is forward. The weight is on the toes, and the knees are slightly flexed. The arms can be down or hanging slightly back.

Standing Start

Norwegian Start

The Norwegians use the standing start in a novel way.

Command Action
"On your mark," Runner takes a position at the starting line with left foot forward.
"get set," Right hand is placed on the left knee and the left hand is carried back for a thrust.
"go." Left hand comes forward, coupled with a drive by the right foot.

Norwegian Start

The advantages claimed for this start are that it forces a body lean and makes use of the forward thrust of the arm coordinated with the step of the opposite foot.

Sprinter's Starts

There are several different kinds of sprinter's starts, but it is best to concentrate on a single type. To take the "on the mark" position the toe of the front foot is placed from 4 to 12 inches behind the starting line. The thumb and first finger are placed just behind the line, with the other fingers adding support. The knee of the rear leg is placed just opposite the front foot or ankle.

"On Your Mark"

"Get Set"

For the "get set" position, the seat is raised so it is slightly higher than the shoulders, the knee of the rear leg is raised off the ground, and the shoulders are moved forward over the hands. The weight is evenly distributed over the hands and feet.

On the "go" signal, push sharply off with both feet, with the front leg straightening, as the back leg comes forward for a step. The body should rise gradually and not pop up suddenly.

The instructor should watch for stumbling action on the first few steps. This is due to too much weight being on the hands during the "get set" position.

Sprinting Form

The body leans forward, with the arms swinging in opposition to the legs. The arms are bent at the elbows and swing from the shoulders in a forward and backward plane, not across the body. Forceful arm action aids sprinting action. The knees are lifted sharply forward and upward and brought down with a vigorous pushing motion, with a forceful push by the toes. Sprinting should be a driving and striding motion as opposed to the inefficient pulling action shown by some runners.

Good Sprinting Form

Running Form

In running form, as compared to sprinting techniques, the body is more erect and the motion of the arms more or less takes care of itself. Pace is an important consideration. In running, concentrate on the following: the quality of lightness and ease, the quality of relaxation and looseness, good striding action, and slight body lean and good head position.

How the foot meets the ground generally takes care of itself. Some children like to run up on their toes; others use more of the foot.

Good Running Form

Baton Passing

The runner exchanges the baton from his or her left hand to the right hand of the runner ahead. The runner should carry the baton like a candle when passing. The receiver reaches back with his or her right hand, with the fingers pointed down and thumb to the inside, and begins to move ahead when the coming runner is 3 to 5 yards back of him or her. The receiver grasps the baton and immediately shifts it to the left hand while moving. The exchange to the next runner should be made on the move, with the front runner timing his or her start and increase of speed to the pace of the runner coming in. If the baton is dropped, it must be picked up or the team is disqualified.

An alternate way of receiving the baton is to reach back with the hand facing up. The first method is considered more suitable for sprint relays.

With either method, the initial runner has the baton in his left hand as he or she starts the race.

Standing Long Jump

In both the standing and running long jump, the measurement is made from the takeoff board or line to the nearest point on the ground touched by the jumper. It is important for the children not to fall or step backward after making the jump. In the standing long jump, the performer toes the line with the feet flat on the ground and fairly close together. His or her arms are brought forward in a preliminary swing and then swung down and back. The jump is made with both feet as the arms are swung forcibly forward to assist in lifting the body upward and forward. While in the air, the knees should be brought upward and forward with the arms forward to sustain balance.

Standing Long Jump (note hands and arms well back)

Long Jump

A short run is needed and should be planned so that the toes of the jumping foot contact the board in a natural stride. The jumper takes off with one foot and should strive for height. The landing is made on both feet after the knees have been brought forward. The landing should be made in a forward direction, not sideward.

More efficient jumping is done when a check point is used. The check point can be established about halfway down the run. Competitors can help each other by marking the check point for a jumper during the run prior to the jump. Each jumper should know how many steps back from the takeoff board his or her check point is located. On the run for the jump he or she hits the mark with the appropriate foot (right or left), so he or she reaches the board with the correct foot in normal stride for the jump.

The jumper should be at full speed when he or she arrives at his or her check point. The last four strides taken before the board should be relaxed and in readiness for the takeoff to be made. The last stride can be shortened somewhat.

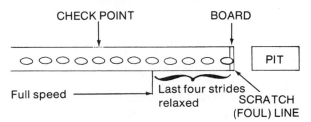

A fair jump is made back of the scratch line. A foul (scratch) jump is called if the jumping step is beyond the scratch line or the jumper runs into or through the pit. Each contestant is given a certain number of trials (jumps). If a jumper runs into the pit or steps over the scratch line while jumping, this counts as one of the trials. Measurement is from the scratch line to the nearest point of touch.

Hop-Step-and-Jump

This event is increasing in popularity, particularly because it is included in Olympic competition. A takeoff board and a jumping pit are needed. The distance from the takeoff board to the pit should be a distance that the poorer jumpers can make. The event begins with a run, similar to the broad jump. The takeoff is with one foot, and the jumper must light on the same foot to complete the hop. He or she then takes a step followed by a jump. The event finishes like the long jump with a landing on both feet.

The pattern can be changed to begin with the left foot. A check point should be used, similar to that for the long jump.

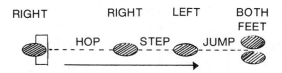

The jumper must not step over the takeoff board in the first hop, under penalty of fouling. Distance is measured from the front of the takeoff board to the closest place where the body touches. This is usually a mark made by one of the heels, but it could be a mark made by an arm or another part of the body if the jumper landed poorly and fell backward toward the takeoff board.

Jump Combinations

Different jumping combinations can be set up to challenge the children. Combinations such as two or three standing long jumps and up to five hops in succession can be used.

Working with the High Jump

Three styles of high jumping are presented. There has been some debate regarding the desirability of teaching the scissors style. Some maintain that this is a logical and relatively easy way for the children to jump and that the technique has utilitarian value outside of track and field work, while others believe that a youngster trained to jump this way would have to change his or her technique if he or she became seriously interested in high jumping.

High jump techniques are developed by effective practice. The bar should be at a height that offers some challenge but allows concentration on technique rather than on height. Too much emphasis on competition for height quickly eliminates the poorer jumpers, who are the ones who need the practice the most. The practice of keeping the entire class together on a single high jump facility is poor methodology. This concentrated arrangement determines who are the best jumpers in the class but does little else.

High Jump – Scissors Style

The high jump bar is approached from a slight angle. The takeoff is by the outside leg (the one farthest from the bar). The near leg is lifted and goes over first, followed quickly by the rear leg in a looping movement. There should be a good upward kick with the front leg, together with an upward thrust of the arms. The knees should be straightened at the highest point of the jump. The landing is made on the lead foot followed by the rear foot.

High Jump – Straddle Roll

Approach should be made from the left side at an angle of no more than 45 degrees. There are four parts to the jump, with respect to coaching.

1. The Gather: The last three steps must be fast and vigorous, with the body leaning back a bit. The takeoff is on the left foot.

2. The Kick: The right leg is kicked vigorously, as the plant with the jumping foot is made.

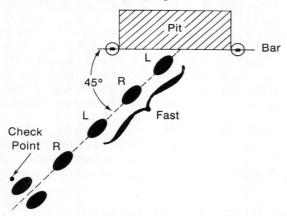

3. Arm Movement: An abrupt lift with both arms is made, with the left arm reaching over the bar and the right moving straight up. This puts the jumper in straddle position as he or she goes over.

4. The Back Leg Clearance: This is accomplished by straightening the body, rolling the hips to the right (over the bar), or dropping the right shoulder.

Good pit protection is needed in the form of mats or foam rubber pads to cushion the fall. While the basics are presented, each jumper should attempt to develop his or her own unique style.

High Jump – Western Roll

The approach, gather, and kick are the same as for the Straddle Roll. The jumper in the Western Roll, instead of being face down to the bar, clears the bar by lying parallel to the bar on his or her side. The left arm is pointed down at the legs just at crossing and then lowered. The head is turned toward the pit after clearance and the landing is made on both hands and the left (takeoff) foot.

Hurdling

Hurdling is an interesting activity, but it poses equipment problems. Hurdles can be formed by shaping electric conduit pipe (see page 564 for diagram). Hurdles using wands supported on blocks or cones also can be used. Hurdles should begin at low heights (12 inches) and move to the 18-inch height. They should be placed about 25 feet apart. A 60-yard course can be established as diagrammed, using six hurdles.

Start X | 25′ | 25′ | 25′ | 25′ | 25′ | 25′ | 30′ | Finish

←————————180′ (60 yds.)————————→

A single or double hurdle course can be set up, primarily for practice. If there is competition, then it should be on a time basis. If regular hurdles are available, then practice on the lower temporary hurdles should precede work on regular hurdles.

Children should recognize that hurdling is akin to sprinting and that speed is essential. The child should go over the hurdle with the same leading foot each time.

A hurdles course or practice area can be set up in a place other than on the track. In this way, the hurdles can be left in place for more concentrated use.

Potato Shuttle Race

This race is an adaptation of an old American custom during frontier harvest celebrations; a number of potatoes were placed in a line at various distances for each competitor, who was at a starting line. The winner was the one who brought in his or her potatoes first, one at a time. He or she won a sack of potatoes for the effort.

The modern version of this race uses blocks instead of potatoes, and each runner runs the following course.

Start   Box

X | □   ○   ○   ○   ○

(all distances between the start, box, and blocks—15′)

A box is placed 15 feet in front of the starting line, with four blocks in individual circles the same distance apart. The runner begins behind the starting line. He or she puts the blocks, one at a time, in the box and finishes across the original line. He or she can bring the blocks back one at a time to the box in any order he or she wishes. All blocks must be put inside the box. The box should be 12 by 12 inches, with a depth of 3 to 6 inches. Blocks must be placed or dropped, not thrown, into the box.

Teaching Suggestions: The most practical way to organize competition in this race is to time each individual and award places on the basis of elapsed time, since the race is physically challenging. Be sure to make clear to the competitors that each is running individually and should strive for his or her best time, regardless of his or her position or finish in the race. Timers should act as judges to see that the blocks are placed or dropped inside the box. A block that lands outside the box must be placed inside the box before the student goes after another block. Blocks should be about 2 inches on a side, but this can vary.

When a runner picks up a block, it is best that he or she changes it to the other hand immediately. This avoids making an unnecessary turn when dropping the block into the box.

The race can be run as a relay. The first runner of the relay brings all the blocks in one at a time and tags off the second member of the relay team, who returns the blocks one at a time to the respective spots. The third relay member brings the blocks in, and the fourth puts them out again. For this race, it is necessary to have pie tins, floor tiles (9 by 9 inches), or some other items in addition to the box, so, when the blocks are put out by the second and fourth runners, it can be determined definitely that a block rests on its proper spot. A block must be on its spot in proper fashion before the runner brings out the next block.

Pace Running

Children should get some experience in running for moderate distances in an effort to acquire some knowledge of pace. The running should be loose and relaxed. Distances up to 1600 meters may be a part of the work.

A fun activity is allowing children to estimate pace and time. On a circular track, at a set distance, let each runner stipulate a target time and have him or her see how close he or she can come to it.

To check time, each runner has a partner. Someone with a stopwatch counts out loudly the elapsed time second by second, and the partner notes the runner's time as he or she crosses the finish line.

Jogging

Jogging principles and development were covered in chapter eight.

Relays

Two types of relays are generally included in a program of track and field for children.

Circular Relays

These relays make use of the regular circular track. The baton exchange technique is important, and practice is needed for this technique.

On a 200-meter or 220-yard track (see diagrams), relays can be organized in a number of ways, depending upon how many runners are spaced for one lap. The relay can be organized with four runners to each lap, each running one-quarter of the way; two to a lap, each running one-half the distance; or each runner running one complete lap. In these races, each member of the relay team runs the same distance. Relays also can be organized so that members run different distances. Batons should be used.

Shuttle Relays

Since the children are running toward each other, one great difficulty in running relays is control of the exchange. In the excitement, the next runner may leave too early, and the tag or exchange is made ahead of the restraining line. A high jump standard can be used to prevent early exchanges by having the runner await the tag with his or her arm held around the standard. A difficulty with this is the provision of enough standards for all the teams.

For this type of relay, a track facility is not needed. These relays can be run on most any flat area.

A SUGGESTED TRACK FACILITY

The presence of a track facility is a boon to the track program. Few elementary schools have the funds or space for a quarter-mile track. A shorter track facility that can be installed permanently with curbs or temporarily with marking lime is suggested. Discarded fire hoses could be used to

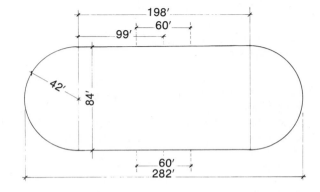

One-Eighth-Mile Track (220 yards)

mark the curbs and could be installed each spring with spikes.

The facility is one-eighth mile in length and has a straightaway of 66 yards in length, which is ample for the 60-yard dash. It allows flexibility in relays, since relay legs of 55, 110, and 220 yards are possible.

Since the United States is converting to the metric system, a 200-meter track (see the diagram) may be preferable to the 220-yard track.

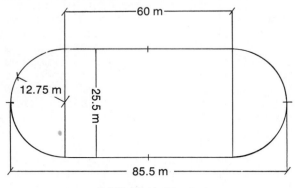

A 200-Meter Track

Sixth-grade classes could profit in number concepts by helping lay out the track and calculating the distances from the dimensions.

INTERVAL TRAINING

A track of the smaller size facilitates the interval type of training. Children should know this technique, which consists of running at a set speed for a stipulated distance and then walking around back to the starting point. Children on the one-eighth-mile track could run for 110 yards and then walk the remainder of the distance back to the starting point. This should be repeated a number of times. Or the child could run the entire 220 yards and then take a timed rest, after which he or she could repeat the performance. Breathing should return to near normal before he or she attempts the next 220-yard chore.

CONDUCTING TRACK AND FIELD DAYS

Track and field days can range in organization from competition within a single classroom to competition between selected classes, from an all-school playday type of meet, between representatives of different schools, to an area or all-city meet. In informal meets within a class or between a few classes, all children should participate in one or more events. Each student can be limited to two individual events plus one relay event, with no substitutions permitted. An additional condition

could be imposed that the competitor for the individual events enter only one track event and one field event.

For larger meets, boys and girls should qualify separately, since competition should not be mixed. Two means of qualification are suggested.
1. Qualifying times and performance standards can be set at the start of the season. Any student meeting or bettering these times or performances is qualified to compete.
2. In an all-school meet, first- and second-place winners in each class competition qualify for entry. For a district or an all-city meet, first- and second-place winners from each all-school meet become eligible.

Generally, competition is organized in each event by sex and grade. This does not eliminate mixed teams competing against mixed teams in relays. Height and weight classifications are used sometimes.

Planning the Meet

The order of events should be determined by the type of competition. Generally, relays are last on the program. If preliminary heats are necessary, these are run off first. Color-coded cards should be given the heat qualifiers; this helps get them into the correct final race.

Advice should be secured from the local track coach about details of the meet. Sufficient help must be present. Helpers can be secured from a number of volunteers, such as school patrons, secondary students, teacher-training students, and service clubs. Adequate and properly instructed help is an essential factor. A list of key officials and their duties follows.

The meet director: This person should be located at a convenient point near the finish line, with a table on which all official papers are kept.

The announcer: This person could be in charge of the public address system. Much of the success of the meet depends upon his or her abilities. He or she is stationed at the director's table.

The clerk of the course: The clerk of the course has charge of the entries and places the competitors in their proper starting slots.

The starter: The starter works closely with the clerk of the course. He or she should use a starter's gun. A second gun in reserve, in case of failure, is a sound idea.

Head and finish-line judges: There should be one finish judge for each awarded place, plus one more. The first competitor "out of the money" is identified in case there is a disqualification. The head judge can cast the deciding vote if there is doubt about the first- and second-place winners.

Timers: Three timers should time first place, though fewer can be used. If another timer is available, he or she can time second place. Timers report their times to the head timer, who determines the correct winning time. Accurate timing and enough timers are important if records are a factor.

Messengers: A messenger takes the entry card from the clerk of the course to the finish judge, who records the correct finish places and the winner's time after the race has been completed. The messenger then takes the complete record of the race to the meet director's table.

Field judges and officials: Each field event should be manned by a sufficient crew, headed by a designated individual. Each head judge should be given a clipboard with fully explained rules for the event he or she is judging.

The marshall: Several marshalls should be appointed to keep general order. They are responsible for keeping noncompetitors from interfering with or getting in the way of the events. Competitors can be kept under better control if each unit has an assigned place, either in the infield or in the stands. Only assigned officials and competitors should be present at the scenes of competition.

Other Details

In smaller meets, first, second, and third places are the usual number, with the scoring on a five-, three-, and one-point base. Relays, because of multiple participation, should count double the individual place point score. For larger meets, more places can be awarded and the individual point scores can be adjusted.

Ribbons can be awarded but need not be elaborate. The name of the meet should be printed on the ribbons, but place and individual event designation on the ribbons is expensive. The ribbons are given with blue for first place, red for second, and white for third. They usually are awarded after each event. Awarding ribbons at the conclusion of a large interschool meet is anticlimactic, since many spectators have already left. Certificates of participation can be issued at such an affair to the nonwinners. This assures that all children receive recognition for participation.

In an all-school track and field day, an award convocation provides desirable recognition. Both place awards and certificates of participation can be given, with all the children in the school present.

Trophies are desirable for larger interschool meets but should be modest and limited to team performance. In an intraschool meet, a traveling trophy, plaque, or pennant to be displayed in the classroom of the winner stimulates effort.

An opening ceremony is desirable for larger meets; it would include the salute to the flag. Competitors from each unit can be introduced as a group, with announcements and instructions emphasized or clarified at this time.

Holding the event on a school morning or afternoon gives status to the affair and allows all children to participate.

It is of help if the competitors wear numbers. Safety pins, rather than straight pins, should be used to keep the numbers in place. Numbers can be made at the individual schools when they have been given well-defined instructions pertaining to materials, colors, and sizes.

Organizing the Competition

Competition in elementary school track and field days can take many forms, depending upon the focus of the meet. Inherent are the goals that many children should take part and many should reach a measure of success. On a lower priority is the determination of individual champions and meet winners. Meets can take the following patterns.

Informal Competition

Competitors are assigned to different races and compete only in that race. There are no heats as such, nor is there advancement to a final race. Races are chosen so that individuals on the same team usually do not run against each other. Points may or may not be given toward an overall meet winner. This type of meet is more like a playday and can take many different forms. Other nontrack events, such as the softball throw, the football kick, and Frisbee throwing, can be included.

Individual Competition

Winners and place finishers are determined for all events, with no team scoring or meet winner.

Team Competition

Individual winners are determined, and each contributes his or her earned point score toward a team score. The team with the highest score wins. Different team winners can be determined for grade levels and for boys and girls.

Relay Competition

This is in the nature of a relay carnival, in which a number of relays comprise the program. Field event performances can be combined for several individuals to serve the same purpose. Few, if any, individual events are scheduled.

Relays are fun events, and a number should be a part of track and field days under any plan. Relays increase the desirable element of student participation. Mixed relays should be a consideration.

CROSS-COUNTRY MEETS

Cross-country meets are interesting for children and provide a culminating activity for youngsters interested in jogging and distance running. The following represent suggested competitive divisions and distances to be run.

Division	Age	Sex	Distance
1	8-9	M	1 mile
2	8-9	F	1 mile
3	10-11	M	1¼ miles
4	10-11	F	1¼ miles
5	12-13	M	1½ miles
6	12-13	F	1½ miles

Divisions 5 and 6 are classed as open divisions, and any child in elementary school may enter, even if he or she has not reached the age of 12. Ages are defined by birthdays, and a child is regarded as being of a certain age until he or she reaches the next birthday.

The primary concerns should be that the child is able to gauge his or her pace to finish the race, with his or her finishing rank a secondary goal. Individual time comparisons are desirable, so a child can determine his or her progress. In most cross-country meets in which large numbers of children are entered, establishing individual times for other than a few of the first finishers is difficult.

In team competition, a simple means of determining a winner is to give first place to the team that has five children finishing before the same number from another class cross the line. This provides a quick and definite determination of team rank.

Schools or classes can make their own numbers and outfit themselves with some kind of uniforms, or identifications. Placement certificates could go to the first 10 finishers by place, and participation certificates could go to all others who finish the race. Each child should know his or her finishing rank.

Thirty-two

Volleyball and Related Activities

Volleyball is an excellent recreational activity that is important to the program, because it is one of the few sports that can be conducted coeducationally. In many gymnasiums, the lack of more than one court means playing 12 to 15 children on a side, which provides relatively little activity for some of the children. These games usually are dominated by 3 or 4 skillful children on each side, with the others taking only a minor part.

Volleyball cannot be played with much success unless a good basis of skills is established. There must be concentration on the skills, with attention to proper technique. Hand-eye coordination in volleyball leading to good ball control comes slowly, and patience is needed.

The game of Newcomb has been removed from volleyball lead-up activities because of the emphasis on throwing and catching skills, which are not part of volleyball. Newcomb has value for children but not as a lead-up game to volleyball. It is found on page 398.

EMPHASIS IN EACH GRADE LEVEL

In the physical education lesson, attention should be centered on keeping the ball in play and thus on increasing both enjoyment and skill development. The skills of the overhand serve, the setup, spiking, and blocking should be introduced only when there is a competitive situation, such as

Suggested Volleyball Program

GRADE	FOURTH	FIFTH	SIXTH
Skills	Serve—underhanded Simple returns	Overhand pass Forearm pass	Overhand serve Setup Spiking Blocking
Knowledges	Simple rules Rotation	Basic game rules	Game strategy Additional rules
Activities to be stressed	Beach Ball Volleyball One-Bounce Volleyball Shower Service Ball	Keep-it-up Cage Volleyball Volleyball	Volleyball Three-and-Over Volleyball Four-Square Volleyball
Testing		Simplified serve test Wall test	Serve scoring test Wall test

533

in the intramural program or in interschool competition, wherein the emphasis shifts to one of winning. Most teachers find that only a few of the more skilled children can achieve success in these more advanced skills. This does not preclude orientation and explanation to all children of the place these advanced skills have in the game of volleyball, but heavy emphasis on these skills for all children makes for a frustrating experience.

In the primary grades, children should have had ball-handling experiences generally related to volleyball skills. Rebounding and controlling balloons are excellent related experiences, particularly for younger children. Included in the ball-handling experiences with the rubber playground ball (8½ inch) should be exploratory work in batting the ball with the hands and rebounding the ball from the hands and other parts of the body. This preliminary experience in visual tracking is advantageous.

Fourth Grade

Fourth-grade experiences should be based on the use of the beach ball and should culminate in the game of Beach Ball Volleyball. The beach ball is larger and more easily handled than a volleyball and achieves a level of success not possible with a

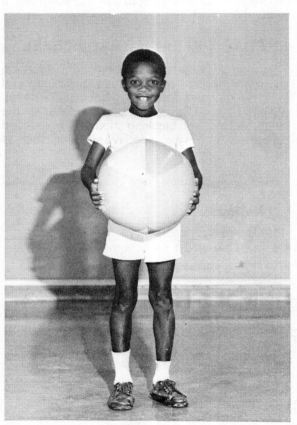

A Beach Ball

smaller ball. Volleyball for the handicapped is described on page 542.

Simple returns and underhanded serves can be practiced with beach balls. Later in the instructional sequence, serving the volleyballs should be introduced.

The game of One-Bounce Volleyball can be played with a beach ball or a volleyball. The game of Shower Service Ball should be played with volleyballs.

Fifth Grade

Beach balls can be used in the early stages of the instruction, but there should be a shift to volleyballs as soon as it is practical in the fifth grade. Students in this grade should begin to exhibit good basic mechanics in handling high and low passes. They should review the serve and polish up this skill. Basic game rules should be used in volleyball modified for this age group. The game of Keep-it-up calls for controlled passing. Cage Volleyball is an interesting variation of the regular game.

Sixth Grade

For sixth-grade students, the program should add practice in the overhand serve, the setup, spiking, and blocking when there is intramural or interschool competition and then only for those students taking part in such competition. Game rules that affect these phases of the game should be covered. An introduction to elementary strategy should be part of the instruction.

Four-Square Volleyball provides an interesting form of competitive volleyball. The game Three-and-Over Volleyball should be the basic game for the physical education instructional program.

BASIC VOLLEYBALL RULES

Officially, six players make up a team under the rules. However, any number from six to nine make suitable teams in elementary school programs.

To begin, captains toss a coin for the order of choices. The winner can choose either to serve or to take a choice of courts. Whichever option the winner selects, the opposing captain takes the other.

At the completion of any game, the teams change courts, and the losing side serves.

To be in position to serve, the player must have both feet behind the right one-third of the end line. He or she must not step on the end line during the serve. The server is in what is known as right back position.

Only the serving team scores. The server retains his or her serve, scoring consecutive points, until his or her side loses and is put out. Members of each team take turns serving, the sequence being determined by the plan of rotation.

Official rules allow the server only one serve to get the ball completely over the net and into the opponent's court. Even if the ball touches the net (net ball) and goes into the correct court, the serve is lost.

The lines bounding the court are considered to be in the court. Balls landing on the lines are counted as good. Any ball that touches or is touched by a player is considered to be in, even though the player who touched the ball was clearly outside the boundaries at the time. He or she is considered to have played the ball if he or she touches it.

The ball must be returned over the net at least by the third volley, which means that the team has a maximum of three volleys to make a good return.

Chief violations causing loss of the point or serve are:

1. Touching the net during play.
2. Not clearly batting the ball. This is sometimes called palming or lofting the ball.
3. Reaching over the net during play.
4. Stepping *over* the center line. Contact with the line is not a violation.

A ball going into the net may be recovered and played, provided no player touches the net.

The first team to reach a score of 15 points wins the game, *provided* the team is at least 2 points ahead of the opponent. If not, play continues until one team secures a 2-point lead.

Only players in the front line may spike, but all players may block. No player may volley the ball twice in succession.

VOLLEYBALL SKILLS

Underhand Serve

There are many different serves in volleyball, but best results are obtained when the instruction is concentrated first on the simple, basic underhand serve. The description is for a right-handed player. Stand with the left foot forward and pointed

Underhand Serving Position

Underhand Serve

toward the net. The ball is held in the left hand, with the arm across the body so the ball may be struck with the right hand moving straight forward. The fingers are spread, and the ball rests on the pads of the fingers. The right hand forms a partial fist, with the knuckles toward the ball. Swing the right hand forward in an underhanded motion, striking the ball out of the left palm.

Children should explore other hand positions for contacting the ball. Experiment with the heel of the hand, the side of the fist, and others as they wish. Each student then can select the best way for him or her to make a successful serve.

Overhand Pass or Return

The overhand pass must be mastered if there is to be interesting, competitive play. Otherwise, if the ball is served and not returned well or often, the game is dull.

Partial Fist for Serving

Side of the Fist for Serving

Move directly underneath the ball and contact it with cupped hands and fingertip control. Feet should be in an easy, comfortable position, with knees bent. The cup of the fingers is made so the thumbs and forefingers are close together and the other fingers are spread. The hands are held forehead high, with the elbows out and level to the floor. The player, when he or she is in receiving position, looks as if he or she is about ready to shout upward through his or her cupped hands.

Contact the ball just above eye level and propel it with the force of the spread fingers, not the palms. At the moment of contact, straighten out the legs and follow through well with the hands and arms.

If the ball is a pass to a teammate, it should reach good height to allow for control. If the pass is a return to the other side, it can be projected forward with more force. The tendency of some children to jump as they volley the ball should be discouraged.

Forearm Pass (Underhand Pass)

While this pass is more logically termed the forearm pass, some like to call it the underhand pass. It takes the place of the old underhand pass, where the ball was contacted with the hands. The body must be in good position in order to assure a

Overhand Pass

Forearm Pass (Underhand Pass) Position

proper volley. The player must move rapidly to the spot where the ball is descending to prepare himself or herself for the pass.

Body position is important. The trunk leans forward and the back is straight, with about a 90-degree angle between the thighs and body. The legs are bent and the body is in a partially crouched position, with the feet shoulder width apart.

The hands are clasped together, so the forearms are kept parallel. The clasp should be relaxed, with the type of handclasp a matter of choice. The thumbs are kept parallel and together in one method. The fingers of one hand make a partially cupped fist, and the fingers of the other hand overlap the fist. Another method is to cup both hands and turn the hands out a little, so the thumbs are apart. The wrists in either case are turned downward and the elbow joints are reasonably locked.

The forearms are held at the proper angle to rebound the ball, with the contact made with the fists or forearms between the knees as the receiver crouches.

Dig Pass

This is used as an emergency return when neither the overhand nor the forearm pass is possible. It should be a stiffened rebound from one arm, rebounding the ball from one of the following: cupped fist, heel of the hand, or inside or outside of the forearm. Remember, the dig pass is an emergency pass that should not be employed as a standard return.

Setup

The name *setup* applies to a pass that sets up the ball for a possible spike. The object is to raise the ball with a soft, easy pass to a position 1 or 2 feet above the net and about 1 foot from the net. The setup is generally the second pass in a series of three. An overhand pass is used for the setup. It

is important for the back line player, who has to tap to the setter, to make an accurate and easily handled pass.

Spike

Spiking is the most effective play in volleyball and, when properly done, is extremely difficult to return properly. It depends a great deal upon the ability of a teammate to set it up properly. On the elementary school level, spiking should be done by jumping high into the air and striking the ball above the net, driving it into the opponent's court. It is the kill shot in volleyball. Experienced players may back up for a short run. However, the jump must be made straight up so as not to touch the net, and the striking hand must not go over the net.

Overhand Serve

The overhand serve requires more practice than the underhand, but it is considered a more effective serve. The most commonly used overhand serve is the floater, that is, sending the ball across the net in such a fashion that it has no spin.

The server stands with a slightly staggered stance, with the left foot forward (right-handed server). The knees are relaxed for comfort and ease, with the body slightly turned as governed by the position of the feet. The ball should be held with the left hand.

Beginning an Overhead Serve

Dig Pass

Overhead Serve—Contacting the Ball

The ball is tossed lightly about 2 to 3 feet above the head so that it descends a foot or more in front of the shoulder of the striking hand. On the toss, the body weight is transferred to the back foot.

Contact is made with the ball in a motion resembling a baseball catcher's throw to second base. The arm is flexed and cocked, with the hand drawn back near the ear. The upper body rotates slightly to the right in a preparatory move.

As the ball drops, the body weight transfers to the front foot with either a short step or a slide. The striking arm snaps forward from its cocked position. To assure a floater, little follow-through of the arm is made.

Hand contact can be made in several ways: the open hand, the cupped hand with knuckle contact, or the clenched hand (fist). The wrist remains rigid in all hand contact methods. Contact should be made in the center of the ball with the hand.

INSTRUCTIONAL PROCEDURES

1. For a class of about 30 students, two volleyball courts are needed. Not more than 6 to 9 children should be on a team. In elementary school gymnasiums, where a basketball court is present, the volleyball nets should be stretched lengthwise, each utilizing half of the basketball court as a volleyball court.

2. Courts generally should be 25 by 50 feet but can vary in size and shape. Net height can vary from 6 feet for fourth graders to a maximum of 7 feet. Standards or wall brackets should be constructed, so various net heights are possible. A line, called the center line, should be drawn on the floor directly under the net, dividing the court into two halves. Where possible, nets should be stretched with proper tension, permitting ball recovery from the lower part of the net. A net that just hangs does not permit this.

3. Regular volleyball rules call for one chance to serve the ball over the net *without* touching the net. In learning stages, the teacher can modify the rules to allow a second chance. Another modification is to move the server forward from the base line to a point where he or she can serve the ball over the net successfully.

   This is particularly true when serving beach balls. One assist may be allowed to get the beach ball over the net on a serve.

4. At the net, the players should stand an arm's length away for best play. Other players should play their positions rather than ganging up on the ball.

5. To save time, children should be taught to roll the ball to the server. Other players should let the ball roll to its destination without intercepting it.

6. The use of the fist to hit the ball on normal returns causes poor control and interrupts the play. Both hands should be used to hit the ball. If difficulty occurs with enforcement, the teacher can rule hitting with the fist a foul that causes a loss of a point. The fist should be used only for difficult, emergency recoveries.

7. A referee should be appointed, since violations of rules occur in the heat of the game. A referee positioned near the net can call violations effectively.

8. Effective instruction is possible only when properly inflated balls (beach balls, volleyballs, and similar balls) are of the type that can be rebounded easily from the hands and arms without pain. A heavy, flabby ball takes much away from the enjoyment of the game.

9. Rotation should be introduced in the fourth grade and used in lead-up games.

10. Spiking and blocking skills should be introduced mostly as a matter of orientation. Better skilled students will be able to absorb some of these techniques, but to expect all students to reach a skill level where spiking and blocking can be employed as regular parts of the game is unrealistic. This is also true of the overhand serve.

TWO LINES

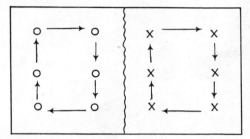

THREE LINES

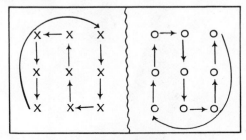

Rotation Plans

ORGANIZING FOR INSTRUCTION

Small-group instruction should be used where three or four children comprise a group. Eight or more beach balls should be used for introductory work in the fourth grade. The 15- to 16-inch beach ball seems to be the more practical ball. Beach balls are comparatively less expensive than other balls.

For more critical skills, it is best to have a volleyball (or similar ball) for every two children. Outdoor play provides needed practice space when indoor space is limited. Wind, however, is a factor in outdoor play.

When beach balls are used, controlled tossing by one player to the others of his or her group is desirable for practicing specific volleys. The most effective feeding toss is usually underhanded, providing a soft, high pass that permits practice of the desired return. The leader and semicircle formation is appropriate for this type of practice.

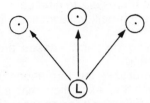

Serving should emphasize successful serves, beginning with short distances and increasing as skill is acquired. Serving practice should first be done back and forth between individuals and later across a net.

VOLLEYBALL DRILLS

In addition to the informal organization of the two to four children practicing skills, the following drills can supplement the unit.

Serving

Two teams face each other from opposite sides of a volleyball court. All players serve from behind the baselines. The ball is served back and forth across the net. There should be some method of taking turns, but a rigid order is not required. Two or more volleyballs should be used in the drill.

Wall Volley

A smooth wall is needed. A line is drawn on the wall 6½ feet above and parallel to the floor. One player begins by tossing the ball above the line on the wall and attempts to keep it in play by volleying. Players should change frequently or can change after a miss.

Spiking

A leader and file formation is needed, or this can be done informally. The leader stands about 3 feet from the net and tosses the ball (setup) for spiking. The toss also should be about 2 feet above the net, so the ball just hangs there for an easy spike. Some care is needed in the toss if the drill is to be successful.

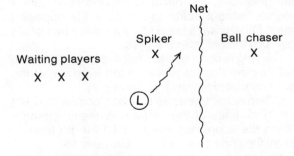

Setup and Spiking

A second stage of the spiking drill adds a setup player and a regular setup pass in place of the toss by the leader. Problems will occur with the drill,

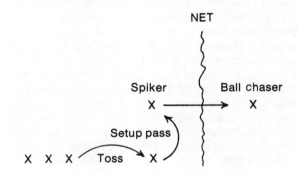

since an accurate setup pass cannot be made repeatedly so the spiker gets a fair chance to spike. Specialized practice in making proper setup passes should be held.

Recovery from the Net

If the net is stretched properly, recovery drills can be instituted. One player throws the ball into the net and another attempts to recover with an underhand pass.

VOLLEYBALL ACTIVITIES

Fourth Grade

Beach Ball Volleyball

Playing Area: Volleyball court.
Players: Two teams, six to nine each.
Supplies: A beach ball, 12 to 15 inches in diameter.
Skills: Most passing skills, modified serving.

There are two versions of this game.

Simplified Version: The players of each team are in two lines on their respective sides of the net. The ball is put in play by one player in the front line, who throws the ball into the air to himself or herself and then hits it over the net. Play continues until the ball touches the floor. The ball may be volleyed any number of times before crossing the net.

A team loses a point to the other team when the ball goes over the net and hits the floor out-of-bounds without being touched by the opposing team. Otherwise, a team loses a point when it fails to return the ball over the net.

Serving is done by the front line only. When the ball hits the floor, a player in the front line of the team on that side puts the ball in play.

When either team has scored 5 points, the front and back lines of the respective teams change. When the score has reached 10 for the leading team, the lines change back. Game is 15.

Variation: Any player in the back line may catch the ball as it initially comes from the opposing team. He or she immediately makes a little toss to himself or herself and passes the ball with a volleyball pass to a teammate. The player who catches the ball and bats it cannot send it across the net before a teammate has touched it.

Beach Ball Volleyball: This game approximates regular volleyball and differs from the simplified game just described in the following ways.

Serving: Serving is done, as in volleyball, by the player on the right of the back line. However, the distance is shortened, since it is difficult to serve a beach ball successfully from the normal volleyball serving distance. The player serves from his or her normal playing position *on the court* in the right back position.

Volleying the Beach Ball

Scoring: As in volleyball. Server continues serving as long as he or she scores.
Rotation: As in volleyball.
Volleying: Ball must go over the net at least by the third volley.
Teaching Suggestion: Be sure the server positions himself or herself as close to the net as he or she can (about the middle) and still remains in the right back position on the court. Successful serving is an important factor in providing an enjoyable game.

One-Bounce Volleyball

Playing Area: Volleyball court.
Players: Two teams, six to nine each.
Supplies: Beach ball, volleyball, or another suitable ball.
Skills: Passing (forearm passes are used frequently), serving.

The game utilizes the formations and rules of volleyball, with the exception that the ball may bounce once between hits or passes. Play begins with the regular serve, as in volleyball. The served ball may be played as in volleyball, or the team can allow the ball to bounce once between passes.

In the early stages of the game, there can be any number of hits and bounces, provided the ball does not bounce more than once between hits. Later, allow only three players to handle the ball before it must be returned across the net.

Shower Service Ball

Playing Area: A volleyball court, each half occupied by one team. Players are scattered in no particular formation. A line, parallel to the net, is drawn through the middle of each court.
Players: 6 to 12 on each team.
Supplies: Four to six volleyballs.
Skills: Serving, catching.

The game involves the skills of serving and catching. To start the game, the volleyballs are divided between the teams and are handled by players in the serving area. The serving area is between the base line and the line drawn through the middle of each court.

Balls may be served at any time in any order, just so the server is in the serving area (back half) of his or her court. Any ball that is served across the net is to be caught by any player near the ball. The person catching or retrieving a ball from the floor moves quickly to his or her serving area and serves. A point is scored *for* a team whenever a served ball hits the floor in the other court or is dropped by a receiver. Two scorers are needed, one for each side.

Teaching Suggestion: As the children improve, all serves should be made from back of the base line.

Fifth Grade

Keep-it-up

Playing Area: Playground, gymnasium.
Players: Five to eight players on each team.
Supplies: Volleyball for each team.
Skills: Overhand, forearm, and dig passes.

Each team forms a small circle of not more than eight players. The object of the game is to see which team can make the greater number of vol-

leys in a specified time or which team can sustain the ball in the air for the greater number of consecutive volleys without error.

Directions

1. Game is started with a volley by one of the players on the signal "go."
2. Balls are volleyed back and forth with no specific order of turns, except the ball cannot be returned to the player from whom it came.
3. A player may not volley a ball twice in succession.
4. Any ball touching the ground does not count and ends the count.

Teaching Suggestions: Players should take the responsibility for calling illegal returns on themselves thus interrupting the consecutive volley count. The balls should be of equal quality, so no team can claim a disadvantage. Groups should be taught to count out loud, so that their progress is known.

Cageball Volleyball

Cageball Volleyball is a variation of regular volleyball. The ball used is a cageball, 18 to 24 inches in diameter. The following special rules govern this game.

1. The serve is made by a player in the back line in his or her normal playing position by tossing the cageball into the air and then batting it toward the net. Other players can assist the ball on its way over.
2. Any number of hits may be made in any combination or order by the players, but the ball must be clearly batted and not lofted or carried.
3. Scoring and rotation follow volleyball rules.

Teaching Suggestions

1. A 24-inch ball is about the largest one that can be used for this game, since a larger ball is difficult to handle legally by volleyball rules.
2. The referee must be alert to call violations involving momentarily resting or supporting the ball to keep it from hitting the floor.

Regular Volleyball

Regular volleyball should be played in the fifth grade, with one possible exception in the rules. In the early experiences, it is suggested the server be allowed a second chance if he or she fails to get the first attempt over and into play. This should be only on the initial serve. If he or she fails a second time, regular rules prevail.

Some instructors like to shorten the serving distance during the introductory phases of the game. It is important for the serving to be done well enough to keep the game moving.

The rules for volleyball are listed in the early part of the unit (page 534). A referee should supervise the game. He or she generally has three calls.

1. "Side out"—the serving team fails to serve the ball successfully to the other court, fails to make a good return of a volley, or makes a rule violation.
2. "Point"—the receiving team fails to make a legal return or is guilty of a rule violation.
3. "Double foul"—fouls are made by both teams on the same play, in which case the point is replayed. No score or side out results.

There should be some emphasis on team play. Back court players should be encouraged to pass to front court players rather than merely batting the ball back and forth across the net.

Variation: Allow the receiver in the back court to catch the serve, toss it to himself or herself, and propel it to a teammate. The catch should be limited to the serve and the pass must go to a teammate, not over the net. This counteracts the problem of children in the back court being unable to handle the serve to keep the ball in play if the served volleyball is spinning, curving, and approaching with such force that it is difficult to control.

Sixth Grade

Three-and-Over Volleyball

The game Three-and-Over serves to emphasize the basic offensive strategy of volleyball. The game follows the regular rules of volleyball, with the exception that the ball must be played three times before going over. The team loses the serve or point if the ball is not played three times.

Four-Square Volleyball

Playing Area: A regular volleyball court with a second net at right angles to the original net, dividing the playing area into four equal courts.

Players: Two to four on each of four teams. An extra team can be off, awaiting rotation to the #4 court.

Supplies: Volleyball.

Skills: All volleyball skills.

The courts are numbered as in the diagram. The object of the game is to force one of the teams to commit an error. Whenever a team makes an error, it moves down to the #4 court, or off in case there is a waiting team. A team errs by not returning the ball to another court within the prescribed three volleys or by causing the ball to go out-of-bounds.

The ball is always put in play by a serve by a player from the #1 team, the serve being made from any point behind the end line of that team. Players must rotate for each serve. The serve must be made into court #3 or #4. Play then is as in volleyball, but the ball may be volleyed into any of the other three courts.

No score is kept. The object of the game is for the #1 team to retain its position.

Teaching Suggestions: The game seems to play best with five or more teams. With four teams, the team occupying court #4 has no penalty for an error, since it already is in the lowest spot and cannot be penalized.

Regular Volleyball

There should be continued play in regular volleyball, with increased attention to team play. The concept of offensive volleyball should be introduced, with some attention to the skill of spiking. However, the emphasis on setting up and spiking should not be overriding considerations. Continued practice on the fundamental skills of serving and volleying should be an important part of the instruction. Closer attention to the details of good technique makes for more efficient play.

Wheelchair Volleyball

Children in wheelchairs can participate successfully in some phases of volleyball. For example, a child confined to a wheelchair can compete against a nonhandicapped child on a one-on-one basis when the courts are laid out in this fashion. The net should be about 6 feet in height. The differences in size of the playing areas should be such that the mobility factor is equalized. Serving by the normal child is done from behind the back line and by the handicapped child with his or her wheels on the back line. Rules should be adjusted as necessary.

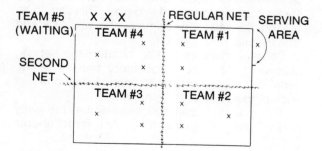

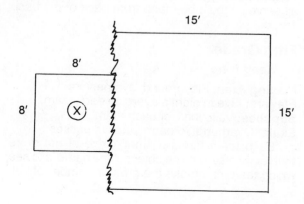

TESTS FOR VOLLEYBALL SKILLS

Serving and volleying are the skills to be tested in volleyball. Serving is tested in two ways, one with a simple serve and one with an accuracy score.

Simplified Serve Test

The child to be tested stands in the normal serving position behind the end line on the right side. He or she is given a specific number of trials in serving. His or her score is the number of times he or she serves successfully out of his or her trials (10). The serve must clear the net without touching and land in the opponent's court. A ball touching a line is counted as good.

Serve Accuracy Test

A line is drawn parallel to the net through the middle of one of the courts. Each half is further subdivided into three equal areas by lines parallel

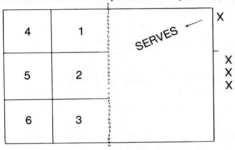

to the sidelines. This makes a total of six areas, which correspond to the six positions of members of a volleyball team. The areas are numbered from 1 to 6.

Each child is allotted one service attempt to serve the ball into each of the six areas in turn. Scoring is as follows.

Two points—serving into the designated court area.

One point—missing the designated area but landing in an adjacent area to the target area.

No points—failing to serve into the target or adjacent area.

Wall Test for Volleying

The player stands behind a restraining line 4 feet away from a wall. A line is drawn on the wall parallel to the floor and 6½ feet up, representing the height of the net. A player is allowed 30 seconds to make as many volleys as he or she can above the 6½-foot line, while keeping behind the restraining line. A counter is assigned to each testing station to count the successive volleys.

To start, the child makes a short toss to himself or herself for the first volley. If time permits, more than one opportunity can be allowed, and the best count from any of the 30-second periods is his or her score.

Mats can be placed to serve as a restraining line. Stepping on top of the mat makes that volley illegal.

Thirty-three

Miscellaneous Sports-Type and Playground Activities

The activities covered in this chapter sometimes are classified as sports, but they are played most often on school playgrounds in various parts of the United States. Quite often, these traditional activities have been modified to meet the needs and preferences of local areas, and so they may not be played everywhere in the ways described in this textbook. The main purpose for including these materials in the text is to give the teacher some background and rules for the activities, so the children can have some experience with these time-honored games.

Basic instruction for these activities can be carried on during the physical education program to give the children the knowledge and skill necessary for success. Children can select the activity in which they wish to participate during recess or the noon hour, after school, or at home. It is hoped that these activities will provide a start for children in learning how to use their leisure time effectively, as well as giving them the joy of participating in physical activity.

Beanbag Horseshoes (All Grades)

This activity is played just as regular horseshoes is, except that beanbags and old car tires are used. Two tires are placed 15 to 30 feet apart and are used as the targets. Players must stay behind the tires when throwing. They get three throws each. A beanbag that lands in the center of the tire counts 3 points, and a beanbag that lands and stays on top the sidewall of the tire counts 1 point. The first person to score 15 points is declared the winner.

Deck Tennis (Grades Three through Six)

Deck tennis is played with a deck tennis ring made either of rope or rubber. Either two or four players can participate. Rules are somewhat similar to volleyball, and the server continues to serve as long as he or she scores points. Serving is made from a position behind the baseline by throwing the ring underhanded into the opposite half-court, diagonally from the server. The toss is made underhanded from the side.

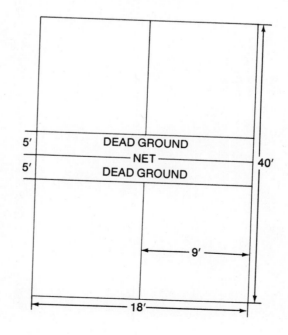

The ring may be caught only with one hand and must be returned immediately from the area where it was caught. The server scores a point if the receiver fails at any time to return the ring properly or in so returning causes it to light outside the court or in the dead ground. A ring that lights in the court is counted as good for the thrower. When the server errs, the receiver becomes the server and no points are scored.

The diagram on the opposite page illustrates a doubles court used with diagonal services. For a singles game where a single court is used, diagonal serving is not employed.

Four Square (Grades Three through Six)

Playing Area: Usually outside on a hard surface, according to the following diagram.
Players: Four players play the game, but others are in line for a turn.
Supplies: Playground ball or volleyball.

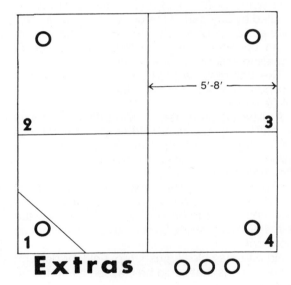

The squares are numbered 1, 2, 3, and 4. A service line is drawn diagonally across the far corner of square #1. The player in the #1 square must stay behind this line when he or she serves. The serve always starts from the #1 square.

The ball is served by dropping it and serving it underhanded from the bounce. If the serve hits a line, the server is out. The server can hit the ball to any of the other three courts. The player receiving the ball must keep it in play by striking the ball after it has bounced once in his or her square. The receiver directs it to any other square with an underhand hit. Play continues until one player fails to return the ball or commits a fault.

The following are faults.
1. Hitting the ball sidearm or overhand.
2. Ball landing on a line between the squares. (Ball landing on an outer boundary is considered good.)
3. Stepping in another square to play the ball.
4. Catching or carrying a return volley.
5. Allowing ball to touch any part of the body except the hands.

When a player misses or commits a fault, he or she goes to the end of the waiting line and all players move up. The player at the head of the waiting line moves into square #4.

Variations
1. A 2-foot circle into which the ball cannot be hit without scoring an error can be drawn at the center of the area.
2. The game can be changed by varying the method of propelling the ball. The leader sets the means. The ball can be hit with a partially closed fist, a back of a hand, or an elbow. Also, a foot or a knee can be used to return the ball. Call out "fisties," "elbows," "footsies," or "kneesies" to set the pattern.
3. *Chain Spelling:* The server names a word, and each player in returning the ball must spell the correct letter in proper rotation.

Two Square (Grades Three through Six)

Playing Area: Generally outside on a hard surface according to the Four Square diagram.
Players: Two players, but others may be in line for a turn.
Supplies: Playground or volleyball.

The basic rules are the same as for Four Square, except that only two players are involved and two squares are used. If there are players waiting for a turn, the active player who misses or fouls can be eliminated, as in Four Square. If only two players wish to play, a score can be kept.

In Two Square, the ball must be served from behind the base line.

European Handball (Team Handball) (Grades Five and Six)

European Handball is a game fast growing in popularity, since it is now an official Olympic sport. Basically, it is an outdoor game in the United States, but in Europe it also is played indoors in what are known as sports halls. The game is also called Team Handball and Danish Handball. Rules vary in different locales. The format presented is suitable for elementary school participation.
Playing Area: A rectangular field 50 by 100 to 70 by 140 feet. In the middle of each goal line is a goal

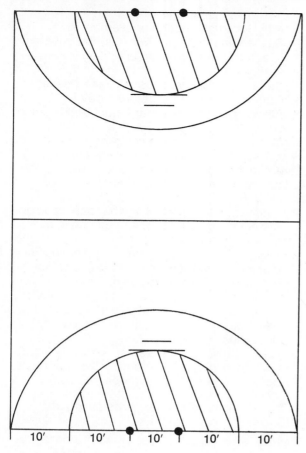

10 feet wide and 6 feet high. This can be outlined by standards and some type of crossbar. A goal area is marked off as diagrammed by a goal area line. Ten feet farther out is another line, the free-throw line. Directly in front of the goal and 22 feet away is a penalty line. A center line (onside line) divides the court. The playing field is the entire court less the two goal areas.

Players: Seven players on each side, one of whom is a goalie. The number of players can vary for elementary school play. Three players are designated as offense and three as defense.

Supplies: The official ball is a little smaller than a soccer ball. Team identification is important.

Scoring: One point is scored from each goal, which is made when an attacking player throws the ball from the playing field past the goalie into the goal.

Timing: The game is played in two halves, 10 to 20 minutes each. Teams change goals at the start of the second half. The clock is stopped after a goal or a violation and started again when the ball is put in play.

Time-outs: No time-outs are permitted, except for injury or substitution. Substitutions may be made only when the ball is not in play.

Area Restrictions: The goal area belongs to the goalie. No one may enter the area to play the ball. An offensive player may enter the area as part of his or her throwing action, provided that the ball has clearly left his or her hand before he or she makes contact in the goal area. The line defining the area is a part of the area.

All players must be onside in their respective halves of the playing field when the ball is put in play at the start of the game or after a score. After the throw-in, players may go anywhere in the playing field.

Starting the Game: The team that wins the toss may decide to put the ball in play or select which goal it wishes to defend. The loser of the toss exercises whichever option is not taken by the team winning the toss. To put the ball in play, a member of the team takes the ball out-of-bounds near the center line with a throw-in.

After a Score: Similarly, after a score, a throw-in resumes play at the center line by the team that did not score.

Throwing and Catching: The ball may be handled by any part of the body above the knees. Mere accidental hits below the knees from a throw by an opponent are permitted, but stopping or propelling actions are violations.

The ball may be held by a player only for 3 seconds. A player may take three steps with the ball held in hand.

A player is permitted to take one bounce with the ball, using one hand. He or she may take as many steps during the bounce as he or she wishes. He or she can catch the ball in both hands after the bounce.

Guarding and Ball Recovery: In playing the ball in another player's hands, only one hand may be used and this is to be kept open. No tie-ups are permitted, nor may the ball be pulled away from an opponent.

No one may block, push, trip, hold, or perform similar actions that could be classed as unnecessary roughness.

A player may not touch a ball a second time unless he or she performs a bounce. An intervening player must touch the ball before the player can touch it again.

The Goalie: The goalie may stop the ball with any part of his or her body. Any ball that touches the goal area, the goalie, or the goal line belongs to the goalie, except when it rolls back into the playing field. He or she may move around in the goal area without time or step restrictions. However, he or she must get rid of the ball promptly or be subject to a penalty for unsportsmanlike conduct.

The goalie cannot leave the area with the ball, nor can he or she bring the ball into the goal area from the playing field. If he or she enters the playing field, he or she becomes just another player until he or she returns to goal area. The goalie may throw the ball into the playing field after a goal attempt but cannot use a kick.

Throw-in: Throw-ins occur at the start of the game, after a score, and as the result of an out-of-bounds. The out-of-bounds throw-in is from the spot where the ball went out-of-bounds. No score can result directly from a throw-in. This must be a two-handed overhead throw similar to that used in soccer.

Corner Throw-in: This is similar to the soccer corner kick, where the ball is put in play at the corner where the defenders (not the goalie) touched the ball last before it went out-of-bounds over the goal line. The ball may be thrown with any kind of a throw.

Free Throw: A free throw is awarded at the spot of the fault, except when the violation is between the goal-area line and the free-throw line, in which case it is thrown from the free-throw line. All defenders are to be 10 feet back of the free-throw spot. If the ball is thrown by the offensive from the free-throw line, the defenders stand just ahead of the goal-area line. A free throw is awarded for traveling (more than three steps), holding the ball longer than 3 seconds, offside, illegally entering the goal area, illegal guarding, and playing the ball with the feet.

Penalty Shot: A penalty shot is taken from the penalty line with only the goalie defending. All others must be behind the free-throw line. If missed, the ball is in play. Penalty shots are awarded for rough play, player entering the goal area to block an attempt, purposely throwing the ball into goal area one is defending, goalie bringing the ball into the playing field, pushing a player into the goal area, or unsportsmanlike conduct.

Disqualification: A penalty shot and 2-minute disqualification may be awarded for flagrant fouls. This is a judged situation by the official.

Tied Ball: A tied ball is called when two players of opposite teams commit faults. All players must be 10 feet away from the official who bounces the ball into play.

Teaching Suggestion: Some attention to defensive formation is important. The following defenses are suggested.

1. *6-0 Defense:* In this all six field players form a defensive line just outside the goal area they are defending.
2. *5-1 Defense:* One player is designated as a rover, and he or she attempts to harass the team and tries to steal the ball. The other five form the defensive line just outside the goal area.
3. *4-2 Defense:* This is similar to #2 but employs two rovers.

As soon as one team recovers the ball, they should move the ball rapidly down the court before the defense can get set. Most of the scoring attempts are made from a leap into the air and throwing from a high point. Effective throws are made from a leap into the goal area that releases the ball before contact with the goal area is made.

Hopscotch (All Grades)

Playing Area: Diagram drawn on a hard-surfaced area.

Players: Not more than four or five to any one game.

Supplies: A lagger for each player (a stone makes a good lagger).

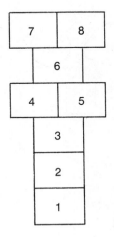

In the first example shown, the first player starts the game by tossing his or her lagger into the first (#1) box. He or she then hops *over* the first box into the second box. He or she then hops into box #3 on the same foot. The general rule is to hop on one foot in the single boxes and both feet (one in each) into the double boxes. When he or she reaches boxes #7 and #8, he or she turns around completely in place with a jump exchange of the feet into the opposite boxes. He or she hops back with a jump into boxes #4 and #5. When he or she reaches box #2, he or she reaches over and picks up his or her lagger, hops into box #1 and out. He or she then tosses his or her lagger into box #2 and repeats the routine. He or she continues jumping into the other boxes with his or her lagger until he or she has covered all eight. Certain rules are basic.

1. The player may not hop into the box where his or her lagger has been tossed. He or she picks up the lagger on the way back by stopping in the box immediately in front. After he or she has picked up the lagger, he or she can hop into the box.
2. A player loses his or her turn when his or her lagger is not tossed into the correct box or rests on a line.
3. Stepping on a line, missing a box, falling, and

stepping into a box where the lagger rests are fouls and stop the turn at that point.

4. After a player has gone completely through the boxes (through the "eighties"), he or she may write his or her name in any box, and no one but that player may step in that box. The player whose name is in the most boxes wins.

There are innumerable forms of hopscotch and each area has its favorites. Hopscotch formations take the forms of simple lines of boxes, crosses, squares, snails, and other varied figures. It is truly an international game, played in almost every country. The following diagrams can be used to add variety to the hopscotch pattern.

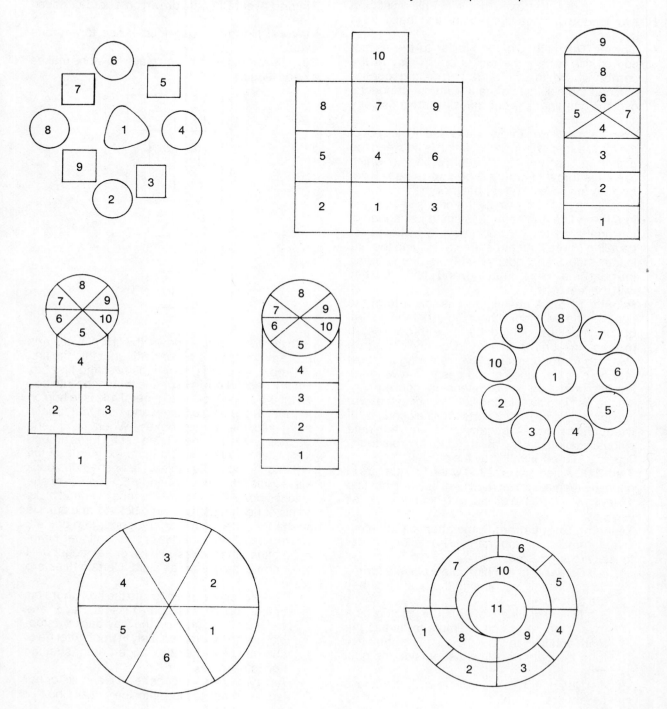

O'Leary (Grades Two through Six)

O'Leary is an individual contest played with each child having a small ball, or it can be played with a number of children taking turns when a player makes an error. The child chants the following to the tune of "Ten Little Indians": "1-2-3 O'Leary, 4-5-6 O'Leary, 7-8-9 O'Leary, 10 O'Leary, Postman." He or she bats the ball with the open hand to the ground (as in basketball dribbling), keeping time to the counting. On the word *O'Leary,* he or she gives a harder bounce and performs a stipulated task. This means that the task is repeated four times during the course of one routine. On the word *postman,* the child catches the ball. The tasks can vary, but they should have the same established order for each game. The following progression is suggested for the game with each task being done on the word *O'Leary.*

1. Swing the right leg outward over the ball.
2. Swing the left leg outward over the ball.
3. Swing the right leg inward over the ball.
4. Swing the left leg inward over the ball.
5. Grasp hands together, forming a circle with the arms. Ball passes through arms from below.
6. Same as #5, but the ball passes through from above.
7. Form a circle with the forefingers and thumbs. The ball passes upward through the circle.
8. Same as #7, but the ball passes downward through the hands.
9. Alternate #1 and #2 on each *O'Leary.*
10. Alternate #3 and #4.
11. Alternate #5 and #6.
12. Alternate #7 and #8.
13. Do #1, #2, #3, and #4 in order.
14. Do #5, #6, #7, and #8 in order.
15. Finish with a complete turn around on each *O'Leary.*

Rope Quoits (Grades Three through Six)

Any number of players may play in a game. High score wins. The distance from foul line or shooting line to the rope quoit base should be as close to 15 feet as possible.

Each player shoots four quoits per frame when it is his or her time to shoot. Opponents then shoot four quoits, in the same manner. Ringers count five points each. All other quoits remaining on the base count one point each. Quoits that go off the board are lost and do not score any points. A game consists of 10 frames for each player in the game.

Diagrams of rope quoit base and quoits are found in chapter thirty-four.

Kick Shuffle (Grades Three through Six)

Playing Area: Diagram is illustrated below, on a hard surface.
Players: Two to four.
Supplies: Three kicking blocks (2 by 4 by 4 inches).

The target can be laid out permanently with paint or temporarily with chalk. The blocks are made from regular 2-by-4-inch lumber. They should be cut a little short of 4 inches in order to match the width of the lumber.

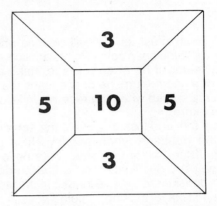

The first player stands at a kicking line drawn about 15 feet from the front of the target. He or she stands at the line with the forward foot and with the other slides or kicks the blocks, one at a time, at the court. He or she scores the points as listed when the block rests in a particular space. If the block is on a line *between* two spaces, he or she scores the lower figure. If the block stops on an outside line, it scores nothing.

The game can be played by two or three players, who take turns at a target. With larger numbers or with partners, it would be better to lay out a court with two targets, one at each end, similar to shuffleboard courts.

Other diagrams could be arranged.

Sidewalk Tennis (Grades Two through Six)

Playing Area: On any sidewalk, four cement squares in a row can be used. Areas can be drawn on the gymnasium floor or other surfaced area.
Players: Two.
Supplies: Tennis ball or rubber ball that bounces well. Paddles can be used.

The game is between two players, one in each court. The object is for the server to serve the ball over the net line into the other court. The server must bounce the ball behind the baseline and hit the ball underhanded into the opponent's court.

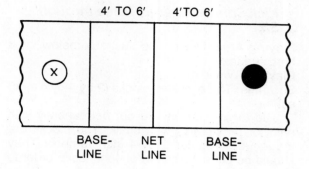

4' TO 6'   4'TO 6'

BASE-   NET   BASE-
LINE   LINE   LINE

The receiver must let the ball bounce and then return it with the open palm. Points are scored only by the server. If he or she fails to make a good serve or a good return, he or she loses the serve. Points are scored when the receiver fails to make a good return.

It is a foul and loss of serve if the server steps over the baseline when serving. It is out-of-bounds if the ball at any time lights beyond the baseline. Any ball lighting on a line bordering a court is considered to have landed in that court.

The first player scoring 11 points wins, provided he or she is 2 points ahead. If either player does not have a 2-point advantage when his or her score totals 11, the game continues until one player is 2 points ahead.

Variation: The game can be played as doubles. Partners alternate on returns.

Tetherball (Grades Two through Six)

Tetherball is a popular game and is a natural where space is limited. The equipment consists of a pole and a tetherball attached to the pole by a length of rope. Pole assemblies outside are generally put in permanently with a concrete installation.

Two to four players can participate, but the game is generally played by two children.

The first server is picked by lot. One player stands on each side of the pole. The server puts the ball in play by tossing it into the air and hitting it in the direction he or she chooses. The opponent must not strike the ball on the first swing around the pole. On its second time around the pole, he or she hits the ball back in the opposite direction. As the ball is hit back and forth, each player tries to hit the ball so that the rope winds completely around the pole in the direction in which he or she has been hitting the ball. The game is won by the player who succeeds in doing this or whose opponent forfeits the game by making any of the following fouls:

1. Hitting ball with any part of the body other than the hands or forearms.
2. Catching or holding the ball during play.
3. Touching the pole.
4. Hitting the rope with the forearm or hands.
5. Throwing the ball.
6. Winding the ball around the pole below the 5-foot mark.

After the opening game, the winner of the preceding game serves. Winning four games wins the set.

Tennis Volleyball (Grades Four through Six)

Playing Area: A court 20 by 40 feet or 25 by 50 feet on a hard surface. A net 3 feet high is across the center.

Players: Two teams with two to six players on each team.

Supplies: A volleyball or a similar ball.

This game combines some of the features of volleyball and tennis. The players on each team are positioned usually in two lines, front and back. Play is started with a serve from the right side of the backcourt line of the team serving. Only the team serving scores. The same server continues serving until his or her side has made a fault, at which time the serve goes to the other team. A team rotates positions when it receives the serve privilege.

The server drops the ball and bats it with his or her hand after the bounce so that it goes over the net and into the opposite court, where it must bounce before it can be played. The serve must not touch the net or it is a fault. On any other play, the ball may touch the net and drop over and then be played by the receiving team. The ball may be played after the serve and on any other play by batting it with the hand after it bounces or by volleying it, as in volleyball. After three touches by the receiving team, the ball must go over the net on the fly to be a good ball. Players may volley or bounce the ball to each other before sending it over the net, subject to the three-touch rule. Any ball touching a line is counted as in the court that is bounded by the line touched.

To count as a good return across the net, the ball must go directly (not bounce) across the net and land in the opponent's court. However, if it touches any player before it touches the court's surface, it is counted as a good play. A ball bouncing twice before it is hit or between hits is a fault.

Play is usually to 15 points, but it can be otherwise. A team must win by at least 2 points, and play is continued until this occurs. If the score were tied at 14 to 14, for example, play would continue until one team was 2 points ahead.

Thirty-four

Facilities, Equipment, and Supplies

The facilities for physical education can be considered in two classifications—outdoor areas and indoor facilities. Climatic conditions should determine which type of facility is more important for the school. Usually, outdoor space provides enough room for several classes to work simultaneously. Where weather conditions require frequent use of indoor space, a minimum of one indoor teaching station for each eight classrooms is needed.

In addition, for taking care of the needs of the handicapped, as required by federal regulations (Public Law 94-142), another indoor play area, separate from, but close to, the regular indoor facility, is required.

Planning facilities for physical education should be done in terms of maximum projected enrollment. Too often, the planning is done in terms of the present situation. Later, when it becomes convenient to add classrooms to the school, they are added without changes in the physical education teaching areas. What was an adequate and suitable teaching situation then creates a scheduling problem. Adding physical education facilities is difficult because of escalating costs coupled with the relatively high cost of physical education facilities in comparison to regular classroom space.

OUTDOOR AREAS

Standards for play areas call for a minimum of 10 acres for the school itself, with an additional acre for each 100 pupils in the maximum projected enrollment. Parking areas, cycle racks, and entry roads are not allowed for in these standards. The outdoor area should include field space for games, a track, hard-surfaced areas, apparatus areas, play courts, age-group play areas, covered play spaces, and a jogging trail.

Fields should be leveled, drained, and turfed, since grass is the most usable field surface. An automatic sprinkler is desirable, but the sprinkler heads should not protrude and become safety hazards. Such installations permit sprinkling during the evening and the night, so the fields are not too soggy for play the next day.

A hardtop area should be marked with a variety of games, and it could include tetherball, volleyball, and basketball courts. Four Square courts, hopscotch layouts, and circles for games are examples of other markings that can be put on these surfaces. Simple movement pattern courses also can be marked out.

Some administrators like to hard surface the entire play area, since this eliminates the mud problem and the need for sprinkling and lowers maintenance costs. This is usually done in areas where play space is limited, and the number of students makes keeping a good turf surface very difficult. However, there are likely to be many more injuries on a hard surface than on grass.

An official track, 440 yards or 400 meters, may be installed when interest in track and field is high. However, space should be provided for a smaller track, 220 yards or 200 meters, in any case, and the track should be built in an area where it would not interfere with other activities. A temporary track can be laid out every spring (see pages 529-530) for schools where a permanent installation is not practical.

Separate play spaces for different age groups should be included in the planning. Such areas should contain apparatus designed for each age group. The location of the play area for primary-level children should be well away from play areas where footballs and softballs are used, so that the play of the older children is not likely to threaten the younger children.

Small hard-surfaced play courts may be strategically located near the edges of the outdoor area, thus spreading out the children. Small courts approximately 40 by 60 feet can be equipped for basketball and/or volleyball.

A covered shed can be divided for use by different age groups. Climatic conditions would dictate the necessity of such facilities.

A jogging trail can stimulate interest in jogging. Small signs indicating distances covered and markers outlining the trail are all that is needed.

Providing for an area set aside for a developmental playground should be an important part of planning the total play space. The area that contains equipment and apparatus should be landscaped so that it contains small hills, valleys, and tunnels for the children. A recommended approach is to develop the playground into various developmental areas, so the children can develop different body parts in different areas of the play space. For example, one area might contain a great deal of climbing equipment for arm-and-shoulder-girdle development, and another area might challenge the leg and trunk region. Equipment and apparatus should be abstract in nature, so creation and imagination are left to the children. Apparatus that are enjoyable for the children can be manipulated and changed to suit the needs and desires of the youngsters.

INDOOR FACILITIES

The gymnasium must be well planned if maximum utility is to be derived from it. The combination gymnasium-auditorium-cafeteria facility leaves much to be desired and creates more problems than it solves. Although it is labeled a multipurpose room, a better term probably would be multiuseless. The cafeteria is a particular problem. The gymnasium must be vacated before the lunch hour so that chairs and tables can be set up, and it is not available for activities until the facility has been cleaned, which usually involves mopping. This eliminates any noon-hour recreational use, leaving little play area for children during inclement weather. In extreme cases, the lack of

help takes the gymnasium out of use during the early part of the afternoon until the custodian has completed his or her cleaning chores.

Play and special events practice is hardly compatible with the free atmosphere of physical education activities. Special programs, movies, and other events necessitating chairs also complicate the situation.

The gymnasium should be located in a separate wing connected to the classrooms by a covered corridor. It should provide ready access to play areas. Isolating the gym from the remainder of the school minimizes the noise problem and allows afterschool and community groups to use the facilities without having access to other parts of the school.

The indoor facility should be planned as a physical education facility in which athletic contests may be scheduled at times, not predominantly as an athletic facility with consideration for spectators. The latter approach is acceptable when the physical education needs have been met, however.

In the gymnasium, floor markings and boundaries should be placed on the floor to provide convenient areas for the more common activities. The markings should be painted on the floor after the first or second sealer coat has been put on. A finish coat then should be put over the lines. The diagram on the next page is an example of how floor markings can be placed in order to maximize the usefulness of the facility.

Temporary lines needed during the year can be marked with pressure-sensitive tape. However, these tapes have disadvantages in that they are difficult to remove completely and are apt to take off some of the finish when they are removed.

A hardwood, preferably maple, gym floor is recommended. Other surfaces limit community use and create both safety and maintenance problems.

Walls should have a smooth surface 8 to 10 feet up from the floor for safety and for ball rebound practice. Walls and ceilings should have acoustical treatment. In original construction, a recess for each set of ropes on tracks is excellent.

Lights should be of sufficient intensity, and they should be recessed to prevent damage. The lights should be arranged so that they can be serviced from the floor. Exposed beams should be available for attaching apparatus.

Electrical outlets should be available on all walls. A permanent overhead public address system is desirable, permitting a permanent installation of the record player for easy and quick access. In original construction, this cabinet can be recessed.

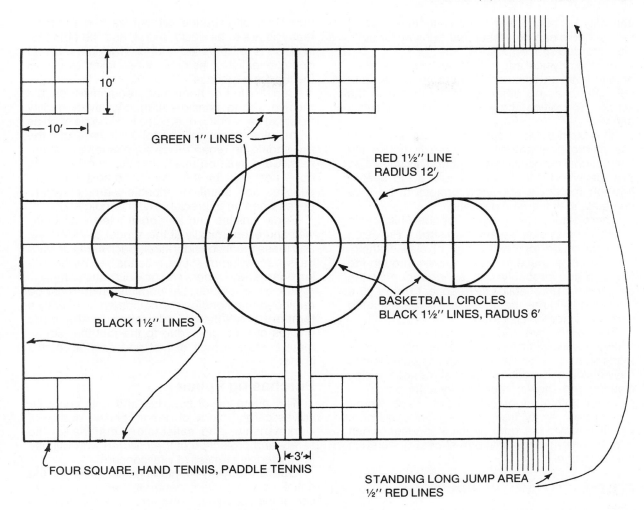

GREEN 1″ LINES

RED 1½″ LINE
RADIUS 12′

BLACK 1½″ LINES

BASKETBALL CIRCLES
BLACK 1½″ LINES, RADIUS 6′

FOUR SQUARE, HAND TENNIS, PADDLE TENNIS

STANDING LONG JUMP AREA
½″ RED LINES

Windows should be placed high on the long sides of the gymnasium. Skylights are not recommended. Protection from glare and direct sun rays should be provided.

If the baskets and backboards need to be raised and lowered often, a motor-driven system eliminates laborious hand cranking. Its switch should be activated with a key.

Adequate storage space is something that must be given careful thought. Storage space for the sheer bulk of equipment and instructional supplies used in present-day physical education must be considerable, and the storage area must be designed so that the materials are easily available.

One problem frequently associated with a combination auditorium-gymnasium facility is the use of the physical education storeroom for the storage of such bulky auditorium equipment as portable chairs on chair trucks and portable stages, to say nothing of lighting fixtures and other paraphernalia for dramatic productions. Unless the storage facility is large enough—and most of them are not—an unworkable and cluttered facility is the result. The best solution is two separate storerooms for the dual-purpose facility, or at least one storeroom that is large enough should be allowed for.

A separate storage area or cabinet is essential for outside groups if they use the facility. They should not have access to the regular physical education supply room, since this only leads to trouble. If they are permitted to use school equipment, it should be checked out to the group and later checked in.

Many storage areas in European schools have doors on tracks similar to American overhead garage doors. This system has a number of advantages, since the larger opening makes the handling of large apparatus much easier.

Most architects are not aware of the storage needs of a modern physical education program. It can only be hoped that the architects designing new schools can be persuaded to allow for sufficient storage space.

For the physical education specialist, it is desirable to have an office-dressing room, since he or she often has no other assigned space in the school. The office should contain a toilet and a shower.

If contract or task approaches are important in the instructional process, an area to house the instructional materials is desirable. This should be a place where the children could go to search through materials and view projectors as they complete their learning packets.

There should be a place for the children to change to play clothing and gym shoes. Provision must be made for the storage of play clothing. Such storage space for kindergarten through the fourth grade probably can be arranged in the classroom, thus enabling the teacher to make sure that each child has the necessary items when the class starts for the play area.

For grades five and six dressing rooms and shower facilities large enough to take care of peak loads should be available. Since it is advisable to have children in grades five and six change to play clothing and shower after activity, different provisions for clothing storage should be made. A storage system away from the regular classroom would remove the odor problem present when play clothing (particularly gym shoes) is stored in the classroom.

EQUIPMENT AND SUPPLIES

Equipment includes those items of a more or less fixed nature. Supplies include those nondurable materials that have a limited time of use. To illustrate the difference—a softball is listed under supplies, while the longer-lasting softball backstop comes under the category of equipment. Equipment needs periodic replacement, and budgetary planning must consider the usable life span of each piece of equipment. Supplies generally are purchased on a yearly basis. It is important not only to have adequate financing for equipment and supplies but also to expend funds wisely.

If the objectives of physical education are to be fulfilled, instructional materials must be available in sufficient quantity. Enough equipment should be present so that there is little waiting for turns. In handling manipulative items, the one-for-one principle should prevail. Each child should have an object of his or her own to work with. This is also true of individual mats. In partner work, there should be one object for each two children.

Policies covering the purchase, storage, issue, care and maintenance, records, and inventory of supplies are necessary if maximum use and return

from the allotted budget is to be realized. Program features are to be decided first, and the purchasing plan is to be based on this. Having a minimal operational list of instructional supplies stabilizes the teaching process.

Constructed or homemade equipment should receive strong consideration. However, quality must not be sacrificed. Articles from home such as empty plastic jugs, milk cartons, old tires, and the like should be regarded as supplementary materials. Care must be taken that the administration does not look for the cheap, no-cost route for supplies and sacrifice valuable learning experiences when an appreciable cost is indicated.

Some articles can be constructed sufficiently well and economically at the school or the home, and these merit consideration. Such items as yarn balls, hoops, lummi sticks, balance beams, bounding boards, and others can be built satisfactorily.

For other articles, the administration must be reminded that constructed equipment is usually a temporary solution, undertaken in the early phases of a program due to the fact that equipment costs are high at first and cannot be met immediately.

Purchasing Policies

The purchase of supplies and equipment involves careful study of needs, prices, quality of workmanship, and satisfactory materials. The safety and protection of the children who will use the materials are also of vital concern.

Quantity buying by pooling the needs of the entire school system generally results in better use of the tax dollar. However, there may need to be some compromises on the types and brands of materials in order to satisfy different users within a school system. If bids are asked, there is need to make careful specifications for materials. Bids should be asked only on those items specified, and "just as good" merchandise should not be accepted as substitutes.

One individual within a school should be made responsible for the physical education supplies and for keeping records of equipment and supplies and purchasing. Needs vary from school to school, and it is practical for school district authorities to deal with a single individual within each school. Prompt attention to repair and replacement of supplies is more likely under this system. The designated individual also should be responsible for testing various competitive products to determine which will give the best service over time. Some kind of labeling or marking of the materials is needed if this is to be accomplished.

An accurate inventory of equipment should be undertaken at the start and the end of the school year. Through a sound system of inventorying, the durability of equipment and supplies and the amount of supplies lost or misplaced can be established.

The ordering of supplies and equipment should be done at the end of the school year and be completed no later than July 1, and earlier if possible. A delivery date in August should be specified, so the orders can be checked and adjustments made, if needed, before the school year begins in the fall.

Equipment of good quality should be purchased, since most of it will last from 7 to 10 years, thus holding replacement costs to a minimum. The policy of some purchasing agents of selecting items of low cost with little regard to quality in order to stretch the budget dollar is unsound.

Budgetary practices need to consider the yearly procurement of instructional supplies, as well as major replacement and procurement of large items, usually staggered over a number of years. Once sufficient equipment and supplies have been procured, the budget problem becomes one of replacement and repair.

Recommended Equipment

Outdoor Equipment

Two criteria are important for selecting equipment for the outdoor setting for physical education. The first is that each piece of equipment must contribute to the development of the child. For this reason, items that involve only "sit and ride" experiences (such as swings, teeters, and merry-go-rounds) are not recommended. In addition, the value of the slide is questionable, but some educators feel that there is value in the climbing part and that the slide is a challenge to overcoming fear. The second criterion is the safety factor. Many of the circular, hanging types like the giant stride often prove dangerous.

Climbing Structures: There are many brands and many good varieties. Various types such as jungle gyms and castle towers have value in physical fitness.

Horizontal Ladders: Horizontal ladders are valuable pieces of equipment on the playground. They come in a variety of combinations and forms. Arched ladders are quite popular, and they allow children to reach the rungs easily. Uniladders, consisting of a single beam with pegs on each side, offer good challenge for children. A set comprising two arched ladders, crossing each other at the center at right angles, offers the potential for numerous types of movement experiences.

Climbing Ropes: In some climates where the weather is not too severe, schools are installing climbing ropes outside. These should not be over 12 to 14 feet in height and should be equipped with circular stops at the top.

Arched Ladders

Balance Beams: Beams made from 4-by-4-inch beams can be put in permanent installations. These can be arranged in various patterns but should not be more than 12 to 18 inches above the surface. Outdoor balance beams provide an extension of the instructional activities of the program.

Turning Bars: Turning bars made from 3-inch galvanized pipe offer exciting possibilities for children. The bars can be from 6 to 10 feet in length and positioned 30 to 36 inches above the ground.

Horizontal Bar Combinations: A set of three horizontal bars together at different heights is a valuable piece of apparatus for physical education.

Basketball Goals: These may or may not be combined with a court. Youngsters play a great deal of one-goal basketball, and a regulation court is not needed for this game. These should be in a surfaced area, however. Outdoor baskets for elementary school use should be 8 to 9 feet off the ground. This lowered height (regulation is 10 feet) poses a problem, since children can more easily jump up and grasp the front of the rim and damage the basket or tear it loose. Strong construction that withstands this abuse is one solution. Some schools revert back to the 10-foot-high basket, thus putting it out of reach of most children.

Volleyball Standards: Volleyball standards should have flexible height adjustments, including a low height of 30 inches for use with paddle ball.

Softball Backstops: Softball backstops can be either fixed or portable.

Tetherball Courts: Tetherball courts should have fastening devices for the cord and ball so that these can be removed from the post for safe keeping.

Track and Field Equipment: Jumping standards, bars, and pits should be available. These must be properly maintained.

Challenge Courses: Considerable choice is available in setting up outdoor Challenge

Courses, a new development on the equipment market. Many interesting and challenging obstacles can be put together in an effective course.

Other Playground Equipment

Many other items can be used as part of the outdoor playground plan. These include large concrete sewer pipes (24 inches or more in diameter) placed variously, posts in combination for stepping stones, forts made of railroad ties or building blocks, tractor tires placed in pyramid fashion, a giant tractor tire placed flat, a series of jumping blocks for Leapfrog, steps and platforms from which to jump, and simulated locomotives and trains. Truck tires embedded about half their diameter into the ground make interesting objects for play.

There is much emphasis today on the creative playground. Many creative and imaginative pieces of playground apparatus are available for this purpose from commercial sources.

Indoor Equipment

Several principles should govern the choice of indoor equipment. First, a good variety of equipment should be available in sufficient numbers to keep the children active. Standing around and waiting for turns should be minimized. Included should be items to challenge arm-shoulder-girdle development (climbing ropes, climbing frames, ladders, and similar apparatus). A criterion for selection should be that most, if not all, equipment is of the type that the children themselves can carry, assemble, and disassemble. A regular trampoline, for example, would not meet this test. Items suggested for equipping an indoor facility follow.

Mats for Tumbling and Safety: Mats are basic to any physical education program and at least eight should be present. Enough mats must be available to provide safety flooring for climbing apparatus. The light, folding mats are preferable because of their ease of handling and storing. Folding mats stack better and can be moved with the appropriate carts. Mats should have fasteners so that two or more can be joined together. The covers are plastic and can be cleaned easily. The

one objection is that they are not as soft as the type used for wrestling. Mats should be 4 feet wide and 7 or 8 feet long. Heavy hand-me-down mats from the high school program, some with canvas covers, may prove counterproductive, because they are hard to handle and store.

Other mats that can be considered are thick, soft mats (somewhat similar to mattresses) and inclined mats. Soft mats are generally 4 inches or more thick and so they entice the timid into activities that otherwise they would not try. Inclined mats are wedge shaped and provide downhill momentum for rolls. Both types of mats are excellent for the program for the handicapped.

Individual Mats: Strong consideration should be given to a supply of 30 to 35 individual mats, which are used mostly for the primary program. The mats can be 20 by 40 inches or 24 by 48 inches. They provide the basis for many interesting movement experiences and introductory tumbling activities. However, expense is a factor, since the initial outlay, including that for a carrying cart, is quite high. The mats, however, last indefinitely with care and add much to the program.

Record Player: A good record player with a variable speed control is a must for the program. Pause control is also helpful. The physical education program should have its own record player, since there is enough demand to justify this. Access to a tape recorder is also helpful.

Balance-Beam Benches: These have a double use. They can be used as regular benches for the many types of bench activities, and when they are turned over, they become balance beams. The balance-beam bench should be of sturdy construction to stand up under the various demands. Wooden horses or their supports can be used to provide inclined benches. Six benches are a minimum for class activity.

Balance Beams: A wide beam (4 inches) is recommended for the kindergarten and the first grade. Otherwise, the usual 2-inch beam should be used. Balance beams with alternate surfaces (2 or 4 inches) can be constructed out of common building materials.

Chinning Bar: The chinning bar is especially useful in the testing program for physical fitness,

Outdoor Challenge Course

Climbing Ropes on Tracks

Types of Balance Boards

as well as providing body support activities. The portable chinning bar used in the doorway of the gymnasium is a substitute.

Climbing Ropes: Climbing ropes are essential to the program. At least eight should be present, but more allow for better group instruction. Climbing rope sets on tracks are the most efficient method of handling these pieces of equipment. With little effort or loss of time, the ropes are ready for activity. Ropes are available in a variety of materials, but good-quality manila hemp seems to be the most practical. Ropes should be either 1¼ or 1½ inches in diameter.

Volleyball Standards: The standards should allow for various heights for different grades and also for other games.

Portable Climbing Structures: These portable sets usually are based on wooden or metal horses and include supported bars, ladders, and other equipment for climbing.

Bounding Boards: These are 2 by 6 feet and generally are made of ¾-inch marine plywood. (Knots in poor-quality plywood cause the boards to break.) Useful in the primary program, four boards should be constructed.

Balance Boards: Four to six balance boards of different types are a desirable extension of apparatus experiences. Bongo boards also are useful.

Supply Cart: A cart to hold supplies is quite desirable. Other carts can be utilized for the record player and for regular and individual mats.

Jumping Boxes: Small boxes used for jumping and allied locomotor movements have good value in extending the opportunities for basic movement skills. For kindergarten and the first grade, boxes should be 8 and 16 inches in height. For the older children, boxes of 12 and 24 inches offer sufficient challenge. The shorter box can be 16 by 16 inches and the taller box can be 18 by 18 inches in size. The smaller box can be stored inside the larger box. The top of the box should be padded with carpet padding and covered with leather or durable plastic. Holes drilled through the sides provide fingerholds for ease of handling.

Portable Combination Set

First-Grade Children Using 16-Inch Jumping Boxes

Inclined Climbing Frame

Eight boxes, four of each, are a minimum number for the average-size class.

Horizontal Ladder Sets: Horizontal ladders that fold against the wall make an excellent addition to indoor equipment. The ladder may be combined with other pieces of apparatus in a folding set.

Climbing Frames: Climbing frames, mostly of European origin, are becoming increasingly popular and available in this country. The authors have had excellent success in their programs with the inclined climbing frame.

A type of frame that has been well accepted in this country and in Canada is the Centaur Frame, which can be ordered from Centaur Athletics, Inc., P.O. Box 178, Custer, Wash. 98240.

Other Items

A portable chalkboard is desirable, as is a wall screen for viewing visual aids. There also should be a large bulletin board and a wall chalkboard, both of which should be located near the main

Centaur Climbing Frame

entrance. The wall chalkboard permits quick announcements or notes.

An audiovisual cart or stand for projectors is helpful. It should contain sufficient electric cord to reach wall outlets.

Supplies for Physical Education

A basic list and an optional list of supplies should be established for each program. The basic list stipulates the instructional materials that should be available for teaching. In addition, there should be extra items held in storage for replacement during the year. Optional supplies depend upon personal preferences and the funds available.

Basic Supply List

Ball inflator with gauge (1)
Balloons, rubber (1 for each child)
Balls
    Beach balls, 12 to 16 inches (2-6)
    Cageballs, 24 inches (2)—also an extra bladder
    Playground balls, rubber—mostly 8½ inches (1 for each child)
    Small balls, sponge or tennis, assorted colors (50)
    Sports balls (football, basketball, soccer, volleyball; 8 of each)
    Yarn or fleece balls (1 for each child)
Basketball nets (6 extra)
Batting tees for softball (4-6)
Beanbags, assorted colors (2 for each child)
Cones, rubber—boundary markers (24)
Eyeglass protectors (4 or more)
Gym scooters (4 for relays or 1 for each two children for games)
Hockey sets (2)
Hoops, 36 or 42 inches (1 for each child)
Indian clubs (16 or more)
Individual mats (1 for each child)
Jump ropes, individual (1 for each child), a variety
Jump ropes, long (8)
Jump-the-shot ropes (3)
Lummi sticks (32 pair)
Magic (stretch) ropes (8)
Measuring tape, 50 feet or longer (1)
Paddles, wooden (1 for each child)
Parachute, 24 or 28 foot (1)
Pinnies or other team markers (1 for each two children)
Records (as needed), sufficient supply
Scoops, bottle (1 for each child)
Softball equipment—balls, gloves, masks, bases, bats, protector
Stopwatches, $\frac{1}{5}$ or $\frac{1}{10}$ second (3)
Tambourine (1)
Tetherball sets (as needed)
Tinikling pole sets (6)

Tom-tom or dance drum (1)
Tote bags for balls (12 or more)
Track and field equipment—batons (8), jump boards, hurdles, crossbars or ropes, starter, jump standards
Tug-of-war ropes, individual (1 for each two children)
Volleyball nets (2)
Wands (1 for each child)
Whistles (8)
Wire baskets for holding items (6 or more)

Optional Supply List

Bongo boards (8)
Broom handles (8)
Deck tennis rings (16)
Frisbees (16)
Horseshoes, sets with pegs
Lime—for lining fields
Liner, dry—for lining fields
Microphone for record player
Pitching targets
Pogo sticks (8)
Repair kit for balls
Shuffleboard equipment
Stilts (6 pair)
Table tennis equipment
Tape, colored—for temporary lining
Tires, auto
Tires, bicycle
Tool chest—saw, hammer, pliers, et cetera
Tubes, auto, oversized—inflatable
Tug-of-war rope, large (60 feet or more)
Wooden blocks, 1 by 1 inch for relays (24)

The preceding list represents the kinds of items that can be optional and is meant to be only a representative list. Other items purchased commercially or made at home could be added.

Storage Plans

When a teacher takes a class into the gymnasium for physical education, he or she has the right to expect and be assured of sufficient supplies to conduct his or her class. A master list stipulating the kinds and quantities of supplies that should be in storage should be established. A reasonable turnover should be expected, and supply procedures should reflect this. The supplies in the storage facility should be available for physical education classes and afterschool activities. They should not be used for recess or free play periods, since each classroom should have its own supplies for this purpose.

A systematic procedure should be established for the storage of equipment and supplies. A place for everything and everything in its place is the key to good housekeeping. Bins, shelves, and places where supplies and equipment are to be kept should be labeled.

Equipment Cart

Both teachers and students should accept the responsibility for maintaining good order in the storage facility. Squad leaders or student aides can assume major responsibility. At the end of the week, the teacher in charge of the storage area can assign older children to help tidy up the area, put things back in place, and repair or replace articles as needed. This gets things ready for the start of the following week. A principal certainly is inclined more favorably toward purchase requests when he or she observes the good care the instructional materials are receiving.

Some schools have found it helpful to use small supply carts of the type pictured above. The cart holds the articles most frequently used. It does take up space, but it is quite a time-saver. Carts can be built inexpensively to a personal plan, or an equipment carrier can be purchased. Other carts to hold the record player and to store and move mats are helpful.

An off-season storage area should be established to which articles not in present use can be moved. Reserve new equipment not yet placed in use should be kept in a separate area, perhaps under lock and key.

Care, Repair, and Marking

A definite system should be established for repairing supplies and equipment. A quick decision needs to be made whether they can be repaired locally or need to be sent out. If the repair process is lengthy and not efficient, children and teachers may prefer to use the article until it no longer can be salvaged, rather than be deprived of its use.

Balls need to be inflated to proper pressures. This means using an accurate gauge and periodic checking. The needle should be moistened before it is inserted into the valve. Children should not sit on balls and should only kick balls made specifically for kicking (soccer balls, footballs, and playground balls).

Softball bats and wooden paddles should not be used for hitting rocks, stones, or other hard materials. Neither should bats be knocked against fences, posts, or other objects that will cause damage. Broken bats should be discarded, since they are unsafe even when taped around the break. Children should learn to keep the trademark up when batting. Bats should be taped to prevent slippage.

Cuts, abrasions, and breaks in rubber balls should be immediately repaired. In some cases, this repair can be handled by means of a vulcanizing patch as used for tire tube repairs. In others, the use of a hard-setting rubber preparation is of value. However, some repairs are beyond the scope of the school, and the ball should be sent away for repair.

Mats are expensive and care is needed if they are to last. A place where they can be stacked properly should be provided, or there should be handles for hanging them up. A mat truck is another solution, provided there is space for storing the truck. The newer plastic or plastic-covered mats should be cleaned with a damp, soapy cloth.

For off-season storage, balls should be deflated somewhat, leaving enough air in them to keep their shape. Leather balls should be cleaned with an approved ball conditioner.

For small items, clean ice cream containers make adequate storage receptacles. Most school cafeterias have these and other containers that can be used in the storage room to provide order. Small wire baskets also make good containers for small physical education materials.

An area should be established for the equipment needing repair, so the articles for repair are evident at a glance.

Equipment that will warp should be laid in a flat place.

All equipment and supplies should be marked. This is particularly important for equipment issued to different classrooms. Marking can be done with indelible pencils, paint, or stencil ink. However, few marking systems are permanent and re-marking at regular intervals is necessary. Sporting goods establishments have marking sets available for this purpose. An electric burning pencil or stamp is also useful but must be used with caution so as not to damage the equipment being marked.

Rubber playground balls come in different colors, and an assignment to a classroom can be made on the basis of color. A code scheme with different color paints also can be used. It is possi-ble to devise a color system by which the year of issue can be designated. This offers opportunities for research into equipment use.

RECOMMENDATIONS AND SPECIFICATIONS FOR CONSTRUCTING EQUIPMENT AND SUPPLIES

The following section is divided into two major areas. The first area offers recommendations for sources and materials needed to construct equipment and supplies, as well as recommended usage. The second part consists of diagrams and specifications for building equipment in an economical manner. Thus, if the recommended equipment can be described without an illustration, it will be found in the first section.

Some supplies are designed especially for children in the intermediate grades. Junior-size footballs and basketballs are available and should be used. Rubber-covered balls generally prove more satisfactory than the leather variety for use in the elementary school, particularly during wet weather.

Smaller children can use rubber playground balls for volleyball-type games. When playground balls are used for soccer skills, they work more satisfactorily when slightly deflated.

When children are working on simple bouncing skills, it is imperative for each child to have a ball. The supply of balls can be augmented by tennis balls or sponge balls. Discarded tennis balls from the high school tennis team are a good source. Holes can be poked into the tennis balls if they are too lively for the children to handle. Sponge balls are inexpensive and with care last indefinitely.

A good supply of ropes for jumping is essential. The authors are partial to the newer plastic-link jump ropes, since these have good weight, come in attractive colors, can be shortened easily (by taking out some links), and can be purchased with color-coded handles. The handles provide good leverage for turning momentum. Ropes, however, can be made from cord.

Heavy sashcord or hard-weave polyethylene rope is suitable. The ends should be whipped, heated, or dipped in some type of hardening solution to prevent raveling. Lengths can be color-coded with dye or stain.

The following lengths are recommended.

Grades kindergarten through two: mostly 7 foot, with a few 6-foot and 8-foot lengths.

Grades three through six: mostly 8 foot, with a few 7-foot and 9-foot lengths.

Instructors: 9 or 10 foot.

Enough ropes in the suggested varieties should be present for each child to have a rope of the correct length. The supply of ropes should include 8 to 10 long ropes of 14 or 16 feet in length.

Beanbags can be made easily. Good-quality, bright-colored muslin is suitable. Some teachers have had success in asking parents to save the lower pantlegs of worn-out denim jeans. This material wears extremely well and is free. Some prefer a beanbag with an outer liner that snaps in place to allow for washing. Another idea is to sew three sides of the beanbag permanently. The fourth side is used for filling and has an independent stitch. The beans can be removed through the side when the bag is washed. Beanbags should be about 4 by 4 inches and 6 by 6 inches and can be filled with dried beans, peas, wheat, rice, or even building sand.

For games requiring boundary markers, pieces of rubber matting can be used. In addition, small sticks or boards, painted white, are excellent. A board 1 by 2 inches, 3 or 4 feet in length, makes a satisfactory marker.

Tetherballs should have a snap-on fastener for easy removal.

Softballs can be purchased without stitching (concealed stitch); this eliminates the problem of broken stitches and consequent repair.

A jump-the-shot rope can be made by using an old, completely deflated volleyball tied on the end of a rope.

Old tires, even those from bicycles, can be used. See the chapter on apparatus activities for many ideas for utilizing tires.

Schools near ski areas may be able to get discarded tow ropes. These make excellent tug-of-war ropes.

Indian clubs can be turned in the school woodshop. However, many substitutes can be made. Two-by-two-inch lumber cut into short pieces (6 to 10 inches long) stand satisfactorily. Lumber companies usually have dowels 1 to 1½ inches in diameter. Sections of these make satisfactory Indian clubs. Broken bats also can be made into good substitute clubs.

White shoe polish has numerous uses and will come off the floor with a little scrubbing. Marking lines and making designs are two of the uses for this marking device.

Three-pound coffee cans can be used as targets.

Empty half-gallon milk cartons also have a variety of uses.

Inner tubes can be cut into strips and used as resistive exercise equipment. Cut across the tube in strips about 1½ inches wide.

Old bowling pins can be obtained from most bowling alleys free of charge. Since they are too large for the children to handle easily, cut 6 to 8 inches off the top. Parallel cuts through the body of the pin provide hockey pucks and shuffle board disks. Another way to trim bowling pins is described on page 563.

For kindergarten and first-grade children, improvised balls can be made from crumpled newspaper bound with cellophane tape. Papier-mâché balls are also useful. Light foam rubber cubes can be trimmed to make interesting objects for throwing and catching.

Bamboo poles for making Tinikling poles sometimes can be secured from carpet stores, where they are used to give support to the center of a carpet roll. Plastic Tinikling sticks are also available commercially.

A better value for rubber traffic cones can be realized if these are purchased from a highway department's supply source, since they are usually less expensive than those purchased from physical education equipment supply firms.

Plastic jugs can be utilized in place of traffic cones.

Diagrams and Specifications for Constructed Equipment

Balance Beam

The balance beam is used for many types of activities (see page 299). Two types of stands for a beam utilizing a two-by-four are included here. The beam can be placed with the wide or the narrow side up, depending on the skill of the performer. If the beam is longer than 8 feet, a third stand should be placed in the middle. Care must be taken to sand and apply multiple coats of finish to prevent splintering and cracking.

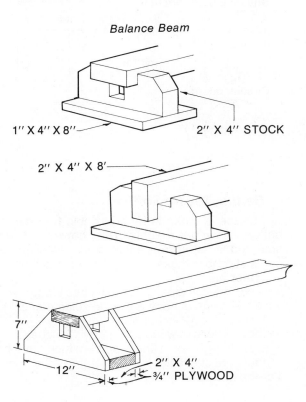

Balance Beam

1″ X 4″ X 8″   2″ X 4″ STOCK

2″ X 4″ X 8′

7″

12″   2″ X 4″
¾″ PLYWOOD

Balance Beam Bench

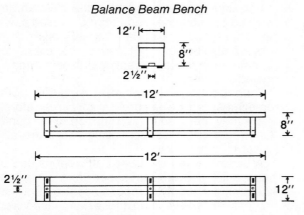

Balance Boards

Many different styles of boards can be constructed, depending on the materials available and individual needs. The board should have a piece of rubber matting glued to the top to prevent slipping. The board should be placed on an individual mat or a piece of heavy rubber matting. A square board is easier to balance than a round one, for its corners touch the floor and give more stability.

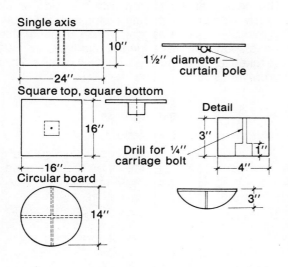

Single axis

1½″ diameter curtain pole

Square top, square bottom

Detail

Drill for ¼″ carriage bolt

Circular board

Batting Tee for Softball

The tee is made to be adjustable to allow for batters of various heights. This, however, takes time and is not always satisfactory. An alternate suggestion is to make tees of different heights.

Materials

1 piece—1-inch pipe, 24 to 28 inches long
1 piece—radiator hose with inside diameter of 1½ inches, 8 to 12 inches long
1 piece—block of wood 3 by 12 by 12 inches
1 pipe flange for 1-inch pipe, which can be mounted on block
Screws and hose cement

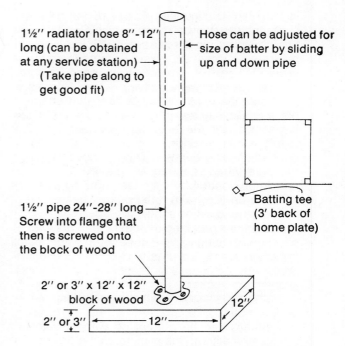

1½″ radiator hose 8″-12″ long (can be obtained at any service station) (Take pipe along to get good fit)

Hose can be adjusted for size of batter by sliding up and down pipe

1½″ pipe 24″-28″ long Screw into flange that then is screwed onto the block of wood

Batting tee (3′ back of home plate)

2″ or 3″ x 12″ x 12″ block of wood

Directions: Mount the flange on the block and screw the pipe into the flange. Place the radiator hose on the pipe. Paint as desired.

To secure a good fit for the radiator hose, take the pipe to the supply source. If the hose is not to slide, then secure it with hose cement.

An alternate method is to drill a hole into the block and mount the pipe directly with mastic or good-quality glue.

Note that 1-inch pipe has an outside diameter of approximately 1½ inches, allowing the proper size hose to fit over it.

Blocks and Cones

Blocks with grooves on the tops and one of the sides are excellent for forming hurdles with wands.

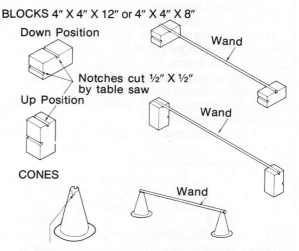

BLOCKS 4″ X 4″ X 12″ or 4″ X 4″ X 8″

Down Position

Wand

Notches cut ½″ X ½″ by table saw

Up Position

Wand

CONES

Wand

Cut a ½″ notch on each side of top lip of cone

A four-by-four, cut into various lengths (6, 12, and 18 inches), gives a variety of hurdle sizes. Cones can be notched and used in place of the blocks.

Bongo Boards

Bongo boards are excellent for helping students learn concepts of static balance. Roller sizes can be increased to make the challenges more difficult. Students can be challenged to balance with their legs in different positions, with body parts at different levels, and while manipulating an object such as a ball, beanbag, or hoop.

Materials

1 piece—¾-inch plywood cut to the dimensions of 8 by 36 inches
3 feet of wood 1 by 2 inches
1 roller, which can vary in diameter from 2 inches to 5 inches

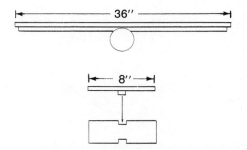

Directions: On the bottom of the plywood board, glue and screw down the 1-by-2-inch piece of lumber. This provides a guide that will keep the roller from moving out from under the board. The roller should be cut so that the guide fits inside the slot on the roller with a clearance of not more than ⅛ inch.

Bounding Board

Bounding boards should be made from good-quality, ¾-inch marine plywood, since this type of plywood is stronger and holds up under repeated bounding. If the board exhibits a tendency to break, a stop can be put under the middle of the board. A 2-by-4-inch padded board the width of the bounding board usually works adequately.

It is not necessary to finish the boards. Different lengths of boards give various amounts of bounce and can be adapted to the size of the student. Heavier students should not bound on boards

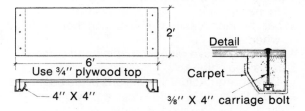

made for younger children. Glue the plywood to the supporting timbers.

Materials

1 piece—¾-inch marine plywood 2 by 6 feet
2 pieces—4-by-4-inch boards, 2 feet long, trimmed as shown
6 carriage bolts—⅜ by 4 inches
2 pieces of carpet about 8 by 24 inches
Glue

Bowling Pins

Bowling alleys give away old tenpins that can be used for many purposes. Suggested uses are for field and gymnasium markers, bowling games, and relays. Cut the bottom 2 inches off the pin, and sand it smooth. Pins can be numbered and decorated with decals, colored tape, or paint to enhance their attractiveness.

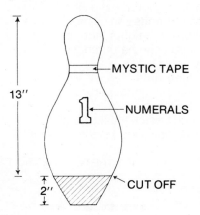

Nylon-Stocking Paddles

Nylon-stocking paddles can substitute quite effectively for wooden paddles when they are used with a light foam rubber or a newspaper ball. They are excellent for primary-age children because of their light weight and the fact they cannot cause injuries. A badminton bird can be used with the paddle for various activities such as hitting over a net and for performing many individual stunts.

Materials

Old nylon stocking
Wire coat hanger

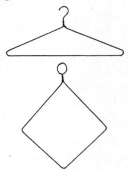

Masking or athletic tape
String or wire

Directions: Bend the hanger into a diamond shape. Bend the hook into a loop, which is to become the handle of the paddle. Pull the stocking over the hanger, beginning away from the handle, until the toe of the nylon is as tight as possible against the point of the hanger. Hold the nylon at the neck of the hanger and stretch it as tight as possible. Tie the nylon tightly with a piece of heavy string or light wire. Wrap the rest of the nylon around the handle and make a smooth, contoured surface. Complete the paddle by wrapping tape around the entire handle to prevent loosening.

Conduit Hurdles

Conduit hurdles are lightweight and easy to store. Since they are not weighted and fall over easily, children have little fear of hitting them. The elastic bands can be moved up and down to create different heights and challenges for students. Conduit can be purchased at most electrical supply houses.

Materials
Electrical conduit pipe ½ inch in diameter, 10 feet long
1-inch stretch elastic tape
Wood doweling ½ inch in diameter

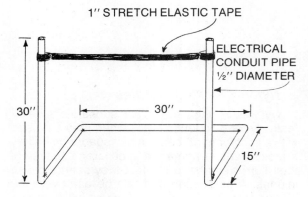

Directions: The piece of conduit 10 feet long should be bent to the following dimensions: uprights—30 inches high; base—30 inches wide; and the sides of the base—15 inches long. A special tool for bending the conduit usually can be purchased from the supply house where the conduit was bought. Loops should be sewn on each end of the elastic tape, so it slides over the ends of the hurdles with a slight amount of tension. Short pieces of doweling can be put in the ends of the conduit to raise the height of the hurdle.

Footsies

Footsies can be made economically by the children. They provide excellent challenge for movement. The activity requires coordination of both feet to keep the footsie rotating properly. Activities such as running in place, running (moving), hopping, and jumping are possible. Children should be challenged to perform with each foot and at different tempos. Routines to music can be developed, and manipulative activities can be performed simultaneously for greater challenge. Students can play catch with balls, juggle beanbags, or work with a paddle and ball.

Materials
Plastic bleach bottle, half-gallon size
⅛-inch clothesline-type rope
Old tennis ball
Large fishing swivel, preferably with ball bearings

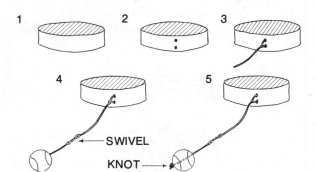

Directions: Cut a circular strip about 2 inches wide out of the bottom of the bleach bottle. Cut two holes in the strip about 1 inch apart. Thread a 3-foot piece of clothesline through the holes, and tie a knot on the outside of the strip. Cut the clothesline in half and tie the swivel to each end of the cut cord. The swivel prevents the rope from becoming twisted.

Puncture the tennis ball with an ice pick, making two holes directly across from each other. Thread the line through the holes with a piece of wire or a large crochet hook. Tie a large enough knot near the outer hole so the line does not slip back through the holes.

Gym Scooters

Scooters are easily constructed from common, available materials. The casters should be checked to see that they do not mark the floor. Scooters have many uses, as previously described. Another use for the scooter is for moving heavy equipment.

Materials
1 piece—2-inch yellow pine board cut 12 by 12 inches square
4 ball bearing casters with 2-inch hard rubber wheels
4 feet of protective rubber stripping and cement
Screws and paint

Directions: Actual dimensions of the board are around 1⅝ by 11⅝ by 11⅝ inches. Two pieces of ¾-inch plywood glued together can be substituted. Cut and round the corners, smoothing them with a power sander. Sand all edges by hand. After two coats of paint, fasten the four casters approximately 1½ inches diagonally in from the corners. For cushioning the impact of scooters on other objects, a rubber strip may be fixed around the edges with staples and cement.

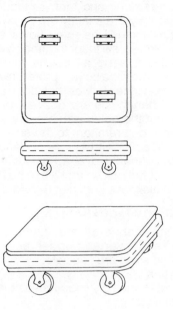

Hoops

Hoops can be constructed from ½-inch plastic water pipe, which unfortunately only comes in drab colors. However, the cost savings are great and override the drab colors. Another advantage is that hoops can be constructed in different sizes. A short piece of doweling, fixed with a power stapler or tacks, can be used to join the ends together. An alternate method is to use special pipe connectors. Weather-strip cement helps make a more permanent joint.

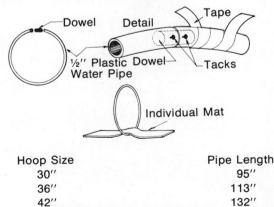

Hoop Size	Pipe Length
30″	95″
36″	113″
42″	132″

Hurdle and High Jump Rope

The weighted hurdle and high jump rope is ideal for beginning hurdlers and high jumpers who have a fear of hitting the bar. The rope can be hung over the pins of the high jump standards and the weights will keep the rope fairly taut.

Materials

10 feet of ⅜-inch rope
Two rubber crutch tips (no. 19)
Tacks (no. 14) and penny shingle nails
Lead (can be purchased at plumbing outlets)

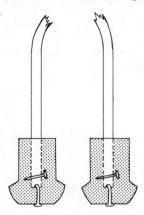

Directions: Take the 10-foot piece of rope and drive carpet tacks through the rope approximately ¾ inch from the ends. Drive three nails into bottom of each of two rubber crutch tips. Place the rope ends into the crutch tips and fill them with hot lead.

Individual Mats

Individual mats can be made from indoor-outdoor carpeting that has a rubber backing. This prevents the mat from sliding on the floor and offers some cushion. Also, the mats can be washed easily when they become soiled. If possible, mats of different colors are preferable, because they can be used for games, for color tag, and for easy division of the class according to the color of mat. Oftentimes, carpet stores have many small pieces and remnants that they sell cheaply or give away.

20″ X 40″ or 24″ X 48″

Individual Tug-of-War Ropes

Individual tug-of-war ropes can be made economically from garden hose and ropes. The cheaper plastic garden hoses (⅝ inch in diameter) work much better than the more expensive rubber hoses. The plastic hose does not crease as easily and gives the hands more protection. The white, soft, braided nylon rope (¼ inch in diameter) offers adequate strength and is much easier to handle. A bowline knot should be used, since it does not slip and tighten around the handle. The ends of the nylon rope should be melted over a flame to prevent them from unraveling.

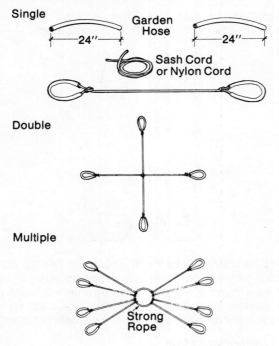

Jumping Boxes

Jumping boxes are used for developing a wide variety of body management skills. The dimensions can be varied to satisfy individual needs, but, if the boxes are made so they fit inside of each other, storage is less of a problem. The boxes also can be used to transport equipment and supplies when they are not being used for their primary purpose.

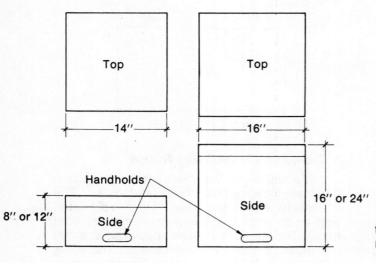

Materials

¾-inch marine plywood
Wood screws, paint, and glue
Carpet pad remnants
Naugahyde or similar material to cover boxes
Upholstery tacks

Directions: The four sides should be cut to similar dimensions and then sanded together to make sure they are exactly the same size. Use a countersink and drill the screw holes, apply glue to the joints, and screw them together. When the box is assembled, sand all edges to remove any sharpness. Paint the boxes, preferably with a latex base paint, since it does not chip as easily as enamel. If handholds are desired, drill the holes and then cut the holes with a saber saw. Finally, cut a carpet pad remnant to the size of the top of the box and cover with a piece of Naugahyde. The Naugahyde should overlap about 4 inches on each side of the box so that it can be folded under to double thickness and then tacked down.

Jumping Standards

Jumping standards are useful for hurdling, jumping, and over-and-under activities. Many shapes and sizes are possible.

Materials

2 pieces of ¾-inch plywood (cut as diagrammed), 25 inches long
2 wood blocks, 2 by 4 by 6 inches
Glue and paint

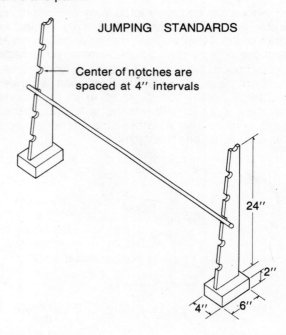

Directions: The wood blocks should be morticed lengthwise about 1 inch deep. After the uprights have been cut to form, set them with glue into the blocks, making sure that the uprights are plumb.

Paint as desired. Small circles of various colors can be placed at each of the corresponding notches of the uprights for better identification.

Ladder

A ladder laid on the floor or on a mat provides a floor target for varied movement experiences and has value in perceptual-motor programs and those for exceptional children. Sizes can vary.

Materials

2 pieces of straight-grained 2-by-4-inch timbers, 9½ feet long

10 pieces of 1¼-inch or 1½-inch dowels 20 inches long

Glue and paint or varnish

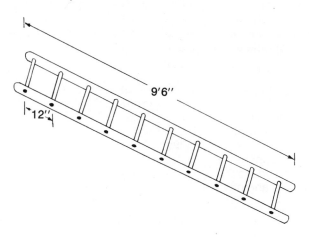

Directions: Round ends and sand edges of the timbers. Center holes for the ladder rungs 12 inches apart, beginning 3 inches from the other end. Cut the holes for the rungs ¹/₁₆ inch smaller than the diameter of the rungs. Put glue into all of the holes on one timber, and drive in all of the rungs. Then, glue the other timber in place. Varnish or paint the ladders.

Lummi Sticks

Lummi sticks are excellent tools for developing rhythmic skill and easily can be used in the classroom. They can be shared with the music teacher, who can use them as rhythm sticks. Classroom isometrics can be performed, using the sticks for resistance (see unit on wands, page 273). It is also possible to use the sticks as relay batons.

Materials

1-inch doweling, cut into 12-inch lengths
Paint and varnish

Directions: The notches and different colors are options, but do make the sticks more attractive. If desired, cut notches ⅛ inch wide and ⅛ inch deep on a table saw. Round off the ends and sand

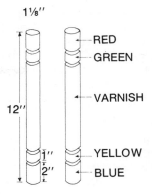

the entire stick. Paint and varnish the stick, as shown in the diagram.

Magic (Stretch) Ropes

Magic, or stretch, ropes can be made by stringing together 25 to 30 large-size rubber bands. Common clothing elastic also can be used to make excellent ropes. Some teachers have had success with shock cord, which usually can be purchased in a boating marina.

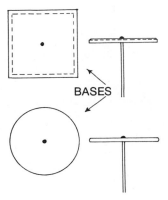

Outdoor Bases

There are many satisfactory methods for constructing bases. They can be made from heavy canvas by folding the canvas over three or four times and stitching it together. Heavy rubber matting can be cut to size. More permanent bases should be made from outdoor plywood and painted as described below.

Materials

Exterior ¾-inch plywood
Carriage bolt, 14 inches long, ½ inch in diameter
Paint

Directions: Cut the plywood into 12-by-12-inch squares. Bevel and sand the top edges. Drill a ½-inch hole in the center of the base and then paint it. When it is dry, place the carriage bolt in the center hole and drive it into the ground. More holes can be used to make the base secure, and large spikes can be substituted for the carriage bolt.

Paddles

Paddles can be made in many sizes and with different thicknesses of plywood. Usually, ¼-inch plywood is best for grades kindergarten through two and ⅜-inch plywood for grades three through six. Paddles can be painted or varnished and the handles taped to give a better grip. Holes can be drilled in the paddle area to make it lighter and decrease air resistance. Good-quality plywood, perhaps marine plywood, is essential.

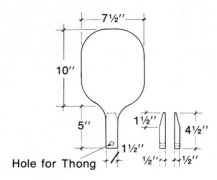

Paddle Tennis Net Supports

The advantage of these sets is that they stand by themselves on the floor and still provide proper net tension. The stands come apart easily and quickly and can be stored in a small space.

For lengths up to 8 feet or so, a single center board, with holes on each end, can be used, eliminating the need for bolting two pieces together.

Materials
2 broomsticks or ¾-inch dowels, 24 inches long
21-by-4-inch boards, 24 inches long
1 or more 1-by-4-inch boards
Glue

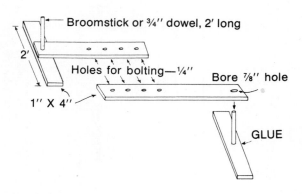

Directions: The upright supports are made by drilling a hole ¹¹/₁₆ inch in diameter in the center of each one-by-four. Drive the dowel into the hole, fixing it with glue. The dowels can be notched at intervals to permit different net heights.

The length of the crosspieces depends upon how much court width is to be covered. If a single crosspiece is to be used, holes should be bored in each end. The holes should be big enough (⅞ inch), so the dowel slides through easily.

If the crosspiece is in two halves, then ¼-inch bolts are needed to bolt them together, as indicated in the diagram.

Plastic Markers and Ball Catchers (Scoops)

Gallon plastic jugs filled halfway with sand and recapped make fine boundary markers. The markers can be painted different colors to signify goal, out-of-bounds, and division lines. The jugs also can be numbered and used to designate different teaching stations. There are many possibilities for activities when the plastic bottles are cut down to make ball catchers.

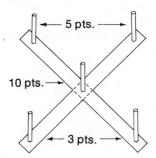

Ring Toss Target

Many ring toss targets can be made from 1-by-4-inch lumber and old broom or mop handles. They can be made to hang on the wall or to lie flat on the ground. The quoits made from garden hose are excellent for throwing to the targets. Children can throw from different positions as well as overhand, underhand, or from behind the back. The pegs can be painted different colors to signify different point values.

Materials
2 one-by-fours, 18 to 20 inches long
5 pegs, 6 inches long (old broom handles)
Screws and paint

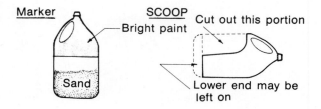

Directions: Glue and screw the 1-by-4-inch boards together, as shown. Bore the proper size holes in the boards with a brace and bit, and glue or screw the pegs into the holes. Paint the base and sticks, and, if desired, number the sticks according to their point values.

Quoits or Deck Tennis Rings

Deck tennis is a popular recreational net game that requires only a ring as basic equipment. The rings are easily made by students and can be used for playing catch and target throwing. The rings can be made from heavy rope by braiding the ends together, but usually the following method is easier. Weather-strip cement helps strengthen the joints.

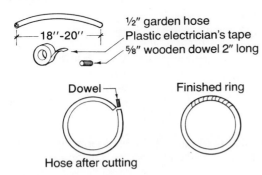

½" garden hose
Plastic electrician's tape
⅝" wooden dowel 2" long

Dowel — Finished ring

Hose after cutting

Tire Stands

Tire stands can be used to keep tires in an upright position. The tires can be used for movement problems, over-and-through relays, and vaulting activities and as targets. Tires are much cleaner and more attractive when they are painted inside and outside.

Materials
2 side pieces (boards 1 by 6 by 24 inches)
2 end pieces (boards 1 by 6 by 13 inches)
4 carriage bolts, ⅜ by 2 inches
Glue, screws, and paint
1 used tire

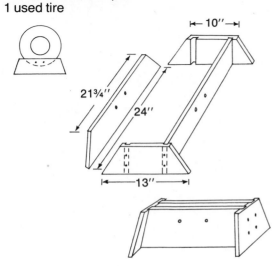

Directions: Cut the ends of the side boards at an angle of 70 degrees. Dado each end piece with two grooves ¾ inch wide and ¼ inch deep. The distance between the grooves is determined by the width of the tire. Round off corners, and sand edges. Glue and screw the stand together. Install tire into frame by drilling two ⅜-inch holes in each side of the frame and tire. Secure the tire to the frame with the bolts. Paint both tire and frame a bright color.

Note: Dimensions of the frame vary according to the size of the tire, making it necessary to adjust the frame dimensions to the tire.

Track Starter

The track starter is an ingenious device that simulates a gun report. Many of the starters can be made, so the children can start their own races.

Materials
2 boards (2 by 4 by 11 inches)
2 small strap hinges
2 small cabinet handles

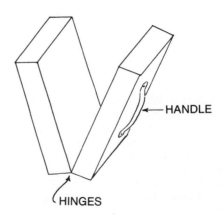

←—HANDLE

HINGES

Directions: Cut the boards to size, and sand off any rough edges. Place the two blocks together, and apply the two hinges with screws. Add the two handles near the top of the boards. Open the boards and then quickly slam them together to obtain a loud bang.

Wands

Handles from old brooms or mops can make excellent wands. These generally come in different diameters, but this is not an important factor. The ends can be sanded and the wands painted different colors. If noise is a concern, rubber crutch tips can be placed on the ends.

⅝" or ¾" Doweling

Lengths: K-1 = 30", 2-3 = 36", 4-6 = 42" or 1 meter

Yarn Balls

Yarn balls are useful pieces of equipment that can be used to enhance throwing and catching skills and for many games. They have an advantage over balls in that they do not hurt the children when they are hit by them and they can be used in the classroom or other limited areas. They can be made by older children or by the PTA. Two methods of making yarn balls are offered here; both work well. When possible, wool or cotton yarns should be used, since they shrink when soaked in hot water or steamed and make tight, effective balls. Nylon and other synthetic yarns are impervious to water and so do not shrink.

Materials for Method #1

One skein of yarn (wool) per ball
Piece of box cardboard 5 inches wide and 10 inches or so long
Strong light cord for binding

Directions: Wrap the yarn 20 to 25 times around the 5-inch-wide side of the cardboard. Slide the yarn off the cardboard, and wrap it in the middle with the cord, forming a tied loop of yarn. Continue until all the yarn is used up.

Take two of the tied loops and tie them together at the centers, using several turns of the cord. This forms a bundle of two tied loops, as illustrated.

Next, tie the bundles together until all the bundles are used.

The final step is to cut and trim the formed ball. Cutting should be done carefully, so that the lengths are reasonably even or considerable trimming will be needed.

Materials for Method #2

Two skeins of yarn (wool) per ball
Two cardboard doughnuts (see dimensions below)
Strong, light cord for tying

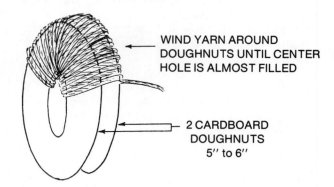

WIND YARN AROUND DOUGHNUTS UNTIL CENTER HOLE IS ALMOST FILLED

2 CARDBOARD DOUGHNUTS 5″ to 6″

Directions: Make a slit in the doughnuts, so the yarn can be wrapped around the cardboard. Holding strands from both skeins, wrap the yarn around the doughnut until the center hole is almost completely filled with yarn. Lay the doughnut of wrapped yarn on a flat surface, insert scissors between the two doughnuts, and cut around the entire outer edge. Carefully insert a double strand of the light cord between the two doughnuts and catch all of the individual strands around the middle. Tie as tightly as possible with a double knot. Remove the doughnuts, and trim the ball, if necessary.

Appendix I

Sources for Records for Rhythmic Programs in Elementary Schools

The following sources, in most cases, handle a variety of records. It is suggested that the teacher write and ask for descriptive literature. The request should include the type of rhythmic program and the grade level for which the records are going to be used.

Bowmar Records
622 Rodier Dr.
Glendale, Calif. 91201

Canadian F.D.S.
Educational Recordings
605 King Street
W. Toronto, 2B, Canada

Children's Music Center
5373 W. Pico Blvd.
Los Angeles, Calif. 90019

Dance Record Center
1161 Broad Street
Newark, N.J. 07114

David McKay, Inc.
750 Third Ave.
New York, N.Y. 10017

Educational Activities, Inc.
P.O. Box 392
Freeport, N.Y. 11520

Educational Recordings of America, Inc.
P.O. Box 231
Monroe, Conn. 06468

Educational Record Sales
157 Chambers Street
New York, N.Y. 10007

Folkraft Records
1159 Broad Street
Newark, N.J. 07714

Freda Miller Records for Dance
Department J, Box 383
Northport, Long Island, N.Y. 11768

Hoctor Educational Records, Inc.
Waldwick, N.J. 07463

Instructor Publications, Inc.
Dansville, N.Y. 14437

Kimbo Educational Records
P.O. Box 246
Deal, N.J. 07723

Leo's Advance Theatrical Co.
2451 N. Sacramento Ave.
Chicago, Ill. 60647

Loshin's
215 East Eighth St.
Cincinnati, Ohio 45202

Master Record Service
708 East Garfield
Phoenix, Ariz. 85000

Merrback Records Service
P.O. Box 7308
Houston, Tex. 77000

RCA Victor Education Dept. J
155 E. 24th Street
New York, N.Y. 10010

Record Center
2581 Piedmont Road N.E.
Atlanta, Ga. 30324

Rhythms Productions Records
Dept. J., Box 34485
Los Angeles, Calif. 90034

Rhythm Record Co.
9203 Nichols Road
Oklahoma City, Okla. 73120

Russell Records
P.O. Box 3318
Ventura, Calif. 93003

Selva and Sons, Inc.
Dept. J, 1607 Broadway
New York, N.Y. 10019

Square Dance Square
P.O. Box 689
Santa Barbara, Calif. 93100

Standard Records & Hi Fi Co.
1028 N.E. 65th
Seattle, Wash. 98115

Windsor Records
5530 N. Rosemead Boulevard
Temple City, Calif. 91780

Observing a Lesson and Assessing the Performance of an Instructor

A more effective observation and critique of a lesson presentation in physical education can be made if a check list of pertinent teaching factors to be observed is available. The supervisor or teacher doing the critique can make notes on the form and discuss the results later with the teacher. In evaluating a teacher's performance, four major areas should be considered.

1. The Teacher as a Person: Is his or her appearance that of a professional person? What is his or her bearing in front of the children? Does he or she put something (effort) into his or her teaching? Is his or her voice appropriate for teaching physical education?

2. Teaching Skills and Class Management: Has the facility been made ready for the lesson? Are the instructional materials well handled? Does the setting have appropriate educational guidance? Are a safe environment and instructional safety factors present? Have safety precautions been taught and observed? Is there effective balance between verbalization and movement, or does the instructor waste valuable learning time with too much talk? Is there effective movement and handling of children with respect to changes of activity and utilization of available space?

3. Communication Skills and Rapport with Students: Can the teacher convey his or her ideas clearly on the level of the children? Are the children working industriously with enthusiasm and exhibiting a good level of interest? Is the instructional process a two-way street, wherein the students' ideas and suggestions are sought, considered, and utilized? Is there consideration for individual students and their special needs? Does the instructor see and act when a student appears to need help? Does the instructor move among the students, interacting with each? Does the instructor provide positive reinforcement and encouragement, with a minimum of criticism and negative approaches?

4. The Lesson: Does the lesson show good planning and preparation based on a written lesson plan? Are the teaching methods appropriate to the activity and the children? As the lesson unfolds, does the teacher adapt and adjust to the children's abilities? Is there evidence of good progression? Does the instruction review prior material and begin at a level where all children are comfortable and can meet with success? Are each of the steps in progression developed sufficiently before moving to the next step? Among the students, is there provision for maximum participation? Is the student activity level appropriate, with little standing around and waiting for turns? Have the lesson objectives been accomplished? Has opportunity been provided for exploration and creativity? Have students had a chance to come up with movement patterns and "do their thing"? Is there opportunity provided for the students to critique and evaluate the lesson?

Lesson Observation/Instructor Assessment

Rating Scale
   3 *Competent, good, high level*
   2 *Moderate, satisfactory*
   1 *Needs improvement*
   X *Not observed or applicable*

Date_____

Instructor_____

Evaluator_____

Grade Level_____

Activities_____

Personal Qualifications   *Comments*

___ 1. Appearance: neatness, appropriate dress

___ 2. Poise, confidence, self-control

___ 3. Enthusiasm, energy

___ 4. Voice: clarity, force, effectiveness

Teaching Skills – Classroom Management   *Comments*

___ 1. Facilities and equipment prepared

___ 2. Supplies: efficient handling

___ 3. Effective behavior level and control

___ 4. Safety precautions: taught, observed

___ 5. Effective use of time: verbal/movement

___ 6. Efficient movement of students, use of space

Communication Skills – Rapport with Students   *Comments*

___ 1. Conveys ideas clearly and effectively

___ 2. Maintains student interest and enthusiasm

___ 3. Utilizes student ideas and suggestions

___ 4. Sensitive to student needs

___ 5. Interacts with students

___ 6. Provides positive reinforcement, encourages

The Lesson   *Comments*

___ 1. Shows good planning, preparation

___ 2. Teaching methods appropriate to content

___ 3. Adapts, adjusts to students' abilities

___ 4. Appropriate progressions

___ 5. Provides for maximum participation

___ 6. Accomplishes objectives

___ 7. Allows for exploration, creativity

___ 8. Provides for critique, evaluation

General Comments

What were the strong points or commendable aspects of the lesson presentation?
What suggestions are made for improving or strengthening the quality of the presentation?

Two questions at the completion of the specific items of the assessment form allow for general comments. It is recognized that not all of the specifics in the form may be available for observation.

Bibliography and Related Materials Resources

For the reader's convenience, this bibliography is divided into major subject areas. Addresses of the various publishers can be obtained at most libraries and from the *Publishers' Trade List Annual* and *Books in Print.* A listing of card packets for games, rhythms, and stunts also has been included. It should be noted that, in some instances, titles include more than one area; however, these were classified under the area of greatest emphasis.

AAHPER refers to the American Alliance for Health, Physical Education and Recreation, 1201 Sixteenth Street N. W., Washington, D.C. 20036.

The bibliography is organized as follows:

1. Curriculum in Elementary School Physical Education
2. Fitness and Exercise
3. Games and Similar Activities
4. Rhythms, Songs, and Dances
5. Stunts and Tumbling, Apparatus, and Rope Jumping
6. Health, Safety, and Posture
7. Perceptual-Motor Development
8. Card Packets for Physical Education Activities
9. English Books on Movement
10. Miscellaneous

1. CURRICULUM IN ELEMENTARY SCHOOL PHYSICAL EDUCATION

AAHPER. *Echoes of Influence for Elementary School Physical Education.* Washington, D.C., 1977.

_____. *Essentials of a Quality Elementary School Physical Education Program.* Washington, D.C., 1970.

_____. *Knowledges and Understandings in Physical Education.* Washington, D.C., 1973.

_____. *Movement Activities for Places and Spaces.* Washington, D.C., 1977.

_____. *Personalized Learning in Physical Education.* Washington, D.C., 1976.

_____. *Who Can.* Washington, D.C., 1977.

Aitken, Margaret H. *Play Environment for Children: Play, Space, Improvised Equipment and Facilities.* Bellingham, Wash.: Educational Designs and Consultants, 1972.

Arnheim, Daniel D., and Pestolesi, Robert A. *Elementary Physical Education.* St. Louis: C. V. Mosby, 1978.

Arra, Carl. *Physical Education in the Elementary School.* Cranbury, N.J.: A. S. Barnes, 1970.

Association for Childhood Education International. *Physical Education for Children's Healthful Living.* Washington, D.C., 1968.

Block, Susan Dimond. *"Me and I'm Great": Physical Education for Children Three through Eight.* Minneapolis: Burgess, 1977.

Brink, Edward F., and Rada, Roger L. *Experiences in Movement: Movement Activities for the Elementary School.* Dubuque, Iowa: Kendall/Hunt, 1975.

Brown, Margaret C., and Sommer, Betty K. *Movement Education: Its Evolution and a Modern Approach.* Reading, Mass.: Addison-Wesley, 1969.

Bryant, R., and Oliver, E. *Fun and Fitness through Elementary Physical Education.* West Nyack, N.Y.: Parker, 1967.

Bucher, Charles A., and Reade, Evelyn M. *Physical Education and Health in the Elementary School.* New York: Macmillan, 1971.

Burton, Elsie Carter. *The New Physical Education for Elementary School Children.* Boston: Houghton Mifflin, 1977.

Canadian Association for Health, Physical Education and Recreation. *New Perspectives for Elementary School Physical Education Programs in Canada.* Ottawa, Canada, 1976.

Cherry, Clare. *Creative Movement for the Developing Child.* Belmont, Calif: Fearon, 1971.

Christian, Quentin A. *The Beanbag Curriculum.* Wolfe City, Texas: The University Press, 1973.

Cochran, Norman; Wilkinson, Lloyd C.; and Furlow, John J. *A Teacher's*

Guide to Elementary School Physical Education. 3rd ed. Dubuque, Iowa: Kendall/Hunt, 1976.

Colvell, Lida C. *Jump to Learn.* San Diego, Calif.: Pennant Educational Materials, 1975.

Corbin, C. *Becoming Physically Educated in the Elementary School.* 2nd ed. Philadelphia: Lea & Febiger, 1976.

Cratty, Bryant J. *Intelligence in Action, Physical Activities for Enhancing Intellectual Abilities.* Englewood Cliffs, N.J.: Prentice-Hall, 1973.

Cratty, Bryant, et al. *Movement Activities, Motor Ability and the Education of Children.* Springfield, Ill.: Charles C. Thomas, 1970.

Dauer, Victor P. *Essential Movement Experiences for Preschool and Primary Children.* Minneapolis: Burgess, 1972.

Demeter, Rose. *Hop-Run-Jump: We Exercise with Our Children.* Edited by M. Wuest and M. Moskin. New York: John Day, 1968.

Department of Education, N.S.W. *Physical Education in Primary Schools.* Sydney, N.S.W., Australia: Minister for Education, n.d.

Doray, May B. *See What I Can Do! A Book of Creative Movement.* Englewood Cliffs, N.J.: Prentice-Hall, 1973.

Dutton, Marion. *Movement Education.* New York: E. P. Dutton, 1973.

Elliot, Margaret E.; Anderson, Marion H.; and LaBerge, Jeanne. *Play with a Purpose.* New York: Harper & Row, 1978.

Espenschade, Anna S. *Physical Education in the Elementary Schools* (#27 of the series *What Research Says to the Teacher*). Washington, D.C.: National Education Association, 1963.

Fabricius, Helen. *Physical Education for the Classroom Teacher.* Dubuque, Iowa: Wm. C. Brown, 1971.

Fait, Hollis F. *Physical Education for the Elementary School Child.* 3rd ed. Philadelphia: Saunders, 1976.

Fandek, Ruth W. *Classroom Capers—An Exploratory Approach to Movement Education in the Classroom.* Bellingham, Wash.: Department of Physical Education, Western Washington State College, 1969.

Frostig, Marianna, and Maslow, Phyllis. *Move-Grow-Learn.* Chicago: Follett Education Corp., 1969.

Gallahue, David L. *Motor Development and Movement Experiences for Young Children (3-7).* New York: Wiley, 1976.

Gallahue, David L.; Werner, Peter H.; and Luedke, George C. *A Conceptual Approach to Moving and Learning.* New York: Wiley, 1975.

Georgia Department of Education. *Every Child a Winner: With Improved Physical Education Equipment.* Atlanta, 1973.

Gerhardt, Lydia A. *Moving and Knowing: The Young Child Orients Himself in Space.* Englewood Cliffs, N.J.: Prentice-Hall, 1973.

Gilliom, Bonnie Cherp. *Basic Movement Education for Children: Rationale and Teaching Units.* Reading, Mass.: Addison-Wesley, 1970.

Glass, Henry "Buzz." *Exploring Movement.* Freeport, N.Y.: Educational Activities, 1966.

Hackett, Layne C., and Jenson, Robert C. *A Guide to Movement Exploration.* Palo Alto, Calif.: Peek Publications, 1966.

Hall, J. Tillman; Sweeny, Nancy Hall; and Esser, Jody Hall. *Until the Whistle Blows: A Collection of Games, Dances, and Activities for Four- to Eight-Year-Olds.* Santa Monica, Calif.: Goodyear, 1976.

Hatcher, Caro, and Mullin, Hilda. *More Than Words—Movement Activities for Children.* Pasadena, Calif.: Parents for Movement Publications, 1969.

Herron, R. E., and Sutton-Smith, Brian. *Child's Play.* New York: Wiley, 1971.

Humphrey, James H. *Child Learning through Elementary School Physical Education.* Dubuque, Iowa: Wm. C. Brown, 1974.

Jones, Genevieve. *Seeds of Movement (Book One).* Pittsburgh: Volkwein Brothers, 1971.

Jordan, Diana. *Children and Movement.* New Rochelle, N.Y.: Sportshelf, 1968.

Kirchner, Glenn. *Physical Education for Elementary School Children.* 4th ed. Dubuque, Iowa: Wm. C. Brown, 1978.

Kirchner, Glenn; Cunningham, Jean; and Warrell, Eileen. *Introduction to Movement Education.* 2nd ed. Dubuque, Iowa: Wm. C. Brown, 1977.

Kruger, Hayes, and Kruger, Jane Myers. *Movement Education in Physical Education.* Dubuque, Iowa: Wm. C. Brown, 1977.

Latchaw, Marjorie. *A Pocket Guide of Movement Activities for the Elementary School.* Englewood Cliffs, N.J.: Prentice-Hall, 1970.

Latchaw, Marjorie, and Egstrom, G. *Human Movement: With Concepts Applied to Children's Movement Activities.* Englewood Cliffs, N.J.: Prentice-Hall, 1970.

Logsdon, Bette J., et al. *Physical Education for Children – A Focus on the Teaching Process.* Philadelphia: Lea & Febiger, 1977.

Marzollo, Jean, and Lloyd, Janice. *Learning through Play.* New York: Harper & Row, 1972.

Means, Louis E., and Applequist, Harry A. *Dynamic Movement Experiences for Elementary School Children.* Springfield, Ill.: Charles C. Thomas, 1974.

Miller, Arthur G., and Whitcomb, Virginia. *Physical Education in the Elementary School Curriculum.* Englewood Cliffs, N.J.: Prentice-Hall, 1974.

Montgomery County Community College, Blue Bell, Pa. *Concepts in Human Movement.* Edited by Marian H. Rockwell and David G. Yeo. Dubuque, Iowa: Kendall/Hunt, 1977.

Moran, Joan M., and Kalakian, Leonard H. *Movement Experiences for the Mentally Retarded or Emotionally Disturbed Child.* 2nd ed. Minneapolis: Burgess, 1977.

Mosston, Muska. *Developmental Movement.* Columbus, Ohio: Charles E. Merrill, 1965.

Ontario Department of Education. *Physical and Health Education Interim Revision–Movement and Growth.* Toronto, Ontario, 1967.

Porter, Lorena. *Movement Education for Children.* Washington, D.C.: AAHPER, 1969.

Schurr, Evelyn L. *Movement Experiences for Children.* 2nd ed. Englewood Cliffs, N.J.: Prentice-Hall, 1975.

Smalley, Jeannette. *Physical Education Activities for the Elementary School.* Palo Alto, Calif.: National Press Publications, n.d.

Society of State Directors of Health, Physical Education, and Recreation. *A Statement of Basic Beliefs.* Washington, D.C., 1964.

Stanley, Sheila. *Physical Education: A Movement Orientation.* Scarborough, Ontario: McGraw-Hill, 1969.

Sweeney, Robert T. *Selected Readings in Movement Education.* Reading, Mass.: Addison-Wesley, 1970.

Tillotson, Joan, et al. *A Program of Movement Education for the Plattsburgh Elementary Public Schools.* Plattsburgh, N.Y., 1969.

Turner, Lowell F., and Turner, Susan Lilliman. *Elementary Physical Education: More Than Just Games.* Palo Alto, Calif.: Peek Publications, 1976.

Van Holst, Auke. *Physical Education Curriculum for Elementary Grades.* London, Canada: The London Free Press, 1973. (A set of four volumes for grades one through four.)

Vannier, Maryhelen, et al. *Teaching Physical Education in Elementary Schools.* Philadelphia: Saunders, 1978.

Werner, Peter H., and Simmons, Richard A. *Do It Yourself: Creative Movement with Innovative Physical Education Equipment.* Dubuque, Iowa: Kendall-Hunt, 1973.

Wickstrom, Ralph L. *Fundamental Motor Patterns.* Philadelphia: Lea & Febiger, 1977.

2. FITNESS AND EXERCISE

AAHPER. *Fitness Test Manual.* Washington, D.C.: 1976. Also available from the AAHPER is a variety of fitness materials, including record forms, certificates, emblems, and bar patches. Write for descriptive literature. Available from the President's Council on Physical Fitness. Write to Superintendent of Documents, U.S. Government Printing Office, Washington, D.C. 20201. *Youth Physical Fitness: Suggestions for School Programs.* 1973.

Bowerman, William J., and Harris, W. E. *Jogging.* New York: Grosset & Dunlap, 1967.

Cooper, Kenneth. *Aerobics.* New York: Grosset & Dunlap, 1968.

Fixx, James F. *The Complete Book of Running.* New York: Random House, 1978.

Hafen, Brent Q., ed. *Weight and Obesity: Causes, Fallacies, Treatment.* Provo, Utah: Brigham Young University Press, 1975.

Morehouse, Laurence E., and Gross, Leonard. *Maximum Performance.* New York: Simon and Schuster, 1977.

Royal Canadian Air Force. *Exercise Plans for Physical Fitness.* New York: Pocket Books, 1962.

Wallis, Earl L., and Logan, Gene A. *Exercises for Children.* Englewood Cliffs, N.J.: Prentice-Hall, 1966.

3. GAMES AND SIMILAR ACTIVITIES

AAHPER. *Games Teaching.* Washington, D.C., 1977.

_____. *ICHPER Book of Worldwide Games and Dances.* Washington, D.C., 1967.

_____. *Youth Sports Guide—For Coaches and Parents.* Washington, D.C., 1977.

Arnold, Arnold. *The World Book of Children's Games.* New York: World Publishing, 1972.

Athletic Institute. *How to Improve Your Track and Field for Elementary School Children and Junior High School Girls.* Chicago: Athletic Institute, n.d.

Bancroft, Jessie H. *Games.* Rev. ed. New York: Macmillan, n.d.

Cratty, Bryant J. *Learning about Human Behavior through Active Games.* Englewood Cliffs, N.J.: Prentice-Hall, 1975.

Heaton, Alma. *Double Fun: 100 Outdoor and Indoor Games.* Provo, Utah: Brigham Young University Press, 1975.

Hofsinde, Robert. *Indian Games and Crafts.* New York: Morrow, 1957.

Lincoln, Eric. *Backyard Games.* New York: Stadia Sports Publishing, 1973.

Macfarlan, Allan A. *Book of American Indian Games.* New York: Association Press, 1958.

Milberg, Alan. *Street Games.* New York: McGraw-Hill, 1976.

Morris, G. S. Don. *How to Change the Games Children Play.* Minneapolis: Burgess, 1976.

Nelson, Esther L. *Movement Games for Children of All Ages.* New York: Sterling, 1975.

New Games Foundation. *The New Games Book.* Edited by Andrew Fluegelman. Garden City, N.Y.: Doubleday, 1976.

Reader's Digest. *Book of 1000 Family Games.* Pleasantville, N.Y.: The Reader's Digest Association, 1971.

Rockwell, Anne. *Games (and How to Play Them).* New York: Thomas Y. Crowell, 1973.

Spencer, Zane A. *150 Plus! Games and Activities for Early Childhood.* Belmont, Calif.: Fearon, 1976.

Sullivan, George. *Sports for Your Child.* New York: Winchester Press, 1973.

4. RHYTHMS, SONGS, AND DANCES

AAHPER. *Children's Dance.* Washington, D.C., 1973.

_____. *Choosing and Using Phonograph Records for Physical Education, Recreation and Related Activities.* Washington, D.C., 1977.

Barlin, Anne, and Barlin, Paul. *Dance-a-Folk Song.* Los Angeles: Bowmar, 1974.

Bley, Edgar S. *The Best Singing Games for Children of All Ages.* New York: Sterling, 1957.

Boorman, Joyce. *Creative Dance in the First Three Grades.* New York: McKay, 1969.

_____. *Dance and Language Experiences with Children.* Hamilton, Ontario: Longman Canada, 1973.

Carroll, Jean, and Lofthouse, Peter. *Creative Dance for Boys.* New York: International Publications Service, 1969.

Doll, Edna, and Nelson, Mary Jarman. *Rhythms Today.* Morristown, N.J.: Silver, 1965.

Evans, Ruth. *40 Basic Rhythms for Children.* Putnam, Conn.: U.S. Textbook Company, 1958.

Gelineau, R. Phyllis. *Songs in Action.* New York: McGraw-Hill, 1974.

Gilbert, Cecile. *International Folk Dance at a Glance.* 2d ed. Minneapolis: Burgess, 1974.

Harris, Jane; Pittman, Anne; and Waller, Marlys. *Dance a While.* Minneapolis: Burgess, 1978.

Heaton, Alma. *Fun Dance Rhythms.* Provo, Utah: Brigham Young University Press, 1976.

Jensen, Mary Bee, and Jensen, Clayne R. *Square Dancing.* Provo, Utah: Brigham Young University Press, 1973.

Jernigan, Sara Staff, and Vendien, C. Lynn. *Playtime—A World Recreation Handbook of Games, Dances, and Songs.* New York: McGraw-Hill, 1972.

Joyce, Mary. *First Steps in Teaching Creative Dance.* Palo Alto, Calif.: National Press Books, 1973.

Mason, Bernard S. *Dances and Stories of the American Indian.* New York: Ronald Press, 1944.

Murray, Ruth Lovell. *Dance in Elementary Education.* New York: Harper & Row, 1963.

Nelson, Esther L. *Dancing Games for Children of All Ages.* New York: Sterling, 1973.

_____. *Musical Games for Children of All Ages.* New York: Sterling, 1976.

Russell, Joan. *Creative Dance in the Primary School.* London: McDonald & Evans, 1965.

Taylor, Carla. *Rhythm: A Guide for Creative Movement.* Mountain View, Calif.: Peek Publications, 1973.

Tobitt, Janet. *Red Book of Singing Games and Dances from the Americas.* Evanston, Ill.: Summy-Birchard, n.d.

_____. *Yellow Book of Singing Games and Dances from Around the World.* Evanston, Ill.: Summy-Birchard, n.d.

Wiener, Jack, and Lidstone, John. *Creative Movement for Children: A Dance Program for the Classroom.* New York: Van Nostrand-Reinhold, 1969.

Winters, Shirley. *Creative Rhythmic Movement for Children of Elementary School Age.* Dubuque, Iowa: Wm. C. Brown, 1974.

5. STUNTS AND TUMBLING, APPARATUS, AND ROPE JUMPING

Bailie, Sam, and Bailie, Avelyn. *Elementary School Gymnastics.* St. Louis: Atlas Athletic Equipment, Co., 1969.

Baley, James A. *Gymnastics in the Schools.* Boston: Allyn & Bacon, 1965.

Drehman, Vera L. *Head Over Heels.* New York: Harper & Row, 1970.

Harris, Rich. *Introducing Gymnastics.* Napa, Calif.: Physical Education Aids, 1964.

Keeney, Charles J. *Fundamental Tumbling Skills Illustrated.* New York: Ronald Press, 1966.

O'Quinn, Garland, Jr. *Gymnastics for Elementary School Children.* Dubuque, Iowa: Wm. C. Brown, 1967.

Skolnik, Peter L. *Jump Rope.* New York: W. P. Workman, 1974.

Smith, Paul. *Rope Skipping—Rhythms, Routines, Rhymes.* Freeport, N.Y.: Educational Activities, 1969.

6. HEALTH, SAFETY, AND POSTURE

AAHPER. *Answers to Health Questions in Physical Education.* Washington, D.C., 1970.

———. *Health Appraisal of School Children.* Washington, D.C., 1970.

———. *Healthful School Environment.* Washington, D.C., 1969.

———. *Physical Growth Chart for Boys.* Washington, D.C., 1960.

———. *Physical Growth Chart for Girls.* Washington, D.C.: 1960.

———. *Teaching Safety in the Elementary School (Classroom Teachers Series).* Washington, D.C., 1972.

Davies, Evelyn A. *The Elementary School Child and His Posture Patterns.* New York: Appleton-Century-Crofts, 1958.

Lilly, Luella J. *An Overview of Body Mechanics.* Mountain View, Calif.: Peek Publications, 1973.

Lowman, Charles, and Young, Carl Hansen. *Postural Fitness: Significance and Variances.* Philadelphia: Lea & Febiger, 1960.

U.S. Consumer Product Safety Commission. *Hazard Analysis: Playground Equipment.* Washington, D.C., 1975.

Vannier, Maryhelen. *Teaching Health in Elementary Schools.* Philadelphia: Lea & Febiger, 1974.

Wells, Katherine F. *Posture Exercise Handbook.* New York: Ronald Press, 1963.

Willgoose, Carl E. *Health Education in the Elementary Schools.* Philadelphia: Saunders, 1974.

7. PERCEPTUAL-MOTOR DEVELOPMENT

AAHPER. *Annotated Bibliography on Perceptual-Motor Development.* Washington, D.C., 1970.

———. *Foundations and Practices in Perceptual-Motor Learning—A Quest for Understanding.* Washington, D.C., 1971.

———. *Motor Activity and Perceptual Development—Some Implications for Physical Educators.* Washington, D.C., 1968.

———. *Perceptual Motor Foundations: A Multidisciplinary Concern.* Washington, D.C., 1969.

Auxter, David. *Perceptual Motor Development Programs for an Individually Prescribed Instructional System.* Slippery Rock, Pa.: David Auxter, 1971.

Braley, William T.; Konicki, Geraldine; and Leedy, Catherine. *Daily Sensorimotor Training Activities.* Freeport, N.Y.: Educational Activities, 1968.

Cratty, Bryant J. *Developmental Sequences of Perceptual-Motor Tasks.* Mountain View, Calif.: Peek Publications, 1970.

———. *Movement Behavior and Motor Learning.* Philadelphia: Lea & Febiger, 1973.

———. *Movement, Perception and Thought.* Mountain View, Calif.: Peek Publications, 1969.

———. *Perceptual-Motor Behavior and Educational Processes.* Springfield, Ill.: Charles C. Thomas, 1969.

Cratty, Bryant J., and Martin, Sister M. M. *Perceptual-Motor Efficiency in Children.* Philadelphia: Lea & Febiger, 1969.

Delacato, Carl W. *The Diagnosis and Treatment of Speech and Reading Problems.* Springfield, Ill.: Charles C. Thomas, 1963.

———. *The Treatment and Prevention of Reading Problems.* Springfield, Ill.: Charles C. Thomas, 1959.

Flinchum, Betty M. *Motor Development in Early Childhood.* St. Louis: C. V. Mosby, 1975.

Godfrey, Barbara, and Kephart, N. C. *Movement Patterns and Motor Education.* New York, Appleton-Century-Crofts, 1969.

Kephart, Newell C. *The Slow Learner in the Classroom.* Columbus, Ohio: Charles E. Merrill, 1960.

LeCrone, Harold, and LeCrone, Mary Jane. *Let's Play a Learning Game.* Oklahoma City, Okla.: Harold and Mary Jane LeCrone, 1966.

Mafex Associates. *Manual of Perceptual-Motor Activities.* Johnstown, Pa., n.d.

Portland Public Schools. *Improving Motor-Perceptual Skills.* Corvallis, Ore.: Continuing Education Publications, 1970.

Roach, Eugene, and Kephart, Newell C. *The Purdue Perceptual-Motor Survey.* Columbus, Ohio: Charles E. Merrill, 1966.

Smith, Paul. *Perceptual Motor Test.* Mountain View, Calif.: Peek Publications, 1973.

Van Whitsen, Betty. *Perceptual Training Activities Handbook.* New York: Teacher's College Press, 1967.

8. CARD PACKETS FOR PHYSICAL EDUCATION ACTIVITIES

The card packets are available from Burgess Publishing Company, 7108 Ohms Lane, Minneapolis, Minn. 55435.

Berger, H. Jean. *Program Activities for Camps.* 2nd ed. 1969.

Harris, Jane A. *File O' Fun: Card File for Social Recreation.* 2nd ed. 1970.

Richardson, Hazel A. *Games for the Elementary School Grades,* 2nd ed. 1951.

Vick, Marie, and Cox, Rosann McLaughlin. *A Collection of Dances for Children.* 1970.

9. ENGLISH BOOKS ON MOVEMENT

Most English books on movement may be secured from the Ling Book Shop, 10 Nottingham Place, London, W. I., England. The authors recommend the books by Bilbrough and Jones, which present a middle-of-the-road approach of English programs.

Bilbrough, A., and Jones, P. *Developing Patterns in Physical Education.* New York: International Publications, 1973.

———. *Physical Education in the Primary School.* London: London Press, 1967.

Cameron, W. McD., and Pleasance, Peggy. *Education in Movement.* Oxford: Basic, Blackwell, and Mott, 1963.

Cope, John. *Discovery Methods in Physical Education.* London: Thomas Nelson and Sons, 1967.

Edmundson, Joseph. *P.E. Teachers' Handbook for Primary Schools.* London: Evans Brothers, 1960.

Laban, Rudolph. *The Mastery of Movement.* Boston: Plays, 1971.

———. (Revised by Lisa Ullmann.) *Modern Educational Dance.* London: McDonald & Evans, 1963.

London City Council. *Educational Gymnastics.* London: London City Council, 1964.

Ministry of Education. *Physical Education in the Primary School.* Part 1: "Moving and Growing," Part 2: "Planning the Programme." London: Her Majesty's Stationery Office, 1952.

Randall, Marjorie. *Basic Movement.* London: G. Bell & Sons, 1963.

Thornton, Samuel. *Laban's Theory of Movement: A New Perspective.* Boston: Plays, 1971.

10. MISCELLANEOUS

AAHPER. *Adapted Education.* Washington, D.C., 1969.

———. *Complying with Title IX in Physical Education and Sports.* Washington, D.C., 1976.

———. *Desirable Athletic Competition for Children of Elementary School Age.* Washington, D.C., 1968.

———. *Planning Facilities for Health, Physical Education, and Recreation.* Washington, D.C., 1974.

———. *Preparing Teachers for a Chang-*

ing Society. Washington, D.C., 1970.

_____. *Preparing the Elementary Specialist*. Washington, D.C., 1973.

_____. *Professional Preparation of the Elementary School Physical Education Teacher*. Washington, D.C., 1969.

Association for Child Education International. *Play: Children's Business*. Washington, D.C., 1974.

Bell, Virginia Lee. *Sensorimotor Learning*. Pacific Palisades, Calif.: Goodyear, 1970.

Corbin, Charles B. *Inexpensive Equipment for Games, Play, and Physical Activity*. Dubuque, Iowa: Wm. C. Brown, 1972.

Cratty, Bryant J. *Developmental Games for Physically Handicapped Children*. Mountain View, Calif.: Peek Publications, 1971.

_____. *Movement Behavior and Motor Learning*. Philadelphia: Lea & Febiger, 1973.

Doll, Edgar A. *Oseretsky Motor Proficiency Tests*. Minneapolis: American Guidance Services, 1946.

Felker, Donald W. *Building Positive Self-Concepts*. Minneapolis: Burgess, 1974.

Gallahue, David L. *Developmental Play Equipment for Home and School*. New York: Wiley, 1975.

Gilbert, Anne Green. *Teaching the Three R's through Movement Experiences*. Minneapolis: Burgess, 1977.

Hackett, Layne. *Movement Exploration and Games for the Mentally Retarded*. Mountain View, Calif.: Peek Publications, 1970.

Humphrey, James H. *Improving Learning Ability through Compensatory Physical Education*. Springfield, Ill.: Charles C. Thomas, 1976.

Johnson, Barry L., and Nelson, Jack K. *Practical Measurements for Evaluation in Physical Education*. 2nd ed. Minneapolis: Burgess, 1974.

Kryspin, William J., and Feldhusen, John F. *Writing Behavioral Objectives*. Minneapolis: Burgess, 1974.

Lawther, John D. *The Learning of Physical Skills*. Englewood Cliffs, N.J.: Prentice-Hall, 1968.

Moran, Joan M., and Kalakian, Leonard H. *Movement Experiences for the Mentally Retarded or Emotionally Disturbed Child*. 2nd ed. Minneapolis: Burgess, 1977.

Play Schools Association. *Materials and Equipment for Learning in Play Activities*. New York, n.d.

Poteet, James A. *Behavior Modification: A Practical Guide for Teachers*. Minneapolis: Burgess, 1973.

Sapora, Allen V., and Mitchell, Elmer D. *The Theory of Play and Recreation*. New York: Ronald Press, 1961.

Singer, Robert. *Motor Learning and Human Performance*. New York: Macmillan, 1968.

Stallings, Loretta M. *Motor Skills Development and Learning*. Dubuque, Iowa: Wm. C. Brown, 1973.

Sullivan, Dorothy D., and Humphrey, James H. *Teaching Reading through Motor Learning*. Springfield, Ill.: Charles C. Thomas, 1973.

Werner, Peter, and Simmons, Richard A. *Inexpensive Physical Education Equipment for Children*. Minneapolis: Burgess, 1976.

AVAILABLE FILMS

The authors have produced four films that illustrate rather closely and accurately basic theory and activities that are recommended in this guide.

Innovation in Elementary Physical Education. 16 mm. Sound/Color. 30 minutes.

This film presents the program activities of the Pullman (Washington) Elementary Physical Education Project, in which Dr. Dauer served as program director and Dr. Pangrazi as physical education specialist. The project was funded under Title III of the Elementary and Secondary Education Act and has received national recognition, including several honors.

The film is an excellent orientation presentation for teacher-training classes and teacher groups, since it presents broad program outlines and illustrates many diverse activities. It also provides valuable illustrative material for community groups.

Movement Experiences — Parachutes. 16mm. Sound/Color. 10 minutes.

Shows parachute sequences and activities as experienced by fifth-grade boys and girls.

Movement Experiences — Wand Activities. 16mm. Sound/Color. 10 minutes.

Three sixth-graders show the types of activities that can be done with wands. The film finishes with a fifth-grade group illustrating wand activities.

Movement Experiences — Hoops and Individual Mats. 16 mm. Sound/Color. 10 minutes.

This film illustrates two physical education activities. Selected intermediate children show hoop activities both individually and in a class setting. Individual mat activity features first-grade children as subjects, with activities and sequences presented. A class of second-grade children show how the activities can be utilized in a physical education lesson.

Films are available for sale or rental. Write to:

Pan-Dau Films
108 W. Fairmont
Tempe, Ariz. 85282

Physical Fitness Tests

Two types of fitness tests are suggested for the elementary level. The first is the screening test, which is designed to measure basic minimums in a quick, easily administered procedure.

The second type of test is a diagnostic test that can be used to evaluate a student's fitness level in relation to other students'. Another use is for evaluating the effectiveness of a program in terms of developing physical fitness. Students can be tested at the start and the end of the school year to see whether their level of fitness has been significantly raised and whether the program can be deemed effective. The Dynamic Physical Education Revision of the 1966 National Physical Fitness Test is offered as an example of a diagnostic test.

A. A SCREENING TEST FOR IDENTIFYING THE PHYSICALLY UNDERDEVELOPED CHILD

A screening test generally establishes basic minimums that must be met or the child is screened out for further investigation. It is not to be regarded as a diagnostic tool but merely as a device to identify quickly the more deficient children. In some cases, the borderline student can meet the basic physical minimums and is not so identified. However, those children with serious deficiencies can be readily identified by a screening test. The regular physical fitness test gives more detailed and relative information about fitness levels of all children, including those who are physically underdeveloped.

A feasible screening test[1] for identifying the physically underdeveloped child is recommended by the President's Council on Physical Fitness and Sports. It is designed to measure basic minimums of strength, flexibility, and agility, with three simple items that make up the test: (1) arm and shoulder strength (girls—Flexed-Arm Hang; boys—Pull-ups), (2) abdominal strength (Sit-ups), (3) agility (Squat Thrusts).

Administration of the Screening Test

It is recommended that all pupils be screened at the beginning of the school year. Those who fail should be given a diagnostic test for further information.

Divide the class into pairs, with one pupil of each pair acting as a scorer for his or her partner. After each test, results can be recorded by the teacher on a class record form.

Equipment needed includes at least two chinning bars. For the girls, the height of the chinning bar should be adjustable. Begin with the taller girls and lower the height of the bar as needed. This keeps the adjustment process to a minimum.

Flexed-Arm Hang (Girls)

Equipment: A stopwatch and a sturdy bar, comfortable to grip and adjustable in height (height should be approximately the same as the girl tested).
Starting Position: Using an overhand grip, the

[1]*Youth Physical Fitness* (Washington, D.C.: U.S. Government Printing Office, 1973) pp. 12-14.

pupil hangs with chin above bar and elbows flexed. Legs must be straight and feet free of floor.
Action: Hold position as long as possible.
Rules: Timing should start as soon as pupil is in position and released from any support other than her own. Timing should stop when the pupil's chin touches or drops below the bar. Knees must not be raised and kicking is not permitted.
To Pass: Hold position for 3 seconds.

Note: In case an adjustable bar is not available, different sizes of boxes can be used to position the girls. Another method is to have someone lift each girl into the hanging position.

Pull-ups (Boys)

Equipment: A bar of sufficient height, comfortable to grip.
Starting Position: Grasp the bar with the palms facing forward; hang with the arms and legs fully extended.
Action: Pull the body up with the arms until the chin is higher than the bar. Lower body until arms are fully extended.
Rules: The Pull-up must be smooth and not a snappy movement; legs must be kept straight and not kicked. One Pull-up is counted each time the pupil raises his chin above the bar.
To Pass: Perform one Pull-up.

Sit-ups (Boys and Girls)[2]

Equipment: None. However, a mat or other soft (grass) surface is preferred.
Starting Position: Pupil lies on back with knees flexed, feet about 1 foot apart. The hands, with fingers laced, are grasped behind the head. A partner holds the performer's ankles and keeps his or her heels in contact with the floor while counting each successive Sit-up.
Action: Sit up and turn the trunk to the left, touching right elbow to left knee. Return to starting position. Repeat, touching left elbow to right knee.
To Pass: Boys do the following number of Sit-ups: age 10—25; age 11—26; age 12—30; age 13—38. Girls, ages 10-13, do 20 Sit-ups.

Note: No resting is permitted. The Sit-ups must be continuous. The body should return completely to the floor each time in the return position.

Squat Thrust (Boys and Girls)

Equipment: A stopwatch or a watch with a sweep second hand.
Starting Position: Pupil stands erect.
Action: One complete Squat Thrust is a four-part movement.

---

[2]The authors prefer the name Curl-up for this activity, but the President's Council on Physical Fitness and Sports uses the term Sit-up.

Count 1: Bend knees and place hands on floor in front of feet. Arms may be between, outside, or in front of the knees.
Count 2: Thrust legs back until the body is straight from shoulders to feet (push-up position).
Count 3: Return to squat position (as in count 1).
Count 4: Return to erect position.
To Pass: girls—three Squat Thrusts in a 10-second time; boys—four Squat Thrusts in a 10-second time.

Note: Be sure the body comes to a fully erect position each time. Also, the body should be in a straight line in the push-up position. There is a tendency by some to cut short these two positions in the race against time.

B. THE DYNAMIC PHYSICAL EDUCATION REVISION OF THE NATIONAL PHYSICAL FITNESS TEST

The test presented is a modification of the one adopted by the President's Council on Physical Fitness and Sports in 1966. The revision includes an updating of norms, which are stated in both American and metric equivalents, and a deletion of the softball throw and shuttle run. The 600-yard run/walk also has been deleted and a mile or 1600-meter run/walk substituted.

Norms are stated in categories rather than in percentiles, since this approach seems to be more meaningful to parents and children. The events included in the test are these.
1. Pull-ups for boys and Flexed-Arm Hangs for girls.
2. Sit-ups.
3. Standing long jump.
4. Fifty-yard dash or 50-meter dash.
5. Mile run/walk or 1600-meter run/walk.

A program for the test items could follow this plan:
First day: Pull-ups or Flexed-Arm Hangs and Sit-ups.
Second day: Standing long jump, 50-yard or 50-meter dash.
Third day: Mile or 1600-meter run/walk.

During the first two days of testing, the children can be divided into three groups, each of which takes position at one of the test stations. At the conclusion of the testing for the station, the groups rotate to the next station.

Three groups can be used for the final day's testing for the mile or 1600-meter run/walk. However, only two groups are necessary for administration of this test, since each runner has a scorer.

Pull-ups (Boys)

The technique for the Pull-up is described in the screening test, presented on page 581.

Standards for Pull-ups (Boys)

Age	9	10	11	12
Excellent	8	8	8	9
Good	4	4	4	5
Satisfactory	2	2	2	3
Poor	1	1	1	1

Flexed-Arm Hang (Girls)

The technique for the Flexed-Arm Hang is described in the screening test (page 580).

Standards for Flexed-Arm Hangs (Girls)
(In seconds)

Age	9	10	11	12
Excellent	35	37	40	38
Good	18	18	22	18
Satisfactory	12	11	12	12
Poor	7	7	8	7

Sit-ups

Like the Pull-up and the Flexed-Arm Hang, the Sit-up is a part of the screening test and is described under that topic on page 581.

Standards for the Sit-ups

	Boys			
Age	9	10	11	12
Excellent	48	50	50	50
Good	39	42	42	43
Satisfactory	33	36	37	36
Poor	28	31	31	32
	Girls			
Excellent	43	45	48	47
Good	36	37	38	38
Satisfactory	30	32	31	32
Poor	25	26	26	26

Standing Long Jump

Equipment: Any level surface and tape measure.
Starting Position: Pupil stands ready to jump just behind the takeoff line. Preparatory to jumping, the pupil should have knees flexed and should swing the arms backward and forward in a rhythmical motion.
Action: The jump is made with the arms swung forcefully forward and upward, taking off on the balls of the feet.
Rules: Three trials are allowed, with the best scored in feet and the nearest inch. Measure from the takeoff line to the heel or the part of the body that touches nearest to the takeoff line.

Standards for the Standing Long Jump
(In inches)

	Boys			
Age	9	10	11	12
Excellent	70	72	74	80
Good	64	67	70	73
Satisfactory	59	63	65	67
Poor	56	59	60	62
	Girls			
Excellent	65	69	73	75
Good	59	62	66	68
Satisfactory	55	58	61	63
Poor	52	54	58	60

Standards for the Standing Long Jump
(In centimeters)

	Boys			
Age	9	10	11	12
Excellent	178	183	188	203
Good	163	170	178	185
Satisfactory	150	160	165	170
Poor	142	150	152	157
	Girls			
Excellent	165	175	185	191
Good	150	157	168	173
Satisfactory	140	147	155	160
Poor	132	137	147	152

50-Yard or 50-Meter Dash

Equipment: Stopwatch.
Starting Position: Pupil stands behind the starting line. The starter takes a position at the finish line with a stopwatch. He or she raises one hand preparatory to giving the starting signal.
Action: When the starter brings down his or her hand quickly and hits his or her thigh, the pupil leaves his or her mark. The time is noted and recorded.
Rules: One trial is allowed unless it is obvious that the child did not have a fair trial. Time is recorded to the nearest tenth of a second.

Standards for 50-Yard Dash
(In seconds to the nearest tenth)

	Boys			
Age	9	10	11	12
Excellent	7.8	7.5	7.3	7.2
Good	8.1	8.0	7.8	7.6
Satisfactory	8.6	8.4	8.2	7.9
Poor	9.1	8.7	8.5	8.4
	Girls			
Excellent	7.9	7.9	7.5	7.4
Good	8.5	8.3	8.0	8.0
Satisfactory	9.0	8.7	8.4	8.3
Poor	9.4	9.1	8.9	8.7

Standards for 50-Meter Dash
(In seconds to the nearest tenth)

	Boys			
Age	*9*	*10*	*11*	*12*
Excellent	8.5	8.2	8.0	7.9
Good	8.7	8.6	8.5	8.3
Satisfactory	9.4	9.2	9.0	8.6
Poor	10.0	9.5	9.3	9.2
	Girls			
Excellent	8.6	8.6	8.2	8.1
Good	9.3	9.1	8.6	8.6
Satisfactory	9.8	9.5	9.2	9.1
Poor	10.3	10.0	9.7	9.5

Mile or 1600-Meter Run/Walk

Equipment: Stopwatch, running area with starting and finishing lines to cover the desired distance (see note).

Starting Position: Pupils are divided into pairs. While one runs, the other stands near the timer and listens for the finishing time. The timer calls out the time on a continuous basis, until all the runners have crossed the finish line.

Action: On the signal to start, the pupil starts running the distance. Students should be cautioned to pace themselves.

Standards for the Mile Run/Walk
(In minutes and seconds)

	Boys			
Age	*9*	*10*	*11*	*12*
Excellent	7:18	7:00	6:54	6:38
Good	8:12	7:54	7:30	7:12
Satisfactory	9:12	8:42	8:18	7:48
Poor	10:12	9:30	9:06	8:48
	Girls			
Excellent	8:36	8:18	7:36	7:36
Good	9:36	9:30	8:48	8:36
Satisfactory	11:00	10:24	9:48	9:48
Poor	12:06	11:36	10:48	10:48

Standards for the 1600-Meter Run/Walk
(In minutes and seconds)

	Boys			
Age	*9*	*10*	*11*	*12*
Excellent	7:15	6:58	6:52	6:34
Good	8:09	7:51	7:27	7:09
Satisfactory	9:09	8:39	8:15	7:45
Poor	10:08	9:27	9:03	8:45
	Girls			
Excellent	8:33	8:15	7:33	7:33
Good	9:33	9:27	8:45	8:33
Satisfactory	10:56	10:20	9:44	9:44
Poor	12:02	11:32	10:44	10:44

Rules: The time is recorded in minutes and seconds. Walking is permitted but the object is to cover the distance in the shortest time.

Note: See page 529 for a diagram of a 220-yard and page 530 for a 200-meter track.

C. TEST ADMINISTRATION

Throughout the school year, testing should be done at least twice. Testing should be done at the beginning of the school year to select the low-fitness children and to point out directions the program should take. Testing at the end of the year can provide information with respect to what has been accomplished. Another testing period can be scheduled midway (January or February) to provide an indication of progress at that point.

Testing is always a problem for the individual teacher without help. It is difficult for children to supervise each other and secure reliable measurements.

The authors would recommend a plan by which the school secures the help of the community-school organization in the testing program. Interested parents make excellent testers. A team of parents for testing can be established on a school, group of schools, or school district basis, depending upon the situation. Where such a plan is in operation, school districts report enthusiastic support of the testing and of the entire physical education program.

The testers must first undergo orientation and training in the testing procedures. A trial run with one class or a small group helps iron out most difficulties. The testing program should be organized efficiently, with good testing procedures. Each tester should have detailed instructions for each station.

If enough parents are available, it is good to have two testers at each station. One has a clipboard and does the recording, while the other does the measuring.

Two systems of recording the information can be used. One is to have class lists at each station for recording. The second is for each child to have an individual record card, which he or she carries from station to station. The first method is speedier, but care must be taken to match the correct name with the performance. The class lists have to be transferred to the individual cards after the testing is over.

Some school districts are successfully recording data on IBM cards. This provides a ready and easy means of analyzing the data. Laborious hand tabulation of the results is eliminated.

The test results, or at least the interpretation thereof, should be a part of the child's health records and should be included in the periodic progress report to the parents. The school report card should contain a section devoted to the physical fitness of the student.

Test results for a class and for the school should be interpreted in the light of national norms and in comparison with local achievement. Testing is meaningless unless the real concern is for upgrading the physical education program and raising the physical standards of the children to desirable levels.

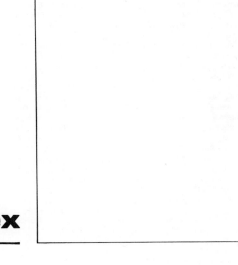

Index

STUDENTS, TELL THE AUTHORS
AND THE PUBLISHER WHAT YOU THINK!

Students are shaping the curricula, texts, and materials which have a role in determining the effectiveness of their education. Both the authors and Burgess Publishing want your opinion of this book. We want to develop better textbooks. Please tell us what you like about this book. Please tell us about improvements you feel should be made. We'll be grateful. And, if you give your mailing address, WE WILL REFUND DOUBLE YOUR POSTAGE.

Your name (optional)_____

School_____ Your mailing address _____

City and state _____ Zip code_____

Course title_____Instructor's name_____

1. How does *Dynamic Physical Education for Elementary School Children* compare with other texts you have used? Circle one.

    better than any other   better than most   about the same as the rest

    worse than most   worst I've ever used

2. Circle those chapters you especially liked:

    Chapter: 1 2 3 4 5 6 7 8 9 10 11 12 13 14 15 16 17 18 19
             20 21 22 23 24 25 26 27 28 29 30 31 32 33 34

    Comments:_____

    _____

3. Circle those chapters you feel could be improved:

    Chapter: 1 2 3 4 5 6 7 8 9 10 11 12 13 14 15 16 17 18 19
             20 21 22 23 24 25 26 27 28 29 30 31 32 33 34

    Comments:_____

    _____

4. Please list any chapters which were not assigned by your instructor.

5. What additional topics did your instructor discuss which were not covered in this text?

OVER, PLEASE!

6. After taking this course, are you interested in taking more courses in this field? ( ) yes ( ) no

7. If you want to teach, would you find this text useful in your profession? ( ) yes ( ) no

8. Have you any suggestions to help us improve this textbook?

9. Please give us your impressions of the text.
   Rate the following:

	Excellent		Average		Poor	No opinion
Logical organization	5	4	3	2	1	( )
Readability of text material	5	4	3	2	1	( )
General layout and design	5	4	3	2	1	( )
Match with instructor's course organization	5	4	3	2	1	( )
Illustrations which clarify the text	5	4	3	2	1	( )
Up-to-date treatment of subject	5	4	3	2	1	( )
Explanation of difficult concepts	5	4	3	2	1	( )
Selection of topics in the text	5	4	3	2	1	( )

10. Do you plan to keep the book or sell it? ( ) keep it ( ) sell it

11. Did you purchase the Pangrazi-Dauer *Lesson Plans* to accompany the text? ( ) yes ( ) no

    ( ) not available in the bookstore

12. General Comments:

Please check here if you have any objections to being quoted in our advertising. ( )

To mail, remove this page from the book and mail to:

WE WILL REFUND DOUBLE YOUR POSTAGE!

(We are sorry, but postal regulations make it difficult for us to use a postage return permit.)

Wayne Schotanus
Physical Education Editor
Burgess Publishing Company
7108 Ohms Lane
Minneapolis, MN 55435

Both the authors and the publisher thank you.